Word & Worship Workbook

for Year A

For Ministry in Initiation, Preaching, Religious Education and Formation

Mary Birmingham

Paulist Press
New York, N.Y. • Mahwah, N.J.

Acknowledgments

Excerpts from the *New Jerome Biblical Commentary,* edited by Raymond E. Brown and Joseph A. Fitzmyer, copyright © 1989, are reprinted by permission of Prentice Hall Inc., Upper Saddle River, N.J. The English translation of Eucharistic Prayer IV, opening prayers, antiphons, solemn blessings, prefaces and other texts from *The Roman Missal* © 1973, International Committee on English in the Liturgy (ICEL); excerpts from the English translation of *Documents on the Liturgy, 1963–1979: Conciliar, Papal and Curial Texts* © 1982, ICEL; excerpts from the English translation of the *Rite of Christian Initiation of Adults* © 1985, ICEL, are reprinted by permission. All rights reserved. Selections from *Matthew Interpretation: A Bible Commentary for Preaching and Teaching* by Douglas R. A. Hare, © 1993 by John Knox Press, are used by permission of Westminster John Knox Press. Material from *Sharing the Word through the Liturgical Year* by Gustavo Gutiérrez, © 1997 by Orbis Books, is reprinted by permission of Orbis Books. Excerpts from *Sharing the Light of Faith, National Catechetical Directory for Catholics of the United States* and *Sharing the Light of Faith, An Official Commentary* are reprinted by permission of the United States Catholic Conference. Excerpts from *The Liturgical Year* by Adolph Adam, translated by Matthew J. O'Connell, © 1981 by Pueblo Publishing Co., Inc., © 1990 by The Order of St. Benedict, Inc., from *Days of the Lord,* volumes 1–7, copyright 1991 by The Order of St. Benedict, Inc., from *Preaching the Lectionary* by Reginald H. Fuller, © 1974 by The Order of St. Benedict, Inc., and from *The Cultural World of Jesus* by John Pilch, © 1995 by The Order of St. Benedict, Inc., are reprinted by permission of The Liturgical Press, Collegeville, MN. Excerpts from *Reading the Old Testament* by Lawrence Boadt, © 1984 by Paulist Press, Inc., are reprinted by permission of Paulist Press. Material from *Invitation to Matthew* by Donald Senior, C.P. is reprinted by permission of the author.

Book design by Céline Allen. Cover design by Tim McKeen. Cover illustration by Julie Lonneman.

Library of Congress Cataloging-in-Publication Data

Birmingham, Mary.
Word & worship workbook : for ministry in initiation, preaching, religious education, and Formation / Mary Birmingham.
viii, 736 p. ; 28 cm.
Includes bibliographical references and index.
Contents: [1] For year A — [3] For year C.
ISBN 0-8091-3826-3 (alk. paper)
1. Catechetics—Catholic Church. 2. Church year—Study and teaching. 3. Catholic Church. Lectionary for Mass (U.S.) Year C. I. Title. II. Title: Word and worship workbook.
BX1968.B54 1999
268'.82—DC21 97-22382
r98

Published by Paulist Press
997 Macarthur Blvd.
Mahwah, N.J. 07430

Printed and bound in the United States of America

Contents

1. Introduction

> If you hope to become part of God's reign, you must let yourself be overtaken, knocked breathless, by a Presence, a Reality you can neither invent nor control. In a word, you have to open your life to the holy violence of conversion—a tumultuous experience that is liable to leave you feeling drenched and exhausted, as though the seas had seized, swallowed and spat you back alive on the shore. Newborn and salted, you sense that nothing looks the same, nothing can ever be the same.[1]

Nathan Mitchell's metaphor captures the heart of this book's purpose or, more humbly, its hope! While you may not find yourself spat back salted and drenched on the local beach, it is hoped that through the use of the methods and proposed sessions, you, as a catechist or small group facilitator, will share in the experience of empowering and being awed by the conversion of the adults and children with and to whom you minister and perhaps even by your own heightened faith life. Hope springs eternal in the human heart. One might therefore hope to light a spark, fan a flame, or at the very least prompt bold new questions to be raised regarding our Christian/Catholic story.

What was the experience and understanding of bread and gospel to the generations who went before us? Where work needs to begin and proceed is in helping people ask the right questions in finding meaning for their lives.

The genesis of this resource flows from the conviction that "...as many ministers of the divine word as possible will be able to effectively provide the nourishment of the Scriptures for the People of God, thereby enlightening their minds, strengthening their wills, and setting their hearts on fire with the love of God."[2] Catechists are ministers of that divine word. "The study of the sacred page is the soul of sacred theology. Sacred theology rests on the written word of God, together with sacred tradition, as its primary and perpetual foundation."[3] Catechesis that enlightens, strengthens, and inflames the love of God leads to deep conversion, which in turn leads to transformation of people's lives. This catechesis begins with the lived experience of people. It helps them celebrate and reflect on the presence of Christ in word and sacrament, in one another, and in the life and mission of the church. Hopefully this resource will assist in that noble endeavor.

This book is intended to help catechists plan engaging sessions for adults and children around the Sunday experience of word and worship. You, the catechist or group leader, may use this as a resource for planning your sessions or working with your specific group.

The structure of *Word & Worship Workbook* is based on the liturgical calendar. There are weekly planning sessions that include prayers and blessings from the liturgy, scholarly exegesis of the Lectionary scriptures, reflection questions, and suggestions for doctrinal themes. A doctrinal appendix is included for the catechist's reference.

One might ask, "How is this different from other resources that provide exegetical or catechetical material?" The answer is three-fold:

1. This book provides, under one jacket cover, condensed, scholarly exegetical material relating to both scripture and tradition and drawn from multiple and varied sources.
2. It includes ritual prayers and blessings, as well as questions, options, and possibilities for "unpacking" the experience of worship in the liturgical year.
3. It suggests themes from among the repertoire of hierarchical truths that naturally flow from interpreted texts of the Lectionary.

---

[1]Nathan Mitchell, "The Kingdom of Justice," in *Modern Liturgy,* 18: 8.

[2]*Dogmatic Constitution on Divine Revelation* (*Dei Verbum*), #23, in *DVII.*

[3]Ibid., #24.

Jim Dunning, in his book, *Echoing God's Word,* challenged us to view liturgical catechesis from a new perspective. Jim asserted that we as ministers must allow ourselves to be transformed by such catechesis if we are to pass it on to others. For this reason, *Word & Worship Workbook* is not a book of lesson plans. It is a resource that committed Christians can use to prayerfully, ritually, and in an informed manner prepare for ministry in the church.

> We need formation and transformation, not just information. We need to take the journey ourselves. As ministers we need both the what (such as the vision of the church, faith, conversion, liturgical catechesis in these rites) and also some how's (some practical ways for pastoral ministers and catechumens to do that liturgical catechesis). We need methods, especially for catechists and homilists, that bring the word of God to echo in and through our lives in the community and that situate doctrine and law within the good news.[4]

This book is an attempt to provide such a method. It also seeks to tap into the current phenomenon of people's need for conversion and for renewed interest in scripture and in Jesus.

How might *Word & Worship Workbook* be used in a parish setting? The possibilities require only imagination. Obvious applications include:

1. Initiation Ministry
Catechists who work with catechumens and candidates could use this workbook to prepare sessions in which the central task is formation of the catechumen or candidate into the mystery of absorption in the paschal mystery of Christ as it unfolds in one liturgical cycle. "By means of the yearly cycle the Church celebrates the whole mystery of Christ, from his incarnation until the day of Pentecost and the expectation of his coming again."[5]

2. Small Christian Communities
Facilitators could use this workbook to plan group sessions. Liturgy is about life. Reflection on the experience of liturgy is a wonderful way to share life in the context of our Catholic Christian experience. In order to be *community,* one must reflect on what it is the community celebrates as well as on what it believes, professes, and holds to be true.

3. Formation in Ministry
This workbook could be used by facilitators working with parish catechists who minister to adults and children through catechumenal ministry, scripture study, and adult enrichment.

4. Liturgy Teams
Liturgy teams could use *Word & Worship Workbook* as a source of reflection as they engage in planning liturgies, celebrations, and rituals for the parish.

5. Religious Education for Young People
There is much talk today regarding Lectionary-based catechesis in our schools and religious education programs. *Word & Worship Workbook* could assist religious educators in preparing Lectionary-based catechesis for their young people. At the very least it would help all who catechize be more informed about the "work" (read "liturgy") that we, as the people of God, do every Sunday throughout the liturgical cycle.

There are two final points. First, you will notice that there is an "agenda" in each of the weekly sessions. While attempting to avoid scriptural and doctrinal fundamentalism, there is nevertheless one constant lens through which the information contained in these pages has been redacted. This agenda is a radical option for the poor, the marginalized, and the less fortunate. In their document, *Communities of Salt and Light: Reflection on the Social Mission of the Parish,* the U.S. bishops state that

> The parish is where the church lives. Parishes are communities of faith, of action, and of hope. They are where the gospel is proclaimed and celebrated, where believers are formed and sent to renew the earth. Communities are measured by how they serve the "least of these" in our parish and beyond its boundaries—the hungry, the homeless, the sick, those in prison, the stranger. The Church teaches that social justice is an integral part of evangelization, a constitutive dimension of preaching the gospel, and an essential part of the Church's mission.[6]

---

[4] *EGW,* 20.
[5] *GNLY,* #17.
[6] *Communities of Salt and Light: Reflection on the Social Mission of the Parish* (Washington: NCCB, 1993), 1–3.

If this is true, it follows that justice is at the very heart of the gospel. The Hebrew understanding of justice (*hesed*) is right relationship. To be in right relationship with God means that one must show care and concern for God's *anawim*—the poor, the powerless, widows, orphans, and the marginalized. Thus, every weekly session is crafted in such a way as to raise questions of social responsibility. Justice is truly the agenda of the gospels. It is truly the agenda of this workbook.

Second, to be Catholic, says James Joyce, means, "Here comes everybody." We are diverse and we are to be inclusive. There is to be no "Jesus and me" mentality in the Catholic experience. Catholicism assumes community. We inherited the understanding that we are in relationship to God "as a people" from our Jewish ancestors. A personal relationship with God is essential. But we are corporate by nature and by intention. Thus, the first perspective in each session will be communal. The first question will always be, "What are the implications and challenges for our community, for the wider community?" Only after this question has been addressed is there movement toward the personal context, "What do the gospel and the liturgy call me to as a member of that corporate body?"

There is no doubt that Jesus maintained a radical stance toward the inclusion of all people. Language expresses our deepest held beliefs, convictions, and biases. To use exclusive language is against the spirit of the basic message of Jesus' gospel. Thus, I have tried to be as inclusive as possible throughout this text.

Since God is neither male nor female, our descriptive language is extremely limited. There are no adequate pronouns. The ancients struggled with naming God too, thus their designation, *YHWH.* However, I am a product of my own cultural and religious conditioning. While I desperately tried to avoid specific male pronouns in reference to the Transcendent Other, I found my efforts futile. Suffice it to say that the use of "him" when it comes to God is solely a literary concession. There were no other choices that allowed the text to make sense and to flow smoothly. Also, quoted material was included as originally written; there were no changes made to texts from other sources.

Finally, the springboard for jumping into these often uncharted waters with both feet is to proceed with courage. As we embark on this sometimes perilous voyage, may we be seized, salted, drenched, swallowed, and spat back alive on that not so distant shore we call "the Kingdom of God."

I would like to acknowledge those special people in my life who made the writing of this book possible. My first thanks and heartfelt appreciation go to my loving family and friends, especially my husband, who held down the family fort during the last year. Their support, love, and encouragement kept me going, especially in those rare moments when being spat out on the local beach looked far more inviting than spending one more hour at the computer. Without them this book would have been nothing more than a dream. I also extend my appreciation to all who have been a part of my life, and to the wonderful community of Our Saviour's Parish who have taught me what it means to be a disciple.

Mary Birmingham, 1998

2. The Substance of Catechesis

Before proceeding further, it is important to understand *catechesis* as it is referred to in *Word & Worship Workbook.* The *catechesis* of subsequent pages embodies a broader interpretation than just the "Catholic stuff" that many have traditionally assumed is its definition. Catechesis refers to a radical relationship with Jesus Christ. Catechesis explores and recognizes God's action and presence in our natural lives, in scripture, and in the life, faith, and worship of the church. This chapter will dissect what that means in practical terms. Whether you are a small group facilitator with little or no formal catechetical training or a learned catechist, *Word & Worship Workbook* could be a useful tool as you "do" the work of catechesis.

CATECHESIS

Many people operate out of an erroneous assumption that catechesis refers to subject matter such as specific doctrines or theologies. In other words, catechesis implies content or head knowledge. However, catechesis supersedes that narrow interpretation. What, then, is it? One need look no further than church documents and the teaching authority of the church to gain insight.

The literal translation of the Greek word *catechesis* is "a sounding down, a resounding, and re-echoing." What and who is the object of this resounding? The "Who" is Jesus Christ. The "What" is the Good News of salvation offered by his life, death, and resurrection. Pope John Paul II, in his apostolic exhortation, *Catechesi tradendae,* states that "the heart of catechesis is in essence a Person, the Person of Jesus of Nazareth, the only Son from the Father...who suffered and died for us, and who now, after rising, is living with us forever."[1] When people catechize, they reveal God's plan of salvation realized in the person of Jesus. Catechesis explores the meaning of Jesus' life, his words, and the marvelous works (signs) he accomplished. Catechesis is about relationship. It concerns a radical, personal, communal relationship with the living God encountered in Jesus Christ through the Holy Spirit. Catechesis helps us interpret the story of our lives in dialogue with the story of the scriptures and the story of the church throughout the ages.

The *National Catechetical Directory* (NCD) asserts that catechesis is God's word revealed through Jesus and operative in the lives of people exercising their faith. Catechesis supports the mission of the church to proclaim and teach God's message, to celebrate the sacred mysteries and to serve God's people.[2] In this way the church establishes the reign of God on earth. The aim of catechesis is to nurture a mature faith in adults, who will in turn help nurture a growing faith in children. "The content of catechesis, then, is no more (but no less) than God's self revelation."[3]

THE FOUR SIGNS OF CATECHESIS

The catechesis referred to above is experienced through four signs of God's presence. God manifests the divine presence to humanity through signs. There are four signs of God's communication with humanity. God is present through natural, biblical, ecclesial, and liturgical signs.

I: Natural Signs

God, through Jesus Christ, is revealed in everyday life through natural signs. God resides and is revealed in the very substances of nature: creation, symbols, and our sensory world. God presides at the banquet of everyday life! God communicates to us through our own experience of life: through science, technology, and the arts, through all that is human and all that supports or enhances human life. Our first awareness of God comes to us through *natural signs.*

---

[1]John Paul II, *Catechesi tradendae,* #43.

[2]*Sharing the Light of Faith, National Catechetical Directory for Catholics of the United States* (NCD), USCC, 1979, #30.

[3]*Sharing the Light of Faith, An Official Commentary* (Washington: USCC/NCCB, 1981), 19.

The elements of life such as water, light, fire, bread, and oil reveal and point to God. For example, we know that water is necessary for life. We cannot survive without it. God created this life-sustaining element. Through the natural properties of water we are reminded that God is necessary for life. Humanity depends on the benevolence of God.

God is revealed through the gift of science. God is encountered through the intervention of medical science and the healing arts. Believers recognize God's presence in the fields of science and technology. We are called to use the insights of secular sciences and appropriate them into catechetics. For example, catechetics is in great debt to the human secular sciences for a contemporary understanding of adult faith development, stages of faith, and childhood spirituality and faith development.[4]

This resource celebrates the God of everyday life. *Word & Worship Workbook* hopes to assist people to recognize God's presence in the natural order by providing questions that probe the awareness of God in the normal routine of life and its environment. At the heart of the natural sign is the realization that Christ is present in all things and throughout all creation. The task of catechesis is to help people become aware of his presence.

II: Biblical Signs

God, in Jesus Christ, through the Spirit, is revealed through *biblical signs.* Through the proclamation of God's word in worship and through the study of sacred scripture we are able to more fully live the Christian message. The gospel is the "principal witness of the life and teachings of Jesus."[5] Thus, in the course of one complete liturgical cycle, Christ of the gospels is encountered in the liturgical proclamation of the word. "By means of the yearly cycle the Church celebrates the whole mystery of Christ, from his incarnation until the day of Pentecost and the expectation of his coming again."[6] Christ is present to us through *biblical signs* when we proclaim, listen, study, and live the sacred word.

First and foremost, scripture is experienced as the sacramental presence of God alive in the proclamation of the word. Every time the word is proclaimed in liturgy, Christ is truly present.[7] Scripture is the story of people in covenant relationship with their God. The task of Christians is to connect the story of their everyday lives with the story of Christ in the scriptures. There are a few basic, high priority themes that are woven through the Hebrew scriptures (Old Testament) and the New Testament. These biblical themes show us how God has been present and attentive to the work of salvation throughout all of human history. They give us a glimpse of how God views his relationship with us and how we, in turn, are to view our relationship with God. These basic themes are Creation, Covenant, Exodus, and People of God (community). These recurring themes emphasize the manner in which God has been present to us. They are standard themes that occur in both testaments.

Biblical Themes

a. Creation

God's power and divinity are witnessed through the things God has made, through *creation.* "Ever since the creation of the world, his invisible attributes of eternal power and divinity have been able to be understood and perceived in what he has made" (Rom 1:20). One need only gaze through the window of a 747 jetliner to be awesomely jolted by the explosive, generative, and creative power of the Almighty. Conversely, a quiet repose while watching bugs making trails on the shimmering waves of a gurgling brook serves as a peaceful reminder of God's order, symmetry, and artistry in the creation of nature's intricate designs.

During the Easter Vigil the story of creation is told to remind us that the Easter event, the paschal mystery, was part of God's plan from the beginning. What God accomplished through Jesus began with the creation of the world. Creation was not a one-time event; it is not static, but

[4]Linda Gaupin, "Special Certification in Sacramental Catechesis," class session I, Diocese of Orlando, Florida, October 23, 1996.

[5]NCD, #60a; I.

[6]*GNLY,* #17.

[7]Gaupin, "Special Certification in Sacramental Catechesis."

exists on a continuum. It continues through history. God's creative power continues in the process of transformation. God's evolving work of creation continues in the presence of the risen Christ in the church today in the lives of men and women. All creation groans in grateful praise of the Creator.

b. Covenant

The theme of *covenant* began with the promise made to Abraham, continued on with Moses, and was fully revealed in the life and person of Jesus Christ. God is in covenant relationship with us today. It is the same covenant that began with Abraham, was fulfilled in Jesus, and continues to be lived by people of faith throughout the ages. *God promises to be with us.* That covenant relationship is experienced each day as people of faith live in the risen presence of Jesus. One need look no further than the sick bed of a dying child to find a mother sustained by the presence of her living God.

The covenant made with Abraham and Moses and fulfilled through Jesus continues today as people live in radical, reciprocal relationship with the living God. This relationship is ratified and renewed as people live in biblical justice. Biblical justice demands that one love the Lord God with one's whole heart, soul, and entire being and extend that same love to others and to self. Thus, people are to be treated as God would treat them: as children of God who deserve the highest dignity. To be in covenant with God means that the disciple has a duty to respect the dignity of all human persons. The poor, marginalized, oppressed, and powerless become the object of the disciple's care, concern, and love. Catechesis seeks to help people encounter the abiding presence of their covenant God and to instill in them zeal for a life of loving, apostolic service.

c. Exodus

The *exodus*, the premier symbol of God's saving love for the Hebrew people, ultimately reaches perfect fulfillment and profundity in the "passage from death to life accomplished by Christ's paschal mystery."[8] This sign so clearly defines the Christian life that nearly every catechetical encounter addresses the mystery it contains. The ultimate goal of catechesis is transformation. Exodus asks the question, "How have I/you/we been transformed, changed, brought from death to life, in the story we just shared?" Every Christian has an exodus, a passover story; it is the heart of conversion. Each Christian's exodus story constitutes participation in the cherished life, death, and resurrection of Jesus Christ, the paschal mystery.

d. People of God

Another important sign throughout the scriptures is the image of God in relationship to a "people." In the Hebrew scriptures the community was a tangible sign of God's presence. In the New Testament that same sign was transferred to the church, the people of God. By remembering this sign we are better able to move beyond an individualistic "Jesus and me" mentality and embrace the God of Inclusion who is in relationship to us as a "people." The first perspective in scripture's challenge is communal: How does this word challenge "us" as a community? What is the parish, diocesan, universal church's response in the civic, local, and national world? Are parishes responding to the culture as Christ would respond?

The people of God, the church, is in covenant relationship with God. The people of God, the church, is *one body* and is often called the sacrament of Christ. "As a divine reality inserted into human history, the Church is a kind of sacrament. Its unique relationship with Christ makes it both sign and instrument of God's unfathomable union with humanity and of the unity of human beings among themselves."[9] God is in intimate union with the church. Do our communities reveal the story of a people responding in faith to a God who is in relationship with and living within *them?* God's word is spoken first to a people. Every page of the Hebrew scriptures unveils God's self communication to *Israel.* Formation in the word of God assumes a communal relationship. The church is to respond to the world and the culture as a corporate body.

The biblical themes of creation, covenant, exodus, and community are like yeast is to bread.

[8] NCD, #43.

[9] Ibid., #63.

They are the leaven that allows the meaning of God's relationship with humanity to rise to fullness. Effective ministry of the word remembers and makes present the God of all creation and new life, the God of exodus who leads us out of slavery into that new life, and the God who invites the people of God into radical, reciprocal, covenant relationship.

III: Ecclesial Signs

Ecclesial signs usually are assumed to be the "content" of catechesis. Biblical signs help us encounter the presence of God in the proclamation of the word and remember and make present the saving works of God throughout salvation history. Ecclesial signs uncover the presence of God throughout the history of the church through its creed and through the way it lives its faith. Ecclesial signs get us in touch with the manner in which people lived the gospel message and celebrated their experience of God's revelation to the church. Over time, these people formulated their creed and the principles that would define behavior (tradition).

The Second Vatican Council's document on divine revelation, *Dei Verbum*, states:

> In His gracious goodness, God has seen to it that what He had revealed for the salvation of all nations would abide perpetually in its full integrity and be handed on to all generations.... This sacred tradition, therefore, and Sacred Scripture of both the Old and New Testament are like a mirror in which the pilgrim Church on earth looks at God, from whom she has received everything, until she is brought to see Him as He is, face to face (cf. 1 Jn. 3:2). ...Now what was handed on by the apostles includes everything which contributes to the holiness of life, and the increase of faith of the People of God; and so the Church, in her teaching, life, and worship, perpetuates and hands on to all generations all that she herself is, all that she believes.[10]

Catechesis continues what began with the apostles: handing down the tradition to present and future generations. That tradition encompasses the revelation of Jesus Christ as handed down through history, through faith, creed, worship, and way of life. Catechesis encompasses not only natural and biblical signs of God's presence, but also the witness of God in the life of the church in its creed, code, and cult.[11]

Ecclesial signs (tradition) are but one of four ways God is revealed to us. There is often a tendency to believe that to be a good practicing Catholic is to know all the "Catholic stuff" from treatises on the Trinity to the historical development and understanding of indulgences. Many well-intentioned parish catechumenates, for example, are more concerned with the *information* about Catholic beliefs and practices (ecclesial signs) than they are with *formation* in the Christian/Catholic experience (all four signs). There is an assumption that *knowing* the Catholic information will automatically make good disciples. While not wishing to minimize the necessity of passing on Catholic teaching in its entirety, catechesis is the work of an entire lifetime. How many average Catholics know "all Catholic teaching in its entirety?"

The *Rite of Christian Initiation of Adults* states that there must be a "suitable catechesis, accommodated to the liturgical year...."[12] Too often that has been translated, "every jot and title of Catholicity." The question should not be, "Do they know everything?" Rather, the questions should be, "Have they encountered Christ in word, worship, and sacrament? Have they encountered Christ in the life and mission of the church? How does post-biblical teaching (doctrine) impact the Christian life? Where is the challenge for the community, the individual?"

Foundational issues deserve the highest priority as they help move adults toward a mature, faith-filled Christian life. St. Augustine was once asked for a handbook of Christian doctrine. He complied by making his own handbook of basic beliefs. It includes an explanation of the creed, the Lord's Prayer, and the two great commandments—love of

[10] *Dei Verbum* #7, #8, in *DVII*.

[11] NCD, #45.

[12] *RCIA*, #75.

God and love of neighbor. Augustine asserted that "what we are to believe, what we are to hope for, and what we are to love, is the sum total of Christian doctrine."

The church recognizes that there is a hierarchy of truths around which other truths are rooted. There are many teachings that comprise the Catholic story. The focus of *Word & Worship Workbook* will be those foundational truths that form and flow from the core content of the Catholic/Christian experience. Both the *General Catechetical Directory* and the *National Catechetical Directory* name four basic truths that hold priority of place within the tradition and are the norm for catechesis. They are: "[1] the mystery of the Father, the Son and the Holy Spirit, Creator of all things; [2] the mystery of Jesus Christ, the incarnate Word, who was born of the Virgin Mary, and who suffered, died, and rose for our salvation; [3] the mystery of the Holy Spirit, who is present in the Church, sanctifying it and guiding it until the glorious coming of Christ, our Savior and Judge; and [4] the mystery of the Church, which is Christ's Mystical Body, in which the Virgin Mary holds the preeminent place."[13]

However, lest I give the impression that mature Catholics need not grow in the fullness of Catholic faith and life, I would suggest that we allow Richard McBrien's distinction between catechesis and theology to give us serious food for thought as we approach our various ministries of the word.

> A doctrine is an official teaching that derives from theology, not from direct inspiration of the Holy Spirit. Before the official Church can propose a statement of faith for the acceptance of its members, it must first think about and struggle with its possible meanings and with various possible expressions of meaning. That process of struggle to understand faith, leading to some official expression of faith, is called theology.... Theology, however, does not consist simply of a listing, explanation, and defense of doctrines. The theologian's task is not only explicative, but critical—critical even of doctrines, or at least of a doctrine's language and conceptual framework so that the doctrine's truth can become accessible anew in a fresh formulation....
>
> Theology is not catechesis. Catechesis is, literally, an "echoing" of the faith. Unlike theology, catechesis is for the potential member (known as the catechumen) or for a newly initiated member of the Church (whether a young child or an adult convert). Catechesis teaches the faith by highlighting and explaining the main elements of the faith-tradition and their relationships, as well as their personal and pastoral implications.
>
> The catechist's task is not to invite potential or new members of the Church to think critically about their faith, but rather to understand and appropriate it in as clear and spiritually fruitful a way as possible. The theologian's task, by contrast, is critical. The mature member of the Church is invited to think critically, to question, even to challenge certain elements of the faith-tradition.[14]

Many good people in the church have not had the opportunities to know and grapple with the basic, core elements of our faith and the implication for living the Christian life. Catechesis must, then, be the starting point.

Located in the Doctrinal Appendix of this workbook is a list of the priority tenets of faith that *flow from* the hierarchy of truths and that are experienced in the liturgical cycle. Included with each post-biblical teaching are reflection questions that help connect ecclesial signs (tradition) and everyday life. Like biblical, natural, and liturgical signs, ecclesial signs intrinsically require a response. Such signs pave the way and point out the path toward bringing about God's reign on earth. This reign proclaims the Good News and demands liberty for those still held captive to oppression's grip.

---

[13]NCD, #47.

[14]Richard P. McBrien, "On What Theology Is and Is Not," excerpted in *America*, June 8, 1996, pp. 14–15. [Excerpts reprinted with permission from *The Tidings* (Southern California's Catholic weekly) of April 12 and 26, 1996.]

IV: Liturgical Signs

God, through Jesus Christ, is revealed and encountered in the celebration of liturgy, the liturgical year, and the sacramental rites of the church. God, through Jesus Christ, is manifest through the church (ecclesial signs) by the way she appropriates her theology, formulates her creed, and lives her mission in the world.[15] Liturgical signs have their home in ecclesial signs, just as ecclesial signs reside within liturgical signs. All four signs are not independent of each other, though they are distinct. Liturgy, through ritual, symbols, and gestures, celebrates, remembers, and manifests God in the natural elements of life: fire, light, water, oil, bread, and wine. Liturgy celebrates, remembers, and makes present the signs of God in scripture. It is a living, ongoing testimony to the scriptural themes of creation, covenant, exodus, and community. Every time the church gathers for eucharist, those themes embody the language of God's continued relationship to the church. Liturgy proclaims the core creed of Christian faith. The church prays and from her prayer flows her belief: *lex orandi, lex credendi.* The creed is a living testimony to the faith and life of men and women of all generations, past, present, and future, the *communion of saints.* Liturgy, then, sends forth the church with a mission to live that faith, life, and creed for the transformation of the world.

One precious contribution of the Second Vatican Council was to describe liturgy as "the source and summit toward which the activity of the Church is directed and the font from which her power flows."[16] If the aim of catechesis is to reveal Jesus Christ, the gospel that is proclaimed in the liturgy is the "principal witness of the life and teachings of Jesus."[17] Jesus is truly present in proclamation of sacred scripture and in the eucharist, in the elements of bread and wine, transformed to body and blood, as well as in the celebrating assembly. Catechesis prepares the community to celebrate and ritualize partnership with Jesus in the paschal mystery (his life, death, and resurrection) and to be sent as a sign into the world.

[15]NCD, #41–46.

[16]*Constitution on the Sacred Liturgy (CSL),* #10, in *DVII.*

[17]NCD, #60.

Catechesis is intrinsically connected to liturgical and sacramental activity. In the Apostolic Exhortation, *Catechesi tradendae* (#23), Pope John Paul II asserts that Christ works for the transformation of humanity in the sacraments, especially the eucharist. Catechesis has the power to change and originates in the liturgy. Liturgical catechesis has as its aim initiating people into the mystery of Christ. Catechesis helps the community reflect on the meaning and implication of the liturgy and sacraments. The purpose of catechesis is to assist believers so that their faith can "become living, conscious and active, through the light of instruction."[18]

God is present in the church as it gathers for prayer. The task of the church, then, is to reflect upon the deeper meaning of the experience of the risen Christ in the liturgy and the sacraments and to make appropriate life connections. Liturgy is the privileged environment for catechesis. It is where the people of God gather to encounter the biblical, ecclesial, and liturgical signs of God's presence during the liturgical year. From that encounter flow action and the mandate to go, do, and be what was just celebrated.

Liturgical Catechesis

The type of catechesis explored in this workbook is often referred to as liturgical catechesis. Liturgical catechesis uses as its source the liturgy, the sacramental rites of the church, and the church year.[19] Liturgical prayer is the church's official, public prayer celebrated in the midst of community. It is the way we are "church." The *Constitution on the Sacred Liturgy* states that "Liturgical services are not private functions, but are celebrations belonging to the Church" (#26). Through liturgy we celebrate the seasons of the church year and we ritualize the significant transition moments in the lives of individuals and the community (baptisms, funerals, weddings, etc.).

While liturgical catechesis admittedly does not give a syllabus for doctrinal curriculum, it seeks to reveal and uncover the basic truths of our faith inherent in the celebration of the liturgy. "Although the liturgy is above all things the worship

[18]NCD, #5.

[19]NCD, #44.

of divine majesty, it likewise contains rich instruction for the faithful."[20] As the church prays the scriptures and ritual prayers in the context of the liturgical year, as she shares eucharist and is sent forth, she internalizes, professes, and celebrates her creed about God, Jesus, and Spirit, the profound mystery of the church, and Mary's preeminent role.

The church at prayer ritualizes, lives, and celebrates the life and mission of Jesus. Liturgical prayer teaches us what it means to be Christian, Catholic, and disciples. Liturgical catechesis helps us articulate and enflesh it for our lives.

The Second Vatican Council's vision was for all people to be instructed and prepared for full participation in the church's liturgy. Since one of the principal signs of catechesis is liturgy, the church holds that catechesis begins with liturgical prayer and flows from it. "While every liturgical celebration has educative and formative value, liturgy should not be treated as subservient to catechesis."[21] There is a complementarity between liturgy and catechesis. Catechesis serves the liturgy and prepares people for full and engaging participation in it. Liturgy, on the other hand, provides rich food for the substance and basis of catechesis.

Every catechetical endeavor of the church must have liturgy as its anchor. The weekly sessions contained in this workbook are centered in liturgy. Catechist preparation sessions and the sample catechetical session take place within a liturgy of the word format. The ritual prayers of the church and the readings from the Sunday liturgy are formally and ritually proclaimed.

Many think of liturgy only in terms of the Sunday experience, but our church enjoys a vast repertoire of liturgical prayers and blessings: eucharistic celebrations, liturgies of the word, liturgy of the hours, blessings,[22] the Rite of Christian Initiation of Adults, the Rite of Baptism for Children, the Order of Christian Funerals, sacramental rites such as penance, marriage, ordination, confirmation, anointing of the sick and viaticum. In the midst of such liturgy, the living, dying, and rising Christ is encountered. Liturgical catechesis gives us a language with which to express the encounter.

Liturgical catechesis encourages people to name their experience of liturgy and ritual, articulate an understanding of the experience, and then make appropriate, informed decisions to live the message and become agents of change in the world. Thus, liturgical prayer is transformative. Like bread and wine, liturgy seeks to change us into a new reality: vibrant life-giving disciples.

Thus, the catechesis within the pages of *Word & Worship Workbook* is situated in the liturgical cycle: the Sundays, seasons, solemnities, and feasts of the year. As liturgy is the source and summit of all we do, and since catechesis prepares people for full and active participation in and reflection on the experience of liturgy, conversation in this workbook always begins with the presence of Christ encountered in people's experience of liturgical worship. This experience is on two levels: the liturgical worship of the catechetical gathering and reflection on and preparation for the Sunday experience of liturgy—the place from which the church's power flows.

In summary, then, catechesis echoes the four ways God makes his presence known to humanity—through natural, biblical, ecclesial, and liturgical signs. Catechesis is not solely a cognitive rendering of the articles of faith. Catechesis initiates an encounter with the risen Christ of biblical history and helps express an understanding of that encounter. Catechesis shows how the Christ encounter is celebrated in ritual and how the church remains a perpetual institution of living faith expressed in precept, dogma, life, and mission.

---

[20] *CSL*, #33.

[21] NCD, #36.

[22] Between *The Book of Blessings* and the *Catholic Household Blessings and Prayers*, there is a blessing for nearly every circumstance in life.

3. Scripture

PART ONE: THE LECTIONARY

The Lectionary is the book that contains the chosen scriptural texts from the Old and New Testaments for proclamation in the liturgy throughout the liturgical cycle. The Lectionary begins with the readings from the three cycles of the First Sunday of Advent, continues through all the liturgical seasons, the Sundays of Ordinary Time, solemnities, weekdays, feasts, ritual and votive masses, and readings for masses for various needs and occasions. The Lectionary is the way Catholics encounter the bible, the living word of God, in their worship.

The liturgy by nature is biblical. The eucharistic liturgy is no exception. Most of the ritual prayers of the mass are inspired by biblical passages or images. "The Lord's Supper is an act of obedience to a biblical injunction (Lk 22:14c). From the opening sign of the cross (Mt 28:19) to the final dismissal (Ps 29:11b; Jdt 8:35), the participants are invited to live in the world of the Bible as one people with its people."[1]

The word of God is the heart of all liturgical gatherings. The mystery of Christ is unfolded during the liturgical year in the celebration of the church's sacraments and sacramentals. As each celebration is built upon the word of God "and sustained by it," every time the church gathers for liturgical prayer it "becomes a new event and enriches the word itself with new meaning and power."[2] In other words, Christ is sacramentally present to us in the proclamation of the biblical texts and continues to teach, form us, and provide new, life-changing insight into the living word of God.

The first and second (Old and New) Testaments are both proclaimed in order to demonstrate that there is continuity in God's plan of salvation begun with Israel and brought to completion through Jesus Christ.

We are to respond with assent and commit our lives to God's word in the person of Jesus experienced in the proclamation of the word and the celebration of the eucharist. The word brings us to the awareness of the paschal mystery of Christ we celebrate and make present in every celebration of the eucharist.

The Cycles

There are three liturgical cycles: A, B and C. Each new liturgical cycle begins on the first Sunday of Advent each year and lasts for one complete year. The three cycles make it possible for the fullness of the biblical texts to be proclaimed in the assembly over a three-year period. Each cycle's primary vehicle for encountering the mystery of Christ is one of the synoptic gospels: Matthew (A), Mark (B), Luke (C).[3] The gospel of John is interspersed in each cycle. At the beginning of the liturgical cycle the readings are concerned with the inauguration of Christ's manifestation and the beginning of his ministry. The end of the year focuses on chapters leading up to the passion.

How and Why the Readings Were Chosen

The biblical texts chosen for use at liturgy are intended to proclaim God's word so that the faithful may grow in the faith they profess. The history of salvation is broken open, especially during the seasons of Easter, Lent, and Advent, but also throughout the entire liturgical year. The readings correspond to the purpose and focus of the liturgical seasons and the principles of scriptural interpretation.

The Sundays and solemnities contain the most important biblical passages so that the faithful may experience God's revealed Word and plan of salvation over a reasonable period of time. The week-

---

[1] Gerard S. Sloyan, "Overview of the Lectionary for Mass: Introduction," in *TLD,* 118.

[2] "Lectionary for Mass: Introduction," Chapter 1, #3, in *TLD,* 127–128.

[3] Refer to chapter 9 on this year's liturgical cycle.

day readings contain a second series of readings that complement but are independent of the Sunday readings. "The Order of Readings for Sunday and the solemnities of the Lord extends over three years; for weekdays, over two. Thus, each runs its course independently."[4]

In addition, there are other sets of readings that follow their own set of rules depending upon their use, such as readings for celebrations of the saints, ritual masses, masses for various needs and occasions, votive masses, or masses for the dead.

Structure of Readings for Sundays, Seasons, and Solemnities

Each Sunday mass has three readings. The first reading is generally taken from the Hebrew scriptures (Old Testament). The second reading is from one of the apostles (either a letter or the book of Revelation, depending on the season), and the third reading is from the gospel. The responsorial psalm is a chant response following the first reading. It is from the psalter and usually is directly related to the first reading. However, there is allowance for the use of psalms common to a particular season, feast, or celebration. The psalm is generally sung, as the psalms were written as songs and best fit that mode of expression. The gospel acclamation (the Alleluia or the Lenten acclamation) is "a shout of joy which arises from the whole assembly as a forceful assent to God's Word and Action."[5] It is an acclamation of praise in preparation for the proclamation of the gospel.

There is a continuity between the Old and New Testaments that is best demonstrated when the first reading is directly related to the readings and the liturgy of the day, particularly the gospel. The Old Testament texts were chosen with that perspective in mind.

The order of proclamation is: first reading (Old Testament), responsorial psalm, second reading (from apostolic letters or Revelation), gospel acclamation, gospel.

There is also a unity and harmony evident in the readings chosen for liturgical seasons. The seasonal readings reflect the meaning of the seasons of Advent, Christmas, Lent, and Easter, which have their own distinctive character.

The Readings for the Seasons of the Year

Advent Season
The gospels for the Sundays of Advent are concerned with the theme of Jesus' coming at the end of time and preparation for his birth at Christmas. The Old Testament readings are prophecies about the future messiah and messianic age. The apostolic letters are exhortations and proclamations that center around the themes of Advent. There are two series of readings for use during the weekdays of Advent. During the early weeks (first Sunday through Dec. 16) we hear from John the Baptist and extensively from the prophet Isaiah.The last weeks are concerned with events that immediately prepared for Jesus' birth (chapter 1 from Luke and Matthew).

Christmas Season
The readings of Christmas reflect important themes in the Christian tradition. On the feast of the Holy Family the readings are about the childhood of Jesus and the virtues of family life. The readings for the octave of Christmas, the solemnity of Mary, Mother of God, are about the Virgin Mother of God and the giving of the holy Name of Jesus. The readings for the Second Sunday after Christmas profess our belief in the Incarnation; the Epiphany readings are about the calling of all people to salvation. The texts for the feast of the Lord's baptism reflect the mystery of that event. The weekday readings center around themes of the Lord's manifestation.

Lenten Season
The first and second Sundays recount the Lord's temptation in the desert and the transfiguration. The third, fourth, and fifth weeks in Cycle A tell the story of the Samaritan woman, the man born blind, and the raising of Lazarus from the dead. These gospels may be used in place of the readings of Cycle B and C every year, as they are especially important to the Christian initiation process.

Passion (Palm) Sunday's gospel preceding the procession is a passage from the synoptic gospels that relates the story of Jesus' triumphant entry

[4]"Lectionary for Mass: Introduction," #65, in *TLD*, 140.
[5]"Music in Catholic Worship," #53, in *TLD*, 286.

into Jerusalem. An account of the Lord's passion from one of the synoptics is read during the mass.

During Lent, the first readings are about the main aspects of our salvation history from the beginning up until the new covenant in Christ. The apostolic letters were chosen to reflect the first reading and the gospel.

The weekday readings from the Old Testament and gospel readings are related to each other. Readings that highlight proper Lenten spirituality and catechesis are used throughout the season during the week. The early days of Holy Week center around the mystery of the passion; the chrism mass celebrates Jesus' messianic mission and its continuation in the church by means of the sacraments.

Easter Triduum
Holy Thursday recounts the story of the last supper and its implication in the washing of the disciples' feet as well as Paul's telling of the institution of the eucharist, the new Passover in Christ. Good Friday always proclaims the passion event from John's perspective. Jesus as the prophesied suffering servant of Isaiah is the high priest who offered himself in sacrifice for all. The Easter Vigil's Old Testament readings (there are seven) tell the wondrous deeds of our salvation history beginning with the creation of the world. The resurrection story from one of the synoptic gospels and St. Paul's letter to the Romans about Christian baptism as the sacrament of Christ's resurrection are the two New Testament readings proclaimed at the Vigil.

Easter Sunday's gospel is from John and is about the finding of the empty tomb. However, we are allowed to use the gospel from one of the synoptics. If there is an Easter Sunday evening mass, the story of the disciples on the road to Emmaus may be used. The apostolic letter is from Paul and is concerned with living the paschal mystery.

Easter Season
The gospels for the first three Sundays of the season center around post-resurrection appearances of Jesus. The fourth Sunday is about Jesus, the Good Shepherd, and the fifth, sixth, and seventh Sunday gospels are taken from the teaching, conversation, and prayer of Jesus at the last supper. Throughout the Easter season the Old Testament reading is replaced by passages from the Acts of the Apostles in which the life, witness, and growth of the early church are unfolded. The apostolic readings that best reflect the spirit, faith, hope, and joy of the Easter season are taken from: year A–1 Peter; year B–1 John; year C–Revelation. During the first week (octave) of Easter, Acts is read semi-continuously at the weekday liturgies. The weekday gospel recounts the appearance of the risen Christ. The rest of the season proclaims John's gospel of the last supper discourse, especially themes that emphasize the paschal mystery.

Solemnity of Ascension
The first reading is a proclamation of the Ascension of Christ as described in the Acts of the Apostles. The apostolic letters are about Christ who sits at the Father's right hand in glory and the gospel proclaims the Ascension event from the view of a particular year's synoptic gospel.

Solemnity of Pentecost
The vigil readings for Pentecost give us the choice of four possible readings from the Old Testament that best reflect the many dimensions of the mystery of Pentecost. The apostolic readings depict the Holy Spirit alive and working in the church and the gospel remembers Christ's promise to send the Spirit. Pentecost day has us immersed in the account of Pentecost taken from the Acts of the Apostles (first reading). The apostolic letter from Paul highlights the workings of the Spirit in the church and the gospel remembers Jesus' gift of the Spirit to the disciples on Easter night.

Ordinary Time
Ordinary Time is not really a liturgical season, but it is the thirty-three to thirty-four Sundays of the year in which the fullness of the paschal mystery is unfolded through the life and mission of Jesus proclaimed in the Sunday gospel. Thus, even though Easter is the "mother of all feasts" and the pinnacle of the liturgical year (the very axis upon which it spins), each Sunday is a remembrance and celebration of Easter. Every liturgical celebration is an Easter, paschal event.

During Ordinary Time there is no distinctive character to the readings. The arrangement of the apostolic readings and the gospel is semi-continuous, and, as stated before, the first reading is chosen for its connection to the gospel.

The Second Sunday of Ordinary Time centers on the manifestation of the Lord (which Epiphany also celebrates) with the story of the wedding feast of Cana. The Third Sunday begins a semi-continuous reading of the synoptic gospels in which Jesus' life, mission, and work are unfolded in their fullness according to the perspective of each gospel. The readings form a continuity with the liturgical cycle. For example, the beginning of the year is concerned with the beginning of Jesus' life and work and develops from there accordingly as his story is proclaimed and celebrated throughout the year. The end of the year moves us toward endings and last things. It centers around the ending of Jesus' earthly life and work and eschatological considerations.

Solemnities of the Lord During Ordinary Time
The feasts of Holy Trinity, Corpus Christi, and the Sacred Heart (some call them idea feasts, as they do not celebrate an event in Jesus' life) all have biblical texts that express the meaning particular to each celebration.

Weekdays of Ordinary Time
During weeks one through nine, the gospel of Mark is proclaimed at the weekday masses. Matthew is read from the tenth to the twenty-first week; Luke is read from the twenty-second to the thirty-fourth week. Mark is read in its entirety with the exception of two passages that are read during a different season. Matthew and Luke contain all the passages not included in Mark. The first readings of the weekday masses are continuous readings that are taken first from the Old Testament books, then from the New Testament books. The number of weeks depends on how long it takes to get through a particular book.

The Old Testament passages were selected to recount the overall story of our salvation history and to reflect the general character of the individual books. The only Old Testament books that do not appear in some form in the Lectionary in the weekday cycle are two small prophetic books, Obadiah and Zephaniah, Esther, Judith, and the poetic Song of Solomon. Esther and Judith are read on Sundays and weekdays at other times of the year, however.

The readings from apostolic letters were chosen in order that the basic intent, message, and teaching of each letter be presented. Keeping in the spirit of beginning and last things, the end of the year weekday readings are from Daniel and Revelation and reflect the eschatological nature of the end of the liturgical cycle.

Lectionary-based Catechesis

This phrase is used to describe a method of catechesis based on the word of God proclaimed at the Sunday liturgy. In practice it is sometimes reduced to a simplistic approach that listens to the word of God and appropriates personal meaning from the word, and then chooses a doctrine that best complements our personal understanding. Often, however, the doctrinal teaching has little to do with the spirit of the season, solemnity, feast, or Sunday of the year.

The church, however, has left us a marvelous tool for the ordering of catechesis: the Lectionary and the liturgical cycle. As one can see from the above descriptions of the readings chosen for use in liturgy through the seasons and Ordinary Time, the liturgy itself dictates what issues of doctrine emanate from our worship.

The liturgical year provides the vehicle for the ordering of doctrine through the selected biblical texts for a specific season, Sunday, solemnity, feast, sacrament, or celebration. The readings, liturgical prayers, and gestures and symbols reflect the meaning of the celebration and the doctrine that flows from it. For example, during the Christmas season, the readings express our belief in the Incarnation, the manifestation of God, Mary as Mother of God, and the salvation offered to all people. The liturgy suggests and sets forth the thematic content of our catechesis during the season of Christmas: Incarnation, soteriology (salvation), manifestation, Mary Mother of God.

It is evident from the description, structure, and ordering of readings throughout the liturgical cycle that the major tenets of the Christian faith are unfolded in the readings and liturgies of the liturgical year. The liturgy provides us with the basis of catechesis. The implication, then, is that catechists must become very familiar with what the liturgy truly expresses, rather than with what they think it appears to be saying, or what seems to be compatible with our personal (often fundamentalist) interpretation of the readings of a particular Sunday.

Thus, catechists need to be familiar with documents such as the Introduction to the Lectionary, General Norms for the Liturgical Year, and all liturgical documents that define and express what it is we celebrate. This is one reason why a resource such as this is an important tool. While it does not answer all questions, it does provide interpretation of the biblical texts and it proposes inherent meaning in the liturgical celebration itself. It is in no way a substitute for the primary documents that truly inform and provide the praxis and rationale for the practice of our worship, faith, and life.

PART TWO: THE INTERPRETATION OF SCRIPTURE

A word about the interpretation of scripture is in order at this juncture. *Word & Worship Workbook* is centered around the interpreted texts of the Lectionary scriptures. When I first entered the world of scriptural interpretation I had many questions. How can one scholar propose one interpretation, and another propose something altogether different? If these are respected scholars, who is right and who is wrong? Which interpretation is the most authentic? Do I really have the authority to present interpretations that are boldly new and unfamiliar to our common literal understanding of the texts?

Recently a man challenged me, "How is it possible that we could have heard a scripture in a certain way all our lives, and yet the discovery of the possible mistranslation of one word might change the entire meaning of a text? How can that be?" It is a valid question, one that I asked myself many times over in the early days. Hopefully, this chapter will answer some of those questions.

I make no claims to be a scripture scholar. In my role as catechist I have worked with scriptural exegesis in a parish setting for a long time and have used multiple resources and commentaries by various respected biblical scholars. As a compiler and redactor (editor), I have chosen exegeses according to a certain point of view. As a human person, I bring my own personality, beliefs, biases, and heart's desires to every reading of scripture. My first hearing of the scriptures is influenced by my limited perspective. Awareness of this limited perspective grew as the role of facilitating exegesis in our community was shared by members of a team. Each interpretation bore the personality traits of the facilitator who prepared it. The material might have been the same, but it was always nuanced from the perspective of the facilitator.

Bernard Lee maintains that we all enter every experience biased, "that is, with presuppositions, and rarely with much self consciousness about our ideological convictions. It is not wrong to have them. It is natural. It is disastrous not to know we have them."[6] Lee suggests that our safeguard is the Christian community as this is where discernment takes place. Thus, my effort to interpret the interpreters and to choose which interpretations to use comes with no official approbation. It is the result of one pastoral minister/liturgist's attempts to struggle with the insights of such interpretation in the midst of a faith-filled, life-giving Christian community. The efficacy of the redacted exegeses in this text will only be borne out (or not) in the midst of communities that seek to find God's compelling word in the midst of praying, studying, celebrating, and sharing the scriptures.

There is comfort in Jim Dunning's citation of Bernard Lee's[7] encouragement to ministers of the word:

> If we truly converse with scripture and allow the texts in their strangeness to interpret, change, challenge and call us to conversion, we need some guides to invite us

[6] *TFC*, 64–65.

[7] Bernard J. Lee, "Shared Homily: Conversation that Puts Communities at Risk," in *Alternative Futures for Worship, Volume 3: The Eucharist*, ed. Bernard J. Lee (Collegeville: The Liturgical Press, 1987), 157.

> into their world. Lee insists that the model for such guides is not the scholar who knows all the nuances of form criticism, redaction criticism, literary criticism and structural analysis but who cannot lead us toward any pastoral "so what's." We require, rather, a new kind of minister of the word and a new sense of community urgency to have someone prepared to help us converse with the word in our own world.[8]

This workbook's purpose is to assist people in the art of conversing with the word "in our own world." Such conversation leads to conversion that is at the heart of the liturgy and the scriptures.

Different models of biblical criticism (historical critical, literary, redaction, and others) are employed in some form or another throughout all the exegeses in this workbook. Different scholars employ different methods in their analyses. The vehicle used to travel the road of exegesis is far less important than the destination. What is important is the heart and soul of the text: "How have we/I been transformed as a result of our conversation with the scriptures?" To simply read the information within these pages without grappling with the interpretive questions in a communal setting of some sort is to miss the opportunity to allow the texts to overtake us. To reiterate this book's opening hope, "We miss the chance to be knocked breathless by the holy violence of conversion that will leave us drenched and exhausted as though swallowed by the sea and spat back newly salted upon the shore"[9] never to be the same again. Interpretation allows the texts to interpret us, to tell us who we are: God's beloved and chosen people.

The type of agenda, interpretation, and reflection process used in this workbook is pastoral and theological and employs historical and literary criticism. It is pastoral as it deals with real issues from real people's lives in the midst of their everyday existence. It is theological as it seeks to answer the question: "Who is the God of Jesus and what is the meaning of human life lived in the Spirit?" Historical criticism allows us to listen with the ears and cultural experience of a first-century Palestinian in order to better illuminate the meaning for listeners of the twenty-first century. The historical critical method allows us to move beyond a fundamental or purely historical meaning of the texts. The historical critical method studies scripture in the context of the history, culture, customs, religious beliefs, and economy of the original community for which the word was written. This methodology recovers and discovers the past of the text in order to bring it into today. "Since the Bible points to the mystery of God and of the divine-human relationship, it makes claims not simply on its original audience but on subsequent generations."[10] We not only strive to understand biblical interpretation historically, but we also engage in a hermeneutic to translate or explain it for today. Scripture is not approached as an historical, literally interpreted representation of the events that took place and the people who were involved. Rather, it uncovers the heart and soul of the message, the reason and meaning for the retold event.

Through literary criticism, the nuances and translations of language, cultural idioms, past and present meanings, and literary devices are explored. Literary criticism helps us get inside the storyworld of the text to allow the drama to touch, impact, and transform us.[11]

Scriptural interpretation draws on the wisdom and lived experience of past Christian communities through the centuries of the church's existence. Such communities struggled to live the gospel as it was passed on to them. Because of the struggle, the church today is the beneficiary of a rich deposit of faith emanating from the scriptures. Biblical archaeology and study over the past forty years have contributed greatly to our understanding of the sacred text.

The doors to biblical scholarship were opened on September 30, 1943 by Pope Pius XII's encyclical, *Divino Afflante Spiritu* ("Inspired by the Holy Spirit"). The encyclical exhorted the church and biblical scholars to use the modern methods of in-

[8]*EGW,* 180.

[9]Refer to opening sentence of chapter 1: quote by Nathan Mitchell.

[10]*EGW,* 166.

[11]Ibid., 177.

terpretation that Protestant churches had already been using. The intent was to "describe the literal sense of the scriptures, i.e. 'what the writer intended to express.'"[12] Prior to this time, much of our understanding of scripture had been figurative and allegorical. The encyclical moved us beyond allegory to the story-world of the text. *Divino Afflante Spiritu* challenged exegetes to uncover what the scriptures meant to the original authors and hearers of the texts.

Raymond Brown reminds us that the Roman Catholic Church issued a pronouncement on the historical accuracy of the gospels. Citing the Pontifical Commission's Instruction on *The Historical Truth of the Gospels* issued in 1964, Brown tells us:

> Rome has insisted that one should speak of the Gospels as historical in the sense that the four accounts of the ministry of Jesus took their origin in words that Jesus spoke and deeds that he performed. Nevertheless, the pronouncement made clear that those words and deeds underwent considerable adaptation from the time of Jesus' ministry until the time when they were written down in the Gospels. For instance, there was a period of oral transmission wherein the apostles preached what Jesus had said and done; but they infused their accounts of Jesus with a post-resurrectional insight into his divinity—an insight they had not had when he was alive. Then in the commission to writing by the evangelists there was a further selection, synthesis and explication of the accounts that had come down from apostolic preaching with the result that the final Gospel narratives of the ministry are not necessarily literal accounts of what Jesus did and said.[13]

Brown cites the Roman document's position that the inherent truth of the story is not affected by the fact that the authors relate the words and actions of Christ in a different order and that they do not recount his sayings literally, but rather differently, while still preserving their sense.

[12]*HCEC,* 423.
[13]*ACC,* 2.

Brown also reminds us that most Catholics are not aware of this position of the church and are still uneasy when someone suggests that "a particular section dealing with Jesus' ministry is not literal history."[14] Contemporary students of the scriptures must keep in mind that "in the course of transmission from Jesus to the evangelists, all Gospel material has been colored by the faith and experience of the Church of the first century."[15]

Matthew, Mark, and Luke are called synoptic gospels. Their overall vision of Jesus is fairly similar. In the synoptic gospels Jesus is very busy establishing his reign and teaching his disciples what it means to live and work toward building that reign. Thus, there is little time or concern for proclaiming a theology about himself. John's Jesus, on the other hand, provides us with a refined christology. Each gospel was written from the vantage point of the community for which it was written. There was a significant difference in the way a story was told depending on the economic and class status of the listener. The stories were told with the community in mind, according to their needs and life situation. Since each evangelist was writing for his own community and from his own perspectives, each gospel is marked by the distinctive personality and specific agenda of its author.

It was once thought that Matthew was the earliest gospel. However, research has shown that Mark was the first evangelist, since his text appears in both Matthew and Luke. Matthew and Luke also share similar material that is not included in Mark. Thus, most scholars would agree that there must have been another source that was familiar to both Matthew and Luke. This lost reference is called *Quelle* (German for source) or "Q."

As the Hellenized, Greek speaking world became Christianized, the original biblical texts were translated into Greek. Translation from one language to another automatically involves interpretation. Jesus spoke Aramaic, not Greek. Every gospel was interpreted not only in a new language, but in a different cultural system and world view as well. By the time the Greek texts were compiled, Christian culture had already embraced Greek

[14]Ibid.
[15]Ibid., 3.

philosophical thought that colored the translations according to Greek constructs.

Very often there are no words that capture the complexity of meaning in the original language, so the translator opts for an approximation. Language is limited. Scholarship, study, and archaeological efforts have advanced the quest to unearth authentic interpretation of the ancient texts. Exegesis is not an exact science. Yet that need not shake our faith too greatly, as the synoptic gospels are not always consonant with one another either. In many instances they contradict each other. For example, Luke's Jesus dies on the cross with a sense of peaceful confidence (23:46; cf. 23:34, 43) whereas Mark's Jesus cries out in desolation (15:34ff.).

Each evangelist has his own perspective and all draw upon the corporate memory of their different communities. New Testament scholarship recognizes that "the Gospels themselves are not histories of Jesus but the record of how communities remembered Jesus and taught new generations what and how they remembered."[16]

All scriptural interpretation is biased in one way or another. There is no such thing as an uninterpreted fact. History, for example, is shaded according to the bias of the historian. I was once struck by a comment made by a school principal who said that she would not use the Encyclopaedia Britannica in her school as it colored the events of the American Revolution according to a British bias. It was an eye-opening moment for me. Of course, it made perfect sense. Historians would naturally portray the "facts" of their history from a biased viewpoint. Facts, no matter how certain they are, are interpreted through the lens of the messenger, scribe, or historian.

Most scholars agree that none of the evangelists were eyewitnesses to Jesus' life and ministry. They had to rely on an oral account (a previous tradition) of his life. Raymond Brown asserts that the gospels developed over a long period of time and were based on the memory and tradition of communities that lived and celebrated Jesus' words and deeds. "Apostolic faith and preaching has reshaped those memories, as has also the individual viewpoint of each evangelist who selected, synthesized and explicated the traditions that came down to him."[17] The implication for our understanding of the gospels is that each evangelist gives us a multi-faceted prism's view of the God/man called Jesus. Brown suggests that we should not be disconcerted when we read the contrasting views of Jesus in the gospels. Nor should we attempt to decide which view is the most correct. Each view is given to us "by the inspiring Spirit, and no one of them exhausts the meaning of Jesus. It is as if one walks around a large diamond to look at it from three different angles. A true picture of the whole emerges only because the viewpoints are different."[18]

What does all this mean for the average minister of the word in a parish? An effective minister of the word is armed not only with a personal understanding of scripture, but also with "the work of biblical scholars... [who] provide historical and literary insights which help uncover the meaning of the sacred texts."[19] When reflecting upon the scriptures people often focus on an affective, "warm fuzzy," personalist/literalist/fundamentalist hearing and understanding. "This is what it must mean because this is what it says," or "How did it make me *feel*?" There is nothing wrong with approaching the scriptures this way. It is the first way we are to approach the bible, as a hermeneutic of experience. It is beneficial insofar as it touches the person's lived experience (natural sign). However, sometimes this initial reaction becomes the final perspective and people unwittingly are left with a fundamentalist understanding of the text. "This is what it means because this is what it says and since it is in the bible it must be right." They are not challenged to move beyond their basic assumptions regarding the meanings of texts and the implications for Christian living. The opportunity to be challenged by the heart and soul of the text is often missed. The role of the minister of the word is to move people beyond this initial literal understanding to one that provides the foundation for a renewed praxis of Christian living.

[16] *TFC*, 38.

[17] *CCHW*, 68.

[18] Ibid., 71.

[19] *Sharing the Light of Faith, An Official Commentary*, 20.

For example, on the sixth Sunday of Ordinary time, Cycle C, we hear Luke's version of the beatitudes. "Blest are you poor; the reign of God is yours" (6:20). An exclusively personal hearing of this scripture might prompt someone who is not literally poor to identify with the poor of Luke. They might think, "Surely, this means all who are poor in any way, such as the lonely, the stressed, those who are poor in spirit. I certainly am in that category." While Matthew's gospel does indeed make this extension, Luke's does not. The person's identification with the poor and assigning of personal meaning to the text perhaps is due to a life situation such as stress, sorrow, or grief, etc. This identification is not only logical, but desirable. It helps the person encounter God's love and compassion.

However, exegesis on the text presents a challenge. After conversing with the interpretation of the passage, that same person, given the opportunity, is invited to move beyond self, to a world view that embraces the heart of Luke's gospel: radical concern for the poor and the marginalized. Raymond Brown suggests:

> Luke's poor are the real "have-nots" of this world; his hungry know the misery of an empty stomach; his unfortunate are weeping. And just so that we do not miss the realism of the beatitudes, Luke narrates a series of corresponding "woes," stark anathemas hurled against the rich and the content who do not know the meaning of need.[20]

After such reflection on Luke's beatitudes, the person's original understanding is challenged. A decision is in order. He or she must make a decision: Am I willing to have my original assumption and understanding challenged? Is it in harmony with the exegesis? If not, where is the difficulty? Transformation takes place through honest conversation with the interpretation. Concern for self moves to concern for others, in this case, the poor and marginalized. Conversion moves us beyond the personal (me only) to the corporate and/or the global (us together). Herein lies the impetus for Christian apostolic action. Catechesis of this sort always asks the communal question: How is the community and how am I challenged by such a word?

There is one powerful bias in the gospels: the thread that weaves their intricate design. This bias, which permeates all of scripture, is a radical option for the oppressed, the poor, and those without power or use of the world's resources. One cannot ignore it or deny it. It is so blatant that one would have to fall over it, were it to be in one's path. A preferential option for the poor (in the words of the bishops) influences the way we are to hear the word of God. Love of God and love of neighbor demand that we be responsible for all members of the human family. For many, however, this bias is the biggest stumbling block in the scriptures. It is extremely counter-cultural and very politically incorrect. In an individualistic society such as ours, our creed often becomes, "Just pick yourself up by the bootstraps and take care of yourself." While such a platitude is grounded in the American work ethic, it ignores those factors that make it all but impossible for today's marginalized to even find their boots in the first place! To be Christian today means that we are to become bootmakers. Then and only then will the disenfranchised gain access to the world's possibilities. The decision ("so-what") questions, therefore, are critical to this process. When one is faced with having to commit to a transformed world view by the assent of one's actions, true metanoia is possible.

We are taught that the word of God proclaimed at liturgy is one of our primary symbols. What is the function of symbol? Symbols provide a language system between God and humanity. Symbols speak to us in ways that words cannot. Symbols convey many different layers of meaning. Water as symbol evokes images of life giving, thirst quenching, and death-dealing all at the same time. Some have called the Vietnam wall a national symbol. Imagine a war protester and a U. S. Army officer standing before that symbol. The wall no doubt speaks two different things to both men. One can only imagine. But a loud word it speaks!

A comparison between sign and symbol helps us understand the complexities of the word of God as symbol. A sign is uni-dimensional. It points to

[20] *BAL*, 336.

one reality. A stop sign has one literal meaning: STOP. There is no other way to read STOP. One had better heed the sign. It means what it expresses. There are no ambiguities regarding the meaning of sign. A symbol, on the other hand, is complex, ambiguous, and powerfully enriches our lives. Symbols do not mean the same thing to every person who encounters them. Symbols touch the inner recesses of our being. They provide a vehicle for divine communication. A woman whose husband had just committed suicide was particularly moved by the symbol of breaking bread at her husband's funeral. She fully understood the meaning of one of the liturgy's primary symbols as if she had encountered it for the first time. The breaking bread recalled Christ's broken body. That day, the torn bread recalled her broken body as well. The symbol of breaking bread communicated a new truth to her. God spoke thunderous words through that symbol. Christ would have died on the cross even if she, in her unbearable grief, had been the only person in the world.

The linguistic symbol world of the gospel touches us on many different levels. How it touches us depends on the events of our lives. The story of Jesus healing the widow's son is going to speak something entirely different to a woman who has just lost her teenage son than it will to someone whose life experience is altogether different. Symbols never get exhausted of possible meanings.

The word *love* is a linguistic symbol. Its meaning will never be exhausted. We celebrate eucharist over and over because we have not experienced all there is to experience in the eucharist. What speaks to us today may not speak to us tomorrow. The word of God is living word. We are living people. Living things are fluid. Through the will of the Spirit, we move, change, and await new possibilities at the horizon of each new day. Symbols evolve. So do we. Consequently, we will never exhaust the symbol world of the scriptures. It is why we can return to Matthew, three cycles later, and hear a word in a way that we never heard it before.

Sunday to Sunday and celebration to celebration, we encounter the sacramental, risen presence of Christ. How will we interpret the experience for our lives? Ancient wisdom assumed that Christians would engage in mystagogical reflection that would give meaning to their lives. Liturgy leads us to reflection. From the experience of Christ present in word and sacrament we order our Christian life. Mystagogical reflection as it is envisioned in this resource begins and begins again with the experience of Christ present in eucharistic liturgy; in the community of believers; in the church, *called and sent*; in the word, first experienced, then illuminated by informed scholarship and in the handed-down tradition of previous generations.

Catechists are charged with planting seeds. They are to plant the interpreted experience of liturgy, scripture, and tradition. God, the Creator/Harvester, then, will water, fertilize, and bring to fullness of life those who seek authentic worship and life in Spirit and in truth.

4. The Catechist

Many unsuspecting persons find themselves in the role of catechist quite by accident. We have all heard the whimsical story of the person who comes to the church office to buy a mass card and is asked to be the Director of Religious Education. While this story is more myth and mirth than fact (we hope!), there are still many eager ministers who have not had the opportunity to pursue advanced instruction to prepare for catechetical ministry. In order to "re-echo" the person of Christ encountered in everyday life, in scripture, in the faith and belief of the church, and in liturgical celebrations, catechists need hearts that are on fire with the love of God and the desire to share that love with others.

However, more is needed. Catechists must be familiar with the authentic Christian/Catholic story: scripture and tradition. Formal instruction is important. Many, if not most diocesan offices provide good catechist training. Most people who will use this resource are probably familiar with the principles of catechesis articulated in previous chapters. However, review is often an enlightening and renewing endeavor.

Catechists should be confident that the heritage they are "handing down" is truly the official understanding of the church's tradition. Many folks make assumptions regarding church teaching, when in fact their assumptions are incorrect. For example, the church has no official position regarding recent Marian apparitions. While making no judgment one way or another regarding the authenticity of such apparitions, it is not necessary for a Catholic to consider them a part of the deposit of faith. To teach such apparitions as fact and precept would be grossly incorrect. It is one thing to share a personal and private experience of faith enrichment; it is quite another for a minister of the church to pass it on as divinely inspired revelation. Such apparitions come under the heading of private revelation and do not constitute "...all that the Catholic Church believes, teaches, and proclaims to be revealed by God."[1]

[1] *RCIA*, #491, #585.

Also, while there is certainly disagreement and tension regarding the use of "male" centered God language, the church teaches that God transcends the human limitations of male and female. If one were to insist that the church teach that God is male, that person would be wrong.

Therefore, it is always wise to check with primary sources to either affirm or challenge one's understanding of church teaching. It is always good to seek out and refer to sources such as the Vatican II documents, the *General Catechetical Directory,* the *National Catechetical Directory, Sharing the Light of Faith,* and its companion, *Sharing the Light of Faith: An Official Commentary,*[2] the *Catechism of the Catholic Church,* and other catechetical documents, liturgical documents, encyclicals, apostolic exhortations, pastoral letters, canon law, etc. Secondary resources would include various works and commentaries of respected scholars and theologians.

Finally, catechists must be willing to enter into and immerse themselves in the conversion world of catechesis. It is a lifelong pursuit. The Christian life is not static. It is a life. To live is to grow. To grow means one has to learn. To learn means to live in a new way. "Catechesis is a lifelong process for the individual and a constant and concerted pastoral activity of the Christian community."[3]

Catechesis empowers men, women, and children and brings the light of faith to life. A noted atheist once mused that he might consider Christianity if

[2] The *National Catechetical Directory* (NCD), *Sharing the Light of Faith,* was formulated in response to the urging of the Sacred Congregation for the Clergy following formulation of the *General Catechetical Directory.* The GCD was prepared by that same Congregation after the Second Vatican Council called for a document that would provide the basic fundamentals of catechesis for the universal church. The intent of the Council was to assist Catholics in an informed and living faith. The bishop's conferences were urged to prepare national directories in order to apply the principles and guidelines of the *General Catechetical Directory.*

[3] NCD, #32.

he were to observe disciples truly living the message they allege to proclaim. It is a sad critique that he has not encountered such disciples (if, indeed, his observation constitutes more than a tongue in cheek commentary!)

The church's vision of catechesis seeks to create living, conscious, and active followers of Christ evidenced by the way they live their lives. Enormous gratitude goes to all faithful servants who strive to bring that life to birth in the people they serve. May your lives be richly blessed as you encounter Christ in this catechesis of transformation.

5. A Story of Transformative Catechesis

Credos often have little life of their own. It takes the power of the human person to bring them to life. Stories put flesh and bones on the catechesis we profess. The following vignette is a real, though composite story that takes place in the context of Christian initiation. It is a story that is or should be repeated in the lives of all Catholics who walk the ongoing journey of faith.

Her name was Rita. She was preparing for the sacraments of initiation. Rita's preparation, her "suitable catechesis"[1] consisted in helping her strengthen the relationship she was developing with God by sharing common stories and experiences of Jesus' presence. She reflected upon the life of Jesus found in the Lectionary scriptures and the church's understanding of those scriptures. There were also stories of Christians and saints throughout the ages who tried to live the message of Jesus in their daily lives, some by offering their lives for others.

Folks shared with Rita how, in their struggle to live a gospel life, those earlier Christians wisely formulated and handed down the beliefs and practices that helped conform them to the life of Christ. Christians from the very beginning gathered to celebrate their common faith in Jesus and to be strengthened and nourished for mission in their world. Early Christians had inherited a tradition from their ancestors, the Hebrew people. To be in right relationship (*hesed*) with the God of Abraham and Moses assumed an action, a response. This response involved inclusive care and concern for the poor, widows and orphans, outcasts, and the marginalized.

Jesus lived *hesed* in word and practice. It was the hallmark of his ministry and was to be the hallmark of the Christian life. While often falling short of the mark, Christians relied on Jesus' two great commandments: love of God and love of neighbor. They gathered together to worship and be strengthened to go out and strengthen others. Rita was told how the same thing still happens today when the community gathers for liturgy. Rita understood what that meant. She, too, received similar strength in her encounter with Christ and his people in the celebration of the word each Sunday.

Over time Rita shared her experience of God. She had come to know that God was always a part of her life. She felt personally called into relationship with Jesus. This relationship brought her to the doors of the Catholic Church. Her faith was personal. The communal dimension frightened her, however, as it might ask more than she was willing to give.

Over time Rita's relationship with Jesus grew and her life began to change. Her angry, bitter edge began to melt away with the passing of each Sunday. The Christ of word and worship was impacting her life. She began to see areas and attitudes that were not in conformity with Jesus of the gospels. The Christ she encountered was reconciling and inclusive. The church she sought celebrated reconciliation and challenged one to conversion and transformation. The church was a vision and a source of biblical justice.

The social teaching of this church became Rita's proverbial thorn in the flesh, however. Jesus was far more inclusive of others than she was. Rita's new church insisted that *all* persons deserve to be treated with rightful, equal human dignity and respect. She wanted to change her inner disposition, but letting go was difficult. There was a cloud of darkness hanging over her. She tried to ignore it, but the gospel was persistent. Something was wrong. Denial is illusion's safety net. The "so-what" questions of each week began to haunt her. She responded to her new Christian life by working with needy mothers and their children. Yet, something was still wrong.

In the lenten season, those preparing for baptism—along with all the faithful—enter a period of purification and renewal. During the ritual celebration of scrutiny, Rita became conscious of the barrier that still existed in her life. In the procla-

[1] *RCIA*, #75.

mation and preaching of the story about the man born blind, Rita became aware of her own "blindness from birth." It was a blindness that had its roots in her family system. Rita was raised in a climate of hate, prejudice, and racial bigotry. This hatred was normative behavior for her and her entire family. It was the "code and creed" she knew. The response of hate is to act hatefully, just as the response of love is to act lovingly. There had been responses of hate in her life. How could she reconcile such hatred? There was obviously no room for hatred in Jesus' reign. Jesus preached a gospel of reconciliation and inclusion.

Through catechesis that echoed Jesus' life to Rita, she was able to listen and respond to God's word. Scripture and tradition had been forming her. In spite of her environmentally conditioned hatred, Rita was captured by the inclusive God of scripture and a church struggling to live the gospel. She resolved to release the hatred.

After the Vigil's cleansing bath of baptism, the slathered, scented, and sealed anointing of the Spirit in confirmation, and the uniting, healing, and nourishing reception of Jesus in the eucharist, Rita was drained of emotion. She was well aware of her personal story of creation, covenant, exodus, and community experienced throughout her life's journey. Rita was not to remain in the safe haven of the Sunday table. She was sent forth to become the gift she had received.

The Vigil was not the end for Rita. Nor is any celebration of sacrament a port of arrival rather than departure. Rita realized a deeper reality. She was empowered for action in response to the Christ encountered in *word, eucharist,* and *community*. Her role was one of servanthood. Her mission was clear. She would do what she could to right the wrong that had been so much a part of the life she knew before. Christ had brought something to birth in her. Her exodus from death to life meant that she had to bury the seeds of hatred she had known. Rita's heart would permanently change through her decision to act. She resolved to become a voice for those she had once hated. Her most feared platform would be her family's own front porch. She was well aware of what it might cost. Yet she was willing. "Lord, help my unwillingness." A new joy crept into her life.

Rita's catechesis not only prepared her for full and vibrant celebration of the liturgy, but it also helped her realize that she was changed because of it. Rita could not wait to share her new life with the community that had nurtured her and assisted in God's creative work in her life. Rita unabashedly shared her passover story with the Sunday assembly during the Easter season. Rita had presided over the death of *hatred* at the Easter Vigil. In its place was resurrection of *love*: the new life of Christ's healing, sacramental joy. She thanked the community for nurturing her in her many months of formation. She credited God's word, the Catholic story, and her new family of friends for assisting in birthing her transformation.

The meaning Rita extracted from her experience was nothing less than a refined articulation of the church's foundational belief: the paschal mystery of Jesus Christ. Rita engaged in liturgical catechesis with the community. She recalled the threshold moments of the Easter Vigil. As she was immersed for the first time, gasping for air in the stirring waters, Rita experienced an interior cleansing. She waged her last battle with *hatred.* That old demon was being washed away while frantically holding on for one last breath of life. On the third plunge Rita thought of what it meant to die. "I came up the third time gasping for air." In those split seconds she sensed the fear of the Israelites sloshing through the watery wall toward an unknown land of promised freedom, leaving behind their despised, yet familiar life of bondage.

Water soaked and Spirit drenched, Rita exited the font aware that it was more than excess moisture dripping off her waterlogged robe. Her familiar, nasty companion was slithering back into the murky waters, never to surface again. She sensed new life. "If Jesus died for me and for everybody else, then I have to do the same. I have to let hatred die and I have to live for other people, just like Jesus did."

Rita's experience of baptism taught her more about the theology of baptism than any creedal statement could ever articulate. When the church teaches that baptism is the washing of sin, incorporation into the Body of Christ and the mission of discipleship, it is because generation after generation has experienced what Rita experienced.

Theology is not as lofty as it sometimes appears to be. It is simply a vehicle for the expression of faith.

Rita was catechized by the belief, story, and tradition of a people (both present and past) who share a common faith in Jesus Christ. She was further catechized by a rich, sensory ritual experience (liturgy) laden with meaning. With the entire church, Rita began the life-long process of experiencing celebration that leads to reflection that leads to meaning for life. The ancients called it mystagogical catechesis, uncovering the deep layers of mystery.

The *Rite of Christian Initiation of Adults* points out that catechesis for catechumens "enlightens faith, directs the heart toward God, fosters participation in the liturgy, inspires apostolic activity and nurtures a life completely in accord with the Spirit of God."[2] Rita experienced a suitable catechesis. Such catechesis should be the agenda of the entire Christian dispensation. It is not reserved only for those seeking entry into the church. Initiation is only the gateway, the beginning. Sacramental/liturgical/ritual catechesis is the conversion work of an entire lifetime.

[2] *RCIA*, #78.

6. Format for Catechist's Planning Session

Catechists participate in the following reflection process prior to the Sunday liturgy in order to prepare catechesis for their particular ministry group.

The weekly sessions in this book are intended to help prepare facilitators to lead a "Breaking Open the Word" session that begins with a liturgy of the word and is followed by an adult learning session that explores the word just celebrated. Refer to chapter 7, "Preparing the Catechetical Session," for assistance in crafting catechetical sessions after participating in the weekly sessions provided in this workbook.

The prayers provided in the weekly sessions are the ritual prayers from the Sacramentary for that particular Sunday or feast. The entrance antiphon, opening prayers, prayers over the gifts, preface, prayer after communion, and final blessings serve to reveal the meaning inherent in the liturgy and the scriptures. Thus, the prayers chosen for the weekly preparation session might be any one of the prayers from the liturgy of the day and are chosen for their connection to the liturgy's obvious themes. The closing prayer of the weekly session, you will discover, is not necessarily the closing prayer of the liturgy.

PREPARATION

Liturgical Prayer

The entrance antiphon, the opening prayer, the final prayer, and assorted blessings are taken from the liturgy of the coming Sunday or feast. Other ritual prayers are also included throughout the workbook as appropriate and are taken from the Roman Missal, the *Rite of Christian Initiation of Adults,* the Liturgy of the Hours, or approved books of blessing such as *The Book of Blessings* and *Catholic Household Blessings and Prayers.*

Environment

As the preparation session occurs in the context of a liturgy of the word, it is worthy of a prayerful space decorated with the symbols of the liturgical season. Suggestions and available directives regarding the liturgical space are given at the start of each new liturgical season to assist you in creating a prayerful place for your gathering.

Music

While musical selections are not suggested in this workbook, it is nevertheless important to begin each gathering with music that is familiar to all gathered. Simple refrains are easily mastered by even the most challenged singer. Music is important to the catechetical gathering as it serves a critical function in the celebration of liturgy.[1] The psalm refrain could be chanted on one tone and ended on a lower note than the central tone, much like the chanting of the presider/celebrant when he chants, "The Lord be with you," and all respond, "And also with you." The entrance antiphon could be chanted in the same manner.

LITURGY OF THE WORD

The readings are proclaimed in a brief liturgy of the word format with song, proclamation, and gesture (standing, sitting, sign of the cross, etc.).

Proclaim the Readings from the Lectionary

(Perhaps a copy of the text can be made available and given to each person *after* the proclamation.

[1]"Among the many signs and symbols used by the church to celebrate its faith, music is of preeminent importance. As sacred song unites to words, it forms a necessary or integral part of the solemn liturgy" (*Constitution on the Sacred Liturgy,* #112, in *TLD*). "The quality of joy and enthusiasm which music adds to community worship cannot be gained in any other way. It imparts a sense of unity to the congregation and sets the appropriate tone for a particular celebration. In addition to expressing texts, music can also unveil a dimension of meaning and feeling, a communication of ideas and intuitions which words alone cannot yield. This dimension is integral to human personality and to growth in faith. It cannot be ignored if the signs of worship are to speak to the whole person" ("Music in Catholic Worship," #23, #24, in *TLD*).

Some like to make notes on the text during the exegesis.

Step 1
Naming One's Experience

All share their initial impressions. All listen without agreeing or disagreeing. In this case, the hearing of scripture constitutes the experience. What are your initial impressions? What were the feelings, mood, words that captured your attention? How did the readings (particularly the gospel) affect you? Stay with your initial feelings. Do not try to explain or give a rationale at this point. This first exercise is an attempt to name your initial experience.

Step 2
Understanding the Experience

Why did the text touch you? Were there any experiences in your life that may have shaped the way you heard the story? What understanding of this gospel or readings do you already bring with you to this dialogue? What are your biases? What do you think the gospel readings are trying to convey? In your opinion, what does it mean?

Step 3
Input from Vision/Story/Tradition

The readings are interpreted in the context and from the vantage point of their original setting, culture, time, and hearers.

Liturgical Context

The facilitator gives *brief* input regarding the liturgical context of the readings. In a few sentences the facilitator explains why this reading occurs where it does in the liturgy in the present cycle. Most often the ritual prayers of the liturgy support the intent of the readings. Readings point to and focus the season, cycle, sacrament, feast, or theology.[2] The readings are interconnected with the liturgy and shed light on the celebration. Similarly, the liturgy being celebrated also helps focus the readings. The liturgy is not only the liturgy of the word. It is much more. There are four equal signs of God's presence in the liturgy: God's presence in the assembly, the word, the eucharist, and the presider/celebrant. The readings, therefore, and all the elements of liturgy are interdependent. To provide biblical interpretation without the liturgical context is to present a distorted view of the liturgy.

Gospel Exegesis

The facilitator provides the critical biblical scholarship, using the insights of various biblical scholars. The world of the text is penetrated by looking at its structure, context, and literary devices, as well as by deepening our understanding of the author's intent or the church's reasons for using the text. What was the text saying to the early Palestinian community? Why was it said? Who was the audience and what was the background?

We ask: What does critical biblical scholarship have to say about this text? How would people have heard it in Jesus' time? Sometimes the meaning of the text is crystal clear and obvious. However, very often help is needed to appreciate the story-world, biases, and agenda of the original teller and listeners of the stories.

Proclaim the gospel again.

Listening to the gospel following the presentation of biblical interpretation often allows the text to be heard with new ears. The exegesis is brought to bear on this second reading of the gospel and helps implant (or perhaps cast doubt on) the insights that were shared.

Step 4
Testing Original Assumptions

This conversation gets the meaning out in front. Testing helps make the connection between the

[2]In the Rite of Confirmation there is a list of scripture citations for use in the ritual celebration. All of the citations, taken together, shed light on the meaning of the sacrament, making it beneficial to include and use all of the readings in preparation for confirmation. The suggested readings are not simply for the purpose of choosing texts for the liturgical celebration. They help express the meaning as well.

original story and the listener's initial assumptions and understanding. It either strengthens or challenges first impressions. Initial impressions are contrasted with or related to the exegesis. A person may experience excitement, challenge, discomfort, surprise, disagreement, vulnerability, or affirmation. It is at this point that we test our earliest assumptions and prior understandings in order to allow the text to transform us. Sometimes it is very difficult to let go of our previous biases, particularly when they have been informed by a prior fundamentalist hearing of the scriptures. It is at this juncture in the process that the adult is gently led toward a new outlook. As said earlier, the stories of scripture are like a prism; they can be viewed from various perspectives depending on how the light hits the prism at a given moment. People are asked: Now that you've heard the biblical scholarship concerning this text, how do you feel about it? How does your original interpretation fit with the opinions of scholars? What was the message to the community then and now? How would you articulate an understanding of the readings now?

Step 5
Decision

After an in-depth dialogue with the scriptural exegesis, a decision is in order. We decide if our original understanding is adequate or if it is in need of transformation. If the latter is true, opportunity is given to articulate a new or renewed course of action, practice, and/or attitude for the future. Scripture and tradition demand a response. Discipleship demands action. We are called to and empowered for service by the word of God and by the mission of the church. *This step is critical.* Transformation is observable in the life one lives, in the attitudes one professes, and in one's work of service in the world. "The proof is in the pudding."[3]

If people are not given the chance to move beyond steps one and two (naming their experience and articulating an understanding of the experience), there is a tendency to unwittingly engage in their own form of scriptural or doctrinal fundamentalism.

Reflection, study, and dialogue of this sort demand a decision, even if the decision is not to decide. If one has difficulty or disagrees with a particular interpretation, then the decision is to disagree. The decision then becomes a conscious resolution to ignore or be unaffected by what was shared. This is not a value judgment. Again, there is nothing that states that every biblical interpretation must be accepted as fact. That is one reason why it is wise to consult multiple commentators.[4] One scholar may shed light on one piece of the puzzle, while another sheds light on a different piece. Scripture scholarship is a growing, evolving discipline and unfolds as advances in biblical scholarship and biblical archaeology continue.

People are asked: How does this biblical scholarship challenge our community's (church's, parish's, neighborhood's, world's) attitudes and apostolic works? In what practical way can our parish respond to this biblical challenge? How has this biblical scholarship changed or challenged my attitudes and apostolic action? In what practical way can we/I respond to this biblical challenge?

DOCTRINAL ISSUES

Following the scriptural and liturgical segment of the preparation session, participants engage in dialogue and conversation with an issue from tradition, a doctrinal issue. Participants begin by suggesting possible doctrinal themes that flow from the readings. Whether or not this exercise results in choosing the actual topic for discussion, it is a worthwhile exercise. It helps people realize that there are connections to be made between the

[3]While Christian life is not all action and no "being," one cannot ignore the gospel imperative to live the gospel we profess. As in all things, there is to be balance, however. Action is balanced with prayer. Also, action may simply mean living a life of love in our home environments or changing an attitude or perspective and having the courage to speak up for what we believe. Some people are definitely called to public, active, pavement-pounding ministry. Others are called to ministry in the home and the marketplace. We are all invited to take the gospel with us to inform our posture, our actions, and our attitudes wherever we practice our ministry.

[4]You will note that each week's exegesis in this workbook contains insights from a variety of respected biblical scholars.

liturgy and the basic truths of our faith. Often multiple themes surface. Some are listed at the end of each week's session.

There are two possible approaches to choosing a topic for discussion.

a) The facilitator invites participants to name and list possible doctrinal issues/themes. Participants choose an appropriate topic for their particular parish and ministry group. Once the topic is chosen, they consult primary sources (such as catechetical and liturgical documents and/or *The Catechism of the Catholic Church,* etc.) and/or read a doctrinal issue from the Doctrinal Appendix. All then respond to questions like the questions found in each topic of the Doctrinal Appendix. Or
b) A facilitator prepares and presents a specific doctrinal theme of his or her choosing.

Participants respond using the same five-step process described above.

The prepared doctrinal material should include the church's understanding of a particular doctrinal issue, including appropriate church documents, the perspective of the *Catechism of the Catholic Church,* expansion material by respected theologians, perhaps some background on historical context. The doctrinal segment is not "everything you ever wanted to know about a topic"; it is, rather, ***brief input*** on a particular post-biblical teaching, creed, or practice. Doctrine comes to us from the lived experience of past communities. Much of it comes to us from the scriptures; the rest comes to us from post-biblical generations[5] that struggled to live the gospel in the presence of the risen Christ, and as a result formulated their creed out of their experience and understanding.

The hierarchy of truths is proclaimed at liturgy every time the church gathers. Either the liturgy itself or the readings from scripture address the principal tenets of our faith.[6] From the church's prayer comes her rule of faith (*lex orandi, lex credendi).*

The Doctrinal Appendix provides *some* core doctrinal material. A resource of this size could not possibly address all doctrinal issues. *Word & Worship Workbook* is not intended to be a sole resource. However, by providing a sampling of core material, we hope that catechists will become familiar with the kinds of issues that need to be addressed, and that they will be able to use church documents in addressing any subjects not included in this workbook. The doctrinal material is presented in a reflection process format to facilitate dialogue with the material. The five-step reflection process (Naming, Understanding, Input, Testing, Decision) provides a framework for sharing. Following each doctrinal session there are instructions to return to the planning guide chapter that will assist you in preparing the catechetical session.

[5]Doctrine (tradition) is and has been formulated by the teaching authority of the church, the magisterium including the *sensus fidelium,* the sense of the faithful. The Second Vatican Council document, *Dogmatic Constitution on Divine Revelation (Dei Verbum)* asserts: "The tradition which comes from the apostles develops in the Church with the help of the Holy Spirit. For there is a growth in understanding of the realities and the words which have been handed down. This happens through the contemplation and the study made by believers who treasure these things in their heart (cf. Lk 2:19, 51), through the intimate understanding of spiritual things they experience, and through the preaching of those who have received through episcopal succession the sure gift of truth." *(Dei Verbum* #8, in *DVII.)*

[6]For further expansion on the topic of doctrine, refer to the Doctrinal Appendix. Also see the list of doctrinal issues that are encountered in the liturgical year.

7. PREPARING THE CATECHETICAL SESSION

At the end of each doctrinal teaching in the Doctrinal Appendix you will be instructed to refer to this chapter. This guide assists in planning an actual catechetical session. It provides general suggestions and ideas (painted with broad strokes) for crafting your session. It is in no way exhaustive, nor is it the *only way* to work with your group. It is merely the impetus and launching pad for using your own gifts of creativity as you work with your particular ministry group. This chapter is merely a suggested outline. Use as little or as much of it as suits your needs. Be sure that your planning considers the emotional, developmental, and age appropriate abilities of various groups within a ministerial setting.[1]

If your ministry is with adults, the same five-step reflection process is used: Naming, Understanding, Input, Testing, Decision.

THE LITURGY OF THE WORD

When a catechetical session for some reason does not follow directly upon the liturgy of the word at mass (if, for example, the catechumens are *not* dismissed following the liturgy of the word to break open the word), the session that meets during the following week should begin with a liturgy of the word as outlined on the right, followed by extended catechesis (see steps 1–8). It is not necessary to do all three readings. Perhaps the Old Testament reading, a psalm, and the gospel are all you will need to proclaim for that session. Or perhaps only the gospel is necessary. Adapt the outline to your particular needs for each specific session.[2]

[1]It would be beneficial for people in ministry to be familiar with the study of faith development in children and adults. Basic resources might be James Fowler's *Stages of Faith*, and *Becoming Adult, Becoming Christian* (Harper SanFrancisco).

[2]Please note that if the catechetical session follows directly upon the Sunday liturgy of the word, *there is no need to repeat a complete liturgy of the word.* The liturgy continues for them. Thus a brief centering prayer (perhaps taken from that day's liturgy), or psalm refrain and the proclamation or recall of the gospel are all that is necessary (refer to steps 1–8).

A MODEL LITURGY OF THE WORD

When gathering for a liturgy of the word, the following format is used or is adapted for your particular group. It is important to prepare a liturgical environment with appropriate symbols, music, and gestures.

Introductory Rites

Entrance Antiphon (sung) or

Psalm (sung) or

Appropriate Song

Entrance Procession
- Reader carries Lectionary or the Book of the Gospels.

Greeting
- Sign of the Cross

Opening Prayer
- The Opening Prayer from the Sunday or feast may be used.

Word of God

Reading (from Old Testament, Sunday or feast, or sacramental celebration)

Responsorial Psalm (always sung)

Reading (from apostolic letters of the Sunday, feast, or sacramental celebration)

Gospel Acclamation (always sung)

Gospel (from Sunday, feast, or sacramental celebration)

Homily

General Intercessions (adapted to occasion)

Lord's Prayer

Concluding Rites

Prayer/Blessing

Sign of Peace

Dismissal

FORMAT FOR CATECHETICAL SESSIONS WITH A MINISTRY GROUP

1. *Breaking Open the Word.* When catechumens are dismissed following the liturgy of the word to further reflect on the word of God in a different space, they begin the session with a brief centering prayer or psalm refrain. (RCIA # 81–101 suggests that the minor rites can be used to open or close a catechetical gathering.) The gospel is then proclaimed or recalled. Remember that their session is a continuation of the liturgy from which they were just dismissed. Their worship resumes.

   Cetechumenal groups (and/or other ministry groups such as small Christian communities) that meet during the week rather than following the liturgy of the word at the Sunday liturgy, celebrate the liturgy of the word (using last week's readings) as outlined above before they break open the scriptures.

   Participants then crack open the liturgy of the word. They name their experience of the gospel (there is generally not enough time to address all three readings) and articulate their understanding of it. *Brief* input is then provided regarding the liturgical context and the exegesis of the gospel.

2. *Testing the Scriptures.* The participants then enter into dialogue with their own experience and the exegesis. Participants name any new or renewed insights that may have resulted from their conversation.

3. *Catechumens Reconnect with Sponsors and Community.* In a catechetical setting it is at this point that the session stops and the group joins the community and their sponsors for hospitality (coffee and doughnuts) after mass. Sponsors then join the catechumens and candidates for extended catechesis. If the ministry group is not catechumenal, step 3 is obviously omitted.

4. *Extended Catechesis.* The church's tradition is presented. The catechist helps make the connection between the scriptures, the liturgy, and the doctrinal material that is presented: How does this particular doctrinal issue flow from the celebration of the liturgy? Elements of the four signs of catechesis—the person's personal experience (natural sign), possible scriptural connections (scriptural sign), the church's perspective, teaching and/or way of life (ecclesial sign), and the way in which the tradition is celebrated or reflected in the liturgy (liturgical sign), are included in the *brief* presentation.

5. *Testing the Tradition.* The group discusses the doctrinal issue, and tests it against their previous assumptions. They articulate any new or renewed insights or experiences of transformation that resulted from their sharing.

6. *Making the Appropriate Life Connections.* Participants share an experience from their lives. How do their new or renewed insights, their experience of the liturgy of the word, the scriptures, and tradition relate to an experience in their lives?

7. *Decision.* Participants articulate the implications of their sharing and what, if any, decisions for action, transformation, or commitment they are considering.

8. *Closing Prayer.* For catechumenal groups, the session might close with one of the minor rites: a blessing or exorcism. For other ministry groups, the session closes with any prayer form of their choosing: blessings, prayers from the liturgy, intercessions, etc.

CLARIFICATIONS

Scripture

Simplify the exegesis as much as possible. Be brief. The same or similar reflection questions used in your preparation session may be used, if they are appropriate for your specific group. Sessions take place *after* the experience of Sunday liturgy. Reflection takes place in light of the liturgical experience of the word. Remember to include insights and memories gleaned from the ritual experience of the community's liturgy, including symbols, homily, music, etc. Consider the questions you will use in light of the composition of your group. For example, you might not use the same language or questions for people in the catechumenate as you would for catechists or someone in a small Christian community. Avoid "churchy" language. Make no assumptions that people know what you are talking about. Remember that this is formation, not religious education.

Tradition

Present the doctrinal material in the same dialogical, formational fashion as scripture was presented. Allow people time to reflect, observe, and react. Allow them the opportunity to articulate the meaning for themselves. Provide accurate, informed input regarding the issue (church documents). Be careful to keep the input section brief, no more than ten minutes. It is not meant to be an exhaustive study of the church's theology. It is a sharing of the church's story in light of our own story and the implications for living the Christian life. The purpose of passing on the church's tradition is to help people live the life of faith encountered through God's presence in community, word, and eucharist and apply it to the Christian life. Doctrine often points the way. Make sure that *transformation* rather than *information* is a primary focus.[3]

Allow testing and discussion with the doctrinal input piece in order to challenge original assumptions and understanding of the issue. Encourage people to grapple with the "decision for action" questions. There is a common tendency to reduce challenge questions to ethereal mind-sets rather than praxis (practice informed by theory/theology). "What difference does this issue make in my life?" "In what way am I/we called to change due to the scriptural and doctrinal material we have shared today?"

[3]Please make no mistake in regard to my bias concerning transformation vs. information. Information is not bad; it is desirable and laudable. Catholics should be doctrinally literate. I am not only in favor of passing on information, I love teaching Catholic doctrine. However, in the past, most of our efforts were centered around imparting information while assuming the information would provide the impetus for transformation. Experience has taught me that most people encounter the living God before doctrine impacts them on any meaningful level. Thus, balance is imperative: transformation and information.

The Planning Session:
Things to remember as you plan your session.

1. Try to make connections with the previous week's liturgy. Where were we last week and where are we going today? What are the connections?

   Is there something that can be brought over into the sharing today? In a brief statement, how was your life different as a result of our sharing last week? Is there any unfinished business? Is there an overall thematic statement we can make as we move into this session?

2. Decide what direction to take in light of the sharing that took place in your preparation session.

   How does what we just shared [in our preparation session] specifically impact and affect the people in our ministry group? Is there a specific aspect of biblical scholarship that is more pertinent to their journey? Can all the material that we shared be covered? If so, how? If not, what are priority issues?

3. Decide what areas might be problematic.

   Are there issues we have discussed that will cause unnecessary tension and difficulty for the group? If so, how do we deal with that?

4. Decide what questions need to be asked in order to effectively and concretely move group members through the reflection process.

   What questions should we ask to help them move, as we did, from naming their initial impressions and understanding to allowing the scholarship to test their assumptions and biases in order to appropriate renewed meaning and praxis (practice informed by theology) for action? What challenge questions need to be asked? What are the implications for the community and for the individual?

5. Decide on the practical format and techniques.

   How should the material be presented? What is the format for the questions: write in journal, one-to-one sharing, wider group, small group sharing, etc? What equipment (e.g., flip chart, paper, pencils, markers, overhead projector, journals, bibles, etc.) is needed?

6. Decide on supplementary materials.

   Are there any supplementary materials that we would like to use such as Catholic Updates, bulletin inserts, articles, books, etc.?

7. Discuss current issues and events that might impact the group's sharing.

   What are the current, pertinent issues in the church, neighborhood, civic community, and world that might enter the conversation? (Never ignore a local crisis issue that is weighing heavily on the community. It impacts people's lives and so should be included in their dialogue with the gospel.)

   For example, the major employer in my parish is the Kennedy Space Center. It would have been an affront not to spend considerable time lamenting the Challenger explosion so many years ago. There was not a person in the parish who was not impacted in some way either directly (having worked on the Challenger) or indirectly. Liturgy, the gospel, and worship are connected to our everyday lives. That event impacted our community in untold ways for years as we lamented, prayed, and celebrated the resumption of the suspended shuttle program in our Sunday gatherings. While that is a dramatic example, be sure to pay attention to what is happening in the local civic community that will impact those in your ministry groups.

8. Determine what doctrinal issues might surface from within the group other than the issue being prepared.

   What issues of post-biblical teaching might surface in addition to, or other than, what we have prepared? Would we be ready to address those issues?

9. Remember to connect the doctrinal material to everyday life.

   How do we connect the post-biblical teaching (doctrine) to the lived experience of those in our ministry group? What are the appropriate questions to help them see the relevance for their lives?

10. Determine what types of prayers and/or blessings will be used.

    What prayer experiences are we going to incorporate: rituals, prayers, spontaneous prayer, prayers from *The Book of Blessings* or *Catholic Household Blessings and Prayers,* catechumenal minor rites such as blessings, exorcisms, and anointing? (The Minor Rites of the RCIA, #81–101, are normative closing and opening prayers for the catechumenate and should be used over and over as they, like liturgy, are formative.)

11. Invite (when appropriate and possible) other parishioners to share their stories and lives with the ministry group.

    Should others from the community be invited to share their story or experience with the ministry group? Who are they and why should they be present?

12. Invite the people to serve in apostolic ministry.

    In what ways are we encouraging and challenging the mission activities in the lives of people in our group? When did we last address those questions? Are we asking concrete questions that require a practical response?

13. Determine the foundational issue.

    Did we ask the bottom-line question: What are the "so what's" of this session? In what way does this experience of liturgy, scripture, and tradition challenge the community and the individual? What action will be taken?

14. Remember the ongoing issues.

    Did we remember to: a) include questions that center on the four signs of catechesis:

natural, biblical, liturgical, and ecclesial, and b) include questions that touch the basic themes of the scripture: covenant, creation, exodus, and community?

15. Determine necessary praxis for working with children.

    If our work is with children, have we chosen age and developmentally appropriate as well as sensory and concrete ways of passing on the message of what has just been shared?

16. Determine music and environment questions.

    What music will we use in our session? Where and when will we use it? Are books or song sheets to be used? How will we create a prayerful environment that will enhance and highlight the symbols of the season?

8. Time and the Liturgical Cycle

Sacred Time

God resides in the space of our temporal lives. Our daily lives are ordered by the sequence of time. It marks our coming and our going. Time determines when we will work, when we will play, and when we will pray. Time is sacred. Our lives as Catholic Christians are ordered by the sacred observance of time. Each day is holy. Each day, each hour, brings a renewed encounter with the Morning Star, the Dawn of Salvation, our Evening Light, the Prince of Peace. The hand of God at creation sanctified all created things, among them, the ordering of days and nights. God, the Master Artist, captured the fleeting moment and fixed it with other moments to form the hour. The hour was multiplied to fix the day, the day to form the week, the week to order the year. In order to understand the significance of our own liturgical calendar and what it expresses, it would be helpful to plumb the religious history of how our ancestors understood the division and ordering of time.

In the Hebrew scriptures time was regarded in a way that was far different from the way in which we regard it in modern times. There was no Hebrew word for *time* meaning duration. Time was seen as the "moment or period during which something happens."[1] Human life was a compilation of the events of time. "There is a time for everything under the sun; a time to be born and a time to die" (Eccl 3:13).

There were various perceptions of time: enduring time, appointed time, liturgical time, and measuring time. *Enduring time* was the measuring of time that formed a beginning and an ending, time that resembled eternity, an abstract sense of timelessness.[2] Current events were "perceived as stretching backward or forward or as continuing indefinitely, but this is not the same as eternity, as a life or event outside of time."[3] *Appointed time* was a reference term to identify a specific event, particularly the "prescribed feasts."[4] At the *appointed time* the assembly would gather for celebration of ritual feasts. *Measuring time* viewed the work of God at creation as that of ordering time into fixed hours, days, months, and years. God was the creator of time and sustained and ordained every facet of life. Time was the servant of God's purpose. Human beings were to use time for establishing God's shalom and justice as they ordered their lives and relationships in tune with God's will. The Israelites eventually moved toward an understanding of time as historical. Time was seen in relationship to the saving events of Yahweh.

The New Testament viewed time through the lens of Judaism. A day extended from sundown on one day to sundown the next. Thus, the Last Supper and the crucifixion took place on the same day. In first-century Palestine, time was measured in far less stressful terms than today. Time seemed to stand suspended in an extended *present.* There was no rush or anxiety about the future. The moment had its own concerns. Time in the New Testament was seen in terms of its eternal or everlasting quality (*aion*—the modern word "eon" comes from this Greek origin). Everlasting time had already begun for the Christian *in this life.* It began at the paschal event of Jesus. Even though the synoptic gospels looked at everlasting time as a future event, John referred to it as a present reality. For John, "eternal life begins now, as soon as one turns to Jesus in faith."[5]

Another concept of time in the New Testament is that which refers to a determined, specific, set time, "ordinary calendar time as a quantity" (Greek—*chronos*). Chronos time ruled the ancients' daily lives and kept society functioning. A spiritual rendering of time in the New Testament

[1]Kathleen O'Connor, "Time," in *CPD*, 998.

[2]However, the concept of eternity as life after death, everlasting life, did not evolve until much later in Israel's history. The timelessness of enduring time was *not* an allusion to life after death or eternity as we understand it. It had more to do with extended time; time that stood still, suspended in the timelessness of God.

[3]O'Connor, "Time," in *CPD*, 999.

[4]Ibid., 1001.

[5]Sean P. Kealy, C.S.S.P., "Time," in *CPD*, 1000–1002.

is referred to as *kairos*. *Kairos* refers to those moments of spiritual significance, such as Jesus' coming and the moments and events of his life. It also refers to the circumstances in an individual's or community's life that are transitional, significant moments in the faith journey. All time was seen in relationship to Jesus Christ.

Historical time moved from the past to the present fulfillment in Jesus. Early Christians saw themselves as living in the last age; that is, they lived in the future. The future began with Christ's death and resurrection while they awaited the day of his second coming (as do we in this last age). The resurrection launched eternity. *Kairos* time envisions time and all the events of history in relationship to the Christ event.

Judaism understood time as cyclic. The events of God's intervention in human history were remembered and made present for each generation. They could not be repeated, but in the remembering, God's action was made effective for each succeeding age. Christians celebrate, recall, and make present the saving acts of Jesus every time they gather. The paschal mystery—Jesus' life, death, and resurrection—was considered the hallmark event of history. Through the paschal mystery humanity shares in Jesus' special relationship to the Father through the Holy Spirit as well as in his passion, death, and resurrection. We unite our lives to Christ's in order to share in the Father's community of love with the Son and the Holy Spirit. We seek to model our lives after Christ's and thus offer our lives as Christ offered his: then, today, and in the future. We do this when we remember (*anamnesis*) Jesus' saving events. Those same events are made present for each generation.

The early Christians ordered their entire lives around Jesus' *pasch*. The *pasch* identified who they were, how they were to live, how they were to wait for his return. Time was seen as a memorial to his passion, death, and resurrection. The morning and evening temple sacrifices were "reinterpreted as symbols of Jesus' own sacrifice."[6] The sun's slumber and awakening were seen in terms of Jesus' death and resurrection. Sundown symbolized Jesus' death and our hope for his return and for everlasting life. Sunup symbolized his resurrection. Israel's feasts were transposed into a Christian re-ordering. The yearly Passover became a metaphor for Jesus' passage from death to life.[7]

The early Christian community celebrated an annual *pasch* in which they remembered Jesus' passion, death, and resurrection. Otherwise, the only set time for prayer and worship in the first two centuries occurred on Sunday. A shift took place in the third century. As it became apparent that Jesus' return was not as immanent as once thought, there was a need to establish regulated practices of worship for the expanding church. A new ordering of time emerged.

As a response to scripture's exhortation to pray always, there emerged the practice of praying at various hours of the day. In the sixth century, monastic communities gathered for prayer at eight fixed times throughout a twenty-four hour period (the liturgy of the hours). The Middle Ages experienced a diminishment of natural symbols and metaphors. Symbols of sun and dawn in relationship to death and resurrection gave way to recitation of the Divine Office at no specific, fixed time during the day.

The liturgical year developed in similar manner. In the very early days of the church, Christians celebrated a yearly commemoration of the *pasch* and gathered only on Sunday. By the third century, Epiphany and commemorations of martyrs were added to the Christian observance. By the fourth century other remembrances of Christian events were added to the repertoire of observable feasts with the inclusion of the Nativity, the Ascension, Pentecost, and martyrs' feasts. Each of these feasts celebrated the entire mystery of Jesus' life, death, and resurrection. "At their inception these feasts were unitive feasts, each embracing the whole paschal mystery through the prism of a particular faith symbol or event. Thus, Augustine (d. 430) could call them sacraments."[8]

All ritual observances had been celebrated as remembrances and symbols of the paschal mystery.

[6]Edward Foley, O.F.M.Cap., "Time," in *CPD*, 1003.

[7]Ibid.

[8]Ibid., 1005.

However, usage of symbols and metaphors waned during the Middle Ages. Efforts were made to determine literal historical times, dates, and places of the circumstances of Jesus' life. Time was marked by literal observances of events in his ministry, passion, death, and resurrection. (For example, the secular calendar proceeds from the date of Jesus' birth.)

Nature's rhythms (light and darkness) provide obvious metaphors for the paschal mystery. The light and darkness of day and night are cohesive with body rhythms of the human person. The slumber of night awakens in us the desire for the resurrection brightness of a new day. All parts of creation, its images and its life cycles, are metaphors of life and death. Recent reforms sought to restore the obvious, natural symbols that speak of Christ's paschal mystery: light, darkness, seasons, and feasts. In this way we immerse ourselves in the mystery of Christ's greatest act of redemption as we wait in hope for his return.

The Liturgical Calendar

Due to the reform of the liturgical calendar, Christian observances have been restored to their original context through the renewed, ritual ordering of time. All time is sanctified. The paschal mystery is the centerpiece of all liturgical celebration and ritual observances. "Christ's saving work is celebrated in sacred memory by the Church on fixed days throughout the year. Each week on the day called the Lord's Day, the Church commemorates the Lord's resurrection. Once a year at Easter the Church honors this resurrection and passion with utmost solemnity. Through the yearly cycle the Church unfolds the entire mystery of Christ and keeps the anniversaries of the saints."[9] Thus, the paschal mystery is the root and the heart of the liturgical cycle. "By means of the liturgical cycle the Church celebrates the whole mystery of Christ, from his incarnation until the day of Pentecost and the expectation of his coming again."[10] The Lord's day, Sunday, commemorates this mystery each week even though the entire Easter season is devoted to its celebration and commemoration.

[9]*GNLY,* #1, in *TLD.*

[10]Ibid., #17

The church declares that each day is holy,[11] particularly as it gathers for daily worship. Our observance of Sunday is the earliest tradition of worship handed to us from the apostles. This day of the Lord is a weekly paschal event. "Thus Sunday must be ranked as the first holy day of all."[12] Since Sunday is held in such high esteem, nothing preempts it except solemnities and feasts of the Lord. "Only nine festivals can displace the celebration of the Sunday itself."[13] The Sundays of Advent, Lent, and Easter, however, "take precedence over all solemnities and feasts of the Lord."[14] Easter is an extended meditation on the multifaceted dimensions of the paschal mystery and each Sunday is our ongoing remembrance and expression of devotion to it. We live our lives in the shadow of the cross and resurrection.

Thus, the "mother of all feasts" is Easter. Easter is to the liturgical year what Sunday is to the week. It is the premier ritual, whose life blood flows throughout the year to each and every ritual celebration. The Easter Triduum is the "culmination of the entire liturgical year."[15] The Triduum begins with the celebration of the Lord's Supper on Holy Thursday, continues with the celebration of the Lord's Passion on Good Friday, and culminates at the Easter Vigil in the darkness of night.

The Easter season continues for fifty days and culminates on the feast of Pentecost. Forty days after Easter, the feast of the Ascension is celebrated. The days from Ascension until Pentecost anticipate the coming of the Holy Spirit.

Lent is a time of preparation for the celebration of Easter.[16] It is also a time of preparation for baptism. Catechumens prepare for celebration of the sacrament itself and the faithful prepare to renew their baptismal promises at Easter. It is also a time of renewal and penitence.

[11]Ibid., #3.

[12]*Constitution on the Sacred Liturgy (Sacrosanctum Concilium),* #106, in *TLD.*

[13]Laurence E. Mick, Timothy Fitzgerald DiCello, Kathleen Hughes, RSCJ, *Sourcebook for Sundays and Seasons* (Chicago: Liturgy Training Publications, 1995), 61.

[14]*GNLY,* #5.

[15]Ibid., #18.

[16]Ibid., #27.

Christmas is second only to Easter and celebrates the Incarnation and manifestation of Christ/Spirit/God to the world. "Advent has a twofold character: as a season of preparation for Christmas when Christ's first coming to us is remembered, as a season when that remembrance directs the mind and heart to await Christ's second coming at the end of time. Advent is thus a period of devout and joyful expectation."[17]

Separate from the seasons that remember a particular aspect of Christ's salvific action, there are thirty-three or thirty-four weeks that are not devoted to any one facet of the Christian mystery. For those extended Sundays of the year, the church unfolds and observes all aspects of the mystery of Christ. Those Sundays are referred to as Ordinary Time.

Ordinary Time begins on the Monday after January 6 and continues until the Tuesday before Ash Wednesday. It resumes on the Monday after Pentecost and ends with the First Sunday of Advent.

Throughout the liturgical cycle, the church also remembers and venerates Mary, the mother of God, and commemorates the feasts of various saints and martyrs. The way the importance and significance of the celebration are determined is by its classification as a solemnity, feast, or memorial. Solemnities are principal celebrations of the church. Easter and Christmas are the most important solemnities and continue for eight days (octave).[18]

Feasts are next in importance and they generally fall on the natural days unless they fall on Sunday and commemorate the Lord during Ordinary Time and the Christmas season.[19] Memorials are observances that fall on weekdays. They are either obligatory or optional. Obligatory memorials must be celebrated on the designated day.

All ritual celebrations of the church cycle recall and make present the saving event of Jesus Christ through his life, death, and resurrection. "In the last analysis the paschal mystery is celebrated in every liturgical feast and in every feast the Lord who emptied himself, sacrificed himself in obedience unto death, and is now glorified, is present to his community and acts efficaciously in it."[20]

[17]Ibid., #39.

[18]Ibid., #11.

[19]Ibid., #13.

[20]*LY*, 31.

9. Liturgical Cycle A: Overview of Matthew's Gospel

Matthew is the evangelist of the church's first liturgical cycle—Cycle A. Matthew's gospel is used thirty-two times over the course of the year. "This gospel consists of twenty-eight chapters divided into 1,064 verses; 593, or a little more than half, are read in the Sunday liturgies."[1] Beginning on the Third Sunday in Ordinary Time, Matthew's gospel begins with the inauguration of Jesus' public ministry in Capernaum and ends with the discourse on the final judgment.

The pen of the artful evangelist Matthew offers us an encounter with the Christ of faith and of history. What do we know about him, his community, and his culture? Matthew was a scribe. It is doubtful that he was the Matthew of tax collector fame. It is fairly safe to ascertain that Matthew was from a Hellenized Jewish culture. His gospel was written in Greek and he was very familiar with the scriptures. He was obviously writing to a Jewish community because he took it for granted that the Jewish laws and customs were known by his readers. Donald Senior calls this an ecclesial gospel as Matthew shows concern for the community.[2] Matthew used the medium of story to punctuate the message of salvation through Jesus. However, it was not Matthew's concern to write a biographical sketch of Jesus. The message was more important than the facts of history. "Matthew is not an archivist—rather, he is a preacher."[3]

Senior maintains that there is a consensus among scholars that Matthew's community was a mixed population of Jews and Gentiles. Matthew wrote from a major metropolitan area very much like Antioch, probably in Syria. Most scholars believe that the gospel was written after the Jewish revolt in 70 C.E.

The Jewish structure had changed. The Temple was no more. The Jews were no longer formed by the Temple rituals as had been the case prior to the revolt. There was a major shift in what it meant to be Jewish.

Tension abounded regarding Jewish identity. What did it mean to be a Jewish Christian? What should be the posture of a Jewish Christian toward a Gentile convert to Christianity? In light of rigid purity laws, how could a Jewish Christian live in agape love with a non-Jewish Christian?

Paul was incredulous at the thought that Judaism would not accept the Messiah. He believed that Israel would eventually be won over, and that Jews would embrace Christ—they would and they must. Matthew's reality was certainly not Paul's hope. Matthew lived with a Judaism that did not accept Jesus as Messiah. Rather than to completely break away from one another, Judaism and Christianity took different paths following the Jewish revolt. Diverging from one common origin and relationally like "siblings," rabbinic Judaism and Christianity were two different responses to the effects of the religious and social conditions caused by the revolt.

The Judaism that Jesus knew was no longer a reality by the time Matthew wrote his gospel. The synagogue was the prime religious center. The synagogues were in villages. They were not places of worship.

Formal Judaism lost its cultic center—the priestly families. Temple worship was transferred to the home. Prior cultic observances were celebrated in the home. The pilgrimage feast moved into the home. The mother represented the priestly role as she carefully washed the vessels for the ritual meal. The father assumed the priestly role as the leader of prayer and the presider of the home rituals.

Matthew reveals a tension between Christians and the synagogue. The leaders of rabbinic Judaism were the scribes and Pharisees. Much like the unifying and consolidation efforts of Ezra and Nehemiah after the exile, the scribes and Pharisees were concerned with consolidating and bolstering

[1]*DL* (IV), 14.

[2]Donald Senior, "Gospel of Matthew," Workshop—Our Saviour's Parish, Cocoa Beach, Florida, October, 1995.

[3]Ibid.

their Jewish identity. Diversity would not be tolerated—status quo was critical.

Mark's gospel did not address the tensions that existed in Matthew's community. Matthew asks and responds to the questions concerning what it means to be a Jewish Christian: How are we to accept the Gentile converts? The Greeks do not know our dietary laws. How are we to respond? What if we lose our Jewish identity? Who will remember our heritage?

The beginning point for Matthew's community was the belief that *they must be Jewish.* Matthew understood his role as one of getting to the heart of their Jewish tradition, while breathing new life into the tradition they regarded as sacrosanct. His gospel is a response to a community in transition. The transition was of astronomical proportions for those living in Matthew's ancient cultural milieu. The transition involved movement of the community from one age, imbedded in Palestinian Judaism, to a new, expanded, religious and social world—"moving in Spirit to new unexpected worlds."[4]

People in Matthew's cultural world were in dire need. They understood impoverishment and what it meant to be completely dependent. Coming from their experience of hopelessness, Gentiles encountered the Source of life—the living God. They would not be kept from this encounter. They had found it; they wanted it; they would have it. They would move heaven and earth to live in relationship with the Source of all life. The Jews would have to get used to it; the Gentiles had a place in the community. The community would simply need to adjust. Remember how the Canaanite woman who asked for the scraps from Jesus' Jewish table would not be stopped? In Matthew's gospel, Jesus responded to her, an unclean Canaanite woman, in typical rabbinic Pharisee style, in effect telling her to go away because she was not worthy of the scraps from the table of Jewish identity. But she was cause for a moment of awareness for Jesus—an *aha!* moment of revelation. Something new was afoot and even Jesus was growing in awareness of what God was doing!

[4]Ibid.

Matthew views past, present, and future eschatology in light of the Jesus event, and reminds the reader of previous salvation history. He insists that faith in Jesus affirms what it means to be elected by God—to be *the People of God.* Matthew paints a picture of Jesus as the fulfillment of Hebraic messianic prophecy. Jesus' teaching and ministry fulfill the heart of the Law and the Prophets. Jesus' death inaugurates the promised messianic age. Matthew demands faithfulness to the Jewish heritage, but also to the movement of the Spirit in the messianic age—*both now and not yet.*

Matthew reminds the Jewish audience of the many ways that God painted Israel's history with very crooked lines. His genealogy is a testament to the way God had always used unseemly characters and events to bring salvation history toward its fulfillment. His gospel is filled with stories of outsiders (the unclean and the sinner) who would participate in God's plan of salvation, accomplished through the life, death, and resurrection of Jesus Christ.

In Matthew's gospel, actions speak louder than words. He demands a response that gives more than lip service to the gospel's moral imperatives. The Beatitudes are the barometer by which commitment to Christ is to be judged. To be a member of God's people meant a radical shift in behavior. "What has made Matthew so precious to generation after generation of Christians is . . . its fusion of gospel and ethics, of faith and morality. The dominant characteristic of the First Gospel is its moral earnestness."[5]

According to Donald Senior, there are six fundamental dimensions of Matthew's portrayal of Jesus and his mission:

1. Matthew's Jesus proclaims the coming reign of God. *(So does Luke's and Mark's)*

2. Matthew's Jesus puts love, compassion, and respect for human life at its center. *(5:17; 22:34–40; 12:7; 5:43–48 [Matthew only])*

3. Matthew's Jesus is portrayed as God's Servant, committed to lifting the physical and social bur-

[5]*MI,* 1.

dens of humanity. *(1:21; 4:24–5:1; chps 8–9; 12:18–21; 15:29–31)*

4. Matthew's Jesus is in solidarity with and identifies with the poor and marginalized. *(1:23; 9:9–13; 8:5–13; 15:21–28; 21:14; 25:31–46)*

5. Matthew's Jesus stressed human responsibility, called for action and not mere words, and condemned religious hypocrisy. *(3:15; 5:19; 7:21–27; 21:28–32; chps 23–25)*

6. Matthew's Jesus empowered his community and sent them on an inclusive and universal mission of justice and healing in the world. *(10:7–8; 28:16–20 [movement from Judaism to the world—only in Matthew])*[6]

While there is debate concerning which gospel was first, most scholars agree that Matthew was written after Mark and that Matthew used the gospel of Mark and the Q *(quelle)* as his source. However, some scholars suggest that the acceptance of Mark as the first gospel was too hasty—that Matthew was indeed the first evangelist as once thought, particularly in light of its obvious Jewish orientation and other more detailed concerns. David E. Garland maintains that those who believe in the primacy of Matthew have insufficiently proven their case: "Proponents of Matthean priority have also never satisfactorily answered the question of why, if one has Matthew and Luke [as the original source], would one create a gospel like Mark?"[7] Suffice it to say that most contemporary scholarship accepts the belief that the gospel of Mark was written first; that Matthew used Mark and the Q as primary source material. How else does one explain the huge sections of Mark's gospel found in Matthew (about 90%)?[8] Perhaps the reason for another gospel besides Mark lies in the fact that Mark did not address many of the needs of Matthew's diverse transitional community.

Garland suggests that Matthew's reason for writing the gospel cannot be so easily deciphered. He contends that the best analysis is to assume that it was "intended for broad circulation in a variety of Christian communities with a variety of needs and issues, and that it was motivated simply by 'a general desire to tell others about Jesus, who he was, what he did and what happened to him in the end' (R.A. Burridge, *What are the Gospels? A Comparison with Graeco-Roman Biography,* SNTSMS 70 [Cambridge University Press, 1992], 214). The assumptions that Matthew used Mark and Q and that the Gospel belongs in the overall genre of 'lives'[9]—both of which are debated—would support this more general conclusion about why it was penned."[10]

Garland suggests that the gospel's purpose is to tell the story of Jesus, to bolster faith in him and his mission, to convince and refute, to explain present circumstances, to exhort the community, and to arm disciples for apostolic mission.[11] Whatever the reason for writing *The Gospel According to Matthew,* we, as church, will spend the next year encountering the life and mission of Jesus Christ through the eyes, heart, and pen of this artful scribe.

[6]Ibid.

[7]*RM,* 3.

[8]For a resource that suggests a Matthean priority refer to: *The Gospel of Jesus: The Pastoral Relevance of the Synoptic Problem,* by William R. Farmer (Westminster/John Knox, 1994).

[9]"Lives" refers to a literary genre in which anecdotes were selected from the life of an individual and everything about the anecdote was for the purpose of portraying the person's whole essence or character.

[10]*RM,* 5.

[11]Ibid., 6–10.

The Season of Advent

The Season of Advent: An Overview

"Advent begins with the first evening prayer of the Sunday that falls closest to November 30 and ends before the first evening prayer of Christmas."[1] The document *General Norms for the Liturgical Year and the Calendar* states: "The season of Advent has a twofold character. It is a time of preparation for Christmas when the first coming of God's son to men is recalled. It is also a season when minds are directed by this memorial to Christ's second coming at the end of time. It is thus a time of joyful and spiritual expectation."[2]

The origin of Advent dates back to the fifth century and is influenced by the Eastern Church. The primary focus of this liturgy was expectation of the Lord's birth at Christmas. The first evidence of Roman observance of the season occurred around the sixth century. There was little emphasis placed on the parousia. The focus was on preparation for the celebration of Christ's birth.

At the same time, however, there were other shifts taking place that would eventually impact Advent's original focus. The Irish missionaries had descended upon Gaul with a compelling message concerning the final judgment of humanity. They exhorted people to repent in the face of eventual judgment. Thus, Advent became laden with penitential overtones. This influence reached the Roman church by the twelfth century as evidenced by the wearing of purple vestments and the exclusion of the Gloria during the liturgy. Yet, in spite of this, the penitential character of Advent was different in tone from that of Lent. There was an inherent joy to the penitential observance. There was clear intention that omission of the Gloria was an anticipatory gesture rather than a penitential gesture. "It is not omitted for the same reason as it is omitted in Lent, but in order that on the night of Christmas the angels' song may ring out again in all its newness."[3]

[1] *GNLY,* #40.

[2] Ibid., #39.

The first Sunday of Advent begins a new liturgical year and liturgical cycle: CYCLE A. During this year we encounter Jesus through the eyes of Matthew, the evangelist. Matthew was writing to a Jewish and Gentile Christian audience. For more information on the context and perspective of the gospel according to Matthew, see the chapter entitled "Overview of Matthew's Gospel."

Advent prepares us for the coming of the Savior. We must ask ourselves, "From what do we need saving?" The scriptures of Advent challenge us to wait for the day of the Lord, but they also demand that justice reign. In the biblical sense, justice (Hebrew: *hesed*) refers to right relationship with God as evidenced by one's behavior toward God and God's people. The demands of justice are not suggestions; they are commands. Advent asks the tough question: How are we living *hesed* relationship with our God? If we are God's people, if we are in covenant relationship with God, then we must be advocates of justice wherever injustice takes center stage.

Another theme that echoes through the season is penitential. God's people are to recognize, name, and lament over the evil that permeates the world and work to eradicate it. Throughout Advent we hear from the ancient prophets who cry, "Repent and change your lives!" The prophets' cry is as relevant today as it was then. They foretold the light that would shine in the midst of darkness. Christ is that light. We are to embrace the light and become the light of Christ in the world.

[3] *Commetarius In Annum Liturgicum Instauratum,* chap. I, sect. II, 2 (p. 61), published by the Consilium for the Implementation of the Constitution on the Sacred Liturgy.

Advent explores two realities: the kingdom *here and now* and the kingdom *yet to come.* We live in the midst of that tension. We struggle to maintain the proper balance between passive waiting and proactive waiting. When we are proactive we cooperate in the work of *history making.* We enter salvation history with God and seek to alter injustice when we see it. We enter the struggle of the kingdom *here and now* with a vigilant eye and hopeful anticipation of the kingdom *yet to come.*

As consumerism seems to preoccupy the culture in the waning days of Advent, our liturgy seeks to bring us back to the "reason for the season." Advent is a wake-up call to the world. Advent's message is a counter-cultural plea to engage in the deeper meaning of the season. It is a mandate to reflect upon and prepare for the second coming of Christ, while looking forward to the celebration of the Incarnation, the ultimate gift of God's personhood to the world. We can do nothing less than ask ourselves the questions of human response and responsibility in the face of such a gratuitous gift.

St. Bernard (1090–1153) gave us a wonderful summation of the meaning of Advent when he wrote:

> We know that there are three comings of the Lord. The third lies between the other two. It is invisible, while the other two are visible. In the first coming he was seen on earth, dwelling among men [and women]; he himself testifies that they saw him and hated him. In the final coming "all flesh will see the salvation of our God," and "they will look on him whom they pierced." The intermediate coming is a hidden one; in it only the elect see the Lord within their own selves, and they are saved. In his first coming our Lord came in the flesh and in our weakness; in this middle coming he comes in spirit and in power; in the final coming he will be seen in glory and majesty. Because this coming lies between the other two, it is like a road on which we travel from the first coming to the last. In the first, Christ was our redemption; in the last, he will appear as our life; in this middle coming, he is our rest and consolation.[4]

The First and Second Sunday of Advent center around the future coming of Christ. The Third Sunday's focus is on the present coming and the Fourth Sunday is on the birth of Jesus, the past coming.

Advent and Christmas form a unity. We cannot engage in one season without reflection upon the other. Both seasons complement one another and do not stand alone. Yet Advent and Christmas are also viewed through the lens of Lent and Easter. Advent/Christmas looks toward the fulfillment of the Incarnation that is celebrated through the paschal mystery at Easter.

As in all good liturgy, we are to properly prepare ourselves for full and vibrant participation. Advent prepares the heart and the church for just such participation in the mystery of Christ's Incarnation.

[4] *Homelie pour l'Advent,* 5:1–3, *Edition cistercienne,* 4, 1966, pp. 188–190, in *Liturgy of the Hours* (New York: Catholic Book Publishing Co., 1975), p. 169.

First Sunday of Advent

Liturgy of the Word Format: opening song, sign of the cross, opening prayer, reading, responsorial psalm, reading, gospel acclamation, gospel, general intercessions, Lord's Prayer, concluding rites-prayer, and blessing.[1]

Environment

Advent is more than a time of personal conversion and preparation. The scriptures of Advent remind us that we are preparing for a renewal of cosmic proportions. The universe groans in longing anticipation for the *One Who Came,* the *One Who Comes,* and the *One Who Will Come Again.* The worship space and meeting space for catechesis should immediately awaken us from the slumber of complacency and speak to us through the thunderous silence of symbols, color, wreath, and candle. The possibilities are limited only by the imagination. Not only should the Advent environment reflect the hopeful, anticipatory images of the season, but also the harsh, Baptist-like demand for justice and reformation. The theme of final judgment resounds throughout the season. How might an environment be crafted to help disquiet the comfortable, and ignite the complacent? One way to remain true to the spirit of Advent is to avoid trite images and saccharin art; to clothe the space in Advent's liturgical color, the violet hues of purple; and to simply and starkly use symbols or art that reflect anticipation, justice, and the final eschaton. Perhaps the bold use of color (purples laced with traces of navy, black, and the silver of the midnight sky) alongside an austere, but striking Advent wreath is all that is needed to convey the cosmic nature of the season. The symbolism of the Advent wreath "lies in the tension between light and darkness.... It represents the long time when people lived in spiritual darkness, waiting for the coming of the Messiah, the light of the world."[2] Each week a new candle is lit: "... light increases, pushing out darkness... until all four are burning."[3] The Advent wreath cradles our primary symbols—wood and light. "The wood refers to the 'living greens' that are used to make the wreath.... The wood or pine embodies the primary symbol of the cross. It is the wood of the cross which will become the sign of our salvation at Easter whereby all are saved by the 'wood of the cross'.... The four candles represent Christ, the Light of the World!"[4] A carved-out log or a grouping of branches laced with evergreens could be used to cradle the four candles. Four purple candles, or three purple candles and one rose candle (for *Gaudete* Sunday, the Third Sunday of Advent), or four white candles, may be used in the wreath.

Mary certainly plays a supporting role in Advent's unfolding drama. However, she waits in the wings (careful not to upstage the season's central themes) for her center stage arrival and the role she will play during the latter days of the season. Perhaps iconography might be the medium to bring appropriate images of Mary's role in the history of salvation into the environment during the waning days of the season. John the Baptist leaps front and center on the first Sunday and screams to us from art both ancient and contemporary: "Repent, change your lives!" An artist's rendering (i.e. an icon) of the Baptist would be a wonderful addition to your Advent meeting space. The four archangels are also Advent images: "Gabriel blowing the trumpet, Michael with the scales of justice, Raphael with healing gall, and Uriel darkening the sun and moon—all assisting in the resurrection of the dead."[5] Icons of the archangels or of John the Baptist, pictured with wings (because he is God's messenger) might be artistically incorporated.

Flowers, while not prohibited, should be used sparingly and simply. Advent does reflect a spirit of joy. However, the joy is minimized in compari-

[1]These weekly sessions are situated in a Liturgy of the Word format. It is assumed that the catechists will enter the reflection process in the context of a Liturgy of the Word, using the readings for the coming liturgy and session they are preparing. The format includes all the pieces that make up a Liturgy of the Word. Adapt it according to your needs.

[2]*CCT,* 49.

[3]Ibid.

[4]Linda Gaupin, *Catechesis and Liturgy,* Course Text, 52.

[5]*TCY,* 210.

son to the cosmic bliss of Christmas. Thus, the Advent environment should never overpower the Christmas environment to come. Christmas and Advent are understood as unified and complementary. Christmas, and its environment, should build upon Advent.

Blessing of an Advent Wreath

Before your group lights the first candle of the Advent wreath, the following blessing, taken from *Catholic Household Blessings and Prayers* (NCCB, 1988), may be used.

All make the sign of the cross.

Leader: Our help is in the name of the Lord.

All respond: Who made heaven and earth.

Leader: In the short days and long nights of Advent, we realize how we are always waiting for deliverance, always needing salvation by our God. Around this wreath, we shall remember God's promise.

Scripture is read.

Listen to the words of the prophet Isaiah:
the people who walked in darkness have seen a great light;
Upon those who dwelt in the land of gloom a light has shown.
You have brought them abundant joy and great rejoicing.
The word of the Lord.

All respond: Thanks be to God.

After a time of silence, all join in prayers of intercessions and in the Lord's Prayer.

Then the leader invites:
Let us now pray for God's blessing upon us and this wreath.

After a short silence, the leader prays:

Lord our God,
we praise you for your Son, Jesus Christ:
he is Emmanuel, the hope of the peoples,
he is the wisdom that teaches and guides us,
he is the Savior of every nation.
Lord God,
let your blessing come upon us
as we light the candles of this wreath.
May the wreath and its light
be a sign of Christ's promise to bring salvation.
May he come quickly and not delay.
We ask this through Christ our Lord.

The first candle is then lighted.

Leader: Let us bless the Lord.

All respond, making the sign of the cross:
Thanks be to God.

The blessing concludes with a verse from "O Come O Come, Emmanuel."[6]

INTRODUCTORY RITES

Opening Song (or Entrance Antiphon[7])

To you, my God, I lift my soul, I trust in you; let me never come to shame. Do not let my enemies laugh at me. No one who waits for you is ever put to shame. (Ps 24:1–3)[8]

Opening Prayer

The facilitator of the session may lead the prayer. Others in the group may be asked to proclaim the readings.

Let us pray
[that we may take Christ's coming seriously]

---

[6] *CHBP,* 64.

[7] Each mass has an assigned "entrance antiphon." This is usually a couple of sentences from the scriptures (most often psalmody, intended to be sung) and, in a sense, is considered the official part of the liturgy, and thus its opening song. However, very often the general practice in this country has been to sing a hymn since the appropriate antiphon or psalm was not yet set to music. Thus, the first option is to sing the assigned psalm or antiphon of the liturgy. The choice of a hymn is the last option. It used to be that each Sunday liturgy was given a title. The title was in Latin and was the first word of the entrance antiphon.

[8] First Sunday of Advent: "Entrance Antiphon," *The Sacramentary.*

Pause for silent prayer.

All-powerful God,
increase our strength of will for doing good
that Christ may find an eager welcome at his coming
and call us to his side in the
kingdom of heaven,
where he lives and reigns with you and the Holy Spirit,
one God, for ever and ever. Amen.[9]

LITURGY OF THE WORD

The readings are proclaimed.

First Reading[10]
Isaiah 2:1–5

Overview of Isaiah: Isaiah was a prophet of the southern kingdom of Judah who served in that role for over forty years (c. 740–700 B.C.E.). The book bearing his name is the largest prophetic work in the Bible. Isaiah of Jerusalem is believed to be the author of the first thirty-nine chapters (First Isaiah: chapters 1–39; Deutero-Isaiah: chapters 40–66). It is probable that Isaiah came from privileged roots as he seems to have had free access to the royal courts and to the king himself. Isaiah was intensely involved in the political life of the day. Two events during those forty years consumed much of Isaiah's attention. In the year 734 the northern kingdom, under the rule of King Hoshea, joined forces with Damascus against Assyria. Both Israel and Damascus were afraid that Judah would not go along with the plan, so they attacked Judah first. Desperate to defend itself, Judah joined forces with Assyria and thus became Assyria's vassal. Isaiah found King Ahaz's decision to align with pagan Assyria repugnant. The defeat delivered a disastrous blow to Israel and Damascus. Damascus was destroyed and Israel was divided into three provinces under the control of an Assyrian governor. Only a small area near the capital city of Samaria was left for King Hoshea to govern. Isaiah begged the people of Judah not to get involved with Assyria, but no one would listen. Chapters 6–11 deal with this tragic situation in great detail.

The second event that concerned Isaiah was the attempt by King Ahaz's son, King Hezekiah, to free Judah from Assyrian domination. Hezekiah led the revolt and won Judah's liberation in 705 B.C.E. against the Assyrian king's son, Sennacherib. Four years later Sennacherib attacked Judah. Isaiah tells us that a plague destroyed the Assyrian army, forcing them to return to their homeland. However, nearly every Judean city was destroyed except Jerusalem. Hezekiah paid a huge booty to Assyria to keep them from attacking again.

Isaiah's agenda is ardently set forth in his oracles. He railed against injustice, oppression, and idolatry. He implored the people to turn from their wicked ways and return to Yahweh. Isaiah proclaimed a God who was in control of the whole world, a God who blessed and disciplined those who were in covenant with him. Isaiah exhorted Israel and Judah to subject themselves only to Yahweh and not to the domination of foreign powers. In spite of Isaiah's warnings, Israel's kings did not heed his advice. They refused to believe the promise that Yahweh would protect and defend their nation. "As a result, Isaiah turned his hopes to a future king who would obey Yahweh. From this moment, the words of Isaiah inspired hopes of a messiah, a new king in Israel's future who would better serve God and bring about a full measure of the divine blessing on the land (see Is 9:1–6 and 11:1–9)."[11]

Isaiah also proclaimed the holiness of God. Yahweh, creator of the universe, ruled his people in splendor and majesty and was worthy of honor and praise. Yahweh resided in the midst of Israel and as a result the people were to live in holiness. This holiness was evidenced by the ethical demands of a well-lived life, committed to the justice

---

[9]First Sunday of Advent: "Opening Prayer," *The Sacramentary.*

[10]The exegesis for the first and second readings may or may not be the focus of your group's reflection, as there may only be time to give adequate attention to the gospel, your primary concern. However, the exegesis is included here in order to provide a thorough investigation of the entire liturgy of the word as there may be parts (or all) that would be necessary to the direction you wish to take with your particular ministry group.

[11]*ROT,* 329.

of God. Nothing disrupts the way of this holiness like human pride. Such pride invites God's discipline. But the God who punishes also forgives and restores. Isaiah prophesied about the destruction of Israel and Judah. However, he promised that a remnant would survive that would be the source of Israel's hope.

Today's Pericope:[12] Today's prophecy in Isaiah is almost identical to the prophecy in Micah 4. Though not certain, scholars generally agree that both prophets borrowed the oracle from a common source. It is probably an excerpt from an ancient liturgy.

Today's passage proclaims the coming of the *Future One.* While at prayer Isaiah had a vision. He could see into the future—the end of history. All the nations of the earth make a royal pilgrimage to the gates of heaven on the great and final day. Yahweh, the just judge, will settle strife between them and establish lasting peace. Isaiah's eschatological vision looks to the day when physical history will end. In that new reality there will be no more war. The *One Who is to Come* will usher in the manifestation of God's new rule, "an era of utterly pure peace."[13] The era of peace will take place when God's plan triumphs at the final eschaton. On the earthly plane of existence we will know war. However, that is not to deter us from working diligently for realization of Yahweh's future promise. "The Lord is at the center of history attracting and energizing the path of his people. We should ask ourselves: In what direction are we going? Hopefully, our answer will be: toward peace and solidarity for everyone, a desire we all share."[14] In Isaiah's vision the nations must learn what it means to walk in the light of the Lord—to follow the path God ordains. Only then is peace possible. Our world spends vast reservoirs of money that could be used to feed its starving inhabitants on the methods and means of war, destruction, and death. "Isaiah's text suggests a total disarmament, from our hearts where unjust violence begins to the structures preparing for war."[15] The bottom line: peace is possible only in God.

[12]A pericope is the particular portion or segment of scripture that is chosen for a specific proclamation.

[13]*DL* (I), 33.

[14]*SWTLY,* 4.

[15]Ibid.

Responsorial Psalm
Psalm 122:1–9

Psalm 122 is an "ascent psalm" used by pilgrims as they ascended into Jerusalem for festivals. This psalm also speaks of a pilgrimage that results in lasting peace and exults over the unity that is expressed in the gathering of all the tribes in the holy city. Reginald Fuller contends that part of the eschatological hope of post-exilic Judaism looked toward the day when all the nations would gather in Jerusalem. The early church understood this to be fulfilled in the admission of the Gentiles into the church, he says, and will be finally realized when Christ comes again.[16]

Second Reading
Romans 13:11–14

Overview of Paul's Letter to the Romans: Paul wrote his letter to the Romans before he made his last trip to Jerusalem, as indicated in 15:25. It was written around 57–58 C.E., probably in Corinth. Paul sought to expand his missionary base to the west toward Spain. His plan was to visit the Roman church on the way, his lifelong ambition. Before his trek could begin he needed to make one last trip to Jerusalem to hand deliver the offering collected by his newly-founded Gentile churches. His intent was to express solidarity between the poor of the new Gentile churches and the Jewish Christian church in Jerusalem. Thus, before he left for Jerusalem he wrote to the Romans to inform them of his impending arrival, asking them to pray that the collection would be well received by the Jerusalem church.

One school of thought suggests that the letter to the Romans is Paul's catechism of Christian doctrine. Another school supports the supposition that it is his last will and testament, and still another that it is the formulation of Paul's own doctrine. Since much of Christian doctrine is missing from Romans, Joseph Fitzmyer maintains that it is none of the above, but rather an essay letter stating "his missionary reflections on the historical possibility of salvation, rooted in God's uprightness and love, now offered to all human beings through faith in Christ Jesus."[17]

[16]*PL,* 2.

[17]Joseph A. Fitzmyer, S.J., "The Letter to the Romans," *NJBC,* 830.

Paul's conflict with the Judaizers made him come to see that justification and salvation are not offered through adherence to the law, but rather to faith in Jesus Christ crucified. Through faith and baptism we are all heirs to what Jesus accomplished through his death and resurrection. The Jerusalem church distrusted Paul because of his anti-Law sentiments. The money offering was a sign of good will between the Gentile and Jewish Christian church.

The letter to the Galatians began Paul's reflection on the meaning of the Christian kerygma. He was forced to seriously formulate his theology. The more he grappled with the truths of the Christian faith, the more he was certain that human beings are justified by faith, not their own merits. It was a difficult message to accept. Justification through the Law was ingrained in the people's consciousness and history.

Paul was afraid that people would simply not believe they were forgiven. He had an urgency to proclaim the good news to the entire world! While the message of Paul's letter to the Galatians is similar in content, the tone of his Romans letter is less defensive. Romans was well articulated, perhaps dictated to a scribe and written in the style of Greek literature. Galatians was written from the perspective of the jail cell and reflected his frantic situation. For Paul, all one needed was to accept the message of Christ to become transformed.

Paul's problems with the Judaizers was past history by the time he wrote to the Romans. He was probably aware of the problem that existed between the Jewish Christians (exiled by Claudius and later returned under Nero) and the Gentile church. The Gentile church was not concerned with dietary laws, and thus, during the Jewish exile, was quite comfortable in practicing the Christian discipline without paying heed to such long-held cherished regulations. This obviously did not set well with the returning Jews. The Gentiles were the "strong" ones because they were not bound by such regulations and the Jews were the "weak" ones because they were so compelled. Paul addressed this situation in his letter. Paul's letter to the Romans has had a greater impact on Christian theology than any other New Testament letter.

Today's Pericope: Paul sets up a cosmic tension between light/darkness, night/day, sleeping/awake, hourly/fulltime. This section reflects the early Christian belief that they resided with their feet squarely planted between two doors—their present evil age and the one yet to unfold. "Christians stand in the dark with their faces lit by the coming dawn."[18] Thus they could live in the reality of the future age while residing in the present. The implication, of course, is that Christians were to live their baptismal commitment as children who reside in the full brilliance of Christ's light. Christians were called to show by their actions that they were indeed Christian and standing on the precipice of the last age, ushered in by the death and resurrection of their Master. Love is the key. As they became more imbued with Christian living, their life became rooted in love, and more and more they turned away from sin. Sin lost its choke-hold.

Paul believed that the final eschaton would happen in his lifetime—indeed soon! We are living testimony to the error of his assumption. We are nonetheless to live each day as if the consummation of the world might take place before tonight's evening news. Thus we are to put on the armor of light and, as Paul tells us, "not the armor which creates violence, lies, and despair, but rather the armor which secures peace, establishes justice, and creates solidarity among peoples."[19] Jesus Christ who came, who comes, and who will come again, is the light in which we bathe. May our actions reflect his light in our lives.

The gospel is proclaimed.

Gospel[20]

Matthew 24: 37–44. Jesus speaks of the end of time.

---

[18] *PL,* 2.

[19] *SWTLY,* 3.

[20] The gospel exegesis is provided later in this session so that it may be presented in the proper sequence where it occurs in the adult five-step reflection process. The exegesis is provided for the first and second readings for your information and edification, and for you to use at your discretion. Once again, the gospel is the primary source of reflection. If there is time for reflection on the other readings, all the better.

STEP 1
NAMING ONE'S EXPERIENCE

What were your first impressions? What was your first response to the gospel (or the other readings)?[21] What captured your attention?

Each person names his or her initial impression. Statements should be brief. No reasons should be given at this time. All simply listen without agreeing or disagreeing.

STEP 2
UNDERSTANDING

In a brief statement, what do you think this gospel is trying to convey?

STEP 3
INPUT FROM VISION/STORY/TRADITION

Liturgical Context[22]

The First and Second Sunday of Advent open the unfolding drama of history's premier event on an eschatological tone. The scope transcends the immanent expectation of the coming of Christ in history as well as the Christ who dwells in our midst and who will one day return in glory. The first two Sundays bespeak the cosmic liturgy that will usher in the culmination of all history and the final eschaton. "The prophetic oracles glimpse the day when the Lord will call together all nations in eternal peace of the kingdom of God (Is 2:1–5: First Sunday, year A), when God will judge the poor with justice (Is 11:1–10: Second Sunday, year A), when he will manifest his glory (Bar 5:1–9: Second Sunday, year C)."[23]

The Baptist exhorts us to prepare for the coming reign of God. We are to be as watchful as a sentry at his post. The entrance antiphon reminds us that no one who waits on the Lord will be disappointed. While ever mindful of the earthly reality of God's reign, we are not to forget that we live in the constant tension between the reign of God *now and not yet* reflected in today's communion antiphon:

> Father,
> May our communion teach us to love heaven.
> May its promise guide our way on earth.[24]

We can look to the preface of the liturgy for an understanding of what it is we believe about a feast or season. The Prefaces for Advent remind us that Jesus fulfilled the plan of salvation inaugurated by God at the creation of the world. We wait now for the final fulfillment when Christ returns again (Advent Preface I, for use until December 16). We are reminded that Christ's coming was foretold by the prophets, that the Virgin Mary bore him with the greatest love and that the Baptist paved the way for and announced his coming. We are to be confident as we prepare to celebrate his birth because Christ himself fills us with joy so that we may be watchful and ready when he returns (Advent Preface II, for use the last eight days, December 17–24.).

The liturgies of Advent begin in preparation for the Lord's second coming. By the third week and fourth week the focus is on the immediate preparation for the feast of the Incarnation of Christ at Christmas.

Advent prepares us to enter fully into the mystery of the Incarnation. Jesus dwells among us as we remember and celebrate his historical coming and anticipate his second coming at the end of time. We are immersed in Christ's explosion into human history. The liturgy engages in a sacred re-

[21]Once again, the primary focus of reflection is the gospel. However, very often the other readings demand attention and must be brought into the dialogue.

[22]The scriptures in the Lectionary, the seasons of the year, and the ritual prayers of the mass are interrelated and form the basis for liturgical catechesis. The *liturgical context* attempts to explore and clarify the themes and this interrelatedness.

[23]*DL* (I), 25.

[24]First Sunday of Advent: "Communion Antiphon," *The Sacramentary.*

membering *(anamnesis)* of God's salvific action in history and the role of humanity in that action. The prophets of old cry to us from their ancient graves with the same plea we hear from contemporary prophetic voices: "Reform your lives, the day of the Lord is near." Whether that final day comes in our lifetime or in the future makes no difference. Our lives are to reflect prayerful diligence and attentiveness to the task of waiting in joyful hope. The liturgies of Advent give us the opportunity to observe and reflect upon that future kingdom as well as the kingdom of God in our midst. The Advent liturgies powerfully remind us of our need to conform our lives to the will of God. According to Karl Rahner, Advent is the time of "*... the secret experience of the apparently inexperienceable....*"[25] "So the period of Advent is actually not simply just the time before something that has not occurred yet. But just as well it can be understood as the period for the quiet growth of a life already given; and it works just like the time when, like the seed long since sown in springtime, God's inward arrival comes through unobtrusively and slowly, but with terrific force and becomes manifest in all the seeming banality of our lives."[26]

Gospel Exegesis

The facilitator provides input from critical biblical scholarship. This input includes insights as to how people would have heard the gospel in Jesus' time.

Matthew 24: 37–44: Today's gospel is Matthew's rendering of the synoptic apocalypse found also in Matthew 24, Mark 13, and Luke 21. Following the pattern of Jewish apocalypses, the synoptic apocalypses relate events that happened before the Jewish revolt of c. 70 C.E. It was understood that such events would signal the inauguration of the Son of Man's return, the final eschaton and the new age.

Within the framework of this apocalypse, Mark inserted segments of Jesus' sayings. The sayings suggest that rather than the end coming in the form of a stylized timetable (which Matthew, Mark, and Luke suggest in the traditional apocalypse), it comes rather when one least expects it. The end will ultimately result in the judgment and subsequent separation between the saved and the unsaved. Some will be escorted to the new realm, others will be left behind. Thus, the posture is one of watchfulness. The synoptic apocalypses seem to suggest that there will be a schedule of events to watch for. The sayings of Jesus found in this pericope probably more accurately describe Christ's overall eschatological teaching, however. We do not know the day or the hour. It will come upon us all of a sudden—so we should be prepared.

Just like Paul was mistaken about when the end would occur, it is interesting to note that in this passage, so is Jesus. Jesus also thought the events he described would take place very soon. The fact that they did not occur leads some scholars to interpret that as Christ's acknowledgment that the will of God is open to change. It is not written in stone. God's will is not necessarily fixed or unchangeable. "God can shorten the days for the sake of the elect (Luke 18: 7–8), and he can also lengthen the period of grace (Luke 13:6–9) as a free act of mercy."[27]

The fact that Jesus was mistaken also points to a reality that is often missed even in today's enlightened world. We say we believe that Jesus was fully human and fully divine. But do we really? The Councils of Nicea and Chalcedon definitively counteracted the heresy of Docetism which declared that Jesus was not really human, but that he possessed supernatural future knowledge unlike other human beings. It seems very easy for many of us to accept the divinity of Christ but to be suspicious of his humanity. How could he have been subject to the same base temptations that the rest of us encounter? Yet we profess and believe that Jesus Christ, Son of God, is truly human and truly divine. "He was a genuine human being like us, or his death on the cross was a cruelly deceptive sham. The gospel testimony provides strong support for this view: Jesus did not know all things."[28]

The mandate, then, is to be alert and ready for Christ's arrival, even at a time when we least expect it. How will Christ find us? Gutierrez suggests that this watchfulness demands that we pay attention to the brothers and sisters in our midst and

[25] *GCY*, 9.
[26] Ibid., 10.
[27] *PL*, 4.
[28] *MI*, 282.

listen to their "... clamor for liberation, supporting our people's deepest hopes. Waiting does not bring us out of history; it involves us with it since we are hoping for the God who has come and is in our midst."[29] Such hope is difficult to maintain at best. Yet maintain it we must. For it is in the striving and hopeful waiting that we are given the opportunity to observe our actions: "... what is deceptive and underhanded in our personal lives... also what is hopeful in our efforts to defend life and justice."[30] Hopeful waiting acts on our souls like the refiner's fire purifies and melts the jeweler's gold.

We are clearly not to presume to know the hour or the day of the consummation of the world. Not even Jesus or the angels are privy to such inside information. Yet generation upon generation continues to try and pry the intention of God right out of him—as if we were capable of such arrogant control. A recent supermarket tabloid's headlines reveals our fascination with the End Times:

> Scrolls unearthed in Turkey reveal God's warning of a second Great Flood... Also revealed: Christ about to return to Earth! The true date of Doomsday! Secrets of daily life in heaven! You have a last chance to repent! Other Miracles Ahead! Herbs to cure all diseases! Sins of past forgiven! Downfall of all tyrants! Another Garden of Eden! (*Sun* Newspaper, October 14, 1997)

Try as we may to pinpoint our God, the fact remains that as far as the parousia and the great eschaton are concerned, the only thing we know two thousand years later that Jesus did not know is that ***soon*** can be a very long time! Obviously, whenever concerns such as these take up our attention we are not on the track that God would chart for us. Today's gospel reminds us that Advent calls for a response of faith. "Whoever can wake up and be quiet and wait can already experience right now how Advent mysteriously lets the inexperienceable God be experienced."[31] So we do not know the hour or day. So what? What difference does it make? What *does* make a difference is the way we live our lives in hopeful anticipation. How are we nurturing our relationship with the living God in our midst? How are the *least of our brothers and sisters* cared for?

Matthew's community was struggling fifty years after the death of Jesus. The culture of Jesus' day could not see past the events of each day—they were present-oriented people (unlike our own American culture that thinks mostly in terms of *nothing but the future*—my future retirement, my future job, when I get my life under control, when my children grow up, etc.). Matthew's community expected Jesus' immediate return. What happened? Where was he? Were the rest of his promises a hoax too? For a culture that could only think in terms of the present moment, the concept of waiting for a future day was out of their contextual understanding. In today's gospel Matthew borrows some of Jesus' earlier sayings in order to console a confused, bewildered, and beleaguered community. He helps them to see beyond today (for them a difficult task) to a future day of glory. The challenge for Matthew's community was one thing. The challenge for us today is quite another. "Americans are so terminally future oriented... that they frequently miss the present entirely."[32] If not careful we might miss what Karl Rahner suggests is Advent's invitation: "Of course only one who can be still and pray; only one who is patient and does not drown out the frightening silence in which God dwells, and which often comes over us, with the racket of everyday life and the shouts coming from the amusement park of the world, can already hear with ease and already discreetly appreciate something of the eternal life that is already inwardly given to us in this fragmenting time as the indwelling of God in us."[33] Advent invites us to discover the delicate balance between contemplation and action "as we wait in joyful hope for the coming of our Savior Jesus Christ!"

Proclaim the gospel again.

Sometimes we gain new insights when we hear the text after the interpretation is given. Someone from the group proclaims the gospel a second time.

---

[29] *SWTLY,* 3.

[30] Ibid.

[31] *GCY,* 10.

[32] *CWJ,* 3.

[33] *GCY,* 10.

Step 4
Testing

Conversation with the Liturgy and the Scriptures

Test your original understanding in dialogue with the interpretation.

(You might consider breaking into smaller groups.)

Now that you've heard what the scholars have to say about this passage, how do you feel about it? How does your original understanding of this gospel compare with what we just shared? Were there any new insights for you? What seems to resonate as an issue in your particular community? In what way does your community 1) Live fully in the present? 2) Act in a diligent and watchful manner in hopeful anticipation of the future? 3) Live the delicate balance between contemplation and action? How might you be called to do the same in your personal life? How does this story speak to your life?

Sharing Life Experience

I am reminded of the example of my father. He loved my mother dearly. At one point in their life she became seriously ill. It was an extended illness—four months of hospitalization, and a year and a half of outpatient care. Dad had one pre-teen and two teenage daughters to "ride herd on," as he used to say. Having just sent my "baby" off to college, I can fully appreciate the fulltime job that the care and nurturing of teenagers involves. One of my fondest memories is of dad sitting at the picnic table outside, head in his hands, crying as he asked God for guidance and healing. He told me that God was his buddy and that no matter what happened he would take care of us. Dad lived each moment and gave the trials of each moment his undivided attention. He tended to the matters at hand. He loved and nurtured my mother through her illness and he was there for his daughters, all the while keeping the family running midst the pressures of his daughters' ongoing teenage life. But we were all very aware of what drove his engine. My father spent every Wednesday night from midnight to one in the morning on his knees before his God at our parish church's perpetual adoration. He spent every morning before work praying his morning offering. He never ceased to tell us how much we were loved and how much God loved us. He took us by the hand and led us into a personal relationship with our God. We knew God because my father and mother knew him intimately. Attentiveness to the concerns at hand, faith in the living God, and love kept my father going during those dark days as he waited for the healing he so desperately sought for my mother. The faith of my dad and mother was rock solid. It was an Advent faith that demanded that they live in the present, fully aware of the God who guided, strengthened, and uplifted their lives. It was a faith that looked to the future, confident that God would continue to be with our family no matter what circumstances befell us. Dad exuded his loving self to everyone he met.

Dad was not called to evangelize on the streets or run a soup kitchen. But he was called to teach his family how to love with a passion that could not help but spill out to the world's poor, oppressed, and downtrodden. That dark time for my parents was one of life's time-outs. It was a time-out to discover what was really important in life and to encounter the action and loving presence of the living God in their lives. It was a time-out to love even when love was difficult. It was a time that demanded attention to the present, but invited hope for the future.

Advent is a time-out from life's rat race to contemplate the God who dwells within and who continues to crash into our lives. It is a time to access our relationship with God and our relationship with the world around us as we wait for the constant Incarnation of Christ amidst the mud and muck of our own lives and the lives of the world's forsaken.

Participants share an experience from their lives that connects with the biblical interpretation just shared.

What was Matthew trying to tell his community? What does he have to say to your community and to you today? How are the biblical themes of covenant, exodus, creation, and community evident in today's readings? (In the gospel and readings for this first Sunday of Advent, is there evidence of God's promise to be with us [covenant], the passage from death to life-transformation [exodus], God's continuing action of creation and recreation [creation], and the presence of God in the community of believers [community]?) Do you still feel the same way about this text as when you began? Has your original understanding been stretched, challenged, or affirmed?

STEP 5
DECISION

The gospel demands a response.

How does our understanding of these scriptures and today's liturgy call us to transformation? In what way does our community need to grow in the fullness of today's scriptures? In what concrete ways is our parish called to respond? How have I been challenged to grow as a result of our sharing? What is one concrete action I will take this week as a response to the liturgy today?

Pastoral Considerations: Advent is a time of spiritual preparation and conversion. How might we assist families in keeping the spirituality of Advent in the fore, in light of the season's rampant consumerism? Every household might be encouraged to have a copy of *Catholic Household Blessings and Prayers* (NCCB) that includes pertinent prayers and blessings for use in the Advent season: "At Table During Advent," 64–69, "Blessing of an Advent Wreath," 110–12, "Blessing of a Christmas Tree," 113, "Blessing of a Christmas Crèche or Manger Scene," 117. A beautiful, scripturally-based Advent calendar is available from Liturgy Training Publications for use in homes and classrooms.

Advent is a time for increased efforts to uphold the values of justice that we should be emphasizing throughout the year. What are some creative ways to call attention to the ongoing ministries of justice in your parish? Who are the poor in our midst? In what way are the needs of the poor addressed in our parishes? If there are no organized efforts, perhaps groups might join forces with civic groups dedicated to providing necessities, meals, and gifts for the poor. What local agencies might benefit from our increased participation?

Christian Initiation: What rites might be celebrated during Advent? The RCIA insists that the catechumenate proper should last at least one year from the rite of acceptance until initiation at the Easter Vigil (National Statutes #6). Catechumens are thus formed in the life, death, and resurrection of Christ as it unfolds in the gospel proclaimed in the liturgy in one complete liturgical cycle. Parishes that celebrate the rite of acceptance on the First Sunday of Advent and initiation at the vigil, have a catechumenate that lasts only four months at best. Catechumens are thus formed in only a third of the paschal mystery of Jesus Christ! This deserves serious reflection, discernment, and attention and invites us to ask ourselves what informs our pastoral practices. In a year-round catechumenate the rite of acceptance is celebrated about four times a year, thus giving people the opportunity to move in and out of the process according to *their* timetable, not ours.

One rite that might be celebrated is the *anointing of catechumens.* This rite "symbolizes their need for God's help and strength so that, undeterred by the bonds of the past and overcoming the opposition of the devil, they will forthrightly take the step of professing their faith and will hold fast to it unfalteringly throughout their lives (RCIA 99)." Advent, with its emphasis on repentance and conversion, might be an excellent time to celebrate it.

The blessings (RCIA 95–96) and minor exorcisms (RCIA 90–93) should be used regularly (perhaps each time) as the catechumens gather. If blessings are used with baptized candidates, remember to adapt the blessings to reflect that they are one with us by virtue of the baptism we share.

DOCTRINAL ISSUES

What church truth/teaching/doctrinal issue could be drawn from the gospel for the first Sunday of Advent?

Participants suggest possible doctrinal themes that flow from the readings.

Possible Doctrinal Themes

Advent; eschatology; kingdom of God; discipleship; repentance and reconciliation; Christ's coming: future, present, past; Son of Man; parousia

Present the doctrinal material at this time.

1. The facilitator gives input on a particular doctrinal issue of his/her prior choosing. OR

2. Group members choose a doctrinal issue from the list they created. They read together from appropriate church documents or the Doctrinal Appendix.

(The doctrinal issues are found in the Doctrinal Appendix in the back of this workbook. If you are choosing an issue from this resource, please refer to it now.)

Reflection questions centered around the chosen doctrinal theme can be found at the end of each topic in the Doctrinal Appendix. The questions are based on the five-step reflection process. If you choose a topic not included in the Doctrinal Appendix, craft your own questions according to the same five-step process.

Following the reflection questions you will be reminded to return to Chapter 7, "Preparing the Catechetical Session," to assist you in crafting your own session.

Closing Prayer

Faithful Covenant God,
During this Advent time of prayer and recollection,
we turn our gaze toward you.
We acknowledge our total dependence on your mercy.
Look with kindness on your people.
Nourish us with the food of expectant faith,
Allow our hidden hopes to discover the possibilities that lie within.
Help us to risk, to reach beyond our normal, safe solutions to life's queries.
O Father and Mother of the Universe, your Son is coming and will not delay.
You will bring every hidden hope to light and reveal yourself in our secret desires.
Lead us deeper into the dim lit shadows of winter's dusk and have pity on us.
We ask this through your Son, Jesus Christ, our Savior and Lord. Amen.[34]

[34]Inspired by: Carroll Stuhlmueller, C.P. *Biblical Meditations for Advent and the Christmas Season* (New York/Ramsey, Paulist Press, 1980.)

SECOND SUNDAY OF ADVENT

Environment (see First Sunday of Advent)

John the Baptist is a primary character in today's gospel. Perhaps an icon bearing his image might be included in the gathering space.

Lighting the Advent Candles

Prayer to accompany the lighting of the remaining candles throughout Advent:

The following prayer may be used each time your group gathers and a new candle is lit each week.

Two Advent candles are lighted as the leader says:
Blessed are you, Lord God of all creation:
in the darkness and in the light.
Blessed are you as we wait in joyful hope
for the coming of our savior, Jesus Christ.

All respond:
For the kingdom, the power, and the glory are yours, now and forever.

The leader says:
Come, Lord Jesus!

All respond:
Come quickly!

The leader says:
Let us live soberly, justly, and devoutly in this world
as we wait in joyful hope
for the coming of our Savior, Jesus Christ.

All respond:
For the kingdom, the power, and the glory are yours, now and forever.

(Adapted from *Catholic Household Blessings and Prayers,* NCCB, 1988, 64–67.)

INTRODUCTORY RITES

Opening Song (or Entrance Antiphon)

People of Zion, the Lord will come to save all the nations, and your hearts will exult to hear his majestic voice (see Is 30:19, 20).

Opening Prayer

The facilitator of the session may lead the prayer. Others in the group may be asked to proclaim the readings.

Let us pray
[in Advent time for the coming Savior to teach us wisdom]

Pause for silent prayer.

Father in heaven,
the day draws near when the glory of your Son
will make radiant the night of the waiting world.
May the lure of greed not impede us from the joy
which moves the hearts of those who seek him.
May the darkness not blind us
to the vision of wisdom
which fills the minds of those who find him.
We ask this in the name of Jesus the Lord.[1]

LITURGY OF THE WORD

The readings are proclaimed.

First Reading[2]
Isaiah 11: 1–10

---

[1]Second Sunday of Advent: "Alternative Opening Prayer," *The Sacramentary.*

[2]The exegesis for the first and second readings may or may not be the focus of your group's reflection as there may only be time to give adequate attention to the gospel, your primary concern. However, the exegesis is included here in order to provide a thorough investigation of the entire liturgy of the word as there may be parts (or all) that would be necessary to the direction you wish to take with your particular ministry group.

(See First Sunday of Advent for overview of the Book of Isaiah.)

In the overview of Isaiah from last week we noticed how Isaiah's prophecy about a future messiah evolved. It arose in response to the refusal of the kings of Israel to obey and yield to Yahweh's rule over their nation.

Today's pericope from a section called "Book of Emmanuel" (7:1–12:6) introduces us to the image of an ideal future king who can trace his origins to the family of David. This future king would be endowed with the spirit of God and would be richly gifted. This king would reestablish Israel's proper political place in the world. According to Reginald Fuller, the benefits of this king's reign are described in three pairs: "... 'wisdom and understanding' are powers of the intellect; 'counsel and might' denote practical ability; 'knowledge and fear of the Lord' are gifts of piety."[3] This messiah to come will usher in a world that is "clearly not of this world."[4]

Throughout scripture the tree is associated with images of a royal dynasty. Isaiah compares David's dynasty to a "'stump' (vs.1), that seemingly lifeless vestige of what had once been a flourishing tree. But he encouraged his contemporaries not to lose heart, because even from the stump of 'Jesse' (David's father) the Lord could bring forth a new shoot."[5] Isaiah seems to be holding out to the world the dream of a universal paradise. He envisions the reestablishment of Eden's paradise, where God willed that all creation live in peaceful harmony. The intention of Isaiah's oracle was to comfort the people with future hope of a messianic reign in which all people would live in peace and harmony rather than in discord and the destruction of war. Evildoers would have no control over people in Isaiah's future messianic world.

If Christ then is the messiah and we are living in this messianic age, how do we respond to the skeptics who say to us: "Where is this messiah of yours? It does not take a rocket scientist to see that Isaiah's utopian paradise did not arrive with his Advent. Where is this kingdom of peace on earth? We see no lions and lambs enjoying idyllic harmony. We are still faced with sin, violence, and injustice." The just shoot of Isaiah is truly Christ, *The One Who Is To Come.* However, Advent reminds us that Christ ushered in the reign of *now and not yet.* No, we have not reached Isaiah's paradise. As long as there is pain, suffering, and injustice we will continue to be in the process of becoming what and who we were created to be. But when two or more are gathered in Christ's name and *truly* living the message he came to proclaim, there *is* peace, harmony, and the restored order of creation. Only then will we be living in covenant relationship with God evidenced by our behavior *(hesed)*—the way we take care of God's people and God's world. When two or more are gathered and living in right relationship, then are the hungry fed and justice given to the oppressed. The small ways we live Christianity here on earth gives us a brief glimpse of future life in the new and eternal city.

Responsorial Psalm
Psalm 72:1–2, 7–8, 12–13, 17

This psalm is the prayer of a monarch during times of prosperity and peace. It was later understood in terms of the messianic prophecy, both from a Jewish and Christian perspective.

Second Reading
Romans 15:4–9

(See First Sunday of Advent for the overview of Paul's letter to the Romans.)

While Isaiah envisioned the human community living in peaceful harmony, Paul insisted that it be realized in the Christian community. In Romans 14:1–15:13, Paul invites discernment and love when it comes to the difficulties within the community. Christians who commit to Christ are expected to live in peace with one another. The antidote for discord is love. The tension Paul addresses is due to the factions (the weak *and* the strong) within the Roman community. Paul aligned himself with the strong and agreed with them that God's reign does not demand strict observance of

[3] *PL,* 5.
[4] *DL* (I), 67.
[5] *WWC,* 4.

the law. They did not see the need to participate in the religious practices of the former age. Their life in Christ was all that mattered. The *weak* brought their former traditions with them and were not ready to forego them. Paul, therefore, permitted diversity in the community's ritual practices. Most of chapter fourteen provides instruction for living in harmony within the Christian community. Paul's model for living in right Christian relationship is Jesus Christ crucified. Christ is the reason we are accepted by God and "the model of how they [we] are to accept one another in mutual service: 'Welcome one another, then, as Christ has welcomed you, for the glory of God.'"[6]

It is important to remember that when a New Testament passage refers to *scriptures* it is a reference to the Old Testament. The New Testament had yet to be written. The Advent readings reflect an image of God's word as a book of hope, especially evident in today's pericope. The *scriptures* of the Old Testament looked to the day of fulfillment in the person of the *Messiah To Come* and the completion of God's action in history at the end of the world. He expected the strong to support the weak and "bear the burden of their scruples and baggage from the past."[7] Paul invited his churches to search the scriptures for the strength and wisdom to avoid behavior that would cause discord among disciples. Paul no doubt is speaking a powerful word for the Roman community, but it is also a word for the church today. Division is rampant and seeks to destroy the unity Christ demands. Paul insists that we consciously work for the unity that is expected of us. Love, acceptance, and self-sacrifice are the key.

Paul insists that the scriptures were written to instill hope. Inherent within hope lies the promise that when God acts, seeds of even more hope lie within the action. For example, when God sent his Son, **the fulfillment of our hope,** there was, within that event, hope for more of God's unfolding love as Christ continued and still continues to direct the ongoing drama of human life. The ultimate hope, however, lies in that future hope which ignites our ongoing Christian life—the great eschaton and Christ's second coming.

[6]*WNT,* 335.

[7]*WWC,* 4.

Gospel[8]
Matthew 3:1–12

John the Baptist appeared in the desert of Judea preaching a message of repentance.

STEP 1
NAMING ONE'S EXPERIENCE

What were your first impressions, your first response to the gospel (or the other readings)?[9] What captured your attention?

Each person names his or her initial impression. Statements should be brief. No reasons should be given at this time. All simply listen without agreeing or disagreeing.

STEP 2
UNDERSTANDING

In a brief statement, what do you think this gospel is trying to convey? In your opinion, what does it mean?

All share their understanding of what the text is trying to convey.

STEP 3
INPUT FROM VISION/STORY/TRADITION

Liturgical Context[10]

The second Sunday of Advent begins the movement from a future-oriented eschatology and

[8]The gospel exegesis is provided later in this session so that it may be presented in the proper sequence where it occurs in the adult five-step reflection process. The exegesis is provided for the first and second readings for your information and edification, and for you to use at your discretion. Once again, the gospel is the primary source of reflection. If there is time for reflection on the other readings, all the better.

[9]The primary focus of reflection is the gospel. However, very often the other readings demand attention and must be brought into the dialogue.

[10]The scriptures in the Lectionary, the seasons of the year, and the ritual prayers of the mass are interrelated and

moves into preparation for the Incarnation of Christ. Reginald Fuller reminds us that this shift is evident in all three readings, and also that hints of a future-oriented eschatology are evident in the second readings for both this Sunday and next. The Second and Third Sundays of Advent focus on the character of John the Baptist and his theme of repentance and conversion to Christ. John's preaching is a living word today as we too prepare our hearts for Christ's coming.

Conversion, repentance, and justice are themes that jump from the pages of today's scriptures. The opening prayer invites this conversion when it asks the God of power and mercy to remove all obstacles to our receiving Christ with joy.

Gospel Exegesis

The facilitator provides input regarding critical biblical scholarship on this text. The input includes insights as to how people would have heard the gospel in Jesus' time.

Matthew 3:1–12: This Sunday our attention turns to immediate preparation for the Incarnation of Jesus Christ. It is interesting that the first character we hear from proclaims Jesus' life and work, not necessarily his birth. John the Baptist points to the church's wider perspective of the Incarnation. The Incarnation is far more than the singular reality of Christ's nativity. The Incarnation, in the eyes of contemporary biblical scholarship, includes the entire mystery of Christ: his life, death, resurrection, ascension, and the coming of the Spirit at Pentecost. The Incarnation envelops the entire Christ-event. It is quite fitting that the Baptist proclaimed Jesus' overall message of repentance and the establishment of God's reign—here and now. The advent of Christ "is not just his nativity but rather his total coming."[11]

The issue of the *kingdom of God* is a primary focus for Matthew. It was one of Jesus' fundamental themes. Over and over Jesus announced the establishment of God's *kingdom.* He announced it in story and parable. In order to fully appreciate the impact and urgency of his message it is important to understand the history and symbolism associated with the term. *Kingdom of God* was laced with meaning and metaphors that track the salvation history of a people in relationship with their God. Prior to the Babylonian Exile there was a common myth (story) about God and his reign. This myth came out of the people's political and national experience of monarchy. This is how it went: God was so powerful that he created the heavens and the earth; God delivered the people out of bondage into a land of milk and honey; God "defeated their enemies like a conquering warrior, and gave them the promised land. He was universal king, judging the nations, and his 'reign' was thought to encompass his whole creation."[12] This reign was understood as the Kingdom of God. The myth of this Warrior God who would protect, defend, and judge the people was the foundation for ancient Israel.

But then their worst nightmare became a reality. Israel's political applecart was turned on its end and the people were taken into exile in Babylonia. Their present world-view shifted and the basis for their national solidarity had to be reordered. The notion of *Kingdom of God* became an eschatological myth used to uphold people in times of despair, destruction, and persecution. In the years before Christ's birth an apocalyptic fervor existed that understood the myth in terms of their present evil age and the good age to come. The present evil age was to be overthrown in one last great action of God. God would overthrow and judge the present evil kingdoms and in so doing reestablish a reign of peace like the peace of Eden at the creation of the world. The more horrible the situation of the world, the surer was the sign that the end was near. The political and cosmic sign of the times would let the people know that the time was at hand.

Not every Jewish person of the time understood such things in the literal sense, but some did. Regardless of whether it was understood literally or not, the phrase *Kingdom of God* immediately evoked images of Israel's corporate story. "It was a *symbolic phrase recalling the kingdom myth,* the myth in which

---

form the basis for liturgical catechesis. The *liturgical context* attempts to explore and clarify the themes and this interrelatedness.

[11] *PL,* 6.

[12] *NTI,* 413.

God created the world and his people, protected and sustained all that he had created, judging and defeating enemies, even judging the people when they did not conform to the covenant."[13] The symbolic phrase, *Kingdom of God,* would spark and incite the hope of Israel during Jesus' time—the establishment of God's reign.

As alluded to before, such mythical language conjures meaning that expands the literal understanding. In today's gospel John proclaimed that the *kingdom of God is at hand.* The Jew of that culture would have understood that to mean that the anticipated eschatological kingdom had already begun. In their time and in that place they were participants in the fulfillment of what they understood to be a future hope. John the Baptist and Jesus were saying: the future is now. No longer was it necessary to anticipate it; now was the time to respond to it. *"There is no need to look for signs. It is not necessary—the kingdom of God as envisioned by Israel is already in your midst!"* Perhaps for them it was as awesome a proclamation as it would be for us today if we were told that Jesus had returned and was speaking to crowds down at the civic arena! How many of us would jump on the first bus?

Let us take a closer look at this character called John. We would hardly take him seriously were he to arrive on the scene today! John comes to us from the desert, a place of testing and encounter with God. In that great sojourn of former days his ancestors crossed the desert before entering the promised land. Like their ancestors before them, would the Jewish people dare accept John's invitation to cross into a new promised land? Would they take that bold new step? Were they ready for a new sojourn? A new kingdom? The choice lay before them.

John demanded a complete turning away from sin and the changing of the mind, heart, and soul toward God (*metanoia*). "Outside this use of the word (*metanoia*) for an individual's 'conversion,' when the first gospel mentions the word it usually refers to the need for communal or social reconstruction (3:2, 8, 11; 4:17; 11:20–21; 12:41; 17:17; 23:37)."[14] John expected no less than complete communal and individual conversion. He preached repentance, baptism, and the end of time.

Many who followed John and his teaching believed him to be the messiah. Because of John's martyrdom and the admiration Jesus had for him, the early Christian community regarded him as the forerunner of Jesus. "Matthew goes farther than other evangelists by making John a 'little Jesus,' putting Jesus' own central message in his mouth. . . ."[15] In that same vein, Matthew even identified John with Elijah. However, we are not to miss the point—there is to be no mistake. Matthew pulls no punches. The scriptures are definitive about John's role: **he was not the messiah.** John simply (or not so simply) paved the way for the *One whose sandals he was not fit to tie.*

By word and symbol John preached his message of corporate reform to Israel. Even his clothing lent a silent credibility and authority to his preaching. Camel's hair, cinched with a leather belt, was the clothing of the prophets—especially Elijah. Locusts and wild honey were the food of the wilderness. These connected John to Samson, Samuel, and Elijah of "the Old Testament tradition of resistance to injustice and the revolutionary model of renewing society."[16]

John's preaching invited reformation of the culture. Obviously John and his crowd were unhappy with the way things were. He challenged the elite of his day, calling them (the Pharisees and Sadducees) a "brood of vipers." In essence he linked their paternity to that of snakes—an insult of the highest order in a shame-based culture such as that of early Palestine. The moniker he attached to them was intended to point a finger and directly challenge the customary way that honor and status were tied to a person's circumstance of birth. Heading off their response, John insisted that honor should be based on moral, not prestigious grounds. One's actions were to hold far more weight than one's pedigree. The Pharisees and Sadducees did not accept his revolutionary message. "John does not find in them (who are economically and politically powerful) the will to change."[17]

[13]Ibid., 414.

[14]*HD,* 196.

[15]Benedict T. Viviano, O.P., "The Gospel According to Matthew," *NJBC,* 637.

[16]*CWJ,* 5.

[17]*SWTLY,* 7.

John also confronted the high priesthood of Jerusalem that levied exorbitant temple taxes, seized properties, and caused scarcities in the food supply. The ordinary priests and the people of the outlying villages fell prey to the burden imposed by the priestly hierarchy in Jerusalem. John was once an ordinary priest himself and therefore knew well the intolerable conditions that contributed to the social climate of dis-ease. Prophets always championed the cause of the poor and downtrodden. John followed the hallowed tradition that preceded him.

John's message demands that listeners ancient and contemporary take notice. Those who do not heed the Baptist's message will endure the fires of judgment. The conversion and reordering of relationships demanded by John's new repentance will be evident through our behavior. There is no middle ground. We will either comply or we will be divided at the end. We will either give ourselves over completely to God, uphold the rights of the downtrodden or we will be cast off like the chaff and the wheat. It is a sobering, frightening word! Have we watered it down to accommodate our twentieth century sensibilities? When there are brothers and sisters the world over fighting for justice and peace, where do we stand? Are we so caught up in the concerns of our lives that we, like the Pharisees of John's day, fail to stand in solidarity with the marginalized of the world? We cannot look at John without asking ourselves such questions. "Those who have given their lives [for the cause of justice and peace] are also precursors of Jesus in some way. They are calling us to convert and to prepare the way for the advent of the Lord."[18]

The reign of God, the justice of God, *metanoia,* conversion—there is so much in today's gospel to consume, chew, and savor. Even though our attention turns to the immediate preparation for the Christ-event at Christmas, gospels such as the one for the Second Sunday of Advent will not allow us to indulge in sentimental piety. We are forced to look at John the herald and ask how we either follow in his steps or hide in his shadow. "We must not speak of God's love coming down at Christmas without remembering that the divine love is fierce in its judgment of those who resist love's demands. John the Baptist warns us that repentance must not be procrastinated."[19]

Proclaim the gospel again.

Sometimes we gain new insights when we hear the text after the interpretation has been given. Someone from the group proclaims the gospel a second time.

STEP 4
TESTING

Conversation with the Liturgy and the Scriptures

Test your original understanding in dialogue with the text. (You might consider breaking into smaller groups.)

Now that you've heard what the scholars have to say about this passage, how do you feel about it? How does your original understanding of this gospel compare with what we just shared? Were there any new insights for you? How does this story speak to your life?

Sharing Life Experience

> *The other day a beautiful African-American woman shared a story of conversion,* metanoia, *and healing with me. She told me how for most of her adult life she found herself in predominantly white parish communities. She shared an experience of incredible healing centered around the eucharist. It happened during the Rodney King affair. She found herself filled with rage over the whole incident. She felt the piercing hatred of the white community. It made her take a look at her rage, her pain, and her own prejudice. "Do they all hate us?"*
>
> *The week "all hell broke loose" her pastor did not even mention the situation in so much as a prayer of the faithful, which further compounded her anguish. Then it was time to go to communion. She could not go. Her feet were like cement. "I cannot stand in solidarity with these people." She had to face her rage and her corporate wounds head-on. She*

[18]Ibid., 8.

[19]*MI,* 20.

asked God to heal her brokenness. She could not—would not move. But then slowly, she took that first step. From that moment, the rest was easy. As she approached the table she was overwhelmed by the healing love of God for her and for all those in her community. She could come to the table in unity because of Christ's sacrifice. He understood the prejudice and misunderstanding because he had once walked in her shoes.

This beautiful woman and I stood in tearful embrace. I asked her forgiveness for the injustice, prejudice, and hate she and all her brothers and sisters have had to endure because of white prejudice. I asked her for forgiveness for the subliminal ways I have contributed to racial prejudice, while believing I was enlightened. I was so ashamed.

Together we shared a moment of solidarity. I could not begin to know this woman's pain. I could own my participation in it, however. John the Baptist demands metanoia. *I never considered myself a prejudiced person, but upon careful examination I could share with her how insidious the seeds of prejudice are within a culture. The stereotypes, the media propaganda—we are impacted by it whether we care to admit it or not.*

If I am to follow John's mandate, then I must be a strong voice of unity and reconciliation. If the reign of God is **now** *and* **not yet,** *I can participate in the* **not yet** *by living fully in the* **now.** *If paradise means that the lion and the lamb rest in harmony, then I must initiate a similar paradise wherever and whenever I can. If Advent prepares for the coming of Christ at Christmas, in our everyday lives and upon his return, how will I ever be ready if I cannot fully embrace the Christ that lives within all my brothers and sisters in the human family? There is no Greek or Jew, slave or free in the kingdom of God. There are only citizens. Wherever the perfidious evil of prejudice lurks, the judgment of God is not far behind.*

Participants share an experience from their own lives that connect with the biblical interpretation just shared.

What was Matthew trying to tell his community? In what way is the *kingdom of God,* as envisioned in today's gospel, a reality (or not) in your parish community? How might John's word to the "brood of vipers" be a challenge to the contemporary church or your parish? How is it a challenge for you personally?

How does your parish live the mandate of justice in John's gospel? Who are the marginalized in your community, parish, or family? Who are those whose worthiness (pedigree) is suspect? What are you going to do about it? What are the areas in our communal and personal life that are in most need of conversion? Do you still feel the same way about this text as when you began? Has your original understanding been stretched, challenged, or affirmed?

Step 5
Decision

The gospel demands a response.

How does our understanding of these scriptures and today's liturgy call us to transformation? In what concrete ways might our parish respond to the Baptist's call for repentance? Has this conversation with the exegesis changed or stretched my personal attitudes? What are the implications of this gospel in my life? What is one concrete action I will take this week as a response to the liturgy today?

Pastoral Considerations: If your parish is not celebrating the sacrament of reconciliation during Advent, you might consider celebrating a non-sacramental penitential service (chapter V, Rite of Penance). How is your parish exercising a preferential option for the poor? In what way is your parish reaching out to the poor in your community? What kind of outreach is available to the poor in third world countries? Who are the marginalized in your community (those without a voice or those who seem to have little credibility)? What might you do to reach out and include them in the life of your community?

Christian Initiation: The minor rites, blessings, and exorcisms are intended for use throughout the catechumenate, whenever catechumens gather. (Remember to adapt your language to respect the status of the baptized when using a blessing.)

What might your strategies be for including those in your initiation process in the ministries of justice and the apostolate in your parish? Perhaps those who minister to the sick and the poor in your parish would be willing to invite a catechumen to join them. How are you welcoming inquirers who come to you at this time? If you do not have an ongoing process, are you ministering to them or asking them to wait until next year? This issue needs your serious consideration.

DOCTRINAL ISSUES

What church truth/teaching/doctrinal issue could be drawn from the gospel for the Second Sunday of Advent?

Participants suggest possible doctrinal themes that flow from the readings.

Possible Doctrinal Themes

Advent; eschatology; kingdom of God; discipleship; repentance and reconciliation; Christ's coming: future, present, past; Son of Man; parousia

Present the doctrinal material at this time.

1. The facilitator gives input on a particular doctrinal issue of his/her prior choosing. OR

2. The group chooses a doctrinal issue from the list they created. They read together from appropriate church documents or the Doctrinal Appendix.

(The doctrinal issues are found in the Doctrinal Appendix in the back of this workbook. If you are choosing an issue from this resource, please refer to it now.)

Reflection questions centered around the chosen doctrinal theme can be found at the end of each topic in the Doctrinal Appendix. The questions are based on the five-step reflection process. If you choose a topic not included in the Doctrinal Appendix, craft your own questions according to the same five-step process.

Following the reflection questions you will be reminded to return to Chapter 7, "Preparing the Catechetical Session," to assist you in crafting your own session.

Closing Prayer

Father, all-powerful and ever-living God,
we do well always and everywhere to give you
thanks
through Jesus Christ our Lord.
When he humbled himself to come among us as a
man,
he fulfilled the plan you formed long ago
and opened for us the way to salvation.
Now we watch for the day,
hoping that the salvation promised us will be ours
when Christ our Lord will come again in his
glory.[20]

[20]"Preface—Advent I," *The Sacramentary.*

Third Sunday of Advent

Environment

John the Baptist is still a figure in today's gospel. Today is Gaudete Sunday. The name comes from the entrance antiphon from today's liturgy. Every mass has an entrance antiphon (usually a phrase from scripture) assigned to it, and it used to be a custom to assign a title to every Sunday mass. The title was a Latin word taken from the first word of the entrance antiphon. The first word today is rejoice—Gaudete! The color of vestments for today's liturgy is rose, which might be creatively incorporated into the gathering space.

Lighting the Advent Candles

Prayer to accompany the lighting of the remaining candles throughout Advent:

The following prayer may be used each time your group gathers and a new candle is lit each week.

Three Advent candles are lighted as the leader says:
Blessed are you, Lord God of all creation:
in the darkness and in the light.
Blessed are you as we wait in joyful hope
for the coming of our savior, Jesus Christ.

All respond:
For the kingdom, the power, and the glory are
yours, now and forever.

The leader says:
Come, Lord Jesus!

All respond:
Come quickly!

The leader says:
Let us live soberly, justly, and devoutly in this world
as we wait in joyful hope
for the coming of our Savior, Jesus Christ.

All respond:
For the kingdom, the power, and the glory are
yours, now and forever.

(Adapted from *Catholic Household Blessings and Prayers,* NCCB, 1988, 64–67.)

INTRODUCTORY RITES

Opening Song (or Entrance Antiphon)

Rejoice in the Lord always; again I say, rejoice!
The Lord is near. (Phil 4:4, 5)[1]

Opening Prayer

The facilitator of the session may lead the prayer. Others in the group may be asked to proclaim the readings.

Let us pray
[that God will fill us with joy at the coming of Christ]

Pause for silent prayer.

Lord God, may we, your people,
who look forward to the birthday of Christ
experience the joy of salvation
and celebrate that feast with love and thanksgiving.
We ask this through our Lord Jesus Christ, your
Son,
who lives and reigns with you and the Holy Spirit,
one God forever and ever. Amen.[2]

LITURGY OF THE WORD

The readings are proclaimed.

First Reading[3]
Isaiah 35:1–6, 10[4]

---

[1]Third Sunday of Advent: "Entrance Antiphon," *The Sacramentary.*

[2]Third Sunday of Advent: "Opening Prayer," *The Sacramentary.*

[3]The exegesis for the first and second readings may or may not be the focus of your group's reflection as there may only be time to give adequate attention to the gospel, your primary concern. However, the exegesis is included here in order to provide a thorough investigation of the entire liturgy of the word as there may be parts (or all) that would be necessary to the direction you wish to take with your particular ministry group.

[4]See the First Sunday of Advent for an overview of the Book of Isaiah.

Today's reading nestled in the first section of Isaiah (ch. 1–39), is believed to have been penned by the writer of Deutero-Isaiah (ch. 40–) and inserted in the earlier chapters. The reading speaks of the return from the Babylonian exile in the context of the Exodus. The desert will bloom as it did in the Exodus and "the ransomed of the Lord will return and come to Zion."[5] In this triumphant return there will be signs. The blind will see, the deaf will hear, and the lame will walk. The prophet is a bearer of hope to a people steeped in the hopelessness of exile. The people were not to fear; they were to rejoice and be hopeful as Yahweh would see them through the arduous journey back home, through the desert to their homeland.

All nature would rejoice over the saving works of God. Such rejoicing in the cosmos had always been associated with the arrival of the exemplary king and the messianic age. Those returning would be richly blessed. The weak would be made strong and the frightened would find courage. All would congregate joyfully in Zion because of the great works of the Lord.

This passage reflects hopes for the return to the paradise of creation. It was understood that the messianic age would usher in the perfect harmony envisioned by God at the creation of the world. In the New Testament the signs and wonders of today's reading became associated with the miraculous works of Christ. Christ was understood as the ideal king and the messianic age was understood to be fulfilled and ushered in by Jesus Christ.

In the gospel for the Third Sunday of Advent, Jesus exhorts his disciples to go to John in prison and tell him that the deeds foretold in the Old Testament prophetic texts are fulfilled in the person of none other than himself—Jesus Christ, Son of the Father.

Responsorial Psalm
Psalm 146:6–7, 8–9, 9–10

This is a "Halley" (Halleluia) psalm. It praises the wonderful works of Yahweh in salvation history. It picks up the same themes reminiscent of the messianic age found in the first reading.

[5]*PL*, 7.

Second Reading
James 5:7–10

Overview of James: The letter of James is not a letter at all, but a parenesis—a moral exhortation or instruction. Parenesis is a common literary form of the ancient Hellenistic, Christian, and Jewish worlds. Christian tradition freely employed this common form of moral imperative. James used common Hellenistic literary techniques such as plays on words and the diatribe in which there is an imaginary conversation between the writer and an imaginary person.

Tradition maintained that James is the James identified as the brother of Jesus. However, there is much to discount that assertion. The date of the text antedates him; the text uses later Greek literary devices; the text makes little reference to Jesus, and the letter does not reflect James' conservative approach to the Law.[6]

One distinctive characteristic of the letter is the insistence that faith not be a matter of abstract theory, but be put into concrete everyday action. James exhorts the poor and those who experience trials and tribulations to be joyful, and to patiently endure. He called for prayer, wisdom, confidence, and faithfulness to the word of God until the Lord comes. The audience was probably a Jewish-Christian community in the outlying area of Palestine. The probable date of the letter is around 60 C.E., before Paul's teaching on faith and works and before the destruction of the temple in Jerusalem in 70 C.E.

Today's Pericope: The *coming of the Lord* referred to in today's reading is not a reference to the first coming of Jesus, but rather the final judgment. It is reminiscent of Advent's overall theme of the reign of God *now* and *not yet.* We prepare for the Christ of history, the Christ present in our midst, and the Christ who will come again. The theme of joy is tempered with the caution to be watchful and patient as we await the Lord's return.

In the verses before today's segment, James challenged the rich for showing little concern for the poor in their midst. James then turned to the poor and reminded them that they were not for-

[6]*NTI*, 374.

gotten by God. He exhorted the community to wait patiently for the Lord's return, just as the farmer waited for the harvest. The Old Testament prophets were to be a model for the endurance James was demanding. The prophets sowed the seeds of God's word and then patiently waited for God to bring the seeds to harvest.

James proclaimed a relevant word for our contemporary society. Patience is not a common virtue in our modern culture. However, it is a virtue that fosters hope which results in faith in the salvation and eternal reward promised by Christ. "Patience is not resignation but it is the fruit of a loving faith that is content to discover God's gifts in the manner and in the moment he reveals them."[7]

Gospel[8]
Matthew 11:2–11

Jesus sent his disciples to John in prison to tell him that he [Jesus] was the One John had been heralding. Jesus then told the crowds about the greatness of John.

STEP 1
NAMING ONE'S EXPERIENCE

What were your first impressions? What was your first response to the gospel (or the other readings)?[9] What captured your attention?

Each person names his or her initial impression. Statements should be brief. No reasons should be given at this time. All simply listen without agreeing or disagreeing.

[7]*WWC,* 7.

[8]The gospel exegesis is provided later in this session so that it may be presented in the proper sequence where it occurs in the adult five-step reflection process. The exegesis is provided for the first and second readings for your information and edification, and for you to use at your discretion. Once again, the gospel is the primary source of reflection. If there is time for reflection on the other readings, all the better.

[9]The primary focus of reflection is the gospel. However, very often the other readings demand attention and must be brought into the dialogue.

STEP 2
UNDERSTANDING

In a brief statement, what do you think this gospel is trying to convey?

STEP 3
INPUT FROM VISION/STORY/TRADITION

Liturgical Context[10]

As mentioned above, today is Gaudete Sunday and *Gaudete* means *rejoice.* The entrance antiphon for today's liturgy echoes Isaiah, "The desert and the parched land will exult; the steppe will rejoice and bloom." In this midpoint through Advent, the sense of anticipated joy heightens. The purple hues reminiscent of Lenten repentance are not so subtle as to be missed altogether. However, always at the center of Advent's repentance is the undercurrent of joyful expectation. "It is a joy that guards against anxiety... that frequently goes hand in hand with the unshakable feeling of being abandoned by God. Above all, it is an interior peace 'in the Lord,' a surrendering to his providence and love, which Jesus, in the Sermon on the Mount, makes a fundamental requirement for the kingdom (Mt 6:24–34)."[11] The reserved joy of this transition point in Advent is evidenced by the plea that all be prepared and sadness removed; for it "hinders us from feeling the joy and hope which his presence will bestow."[12]

John is the prophet who explodes onto the scene during Advent and Lent in the readings as the one who exhorts us to repent and tells us of our need for God's forgiveness and redemption. John is a symbol of the preaching ministry, and reminds us that we are all called to preach the living word

[10]The scriptures in the Lectionary, the seasons of the year, and the ritual prayers of the mass are interrelated and form the basis for liturgical catechesis. The *liturgical context* attempts to explore and clarify the themes and this interrelatedness.

[11]*DL* (I), 117.

[12]Third Sunday of Advent, "Alternative Opening Prayer," *The Sacramentary.*

of God. John is the prophet who heralds the Savior and reminds us of our appointed task in this day and age. We too are to herald the Christ in our everyday lives.

In addition to repentance we are reminded that through the eucharist we are given God's help and freedom from sin. The eucharist, too, prepares us for the Incarnation, the coming of Christ in our lives. "...may this Eucharist bring us your divine help, free us from our sins, and prepare us for the birthday of Our Savior...."[13] We must not forget that Advent celebrates the *kingdom here and now and the kingdom not yet.* We look forward to the day when Jesus will return as we recall his first coming and prepare for his present coming that will explode anew at Christmas but is ongoing throughout our Christian lives.

Gospel Exegesis

The facilitator gives input regarding what critical biblical scholarship has to say about this text. The input includes insights as to how people would have heard the gospel in Jesus' time.

What a character, this John! He was in prison. Had he been stupid enough to stand for the truth? Surely he had to know what it would cost him! Was he a fool? Where were all his friends? He sat there alone. Did he wonder if it had all been a hoax? Was he depressed? Why did he ask the question: "Are you the One?" Didn't he already know the answer? He baptized Jesus, didn't he? Was he expecting a different kind of messiah? Did Jesus throw him off guard? Rather than give easy answers, Jesus sent word back to John that demanded the same response from John that he asks from us today. Jesus told John to observe the signs and figure it out for himself. The blind see, the lame walk, the deaf hear, the dead are raised to life and the poor have the good news preached to them. Of course John would know that these were the very things the scriptures of old foretold as evidence of the reign of God. God's wonderful works! God's marvelous deeds! Truly the reign of God was in his midst—in *our* midst! There is always enough evidence to proclaim the reign of God, but there is also always a fragment or a piece of ambiguity that demands that we accept the good news on faith. Who and where are the signs of God's reign in our modern world: the blind, deaf, lame, dead, and the poor? Do we recognize the signs, or are we blind to them?

Jesus did not rescue John from death row. His miracles didn't help John. Yet John still believed. He was the messenger who paved the way, after all. "He is the messenger preparing the way for the God who takes such an inhumanly long time to come and does not even hurry when his prophet is perishing, the God who always makes his point, that he wins by losing, that he is living and gives life by being put to death himself, that he is the future which seems to have no future."[14] The question from John's heart sounded like the mournful uncertainty of a disheartened prophet. Might it even echo the future anguish of One who would one day question his own Father in that famous garden: "My God, my God, why have you abandoned me?" Yet Jesus heard John's anguish and reached out to him. Jesus heard John's prayer. "In *prayer* we may show even a frightened heart to God, a heart that can practically do no more and no longer knows how long its strength will hold out. In a heart that prays there still remains faith and this receives a sufficient answer: 'Go and tell John what you see'... and 'blessed is he who takes no offense at me' even if he sits abandoned in prison."[15]

All of the speculation about what might have been the feelings and the motivation behind John's question of Jesus is, in reality, just that—speculation. We have no way of knowing for sure what was going on in John's mind and heart as he formulated his question to Jesus. We can use his question today, however, to enter the world of imagination, and in doing so, touch our own areas of doubt, fear, and uncertainty. Scholars remind us that Matthew had little concern for the historical details of the reasons for John's query. "The narrative shows no interest in the questioning as a historical event, since it has no sequel; nothing is said about what John's disciples reported or how he re-

[13]Third Sunday of Advent, "Prayer After Communion," *The Sacramentary.*

[14]*GCY,* 29.

[15]Ibid.

sponded. This is beside the point for Matthew. All weight lies on *Jesus'* response to the question."[16] Jesus' answer says more to us about his activity than it does about who he is. John asked his question on behalf of Israel. John does not speak as prophet "but as a representative member of his people (note the 'we' of the second clause)."[17] Matthew places Jesus' response in the present tense ("what you see and hear"[18]) and demands that before we can appreciate the actions of Christ the messiah, we must first appreciate the word he came to preach. Jesus preached good news to the poor and liberty to the captives. Jesus is the promised One of Israel. He announced the reign of God first in word, then in action. God was bringing to fulfillment in Jesus Christ his ultimate reign. It is not the reign Israel expected, but it is God's reign fulfilled in word and deed through God's son, Jesus, the Christ.

No wonder it was difficult for many to see Christ for who he was! He even upset simple cultural norms. Jesus' response to John would have been regarded as boastful. "Isn't Jesus boasting and thereby violating the honor rules of his culture? Isn't a Mediterranean person obliged to deny compliments (Mt 20:29–31) and avoid the appearance of grasping for honor (Mt 10:24–25) in order not to impinge on someone else's honor?"[19] Jesus asserted his rightful authority and identity and anticipated a new charge against him by "concluding with a beatitude: 'Truly honorable is the one who takes no offense at my rightful claim to honor! (V. 6).'"[20] This gospel is a polemic against all the negative responses to Jesus' ministry. Matthew is strong and clear. Jesus stands on his authority. The reader or listener is faced with a choice. God is ushering in the reign of God through the word and deeds of Jesus Christ. Will I accept it or reject it? The question is as relevant today as it was then.

In today's pericope Jesus also affirms John's place of honor in salvation history. However, there is within this affirmation a continuation of the good news he came to preach. Inherent within verse 11 is a promise. As great as John the Baptist, Christ's messenger, truly is, simple followers who believe in Christ will have an equal standing with this hero of heroes, this witness of God's definitive action in salvation history. The act of simple belief is as great as the prophetic action of John! God's *anawim* will again stand first in the reign of God.

We cannot ignore the one constant in Jesus' preaching. Jesus will not allow the poor to be forgotten. We dare not miss the point! The sign of God's reign is the poor having the good news preached to them. "Works for the sake of the poor and needy identify Jesus as the Messiah."[21] Jesus' message is the same message that God proclaimed at the creation of the world. The ideal kingdom, the paradise God intended at the creation of the world, is a kingdom where biblical justice reigns. God demanded that his children love the Lord their God with their whole heart, mind, and soul, evidenced by the love, care, and concern shown for one another and for the poor and oppressed of the world! Jesus, the realization of God's promised kingdom, reminds the poor that they are the beneficiaries of this promised reign of God!

Today's gospel poses a challenge and an invitation. We are all invited and called to be messengers of the Lord. We are all invited and called to witness to God's mighty deeds in our everyday lives. And it is to the poor that we must turn our attention. Like Jesus we must announce the good news to them. Even today the blind see, the deaf hear, the lame walk, and the sick are healed. Even today God cares for the poor—the hungry poor and the lonely poor, the homeless poor, and the empty poor. Therefore Rejoice! Gaudete! the reign of God is at hand! Look at the great and mighty deeds of the Lord.

Proclaim the gospel again.

Sometimes we gain new insights when we hear the text after the interpretation has been given. Someone from the group proclaims the gospel a second time.

[16] *MI*, 121.

[17] Ibid., 120.

[18] Contrast the present tense of Matthew with the past tense of Luke: "what you have seen and heard" (Lk 7:22).

[19] *CWJ*, 8.

[20] Ibid.

[21] *SWTLY*, 12.

Step 4
Testing

Conversation with the Liturgy and the Scriptures

Test your original understanding in dialogue with the text.

(You might consider breaking into smaller groups.)

Now that you've heard what the scholars have to say about this passage, how do you feel about it? How does your original understanding of this gospel compare with what we just shared? Were there any new insights for you? How does this story speak to your life?

Sharing Life Experience

I cannot reflect on this gospel without my thoughts and my heart turning to a beautiful young couple in our catechumenate. The husband recently got news that his father was dying of cancer. This was a difficult enough blow. A few weeks later they both received word that their six-months-old infant has an extremely rare genetic disease that usually claims its victims within the first year and a half. This is an infant who arrived after a problem pregnancy and three previous miscarriages. The child is a picture of health, so it does not seem possible that this evil omen is lurking just months around the corner! They are devastated and ask the typical questions: "Why has God done this to us? What have we done?" Our catechumens also ask: "Why do good people like this have to suffer so terribly? If God can heal the blind and the deaf, surely he will heal this precious baby, right?"

This tremendous pain has united our catechumenal community like fire that forges steel. We have explored all the scriptures that shed light on matters so crucial. Our answers still do not quell the searching, doubting, anguished hearts of this young family or the community that embraces them in love. Yet in the midst of this horror the good news is preached. The reign of God is near! Hope reigns eternal. Prayer is rising to heaven like a billowing mushroom cloud of smoke. Anguished cries go up, pleading for one of the miraculous signs we heard about in today's gospel—oh God, give us such a miracle!

Yet a miracle lies obscurely in our presence already. In the midst of this suffering, our wonderful community has become the hands, heart, and face of God to this anguished young couple. Catechumens, sponsors, and others in the parish have embraced them like a parent at the bedside of a dying child. People in the catechumenal community and beyond take meals to their home, mow their lawn, and offer prayers and encouragement. Every waking, precious moment is made available to spend with their fragile baby boy. Love is oozing out of God's people. Their love has been the presence of God for this family, which has humbly and willingly accepted the outpouring of love. The community has been a visible sign that God is walking with them in their hour of agony.

The mother called me and shared how she was reflecting on the story of the blind man. Jesus reminded the people that it was no sin that caused the blindness and that he would heal him so the glory of God could be revealed. This sorrowing mother shared that, no matter what, God's glory would be revealed through her infant son! If her baby is healed, God's power and incredible might would be manifest to a praying world. If her baby died, God's glory would be revealed through the love manifested in the community and the way it has bound us all together. They are overwhelmed by the incredible compassion of God evident in God's people.

Like John in today's gospel, this couple and our community are compelled to ask the question: "Jesus, are you the One? What signs have we been given to know that the reign of God is in the midst of this anguish?" Our answer for now is: "Look at the way we love one another!" We are standing on the word of God and entrusting this baby to the cross of the suffering Christ. But God's prompted action in our community reveals with unspoken certitude that the reign of God is in our midst.

Mother, father, and baby now wait. Our community waits with them. But it is a waiting that is bolstered by hope—hope in a God who weeps when we weep and suffers when we suffer. We wait for the God who died for us and rose for us; the God who came crashing once, who continues to crash even now, and will always crash into the lives of those who seek him with simple faith.

Participants share experiences from their own lives that connect with the biblical interpretation just shared.

What was Jesus trying to say to the community of his day? What is the relevance for us? In what way do you relate to the figure of John the Baptist in today's gospel? Jesus proclaimed the reign of God by pointing to signs of that reign. What signs of God's reign are in your midst? Do you still feel the same way about this text as when you began? Has your original understanding been stretched, challenged, or affirmed?

STEP 5
DECISION

The gospel demands a response.

How does our understanding of these scriptures and today's liturgy call us to transformation? Was there anything in this text that particularly challenged you to live in a new way? How might your parish respond to today's scriptures? Has this conversation with the exegesis invited you to think or behave in a new way? What one concrete action will you take this week as a response to today's liturgy?

Christian Initiation: Perhaps this would be a good time to invite parishioners, catechumens, and candidates to witness to the marvelous works of God in their lives. In what way are the catechumens, candidates, and sponsors invited to participate in the ministry of the word and in the ministry of action? Today's liturgy is a proclamation of the reign of God. How do we invite people to proclaim the reign of God in our midst? Explore the opportunities available in your parish.

Penitential Celebrations: Perhaps in preparation for the celebration of the mystery of Incarnation, catechumens, candidates, sponsors, and the faithful might gather for a non-sacramental penitential celebration (Chapter V–Rite of Penance). "Penitential celebrations are gatherings of the people of God to hear the proclamation of God's word. This invites them to conversion and renewal of life and announces our freedom from sin through the death and resurrection of Christ. The structure of these services is the same as that usually followed in celebrations of the word of God and given in the *Rite for Reconciliation of Several Penitents.*"[22] Refer to #36 in the Rite of Penance for the nature and structure of the Rite. It is important to consider the exhortation in # 37: "Care should be taken that the faithful do not confuse these celebrations with the celebration of the sacrament of penance. Penitential celebrations are very helpful in promoting conversion of life and purification of heart. It is desirable to arrange such services especially for these purposes:

- to foster the spirit of penance within the Christian community;
- to help the faithful to prepare for confession that can be made individually later at a convenient time;
- to help children gradually form their conscience about sin in human life and about freedom from sin through Christ;
- to help catechumens during their conversion.

Penitential celebrations, moreover, are very useful in places where no priest is available to give sacramental absolution. . . ."[23] The opening prayers and the readings from "Penitential Celebrations During Advent" [Appendix II] might be a good choice.

DOCTRINAL ISSUES

What church truth/teaching/doctrinal issue could be drawn from the gospel for the Third Sunday of Advent?

Participants suggest possible doctrinal themes that flow from the readings.

Possible Doctrinal Themes:

Advent; kingdom of God; eschatology; biblical justice; discipleship; repentance and reconciliation; Christ's coming: future, present, past; Son of Man; parousia

[22]Rites of the Catholic Church, "Rite of Penance," #36, p. 358.

[23]Ibid., #37, p. 358.

Present the doctrinal material at this time.

1. The facilitator gives input on a particular doctrinal issue of his/her prior choosing. OR

2. The group chooses a doctrinal issue from the list they created. They read together from appropriate church documents or the Doctrinal Appendix.

(The doctrinal issues are found in the Doctrinal Appendix in the back of this workbook. If you are choosing an issue from this resource, please refer to it now.)

Reflection questions centered around the chosen doctrinal theme can be found at the end of each topic in the Doctrinal Appendix. The questions are based on the five-step reflection process. If you choose a topic not included in the Doctrinal Appendix, craft your own questions according to the same five-step process.

Following the reflection questions you will be reminded to return to Chapter 7, "Preparing the Catechetical Session," to assist you in crafting your own session.

Closing Prayer

Father, all powerful and ever-living God,
we do well always and everywhere to give you thanks
through Jesus Christ our Lord.
His future coming was proclaimed by all the prophets.
The virgin mother bore him in her womb with love beyond all telling.
John the Baptist was his herald
and made him known when at last he came.
In his love Christ has filled us with joy
as we prepare to celebrate his birth,
so that when he comes he may find us watching in prayer,
our hearts filled with wonder and praise.[24]

[24]"Preface—Advent II," *The Sacramentary.*

Fourth Sunday of Advent

Environment

All four candles are lit today as Advent reaches fulfillment in the Christ event. Perhaps an anticipatory manger of empty straw might be added as the final preparatory gesture. Our hope, longing, and conversion have created this straw berth for the Lord who comes continuously and who will come again on the last day.

Lighting the Advent Candles

Prayer to accompany the lighting of the remaining candles throughout Advent:

The following prayer may be used each time your group gathers and a new candle is lit each week.

Four Advent candles are lighted as the leader says:
Blessed are you, Lord God of all creation:
in the darkness and in the light.
Blessed are you as we wait in joyful hope
for the coming of our savior, Jesus Christ.

All respond:
For the kingdom, the power, and the glory are yours, now and forever.

The leader says:
Come, Lord Jesus!

All respond:
Come quickly!

The leader says:
Let us live soberly, justly, and devoutly in this world
as we wait in joyful hope
for the coming of our Savior, Jesus Christ.

All respond:
For the kingdom, the power, and the glory are yours, now and forever.

(Adapted from *Catholic Household Blessings and Prayers,* NCCB, 1988, 64–67)

INTRODUCTORY RITES

Opening Song (or Entrance Antiphon)

Let the clouds rain down the Just One, and the earth bring forth a Savior (Is 45:8)[1]

Opening Prayer

The facilitator of the session may lead the prayer. Others in the group may be asked to proclaim the readings.

Let us pray
[as Advent draws to a close
for the faith that opens our lives
to the Spirit of God]

Pause for silent prayer.

Father, all-powerful God,
your eternal Word took flesh on our earth
when the Virgin Mary placed her life
at the service of your plan.
Lift our minds in watchful hope
to hear the voice which announces Christ's glory
and opens our minds to receive the Spirit
who prepares us for his coming.
We ask this through Christ our Lord.[2]

LITURGY OF THE WORD

The readings are proclaimed.

First Reading[3]
Isaiah 7:10–14

[1]Fourth Sunday of Advent, "Entrance Antiphon," *The Sacramentary.*

[2]First Sunday of Advent, "Opening Prayer," *The Sacramentary.*

[3]The exegesis for the first and second readings may or may not be the focus of your group's reflection as there may only be time to give adequate attention to the gospel, your primary concern. However, the exegesis is included here in order to provide a thorough investigation of the entire liturgy of the word as there may be parts (or all) that would be necessary to the direction you wish to take with your particular ministry group.

(See First Sunday of Advent for overview of the Book of Isaiah.)

There are two lens with which to view the reading from Isaiah. The first lens concerns the historical situation of the reading. Isaiah tries unsuccessfully to convince King Ahaz of the southern kingdom that everything will turn out successfully in the face of impending defeat by the northern kingdom and Syria. Isaiah tells Ahaz to *just hold tight* and to prove what he says, and Yahweh will give him a sign. Even though Ahaz refuses to listen to Isaiah, Isaiah gives him the sign anyway. The sign is a young woman who will bear a son to be called Emmanuel (God is with us). Some scholars speculate that the child in question was the future son of Ahaz and the queen, Hezekiah. The sign would definitely prove that God was with his people and that the Davidic dynasty would endure. Even before the child in the womb of Ahaz's wife would reach adulthood, the northern alliance would be defeated. Judah would be reduced in size and stature. There would be a Band-Aid approach to the immediate situation, but in the long run, the capitulation of Ahaz would lead to future disaster for Judah.

For ancient Israel a sign was understood as tangible evidence of the presence and the will of God. We are not to think of a sign in modern terms such as the distinction between natural vs. supernatural. Israel believed that even ordinary events could be a sign from Yahweh. A sign was Israel's way to understand that God was interested in human affairs. "The Israelites had a sense of the immediacy of God's presence. They believed that any event—ordinary or extraordinary—could be a sign that God was in their midst. To them an event was *wonder*-ful, or *sign*-nificant not because it abrogated a natural law, but because it testified to God's presence and activity in their midst."[4] The purpose of a sign is to give credence and authority to Yahweh's word spoken through the prophets. The significance of a sign is that not only can God's word be heard, but it can be *seen* through the action of the sign. It does not have to be miraculous; it just has to confirm the prophecy spoken as a threat or a promise.

Isaiah prophesied to a people who would not hear the word of God or see God's activity. Ahaz could have had a sign of his choosing, but he decided to go his own way. Under a pious pretense he retorted that he would not put Yahweh to the test. Frustrated, Isaiah offered a sign to the house of David. The promise made to David would stand firm. Isaiah paints the picture of "a child-king who in due time will *faithfully* exercise the task of government."[5] In the beginning this Emmanuel child would live in a time of great sorrow. The Assyrians would ravage the land, transforming it into a wasteland. Yet for those with the vision to understand, the presence of the child was to be a sign that God was leading the people through "divine judgment to the dawn of a new day."[6] This judgment was an opportunity for a new beginning. The child was a sign that God was with them in their promise-filled future that those remnant few believers would share on the other side of dark days. The child would then ascend his rightful throne and in the name of Yahweh rule the people in equity. Even though Isaiah was not looking to the distant future, there is a great temptation to see the Emmanuel child in messianic terms.

The second lens, mentioned earlier, fast forwards to the evangelists of the gospels. In the translation of the gospels used by the evangelists, the word for young woman was *virgin* (*parthenos*). The only thing on Isaiah's mind was the fact that God would have his way and Judah would eventually enjoy peace. However, when Isaiah attached his expectation of success to the promise that David's heritage would last forever, all of Israel continued to keep that hope alive. Christianity believed that Isaiah's prophetic word was fulfilled in Jesus Christ.

Responsorial Psalm

Psalm 24:1–2, 3–4, 5–6

This psalm was composed as a processional for the king as he entered the temple. In the Christian sense it can be applied to the Christ who comes triumphantly into human history through the mystery of his Incarnation.

[4] *UOT,* 74.

[5] Ibid., 334.

[6] Ibid.

Second Reading
Romans 1:1–7

(See the First Sunday of Advent for an overview of St. Paul's letter to the Romans.)

Paul extends the customary greeting to include a definition of the gospel that was the traditional (not necessarily Pauline) understanding. Paul's proclamation of the creedal statements inherent in this portion of the letter is to assure the Romans that the message Paul came to preach was a message that had already been handed on to them.

Paul made reference to the fact that Jesus was descended from David. Jesus shied away from that association as he did not want to affiliate himself with contemporary notions of a political messiah. The early church, however, when preaching to Jewish Christians, had to make such associations in order to prove that Christ was the long-awaited messiah. Davidic descent was an absolute criterion. Interestingly, the referral of Jesus' relation to David is used here by Paul to stress Jesus' humanity. Here was this man Jesus, referred to in this instance not as the exalted, ascended Christ, but the "lowly" human being descended from another "lowly" human being, the "lowly" King David. One cannot miss the touch of irony. "The Davidic descent of Jesus stresses, not his exalted majesty, but his terrestrial lowliness."[7]

Gospel[8]
Matthew 1:18–24

STEP 1
NAMING ONE'S EXPERIENCE

What were your first impressions? What was your first response to the gospel (or the other readings)?[9] What captured your attention?

Each person names his or her initial impression. Statements should be brief. No reasons should be given at this time. All simply listen without agreeing or disagreeing.

STEP 2
UNDERSTANDING

In a brief statement, what do you think this gospel is trying to convey?

STEP 3
INPUT FROM VISION/STORY/TRADITION

Liturgical Context[10]

In today's liturgy Mary takes her humble center stage role in order to point us to the reason for the Christmas event—the Incarnation of God's Son, Jesus Christ. Mary always points us to Christ, and indeed that is her role on this Fourth Sunday of Advent. The liturgy increases its energy in proclaiming the coming of Christ in anticipation of the Christmas feast. Mary's visit to her cousin Elizabeth is a reminder to us that we are to bear Christ within us, and that to do so ultimately leads us to lay down our lives in love and service of others.

The Opening Prayer for today's liturgy reminds us of the paschal nature of the Incarnation of Christ, to "... lead us through his suffering and death to the glory of the resurrection...." In this season of sentimental songs about manger babies

[7] *PL*, 12–13.

[8] The gospel exegesis is provided later in this session so that it may be presented in the proper sequence where it occurs in the adult five-step reflection process. The exegesis is provided for the first and second readings for your information and edification, and for you to use at your discretion. Once again, the gospel is the primary source of reflection. If there is time for reflection on the other readings, all the better.

[9] The primary focus of reflection is the gospel. However, very often the other readings demand attention and must be brought into the dialogue.

[10] The scriptures in the Lectionary, the seasons of the year, and the ritual prayers of the mass are interrelated and form the basis for liturgical catechesis. The *liturgical context* attempts to explore and clarify the themes and this interrelatedness.

and straw pillows, we must not forget that the reason Christmas has captured the hearts of humankind often gets obscured in its secularization. Jesus came to die and rise for us. We are to follow him and do what he did. It is driven by joy, but it is not sentimental piety. Suffering, dying, and rising are sobering reality—the real stuff of life. The liturgy offers us a reality check in the midst of our over-secularized remembrance of this feast. The Christmas event is about our salvation. "But one cannot lose sight of the fact that this birth is but the first step to Easter, and that its ultimate importance lies in the mystery of salvation in which we share."[11] In the Alternative Opening Prayer we ask that we, like Mary, be given the strength and the open hearts to place our lives in the service of God's plan. Do we really mean it? This is the question that resounds on the Fourth Sunday of Advent.

Gospel Exegesis

The facilitator provides input regarding what critical biblical scholarship has to say about this text. The input includes insights as to how people would have heard the gospel in Jesus' time.

In order to fully appreciate the impact of today's gospel we must turn our attention to the ancient Mediterranean culture and customs. Betrothal was not exactly like our common understanding of engagement. Betrothal merely meant that the couple were set aside and secured for each other. It was decided by family contract that two persons would be married for either economic or political reasons. Marriage was intended to better the family or community system. Love had little to do with it. The father of the bride entered into contract with the father of the groom's family. The betrothed couple thus began the initial process of marriage, but were not yet living together. In true fashion, Joseph might have been the last to know that something was wrong with Mary. Since she would not have been living with him, only the women of the village would have been aware that she was no longer taking part in the monthly ritual purification rites.

[11]*DL* (I), 137.

Joseph, an honorable man, loved God. He was required to demonstrate that love by following God's law and divorcing Mary. His love for God and God's just law would not allow him to turn a blind eye to her assumed indiscretion, so he knew he must divorce her. But he chose the way of mercy. Joseph decided to divorce Mary in secret so as to avoid her public humiliation. Mary's baby would not have been Joseph's. The honor code of ancient Palestine would have insisted that one man not take something that belonged to another. The baby obviously belonged to another man. By law Joseph could have exposed Mary and risked her death. Instead, being the honorable man that he was, Joseph chose to quietly divorce her in order to give the real father a chance to step forward, claim the child, and enter into marriage with Mary.

God intervened and revealed his plan to Joseph who then became an instrument in God's plan of salvation. God elevated Jesus to a position of honor when he announced to Joseph that the child would be male (considered a special gift from God) and his name would be Jesus. This piece of the story "enhance[d] Joseph's honorable reputation, for God would not honor a shameful person."[12] God wrote the story with crooked lines. Joseph reminds us that God's plan does not always fit within the confines of human laws or design. God is beyond all time and history and intervened in human events to realize his purpose.

Matthew's intention in today's pericope is to affirm our belief in the divine origin of Jesus Christ. Jesus is God's Son. The virgin birth serves as the exclamation point on the end of that sentence. Jesus is the *Anticipated One.* Jesus is the Son of God, the One sent to save the world. Jesus is Emmanuel—God is with us—the ultimate sign of God's action of salvation in the world. Jesus is the divine and the human One—fully divine and fully human. Jesus is the *Expected One* descended from David's line. "Jesus, son of Joseph" is a testament to that reality. Joseph was the true descendant of David. As Joseph's son, Jesus was the legitimate heir to the Davidic dynasty. While not negating the Holy Spirit's role in the conception of Jesus,

[12]*CWJ*, 12.

Joseph served as another sign of God's miraculous intervention. Joseph was an actor in God's unfolding drama. Joseph's role was to legitimate Jesus by naming him. It was traditionally the role of women to name their babies. Joseph assumed this role in order to legally and legitimately acknowledge that Jesus was his son, thereby making Jesus a descendant of David.

In Luke's gospel Mary is the humble, submissive receptor of God's plan. In Matthew's version of the gospel we are given a glimpse of Joseph's role. Matthew highlights Joseph, the human agent who responds to the initiative. "... Luke emphasizes the essential passivity of the human response to God's action: 'Let it be done to me according to your word' (Luke 1:38). Matthew, on the other hand, by selecting Joseph as his leading actor, stresses the active component in the human response."[13] Joseph was instructed three times to *do something*. He did as he was instructed. The point is not to be missed. Matthew demands that human beings must respond to God's initiative and grace.

Traditionally miraculous birth events in scripture point to God's role in salvation history. Whenever there are miraculous events surrounding the birth of an individual, it is meant to highlight the role the child would one day assume in God's plan. "Just as God had miraculously created Moses to be his people's deliverer, so now God raised up Jesus to be the new and greater Moses, the ultimate savior."[14] The miraculous circumstances of Jesus' birth would immediately alert peoples in antiquity that this child was destined for a great role in God's plan.

By naming Jesus "Emmanuel—God is with us," Matthew reminds us of the greatest truth of the Incarnation. God through Christ is present in our lives. God through Christ continues to reveal Godself to us. In perfect freedom God, through Christ, invites us into intimate relationship. When humanity sins, it does not just turn against God's will, but turns its face on the God who dwells within; who desires intimate, living relationship; who spends a lifetime communicating Godself to each individual and to the world. Karl Rahner puts it best: "It is both terrible and comforting to dwell in the incomprehensible nearness of God, and so to be loved by God himself that the first and last gift is infinity and incomprehensibility itself. But we have no choice. God is with us."[15]

Joseph's first response to the mysterious conception was to remove himself from it—to walk away. But God revealed to him that he had a role to fill. He was part of the plan. His first reaction no doubt was shock. "From astonishment to faith and submission of one's life by the reception of the word, extraordinary as it may be—this is the path for all believers and the Church itself to follow to respond to the call of God and his word (Gospel)."[16]

Proclaim the gospel again.

Sometimes we gain new insights when we hear the text after the interpretation has been given. Someone from the group proclaims the gospel a second time.

STEP 4
TESTING

Conversation with the Liturgy and the Scriptures

Test your original understanding in dialogue with the text.

(You might consider breaking into smaller groups.)

Now that you've heard what the scholars have to say about this passage, how do you feel about it? Was there anything in this gospel you had never considered before? Were there new insights? How does this story speak to your life?

Sharing Life Experience

> *There was a time when I knew that God was asking me to do something I did not want to do. My pride*

[13] *MI*, 8.

[14] Ibid., 11.

[15] *GCY*, 43.

[16] *DL* (I), 144.

was at stake and so I began a litany of rationalizations. No matter how much I rationalized, it always came back to the same awareness. God was asking me to stretch beyond myself. I resisted with my entire being. I believed that if I ignored the prompting it would go away. It did not. There would be no rest until I listened to that inner voice and responded to the voice of God. So, kicking, screaming, and dragging my heels, I submitted. Little did I know at the time the wonderful way God would ultimately work through that situation and thus enrich my life. I was similarly surprised at the way God continued to reveal Godself to me following my decision to submit to his will. Joseph had to listen to a dream in order to know God's plan for his life. I don't know if I would trust a dream. I had a difficult enough time trusting the obvious! No doubt if an angel had appeared to me with the same news Mary received I would have been inviting him to don the white coats, but only after I put one on myself for thinking I was talking to an angel in the first place! Mary reminds me that sometimes I have to look at the incredulous and realize that God often comes crashing into our lives not only in obvious, ordinary events, but also in ways we would never expect. Joseph reminds me that life is about the choices I make. I can choose to submit to the grace and voice of God within me, or I can live life on my own initiative.

Advent and Christmas are a reminder that we are in an intimate relationship with the God who dwells within us. We either grow in that relationship or we stagnate. To grow means to actively respond to God's grace and initiative in our lives. To bring Christ to birth in our lives means that we must respond to his presence within us, even when all outward appearances seem to suggest that God is nowhere in sight. The challenge of today's gospel is to accept the Christ who invites us into relationship and to share that relationship with others who long to bring him to birth in their lives, yet need only to be shown the way.

Participants share an experience from their own lives that connects with the biblical interpretation just shared.

What was the purpose of Matthew's rendition of this story? How is Joseph a relevant character for our contemporary lives? What might he have to say to us about our personal relationship with God and with God's people? How does Mary's role in today's liturgy invite us to bring Christ more fully to birth in our lives? How might this gospel challenge us to enter more fully into the paschal mystery (the life, death, and resurrection) of Jesus Christ? What difference does it make to our everyday lives? Keeping in mind Advent's purpose, how does today's liturgy serve as preparation for Christmas? Do you still feel the same way about this gospel as when you began? Has your original understanding been stretched, challenged, or affirmed?

STEP 5
DECISION

The gospel demands a response.

In what way does this gospel and this Advent liturgy invite change in our lives? Be concrete. What is the challenge for your parish community? What word does your community need to hear and how might it be challenged to respond? Has this conversation with the exegesis changed or stretched your personal attitudes? What are the implications of this gospel in your life? What is one concrete action you will take this week as a response to the liturgy today?

Christian Initiation: In what way have the catechumens and candidates been invited to participate in the ministries of justice in the parish? Are there shut-ins to be visited? A soup kitchen to be tended? Sick to be visited? What "Prayers of Exorcism" and "Prayers of Blessing" might be prayed with catechumens that seem to best reflect the spirit of the latter days of Advent and the early days of the Christmas season? Perhaps you might invite catechumens and candidates to purchase *Catholic Household Blessings and Prayers* (NCCB) for use in their homes. Included in this wonderful collection, and particularly appropriate during the Advent/Christmas season, are the following rituals and blessings: "Blessing of an Advent Wreath," "Blessing of a Christmas Tree," "Blessing of a Christmas Crèche or Manger Scene," "Blessing for the New Year," "Blessing of the Home and Household on the Epiphany."

DOCTRINAL ISSUES

What church truth/teaching/doctrinal issue could be drawn from the gospel for the Fourth Sunday of Advent?

Participants suggest possible doctrinal themes that flow from the readings.

Possible Doctrinal Themes:

Advent; eschatology; kingdom of God; discipleship; repentance and reconciliation; Christ's coming: future, present, past; Son of Man; parousia

Present the doctrinal material at this time.

1. The facilitator gives input on a particular doctrinal issue of his/her prior choosing. OR

2. The group chooses a doctrinal issue from the list they created. They read together from appropriate church documents and/or the Doctrinal Appendix.

(The doctrinal issues are found in the Doctrinal Appendix in the back of this workbook. If you are choosing an issue from this resource, please refer to it now.)

Reflection questions centered around the chosen doctrinal theme can be found at the end of each topic in the Doctrinal Appendix. The questions are based on the five-step reflection process. If you choose a topic not included in the Doctrinal Appendix, craft your own questions according to the same five-step process.

Following the reflection questions you will be reminded to return to Chapter 7, "Preparing the Catechetical Session," to assist you in crafting your own session.

Closing Prayer

Father, all powerful and ever-living God,
we do well always and everywhere to give you thanks
through Jesus Christ our Lord.
His future coming was proclaimed by all the prophets.
The virgin mother bore him in her womb with love beyond all telling.
John the Baptist was his herald
and made him known when at last he came.
In his love Christ has filled us with joy
as we prepare to celebrate his birth,
so that when he comes he may find us watching in prayer,
our hearts filled with wonder and praise.[17]

[17] "Preface—Advent II," *The Sacramentary.*

The Christmas Season

The Christmas Season: An Overview

There is no evidence of an official feast celebrating the nativity until the fourth century. There are two hypotheses regarding the origin of this feast. One school of thought suggests that it was adopted in response to a pagan feast inaugurated by the Roman emperor Aurelian in the hopes of strengthening and uniting his empire. The feast, *sol invictus,* was a celebration honoring the shortest day of the year when the sun reaches its lowest point. It reaches this point on December 25, the winter solstice. From that day forward the sun begins its victory over darkness by lengthening the time it will peer through the dimness of an unlit sky. Thus, the days begin to lengthen as the sun processes heavenward toward its ultimate destiny, full brightness and height during the summer solstice. Christians had no difficulty appropriating this feast to their understanding of Jesus who declared himself Light of the World. They could say very righteously to their pagan neighbors that they, in truth, were celebrating the "real" Sun of justice.

The second school of thought centers around the date of December 25 itself as the reason for establishment of the feast. Christians were very aware of the solstices and equinoxes because of the constant references to Christ as Light. Some hypothesized that John the Baptist was conceived during the autumn equinox and born during the summer solstice. As Jesus was to have been born six months later, that put his birth right at December 25th. It was once again evidence of God's incredible timing and wisdom. It seemed to be no accident that God's mighty work coincided with the temporal world's celebration of the symbols of light and darkness.

The feast spread rapidly due to the influence of the Arian heresy that "made the Son of God the highest of creatures, greater than we but less than God."[1] The Council of Nicea refuted the heresy and formulated the Nicene Creed. Through celebration of Jesus' birth, people would have an opportunity in their liturgy to proclaim what the council set out to accomplish.

There is an historical progression to the eventual celebration of the three masses of Christmas: night, dawn, and during the day. The first celebration of the feast of the nativity was a small papal mass. The prologue of John was proclaimed at this mass, the forerunner to our mass during the day. Jesus was honored as the Word of God made flesh. God revealed the Eternal Word to prophets throughout salvation history. The *Word* reached fulfillment in the Incarnation of the Son of God. The gospel and the celebration itself are highly christological.

Underneath the church of St. Mary Major in Rome is a small chapel designed as a replica of the cave at Bethlehem where Jesus was born. Wood was brought to the space, thus the name "mass near the crèche." The story of Jesus' birth was read at this liturgy, the forerunner of the midnight mass. The symbol of the *Christ, our Light* is highlighted in the opening prayer. In the renewed liturgical calendar, the mass at night is patterned after this early St. Mary Major observance.

On December 25, the pope went in the early morning to St. Anastasia's Church in honor of the Greek feast day honoring the church's patroness, a martyr highly venerated in the East. The story of the shepherds who arrive at the crèche seeking the heralded Child is proclaimed at this early morning liturgy, the mass at dawn. There is more reference to the "Light that will shine" in this liturgy than there is in the midnight liturgy.

In addition to the theme of Christ's manifestation to the world through the Incarnation, the liturgies of Christmas proclaim another truth that is evidenced in the opening prayer for the mass during the day and the third Christmas preface. A holy exchange takes place and humanity is elevated to the status of God's child. We share in Jesus' divine

[1] *CSM,* xxxiv.

nature. "Your Son shared our weakness [literally: our humanity]: may we share his glory [literally: his divinity]." "Your eternal Word has taken upon himself our human weakness, giving our mortal nature immortal value."[2]

The texts of Christmas, while not directly referring to the paschal mystery, have strong underpinnings of Christ's act of redemption. It is through the life, death, and resurrection of Jesus that we are saved. We cannot look at Christmas without remembering Easter. The Christmas season celebrates the Incarnation of Christ that ushers in God's fulfillment of salvation history. It also honors Christ's manifestation to us in human form. These two realities define and give meaning and expression to the content of our Christian theology. One liturgy cannot possibly capture all the dimensions contained within the mystery of the Incarnation. The fact that so many texts are offered to us for celebration and reflection denotes the richness and complexity of the season. Like the view through a prism, all the readings together help reflect the many facets of the profound mystery of Christ's Incarnation.[3]

The primary symbol of the Christmas liturgy is light. Christ, the light, has ushered in the messianic age. Christmas without magnificent, abundant light is like Easter without the paschal candle. Christmas without paschal themes is akin to baptism without water. Many traditional symbols from our culture remind us that Christmas draws its true meaning from Easter. Eucharistic overtones can be found in the symbol of the manger. Jesus was placed in a feed-box; he is to be our spiritual food. He was wrapped in swaddling clothes and placed in the manger. He would one day be wrapped in burial cloths and placed in a rock-carved tomb. Jesus' manifestation to the shepherds, society's lowest, reminds us that Jesus came to preach the good news to the poor. The Christmas tree was understood in its earliest conception as reminiscent of the woods of the cross. Holly is a Christmas symbol because its thorns and red berries remind us of the suffering of Christ. The wreath, an ancient symbol of victory, reminds us of Christ's victory over death.

[2]*LY*, 127.
[3]*DL* (1), 191–192.

Holy Family

The feast of the Holy Family falls on the Sunday within the octave of Christmas. This relatively new feast originated in Canada. The feast of the Holy Family lifts up the family of Nazareth as a model for struggling Christian families. Pope Leo XIII promulgated this celebration of the family of Mary, Jesus, and Joseph.

Epiphany

Epiphany means "showing forth" or manifestation. It was considered a primary feast in the area of Gaul around the third and fourth century. Epiphany, "from the Greek (*ephiphaneia*, or *theophoneia*, 'appearance or manifestation of God'), was the original feast of Christ's birth."[4] In the ancient world an epiphany referred to a visit from a god or one who was revered as a god, such as a king.

In the East, Jesus' birth and his baptism were celebrated on this day. Thus, new members were baptized on this feast. The wedding feast at Cana, where Jesus manifested his power for the first time, was also commemorated on Epiphany.

"In the second half of the fourth century East and West took over each other's birthday feast of Jesus. While the East celebrated on December 25 not only the birth of Jesus but also the coming of the Magi, and reserved January 6 for the commemoration of Jesus' baptism and his miracle at Cana and for the conferral of baptism, the West on January 6 celebrated the Epiphany of the redeemer in connection with the coming of the wise men, the baptism of Jesus, and the wedding feast at Cana."[5]

J. A. Jungman unites both feasts thematically when he states: "The mystery of the Incarnation is the proper subject of them both; but at Christmas we consider chiefly the coming down of the Son of God who became one of the poor children of men, while on the Epiphany we direct our attention to this Child's divine dignity which already is beginning to manifest itself in the world."[6]

[4]*LY*, 144.
[5]Ibid, 145.
[6]*PW*, 208.

Epiphany is also the day we remember the three magi. However, the focus is still on Christ and not the magi. In the gospel, wise men from the East come to exalt the newborn king of the Jews. The point of the story rests with Christ who comes to save the whole world, pagans and all.

Adolf Adam suggests that Epiphany is the premier celebration of Christ, the King. He proposes that the other feast designated by that title has more to do with reverence for the title, the theological concept, than it does with the inherent reality of Christ's kingship. "It is essential to the liturgical feast of Epiphany that it brings before us, in a concrete way, a royal action of Christ, an event that is an essential part of the process of salvation."[7]

Baptism of the Lord

The feast of the baptism of the Lord is celebrated on the Sunday following Epiphany. If the Sunday of Epiphany falls after January 6, then the feast of the Lord's baptism is celebrated on Monday that year. During Cycle C the gospel that is read is that of the wedding feast at Cana. During Cycle A the gospel is the account of Jesus' baptism.

This feast is important for three reasons. Jesus is named by the voice of God who calls him "Son." The Holy Spirit descends upon Jesus and thus anoints him for the destiny he is to fulfil. Since it is John who baptizes, Jesus shows his partnership with sinful humanity. This feast brings the Christmas season to an end.

Octave of Christmas

Following Christmas (and Easter) there is an entire week of liturgical feasts called an octave. The feast of St. Stephen, the first martyr (model of love for enemies and fearless witness to the faith), is on December 26. The feast of John the Apostle and Evangelist is celebrated on December 27. The feast of the Holy Innocents, the children killed by Herod, occurs on December 28. Other martyrs' feasts are celebrated on the remaining days of the week.

Christmas celebrates the manifestation of Christ, the Light of the world. The feasts of the octave lead us into the sobering reality of what happens when one becomes a child of the Light. For the Christian there can be no complacent lapses into nostalgic reminiscence of roasted chestnuts, pine scented rooms, or cozy hearths near an open fire. The Christmas octave feasts of St. Stephen, John the Apostle, and the Holy Innocents serve as a reminder that the only open fire a true disciple can expect is that of the martyr's stake. It has been said that the three feasts are examples of the three possible forms of martyrdom: voluntary and executed (St. Stephen), voluntary, but not executed (John the Apostle), and executed but not voluntary (the Innocents). However, regardless of how martyrs offer their lives, these feasts remind the believer that the cost of discipleship is very high. The Incarnation of Christ, the Light of the world, often requires nothing less than the complete self-offering of one's life.

The first reading of the feast of St. Stephen recounts the story of his ministry and his martyrdom. Christians are reminded of the persecutions they must endure for the sake of the gospel.[8] Stephen was chosen by the apostles to help them because "he was trusted by everyone."[9] Stephen distributed food to the poor and was the first deacon because of his great charism of service. St. Stephen's commemoration is one reason for the custom of giving gifts to the poor at Christmas.

The root meaning of the word *martyr* is "witness." Stephen gave witness to Christ by the gift of his life. The etymology of Stephen's name is "wreath." War heroes and famous athletes of his day were given wreaths in honor of their achievements. Art depicting martyrs often portrays them wearing wreaths around their heads. The Christmas wreath "announces the victory of Christ who brings justice, love and peace. We remember deacon Stephen, the first witness to lay down his life for Christ."[10]

The feast of John the Apostle, celebrated first in the East, dates to the fourth century. Tradition emanating from Irenaeus holds that John ministered in Ephesus and was later banished to the island of Patmos where he wrote the book of Reve-

[7] *LY*, 147.

[8] Ibid., 142.

[9] *CC*, 191.

[10] Ibid., 191.

lation. He subsequently returned to Ephesus where he composed the gospel of John and died at an old age.[11] "The symbol of John's gospel is that of the eagle that flies to the heights."[12] The liturgy of this feast stresses that God was announced to humanity through the revelation given to John. John the Apostle, the Evangelist, manifested the Word of God, the Logos, to the world. The liturgy of this feast names him a credible eyewitness to the life of Jesus.

The origin of the feast of the Holy Innocents dates to the sixth century in North Africa. This date was chosen for the feast because of its connection to the Christmas story. The liturgy of the day tells the story of the flight into Egypt and the slaughtering of the innocent children by Herod who was in search of the prophesied Child. These children are remembered and praised for their innocent martyrdom.

Very often catechetical groups do not meet during the Christmas season. While this is understandable, it is somewhat regrettable. A great part of our Christian tradition is celebrated in the days and the feasts of the Christmas season. Every attempt should be made to break open the Christmas season liturgies with groups participating in liturgical catechesis. The liturgies and feasts of Christmas are integral to complete acquaintance with the entire rich deposit of faith. The liturgies of the Christmas season celebrate and emphasize each hierarchical truth of Catholic teaching. A great deal of flexibility and creativity is needed to ensure that adequate reflection is given to this great season.

There are four liturgies of Christmas: the Christmas vigil, the mass at midnight, the mass at dawn, and the mass during the day. As a result, people will be attending different masses and will not necessarily be experiencing the same readings. It will take a great deal of imagination to effectively incorporate all the readings into a catechetical session. Perhaps it will be next to impossible, considering people's busy lives and time constraints. If there is time for reflection on the readings from only one specific mass, it would be important that the other readings be made available to participants for their personal reflection. However, all the readings of the Christmas liturgies taken as a whole reflect the broader mystery of the Incarnation. A possible solution might be to provide a Christmas season retreat in which all the readings of Christmas would be reviewed and participants would be offered an opportunity to experience the entire rich fare in the treasury of our Christmas liturgical repertoire.

> ...Despite all the liturgical formularies, one thing remains: it is impossible to encompass and express in only one liturgy the richness and complexity of the mystery that it celebrates. The good liturgies are those that are not limited to one perspective. This accounts for the diversity of scriptural texts that are offered for reading and meditation. They are not as distracting as one might think: they open up, rather, a greater awareness of what is being celebrated.[13]

[11] *LY*, 142.
[12] *CC*, 191.

[13] *DL* (I), 193.

Christmas

Vigil Mass, Mass at Midnight, Mass at Dawn, Mass During the Day

The liturgies of Christmas are presented here: the vigil mass, mass at midnight, mass at dawn, and mass during the day. Perhaps you will have time to reflect upon only one of the liturgies. However, all of the readings shed light on the fullness of Christmas and help to unfold the meaning of the Incarnation.

The Infancy Narratives of the New Testament

Matthew and Luke are the only evangelists who tell of Jesus' birth. Raymond Brown suggests that it was not for historical purposes, but for religious reasons that the infancy narratives are told in the first place. These religious reasons are: "first, the identity of Jesus, second, his role as dramatic embodiment of the whole of history."[1] Matthew and Luke use the birth stories as a bridge between the old law, the prophets, and other scriptural books. Matthew and Luke felt that an understanding of Jesus' life and mission could be grasped only in light of the major themes and stories of the Hebrew scriptures.

One cannot help but notice that the two accounts differ considerably. Today's Christmas crèche is a combination of both stories put together. Brown warns against trying to make the stories mesh by explaining away the differences. "A greater fidelity to Scripture as we have received it would recognize that the Holy Spirit was content to give us two different accounts and that the way to interpret them faithfully is to treat them separately."[2] There is no accurate way to know where and how the two evangelists received their information. Brown suggests that when there is excessive concern for historical accuracy we are distracted from the inspired meaning of the biblical text: the identity of Jesus and his role in the fulfillment of salvation history.

Raymond Brown further reminds us that the infancy narratives had a different genesis than the stories about Jesus' life and ministry. The apostles attested to the latter. However, we have no idea where the stories of the magi and the star came from. Some suggest that such stories were orally transmitted from family sources such as Mary and Joseph. However, that is merely a supposition.

Historical accuracy becomes a problem when one considers that Matthew and Luke differ considerably in their accounts and sometimes they come close to contradiction. Another mitigating factor lies in the fact that there is no public record of the startling event of the star in the sky which should have prompted some kind of a public record—"for example, a star that moved through the heavens in a totally irregular way but left no astronomical record."[3]

Adding to the doubts about historical accuracy is the fact that nowhere else in the gospels is there a parallel between the stories of the gospels and the Old Testament like there is a parallel between the birth stories and the Old Testament. Some scholars suggest that the birth narratives were an extended meditation on stories, images, and themes from the Old Testament (a midrash).

In spite of these problems, Brown insists that scholarship has entered a positive new stage and, rather than stressing the difficulties inherent in the texts, focuses on the theology that the texts express. This new stage of biblical scholarship now asks why Matthew and Luke included the stories in the first place. How does each infancy narrative accord with the respective evangelist's theology? How do the infancy narratives convey the good news of salvation, so that they are truly and literally "gospel"?

One reason that Matthew and Luke begin their gospel with the birth story is to remind their readers that it was at Jesus' conception and birth that God revealed the identity of Jesus to the world.

Environment

While the seasonal color of Christmas is red and green in the culture, the liturgical color of Christ-

[1] *CCA*, 10–26.

[2] Ibid., 9.

[3] Ibid., 9–10.

mas is white. The traditional Christmas tree and crèche are appropriate adornments for the catechetical environment. Holly, a plant associated with Christmas, not only adds to the environment but carries symbolic meaning as well; the berries are reminiscent of Christ shedding his blood and the prickly leaves are an allusion to the crown of thorns. The primary symbol of the Incarnation is light. Christ, the Light of the world, came to dispel the darkness. Every environment should include ample use of candles to reflect the light that always shines.

The following blessings may be used to bless the tree and the crib. They are adapted from *Catholic Household Blessings and Prayers.*

Christmas Tree Blessing

This tree is a blessing to our space.
It reminds us of all that is filled with the gentleness and the promise of God.
It stands in our midst as a tree of light
that we might promise such beauty to one another and to our world.
It stands like the tree of paradise that God made into the tree of life, the cross of Jesus.
Lord God, let your blessing come upon us as we illumine this tree.
May the light and cheer it gives be a sign of the joy that fills our hearts.
May all who delight in this tree come to the knowledge and joy of salvation.

Blessing of a Christmas Crèche

We are at the beginning of the days of Christmas.
All through the season we will look upon these images of sheep and cattle,
of shepherds, of Mary and Joseph and of Jesus.
God of Mary and Joseph, of shepherds and animals,
bless us whenever we gaze on this manger scene.
Through all the days of Christmas
may these figures tell the story of how humans, angels, and animals
found Christ in this poor place.
Fill this place with hospitality, joy, gentleness and thanksgiving
and guide our steps in the way of peace.
We ask this through Jesus Christ the Lord.

VIGIL MASS

INTRODUCTORY RITES

Opening Song (or Entrance Antiphon)

Today you will know the glory that the Lord is coming to save us, and in the morning you will see his glory (see Ex 16:6–7).[4]

Opening Prayer

Let us pray
[that Christmas morning will find us at peace]

Pause for silent prayer.

God our Father,
every year we rejoice
as we look forward to this feast of our salvation.
May we welcome Christ as our Redeemer,
and meet him with confidence when he comes to be our judge,
who lives and reigns with you and the Holy Spirit,
one God, for ever and ever.[5]

LITURGY OF THE WORD

First Reading[6]
Isaiah 62:1–5

This was probably a song used to accompany a pilgrimage to Jerusalem. It is quite appropriate that this reading begins the Christmas celebration. It is a joyful exclamation that the day of salvation has arrived. Obviously, Christianity connected the object of Israel's joy to that which is celebrated today, the Incarnation of God's Son. The conferral of a new name designated God's almighty power over creation. When one was given a new name, that

[4]Christmas Vigil Mass: "Entrance Antiphon," *The Sacramentary.*

[5]Christmas Vigil Mass: "Opening Prayer," *The Sacramentary.*

[6]The exegesis for the first and second readings may or may not be the focus of your group's reflection as there may only be time to give adequate attention to the gospel, your primary concern. However, the exegesis is included here in order to provide a thorough investigation of the entire liturgy of the word as there may be parts (or all) that would be necessary to the direction you wish to take with your particular ministry group.

person was made a new creation. "To give a name is also to take possession."[7]

Responsorial Psalm
Psalm 89:4–5, 16–17, 27–29

In the first reading, Isaiah proclaims the covenant love between Yahweh and his people. The vigil of Christmas hearkens back to this covenant as it is fulfilled in the nativity of the messiah. The responsorial psalm sings of the covenant Yahweh made with Israel. This covenant is fulfilled in and through the Incarnation of Christ.

Second Reading
Acts 13:16–17, 22–25

Today's pericope consists of portions from Paul's speech in which Paul recaps Israel's salvation history and the arrival of the promised messianic era. Paul insists that Jesus and the message he came to preach belong to Israel's history. Jesus was the fulfillment of Israel's messianic hopes. Therefore, as rightful heirs of the messianic promise, Israel was entitled to be the first recipient of the good news. Paul acknowledges the election of Israel by Yahweh. He makes the case that the salvation history begun in the Old Testament is fulfilled in Christ. The Baptist played a role similar to Samuel's when he inaugurated the first of the line of ancient kings. John heralded the messiah who was foretold of old and who was the rightful heir to the messianic throne.

Gospel
Matthew 1:1–25

The genealogy of Jesus is proclaimed.

STEP 1
NAMING ONE'S EXPERIENCE

What were your first impressions? What was your first response? What captured your attention? How did the readings affect you?

Each person names his or her initial impression. Statements should be brief. No reasons should be given at this time. All simply listen without agreeing or disagreeing.

[7]*DL* (I), 196.

STEP 2
UNDERSTANDING

In a brief statement, what do you think this gospel is trying to convey?

STEP 3
INPUT FROM VISION/STORY/TRADITION

Liturgical Context[8]

The vigil mass is the least celebrated. It may be celebrated before or after the first vespers of Christmas. If this mass is not celebrated, the readings and prayers may be used for prayer and meditation in preparation for celebration of the feast.

A brief background will be given for the readings. Since the genealogy from Matthew's gospel is rarely heard by a gathered assembly, it is important to note that its message is worthy of serious consideration and contemplation.

In the first reading we hear that God espouses Israel. God weds humanity. One is reminded of a similar marriage metaphor sung at the Easter Vigil, the "mother of all feasts." God's betrothal to Israel culminates in the wedding event of salvation. God espouses his people. The song of the Easter Vigil is: "This is the night when heaven is wedded to earth and humanity is reconciled with God!" (Exsultet). The vigil announces the inauguration of that paschal event.

Gospel Exegesis

The facilitator gives input regarding what critical biblical scholarship has to say about this text. The input includes insights as to how people would have heard the gospel in Jesus' time.

[8]The scriptures in the Lectionary, the seasons of the year, and the ritual prayers of the mass are interrelated and form the basis for liturgical catechesis. The liturgical context attempts to explore and clarify the themes and this interrelatedness.

Genealogies are rarely read at liturgies. According to Raymond Brown, we miss a very important piece of salvation history if we ignore the genealogy of Jesus. Matthew's intent is to trace Jesus' origins to the house of David through Joseph. Even though Joseph was not the biological father of Jesus (the Holy Spirit is the creative power behind the conception of Christ), he was the legal[9] father because of his betrothal to Mary. Jesus, then, is rightful heir to the house of David. He possesses the necessary pedigree to claim the messianic title.

Brown asserts that the genealogy is told in order to highlight the paradox of a God who writes the story of salvation with "crooked lines." "A God who did not hesitate to use the scheming as well as the noble, the impure as well as the pure, men to whom the world hearkened and women upon whom the world frowned—this God continues to work in the same mélange."[10] The genealogy shows that God used ordinary, unknown men and women to be part of the greatest story ever told. "The message of the genealogy is an enabling invitation."[11]

God chose scoundrels and saints to be in this many-act play called salvation. There was one who pilfered his brother's birthright and one who sold his brother into slavery. God used people who would never stand up to human scrutiny. From the very beginning, God used questionable people to participate in the grand design, just like Jesus would do in his ministry to the prostitutes and tax collectors. The cast of characters in Matthew's genealogy includes scoundrel kings and the famous King David (who was not a paragon of virtue). Also included is a cast of extras, the long list of names we know nothing about. They remind us of our own minuscule place on the continuum of salvation history's time-line.

The genealogy names foreign prostitutes. It names women who give birth in questionable circumstances, and the last of these is Mary, pregnant and husband-less. God's design is certainly out of the imaginative world of human consciousness.

Yet, it stands as a clarion call, an invitation of immense significance for our lives. This God who used fallible, crafty, wily, saintly, and not-so-saintly human beings to usher in his reign continues to work with our frailty and our shortcomings.

Jesus entered our world with the intention of getting his hands dirty. He is not the image portrayed in saccharine art that shows him as a sweet, otherworldly, haloed being who exists out of our grasp or realm of understanding. Rather, the Jesus of Matthew's genealogy has a sordid family tree. He understands the "drunk uncle" hidden in everyone's closet. He understands the inherited sins of past generations. His ancestry includes the famed Davidic monarchy that, like the sinful church of any age, was used by God in spite of its corruption, sin, and vanity. Nevertheless, it was to be a vehicle for God's plan of redemption, just as the church has been and always will be. He stands as a beacon of light in the midst of relational darkness.

The genealogy portrays the unfathomable deeds of God and the gratuitous grace that has been poured out upon the world since the beginning of time, in spite of us and in communion with us. Jesus is the ultimate expression of that grace. Through his life, death, and resurrection Christ pours out a newer and fuller portion to sustain the church until his promised return.

One cannot miss the Old Testament parallels in the Matthean account of the infancy narrative. Joseph went to Egypt as a result of a dream. Joseph of the Old Testament went to Egypt for the same reason. Jesus' escape from Herod is like Moses' escape from Pharaoh. Pharaoh was warned by his scribes of the threat the child Moses posed to his throne. Pharaoh killed all the male children as a result. Moses' father was given the revelation in a dream that his pregnant wife would bear a child who would save Israel. The pre-warned parents were able to save the child from slaughter. One need not cite the obvious similarities between Herod and Pharaoh.

In the Old Testament Balaam was summoned from the East by Pharaoh to destroy Moses. David was understood as the *star* prophesied by Balaam. Instead of destroying Moses, Balaam told of the Davidic monarchy that would one day rise. "Just as

---

[9]Legal fatherhood was not a status that required physical fatherhood.

[10]*CCA*, 25.

[11]Ibid.

Balaam saw the star of David rise, the New Testament magi saw the star of the King of the Jews at its rising."[12]

Matthew uses the events of this story to follow a pattern used throughout his gospel: the good news was proclaimed, followed by a response of acceptance or rejection. Matthew begins his story in anticipation of the path that the gospel would take following Jesus' resurrection. The good news would be proclaimed. People would either accept or reject it. The bottom line—God manifested himself to the world; he became "Emmanuel—God is with us." God became one with us through his Son who lived in the midst of the human story. The faithful who accepted Jesus' revelation experienced salvation, while others saw it as offensive and contradictory. Balaam could look to a future king David. The magi could look to a future day when Jesus' kingship would only be understood as he sat victorious at heaven's throne, having vanquished the cross's apparent sign of defeat.

Proclaim the gospel again.

Sometimes we gain new insights when we hear the text after the interpretation has been given. Someone from the group proclaims the gospel a second time.

Step 4
Testing

Conversation with the Liturgy and the Scriptures

Test your original understanding in dialogue with the text.

(You might consider breaking into smaller groups.)

How do you feel about Matthew's genealogy in light of the interpretation just given? Were there any new insights? How does your original understanding of this story compare with what was just shared? How does this story speak to your life?

[12]*ACC,* 12

Sharing Life Experience

I am reminded of the family trees we all bring with us into adulthood. Like Jesus, we all have our share of "drunk uncles" lurking in our dark closets. Yet, when we look at the stories of our lives we are often amazed at how God works in the midst of the darkened spaces in order to bring his light into our lives. I am reminded of the story of a deceased aunt (that I never knew) who had a very sad and sordid history that was the family's deepest, darkest secret. Our mother promised to tell us the secret after the death of one of her other relatives. Unfortunately, this relative outlived my mother and today none of us know this deep, dark secret.

This secret was the source of great shame to the relatives of my mother's generation. Yet I often wonder about Eleanor. What was her story? What was the secret? How was God present to this woman with the sordid past? Did she in any way impact the people in my mother's life? Did she know my mother and in any way influence her life, thereby in some way influencing me? Was her secret really so horrible, or was it nothing more than the judgmental musings of scrutinizing relatives? Rather than a scarlet letter, perhaps Eleanor wore a saint's halo in the mind and heart of God. I will never know the answers to those questions, but I often think about Eleanor when Matthew's genealogy is read. So many unknown saints and sinners were part of Jesus' family tree. Yet even though his lineage is laced with people of shame as well as virtue, God accomplished his will in the midst of Jesus' not-so-perfect family tree. God does not expect perfection. Very often we are ashamed of the "drunk uncles" in our lives and believe that we have to be a "holy family" before God works in our lives. The reading of the genealogy reminds us that God comes to us midst the imperfections. Jesus comes to the shame-filled. Jesus comes for the Eleanors of this world in order to turn their secrets into Good News. I celebrate Eleanor and thank God that Jesus came to shed light on the secrets we all bury in our dark closets. Jesus invites us into the light of his Incarnation where there is no room for shame.

Participants share their life experience in relation to the exegesis at this time.

What was Matthew trying to tell his community? What does he have to say to our community and to me today? How is God's covenant expressed in these readings? How is the theme of liberation and deliverance (exodus) expressed in this gospel? If God is always in the process of creating things anew, how is that expressed in the readings from this liturgy? Where is the challenge in Matthew's story-telling pattern: proclamation of the good news followed by the response of acceptance or rejection? How is God speaking to a people (community)? Do you still feel the same way about this text as you did when you began? Describe your understanding of this story now. Has your original understanding been stretched, challenged, or affirmed?

STEP 5
DECISION

The gospel demands a response.

How can Matthew's rendering of the genealogy possibly speak to a contemporary church? In what concrete way are we called to respond? Have I been changed in any way as a result of this sharing? What are the implications for my life? What is one concrete action I can take this week as a response to what we have learned and shared?

Christian Initiation: As there is little opportunity for most groups to reflect on the powerful implications of the readings in the vigil mass, perhaps a Christmas season retreat could center on all the readings of the Christmas liturgies.

MASS AT MIDNIGHT

INTRODUCTORY RITES

Opening Song (or Entrance Antiphon)

The Lord said to me: You are my Son; this day I have begotten you.[13]

[13]Christmas Mass at Midnight: "Entrance Antiphon," *The Sacramentary.*

Opening Prayer

The facilitator of the session may lead the prayer. Others in the group could be asked to proclaim the readings.

Let us pray
[with joy and hope
as we await the dawning of the Father's Word]

Pause for silent prayer.

Lord our God,
with the birth of your Son,
your glory breaks on the world.
Through the night hours of the darkened earth
we your people watch for the coming of your promised Son.
As we wait, give us a foretaste of the joy that you will grant us
when the fullness of his glory has filled the earth,
who lives and reigns with you for ever and ever.[14]

LITURGY OF THE WORD

The readings are proclaimed.

Let us listen to God's word.

First Reading
Isaiah 9:1–6

In order to appreciate this reading in light of the Christmas event, it is important to look at the situation and the story that defines it in the book of the prophet Isaiah. King Ahaz, the youthful king of Judah (Southern Kingdom), inherited a throne in which the political problems were no match for him. The king of the Northern Kingdom (Israel) had made an alliance with Assyria. This infuriated the people, as it drastically raised their taxes. A group from the western part of the country joined forces with Damascus to overthrow Assyria, which had joined forces with Israel in the north. Thus, the Southern Kingdom, Judah, was a prime target for overthrow. King Ahaz was panic stricken and felt drawn to join forces with the North, and thus with Assyria. Isaiah met Ahaz and told him to trust Yahweh and be calm. He told Ahaz that the only

[14]Christmas Mass at Midnight: "Alternative Opening Prayer," *The Sacramentary.*

way to deal with the crisis was to maintain a relaxed reliance on Yahweh who was far greater than any human power. God was in covenant relationship with Judah and therefore would not abandon them. Nor would God think of abandoning the promise made to David regarding David's everlasting dynasty. Isaiah assured Ahaz that he must have faith. If his faith was secure, his throne would also be secure.

Isaiah was telling Ahaz to be strong and to resist the temptation to unite with Syria and Israel in the north. Yahweh would protect them. Ahaz did not listen to Isaiah. Isaiah promised Ahaz a sign of assurance that Yahweh would do as promised. Ahaz told Isaiah that he was not interested in asking for a sign; he would not think of putting Yahweh to the test. Isaiah became angry and told Ahaz that Yahweh would offer a sign to the house of David—to David's dynasty, not to Ahaz. The sign would confirm that the northern alliance was doomed and that God would be faithful to the promise made to David. "The purpose of a sign [in biblical history] was to make visible and to confirm dramatically the truth and power of Yahweh's word spoken by the prophet. A sign does not necessarily have to be a miracle, in our sense of the word, for its significance is not so much in its unusual character as in its power to confirm a prophetic word spoken in threat or promise."[15] The ability to see signs was an important part of Israel's faith. It enabled them to perceive God acting in human history.

Isaiah's sign was the promised birth of a child whose name was Immanuel (God is with us). Isaiah prophesied that the birth was imminent. He believed the mother to be already pregnant. One might ask how the coming of a child could be a sign for Ahaz. Isaiah attested that, unlike Ahaz, the child would be a faithful, steadfast leader of the people. Isaiah prophesied in response to a current crisis in his time. He had no idea that this prophecy would become the basis for the Jewish hope in a future messiah. Isaiah's song in chapter 7 became a part of the prophetic messianic tradition. This "child to come" was to share the suffering of his people. The child would usher in an age of judgment and an opportunity for new beginnings.

[15]*UOT,* 331–334.

In Isaiah's prophecy the child was feasting on milk and honey, a reference to the milk and honey found in the promised land. Those listening to Isaiah realized from that reference that this child would be a sign of hope following a dismal time of misery and tribulation. "For Yahweh's purpose is not to destroy, but to refine and cleanse a remnant people. Once the Assyrian yoke is overturned the child will ascend the throne as the agent of God's rule over the people. Then the meaning of his name Immanuel will be clearly understood."[16] The early Christian community used this prophecy as the foundation for their belief in Jesus as messiah. This prophetic hymn of Isaiah sings of hope in the messiah, fulfilled in the person of Jesus Christ: Wonder Counselor, Mighty God, Everlasting Father, Prince of Peace!

Responsorial Psalm
Psalm 96:1–2a, 2b–3, 11–12, 13

The new song referred to in the psalm is the song to be sung when the messiah redeems the world. It will replace the old song sung when Moses delivered the people out of bondage.

Second Reading
Titus 2:11–14

The letter to Titus was written not to a community, but rather to an individual in regard to his pastoral duties. There are two other such letters, and they are referred to as the "pastoral epistles." There is some question as to whether Paul wrote these letters. Some believe that the letters might have been written by a disciple(s) who was trying to "publish the sort of letter he thought the master might have written had he still been alive."[17]

The reading of Titus reminds us that Advent prepared us for two comings. We do not forget the second coming of Christ even as we are steeped in celebration and remembrance of his first coming. Christ will come again; we are to live noble lives. Robert Karris asserts: "These verses are fitting for Christmas because they invite us to contemplate the new born babe as God's gracious appearance for our salvation."[18]

[16]Ibid.
[17]*GAP,* 128.
[18]*PE,* 112.

The overall theme of the letter to Titus is that we are not to retreat from the world. We are to be a sign in the world. We are to live upright lives as we go about the task of life, remembering as we go that our final fulfillment will take place when Christ comes again.

Gospel
Luke 2:1–14

The angels appear to the shepherds and the heavenly hosts sing God's praises and announce the arrival of the messiah.

STEP 1
NAMING ONE'S EXPERIENCE

What were your first impressions? What was your first response? What understanding of this story did you bring with you to this conversation? How did the readings affect you?

Each person names his or her initial impression. Statements should be brief. No reasons should be given at this time. All simply listen without agreeing or disagreeing.

STEP 2
UNDERSTANDING

In a brief statement, what do you think this gospel is trying to convey?

STEP 3
INPUT FROM VISION/STORY/TRADITION

Liturgical Context

Read the overview of Christmas. The Christmas readings proclaim for us the reason we gather to remember the nativity event. They unfold for us a refined Christian understanding of the Incarnation. The opening prayer and the prefaces help us focus on the theological meaning of the celebration. God sent his Son as a human being to the world to redeem the world. Jesus is both fully human and fully divine. We became heirs to Christ's divinity through his Incarnation and subsequent life, death, and resurrection. We will share eternal life with him because of the nativity and the event for which he was born: his death and resurrection. We still wait in hope for his return.

Gospel Exegesis

The facilitator gives input regarding what critical biblical scholarship has to say about this text. The input includes insights as to how people would have heard the gospel in Jesus' time.

Our culture has so romanticized and consumerized Christmas that it is difficult to remember that the scriptures of the Christmas liturgies are not intended as detailed historical narratives (while they are nonetheless historical), but as a means of communicating the awesome reality of God's explosion into human history through the person of Jesus Christ.

The story of Jesus' birth is told as good news. Why good news? Charles Talbert tells us that in the Mediterranean world every time a great ruler was born, the benefits to the people were announced. The newborn ruler was often called a savior who would bring peace. Jesus, the new ruler, the one who came to fulfill the ancient prophecies, "who has on his birthday a proclamation of the benefits of his birth,"[19] is truly good news.

Shalom (peace), according to Hebrew understanding, meant wholeness, the right ordering of relationships with one another, with God, with the earth, and with oneself. "Peace became an eschatological hope."[20] To be at peace meant that one was in complete harmony with God, neighbor, creation, and self. Obviously, the only place where the perfection of such harmony is realized is in the eternal hereafter.

Luke situates his gospel in the context of the current political situation. Persecutions were taking place when Luke was writing his account. In Luke's gospel, the origin of the child Jesus is

[19] *RL*, 32.

[20] Ibid.

traced back to two small inconsequential towns, Nazareth and Bethlehem. Jesus was born to poor parents. He was not what one would consider "royal material" in the earthly sense of the word. Certainly, it would be difficult to imagine one so lowly laying claim to the political power of the reigning imperial authority. Luke made it clear that the kingship of Jesus has more to do with spiritual realities than with governmental overthrow. The logical extension to this carefully devised genesis is that Jesus' followers are part of his heritage and thus are not a threat to political authority. Read: there is no reason to persecute the church.

The image of shepherds has been over-sentimentalized throughout history. Shepherds were despised individuals and considered to be in the same category as tax collectors and prostitutes. "Their testimony was not considered valid because of their reputation for dishonesty."[21] The message cannot be missed. God comes for the outcast, for those everyone hates, disregards, and leaves behind as useless. God's salvation is for everybody. The shepherds are the first to whom the message is told. Perhaps they needed it the most. This is not the last time we will hear this message from Luke.

"Angels who bring messages to accompany events are the biblical way of expressing the meaning of salvation as an act of God."[22] There are two visitations from angels in Luke's story. The first announces the birth of the messiah. The second appearance comes in the form of the heavenly host. They announce that God's favor has come to people of good will. Reginald Fuller tells us that "people of good will" is not a term of exclusion. In Hebrew, "people of good will" referred to all people who, because of this event, were the object of divine favor.[23] It also appears as if the angels came to proclaim Jesus' name and his identity. However, Eugene LaVerdiere tells us that "Luke's main point, which links God's glory in the highest with peace on earth for the humble, would have been lost had the passage merely raised the matter of Jesus' identity. The narrative called for a manifestation of Jesus' life and mission, a statement which would anticipate the actual unfolding of the implications of his name."[24] Luke's purpose is christological and ecclesial. Christ's mission is named and the church "is identified as the humble recipient and proclaimer of the gospel."[25]

Proclaim the gospel again.

Sometimes we gain new insights when we hear the text after the interpretation is given. Someone from the group proclaims the gospel a second time.

Step 4
Testing

Conversation with the Liturgy and the Scriptures

Test your original understanding in dialogue with the text.

(You might consider breaking into smaller groups.)

Now that you've heard what the scholars have to say about Luke's version of the nativity narrative, how do you feel about it? Were there any new insights? Was there anything you had not considered before? How does your original understanding of this story compare with what was just shared? How does this story speak to your life?

Sharing Life Experience

Participants share something from their lives that connects with the exegesis just given.

> *I am reminded of the Christmas season a few years ago when, as part of an evening of music and poetry, a group of beautiful liturgical dancers artistically pirouetted their way to the Christmas crèche accompanied by angelic voices blended in harmonious exultation of the God who comes to us in the flesh. It all sounds very beautiful and holy, doesn't it? Well it was; that is, until we spotted something happening in the back of the dancers' line. Someone (who was certainly not wrapped in the swaddling garb of angelic chiffon) decided it was appropriate to join the dancers in their gestures of praise. Bringing up the rear behind six beautiful young women*

[21]Ibid., 33.
[22]*PNL*, 467.
[23]Ibid.

[24]*LK*, 33.
[25]Ibid.

was one slovenly drunk who not-so-gracefully joined the parade—pirouettes, twists, turns, and all. I was horrified that such a beautifully choreographed work was being destroyed so haphazardly and with unconscious, alcoholic disdain. Later in the evening, there was a piece of poetry that echoed in wretched despair for those who, on Christmas night and every night, have no place to call home. Is there no place to be found where human choruses welcome the world's homeless into the sacred halls of their incense-soaked cathedrals? Suddenly, there was something very paradoxical about the scene. Christ exploded into the world for this very outcast, society's lowest. If our drunken visitor had been the only one, Christ still would have come. We cannot imagine and feel we do not deserve love like that! Who would listen, if he, like the shepherds, were to be visited by heavenly hosts with tidings of great joy? Would anybody listen?

All share at this time.

What was Luke trying to tell his community? How does the image of the shepherds resonate with our experience of the Christmas story? How does it feel to have our sentimental understanding of the Christmas story challenged? If the shepherds were unsavory characters, yet the angels appeared first to them, what is the message for our community? How would it be received? Do we still feel the same way about this text as we did when we began? What is our understanding of this story now? Has our original understanding been stretched, challenged, or affirmed?

Step 5
Decision

The gospel demands a response.

What would be the contemporary implications of the angels' message to the shepherds? What would be the implication for our communities today? In what concrete ways should we respond? Has this conversation with the exegesis of this Christmas gospel changed or stretched my personal attitudes? What are the implications of Jesus' Incarnation for my own life? What should be my/our response?

Mass at Dawn

Proclaim the readings from the mass at dawn. If time is limited, focus on the gospel.

First Reading
Isaiah 62:11–12

Trito-Isaiah, the third book of Isaiah, is concerned with the sin of the people. Their sin delays salvation. Nevertheless, they still believe that salvation is not far off. Trito-Isaiah sees salvation as a new creation very much like the creation of Genesis. Judgment is harsh. In this brief pericope for use at the mass at dawn we experience the joy of the new Israel at the arrival of "messianic salvation."[26]

Responsorial Psalm
Psalm 97:1, 6, 11–12

This is an enthronement psalm. One cannot miss the light imagery and its connection with the Christmas theme of the dawning of light.

Second Reading
Titus 3:4–7

Hubert Richards cites this passage from Titus as a "fine summary of the gospel Paul made his own; it is no wonder it has been chosen as one of the readings for the Christmas liturgy. It has a lyric quality...."[27] In this third chapter of Titus, Paul points out the wonders of God. He proclaims that God is all good and wishes nothing less than the very best for his children: wholeness and salvation. Paul insists that we are to imitate God's love for us and treat others accordingly. Because we have been so gratuitously loved, we in turn must live in love and give in love. God would do no less for us. It is what God would want us to do. Paul echoes what appears to be a familiar understanding of Jewish spirituality. Covenant people are to work toward the ordering of right relationships (*hesed*). We are in *hesed* relationship when our relationships with God, one another, ourselves, and the earth are in right order. These relationships, of course, are informed by the great law of love, evidenced by our behavior to the least of God's people.

[26] *PNL*, 467.
[27] *GAP*, 133.

Paul provides us with a familiar schema. Robert Karris suggests that there is a movement of transformation in the *then/now* assumption apparent in this text. We were once this way, but now we are a different way. We have been made a new creation through our baptism in Jesus. We were once children in darkness, but not anymore. Now we are children in the light. Citing its use of the pronouns *we/us* rather than *you,* Karris also suggests that this pericope was once a ritual prayer used in liturgy. Titus 3:4–7 is believed to be part of an ancient baptismal hymn of thanksgiving. We give thanks that we have been made new creations in Christ through the refreshing waters of baptism. At baptism we receive the Spirit and wait in hope for the life we will share in eternity. At our baptism we share in what God accomplished through Jesus' entrance into human history at his nativity and subsequent pasch: the salvation of the world. We are to go forth transformed and make a difference in our respective worlds. "Paul insists that liturgy begets daily Christian life."[28] Paul stated that we are justified by faith and are heirs of eternal life (Ti 3:7). Through the Incarnation, we share in Jesus' divinity.

Gospel
Luke 2:15–20

The shepherds speak among themselves of the wonderful good news and decide to go and see for themselves.

Step 1
Naming One's Experience

What were your first impressions? What was your first response? What grabbed your attention? How did you feel?

Each person names his or her initial impression. Statements should be brief. No reasons should be given at this time. All simply listen without agreeing or disagreeing.

Step 2
Understanding

In a brief statement, what do you think this gospel is trying to convey?

Step 3
Input from Vision/Tradition/Story

Liturgical Context

The light motif is even more prominent in the liturgy for the mass at dawn than it is at the midnight mass. The responsorial psalm, the entrance antiphon, and the opening prayer speak of the light that will shine this day on us and on our actions.

Gospel Exegesis

The facilitator gives input regarding what critical biblical scholarship has to say about this text. The input includes insights as to how people would have heard the gospel in Jesus' time.

This gospel is an extension of the story begun at the midnight mass. Again, we know these culturally sentimentalized stories so well that it is often easy to be blinded by their significance. Jesus came for the outcast. Shepherds were outcasts, despised and considered dishonest. Yet they were the ones who saw the Christ child. They were the ones who heard the heavenly hosts singing the hymn of praise and announcing *shalom*/peace (wholeness, *hesed*). Perhaps we could call these outcasts the first evangelists. They were the first to spread and tell the good news. Would anybody believe their testimony?

Proclaim the gospel again.

Sometimes we gain new insights when we hear the text after the interpretation is given. Someone from the group proclaims the gospel a second time.

[28] *PE,* 124.

STEP 4
TESTING

Conversation with the Liturgy and the Scriptures

Test your original understanding in dialogue with the text.

(You might consider breaking into smaller groups.)

How does it feel that some of our traditional assumptions about the Christmas story are brought into question by contemporary scholarship? How do you feel about the image of the shepherds portrayed by the scholars? How does this story speak to your life? What was Luke trying to tell his community? What does he have to say to you and to your community today? What do the Christmas readings say about God/Jesus? Do you still feel the same way about this text as you did when you began? Describe your understanding of this story now. Has your original understanding been stretched, challenged, or affirmed?

STEP 5
DECISION

The gospel demands a response.

How do these readings for Christmas challenge me and the community to action? Where is growth needed in my community, in me? What am I going to do about it?

MASS DURING THE DAY

Proclaim the readings from the mass during the day. If time is limited, focus on the gospel.

First Reading
Isaiah 52:7–10

The people of Israel had the ability to view their lives in relationship to the mighty acts of God. They possessed a corporate conscience that allowed them to see the events of their lives in relationship to the Yahweh who saved, judged, forgave, punished, rewarded, and ordained their very life breath. Their optimism in the face of despair and oppression was of heroic proportions. Even though their exile was moving into a second generation, their hope for restoration was not to be squelched. The bondage that had ravaged their identity had the purging, yet freeing effect of giving definition to their lives.

Prophets such as Deutero-Isaiah helped them examine themselves and in the process they were formed in the heart and will of God. When it was time for their deliverance, joy overflowed and exultation filled the heart of a nation. It is this joyful song we hear from the prophet on Christmas morn. Their vindication had arrived. They were delivered from bondage. The dawn of God's saving might was upon the earth.

One need not wonder why Isaiah was chosen to sing this privileged song of joy in the liturgy of Christmas morning. It was this very event, the Christ event, that he foreshadowed in his eschatological hymn. During the time of Deutero-Isaiah, messianic prophecies began to include an eschatological element, a future hope of deliverance at the consummation of the world. Jesus ushers in the last days through his Incarnation. There was reason for joy.

Responsorial Psalm
Psalm 98:1, 2–3, 3–4, 5–6

All of the psalms of Christmas are enthronement psalms. They praise God for the acts of salvation and are most appropriate on this day of salvation.

Second Reading
Hebrews 1:1–6

St. Paul's letter to the Hebrews is not a letter at all, but rather, a *logos* of encouragement for the community. A logos was a public address, very much like a homily. This opening address is a christological hymn of praise with roots in Jewish praise of Lady Wisdom. Wisdom was personified and considered to be with God in the act of creation. Wisdom also was the agent of God's revelation of self to Israel. The early Christian community appropriated that understanding to Jesus. Jesus assumes the role of One who was with God from the beginning in the work of salvation.

Gospel
John 1:1–18 or 1:1–5, 9–14

STEP 1
NAMING ONE'S EXPERIENCE

What were your first impressions? What captured your attention?

Each person names his or her initial impression. Statements should be brief. No reasons should be given at this time. All simply listen without agreeing or disagreeing.

STEP 2
UNDERSTANDING

In a brief statement, what do you think this gospel is trying to convey?

STEP 3
INPUT FROM VISION/STORY/TRADITION

Liturgical Context

Prior to Vatican II, the prologue to John's gospel was read at the end of every mass, thus recalling for the faithful the salvation event of God through the Incarnation of the Son.

"Christmas is a feast that celebrates our redemption even though the focus of attention is on the Incarnation and the 'marvelous exchange' and not on the passion and resurrection."[29] This is clearly expressed in the second reading: "He cleansed us from our sins and took his seat at the right hand of the majesty in Heaven . . ."(Heb 1:3). The gospel for the mass during the day uses John's prologue to proclaim the mystery of the Incarnation. God speaks a definitive *Word* to the world and to Israel. Salvation was at hand. The *Word* had been spoken. John's prologue and the letter to the Hebrews emphasize that the Christmas liturgy is more than a mere celebration of a baby's birth. It is God's center-stage act of communication with the world. (On this day, one might consider using the shorter form of the reading, since the longer form, including reference to John the Baptist, contains what is believed to be a later addition to the original hymn.)

This liturgy celebrates the great expression of joy inherent in all of the Christmas readings. The mystery of Jesus' Incarnation is raised to a cosmic level. John reminds us in his prologue that we must return to the beginning and remember that God began the Christmas story at the creation of the world. God had always intended that humanity be heirs of eternal life with him. We must look at the nativity alongside the cross and resurrection. Christmas is viewed through the lens of Easter.

Gospel Exegesis

The facilitator gives input regarding what critical biblical scholarship has to say about this text. The input includes insights as to how people would have heard the gospel in Jesus' time.

The prologue serves as a preface to John's gospel. It is theological and its purpose is to establish the thesis for the entire book. John's gospel tells the stories of Christ from the perspective that God, even from the beginning, from before time, from the eternal past, had been in the process of communicating. To be God means to reveal God. Creation was an act of God's self-communication. God's revelation to Israel was a continuation of his continuous activity of self-revelation. Jesus, then, was the definitive, incarnate expression of God's self-communication to Israel.

Reginald Fuller suggests that the Word became flesh throughout Jesus' entire ministry. Through Jesus' life and miracles God continued the process of revealing self to the world. Jesus manifested God to humanity. In John's prologue, *flesh* refers to all human history since the very beginning, the creation of the world. All that God had done *for* and *with* Israel is brought to this moment, to this

[29] *DL* (I), 128.

defining moment of salvation. All of God's deeds up to this point are understood in light of God's premier saving event: the spoken Word of God, in human form, given as ultimate gift of self, to suffer for the sins of the world.

John's gospel was written in response to the situation at the end of the century in which belief in Christ's divinity was questioned. John made his case by proclaiming that Christ was a part of God's action at creation. Jesus was present at God's first act of salvation (creation) and awaited his entrance into the world (Incarnation) to inaugurate God's last, conclusive act of salvation.

Patricia Datchuck Sanchez offers an interesting observation. The Semitic understanding of the word *logos* was "a challenge a believer can accept or reject."[30] A *logos* from God could be accepted or rejected. Thus the believer was faced with a decision and a response. The Greek understanding of *logos* was "an intermediary between God and the created universe."[31] The *logos* brought order to the universe. Therefore, according to Hellenistic thought, the one who embraced the *logos* would have access to the mysteries of the heavens. John is familiar with both constructs and cleverly uses both meanings in defining the ultimate mystery of Christ. Christ is the one who invites and calls people to faith, but he is also the one who reveals the face of God to the world.

Proclaim the gospel again.

Sometimes we gain new insights when we hear the text after the interpretation has been given. Someone from the group proclaims the gospel a second time.

STEP 4
TESTING

Conversation with the Liturgy and the Scriptures

Test your original understanding in dialogue with the text.

(You might consider breaking into smaller groups.)

How does John's prologue speak to you? Did the exegesis offer any new insights? How does your original understanding of this Christmas gospel compare with the interpretation? Does John's description of Christ as the eternal spoken Word of God have anything to do with your life? If so, how? What relevance does it have today? What was John trying to say to his community? What does he have to say to your community and to you today? Do you still feel the same way about this text as you did at the beginning? Describe your understanding of this story now.

STEP 5
DECISION

The gospel demands a response.

How should our community respond to this word from John? If we accept the Semitic understanding of *logos,* how might Christ be challenging us in this reading, or in all of the readings of Christmas? What one specific, concrete thing can I do during this season to respond to the word spoken today?

DOCTRINAL ISSUES

What church truth/teaching/doctrinal issue could be drawn from the readings for Christmas ?

Participants suggest possible doctrinal themes that flow from the readings.

Possible Doctrinal Themes

Incarnation; christology; manifestation; salvation; soteriology

Present the doctrinal material at this time.

1. The facilitator gives input on a particular doctrinal issue of his/her prior choosing. OR
2. The group chooses a doctrinal issue from the list they created. They read together from the Doctrinal Appendix.

---

[30] *WWC,* 274.
[31] Ibid.

(The doctrinal issues are found in the Doctrinal Appendix in the back of this workbook. If you are choosing an issue from this resource, please refer to it now.)

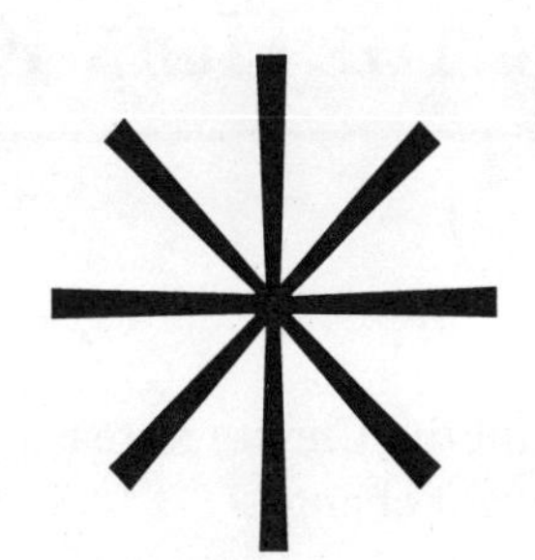

Reflection questions centered around the chosen doctrinal theme can be found at the end of each topic in the Doctrinal Appendix. The questions are based on the five-step reflection process. If you choose a topic not included in the Doctrinal Appendix, craft your own questions according to the same five-step process.

Following the reflection questions you will be reminded to return to chapter 7, "Preparing the Catechetical Session," to assist you in crafting your own session.

Closing Prayer

Father, all powerful and ever living God,
we do well always and everywhere to give you thanks
through Jesus Christ our Lord.
Today in him a new light has dawned upon the
world:
God has become one with man,
and man has become one again with God.
Your eternal Word has taken upon himself our
human weakness,
giving our mortal nature immortal value.
So marvelous is this oneness between God and
man
that in Christ man restores to man the gift of everlasting life.
In our joy we sing to your glory
with all the choirs of angels:
All sing or say: Holy, holy, holy, Lord, God of
power and might,
heaven and earth are full of your glory.
Hosanna in the highest.
Blessed is he who comes in the name of the Lord.
Hosanna in the highest.[32]

[32]Christmas Preface III, *The Sacramentary*.

Feast of the Holy Family

Environment

Because it is still the Christmas season, the environment does not change.

INTRODUCTORY RITES

Opening Song (or Entrance Antiphon)

The shepherds hastened to Bethlehem, where they found Mary and Joseph, and the baby lying in a manger.[1]

Opening Prayer

The facilitator of the session may lead the prayer. Others in the group may be asked to proclaim the readings.

Let us pray
[for peace in our families]

Pause for silent prayer.

Father in heaven, creator of all,
you ordered the earth to bring forth life
and crowned its goodness by creating the family of man.
In history's moment when all was ready,
you sent your Son to dwell in time,
obedient to the laws of life in our world.
Teach us the sanctity of human love,
show us the value of family life,
and help us to live in peace with all men
that we may share in your life for ever.
We ask this through Christ our Lord.[2]

LITURGY OF THE WORD

Today it would be important to pay attention to all of the readings. Taken together they better express the meaning of this feast. You might want to give particular attention to the second reading.

[1]Holy Family: "Entrance Antiphon," *The Sacramentary.*

[2]Holy Family: "Alternative Opening Prayer," *The Sacramentary.*

Let us listen to God's word.

First Reading
Sirach 3:2–6, 12–14

Overview of Sirach: The wisdom literature contained in the Book of Sirach was written by the person it was named after—a rare occurrence in biblical literature. It is one of the longest works in the Bible. In some translations it is referred to as "Ecclesiasticus," probably meaning the ecclesiastical book or the church book.

Ben Sira wrote Sirach around 180 B.C.E He was an educated man whose main writing concerns were reflection on the Torah and practical suggestions for upright living. He studied the Law, Prophets, and Writings and as scribe and teacher ran a school for young Jewish men. [3] Ben Sira also traveled extensively and studied the cultures of the places he visited. He gleaned much from the wisdom traditions of those places. He included and incorporated the best of what he learned (as long as it did not compromise his Jewish beliefs, tradition, or heritage) into his teaching.

Sirach wrote his treatise on wisdom not for personal gain, but for those who sought after it. Even though the pagan philosophies of Hellenism were on the rise, his aim was not to argue against the emerging cultural trends. He simply wished to show that the Jewish life was far superior to the emerging Hellenistic culture. True wisdom had its center in Jerusalem, not Athens. Thus, good Jews should avoid the influence and lure of the new philosophies and temptations of the Greek culture.

The book of Sirach was not accepted in the Hebrew and Protestant canons. The cause for its omission in the Jewish canon is probably due to the first century Pharisees' dislike of the theology it contained (such as Sirach's denial of retribution in the afterlife). It was nevertheless much quoted by later rabbis. The early church fathers strongly

[3]Alexander A. Di Lella, O.F.M., *NJBC,* 496.

attested to its canonicity. The Sirach text was used in Christian worship more than any other text, with the exception of the psalms.

Today's Pericope: Sirach offers a commentary on the fifth commandment—to honor one's parents. When one follows this command, a multitude of sins are forgotten. Sirach was so serious about the law's exhortation, that to break the law was considered tantamount to breaking the covenant relationship with God.

Israel was in covenant relationship with Yahweh (*hesed*). This *hesed* assumed a reciprocity in which love of one another flowed out of the love of God. The first person or group deserving of *hesed* was one's parents. When a person uprightly and justly followed the law, he or she could expect mercy, blessings, and God's forgiveness. Children were to respect and care for their parents. Parents who raised their children in righteousness could expect their children to be firmly planted in the faith of Israel. Children that do not heed their parents can expect to be uprooted from their firm foundation.

It was suggested in the Law that anyone who does not treat the aged with care and concern is guilty of blasphemy. The challenge of this scripture is very clear. Dysfunctional family systems were not tolerated in ancient Israel. It was assumed that all people would live in the harmony God expected.

Family was a very important reality for Israel. The clan, the tribe, the extended family, the people of God, all represented a form of family that was in covenant relationship with Yahweh. Covenant relationship requires a great respect and care for one another.

Responsorial Psalm
Psalm 128:1–2, 3, 4–5

This wisdom psalm calls on God to bless human efforts. Psalm 128 insists that the prosperity of family and society begins with a basic fear of the Lord. Prosperity and harmony as interchangeable terms are possible only when a person lives in submission to God's will, loves God with heart and soul, and extends that love to others. Herein lies the basis for fear of the Lord. This wisdom psalm beseeches the blessings of God in human efforts. "Happy" refers to the blessing of many sons. The reference to "house" ("home" NAB) is a reflection on human effort. All who do what is upright in God's eyes will be blessed with many children.

Second Reading
Colossians 3:12–21

Overview of St. Paul's Letter to the Colossians: Colossae was a city in Asia Minor, the present day Turkey. It was a thriving center for wool and textiles. Its name comes from the dark red dye used in wool. During the time of the early church, Colossae was eclipsed by the prominence of nearby Laodicea. Colossae was ruined by an earthquake (c. 60 C.E.) and was probably not rebuilt.

The Christian community in Colossae was comprised mostly of Gentiles and was founded by Epaphras, one of its natives. The purpose of the letter was to strengthen the faith of the community and to correct the errors that had plagued the Christian community. The errors in question centered around prevalent false teaching. "According to the letter, the false teaching is a philosophy and an empty deceit (2:8), a human tradition (2:8); it concerns the elemental spirits of the universe (2:8), and angels (2:18); it demanded observance of food regulations and festivals, new moons, and sabbath (2:14, 16, 20, 21); and it encourages ascetic practices."[4] It appears that the Christian community incorporated pagan philosophies such as gnosticism, astrology, magic, and the mystery religions into their religious practices.

Another major error was an implied denial of Jesus as the sole redeemer and mediator of the world. Paul defends the Christian position by emphatically affirming Jesus "both as savior and as a creative and cosmic principle."[5] The letter affirms the central role of Christ in salvation and refutes the gnosticism prevalent in the church of Colossae.

Colossae experienced division in the community over the inclusion of Gentiles. Aberrant religious

[4]Maurya P. Horgan, "The Letter to the Colossians," *NJBC,* 877.

[5]*DB,* 146.

practices threatened the Colossian church. Epaphras called on Paul in prison to chastise and challenge his community to fidelity in Christ. Paul willingly wrote to his Colossian brothers and sisters and stressed that they must remain steadfast to the Christ who is above any pagan, philosophical, or religious practice that humans might construct. Jesus is the center of the universe, our primary reality. Any other spiritual quest is idolatry.

Some contemporary biblical scholars question the Pauline authorship of this letter. There are too many differences between this letter and other confirmed Pauline letters, they insist. "Colossians contains 86 words not found in the uncontested Pauline writings, of which 34 are not found elsewhere in the New Testament."[6] It seems that the articulation of Christology is different in this letter than in other letters. "Colossians exhibits a more elaborate theology of the Church, particularly the Church as the body and Christ as the head; Colossians uses the term mystery for the plan of salvation; the idea of knowledge becomes prominent; and the cosmological-Christological synthesis, while not unparalleled in earlier writings, is here much more complex."[7] Scholars who maintain that Paul did write the letter are not disturbed by the differences. They suggest that the language difference is simply an attempt by Paul to use terms and speak in the language of the very philosophies he was attempting to combat, by incorporating that language into his Christian defense. Those who insist on Pauline authorship state that the summary of Christian belief found in the letter reflects the brilliance only Paul could expound. The letter is believed to have been written during his captivity in prison.

Some scholars believe this pericope is part of a baptismal teaching. When Paul exhorts the Colossians to "put on love," he references the baptismal liturgy in which a new garment is put on as a symbol of new life in Christ. The old self dies to sin and the white color of the garment represents triumphing over death and sin.

Today's Pericope: There is often great controversy over the latter verses of this pericope. Some people believe that the piece regarding the submission of wives should be left out of the text for the same reasons that the verses regarding the submission of slaves were deleted. The verses regarding slavery were deleted because of society's changed view of slavery. It is a thing of the past and is intrinsically evil. Some believe the verses about "submissive wives" should be deleted for the same reason. Proponents of deleting the text suggest that it was a reality of a former time and culture. Today Christian marriage is seen as a community of covenant love, rooted in mutuality and reciprocity. Further, there is an even more more compelling argument against reading the verses. Many times they have been cited as an apologetic for dominance over wives by controlling, abusive husbands.

However, Raymond F. Collins suggests a different approach. He asserts that these and similar readings were part of early Christian *Haustafel* or household codes (compendiums of household duties).[8] There were political reasons for such codes. Christians were believed to be disruptive of the social order. They refused submission to the gods of the state. "On the domestic scene, various women, young people, and slaves had become Christians. Such phenomena led to widespread suspicion of Christians and even to the persecution of Christians, considered people who disrupted social order and disturbed domestic harmony."[9] The household codes were a way for Christians to assert their compliance with the family values of the day. Collins suggests that there is merit in proclaiming these readings. We should read the "submissive wives" text as presenting the world view of a former time, a former culture, and a former reality. Their value to us today is the deeper meaning they suggest. He submits that these readings affirm the concern that God has for the human family within the social culture in which it exists. "One cannot make of any given society's family structures the norm for all families of all times and places. We can, however, affirm that God is not indifferent to family life, as it is actually structured within any given society."[10] He suggests that the household codes point to God's care for the family as it is lived—not as it is idealized by some

[6]Ibid.
[7]Ibid.

[8]*WWC*, 276.
[9]*TE*, 81–84.
[10]Ibid.

outside agency. Collins asserts that the basic message of the text should not be overlooked. The household codes affirm that there must be some order for a family to function well. He maintains that their use in the liturgy affirms that the Christian family has been and always will be a concern of the church. "The well-being of families who belong to the church is important for the well-being of the church itself."[11]

Although twentieth-century America has little resemblance to early Christian communities, there are corollaries to be drawn. Even the piece regarding slaves and masters has its present-day corollary. Both "submissive wives" and "obedient slaves" point to a reciprocity of relationships that is expected even today. When people work, they expect a fair wage for their labor and to be treated with respect and concern by their employers. Employers expect a fair day's work for a fair day's wage. It all boils down to the right ordering of relationships. We are all to "do right by one another."

Collins offers a caution. He says that there is a strength and a liability to the contemporary proclamation of the household codes of early Christian communities.

> It is a strength insofar as it recalls that one must live the Christian life within the context of a socially conditioned set of human relationships. It is a liability when one attempts to make the social relationships of yesteryear a norm for the social relationships of today. *When preaching household codes, the homilist should NOT proclaim that wives should be submissive to their husbands.* Such submission is no longer culturally acceptable; indeed, in our times, it may well be antithetical to the gospel itself. On the other hand, the liturgical reading of the household codes may provide a pastorally sensitive homilist with an opportune occasion for reflecting on the changing nature of the family structure.[12]

Collins suggests that there be serious reflection regarding our assumed norms for the human family. The nuclear family of the past is not the present norm. Nor was it the norm for all time. The extended family system was around long before the "Quaker, child centered family of the middle colonies."[13] He also notes that in the seventeenth and eighteenth centuries the father was the primary care giver following the baby's nursing period. Before we canonize the "'typical' twentieth century white American family" we should rather reflect on God's presence in every family, no matter what social circumstances it finds itself in. Perhaps the atypical family is pure gift in our midst. It is a reminder of our responsibility to God's *anawim,* to one another, and to those who struggle just to keep themselves afloat in turbulent, often violent and dysfunctional family systems. It is the responsibility of the church, the people of God, to reflect God's care for all families, those considered typical and especially those considered atypical.

[11]Ibid., 83

[12]Ibid., 84.

Gospel
Matthew 2:13–15, 19–23

The angel appeared to Joseph in a dream and told him to take the child to Egypt.

Step 1
Naming One's Experience

What were your first impressions? What was your first response? What captured your attention? How did you feel?[14]

Each person names his or her initial impression. Statements should be brief. No reasons should be given at this time. All simply listen without agreeing or disagreeing.

Step 2
Understanding

In a brief statement, what do you think this gospel is trying to convey?

[13]Ibid., 85.

[14]The primary focus of reflection is the gospel. However, very often the other readings demand attention and must be brought into the dialogue.

Step 3
Input from Vision/Story/Tradition

Liturgical Context[15]

Like other readings of the Christmas season, the gospel for this Sunday is another manifestation of Christ, the Son of God to the world. Today it is Jesus' wisdom that becomes manifest. The liturgy allows us to gaze upon this Christ who, though fully human, is the personification of divine wisdom.

The church has set aside this day to uplift and reflect upon the Christian family. The holy family is offered as a model. The first and second readings provide insights into familial relationships. Perhaps after reflecting upon what it means to love in the context of family, family systems, and societal structures, we then can turn to the gospel to remind us that we have one who is filled with wisdom, who lavishly showers us with love, who promises to be with us, even as we struggle to live in love in difficult situations. Perhaps the gospel reminds us that we must turn our children and their futures over to the providential care of God. Perhaps it tells us that we must be content to live in the mystery of God's revelation in our lives, even when we are faced with difficult family experiences. Perhaps we can view Mary and Joseph as willing to accept the ambiguity that life often presents. Perhaps they can serve as reminders to us that if we ponder the marvels of God in our heart and watch God's plan unfold in our lives, we will one day be able to look back and discern the mighty hand of God in the most trying situations.

The prayers of today's liturgy ask God for the intercession of Mary and Joseph for the peace and unification of families. The Prayer over the Gifts states: "Lord, accept this sacrifice and through the prayers of Mary, the virgin Mother of God, and of her husband, Joseph, unite our families in peace and love." The liturgy reflects great concern for the Christian family. On this day, this Christmas-season feast, we once again celebrate God's manifestation to the human race. Let us put it in the context of what can often be a most difficult place to experience such manifestation: the human family. We pray for and uplift families who struggle to submit their lives to the will of God. We thank God for the witness of their lives. We pray for those who suffer violence, hatred, and animosity within the walls of their own homes.

Gospel Exegesis

The facilitator gives input regarding what critical biblical scholarship has to say about this text. The input includes insights as to how people would have heard the gospel in Jesus' time.

The original intention of this gospel has little to do with the theme of family. "Matthew's concern rather is to present Jesus as recapitulating in his life the history of Israel."[16] Jesus was frequently looked upon by Matthew as another Moses. The correlation is obvious. Pharaoh decreed that Moses and all male children be slaughtered. Moses was saved from the slaughter by Pharaoh's daughter. As a young adult, Moses killed an Egyptian and was forced to flee to Midian until after the death of Pharaoh, when Yahweh commanded him to return to Egypt. The evangelist wants his readers to see the similarities between Moses, the great liberator of his people, and Jesus, the great liberator of all the world. Were not their humble origins conspicuously similar? Matthew used practically the same language in telling the story of Joseph's flight into Egypt as was used in relating God's command to Moses to return to Egypt from Meridian with his sons. "The double connection that Matthew obviously intends is to make us decode the message. The history of the new people of God begins with Jesus' departure into Egypt and his return to the land of Israel. This pilgrimage is similar to the one Jacob made. Jesus was the instrument of the freedom that God initiated, hinted at by the freedom for which Moses was protagonist".[17]

[15]The scriptures in the Lectionary, the seasons of the year, and the ritual prayers of the mass are interrelated and form the basis for liturgical catechesis. The *liturgical context* attempts to explore and clarify the themes and this interrelatedness.

[16]*PL*, 25.

[17]*DL* (I), 227.

Jesus' return to Israel from Egypt fulfills an unknown biblical passage. However, the text reference reminds the reader that God's will is the driving force behind the action of Joseph and the subsequent return of Jesus to Israel from Egypt. Moses died before entering the promised land. Lawrence Boadt maintains that the reason for Moses' death is pragmatic. Had Moses led his people into the promised land, the temptation of the people would have been to credit Moses and not Yahweh, the ultimate liberator and deliverer of the people.[18] Jesus, however, entered the promised land, Israel, in the region of Galilee, and would live to fulfill God's final plan of salvation and liberation. Matthew's intention is to show that Jesus is indeed the One whom the prophets foretold. Jesus is the fulfillment of the Hebrew Scriptures.

Due to miscalculations in the formulation of the ancient calendar, Jesus was actually born in 6 B.C.E. and Herod died in 4 B.C.E. Herod's obsessive control and fear led him to his heinous, murderous plan. Joseph discovered Herod's obsession and thus followed the directive given to him by God in a dream to take Jesus to Egypt. Egypt had long been established as a place of refuge for Judeans, because it was not under Herod's control. The holy family quite possibly settled in Galilee because of the safety it provided. Judeans under Herod's control were often in grave danger, and Galilee provided a safer place for them.

How does what Matthew wanted to convey in this gospel passage have anything to do with the Feast of the Holy Family? Explicitly it does not. Implicitly we can be reminded of the hardships the holy family endured. The first two readings, taken together, set the stage for the way we may experience the gospel on this feast. They peer into the mystery of family relationships and perhaps hint that a model for these family relationships can be found in the holy family who, in this pericope, face danger, fear, and an unknown future. Mary and Joseph packed up their family and moved in response to Joseph's dream. They responded in faith to the will and word of God; they endured hardship and poverty; they faced struggles and frustration. This family was the haven that would nurture the Christ, God made flesh. We cannot miss the point that Jesus was born as a human in the context of the human struggle. No wonder Christ hated human suffering. He knew all too well the frustrations of life. Yet in the midst of this life's travails, Jesus was perfectly faithful to his Father. He did not waver in his steadfast obedience. He followed God's plan for his life and for the salvation of the world—even though it led to his death.

The holy family was perhaps the first family to live in the reality of the Incarnation. We make the holy family an American construct if we think of them in terms of mother, father, and son. The ancient Middle Eastern family consisted of the large extended family. It is quite possible that all the inhabitants of the small hamlet of Nazareth were Jesus' relatives. The nuclear family interrelationships were different in the ancient setting as well. The mother and eldest son shared a close bond, whereas the bond between husband and wife was weak. While we may look to the holy family as model, it would be a mistake to romanticize them into a life situation that has very little to do with reality. The model they provide for us has more to do with the fact that they were the first family to live in the reality of the Incarnation. They were the first to struggle with the realization of what God was doing in Christ, even though it caused much confusion. They lived their life ordered by the will and the word of God. Herein lies the basis of our imitation. Pope Paul VI said it eloquently:

> Nazareth is a kind of school where we may begin to discover what Christ's life was like and even to understand his gospel. Here we can observe and ponder the simple appeal of the way God's Son came to be known, profound yet full of hidden meaning. And gradually we may even learn to imitate him.
>
> Here we can learn to realize who Christ really is. And here we can sense and take account of the conditions and circumstances that surrounded and affected his life on earth: the places, the tenor of the times, the culture, the language, religious customs, in brief everything which Jesus used to make himself known to the world.

[18]Lawrence Boadt, Workshop—"The Letters of Paul," given at the Church of Our Saviour, Cocoa Beach, Florida, October 1997.

Here everything speaks to us, everything has meaning. Here we can learn the importance of spiritual discipline for all who wish to follow Christ and live by the teachings of his gospel.

How I would like to return to my childhood and attend the simple yet profound school that is Nazareth! How wonderful to be close to Mary, learning again the lesson of the true meaning of life, learning again God's truths."[19]

Matthew suggests that the flight into Egypt is directed or connected with passages from scripture. His point is not to be missed. "This suggests that Jesus' family directed him toward his destiny 'according to the Scriptures,' that is, in harmony with God's will as revealed in the Bible. Oh that this might be true for contemporary families as well!"[20]

Proclaim the gospel again.

Sometimes we gain new insights when we hear the text after the interpretation has been given. Someone from the group proclaims the gospel a second time.

STEP 4
TESTING

Conversation with the Liturgy and the Scriptures

Test your original understanding in dialogue with the text.

(You might consider breaking into smaller groups.)

How do the readings for the Feast of the Holy Family speak to you today? Are there any new insights? What message in these readings do contemporary families most need to hear? What is the most pressing message for your parish family? Your nuclear family? How does this story speak to your life?

[19]Paul VI, "Homélie prononcée à Nazareth le 5 janvier 1964," in La Liturgie des Heures, 1980, p. 251 (Office of Readings for the Holy Family).

[20]*CWJ*, 15.

Sharing Life Experience

Participants share an experience from their lives that connects with the biblical interpretation just shared.

I am reminded of when we moved our family to Florida. I did not want to move. I knew it was right for our lives, but I did not want to leave the security of the known world for the unknown. Much prayer and discernment went into our decision. We did not receive a mandate in a dream—but it seemed like a dream to me. The events fell so quickly into place (we sold a house, I found a job, and we moved four kids, a dog, and a cat in a matter of three weeks). But it was difficult. Knowing that it was God's plan for our lives did not make it easier. It was the greatest challenge of my life up to that point. I was leaving the security of my Midwestern roots for what only God knew for sure! Yet, when I look back, I marvel at the ways God fulfilled the purpose of our lives through that move. Such decisions are not easy. Family relationships can be the most trying relationships we will ever know. Yet in families is where the paschal mystery is lived, day in and day out.

I don't know what turn our lives would have taken had we not responded to that gentle nudge from God. What we learned from that situation in our life sustained us as we raised our family through the difficult years. We knew that ultimately God is with us. The Incarnation is a reality in our lives.

We suffered the trials that most families endure—the teenage years, near-death accidents, near-death illnesses, financial losses—all of those frustrations that prompt contemporary families to say with St. Theresa, "Lord, if this is how you treat your friends, it's no wonder you have so few!" However, the truth of the Incarnation is that we were never alone in any of it. We are strong because of it. And our family is better for it. Our job was to listen and trust. Sometimes we did; sometimes we fell short. But God was and is present—not only in the joys, but in the heart-wrenching sorrows. God drives our lives. God shows us what it means to love. God reminds us that the love he shows us is not only to be poured out in the midst of our families, but is to extend to others in the world—especially to the poor and the marginalized.

All share their life experience.

What was Matthew trying to tell his community? How do today's readings reflect God's promise to be in relationship with humanity [covenant]? In what way do the readings speak of liberation [exodus]? In what way do today's readings invite us to participate in God's work of creation [creation]? What is the ultimate message for today's contemporary world [community]? Do you still feel the same way about these readings as when you began? Was your original understanding of today's readings affirmed or challenged?

Step 5
Decision

The gospel demands a response.

How does our understanding of these scriptures and today's liturgy invite us into deeper conversion? In what concrete ways is our parish called to respond? Has this conversation with the exegesis changed my personal attitudes or behavior? What are the implications of this gospel in my life? What is one concrete action I will take this week as a response to the liturgy today?

Pastoral Considerations: Perhaps this would be a good time to bless expectant parents, and families of all shapes, sizes, races, and cultures. Refer to the *Book of Blessings.*

Christian Initiation: Perhaps there are candidates ready to celebrate a Rite of Acceptance or Welcome. Also, very often the initiation process stretches relationships in some family situations. Since the "anointing of catechumens" is intended to strengthen catechumens it might be a good time to celebrate the rite.

DOCTRINAL ISSUES

What church truth/teaching/doctrinal issue could be drawn from the gospel for the Feast of the Holy Family?

Participants suggest possible doctrinal themes that flow from the readings.

Possible Doctrinal Themes

Christian family; Incarnation; manifestation; charity; salvation–soteriology

Present the doctrinal material at this time.

1. The facilitator gives input on a particular doctrinal issue of his/her prior choosing. OR
2. The group chooses a doctrinal issue from the list they created. They read together from the Doctrinal Appendix.

(The doctrinal issues are found in the Doctrinal Appendix in the back of this workbook. If you are choosing an issue from this resource, please refer to it now.)

Reflection questions centered around the chosen doctrinal theme can be found at the end of each topic in the Doctrinal Appendix. The questions are based on the five-step reflection process. If you choose a topic not included in the Doctrinal Appendix, craft your own questions according to the same five-step process.

Following the reflection questions you will be reminded to return to chapter 7, "Preparing the Catechetical Session," to assist you in crafting your own session.

Closing Prayer

Eternal Father,
we want to live as Jesus, Mary and Joseph,
in peace with you and one another.
May this communion strengthen us to face the
troubles of life.
Grant this through Christ, our Lord.[21]

[21]Feast of the Holy Family: "Prayer After Communion," *The Sacramentary.*

Mary, Mother of God

Environment

The Christmas season environment continues.

INTRODUCTORY RITES

Opening Song (or Entrance Antiphon)

A light will shine on us this day, the Lord is born for us: he shall be called Wonderful God, Prince of peace, Father of the world to come; and his kingship will never end (see Is 9:2, 6; Lk 1:33).[1]

Opening Prayer

The facilitator of the session may lead the prayer. Others in the group may be asked to proclaim the readings.

Let us pray...

Pause for silent prayer.

Father, source of light in every age,
the virgin conceived and bore your Son
who is called Wonderful God, Prince of Peace.
May her prayer, the gift of a mother's love,
be your people's joy through all ages.
May her response, born of a humble heart,
draw your Spirit to rest on your people.
Grant this through Christ, our Lord.[2]

LITURGY OF THE WORD

First Reading[3]

Numbers 6:22–27

Overview of the Book of Numbers: The name "Numbers" comes from the description of the census in chapter one. The laws contained in the Book of Numbers are directed to a people on a journey through the promised land. The material in the Book of Numbers extends over multiple centuries and from various ancient biblical sources. The narrative portion of Numbers belongs to an earlier period, while the laws were written during a later time in Israel's history. A portion of Numbers parallels the story of Exodus, especially stories of the grumbling, rebellious Israelites in the desert. "The incidents in Exodus stress the patience of Yahweh, who always listens to Israel's needs and intervenes to help. Numbers 11–21, on the other hand, stresses that the people's constant rebellion led Yahweh to **punish** them time and again. But each time Moses intervenes and begs for the sake of the people, and God softens his anger and turns back his punishments or heals the victims."[4]

Later biblical authors of Numbers looked back on the rebellion and failures of their ancestors. They believed that the trials and hardships they endured were God's punishment for rebellious behavior. "They could look back on the centuries of injustice, disobedience, and false worship, the condemnations of the prophets, the failures of the kings, and know that the loss of their freedom and land in exile had been richly deserved. God cannot be pushed too far without asserting his own justice and honor. Yet even at a late hour, he could turn from his anger and spare them, if they would only turn to him."[5] It was a constant theme for Israel: Israel sinned; God punished. Israel repented; God forgave and restored.

---

[1]Solemnity of Mary, Mother of God: "Entrance Antiphon," *The Sacramentary.*

[2]Solemnity of Mary, Mother of God: "Alternate Opening Prayer," *The Sacramentary.*

[3]The exegesis for the first and second readings may or may not be the focus of your group's reflection as there may only be time to give adequate attention to the gospel, your primary concern. However, the exegesis is included here in order to provide a thorough investigation of the entire liturgy of the word as there may be parts (or all) that would be necessary to the direction you wish to take with your particular ministry group.

[4]*ROT,* 192.

[5]Ibid, 193.

It is at the end of Numbers that leadership of Israel is passed on to Joshua at the death of Moses, and Israel begins its conquest of the promised land.

Today's Pericope: Today's reading contains Aaron's blessing, which is an amazing anticipation of Christian belief in the Trinity. The last verse is the key verse for our purposes in this liturgy. God's name is invoked. In biblical tradition the "name" implies the totality of the person. All God is and has done throughout salvation history is brought to bear in this blessing. "To 'bless' means to invoke upon the faithful all that God is and all that he has done for his people."[6] Christians have extended this understanding to include all that has been accomplished through Jesus. "The name of Jesus is the name of the triune God made manifest and present in saving power."[7]

Responsorial Psalm
Psalm 67:2–3, 5, 6, 8

The theme of the first reading is resounded in the psalm. The psalmist asks for God's mercy. The Christian sees God's blessing fulfilled in the person of Jesus.

Second Reading
Galatians 4:4–7

Overview of Galatians: The word *Galatians* is another word for *Celtic* or *Gallic.* Galatians were from a Celtic tribe near France. The Greeks referred to it as Galatia. The Galatians eventually migrated east and settled near northern Turkey. The Romans combined other tribes in Turkey and thus formed the Province of Galatia.

Paul's letter to the Galatians is similar in tone and content to the letter written to the Romans. However, the difference between Galatians and Romans is that one was written in the heat of the moment and the other was carefully planned and crafted with deliberate intention.

Paul's agenda was to answer the religious dilemmas facing the emerging Christian church. Scholars believe it was written in response to the problems going on in Corinth. Jewish Christians were insistent that Gentile converts follow Jewish ritual requirements. The problem raised questions and difficulties in the community. Should they remain strictly Jewish and observe all the practices and rituals of Judaism, or "was their Christian experience so distinctive, and [were] their claims for Jesus so absolute, that they could no longer be contained within Judaism?"[8] Unlike the first believers who saw Christianity in strictly Jewish terms (and as a sect within Judaism), the new pagan converts radically challenged the status quo. The implications were serious. How could they claim to be the heirs of the Old Testament covenant if they were no longer a part of Israel?

In the beginning Paul was sure that Jesus was doing something radically new and distinct. Thus, he felt that new converts should not be saddled with former binding, covenant rituals. This was scandalous to observant Jewish Christians. Their practice of the Christian faith was rooted in their Jewish heritage. Judaism was the foundation upon which Jesus established his reign. Jesus asserted that he had not come to abolish the law but to fulfill it. Then why were these Corinthian converts excused from Jewish formation? It did not make sense. It only proved to them that the heresies and godless practices would never have happened in the first place if these converts had been well grounded in the ethics of Judaism.

Paul was furious, but it forced him into further discernment. The issue of circumcision further exacerbated the controversy. It was only through circumcision that people were in covenant relationship with Yahweh. It was a sign of membership in the People of God (one of Israel's primary motifs). Paul was hurt and angry over the attacks by other Christians. He was not as informed as the "real" apostles. He had not known the historical Jesus. How could he be right and the others wrong? So the arguments continued. Paul dug in his heels, typically overreacting, and boldly maintained that his position was the only correct one.

Paul's rhetoric was so divisive that he polarized the community. He cut to the heart of religious obser-

[6] *PL*, 27.
[7] Ibid.

[8] *GAP*, 81.

vance. He professed Christianity to be on one side of the religious pole and Judaism to be on the other. Only one was absolutely correct, so the other was absolutely incorrect. We need not guess where Judaism fell. (Finesse was certainly not one of Paul's strong suits!)

He wisely named the potential dispositions inherent in all religious traditions and religious people. They will either be obedient or not; sincere or not; aware or blind; mature or childish. So far so good; we can all agree. However, Paul's conclusion sent chills through even the most lackadaisical Jew. Paul asserted that Christianity completely adhered to the virtuous side of those determinants while Judaism was absolutely the opposite. (Not a way to win friends and influence people!)

Paul suggested that circumcision was no more than an act of savage brutality and almost implied that he was ashamed of his own permanent Jewish branding. While his methods left a lot to be desired, Paul's intentions were to hold fast to the central gospel message.

Salvation was freely won by Christ's death and resurrection and could not be earned by one's own merit. Paul maintained that the Jewish perspective of right relationship with God (during Paul's time) evolved into total adherence to the law. This implied that salvation could be merited by one's own efforts. Paul vehemently protested. Salvation was a free, utterly gratuitous gift from God. "People do not need to prove themselves. God accepts them as they are, with all their sins. When they acknowledge this is so, of course, they will make every effort to live a life of union with God. Still it is God's unearned love, not their own effort, that puts them right with God. They become good because God is good."[9]

The way of the law, on the other hand, stressed human responsibility. Serving God was synonymous with rule-keeping. Such a perspective breeds the notion that if I am good enough, and follow the rules to the end, then God is obliged to save me.

Paul's way is not without its own set of dangers. Blindness, carelessness, and benign neglect could easily creep into the equation and prompt a person to sit on his or her laurels and passively respond to the demands of discipleship. However, Paul's vision put God in charge and offered disciples the necessary freedom to respond to God, not to restrictive religious systems. Paul's letter to the Galatians reasserts belief in the paschal mystery. Jesus suffered, died, and rose again for the sins of the world. This reality has the power to change lives.

Paul so impulsively cranked out his letter that he did not even take the time to offer the customary introductory prayers of praise. The Galatians had questioned Paul's teaching. He had to set them straight. Paul's letter defended his ministry and his position. He had not been wrong. Faith was all that was required for salvation. Jesus had paid the price; humanity reaped the benefits. The law and all the ritual requirements of the law were no longer necessary. Furthermore, his right to apostolic succession was given credence by Jesus' post-resurrection appearance to Paul.

This was a significant shift for the early church. One position embraced works as a means of salvation; the other maintained that salvation through faith automatically leads to good works. Early Christians were put in a position of having to make a choice.

Paul's letter to the Romans took up the same passionate conviction. However, it was more thoughtfully crafted and was not as influenced by his "knee jerk" reaction to the accusations leveled against him.[10]

***Implications for This Feast*:** St. Paul is particularly relevant on this New Year's Day as a reminder that we are children of God and heirs to the salvation won through the paschal mystery of Christ. We inaugurate the new year with the resolve to live in the fullness of Christ's light. His letter to the Galatians reminds us that since we have been elevated to God's divine life through the coming of Jesus, we must own that divine heritage and live accordingly.

[9]Ibid, 84.

[10]The primary source for the exegesis concerning Paul's letter is taken from *The Gospel According to St. Paul* (*GAP*) by Hubert Richards.

Gospel[11]
Luke 2:16–21

The shepherds go to Bethlehem in haste to see the babe they had been told about. Mary treasures it all in her heart and on the eighth day they took Jesus to be circumcised and to be given his name.

STEP 1
NAMING ONE'S EXPERIENCE

What were your first impressions? What was your first response?

Each person names his or her initial impression. Statements should be brief. No reasons should be given at this time. All simply listen without agreeing or disagreeing.

STEP 2
UNDERSTANDING

In a brief statement, what do you think this gospel is trying to convey?

STEP 3
INPUT FROM VISION/STORY/TRADITION

Liturgical Context

The Solemnity of Mary is the oldest of Marian feasts. This feast is christological and defines Mary's role in the church. It also defines Marian devotion. The Vatican II document *Lumen Gentium* states:

> Devotion to Mary as it has always existed in the Church, even though it is altogether special, is essentially distinct from the worship of adoration paid equally to the Word incarnate, the Father, and the Holy Spirit. For the various forms of Marian devotions sanctioned by the Church, within the limits of sound orthodoxy and suited circumstances of time and place as well as to the character and cultures of peoples, have the effect that as we honor the Mother we also truly know the Son and give love, glory and obedience through him, through whom all things have their being (see Col 1:15–16) and in whom it has pleased the eternal Father that all fullness should dwell.[12]

To reiterate: this feast is christological. It is primarily about the birth of Christ, the fulfillment of God's plan of salvation. However, it also points to Mary as an example of faith. She is a model for all believers and exemplifies the true Israel. Mary was a willing vessel, ready to receive God's grace. We too are to be such vessels.

The prayers of the liturgy today ask for her intercession. The liturgy itself shows us Mary's role in the church.

> God our Father,
> may we always profit by the prayers
> of the Virgin Mary,
> for you bring us life and salvation
> through Jesus Christ, her Son.
> (Opening Prayer)

> God our Father,
> we celebrate this season
> the beginning of our salvation.
> On this feast of Mary, the Mother of God,
> we ask that our salvation
> will be brought to its fulfillment.
> (Prayer over the Gifts)

> Father,
> as we proclaim the Virgin Mary
> to be the mother of Christ and the mother of the Church,
> may our communion with her Son
> bring us salvation.
> (Prayer after Communion)

[11]The gospel exegesis is provided later in this session so that it may be presented in the proper sequence where it occurs in the adult five-step reflection process. The exegesis is provided for the first and second readings for your information and edification, and for you to use at your discretion. Once again, the gospel is the primary source of reflection. If there is time for reflection on the other readings, all the better.

[12]*Lumen gentium* #31, in *DVII.*

Mary is our intercessor. She stands with the pilgrim church as we wait in hope for Jesus' return.

We cannot ignore the fact that this feast also initiates the new year. As each new year brings solemn promises of transformation, the feast of Mary, Mother of God, reminds us that Christian discipline involves striving to live in harmony with God's will. Mary opened herself to receive God's grace and blessing. In this new year, we, too, ask for God's grace and blessing. Our prayer is for the openness to embrace salvation when it comes our way.

If catechetical groups are unable to center a session around this solemnity, it would be very important to address the themes and truths inherent in this celebration during another session.

Gospel Exegesis

The facilitator provides input regarding critical biblical scholarship on this text. The input includes insights as to how people would have heard the gospel in Jesus' time.

This gospel is almost identical to the gospel for the mass at dawn of Christmas day. It adds the event of Jesus' circumcision and the conferral of his name. Mary follows the prescriptions of the law by having Jesus baptized according to the law. In biblical tradition, the "name" often designated the person's mission. The name "Jesus" means "the one who saves." Thus, his very name identifies his role and his destiny. Throughout the Christian scriptures we are shown the power of Jesus' name to heal, expel demons, and liberate people. Jesus' name is to be used in faith.

However, in and of themselves, the events of today's gospel were not extraordinary. Many biblical figures have been given a new name; Jesus' name was not exceedingly significant in biblical times, as there were others with the same name; presenting Jesus at the temple for the circumcision was prescribed by the law. Thus, the intent is to show that Mary did all that the angel told her to do. She was a willing, obedient servant.

Yet Christians know the story and they know well that the name indeed tells us who Jesus is: "the one who saves." We know from this story and beyond this story that Jesus' mission is extraordinary and is the fulfillment of all that was promised by the prophets of old. Jesus' name was power. His healing ministry was evidence of that power. When we call on Jesus in faith, we invoke the power of his name and place our lives under his care. It requires a great leap of faith. Mary did not ask how her son would become great as the angel had proclaimed. Hers was not to question or to know, but simply to accept in trust.

God's grace was shown to sinners in the revelation given to the shepherds. The peace offered is offered freely for all people, equally, not just for the pious righteous. We recall from a previous Sunday that peace implies wholeness, all things in right relationship, harmony. The peace brought by God's Son is a peace whereby people live in *hesed* love. Relationships are brought under the dominion of God. "The recovery of wholeness in human relationships, which is due to God's acts in Jesus, reflects honor to God."[13] This is understood in terms of our relationship to the human race, to one another, to the stranger, the lost, the alien, the misfit, and the outcast. Gustavo Gutierrez expresses it beautifully: "By becoming human, the Son of God transforms every human face into the expression of God's presence and exigency."[14] He further added comments by the Latin American bishops in Puebla, Mexico in which they exhorted the faithful to discover the presence of Jesus in the faces of the world's poor. Gutierrez tells us that such faces serve as a reminder and an invitation to us all to become more faithful to living the gospel of Christ. If we, like Mary, ponder such things in our heart, perhaps then will the "insignificant and the excluded of this world become an epiphany (a revelation) of God for us."[15]

Mary accepted in faith what she had been told. She did not question. She allowed the events to unfold and was a willing, obedient servant in God's grand design. We are called to the same mission.

Proclaim the gospel again.

[13] *RL*, 34.
[14] *SWTLY*, 34.
[15] Ibid.

Sometimes we gain new insights when we hear the text after the interpretation has been given. Someone from the group proclaims the gospel a second time.

STEP 4
TESTING

Conversation with the Liturgy and the Scriptures

Test your original understanding in dialogue with the text.

(You might consider breaking into smaller groups.)

How does the feast of Mary the Mother of God touch your life? Does this feast have any relevance for the church today? Were there any new insights? How does your original understanding of this story compare with what we just shared?

How does this story speak to your life?

Sharing Life Experience

Parish life is the incredible, living sign of God's presence in the world. It is filled with faith-filled people who, like Mary, trust God in the midst of life's difficulties and ambiguities. The week before and after Christmas this year, a forty-six-year-old woman (and friend) died suddenly in the shower, another woman died unexpectedly on a family outing, another woman's son was stabbed to death, and another parishioner's sister committed suicide. It is so difficult to lose loved ones, especially in untimely, unexpected ways, and especially during the holidays. In the midst of such tragedy it would be easy to wonder where God is. Yet over and over I experience the living faith of people who face such pain with courage—people who have the assurance that God is in control of their lives and will give them the strength that will see them through their grief. I am awestruck by the presence and compassion of the community as it embraces families through the tragedies of their lives.

On this day, New Year's Day, I am reminded that life is a precious gift. The death of my friend, and of the other parishioners who died so unexpectedly over the holidays, is a stark reminder of how tenuous life is. Mary did not question the future. She simply put her trust in God and walked into it with the assurance that God would lead her. We may only have today to live the love that God invites us to live. Mary walked into her future with a willing, obedient heart.

Mary is a model for all mothers who worry about their children, and for families who worry about their loved ones. Ancient Palestinian existence was fraught with danger, yet Mary trusted. She trusted even when she knew that her pregnancy might, at the very least, cause public scandal. Mary is our anchor whenever concerns over family, friends, and loved ones lead us to the brink of despair.

Today's liturgy is a wake-up call for me to live each day to the fullest, to trust God to lead and guide me through life's difficulties, and to respond in love to the world's suffering, poor, and downcast. Today might be the day God wants to use me as a vessel of his love. Perhaps there is someone in dire need of God's love (maybe even someone the world judges as unworthy of that love). Will I respond?

Participants share an experience from their lives that connects with the biblical interpretation just shared.

What was Luke trying to tell his community? What does he have to say to your community and to you today? The biblical themes of covenant, exodus, creation, and community are in full expression in the readings for today's liturgy. What difference does it make? Do you still feel the same way about this text as you did when you began? Has your original understanding been stretched, challenged, or affirmed?

STEP 5
DECISION

The gospel demands a response.

How does our understanding of these scriptures and today's liturgy call us to transformation? In what way are we, like Mary, to grow in faith? In what way does our community need to grow in the fullness of today's scriptures? In what concrete ways is our parish called to respond? Has this conversation with the exegesis changed or stretched my personal attitudes? What are the implications of this gospel in my life? What is one concrete action I will take this week as a response to the liturgy today?

DOCTRINAL ISSUES

What church truth/teaching/doctrinal issue could be drawn from the gospel for the Solemnity of Mary, Mother of God?

Participants suggest possible doctrinal themes that flow from the readings.

Possible Doctrinal Themes

Christology; salvation; Mary's role as disciple; Mary as model of church; Incarnation

Present the doctrinal material at this time.

1. The facilitator gives input on a particular doctrinal issue of his/her prior choosing. OR
2. The group chooses a doctrinal issue from the list they created. They read together from the Doctrinal Appendix.

(The doctrinal issues are found in the Doctrinal Appendix in the back of this workbook. If you are choosing an issue from this resource, please refer to it now.)

Reflection questions centered around the chosen doctrinal theme can be found at the end of each topic in the Doctrinal Appendix. The questions are based on the five-step reflection process. If you choose a topic not included in the Doctrinal Appendix, craft your own questions according to the same five-step process.

Following the reflection questions you will be reminded to return to chapter 7, "Preparing the Catechetical Session," to assist you in crafting your own session.

Closing Prayer

Father, as we proclaim the Virgin Mary
to be the mother of Christ and the mother of the
Church,
may our communion with her Son bring us to
salvation.
We ask this through Christ, our Lord.[16]

[16]Solemnity of Mary, Mother of God, "Prayer After Communion," *The Sacramentary.*

EPIPHANY

Environment

The liturgical color of the Christmas season is white. This celebration is centered around the manifestation of Christ, the Light. Epiphany is also the day on which we hear about the wise men from the East. Perhaps a Christ candle could be lit as you pray the opening prayer.

INTRODUCTORY RITES

Opening Song (or Entrance Antiphon)

The Lord and ruler is coming: kingship is his, and government and power (see Mal 3:1; 1 Chron 19:12).[1]

Opening Prayer

The facilitator of the session may lead the prayer. Others in the group may be asked to proclaim the readings.

Let us pray
[Grateful for the glory revealed today through God made man]

Pause for silent prayer.

Father of light, unchanging God,
today you reveal to men of faith
the resplendent fact of the Word made flesh.
Your light is strong,
your love is near;
draw us beyond the limits which this world imposes
to the life where your Spirit makes all life
complete.
We ask this through Christ, our Lord.[2]

LITURGY OF THE WORD

The readings are proclaimed.

Let us listen to God's word.

[1]Epiphany: "Entrance Antiphon," *The Sacramentary.*
[2]Epiphany: "Alternative Opening Prayer," *The Sacramentary.*

First Reading
Isaiah 60:1–6

The return from exile in Trito-Isaiah foreshadows the liberation won by Christ through his manifestation to the world. The Gentiles converging upon Jerusalem provide a glimpse of the manifestation of Christ—not just to the chosen people, but to the Gentiles and to the entire world.

In the poems of Trito-Isaiah there is great excitement and expectancy regarding what is about to take place. "It is as if the hell and horror had been left behind, and one is moving up a high, sun drenched summit to the very doors of the Kingdom of God."[3]

Prophets were often gifted by the Spirit to utter oracles that transcended the immediate reality. They were able to understand the meaning of God's plan in the present as well as in the future. When we hear these prophetic utterances over and over in scripture, we begin to see God's plan for the human race. It all makes perfect sense in light of what has been proclaimed throughout the generations. The prophet saw the fulfillment of God's action. He saw the magnificent light that would illumine the darkness created by humanity's sin. He saw the future city in which God's power would be seen by all. The prophet of Isaiah's time knew well about God's manifestation. It was called *shekina* glory, the unveiled, glorious presence of Yahweh. The prophet saw a future where all would live in *shekina* glory. The new city would be illumined for all to see. St. John would also see this prototype city aglow with the magnificence of Yahweh's *shekina* in the prophecies of Revelation. Even though there is an eschatological promise inherent in such prophecies, we know that Christ is the manifestation of God's glory.

We are reminded of the typological aspects of this text when we read of Gentiles riding on camels and bearing gifts of gold, frankincense, and myrrh. When we read of them converging upon the city of

[3]*TKG,* 137.

Jerusalem singing praises, our attention is immediately drawn to the heart of the Christian story.

Responsorial Psalm
Psalm 72:1–2, 7–8, 10–11, 12–13

This psalm, originally a hymn composed for the Davidic monarchy, speaks of the future messiah and describes those bearing gifts and bowing in worship before the messiah who was to come. This psalm was appropriated by the Christian community as a foreshadowing of Jesus. The messiah/ king would come to bring God's justice-liberation and help for the oppressed and the needy.

Second Reading
Ephesians 3:2–3, 5–6

Overview to St. Paul's Letter to the Ephesians: The letter to the Ephesians is directly related to the letter to the Colossians. Duling and Perrin attest that Ephesians quotes and develops the themes found in the letter to the Colossians. Nearly a third of the words from Colossians appear in Ephesians.

There is a question as to the Pauline authorship of both letters. Those who insist on Paul as the author say that it is highly probable that one man could have written the letters in a short amount of time, thus their similarity. Those who argue that Paul did not write the letters suggest that both letters (Colossians and Ephesians) were reiterations of Paul's previous writings. Those former letters were probably used as a reference for the writing of Colossians and Ephesians. Those who do not believe that Paul wrote Ephesians also point to the many words (forty) that are not found in Paul's other letters, but are instead found in later Christian literature.

Another reason scholars deny Pauline authorship lies in the differences between Paul's usual theology and the theology inherent in this letter. In the letter to the Ephesians, the author refers to the "holy apostles" as having special insight. Duling and Perrin suggest that "Paul never distinguishes apostles in this way and never regards them as 'holy' in a way other Christians are not."[4] Ephesians uses the word church exclusively as a term for the universal church (resonant with the theme of the "Great Church" of later centuries). Paul used the word to mean local community as well.

The letter to the Ephesians is also not a letter in the usual Pauline form. Paul usually wrote in response to problems or an occasion in his life. The letter is certainly different from Paul's other letters. Whether it be the work of a calmer, more reflective imprisoned Paul, or the brilliant work of a later disciple of Paul's who was eager to make his master's ideas known, what is certain is the plentiful adherents to both sides of the controversy.

The context for the letters: Paul established a mission in Ephesus and Colossae ten years earlier on his third missionary tour. Ephesus was his headquarters. The letters to the Colossians and Ephesians are known as the "Captivity Epistles" because they were written from his jail cell. Paul had left Corinth for Jerusalem. He was constantly in trouble with his pursuers, the Jewish authorities. They accused him of defacing the temple and he was subsequently thrown into prison. He spent three years in prison in Jerusalem and Caesarea.

A great concern for Paul in Ephesus and Colossae was dilution of the gospel due to the influence of gnosticism. Paul was concerned with promoting an authentic gospel, not one made of people's own agendas and exclusive concerns. Even though Paul passionately preached the universality of the Christ event, he was appalled at the way in which the gnostics distorted his teaching and in the process diluted the Christ-event. They relegated the person of Christ to angelic being or heavenly body. Paul would have none of it. "Christ is no mere angel or semi-god. He is the very image of the invisible God, a window through which men can finally see without distortion God as he really is."[5] To reduce Christ to a mere heavenly body was to deny his role as Savior of the world. The letter to the Ephesians addresses and refutes this gnosticism.

Today's Pericope: Today's reading from Ephesians is read every year in all three cycles on the feast of Epiphany. Today's text resonates with the reading from Isaiah when it asserts that the Gentiles along with the Jews are also heirs to the promise of salvation. All men and women from every nation on

[4] *NTI,* 220.

[5] *GAP,* 113.

earth will converge on the holy city singing God's praise. Matthew picks up the same theme with the arrival of the magi bearing gifts. The message of all three readings is not to be missed. Salvation is for all people. No one is excluded. Jew and Gentile alike share the covenant. Two themes are represented in this pericope: Jesus, the revelation of God and the universal message of salvation.[6]

Gospel
Matthew 2:1–12

Today's gospel tells the story of the magi who come bearing gifts to the messiah who was to be born. Herod tries to trick them into divulging the location of this great event.

STEP 1
NAMING ONE'S EXPERIENCE

What was your first impression? What captured your attention?

Each person names his or her initial impression. Statements should be brief. No reasons should be given at this time. All simply listen without agreeing or disagreeing.

STEP 2
UNDERSTANDING

What understanding did you bring with you to these readings? In a brief statement, what do you think this gospel is trying to convey?

STEP 3
INPUT FROM VISION/STORY/TRADITION

Liturgical Context

Please read the Christmas Overview for background on this feast. The Epiphany texts need to be understood in the context of the entire Christmas season. Epiphany is another celebration of Christ's manifestation to the world. Even though there is great emphasis placed on the story of the magi, the theme of this feast transcends the manifestation of God to the gentiles; it centers on God's self-revelation to humanity in the person of Christ. This is another manifestation in a line of manifestations during the season: to the shepherds, to Mary, the Mother of God, through baptism, and now to all the world.

In the overview of the Christmas season it was stated that the feast of the Epiphany has undergone a few shifts in the Eastern and Western Church. When East and West transposed their feasts, the West preserved Christmas overtones in its observance of Epiphany. "The connection is especially clear in the insertions in the first eucharistic prayer, since they speak of the celebration of this most holy day 'when your only Son, sharing your eternal glory, showed himself in a human body.'"[7] However, Epiphany was also the day to remember the magi. As the magi were considered Gentiles, the feast proclaimed the manifestation of God's mission to the Gentiles and to all nations.

Today's liturgy remembers and makes present the very mystery it celebrates—that is, the manifestation of God's power, God's salvation to the entire human race. The opening prayers of this liturgy exhort us to listen to the readings "as an announcement of a mystery, of the good news, of what is and will be."[8] The celebration calls us to live in the glory that is ours. In the Epiphany liturgy when we pray the "Prayer over the Gifts" we ask God to accept our offerings, not of gold, frankincense, and myrrh, but our very selves—our hearts and our humanity. The preface for Epiphany proclaims the feast's central theme, Christ, the Light of the Nations: "Today you revealed in Christ your eternal plan of salvation and showed him as the light of all peoples. Now that his glory has shown among us you have renewed humanity in his immortal image."

Gospel Exegesis

The facilitator provides input regarding critical biblical scholarship on this text. The input includes insights as to how people would have heard the gospel in Jesus' time.

[6] *PNL*, 478.

[7] *LY*, 147.

[8] *DL* (I), 254.

Detailed historicity is not the object of this story. A far greater concern is the meaning of God's manifestation to the world expressed through the symbolic language of the story. That does not mean that the story is not based on a factual occurrence. Certainly, something happened to elicit such a narrative. However, the author cares little about the details. It is the point of the story that has captured his imagination, and in the process of telling that story he hopes to capture ours.

The way Matthew tells the story is "colored by the faith which enlightened the evangelist when he wrote his work; it expresses and clarifies the faith of the Church at the time; he intended it to be an aid to the faith of those Christians for whom he wrote. But faith is not simply a matter of acknowledging that Jesus is Messiah, Lord and Son of God. It involves obedience to him now. The Gospel is not only 'kerygma,' that is to say, proclamation of faith; it is also 'catechesis,' instruction on how to unify one's faith and life. This part of the message is especially stressed in Matthew."[9]

"After Jesus' birth...." begins the narrative regarding the approaching magi. Matthew puts this story in the context of the wider political arena. Herod was reputed to be compulsive and neurotic with regard to the possible political overthrow of his power. One cannot miss the subtlety of Herod's part in this drama. The scribes and Pharisees in Matthew's gospel quote Micah regarding the messiah's projected birthplace and are unaffected and unimpressed. Herod, on the other hand, takes the story of the "King of the Jews" quite literally and seriously. Those who knew better and *should have gotten it,* ignored it; and those who should have had no understanding or interest *did get it,* and as a result set out to do violence.

The mysterious magi enter the scene. The story tells us little of their origin. However, because of Psalm 72, where kings from Tarshish and the Isles come bearing gifts, it is assumed that the magi are those referred to in the psalm. This puts their place of origin in Persia. The only reason we have assumed there were three is due to the three gifts of frankincense, gold, and myrrh. In later Western tradition they were given the names Balthasar, Melchior, and Caspar. They became symbols of the diversity of the church, of God's manifestation to the Gentile world, to all peoples.

Jesus is called the "King of the Jews" in order to name him the messiah. The *star* is a reference to a messianic prophecy in the Old Testament book of Numbers in which a star was identified with the messiah (Num 24:17). For Matthew, the magi signify that Christ has always manifested his glory to people from distant lands. There is noticeable irony in the fact that it is the very scribes and Pharisees who supply the magi with the scriptures that direct them to the place where their search will end.

The magi find the child and their search ends. They learn of Herod's evil plotting and thus return home by a different route. Having found the child Jesus, their lives were forever touched. They were transformed. Their change in direction alerts us to this transformation. A change in direction in the Bible assumes a change of heart, conversion, a *metanoia.*

In ancient times, people were often attracted to astral religions because of the cold predictability of the stars.[10] These religions were very burdensome as people believed themselves under submission to powers beyond their control. Some early Christians were offended by this story as it appeared to tolerate astrology. However, their problem was not Matthew's problem. The star merely served a purpose. The star was the instrument that would lead people to the One who would break the power of any force that would bind people to a predetermined fate. When people are in God's hands, their fate is secure in and through Jesus.

Later the gifts of gold, frankincense, and myrrh became symbols of Christ's kingship, his divinity, and his suffering. Like Christmas, Epiphany is a feast of redemption. Christ became incarnated in our world and manifested the presence of God in order to save the world from itself. Sin could be conquered only through the life, death, and resurrection of the One who was born and the One who revealed his glory to all the nations. The call

---

[9]J. Dupont, "L'evangile de saint Matthieu: quelques cles de lecture," in *Communautes et liturgies* 57 (1975): 21.

[10]Benedict T. Viviano, O.P., "The Gospel of Matthew," *NJBC,* 636.

of this gospel is to proclaim the *shekina* glory of God through Christ.

This is a feast of manifestation. God manifests himself to the world. He elevates the human heart and offers humanity his divine dignity. God sits on the throne of heaven and earth and is Lord over all the world. God is a God not just for a select few, but for the whole world. This is a missionary feast par excellence. "All nations will come to this light (v. 3); all are called to become disciples of Jesus Christ (Mt 28:19). This is why Epiphany is the great missionary feast. A church which is not missionary is a contradiction as the community of Christ's followers. This is true for all Christians, for faith is not a private and interior matter; rather it impels communication and life in community."[11]

Proclaim the gospel again.

Sometimes we gain new insights when we hear the text after the interpretation has been given. Someone from the group proclaims the gospel a second time.

Step 4
Testing

Conversation with the Liturgy and the Scriptures

Test your original understanding in dialogue with the text.

(You might consider breaking into smaller groups.)

Were there any new insights? Was there anything you had not considered before? There are many levels of meaning in this text, such as inclusivity, the manifestation of God's power, and the fact that the Gentiles appropriated the faith while the chosen ones missed it. How are these themes relevant for our community today? Has your original understanding of these stories been transformed in any way? How? How does this story speak to your life?

Sharing Life Experience

This feast reminds me of a special young man who is on an odyssey of discovery. God is compelling him toward God's incredible light. I am honored to be a part of this young man's life. In willing obedience, he is following a star, not knowing where it will lead. I am awed by his journey (even though I often find myself frustrated by it, as it does not always conform to the norms that society sets out for those preparing for the adult world).

As a young adult he does not come across many peers who understand his faith journey. In some ways it is a lonely road for him. Yet he has heard the voice of God within. It beckons him. The miracle lies in his ability to hear the voice midst the pressures and lures of his everyday experiences. He sees God in all the experiences of his life. He is open to discovery and to the mysteries God reveals to him. This manifestation of God in his life is not the pious imaginings of a dreamer. His epiphany has radically transformed his life. He has been on several wrong roads, and like the magi (and because of the promptings of God) has moved toward his destiny by taking the difficult road of conversion. He listens to God's voice and at age twenty-two works very hard to act on the word he hears. He has allowed God to change his life and is grateful for the gift of divine energy. When dealing with someone who is difficult, he feels that it is his responsibility to offer the gift of God's divine energy to that person, because it is the only thing that has the power to transform. I have seen a huge change in his life and his change invites change within me. I watch his response to the God within and I marvel at his ability to listen, respond, and then to allow his shortcomings to be tested and changed. Evidence of this young sojourner's relationship with God is readily observable. He offers love to everyone—the poor, the outcast, and even those he finds most difficult to love. He believes his life's mission is to offer the gift of himself to the less fortunate. He is not an idyllic, superhuman young adult. He struggles with the same issues of all young people today. Yet he is incredibly and refreshingly unique in his ability to listen to, and be conscious of, the God who is manifested to him in his everyday life. Watching this young man respond to the word and will of God invites change within me. I thank God for his witness in my life.

Epiphany is a reminder that God continues to make his presence known to us and invites us to respond to that presence. This feast also prompts us to share with others the divine energy that has been given to us. There is responsibility attached to our relationship with God.

---

[11] *SWTLY*, 38.

All share their life experience.

What was Matthew's message to his community? Is it relevant today? How do these scriptures speak to you as church and to you personally? Are the biblical images of covenant, creation, exodus, and community in full view in today's liturgy? How? Do you still feel the same way about this text as you did when you began? How would you explain these readings to a stranger?

STEP 5
DECISION

The gospel demands a response.

In what way are we called to respond to this gospel? How are our attitudes challenged in this liturgy? Would there be any contemporary corollary for the issue of Gentile inclusion today? Has this conversation with the exegesis of the Epiphany called for transformation of my actions or attitudes? Name one concrete action we/I will take this week as a response to today's liturgy.

Christian Initiation: The baptism of Jesus was originally associated with the feast of Epiphany. In the East baptisms were celebrated on this day. Since initiation has an historical connection with this feast, perhaps today would be an appropriate time to celebrate the baptism of people with special circumstances (such as catechized, unbaptized persons) or with infants. It might also be a good time to celebrate a rite of full communion in the Catholic Church, or a rite of acceptance, or a rite of welcome.

DOCTRINAL ISSUES

What church truth/teaching/doctrinal issue could be drawn from the gospel for the feast of the Epiphany?

Participants suggest possible doctrinal themes that flow from the readings.

Possible Doctrinal Themes

Epiphany; manifestation; christology; missiology; evangelization; ecumenism

Present the doctrinal material at this time.

1. The facilitator gives input on a particular doctrinal issue of his/her prior choosing. OR
2. The group chooses a doctrinal issue from the list they created. They read together from the Doctrinal Appendix.

(The doctrinal issues are found in the Doctrinal Appendix in the back of this workbook. If you are choosing an issue from this resource, please refer to it now.)

Reflection questions centered around the chosen doctrinal theme can be found at the end of each topic in the Doctrinal Appendix. The questions are based on the five-step reflection process. If you choose a topic not included in the Doctrinal Appendix, craft your own questions according to the same five-step process.

Following the reflection questions you will be reminded to return to chapter 7, "Preparing the Catechetical Session," to assist you in crafting your own session.

Closing Prayer

God has called you out of darkness
into his wonderful light.
May you experience his kindness and blessings,
and be strong in faith, in hope and in love. Amen.
Because you are followers of Christ,
who appeared in this day as a light shining in
darkness,
may he make you a light to all your sisters and
brothers.

Response: Amen.

The wise men followed the star,
and found Christ who is light from light.
May you find the Lord
when your pilgrimage is ended.

Response: Amen.[12]

[12]Epiphany: "Solemn Blessing," *The Sacramentary.*

Baptism of the Lord

Environment

This feast brings the Christmas season to an end.

INTRODUCTORY RITES

Opening Song (or Entrance Antiphon)

When the Lord had been baptized, the heavens opened, and the Spirit came down like a dove to rest on him. Then the voice of the Father thundered: This is my beloved Son, with him I am well pleased (Mt 3:16–17).[1]

Opening Prayer

The facilitator of the session may lead the prayer. Others in the group may be asked to proclaim the readings.

Let us pray
[that we will be faithful to our baptism]

Pause for silent prayer.

Almighty, eternal God,
when the Spirit descended upon Jesus
at his baptism in the Jordan,
you revealed him as your own beloved Son.
Keep us, your children, born of water and the Spirit,
faithful to our calling.
We ask this through our Lord Jesus Christ, your Son,
who lives and reigns with you and the Holy Spirit,
one God, for ever, and ever.[2]

LITURGY OF THE WORD

The readings are proclaimed.

Let us listen to God's word

First Reading[3]
Isaiah 42:1–4, 6–7

Scholars believe that the suffering servant in Deutero-Isaiah represents Israel and its role as covenant people in relationship to Yahweh. There is strong evidence that the writer is referring specifically to Israel. Israel was servant from the very beginning, from its very origins in the womb of Sarah. Servant Israel is Yahweh's agent who quietly brings the idolatrous nations to justice. "Israel's election is for responsibility."[4] The image of suffering servant belongs to Israel who, through its exile, was tried by God for her transgressions and was recreated in order to participate in God's plan of salvation.

Bernhard Anderson suggests that there are flaws in this interpretation. The second poem clearly refers to an *individual* whose mission is *to* Israel. The "servant" of Deutero-Isaiah acclaims that Yahweh called him from the womb to be a light to the nations. Thus, the servant is an individual, not the collective Israel.

Some believe the servant was Moses; others believe the servant was Deutero-Isaiah himself. Some believe the suffering servant was a remnant few who would remain faithful to Yahweh. Others believe the servant was some future messianic person. (Jesus referred to himself as the suffering servant.) The early Christian community believed Deutero-Isaiah to be prophesying about their messiah and Lord, Jesus Christ.

In today's liturgy it makes no difference which hypothesis is correct. Deutero-Isaiah is chosen on this feast to shed light on the mission of Christ.

---

[1]Baptism of the Lord: "Entrance Antiphon," *The Sacramentary.*

[2]Baptism of the Lord: "Opening Prayer," *The Sacramentary.*

[3]The exegesis for the first and second readings may or may not be the focus of your group's reflection as there may only be time to give adequate attention to the gospel, your primary concern. However, the exegesis is included here in order to provide a thorough investigation of the entire liturgy of the word as there may be parts (or all) that would be necessary to the direction you wish to take with your particular ministry group.

[4]*UOT,* 490.

Jesus is the fulfillment of Second Isaiah's word to Israel. It is Jesus who establishes God's justice. It is Jesus who reaches out to the poor and the powerless. It is Christ who, assuming the role of suffering servant, dies for the transgressions of many. Today this reading does not stand on its own. It prefigures Jesus' baptism in the River Jordan.

Responsorial Psalm
Psalm 29:1–4, 9b–10

The "voice above the waters" in the psalm chosen for this liturgy is harmonious with the voice of God from heaven in today's gospel. The psalm proclaims the manifestation of God through Jesus' baptism in the River Jordan.[5]

Second Reading
Acts 10:34–38

This pericope from the Acts of the Apostles attests to the manifestation of God through Jesus Christ. Jesus' baptism is testimony to God's presence through Jesus' words and works. There are a few significant segments in this reading, obviously chosen for its connection to the gospel. First, the story of Cornelius was important for the early church. Cornelius was a Gentile. His conversion opened the door to the Gentile mission and to the inclusion, integration, and incorporation of Gentile Christians with Jewish Christians. Peter proclaimed that God has no favorites, since all are called equally. "Therefore, the door is open to anyone who fears God and works righteousness as Cornelius does (cf. 10:33). Such a person is 'acceptable' to God."[6]

Second, verse 36 reflects evidence of a key theme of both Luke and Acts. Luke's primary message is the proclamation that Jesus is Lord and messiah. "He brings peace to the Jewish people in fulfillment of scriptural promises; it applies to all peoples, for they are invited to share with Israel in this messianic peace."[7] Verse 36 is an echoing of the birth narrative in which God proclaimed to the shepherds that peace had come to all the earth. Robert Tannehill suggests that verses 36–43 are a chronological summary of Luke's gospel from the birth stories through the sending of the apostles to the world. Empowered by the Holy Spirit, Jesus' ministry manifested God's healing and forgiveness and liberated those in bondage. He established a peace that only Yahweh could give. The response to Jesus' life and work was and is apostolic witness to his life, work, and resurrection.

We encounter the story of Christ through events that reflect God's action and presence in and through Jesus' life, his work, and the ultimate fulfillment of God's plan of salvation for the human race. Jesus proclaims God's reign. God tells Mary of her role in salvation history; God tells the shepherds the good news of Jesus' birth; God manifests himself to the magi, to the Gentile world, to all nations; and God manifests the fulfillment of his master plan through Jesus in the baptism at the River Jordan.[8] Reginald Fuller asserts that it is often said that a significant contrast exists between the message of Jesus and the message of the church. "Jesus preached the kingdom, but the church preached Jesus."[9] Fuller maintains that, in essence, there is really little difference. He maintains that Jesus was proclaiming God's action and presence in the lives of human beings through healings, exorcisms, and through his words and works. The church, on the other hand, proclaimed and proclaims that God was and is present through the signs, words, and deeds Jesus performed. God has, is, and will continue to be present in human history.

Gospel[10]
Matthew 3:13–17

Jesus is baptized in the River Jordan and anointed through the power of the Spirit.

---

[5]*PNL*, 132.

[6]*NULA*, 137.

[7]Ibid, 140.

[8]*PNL*, 132.

[9]Ibid.

[10]The gospel exegesis is provided later in this session so that it may be presented in the proper sequence where it occurs in the adult five-step reflection process. The exegesis is provided for the first and second readings for your information and edification, and for you to use at your discretion. Once again, the gospel is the primary source of reflection. If there is time for reflection on the other readings, all the better.

Step 1
Naming One's Experience

What captured your attention in these readings?[11] How did you feel?

Each person names his or her initial impression. Statements should be brief. No reasons should be given at this time. All simply listen without agreeing or disagreeing.

Step 2
Understanding

In a brief statement, what do you think this gospel is trying to convey? What understanding did you bring with you to this discussion?

Step 3
Input from Vision/Story/Tradition

Liturgical Context[12]

The focus of the Christmas season is theological rather than historical. Throughout the season we experience the multi-faceted manifestations of God through Jesus Christ, his Son. Particularly in the East, the entire life of Christ is regarded as repeated manifestations of God, with the baptism of Jesus representing the most important of these manifestations. The East celebrates the Lord's baptism (and the manifestation at Cana) on the feast of the Epiphany. Prior to the renewal of the Roman calendar, this feast was not given the prominence it deserved in the Western church. Thus, without preempting Epiphany, the new calendar restored the feast of the Baptism of the Lord to a prominent place. It now follows Epiphany and closes the Christmas season.

God anointed Jesus for public ministry through the power of the Holy Spirit. The baptism at the River Jordan is Jesus' ritual celebration of empowerment. He is empowered through the authority of the voice of God, lord of the universe. Since John is intimately involved in this ritual event, the church avows that Jesus "shows his solidarity with the guilty human race and gives water the power to forgive sins."[13]

The preface of this liturgy expresses our theology succinctly and is very clear regarding God's role on the stage of salvation history. "You celebrated your new gift of baptism by signs and wonders at the Jordan. Your voice was heard from heaven to awaken faith in the presence among us of the Word made man. Your spirit was seen as a dove, revealing Jesus as your servant, and anointing him with joy as the Christ, sent to bring to the poor the good news of salvation."[14]

Gospel Exegesis

The facilitator provides input regarding what critical biblical scholarship has to say about this text. The input includes insights as to how people would have heard the gospel in Jesus' time.

Matthew's account of Jesus' baptism follows Mark's, with a few exceptions. John baptized people for the forgiveness of sins. Reginald Fuller maintains that some people believe that perhaps Jesus and John have very little to say to each other in Matthew's version because Matthew has a problem with the sinless Jesus submitting to John's baptism. Yet nowhere in the text does the subject of Jesus' sinlessness seem to be an issue. Something else is going on here.

During the time of the evangelists there was an active group of John the Baptist's disciples. They believed that John was the herald of God's final revelation. The historical authenticity of Jesus' baptism can be attested to with great certainty because of the existence of this sect. Obviously, Christians would have had a vested interest in *not*

[11]The primary focus of reflection is the gospel. However, very often the other readings demand attention and must be brought into the dialogue.

[12]The scriptures in the Lectionary, the seasons of the year, and the ritual prayers of the mass are interrelated and form the basis for liturgical catechesis. The *liturgical context* attempts to explore and clarify the themes and this interrelatedness.

[13]*LY*, 148.

[14]Feast of the Baptism of the Lord: "Preface," *The Sacramentary*.

having Jesus be baptized by John. It would only have given credence to the Baptist sect's claims and to John's superiority over Jesus. Matthew, however, solves the dilemma of Jesus' baptism by John.

Jesus gives the reason for submitting to baptism by John. Jesus was baptized in order to fulfill God's plan of salvation. In the first reading, Isaiah professed that the servant is called in *righteousness.* Jesus states that his purpose was to fulfill all *righteousness.* Thus, he was baptized in order that he be revealed as the servant of Yahweh who ushers in the fulfillment of God's plan.

Some scholars have an interesting explanation of the "to fulfill all righteousness" reasoning. Jesus went out to see for himself this John he had heard so much about. John's ministry subsequently ignited a spark in Jesus. John touched Jesus' heart and he experienced his own moment of conversion. Jesus then moved into a deeper awareness of his identity, his mission, and subsequently his destiny. Jesus was baptized because God willed it. He thus went on to assist John in the baptizing ministry (Jn 3:22).

Why would it be God's will that Jesus be baptized? One reason is to show his solidarity with sinners. He became one with the sinners he was destined to save by joining them in the same baptismal bath in the same murky waters of the Jordan. As their leader and their lord, Jesus became one with his people through participation in the same sacrament of renewal with their God. This would be the first step on the road to the cross.[15] Jesus was officially empowered by the Holy Spirit for the task of establishing God's reign on earth.

Another area of distinction between Matthew and Mark can be found in the voice from heaven. Mark's voice is a direct quote from Jesus, as if to suggest that Jesus was commissioned by God for his intended mission. The voice in Matthew's text is intended for the church. "But Matthew wants to make it quite clear that the baptism is rather an epiphany declaring to the Church the true identity of Jesus: he is the servant of Yahweh, fulfilling in his person the mission of the servant as depicted in Second Isaiah."[16]

In the ancient shame- and honor-based Palestinian culture in which Jesus lived, this authoritative voice from heaven would have constituted an important milestone for Jesus. It would have established Jesus' authority and inaugurated his mission. "In the baptism, a public event witnessed by everyone present, God personally proclaims a relationship of father and son, patron and client, with Jesus."[17] The voice from on high would have established Jesus' credibility.

The righteousness referred to in today's text assumes holiness. Holiness in biblical terms is living in right relationship with God and with other people. It involves acknowledging the human dignity of all people, especially those who are on the bottom of society's social heap. Love of God is intrinsically tied to love poured out on others. Isaiah heralded the suffering servant. Jesus is the fulfilment of that herald. As servant he showed us the path of life. Discipleship cannot rest solely in pious concentration on the mystery of God without leading to the offering of self for others. We are all destined to become suffering servants.

The Christmas season expresses our unique calling and dignity. Through the manifestation of God to the world, the Incarnation of his Son, human beings were elevated to a divine nature and to the highest dignity. By virtue of our baptism, it is not only our responsibility to care for the world's poor and oppressed, it is our duty and our divine calling. Just as Jesus entered the waters of the Jordan in solidarity with those he would save, so too are we to jump into those same waters. We have, in fact, already entered those waters. The Lord's baptism is a call to renew our own baptismal commitment. We are baptized as priest, prophet, and king and as such are commissioned to lead others to Christ, to preach his Good News, and to offer the gift of our lives for others in selfless service.

Proclaim the gospel again.

[15] *MJ,* 21.

[16] *PL,* 34.

[17] *CWJ,* 20.

Sometimes we gain new insights when we hear the text after the interpretation has been given. Someone from the group proclaims the gospel a second time.

STEP 4
TESTING

Conversation with the Liturgy and the Scriptures

Test your original understanding in dialogue with the text.

(You might consider breaking into smaller groups.)

What is your first reaction to the exegesis? Were there any new insights for you? How do you feel about the part of the story where Jesus went to John, experienced conversion and was thus empowered to join John in his baptizing ministry of covenant renewal? What do you think about Jesus' baptism being an occasion for his own conversion and a growth in awareness of his identity? How does this story speak to your life?

Sharing Life Experience

Jesus humbled himself in obedience to his father in order to be in solidarity with the sinners he would save. Jesus sought out John and in the process experienced his own moment of conversion. Jesus was righteous and thus lived in the holiness of God. What does all that mean to me as I strive to live this Christian life? I am reminded of the weekly experience of ministering to people in the initiation process. They come seeking God's will for their lives. They bring a simple faith. Perhaps Jesus was not only touched by John, but also by the earnest faith of those who came to John asking for baptism. I am humbled by the faith and the stories of how God manifests himself to the catechumens and candidates through their everyday efforts to live the gospel. Their stories of conversion and healing continue to strengthen my own faith. I feel humbly honored to witness God's powerful transformative action in their lives. As we share the stories of scripture and the stories of our lives, I am amazed at the ways God invites us to change, week after week and day after day. I have seen relationships heal and have watched people turn away from destructive lifestyles. The gospel makes a difference in their lives—in my life. Jesus' life and work make a difference in all our lives. Jesus entered the murky waters of the Jordan just so we could share his life. Week after week I leave those initiation sessions with a firm resolve to change, to be a better disciple, and to live that week's gospel throughout the week. Conversion is not a one-time event. It is ongoing. I can remember many times when I left our Sunday sessions aware that I needed to work at strengthening my marriage, or my relationship with my children, or to change parts of my interior life that were screaming for change. Today is another reminder that I am still in process.

Jesus' mission was inaugurated at the event of his baptism by John. He became one with sinners. He lived with them, got his hands dirty, and showed them (and us) what love truly means. Whenever I share a story of God's grace and healing in my own life, and whenever others share their story with me, we are reminded of the implications of Jesus' baptism. He became one with us; he chose to submit to his father's will in holiness in order to show us how to do the same. We share in Jesus' saving mission when we reach out to others—when we comfort the sorrowing, feed the hungry, and tell others of God's marvelous deeds. Whenever the catechumens and candidates serve dinner to the homeless, or reach out to others in the group or other people in their lives, I am touched by their willingness to serve. One young man in the process recently purchased twenty daily meditation books so he could give one to each member of the group. The book had helped him encounter the living God in his everyday life and he wanted to share it. This same young man asked the soup kitchen personnel if he could purchase bulk quantities of meat to serve to the homeless. He also started a daily prayer and meditation group with his co-construction workers. God's incredible, transformative love continues to pour out of the catechumens and I feel blessed to stand in the fallout.

Participants share an experience from their lives that connects with the biblical interpretation just shared.

What was Matthew trying to tell his community? Is there a relevant word for our community today? Do you still feel the same way about this text as when you began? Has your original understanding been stretched, challenged, or affirmed?

STEP 5
DECISION

The gospel demands a response.

How do these readings and this liturgy invite change? In our community? In you? How might our parish be called to respond to today's liturgy? In what way, if any, has this conversation invited you to think or behave in a different way? What are the implications of this gospel in your life? What is one concrete action you will take this week as a response to today's liturgy?

Pastoral Considerations: No doubt this would be an excellent time for the parish to celebrate a rite of sprinkling so that all the faithful, including baptized candidates, are given an opportunity to reflect on the implications of their baptism.

Christian Initiation: This might be a good time for the anointing of catechumens. As usual, the minor blessings and exorcisms can be prayed with them each week. This might also be an opportune time to once again remind baptized candidates preparing for full communion of the Catholic Church that we share one baptism and that we are already one with them by virtue of our baptism.

DOCTRINAL ISSUES

What church truth/teaching/doctrinal issue could be drawn from the Baptism of the Lord gospel?

Participants suggest possible doctrinal themes that flow from the readings.

Possible Doctrinal Themes

Baptism of the Lord; soteriology/salvation; manifestation; baptism; conversion; paschal mystery

Present the doctrinal material at this time.

1. The facilitator gives input on a particular doctrinal issue of his/her prior choosing. OR
2. The group chooses a doctrinal issue from the list they created. They read together from the Doctrinal Appendix.

(The doctrinal issues are found in the Doctrinal Appendix in the back of this workbook. If you are choosing an issue from this resource, please refer to it now.)

Reflection questions centered around the chosen doctrinal theme can be found at the end of each topic in the Doctrinal Appendix. The questions are based on the five-step reflection process. If you choose a topic not included in the Doctrinal Appendix, craft your own questions according to the same five-step process.

Following the reflection questions you will be reminded to return to chapter 7, "Preparing the Catechetical Session," to assist you in crafting your own session.

Closing Prayer

Almighty, eternal God,
when the Spirit descended upon Jesus
at his baptism in the Jordan,
you revealed him as your own beloved Son.
Keep us, your children born of water and the Spirit,
faithful to your calling.
We ask this through our Lord Jesus Christ, your Son,
who lives and reigns with you and the Holy Spirit,
one God, forever and ever.[18]

[18]Feast of the Baptism of the Lord: "Evening Prayer," *Christian Prayer: Liturgy of the Hours* (New York, Catholic Book Publishing Co., 1976).

THE SEASON OF LENT

The Season of Lent: An Overview

The rich, liturgical color of royal purple cloaks the season in its penitential vesture. Simplicity and austerity quietly whisper images of the barren desert. Flowers are absent; music is sparse and the church quietly, but firmly, heralds its reflective "time out." Things have noticeably changed. As people and as church, we enter the poustinia of serious penitential and baptismal reflection. We take stock and assess our growth in the Christian life. We ask ourselves, "Where is there need for healing and reconciliation in our lives?"

> Lent is a preparation for the celebration of Easter. For the Lenten liturgy disposes both catechumens and the faithful to celebrate the paschal mystery: catechumens, through several stages of Christian initiation; the faithful, through reminders of their own baptism and through penitential practices.[1]

History of Lent

The history of Lent evolved over the centuries from varied and sometimes blended sources. Very early in the church's history, the Jewish Christians superimposed their worship of Jesus, the new Passover, on the annual celebration and understanding of Jewish Passover. Once this was established as an annual Christian feast, it was preceded by a day of fasting. At the same time, gentile Christians fasted on Wednesdays and Fridays, and celebrated the breaking of the bread after Sabbath, on the first day of the week. Eventually both traditions merged, and the annual Easter feast was celebrated on the Sunday closest to the Jewish Passover. The Saturday before Easter Sunday was designated a fast day and, since the Friday fast was already in observance, there emerged a two-day, pre-Easter fast. Eventually the fasting period was extended to begin the Sunday before Easter (a week-long fast).

Early in the church's history, the Christian initiation of adults was a focus of the pre-Easter fast. By the third century, more was required for an adult to become a Christian than simply converting to belief in Jesus Christ. A process of initiation emerged that extended over a period of time and included several stages marked by ritual celebrations. There was no time limit imposed and eventually the process extended over a period of three years. Initially, baptisms were not specifically assigned to the Easter celebration, but rather, were most often celebrated during the fifty days between Passover and Pentecost.

Scrolling through time to the fifth century, we find the observance of a three-week preparatory fast for baptism. By the eighth century, three scrutinies were celebrated with those preparing for baptism. The scrutinies, which took place on three consecutive Sundays, are believed to have evolved from the three-week preparatory fast of previous centuries.

The history of a defined lenten season may be loosely divided into three periods: 1. the Council of Nicea (325) until the Middle Ages; 2. Middle Ages until the Second Vatican Council; 3. the promulgation of the Missal, Lectionary, and Roman Calendar by Paul VI in 1969 until the present.[2] The Council of Nicea set forth a forty-day preparatory fast and determined a fixed date for the celebration of Easter.

At one time, the Alexandrian church (in the East) celebrated the Lord's birth and began its liturgical year on January 6. Alexandria's new year began with the proclamation of the Lord's baptism, the beginning passage from the gospel of Mark. St. Mark was considered the founding father of the

[1] *GNLY*, #27.

[2] *DL* (II), 1.

Eastern church. Since the next passage in Mark's gospel was the story of Jesus' forty-day trial in the desert, the Alexandrian church established a similar forty-day fast (the "Fast of Jesus") beginning on January 7th. This fast had no connection to the week-long pre-Easter fast. Once the forty-day preparatory fast before Easter was established by the Council of Nicea, it collided with Alexandria's "Jesus fast" following the feast of the Lord's baptism. Adjustments, therefore, had to be made. Some monasteries observed a hundred-day fast in order to unify the two traditions of the East and the West.

Modern scholarship suggests that the penitential nature of the Lenten season emerged and grew stronger because of the influence of Alexandria's forty-day fast which was inspired by Jesus' temptations in the desert. The baptismal nature of Lent weakened with the decline of adult initiation in the fifth and sixth centuries. The heightened sense of penitence gave rise to the observance of three penitential Sundays prior to the first Sunday of Lent. These Sundays were called Septuagesima, Sexagesima, and Quinquagesima Sundays (seventy, sixty, and fifty days before Easter) and were observed until the Second Vatican Council.

Early in the fourth century, Lent lasted six weeks, beginning on the First Sunday of Lent. However, since Sundays were not fast days, the six weeks allowed for only thirty-six, rather than forty days of fasting. Thus, in the sixth century, Wednesday, Thursday, Friday, and Saturday before the First Sunday of Lent were added to the season in order to complete the forty days of fasting.

The Second Vatican Council restored a simpler, earlier version of Lenten observance. The Council halted the observance of three penitential Sundays prior to Lent. Lent begins on Ash Wednesday and continues until the Mass of Holy Thursday (which begins the Easter Triduum). Thus, there are five Sundays of Lent, followed by Palm Sunday (also called Passion Sunday). Lent begins on a day between February 10 and March 10, depending on the year and the occurrence of the spring equinox. It ends between March 19 and April 22. Lent is the only season that begins on a weekday (Ash Wednesday).

From the very earliest days, the season of Lent prepared the church for Easter. Lent fortifies God's people for immersion into the Lord's passion, death, and glorious resurrection. The ancient stories of God's salvation history with Israel were only a prelude to the ultimate event of all time—Jesus' paschal mystery. Each Sunday during Lent, the first reading takes us on a journey back to ancient Israel and brings forward the saving benefits of God's redemptive actions into our present day experience.

Themes of Lent

The season of Lent is highly charged with images of the exodus, Israel's premier, identifying moment. Passover is for Jews what the eucharist is for Catholics. Yahweh's action of delivering Israel out of Egyptian bondage was so essential to its consciousness and identity that it was instructed to commemorate it each year as a living memorial of God's great covenant with his people. The angel of death passed over the houses of the Israelites; they were delivered out of bondage and given possession of the promised land. The covenant was forged, and a *people,* a *holy nation* was brought to birth. Lent serves as the womb for the elect who await new birth into Christ's new covenant.

Lent is penitential, baptismal, and eucharistic by its very nature. The Second Vatican Council restored the early baptismal focus of Lent. The *Constitution on the Sacred Liturgy* restored the two-fold baptismal and penitential nature of Lent. "By recalling or preparing for baptism and by repentance, this season disposes the faithful, as they more diligently listen to the word of God and devote themselves to prayer, to celebrate the paschal mystery" (#109). Both baptism and repentance were to "be given greater prominence in both the liturgy and liturgical catechesis" (#109). This is to take place in the liturgy through homilies and catechesis that emphasize the two-fold nature of the season.

Penitential Nature of Lent

Lent is an extended time of self examination. "During Lent penance should be not only inward and individual, but also outward and social."[3] In the Rite of Christian Initiation of Adults, Lent coincides with the period of purification and enlightenment for catechumens. The elect[4] enter a process of purification in which they examine their heart, mind, and intentions. They ask God to enlighten the areas of sin and darkness with the light of Christ's healing presence. The elect preparing for baptism (along with the rest of the faithful) scrutinize and uncover *(enlighten)* what is weak and sinful and ask God to heal, strengthen, and liberate us from the power of evil *(purify)*. The elect are a symbol of the penitential posture we are all to assume during the season. The elect stand before the community in the celebration of the scrutinies on the Third, Fourth, and Fifth Sundays of Lent as the premier sign of Christ's *deliverance from* and *victory over* the power of evil.

During Lent's extended penitential period, the church examines the dimension, power, and impact of personal, social, and systemic sin. It asks to be delivered from sin's illusionary power and control. Since the scrutinies are an important part of the church's lenten observance, it is important to explore the meaning of the ritual and our participation in it. The following is an extract from my article in *Christian Initiation Magazine* regarding the scrutinies.

> In the scrutinies we name and uncover the sinister reality of sin; the personal sin that we commit when we reject God and fail to love; the social sin that we participate in when we do nothing to change the systems and structures that keep members of God's family oppressed, marginalized, hungry, and poor; and finally the systemic sin that encompasses total hopelessness and despair. Systemic sin is sin in which the only solution is God alone. Death already reigns in the situation and nothing short of a miracle is required to heal it. "Sin and its effects are visible everywhere: in exploitive relationships, loveless families, unjust social structures and policies, crimes by and against individuals and against creation, the oppression of the weak and the manipulation of the vulnerable, explosive tensions among nations and among ideological, racial and religious groups and social classes, the scandalous gulf between those who waste goods and resources and those who live and die amid deprivation and underdevelopment, wars and preparation for war. Sin is a reality in the world."[5]
>
> Lest we be brought low by its devastating effects we must not lose sight of the most important element of the scrutinies: enlightenment or grace. Grace is union with God and a share in his life. The *National Catechetical Directory* reminds us that we are unconditionally loved, adopted children and that we live in the reality of being forgiven our sins.[6] Thus, the elect are filled with the presence of Christ the Liberator, who won the victory over evil and its consequences. In the Trinitarian prayer of exorcism, God the Father is invoked and asked for strength and protection. Through the power of the Holy Spirit (the epicletic action of laying on of hands), Jesus exercises his healing and liberating power over the effects of evil. Thus, the power and presence of Christ in Word and Exorcism are the primary symbols of the scrutinies.

Lent is a time of conversion, of *metanoia*, a compete turning away from sin into the loving arms of our loving God. "What we are about when we observe this liturgical time is the correction of our habits in order to relearn normative Christian behavior,"[7] first as a church, then as individuals. While it is a somber time, it is nevertheless marked by a spirit of joy. As Christians we know the rest of the story. Christ was victorious over the power of sin and death. While it is no doubt a time of serious reflection and interior conversion, we are joyful because we know that Easter joy awaits us. Christ the Liberator continues to heal, strengthen,

[3] *Constitution on the Sacred Liturgy*, #110, in *TLD*.

[4] Catechumens are called *the elect* after celebration of the rite of election on the First Sunday of Lent.

[5] *NCD*, #98, in *TCD*.

[6] Ibid.

[7] *DL* (II), 6.

and free us from the bondage imposed by ourselves and by the world.

Baptismal Nature of Lent

Lent is baptismal in nature. It is the time when the *elect* prepare to be fully initiated at the Easter Vigil through the sacraments of baptism, confirmation, and eucharist. During Lent, the faithful prepare to ritually remember their baptism and their baptismal commitment. Whether the newly baptized are present or not, the faithful will recall their baptism and renew their profession of faith at the Easter liturgies.

In the earliest days of the church, the Christian community walked hand in hand with the elect in their preparation for baptism—they were in it together. In his book, *The Liturgical Year,* Adolf Adam suggests that pre-Easter fasting was a way to prepare for the reception of the Spirit and the Easter sacraments of baptism and eucharist. It was a weapon against evil spirits, and a means to help the poor with money that would otherwise have been spent on food. What the church required of candidates for baptism by way of liturgical and spiritual effort was also done by the faithful in solidarity of spirit. "An atmosphere of cooperation and reciprocity was thus established that benefited the entire community."[8]

Eucharistic Nature of Lent

The season of Lent also prepares the elect and faithful for eucharist. While focusing on the baptismal nature of the season, we must not forget that baptism is the gateway, the door that leads to the table. The goal of initiation is not baptism; it is eucharist. The eucharist is the fullest sign of incorporation into the Body of Christ; it is the ultimate sacrament of unity. Through our participation in Christ's Body we become one people. The entire Christian life is somewhat catechumenal in nature. Christians are never finished; they never arrive; they are always on the journey. St. Augustine called the eucharist the repeatable sacrament of initiation. Eucharist is always a new encounter with the risen Christ. Jesus gave us his Body and Blood for the forgiveness of sins. Thus, whenever we eat Jesus' Body and drink his Blood at the communal feast we are made a new creation.

[8] *LY,* 91–113.

Each time we partake of Christ's Body and Blood, we recommit our lives to the ongoing incorporation into his life, death, and resurrection, the paschal mystery. We receive the necessary nourishment to take up our cross, to go out to the world, *to be fed off of,* and to become food for others. We come back to the table depleted; we are nourished again so that we can go out again.

The Disciplines of Lent: Prayer, Fasting, and Almsgiving

During the fifth century the church gathered for liturgical prayer on Mondays, Wednesdays, and Fridays. It was not until the sixth century that the other days of the week were added as eucharistic observances. Thus, from the earliest stages of the season, Lent was marked by prayer and communal worship. The people gathered to celebrate special "Liturgies of the Word, homilies and prayer.... Lent is a time characterized by more assiduous observance of prayer and liturgy."[9]

Fasting is regarded as the hallmark discipline of Lent. No doubt most Christians would immediately identify fasting with Lent. However, fasting is not just a lenten discipline. It should be a habit common to the Christian's entire life. Fasting does not have its origin in Christianity. The Jews fasted throughout their history. Fasting was a discipline of other pagan religions as well.

Fasting is *always* observed in tandem with prayer and almsgiving. The early Fathers of the Church considered fasting an exercise of compassion. It is expressed best in the following ancient sermon.

> There are three things, my brethren, by which faith stands firm, devotion remains constant, and virtue endures. They are prayer, fasting and mercy (almsgiving). Prayer knocks at the door, fasting obtains, mercy receives. Prayer, mercy and fasting: these three are one, and they give life to each other.

[9] *DL* (II), 4.

Fasting is the soul of prayer, mercy is the lifeblood of fasting. Let no one try to separate them; they cannot be separated. If you have only one of them or not all together, you have nothing. So if you pray, fast; if you fast, show mercy; if you want your petition to be heard, hear the petition of others. If you do not close your ear to others, you open God's ear to yourself.

When you fast, see the fasting of others. If you want God to know that you are hungry, know that another is hungry. If you hope for mercy, show mercy. If you look for kindness, show kindness. If you want to receive, give. If you ask for yourself what you deny to others, your asking is a mockery...

...Fasting bears no fruit unless it is watered by mercy. Fasting dries up when mercy dries up. Mercy is to fasting as rain to the earth. However much you cultivate your heart, clear the soil of your nature, root out vices, show virtues, if you do not release the springs of mercy, your fasting will bear no fruit.

When you fast, if your mercy is thin your harvest will be thin; when you fast, what you pour out in mercy overflows into your barn. Therefore, do not lose by saving, but gather in by scattering. Give to the poor, and you give to yourself. You will not be allowed to keep what you have refused to give to others.[10]

Prayer, fasting, and almsgiving are communal disciplines of Lent. The lenten disciplines are not for private edification but are to build up the entire church. One fasts in order to share. In antiquity, those who did not have enough to share were instructed to fast and use the money they saved on food to give to the poor. Prayer, fasting, and sharing are the agenda of the entire community. Many parishes gather during Lent for light soup suppers in which the money normally spent on a hearty meal is given instead to the poor.[11]

Prayer, fasting, and sharing must include reflection on the social dimensions of sin in our world where many people do not have an adequate share of the world's resources. Our commitment to prayer and fasting must include a commitment to issues of justice and equality for all people. It is hypocrisy to pray and fast and then assert that the poor of the world are not our problem, but are, instead, the problem of politicians and other nations.

The only obligatory fast days are Ash Wednesday and Good Friday. Some dioceses have included the Fridays during Lent as days of fast and abstinence.

The Lenten Lectionary

The Old Testament readings of Lent proclaim the salvation events wrought by Yahweh, especially the exodus. Christianity understands the readings from the Hebrew scriptures to be the foreshadowing of the salvation accomplished through Jesus Christ. Reginald Fuller maintains that during Lent, the New Testament letters profess the Christian kerygma and participation in the passion, death, and resurrection of Christ through baptism. The lenten gospels are stories from Jesus' life that foreshadow his impending death and resurrection. The scriptures of Lent are intended to prepare us to celebrate our redemption in Christ. "The emphasis of the Lenten readings is the new life to which the baptized are called and its ethical demands."[12]

Fuller also suggests that the lenten readings are penitential, but are placed in the context of the missionary implications of the gospel. On the First Sunday of Lent, the focus is the fasting of Jesus and his temptation in the desert. The Second Sunday of Lent takes us to the mountain of Jesus'

[10]St. Peter Chrysologus (ca. 380–450), "Sermon 43," Patrologia Latina 52, ed. J.P. Migne, in *The Liturgy of the Hours,* Vol. 2 (New York: Catholic Book Publishing Co., 1976), Office of Readings, Tuesday in the Third Week of Lent, 231–232.

[11]However, to reserve these activities only to the season of Lent diminishes Jesus' ongoing call to prayer, fasting, and sharing, the hallmarks of biblical justice. Lent serves as a reminder of what we should be doing as a matter of course throughout the entire Christian life.

[12]*PNL,* xxix.

transfiguration where we will hear the story from Matthew, Mark, or Luke's perspective. Thus, the First and Second Sundays of Lent in each cycle proclaim the same gospel event: temptation in the desert and the transfiguration. The gospels for the remaining Sundays of Lent are not the same for each cycle.

During Cycle A, we hear the powerful stories of the Samaritan woman at the well (Third Sunday of Lent, first scrutiny), the man born blind (Fourth Sunday of Lent, second scrutiny) and the raising of Lazarus (Fifth Sunday of Lent, third scrutiny). These Johannine gospels are catechumenal in nature as they best reflect the baptismal and penitential nature of the season. Through these stories we encounter sin (personal, social, and systemic) head on and are filled with "Christ the Redeemer, who is living water, the light of the world, and the resurrection and the life."[13]

The Cycle A readings are known as "the Johannine signs" and were "long viewed as symbols of the Christian experience of baptism."[14] When baptismal preparation was only three weeks long, the three Johannine gospels were used as primary catechesis because of their strong baptismal images: "water and spirit, the light of faith, and death and life."[15] Whenever there are catechumens, the Cycle A readings are to be used, regardless of the liturgical cycle. Since they were for use in catechumenal ministry and were intended to "arouse the baptismal faith" of the faithful, there is an option to use the Cycle A readings each year.

During Cycle B, the Third Sunday's gospel is John's account of the destruction of the temple and its subsequent rebuilding in three days. The Fourth Sunday's gospel (also from John) professes the Son of Man who will be raised for the salvation of all. The Fifth Sunday is about the grain that dies and bears much fruit.

The Cycle C gospel for the Third Sunday of Lent is about the need for repentance and conversion. The Fourth Sunday is the story of the prodigal son and the Fifth Sunday is the story of the woman accused of adultery.

The second reading during Lent is chosen to support the gospel. The first reading, however, is concerned with recounting significant events in salvation history. On Palm Sunday, the first and second readings are the same every year. The gospel is the passion narrative from one of the synoptic gospels. (For more on the lenten lectionary, see chapter 3 on scripture.)

As a springboard for lenten reflection, the following poem captures the heart of Lent's purpose. The protagonist of the poem is a catechumen who has journeyed with a community of faith for over a year. The catechumen has just celebrated the rite of election and has moved into the final preparatory period of purification and enlightenment. The person in this poem has encountered Jesus through the prayer and worship of his or her celebrating community in one complete liturgical cycle. This person speaks for us all.

*so what **could** be left, sister lent?*

I thought I had uncovered it all . . . layer by layer I shed it all away . . .
*so what **could** be left, sister lent?*
like a snake squirming from the casing of his former self
and the butterfly wrestling from the safe bondage of her quiet hibernation . . .
I stand empty . . .
a wonderful, curious, new creation,
chosen of god . . .
nakedly I gaze before discernment's interior mirror . . .
*so what **could** be left, sister lent?*
Sunday after Sunday, story after story, decision after decision,
gave way to an empty, vulnerable vessel, ready for easter filling . . .
*so what **could** be left, sister lent?*
like an air-dried sponge I stand waiting . . .
for what do I wait?
for fire light's illumination . . .
for baptismal water's soaking immersion . . .
for confirmation oil's sealing configuration . . .
for eucharist bread and wine's sumptuous celebration
for dying, rising, famine, for feasting,
for those who are *out* to be one with the *in* . . .
to eat, to be broken, to be poured, to be filled,
to live by example, to die, to be food . . .

[13]*RCIA*, #143.
[14]*PNL*, xxix.
[15]*DL* (II), 35.

for the hungry, the lost, the blind and the obstinate...
I wait to give more of the gift already given,
the sacrament of life for the sake of the kingdom...
so, forty more days of repentance and ashes
to renew, to strengthen and prepare for the banquet...
is there more? could there be?
one forgotten remnant
of a life not yet surrendered, of blindness, repression?
be it sojourn, or Passover or exodus event
I stand with eyes opened, my heart in my hand...
what could be left? only ***YOU*** know for sure...
so do what ***YOU*** will, root out from the core
all that might keep me from the life ***YOU*** intend
of thanksgiving, of service and praise till the end...

Mary Birmingham

Ash Wednesday

Environment

The catechetical space may be adorned simply with a cross, the Lectionary, and a candle; you might want to use hints of the color purple. A clay pot filled with ashes may be included as a sign of our need for repentance. Barren branches simply arranged speak of that buried seed, hibernating in its preparatory earthen cocoon awaiting the new life of Easter. Since Lent is a time of preparation for baptism, holy water fonts should be emptied.

The names and pictures of catechumens who will be initiated at the Easter Vigil might be placed in a basket nearby so all can be united with them in prayer and solidarity throughout the season.

The cross might be surrounded by purple cloth and then in the later weeks shrouded with that same purple cloth. This ancient practice is reminiscent of Isaiah's prophecy concerning the future day of the Lord: the new heaven and new earth. The veil that covers our eyes will be torn down and all will see the glory of God. Sin shrouds us from the *shekina* glory of God. The custom of veiling statues was stopped after the Second Vatican Council. However, it was reinstated in 1985 for use in the last weeks of Lent.[1]

The following ritual prayer from *Catholic Household Blessings and Prayers* may be used to bless the lenten environment:

INTRODUCTORY RITES

Opening Song (or Entrance Antiphon)

Lord, you are merciful to all, and hate nothing you have created. You overlook the sins of men to bring them to repentance. You are the Lord our God. (See Wisdom 11:24–25, 27.)[2]

[1] *TCY*, 42–69.

[2] Ash Wednesday: "Entrance Antiphon," *The Sacramentary.*

Ash Wednesday Blessing of the Season and of a Place of Prayer

All make the sign of the cross as the leader begins:
The Lord calls us to days of penance and mercy.
Blessed be the name of the Lord.

All respond:
Now and for ever.

Leader: Remember that we are but dust and ashes, yet by God's grace we have died in baptism and have put on the Lord Jesus Christ. Each year we keep these forty days with prayer and penance and the practice of charity so that we may come to the Easter festival ready to renew once more the life-giving commitment of our baptism. Throughout this Lent we shall gather here to read the Scriptures and ponder them and to intercede with God for the needs of the world.

Scripture
Isaiah 58:5–10

(Someone proclaims the reading from the prophet Isaiah.)

After a time of silence, members of the household offer prayers of intercession for the world, the church and its catechumens, and themselves. The leader then invites:

Let us kneel and ask for God's blessing on us and this holy season.
Merciful God,
you called us forth from the dust of the earth;
you claimed us for Christ in the waters of baptism.
Look upon us as we enter these Forty Days
bearing the mark of ashes,
and bless our journey through the desert of Lent
to the font of rebirth.
May our fasting be hunger for justice;
our alms, a making of peace;
our prayer, the chant of humble and grateful hearts.
All that we do and pray is in the name of Jesus.

Each person then kisses the cross.

All then stand, and the leader concludes.

All through these days let us be quiet and prayerful,
pondering the mysteries told in the Scriptures.
In the cross, we have been claimed for Christ.
In Christ, we make the prayer that fills these days of mercy:

Our Father...

The leader says:
Let us bless the Lord.

All respond, making the sign of the cross:
Thanks be to God.[3]

Opening Prayer

The facilitator of the session may lead the prayer. Others in the group may be asked to proclaim the readings.

Let us pray
[in quiet remembrance of our need for redemption]

Pause for silent prayer.

Father in heaven,
the light of your truth bestows sight
to the darkness of sinful eyes.
May this season of repentance bring us the blessing of your forgiveness
and the gift of your light.
Grant this through Christ our Lord.[4]

LITURGY OF THE WORD

Let us listen to God's word.

The readings are proclaimed.

First Reading
Joel 2:12–18

[3]"Ash Wednesday Blessing of the Season and of a Place of Prayer," *CHBP,* 132–135.

[4]Ash Wednesday: "Alternative Opening Prayer," *The Sacramentary.*

Joel's book is heavily centered in the language of temple worship. He speaks of vegetable offerings, libations, the fast, and a solemn assembly—the things of ritual worship. Temple priests, ministers of Yahweh, and ministers of the altar were part of Joel's cast of characters. Joel was one of the twelve minor prophets. Most scholars believe that the book of Joel was written after the exile and after the temple had been rebuilt (ca. 515 B.C.E.).

In chapters 1 and 2, Joel tells of a devastating drought and locust plague and thus sets the tone for his manuscript. His primary agenda concerns the reversal of fortunes. The first chapters depict the effects of the drought and plague on the people and on their worship. First, those directly involved by the effects of the plague (such as farmers) were called to lament. The effects of the invading army of locusts were so horrific, however, that the entire community was summoned to publicly lament.

Scholars believe that the book's main theme flows from verse 18. There was a corporate summons to grieve and lament. Israel was in devastation; there was pending doom. One can almost imagine the scene in true epic style. The ground rumbled, the earth shook, and the invading creatures blackened the sky. The people pleaded and Yahweh responded—a miracle happened! Yahweh intervened; the drought and plague were lifted. Their fortunes were reversed; Yahweh saved the day. This day was to be remembered.

Later in the book, Joel assigned this story to the community's corporate memory so that when all seemed lost, Israel would remember Yahweh's mercy. They would count on Yahweh to usher Israel into that final victorious battle. Herein lies an important lesson regarding the power of storytelling. Our stories of faith sustain us through the difficult times. We remember God's action, and are encouraged to be steadfast.

Yahweh does not act because of the ritual offerings. Yahweh acts because of his kindness and mercy and because of "who God is." For God, doing and being are the same thing. People repent because they are confident of his mercy. *Everyone* is called to fast—no one is excluded!

Responsorial Psalm
Psalm 51

Psalm 51 is the psalm of repentance. Humans acknowledge their utter guilt before God. God not only forgives the sin and guilt, but he restores the relationship.

Second Reading
2 Corinthians 5:20–6:2

Paul expounds a beautiful theology regarding the effects of Christ's death and resurrection upon the sin of the world. When Christ died, the veil on the temple was ripped in two. Humanity was given access to the holy of holies; God was now approachable. Christ *became* the very sin he came to destroy. He lifted the weight of sin from humanity's shoulder. Jesus' act was the ultimate gift of grace. Now is the time to rejoice in the grace that was won for all the world! Like Joel, we must shout it from the rooftops—the day of salvation is upon us! It is Good News; we can do no less than share it.

Gospel
Matthew 6:1–6, 16–18

Jesus warns about ostentatious displays of prayer and fasting.

Step 1
Naming One's Experience

What were your first impressions? What was your first response? What grabbed your attention? How did you feel?

Each person names his or her initial impression. Statements should be brief. No reasons should be given at this time. All simply listen without agreeing or disagreeing.

Step 2
Understanding

In a brief statement, what do you think this gospel is trying to convey?

Step 3
Input from Vision/Story/Tradition

Liturgical Context

On Ash Wednesday we receive ashes as a sign of our willingness to repent. We are sorry for our sins. At one time ashes were a public sign of repentance. They were not used in official liturgy until the thirteenth century. Until the reform of the liturgy, the ritual took place before mass. Since the reform, the blessing and distribution of ashes take place following the liturgy of the word. If mass is not celebrated, it takes place in the context of the liturgy of the word.

The ashes are given with the words, "Remember, man, that you are dust and to dust you shall return," or "Turn away from sin and be faithful to the gospel."[5] (See also "Dust," Appendix II.) The ritual prayers that accompany the blessing of ashes place the season in its appropriate pre-Easter perspective:

> Lord,
> bless the sinner who asks for your forgiveness
> and bless + all those who receive these ashes.
> May they keep this Lenten season
> in preparation for the joy of Easter.
> We ask this through Christ, our Lord.
> Bless these ashes+
> by which we show we are dust.
> Pardon our sins
> and keep us faithful to the discipline of Lent,
> for you do not want sinners to die
> but to live with the risen Christ,
> who reigns with you forever.[6]

On Ash Wednesday we humbly come before God seeking *metanoia*, conversion, and complete repentance. Our repentance is an act of faith because we repent trusting in God's kindness and mercy. Today's liturgy is a call to repentance for the

[5] Ash Wednesday: "Blessing and Distribution of Ashes," *The Sacramentary.*

[6] Ibid.

whole church. Joel sets the stage. "Proclaim a fast, call an assembly!" This is not a "Jesus and me" event. The entire community is called. Together we recognize our need for God's mercy.

We engage in a process of reflection and renewal as a community. Joel summoned the nation, the church summons its people. Fasting increases our hunger. For whom do we hunger? The resurrected Christ. What is the living memorial of his resurrected presence? The eucharist.

Gospel Exegesis

The facilitator gives input regarding what critical biblical scholarship has to say about this text. The input includes insights as to how people would have heard the gospel in Jesus' time.

Jesus' words are part of the discourse on the Mount. They are part of the evangelical section of the sermon. We must read this gospel in its evangelical context, as well as in the obvious context of prayer, fasting, and almsgiving. To live as Jesus commanded is to live according to the demands of the law, according to God's justice. God's justice (*hesed*) embodies right relationship with God as evidenced by care and concern for the poor and oppressed. Our prayer, fasting, and almsgiving must be in the spirit of the gospel and its mission orientation. Our light must shine before all, but it must shine with integrity. There can be no false airs, no hypocrisy. We are not to perform the lenten disciplines to gain the admiration of others.

The good deeds of a righteous person will cause people to see the light of Christ. Jesus invites us to look within and judge our motives. As community and as individuals we are to examine our hearts and judge our motivation for worship, prayer, fasting, and devotional practices.

Christians are to be joyful in the midst of their trials. In spite of life's difficulties they know what awaits them. Believers are to act in love toward their neighbors and invite others to Christ by the way they live their lives.

Proclaim the gospel again.

Sometimes we gain new insights when we hear the text after the interpretation has been given. Someone from the group proclaims the gospel a second time.

STEP 4
TESTING

Conversation with the Liturgy and the Scriptures

Test your original understanding in dialogue with the text.

(You might consider breaking into smaller groups.)

Were there any new insights? Was there anything you had not considered before? How do the readings for Ash Wednesday speak to your life?

Sharing Life Experience

Participants share an experience from their lives that connects with the biblical interpretation just shared.

> *I see people in my parish who live their lives in the spirit of Jesus' gospel. They live it not only during Lent, but also throughout the year. They are the real saints. They live their lives in humble submission to the word of God. They pray, fast, and reach out to the sick, the sorrowing, the infirm, the lonely, and the aged. One woman exemplifies the life Jesus calls us to live in today's gospel. She ministers to the sick and the elderly. She ministers the word of God everywhere she goes. She seeks God with every breath she takes. She speaks for truth and will not listen to gossip or destructive conversation. She exudes joy and typifies the humility demanded in today's gospel. Few people know how much she does for the reign of God. I look to her this Lent to remind me of the spirit and challenge of the season. My lenten repentance and conversion must lead me to grow more like the woman I admire so.*

All share their life experience.

What was Matthew trying to tell his community? What does he have to say to our community and to me today? What might God be creating in us through this experience of Jesus in the gospel and the lenten liturgy? In what way does this gospel point to God's promise to be with us? In what way have I/we known death/resurrection in my/our experience and understanding of this gospel? How is God speaking to us as a community? Has our original understanding been stretched, challenged, or affirmed?

STEP 5
DECISION

The gospel demands a response.

How does your sharing and this biblical interpretation challenge your community's attitudes? What will you/your community/your parish be called to do in response? Name one concrete action you will take this week as a response to what was learned and shared today.

DOCTRINAL ISSUES

What church truth/teaching/doctrinal issue could be drawn from the gospel for Ash Wednesday?

Participants suggest possible doctrinal themes that flow from the readings.

Possible Doctrinal Themes

Lent, conversion, repentance, fasting

Present the doctrinal material at this time.

1. The facilitator gives input on a particular doctrinal issue of his/her prior choosing. OR
2. The group chooses a doctrinal issue from the list they created. They read together from the Doctrinal Appendix.

(The doctrinal issues are found in the Doctrinal Appendix in the back of this workbook. If you are choosing an issue from this resource, please refer to it now.)

Reflection questions centered around the chosen doctrinal theme can be found at the end of each topic in the Doctrinal Appendix. The questions are based on the five-step reflection process. If you choose a topic not included in the Doctrinal Appendix, craft your own questions according to the same five-step process.

Following the reflection questions you will be reminded to return to chapter 7, "Preparing the Catechetical Session," to assist you in crafting your own session.

Closing Prayer

Come back to the Lord with all your heart;
leave the past in ashes,
and turn to God with tears and fasting,
for he is slow to anger and ready to forgive.
(Joel 2:13)

Let the priests and ministers of the Lord
lament before his altar, and say:
Spare us, Lord, spare your people!
Do not let us die for we are crying out to you.
(Joel 2:17; Est 13:17)[7]

[7]Ash Wednesday: "Antiphon 1 and 2," *The Sacramentary.*

First Sunday of Lent

Environment

Refer to Ash Wednesday. If not meeting on Ash Wednesday, the first Sunday of Lent would be an appropriate time to bless your catechetical space with the "Ash Wednesday Blessing of the Season and of a Place of Prayer" found in the previous session.

INTRODUCTORY RITES

Opening Song (or Entrance Antiphon)

When he calls me, I will answer; I will rescue him and give him honor. Long life and contentment will be his. (Ps 90:15–16)[1]

Opening Prayer

The facilitator of the session may lead the prayer. Others in the group may be asked to proclaim the readings.

Let us pray
[at the beginning of Lent for the spirit of repentance]

Pause for silent prayer.

Lord our God,
you formed man from the clay of the earth
and breathed into him the spirit of life,
but he turned from your face and sinned.
In this time of repentance
we call out for your mercy.
Bring us back to you
and to the life your Son won for us
by his death on the cross,
for he lives and reigns for ever and ever.[2]

LITURGY OF THE WORD

The readings are proclaimed.

[1]First Sunday of Lent: "Entrance Antiphon," *The Sacramentary.*

[2]First Sunday of Lent: "Alternative Opening Prayer," *The Sacramentary.*

First Reading[3]
Genesis 2:7–9; 3:1–7

Overview of the Book of Genesis: Genesis, from the Greek *genesis,* means beginning or origin. Genesis is the first book in the Bible and the first book of the Pentateuch [the first five books of the Bible]. The Book of Genesis spans a vast period of time from the creation of the world to about 1500 B.C.E. The writers were hardly concerned about (or aware of) the world's two-million-year history, or the inherent details. What concerned the authors of Genesis was to record the religious significance of the events of human history from the very beginning. The authors were also concerned with helping Israel remember its past, and thus to reflect and understand how they were formed as "a people." A small portion of the book is devoted to the origins of creation and the rest is concerned with the life, deeds, and stories of the patriarchs. Israel believed that God was in a special covenant relationship with them as a people. Israel believed that when God chose Abraham and the patriarchs he was choosing an "historical people for the realization of his purposes.... In Israelite tradition these patriarchs were presented as the first to hear Yahweh's promises for the future."[4] God's dealings with the patriarchs was understood as the covenant God made with Israel as a people.

Genesis is not understood as the history of the nation—that began with the liberation of Israel in the exodus event. Genesis is a "pre-history, a collection of remembrances and theological reflections that help throw light on the exodus."[5] God

[3]The exegesis for the first and second readings may or may not be the focus of your group's reflection as there may only be time to give adequate attention to the gospel, your primary concern. However, the exegesis is included here in order to provide a thorough investigation of the entire liturgy of the word as there may be parts (or all) that would be necessary to the direction you wish to take with your particular ministry group.

[4]*PAI,* 55.

[5]*ROT,* 110.

acted mightily in the exodus event. Genesis seeks to show that God was in relationship with them as a people and had planned for the momentous exodus from the very beginning of the world.

Scholars define four different traditions or sources that were responsible for the first books of the Bible. Some of the traditions were older than others. Two sources were named for the way the writer referred to God. The Yahwist ["J"] source, believed to be the oldest (c. 10th century B.C.E.), referred to God as Yahweh. The Elohist ["E"] source (c. 9th century B.C.E.) referred to God as Elohim. Originally it was believed that there were only two sources, the Yahwist and Elohist. Although the books of Genesis and Exodus contain passages that refer to God as Elohim, they clearly were written by two separate authors. This led to the belief in a third source that also referred to God as Elohim, but contained overtones that reflected a priestly focus (interest in rituals, genealogy, laws, and liturgical concerns). This source is referred to as the Priestly ["P"] source. A fourth and independent source is the Deuteronomic ["D"] source. It is believed that the unique and distinctive Book of Deuteronomy, noted for long speeches and sermons, was written by an author other than the Yahwist, Elohist, or Priestly writers. Biblical scholarship usually refers to the four traditions by the abbreviations J, E, P, and D.

The Yahwist tradition forms the "heart" of the first books of the Bible. The Yahwist is primarily concerned with the continuous story of God's action in salvation history. As artisan and theologian, the Yahwist wove together stories, songs, and poems that had been handed down in the life of the community. He was a master storyteller. The Yahwist has God engaged in grand dialogue with those in the stories and even with himself, thus illustrating that God orders and is in charge of all human events. There is a quality of the modern epic inherent in the Yahwist tradition. "The Yahwist created more than a story of Israel's past; he created a theology and a purpose that explained the religious faith and special spirit of the nation. It became the foundation for Israel's future meditation upon Yahweh's love."[6]

[6]Ibid., 101.

The Yahwist tradition is also the dominant tradition in the book of Genesis. The Yahwist is the only source that tells the story of the fall of humanity and the parallel story of the tower of Babel. The flood, believed to be of Priestly origin, probably served the same theological purpose as the story of the fall. Some stories were recorded by more than one tradition. One such story was the covenant of Abraham.

Genesis introduces the pre-history of Israel, beginning with the origins of the human race, the subsequent fall and alienation from God "followed by his [man's] progressive degeneration."[7] Genesis begins Israel's understanding of promise and covenant with the emergence of Abraham. At first it appears that the promise simply involves the promise of a new land and multiple descendants. However, it was the Abraham covenant that eventually gave birth to Israel's messianic hope.

Today's Pericope: The story from Genesis catapults us center stage to the unfolding drama of humanity's origins and first experience of sin and death. While the genre of Genesis is often referred to as "story," it really transcends mere narration. More than story, Genesis is an extended meditation on the mystery of sin and evil and the origins of life and death. It is born of the wisdom of ancient sages. Rather than postulating a literal, historical chronology of the *world's first events,* Genesis instead uses the legend and "vestiges of the Babylonian creation myth (*Enuma Elish*) as well as the Saga of Eden, a popular Canaanite and Akkadian tale"[8] as the vehicle to reflect upon the creation of humanity, its fall from grace, and God's self-revelation to the world. Such tales and legends were used to reveal the deeper truths of the Genesis events. It is believed that the story of the serpent and forbidden fruit may have been directed at the Canaanite fertility cults of the day.

In today's narrative, God creates the human person and builds a new world for his new creation.[9] In this very ancient culture it was believed that without the life-breath of God blown into the nostrils of every human person, life would cease. At

[7]*DOB,* 302.
[8]*WWC,* 21–22.
[9]*ROT,* 118.

this point in anthropological development, there was no understanding of the human soul. Without God's life-breath, all would simply return to dust.

The world fashioned by God at creation was a world of peace, harmony, and perfect order—all things in right relationship. In this created order, God was in perfect relationship with humanity, and humanity was in right relationship with God and one another. But something went terribly awry.

Humanity's saga of sin and conversion was inaugurated in the Genesis story. Human beings were God's creation, precious and holy, yet they turned away from their reliance on God. Humanity destroyed the shalom of Eden! They disrupted the peace that was intended at the creation of the world. This disruption was sin—the ultimate form of idolatry. Sin denies our need for God. Through sin we rupture the covenant relationship God established with us at the beginning of the world. "Humanity is not what God intended it to be."[10] Nevertheless, God placed man and woman at the center of God's plan for the salvation of the world. Genesis invites us to reflect upon the implications of that reality.

The author's use of the name Adam was a reference to and was understood as "Everyman." When we meditate upon the wisdom of Genesis we cannot help but place ourselves as the person of Adam—Everyman. Adam's story is our story. The same threads run through both.

Reginald Fuller exhorts us not to place too much emphasis on Eve as the culprit of Adam's first sin. He reminds us that the apostle Paul does not even mention Eve (1 Tim 2:13–14), but rather places the blame squarely on Adam's shoulders. This is not a diatribe about which sex is responsible for which sin. Both men and women sin, each in his or her own unique, distinctive way. There is no such thing as an "abuse excuse" or "copout" in Genesis. Human beings alone bear responsibility for their sins. They cannot blame God, nor the proverbial "other guy." All share corporate responsibility for the condition of sin and evil in the world. Sin is a choice. The more we choose sin, the more difficult it is to choose the *habit of grace.*

[10]*PL,* 38.

Adam and Eve's awareness of their nakedness was not only an awareness of sex, but was also a reminder of their shame.[11] They chose to be duped into thinking that they could be like gods! They already knew the God of *Ultimate Providence,* yet they turned away and sought their own glorification instead.

However, all was not lost. There was hope. Humanity could repent and God would listen. Humanity would remember Eden and their promised shalom. They could repent from their former ways, begin anew and return to the original covenant of peace and harmony with God and the created order. The Genesis meditation is not an exercise in despair, but rather a reflection of hope: hope in the God of mercy and compassion. "This is why the meditation over the origin of sin and its entrance into the world is not followed by a song of lament and mourning, but by a psalm of repentance, that is, a confession of the Lord's merciful love, a song of humble trust and hope: 'Be merciful, O Lord, for we have sinned.'"[12]

Responsorial Psalm
Psalm 51:3–4, 5–6, 12–13, 14, 17

This psalm expresses the sinfulness of human beings. In today's psalm the people take responsibility for their sins and turn to God in repentance. "Psalm 51 is the classic treatment of repentance. It passes beyond mere shame at the consequences of sin (attrition) to an acknowledgment of guilt before God (contrition): 'Against thee, thee only, have I sinned.' It sees forgiveness not only as the removal of guilt but as the restoration of the right relationship to God...."[13]

Second Reading
Romans 5:12–19

Refer to the Fourth Sunday of Advent for an overview of St. Paul's letter to the Romans.

In today's pericope, Paul asserts that Adam began humanity's descent into sin and death, but Christ inaugurated humanity's ascent into vindication, freedom, and new life. Adam initiated sin and

[11]*WWC,* 22.
[12]*DL* (II), 42.
[13]*PL,* 39.

death. Death means bondage. Christ initiated liberation and life. Life means freedom. Paul's letter could almost serve as a response to today's first reading. Adam started the spiral fall into sin. Christ restored the human race from the consequence of Adam's fault. "O happy fault, O necessary sin of Adam!"

The first five chapters of Romans is a meditation on the "human condition before and after Christ's coming."[14] Sin and darkness prevailed before Christ. Light and life explode into the world through the messianic reign of Christ. Grace has won the definitive victory for the human race. The grace of Christ will endure. Ultimately Paul's letter celebrates the destiny we share because of the sacrifice of Jesus on the cross. One person's sin (Adam's) established all human beings as sinners: "Jesus' obedience leads to the possibility and reality ('they will be established') of being righteous people."[15] This is truly good news!

Gospel[16]
Matthew 4:1–11

Jesus fasts for forty days and forty nights in the desert.

STEP 1
NAMING ONE'S EXPERIENCE

What were your first impressions? What was your first response to the gospel (or the other readings)?[17] What captured your attention?

Each person names his or her initial impression. Statements should be brief. No reasons should be given at this time. All simply listen without agreeing or disagreeing.

STEP 2
UNDERSTANDING

In a brief statement, what do you think this gospel is trying to convey?

STEP 3
INPUT FROM VISION/STORY/TRADITION

Liturgical Context[18]

The origin of the first two Sundays of Lent (temptation and transfiguration) dates back to the fourth century. The First Sunday of Lent recalls Jesus in the desert, the place of his temptation and Israel's unfaithfulness (as well as its faithfulness). The symbol of the desert has ancient roots in the church. It was seen as a quiet place, free from distractions, where people could commune with God. Monasticism emerged out of the desert motif.

The first reading on the First Sunday of Lent in all three cycles remembers God's self-revelation to humanity through the prism of salvation history. This history allows us to view the paschal mystery from the vantage point of God's saving action from the very beginning of God's relationship with the human race. What God began at the creation of the world was the first step in the forward movement toward what he would ultimately accomplish through the life, death, and resurrection of his Son.

[14] *DL* (II), 43.

[15] *WNT*, 326.

[16] The gospel exegesis is provided later in this session so that it may be presented in the proper sequence where it occurs in the adult five-step reflection process. The exegesis is provided for the first and second readings for your information and edification. Use at your discretion. Once again, the gospel is the primary source of reflection. If there is time for reflection on the other readings, all the better.

[17] The primary focus of reflection is the gospel. However, very often the other readings demand attention and must be brought into the dialogue.

[18] The scriptures in the Lectionary, the seasons of the year, and the ritual prayers of the mass are interrelated and form the basis for liturgical catechesis. The *liturgical context* attempts to explore and clarify the themes and this interrelatedness.

> God, who wishes all men to be saved and come to the knowledge of truth (1 Tm 2:4), in many and various ways... spoke of old to our fathers by the prophets (Heb 1:1). When the fullness of time had come He sent His Son, the Word made flesh, anointed by the Holy Spirit, to preach the gospel to the poor, to heal the contrite of heart (cf. Is 61:1; Lk 4:18), to be a "bodily and spiritual medicine,"[19] the Mediator between God and man (cf. 1 Tm 2:5). For His humanity, united with the person of the Word, was the instrument of our salvation.... The wonders wrought by God among the people of the Old Testament were but a prelude to the work of Christ the Lord in redeeming mankind and giving perfect glory to God. He achieved his task principally by the paschal mystery of his blessed passion, resurrection from the dead, and glorious ascension, whereby dying, he destroyed our death and, rising, he restored our life. For it was from the side of Christ as He slept the sleep of death upon the cross that there came forth the wondrous sacrament which is the whole Church.[20]

Jesus' temptation in the desert, proclaimed on every First Sunday of Lent in all three cycles, heralds Jesus' triumph over Satan as well as the mandate that we all enter with Christ into the fight against evil.[21]

"At Sunday Masses in Lent, the first reading is independent from the other two. Each of the three series constitutes a catechetical unity, as do the seven Old Testament readings at the Easter vigil. Hence their importance during the first five Sundays of Lent."[22] The readings serve as a stark reminder of who we are, where we came from, and where we ought to be going. They prepare us for the renewal of our baptismal promises at Easter and they help us to reflect on the dimensions of sin and grace in our lives.

The lenten theme of *conversion* is highlighted in the liturgical prayers of each Sunday. Note the "Alternative Opening Prayer" for today's liturgy: "In this time of repentance we call out for your mercy. Bring us *back to you* [italics mine] and to the life your Son won for us by his death on the cross...." The "Prayer Over the Gifts" asks that the sacrifice we offer will help *to change our lives;* and the "Prayer After Communion" invites us to *live by the word* and to seek the Bread of Life. The call to conversion cannot be clearer either in scripture or in the liturgy.

Lent highlights and illumines that which should be the agenda of every day of our lives: a complete turning of our lives and our hearts to God, a true sense of sorrow for sin, and participation in our baptismal life which is, ultimately, participation in the paschal mystery of Jesus Christ. "Lent is the explicitness of that period of 'fast' and 'passion' which extends over our whole lives. Today's welfare and consumer state has accommodated itself to a permanent lie: the impression is universally given that serene happiness is everywhere the rule, or if that is not strictly true in every case, it soon will be with goodwill and the irresistible progress of humankind."[23] Yet, how can we ignore the reality of suffering in this world? Pain, death, old age, and sickness are with us forever. We cannot deny or ignore this somber reality. One thing we can do, however, is to ask how to cope with it. "Cynicism and stoicism do not go very far. In faith, hope and love a Christian understands this aspect of her life as a sharing in the Lord's passion. The acceptance in belief and hope of one's own passion is exercised by what in Christian asceticism is called 'voluntary renunciation.' In Lent, however, that which one must necessarily suffer in life in sober realism and can live in hope as a *Christian* passion becomes publicly known, in ecclesial, liturgical, and sacramental explicitness, as a freely loving participation in the passion of Christ."[24]

Jesus' ordeal on the Temple parapet in Jerusalem was a foreshadowing of the cross he would endure. Jesus' temptation is an invitation and a challenge. The elect and the entire church are invited to the temple parapet as a prelude to the journey

[19]St. Ignatius of Antioch, "To the Ephesians," 7, 2; ed. F.X. Funk, *Patres Apostolici* I, Tubingen, 1901, p. 218.

[20]*CL,* #105.

[21]*DL* (II), 37.

[22]Ibid., 36.

[23]*GCY,* 120–121.

[24]Ibid.

to Jerusalem and the challenge of the cross. Lent marks the way for us all.

Rite of Election and Rite of Sending

By the fourth century, Easter was the customary time for the celebration of baptisms. However, there is evidence that Pentecost was another suitable time.[25] At the beginning of Lent, the catechumens who desired baptism handed over their names as a request for baptism. To "give in their names" became the technical language for their request to be baptized. "Candidates whose application was accepted were called 'applicants' (*competentes*), 'chosen' (*electi*), or 'destined for illumination' (*photizomenoi*)."[26] A description of the rite was handed down to us by the Gallican or Spanish nun, Egeria (4th century) who, on a pilgrimage to Jerusalem, wrote down her experiences.

> I think I ought to tell you how instruction is given to those who are baptized at Easter. Those who give in their names do so the day before Lent begins; the presbyter writes down the names of all of them. This takes place before the eight weeks during which, as I told you, Lent is observed here. When the presbyter has made a note of all the names, later on another day in Lent, the day on which the eight weeks begin, the bishop's chair is set up in the middle of the great church, the church of the Martyrium. The presbyter sits on either side on chairs and all the clerics stand. Then the candidates are brought in one by one, the men with their "fathers," the women with their "mothers." Then the bishop one by one asks their neighbors: Is he a good-living man? Does he respect his parents? Is he a drunkard or trustworthy? He asks them like this about every vice, at least the more serious ones. If the bishop finds that the candidate is free from all these faults about which he has questioned the witnesses, he writes down the candidate's name with his own hand.[27]

[25]St. Siricius [pope, 384–399] was known to have baptized people at Pentecost.

[26]Edward Yarnold, S.J., *AIRI,* 8.

[27]Egeria, *Peregrinatio,* 45, in Edward Yarnold, S.J., *AIRI,* 8.

The rite of election that is presently celebrated is an adaptation of the ancient rite.

Today begins the period of purification and enlightenment for catechumens. This marks the beginning of the final, more intense preparation for the Easter sacraments of initiation. The celebration of the rite of election and the enrollment of names is the liturgical rite that marks entry into this final period that coincides with the season of Lent. The principal celebrant for the rite of election is the bishop and it generally takes place at the diocesan cathedral. However, the great enthusiasm and ownership of the rite at the parish level has prompted an adaptation known as the rite of sending.

The rite of sending allows the parish to send their catechumens to the bishop for election and enrollment of names. The preliminary judgment of the catechumens' readiness takes place within the parish. The parish is the spiritual mother who now wishes to send her fledglings to election with assurances of love, support, and prayers. Baptized candidates are also sent to the bishop for recognition of their call to continuing conversion during this time of preparation for completion of their initiation.

At the rite of election, the catechumens make a transition into their final preparation for initiation and are conferred with a new name: the *elect.* In scripture, the conferral of a new name signified a changed status or a new mission or vocation. The church accepts the catechumens as chosen of God; they are elected by God. On the basis of the testimony of the godparents and the catechists, as well as the catechumens' own reaffirmation, the church judges their state of readiness to go forward for initiation at the Easter Vigil. The church testifies to God's grace at work in the lives of the catechumens. The catechumens, then, hand their names over, and enroll for baptism.

Election is about being chosen. To be chosen assumes that one is in reciprocal covenant relationship with God. It is a relationship rooted in biblical justice. "Election as people of God requires a style of life that reflects this office. It is as much a responsibility as it is a privilege."[28] Election is a

[28]Marilyn M. Schaub, "Election," *CPDBT,* 250.

radical call to intimate relationship with God and unconditional love toward all of God's creation. In the Old Testament, election assumed that those chosen believed in their hearts and professed with their voices the ancient Shema: "The Lord God is One. We are to love the Lord God with all our heart, mind and soul, and love our neighbor as ourselves."

Election is God's free act of gratuitous, unmerited love. However, there is always an inherent obligation on the part of the person or group chosen. "To belong to God in the special relationship of election demands that one imitate the very character and qualities of God."[29] Election reminds us that God is in charge; we are not. Election is freely given, but it is also freely received. Barbara Bowe suggests that a person's membership among the elect depends on the extent to which a person is faithful to God throughout life, especially during times of distress and tribulation. Thus, there is an eschatological dimension inherent within election. Election is participation in the messianic reign in this world and anticipation of God's reign to come.

Election is understood as vocation and responsibility rather than privilege and superiority. Election assumes a special intimacy and full communion with God as well as the vocation to witness to the marvels of God in the world.[30]

Today's gospel is a wonderful testament to election. The first Christians compared Jesus to the suffering servant of Isaiah, the "chosen one of God" (Is 42–53). Jesus, as God's beloved, stands chosen above all others as God's elect. Prior to Jesus' temptation scene, he was baptized by the Holy Spirit in the Jordan River. The Spirit called and empowered Jesus for mission. The Spirit then led Jesus to the desert where he was tempted. The temptation was a prelude and preparation for Jesus' ministry; it was intended to show Jesus the scope of his mission. His reign was to be a reign of service, not power. Jesus, "Beloved," "Elect of God," was shown what his ministry was to be by being shown what it was not to be. Jesus' ministry was rooted in service, self-offering, and reliance on the word of God.

Jesus, as God's chosen and God's elect, was faithful to his call and mission. His call ultimately led him to the desert where his ancestors had failed miserably. They failed in their call to covenant relationship. Jesus not only succeeded in this, but also offered us a new covenant. Jesus invites us all into the desert of Lent. On this First Sunday of Lent, Jesus shows the elect what the call of discipleship means. It is fraught with dangers; it is the emptying of self; it is a mission of service that leads ultimately to the cross. Jesus does not leave us alone in our testing; rather, he gives us the sword of God's word as our protection. He shows us and the elect the way through purification to enlightenment.

At the rite of election, the godparents testify to the catechumens' readiness to accept God's call and subsequent challenge of election. The church, then, declares the catechumens chosen and ready to go forward for initiation.

Gospel Exegesis

The facilitator gives input regarding what critical biblical scholarship has to say about this text. The input includes insights as to how people would have heard the gospel in Jesus' time.

The intention of today's gospel is not to provide an accurate historical account of the events of Jesus' temptation by Satan. Nor is it primarily about Jesus' confrontation and subsequent vanquishing of Satan. It was written as a story about the testing of God's Son. "God, through the Spirit, intends to *test* Jesus; Satan, God's indirect agent, seeks to tempt the Messiah designate."[31]

In today's pericope there are elements of haggadic midrash in which a fanciful story is told "whose purpose it is to interpret Scripture. There may well be an underlying kernel of historical truth, since other passages suggest that Jesus regarded himself as involved in a struggle against Satan (see Mt 12:29; Lk 10:18)."[32] However, the

[29]Barbara E. Bowe, R.S.C.J., "Election: New Testament," *CPDBT,* 251.

[30]Robert J. Schreiter, C.PP.S., "Election: Pastoral Liturgical Tradition," *CPDBT,* 254.

[31]*MI,* 23.

[32]Ibid.

primary concern of this story is a theological midrash (a reflection) on the meaning of Jesus' divine Sonship.

The ancient Mediterranean culture lived in the world of spirits as much as in the ordinary plane of existence. The culture believed that spirits abounded and that they interfered in human affairs. When the voice of God from heaven named Jesus his Beloved Son, the highly-charged, spirit-sensitive culture of the then-known world would have fully understood the implications of that event. The compliment paid to Jesus would have captured the attention of the underworld. The spirits would be compelled to test Jesus to see if the voice from heaven proclaimed the truth. They would try to trip him up in the event that the voice was speaking the truth. Jesus was then led into the place where the spirits lived, the place of testing—the desert. Jesus, full of the Holy Spirit, would then do battle with the evil one.[33]

The testing of Jesus parallels the testing of Abraham. The temptation story has a parallel with the testing of Abraham in the Old Testament. Jesus became both Abraham and Isaac because he eventually placed himself upon the altar of sacrifice.

The testing of Jesus parallels the testing of Israel. Connections can also be made between the temptation of Jesus in today's gospel with the testing of the Hebrews in the wilderness. The forty days and forty nights are reminiscent not only of Moses' fast, but also of the forty years in the desert. Israel failed; Jesus did not.

In today's gospel Matthew plays upon the three tests of Israel. The first test of Israel is "the first of many stories of Yahweh testing the people in the wilderness. God puts humans in a position where they must show their true allegiance; God may test humans but humans may not test God. All the tests in the wilderness concern either food and drink for the people or Moses' authority."[34]

The first test, then, involved hunger. Israel was hungry. Yahweh tested the faithfulness of the people before he graced them with manna from heaven. Israel doubted God's providence. The people betrayed the covenant relationship they shared with Yahweh. God entered into a covenant relationship with Israel in which he promised that their needs and concerns would be met. In return, Israel promised reliance on God's benevolence and promised to offer reciprocal care for one another, and especially for those in need.

Jesus, on the other hand, did not submit to the manipulation of God's power in order to satisfy his hunger. He had no doubt that God *could* change the stones to bread, but he was satisfied in waiting for God to provide the bread he needed to satisfy his hunger. We live by the power of God alone. The source of all life and breath comes from God. "It is noteworthy in these reflections of the sacred authors that temptation is a test of understanding and of faith in the power of God."[35]

The second test involved testing God. The second test of Jesus parallels the event in Exodus (17:1–7) in which the Israelites questioned whether God was with them. They were thirsty. In an earlier story, the people could not drink the bitter water; in this situation, there was no water at all. They attacked Moses in their demand for water. They quarreled with God; they did not believe that God would take care of them. Yahweh instructed them to strike the rock and draw water. The site of this miracle was named Meribah (Hebrew "to quarrel") and Massah (Hebrew "to test"). "Yahweh gives bread from heaven and water from this rock to this people in the wilderness; he thus proves his mastery over the hostile environment."[36] The rebellious people challenged their God and in so doing demonstrated their own unworthiness of the covenant they shared.

Conversely, Jesus refused to manipulate God's power by calling on it to save him in the event that he would jump from the temple's parapet. He knew well that God would take care of him and that God could indeed save him were he to jump. But Jesus would not succumb to a showy demonstration of power. He would not be enticed into Satan's game of power manipulation, nor would Jesus in turn manipulate God into action.

---

[33] *CWJ,* 49–51.

[34] Richard J. Clifford, "Exodus," in *NJBC,* 50.

[35] James A. Fischer, C.M., "Temptation," in *CPDBT,* 984.

[36] Ibid., 51.

Jesus' third temptation dealt with the issue of idolatry. Jesus responded to the temptation with a command from Deuteronomy that demanded that people fear the Lord, serve the Lord, and swear by the Lord's name (6:13–14). According to Douglas Hare, the Jews believed that the gods of the Graeco-Roman pantheon were demons and therefore were agents of Satan. There was a great temptation for the Jews to embrace the pagan gods for political and economic reasons. There were well-known cases of famous Jews who left Judaism to feather their political nests. Some Jews were "willing to accept a 'pinch of idolatry' to further their political careers."[37] The third temptation of Jesus reminds us that he would never be tempted to "sell out" for political or personal gain. He would give humanity his undivided loyalty. He would not be compromised. He would serve and worship God and God alone.

Douglas Hare suggests that even though this reading is assigned to the First Sunday of Lent as an invitation to meditate on sin and temptation in our lives, devils on rooftops do not immediately capture the attention or the imagination of modern readers. There is little in the story that relates to modern life—or so it might seem. People still ask the question: How could Jesus really know what it is like to walk in our shoes? Perhaps he could tell us how to spar with a steeple-perched devil over mind games and power plays, but how can he speak to the real temptations we face in our complex world? "What did Jesus know of the temptations that are faced daily by the recovering alcoholic and substance abuser? The lonely divorcee? The struggling business owner? The teenager who covets peer acceptance above all? There is, however, a common denominator that links all of these with the temptations ascribed to Jesus. The basic, underlying temptation that Jesus shared with us is the temptation to treat God as less than God."[38] Today's story reminds us of the greatest void in our culture—God-less-ness. God is not allowed to be God, because he is denied, spurned, and ridiculed.

We might not be tempted as Jesus was tempted. We may never struggle with the devil over whether we are going to bungee-jump off the nearest skyscraper; but we may wrestle furiously over whether we should support systems that keep people in the throes of poverty. We will often be tempted to mistrust the experience of God in our lives and his willingness to encourage us to face our trials. It is doubtful that any of us would be lured by a modern-day version of Baal, but seduction by consumerism is not an unthinkable possibility. There are many things in today's world that serve as a stumbling block to love, serve, and worship God alone. Today's gospel reminds us that Christ is the One who went before us and continues to show us the way. To follow Christ means to acknowledge his sovereignty and to revere and live by his word.

Jesus' third temptation on the mountain was significant for another reason. Mountains were places of God's revelation. They are "places where the Father of the Son gives teachings to human beings."[39] The mountain was the place where Jesus was offered the world if he would worship the one whose plan was antithetic to God's. Matthew is emphatic. Contrary to the disobedient son, Israel, Jesus is the obedient, faithful Son of God. Jesus waged battle with the devil and was victorious. Jesus avoided shame and upheld his important honor. Until his arrest, no one would get the better of him. He would not be shamed or tricked.

Reginald Fuller asserts that Matthew and Luke tell almost identical stories, but Matthew rearranged the order of temptations as found in the gospel of Luke. Luke's order was bread-mountain-temple. Matthew rearranged it to bread-temple-mountain. Fuller suggests that Matthew rearranged the order to emphasize that Jesus was the Son of God and that the temptations "were messianic in character."[40] Luke's version emphasized that Jesus was the new Adam. The old Adam fell when tempted—Jesus did not. The temptations of Jesus are the temptations of the new Adam.

Fuller states that it is difficult not to read the Lucan interpretation into today's gospel when taken in tandem with the first and second readings from Genesis and Romans. The latter certainly promote and support the Lucan theme.

[37] *MI*, 25.

[38] Ibid., 26.

[39] *CWJ*, 50.

[40] *PL*, 40.

An American lenten meditation on this gospel might logically begin with a reflection on the use and abuse of power. Power is an aphrodisiac that is present in many overt as well as subtle forms, not only in systems and governments, but in the marketplace, the church, and within families. Today's gospel is an opportunity to discover its seductive lure.

Proclaim the gospel again.

Sometimes we gain new insights when we hear the text after the interpretation has been given. Someone from the group proclaims the gospel a second time.

Step 4
Testing

Conversation with the Liturgy and the Scriptures

Test your original understanding in dialogue with the text.

(You might consider breaking into smaller groups.)

Now that you've heard what the scholars have to say about this passage, how do you feel about it? How does your original understanding of this gospel compare with what we just shared? Were there any new insights for you? How does this story speak to your life?

Sharing Life Experience

Participants share an experience from their lives that connects with the biblical interpretation just shared.

> *There are two ways for me to respond to the readings today—personally and as a member of society. I am, like Adam, a human being prone to sin. I am tempted and often fail. Sometimes I resist temptation. On a personal level this gospel speaks to me every time I do not allow God to be God. When I spend an inordinate amount of time worrying about my children and about the circumstance of my life, I place myself in the driver's seat and I relegate God to the bumper seat. On more than one difficult occasion in my life I have been known to grumble like the Israelites: Are you in this with me or not, God? Whenever I try to control those around me, or the situations of my life, I take God out of the equation and choose instead to be my own god. Not only do I act like God, but when I try to control others, it is a serious abuse of power—even when it is my own young adult children. Control and domination are abuses of power, even when subtle and well-intentioned. I recently tried to meddle and insist on a course of direction for one of my young adult children. If my parents had been so presumptuous with me when I was the same age, I would have bristled and chosen an opposite course simply out of contrariness. My adult children continue to teach me that God is leading their lives—it is no longer my job. They often do a better job of listening to the voice of God than I do. I have even been presumptuous enough to think that I know God's will for them better than they do! Today's gospel reminds me that I may not exert power and control over anyone—husband, children, friends, or coworkers.*
>
> *We are lured by many seductive gods in today's culture. Those seductions often take the form of addictions and an inordinate flirtation with consumerism. Addictions and compulsions are the result of control gone amuck in our lives. When food, alcohol, work, drugs, cigarettes, the compulsion to succeed at all costs, and the myriad of other addictions that dot our landscape consume much of our attention, we have relinquished God's control of our lives. The poor addict on the street very obviously wears his or her shame. The whole world knows of their abdication from life. The rest of us with silent addictions (food, work, etc.) may or may not have to face the public shame or humiliation caused by our unresisted temptations.*[41] *When God is not the center of my life, balance is also gone and I pay the price. Today's gospel reminds me that there is One who knows my struggle and is there to help me when I do not allow God to be God in my life. I am challenged to let go of the gods of addiction, no matter where they rear their ugly heads.*
>
> *On a communal level, I participate in the idolatry of the society when, through my silence or neglect, I support systems that keep people under domination and control. My responsibility is to search out those*

[41] A food addict certainly wears his or her addiction, whereas a work addict is often upheld as a paragon of virtue. Addiction places the self in center stage rather than God, no matter what form it takes.

areas where structures continue to oppress people and do what I can to change the situations. There is one area of power and oppression in our civic community that few would even deem worthy of addressing. The homeless of our beach are harrassed. No doubt there are often good reasons for police consternation. However, there is no place on the beach where they are free to exist. Recently one of our homeless fellows was arrested and spent three months in jail for an offense that was punishable by two weeks. You and I would have been adjudicated swiftly. The homeless, however, have no advocates and no means of swift adjudication and therefore often spend months in jail for an offense as simple as littering the beach with an open container. In a geographical location where we must justify the continuous building of new jails, such unwilling residents help underline our jail over-crowding problem with red ink! The homeless are exploited in the interest of building new jails. While I am sure there is oversimplification in my analysis, there is enough reality in it to acknowledge that the abuse of power often takes place right under our noses—and we often couldn't care less. We might even think the homeless have it coming to them. Yet when any group of people is exploited for any reason, the human family has somehow been stripped of its dignity. When I do nothing to help the situation by at least bringing it to public attention, I participate in the structures that continue to oppress. We could all cite many instances where we participate in the world's oppression of people. Today's gospel invites us to turn over those rocks and dare to uncover the sinister realities of power, domination, control, and idolatry in all its subtle forms.

All share their life experience.

What was Matthew trying to tell his community? What was the ultimate point of the temptation story? How does that have any relevance for our community today? Even though wrestling with Satan is not an activity we are consciously aware of in twentieth-century parlance, how can Satan's tempting of Jesus challenge us on any meaningful level? The biblical themes of creation, covenant, exodus, and community are very prevalent in today's readings. How do they relate to your everyday life? How is your community

a. being recreated,
b. living the covenant and promise with God in Christ,
c. experiencing death and resurrection, and
d. understanding its role as a community?

What is your collective and personal response to all of the above questions? Do you still feel the same way about this text as you did when we began? Has your original understanding been stretched, challenged, or affirmed?

Step 5
Decision

The gospel demands a response.

In what way are we invited to change as a result of today's readings, gospel, liturgy? What is the primary challenge for our community? Where is transformation most needed in relation to today's gospel? Are there subtle and not-so-subtle areas of control and domination that need to be addressed? In what concrete ways is our parish called to respond? What are the implications of this gospel [liturgy] for my life? What is one concrete action I will take this week as a response to today's liturgy?

Pastoral Considerations: Today's liturgy reminds us that issues of justice demand attention. What is happening in your civic community that needs the attention of the Christian community? Are there areas where advocates are needed to speak for the rights of the poor? In what ways might your parish participate in the lenten discipline of almsgiving—a soup kitchen, soup suppers where the profits are given to the poor, food drives, clothing drives, a project to assist the poor in Third World countries to help themselves? How is your parish addressing multicultural issues? Are there factions and divisions within the parish community that are crying out for healing? Perhaps Lent is the appropriate time to face those issues head-on.

Christian Initiation: The rite of election is celebrated more than likely at the diocesan cathedral. The parish perhaps will celebrate the rite of sending catechumens for election and candidates for recognition by the bishop. Those in the catechumenate *who will not be initiated at the Easter Vigil* continue in the period of the catechumenate. The elect begin the period of purification and enlightenment—retreat time. It is a time of discernment in which they are prepared for baptism, reflect on sin and grace, and prepare to celebrate the scrutinies. In what ways can the disciplines of prayer, fasting, and almsgiving be highlighted in the catechumenate community? Are there opportunities for catechumens, candidates, and the elect to participate in issues of justice?

Reconciliation. Perhaps baptized candidates, who will enter into full communion with the Catholic Church during the Easter season, might be prepared to celebrate the sacrament of reconciliation during the parish's lenten celebration. The elect might join in the preparation so they can celebrate the sacrament at a later time, after they are initiated. If your parish is not celebrating the sacrament of reconciliation this Lent, perhaps a non-sacramental penitential celebration (found in the Rite of Penance) could be celebrated with catechumens still in process.

DOCTRINAL ISSUES

What church truth/teaching/doctrinal issue could be drawn from the gospel for the First Sunday of Lent?

Participants suggest possible doctrinal themes that flow from the readings.

Possible Doctrinal Themes

Lent, conversion, sin (personal, social, and systemic), grace, paschal mystery, repentance and reconciliation, preparation for baptism, prayer, fasting, almsgiving

Present the doctrinal material at this time.

1. The facilitator gives input on a particular doctrinal issue of his/her prior choosing. OR
2. The group chooses a doctrinal issue from the list they created. They read together from the Doctrinal Appendix.

(The doctrinal issues are found in the Doctrinal Appendix in the back of this workbook. If you are choosing an issue from this resource, please refer to it now.)

Reflection questions centered around the chosen doctrinal theme can be found at the end of each topic in the Doctrinal Appendix. The questions are based on the five-step reflection process. If you choose a topic not included in the Doctrinal Appendix, craft your own questions according to the same five-step process.

Following the reflection questions you will be reminded to return to chapter 7, "Preparing the Catechetical Session," to assist you in crafting your own session.

Closing Prayer

Opening Prayer: First Sunday of Lent

Father,
through the observances of Lent,
help us to understand the meaning
of your Son's death and resurrection,
and teach us to reflect it in our lives.
Grant this through our Lord
Jesus Christ, your Son,
who lives and reigns with you and the Holy Spirit,
one God, for ever and ever.[42]

[42]First Sunday of Lent: "Opening Prayer," *The Sacramentary.*

Second Sunday of Lent

Environment

Refer to Ash Wednesday

INTRODUCTORY RITES

Opening Song (or Entrance Antiphon)

My heart has prompted me to seek your face; I seek it, Lord; so do not hide from me.[1]

Opening Prayer

The facilitator of the session may lead the prayer. Others in the group may be asked to proclaim the readings.

Let us pray
[for the grace to respond to the Word of God]

Pause for silent prayer.

God our Father,
help us to hear your Son.
Enlighten us with your word,
that we may find the way to your glory.
We ask this through our Lord
Jesus Christ, your Son,
who lives and reigns with you
and the Holy Spirit,
one God, for ever and ever.[2]

LITURGY OF THE WORD

The readings are proclaimed.

First Reading[3]
Genesis 12:1–4

[Refer to the *Overview of the Book of Genesis,* First Sunday of Lent.]

Abraham was probably the chief of a wealthy nomadic clan in the south near Hebron. The clan raised sheep and goats and settled near major urban areas when they were not on the move to greener, wetter pastures during the dry season.

We are suddenly and dramatically introduced to this notable character. He appears out of nowhere and is climactically sent to lead a great nation. God wasted no time. He sent Abraham to a new land. This signaled a shift in God's movement. "The world as a whole is no longer the stage of action, but one small corner of it."[4] Now God would focus his attention on Abraham, and the new land he would give him. So began Abraham's journey, led and ordained by God.

According to Lawrence Boadt, there are two important themes in the Abraham story. God made a promise to Abraham. Fulfillment of that promise would begin in Abraham's lifetime and would ultimately impact all the events in the Pentateuch. Abraham was faithful to God and, as a result, God blessed him and made him his specially chosen friend.[5] God's promises to Abraham signaled a formal agreement between the two. God appeared to Abraham in a theophany, demonstrating the "overwhelming personal experience of God's presence that affects the entire direction and quality of a person's life."[6]

God promised to make Abraham the leader of a great nation, but there was a condition: Abraham and Sarah must demonstrate steadfast trust. Abraham was faithful, but the "rest of the story"

[1] First Sunday of Advent: "Entrance Antiphon," *The Sacramentary.*

[2] Second Sunday of Lent: "Opening Prayer," *The Sacramentary.*

[3] The exegesis for the first and second readings may or may not be the focus of your group's reflection as there may only be time to give adequate attention to the gospel, your primary concern. However, the exegesis is included here in order to provide a thorough investigation of the entire liturgy of the word as there may be parts (or all) that would be necessary to the direction you wish to take with your particular ministry group.

[4] *ROT,* 137.

[5] Ibid., 138.

[6] Ibid.

shows that he was not without his momentary digressions (in chapter 17 he took a slave girl because he did not believe that Sarah would have a child). However, it was Abraham's "habit of faithfulness" that was the consistent thread woven throughout his entire life. This habit of faithfulness would ultimately sustain him in the greatest test of his life, the proposed sacrifice of his son Isaac.

The Abraham story is a revelation of God's action and God's faithfulness. God commanded, Abraham responded. God expects no less in response to his self-revelation. The human response of faith, obedience, and hope "opens channels for the redemptive action of God in history and in the world."[7]

God blessed Abraham. Because of sin, the world was destroyed by flood. Abraham signaled a reversal in sacred history. God appointed and commissioned him as the father of a new people. The blessing of Abraham would extend to all believers. "The blessing will be shared by 'all the communities of the earth' which will stand behind Abraham, the prototype of the believer and of the blessed one, whose name will become synonymous with benediction. Abraham is, so to speak, the believer from whom blessing will spread."[8]

Responsorial Psalm
Psalm 33:4–5, 18–19, 20, 22

Today's psalm complements the call of Abraham. God works in human history as people respond in obedience, trust, and hope.

Second Reading
2 Timothy 1:8–10

Overview of Paul's Second Letter to Timothy: Timothy was a disciple of Paul's. He was the son of a Christian mother and a Greek father. Timothy became a disciple of Paul on his second missionary journey. Paul sent Timothy to Macedonia before his third missionary tour. Timothy returned with Paul at the end of that tour. Paul and Timothy were intimate and trusting friends. Paul's first and second letter to Timothy and his letter to Titus are known as the "Pastoral Epistles." St. Thomas Aquinas named them the "Pastoral Epistles" in the thirteenth century. "They are cast as letters from Paul to his associates Timothy and Titus about how they should conduct their ministry as 'elders' of local churches."[9] They are similar in theology, content, and style. Some scholars question Pauline authorship, as the epistles seem to reflect a much later, more refined hierarchical church structure. Those who believe that Paul is the author of the epistles suggest that the letters are consistent with Pauline rhetoric and theology. And they believe that the letters can be attributed to the period following his captivity, in which he was concerned with preserving theology and building and strengthening the developing churches. The Pontifical Biblical Commission of 1913 affirmed Pauline authorship. There is, nevertheless, overwhelming scholarly evidence to the contrary.

2 Timothy is very different from 1 Timothy and Titus. The latter are more concerned with church organization and governance. The former portrays a suffering Paul—an imprisoned, ready-to-be executed Paul who continues to preach the gospel.

Today's Pericope: The first verse of today's reading exhorts Timothy to endure, to challenge false teaching, and to preach the gospel with a vengeance. Paul is exalted as a model to follow in pursuit of that goal. Paul is a model for all church leaders "who by their steadfast preaching will be a bulwark against false teaching."[10]

Drawing upon the "call" theme in today's first reading, the letter to Timothy reminds the reader that those who respond to the call of God can expect suffering. Paul demonstrated steadfast faithfulness and tenacity in the face of suffering and persecution. He suffered because of false teaching, heresies, and political persecution. Verses six through eight read like a deathbed farewell to his beloved community. His words are "to be cherished, remembered, and reflected upon. They are a beacon for life and an endless source of encouragement."[11] Paul heralded the centrality of Christ

[7] *PL,* 42.
[8] *DL* (II), 74.

[9] *RNT,* 281.
[10] *PE,* 37.
[11] Ibid., 38.

crucified. The author of Timothy exalts *Christ who conquered sin and death.* Christ freely offers the grace to overcome and endure in the midst of trials, tribulations, sin, and death.

Gospel
Matthew 17:1–9

Jesus was transfigured on Mount Tabor.

STEP 1
NAMING ONE'S EXPERIENCE

What were your first impressions? What was your first response? What grabbed your attention? How did you feel?

Each person names his or her initial impression. Statements should be brief. No reasons should be given at this time. All simply listen without agreeing or disagreeing.

STEP 2
UNDERSTANDING

In a brief statement, what do you think this gospel is trying to convey?

STEP 3
INPUT FROM VISION/STORY/TRADITION

Liturgical Context

The liturgies of the first two Sundays of Lent date back to the fourth century, making them the oldest lenten observance. From the fourth until the mid-sixth century, Lent was the beginning of the liturgical year and the continuous reading of the Bible.[12] Abraham, the father of Jewish, Muslim, and Christian believers is remembered every Second Sunday of Lent. Abraham was so important to the ancient writers that thirteen chapters were devoted to his life, deeds, and story. Today's scriptures celebrate the call of Abraham. He is a reminder for believers of all generations that each person is called by God and has a role in history's continuous drama.

The blessing given to Abraham was extended to all generations. This blessing is remembered and actualized in the person and mission of Jesus Christ. Abraham is a reminder for us today that it is Christ Jesus who blesses us with "every spiritual blessing in the heavens" (Eph 1:3).

With Abraham was born the People of God. God formed a people to be his own, a chosen race, a holy people, a people set apart to participate in God's own purposes. God was present to Israel. We continue to celebrate that presence in the community of believers today.

The story of the Lord's transfiguration is the gospel for the Second Sunday of Lent. All three gospels place this event immediately after Peter's confession of Jesus, the prediction of his death and passion, the cost of discipleship, and the promise of the parousia. However, the liturgy for this Sunday does not address those themes. The transfiguration event stands on its own, for its own sake and meaning, as a Sunday in Lent. The carry-over of these passages into a liturgical context is not contrary to the spirit of the gospel, however.

> With an unerring instinct, the Lenten liturgy proposes the mystery of Jesus' transfiguration to the contemplation of the faithful who are slowly moving toward the feast of Easter, that is, toward the mysteries—apparently separated but forming a deep unity—of the passion and the resurrection. The liturgy thus transposes the teaching that the three Synoptic Gospels sought to impart.[13]

The Second Sunday of Lent and the transfiguration gospel are intended to accompany the church on our own ascent to Jerusalem and the resurrec-

[12]*DL* (II), 40.

[13]X. Leon-Daffier, "La Transfiguration de Jesus (Mt. 17, 1–9)," *Assemble du Seigneur,* St. series, No 28 (Brutes: Publications de Saint-André, 1962) 27, in *DL* (II), 76.

tion of Easter. The transfiguration serves as a shining beacon of hope to strengthen the church and increase its zeal as it follows Christ to the cross and subsequent glory.[14]

"The mystery of the transfiguration concerns the entire Church—all Christians! The voice is addressed to us with a particular force during Lent when the insistent call to conversion resounds."[15]

The preface for today's liturgy reminds us of the importance of this event. "He had wanted to teach them through the Law and the Prophets that the promised Christ had first to suffer and so come to the glory of his resurrection" (Preface: Second Sunday of Lent). The transfiguration was intended to strengthen the disciples for the ominous trial that lay just beyond the horizon. It was also a message of hope to believers that they would one day share in the glory Christ revealed on that high mountain. This hope is reflected in the "Opening Prayer": "Enlighten us with your word, that we may find the way to your glory"; and in the "Prayer After Communion": "Lord we give you thanks for these holy mysteries which bring to us here on earth, a share in the life to come...."

Gospel Exegesis

The facilitator gives input regarding what critical biblical scholarship has to say about this text. The input includes insights as to how people would have heard the gospel in Jesus' time.

The awesome transfiguration. What was going on? On the surface it appears so surrealistic that it is natural fodder for those prone to be skeptical. Yet the event is found in all three synoptic gospels—a sure sign that the early Christian communities accepted its complete authenticity.

In Mark's gospel, Jesus' identity was constantly in question. The transfiguration was to expand the disciples' understanding of Jesus. It called for a response of obedience, even in the midst of their lack of understanding.

[14]*DL* (II), 76.
[15]Ibid, 79.

Luke posited the event as an experience for both Jesus and his disciples.[16] Luke does not use the same language of transfiguration utilized by Mark and Matthew. Only Luke relates the conversation between Jesus and the guests. Moses and Elijah pointed to Jesus' coming exodus. Jesus would lead the people to freedom, just as a previous generation had once been led. Luke's event proclaimed Jesus as a prophet "great in word and deed"[17] who would suffer and later be vindicated by God. Jesus stood on the threshold of the new, final age. Luke affirms Jesus as Messiah and reminds the disciples of the sobering implications of that reality: suffering, death, glory. The disciples would ultimately follow the same path.

Matthew's version is an "in-house" experience for the benefit of the three disciples. Matthew exalts Jesus as Lord and throughout the gospel is concerned with showing Jesus' superiority to Moses. Moses' and Elijah's part in this one-act encounter demonstrates that Jesus superseded and was the fulfillment of the Law and the Prophets.[18] Matthew insists that disciples should hear, respond, and act on the word of Jesus. Matthew's disciples do not misunderstand. They listen to him.

Matthew calls the event a "vision."[19] This is not to be confused with the paranormal phenomena of the *X-Files* genre, nor is it to be reduced to an inner psycho-spiritual experience (since there are "four persons presented as independent witnesses"[20]). Douglas Hare suggests that Matthew's "vision" refers to God's gift of being able to see what otherwise would have been impossible for mortal perception. The disciples were gifted with such sight.

Altered states of consciousness, like visions and dreams, were not and are not uncommon human experiences in Mediterranean cultures.[21] Our pragmatic "show me" society looks askance at such

[16]Barbara E. Reid, O.P., "Transfiguration," *CPDBT,* 1013.
[17]Ibid.
[18]Ibid.
[19]In the Acts of the Apostles (7:31) Luke used the same word, *sight,* when referring to Moses' experience of the burning bush.
[20]*MI,* 198.
[21]*CWJ,* 53.

phenomena. However, Jesus and his disciples experienced just such a vision. There is much to learn from it. Jesus was considered a disgrace in many circles of his community. The transfigured Jesus experienced a reversal and an advent. While not a parable, the story's meaning functions like a parable. The disgraced Jesus finds favor with the Father and communes with him. It is the ultimate reversal of fortunes and the advent [manifestation] of God's presence and favor. The one who was shamed was vindicated by the Father. Through this inter-communication with his Father, Jesus was immersed in a love that would assure him of exoneration.

The cross was a stumbling block for many earlier believers. If Jesus was really the Messiah, how could the Lord God have forsaken him? According to John Pilch, the transfiguration shows unequivocally that God no more abandoned Jesus than he did his predecessor, Moses. Jesus trusted his Father against all odds. When the world thought of him as dwelling in shame and disgrace, Jesus trusted his Father. Believers are to do no less. We are to trust God; we are to be subject to the Lordship of Christ, the new Moses and Lawgiver.

It is generally believed that the mountain in the story is Mount Tabor in southern Galilee. "The high mountain symbolizes the border zone between earth and heaven, between the material and the spiritual."[22] As one who stood atop that mountain on the feast of the transfiguration, I can readily understand the allegory. The visitor stands transfixed as the panoramic lushness of the valley glistens like the jewels that adorn the new and eternal city, the heavenly Jerusalem. I felt I could reach out and touch the heavenly realm, which seemed at a mere arm's length!

In the doctrine of later generations, the transfiguration was understandably interpreted as the revelation of Christ's divinity. However, the first communities were not so developed in their theology. Matthew's community understood the transfiguration as a proclamation of Jesus as Messiah.

[22]Ibid.

David Garland points out to his readers that the transfiguration is a preview of Christ's resurrected glory and rule from the heavenly throne. On the holy mountain of authority he will rule heaven and earth. It foreshadows the resurrection.

Moses and Elijah are integral to the scene. Moses foretold a prophet that would one day reveal God's will to the world. Elijah was understood as a precursor to the day of the final eschaton. Both characters signal the world that the last age has finally arrived.

True to form, the impetuous Peter responds according to his limited human perspective. He is cut short by the Divine Voice. The disciples were afraid of the Voice—a sign of "Jesus' supreme teaching authority."[23] Jesus touched them and invited them to rise, and in so doing foreshadowed their own resurrection. "Jesus comes forward and soothes their terror with a healing touch: 'Stand up, do not be afraid.' In Jesus divine majesty and gentle compassion meet."[24]

David Garland reminds us of the paradox of the moment. Jesus, on this mountain, is surrounded by hero-saints of old. On the hill of Golgotha he will be surrounded by criminals. On this holy mountain Jesus' clothes shine brilliantly. On the hill of Golgotha they are torn from his body in disgrace. The Divine Voice heralds Jesus as Son. His executioners do the same at his murder.

The vision of transcendent glory was to be balanced with the specter of future suffering. There can be no resurrection, no power from on high, to rule supreme over the earth in resurrected glory without the cross. "His suffering was part and parcel of his glory."[25]

Proclaim the gospel again.

Sometimes we gain new insights when we hear the text after the interpretation has been given. Someone from the group proclaims the gospel a second time.

[23]*RM,* 183.
[24]*IM,* 171.
[25]Ibid., 184.

Step 4
Testing

Conversation with the Liturgy and the Scriptures

Test your original understanding in dialogue with the text.

(You might consider breaking into smaller groups.)

How do you feel about these scriptures? How does your original understanding compare with what we just shared? Were there any new insights for you? How does this story speak to your life?

Sharing Life Experience

Participants share an experience from their lives that connects with the biblical interpretation just shared.

> *Today's liturgy is a celebration of call and response. Lent is a time for me to look within to see where I need to grow as I prepare to renew my baptismal promises at Easter. Abraham was called and in a grand way responded to the call. As a result, an entire nation was formed. He had a pivotal role in salvation history. I will not be leading any great nations in the near future, but I* will *be called upon to bring Christ to my own world—wherever that may be.*
>
> *Jesus showed his disciples the incredible glory of God, the One whom we can quite confidently put our trust in—no matter what. This is a God who vindicates those who are shamed. This is a God who reveals the mysteries of the heavens to a mere clod like Peter. Thank God for Peter. He truly was a clod, the proverbial bull in a china closet. But he jumped into his relationship with Jesus with both feet. He was not afraid to risk or to make a mistake. He was so zealous that he often got it wrong. Yet he was named rock, and told to found an entire church on this rock!*
>
> *Today's liturgy reminds me that the phone is ringing and God is on the other end of the line. He continues to invite me into deeper relationship. He continues to ask that I follow his will for my life. I know that the next few years will bring many changes in my life: empty nest, career shifts, and the like. My inclination is to stay where I am, where it is safe and comfortable. (A pitched tent surrounded by a cloud of brilliant light sounds quite appealing.) Yet God continues to invite me into uncharted waters. He takes me by the hand and asks if I will take the plunge and jump in with both feet.*
>
> *Once, when the call was to move to Florida, I said, "No, we have a house to sell." It was disposed of in three weeks and we were in Florida in four. Once the call was to be a teacher. I said, "No, I am not bold enough." Now I'm bold enough. I recently heard the call to ignore what I had earlier thought the call was, and in so doing averted a major transitional move to another state. In his most amused tone of voice I heard God say, "Just kidding—that was a test!"*
>
> *The transfiguration reminds me that I share God's wonderful glory and his life. But paradoxically, I share his suffering too. Today Jesus reminds me of who I am and where I am headed. He asks me not to get so caught up in pitching my tent that I forget to go where I am sent and needed. It is a journey with many roadblocks, dangers, sorrows, and joys. The transfiguration reminds me that I can make it all the way—even when the late-night calls come in regarding the life and death emergencies of our teenage children, even when there is too much month left after the money has run out, even when the body has decided to go downhill, and when, no matter how well-intentioned I might be, I sometimes find myself misunderstood or misjudged. Peter is a reminder that everything will be okay if I am faithful and sincere about the conversion Jesus invites in my life. If Peter didn't get it perfectly, at least he got it! Someone once said that anything worth doing is worth doing poorly. For me that phrase reads like a fingernail in slow motion across a blackboard! But it is so true. Living the Christ-life is worth doing—even when I fall short. It is okay to stumble through the ambiguities of life as long as I faithfully stay in the struggle. Today's liturgy gives me hope to set out on the trail again—to be willing to risk, to live with and in the midst of the passion and beyond the passion of Jesus Christ.*
>
> *No doubt Jesus was preparing his friends to go out and do as he was about to do—to die for the world. When I remember that my mission as a baptized person is to lay down my life for others, I thank God for the eucharist I share each Sunday with the Body of Christ. It is a taste of that future banquet—the future glory that sustains us in this earthly reality. The catechism tells us that eucharist commits us to*

the poor. No doubt the poor were on Christ's shoulders at Calvary.

There is a young man, very connected to our parish, who gave up a lucrative job as an engineer in a leading computer firm to create and develop a water purifying system for people in underdeveloped Third World countries. It required incredible trust. There were times he questioned the call. His initial fervor and assurance led him through the murky time of testing. Today his purifying system is all over the Third World. His life, and consequently the life of his family, changed drastically. I am not presently being called to the Third World. But I am called to be a voice for and to maintain an option for the poor. I am called to remember that ministry is participation in the death and resurrection of Jesus for the sins of the world. Will I stand firm when the ultimate test comes my way? Please God, strengthen me like you strengthened Abraham and Peter.

All share their life experience.

What was Matthew trying to tell his community? What does he have to say to your community and to you today? How does the story of Abraham and the transfiguration of Jesus reflect God's promise to his people [biblical theme of covenant], God's desire to create a new heart in us [creation], God's desire to free us from the slavery of sin [exodus], and God's presence in our lives [community]?

What difference do these readings make in your life? And in the life of the community? What are the implications? Do you still feel the same way about this text as when you began? How does this conversation with the scriptures and the liturgy invite growth and change in your life? What are the unredeemed areas that cry out for such growth and change? How do these scriptures invite you to respond to the needs of others?

STEP 5
DECISION

The gospel demands a response.

What is the challenge of this liturgy for your community? In what way does your community need to grow in the fullness of today's scriptures? In what concrete ways might your parish be invited to respond? How are you personally challenged and what will be your personal response to today's liturgy? What decision for change are you willing to make?

Pastoral Considerations: In what way are you and your parish responding to the lenten disciplines of prayer, fasting, and almsgiving? [See lenten Overview] What issues of social justice need the attention of your community? Are there any situations in your parish, civic community, state, or national political scene that call for a gospel voice? How are the needs of the poor in your area being addressed? In what way is your community responding to the needs of the sick, the lonely, the grieving, and the marginalized? What about multicultural issues? Will your community be gathering for the celebration of the sacrament of reconciliation? If not, perhaps you might celebrate a *non-sacramental* celebration of reconciliation found in the Rite of Penance. This may be presided over by a non-ordained person.

Christian Initiation: The RCIA designates the Second Sunday of Lent for the optional penitential rite for baptized candidates. The elect continue to be dismissed to break open the Sunday scriptures, but their period of catechesis is officially over. The First Sunday of Lent began their process of purification and enlightenment. This week the elect gather to prepare to celebrate the first scrutiny next week. Catechumens who will not be baptized at the Easter Vigil continue to be dismissed from the Sunday liturgy and participate in extended catechesis.

DOCTRINAL ISSUES

What church truth/teaching/doctrinal issue could be drawn from the gospel for the Second Sunday of Lent?

Participants suggest possible doctrinal themes that flow from the readings.

Possible Doctrinal Themes

Transfiguration, conversion, prayer, fasting and almsgiving, call and response, call of baptism, sin, paschal mystery, repentance and reconciliation

Present the doctrinal material at this time.

1. The facilitator gives input on a particular doctrinal issue of his/her prior choosing. OR
2. The group chooses a doctrinal issue from the list they created. They read together from the Doctrinal Appendix.

(The doctrinal issues are found in the Doctrinal Appendix in the back of this workbook. If you are choosing an issue from this resource, please refer to it now.)

Reflection questions centered around the chosen doctrinal theme can be found at the end of each topic in the Doctrinal Appendix. The questions are based on the five-step reflection process. If you choose a topic not included in the Doctrinal Appendix, craft your own questions according to the same five-step process.

Following the reflection questions you will be reminded to return to chapter 7, "Preparing the Catechetical Session," to assist you in crafting your own session.

Closing Prayer

Father, all powerful and ever-living God,
we do well always and everywhere to give you thanks
through Jesus Christ our Lord.
On your holy mountain he revealed himself in glory
in the presence of his disciples.
He had already prepared them for his approaching death.
He wanted to teach them through the Law and the Prophets
that the promised Christ had to first suffer
and so come to the glory of his resurrection.
In our unending joy we echo on earth
the song of the angels in heaven
as they praise your glory forever.[26]

[26]Roman Missal, *Preface 13: Transfiguration, Second Sunday of Lent.*

Third Sunday of Lent

Environment

Today's liturgy contains strong images of water:

The Entrance Antiphon: "I will pour clean water on you and wash away all your sins..."
The First Reading: "Yahweh instructed Moses to strike the rock and water flowed..."
The Gospel: "But whoever drinks the water I give will never be thirsty..."
The Communion Rite: "Whoever drinks the water I give...will have a spring inside..."

Imaginative display of this powerful symbol in the catechetical environment might be appropriate for today's session.

INTRODUCTORY RITES

Opening Song (or Entrance Antiphon)

I will prove my holiness through you. I will gather you from the ends of the earth; I will pour clean water on you and wash away all your sins. I will give you a new spirit within you, says the Lord. (Ez 36:23–26)[1]

Opening Prayer

The facilitator of the session may lead the prayer. Others in the group may be asked to proclaim the readings.

Let us pray
[to the Father and ask him
to form a new heart within us]

Pause for silent prayer.

God of all compassion, Father of all goodness,
to heal the wounds our sins and selfishness bring upon us
you bid us turn to fasting, prayer, and sharing with our brothers.
We acknowledge our sinfulness, our guilt is ever before us:
when our weakness causes discouragement,
let your compassion fill us with hope
and lead us through a Lent of repentance
to the beauty of Easter joy.
Grant this through Christ, our Lord.[2]

LITURGY OF THE WORD

Let us listen to God's word.

The readings are proclaimed

First Reading
Exodus 17:3–7

Today's reading refers to Israel's defining event: the exodus and the wanderings in the desert. Moses was instructed to strike the rock and water sprang forth. Water was a powerful symbol of God's activity. Water was a sign of life. At creation God hovered over the waters and breathed life into them. Water was a sign of destruction, purification, and God's awesome power. God sent down the rain for forty days and forty nights and submerged the earth because of the sin of human beings. Water was a sign of salvation. When the Israelites thirsted in the desert, water flowed through the power of God. In an arid land, water is an absolute need. Water is a symbol of liberation and passage from death to life. God held back the water for the Israelites to pass through.

Through the water sign there is allusion to the sacraments: water as salvation; water as sign of baptism. Lent is both penitential and baptismal in nature. The first reading touches on both themes.

The psalm for this liturgy exhorts us "not to harden our hearts." Meribah and Massah were the places where the people had sinned. This first reading reminds us of our total dependence on the God who saves, Christ who liberates, and the Spirit who leads us to the life-giving water.

---

[1]Third Sunday of Lent: "Entrance Antiphon," *The Sacramentary.*

[2]Third Sunday of Lent: "Alternative Opening Prayer," *The Sacramentary.*

Responsorial Psalm
Psalm 95

This psalm was chosen for its connection to the first reading. It especially helps focus the meaning for the first reading: "Harden not your hearts."

Second Reading
Romans 5:1–2, 5–8

Up to this point in his letter to the Romans, Paul has expressed his assurance that human beings were justified through the redeeming death of Christ. Today's pericope is concerned with the implications of our justification. Since we are justified, we share the peace of Christ. Our faith in the paschal mystery gives us free access to God's grace as we wait in hope for our future glory. Paul reminds us that the Spirit continues to shower us with the living, ever-present love of God. Reginald Fuller maintains that Paul related justification to the indwelling of the Spirit. The Spirit of God initiates and continues the work of healing transformation within those the Spirit justifies. Each person is thus raised to a state of created grace. God pours out gratuitous love through the gift of the Spirit and through the sacrifice on the cross by God's Son, Jesus Christ. The veil of the curtain was torn at the death of Jesus and sinners were given access to God. That access is the Spirit of God. The gift of the cross is God's Holy Spirit dwelling within human beings to transform them into the elevated state they were destined to attain. We also hear in Paul's letter the roots of our belief in the Holy Trinity.

Gospel
John 4:5–42

Jesus encounters the woman of Samaria.

Step 1
Naming One's Experience

What were your first impressions? What was your first response? What grabbed your attention? How did you feel?

Each person names his or her initial impression. Statements should be brief. No reasons should be given at this time. All simply listen without agreeing or disagreeing.

Step 2
Understanding

In a brief statement, what do you think this gospel is trying to convey?

Step 3
Input from Vision/Story/Tradition

Liturgical Context

As stated in the lenten overview, the Johannine gospels for the three Sundays of Cycle A were used as immediate preparation for those preparing for baptism. Thematically they address the baptismal issues and symbols of water, light, and the passage from death into life. Today's readings are viewed through the lens of baptismal preparation.

The Communion Antiphon (from today's gospel) serves as a summary text for today's liturgy: "Whoever drinks the water that I shall give . . . will have a spring inside . . . welling up for eternal life" (Jn 4:13–14). Today's readings ask us where the areas of sin reside in our society, in the world, in the church, and in our personal lives. Where and how do we thirst? Where in our society, in the church, and in our personal lives, is there a need for Christ's healing liberation? When we scrutinize sin through the eyes of faith, Christ refreshes us and gives us the water of new life that springs up as a fountain within us.

Scrutinies

The Cycle A readings are designated for use when there are catechumens preparing for initiation at the Easter Vigil. In the Rite of Christian Initiation of Adults, Lent coincides with the period of *purification and enlightenment.* It is a period of final preparation for the elect. They (along with the entire church) are to seriously discern the areas of sin and weakness [purification] and allow those areas to be healed and illumined by Christ, the Liberator [enlightenment]. The church celebrates three scrutinies with the elect beginning on the Third Sunday of Lent. Scrutinies are intended to heal what is weak, defective, and sinful, to protect the elect from temptation, and to strengthen them in Christ (RCIA, #141–146). The magnitude of sin in all its forms—personal, social, and systemic—is laid bare. The elect are filled with the presence of Christ the Liberator who won the victory over evil and its consequences. God the Father is invoked and asked for strength and protection in the trinitarian prayer of exorcism. "Through the power of the Holy Spirit (the epicletic action of the laying on of hands), Jesus exercises his healing and liberating power over the effects of evil. Thus, the power and presence of Christ in word and exorcism are the primary symbols of the scrutinies." Preparation for the elect's celebration of the scrutinies includes reflection upon the scriptures from today's readings. The elect seek to uncover the many layers of sin as well as to reflect upon the ultimate source of power and grace. They explore the question, "Where does sin exist and where is liberation needed in the world, in the community, and in my life?" They search the scrutiny gospel for ways that Christ, the great Liberator, is proclaimed and imaged. They come to the scrutiny as expectant, vulnerable, and willing vessels eager to approach the freedom that awaits them.

While scrutinies are celebrated with the elect, they are also for the entire church. We and the elect are on this journey toward liberation and wholeness together. The scrutinies prepare the elect for the sacraments of initiation and they serve as preparation for our own recommitment to the baptismal promises we will profess anew at Easter.

Presentation of the Creed

The presentation of the creed generally takes place during the week following the first scrutiny, "preferably in the presence of a community of the faithful, within Mass after the homily" (RCIA, #157). The elect are to commit the creed to memory and profess it publicly prior to their official profession of faith at their baptism (RCIA, #148). The creed and the Lord's Prayer have always been considered central to Christian faith and prayer. The creed is intended to enlighten the elect with the light of faith. God's wondrous salvation deeds (of which the human race is beneficiary) are professed. The RCIA does allow the presentations to take place during the catechumenate period as the season of Lent is rather brief and packed with multiple spiritual riches. Thus, some parishes celebrate and anticipate the presentations with their catechumens before Lent.

Gospel Exegesis

The facilitator gives input regarding what critical biblical scholarship has to say about this text. The input includes insights as to how people would have heard the gospel in Jesus' time.

The exegesis for the gospel of the Samaritan woman at the well will utilize the insights of Sandra Schneider, a biblical scholar. In my opinion, her interpretation most thoroughly uncovers the heart and soul, not only of the text, but of its place in baptismal and lenten catechesis. At a recent workshop, Donald Senior, one of this country's most respected biblical scholars, asserted that the scholarly work of Schneider in relation to this gospel is masterful and right on the mark. He was surprised that no one had stumbled across it before. He surmised that it was because most biblical scholars have been male. As male members of the community, they approach the texts primarily with a masculine hermeneutic. Biblical texts are to be interpreted not only through the science of biblical criticism, but also through the discerning wisdom of the community. For most of its history, the church has not had the privilege of the discernment of half of her members—the female half.[3] The scholar further noted that the feminine consciousness has not had the opportunity to interpret the texts. That is presently chang-

[3]Barbara Reid, in her book, *Choosing the Better Part* (Collegeville: The Liturgical Press, 1996), describes the vision that best informs the exegesis for this liturgy. "Patriarchy is 'any system, organization, or institution in which the men own, administer, shape, or control a major portion of all the facets of society.' [Joan Chittister, "Yesterday's Dangerous Vision: Christian Feminism in the Catholic Church," *Sojourners* (July 1987): 18.] The world of Jesus was a patriarchal world, as is our own, although that is beginning to change. Feminism, as a response to patriarchy, 'is a commitment to the humanity, dignity, and equality of all persons to such a degree that one is willing to work for changes in structures and in relationship patterns so that these occur to the

ing with the emergence of many female biblical scholars.

Schneider approaches the text with a hermeneutic of suspicion.[4] She confronts the story, suspicious of its obvious moral dilemma: a woman chastised for her sexual indiscretions. It appears as though Schneider side-steps the patriarchal literal meaning, turning instead to the images, symbols, and typology common to the time and to the Johannine community, in order to appropriate a more inclusive interpretation.

Some scholars suggest that the story of the Samaritan woman probably was not an historical story. The story served as legitimization "of the Samaritan mission in John's community; to establish full equality between Samaritan and Jewish Christians, and to affirm Jewish legitimacy as bearer of covenant faith but with a surprising recognition of the essential validity of Samaritan faith and inclusion in the covenant."[5]

Samaria was a territory north of Jerusalem. It was part of the Assyrian and Persian empire in 721–612 B.C.E. The Assyrians imported foreign colonists and deported many of Samaria's native citizens; others sought refuge in Judea. A Yahwism influenced by other religions developed that led to animosity from traditional Jews. The bad feeling between the two groups was further exacerbated when the Samaritans offered to help rebuild the temple after the exile and were turned down by their Jewish brothers and sisters. This added fuel to the already smoldering fires of resentment. Another revolt forced the Samaritans to move to Shechem where they built a temple on Mount Gerizim.[6] Samaritans anticipated a prophet like Moses who would restore worship on Mount Gerizim in northern Israel. The Jews, on the other hand, believed the messiah would be a descendant of David who would restore worship in the Jerusalem temple. It is obvious that resentments ran deep and permeated the consciousness of the two peoples. They were bitter enemies.

In the story of the Samaritan woman, it is the unspoken text between the lines that captures our attention and imagination. The woman is nameless. Nameless people in scripture often represent more than the literal eye can see, especially in John's gospel (the beloved disciple, the royal official, the paralytic at the pool, and the man born blind). This woman is a symbolic figure who represents the Samaritan people and the New Israel (the new kingdom).

The woman was at a well—not just any well, but a famous well. Wells were important symbolic places in biblical literature. Important events in salvation history began with unions initiated at famous wells. Rebecca was found for Isaac at a well; Rachel met Jacob at the very well in this story. Before this scene in John's gospel, at the wedding in Cana, Jesus was called the new Bridegroom. Our attention in this reading, then, turns to Jesus, the new Bridegroom, present at the well of famous weddings to "claim Samaria as beloved in the New Israel."[7]

There is more to consider about the heroine of the story. She was a woman and a Samaritan, the lowest on society's totem pole. Even the pagans hated Samaritans. She was an outcast's outcast! Yet this outcast, woman and Samaritan, encountered Christ. Jesus, a Jew, not only spoke to her and noticed her, but he drank from her bucket (making him ritually unclean). The woman was trained by her culture to believe she was worthless. Yet this Jew offered her acceptance, dignity, compassion, a way out, and a way in! Donald Senior suggests that

---

equal good of all' (Chittister, 18)....Feminism advocates a community of equals that provides for all the members, women and men alike, to use their God-given gifts to the benefit of all. Christian feminists are women and men committed to eliminating sexism in their relations with one another, in the structures of their faith communities and in society. They see this as a work of justice that is truly faithful to the teaching and life of Jesus...." (Reid, 7)

[4]"...A hermeneutic of suspicion recognizes that the biblical texts have been written, for the most part, by men, for men, and about men, and that they serve the interests of patriarchy. One who reads with a hermeneutic of suspicion is wary that the text can be oppressive for women. This does not deny the inspiration of Scripture, but recognizes the limitations of the human authors that set forth God's word." (Reid, 9)

[5]*EGW*, 306.

[6]For further information, refer to: Robert F. O'Toole, S.J., "Samaria/Samaritan," in *CPDBT*, 872–873.

[7]*EGW*, 306.

this woman has much more to teach us than a lesson on morality. It is the story between the lines we dare to hear.

During the exile the Samaritans remained faithful to Yahweh, but became inculturated by their conquerors. While they still loved Yahweh, they nevertheless dabbled in the local worship of the Samaritan gods. The result was that Jews hated the Samaritans whom they judged unfaithful. Samaritans were outcasts and ritually unclean. No good Jew would drink from this woman's bucket. Yet Jesus drank from her bucket. In his encounter with her, Jesus welcomed the lost and included the sinner, the outsider.

She entered into a theological discussion with him. She interrogated him about his action toward her. He had broken Jewish tradition by speaking to her (a woman) and by using the same utensils she had used. She was dumbfounded. Samaritans would have been shocked to hear anyone claiming to be on the same plane as their patriarch Jacob who had given the well to Israel in the first place. Jesus acknowledged Samaria's rightful place in salvation history while still affirming Yahweh's covenant with the Jews. Yet he made it very clear that they had each missed the boat—both the Jews and the Samaritans. Neither had a monopoly on the truth. God was doing something new. While defending the Jewish claim to the covenant tradition, Jesus made no distinctions regarding the *territory* people worshiped in. What was important was the worship Jesus would inaugurate as messiah—worship in spirit and truth, authentic worship. The gospel would guide the worship. In the new kingdom people would live in biblical justice, in right relationship with God. They would live the law of love.

Centered in the middle of Jesus' theological discussion with the woman is his scrutiny of her adulterous liaisons—her five husbands. That she had had five husbands was unusual in the religious society of her day. "Either this is totally out of place, a trivial bit of moralism or even a shallow display of preternatural knowledge on the part of Jesus, or it is an integral part of this highly theological exchange."[8] This story is about the *inclusion* of Samaria into the New Israel. Jesus scrutinized the woman's (Samaria's) adulterous (idolatrous) union with the gods of the five tribes. "Jesus' declaration that Samaria 'has no husband' is a classic prophetic denunciation of false worship, like Hosea's oracle in which the prophet expresses God's sentiment toward unfaithful Israel" (Hosea 2:2).[9] Thus, Jesus suggests that Samaria's relationship to Yahweh in the past was colored by her adulterous flirtations with other gods. Jesus scrutinized the false worship, named the sin, and invited repentance as he included Samaria in his New Israel.

At this wedding well, in broad daylight and at high noon so that all could see, Jesus, the new *Bridegroom*, wed Samaria and included her in the kingdom.[10] "Now the new Bridegroom who assumes the role of Yahweh, bridegroom of ancient Israel, comes to claim Samaria as an integral part of the New Israel, namely, the Christian community and specifically the Johannine community."[11]

What, then, was the woman's response? She recognized Jesus for who he was, messiah and lord. She could do no less than "go and tell everyone . . . and they all came to believe on her testimony." She was the first evangelist and the only person to bring an entire group of people to faith in Jesus. No wonder women had an important ministerial role in John's community.[12]

The implications? Jesus extended reconciliation, inclusion, and healing to alienated Samaria; everyone is included in the reign of God. Jesus shared this revelation with a woman—society's outcast (then and in many places today).[13] He treated her as he would have treated any member of his soci-

[8]*RT,* 190.

[9]Ibid.

[10]Contrast the woman coming to the well at high noon, in the light of day for all to see, with Nicodemus, who came in the dead of night. John's gospel is filled with the metaphor of night and day, light and darkness.

[11]*RT,* 187.

[12]See Sixteenth Sunday in Ordinary Time: the story of Martha and Mary.

[13]At the time of Christ, in order for something to be attested and affirmed, it had to be verified in a court of law. I find it very interesting that first-hand testimony and events often occurred to people who could not legally witness to them in the courts. Women could not serve as verifiable

ety—with respect and dignity. We are, by extension, invited to cast aside any idols of our making that get in the way of our authentic worship of God, and we are to welcome all who are on the bottom rung of society.

This is a story about the kingdom in which there are no outcasts and no strangers, only repentant, welcomed sinners. "In summary, the entire dialogue between Jesus and the woman is the 'wooing' of Samaria to full covenant fidelity in the New Israel by Jesus, the New Bridegroom. It has nothing to do with the woman's private moral life, but with the covenant life of the community. Nowhere in the fourth gospel is there a dialogue of such theological depth and intensity."[14]

In light of the celebration of the scrutinies, this gospel helps us name the social and personal sin that keeps us from an intimate relationship with God. We are reminded that it is God who names our sin, who scrutinizes the evil in our lives, and who invites us to turn away from anything (our personal and corporate idols) that keeps us from a full liberated life in Christ. Today's liturgy highlights the evil of exclusion on any level: in our personal lives, in our society, and in our religious structures. It demands that we ask the questions: *Who is out?* and *Who is in?* Like the woman, we are to go out and invite others in. Today's gospel invites *metanoia*—a complete turning away *from* sin *toward* the Healer, Liberator, Victor, and One who offers living water through the refreshing waters of baptism. This is the victory Christ holds out to us in today's liturgy.

witnesses unless the issue pertained to a household matter. Shepherds were also not allowed to testify as valid witnesses, since they were considered too untrustworthy to give truthful testimony. Yet, is it not God's irony (or perhaps humor) that the two premier events of redemptive salvation were witnessed by people who, by human standards, were not able to verify or testify to what they had witnessed? Shepherds were the first to witness the Incarnation and a woman was first on the scene following the resurrection. Once again, God writes salvation history with crooked lines and refuses to be boxed in by humanity's standards of convention. In today's story, a woman experienced the messiah. Her experience and her story alone had the power to invite people to faith.

[14] *RT,* 191.

Proclaim the gospel again.

Sometimes we gain new insights when we hear the text after the interpretation has been given. Someone from the group proclaims the gospel a second time.

Step 4
Testing

Conversation with the Liturgy and the Scriptures

Test your original understanding in dialogue with the text.

(You might consider breaking into smaller groups.)

Were there any new insights? How do you feel? Comfortable or uncomfortable? Why? How does your original understanding of this story compare with what was just shared? How does this story speak to your life?

Sharing Life Experience

Participants share an experience from their lives that connects with the biblical interpretation just shared.

> *A few years ago I had an encounter with this scripture. It caught my attention, challenged my attitudes, and invited me to change. This story summoned me to let go of the idol I had made of "being right." I had mentally and spiritually excluded some folks who held different points of view than I. They were my outcasts. They were wrong and I was right. Of this I was certain! I had been hurt by them and was not willing to consider how I had excluded them as a group. After wrestling with the angel of this text, I was forced to look at my idol and at the people that I had cut off and excluded. Through an interesting process of not-so-gentle persuasions, the Lord God insisted that I offer a hand in reconciliation to a person that best represented those I had discarded. Our reconciliation began a lasting bond of friendship.*
>
> *This word is a powerful word for communities today. Yet it is a word that often invites the greatest challenge. Try though we may, there are still many excluded people in our communities. Our hierarchical structure excludes, our parish structures exclude,*

and our personal relationships are often exclusive. The gospel continues to invite us to scrutinize the areas of elusion, sin, and idolatry, and ask Christ, the liberator, to deliver us from evil.

All share their life experience.

What was John's message to his community? What are the implications for our communities today? Is there any situation in our community that needs to be enlightened by this gospel? In what way (if at all) did the experience of God's word:

1. affirm God's promise to be with us *(covenant)*
2. lead us through a death/resurrection experience in our attitudes *(exodus)*
3. speak to us as a community *(people of God)*
4. call us to new life *(creation)*?

Do we still feel the same way about this text as we did when we began? Has our original understanding been stretched, challenged, or affirmed?

STEP 5
DECISION

The gospel demands a response.

In what concrete way does this gospel call our parish to action in the church, parish, neighborhood, or world? Has this conversation with the exegesis changed or stretched my personal attitudes? What am I /we/community/parish called to do in response? What is one concrete action I will take this week as a response to what was learned and shared today?

DOCTRINAL ISSUES

What church truth/teaching/doctrinal issue could be drawn from the gospel for the Third Sunday in Lent?

Participants suggest possible doctrinal themes that flow from the readings.

Possible Doctrinal Themes

Grace and sin, baptism, social dimension of sin, Jesus the messiah, reconciliation

Present the doctrinal material at this time.

1. The facilitator gives input on a particular doctrinal issue of his/her prior choosing. OR
2. The group chooses a doctrinal issue from the list they created. They read together from the Doctrinal Appendix.

(The doctrinal issues are found in the Doctrinal Appendix in the back of this workbook. If you are choosing an issue from this resource, please refer to it now.)

Reflection questions centered around the chosen doctrinal theme can be found at the end of each topic in the Doctrinal Appendix. The questions are based on the five-step reflection process. If you choose a topic not included in the Doctrinal Appendix, craft your own questions according to the same five-step process.

Following the reflection questions you will be reminded to return to chapter 7, "Preparing the Catechetical Session," to assist you in crafting your own session.

Closing Prayer

First Scrutiny: Exorcism

All merciful Father,
through your Son you revealed your mercy
to the woman of Samaria;
and moved by that same care
you have offered salvation to all sinners.
Look favorably on these elect,
who desire to become your adopted children
through the power of your sacraments.
Free them from the slavery of sin,
and for Satan's crushing yoke
exchange the gentle yoke of Jesus.
Protect them in every danger,
That they may serve you faithfully in peace and joy
And render you thanks forever. Amen.

Laying on of hands

Hands outstretched over the elect:

Lord Jesus,
in your merciful wisdom

you touched the heart of the sinful woman
and taught her to worship the Father
in spirit and in truth.
Now, by your power,
free these elect from the cunning of Satan,
as they draw near to the fountain of living water.
Touch their hearts with the power of the Holy Spirit,
that they may come to know the Father
in true faith, which expresses itself in love,
for you live and reign for ever and ever.
Amen.[15]

[15]Prayer of Exorcism, "First Scrutiny," *RCIA*.

Fourth Sunday of Lent

Environment

Today's gospel speaks of Christ, the Light of the World. If the environment is not normally adorned with a light symbol, today would certainly be a day to incorporate a Christ candle.

INTRODUCTORY RITES

Opening Song (or Entrance Antiphon)

Rejoice, Jerusalem! Be glad for her, you who love her; rejoice with her, you who mourned for her, and you will find contentment at her consoling breast. (See Isaiah 66:10–11.)[1]

Opening Prayer

The facilitator of the session may lead the prayer. Others in the group may be asked to proclaim the readings.

Father, all powerful and ever-living God,
we do well always and everywhere to give you thanks
through Jesus Christ our Lord.

He came among us as a man,
to lead mankind from darkness
into the light of faith.

Through Adam's fall we were born slaves of sin,
but now through baptism in Christ
we are reborn as your adopted children.

Earth unites with heaven
to sing the new song of creation,
as we adore and praise you for ever:

Holy, holy, holy Lord, God of power and might,
heaven and earth are full of your glory.
Hosanna in the highest.
Blessed is he who comes in the name of the Lord.
Hosanna in the highest.
(Preface, Fourth Sunday of Lent)

[1]Fourth Sunday of Lent: "Entrance Antiphon," *The Sacramentary.*

LITURGY OF THE WORD

Let us listen to God's word.

The readings are proclaimed.

First Reading
1 Samuel 16:6–7, 10–13

In today's reading David is chosen to be king by Yahweh from among Jesse's sons. Throughout all of scripture, it is very clear that God's election is God's own. Humans can do nothing on their own merit to achieve it. God often painted history with crooked lines by choosing people to fulfill his designs who would normally have difficulty passing human scrutiny. David was the least likely character from among Jesse's sons.

Saul anointed David king, thereby signifying the abiding, and guiding presence of God's Spirit. "Anointing means to touch some person or thing with a substance (oil, water, blood, fat, mud) to effect a change, either external or internal."[2] To be anointed by the Lord as king meant that the person was commissioned for a special mission. The new designation required protection and respect. David's anointing also signaled that he was divinely elected and was thus deserving of divine protection.

Today's reading was perhaps chosen for its baptismal images: David was elected by God and anointed for a new life in Yahweh's service.

Responsorial Psalm
Psalm 23:1–3, 3–4, 5, 6

The reasons for the choice of this psalm are ambiguous. One scholar has suggested that it could have been used because of its vague reference to the anointing of David.

Second Reading
Ephesians 5:8–14

[2]John C. Endres, S.J., "Anointing," in *CPDBT,* 28.

Some question Pauline authorship of this letter. However, if Paul was the author, it was written around 60 C.E. This would correspond with Paul's stint in the Roman jail. The letter contains allusions to gnostic influences that were plaguing the first-century church. Chapters four through six describe the difference between the pagan and Christian way of life. It is the difference between life and death, light and darkness.

Today's subject is a primary theme of our Lenten reflection: conversion. The pericope suggests a complete metanoia—a turning away from all that is darkness into the marvelous light of Christ. Some suggest that today's letter was part of an ancient baptismal liturgy because of its use of the light and darkness baptismal metaphor.

Gospel
John 9:1–41

STEP 1
NAMING ONE'S EXPERIENCE

What were your first impressions? What was your first response? What grabbed your attention? How did you feel?

Each person names his or her initial impression. Statements should be brief. No reasons should be given at this time. All simply listen without agreeing or disagreeing.

STEP 2
UNDERSTANDING

In a brief statement, what do you think this gospel is trying to convey?

STEP 3
INPUT FROM VISION/STORY/TRADITION

Liturgical Context

The Fourth Sunday of Lent is highly charged with baptismal themes. Jesus healed the man born blind and then instructed him to wash in the pool of Siloam. The man came to believe in Jesus. On this Fourth Sunday, during the period of purification and enlightenment, the elect celebrate the second scrutiny. (Refer to the overview of Lent and Third Sunday of Lent, Cycle A for further explanation of the scrutinies.) We, along with the elect, seek enlightenment. "The early church referred to baptism as 'enlightenment' and spoke of the candidates as being enlightened."[3]

The three scrutiny gospels were used to prepare people for baptism when preparation lasted only three weeks. Today these readings are still used for penitential and baptismal preparation for the Easter sacraments. Jesus, Light of the World, is important catechesis for those preparing for enlightenment (baptism).

The first reading from Samuel, the anointing of David, may also be connected to baptism. The initiation corollaries are obvious. At baptism we are given (anointed with) the gift of the Holy Spirit. We are anointed priest, prophet, and king. "Baptism is a freely given call from God; it is a gift of the Spirit and brings participation in the royal priesthood of Christ."[4] In today's first reading, Saul anoints David king, symbolizing the presence of the Spirit in his life and mission. The anointing of David signals a changed reality for him. Baptism changes our reality—we change from children of the darkness to children of the light. (The second reading from Ephesians also points to today's baptismal focus when it speaks of those who had once lived in darkness but are now children of the light.) David was anointed for a special mission. Baptism anoints us for the reconciling, evangelizing mission of Jesus Christ. David's new identity entitled him to rights and privileges: he received divine protection and was respected. Through baptism we are protected from the snares of the devil and are entitled to rights and privileges as adopted daughters and sons of God. David's anointing was a sign of God's divine election. We, too, are baptized by God's divine election. We can do nothing on our own to merit salvation.

---

[3]*LY*, 102.
[4]Ibid., 103.

Today's liturgy is filled with anticipatory images of baptism as Easter fast approaches. The preface for this liturgy also speaks of being led out of darkness into the light. The prayer after communion seeks enlightenment from the light of the gospel.

Gospel Exegesis

The facilitator gives input regarding what critical biblical scholarship has to say about this text. The input includes insights as to how people would have heard the gospel in Jesus' time.

Today's gospel is a commentary on Jesus' earlier assertion that he is the Light of the World (Jn 8:12).[5] Jesus contrasts the growing vision of the blind man with the increasing blindness of the ones who claim they already see. This story is placed in the context of the controversies between Christians and the synagogue Jews in John's community. There are seven stories in John's gospel that serve to prove that Jesus was who he said he was—the messiah. They also attest to Jesus as the fulfillment of all prior Jewish worship (in this case, the water and light rituals of the Feast of Tabernacles), thus providing the rationale and the credence for the *new worship* of the Christian community. In other words, the stories gave permission to the Christian community to break away from the rituals of the past in order to embrace the new liturgy of Christ.

Jesus met the blind man after he left the temple area during the Feast of Tabernacles. It was a huge feast that attracted many pilgrims to Jerusalem. For a solid week there was great celebrating as all joyously waved their palm fronds.

The feast was at the end of the harvest. Booths had been erected and there was jubilant dancing, song, and festivity. The feast commemorated the entrance into the promised land and the future hope of the messiah at the end of the world. Priests would go to the pool of Siloam each day, draw a golden pitcher of water, and recite their ritual prayers. "Rivers of living water will flow from within him" (Jn 7:37–38). "I am the light of the world. Whoever follows me will not walk in darkness but will have the light of life" (8:12). They poured the water on the corner of the altar at night in the brilliantly illuminated courtyard of the women. The gospel of the man born blind is told in the contextual framework of this feast.

The collection of miracle stories in John is often referred to as the "Book of Signs." This is because, rather than referring to miracles, John speaks of signs. The stories describe the healing signs Jesus performed in his ministry and then discuss their significance (a forerunner of liturgical catechesis, to be sure!). The signs serve as windows to eternity for those who have faith: "... the man born blind truly sees the sign of Jesus as light of the world and the Pharisees remain in the darkness of their stubborn refusal of faith."[6]

The progression of the miracle begins with a theological discussion stating the nature of the problem. The man born blind from birth enters the scene. The disciples ask Jesus whose sin has caused the man's blindness. It was Jewish belief that sin—either of the individual or the parents—caused suffering. Jesus asserts that blindness is not due to human sin, but that God's glory will be seen through the man's blindness.

The next section of the story describes the miracle. Jesus spits into the dirt, makes a clay compress, and places it on the man's eyes, telling him to go and wash in the Siloam pool—the pool from which the water for the Feast of Tabernacles has just been drawn. The man does as he has been told and returns with his sight restored.

The story progresses to a description of reactions to the miracle. The man's neighbors are incredulous and can hardly believe this is the blind man they have always known. The blind man confesses Jesus' identity and answers their queries by reporting what Jesus instructed him to do. The Pharisees ask the man how his sight was restored. The man responds by relating the details again. Some Pharisees accuse Jesus of healing on the Sabbath. The

[5]For further elaboration, refer to *RJ*, 158.

[6]*WWC*, 26.

Pharisees then approach the man's parents. Fearful of expulsion from the synagogue, they send the Pharisees back to the son. Finally, the Pharisees believe the man was healed.

The Pharisees challenge the man. They state that Jesus is a sinner. The man says that he does not know whether Jesus is a sinner or not, but perhaps they should go and ask Jesus themselves; *perhaps they, too, would like to be his disciples.* This lets the reader know that the newly sighted man is now a disciple. His healing has caused conversion.

Jesus is now elevated to the status of prophet. The man pleads Jesus' case. Never has there been a known case of someone healing a person blind from birth. The man reminds the Pharisees that everyone knows that God does not hear the prayers of sinners; yet this man's prayers were heard. He recalls and names a foundational scriptural truth that God hears the prayers of those who do the will of God and who are devout. The man confesses his christology (the main agenda of John's gospel) *as a result of his experience of Jesus*: Jesus is a prophet, the Master; he comes from God; he does God's will and God hears his prayers in ways that no one has ever before experienced.

The man is then thrown out of the synagogue. His expulsion is connected to his profession of faith in Jesus and his status as disciple. Jesus hears of the man's expulsion and looks for him. Some scholars believe that the next section of this gospel is an ancient liturgical text used at baptism. The man professes belief in Jesus and then worships him. "With this, the process of conversion is complete. For him, light means salvation/sight."[7]

Jesus then challenges the Pharisees. He asserts that his ministry is to bring light to those who cannot see. The Pharisees goad Jesus: "Do you presume to consider us among the sightless?" Jesus accepts their challenge and tells them that to be given sight means they must believe that they are blind in the first place. The Pharisees very self-righteously believe themselves among the fully sighted, thus not in need of Jesus' marvelous sign. "If people can feel the need for light, the help can be forthcoming. But if they absolutize their blindness as sight, then help is impossible. For them, light means judgment/blindness."[8]

While there is progression in the story, there is also progression in the stages of awareness about Jesus's identity: first he was light, then the one sent, then prophet and Son of Man, and finally, Lord. In the first chapter of John, Jesus was named as the "Light that has come into the world." Today's story shows Jesus *in the process of doing* what God sent him to do: his mission as Light of the world. *The gospel asserts that we will know that Jesus is who he says he is by the signs he performs.*

Talbert maintains that the miracle functions as a sign—it is instruction. Miracles have three purposes. They serve as a way to legitimate and give authority to the person of Jesus. The miracle stories are also a means of evangelization—they bring people to faith. Third, they serve as a means of teaching. The story of Jesus' giving sight to the man born blind is a teaching on Jesus, the Light of the world.

Today's gospel prompts serious examination of our inner integrity and self deceptions. Where are we blind and yet think we see? Are any of our firmly held beliefs subject to the discerning challenge of Jesus' illumination?

It is no wonder this gospel was premier catechesis on baptism. The catechumen progresses, like the man born blind, from darkness to light, from unbelief to belief. This gospel reminds those preparing for baptism, as well as those preparing to renew their baptismal profession of faith at Easter, that "all will have to testify to their faith at the risk of being rejected by some or henceforth ignored by others."[9]

Proclaim the gospel again.

Sometimes we gain new insights when we hear the text after the interpretation has been given. Someone from the group proclaims the gospel a second time.

[7] *RJ*, 162.

[8] Ibid.

[9] *DL* (II), 126.

Step 4
Testing

Conversation with the Liturgy and the Scriptures

Test your original understanding in dialogue with the text.

(You might consider breaking into smaller groups.)

Were there any new insights? Was there anything you had not considered before? How does your original understanding of this story compare with what we just shared? How does this story speak to your life?

Sharing Life Experience

Participants share an experience from their lives that connects with the biblical interpretation just shared.

> *The blindness of the Pharisees was a blindness rooted in certainty. The Pharisees were certain that they possessed the light and the only truth. It is a dangerous posture.*
>
> *Our society is steeped in blindness when we continue to perpetrate sins against the world's poor, oppressed, and marginalized. When we continue to foster policies that keep people under the thumb of oppression with the certainty that we are protecting the rights of our own citizenry (e.g., when we do not allow immigrant children access to medical care, etc.), we remain blind to the light of Christ.*
>
> *Our religious structures are steeped in blindness when we treat some of our members as marginalized people with no voice. We are blind when we dismiss members of our communities such as the uninvolved members of our parishes, the homeless, the poor, homosexuals, women, and all those who find themselves "outside the loop," whether that be at the hierarchical, diocesan, parish, or small-group level.*
>
> *I am blind when I hang on to personally held beliefs and positions as if they were written with hammer and chisel on the stone of my very own ego. At times I feel so strongly self-righteous about some issues that there is little room for the possibility of needed conversion, particularly if prayer and discernment helped formulate my position in the first place. Sometimes I call that trust; at other times I call it arrogance. Discernment takes place within the Christian community. If and when I am unwilling to listen to all the voices within the community, my discernment is incomplete. I remain in blindness when I am unwilling to allow God to transform my belligerently held convictions.*
>
> *In my opinion, the primary sin of the Pharisees was idolatry. They presumed to know the mind, heart, and will of God better than God: all things are subject to God's interpretation and intervention. The message for me is: there is a God, and it is not me!*

All share their life experience.

What did I/we hear in this exegesis? What was John's concern for his community in today's gospel? Are there any connections that can be made to our community today? Do the baptismal implications of today's readings have anything to do with our community? What are our collective and personal responses to all of the above questions? Has our original understanding been stretched, challenged, or affirmed?

Step 5
Decision

The gospel demands a response.

How might our community be challenged to change as a result of today's liturgy? In what concrete way does this gospel call our parish to action in the church, parish, neighborhood, or world? Has this conversation changed or stretched my personal attitudes? What is one concrete action I/we will take this week as a response to what we have learned and shared today?

DOCTRINAL ISSUES

What church truth/teaching/doctrinal issue could be drawn from the gospel for the Fourth Sunday in Lent?

Participants suggest possible doctrinal themes that flow from the readings.

Possible Doctrinal Themes

Baptism, conversion, election, sin—personal and corporate

Present the doctrinal material at this time.

1. The facilitator gives input on a particular doctrinal issue of his/her prior choosing. OR
2. The group chooses a doctrinal issue from the list they created. They read together from the Doctrinal Appendix.

(The doctrinal issues are found in the Doctrinal Appendix in the back of this workbook. If you are choosing an issue from this resource, please refer to it now.)

Reflection questions centered around the chosen doctrinal theme can be found at the end of each topic in the Doctrinal Appendix. The questions are based on the five-step reflection process. If you choose a topic not included in the Doctrinal Appendix, craft your own questions according to the same five-step process.

Following the reflection questions you will be reminded to return to chapter 7, "Preparing the Catechetical Session," to assist you in crafting your own session.

Closing Prayer

Second Scrutiny: Exorcism

Father of mercy,
you led the man born blind
to the kingdom of light
through the gift of your Son.
Free these elect from the false values that surround and blind them.
Set them firmly in your truth,
children of the light for ever.
We ask this through Christ our Lord.
Amen.

Laying on of hands

Presider stretches hands over the elect:

Lord Jesus,
you are the true light that enlightens the world.
Through the Spirit of truth
free those who are enslaved by the father of lies.
Stir up the desire for good in these elect,
whom you have chosen for your sacraments.
Let them rejoice in your light, that they may see,
and, like the man born blind whose sight you restored,
let them prove to be staunch and fearless witnesses to the faith,
for you are Lord for ever and ever.
Amen.[10]

[10]Prayer of Exorcism, "Second Scrutiny," *RCIA*.

Fifth Sunday of Lent

INTRODUCTORY RITES

Opening Song (or Entrance Antiphon)

Give me justice, O God, and defend my cause against the wicked; rescue me from deceitful and unjust men. You, O God, are my refuge. (Ps 42: 1–2)[1]

Opening Prayer

The facilitator of the session may lead the prayer. Others in the group may be asked to proclaim the readings.

Let us pray
[for the courage to embrace the
world in the name of Christ]

Pause for silent prayer.

Father in heaven,
the love of your Son led him to accept
the suffering of the cross
that his brothers might glory in new life.
Change our selfishness into self-giving.
Help us to embrace the world you have given us,
that we may transform the darkness of its pain
into the life and joy of Easter.
Grant this through Christ our Lord.[2]

LITURGY OF THE WORD

Let us listen to God's word.

The readings are proclaimed.

First Reading
Ezekiel 37:12–14

The book of Ezekiel is a message of judgment and a message of hope. Ezekiel is considered third in a line of the great writing prophets: Isaiah, Jeremiah, Ezekiel. Ezekiel was a priest and a prophet who was deported to Babylon along with the other inhabitants of Judah (ca. 597–538 B.C.E.). The prophetic ministry of Ezekiel was a testament to the awesome faithfulness and power of Yahweh. Only Yahweh possessed the power to bring life out of the ashes of despair and failure. Israel understood her tribulation and exile as punishment for her sinfulness. The people of Israel believed that God had punished their disobedience and unfaithfulness by inflicting political disaster. The exile was God's divine retribution and only God could breathe life into their hopeless situation. Ezekiel boldly asserted that even though the signs of God's covenant with Israel (promised land, temple, Davidic monarchy) appeared to be dead and gone, Yahweh was still sovereign and in control of their history.

The exile plays a great role in the corporate memory of this people; it is remembered as Israel's time of tribulation. Yahweh punished Israel for her sins. Yet, in spite of Israel's unfaithfulness, Yahweh was steadfast in his love for her. He never broke the covenant, but rather, in his power and love, stood with her to deliver her in her great time of distress.

Ezekiel vehemently professed God to be the sole agent in Israel's liberation. God spoke the word and caused it to be, so that all would know: "I am the Lord." Ezekiel puts these words in the mouth of the Great Author of Life at least eighty-six times throughout the book.

The great age of Israel had collapsed. The people were forced into an alien land (Babylon) without the support of their religious structures to sustain them in the midst of their ordeal. Ezekiel was a revolutionary. He demanded that Israel engage in reform that would see them through their faith-shattering trials.

Ezekiel forged a bold, new path in prophecy. His language and style were unlike those of any prophet before him. The literary text reads like an

---

[1]Fifth Sunday of Lent: "Entrance Antiphon," *The Sacramentary.*

[2]Fifth Sunday of Lent: "Alternative Opening Prayer," *The Sacramentary.*

oratory which suggests that an oral tradition preceded its writing. Ezekiel's message was clear: trust Yahweh, return to the corporate memory and celebration of God's previous saving actions. Worship and observe the law, and faith will be strengthened. Since Ezekiel stressed the Torah as central to his message, he is often called the "father of modern Judaism."

Today's pericope is concerned with the restoration of Israel. Ezekiel assured his audience that the covenant with Israel was still operative (ch. 37). Ezekiel received two visions: one vision was Israel—dead, lifeless, dry bones. In Ezekiel's vision, Yahweh literally breathed life into the dead bones and they were restored to life (37:1–14). The hopeless Israel was given hope and promise for future restoration. Ezekiel's second vision was the convergence of the twelve tribes into one people.

Ezekiel's vision was a summary of his ministry to those in exile: the dead Israel would be restored by the divine breath, wind, spirit (*ruah*) of God. Ezekiel's vision in today's pericope was not intended as a commentary on the resurrection of individuals from the dead.

Ezekiel's vision left nothing to the imagination: death presided over the bone-littered plain. Yahweh and Yahweh alone must intervene if the tables were to turn and if life was to be restored into Israel's breathless corpse.

Responsorial Psalm
Psalm 130

Today's psalm, one of the seven penitential psalms, is an individual lament. The psalmist pleads for deliverance from distress.

Second Reading
Romans 8: 8–11

Paul's letter to the Romans typifies a refined, systematic articulation of Pauline theology. It is considered his greatest theological masterpiece.

Paul insists that God freely *forgives and forgets* people's sins; they are not held against them. Each sinner is welcomed into God's loving arms as a parent would forgive a precious, wayward child. The child is treated as if she or he had never strayed in the first place. The law can never replace the peace, freedom, and relief that only God can give. With the law, human beings work out their own salvation. With Christ, it is already won for those who accept it. Prior to Christ, the law had been a necessary guide. But now, the guide is Christ. We are set free from sin by Jesus' saving action. Jesus' death/resurrection opened the way for the Spirit to reign in the hearts of humankind.

Paul offers us the greatest gift: to see ourselves as God sees us—loved and forgiven. The law does not give us freedom; only Christ gives us freedom. This does not mean that we are no longer bound to an ethical code. Law will always serve as a reminder of our obligations and responsibilities to God, the world, other people, and ourselves. Paul insists that the law does not "capture the will of God."[3] Jesus did not come to create a new set of rigid codes that would replace the old set of rigid codes. Jesus did not denigrate the law; he simply wished to restore its heart.

Jesus came to *show us how to live.* Discipleship consists in living in the pattern of Christ—doing what he did. Thus, Christians are freed from rigid observance of the law. They are, instead, guided by a new motivator—the Spirit of God. When led by the Spirit, Christians participate in a mature, love-based faith. It is a faith based on biblical justice (*hesed*): a reciprocal, covenant relationship with God that is active, alive, and produces every good action because of the demands of love. Loving God with heart, mind, and soul is synonymous with extending that same love to all of God's creation. It is a higher law—one that is not self-determined, but rather Spirit-provoked.

Human nature is flawed because of the sinful, human condition—no one is exempt. However, we must never forget the power and affirmation of our Genesis origins: God created men and women in God's image and saw that "it was good." Thus, we have the ultimate disposition and created potential to be elevated to the divine status that has been our birthright since the beginning of the world. Yet we are nevertheless born into a sinful world and are thus subject to sin. It is sim-

[3] *GAP,* 97.

ply (or not so simply) the way it is. We are human beings and so we are sinners. The indwelling of the Spirit prompts, nudges, and leads us, ever so gently—and sometimes not so gently—toward the created grace that is our destiny. The Spirit gives human beings the possibility of being free from sin. Humanity is to cooperate with the work of creation taking place within each of us. It is not automatic. The Spirit provides the yeast and, out of love, we become what the flour was destined to become: one complete loaf, ready to be broken and shared.

We are new creations in Christ to the extent that we cooperate with the generating work of the Spirit within us. When we live the cycle of death and resurrection and when we lay down our lives for others, we become that which we were created to be. "Paul shows how theology and morality are intimately connected. When we speak of 'Christian being,' we are led to discern what is 'Christian acting.'"[4]

Gospel
John 11:1–45

Jesus raises Lazarus from the dead.

Step 1
Naming One's Experience

What were your first impressions? What was your first response? What grabbed your attention? How did you feel?

Each person names his or her initial impression. Statements should be brief. No reasons should be given at this time. All simply listen without agreeing or disagreeing.

Step 2
Understanding

In a brief statement, what do you think this gospel is trying to convey?

[4]*DL* (II), 129.

Step 3
Input from Vision/Story/Tradition

Liturgical Context

The raising of Lazarus is Jesus' last sign to the world before his impending passion. These are signs because they not only reveal Yahweh, the Almighty, Powerful Creator, but they point to the One who performed the sign, Jesus, the Christ. The signs of Jesus call people to radical faith.

This story is a prelude to the cross. It leads the way; it shows us the meaning of Jesus' coming passion. Lazarus was raised from the dead for a brief respite; Jesus was raised forever. Through Jesus' death and resurrection we all share in the Lazarus sign. The raising of Lazarus prompts every believer to answer the ultimate question: "Do you believe that I am the resurrection and the life?"

Most of John's signs are accompanied by an explanation of the event, except in this instance. This gospel reads more like an unfolding liturgy with a "certain number of declarations made as the action develops.... 'This illness does not end in death, but is for the glory of God, that the Son of Man might be glorified through it'... 'Lazarus has died. And I am glad for you that I was not there, that you may believe'... This sort of composition has been likened to the words of a commentator explaining the unfolding of a liturgy,[5] arousing the attention, spurring the curiosity, and provoking the reflection of the assembly."[6] The declarations made in today's unfolding liturgy prompt assemblies ancient and contemporary to answer the question: "Do you believe in Jesus, the Christ, the One who raised Lazarus from the dead, and the One who can and will raise us from the death of our sinful lives?"

In this liturgy, the elect who are preparing to plunge into the baptismal waters leading to new life stand in the face of impending death and with the entire assembly proclaim with Lazarus,

[5]This image is attributed to M. Moret, *Assemblées du Seigneur,* 2nd series, No 18 (Paris: Publications de Saint-André—Cerf, 1971), 22. In *DL* (II), 131.

[6]Ibid.

Martha, Mary, well wishers, and previous nay-sayers, "Yes, Lord, we do believe that you are the resurrection and the life."

Sin and death reigned in the world. Jesus shattered the choke-hold that death asserted over the neck of a powerless people. Lazarus is a sign and an explanation of the paschal event, of Jesus, the Resurrection and the Life.

The first and second readings attest to God's life-force in the world, the Holy Spirit. Through the power of the indwelling Spirit, we are left a living legacy that entails ongoing participation in the same resurrected life Lazarus was given. In the opening prayer of the Fifth Sunday of Lent, we ask to be inspired and guided by Christ's love and example. In the alternative opening prayer we are reminded of Christ's passion. We ask for the strength to embrace the cross, to work for the transformation of the world, and to be delivered from darkness that blinds us to sin and keeps us from the joy of Easter.

Today the elect celebrate the third and last scrutiny, one of the last steps before they enter into the Lord's ongoing *pasch*—the eucharistic banquet. The elect, with the entire church, celebrate Christ's victory over the systemic evil that keeps people lifeless, like dry, brittle, dead bones rotting in a worldly grave of death and despair. In the celebration of the third scrutiny we pray that the elect be "liberated from the shackles of sin that they may become like Christ by baptism, dead to sin and alive forever in God's sight" and "that they be filled with the hope of the life-giving Spirit and prepare themselves thoroughly for their birth to new life . . . " so the "eucharistic food, which they are soon to receive, may make them one with Christ, the source of life and of resurrection."[7] We thus pray to the Lord—for them and for ourselves.

The third scrutiny on this Fifth Sunday leads us to the premier moment in our liturgical life—the Triduum, the Easter pasch. We are poured out like a libation, ready for Easter filling.

Today brings us to the threshold of Holy Week. Stripped bare of our illusions, confronted with our blindness and insincere motives, the faithful and the elect prepare to enter the tomb of Christ's death and resurrection. We enter the darkened womb of this Holy Week enlightened by Christ who is the "water for which we thirst," the "light of our blindness" and our very "life's breath." We wait to be born anew in the dawn of Easter light. We will then go forth renewed, refreshed, and committed to live the *pasch* until, once again depleted, we will return next year to begin the paschal cycle once again.

Presentation of the Lord's Prayer

The presentation of the Lord's Prayer generally takes place during the week following the third scrutiny, "preferably in the presence of a community of the faithful, within Mass" (RCIA, #178). The Lord's Prayer has always been the prayer "proper to those who in baptism have received the spirit of adoption" (RCIA, #148). The Lord's Prayer gives the elect a better appreciation of God as their Father and thus prepares them to stand in the midst of the celebrating assembly and pray this prayer with confidence. At their baptism they will stand for the first time with the assembly and proclaim this foundational prayer. The creed and the Lord's Prayer have always been considered central to the Christian faith and prayer. The RCIA does allow the presentation of the Lord's Prayer to be deferred until the preparation rites for Holy Saturday.

Gospel Exegesis

The facilitator gives input regarding what critical biblical scholarship has to say about this text. The input includes insights as to how people would have heard the gospel in Jesus' time.

A few verses before this pericope begins, John tells us that "many came to believe in him." This is an excellent springboard for understanding the purpose of the Lazarus sign. Many came to believe in Jesus. Therefore, there was now urgency on the part of the chief priests to put Jesus to death. The stakes were higher. Jesus was having an influence on the people and they were becoming his disciples. Prior to this time, Jesus had had less impact on the Jewish community. People had been rejecting his message and fighting among themselves. Now things were changing, and many Jews were coming

[7] *RCIA*, #174.

to believe in him. Peter Ellis suggests that John may have been mirroring what was taking place in the Johannine community "in the divisions among the people and in the animosity of the Jewish leaders toward those who wanted to accept Jesus and abandon the synagogue" (9:22 and 16:2).[8]

Jesus' greatest "sign," the raising of Lazarus from the dead, leads to the decisive act of unbelief, the formal decision that Jesus must "die for the people" (11:1–57).[9] Thus, the plot thickens and the collaboration of the religious leaders to have Jesus put to death begins. The Lazarus event is the catalyst for their decision to put the plans for his execution into motion.

The miracle stories in chapters 5 and 9 highlight the growing tension between Jesus and the religious authorities and set up this final event. Jesus healed the paralytic in a few short verses and then engaged in a debate with the Pharisees over curing on the Sabbath. Jesus healed the blind man in a brief narrative, and in the rest of the dialogue confronted the blindness of his interrogators. Thus, the miracle signs of chapters 5 and 9 were recounted not only to attest to Jesus' miraculous power to heal (while they indeed served that function), but also as a means of illustrating the judgment Jesus was hurling at the religious establishment.

The evangelist crafted his story around the premise that Jesus' *signs*, especially the gift of life, were gifts from the Father. Ellis believes that, in this instance, the miracle is the point of the story; it demonstrates Jesus' power to raise the dead and offer eternal life.[10] Jesus waited until the fourth day before he went to the side of his grieving friends. At first glance, Jesus' delay seems callous. Perhaps first-century listeners would have thought it more than callous; they may have thought it downright cruel. They would have known without question that by the fourth day Lazarus would have been as dead as those dry, rotted, brittle bones that were littered across Ezekiel's plain. Prior to the fourth day, there might have been hope. "Rabbinical tradition taught that the life breath hovered around the body for three days. After that, all hopes for resuscitation were pointless."[11] Why would Jesus wait so long to go to his dying friend?

By making sure that the reader and the witnesses were fully aware that Lazarus was totally, irrevocably dead, John skillfully crafted the point of the miracle. All hope was lost. There was nothing anyone could do. Like the dead bones in the first reading, only God could breathe life into the situation. It was beyond human imagination and control. ". . . For the Johannine Jesus, the impossible is merely a matter of routine."[12] Jesus' miracle, by his own confession, was to bring people to faith and to reveal and glorify God.

John always refers to life in the eternal sense. Whether human beings are offered the gift of eternal life or not, everyone is subject to the body's mortality. Just as Lazarus was raised to life for a short while only to later die a natural death, so too, are people subject to the same mortality. "As mortal human beings they face the fact of death; but as believers in the Son who possesses the gift of eternal life, here and now, they can confidently look forward to their own resurrection from the dead. Of course, you have to die before you can rise from the dead never to die again; else, the resurrection would merely be a resuscitation."[13] Yet, amidst this mysterious, awe-inspiring gift, there is a lurking dark cloud: the gift of life is also cause for people to maliciously turn against Jesus.

Jesus went to Bethany because of the news of his friend Lazarus' death. Jesus confirmed that the illness would not result in death, but would be for the glory of God. Jesus stayed where he was for two more days in spite of the anxiety and grief of his friends. In typical Johannine style, Jesus' action was a sign that the miracle was going to be at God's initiative, not because of human pressures. "The illness and Jesus' behavior were under divine control."[14]

Pharisees believed in life after death and Martha professed that belief. Jesus asserted that he was the realization of that foundational belief—"I am

[8]*GJ*, 181.
[9]Pheme Perkins, "John," in *NJBC*, 969.
[10]*GJ*, 181.

[11]*WWC*, 29.
[12]Ibid.
[13]*TGJ*, 187.
[14]*RJ*, 172.

the Resurrection and the Life." He was making eternal life possible through the gift of his life.

Jesus arrived at the tomb of Lazarus and wept. Charles Talbert suggests that John was portraying Jesus as a human figure who felt the deepest grief over the loss of a friend, the same grief he experienced over his own impending death and the same grief he experienced knowing that he would be betrayed by a disciple (12:27, 13:21). However, Jesus' weeping is contrasted to the weeping of Mary and the other mourners. Jesus wept sincere tears of sorrow, but did not wail like the other mourners. Wailing was an expression of despair. "Profound grief at such bereavement is natural enough; grief that degenerates into despair, that pours out its loss as if there were no resurrection, is an implicit denial of that resurrection."[15]

However, other scholars suggest a different interpretation of Jesus' emotion at the death of Lazarus. Jesus' weeping does not make much sense if he was aware that he was going to raise Lazarus from the dead. The Greek word *embrimasthai* suggests strong emotion. However, some scholars assert that Jesus' deep emotion is related to his justified anger "at the powers of darkness and evil with whom Jesus is about to do battle. In this emotion and the act which followed it, Jesus' victory over illness, darkness, sin, death and evil is complete and absolute."[16]

Jesus prayed a prayer of thanksgiving over the tomb of Lazarus. It was prayer rooted in ongoing intimacy with his Father. "It is not a prayer of petition, but rather for the purpose of indicating to those assembled his own close relationship with the Father."[17] Jesus' prayer demonstrated that the power he needed depended on God's gift. Jesus summoned Lazarus from the grave and gave the instruction to unbind him from his funeral wrappings. Thus, Jesus, who was called Lord throughout this gospel, completed the revival of the dead man, thereby asserting his sovereignty and authority.[18]

[15] *GAJ*, 416.
[16] *WWC*, 29.
[17] *JGNP*, 37.
[18] Ibid.

The reaction is two-fold: some believed through the sign he performed; others conspired to have him executed (see later verses). Jesus was a threat to the institutional and national Jewish identity. John the Baptist was killed because Herod feared a political uprising of John's followers. The Jewish leaders feared that the hard hand of government would come crashing down on their "holy place" and their "nation" as a result of Jesus' ministry. It would appear as if John was suggesting that the leaders were acting in order to protect the lives and worship of the Jewish community.

Richard Cassidy supports D. A. Carson's position that there were no such noble intentions. When Caiaphas stated that it would be better for one man to die for the many, he was in effect indicting himself and his co-conspirators. What Caiaphas really meant was that it would be better for the one man (Jesus) to die to protect Caiaphas and the Sanhedrin. They were the ones who stood to lose the most because of Jesus' alleged insurrection activities. The Romans might be angered enough to take away what little political, legal, and religious control the Sanhedrin enjoyed. Caiaphas uttered the prophetic oracle that Jesus would die for the whole nation so they would not perish. Indeed, Jesus did die to save all nations—past, present, and yet to come. There is a brilliant piece of irony in this segment. John has Caiaphas utter the prophetic meaning of Jesus' death and yet, from Caiaphas's point of view, he was merely positing the *party line* the Sanhedrin would assume when explaining their intentions to have Jesus killed. Caiaphas was rehearsing for the Sanhedrin what their response might be: "We were simply protecting the nation from Roman intervention and subsequent calamity. If we do not have him killed, the very fiber of our identity, our temple worship, may be threatened."[19]

Chapters 10 and 11 seek to show Jesus as the fulfillment of the Feast of Dedication because of the *signs* he performed. In this way, John's Jesus was authenticating the new worship emerging in the Christian community. This worship would supersede the traditional forms of Israel's worship, such as: temple sacrifices, purification rituals, temple worship on Gerazim or Jerusalem (see Samaritan

[19] Ibid., 43, 107, #8.

woman), the water rituals that promise healing of the body, the feasts of Passover, Tabernacles, and Dedication. The new rituals were seen as the fulfillment of the old.

According to Charles Talbert, in John's gospel, the *disbelief of the people* motif served as a fulfillment of the biblical prophecies such as: "He has blinded their eyes and hardened their heart, lest they should see with their eyes and turn to me to heal them" (Is. 6:10). While human responsibility is not negated in John's gospel, divine sovereignty is a major theme. Thus, God is the architect (planner) of salvation history. Faith is a gift from God generated by divine initiative. Governments are also under the control of God. John maintains that even though God initiates and directs history, human beings are still responsible for their decisions. Those who did not believe in Jesus were responsible for their actions, but these actions were also part of God's plan.[20]

If we make wrong decisions, the implications for our lives are disastrous. We might find ourselves standing with the Sanhedrin in opposition to the saving love of God. Perhaps we will choose our own self interests of power and control while fooling ourselves and others into believing it is for the good of others. Or worse, we may try to stand in the way of God's gift of life by discouraging people in their quest for Jesus Christ, whether by our actions, attitudes or speech, conscious or unconscious. In other words, we have the freedom to choose death over life.

However, life is far more attractive. Jesus offers us life, fulfillment, and joy. We profess and celebrate the gift of life given to us through his paschal mystery. We accept Jesus as Lord of the hopeless, Lord of sinners, and Lord of history. We are heirs to eternal life because of Jesus' saving action and we accept his radical, unconditional love and truth with eyes of faith. Thus, fear loses its control over us. Nevertheless, the ball remains in our court; we are still left with a decision.

Jesus embraced hopelessness and became hope for the world. Jesus became sin and in the process delivered the world. Jesus delivered us from the snares of death and offered us resurrection and eternal life.

[20] *RJ*, 173, 174.

Proclaim the gospel again.

Sometimes we gain new insights when we hear the text after the interpretation has been given. Someone from the group proclaims the gospel a second time.

Step 4:
Testing

Conversation with the Liturgy and the Scriptures

Test your original understanding in dialogue with the text.

(You might consider breaking into smaller groups.)

Were there any new insights? Was there anything you had not considered before? How does your original understanding of this story compare with what we just shared? How does this story speak to your life?

Sharing Life Experience

Participants share an experience from their lives that connects with the biblical interpretation just shared.

> *One night, on the first Friday of Lent, we received the call every parent of teenagers dreads: "Come to the hospital, your son has been in an accident and someone is dead." We rushed to the hospital to discover that our son had been spared, but his best friend since fifth grade had died in his arms. Thus, Adam's family, our son, and the friends of the boys were forced to reflect on the precious gift of life. Some folks would innocently and lovingly say to us: "You are so blessed that God spared your son." I found myself cringing. If God spared my son, then it meant that he had snatched Adam. I had to wrestle with the mystery: "If you ordain all life and if you are the architect of our lives [so went the argument], then you must have willed that Adam die and Joe live." For a time, I even bought into the concept. "God must really have wonderful plans for your life," I horrifically said to my son. He shuddered at the words: "Mom, don't say that. Don't you understand what a burden that puts on me?" I had to retract my untenable position. No, God is not, cannot be like that. God is the author of life; he is not a puppeteer who holds the strings and amuses himself by choosing this life over that life.*

This gospel gives great consolation and meaning to Adam's death. While we grieve over his death (it is now two years later and my son is still grieving), we are assured that Adam's death will not end in despair. Adam knows perfect happiness. We are the ones who are sorrowful. As Christians, we have the eyes of faith to see us through the tragic death of a loved one, particularly a young person. There is no rhyme or reason. Life happens; we are mortal human beings. God is with us in the living of life, but God does not pull all the strings. How it works is a mystery. Death is hideous. If we were not people of faith, despair would be an understandable reaction. It would be difficult to find meaning in a tragic death such as Adam's. We grieve for those who mourn the loss of loved ones, but faith gives us the assurance to know that Adam is far happier in his glorified state than he would have been in this world's sojourn. The Order of Christian Funerals asserts that the bonds of love forged in life do not end with death, but continue into eternity.

There are some who say that faith is this world's opiate for dealing with the tragedies of life. Jesus promised us that we would share eternal life; but he also showed us the price—the cross. So many issues emerged from the experience of Adam's death. The goodness and love of the local teens flowed in the midst of the tragedy. For days they held vigil, told stories, and reflected on the meaning of his death.

Many young people came to the funeral from homes where the word "Jesus" had never been spoken. Others were in their own personal deaths of despair, meaninglessness, and disillusionment because of an adult world that had hurt them. Jesus is the life and the resurrection, but what does that mean to our young people who are hardened by cynicism? My son eulogized his friend, shared how much he cared for Adam and what Adam had meant to him. He offered a challenge. "We have to learn from Adam's death. We have to allow the experience to change us. If we do, his death will have meant something."

The liturgist in me could not help but apply symbolic meaning to the experience. It was a teachable moment for the kids and for us. The name "Adam" means red clay and the first man. Adam, the first young man among their friends to die and return to the red clay of the earth, was also the first to experience the life Jesus promised in today's gospel. He perhaps even paved the way for others. If his death prompted one young person to consider his or her life, then Adam, the first one to return to the red clay of the earth, was like a Christ figure. He paid the price with his life.

While there is no Sanhedrin to taunt us, we face similar enemies when we try to bring life to others. We often find ourselves headed straight for the cross. There is so much death around us. One need only encounter the hopelessness of many young people to observe it first hand. But today's gospel reminds us that we have the gift of life, not only for ourselves, but as a gift to offer all those who find life meaningless and without hope. It is not only Good News, it is the best news.

All share their life experience.

What was John trying to tell his community? Are there any present-day similarities between the issues in John's community and the issues the contemporary church faces? How does this gospel call us (biblical theme of community) or me to be recreated (creation), to experience life, death, and resurrection (exodus) and commitment to my/our relationship with God (covenant)? Do I still feel the same way about this text as I did when we began? Has my original understanding been stretched, challenged, or affirmed?

Step 5
Decision

The gospel demands a response.

What specific thing am I /we/community/parish called to do in response to today's gospel? Has this conversation with the exegesis of the raising of Lazarus changed or stretched my personal attitudes? What are the implications for my life? What is one concrete action I will take this week as a response to what we have learned and shared today?

DOCTRINAL ISSUES

What church truth/teaching/doctrinal issue could be drawn from the gospel for the Fifth Sunday of Lent?

Participants suggest possible doctrinal themes that flow from the readings.

Possible Doctrinal Themes

Eternal life, sin, cross, baptism, soteriology, Jesus the Christ, paschal mystery, death, reconciliation

Present the doctrinal material at this time.

1. The facilitator gives input on a particular doctrinal issue of his/her prior choosing. OR
2. The group chooses a doctrinal issue from the list they created. They read together from the Doctrinal Appendix.

(The doctrinal issues are found in the Doctrinal Appendix in the back of this workbook. If you are choosing an issue from this resource, please refer to it now.)

Reflection questions centered around the chosen doctrinal theme can be found at the end of each topic in the Doctrinal Appendix. The questions are based on the five-step reflection process. If you choose a topic not included in the Doctrinal Appendix, craft your own questions according to the same five-step process.

Following the reflection questions you will be reminded to return to chapter 7, "Preparing the Catechetical Session," to assist you in crafting your own session.

Closing Prayer

Father of life and God not of the dead but of the living,
you sent your Son to proclaim life,
to snatch us from the realm of death,
and to lead us to the resurrection.
Free these elect
from the death-dealing power of the spirit of evil,
so that they may bear witness
to their new life in the risen Christ,
for he lives and reigns for ever and ever.

Laying on of hands

Presider stretches hands over the elect.

Lord Jesus,
by raising Lazarus from the dead
you showed that you came that we might have life
and have it more abundantly.
Free from the grasp of death
those who await your life-giving sacraments
and deliver them from the spirit of corruption.
Through your Spirit, who gives life,
fill them with faith, hope, and charity,
that they may live with you always
in the glory of your resurrection,
for you are Lord for ever and ever.[21]

[21] *RCIA,* #175.

Passion Sunday (Palm Sunday)

On Passion Sunday [Palm Sunday] the Church enters into the mystery of its crucified, buried and risen Lord, who, by his entrance into Jerusalem, gave a glimpse of his own majesty. Christians carry branches as a sign of the royal triumph that Christ won by his acceptance on the cross. Since Saint Paul says: "Provided we suffer with him in order that we may also be glorified with him," the link between these two aspects of the paschal mystery should stand out clearly in the liturgical celebration and catechesis of Palm Sunday.[1]

Environment

The cross is the primary symbol of today's liturgy and should be prominently displayed in the catechetical environment.

INTRODUCTORY RITES

Opening Song (or Entrance Antiphon)

Hosanna to the Son of David,
the king of Israel.
Blessed is he who comes
in the name of the Lord.
Hosanna in the highest. (Mt 21:9)
Let us go forth in peace,
praising Jesus our Messiah,
as did the crowds who welcomed him to
Jerusalem.[2]

Opening Prayer

The facilitator of the session may lead the prayer. Others in the group may be asked to proclaim the readings.

Let us pray
[for a closer union with Christ
during this holy season]

Pause for silent prayer.

Almighty, ever-living God
you have given the human race
Jesus Christ our Savior
as a model of humility.
He fulfilled your will
by becoming man and giving his life on the cross.
Help us to bear witness to you
by following his example of suffering
and make us worthy to share in his resurrection.
We ask this through our Lord
Jesus Christ, your Son,
who lives and reigns with you and the Holy Spirit,
one God, for ever and ever.[3]

LITURGY OF THE WORD

Let us listen to God's word.

The readings are proclaimed.

First Reading
Isaiah 50:4–7

Today's pericope is the second servant song in Deutero-Isaiah. In this song the prophet bemoans the rejection of his message. The people had grown weary of his optimism for the future while they were suffering amid the trials of the exile. However, their frustration would not stop him. He was given a word from the Lord and nothing would keep him from delivering the message. His suffering would result in vindication once Yahweh proved him right. He would not be deterred.

The Christian community thought of Jesus as the suffering servant of Isaiah. Jesus, too, would not be deterred from speaking and living the word he was given. The word he came to preach was one of love and faithfulness. His faithfulness ultimately led him to the cross. This is the fate of all prophets who faithfully proclaim and live their God-given message: a one way ticket to the cross, glory, and ultimate vindication.

[1] *Ceremonial of Bishops,* #263, in *TLD,* 213.

[2] Passion Sunday: "Commemoration of the Lord's Entrance into Jerusalem: The Procession," *The Sacramentary.*

[3] Passion Sunday: "Opening Prayer," *The Sacramentary.*

Responsorial Psalm
22:8–9, 17–18, 19–20, 23–24

This is the first Old Testament scriptural text to have been appropriated for Christian usage. To an innocent onlooker, it seems to have been specifically written with the passion events in mind. This psalm served as a proof text that Jesus indeed was the promised messiah. The psalm speaks of an innocent one's suffering. The details surrounding the suffering servant in the psalm bear an incredible resemblance to the passion and death of Jesus. It is no wonder that the early Christians related this text to the suffering of Christ.

Second Reading
Philippians 2:6–11

It is believed that Paul inserted this beautiful, previously crafted hymn into his letter to the Philippians. Some consider it a perfect expression of Pauline theology regarding the passion and death of Jesus. This hymn was probably used in ancient Christian liturgies and profoundly captures the essence and the paradox of Christian redemption. Jesus, through abject humiliation (see Fourth Sunday of Lent, Cycle C, parable of the prodigal son), offered the free gift of himself. Through such humiliation, salvation was won. Jesus left his rightful throne with Yahweh, descended into the midst of humanity, and took the form of a slave, subject to the suffering and limitations of the human person. He allowed himself to be rejected, misunderstood, and treated like a slave and a criminal. Because of this free gift of self, this abasement, Jesus ascended back to the throne victorious. Because of the resurrection, humanity was and is offered freedom from the ravages of sin and death, and the promise of eternal life. Jesus, the perfect servant, model of all perfect servants, earned the rightful title, Lord, *Kyrios* (Greek), *Adonai* (Hebrew).

Paul was addressing the factions in the Philippian community. He pleaded that all assume the posture of Jesus. If they would only assume the model of Christ's self-abasement, then harmony and peace would be restored to the community. Jesus could have claimed all the rights and privileges of royalty. But he did not. "He became sin." He entered the human condition with all its defects and in the process emptied himself. The Philippian community was exhorted to embrace *kenosis,* a voluntary emptying of self in the manner of Jesus. Paul challenged his community to turn away from the lure of power and control, to assume the humble stance of self-giver. Jesus, emptied and poured-out, went willingly to his passion and death. We are to follow in his footsteps.

Gospel
Matthew 26:14–27:66

The Passion of our Lord Jesus Christ according to Matthew.

STEP 1
NAMING ONE'S EXPERIENCE

What were your first impressions, your first response? What grabbed your attention? How did you feel?

Each person names his or her initial impression. Statements should be brief. No reasons should be given at this time. All simply listen without agreeing or disagreeing.

STEP 2
UNDERSTANDING

In a brief statement, what do you think were the primary concerns of Matthew's version of the passion?

STEP 3
INPUT FROM VISION/STORY/TRADITION

Liturgical Context

The title of today's liturgy expresses its double emphasis: Passion Sunday/Palm Sunday. Today we remember Jesus' triumphant entry into Jerusalem and his passion and death on the cross. "Holy Week has as its purpose the remembrance of Christ's passion, beginning with his Messianic entrance into Jerusalem."[4] The origins of Holy Week began with a yearly celebration of the Lord's

[4] *GNLY,* #31, in *TLD.*

pasch in the spirit of the Jewish Passover. Jesus was celebrated as the new Passover, the one who passed from death into life. The purpose of the celebration was to remember and make present the eschatological implications of Jesus' passion, death, and resurrection. There was very little concern for recording the historical facts. "The redemptive event was a unitary feast, embracing the passion, death and resurrection and exaltation of the Messiah and the outpouring of the Spirit and the anticipation of his coming again."[5]

On the Sunday that began Holy Week, the Jerusalem Christians of the fourth century proceeded to the great church (Anastasis) called the *martyrium* (the place behind Golgotha where the Lord was crucified). Following their morning eucharist and right before the dismissal, the archdeacon announced the beginning of the "Great Week" and summoned Christians to meet each day, "beginning tomorrow" at the ninth hour in the *martyrium.* He instructed them to be ready at the seventh hour (early evening) and to meet at the church on the Mount of Olives. They met at the assigned place and together with the bishop they sang songs, antiphons, and hymns of praise and listened to lessons. At the ninth hour they moved to the place where Jesus ascended into heaven. At the eleventh hour they read the passage of the Lord's triumphant procession into Jerusalem; the bishop then led the procession from the Mount of Olives back to the *martyrium* in the city. Parents carried their small children and all waved their palm branches as they made their holy trek to the city gates. They processed through the city streets until they arrived at the Anastasis at a very late hour. They prayed the *lucernare* together, "with prayer at the cross; after which the people were sent home."[6]

From the earliest days, Passion Week began with the celebration of the eucharist, followed by a procession in honor of Christ the King to the Holy City. Antiphons and hymns were sung and the gospel of the Lord's entry into Jerusalem was proclaimed. With a few minor variations, the celebration of Palm Sunday still contains the same elements and meaning: "While the doors of his city are opened for the King, the Church already celebrates his triumph, being assured of the victory he will gain by his glorious cross."[7]

The church in the East adopted this liturgy with the exception of the procession with palms. Instead, they ritually anointed catechumens while reading John 12, the story of the anointing in Bethany. Following the anointing, they proclaimed the gospel of the entry into Jerusalem. Thus, the name Palm Sunday emerged, even though there was no procession with palm branches at the time.[8]

The *blessing of the palms* in the liturgy did not occur until around the eighth century. Ancient Latin and Greek texts referred to palms as the symbol of life, hope, and victory. However, popular devotion attached a certain magical power to the palms, in part because of the Greek and Roman secular belief that some species of trees carried magical powers. Christians carried over this secular belief by using palms in such practices as eating parts of the blessed palms to deter illness, planting or burning palms in fields to ward off storms, and placing palm branches on livestock to protect them from infestation. People took the blessed branches home in hopes they would ward off evil spirits.

The church responded to this common practice by formulating a blessing ritual for use with the palms. The blessing prayer asks that the branches be blessed and made holy. It is not an invocation of magic; rather—as with all blessings—it is a prayer that God will save us from all threat to our lives, our holiness, and our salvation. "Blessed or consecrated objects are symbols; they express and stimulate faith, hope and love, and do not possess magical power."[9]

The liturgy provides three forms for the entrance rite on Palm Sunday. The first form is reminiscent of the fourth-century liturgy. We are instructed to meet at some other suitable place. All then process to the main church waving palms, not as an historical reenactment, but rather as a sign of loving discipleship. The branches are blessed with holy

[5]*PNL,* 11.

[6]*DL* (II), 210–211.

[7]Ibid., 211.

[8]For further elaboration, refer to *LY,* 107.

[9]Ibid., 108.

water, the entrance gospel is read, a brief homily is given, and—led by cross, incense, and candles—the solemn procession to the church begins.

The second form includes the solemn entrance inside the church before the principal mass of the day. The branches are blessed outside the sanctuary where the gospel is proclaimed. Then the presider and a representative group of the faithful process to the sanctuary.

In the third form, the simple entrance, the entry into Jerusalem is commemorated by singing the prescribed antiphon as the presider processes into the church. However, the Sacramentary suggests holding a bible service the night before to commemorate the triumphant entry into Jerusalem. The church obviously sees great value in not diminishing this important aspect of the Palm Sunday liturgy. However, it is not to overshadow the passion, which is of primary focus. The triumphant entry is significant insofar as it points to the cross.

The ritual prayers of the liturgy including the opening and concluding prayer and the prayer over the gifts reflect the central saving action of Jesus Christ: his victory over death for the reparation of sin. They exalt the death and resurrection of Christ and our ongoing participation in his paschal mystery.

Thus, Palm Sunday brings us to the culmination of Lent's arduous journey. The preparation and emptying of the lenten season have readied us to enter the holy city with Jesus, to die and rise to new life with our Lord and Savior. The triumphant procession has eschatological overtones; it hints of that final day when all will process with Christ into the holy city, the new Jerusalem.

Passion/Palm Sunday is celebrated with full acknowledgment of the ultimate reality: Jesus died and rose from the dead and is now seated at the right hand of God. We do not process as if we do not know the rest of the story. Jesus is addressed as "the Son of David... he who comes in the name of the Lord." This antiphon from Psalm 118 is our joyful testament to the one who came, died, and rose for our sins, the one who is the fulfillment of the law and the prophets. Once again he comes to save in every celebration of the paschal mystery. We proclaim the Lord's passion and we acclaim what we already know to be true: Christ is Victor over sin and death.

In the blessing of the branches we acknowledge Christ's triumph and we ask that he lead us to embrace the cross and to share in the resurrection. The blessing and procession of branches is not an historical reenactment of that first procession. Rather, it is a living memorial to the saints of the past with whom we join in the ongoing dying and rising of people of faith through the centuries. The cross, the book of the gospels, and the presider are signs of the living presence of Christ in our midst as we process together to the Holy City. "It is a presence in absence."[10]

It is important to reiterate that the entrance into Jerusalem is a secondary theme and serves as a preparation for the prominent focus of this liturgy—the passion of our Lord. We are joyful, yet ever mindful of the price paid by our loving Lord to heal the wounded core of humanity. This week reminds us, ever more fully, that the path Jesus chose is also the path of discipleship. It is the path that leads to the light rather than the dark, to salvation rather than death.

The Proclamation of the Passion

Today we read the passion account through the eyes of Matthew. Each year on Passion Sunday we hear from a different evangelist—Luke in Cycle C, Mark in Cycle B, and Matthew in Cycle A. John's account of the passion is read every Good Friday. It is apparent to the observant listener that the passion account read on Passion Sunday and on Good Friday vary considerably. "They do not offer the same outlook of Jesus either in content or outlook."[11]

Thus, contemporary disciples are faced with the awareness that God revealed himself in the words of human beings. Various factors colored their perspectives and the telling of their stories. What family does not have stories of family events, stories that are shaped and colored by the bias or perspective of the teller? "We recall the Catholic

[10] *DL* (II), 213.

[11] *CCHW*, 9.

Church's official teaching that sayings uttered by Jesus have been expanded and interpreted by the apostolic preachers and the evangelists before they were put in the Gospels. . . ."[12]

The fact that there are four different perspectives of the passion accounts serves an unconscious, blessed purpose in the lives of believers that is evident once each gospel is examined on its own ground.

> A true picture of the whole emerges only because the viewpoints are different. In presenting two diverse views of the crucified Jesus every Holy Week, one on Palm/Passion Sunday, one on Good Friday, the Church is bearing witness to that truth and making it possible for people with very different spiritual needs to find meaning in the cross.[13]

Thus, those whose lives cry out like the Jesus of Mark and Matthew, "My God, my God, why have you forsaken me?" find a Christ who resonates with their desperate, yet human pleas for deliverance. Those who need a savior who listens, is present, and can overturn hopelessness find consolation in the cross of those two evangelists. Those who find themselves in need of the tender embrace and loving forgiveness of God will find consolation in Luke's passion narrative. Others may need Christ, the reigning King of heaven and earth, who looks down from the throne of the cross to strengthen and uplift in life's burdensome travail. "To choose one portrayal of the crucified Jesus in a manner that would exclude the other portrayals or to harmonize all the Gospel portrayals into one would deprive the cross of much of its meaning."[14]

The passion narrative is the dramatic portrayal of the most significant event in human history. Its cast of characters reads like a Shakespearean tragedy complete with hero and antagonist. The church allows various readers to proclaim the text. While this serves to heighten the already powerful sense of drama, we are conscious that this is not "theater" provided for our passive enjoyment. We are all fully engaged participants in the proclamation. We are to put ourselves in the place of hero, protagonist, sympathizer, and accuser. In the process, we stand either accused or acquitted.

> The distribution of palm in church may too quickly assure me that I would have been among the crowd that hailed Jesus appreciatively. Is it not more likely that I might have been among the disciples who fled from danger, abandoning him? Or at moments in my life have I not played the role of Peter, denying Jesus, or even of Judas, betraying him? Have I not found myself like the Johannine Pilate, trying to avoid a decision between good and evil? Or, like the Matheean Pilate, have I made a bad decision and then washed my hands so that the record could show that I was blameless? Or, most likely of all, might I not have stood among the religious leaders who condemn Jesus?[15]

Brown insists that the last statement is very probable, since sincerely religious people often have binding, sometimes blinding affiliation with their tradition. However, Jesus challenged fundamentalist adherence to tradition. He always pointed out the human directives and elements that were not in keeping with the will of God. "If Jesus was treated harshly by the literal minded religious people of his time who were Jews, it is quite likely that he would be treated harshly by similar religious people of our time."[16]

Thus, our proclamation of today's passion requires that we become fully engaged, active participants. In so doing, we allow the story to impact our lives and become the leaven for transformation in the fullness of Jesus Christ's paschal mystery.

Entrance Gospel Exegesis
Matthew 21:1–11

The places and events of today's entrance gospel speak to us in far more symbolic ways than first

[12]Ibid., 16.
[13]Ibid., 71.
[14]Ibid.
[15]Ibid., 11.
[16]Ibid., 12.

meet the eye. Assemblies ancient and contemporary are first taken to the Mount of Olives, to the place where the Lord will come triumphantly to gather his people at the end of time (Zech 14:4). We are told that Jesus arrived in Jerusalem from Bethany and returned there. Bethany, "house of the poor," and Bethphage, "the house of figs," are reminders of the judgment against Jerusalem. Jesus, poor and humble, who walked among the poor will not stay in Jerusalem where they kill prophets. Bethphage, the fig tree that did not produce, was Jerusalem's final warning of its unfaithfulness. In this gospel passage, Jerusalem was referred to by its Greek secular name, *Hierosolyma.* It was not deserving of its sacred name, *Jerusalem.*[17] The seat of religious power, this place of holiness through the ages, did not produce the holiness expected of it; instead, it put the savior of the world to death. Judgment was upon it.

The events of the Jerusalem procession are significant for us as we reflect upon the entrance gospel. We enter the week with our eyes on Jesus Christ, *the King.* A cloak thrown on the ground before the king was a sign of royal enthronement. Successors to ancient thrones mounted a donkey to assume their newly ordained royal position. The eschatological messiah of the Old Testament was prophesied to usher in the last days on the back of a donkey (Gen 49:11; Zech 9:9). We are not to miss the symbolism: homage is paid to Christ, the King—to divine royalty.

Since the second century B.C.E. palms had been used in the Feast of Booths as a sign of victory and a symbol of power. The Maccabean revolt took place after the Greeks invaded and occupied Israel. Following the revolt, the temple was purified and the Feast of Booths reinforced the messianic hope for the end times. Today's entrance gospel, with the multitudes waving their palms, proclaims the fulfillment of that messianic hope in the person of Jesus Christ, the one who came to save the world. Thus, "the entry was paradoxically the procession of a king to his coronation—the crown of thorns and the throne of the cross."[18]

[17]I. de La Potterie, "Des deux noms de Jerusalem dans l'évangile de Luc," *Parole de grace: Etudes lucaniennes à la memoire d'Augustin George,* ed. J. Delorme and J. Duplacy (Paris: Recherches de science religieuse, 1981), 70; in *DL* (II), 218.

[18]*PNL,* 12.

Matthew's version of the triumphal entry is for the purpose of exhibiting "Jesus' royal status in a public way."[19] Douglas Hare suggests that it is improbable that the actual event took place as it is recorded. If it had, the Roman authorities would have come crashing on the scene like hornets on unsuspecting targets. There would have been no problem getting witnesses against Jesus for his Jewish trial. There would have been plenty of witnesses. It is more likely that the incident was an interpreted account of a very small scale event that failed to attract public attention. Hare suggests that it well could have been an enacted parable in which Jesus consciously enacted the prophecy of Zechariah (Zec 9:9) by mounting the colt and entering the city. People usually walked into the city. However, little attention would have been given to a man entering on the back of a donkey. The disciples did not even appreciate the significance until after the resurrection (Jn 12:16). Only then did they understand the event as the fulfillment of prophecy.

A few translations have interpreted the word *humble* to make it consonant with the Hebrew of Zechariah's prophecy. As a result, instead of the more appropriate translation, *gentle,* a less than accurate translation, *humble,* resulted. "Matthew, however, is here following the Septuagint, which chose to describe the king as *gentle* rather than humble. The quotation thus reinforces the claim of 11:29, 'I am *gentle* and humble of heart.'"[20] Hare posits that even though the meanings of both words overlap, *humble* should not overshadow *gentle.* "The quotation thus serves to underline the fact that the gentle king arrives in his capital with no sword in hand, vulnerable to whatever his enemies will choose to do to him."[21]

The response of Matthew's crowd reveals Jesus' messianic mission. Their shouts of *Hosanna,* translated from the Hebrew, mean "save now" and can be found in Psalm 118:25. The "Son of David" connects this story with the previous healing of the blind man. In the psalms the word *kyrios* was a title for *Yahweh.* Christians appropriated the term for their risen Lord, their Messiah.

[19]*MI,* 237.

[20]Ibid., 238.

[21]Ibid.

In true dramatic style, Matthew punctuates the event with a cataclysmic event. The city is shaken by an earthquake of supernatural origins. It is possible Matthew's intention is to suggest that the city was shaken to its very core by the arrival of the Holy One.

It is in the irony of the event that we are to find its greatest meaning. "The Son of David enters David's city, but the only throne he finds is a cross."[22] This holy city (of all places) should have acclaimed its king, but chose instead to stand with "all the Herods of this world who maintain the established order."[23] Douglas Hare warns against our own self-righteous Palm Sunday assertions that we, contrary to the holy city Jerusalem, do indeed recognize the King of Kings and Lord of Lords. It was not that many chapters ago that Matthew reminded us that not everyone who calls the Lord "Lord" will enter the reign of God. Only those who do the Father's will (7:21) will enter the kingdom. It is a sober reminder that the gospel is as convicting today as it was then.

Gospel Exegesis

According to Reginald Fuller, the passion narratives possess a different form than the rest of the gospel. All gospel material, other than the passion narratives, was passed on as oral tradition in the short unit format. Those short pieces were preserved as individual units within the gospel. The passion narratives, on the other hand, were told in their complete form from the very beginning. The church continued its early tradition by preserving the pericopes in the Lectionary and keeping the passion narratives in their complete narrative form.[24]

Brown insists that our understanding of the passion narratives must begin with an understanding of the apologetic motives of the evangelists. One concern was to portray a balanced picture of Jesus for the Roman-controlled populace. Jesus was remembered by secular historians as a criminal who had been put to death. The evangelists sought to temper that portrayal, so they depicted Pilate as a fair judge who acknowledged Jesus' innocence. Pilate himself tells the Roman listeners that Jesus is not a criminal.[25]

The second bias of the evangelist centered around the controversy between the early Christians and the synagogue. Many of the gospel perspectives were shaped in relation and in response to that situation. However, Brown also points out that while there were scoundrel "ecclesiastical" politicians intent on getting rid of Jesus for their own selfish reasons, there were also no doubt some very religious men who thought they were honestly safeguarding the people from a liberal, false prophet who was leading the people astray and promoting a lackadaisical adherence to the law of God. Thus, we are prompted to remember that any one of us could stand quite unconsciously and maybe even innocently with the accusers of Jesus at any given time in the story. There were many factors involved in the portrayal handed down to us. Therefore, it behooves us to approach the text with an open mind and heart.

The intent of the evangelists was theological rather than biographical. They were primarily concerned with showing Jesus in relation to the messianic foreshadowing of the Old Testament. "The evangelists were emphasizing that through the Scriptures of Israel God had taught about his Son. Their emphasis also had an apologetic touch against Jews who rejected the crucified Jesus precisely because they did not think he fulfilled Scriptural expectations."[26]

The curtain is about to come up on the drama that will ultimately change the world! It was for this moment that Jesus came into the world. It was for this moment that humanity held its centuries-long breath. It was for this moment that the Word spoke and breathed the world scene into existence. We stand as spectators on the stage of virtual reality. We are there and it is now. Matthew sharpens our senses, puts the players in motion, and catapults us back in time while ever mindful that *we are there and it is now.* We are not to be lulled into the false sense that the "bad guys" are "those guys." The bad guys are those readers ancient and contemporary whose feet fit into the

[22]Ibid., 240.

[23]Ibid.

[24]*PNL*, 15.

[25]*CCHW*, 12.

[26]Ibid., 18.

proverbial shoes portrayed by the antagonists and protagonists in the passion event.

Perhaps the size we wear fits Judas, the one who saw the handwriting on the wall and, concerned with his own self-interests, sold his soul and his relationship with the *Word Incarnate* for thirty pieces of silver. Perhaps many of us easily wear the shoes of those who fled the scene in terror, worrying more about their own skins than the hope of the new kingdom promised by their Master (which by all appearances seemed to have gone up in smoke). Perhaps our feet fit into the sandals of Peter, the one who professed Jesus, but also denied him. Or perhaps we fit snugly into the political shoes of the Pilates of this world who wash their hands and choose to ignore the pervasive systemic evil that looms as a giant blockade and pleads, through its stony silence, for someone to bring it crashing to the ground? "Or, most likely of all, might I [we] not have stood among the religious leaders who condemned Jesus?"[27]

The entire Gospel of Matthew prepares us for this climactic moment. The cross looms large over the reading of each page as we are nudged ever closer to the heart of Christ's redemptive mission. We do not face the passion as shocked and alarmed spectators, but as participants who are fully aware that the road followed in the gospels leads directly to Calvary. "The death and triumph of Jesus are not unexpected or arbitrary endings to the Gospel drama but its inner core."[28]

Donald Senior maintains that the Passion story is a proving ground for fidelity. "Jesus himself is the model; he faces suffering and death with the same integrity and obedience that marked his life."[29] In the shame-based Mediterranean culture in which he lived, Jesus' manliness—his character—was tested. Would he go through his ordeal with head held high or would he grovel in the face of pain, persecution, and torture? Jesus was challenged and withstood the test, demonstrating great heroism. He faced his demons head on and was victorious. The infidelity of the other characters stand in sharp contrast to the faithfulness of the *Anointed One.*

[27]Ibid., 11.

[28]*PJGM,* 18.

[29]*IM,* 249.

Raymond Brown reminds us that the gospel accounts were written by Christian communities, with specific concerns and life situations that impacted their telling of the passion event. "But we must remember that apologetic motives colored the Gospels. Remember our official Catholic teaching (Pontifical Biblical Commission in 1964) that, in the course of apostolic preaching and of Gospel writing, the memory of what happened in Jesus' lifetime was affected by the life-situations of local Christian communities."[30]

An immediate concern was to soft-pedal the portrayal of Jesus in a world governed by Roman law. Brown reminds us that the Roman historian Tacitus remembered Jesus as a condemned criminal who was executed by Pontius Pilate. The Christian account very cleverly uses Pilate to acknowledge Jesus' innocence.

The gospel accounts often reflect the existing tension between the synagogue and the early church. No doubt there were those religious leaders who honestly believed that Jesus was a false prophet and that they were protecting the populace from his influence. On the other hand, there were probably those who were feathering their political nests (as self-serving politicians are wont to do when a public figure appears that might be sacrificed for their self-serving ends).[31] It is with this perspective that we approach the Passion of Jesus Christ according to Matthew.

Most scholars agree that the gospel of Mark was written first. Matthew seems to have included Mark's entire account of the passion with a few added apologetic additions. For example, Matthew includes the death of Judas, Pilate washing his hands, and Pilate's wife's prophetic dream about Jesus' innocence, as well as the guards placed near the tomb. Jesus' former adversaries, the Pharisees, are absent from the crowd of accusers, supporting the Matthean position that the Saducees, the chief priests, were responsible for Jesus' death.

[30]Ibid., 11.

[31]Brown reminds us that the "Annas high priestly family of which Caiaphas was a member gets low marks in Jewish memory," 12.

Matthew's intent is not biographical; it is theological. Jesus came in fulfillment of the Old Testament scriptures. Throughout history the disciples have been accused of crafting the resurrection story in order to prove the messianic prophecies in the Old Testament. In reality, Matthew's intent was to show that Jesus was indeed the *One who was foretold* in those scriptures. The narratives in this unfolding drama serve to place the Passion in the context of salvation history. This was not an isolated event. It was not unrelated to God's plan for the salvation of the world. This was the fulfillment of it. "The voices of the prophets, the anguished prayers of the psalmists, and many other texts of the Hebrew Bible were drawn into the passion story to help the early church detect the pattern of God's presence, even here in what seemed the darkest moment of human history."[32] The invitation to place ourselves squarely in the midst of the narrative events allows us to glean meaning and substance from the suffering and ambiguities in our own lives, even two thousand years after the event. This is a living passion.

The curtain is drawn on the early, somber scenes of the unfolding event. The reader is aware that it is orchestrated by the grand design of God and that the die is cast and will be fulfilled according to God's plan. Jesus is placed in control of the situation. He tells the disciples what to do and they obey him. They are to prepare for the meal. Jesus' time (*kairos*) had arrived. *Kairos* in this sense is a theological reference to the general nature of *kairos* (see Chapter Eight: Time and the Liturgical Calendar), yet it also means the specific time of fulfillment: the fulfillment of God's plan in salvation history. It was time for Jesus to be delivered up.

Jesus reclined at table; he did not sit at the table. The Greek is very clear—the Passover requirements demanded reclining as a sign that they were "free as any in the pagan world."[33]

The betrayal of Judas is made all the more obscene because he had just finished breaking bread with his friend. "Eating together implied 'friendship,' that is, the renunciation of hostile intentions."[34] Matthew's disciples responded to Jesus as "Lord." Only Judas called him "Rabbi," a title often used throughout the gospel by unbelievers.

The Last Supper was obviously a Jewish Passover Seder. "In the narrated events of the meal shared by Jesus and his disciples, the Church recognizes the foundation of its Eucharist."[35] Matthew does not take the reader through all the details of the Seder meal—the four cups of wine, the bitter herbs, the roasted lamb. However, there are important elements that we are to notice.

> There is, however, an allusion to the dipping into the bowl (vs. 23); following the first cup of wine and the recital of the kiddush (sanctification), each participant dipped a vegetable into salt water, as a way of recalling the crossing of the sea in the escape from slavery. A piece of *matzah* (unleavened bread) was then consumed in recollection of the haste with which Israel left Egypt. An indispensable feature of the Seder, then as now, was the interpretation of these various details of the meal, a responsibility that fell to the father of the household or to the host in a larger gathering. Jesus naturally assumed this role. Imagine the startled response of the disciples when the host, taking the *matzah*, made no mention of the ancient exodus, but instead solemnly declared, "This is my body." Implicit in this radical interpretation of the Passover matzah may be seen the announcement, "By means of my imminent death a new exodus will occur."[36]

At the Passover Seder there were four cups. The second cup was the most important. With this cup the exodus and subsequent liberation from slavery were remembered and brought into the present. Included in this ritual remembering was a prayer that those same liberating effects would become operative for the future salvation of Israel. It was a remembering that recalled God's past saving actions, and asked that those same saving actions be brought into the present for the present genera-

[32] *PJGM*, 8.

[33] *MI*, 296.

[34] Ibid.

[35] *IM*, 250.

[36] Ibid., 297.

tion and for future salvation. "A first century rabbi is reported to have said, 'On this night they were saved; on this night we will be saved.'"[37] Usually accompanying this prayer was a prayer for the coming of the Messiah. It was generally believed that the Messiah would arrive during Passover. Hare suggests that it was this second cup that Jesus reinterpreted for his disciples.

The second cup ritually remembered the blood of the lambs sprinkled on the doorpost to alert the angel of death to pass over the house. The "blood of the covenant" was a term used to refer to the covenant God made with Israel on Mount Sinai. Jesus did not make reference to that covenant, but instead inaugurated a new covenant—the blood of the covenant was his blood that would be poured out through his death for the sins of many. "Implicit is a reference to God's future saving act: just as the blood of the passover lambs had been a sign of salvation at the beginning of Israel's history, so Jesus' blood, 'when poured out for many,' would be a the sign of God's end-time saving work. Also implicit is the notion that this covenant will in some sense replace the prior covenant and therefore be 'new' (see 1 Cor 11:25; Jer 31:31–34)."[38] This time the enemy will not be Pharaoh's legions. The enemy will be sin and its ravaging effects. Jesus will die for the sins of many. "Not only is Jesus' death an inauguration of the new covenant promised by Jeremiah (Jer 31:31–34), and not only is it a dying 'for the sake of many,' as Isaiah's suffering servant had prefigured (cf. Is 53:12), but this death is 'for the forgiveness of sins.'"[39] Matthew reiterates a constant theme that runs throughout the gospel: Jesus frees people from sin, heals people from their suffering, and offers his life for humanity.

The meal event ends on a joyful note, reminding disciples that the eucharist is a bond of unity that cannot be broken, not even by death. The next time Jesus would drink with them, they would be drinking the new wine of his messianic reign. The disciples do not understand and they are warned of what is coming. They will deny him and leave him to suffer and die alone.

[37]Ibid.

[38]Ibid., 298.

[39]Ibid., 250.

Douglas Hare points out an important truth inherent in the story of the institution of the eucharist. Theologians speak of the event as the sacrament of the real presence of Christ. Hare reminds us that we must balance this with another stark truth: that it is also the sacrament of the real absence of Christ.

> The eucharistic service forcefully reminds us that Jesus was violently removed from our midst. Despite his spiritual presence (Mt 18:20; 28:20), he is our absent Lord. During his absence we continue to walk the way of the cross, accepting heartache and suffering as unavoidable ingredients of discipleship (see Mt 16:24). We look forward to his coming in the kingdom of his Father, when suffering will be no more (Rv 21:3–4).[40]

Jesus moves to the Mount of Olives. It is important that we not miss the significance of the Mount of Olives. It is here that David fled after being pursued by Absalom. It is here that David wept over the betrayal by his trusted advisor. It is here that the Messiah, descendant of the Davidic monarchy, foretells the denial of his trusted friends and his betrayal by one of his own. It is here that we also come face to face with his humanity. The heresy, Docetism, would have us "divinize" Jesus' human nature, asking us to believe that Jesus somehow did not experience fear or anxiety, or the raw nerve of betrayal by those he loved. To believe this would rob the crucifixion of its significance. "If Jesus was not fully human, the cross was an empty pantomime."[41] Jesus feared his death and asked to be delivered from it. The cup he asked to be delivered from was death. He asked that his father's reign be established some other way. Did he really have to die to accomplish his father's mission? "God is all powerful. Can he not destroy evil without making his Son its victim?"[42] Jesus also prayed that his Father's will be done. It is not the first time we have heard this prayer. It is the prayer Jesus taught his followers; he followed his own teaching. There was no other way. Jesus was obedient unto death. Following the way of Christ can often have extremely serious consequences.

[40]*MI*, 298–299.

[41]Ibid., 300.

[42]Ibid.

We are cautioned against interpreting Jesus' pronouncement about flesh and spirit in the constructs of Greek dualism—flesh is evil and carnal and spirit is soul and spirit, and therefore good. In Hebrew thought, flesh referred to the whole person. Flesh in the sense that Jesus used it was understood as self-sufficiency and a lack of dependence on God. A better understanding of Jesus' proclamation might be: "The spirit inclines us to serve God, but our fleshly minds are intent on serving ourselves."

Gethsemane serves a theological function for Matthew. We are not to miss the point of this exchange in the passion story: Jesus' obedience was his most important sacrifice.[43] The Gethsemane event functions like a parable in action. Jesus, in the garden of Gethsemane, unlike Adam in Eden's garden, is obedient in the face of temptation.

In contrast, Jesus' disciples do not stand up to the test. Unlike Luke, Matthew portrays his disciples professing faith in the fullness of Jesus' identity in the gospel. This makes their abandonment of him at the hour of his greatest need all the more despicable. Judas betrayed Jesus with a kiss. The disciples fell asleep and left Jesus to face his hour of being tested alone. Peter drew his sword and cut off the ear of the high priest's servant, but Jesus put it back on. Matthew uses the event to teach us how Jesus opted for the path of non-violence. More importantly, however, is the christological impact of the scene. Yes, God could have brought the forces of heaven to wreak havoc on this or any other band of enemies, but if he had done so, his plan through Christ would not have been accomplished. God's plan was to be fulfilled through the path of suffering, which was prophesied in the scriptures. "Jesus had access to spectacular power, we are assured, but renounced its use because God's way of dealing with sin is through weakness."[44]

Jesus was arrested and taken before Caiaphas, the high priest. Matthew is the only one that records this piece of information. Even though the trial of Jesus as recorded in Matthew is highly disputed regarding its historical probability, what we learn from it is that Jesus was totally innocent. There is irony in the false, anti-Temple accusations against him. The readers of Matthew are given the account of Jesus' death after the destruction of the Temple. According to Raymond Brown, Matthew invites us to understand the destruction of the Temple as retribution for the death of Christ. One of the charges against Jesus was that he plotted against the Temple. Yet that which Jesus was accused of was fulfilled after his death.[45] Herein lies the irony.

As Jesus stood before his accusers, "nuancing his answers before the high priest,"[46] his earlier prophecies regarding Peter's denial were being fulfilled in the unfolding drama out in the courtyard. Judas fulfilled Jesus' prophecy about him, and the prophecies in Jeremiah and Zechariah. Judas died a violent death as a result of his taking the thirty pieces of blood money. Peter and Judas—the contrast is striking: one wept bitterly over his sin, the other hanged himself.

Matthew's insistence of Jewish guilt for the death of Jesus has served to embitter Christians and Jews for centuries. Brown submits that rather than omit or ignore the references to Jewish guilt, we should address them head on and not succumb to the anti-Jewish bias that was the result of the life situation of Matthew's first-century community. Rabbinic law insisted that a perjurer was responsible for the death of an innocent man until the end of time. It is no wonder that Matthew's community held the Jewish leaders eternally responsible. However, the corporate guilt of the Jewish leaders in hindsight can only be understood in light of Jesus' promise that his blood would be shed for all for the forgiveness of sins. Matthew struggles with an important theological question: "How could Israel reject God's Messiah?... [H]e is not interested in merely reporting but interpreting history."[47]

Jesus was not only found guilty by the Jewish court, but even though pronounced innocent by Pilate and his wife, was also sentenced by a Roman trial. Jews and Gentiles alike rejected Jesus.

---

[43] Ibid., 303.

[44] Ibid., 304.

[45] The hostile portrayal of the Temple leaders should also be understood in light of the tension that existed between Matthew's community and the synagogue.

[46] *CCHW,* 39.

[47] *MI,* 309.

Matthew moves his reader somberly to the closing scene of Jesus' last moments. Again Matthew seeks to portray Jesus as the fulfillment of Old Testament prophecy. Jesus is given gall to drink, a reference to the gall mentioned in Psalm 69:22. Three groups come forward to scoff at the crucified Christ—a reference to Psalm 22:8–9: "All who see me scoff at me. . . ."

Jesus utters his last cry of abandonment. People who insist on divinizing Jesus' humanity have a difficult time with this verse. They claim that in the latter verses uttered by Jesus in Psalm 22, God delivered him from his suffering. Raymond Brown says of this: "That may well be, but the verse that Jesus is portrayed as quoting is not the verse of deliverance but the verse of abandonment—a verse by a suffering psalmist who is puzzled because up to now God has always supported and heard him."[48] Jesus did not despair—it was "my God" he beckoned. However, he did experience the deepest, most profound anguish that comes of feeling forsaken and alone.

Matthew tells us that God did not forsake his Son. Matthew apocalyptically proclaims the immediate effects of Jesus' death. The heavens and the earth stood at attention and all creation shook and rumbled in a cataclysmic groan as it witnessed salvation history's defining moment. The Messianic age was inaugurated. The old passed away [Judaism], and the new—the reign of God in Christ—was born. With Jesus' last breath the dead came forth from their graves and Gentiles were invited into the kingdom. Following Jesus' resurrection to the father's throne, the faithful dead took their long-awaited place in the new Jerusalem. The erupting earth violently announced God's vindication of Jesus.

Matthew placed guards at the tomb (a historical improbability), probably as an apologetic. No one could make the accusation that Jesus' body had been stolen if there were guards at the entrance. The guards could attest that the stone did not move. There were no plots to feign Jesus' resurrection. The chief priests schemed with the guards and told them to lie. They would maintain control of the situation until the end. Matthew used the guards and the scene at the tomb to punctuate his theology. God's power is awesome! Regardless of what people tried to do to keep the events buried, including sealing the tomb, God would have God's way. The earth itself stood as witness to Jesus' death. It would shake again at his resurrection. It would stand at attention as Jesus returned to his place at the right side of his father.

[48] *CCHW*, 44.

Proclaim the gospel again.

Sometimes we gain new insights when we hear the text after the interpretation has been given. Someone from the group proclaims the gospel a second time.

Step 4
Testing

Conversation with the Liturgy and the Scriptures

Test your original understanding in dialogue with the text.

(You might consider breaking into smaller groups.)

Was there anything in the passion narrative you had not considered before? Were there any new insights? How does Matthew's account of Jesus' passion speak to your life?

Sharing Life Experience

Participants share an experience from their lives that connects with the biblical interpretation just shared.

> *I cannot experience a Palm Sunday liturgy without remembering a very defining moment of healing and liberation in my life. It was a moment of passage, of crossing the Red Sea into the promised land. I have told this story before; I will tell it again. The passion, death, and resurrection of Jesus always bring me back to this very personal, yet communal experience of passage and liberation. Two years ago I participated in a retreat and study pilgrimage in Israel. One very defining moment for me occurred on the day we participated in the passion walk that closely resembled the steps of Jesus in his last days. Beginning at the place of the Last Supper, we walked*

down the hillside and across the Kidron Valley to the Mount of Olives. We mirrored the same walk of the fourth-century Christians described above. We stopped and prayed at the Mount of Olives, crossed the Kidron Valley, and processed up the mountainside once again to the holy city and to the Church of the Holy Sepulcher. It was about a four- to five-hour trek and I was not in the best physical shape.

As I labored up the mountainside and down into the valley, I entered the quiet space of sweat-filled, breathless interior reflection. My intention was to enter the heart of Christ as he walked those same steps for far different reasons than I. "Teach me what I need to know; show me your heart," was my earnest prayer. As each step became more strained, things began to change. Rather than centering on my inability to breathe in the hot August Jerusalem sun, I was moved to carry others with me on the burdensome trip. My attention started to shift. How must it have been for Christ as he carried the world on his shoulders that horrible, wonderful day!

"Who am I willing to carry?" Slowly, I became aware of those who suffer and those who cause the suffering. In that land of the Jews I became aware of the millions who had been oppressed, tortured, and murdered at the hands of an evil, distorted, obsessed, and blind Nazi Germany. I was also aware of Arab families from that same ancient land who, after the war to gain Israel's independence, were taken from their homes and led on a death march across Israel. Mothers, fathers, children, grandmothers, and grandfathers had their homes and possessions ripped from them as they were marched to their new settlements. Many died on that horrendous march. How quickly the oppressed had forgotten their own tortuous past and put on the cloak of oppressor.

I invited them all to walk with me, oppressed and oppressor, and together we prayed, "Father, forgive them for they know not what they do. Father, forgive us." The day wore on and my back bent low. As we continued toward the place of freedom, a new group joined my imaginary motley entourage of the world's oppressed. It was this last group that brought me to my knees. They were the children, all the children in the world who were suffering, abused, neglected, and crying out for deliverance. "Climb on," I said, "we'll make it together." We climbed the last mount to Jerusalem huffing with each breath, singing all the way, "Father, forgive them, for they know not what they do."

As we approached the church's courtyard, the holy place where that Final Deliverance was realized, my imaginary companions and I stood still. All of us, the oppressed, the marginalized, the tortured, the poor, the children... all of us stood at the door, aware of who had gone before us. As if struck by lightning, I became aware of just one person—one small girl—who, as a very young child, had cried out to be saved from the horror that was happening to her. If her parents had only known, they would have saved her, but no one knew, no one saved her. She stood frozen at the doors.

It was as if the gentle hand of Jesus, from his nail-ridden wooden throne, reached out his hand to the small girl child and beckoned her into the holy place. Inside the holy of holies, the girl child and her friends stopped motionless at the rock, the earthen rock, split in two and opening into the earth's bowels, the rock that most believe is the very place where Jesus was crucified. On that hot August afternoon, energy-spent, breathless, and emptied, that small girl child and her companions gave it all up to the crucified Christ. They handed it over: the brokenness, the devastation. They left it all on the broken rock of Golgotha. "Father, forgive them, they did not, they do not know what they do."

This girl child was obviously my own wounded inner child. While details are unnecessary, that day Christ walked with me on the steps to Calvary and gave me freedom. He extends that same freedom to every broken person in the world. We are agents of his freedom. It is our job to bring the broken and the wounded to the wooden throne of Jesus.

I left the holy city that day with a new reality. Now whenever I hear the words, "Upon this rock I will build my church," I will think less of Peter and more of the broken, split, fissured rock of Golgotha. It is upon that rock that Jesus built his church—the broken rock of people's lost and forsaken lives, including Peter's. It is Christ who reaches out and says, "I have prepared the way, I have gone before you.... Come, find healing and forgiveness in me... find your freedom."

While this was no doubt a powerful moment of liberation, it is not necessary to go to Israel to encounter the Jesus of Matthew's passion. He is encountered in every life that struggles in the pain and sorrow of life and peacefully submits to the will of God. Jesus' passion finds expression with every person who chooses love over hatred and forgiveness over resentment. As a wife and mother I am asked to live the cross of Christ in the difficult times as well as in the everyday circumstances of life. My family participates in Jesus' passion every time we face a crisis in our lives with a willingness to love, to communicate, to listen, and to put aside our selfish interests and our selfish pride.

Every time we love one another in spite of our angers and our hurts, we live the passion of Christ. Every time we refuse to give in to despair and hopelessness in the difficult times, we live the passion of Christ. We live Christ's passion every time we refuse to submit to hatred, animosity, jealousy, gossip, and self-serving interests, and instead offer love and reconciliation to those who are different from ourselves. Jesus' passion is intimately connected to the living of our lives. As wife and mother I live it every day. As a disciple and parishioner I am given opportunities to live it every day. Jesus' passion helps me face each day with new resolve to extend his reconciling ministry in my family, in my parish, and in the world.

All share their life experience.

What was Matthew's primary agenda in his version of the passion narrative? Have there been times in my life when I have worn the shoes of Peter, Judas, Pilate? In what way? Have I ever walked the way of Jesus? What was Matthew saying to his community, to our community, and to me today? How are we called to live Jesus' passion? What does the cross mean in our lives? In what way do we live the paschal mystery as a community? How do I personally live it? Do I still feel the same way about the passion of our Lord as I did when we began? Has my original understanding been stretched, challenged, or affirmed?

Step 5
Decision

The gospel demands a response.

In what concrete way does the passion of Christ call us (community, parish, me) to respond? Has this conversation with the exegesis of Matthew's passion changed me in any way? What concrete action could I/we take this week as a response to what we have learned and shared today?

DOCTRINAL ISSUES

What church truth/teaching/doctrinal issue could be drawn from the gospel for Passion Sunday ?

Participants suggest possible doctrinal themes that flow from the readings.

Possible Doctrinal Themes

Cross, paschal mystery, redemptive suffering, soteriology

Present the doctrinal material at this time.

1. The facilitator gives input on a particular doctrinal issue of his/her prior choosing. OR
2. The group chooses a doctrinal issue from the list they created. They read together from the Doctrinal Appendix.

(The doctrinal issues are found in the Doctrinal Appendix in the back of this workbook. If you are choosing an issue from this resource, please refer to it now.)

Reflection questions centered around the chosen doctrinal theme can be found at the end of each topic in the Doctrinal Appendix. The questions are based on the five-step reflection process. If you choose a topic not included in the Doctrinal Appendix, craft your own questions according to the same five-step process.

Following the reflection questions you will bc reminded to return to chapter 7, "Preparing the Catechetical Session," to assist you in crafting your own session.

Closing Prayer

Lord,
may the suffering and death of Jesus, your only Son,
make us pleasing to you.
Alone we can do nothing,
but may this perfect sacrifice
win us your mercy and love.
We ask this in the name of Jesus the Lord.[49]

[49]Passion Sunday: "Prayer Over the Gifts," *The Sacramentary*.

HOLY WEEK, EASTER TRIDUUM, THE EASTER SEASON

Holy Week, Easter Triduum, The Easter Season: An Overview

HOLY WEEK

Palm Sunday, while still part of the Lenten season, inaugurates entrance into the liturgical year's holiest, most solemn week. "Holy Week has as its purpose the remembrance of Christ's passion, beginning with his Messianic entrance into Jerusalem. The Sixth Sunday of Lent, which marks the beginning of Holy Week, is called Passion Sunday [Palm Sunday]."[1] The first days of Holy Week, like all of Lent, serve as final preparation for the celebration of Easter. As the Triduum fast approaches, our focus turns toward the suffering of Christ. In the past, Mark's passion was read on Tuesday of Holy Week and Luke's was read on Wednesday. Now the passion narratives from the synoptic gospels are read on Palm Sunday in the three-year cycle.

During the weekdays of Holy Week the scriptures point us toward the Triduum. "In the first half of Holy Week the readings are about the mystery of Christ's passion."[2] We are immersed in the "Servant Songs" of the prophet Isaiah, whose image of the suffering servant finds fulfillment in the suffering of Jesus Christ. The gospel passages relate events from Jesus' last days before his pending passion and death.

Lent does not end with much fanfare. Like a graceful dancer, she makes one last pirouette, solemnly bows, and exits to make way for the grand finale, the showcase piece, the defining moment of the entire movement. Looking back in history, we observe two things that occurred before the Triduum began. The penitents, who on Ash Wednesday entered a period of preparation for reconciliation, were reconciled to the church on Holy Thursday. The oils were blessed on that same day. Thus, before the defining celebration of Christ's premier saving action could begin, the church became whole, complete, and restored again through the reconciliation of its penitents. The oils used in the sacramental, ongoing life of the church were blessed, sent, and received by individual parishes.

[1]*GNLY,* #30, 31, in *TLD.*

[2]"Introduction to the Lectionary for Mass," *The Lectionary for Mass,* #98.

Chrism Mass

Lent ends on the evening of Holy Thursday with the celebration of the Lord's Supper. On the morning of Holy Thursday the Chrism Mass is celebrated by the bishop. For pastoral reasons it may be celebrated on a day prior to Holy Thursday. "At the Chrism Mass on Holy Thursday morning the bishop, concelebrating mass with his body of priests, blesses the oils and consecrates the chrism."[3] The blessing of the oils is a very ancient tradition dating back to Hippolytus and the *Apostolic Tradition* in the third century. Three oils are blessed: oil of chrism, oil of catechumens, and oil of the sick.

The chrism is blessed for the anointing of the newly baptized, for the chrismation of candidates for confirmation, and for the anointing of the hands of priests and the heads of bishops at ordination. Chrism is also used in the dedication of churches and altars.

The oil of catechumens is used to anoint catechumens in their preparation for baptism. "The anointing with oil symbolizes their need for God's help and strength so that, undeterred by the bonds of the past and overcoming the opposition of the devil, they will forthrightly take the step of professing their faith and will hold fast to it unfalteringly throughout their lives."[4]

"The oil of the sick is used to bring comfort and support to the sick in their infirmity."[5] The holy

[3]*GNLY,* #31.

[4]*RCIA,* #99.

[5]"Ceremonial of Bishops," in *TLD,* #274.

oils represent the ministry of the church. Each year we bless the new oils that are used in church life.

The premier focus of the Chrism Mass is the priesthood of Christ. The first reading and the gospel remind us that Jesus was empowered and anointed for this holy priesthood by the Holy Spirit. The second reading for the Chrism Mass from the book of Revelation reminds us that Jesus shares this priesthood with his disciples. "For the Chrism Mass the readings bring out both Christ's messianic mission and its continuation in the Church by means of the sacraments."[6] The Chrism Mass is also an expression of the unity of the priesthood and sacrifice of Jesus, which continues to be a present reality in the church today. All the priests of the diocese come together to concelebrate the Chrism Mass with their bishop and to consecrate the chrism, because they, like the bishop, share in the mission of Christ to sanctify, guide, and build up God's people.[7]

The preface of the Chrism Mass offers praise and thanks for Jesus' priesthood, for our share in it and for those who have been called "to share his sacred ministry by the laying on of hands."[8] The preface outlines the call of ministerial, ordained priesthood:

> He appoints them [presbyters] to renew in his name
> the sacrifice of our redemption
> as they set before your family his paschal meal.
> He calls them to lead your holy people in love,
> nourish them by your word,
> and strengthen them through the sacraments.
> Father, they are to give their lives in your service
> and for the salvation of your people as
> they strive to grow in the likeness of Christ
> and honor you by their courageous witness of faith and love.[9]

The oils are blessed and a renewal of commitment to priestly life may also take place during the liturgy.

[6]"Lectionary for Mass: Introduction," #91, in *TLD*.
[7]"Ceremonial of Bishops," #274.
[8]Chrism Mass: "Preface for Priesthood" (P20), *The Sacramentary*.
[9]Ibid.

While most of the faithful will not be participating in the Chrism Mass, it is an important part of our heritage and a vital piece of our tradition. The scriptures of the Chrism Mass speak to us of Christ's priesthood and our share in his priesthood by virtue of our baptism (according to the ritual text for baptism, we are anointed *priest, prophet,* and *king*). The scriptures and the ritual texts of the Chrism Mass foreshadow and remember the rights, duties, and responsibilities of ordained priesthood. The oils used in the sacramental function of the church are blessed and distributed for use in all diocesan churches throughout the liturgical year.

The Chrism Mass is a pivotal liturgy. Catechesis based on the liturgical year must address the Chrism Mass and what it means for the ongoing life of the church. This workbook does not provide a session for the Chrism liturgy. However, the scriptures and the issues just mentioned should be shared and addressed in catechetical reflections of Holy Week. To completely ignore the Chrism Mass would be tantamount to omitting an integral piece of the church's liturgical life.

THE EASTER TRIDUUM

The Easter Triduum is the "mother of all feasts." All other feasts of the year hinge on this great feast. While each Sunday stands on its own as an observance of the paschal mystery, the entire liturgical year is in forward motion toward the fundamental commemoration of our Christian faith: the redemptive action of Jesus Christ's passion, death, and resurrection. "Theologically and historically the entire liturgical year springs from the paschal redemptive action of Christ and the celebration of this action."[10] Any treatment of the liturgical year should begin and flow from the foundation and celebration of Easter. However, the liturgical year begins on the first Sunday of Advent and liturgical books are ordered according to chronological progression rather than the preeminence of the feast. Thus, in the interest of following the liturgical year and the Lectionary and Sacramentary's layout, *Word & Worship Workbook* begins with the First Sunday of Advent rather than with the logical, primary place—Easter.

[10]*LY*, 57.

It is understood that the early Christians remembered Jesus' saving event in a special way during the annual Jewish celebration of Passover. Jesus, the new paschal lamb, passed from death to life. While the early Christians continued to observe the Jewish Passover, it took on new significance in light of Jesus' saving action. There was probably a gradual break from the traditional Jewish Passover.

However, according to second-century literary evidence, there was debate over the date of the annual celebration, suggesting a probable first-century observance. The earliest recorded celebration consisted of a eucharistic meal, preceded by a period of fasting. According to Adolf Adam, the focus of the feast in Rome was primarily on Christ's resurrection and exaltation. The Council of Nicea (325) definitively set the date on the first Sunday after the first full moon in the spring. This way, Easter would not fall during the annual Jewish Passover feast.

The feast takes its name from the Aramaic and Greek word, *pascha,* which is a translation from the Hebrew, *pesach.* The Hebrew word is translated as a "passing by" or "passing through." The word refers to the primary saving event of Israel. The angel of death passed over the houses of the Israelites. Hebrew slaves were led safely out of bondage through the Red Sea and were given safe passage to the Promised Land. Christians appropriated the feast of Passover to their understanding of Jesus' *pasch:* "He passed through the sea of suffering and death and led the people of God to a communion of grace with the Father."[11]

The word *Easter* has various questionable origins. It was once thought to be a reference to the worship of the spring goddess, *Eostre.* However, modern scholarship refutes that connection. Though scholars are still uncertain, it is probably derived from some connection to or translation of the word *East,* where each day meets the rising sun (an obvious metaphor for "Christ, the sun of justice who will rise again in the East after his descent into death"[12]).

[11]Ibid., 20.

[12]*Patrologia Latina,* ed. J.-P. Migne, Paris, 1878–90, 172:69, in *LY,* 63.

The Triduum:
A Celebration of the Paschal Mystery

Jesus' *pasch* includes his suffering, passion, death, and—most of all—his passage from death to new life through the resurrection. Raniero Cantalamessa expresses it as follows: "The Passover was a pre-existing institution which the Christians inherited from the Old Testament. All its symbolism was directed to immolation, blood sacrifice. Because this was so, it was easy for Christians to make transfer to the passion of Christ."[13] Thus, the term "paschal mystery" was used to express the reality we know as Jesus' suffering, death, and resurrection. According to St. Augustine, "Passover is the day on which we at the same time celebrate the Lord's passion and resurrection."[14] Therefore, Easter is the prime, exalted celebration of the paschal mystery. However, every sacramental celebration is also the ritual remembrance of the same mystery. The Great Feast, however, summons our power of remembering with greater intensity, and rouses within us greater rejoicing, awareness, and corporate memory of the Easter event itself. It brings the paschal experience to full consciousness so that we may enter the mystery of Jesus' death and resurrection with active and vigilant participation. Thus, "Christ's Passover is prolonged in the Church with three rhythms of differing frequency; an annual rhythm which is the feast of Easter; a weekly rhythm which is Sunday; and a daily rhythm which consists in the daily celebration of the Eucharist."[15]

The feast of Easter is the ritual proclamation and embodiment of the saving act of Jesus' resurrection and glorification. This saving reality is remembered and brought into the present. Through this utterly gratuitous act of self-giving love, Jesus conquered sin and death and gave the human race the promise of eternal life and perfect union with Yahweh, the Lord of all creation. Through Jesus' saving act, the church was born. Through the Holy Spirit, the church was empowered to live in perfect union with Christ and to spread his Good News. The feast of Easter cele-

[13]*ME,* 37.

[14]St. Augustine, *Sermo Denis 7 (Miscellanea Agostiniana, 1,* p. 32).

[15]*ME,* 58.

brates the passage from death to life. It inaugurates the church's participation in Christ's redeeming action. The church at Easter remembers past events and makes them present. Easter also prompts the church to look forward to the new and eternal city in the next life as it works for the salvation of the world in this one.

Historical Perspective

Prior to the fourth century all the different aspects of this powerful mystery were separated into specific units that centered on particular features of the mystery. Originally the Easter Vigil was spent in fasting and mourning over the death of Jesus until midnight.[16] The joy of the resurrection thus began at the end of the evening's vigil. At the end of the fourth century there was no Easter Sunday mass, as the Easter liturgy lasted all night long.

Over time, however, the vigil prior to the mass was shortened. In response to the vigil not lasting until the appointed midnight hour, the church of the sixth century initiated an Easter Sunday liturgy. By the eighth century, an early evening vigil emerged, and by the ninth century the rituals that preceded the mass were moved back to noon, thus pushing the mass back to three o'clock. From the Middle Ages on, three o'clock in the afternoon became the starting time for all masses that took place on fast days.

Fasting laws relaxed during the fourteenth century, so masses on fast days were moved to the morning hours. This posed a serious problem, however, for the Easter Vigil. The vigil rituals had to take place in the very early hours of the morning in order for the mass to be celebrated during regular morning hours. This was made obligatory by Pius V. The result: the Easter Candle was carried into the church to the proclamation of *Lumen Christi* in the full light of day, with no one but a few clerics and a handful of the faithful gathered for participation.

Then, in 1951, Pius XII restored the early church's experience of the night vigil and moved it to the night before Easter. The rite was revised and finally made law in 1955. "The Roman Catholic liturgy had rediscovered a lost treasure."[17] Further steps were taken to restore this beautiful, awesome liturgy to its rightful place and status among the liturgies of the church. "During it [the Easter Vigil] the Church keeps watch, awaiting the resurrection of Christ and celebrating it in the sacraments. The entire celebration of this Vigil should take place at night, beginning after nightfall and ending with dawn."[18] "In accord with an ancient tradition, this night is a night of vigil for the Lord, and, as the memorial of the holy night of Christ's resurrection, the Vigil celebrated is the 'mother of all holy vigils.' The Church this night awaits the Lord's resurrection and celebrates the sacrament of initiation."[19]

By the fourth century, pieces of the Triduum gradually developed and merged into one distinct commemoration of the paschal mystery. The Triduum is the word designated for celebration of the Lord's paschal mystery that spans three days. The Triduum is one liturgy that lasts three days. There is no formal closing to the Holy Thursday or Good Friday liturgies. The liturgy continues for three days until its culmination at the Easter Vigil. For three days, the church enters and remains in the tomb with Christ. The Triduum begins with the Mass of the Lord's Supper, continues with the celebration of the Lord's passion on Good Friday, culminates with the Easter Vigil on Holy Saturday, and ends with evening prayer on Easter Sunday.

Holy Thursday

The Mass of the Lord's Supper begins the Triduum. It commemorates the Last Supper and is a living memorial of the institution of the eucharist and of the Lord's Passover in which Jesus left us sacramental signs of his new covenant. In this new covenant, Jesus promised to be with us through the signs he inaugurated (especially the eucharist). Through the *mandatum*, the washing of feet, Jesus reminds us of the self-sacrificing nature of his love. Jesus, servant of the human race, loves

[16] *LY*, 64.

[17] Ibid., 77.

[18] *GNLY*, #21.

[19] "Ceremonial of Bishops," #332.

us to his death. Jesus, servant of all, washes the feet of those he serves and instructs his disciples to go and do the same. We share in the servanthood of Christ. In John's gospel there is no eucharist of bread and wine. John's eucharist *is* the washing of feet. The implication? Go, do this in memory of me! The "Ceremonial of Bishops" asserts that the liturgy of Holy Thursday recalls the unconditional love of God and the height and the depth of that love—even unto death.[20]

We slowly shift into part two of our three-day liturgy as part one quietly fades into the meditative silence of darkness. The liturgy of Holy Thursday draws to its temporary intermission, and the church enters into the silence of meditation as it sets its face toward Jerusalem and the ominous events that will forever change the world.

Good Friday

Celebration of the Lord's Passion on Good Friday commemorates the redemption Jesus won for us through the free gift of his life. Jesus was the messianic fulfillment prefigured by the law and the prophets in the Old Testament scriptures. The redemptive act of the cross was the fulfillment of all the saving acts of Yahweh prior to the Incarnation.

The liturgy of Good Friday begins in silent prayer. There are three parts: the liturgy of the word, with John's account of the passion and the general intercessions; the veneration of the cross; and communion using bread consecrated at the Holy Thursday liturgy. During the liturgy of the word we encounter John's Christ, the royal victor, who is fully aware of his divine preexistence.[21] Jesus' death will return him to his former state, to the state that was his before he was sent to this life's sojourn by his Father. He is not a victim; he is the initiator of events. Jesus freely walks to his death. Jesus is aware of his victory over his enemy, Satan. The Good Friday liturgy is a cause for joyful celebration because of the infinite love of God demonstrated through his Son's passion.[22]

The intercessions of Good Friday are a sign of the priestly function of God's people. All are gathered together in the sacred assembly to offer prayers on behalf of the entire world. The veneration of the cross reminds us of the good news inherent in the cross: this instrument of torture became a sign of salvation and love for all humanity. Part two of this great three-day feast culminates with the reception of communion consecrated the night before at the Holy Thursday Mass of the Lord's Supper. The faithful then leave in silence. The church stands hopeful as it anticipates the night of the great Phoenix rising out of the ashes of sin and death. The church, then, awaits the Passover of the Lord.

The Easter Vigil

The Easter Vigil, in the words of St. Augustine, is the mother of all feasts. It takes center stage in relation to the other liturgies of the Triduum. "During it [the Easter Vigil] the Church keeps watch, awaiting the resurrection of Christ and *celebrating it in the sacraments* [italics mine]. The entire celebration of this Vigil should take place at night, beginning after nightfall and ending with the dawn."[23] There are four parts to the liturgy of this most holy night: the service of fire/light, the liturgy of the word, the service of baptism, and the liturgy of the eucharist.

The Service of Fire/Light

The service of fire/light catapults us back to the journey of the Israelites as they were led by the bright pillar of fire. The radiance of that fire, now dimmed, was replaced by the light of Christ shining in the lives of people. The primordial symbol of fire is blessed anew. The light of the Easter candle is triumphantly carried into the darkened space; the Easter proclamation of *Christ, the Light Who Dispels the Darkness* is shouted, resounded, proclaimed, and heralded in the midst of the great assembly. The *Exultet's* euphoric proclamation elevates the gathering to a communion between the saints of heaven and earth who stand exultant in an assembly of triumphant victory over the crushed head of Satan, the evil arch-villain.

[20]Ibid., #297.
[21]*CCHW*, 57.
[22]*DL* (III), 23.

[23]*GNLY*, #21.

The Liturgy of the Word

The liturgy of the word carries us back to the roots of our Christian genesis: creation, passover, and paschal mystery. The believer is thrust into the drama of the first passover, Israel's liberation from bondage; the second passover, Jesus' passage from death to resurrection; and the third and ongoing passover, the church's passover from sin, darkness, and death to resurrected life both now and for eternity. The Vigil scriptures move us into a world of virtual reality. We are present at the threshold of dawn's first light, water's first flow, the star's first glimmer, the animal's first ravenous howl, the seed's first agonizing rupture from earth's womb and humanity's entrance on the world stage. We are hardly passive spectators as we intimately encounter man's and woman's first cognizance of their own goodness.

We are there and it is now as we stand with Abraham and Sarah in that first perpetual covenant of faith. *We are there and it is now* as we trudge through the parted waters of death, pursued and exhausted by Pharaoh's onslaught, only to be enfolded in the protective mantle of Yahweh's liberating providence. *We are there and it is now* as we call down that great and terrible day of the Lord's visitation, when sin comes to an end and we are gathered as *one people* to process majestically to the gates of the jeweled eternal city. (The first four Old Testament readings.)

The word reminds us that this is a night of genesis, of new life. Life is reborn as we witness the baptismal passage from death to life. Water flows abundantly as it promises to quench our thirst. The God who calls us to repentance pours down the waters of forgiveness on the church. The wisdom who blesses, invites, and leads to the light also delivers us from the stain of defilement. We are sprinkled with fresh water, given new hearts, taken by the hand, and led to the font. (The last three Old Testament readings).

We are then ready to stand in the Roman assembly as Paul definitively acclaims (then and now) that baptism is the "passage from death to sin, to life for God."[24] And finally, as fully engaged, sense-sharpened celebrants, we go with Matthew to the empty tomb, where we, alongside the women witnesses,[25] are the first to hear the wondrous news: "Do not be frightened. I know you are looking for Jesus the crucified, but he is not here. He has been raised, exactly as he promised."

[24]*DL* (III), 43.

The Service of Baptism

Thus, our senses sated and our emotions spent, we escort the elect to the font of life to *do* what we have heard, experienced, professed, and acclaimed. We bring new life to birth and in the process initiate our own rebirth.

As this is a night of new things and new beginnings, the new water is blessed. The water carries symbols and images both ancient and new. As the new water is blessed, the presider-celebrant once again touches our corporate memory. We are reminded of how God's hand once stirred the embryonic waters of creation and deluged the earth with flood, thereby hinting at the purgation of sin through water. Scripture's water images bring us face to face with the God who parted the Red Sea of deliverance. The symbol of water takes us to the shore of the Jordan River where Jesus, the "Beloved Son" whose lanced side would inaugurate the saving flow of his water and his blood, was baptized. Finally, the holy waters of creation, the Red Sea, and the Jordan still flow through the apostolic mission to baptize in the name of the Father, Son, and Holy Spirit.[26] The service of baptism lets us once again plunge into the ancient primordial symbol of water to remind us of who God is, what God did, and what God continues to do in and through the resurrection of Jesus Christ. God immerses us in the purging waters of baptism where death sinks to the bottom and resurrected life gushes to the top, dripping and spilling over at the font's edge. With all the saints—past, present, and future—the church, in its annual ritual, celebrates resurrected life and initiates new members into its hallowed communion.

[25]In order for an event to be proclaimed as authentic, there needed to be two male witnesses. Thus, one can hardly miss the irony that the only witnesses to the empty tomb were not even officially allowed to testify to what they had seen and heard. God does not need a human court to authenticate the greatest act of redemption in salvation history.

[26]*DL* (III), 63.

Together with the elect, we commit and recommit ourselves through our baptismal promises. We pledge to enter and continue in the struggle between good and evil by renouncing evil's lure. We profess our faith in the Father, the resurrected Christ, and the Holy Spirit. Finally, the baptismal liturgy comes to a close as the newly baptized are anointed with confirmation's holy oil, permanently signed and sealed with the Spirit and delivered into God's service. Thus bathed and anointed, neophytes are ready for the joyful, exultant, and long awaited culmination of their journey: incorporation into the Body of Christ through the eucharist, the ongoing participation in Christ's paschal mystery. Purged, reconciled, and renewed through the waters of baptism, the faithful are ready for eucharist, that which St. Augustine called the repeatable sacrament of initiation.

Liturgy of the Eucharist

As the assembly breathes a sigh of intermission, the gifts of bread and wine are brought to the table and the paschal story continues in word and action. Calvary and Easter coexist boldly on our communal table. The *cross* stands triumphant in the brilliant light of the *resurrection* and we, God's people, consume both realities at the eucharistic banquet. Thus fed, we go forth, cross in hand, the resurrection in heart, and take what we have consumed to feed the starving soul of the world.

If this sounds like poetry, so it must. It is only through the language of poets that we dare come close to capturing the mystery of this sacred, awe-filled, holy night.

Symbols of the Vigil

The dominant liturgical symbols of the church—assembly, cross, fire/light, word, water, oil, white garment, laying on of hands, bread, wine—are all manifest at the Easter Vigil. The symbols speak to us of our identity as Catholic Christians. For example, the symbol of light has its genesis in Christ, the light of the world. Since we are to walk as children of the light, light identifies us and we become its reality—we become light, we become bread, etc.

Meaning is conveyed when people encounter symbols, which are repeatable and possess many layers of meaning. They are multi-faceted and have multiple forms and uses. At the Vigil alone, the symbol of light shines forth in the new fire, the Easter candle, the candles of the faithful, the incense, and the sanctuary lamp. Light's power is felt by its absence in the darkened church. The meaning of symbols is expressed in the way they are used and in the background and gestures that define them. Symbols are also understood through the words of the ritual text that are used in relation to them, and through the sacramental proclamation of God's word that accompanies their use.[27]

The Easter Vigil calls forth the symbols that illuminate our existence and that occur in all liturgies. We are people of the cross. We are chrismated into the ecclesial community. We are people of the light and the water of baptism incorporates us into the paschal mystery. We are people of the table: we are eucharistic people.

"Liturgical action depends on symbols because beings cannot be together and communicate without some kind of encounter in words (verbal symbols) and/or in gestures and actions (nonverbal symbols). All knowledge begins with our senses; this means that an encounter with God is only possible by means of sensible signs."[28] In antiquity, a symbol used to be understood as two halves, which when joined became one whole. The person who had one half would thus recognize the other half because the two put together formed the whole entity. By extension, then, a symbol can be regarded as two parts of a whole—the visible and the invisible. Just because the invisible half of the symbol is not readily observable, it is nevertheless half of the reality. When joined with the visible half of the symbol, it constitutes the whole reality. "In the language of religion and theology it is frequently the case that the concept of 'symbol' is reserved for the signs of faith, that is... in addition to their superficial, natural meaning, another and supernatural meaning that is only accessible to

[27]Linda Gaupin, *Sacramental Catechesis,* course text for "Special Certification in Sacramental Catechesis," Diocese of Orlando, Florida, November 1996.

[28]*MSS,* 13.

faith."[29] Through symbols we are able to touch the deep mysteries of our faith in ways that words can never express.

If symbols were to speak, they would say: "I am . . ." rather than "I am like. . . ." Symbols in the sacramental sense *are* the reality they express. Eucharist in the form of bread and wine *is* the Body and Blood of Jesus. We can say with assurance that symbols express our identity. When we consume the precious elements, we become what we have consumed: the Mystical Body of Christ. The symbols of the Easter Vigil, highlighted and set forth, give us the means to communicate with God and for God to communicate with us through our senses. They express all of our sacramental realities. The symbols of the Vigil are food for mystagogical reflection throughout the Easter season and form the basis of our sacramental catechesis.

Easter Sunday

The Easter Sunday liturgy is a later development and thus did not originally have a liturgy of its own. The Easter Vigil is considered the principal mass of the Easter feast.[30] The Easter Sunday mass, however, is a cacophony of jubilation. From the opening prayers to the dismissal alleluia, praise and thanks are rendered for the resurrection of the Lord Jesus Christ. Many people who attend Easter Sunday mass do not attend the Vigil. It is important, therefore, that the homily reflect the unity of the passion and resurrection just as it is reflected in the Easter preface and the communion antiphon. The Vigil should be upheld "as the climax of the liturgical year and thus should be explained."[31] Very often the neophytes return on Easter Sunday and take their rightful place as fully initiated, candle carrying, garmented members of the celebrating assembly. The neophytes themselves are an Easter symbol for the community: a symbol of new, resurrected life in our midst.

[29]Ibid.
[30]*LY,* 83.
[31]Ibid., 84.

OCTAVE OF EASTER

The first eight days after Easter are called the octave. The liturgical calendar names each day a solemnity of the Lord ("General Instruction of the Roman Missal," #24). The observance of the octave dates back to the mid-third to fourth century. Some suggest that celebration of the octave has its roots in the Jewish Passover and the seven days of Unleavened Bread. Each day of the octave was, for the neophytes, a fuller introduction to the mysteries of faith and their initiation sacraments. Observance of the octave was a universal practice of the church (*ecclesiae consensus)* in which all the faithful attended daily liturgy and refrained from work. At one time the octave was referred to as "white week," since the neophytes wore their white baptismal garments to mass. The Eastern church called it a "week of renewal."

Due to the fast-paced life we lead, it is often difficult for the neophytes to attend daily liturgy during the octave. However, the practice should be strongly encouraged. The solemnities of the octave are an integral part of the Easter mystery. Most catechetical groups do not have the opportunity to come together to experience and reflect upon each day of the octave. This workbook will not provide sessions for the days of the octave. However, the octave should not be ignored. Those in catechetical groups—actually, all Catholics—should make every effort to attend daily mass and, when possible, reflect upon the scriptures, ritual prayers, and experience of the liturgies of the octave.

FIFTY DAYS OF EASTER

"The fifty days from Easter Sunday to Pentecost are sometimes called the great 'Sunday.'"[32] Each Sunday is considered a paschal Sunday; the Sundays are called the Second, Third, Fourth, etc. Sundays *of* Easter (not after Easter) until the eighth Sunday, called Pentecost. Forty days after Easter, the Ascension of the Lord into heaven is celebrated except in places where it is not a holy day of obligation, in which case it is moved to the Seventh Sunday of Easter. Following the feast of the Ascension, the weekdays are intended as a

[32]*GNLY,* #22.

preparation for Pentecost. Each Sunday of the Easter season is a solemnity, a Great Feast. Each Sunday exalts an aspect of the paschal mystery.

All three scripture readings of the Sundays are taken from the New Testament. The first reading is always from the Acts of the Apostles. The second reading for Cycle A is from the first letter of Peter. The gospel readings for Cycle A are from John, with the exception of the Third Sunday of Easter, which is Luke's account of the Emmaus story.

The celebration of the fifty days is the church's extended meditation on the paschal mystery as the source, summit, and driving power of the Christian life. The paschal mystery is the heart of all celebration, liturgical and sacramental. The resurrection of Jesus is the hinge on which the doors of faith swing. Without it, the church has no purpose for existence.

The Fifty Days of Easter and the Rite of Christian Initiation

The fifty days of Easter are also called the period of mystagogia (uncovering the mysteries). In the early centuries of the church, there existed an advanced type of religious instruction called mystagogical catechesis, or an introduction to the mysteries. This was usually directed by the bishop after baptism, not before. There was a belief that neophytes were unable to comprehend the church's teaching on eucharist until they had experienced it. Once they had taken part in the ritual celebration, then and only then would they be able to grasp what the awesome mystery was about. In his first address to the neophytes, St. Ambrose began: "I shall begin now to speak of the sacraments which you have received. It was not proper for me to do so before this, because, the Christian faith must come first."[33]

The reality of the risen and crucified Christ was conveyed through the initiation rites and their powerful symbols, thus sparking faith and enthusiasm. Mystagogical catechesis infuses the truths of the faith and the sacraments through the concrete, personal, and vivid memories of water-soaked skin, oil-slathered body, and flowing white robes. St. Cyril said it best to the neophytes: "It has long been my wish to discourse to you on these spiritual, heavenly mysteries. On the principle, however, that seeing is believing, I delayed until the present occasion, calculating that, after what you saw that night, I should find you a readier audience when I am to be your guide to the brighter and more fragrant meadows of this second Eden."[34]

Mystagogical catechesis seeks to make a connection between the events of salvation history (the prefiguring events of the Old Testament and their fulfillment through Christ) and the rites that make those saving events manifest and the benefits operative. Mystagogical catechesis explains the rite in dialogue with the experience of it. Mystagogical catechesis weds truth and experience. During their preparation for baptism, the catechumens immersed themselves in God's word and in the truths of our faith laid out in the celebration of the litugical year. As they unpacked the liturgy week after week, they discovered the truths of salvation history, and with baptism, confirmation, and eucharist they completed the rites of initiation. Now, for the first time, their prior knowledge and their experience come together.

The agenda of mystagogia is ongoing ritual catechesis. What happened? What did it mean? What are the implications and what am I going to do about them? Mystagogy is ongoing, repeated celebration leading to reflection that provides understanding which demands a response, a decision. Mystagogical catechesis is an activity of the entire church. It is what the Easter season is all about. We are *all* to spend the season asking, "What happened, what was my experience, and what does it mean?" The neophytes point to what we should all be doing.

During the season of Easter, the entire church enters a period of mystagogia in which we experience and reflect upon the meaning of the symbols of initiation that express the dying and rising of Jesus for the fifty days between Easter and Pentecost Sunday. "Mystagogy is a time for the community and the neophytes together to grow in deepening their grasp of the paschal mystery and in making it part of their lives through meditation

[33]St. Ambrose, *Catechesis mystagogica* 1.1. (PG 33, 1066).

[34]St. Cyril of Jerusalem 14.10 (PG 33, 836), in *ME*, 65.

on the Gospel, sharing in the Eucharist and doing the works of charity."[35] It is a time for reflection on the way we are called to die and rise and thus fully embrace the paschal mystery in our daily lives. Reflection on the Easter gospels in light of their sacramental experience is the springboard for neophytes to unpack the meaning of the sacraments. This is post-baptismal, sacramental catechesis. Mystagogia is a time to gather with the community for eucharist and to be fed at the paschal table. It is a time to become more immersed in a life of service, outreach, evangelization, and corporal and spiritual works of mercy.

The heart of mystagogy flows from ritual. We pray, we celebrate, we believe; then we seek to find meaning in our prayer, celebration, and belief. What does it mean for our lives? The ritual of mystagogia is eucharist, the "repeatable sacrament of initiation" (Augustine). The neophyte and the worshiping community become immersed in the Easter stories, symbols, and eucharists. Knowledge and understanding of the church's Easter tradition are thus based on experience. The risen Christ is experienced in word, in sacrament, and in symbol. To experience Christ is to "know" Christ.

The fifty days of Easter show us how to live the mystery of the Risen Lord as a result of plunging into the waters of rebirth, of being anointed with the Spirit, and of feasting at the Lord's table. Empty vessels become fully filled. The whole church is catechized, not just the neophytes.

Thus, while post-baptismal catechesis would appear to be only for neophytes, it is indeed the business of everyone; it is a lifelong pursuit. The scriptures and liturgies of the season invite us to engage in this ancient form of catechesis in order to become fully absorbed in the paschal mystery of Jesus Christ. The historical perspective of the fifty days will be covered in the section that deals with Pentecost.

ASCENSION

The feast of the Ascension is a solemnity that focuses on Jesus' second coming (entrance rite) and his continued risen presence in the community (communion antiphon). The liturgy's opening prayer expresses the effects of the resurrection: the elevation of human beings to the glory of Christ. The first two readings are the same every year but the gospel changes according to the cycle.

During the fourth century, the feast of the Ascension was celebrated on the fiftieth day along with the feast of Pentecost. However, there emerged a practice of celebrating the Ascension on the fortieth day after Easter. The reason for this was twofold. First, there was a strong connection to the sacred significance of the number forty. Second, there was reference in the Acts of the Apostles to "appearing during forty days..." and also the witness of the Ascension account in verses 9-11. The decision was made to place the celebration forty days after the resurrection.

The weekdays following Ascension serve as preparation for Pentecost, for the coming of the Holy Spirit. Thus, the old popular devotion, the Pentecost novena, was replaced by an official liturgy. During these pre-Pentecost days, the church enters the room of prayer with Mary, the women, and the disciples as they await the holy fire of the Spirit.

PENTECOST

Pentecost (*pentekoste,* the ordinal form of the number fifty) takes place fifty days after Easter and brings the Easter season to a close. It is the final, dramatic curtain call in which the church is brought on stage, commissioned, and sent out with the fire of the Holy Spirit. Pentecost inaugurates the full manifestation of the Spirit in the messianic age. Pentecost ushers us into the reality of all that was prophesied by the law and the prophets and then fulfilled through Jesus Christ. Pentecost, in its thunderous clamor from the womb of anticipation, celebrates the church's birth on Calvary. Even though Pentecost commemorates the events that took place fifty days after Easter, it continues on through time through the liturgical celebration.[36]

[35] *RCIA,* #244.

[36] *DL* (III), 249.

Pentecost is the day the church celebrates the conferral of the Holy Spirit. "It appears on the fiftieth day, when the Spirit was poured out on the first Christian community, giving it the strength and confidence to testify publicly to the resurrection."[37] The paschal celebration of redemption through Christ took place over the fifty days of Easter and was understood to include the "victorious passion and death, his resurrection and ascension, and the sending of the Spirit upon the Church."[38] Thus, Easter was not just a celebration of the resurrection of Christ, but also an extension of his ministry through the Spirit to the Church: "... Pascha was a total celebration of our redemption...."[39]

The Christian feast of Pentecost has its roots and is to be understood in light of the Jewish celebration by that same name. The Jewish feast of Pentecost, or Weeks, also called *Shabuoth* ("Weeks") was the closing feast for the season of harvest that began with the feast of Unleavened Bread. Thomas Talley speaks of several hypotheses regarding the origin of Pentecost. He suggests that some scholars maintain that Pentecost represents a period of seven weeks measured from the day after Passover. The feast of Passover marked the first day. Thus, seven times a seven-day week equals forty-nine and the addition of one day for festival makes a *pentecontad*, or a period of fifty days.[40] There was dispute over how to count the days and there was an absence of dispute regarding a particular date for the feast of Weeks. Thus, it is suggested that "in the first century it was not simply the fiftieth day that was considered sacred, but the very period between that fiftieth day and the day from which it was counted, a day related in one way or another to Passover."[41] Since pilgrims from Judea and Galilee gathered in Jerusalem for the single-day feast of Pentecost, some scholars suggest that Pentecost was the celebration that brought the entire season, beginning with Passover, to a close. However, Talley maintains that there is also scriptural evidence that the feast stood on its own and was a feast celebrating the renewal of covenant and the giving of the law (Book of Jubilees, ca. 140–100 B.C.E.).[42] During the time of Christ it was probably being observed as a feast of renewal of the covenant.

There is no solid evidence to suggest that the period between Passover and Pentecost was appropriated as one feast of rejoicing by the first-century Christian church. However, by the second century there is evidence (fasting and kneeling in prayer were forbidden during the fifty days) that Christians observed an extended festival from Easter to Pentecost.

As the feast evolved and in places where it was celebrated on Sunday, the feast of Pentecost was counted from Easter-day itself, thus making Pentecost the eighth Sunday after Easter Sunday. Easter to Pentecost was celebrated as one continuous period of rejoicing. However, by the fourth century, the unitive dimension to the fifty days of Easter waned in the Roman church as Ascension and Pentecost were regarded as distinct festivals. Adolf Adam reminds us that the East always regarded Pentecost as the close of the Easter season. The Roman liturgy, on the other hand, "made this day an independent entity and thus a more or less isolated feast of the sending of the Holy Spirit."[43] Like the great feast of Easter, Pentecost was thus afforded an octave that caused liturgical confusion as it coincided with the ember days (days of penance), which had already been established on the liturgical calendar. Thus, this feast of rejoicing over the sending of the Spirit was clouded by days of penance.

In light of historical liturgical studies, the Congregation of Rites restored Pentecost to its unity with Easter and reaffirmed the close connection between the Resurrection, Ascension, and the sending of the Spirit. The "General Norms for the Liturgical Year and the Calendar" states: "The fifty days from Easter Sunday to Pentecost are celebrated in joyful exultation as one feast day, or better as one 'great Sunday'" [#22].

There are two liturgies of Pentecost: the vigil mass and mass during the day. The vigil mass is not

[37]Ibid., 293–294.

[38]*OLY*, 57.

[39]Ibid.

[40]Ibid.

[41]Ibid., 59.

[42]Ibid., 61.

[43]*LY*, 89–90.

widely celebrated as the "mass during the day" is usually chosen for the Saturday evening liturgy prior to Pentecost Sunday. Even though we seldom participate in the vigil mass, the texts are nevertheless a wonderful preparatory meditation in anticipation of the Sunday celebration of Pentecost. The second reading and the gospel are always the same: Romans 8:22–27 and John 7:37–39. The first reading is chosen from among four possibilities: Genesis 11:1–9, Exodus 19:3–8, 16–20, Ezekiel 37:1–14, and Joel 3:1–5.

Pentecost's power is not simply in the recall of a monumental sacred event. While it is indeed just that, it is so much more. Pentecost is an ongoing event. It was inaugurated in the first Christian community, but it still continues to unfold in this messianic era. Pentecost is our eternal hope: it is the perpetual gift of the Spirit to build the Body of Christ. Pentecost celebrates within the community that which takes place in the individual through baptism and eucharist. The Spirit who breathes transforming life into the church is given at baptism and continues to be manifest through the ongoing celebration of eucharist. It is the same Spirit who challenges, teaches, seals us permanently to Christ, and leads us forward in holiness to the new Jerusalem, the holy, eternal city. Pentecost celebrates the reign of God now and not yet; it is a present and future reality. The Spirit of Pentecost continues the work of Christ on earth as we are formed and prepared for the great day of his return. Pentecost is the ongoing renewal of our participation in Christ's new covenant. The liturgy of Pentecost calls us to worship in spirit and in truth. We are strengthened for mission to the world's poor, oppressed, and spiritually hungry.

In summary then, Easter is a living memorial of the primary Christian symbol of deliverance and liberation—Christ's passion, death, and resurrection. Through his ultimate act of sacrifice, Jesus inaugurated the *new covenant.* Jesus, the New Passover, shed his blood, thereby ratifying the new covenant. Jesus' passage from death to life for the forgiveness of sins fulfilled all the promises Yahweh had made with Israel since the creation of the world. Death ultimately lost its power. Christ's death and resurrection would guarantee human beings a place at the eternal banquet. The living memorial of Christ's Passover today is our sharing in the Body and Blood of Christ in the eucharist and our incorporation into and participation in the paschal mystery.

Each year, Easter renews our participation in the paschal mystery. We recall and renew our participation in the life, passion, death, and resurrection of Jesus and the sending of the Spirit to the church. Liturgically and sacramentally we celebrate and exalt the saving effects in our lives. We recommit our lives to cross and resurrection, to dying and rising, and in the process we are renewed in the mandate to go out, teach, and baptize all nations. Such is our faith; so shall it be.

HOLY THURSDAY

INTRODUCTORY RITES

Opening Song (or Entrance Antiphon)

We should glory in the cross of our Lord Jesus Christ, for he is our salvation, our life and our resurrection; through him we are saved and made free.[1]

Opening Prayer

Let us pray.

Pause for silent prayer.

God our Father,
we are gathered here to share in the supper
which your only Son left to his Church to reveal
his love.
He gave it to us when he was about to die
and commanded us to celebrate it as the new and
eternal sacrifice.
We pray that in this eucharist
we may find the fullness of love and life.
Grant this through our Lord Jesus Christ, your Son,
who lives and reigns with you and the Holy Spirit,
one God, for ever and ever.[2]

LITURGY OF THE WORD

Let us listen to God's word.

The readings are proclaimed.

First Reading
Exodus 12:1–8, 11–14

The synoptic gospels place the Last Supper in the context of a Passover meal. John's gospel places it a day before Passover. While the historical facts are not certain, one thing is: the meal was cloaked in the experience and language of Passover. It is very appropriate that the Triduum begin with this reading. The entire experience of Christ's passion, death, and resurrection was understood in light of the passover experience. Jesus naturally was seen as the fulfillment of all the promises inherent in the passover tradition.

As said multiple times throughout this workbook, the Passover was for Israel the hallmark event that celebrated Yahweh's redemptive act of salvation. Then and today every observant Jew remembers the exodus story as if he or she had actually been present for the original event.

The blood on the doorposts was considered a prefiguring of the blood that Christ would shed. This saving blood, shed for the sins of the world, is made real, active, and present at every celebration of eucharist.

This reading remembers the ritual of unleavened bread and passover lamb. Originally, the two rites were separate. Prior to the exodus, the ritual of the sacrificial lamb was used by herders to satisfy the gods as the herders moved their flocks from well-irrigated winter land to dry summer lands. The unleavened bread was used in a ritual for farmers. The rite functioned as a spring cleaning of the previous year's leaven. Tonight's text brings the sacrificial lamb ritual into the exodus story (vv. 11–13). The unleavened bread is established as a living memorial of the actual exodus narrative.[3] Thus, the ritual celebration of the passover lamb and the unleavened bread celebrated in the spring of each new year affords the descendants of the Israelites the opportunity to mark once again the liberation from the yoke of Egyptian bondage. The unleavened bread was a sign that those in bondage had to leave in haste. This urgency evolved through the generations to an expectation of the coming messiah who would return at night.

Our eucharistic bread is unleavened, just as the bread of exodus was unleavened. The nomadic

---

[1] Evening Mass of the Lord's Supper: "Entrance Antiphon," *The Sacramentary.*

[2] Evening Mass of the Lord's Supper: "Opening Prayer," *The Sacramentary.*

[3] Richard J. Clifford, S.J., "Exodus," in *NJBC,* 49.

life was a hurried life; people had to be ready to pick up and leave at a moment's notice. There was no time to wait for the leaven to rise. The Israelites, fleeing from Pharaoh, had no time to wait for the unleavened bread to rise. Eucharistic people are on the move to the new and eternal city. They also have no time to wait around for the bread to rise, but rather, are in a hurry to work for the coming reign of God. For the nomads, for the fleeing Israelites, and for Christians, the unleavened bread was food for their respective journeys.

The shedding of Jesus' blood was easily connected with the Old Testament understanding of blood. Blood was a sign of life. "Blood took on special significance for the Israelites both in the popular imagination and in the official cult.... Blood, as the bearer of life, was offered to God as atonement for humanity's sins."[4] The blood poured out on the altar was a substitute for the human sinner. Thus, an animal that was sacrificed served as a symbol. The animal stood in the place of the sinner who was symbolically offering his own life in order to reestablish the lost covenant relationship with God. The blood of rams was placed on the horns of the altar and on the altar as a sign of the cleansing properties of blood. "The blood removed the impurities which would defile the Israelite community and its cult."[5]

In the ancient agricultural world, blood represented the sharing of all life. Both animals and humans were in relational community. Even though animals had to die for the people to survive, there was a special life relationship with the animals. To shed the blood of an animal was a sacred event. Also, those who shed their own blood to save others were considered sacred people.[6]

The ancient rituals of blood were fulfilled through the shedding of Jesus' blood on the cross. He offered his blood for the sins of the world. In every eucharist we eat Jesus' Body and drink his Blood. Jesus is the new passover; he passed through death to life. Every time we celebrate eucharist we participate in that same passover. With Jesus, we pass from death to sin, to new life in Christ.

[4]Dale Launderville, O.S.B., "Blood," in *CPDBT*, 95.

[5]Ibid., 96.

[6]James A. Fischer, "Blood, New Testament," in *CPDBT*, 97.

Responsorial Psalm
Psalm 116:12–13, 15–16, 17–18

This psalm celebrates the unity of the eucharist: a sacrifice of thanksgiving and a communion among believers.[7] This is a prayer of thanks after a difficult, terrifying ordeal.

Scholars are stumped when it comes to verse 15 in which the death of the faithful ones is precious in the eyes of the Lord. "Difficult. Just why their death should be 'precious' to Yahweh is not easy to see."[8]

Second Reading
1 Corinthians 11:23–26

This is the earliest fragment of Christian tradition preserved in the New Testament. Paul stated that he had received the tradition given in today's letter prior to his dealings with the Corinthians. He used language denoting the *passing on of tradition,* such as that which is passed on through the oral teaching of the rabbis. Paul received his revelation from the oral tradition in which human witnesses, under the inspiration of the risen Christ, shared and passed on their experience.

It is believed that today's pericope is an exegesis of a eucharistic liturgy already being celebrated. It does not completely describe the Last Supper, but rather seeks to define it in light of eucharistic theology. In the earliest celebration of the *breaking of bread,* there was a supper between the bread and the cup (as alluded to in this pericope), thus testifying to the primitive character of this text.[9]

Just as the unleavened bread was a living memorial of the events of Passover, so too is the unleavened bread of eucharist a living memorial of the events of Jesus' *passage through death to life.*

There are strong eschatological overtones in tonight's second reading. Paul reminds us of the Lord's second coming. Eucharist, for Paul and for us, was and is a ritual remembering of the cross

[7]*PNL*, 17.

[8]John S. Kselman and Michael Barré, S.S., "Psalms," in *NJBC*, 546.

[9]*PNL*, 17.

with its effects made real and present. It is an anticipation of Jesus' second coming: "Christ has died, Christ is risen, Christ will come again."

Gospel
John 13:1–15

Jesus washes the feet of his disciples.

STEP 1
NAMING ONE'S EXPERIENCE

What were your first impressions? What was your first response? What grabbed your attention? How did you feel?

Each person names his or her initial impression. Statements should be brief. No reasons should be given at this time. All simply listen without agreeing or disagreeing.

STEP 2
UNDERSTANDING

In a brief statement, what do you think this gospel is trying to convey?

STEP 3
INPUT FROM VISION/STORY/TRADITION

Liturgical Context

Order of Service: Liturgy of the Word, Washing of Feet, Intercessions, Liturgy of Eucharist, Transfer of Eucharist

The observance of Holy Thursday began as a ritual celebration commemorating the Lord's Supper in Jerusalem. The story of the Christ's Last Supper is told and remembered as the event that instituted the eucharist. The Sacramentary defines the homiletic focus of tonight's liturgy: the institution of the eucharist; the institution of the priesthood; and the commandment of filial love. The first and second readings address the institution of the eucharist. The gospel hints at the institution of priesthood[10] and filial love is expressed in all three readings.

The liturgy for Holy Thursday is not unlike every liturgy of the year. However, it does have its own character and is set apart in one particular way. Holy Thursday is understood as the day Jesus was betrayed. This liturgy does *not* attempt to re-create the Last Supper. Jesus is referred to in the third person as if he were absent. "The night he *was* betrayed, he *took* bread," etc. However, the telling makes the actions and words present to us in a very concrete way. At every eucharist, the story we proclaim and the action we perform becomes a reality. The word is *anamnesis,* a remembering that brings the event forward and makes it present. This happens at every liturgy. The Holy Thursday liturgy is the same as every other liturgy in that regard. Where Holy Thursday is unique is that it highlights and exalts the connection between the free offering of Jesus' life through his passion and death and our own present celebration of eucharist.

"Eucharist is the sacrament of the Lord's presence during his absence."[11] We are not participating in an historical reenactment of an event that took place two thousand years ago. The events are historical and they do belong to the past. However, we remember them and they become presently effective. The events of Calvary build up the Body of Christ and are continued today through the sacraments, an ongoing living memorial of those events. We share in Jesus' passion,

[10]Reginald Fuller cautions a careful handling of the issue of priesthood. He suggests that interpreting the command to "do this" as a command for priesthood oversimplifies the meaning for two reasons. First, the Vatican II document, *Decree on the Ministry and Life of Priests,* "set the eucharistic presidency in the wider context of a total pastoral ministry of word and sacrament." Also, there is no solid evidence as to who presided at the first liturgies. It is not until the second century that the bishop presides at liturgy and only later do the priests preside. "The command, 'Do this' (plural) is addressed to the Christian church as a whole. The eucharist is an action of the whole church and the preeminent expression of its priestly character" (1 Peter 2:1–10; Ap 1:6; and perhaps Hebrews 13:15). *PNL,* 18.

[11]*DL* (III), 15.

death, and resurrection and in his saving redemption every time we tell the story and share the meal in his memory. (For further insight, see "Gospel Exegesis," Palm Sunday.)

> Lord, make us worthy to celebrate these mysteries.
> Each time we offer this memorial sacrifice,
> the work of our redemption is accomplished.
> We ask this in the name of Jesus the Lord.[12]

One can understand tonight's liturgy only through the eyes of the Passover. Ancient nomads participated in a ritual to mark the movement of their flocks to summer pastures after the first full spring moon. It was a dangerous journey and, to ward off evil, they marked their tents with the blood of lambs. "The death would propitiate the death-threatening deities."[13]

Later it was very easy to appropriate this rite into the Passover ritual: it gave new meaning to an old rite. Christianity had the same experience: new meaning was given to many of the Old Testament rituals.

The ancient ritual of Passover had two parts: unleavened bread and the sacrifice of the paschal lamb (First Reading). This passover ritual was celebrated by Jesus himself. He prayed the ritual prayers and enacted the ritual actions, perhaps many times over. Jesus was celebrating a passover supper on this night prior to his act of redemption. It was natural that the Christian psyche connect Jesus to the paschal lamb that shed its blood in order to save the Jews from the angel of death in the book of Exodus. The early Christians understood the paschal lamb of Exodus as a foreshadowing of Christ, the Paschal Lamb. John would later declare: "This is the Lamb of God who takes away the sins of the world." Christianity took an old rite and breathed new meaning into it.

So much of the Passover is integral to our understanding of eucharist. Passover was not celebrated alone; it was a family, communal event. Similarly, eucharist is a community event; it is celebrated in communion with other believers. Israel was in relationship to God as a people; so too, are Christians saved as a people. It is not a private affair.

We hear from Paul (tonight's second reading), who received the tradition of the supper from the Lord himself. Today we celebrate the same ritual of breaking bread that Paul's community celebrated. We celebrate eucharist as a living memorial of Jesus' presence in his absence as expressed in the preface for this liturgy:

> Father, all-powerful and ever-living God,
> we do well always and everywhere to give you thanks
> through Jesus Christ our Lord.
> He is the true and eternal priest
> who established this unending sacrifice.
> He offered himself as a victim for our deliverance
> and taught us to make this offering in his memory.
> As we eat his body which he gave for us,
> we grow in strength.
> As we drink his blood which he poured out for us,
> we are washed clean.
> Now, with angels and archangels,
> and the whole company of heaven,
> we sing the unending hymn of your praise.[14]

The gospel for Holy Thursday is John's account of eucharist: washing feet. Some scholars suggest that John's account of the foot-washing scene was a homily given at a eucharistic liturgy in his community. Holy Thursday is the place for us to best understand the meaning of the foot washing (*mandatum*). Holy Thursday used to be called Maundy Thursday, a derivative of the word *mandatum.* The *mandatum* makes sense only in light of Christ's approaching death and resurrection. The *mandatum* flows from Jesus' ultimate act of love: the gift of his life. We, too, are to wash feet by loving and dying for others.

During the Holy Thursday liturgy, people come forward to have their feet washed. The ritual dates back to the fifth century in Jerusalem, the latter

[12]Evening Mass of the Lord's Supper: "Prayer Over the Gifts," *The Sacramentary.*

[13]Launderville, "Blood," 95.

[14]Evening Mass of the Lord's Supper: "Preface of Holy Eucharist," *The Sacramentary.*

part of the seventh century in Gaul and Spain, and the twelfth century in Rome. The *mandatum*, at one time considered a sacrament, was commonly celebrated throughout the year by the early church as a sign of service and Christian charity.

The implication of eucharist is that we share in the paschal mystery. We are called to serve and to wash feet. We are called to love as Christ loved by offering the gift of ourselves for others. The sign of foot washing leads us into the mystery of these three days. Also, Holy Thursday used to be the day on which penitents were reconciled to the church so they could participate in the paschal celebration.

This is the only liturgy in which the church prescribes a hymn during the presentation of the gifts. Gifts for the poor are presented and the antiphon *Ubi Caritas* is sung: "Where charity and love prevail, there is God." The offering of food for the poor is the community's way of ratifying in action the directive of the *mandatum:* "This example I leave you (Antiphon 1) . . . then surely you must wash one another's feet (Antiphon 3) . . . If there is this love among you, all will know that you are my disciples (Antiphon 4) . . . love one another as I have loved you . . ."(Antiphon 5).

Sufficient bread is consecrated so that there is enough for both Holy Thursday and Good Friday. The liturgy ends with a transfer of the eucharist to a different place of reservation. We continue our vigil in prayerful meditation with solemn adoration ending at midnight. Anticipation of Christ's passion begins immediately. There is quiet solemnity as people spend a holy hour in adoration.

After the liturgy, the altar is stripped without any special notice by the assembly. In the past, special meaning was assigned to this action. It was intended to be symbolic of the stripping of Jesus. While this action no longer holds the same meaning, the practice itself was restored after the Second Vatican Council.

Gospel Exegesis

The facilitator gives input regarding what critical biblical scholarship has to say about this text. The input includes insights as to how people would have heard the gospel in Jesus' time.

One scholar calls this story "revelation in action" of the mystery of God, of Jesus and his Passover.[15] The meaning is not apparent at first glance. It unfolds as the story progresses. Jesus laid aside his garment, wrapped a towel around himself, and washed his disciples' feet. Jesus' laying aside his garment in this pericope alerts us to a prophetic symbolism. "Laying aside" is akin to "laying down" as in "laying down one's life." Jesus' action is symbolic of what will happen through his death.

The action of foot washing in Jesus' culture was a very menial task. It was considered too lowly even for Jewish male slaves; only gentile slaves, wives, and children qualified. According to ancient Mediterranean custom, people bathed either at home or in the public baths before attending a dinner party. By the time they arrived at the party, the only washing ritual left was the washing of feet. Verses 6 and 8 refer to the washing of feet. Verses 9–10 refer to the washing of the entire body. Since the body had already been washed before the party, the only remaining washing was that of feet.

Charles Talbert suggests that "the bath of the whole person is linked with becoming a disciple."[16] The foot washing was a preparation for eating with Jesus. John's disciples *were already clean through a bath* (images of baptism). Jesus *made the disciples clean* by his word. Jesus was offering something beyond the cleanliness of the bath. He was offering ongoing, continued cleansing of the dust and dirt of life's everyday journey. This was to be preparation for the meal: disciples were to wash the feet of others. Talbert maintains that the point of the story is that through Jesus' death, the daily sins of disciples (who had already been washed clean earlier from the "principle of sin") were forgiven.[17] Thus, through Jesus' action of selfless love and service, post-baptismal sins are forgiven. After Jesus washed the feet of the disciples he took back his garments and resumed his place. The symbolic meaning in taking back his garments applies to Jesus' taking back his life.

[15]*DL* (III), 19.
[16]*RJ*, 193.
[17]Ibid., 194.

The "do as I have done" command usually is understood to mean: to act as Jesus, the humble servant. One scholar suggests another meaning. If we are to wash one another's feet for the daily forgiveness of sin, an inherent piece of the preparation for eucharist must include forgiveness of our neighbor. There is a specific command to forgive one another's daily sins.

Images of baptism are obvious in tonight's gospel through the cleansing motif. Eucharistic overtones appear in the *mandatum* and preparation for eucharist through the daily forgiveness of sins. On this inaugural night of the Triduum, baptism, confirmation, and eucharist are foreshadowed as the elect wait on the threshold for their reception at the Easter Vigil.

We are reminded that Jesus performs the sign of foot washing right before his passion. As listeners, we expect the gospel to be an account of the institution of the eucharist. However, on this night that celebrates the institution of the eucharist, Jesus invites us into the challenge of living eucharist. John's *mandatum* provides the daily example of offering our lives for others (as Jesus would do the very next day) in service and in forgiveness, as we prepare to dine at his table.

Now we really know how much Jesus loved his disciples. Through the sign of foot washing Jesus took his place among the slaves of the world, humbled himself, and willingly gave up his life. The eucharist is an ongoing remembering of Jesus' passover from death to life. The liturgy jump-starts the Triduum with this solemn reminder: "We shall glory in the cross of our Lord Jesus Christ. Through him we are saved and made free."[18] Just as the Passover was a sign of liberation, so too is the eucharist the sign of liberation for Christians.

Proclaim the gospel again.

Sometimes we gain new insights when we hear the text after the interpretation has been given. Someone from the group proclaims the gospel a second time.

[18]Evening Mass of the Lord's Supper: "Introductory Rites," *The Sacramentary.*

Step 4
Testing

Conversation with the Liturgy and the Scriptures

Test your original understanding in dialogue with the text.

(You might consider breaking into smaller groups.)

Were there any new insights in the readings that you had not considered before? How does your original understanding of this story compare with what was just shared? How does this story speak to your life?

Sharing Life Experience

Participants share an experience from their lives that connects with the biblical interpretation just shared.

> *I can only respond to this Holy Thursday by remembering the example of my sister and her family. Tonight's liturgy invites us to wash feet and to offer our lives in sacrifice for others. Life offers the opportunity to live that in real, often painful ways. I watched my sister and her family respond to the sudden illness of one of their children in the most incredible, sacrificial, paschal way. They put their lives on hold and researched a disease that is so new on the scene that few had ever heard of it. My sister became the epitome of Christ's unbelievable, compassionate love and mercy to her child. Due to a very severe case of this adolescent onslaught chemical disorder, their family endured the test of a lifetime. Many, if not most, would have buckled under the pressure. Each family member had a role to play in the healing that would be gradual and nearly complete. They literally "became the disease," took their beloved child by the hand and walked with her through the Red Sea of desperation to the promised land of healing and liberation. With the help of the medical community, new medical research, and an incredible amount of sacrifice and patience, and an unwillingness to be conquered by the unusual and often embarrassing dimensions of the disease, this child will live a normal life. The family became eucharist, and washed the feet of one of its hurting members in painful and often heroic ways. Wouldn't every family go to similar lengths for one of its members? Sadly this is not always true. Many*

would be tempted to believe in the apparent hopelessness of the situation rather than go to incredible lengths, die the daily deaths, and endure to the end, not knowing if it would work. They are my heroes and a living example in my life of what the power of self-sacrificing love is able to accomplish. They never knew if their efforts would help; there was little research and few who went before them who could help and support them in their trial. They simply had to trust and offer each day, sometimes each moment, to the healing compassion of God and trust that they would safely reach the other side. We celebrate that trust every time we encounter this beautiful child of God.

The Holy Thursday liturgy mandates that same self-sacrificing love to be extended to the least of the least, and the poorest of the poor. "Where charity and love prevail, there God is." What my sister's family offered for one of their children we are invited to offer for all of God's children, especially those whose feet we would rather not wash. We are to become the eucharist of this feast; we are to wash feet and love unto death. It is because of this night that we have the strength to do it.

All share their life experience.

What was John trying to tell his community? What does he have to say to our community and to me today? In what way is our community called to wash feet? Whose feet are we called to wash? How are images of creation, covenant, exodus/death/resurrection and community evident in tonight's readings? Has our original understanding of tonight's liturgy and scriptures been stretched, challenged, or affirmed?

STEP 5
DECISION

The gospel demands a response.

How does our sharing and this biblical interpretation challenge our community's attitudes? In what way does this gospel call our parish to action in the church, parish, neighborhood, or world? What is one concrete action we will take this week as a response to what we have learned and shared today?

DOCTRINAL ISSUES

What church truth/teaching/doctrinal issue could be drawn from the readings for Holy Thursday?

Participants suggest possible doctrinal themes that flow from the readings.

Possible Doctrinal Themes

Eucharist, bread, wine, washing feet, covenant, paschal mystery, charity, Triduum, service

Present the doctrinal material at this time.

1. The facilitator gives input on a particular doctrinal issue of his/her prior choosing. OR
2. The group chooses a doctrinal issue from the list they created. They read together from the Doctrinal Appendix.

(The doctrinal issues are found in the Doctrinal Appendix in the back of this workbook. If you are choosing an issue from this resource, please refer to it now.)

Reflection questions centered around the chosen doctrinal theme can be found at the end of each topic in the Doctrinal Appendix. The questions are based on the five-step reflection process. If you choose a topic not included in the Doctrinal Appendix, craft your own questions according to the same five-step process.

Following the reflection questions you will be reminded to return to chapter 7, "Preparing the Catechetical Session," to assist you in crafting your own session.

Closing Prayer

Almighty God,
we receive new life
from the supper your Son gave us in this world.
May we find full contentment
in the meal we hope to share
in your eternal kingdom.
We ask this through Christ our Lord.[19]

---

[19]Evening Mass of the Lord's Supper: "Prayer after Communion," *The Sacramentary.*

Good Friday

Opening Prayer

Lord,
by shedding his blood for us,
your Son, Jesus Christ,
established the paschal mystery.
In your goodness, make us holy
and watch over us always.
We ask this through Christ our Lord.[1]

LITURGY OF THE WORD

Let us listen to God's word.

The readings are proclaimed.

First Reading
Isaiah 52:13–53:12

The Fourth Servant Song of Isaiah was written while Israel was still in captivity and awaiting deliverance in Babylon. Jerusalem had been destroyed and had not yet been reconstructed.[2] Deutero-Isaiah lamented the plight of the people and offered a message of consolation. Prior to the exile the people had been materialistic, greedy, and overly-prosperous. Once in captivity, that all changed. Deutero-Isaiah portrayed the people as depressed, "dazed, discouraged, and destitute, severely tempted to apostasy."[3] Deutero-Isaiah set out to console, not punish, to offer encouragement, not chastisement, and to strengthen the faith of the people as they awaited deliverance.

The early Christian community believed that Jesus Christ was the suffering servant of the first reading. They believed that Deutero-Isaiah was heralding and foretelling the passion and death of Christ and the inauguration of the messianic age. Jewish scholars are not certain who the suffering servant of Isaiah was. Christians proclaim with faithful assurance: it was Christ, the one who suffered for the many, the one who bore our infirmities. Jewish scholars maintain that the "many" referred to gentiles. It is not certain whether Jesus saw himself as the servant of this Isaian passage. But there is evidence in the scriptures that he embraced Isaiah's servant image as a metaphor for his mission.

The first reading from Isaiah sets the stage for understanding the passion. Jesus, servant of God, who by all appearances was reduced to nothing, was exalted and raised up by the living God. Vindication was his. The passage ends on a note of peace and hope and helps form our understanding and theology of the cross: "Jesus' suffering was innocent, vicarious and redemptive; it is for all people inclusively; the righteous sufferer is finally vindicated."[4]

Responsorial Psalm
Psalm 31:2, 6, 12–13, 15–16, 25

The psalm highlights the suffering of the Just One. It includes the words of Jesus spoken from the cross in Luke's gospel.

Second Reading
Hebrews 4:14–16; 5:7–9

In the letter to the Hebrews, the theme of Jesus, the high priest, is very carefully set forth. "Jesus is the high priest of his own sacrifice, the perfect sacrifice that is ever before his Father, since he dwells eternally in his presence. He is, 'in the heavens,' the eternal and definitive Passover."[5]

This letter consoles us in our humanity. Jesus identifies with our suffering and weaknesses because he was a person, just like us. He was tempted just as we are tempted. "The only difference that the author [of Hebrews] remarks between Jesus' temptations and those of his followers is that he never succumbed to them."[6] He

[1]Good Friday: "Opening Prayer," *The Sacramentary.*

[2]Carroll Stuhlmueller, C.P., "Deutero-Isaiah and Trito-Isaiah," in *NJBC,* 329.

[3]Ibid., 330.

[4]*PNL,* 19.

[5]*DL*(III), 3, 26.

[6]Myles M. Bourke, "The Epistle to the Hebrews," in *NJBC,* 928.

prayed for deliverance *through* his hour to come. Jesus learned obedience through the struggle of his life.[7] Jesus lived his life in complete submission to the will of God. His faithfulness prompted decisions and choices that led him ultimately to the cross.

A major theme of the letter to the Hebrews is *Jesus Christ, the exalted High Priest and Lord, reigns from heaven's throne.* Verses 5–10 are believed to reflect a hymn to "Jesus the High Priest." The author of Hebrews often referred to Jesus as the High Priest in order to accentuate his superiority over the Jewish high priest. Later in the letter to the Hebrews Jesus was contrasted with the high priest in one very important aspect. The priesthood of the Jewish high priest ended upon his death. Jesus' priesthood, on the other hand, required his death in order to be officially inaugurated. Jesus, the resurrected High Priest, reigns from his exalted heavenly throne.

Jesus' throne is a throne of grace because Christ made it possible for the human race to have access to God and to God's grace. Unlike the Jewish high priest, Jesus did not sin, even though he was fully tempted to sin. Jesus offers loud cries, tears, and prayers of supplication (v. 7) to God. In his glorified state, Jesus was no longer subject to the natural struggles of human nature, such as the fear of death.[8] The author of Hebrews maintains that God heard Jesus' cries and saved him from death. Jesus was not saved from death as we understand death. Jesus died a natural death. However, God did hear his cries and God did deliver him from death. Through the resurrection Jesus is no longer dead, but lives eternally. As reigning High Priest, Jesus empathizes with his people because he knows the trials, tribulations, and struggles of life's sojourn. Jesus cried out. He knew pain, weakness, and suffering like any other human being. However, Jesus the High Priest sacrificed the gift of his own life and now sits on heaven's throne as an advocate on our behalf.

Jesus was God's Son (v. 8) in two very distinct ways. "He became Son when exalted; he always was Son because he existed with the Father even before he appeared on earth."[9] The Jesus of John's gospel is aware of his preexistence. Jesus learned obedience through his suffering and was consecrated to the priesthood because of his obedience (v. 8). Thus, he is qualified to "to save those who are obedient to him."[10] The author of Hebrews assures his reader that the follower of Christ will receive eternal salvation because that salvation is based on Jesus' eternal priesthood. In this sense, *eternal* refers to things that exist in the permanence of the heavenly realm rather than the impermanence of the earthly domain.

Gospel

The passion of our Lord Jesus Christ according to John.

Step 1
Naming One's Experience

What were your first impressions? What was your first response? What grabbed your attention? How did you feel?

Each person names his or her initial impression. Statements should be brief. No reasons should be given at this time. All simply listen without agreeing or disagreeing.

Step 2
Understanding

In a brief statement, what do you think this gospel is trying to convey?

Step 3
Input from Vision/Story/Tradition

Liturgical Context

"On this day, when 'Christ our passover was sacrificed' (1 Cor 5:7), the Church meditates on the

[7] *PNL,* 19.

[8] This was probably a reference to Jesus' experience in Gethsemane in Mark 14:35–36. (Bourke, "The Epistle to the Hebrews," 929.)

[9] Bourke, "The Epistle to the Hebrews," 929.

[10] Ibid.

passion of her Lord and Spouse, adores the cross, commemorates her origin from the side of Christ asleep on the cross, and intercedes for the salvation of the whole world."[11]

Scripture scholar Raymond Brown contends that John's Jesus is the all knowing, always in control Savior who conquered sin and death by carefully orchestrated design. Good Friday's message is Good News. St. John Chrysostom very eloquently summed up the reason we gather for this Good Friday feast.

> Today sees our Lord Jesus Christ on the cross; we celebrate, so that we may understand that the cross is a celebration, a solemn, spiritual feast. Before, the cross was synonymous with condemnation; now it is an object of honor. Before, a symbol of death; now, the means of salvation. It has been the source of countless blessings for us: it has delivered us from error, it has shone on us when we were in darkness. We were vanquished, yet it reconciles us with God. We were foes, yet it has regained God's friendship for us. We were estranged, yet it has brought us back to him. . . . We have discovered a wellspring.[12]

The liturgy is not a somber preoccupation with the wounds and suffering of Christ. It is surrounded by anticipatory joy. We do not feign ignorance of the resurrection. Liturgy is truth and authenticity, not historicization. In other words, we do not remember and make present Jesus' passion and death as if we didn't know about the resurrection. It is always a prominent piece of our consciousness, remembrance, and celebration.

There is no intention of minimizing Jesus' suffering. We grieve over his passion, so much so that we fast on this day as an expression of our grief. The Good Friday fast puts us in communion with our brothers and sisters who, from as early as the second century, observed a pre-Easter fast of no food or water. As the centuries wore on, and a definite celebration of Good Friday evolved, the fast was observed on Good Friday and Holy Saturday.

In the very early centuries, there was no official Good Friday liturgy. The observance of Good Friday developed according to the local custom of various places. The liturgy of Good Friday today is a blending of customs, observances, and liturgies that evolved over the centuries from varied sources.

The date of Jesus' death, the 14th of Nisan, which fell on a Friday, was observed as a day of mourning and fasting inspired by compassion (a "grieving fast").[13] By the turn of the fourth century there was a non-eucharistic liturgy that is recorded in the travels of the pilgrim, Egeria (ca. 400). She records multiple liturgies on Good Friday beginning before dawn and continuing through the night. The early dawn service took place at the site where Jesus was scourged. Later in the morning they gathered to venerate the cross. (In the fourth century Empress Helena gave the church in Rome a relic of the holy cross. Any church that possessed a relic of the cross venerated it at this liturgy. The present ritual of veneration developed from these early origins.)

The Christians of Egeria's day then gathered from about noon to three for a liturgy of the word. The celebration consisted of a series of scripture readings including psalms that alluded to Jesus' suffering, the passion of Jesus, and John's account of Jesus' death. Nearly spent from the day-long liturgies, the worshipers gathered again in the evening to listen to the proclamation of Jesus' burial. Following the evening service, there was an all-night vigil for those hearty enough to endure it.

By the seventh century there was a clearly defined Roman liturgy. The pope carried the relic of the cross barefoot from the Lateran Basilica to the Church of the Holy Cross in Jerusalem. The cross was venerated by clergy and laity alike as the scriptures were proclaimed. The intercessions of the faithful ended this liturgy until communion was added in the seventh century.

---

[11] *Circular Letter Concerning the Preparation and Celebration of Easter Feasts,* Congregation for Divine Worship (Rome, USCC, 1988), #58.

[12] John Chrysostom (ca. 350–407), "Homélie pour le Vendredi saint," in *Homiliaire patristique,* Lex Orandi 8 (Paris: Cerf, 1949), 65; in *DL* (III), 27–28.

[13] *LY,* 69.

According to Adolf Adam, the liturgy became far more dramatic during the Middle Ages. The simple communion of the faithful became *missa praesanctificatorum* (mass with previously consecrated gifts). In other words, many parts of the mass, with the exception of the defining element, the eucharistic prayer, were added to this liturgy. The faithful were receiving communion rarely, if at all during those times; thus, only the clergy received the eucharist at the Good Friday liturgy. The Tridentine Mass of 1570 mandated this practice to last for the next four hundred years.

In 1955 the new Order reinstated the traditional three part liturgy: word, veneration of the cross, and communion. After a four-hundred year hiatus, the faithful were once again allowed to receive communion at the Good Friday liturgy. The liturgy was to begin at 3:00 P.M. unless, for pastoral reasons, it could not take place at that time. The liturgical color of the Good Friday liturgy was changed from black to red, the color of martyrs.

The liturgy of Good Friday begins with the very ancient and solemn gesture of prostration by the presiding celebrant and attending priests. The celebrant then moves to the chair and reads the opening prayer followed by the liturgy of the word. The first reading of Good Friday, the fourth Servant Song, was appropriated to the suffering of Christ very early in the Christian tradition. Psalm 31 is a lament and a prayer of trust to the faithful God. The second reading from Paul's letter to the Hebrews exalts Jesus, the great High Priest, the source of salvation. The gospel acclamation introduces the gospel with a proclamation of the exalted, obedient unto death, Jesus Christ crucified. The passion is proclaimed without candles or incense.

The intercessions of Good Friday have their roots in the early Good Friday liturgies. They are the inspiration behind the general intercessions prayed at every liturgy. The intercessions are prayers offered by God's people "for the holy Church, the pope, all states of life in the Church, catechumens, Christian unity, the Jews, all who do not believe in Christ, all who do not believe in God, rulers, those in every kind of need."[14] The intercessions allow the faithful to exercise their "priestly function and intercede for all humanity."[15] Liturgical prayer is universal and missionary. It is not self-centered; it is communal and other-centered. The first intercession is an example of this universal dimension.

Deacon: Let us pray, dear friends,
for the holy Church of God
throughout the world,
that God the almighty Father
guide it and gather it together
so that we may worship him
in peace and tranquility.

Priest: Almighty and eternal God,
you have shown your glory to all nations
in Christ, your Son.
Guide the work of your Church.
Help it to persevere in faith,
proclaim your name,
and bring your salvation to people everywhere.
We ask this through Christ our Lord.[16]

The veneration of the cross is a high point of the Good Friday liturgy: "It expresses the Church's faith in and gratitude to Christ who turned the wood of an instrument of torture into the means of redemption and the sign of God's infinite love. The cross stands as an irresistible call to love God who has loved us so well."[17] The ritual text and antiphons for the veneration proclaim our faith in the cross:

Priest: This is the wood of the cross, on which hung the savior of the world.
All: Come, Let us worship.

Antiphon
We worship you, Lord,
We venerate your cross,
We praise your resurrection.
Through the cross you brought joy to the world.

Psalm 66:2
May God be gracious and bless us;
and let his face shed its light upon us.

[14]Ibid., 73.

[15]General Introduction to the Roman Missal, #45.

[16]Good Friday: "Intercessions for Good Friday," *The Sacramentary.*

[17]*DL* (III), 34.

Antiphon

We worship you, Lord,
We venerate your cross,
We praise your resurrection.
Through the cross you brought joy to the world.[18]

Communion ends the Good Friday liturgy. The Lord's Prayer is recited and communion bread, consecrated the day before, is distributed. The liturgy ends in silence. We keep vigil as we await the Lord's resurrection.

The Office of Readings and Morning Prayer is to be celebrated with the faithful on both Good Friday and Holy Saturday morning.

Gospel Exegesis

The facilitator gives input regarding what critical biblical scholarship has to say about this text. The input includes insights as to how people would have heard the gospel in Jesus' time.

This exegesis of John's passion is based on Raymond E. Brown's *A Crucified Christ in Holy Week.* John's passion narrative is proclaimed every Good Friday. The context for this reading is given in the weeks preceding Holy Week in which other segments of John's gospel are proclaimed. Brown asserts that the Jesus of the Good Friday passion is a far different Jesus from the Jesus portrayed in the synoptic gospels. John's Jesus is aware of his pre-existence. Through Jesus' death he is simply returning to a state he temporarily left during his stay in this world (17:5).[19] The Jesus of Good Friday freely offers his life and freely takes it back again. Jesus is not a victim. There is no struggle. Jesus is confident of the outcome. Satan has no power over Jesus. He is a step ahead of all the characters. He knows what is going to happen. He is in complete control. Brown asserts that John's image and portrayal of Jesus is the one that was most frequently passed on to the faithful. The portrait of Jesus in the synoptic gospels is different: the Jesus of the synoptics was not aware of his pre-existence; he was not so all-knowing, either.

The light-darkness image in John's gospel is a strong sign that appears frequently. Jesus came as Light of the world. Judas arrived with a lantern to arrest Jesus. Judas resided in darkness and needed artificial light in order to see.

John's Jesus is the royal personage who grovels to no one. There are no blood and sweat stained moments in the garden. Jesus does not pray to be delivered from his ordeal (as he does in the reference to Mark's gospel in the second reading from Hebrews). He accepts his appointed task with awareness, purpose, and power. No worldly power has control over Jesus. Jesus Christ, Victor, is in complete control of his destiny.

Brown further points out that the Jewish trial of Jesus is different in John's gospel than it is in the other gospels. Rather than the formal court of the high priest, Caiaphas, Jesus is questioned by the police before Annas, Caiaphas's father-in-law. The interrogators try to determine if there is evidence against Jesus of insurrection, thereby prompting a Roman trial in a Roman court. Jesus is so clever with Annas that his captors abuse him.

Jesus' innocence is written all over his face while Peter's weakness stands out like a rooster's crow at first light. Peter cut off the servant's ear and denied Jesus in the garden. Contrasted with Peter is the beloved disciple of John's gospel. While no one knows for sure who this disciple is, he was nevertheless a hero in the Johannine community. It was the "Beloved Disciple" who was present at the Last Supper, the trial, the foot of the cross, the empty tomb, and the post-resurrection appearances of Jesus. This disciple is *the enlightened one, the witness,* and *the lover* par excellence. It is believed that this disciple was upheld in the Johannine community as the perfect model of discipleship and apostolic witness. The Beloved Disciple, not Peter, is the perfect disciple.

The trial of Jesus reads like a Shakespearean play. Jesus was inside with Pilate; the Jewish community was outside. Pilate was moving back and forth between both and tension was mounting. Pilate was agitated and placating. Jesus was in control, en-

[18]Good Friday: "Veneration of the Cross—Antiphon," *The Sacramentary.*

[19]*CCHW,* 57.

gaged and hardly silent (as in Mark's passion). Jesus assumed his own advocacy. No, he was not a king in the earthly sense, but if Pilate wanted to call him a king, so be it; his kingdom was not of this world. He simply came to testify to the truth—not to preside from a royal throne. Jesus was in control. Pilate was on trial: would he succumb to the political pressure? Pilate was aware of who Jesus was, and he was afraid. He knew who Jesus was, yet he was too afraid to bear witness to the truth.

In Mark and Matthew, Jesus was scourged as a part of his sentence. His cloak was stripped from him and then he was marched off to Calvary. In John's gospel Jesus is scourged before he is brought out from the praetorium to the crowd.

All of the gospels highlight the guilt of the crowd by their own self-recriminating cries to crucify him. However, none of the cries are more intense than those in John's gospel. Jesus, wearing a kingly cloak and crown of thorns, was ultimately abandoned. The Jews favored Caesar over Jesus and in the process abandoned all their hopes for access to the messianic reign. Thus, in the final scene of this Roman court, Pilate extracted fidelity to Caesar from the Jewish crowd and in the process they abdicated their messianic hopes.[20] Pilate then handed Jesus over to the priests to be crucified.

The curtain was about to come down as Jesus, the one who willingly offered his life, carried the cross by himself. According to all four gospels, Pilate put a *titulus* (a charge) on the cross stating that Jesus was a would-be "King of the Jews." John's theology was not without a touch of irony. Jesus, who was rejected as king by his own people, was given the legal title of king by none other than Pilate himself.

[20]Brown alerts us to the anti-Jewish sentiment in John's gospel. He tells us that we are not to ignore it or sugarcoat it. It was real. There was tension between Christians and Jews. It was leveled not just at the leadership, but also at the synagogue. John's community suffered great persecution at the hands of their Jewish brothers and sisters. They were thrown out of the synagogue, which made them very vulnerable. The Romans allowed the Jews to coexist with them, but they were suspicious of Christians. The hostility was deep and it was bitter. However, we are not to use it as a cause and source of anti-Jewish sentiment, but rather to understand it in light of the cultural and religious problems of the first century.

John's Jesus is wearing a seamless garment. The synoptics only make allusions to the division of the garment. Some scholars believe that the seamless garment was the one worn by the high priest. Jesus hangs not simply as king, but as priest as well. Other scholars say the garment was a symbol of unity.

In Mark and Matthew there is no one with Jesus at the cross. John places Mary and the Beloved Disciple at the cross. John uses them in a symbolic way in his narrative. Jesus named Mary the mother of the Beloved Disciple and the disciple was named her son, thus becoming Jesus' brother. "Jesus has constituted a family of preeminent disciples and the Johannine community is already in existence at the cross (which becomes the birthplace of the church)."[21]

John loaded the final verses with further symbolism. Jesus was given wine-soaked hyssop. Hyssop was a type of leaf used to sprinkle the blood of the paschal lamb on the doorposts of Israelite homes in the exodus story. Jesus was sentenced to death at noon, the time when the priests would slaughter the paschal lambs at Passover. With his last breath Jesus fulfilled the Baptist's prophetic proclamation: "Behold the Lamb of God who takes away the sins of the world." Jesus' bones were not broken, again a symbolic connection to the paschal lamb.

Jesus, still in control of his destiny, proclaimed to the world that *"It is finished"* and handed over his spirit. His resurrected spirit, then, was present at his death and at his resurrection. The Spirit was not present until this defining, crowning moment. Jesus breathed the Holy Spirit on the disciples after his resurrection.

Upon Jesus' death he was quietly removed from the cross in a reverent fashion. Contrast this with the synoptics who record all kinds of cataclysmic events upon his death. Blood and water flowed from Jesus' side (the living water that we were told would flow from his side). It is believed that the water signifies the outpouring of the Holy Spirit upon Jesus' glorification. Some scholars suggest that the water and blood are signs of baptism and eucharist. The Spirit was given to the community through baptism (water) and the eu-

[21]*CCHW*, 64.

charist (blood). Thus, the church was born at the foot of the cross through his water of baptism and the blood of eucharist that flowed from his side.

John makes sure that Jesus' burial befits a king; there is plenty of myrrh and oil, and there are cloth wrappings. Nicodemus, a reluctant disciple earlier, now becomes a disciple in full view. At his death, Jesus continued to reconcile sinners to himself. Jesus died as he lived in John's gospel: as a conquering, royal king, in charge of his own destiny, who overcame the sins of the world. Jesus fought the great battle with Satan and was victorious.

The cross then is a sign of victory. Disciples do not stand at this Good Friday cross in sadness or in mourning, but rather in praise and thanksgiving for the incredible mercy of God who loved so greatly that he sent his Son to die for a sinful world.

Proclaim the gospel again.

Sometimes we gain new insights when we hear the text after the interpretation has been given. Someone from the group proclaims the gospel a second time.

STEP 4
TESTING

Conversation with the Liturgy and the Scriptures

Test your original understanding in dialogue with the text.

(You might consider breaking into smaller groups.)

Were there any new insights? Was there anything you had not considered before about this liturgy and/or scriptures? How does your original understanding of Good Friday compare with what we just shared? How does this story speak to your life? Have you ever known a time in your life when the Jesus portrayed in John's gospel was necessary to your situation? How does John's Jesus compare with Matthew's Jesus? What does the Jesus of Matthew and the Jesus of John have to say to our community? To me?

Sharing Life Experience

Participants share an experience from their lives that connects with the biblical interpretation just shared.

Many years ago my husband and I were involved in a parish that gathered regularly to pray for people who were in need of healing. We often encountered people who were broken and beaten down by life's disappointments. They came seeking the healing presence of God in the gathering of our community. I remember one young woman in particular, who was extremely troubled. She had been coming to pray with us for quite some time. Our pastor approached our group with an unusual request. Would we gather to pray particularly for and with this woman? It seemed that she had been actively involved in the occult and was now under the care of a psychiatrist. The doctor had approached our pastor and said, "I am not a Catholic, but I have come up against something in this woman I have never experienced before. It could be auto-suggestion, but I am encountering what this woman believes is the presence of evil. This is new to me. Is there something you can do?" The pastor said he would talk to his bishop. We were reminded that every celebration of the eucharist is a share in the passion, death, and resurrection of Christ, and that every eucharist is an opportunity for healing and liberation. Christ was already victorious. Christ had already conquered sin and death. We know the rest of the story and we celebrate it at every mass.

The Christ of Good Friday is that same victorious, liberating Christ. The woman celebrated the sacrament of reconciliation, and together we, as a community, celebrated eucharist. It was like every other eucharist—a celebration of faith-filled people who gather to take bread, bless it, break it, and share it, and who in the process become broken and shared. The Jesus of John's gospel went to the cross on Good Friday knowing he was in charge and that he would be victorious over sin and death. That same liberating reality is present and operative in our lives today.

Over a period of time, and after continued medical care, and the self-sacrificing pastoral care of our community, the woman experienced profound healing. Today she is a vibrant member of that community. There is no power greater than the power of the

Crucified and Risen Lord! Whether it is something as dramatic as that seemed, or something as normal as the seemingly hopeless situations we often find ourselves in throughout life, today's liturgy is a reminder that Jesus is in control. He knowingly and willingly paid the price. There is no evil in my life or in the world that can erase that reality. Ruptured relationships cannot erase it—not even death can erase it. We continue to live it in our communities when we gather to remember and celebrate the paschal mystery. Today is ***Good*** *Friday; it is such* ***Good*** *News.*

All share their life experience.

What was the message for the Johannine community in the passion narrative? What does he have to say to our community and to me today? How does today's liturgy call us to death and resurrection? What are the implications? What are our collective and personal responses to the Good Friday liturgy? Do I still feel the same way about this text as I did at the beginning? Has our original understanding been stretched, challenged, or affirmed?

STEP 5
DECISION

The gospel demands a response.

In what concrete way does this gospel call our parish to action in the church, parish, neighborhood, or world? Has this conversation with the exegesis of the scriptures and the liturgy for Good Friday called me to change in any way? What am I/we/community/parish called to do in response? What is the challenge of the Good Friday liturgy? What will I/we do about it?

DOCTRINAL ISSUES

What church truth/teaching/doctrinal issue could be drawn from the gospel for Good Friday?

Participants suggest possible doctrinal themes that flow from the readings.

Possible Doctrinal Themes

Cross, redemptive suffering, paschal mystery, christology

Present the doctrinal material at this time.

1. Facilitator gives input on a particular doctrinal issue of his/her prior choosing. OR
2. The group chooses a doctrinal issue from the list they created. They read together from the Doctrinal Appendix.

(The doctrinal issues are found in the Doctrinal Appendix in the back of this workbook. If you are choosing an issue from this resource, please refer to it now.)

Reflection questions centered around the chosen doctrinal theme can be found at the end of each topic in the Doctrinal Appendix. The questions are based on the five-step reflection process. If you choose a topic not included in the Doctrinal Appendix, craft your own questions according to the same five-step process.

Following the reflection questions you will be reminded to return to chapter 7, "Preparing the Catechetical Session," to assist you in crafting your own session.

Closing Prayer

Lord,
send down your abundant blessing
upon your people who have recalled the death of
your Son
in the sure hope of the resurrection.
Grant them pardon; bring them comfort.
May their faith grow stronger
and their eternal salvation be assured.
We ask this through Christ our Lord.[22]

[22] Good Friday: "Prayer Over the People," *The Sacramentary.*

EASTER VIGIL

The Easter Vigil sets out for the church in sign, symbol, word, and gesture the heart of our Catholic Christian faith and identity. The riches contained within the Vigil are nearly impossible to examine in one celebration or catechetical session. The Easter Vigil is the springboard not only for pre-sacramental preparation for the rites of initiation, but also for mystagogical reflection for neophytes and the entire church.[1] Rather than dealing with the segments as individual pearls scattered in other areas of this resource, this session will deal with the pearls as if on a finely crafted string. Therefore, the exegesis of the symbols, words, and ritual pieces in this liturgy will be treated as they occur in the liturgy. Obviously, the format for this session will be different from the formats for other sessions in the book. The gospel, the readings, and each ritual piece of the Vigil are vital to understanding who we are and why we gather on this night. There are enormous riches in this powerful celebration. It would be very difficult to absorb them all in one preparation session. Since the pieces of this liturgy are pivotal to understanding our Catholic heritage, it is essential that they become a benchmark for constant referral. All liturgy flows from this Mother of all Feasts.

This session is crafted in such a way that it can be used for ongoing reflection throughout the Easter season and liturgical year. The meaning, value, and function of symbols, as well as an exegesis of their bibical, ecclesial, and liturgical signs will be explored as they occur in the liturgy. Questions for mystagogical reflection are provided at the end of each section.

[1]The *NCD* asserts that "sacramental catechesis has traditionally been of two kinds: preparation for the initial celebration of the sacraments and continued enrichment following their first reception" (#36). The meaning of the sacraments is set forth in the scriptures assigned to the sacramental rites. Therefore, in order to prepare people for full, conscious, and active participation in the celebrations of the sacraments in the liturgy, the scriptures from those celebrations may be used for prior prayer and meditation. They may also be revisited following the celebration itself for mystagogical reflection and catechesis.

The historical development of the Easter Vigil will not be addressed in this session, as it was covered in the overview of the Easter season.

The symbols will not be repeated in the Doctrinal Appendix as they will be treated extensively in this session. However, symbols are critical to our Catholic tradition and therefore should form a major piece of our catechetical efforts. Thus, there will be questions provided for reflection on them, as well as on the scriptures and the liturgical segments.

This session is divided into seven sections: A. Holy Saturday and Rites of Preparation, B. Symbols, C. Introduction to the Easter Vigil, D. Service of Fire/Light, E. Liturgy of the Word, F. Service of Baptism, G. Liturgy of the Eucharist.

A. HOLY SATURDAY AND RITES OF PREPARATION

We are still in the midst of the Triduum; the liturgy is not over. The church gathers again for celebration of the liturgy of the hours on the morning of Holy Saturday.

Preparatory Rites

The elect are brought together for prayer and reflection in immediate preparation for the sacraments of initiation. If the presentation of the Lord's Prayer was deferred until this time [see #149, #178–180 in RCIA], it is celebrated on Holy Saturday. The "return" or recitation of the creed and the choosing of a baptismal name may also take place at this time (RCIA, #193–196, #200). Another preparatory rite is celebrated with the elect on Holy Saturday. "By the power of its symbolism, the *ephphetha rite*, or rite of opening the ears and mouth, impresses on the elect their need of grace in order that they may hear the word of God and profess it for their salvation" (RCIA, #197).

Blessing of Easter Foods

In some places there is a custom of blessing the foods that will break the lenten fast. Eggs, breads, meats, and produce are brought to the church for a special blessing. These foods used to be forbidden during Lent and blessing them is an indication that the lenten fast is over and Easter has arrived. This was easily understood when the Easter Vigil was celebrated early on Holy Saturday morning and the foods were brought to that celebration. Now, however, the blessing anticipates—rather than celebrates—the arrival of Easter. Gabe Huck suggests that rather than blessing with water (water blessing needs to wait for the Vigil) and incense, a simple extension of hands might be appropriate, if well explained. Another possibility might include inviting people to bring their foods on Easter day. "If such blessings are then given a prominent place in the liturgies of Easter day, with full use of water and incense, the blessings of food might slowly come to be seen—as they originally were—as part of the Easter liturgy."[2]

B. SYMBOLS

The symbols of the Easter Vigil are cross, fire/light, word, water, white garment, oil, laying on of hands, bread, wine, church. The nine dominant liturgical symbols of the church are all manifest at the Easter Vigil. The celebration of liturgy makes use of symbols that speak most appropriately of creation (candle, water, fire), human existence (washing, anointing, breaking bread), and the history of God's saving action in the world (the rites of Passover). The stories and actions of remembrance, the human rituals, and the above mentioned cosmic elements are subsumed into a world of faith and, through the power of the Holy Spirit, they reveal the saving action of Jesus Christ.

Symbols are encountered through the four signs of God's presence (the four signs of catechesis referred to in chapter 2). We encounter symbols through the natural, biblical, ecclesial, and liturgical signs of God's presence. Symbols speak to us of our identity as Catholic Christians. For example, the symbol of light has its genesis in Christ, Light of the World. Since we are to walk as children of the Light, light identifies us and we become its reality—we become light, we become bread, etc.

[2]Gabe Huck, *The Three Days: Parish Prayer in the Paschal Triduum* (Chicago: Liturgy Training Pub., 1981), 53.

Meaning is conveyed when people encounter symbols, which are repeatable and possess many layers of meaning. They are multi-faceted and have multiple forms and uses. At the Easter Vigil, the symbol of light looms in the new fire, the Easter candle, the candles of the faithful, the incense, and the sanctuary lamp. In the darkened church, light's presence is felt in absence. The meaning of symbols is expressed in the way they are used, in the scriptures and ritual prayers that accompany their use, and in the gestures that define them.[3]

The Easter Vigil accentuates the symbols that illumine our existence and that occur in all liturgies. We are people of the cross. We enter the waters and we are chrismated into the ecclesial community. We thus become people of the light and are thereby incorporated into the paschal mystery, which we experience as we gather around the eucharistic table.

"Liturgical action depends on symbols because beings cannot be together and communicate without some kind of encounter in words (verbal symbols) and/or in gestures and actions (nonverbal symbols). All knowledge begins with our senses; this means that an encounter with God is only possible by means of sensible signs."[4] In antiquity, a symbol used to be understood as two halves which, when joined, became one whole. The person who had one half would thus recognize the other half because the two put together equaled the whole. By extension, a symbol was regarded as two parts of a whole—the visible and the invisible. Just because the invisible half of the symbol was not readily observable, it was nevertheless half of the reality. When joined with the visible half of the symbol, it constituted the whole reality. "In the language of religion and theology it is frequently the case that the concept of 'symbol' is reserved for the signs of faith, that is... in addition to their superficial, natural meaning, [they have] another and supernatural meaning that is only accessible to faith."[5] Through symbols we are able to touch the deep mysteries of our faith in ways that words can never express.

[3]Linda Gaupin, *Sacramental Catechesis*, course text for "Specialized Certification in Sacramental Catechesis," Diocese of Orlando Florida, November 1996.

[4]*MSS*, 13.

[5]Ibid., 13.

If symbols were to speak, they would say: "I am..." rather than, "I am like...." Symbols in the sacramental sense *are* the reality they express. Eucharist in the form of bread and wine *is* the Body and Blood of Jesus. We can say with assurance that symbols express our identity. When we consume the precious elements, we become what we have consumed: the Mystical Body of Christ. The symbols of the Easter Vigil, highlighted and set forth, provide the means for us to communicate with God and for God to communicate with us through our senses. The symbols of the Vigil are food for mystagogical reflection throughout the Easter season and form the basis of our sacramental catechesis. Our symbol system connects us to the saints of the past with whom we share the same sacramental signs. When we experience the symbols of water, oil, and bread in their natural, biblical, ecclesial, and liturgical context, we discover new depths of meaning. God speaks to us as we crack open the meanings of the symbols and apply them to our lives. We encounter God in the natural elements of life. Those natural elements point to the hidden mystery of God in our lives. Sirach proclaimed: "Chief of all needs for human life are water and fire, iron and salt, the heart of the wheat, milk and honey, oil, the blood of the grape and cloth." If these are the chief of all human needs, no wonder they form the basis of our entire symbol system. Each one is essential for life just as God is essential for life.

The ecclesial signs provide us with the sources for understanding the nature and purpose of the symbols and rites. Ecclesial signs express what we believe about our symbols, how past communities understood them, and how we live what we believe. The first sources for understanding what the church believes about our signs and symbols are the ritual texts themselves (The Sacramentary, RCIA, rite of baptism, rite of confirmation, rite of penance, etc.).

Liturgical signs provide the vehicle for allowing our symbols to express what they were intended to convey. Liturgical signs occur in the worship of the community, in the liturgical celebration. In the liturgy, we pray the ritual prayers, perform the ritual action, and profess our ritual story. This is the night when new Christians are made in the waters of new birth; when the new oils anoint, seal, and brand the baptized to the image and likeness of Christ; and when the newly consecrated bread incorporates all the faithful in the life, death, and resurrection of Jesus Christ. The liturgy is the theater in which the symbols enact their intended roles and, in so doing, reveal the manifestation of God.

Before proceeding with the Vigil liturgy, let us explore the symbols of church and cross. The symbol of church/people of God is also addressed at this juncture because it is the context within which the Vigil is set. This is the night the church generates itself. We must approach the liturgy of this night from the perspective of church doing the work God has given it.

While the cross is a prominent symbol of this and every liturgy, it is underscored particularly in the liturgies of Good Friday, Palm Sunday, and the feast of the Triumph of the Cross. The cross is a primary symbol of the Easter Vigil as it relates to the resurrection of Christ. Without Christ's death on the cross, there could have been no resurrection. However, this liturgy does not meditate particularly on the cross, per se, but rather on its fulfillment in the resurrection.

Symbol of Church/People of God

One of the clearest symbols of God's presence in the world is the church. There are many interchangeable terms for church—community, church, people of God, assembly—but they are all the same reality. God is present to the world through the visible, tangible sign of God's love, the church. Human beings are, by nature, social beings. Belonging is a basic anthropomorphic need. From its earliest origins, Israel survived because it was *a people*. There was no life outside the community. The ancient world was a treacherous place. Food and water were scarce, and the environment was dangerous. The community was needed for basic survival and protection. The community meant life. The community provided the basic needs of shelter, food, and human companionship. When someone was exiled from the community, it was a death sentence.

One common thread running through all religious symbols is that in some way they speak to something that is essential or meaningful for human life. A symbol mirrors, images, or reflects invisible realities. Symbols provide a way of touching the intangible. God is revealed through a visible, tangible sign, something people can experience, touch, taste, smell, or feel.[6] Since community was essential for life and since there was no life, food, shelter, or protection outside the community, perhaps the community was a sign of who God is, how God acts, and what it means to be God's people. God functions like the community. God is provider, protector, and the One who sustains life.

Our experience of human community colors how we experience and understand the spiritual, biblical sense of community. Community as a symbol of God is a lived reality for people whose primary experience of the family community is nurturing. However, when the contrary is true, community as a sign of God becomes a reality only as it is experienced in the ongoing life of a faith-filled community.

The Easter Vigil celebrates the symbol of church/ people of God in the most visible way through the presence of the elect. After months of loving guidance, care, and nurturing, tender Mother Church gently brings her children to the water's edge for full immersion in the life of the community, the life of God.

Natural Sign

We exist in community. We are part of the human family. We have friends and we are social beings. Groups can be exclusive or inclusive. They can pull together or be divisive. A unified community is capable of accomplishing many common goals. A divisive community is destructive. Community exists on many levels: family, friends, religious groups, ethnic groups, institutional groups, class groups, racial groups, civic groups, cities, states, country, world. Every family is a community. It can be nurturing and speak of the unconditional love of God, or the contrary can be true. Communities have power when they are united; they are powerless when they are not. Communities have the power to change laws and structures.

Questions: Have you ever had an experience of being part of a community other than your church community? What were the things that attracted you to this community? Did you ever have the sense that a community you were part of possessed corporate power?

Biblical Sign

The word *community* is not a term found in either the New Testament or the Old Testament. Israel was formed from tribal origins. Tribes were formed from unions between extended families, parents, brothers, sisters, cousins, in-laws, slaves, and servants. A person's identity was tied to the clan. Kinship was synonymous with tribal identity. Kinship prompted the celebration of rituals that supported the familial tribal bond, such as marriages, burials, and common festival meals. Passover was one such ritual.

In addition, there was a political understanding of community. Tribes were often forced to come together for military purposes or to support political leadership. "The basic Hebrew word for assembly, *qahal*, contains the notion of invited participation or summoning. This suggests that such large gatherings were irregular and exceptional; Israelites gathered at someone's command or request for joint military purposes or raiding."[7] Only hierarchical males in the tribe gathered for such meetings. Such was the tribal, communal structure.

Israel was a unique people, a people set apart. Beginning with Abraham, they were elected by God to become a great nation. Biblical authors be-

[6]This is how sacraments nourish the ongoing life of the church. Sacraments get us in touch with the living God through visible, touchable human symbols. Jesus Christ is called the sacrament of God. The reason God sent the Son to the world is that humanity does not have the capacity to comprehend the mind, heart, and inestimable love of God on its own. Human suspicion and incredulity would have always been a barrier. Unconditional love makes no sense in light of the human condition. Human beings could always say to their maker, "Sure, you love us. Those are empty words. You do not know what it means to struggle, suffer, and live the human condition. Your love is empty until you walk in our shoes. It means nothing." So the Son was sent. His name was Jesus; he walked in our shoes. Made of human flesh, Jesus, the sacrament of God, expressed for us the unfathomable love of God through death on the cross.

[7]Jerome H. Neyrey, S.J., "Community," in *CPDBT*, 151.

lieved Israel was "chosen by God as the means by which a special people were brought into being."[8] Israel was called and elected by God for a special purpose in his plan for the salvation of the world.

The exodus solidified the understanding of Israel's election. God called Moses to deliver *God's people* from slavery in Egypt. He formed an everlasting covenant with them and made them his precious, chosen, endeared children (Ex 19:5–6). God formed a covenant with Israel that was tied to their understanding of the tribal, family system. God would provide, sustain, and protect them. They would enjoy God's blessing, sharing, and peace, *shalom*. In return, they would live *hesed* (biblical justice) and would be obedient to God through adherence to the law and the prophets. Such obedience demanded that God's people extend the same covenant love to one another, especially the weakest members of the clan. Thus, in response to the covenant forged with Israel, they would live in obedience and biblical justice. Every time Israel sinned by going their own way, they understood their sin as disobedience to God's will. Calamity was understood as divine retribution for breaking the covenant.

The New Testament took the understanding of *people of God* one step further. The people of God were all those who were open to God's revelation in Christ, no matter what tribe or clan claimed their membership. "In referring to people of the second covenant, however, it also transcends having a common ancestry and history and is a reality of revelation, faith and historical awareness open to all human beings. This universality stems from the people's relationship to the person of Christ who died and rose in a great Passover event to be Lord of all, as well as from the creative Spirit of God manifested on Pentecost."[9] Thus, the invitation to become the people of God was open to all: Jew, Greek, gentile, who would accept the proclamation of God's reign (Acts 28).

When the Hebrew bible was translated into Greek, the term for *qahal*, an invited gathering, was *ekklesia* or *synagoge*. To the Greeks, the term meant a political gathering. There were many such gatherings that were not religious in orientation. The males would gather in a public square or gathering space for political or other reasons. They may have gathered for reading the Torah on the sabbath, but the *synagoge* was not necessarily religious in purpose.

According to Jerome Neyrey, when the Christian church adapted the term, it understood *ekklesia* (church) to mean the gathering of a new people as citizens of a new political reality—the reign of God. Christians were new citizens of the household of God (Eph 2:19).

People of Jesus' time did belong to groups outside the family structure. Neyrey calls these groups the *fictive* family. The disciples were a fictive family. When Jesus spoke of anyone who does the will of God as being his mother, brother, sister, etc., he was referring to the creation of a new fictive family, the household of God (Mk 3:34–35). Regardless of the social class structure in the tribal or political system, members of Jesus' new fictive family, or households, were to be treated with equal respect, honor, and protection, whether they were slave, servant, woman, or child. They were as deserving as blood relatives. There was no sense of individualism. "Family ideology indicates that individuals should always 'seek the good of the group' (1 Cor 10:24), and not pursue individualistic objectives."[10]

The Christian message of community centered around the eschatological hope of the new, eternal city, the new Jerusalem. It was a message of universality. God's new paradise would be open to all people inclusively without distinctions. "Later in the vision of the new creation (Rev 21:1–22:5), when salvation history is finally fulfilled, God's dwelling will be with the entire human race. 'He will dwell with them and they will be his people' (Rev 21:3)."[11]

Questions: What touched you in the biblical understanding of people of God? Was there any new insight? What does it teach you about God, Christ, Spirit, community, or yourself? What does it mean to you to be part of a com-

[8]Joseph Jensen, O.S.B., "People of God," in *CPDBT*, 720.

[9]Eugene LaVerdiere, S.S.S., "People of God: New Testament," in *CPDBT*, 721.

[10]Neyrey, *CPDBT*, 152.

[11]LaVerdiere, *CPDBT*, 723.

munity comprised of citizens of a new political reality? What are the implications? How does the notion of corporate reality versus individual identity speak to us today? Does your community live the eschatological and universal understanding of community inherent in the New Testament? In what way does your community need to grow in the awareness of its own identity and reality?

Ecclesial Sign

The Second Vatican Council, in its document, *The Dogmatic Constitution on the Church*, recaptured the biblical symbol of the church as people of God. There is a direct bearing and relationship to the scriptural understanding of covenant between God and Israel.

Justin, one of the early church fathers, eventually understood the emergence of the Christian church as coming *from* Israel, but as now being the true Israel. The church continued the work and role of Israel. Augustine described the church as on its way, since the creation of the world, to its final destination in heaven. Since church and state were one during the Middle Ages, there was little need to refer to the church's identity—it was obvious. There was no one to dispute it. During the Reformation there was, however, discussion regarding the role of the church. Rather than using the symbol, *people of God*, the language chosen during the Reformation was *communion of saints*, "the invisible communion of believers who are the true Church."[12]

The symbol did not enjoy a renaissance until the nineteenth century. "The spirit of a people binding them together as a community, works to retrieve the symbol of body of Christ to describe the organic unity of the Church, through the enlivening presence of the Holy Spirit"[13] (per the work of Johann Adam Mohler). This eventually led to the encyclical, *Mystici Corporis* in 1943. With the emergence of the field of biblical studies, the symbol *people of God* was retrieved from the church's earliest foundation, Israel and the Christian community. By 1960, the symbol was a consciously recognized aspect of ecclesiology. This led the way for reformulation of the church's theology.

The Second Vatican Council redefined our understanding of church. The following principles are a summary of our theology as articulated in *Sharing the Light of Faith: The National Catechetical Directory.* "The Church is a mystery. It is a reality imbued with the hidden presence of God" (from Pope Paul VI's opening allocution at the second session, September 19, 1963). "The Church is a gift coming from the love of God, Christ's redeeming action and the power of the Holy Spirit" (*National Catechetical Directory* [NCD], #63). "As a divine reality inserted into human history, the Church is a kind of sacrament. Its unique relationship with Christ makes it both a sign and instrument of God's unfathomable union with humanity and of the unity of human beings among themselves" (NCD, #63). ". . . As a mystery, the Church cannot be totally understood or fully defined. Its nature and mission are best captured in scriptural parables and images, taken from ordinary life, which not only express truth about its nature but challenge the Church: for example, to become more a People of God, a better servant, more faithful and holy, more united around the teaching authority of the hierarchy" (NCD, #63).

The church is a community of believers, the people of God. We are called to become a new people, a royal priesthood, a people claimed by God to proclaim the greatness of God (1 Pet 2:9). Jesus freed us from sin and because of the saving waters of baptism we are called to believe, worship, and witness to his saving works.

We are one body in Christ (Rom 12:5). Through Jesus' death, resurrection, and glorification, he remains a living presence and head of his church, of which we are all members. *We celebrate this identity most especially in the eucharist.* Through the eucharist, we become the Body and Blood of Christ.

The church is servant. The church has a mission to heal and reconcile as Jesus did. The church is to live the gospel through the works of mercy, assisting anyone who is in need of our help. The church as servant acts out of love and concern, not for personal glory. One way the church is servant is through its teaching ministry in which it witnesses to the gospel and the power of God in the world.

[12] Ann Graff, "People of God in the History of Theology," in *CPDBT*, 724.

[13] Ibid.

The church is a sign of the reign of God. The church is evidence that God is alive in our midst. In order to be that sign, the church "must be committed to justice, love and peace, to grace and holiness, truth and life, for these are the hallmarks of the kingdom of God" (NCD, #67).

The church is a pilgrim church. Aware of its sins, the church journeys to its final destination as it repents and overcomes patiently the trials and tribulations that come its way. In this way it demonstrates its steadfast faithfulness to the world.

"As mystery, people, one body in Christ, servant, sign of the kingdom, and pilgrim, the Church is conceived as God's family, whose members are united to Christ and led by the Spirit in their journey to the Father. The Church merits our prayerful reflection and wholehearted response" (NCD, #68).

Questions: Does the church's theology about church resonate with your experience of church in your own community? What are the areas of death/resurrection? What are some specific areas that are in need of growth? What does participation in your community teach you about God, Christ, Spirit, church, or yourself?

Liturgical Sign

The symbol of church as people of God is a primary symbol in the liturgy. The gathered community is a sign of God's presence in our midst. Before the book is opened or the bread shared, God is experienced in the community. "For these people are the people of God, purchased by Christ's blood, gathered together by the Lord, nourished by the word. They are a people called to offer the prayers of the entire human family, a people giving thanks in Christ, for the mystery of salvation by offering his sacrifice. Finally they are a people growing together into unity by sharing Christ's Body and Blood. These people are holy by their origin, but becoming ever more holy by conscious, active and fruitful participation in the mystery of the Eucharist" (*Constitution on the Sacred Liturgy*, #59, "General Instruction of the Roman Missal," #5).

In every liturgical celebration the community is a primary experience of God's presence. We profess the mystery of the church in our ritual prayers and, through the eucharist, we live its reality. Through all the ministries of the church, Christ is present. Thus, when the people participate and celebrate, the lector proclaims, the priest presides, the eucharistic minister serves, the cantor sings, the hospitality people welcome, etc., Christ is made manifest in our midst.

Questions: Have you ever had an experience of the presence of God in the midst of your communal worship? In what ways does your community embody the living presence of Christ in your past worship? What did your experience teach you about God, Christ, Spirit, community, yourself?

Symbol of the Cross

This object of torture and sign of disgrace and horror is a symbol of our salvation. It is the principal Christian symbol of hope. The cross is at the heart of our belief in the paschal mystery and our participation in it. Without the cross there is no resurrection. Tonight's liturgy leads us from the cross to the resurrection. We are transported through time as witnesses of God's great deeds of history and brought to this moment. God fulfilled in Christ what was begun at the creation of the world. We are called to take up our cross and follow Christ. "Apart from the cross there is no other ladder by which we may get to heaven."[14]

The cross was an absurdity to the people of Jesus' time. To imagine the cross as a symbol of salvation, victory, and honor, was as absurd to Jesus' contemporaries as imagining the electric chair as an object worthy of veneration would be in today's culture. The cross is a sign of our redemption. Christ was victorious over sin and death. St. Irenaeus reminds us of the implication of the cross: "By the wood of the Cross the work of the Word of God was made manifest to all: his hands are stretched out to gather every one together."[15]

---

[14]St. Rose of Lima, cf. P. Hansen, *Vita mirabilis* (Louvain, 1668).

[15]Quoted in Henri de Lubac, *Catholicism: A Study of Dogma in Relation to the Corporate Destiny of Mankind* (New York: New American Library, 1964), 210.

Natural Sign

Crucifixion is not a means of execution today. We have no natural concept of cross apart from what has come to us from religious sources. However, the cross is used in our culture as a sign of adornment with little or no meaning attached to it. Some in the counter-cultural strata of today's society have even made a mockery of it. The word *cross* has often been associated with a general understanding of suffering in our culture ("That poor woman has a cross to bear"). The term *cross* is somewhat universally understood to mean the trials in one's life.

Questions: How does "cross" have anything to do with your everyday life? What is your experience of the cross?

Biblical Sign

There was no mention of the cross in the Old Testament. Crucifixion was an oriental means of execution. The Greeks did not use it, but the Romans did. However, Roman citizens were never crucified. Crucifixion on the cross was reserved for slaves, insurrectionists, traitors, and anyone guilty of a grave crime. Jesus alluded to the cross in reference to his own death. The symbol of cross was fostered by Jesus who challenged his disciples to take up their cross and follow him. Cross was understood in that sense to mean the "denial of self." In order to gain one's life, one had to lose it. Disciples had to be willing to give up their personal welfare in response to the reign of God.

Paul gives us a refined theology of the cross as symbol. He preached that the cross was revolting to the Jews and folly to the Gentiles (1 Cor 1:23; 2:2). Through the power of the cross, all people who believe in it are saved. Circumcision is no longer needed; it is replaced by the cross as a sign of God's covenant with the human race (Gal 66:14). The cross is a symbol of unity; it unites Jews and gentiles. Jesus nailed the sins of the world to the cross. He became the victim of their sins (Col 2:14). Jesus freely gave up his life for all. He died once, and for the whole world. We cannot merit salvation. Jesus won it for us, once and for all.

Ecclesial Sign

The symbol of cross is understood to mean the unique sacrifice of Jesus' life for the salvation of the world. Only Christ was able to take unto himself the sins of the world by dying a horrid death on the cross.

St. Augustine exhorted those who were preparing for baptism to understand the significance of the cross: Jesus Christ suffered and died for humanity.

> "Do not hesitate, do not be ashamed. When you first believed, you received the sign of Christ on your forehead, the home of your shame. Remember your forehead and do not be afraid of another man's tongue.... Do not then be afraid of the shame of the Cross."[16]

Since the forehead is where the blush of shame appears, the catechumens were signed with the cross on their forehead as a sign that they should never be ashamed of the cross. There was another reason for signing the candidates with the cross. In antiquity slaves and soldiers were marked on their foreheads or their hands as a sign that they owed allegiance to those they served. The slave was branded with his master's sign whereas the soldier was marked with the name of the Emperor. Catechumens were thus signed as a reminder that they belonged to Christ and his cross. This was referred to as a seal as was the entire rite of initiation. The cross was signed on the forehead once again at the completion of their initiation.[17]

We are united to Jesus' cross and suffering through baptism. The cross is initiatory. We are incorporated into Christ's cross through baptism: we die to sin and are resurrected to new life in Christ. Through confirmation we are branded with the Holy Spirit. We are also sealed and joined to the cross of Christ. Through the eucharist, we share in Jesus' sacrifice of the cross. In the form of bread and wine we once again participate in the breaking, sharing, and pouring out of Jesus' life. We, too, are broken, shared, and poured out. The Christian community shares in the saving effects of Jesus' sacrifice: his paschal mystery, his death and resurrection. Like Jesus on Calvary, paschal Christians are to live, die, and empty themselves, for the sake of others, for the sins of the world.

---

[16] *Sermon* 215.5; *Patrologia Latina*, ed, J.-P. Migne, in *AIRI*, 4.
[17] Ibid.

The sacrifice of the cross continues through the broken bread and the poured cup of the eucharist.

We cannot earn salvation. Jesus won salvation on the cross and through the grace offered by the selfless sacrifice of his life we are all beneficiaries. The cross is a supreme act of love. Jesus' death on the cross fulfilled all the expectations of the old Passover. Salvation history is fulfilled with Jesus' final act of love. All sacraments participate in the cross of Christ. They invite us to live the paschal mystery in our everyday lives and supply the needed grace to do so.

St. John Chrysostom professes it best:

> Today sees our Lord Jesus Christ on the cross; we celebrate, so that we may understand that the cross is a celebration, a solemn, spiritual feast. Before, the cross was synonymous with condemnation; now it is an object of honor. Before, a symbol of death; now, the means of salvation. It has been the source of countless blessings for us: it has delivered us from error, it has shone on us when we were in darkness. We were vanquished, yet it reconciles us with God. We were foes, yet it has regained God's friendship for us. We were estranged, yet it has brought us back to him. . . . We have discovered a wellspring.[18]

Question: In light of your personal experience of the cross, the suffering in your life, can you now perhaps assign a deeper meaning to that suffering in dialogue with our tradition's belief in its saving effects?

Liturgical Sign

The cross forms us as people. Every liturgy, every sacramental celebration has as its primary focus incorporation into the paschal mystery of Jesus Christ. That is, we participate in Jesus' death and resurrection through our participation in the liturgy. Eucharist is a living memorial of that death and resurrection.

Every liturgical gathering remembers the cross of Christ. We begin each liturgy with the sign of our identity, the sign of the cross. We are signed with the cross of Jesus as catechumens and at our baptism. The sign of the cross signifies the grace of salvation won for us through Jesus' passion, death on the cross, and resurrection. We make the sign of the cross before all prayer and as we enter the church.

We remember the cross of Christ especially on Good Friday, Palm Sunday, and the feast of the Triumph of the Cross. The Easter season is a meditation on its saving effects. The entire liturgical year invites us to live the cross each day. The cross is a primary symbol in every blessing, ritual, liturgy, sacrament, and sacramental of the church. (Refer to the Good Friday liturgy for the historical development of the ritual celebration of the cross.)

Questions: Do you remember a time when you were conscious of an experience of the cross in the liturgy? What did it teach you about God, Christ, the church, and yourself? What is the challenge of the cross we celebrate? How are we called to respond to the cross of Christ in our lives?

C. INTRODUCTION TO THE EASTER VIGIL

Huddled around ancient fires, our ancestors told their stories and enacted the rituals that formed them into a holy nation, a consecrated assembly, a people set apart. We, too, gather this night around similar sacred flames to remember our origins, to tell our story, and to "do" the business of making church. The ancient phallic symbol of Easter candle is plunged into the embryonic waters of font. Tonight, the church gives birth. As it labors in love, Mother Church sings its pangs of joy as neophytes are born and hearts are reborn.

This is the night when heavenly hosts gather around their Master's jeweled banquet table in triumphant exultation, awaiting the final great communion. This is the night when Christians of earth look toward their participation in that banquet while rejoicing in the one at hand. It is sacred, earthy work. We dirty our hands in groves of olives, fields of wheat, and vineyards of grapes and

[18] John Chrysostom (ca. 350–407), "Homélie pour le Vendredi saint," in *Homiliaire patristique,* Lex Orandi 8 (Paris: Cerf, 1949), 65; in *DL (III)*, 27–28.

we wash them again and again in the murky waters of life. And somehow the fruit of our labor is sanctified and transports us into the heart of Transcendent Mystery. This is the night when heaven is truly wedded to earth.

This night (the night early Christians believed would be the time and place of Jesus' return) is the high point and premier celebration of our liturgical year. All the liturgies of the year point to this one great feast; it is foundational to our Catholic experience and identity. The Easter Vigil is divided into four parts: 1. Service of Light, 2. Liturgy of the Word, 3. Liturgy of Baptism, 4. Liturgy of the Eucharist.

D. SERVICE OF FIRE/LIGHT

Opening Prayer

Blessing of the Fire

Let us pray.
Father,
we share in the light of your glory
through your Son, the light of the world.
Make this new fire + holy, and inflame us with new hope.
Purify our minds by this Easter celebration
and bring us one day to the feast of eternal light.
We ask this through Christ our Lord.
Let us pray....[19]

Liturgical Context

The liturgy begins with the service of light and the blessing of the new fire. Even though Christ was discovered missing from the tomb at dawn, this liturgy is celebrated in the dark of night, with the blessing of new fire and a procession. The baptized, passing from death to life, darkness to light, were once called the *illuminandi.* The church gathers to celebrate the risen Christ who, on this holy night, dispelled the darkness of death.

This is a night of new things and new beginnings. We bless the new fire that will be used to light all the lights that were extinguished on Holy Thursday. Lit by the flame of the newly blessed fire, the Easter candle is processed into the darkened space as the acclamation of praise resounds: *"Lumen Christi,* Light of Christ, *Deo Gratias,* thanks be to God."

Like our ancestors of old who followed the pillar of light to freedom, we, too, are led to our freedom, the font and table. The procession moves through the church, the light growing brighter with the multiplication of each person's individual candle light. We stand as God's triumphant, liberated people while we listen to our hymn of praise: the Christian story in its grandeur, the mother of all prayers, the Exultet. We boldly, almost shockingly, praise God for the "necessary sin of Adam that gained for us so great a Redeemer" who is Christ our Light, the One who dispelled the darkness. In the dimness of this darkened church we listen as our salvation is unfolded before our sense-sharpened eyes and ears.

There are three ritual moments of light in the service of light: the blessing of the new fire; the procession and passing of light through the congregation with the acclamation, *Lumen Christi, Deo gratias;* and the prayer of blessing in the Exultet. "The fundamental theme of the Exultet is thanksgiving and praise for the light and the event of Easter night: redemption through the paschal mystery."[20]

Questions: How do these introductory moments of the Easter Vigil speak to your community? What do they tell you about God, the church, or you as an individual? What are the implications of blessing the new fire, processing by the light of the Easter candle, and singing our ancient hymn of praise? How does this experience call you to enter the death and resurrection of Christ?

Symbol of Light/Fire

The symbol of light in most religions is a sign of divinity. In the Christian tradition, the symbol of light is a sign of Christ's presence. Darkness symbolizes the converse: God's absence and/or the destructive force of evil. Fire is only used once in

[19]Easter Vigil: "Blessing of the Fire," *The Sacramentary.*

[20]*MSS,* 112.

our tradition—at the Easter Vigil. However, the symbol of fire and light overlap in many ways, so they will be treated together.

Natural Sign

Fire and light order our life. We rise to the light and go to bed in the dark. Light and darkness are known to effect mood shifts. Studies have shown that sunny, bright days impact people in a positive way, whereas repeated dark and gloomy days can cause depression. We need the light to see; we are unable to see in the dark. Too much light can burn us or hurt our eyes. Too much darkness is known to have prompted some suicides. Without light, plants do not grow. If there is too much light they are burned. When the night is illumined with light, it protects us from the unknown shadows of the dark. The light of fire protected ancient communities from intruding marauders. Food is cooked and our homes are heated with the warmth of fire. Fire and hearth are images of cozy comfort. We have no control over the light of day or the darkness of night. We are subject to their benevolence or their tyranny. Forest rangers purposely set fires to prompt new growth in the forest. The giant redwoods cannot procreate without nature's birthing, necessary fire. Fire makes it possible for acorns to gestate through the nutrients found in the charred ash. Fire also destroys.

Question: In what ways do we experience light and fire in our everyday lives? Describe your personal images and experiences of light and fire.

Biblical Sign

The Bible uses fire first in very natural ways, then in symbolic ways. The word "light" appears 257 times in the Bible and the word "fire" 457 times. These are basic, primordial elements, necessary for life. Fire is used in cooking, for heat and light, and as a weapon of war (2 Chr 35:13; Is 44:16, 19; Num 31:10). Fire, as light, is also a means of communication between cities. Fire can be a powerful sign of God's presence and protection: the burning bush (Ex 3:2) and the column of fire that escorted the Israelites (Ex 13:21–22). When fire and light appear in scripture, everyone is to take notice: it means God is present. Fire and light are signs of theophany. A fire was kept burning at the altar as a sign of God's abiding presence (Lev 6:2, 5–6). In addition to being a sign of God's presence, fire is also a sign of God's protection. God protected Elisha with fiery chariots; the three young men who were thrown into the fire by Nebuchadnezzar were not consumed by its flame. A very common Old Testament theme is that God will judge the world by fire (2 Sam 23:7) and test and purify his people by fire (Zech 13:9; Ex 32:20). Light is a reference to Torah or God's law—a lamp to light our feet (Ps 119).

The New Testament uses fire in the same way as the Hebrew scriptures used fire. God appeared to the twelve as tongues of fire. Jesus will test and purify when he baptizes with the Holy Spirit and fire (Mt 3:11). The last judgment is also seen in terms of fire. Jesus is understood as the Light, the new Word that lights our way.

Light is a prime symbol of Christ and his life. Christ is the Light; we are to walk as children of the Light (Mt 4:16; Lk 1:7–9; 2:32; Jn 12:36). For John, the evangelist, Jesus is the *Light* that dispels the darkness. Jesus, the *Light*, is the eternal Word of God. Faith calls people into the *Light*. The reign of God is characterized by light; there is no night in the heavenly sphere (Rev 21:22–27; 22:5).

Questions: What caught your attention in regard to the biblical understanding of fire and light? Why? In what way do you relate to the symbol of light/fire found in scripture? In what way does fire remind you of God's presence? In what way does the symbol of light invite you into the transcendence of God? How does the symbol of light challenge you in your Christian journey? How might light reveal the inclusivity of God? What does it teach you about God, Christ, the church, or yourself? How does it speak to the life of the community, your life?

Ecclesial Sign

The lighting of fire is not, in and of itself, characteristic of Easter. Every evening celebration in the ancient world began with a ritual of lighting. Whenever there is light, God is present: it is cause for our thanks. The blessing prayer over the fire is a prayer of longing for God, the Light that is never extinguished. The ritual of lighting probably has pagan roots. Large bonfires were lighted in the spring in hopes that pagan deities would bless the crops. Christians were forbidden to do this until the emergence of a ritual bonfire associated with Holy Saturday around the sixth century. This eventually became a part of the Easter Vigil liturgy. In the Middle Ages, people observed a custom of extinguishing all fires and lights in or around their homes. They would take a flame from the newly blessed Easter fire to light the extinguished fires in their homes as a sign of new life.

The newly-baptized are presented with a lighted candle as a sign that they have been enlightened by Christ. In antiquity there was reference to "the shining lights" of the neophytes, the "white-robed members of the heavenly kingdom."[21] The use of lighted candles probably originated as a practical necessity in a ritual that took place in the darkened shadows of early dawn. Connection between the lights and the parable of the bridesmaids was made by Gregory Nanzianus in 381: "The lamps which you will light symbolize the torchlight procession in the next world, in which our shining, virgin souls will meet the bridegroom with the shining lights of faith."[22]

Fire and light are signs of the risen Christ. They are also signs of the Holy Spirit. Fire is a symbol of the transforming power and energy of the Holy Spirit. Everything that is touched by the fire of the Spirit is transformed. Tradition understands fire as a sign of hope, consummation, sacrifice, and purification. Fire and light are symbols of sanctification. Light is initiatory in character. It is a symbol of incorporation into Christ's Body: we are to walk as children of the Light. "The presentation of the lighted candle shows that they [neophytes] are called to walk as befits the children of the light" (RCIA, #214). Light is a symbol of Christianity. Jesus is the Light that illumines the world. Light is a sign of wisdom and understanding. Light reminds us of Christ's presence. It is a sign of discipleship and righteousness. Wherever a candle is left burning, Christ is present.

[21]*De Lapsu Virginis*, 5.19, *Patrologia Latina*, ed, J.-P. Migne, in *AIRI*, 34.

[22]*Oratio* 40. 46; cf. 45.2, *Patrologia Gracca*, ed, J.-P. Migne, in *AIRI*, 34.

Questions: How would you articulate the church's understanding of light and fire? In what way does it have anything to do with living the Christian life, our life, your life? How might light speak to you of hope, consummation, sacrifice? What does that mean? In what way do they have relevance for your life? What does tradition's understanding of light and fire teach about God, Christ, the church, or yourself?

Liturgical Sign

The church uses fire, particularly light, extensively in its liturgy. The only time fire is used as a single entity is at the Easter Vigil. Fire is blessed as a sign of the risen Christ. The Easter candle is lit from this new fire and all other candles are lit from the light of that candle. The assembly's individual candles are also signs of the resurrected Christ.

The Easter candle probably originates from the ancient ritual of the *Lucenare*, celebrated at the end of each day. Lamps were lit to ward off the darkness. Light has always been a symbol of the presence of God: Moses and the burning bush, the presence of smoke, the cloud and pillar of fire. Light is such an important symbol and sign of God's presence that it is used in every liturgical celebration. Wherever the Blessed Sacrament is reserved, a sanctuary lamp burns as a sign of Christ's presence. As the neophytes are baptized, they are given lighted candles as a sign of their new status: they now walk as children of the Light. Candles illumine the table of the word and the table of the eucharist as a sign of the living, sacramental presence of Christ. Candles are used for the blessing of throats, Candlemas, and with the sick. The Easter candle is used at baptisms and funerals. Candles are used in processions, in all liturgical celebrations, at evening prayer, weddings, religious professions, and in homes. The symbol of Christ, the *Light*, is present at every liturgy.

Questions: What is your experience of fire and light in liturgy? Has it ever touched you in a conscious way? What does it say to you about God, Christ, church, or yourself? How has the Easter fire spoken to you? What did you experience, feel, and think as you gathered around the new fire at the Easter Vigil, as you carried candles or watched the procession with the Easter candle? What do these signs say to us as a community and what is their challenge?

E. THE LITURGY OF THE WORD

Liturgical Context

The biblical readings for the Easter Vigil are the same in the churches of the East and the West. The first four readings from the Old Testament (Hebrew scriptures) correspond to the Jewish tradition of the "Four Nights." The first night was when the Word of God created the world. The second night was when God appeared to Abraham and Sarah to fulfill the promise that Abraham would father Sarah's child in spite of their very old age. It was also the night when Abraham offered his son, Isaac, in sacrifice to God, thus demonstrating great faith. The third night was the night when the angel of death protected Israel's first-born from the death sentence reserved for Egypt's first-born. Pharaoh released Israel from bondage and Yahweh led the fleeing band through the desert. The fourth night is yet to come and will take place at the end of the world.

Thus, the first four readings are essential to understanding our salvation history already set in motion at the beginning of the world, fulfilled through the Incarnation, and to be culminated through Jesus' second coming.

The next three Old Testament readings are laden with baptismal images. They prepare us for this night when the church opens its fonts to the flowing waters of new birth, death, and resurrection. Paul's letter to the Romans explicitly names baptism as death to sin as the beginning of new life in Christ. The liturgy of the word culminates with the exuberant proclamation of the resurrection. We are taken to the place where death was destroyed forever: we are brought to the empty tomb of Jesus Christ.

The Word as Symbol

The Word embodies the presence of Christ in our midst. We proclaim the word of God as the living, sacramental presence of God. "In the celebration of the liturgy, the word of God is not voiced in only one way nor does it always stir the hearts of the hearers with the same power. Always, however, Christ is present in his word; as he carries out the mystery of salvation, he sanctifies us and offers the Father perfect worship.... That word constantly proclaimed in the liturgy is always, then, a living, active word through the power of the Holy Spirit. It expresses the Father's love that never fails in its effectiveness toward us."[23] When the word is proclaimed, the church is built up and it grows. Through the symbols inherent in the liturgy, salvation events are brought into the present and we are their beneficiaries. Through the proclamation of God's word we are made a new people, heirs of God's covenant.

Natural Sign

Words can build up or tear down. They can affirm or destroy. Words express mystery and reality. Words can be spoken, written, sung, signed, or coded. Words can sell things, teach, regulate, and warn. Words can start wars. Words can create revolutions. Words can change consciousness and political perspectives. Words have power.

Questions: Can you a remember a time when words had a powerful impact on your life, positively or negatively? What did that experience teach you about the power of the word?

Biblical Sign

Word is understood as the self-revelation of God to human beings. The Hebrew word *dabar* means not only the spoken word, but also an event, a happening. The term assumes power, energy, and action. It is dynamic and alive. The word of God connotes God's acts of salvation. The power of God's word is evident in the first reading from tonight's liturgy. God's word created the heavens and the earth: "Let there be light, and there was light" (Gen 1:3). The covenant with Israel comes from the word of the Lord, "Everything the Lord has said, we will do" (Ex 19:8; 24:3, 7). The ten commandments were referred to as the spoken word of God. The word of God is synonymous with God's promises: Abraham and his descendants, the promised land, etc. God's word was spoken through the prophets. God spoke in person to Moses who, in turn, was to speak God's word to Pharaoh (Ex 33:11; Num 12:8; Deut 34:1). Samuel heard the voice of the Lord calling in the night (1 Sam 3:7–14). Prophets spoke

[23] *Lectionary for Mass*: Introduction, #4, in *TLD*, 128.

God's word to David. Nathan assured David that his monarchy would endure forever. Nathan also accused David of having an illicit affair with Bathsheba. Elijah and Elisha are always in dialogue with God's word. When the prophet speaks, Israel listens. What the prophet speaks is as good as accomplished.

In the Wisdom tradition, asserts Irene Nowell, the word is understood as the bearer of good things to God's people and calamity to God's enemies. *Word* is also another term for the law. The wisdom tradition begins to personify the word and give it a divine role. The word, for example, was present at creation and in salvation history (Wis 10–12).

In the New Testament, the term *logos* is used 331 times. It has many possible meanings: a statement, an assertion, a command, a report or story, a proverb, a saying, a prophecy, or a speech. It is used as a reference for the revelation of God, especially revelation as it occurred through Jesus Christ. "In many cases, the 'word of God' is simply the Christian message, the good news."[24] Apostles and preachers speak God's word. Hearers of the word are to listen and respond accordingly.

The evangelist John's use of *logos* is in direct relation to Jesus Christ. In the Jewish story of the Four Nights (the first four readings from the Vigil liturgy), God's word as a personified entity creates the world. Many believe that the identification of Jesus with *logos* comes from this concept. "The hymn in the Prologue is the clearest example in first century Christian literature of both an incarnation and a preexistence of Christology. It affirms both that the logos has become flesh in the person of Jesus of Nazareth and that Jesus of Nazareth existed before the incarnation, indeed before the creation of the world, as God's divine *logos.*"[25]

Toward the end of the New Testament, the word was associated with the written word of God. "The 'good news' came to be seen in the written words of the four evangelists and in the Bible as a whole."[26]

[24]William G. Thompson, S.J. and Gerard S. Sloyan, "Word: New Testament," in *CPDBT*, 1097.

[25]Ibid., 1100.

[26]Anthony Tambasco, "Word of God," in *CPDBT*, 1097.

Questions: Have you ever experienced God's living presence in the scriptures? What did it teach you about God, Christ, the church, or yourself? Was there a call to respond, to action?

Ecclesial Sign

The Church Fathers sought to confirm the dynamic power of God's word through Christ in the church. "Where the Lordship (of God) is proclaimed, the Lord is present" (*Didache*, 4:1). St. Augustine linked the power of preaching to a person's absorption (or lack thereof) in the sacred scriptures. "Caesarius of Arles declared that 'the word of God is not to be treated as inferior to the body of Christ' (Sermon 78:2). For the Father, in fact, the liturgy becomes the fitting place where Jesus as the word of God is fully encountered, first in the scriptural flesh and blood of the *logos* and then in celebration of that word in the bread and wine of the eucharist."[27]

Because of the emergence of various heresies and the rise of the teaching ministry, the church of the Middle Ages was less concerned with the word as the living, dynamic, self-revelation of God and more concerned with the intellectual formulations of doctrines *about* God. Partly due to a concern over this, the Protestant reformers set forth *sola scriptura* (scripture alone) as the only source of God's word, thereby denying the teaching authority of the hierarchy. The Council of Trent insisted that the truth of God's word was in both the written sources and in the unwritten traditions. However, later developments elevated the unwritten source, tradition, to the status of a second, separate source of divine revelation.

Lines were drawn between Protestant and Catholic understandings of God's word. Protestants continued to preach God's word and to assert the importance of its power within each individual. Catholics relied on doctrinal formulations and theologies in relation to God's word. Tradition was placed in a higher position of authority than the biblical sources of God's word.

The Second Vatican Council retrieved the biblical source of God's self-revelation fulfilled through the

[27]Ibid.

person of Jesus Christ. The document *Dei Verbum* asserted the authenticity of scripture and tradition as one source. Thus, God is revealed through the scriptures *and* the tradition of the church. Tradition was redefined in terms of the "faith of the living church which surrounds, preserves and transmits the scriptures and makes them come alive."[28]

Questions: How does the church's experience of God's word throughout its history relate to the life of your community or yourself? What does it teach you about God, Christ, the church, or yourself?

Liturgical Signs

Dei Verbum returned us to our earliest roots in which the living word of God was best experienced in the celebration of the liturgy. Therefore, the Council prompted a renaissance in the preaching ministry of the church. "The primary duty of priests is the proclamation of the Gospel of God to all" (*Decree on Ministry and Life of Priests*). Preaching is characterized by the "proclamation of God's wonderful works in the history of salvation, that is, the mystery of Christ, which is made present and active within us, especially in the eucharistic celebration of the liturgy"(*Constitution on the Sacred Liturgy*, [CSL], #35, 2).

The church teaches that Christ is present in the proclamation of God's word in the liturgy. "He is present in his word, since it is he himself who speaks when the holy Scriptures are read in the Church" (CSL, #7). The word of God proclaimed in the liturgy is efficacious: "and it is from the continued use of Scriptures that the people of God, docile to the Holy Spirit under the light of faith, receive the power to be Christ's living witnesses before the world" (*Lectionary for Mass*: Introduction, #12).

All scripture reveals Jesus Christ. Both Testaments are about the saving work of God in Christ, the *Word* who was present at the creation of the world. God used human authors to reveal his *Word* for the salvation of all. The four gospels hold a preeminent place in the canon of the Bible as they reveal the life and work of Christ, the *Word made Flesh.* [See chapter three and chapter nine.]

[28]Ibid., 1098.

The word and the eucharist are in intimate relationship. "The Church is nourished spiritually at the table of God's word and at the table of the eucharist: from one it grows in wisdom and from the other in holiness. In the word of God the divine covenant is announced; in the eucharist the new and everlasting covenant is renewed. The spoken word of God brings to mind the history of salvation; the eucharist embodies it in the sacramental signs of the liturgy" (*Lectionary for Mass*: Introduction, #10).

Whenever the church gathers for prayer, God's word is primary. Whether the gathering is for sacraments, eucharist, rites, the liturgy of the hours, blessings, or sacramentals, it is the church's intention that the word be a pivotal part of all liturgical celebration.

Questions: Have you ever experienced the presence of Christ in the proclamation of God's word in the liturgy? What did it teach you about God, Christ, the church, or yourself? In what way has the word of God called your community to respond in the past? How is God's word challenging your community now?

THE WORD OF GOD

Proclaim the word of God.

First Reading
Genesis 1:1–2:2

While meditating on the reason for God's incredible action in the lives of human beings, and drawing on Babylonian images of the creation of the world, the ancient author of Genesis (ca. 5th or 6th century B.C.E.) eloquently provided all future generations with refined insight into the creative, loving, and omniscient power of the Creator. The word was spoken and God's generative power created the universe. From creation onward, the generative word of God would have a leading role in human history and experience. (Remember the centurion who told Jesus to say but the word and his servant would be healed.)

"God creates the world for humans in six days and rests on the seventh, the first week of human history; the week of six work days ending in Sabbath observance is thereby hallowed.... In W. Semitic enumerations, the seventh place is often climactic; God's sabbath is therefore the climax of the story, which is primarily about God, not humans."[29] No matter how chaotic the pre-creation order was, God was in control.

Thanks be to God for this inspired author of Genesis. He gave us an anchor that would inspire all generations. Genesis is a constant reference. When we are tempted to accept the hopeless depravity of the human condition, we have something that shakes our sensibilities and reminds us: "Remember? God saw that it was *good.*" "God pronounces the light good, beautiful; the phrase will be repeated six times of created elements, climaxing in the seventh climactic occurrence for the whole universe (v. 31). The declaration is not a deduction from human experience but a divine declaration that all of creation is good."[30] We are created in the image and likeness of God. "The human is a statue of the deity, not by static being, but by action, who will rule over all things previously created (v. 26). In the ancient Near East, the king was often called the image of the deity and was vested with God's authority; royal language is used here for the humans."[31] We are created to be fully alive human beings, imbued with transcendent dignity. "The human being is placed at the summit in the temple of creation: all humanity has value in God's eyes."[32] Men and women are created *equal* in the eyes of God. Men and women are given sacred rights and responsibilities.

In the creation account, men and women are to subdue the earth. They will control their harsh environment by force if necessary, but they are to treat God's creation with proper dignity. Human beings "are to respect the environment; they are not to kill for food but are to treat all life with respect... the world is made for man and woman. Plants will suffice for food for humans and animals; there will be no bloodshed. This prohibition is modified in the renewal of creation after the flood."[33] Thus, the whole created order is good. In Yahweh's world there is no evil; there is only

[29]Richard J. Clifford, S.J. and Roland E. Murphy, O.Carm., "Genesis," in *NJBC*, 11.

[30]Ibid.

[31]Ibid.

[32]*DL* (III), 44.

[33]Clifford and Murphy, *NJBC* 11.

beauty. In an effortless stroke of the Master's brush, God's word painted the heavens and the earth.

The creation story is eschatological as it defines what God intends. "This serene, beautiful world, in which all is ordered to humans, and humans are ordered to God, is how it will be at the end. God's world will triumph."[34] The sin that will follow in subsequent chapters will not reign forever. It will not stand in the way of God's original intent. God will be victorious.

The *word* of God created the world. Christian understanding gives Jesus Christ a star role in this first theater of God's creative drama. Jesus, the spoken *Word* of God (John's prologue), was present and active in this creative, generative moment. Jesus Christ was the *Light* that dispels the darkness and chaos. We share in that light and thus can marvel and proclaim with the psalmist, "Lord, continue to send out your Spirit and renew the face of the earth, continue to create it anew and make it good."

Questions: In what way does God continue the transforming work of creation in our community? Do we really believe in the goodness of creation? What are we going to do about it?

Responsorial Psalm
Psalm 104—Lord, send out your Spirit and renew the face of the earth.
or
Psalm 33—The earth is full of the goodness of the Lord.

Second Reading
Genesis 22:1–18

The Lord God promises Abraham many and great things in this reading. We, however, are shocked by the demand to murder his son. We have a difficult time getting past Abraham's willingness to perform such a heinous act. Someone once raised the question, "If that is an example of the kind of God you wish me to worship, thanks, but no thanks, I want no part of him. What God would ask a father to murder his own son?" It is an hon-

[34]Ibid.

est question. Yet this story is upheld throughout all of biblical literature as a premier story of faith. There has to be and there is more to the story.

In order to understand this story we must stretch ourselves and put our Western mind-sets on hold for a brief period. This story is not about killing one's son; it is about placing one's entire life in the hands of the all-knowing, omniscient God. "The father's life is bound up with that of his child and heir; Abraham entrusts his life and his future unconditionally to the God who calls him."[35]

This is the only time in scripture that God tests one individual rather than the entire nation. Abraham, as the future leader of Israel, must "entrust his entire life and future to God."[36] The reader of this story is aware from the beginning that God is testing Abraham, but Abraham is not aware. Isaac was not Abraham's only son as the text would intimate. Rather, a better translation is: *favored.* God makes sure that in this dialogue, the weight of Isaac's value to Abraham is emphasized.

Abraham and Isaac ascend Mount Moriah, the place believed to be the site of Solomon's first temple. Abraham, then, is the first worshiper on the temple site. Abraham obeys God in silence; Isaac follows and asks the whereabouts of the sacrificial animal. Abraham's reply that God would provide is another example of trusting God to supply all needs. Everything is completely in Yahweh's hands.

The angel arrives to save the day, Isaac is spared, and Abraham proves that his entire life is completely under God's providential care. "He has finally learned to give up control over his own life that he might receive it as grace."[37] God spoke the word to the angel and caused Isaac to be spared. God caused the first-born of Israel to be spared. In Israel it was understood that each new-born child belonged to God and was symbolically sacrificed to God. As a symbolic sign of this sacrifice, a ram (or other animal) was offered in order to redeem the first-born.

[35]Ibid., 25.

[36]Ibid.

[37]Ibid.

Abraham was always understood to prefigure what would be accomplished through Christ. Jesus, God's first-born, would be sacrificed, would stand in as the sacrificial lamb and redeem Israel. We can do no less than respond to such love with the unconditional trust of Abraham. Keep me safe, O God; you are my hope.

Questions: What is your first reaction to God's request to Abraham? How is Abraham a sign for your community? What difference do this reading and its implications make for the life of your community and for your own life? What is the challenge?

Responsorial Psalm
Psalm 16—Keep me safe, O God; you are my hope.

Third Reading
Exodus 14:15–15:1

The Passover is to Jews what the death and resurrection of Jesus is to Christians—the premier saving event of God. It is and has been remembered annually as a living memorial of God's saving, liberating power. It is actualized as it is remembered. Those who remember and celebrate the Passover are, in a manner of speaking, present at the first passover and are beneficiaries of its liberating action.

Thus, the exodus story is told on this night above all nights, when the passover of Jesus Christ was prefigured through the exodus event. This is why the reading from Exodus must be proclaimed at the Vigil.

Whether each detail of this epic event is based on historical fact or on the natural elaboration that goes with the telling of a great moment in the conscious collective memory of a people is not important. What is important is that the exodus event is remembered for generations as a defining moment for the people of God, the supreme initiative of God's loving and liberating action. It is a sign of God's covenant with Israel—a primary theme throughout biblical literature. (Refer to the exegesis on Holy Thursday for a more complete elaboration of the meaning and roots of Passover.)

Jesus is the new Passover, the new covenant. Jesus, the new paschal lamb, was sacrificed for the sins of all, and leads us out of bondage into the promised land of freedom and new life through baptism. The Red Sea was understood in Christian consciousness as an image of baptism. The neophyte passes through the sea of death to new life. It is no wonder that this story of Passover and passage is a baptismal scripture of great importance. We continue to live the benefits of the first Passover and Jesus' Passover from death to life. We must, then, sing triumphantly with Miriam: "Let us sing to the Lord; he has covered himself in glory."

Questions: In what way does your community resemble the Israelite community? How would you describe your communal covenant with God? What can be affirmed and where is growth needed? Are there any areas in your community life that are still in bondage and in need of liberation? How does your community live in covenant relationship with God? What is the evidence that you are in a covenant relationship with God as a community and as an individual? Where does death still reign? Where is there resurrection? What are you going to do about it?

Responsorial Psalm
Exodus 15—Let us sing to the Lord; he has covered himself in glory.

Fourth Reading
Isaiah 54:5–14

This reading is from Second Isaiah (Deutero-Isaiah) and it represents the fourth night—the fourth stage of salvation history. It is the night in which God's own people will be gathered to the heavenly city of eternal life. We are reminded on this Vigil night that lest we become mesmerized by the excitement of tonight and the joy of God's reign in the temporal sphere, there is an important reality always in our consciousness. We live in the reign of God on two planes—*the here and now* and *the not yet.*

This pericope is written from the tenuous situation of captivity. It is a word of consolation to a people in great distress. There is none of the overconfident self-assurance that was evident during the time of First Isaiah when Israel was in its shining glory. Such confidence faded into obscurity in light of domination by a foreign power in the alien land of Babylon.

Isaiah wants his people to know that, no matter what happens, God will not forsake them. No matter how difficult things become, God's covenant with Israel will stand. We are left with the hope and the imagery of that brilliant future city, laid out for us with streets and walls lined with "cornelians, rubies, sapphires and precious stones"—a city in which God's justice will reign eternal. "The word of God emanates from the splendor of the Lord's presence."[38] We pause, then, before our great God and humbly acknowledge in heartfelt response: "I will praise you, Lord, for you have rescued me."

Questions: In what way has your community experienced the consoling love of God? Has there ever been a time in which great distress caused your complete reliance on God? What was the experience like? What does this reading teach you about God, Christ, the church, and yourself? What are you called to do in response?

Responsorial Psalm
Psalm 30—I will praise you, Lord, for you have rescued me.

Fifth Reading
Isaiah 55:1–11

This reading turns our eyes from a backward glance at salvation history to a more present, sacramental stance. We are brought into the presence and action of Christ. Isaiah's conclusion to the "Book of Consolations" speaks of that day in which God's people will be lavished with rich fare and flowing water. "Deutero-Isaiah invites poor people to a joyful banquet."[39] Throughout the Bible, the banquet image is used to demonstrate God's care for Israel. The messianic age and everlasting life in heaven are often described as a banquet.

Yahweh insists that the only requirement for this banquet is thirst for God. People are to seek God who is transcendent and elusive. God is near enough to be troubled by the sin of humanity,

[38]Carroll Stuhlmueller, "Deutero-Isaiah and Trito-Isaiah," in *NJBC*, 343.

[39]Ibid.

however. What Christian does not turn his or her eyes toward baptism and eucharist when hearing of quenched thirsts and rich food, spread for all, rich and poor alike? How could a Christian not think of the eucharistic banquet when hearing of Isaiah's admission-free banquet for the salvation of all people?

The word of God again plays a very important, sacramental role in this reading. "God's word is the initiator: from it comes salvation."[40] Stuhlmueller suggests that, in Isaiah, God's word is not so much a message as it is an event in the mystery of salvation history. God's word is not static, but living; it causes action. God's word will accomplish what God intends. God's word will restore Israel. The world rejoices as God brings Israel home. Sin will be no more in the new Jerusalem. Sin and death will not be invited guests at the eternal banquet; they will be gone forever. The *shalom* peace of God will reside eternally in God's restored Paradise.

Jesus, Word of God, on this night of nights, rises and returns to God. In so doing, Jesus, Word of God, brings salvation to the world. On this night, holier than all other nights, we listen to Isaiah and are invited to remember our baptismal and eucharistic life. We draw deeply and joyfully from the springs of our sacramental salvation.

Questions: Is your community—are you—inclusive? Where are there still areas of death? Where are the areas of resurrection? Do all of God's people have a place at your communal and individual banquet table? Who is not invited? In what way does your community need to grow? What does this reading say to you about God, Christ, the church, and yourself? What is the challenge? What are you going to do about it?

Responsorial Psalm
Isaiah 12—You will draw water joyfully from the springs of salvation.

Sixth Reading
Baruch 3:9–15, 32–4:4

This sixth reading extols the value of wisdom. When we stray (and we will) from God's path, wisdom leads us back. While on this earth, we can never completely know the extent of the mystery of God. What we do know is revealed through the power of wisdom. Wisdom reveals the mind and the heart of God through the Word of God.

Baruch upholds obedience to God's law as the highest value. Israel disobeyed the law and was punished. Prosperity and peace can occur only when the word of God is observed. Baruch understands the Mosaic law as wisdom. In later Judaism, wisdom is "personified and given divine attributes."[41] It is the greatest value, the most prized asset. Without wisdom, all is lost. Only God can offer wisdom; human beings can do nothing on their own to obtain it.

The word of God is the ongoing, sacramental presence of God's wisdom. Through the scriptures we come to know God. In our liturgy we believe that when scriptures are proclaimed we are in the living presence of Christ.

Through baptism, we live within the active, present word of God. We are strengthened and led by God's word in and through Jesus Christ and his Spirit. Thus, with assurance we together proclaim: "Lord, you have the words of everlasting life."

Questions: How is your community responding to God's wisdom? In what way, if any, do you forge ahead without seeking the will of God in your community life? How does your community listen to God? Where is there still death and where is there resurrection? What does this reading say to you about God, Christ, the church, and yourself? What is the challenge?

Responsorial Psalm
Psalm 19—Lord, you have the words of everlasting life.

Seventh Reading
Ezekiel 36:16–28

In tonight's reading from Ezekiel, we are made privy to God's conversation with Ezekiel. God reminded Ezekiel that the people had turned away from Yahweh, thinking they had no need of his providential care. They found themselves in exile

[40] *DL* (III), 52.

[41] Aloysius Fitzgerald, F.S.C., "Baruch," in *NJBC*, 566.

because they had sinned, blasphemed, and acted in depravity. Therefore, God punished them. Only God's power could gather the lost and scattered people.

However, the covenant continues with Israel. God blesses them. This reading is a summary of Ezekiel's theology. Paul resonates the same theology throughout his ministry: salvation is freely offered grace. Salvation and justification are from God.

Ezekiel promises the bestowal of a new heart and a new spirit. "The heart is the seat of thinking and loving, so it will be a new way of looking at life from God's point of view."[42] The new spirit bestowed upon Israel empowers it to live *as a people.* God forms them as a community, not as individuals.

This reading also foreshadows the final eschatological gathering. Before the last gathering, people must be washed clean of their idolatry. Only God is capable of such cleansing. Only God has the power to remove stony hearts and replace them with hearts of love. God's Spirit will breathe new life into these newly gathered children.

On this night of baptisms and rebirth we ask for the new heart and new spirit promised to Ezekiel. Thus, the cries of our heart resound in song: "Create in me a clean heart, O God."

Questions: This reading reminds us why we must ask the communal questions first. God deals with us as a people, yet we often have only the sense that our relationship with God is a "Jesus and me" affair. What are the "stony heart" areas in your community, in your own life? Where is God's transformative healing needed? Where is the death and where is the resurrection? How are you called to change as a community?

Responsorial Psalm
Psalm 42—As the deer longs for running streams, so my soul longs for you, my God.
or
Psalm 51—Create a clean heart in me, O God.

[42]Lawrence Boadt, C.S.P., "Ezekiel," in *NJBC,* 325.

Epistle
Romans 6:3–11

Paul's letter to the Romans is a transition point in the liturgy of the word. We now move from the Hebrew scriptures to the Christian scriptures; from the former age to the messianic age and thus to the present. The Sacramentary instructs us to turn on the lights at this point in the liturgy. This is the moment when we turn from darkness to light. We are led to the font, the place that initiates *bearers of the light.* Baptism assures us that we no longer live in the darkness, but are children of the light.

We are no longer dead. Paul reminds us that through baptism we die to sin and become a new creation in Christ. The neophyte plunges deeply into the waters of death, suffocated by the crushing weight of water and sin, only to come up, gasping for the air of invigorating new life and freedom. (A little sprinkle of water hardly speaks of the same reality.)

"The rite of Christian initiation introduces a human being into union with Christ's suffering and dying."[43] The newly baptized are initiated into Christ's resurrected life. Baptism gives the Christian the power to live the Christian life. Paul asserts that through baptism we are dead to sin; it no longer lives in us. "The destruction of the sinful 'self' through baptism and incorporation into Christ means liberation from enslavement to sin. Hence, one's outlook can no longer be focused on sin."[44]

Reginald Fuller reminds us that the verbs used in Paul's address bring to mind the effects of baptism. When speaking of "dying to ourselves," Paul uses past tense verbs. He uses future tense verbs in relation to the resurrection. Through baptism we *died* (past tense) with Christ.[45] However, our resurrection is our future goal as we live out our baptismal commitment and moral response. We continue to renew our commitment to die to sin each day.

Paul's letter to the Romans prepares us for a key moment of the Easter Vigil liturgy: the renewal of

[43]Joseph A. Fitzmyer, S.J., "The Letter to the Romans," in *NJBC,* 848.
[44]Ibid., 848, 849.
[45]*PNL,* 21, 22.

our baptismal vows. And so, together with the psalmist, we can joyfully sing the triple alleluia as well as our praise, awe, and trust in God's incredible, awesome mighty works!

Questions: How have you died to sin throughout this Lent as a community and as individuals? In what way have you grown? Where is growth still needed? Where is death? Resurrection? What difference has the baptism of neophytes made in your community this year? Is your community prepared to recommit to their baptismal promises? How is growth (resurrection) evident? Where is growth still needed? What is the challenge?

Responsorial Psalm
Psalm 118—Alleluia! Alleluia! Alleluia!

Gospel
Matthew 28:1–10

Herein lies the ultimate reason we gather this night: to remember and bring forward the resurrection of Jesus Christ, the saving event that brings us to this place in time and history. We are a resurrection people. We live in the resurrected presence of the Spirit of Jesus Christ. It is the faith we profess and the power behind our profession. From the very beginning, the liturgy moves us to this moment. Excitement grows, as we are prepared in sense and spirit for the proclamation of the faith we confess with assurance: Christ has died; Christ is risen; Christ will come again. This is where it all began. Matthew takes us back so we can bring it forward.

We are there and it is now. Again the earth rumbles and all creation continues its mournful vigil at the tomb where Jesus was laid. The faithful women are present and witnesses to the scene. Matthew insists on making the earth the final witness to the vindication of God's Son. Cosmic signs have from the very beginning announced the fulfillment of God's plan of salvation in and through Jesus Christ. A star announced his coming, earthquakes punctuated his death and now they punctuate his resurrection. Heaven's messenger dazzles the onlooker amidst the deafening roar of the earth's bowels. We are not to miss the point—and just in case we do, Matthew tells us that even the guards are paralyzed with fear. Once again heaven's messenger announces the glad tidings, reminiscent of a similar announcement some thirty-plus years earlier. That which caused such overwhelming fear in the guards is a source of joy and hope for Jesus' followers. "He is risen." The One who was placed in the tomb of death has risen as he promised he would. Matthew reminds his readers that in this earthly life Jesus was fully confident of his victory over death.[46] (During the Passover meal and his trial before the high priest, Jesus predicted his resurrection.)

Matthew understood the entire event as the dawning of the messianic age and the prelude to the last age. For Matthew, the resurrection of Christ depends on the faith of those who encountered the Risen Christ. "It would be fruitless to try to find 'proofs' in the Gospel that would attest to the truth of the resurrection in a way that would withstand historical scrutiny."[47] Then and now, it is only through the eyes of faith that Jesus' resurrection makes any sense and ultimately offers meaning to our lives. Readers ancient and contemporary are initiated into an encounter with the Risen Christ of all ages—the Alpha and the Omega.

There is one piece of the story that challenges the suspicious among us. According to Raymond Brown, Jesus predicted his passion, death, and resurrection three different times and still the disciples didn't get it. Yet those who plotted to kill him had obviously heard it, and they understood full well what he meant! This is why they took precautions to secure the tomb. Matthew probably used this tidbit to address the skepticism over Jesus' resurrection encountered by the later church. It may have served an apologetic and polemic function. A Matthean agenda has a constant thread woven throughout the passion narrative: human machinations will not thwart the designs of God. God will have God's way!

Matthew's use of irony serves to remind us of the stark contrasts and paradoxes inherent in the Christ event. Jesus had been accused of healing on the Sabbath; the religious leaders tried to block his resurrection on the Sabbath. Jesus lived; those who sought to prevent his resurrection were "as if

[46] *PJGM*, 157.
[47] *DL* (III), 60.

dead." At the birth of Jesus, Herod conspired with the scribes and chief priests to thwart the beginning of Jesus' mission; at his death they strove to prevent its continuance.[48] The point is not to be missed: the power of God is greater than any human force! God will have God's way!

None of the synoptic gospels describe the resurrection. "Matthew's silence about the resurrection itself, similar to the silence of the other canonical gospels, suggests that the resurrection could not be described, for it was an event that touched the other world beyond time and space. When Matthew's angel rolls back the stone, he does not do so to provide an exit for the resurrection but to make it possible to see that Jesus was no longer in the place where he lay (28:6) and that therefore the resurrection had already taken place."[49] The angel interprets the events for them, just as the angels had done at Jesus' birth. They serve a revelatory function. Those who plotted his death will posit one scenario. The angel, on the other hand, reveals the action and the plan of God.

The women are told to go to the disciples (in language reminiscent of Old Testament manifestations: "Go quickly and do not be afraid . . . ," etc.) and tell them to gather for an encounter with Jesus. This occurs only in Matthew's gospel. Donald Senior maintains that Matthew uses this piece of the text to posit his theology. The women were faithful. They stood valiantly by the cross when the disciples did not. Their reward is the announcement by the angel and an appearance from the Lord himself! Jesus appeared to the women who were on their way to their designated mission. Matthew's point? Jesus would always be with his disciples in their missionary efforts to proclaim the crucified and risen Christ. Jesus was and is present in the community as it goes forth. "Matthew is surely presenting virtues that his Christian readers would imitate in receiving and sharing the news of the risen Lord; they were being invited to go quickly with reverential fear and great joy to tell others."[50]

Jesus appeared to the women and they fell down and paid him homage in true liturgical style—an example for all followers in the presence of the Risen One. He calmed their fears and offered the peace and forgiveness he had promised at the Last Supper. The angel had told the women to go in haste to the *disciples*. Jesus tells them to go to his *brothers*. "A new status will emerge for those who hear and believe in the resurrection: they become God's children and thus the brothers and sisters of Jesus."[51] Jesus extends peace to those who deserted him. He takes the initiative. He offers them his love and forgiveness. The Easter Good News is a message of peace and reconciliation. Jesus moves to restore the relationship with his disciples that was broken by their betrayal and denial. Jesus did what he had taught his followers to do throughout his entire ministry.

The official proclamation from heaven, "He is not here, he has risen!" once again resounds throughout heaven and earth. In each liturgy of the church, we remember the cross and resurrection; we bring it into the present and we live it. We continue to live it when we follow Christ's mandate to go out into the world and share the Good News.

The neophytes are escorted to the font as we bring Jesus' saving event to bear in the life of our communities. The newly baptized die and rise in the midst of a community committed to the same dying and rising. Thus, we stand before the exalted throne of the Lamb and profess our baptismal promises. We continue to participate in the ongoing paschal mystery of Christ as we break bread together in the eucharist.

Questions: How does Matthew's account of the resurrection speak to your life? What are some of the key themes that speak to the Christian life? In what way do the women in the scene have anything to do with the community or with your personal life? How do the women challenge us today? How has your community experienced death and resurrection this past year? How does Matthew speak to your community's experience and understanding of the paschal mystery? Put yourself in the women's shoes. How would you react to the appearance of the angel and of Jesus and the mission you are given? What is the challenge of this Easter gospel? What are you called to do in response?

[48] *RCE*, 25.

[49] Ibid., 29.

[50] Ibid., 30.

[51] Ibid., 31

F. SERVICE OF BAPTISM

Following the liturgy of the word is the liturgy of baptism. If there are candidates for baptism, they (the elect) process to the font, singing the Litany of the Saints. The elect and the faithful are in solidarity with the saints of old who went before us and the saints of today who walk with us.

The virgin water is blessed as the candle is plunged three times deeply into it. The intimate union is not to be missed. Water is blessed while remembering past images of God's action through the use of water. We remember the purifying floodwaters, the liberating Red Sea, and the salvation afforded by the water and blood from Jesus' side on the cross. We recall Jesus' mandate to the twelve to go out and baptize in the name of the Father, Son, and Holy Spirit. The blessing of water helps us remember (*anamnesis*) and bring into the present all that God has done throughout human history. We stand with God and the communion of saints as we participate in the ancient and always new and unfolding human and heavenly drama.

Blessing of the Water

Father, you give us grace through sacramental signs,
which tell us of the wonders of your unseen power.
In baptism we use your gift of water,
which you have made a rich symbol
of the grace you give us in this sacrament.
At the very dawn of creation
your Spirit breathed on the waters,
making them the wellspring of all holiness.
The waters of the great flood
you made a sign of the waters of baptism,
that make an end of sin and a new beginning of goodness.
Through the waters of the Red Sea
you led Israel out of slavery,
to be an image of God's holy people,
set free from sin by baptism.
In the waters of the Jordan
your Son was baptized by John
and anointed with the Spirit.
Your Son willed that water and blood
should flow from his side
as he hung upon the cross.
After his resurrection he told his disciples:
"Go out and teach all nations,
baptizing them in the name of the Father
and of the Son and of the Holy Spirit."
Father, look now with love upon your Church,
and unseal for her the fountain of baptism.
By the power of the Holy Spirit
give to the water of this font
the grace of your Son.
You created man in your own likeness:
cleanse him from sin in a new birth of innocence
by water and the Spirit.
We ask you, Father, with your Son,
to send the Holy Spirit upon the waters of this font.
May all who are buried with Christ
in the death of baptism
rise also with him to newness of life.
We ask this through Christ our Lord.[52]

Through our profession of the baptismal promises, we renew the promises made for us at baptism. We agree to continue the process of daily death and resurrection. The elect enter the font of death and resurrection and become the living witness of all that we have shared and heard up to this point. Water soaked and Spirit filled, they take their place in the assembly of believers and await the moment at which the trumpets of heaven announce the culmination of their baptismal journey. They are ushered along with the church triumphant to the banquet table of the Lord. Eucharist—not baptism—is the goal of initiation.

Water-soaked and oil slathered, the newly baptized are presented with the baptismal candle. Through baptism we are called out of darkness to live in the light; we become children of the Light. The Easter candle is a sign of the sacramental presence of Christ, the Light of the World. The fire is a symbol of the transforming energy of the Holy Spirit. Elijah prayed and the fire came down from heaven upon his sacrifice at Mount Carmel. This was a foreshadowing of the Spirit who causes transformation. St. John the Baptist said of Jesus that he would baptize with the Holy Spirit and fire. Jesus would cause great transformation and *metanoia* in his followers. Tongues of fire rested on the disciples at Pentecost. Thus, the symbol of fire has

[52]Easter Vigil: "Blessing of Water," *The Sacramentary.*

been retained as "one of the most expressive images of the Spirit's actions."[53]

As a sign of their new status, of the fact that they are made a new creation, neophytes put on the white garment. In scripture whenever a garment was placed on an individual it was a sign that a new status had been conferred upon that person. The new status for neophytes is that of newly baptized, confirmed children of the Light who await the culmination of their journey as fully initiated members of the community through participation in the eucharist.

Symbol of Water

"Water can cause destruction as well as life and cleansing, lending itself as a symbol of God's judgment as well as of life and forgiveness."[54] The symbol of water speaks to us of multifaceted realities.

Natural Sign

In our natural lives, the experience of water is cleansing, soothing, and thirst quenching. It can be plentiful or in short supply. Water can be smooth and flowing as well as crushingly powerful. It is life-giving and death-dealing. We cannot live without it, and we cannot live in it. The properties of water speak to us of hidden realities. Water reminds us of how God acts and who God is. Like water, God is soothing and God's power is mighty. Immersion in water results in deep cleansing. Immersion in God's love causes deep, interior cleansing. Water is for the body what God is for the soul.

There is another facet to the many dimensions of water's inner realities. Water can be devastating. One can die in water. One is also born in water. No one can control the furious flow of water; no one can control the acts of God. When water is absent, there is thirst. When God is absent, there is parched thirst.

[53]Cf. St. John of the Cross, *The Living Flame of Love,* in *The Collected Works of St. John of the Cross,* trans. K. Kavanaugh, O.C.D., and O. Rodriguez, O.C.D. (Washington DC: Institute of Carmelite Studies, 1979), 577 ff.

[54]Joseph F. Grassi, "Water," in *CPDBT,* 1060.

Biblical Sign

God is present in the biblical signs of water. Water is cited in scripture more than any other natural resource. The authors of biblical texts lived in a dry desert land. They were exposed to the continuous shortage of water. They were naturally preoccupied with finding it and the necessity for it. It is no wonder that our biblical texts use water as the revealer of the "God of Mystery who is its source and faithful dispenser."[55]

At creation, God hovered over the waters; the generative power of the Holy Spirit unleashed God's power and action into the lives of human beings. The great flood of Genesis purged the earth of sin. God's judgment came upon the earth and water purified the human race. "God overcame the primeval waters over the earth (Gen 1:1–10). He unleashed the deluge as a punishment for sin and then brought it to an end, saving Noah, the Hebrew ancestor."[56] God led the Israelites through the Red Sea, drowning Pharaoh in the process. The Israelites were afforded safe passage through the sea to the promised land and, after crossing the hazardous Jordan, were made citizens of a new land.

In scripture, water is a sign of God's providential care. It can be abundantly showered down, or withheld because of sin (Deut 11:14–17). Water, then, is a source of death and of life. As a sign of life it is a sign of God's creative presence.

In scripture water is also a sign of purification. It was used for purification baths before celebrating community rituals. (However, repentance was still necessary for complete forgiveness.) Water is a symbol of the transforming action of the Holy Spirit. The Vigil reading from Ezekiel recalls the power of the Spirit to create transformed minds and hearts.

Water also has a role in the New Testament. Mark uses the image very little. Matthew exhorts everyone to go and baptize all nations. Matthew relates this baptism to the baptism of Jesus in the Jordan. Matthew sees water as a sign of incorpo-

[55]Kathleen Hughes, R.S.C.J., "Water: Pastoral Liturgical Tradition," in *CPDBT,* 1062.

[56]Grassi, "Water," in *CPDBT,* 1060.

ration into Jesus' own baptism. The Acts of the Apostles makes frequent reference to the waters of baptism. Water is a sign of the Holy Spirit. The gospel of John makes abundant use of the symbol of water. The water of Cana represented a repudiation of the old purification rites. The Samaritan woman was offered the new water of Jesus' Spirit. Water was curative in the story of the man born blind from birth who washed in the pool of Siloam. Jesus washed the feet of his disciples as a sign of love, service, and forgiveness. Water and blood came forth from Jesus' side on the cross. This sign was understood as the advent of the Holy Spirit upon the church. The water was a sign of baptism and the blood was the sign of eucharist. (See "Sixth Sunday of Easter.")

Questions: Do the uses of water in scripture have anything to do with your life today? How might contemporary communities relate to the symbolism of water? What does it teach about God, Christ, Spirit, church, or yourself?

Ecclesial Signs

The church's theology of water is many-layered. Even though it is understood that ordinary water may be used for baptisms in an emergency situation, it was always also understood that the water used in baptism must first be consecrated before it can have an initiatory effect. "Not all waters have a curative power; only that water has it which has the grace of Christ.... The water does not heal unless the Spirit descends and consecrates the water."[57]

When the water is blessed at the Easter Vigil, there are two elements to the blessing. The saving action of God in salvation history is remembered, and through the epicletic action the Holy Spirit is invoked to come upon the waters. The Easter candle in plunged into the water as a sign of the power and presence of the Risen Christ. It is also a sign of the Holy Spirit coming upon the water. Cyril of Jerusalem insisted that all baptismal waters are effective because of the action of Christ going down into the Jordan for his own baptism. When the early Christians invoked the Trinity upon any of the sacramental symbols, God became (becomes) present in the symbol. Bread becomes the Body of Christ; water and oil is the Spirit. The Trinity is present in all of the sacraments. Ancient theologians expressed the doctrine of the Spirit's presence in the water by reflecting on the font. "Theodore [of Mopsuestia] saw the font as a womb into which the candidate descended to receive second birth from the Holy Spirit, whose presence impregnates the water. St. Leo the Great compared the Spirit's action of filling the font with his other action of filling the womb of Our Lady."[58] Through the sign of water we are baptized priests, prophets, and rulers; we become adopted children of God and our sins are washed away. (See also "Baptism": Doctrinal Appendix.)

Questions: Does the church's theology of water have anything to do with our lives today? What does it teach us about God, Christ, Spirit, ourselves? What is the challenge? What is the response?

Liturgical Sign

In tracing the roots of baptism's earliest liturgical practice, it appears as if the candidate bent low in humble acceptance, just below the surface of the water, while the bishop pushed on his head. Later archaeological evidence suggests a different practice. Fonts have been discovered that were too small for an adult immersion. The water barely came to the knees of the candidates and had to be poured over their heads. The earliest form of the rite was Trinitarian. The candidate for baptism was plunged three times into the water while the three persons of the Trinity were invoked.

St. Paul understood the immersion as death to sin and incorporation into Christ's death and resurrection. The old person was buried and the font's waters gave birth to the new person in Christ. Ambrose thus made allusion to a tomb-shaped font. Archaeological evidence, however, points to an octagonal-shaped construction. It is believed that running water fed some of those fonts and that some were even heated.

[57]Ambrose, Si. 15. Cf. *The Baptismal Homilies of Theodore of Mopsuestia*, 3.9; E. C. Whitaker, *Documents of the Baptismal Liturgy*, 2nd ed. (London, 1970), p. 7, in *AIRI*, 24.

[58]Ibid.

Two different formulas for baptism were in use at the same time in different locations around the fourth century. In Antioch the formula was Trinitarian: "I baptize you in the name of the Father...," etc. In Jerusalem and Milan the formulas for baptism centered around the profession of faith. "St. Ambrose describes the ceremonies as follows: You were asked: 'Do you believe in God, the Father Almighty?' You replied: 'I believe,' as you were immersed. The ceremony continues with similar acts of faith in the Son and the Holy Spirit."[59] There is further evidence that the Trinitarian model spoken of by Jesus in Matthew's gospel was not strictly adhered to in every place. All of the church Fathers connected baptism with Jesus' baptism in the Jordan.

Liturgy expresses in ritual action the natural, biblical, and ecclesial signs of God's presence through the symbol of water. The waters of baptism are blessed at the Easter Vigil. Through the ritual waters of baptism the neophyte is purified, justified, sanctified, and incorporated into the Body of Christ, the paschal mystery, the communion of saints. Water is used in the rite of sprinkling to remind us of our baptism and thereby recommit us to its call. The casket is blessed with holy water as a reminder that baptism is a share in the eternal life of Christ. People bless themselves with holy water as a sign of their incorporation into the Body of Christ. Water is used in the multiple blessings provided by the church for its ongoing life in Christ such as the dedications of churches, blessings of homes, seminaries, and religious houses, boats, fields, buildings, schools, animals, etc. (Please refer to the RCIA: General Introduction, # 1, 2, Introduction to the Rite of Baptism, and the *Catechism of the Catholic Church,* #694 for further elaboration.)

Questions: Have you ever had a conscious experience of water in the liturgy? How were you impacted? How did it touch you? How does the experience of water call us to transformation as a community?

Symbol of Oil

Once baptized, the new Christian is permanently configured to Christ through the chrism oil of confirmation. Confirmation confers the gift of the Holy Spirit, not the gifts *of* the Spirit. The form of the ritual is "Be sealed with the Holy Spirit." The substance is oil. The baptized person is sealed with the Holy Spirit through the signing with oil.
In antiquity, the seal had the same function that a person's signature has today. A seal formed in wax identified the author of a document. Soldiers were tattooed with the seal of their division. The seal was a sign of ownership, much like a brand on cattle. Confirmation seals the Christian to Christ. The Christian is branded to Christ, marked permanently with the sign of salvation, the cross of Jesus Christ.

Natural Sign

How does oil express the inexpressible? Oil is difficult to rub off, stains clothing when spilled, and can only be rubbed in. Oil has healing, soothing, medicinal qualities. Oil is necessary for life. It is used in cooking, for energy, for lubrication, and for protection from the elements. Oil is a precious commodity; wars are fought over its control. Oil is the agent that holds things together, that unifies the ingredients in a recipe. All those aspects found in the natural world can be used to express the reality of the Spirit.

Our natural experience of oil reminds us of the Spirit. The Spirit stays with us. The Spirit heals and is a soothing, calming presence. The Spirit is balm for our wounded soul and strength in times of need. The Spirit is the unifier that holds God's people together. The Spirit is our life force. Oil expresses the ineffable reality of the Spirit. The Spirit strengthens us when we must lay down our lives for the sake of this precious new commodity: life in Christ.

In the movie, *Lorenzo's Oil,* a young boy discovers that he has a horribly debilitating disease that, without a certain kind of oil in his system, will kill him. The movie begins with a scene from the mother's experience of the Easter Vigil. The Easter candle processes majestically through the church as the boy's mother is observed wrestling with the demon of anger and grief. She will not accept the prognosis that doctors have given her son. The Easter Vigil connection in the movie subliminally suggests that her quest for the holy oil of life is initiated by the Spirit of God, present in the pillar candle of fire leading her through the dangerous journey inaugurated that night. She leaves the Easter scene with

[59] S 2.20; cf. Cyril, MC 2.4, in *AIRI,* 26.

firm resolve and burning determination. Nothing will deter her or her husband. The Spirit is in command and they forge onward. They will find the oil her son, Lorenzo, needs for life. They completely give up their lives for their son.

Through years of tortuous struggle, research, and rejection, they literally lose everything. When scientists rebuff them, they will not take *no* for an answer. Their arduous journey of the cross finally leads them to a cure. It is a simple derivative of the natural, everyday substance found in all kitchens: olive oil.

Lorenzo's family laid down their lives for their son. They loved him unconditionally and completely; they loved him against all odds. They saved their boy's life and the lives of many other children with the same disease. Their selfless act of love resulted in love for others. They "put on Christ" and became Christ for many other suffering children. The oil of chrism is the Spirit's necessary oil. We should be willing to lose all in our quest for it.

The oil of chrism is the necessary oil for the soul. It seals us to Christ. It makes us in his image. We are branded with the sign of his cross. The oil of the Spirit gives us the strength to carry the cross and to bear witness to Christ in our lives.

Questions: What is your experience of oil in everyday life? How might oil remind you of God, the Holy Spirit?

Biblical Signs

Throughout the Hebrew scriptures (Old Testament), oil was used for celebrating and greeting, as well as for preparing a body for burial. Sirach mentions that oil, water, fire, and bread are necessary for life. Oil was used for hygiene and cosmetic purposes and for the healing of wounds. Oil poured on the head of a person signified a changed reality. It meant the person was assigned to a new office. Kings were consecrated to office. Samuel anointed Saul and David for kingly service (1 Sam). It was assumed that God performed the anointing for a special purpose or mission. "So God had brought this person to a new state in life which demanded respect and protection."[60] Prophets were anointed into prophetic service. Elijah anointed Elisha (1 Kgs 19:16). Anointing with oil summons the prophet to hear God's word and sends the prophet to confess it. Priests were anointed or consecrated into God's service. Priestly anointing assumed that the anointed assume "a new role and the imposition of responsibility for effecting and preserving holiness for Israel."[61]

Sacred objects were anointed in scripture. Some oils were reserved for just such anointings (Ex 30:22–33). The tabernacle, the ark, the basin used in the purification rites, the table used for the bread of presence, the menorah, the incense altar, and the liturgical vestments were all anointed with oil.

In the New Testament, the anointings reserved for kings were now assigned to Christ. In the Mary Magdalene incident (Lk 7:50), Jesus connected the anointing of his feet with the forgiveness of sins. The anointing of Jesus by the woman was perceived as an act of anointing in preparation for Jesus' burial. "Matthew shows no interest in naming a motive [for the anointing]. Presumably he, like his readers, ancient and modern, regarded anointing as simply an act of love."[62] Also, since Jesus was anointed by God, this anointing was similarly connected to his consecration as messiah by God. The word *messiah* means anointed of God.

Jesus was anointed prophet by the Holy Spirit. Jesus' ministry of the word and of healing was anointed by God. The letter to the Hebrews asserts that Jesus was anointed high priest by God. Paul's second letter to the Corinthians refers to the Christian as anointed of God. Christ lives and works within the lives of Christians. John later takes up the clarion call and asserts that Christian anointing is realized as the guiding, teaching, and protecting Spirit of God (1 Jn 2:27).

Jesus and the apostles anointed and healed the sick. There are clear directions given in the letter of James for healing the sick; they are to be anointed with oil. As a result, they are healed, sanctified, and forgiven.

Questions: How does your natural experience of oil resonate with scripture's use of oil? Were there any new in-

[60] John C. Endres, S.J., "Anointing," in *CPDBT*, 28.

[61] Ibid., 29.

[62] *MI*, 293.

sights in examining the biblical uses of oil? What does it mean that "oil poured on the heads of a person signified a changed reality"? How can you apply that to your experience of the sacraments of the church? What does oil teach you about God, Christ, Spirit, church, yourself? How do the biblical signs speak to your community?

Ecclesial Sign

The church teaches that oil signifies the conferral of the Holy Spirit. We are sealed with the Spirit at confirmation. Oil configures us to Christ. Oil literally bonds or adheres us to the person of Jesus Christ. Jesus is taken into ourselves. We "put on" Christ. We are branded with Christ himself. We bear the likeness of Christ. We take on Christ's image. We live as Christ would live in the world. The conferral of the Spirit in the oil of confirmation immerses us in the paschal mystery of Christ. We die and rise with Christ. Not only do we plunge into the waters of death and resurrection, but we literally take that death and resurrection into ourselves. We die and rise with the power and strength of the Holy Spirit. The oil of confirmation has an initiatory character; it completes baptism and leads to eucharist. The oil seals us to the mission of Christ and strengthens our priestly, prophetic, and royal role. "By signing us with the gift of the Spirit, confirmation makes us more completely the image of the Lord and fills us with the Holy Spirit, so that we may be witness to him before all the world and work to bring the Body of Christ to its fullness as soon as possible" (RCIA, #2).

(Please refer to "Apostolic Constitution of the Sacrament of Confirmation" and the "Introduction" of the Rite of Confirmation, and the *Catechism of the Catholic Church,* #695.)

Questions: What does the church's use of oil have to do with your community? How does it affect your life? What does it mean that oil seals us to the mission of Christ and strengthens our priestly, prophetic, and royalty role in the mission of Christ? How does the oil of confirmation signify Christ's life? How does the sign of oil relate to your everyday life? What is the challenge?

Liturgical Signs

An ancient practice that has been retained in the modern rite is the three anointings with oil at different stages in the initiation process. The first anointing is a pre-baptismal anointing with the oil of catechumens. The second anointing is post-baptismal and is with chrism. The third anointing is also with chrism and is a sign of the gift of the Holy Spirit.[63] The anointing with the oil of catechumens is understood as a prayer for the candidate to be released from the power of Satan. The candidates also ask for the strength to endure the great contest ahead of them as they prepare for baptism. In the United States this anointing takes place during the period of the catechumenate. In the early church the candidate was rubbed with oil over his entire body, very much like the practice of the wrestler preparing for his match. St. Ambrose reminded the candidates: "You were rubbed with oil like an athlete, Christ's athlete, as though in preparation for an earthly wrestling-match, and you agreed to take on your opponent" (S 1.4).[64] The intention of the anointing is explicitly clear in the *Apostolic Tradition,* where it is explained as the oil of exorcism: "Let all evil spirits depart from you."[65] Cyril paints a different picture. He refers to it as a share in the fullness of Christ. He used the symbolism of the olive tree. The anointing imbues a share in the life of Christ, the true olive. As an exorcism, the oil represents a deterrent to the devil and the removal of sin.[66]

The second anointing mentioned above immediately follows baptism. Jesus Christ was anointed by the Holy Spirit to fulfill his messianic, royal destiny. Baptism was understood by some of the church Fathers as participation in that mission. The ritual anointing emerged as a sign of participation and immersion into Christ's messianic mission. Oil was poured over the heads of the newly baptized and allowed to drip down, reminiscent of the oil that dripped down the beard of Aaron. The pouring of this oil was very much in the tradition of anointing reserved for kings. Ambrose described the anointing as a sign of eternal life and as a sign of the baptized person's share in the messianic mission of Christ in which they are anointed priest, prophet, and king. Theodore posited another view of the anointing. He explained it as a

[63] *AIRI,* 22.

[64] Ibid.

[65] *Apostolic Tradition,* xxi.10, in *AIRI,* 22.

[66] Ibid.

sign of ownership. Those so anointed were inducted as soldiers in Christ's service. He also referred to the newly anointed as branded "sheep of Christ."[67]

The second of the three anointings (the first post-baptismal messianic anointing) is only used when confirmation does not immediately follow baptism, but is deferred to a later date (as is the case in infant baptisms in the West). Obviously the anointing of confirmation takes its place, but what is lost is the language that attests to the newly baptized's new role as priest, prophet, and king.

There were two types of oil used in the ancient liturgical rites—the oil of exorcism and the oil of thanksgiving. The oil of exorcism (oil of catechumens) was used in the first, pre-baptismal anointing. The oil of thanksgiving was used for the two post-baptismal anointings. The latter was laced with a perfume called balsam and was called chrism or *myron.*

There were different interpretations of the significance of chrism in the early church. St. Ambrose described the perfumed chrism as the lure of Christ. "We shall run following the perfume of your robes."[68] Other Fathers referred to the chrism as a sign of a person's understanding of the gospel. John Chrysostom distinguished the two oils by using the image of athlete and bride. The first, pre-baptismal oil is for the athlete; the post-baptismal oil is for the bride. The image of branding as a sign of ownership led to the use of the word *seal* in reference to the signation with oil.

The church uses oil in various ways in its life and ministry. Oils are blessed at the Chrism Mass for use in ministry throughout the diocese. The catechumens are blessed with the oil of catechumens. Oil is used in the dedication of a church. Oil is also used in the sacramental life of the church. Infants are anointed at baptism with the oil of catechumens and chrism. The Spirit is given through the ritual anointing with oil at confirmation. Oil is used in the anointing of the sick and the dying. Priests are anointed for priestly service at their ordination.

Questions: Have you ever experienced the use of oil in liturgy? If so, what do you remember? What did it teach you about God, Spirit, Christ, church, community? What is the challenge for the community?

Symbol of Laying on of Hands

The power of the Holy Spirit is unleashed in the church today by the laying on of hands. The laying on of hands is a sign of the action of the Holy Spirit. It confers the gift of the Spirit in all sacraments.

Natural Sign

The hand can be an instrument of love or an instrument of hate. The touch of a hand can bring comfort and healing in a time of stress. The handshake can express friendship and the hand around another can impart guidance and care. Holding hands is a sign of love. For a child, the hand is a powerful instrument of protection or discipline. The hand used in massage is healing and curative. People clap their hands when happy or excited.

Questions: Do you remember a time when the sense of touch had a particular impact on you? How did it speak to you?

Biblical Sign

According to Dennis Sweetland, the hand has many uses throughout scripture.[69] The hand usually is a sign of God's power. "They assured Joshua, 'The Lord has delivered all this land into our power'" (Jos 2:24). Power is used as a metaphorical substitution for hand. The word *hand* is used over two hundred times in the Hebrew scriptures. When the right hand is mentioned, it usually refers to a place of honor. When the right hand of God is mentioned, it is usually intended to denote incredible, unusual power. "Your right hand, O Lord, magnificent in power... has shattered the enemy" (Ex 15:6).

[67] *Ad Senarium,* 6; Whitaker, p. 157 in *AIRI,* 28.

[68] M 29, translating a text probably based on the LXX version of Cant 1.4, in *AIRI,* 29.

[69] Dennis M. Sweetland, "Hand," in *CPDBT,* 405-407.

The imposition of hands was used ritually in the Old Testament as well as in the New Testament. Hands were extended over offerings in response to the laws of sacrifice (Ex 29:10, Lev 1:4, 4:4, 24, 29, 33, 8:14). When hands were extended over a scapegoat, the guilt was transferred to the animal. The action usually had a direct relation to the acceptability of the sacrifice and the one offering the sacrifice. If the sacrifice was acceptable and pleasing, then the one offering was also acceptable. The sign of hands was intended to set things apart for a sacred purpose.

The laying on of hands is also used in scripture as a gesture of blessing. Hands outstretched over an assembly bless the entire group (Lev 9:22). The same gesture is also understood as a means of consigning power to another person, providing the one doing the consigning has the rightful authority to confer this power. Leaders conferred leadership to others through the action of laying on of hands (Num 27:23).

In the New Testament, the hand was understood in the same way as it was in the Hebrew scriptures. *Hand* was understood as power. The hand of God was not, however, a common New Testament image unless it was referring to an actual Old Testament use of the term (Lk 1:66). The hand was used to heal. Jesus was asked to heal Jairus's daughter by laying his hands on her. The Holy Spirit was conferred at baptism through the laying on of hands (Acts 8:17–19; 19:6). The laying on of hands was also a sign of mission. The apostles laid hands on the seven and they were assigned a special service (Acts 6:6). The laying on of hands was also associated with installation in some office, either as presbyter or apostle (2 Tim 1:6 [See also "Fifth Sunday of Easter: First Reading"]).

Questions: Does the scriptural use of the sign of laying on of hands have anything to do with the life of your community? What does it teach you about God, Christ, the church, or yourself? What are you called to do as a response?

Ecclesial Sign

Traditional theology regarding the laying on of hands is multi-layered. The gesture is believed to be the origin of the sacrament of confirmation. According to Paul VI *(Divinae consortium naturae)*, confirmation (imposition of hands) continues the grace of Pentecost. The action of laying on of hands is the conferral of the Spirit in each of the sacraments. The imposition of hands is used in all the sacraments: baptism, confirmation, eucharist (epiclesis in the eucharistic prayer), healing, penance, marriage, and ordination. The gesture has the same meaning and usage in the church today as it did in the Old and New Testament: it is a sign of power, installation of office, ministry, transfer of authority, healing, and blessing. The laying on of hands is a powerful symbol of the ongoing ministry of Jesus Christ through the power of the Holy Spirit in the church.

Questions: Does Catholic tradition's use of the gesture of laying on hands have anything to do with the life of your community? With your life? What does it say to you about God, God's Spirit, Christ, the church, and yourself?

Liturgical Sign

Every sacrament exercises the epicletic action of calling down the Spirit of God to bless, sanctify, transform, and effect the desired grace. Hands are laid on the elect as they go down into the waters of baptism and are chrismated with the oil of the Holy Spirit, the chrism of salvation. Hands are extended over the gifts of bread and wine as a sign of the Spirit's role in transforming the elements into Christ's Body and Blood. The community is blessed through the laying on of hands at the end of the liturgy. The presider/celebrant extends his hands over the assembly before sending them out to do the work of liturgy in the world. The sacred hand of the Spirit is imposed on the head of those seeking ordination, healing, and forgiveness in the sacraments of orders, anointing the sick, and sacrament of penance. The marriage couple join hands as they enter their solemn covenant and the community extends hands in a gesture of peace and unity at liturgical gatherings. Catechumens experience the hand's ministerial touch frequently throughout the catechumenate through the rituals of acceptance, blessings, anointing, exorcism, and various rites.

Questions: Have you ever experienced the sign of the Spirit at liturgy through the laying on of hands? Describe the experience. How did the experience speak to you?

What did it teach you about God, Christ, the Spirit, the church, or yourself? What are the implications? How is the community challenged? What are you and the community called to do in response?

Symbol of the Garment

The white garment is placed on the neophyte after baptism as a sign of his or her new status: a fully initiated member of the Body of Christ.

Natural Sign

The contemporary adage, "clothing makes the person," is usually a very consumer-oriented idea. When people have no clothes they find it difficult to compete in this consumer-oriented world. Clothes are a sign of status and wealth. In our everyday lives, new clothes have the effect of making us feel like new people. Persons in certain professions are identified by their clothing: judges, nurses, doctors, clergy, police, etc.

Biblical Sign

In the Old Testament, Isaiah 1:18 proclaims that Yahweh "has clothed me with the garment of salvation, and with the robe of gladness he has covered me." The garment represents a new status, a change from a condition previously held. Before they were unsaved; through Yahweh they were now saved and covered with joy. Yahweh's joy covered them completely. The garment represented new life as a saved person. The garment was also a sign of divine royalty. Isaiah portrays the Lord sitting on a lofty throne with the train of his garment filling the temple (6:1). Job insisted that he wore his honesty like a garment (29:14). The garment throughout the Hebrew scriptures was a symbol for a person's interior nature—the inner life. Both Isaiah (51:6) and the author of Hebrews (1:11) use the imagery of the garment to reflect on the transitory nature of life. This life and its earthly concerns will wear out like a garment. Baruch uses the image as a sign of penitence and trust in Yahweh, the Eternal God. "I have taken off the garment of peace and have put on the sackcloth for my prayer of supplication, and while I live I will cry out to the Eternal God" (Bar 4:20, NAB).

In scripture, clothing was a sign of office. Prophets such as Elijah and John the Baptist wore hair garments as a sign of their prophetic ministry (Zech 13:4). As Elijah passed on his prophetic ministry to Elisha, he gave him his cloak. "Clothes are an extension of the person; Elisha is thus assuming Elijah's identity."[70] The ceremonial robe is placed on the prodigal son upon his return as a sign of his father's forgiveness. The garment in this case is a sign of God's mercy and forgiveness of sin. When the garment is placed on the neophytes, we affirm that they are new creations and are clothed in Christ. St. Paul used the expression "putting on Christ" to describe what baptism accomplishes. According to Brendan Byrne, S.J., Paul's expression conjured images from Greek drama. Actors were so completely enveloped in the costume of their character that the audience could see only the character and not the original identity of the actor. Thus, when we observe the newly-baptized, all we are to see is Christ. They have been "clothed in him."

Ecclesial Sign

The white garment is a sign of incorporation into the paschal mystery of Christ through baptism. The white garment is a sign that the newly baptized have put on Christ. They have risen with Christ through the waters of baptism. The clothing with the baptismal garment signifies the new dignity that is theirs.

Liturgical Sign

The neophyte puts on the white garment at baptism. Baptized infants also put on white baptismal garments. Many children who receive their first communion wear a white garment. Some people misunderstand the symbolism of the white communion dress, assuming that it signifies being a bride of Christ. However, since eucharist completes baptism, the white garment of eucharist is the baptismal garment, not a bridal dress. The pall placed on the coffin at funerals is a sign of the baptismal garment and the prescribed garment for liturgical functions is an alb ("General Instruction of the Roman Missal," #80, c), again reminiscent of the baptismal garment.

---

[70]Jerome T. Walsh and Christopher T. Begg, "1–2 Kings," in *NJBC*, 175.

In the very earliest baptismal rites the neophytes were baptized with no clothes on. They were anointed with the oil of the Spirit over their entire bodies; their godparent then helped them don the garment of new life in Christ. The garment signified their incorporation into the paschal mystery and the innocence that was theirs as newborn babes in the Christian life.

St. John Chrysostom alludes to the garment as a uniform, an outward sign of interior reality. The neophytes have put on Christ—they have taken Christ within themselves.

> Men who have undertaken temporal duties often wear on their clothes an imperial badge as a sign to the public of their trustworthiness. They would not permit themselves to do anything unworthy of their uniform; and even if they attempted it, there are many people to stop them. If others wish to harm them, the clothes they wear afford sufficient protection. Now the neophytes carry Christ himself, not on their clothes, but dwelling in their souls with his Father, and the Holy Spirit has descended on them there. They are even more obliged, then, to prove themselves reliable, and show everyone by their scrupulous conduct, and careful lives that they wear the imperial badge.[71]

The early Fathers used other images to portray the significance of the white garment. The garment was compared to the shining garment of Christ at his transfiguration, to the wedding garment, and to the fleece of the Lamb of God.[72]

It was a custom in the West for the neophytes to wear their baptismal garment through the octave of Easter, following which they took their place among the assembled faithful. In addition to wearing his baptismal garment, Emperor Constantine also draped his throne in white. In some places white linen was placed on the head of the newly baptized as a sign of their liberation from slavery. Augustine writes: "Today is called the octave of infants. The veils are due to be removed from their heads and this is a sign of freedom.... Today, as you see, our infants mingle with the faithful and fly as it were from the nest."[73]

G. LITURGY OF THE EUCHARIST

There is not much that sets the Easter Vigil's liturgy of the eucharist apart from every other eucharist celebrated throughout the year. However, it is the night, different from all other nights, when new Christians are born and old Christians are renewed, new fire replaces the old light, new water is blessed, and the newly consecrated bread serves as the new leaven for the renewed missionary activity of the entire church. Our senses are attuned, as on no other night, to the words of the eucharistic prayer,

> Father, all powerful and ever-living God,
> we do well always and everywhere to give you thanks
> through Jesus Christ our Lord.
> We praise you with greater joy than ever on this Easter night,
> when Christ became our paschal sacrifice.[74]

On this Easter night, the trumpets should resound as neophytes triumphantly process to the table for the first time. It is the culmination of their journey. The ritual moment of baptism is not the crowning moment of their experience; it is the gateway. The crowning moment occurs at the table of unity and full participation in the paschal mystery. From the very beginning, the journey of the neophytes has been to the table. All believers come to the table to be nourished by Christ's Body and Blood in order to go out and live their lives in the world. We pour ourselves out for others; we become bread in the world so we can come back to the table again and again, depleted and in need of Easter filling. Every celebration of eucharist is an Easter filling.

[71] St. John Chrysostom, *Baptismal Instructions,* ed. by P. W. Harkins, Ancient Christian Writers, v. 31 (Mahwah: Paulist Press, 1963), in *AIRI,* 32.

[72] Ibid.

[73] *Sermon* 376, *Patrologia Latina,* 39, ed, J.-P. Migne, in *AIRI,* 34.

[74] Eucharistic Prayer: "Preface for Easter I, P 21," *The Sacramentary.*

Bread and Wine

Bread, food for our bodies, and wine, drink of refreshment, celebration, and merriment—are the stuff of life. These symbols assume a new reality in the paschal celebration of eucharist. They are not only reminders of physical nourishment, they become the very sustenance of the soul. We bring our gifts of bread and wine, made by human hands, and we ask God to bless them and make them holy. We ask that the Holy Spirit change these elements into the Body and Blood of Jesus Christ. We believe it happens every time the church gathers to tell the story and pray the blessing prayers of thanks and praise. Bread is and was a sign of God's providence and protection throughout scripture. It was a sign of nourishment, freedom from hunger, and satisfaction of the soul's longing for God. It is a sign of our very sustenance. Thus, bread broken and shared is a sign that we place our lives completely in God's care. The wine, as symbol of Jesus' blood, is a sign of his life force poured out for humanity in atonement for sin. (Refer to the exegesis for Holy Thursday for further elaboration of the biblical symbol of blood.)

We become the bread we receive. We allow ourselves to be poured out as a libation. Christ's broken body was given up; his blood was poured out for the entire world. This happens every time we take the bread, bless it, break it, and share it. Thus, we too become broken, blessed, and shared.

Symbol of Bread

The sign of bread is at the heart of our identity. We are a eucharistic people. Baptism and confirmation lead us to the table and incorporation into Christ's Body and Blood. We consume the Body of Christ and, in so doing, we become the Body of Christ. Each time the Bread of Life is broken, and the Cup of Blood is shared, we become new creations. We take, bless, break, and share Christ's Body. In the taking, blessing, breaking, and sharing, we too are taken by God, blessed and made holy, broken for one another to share ourselves for others in the world. It is through the eucharist that we fully live the paschal mystery of Christ.

Natural Sign

Bread is the staff of life. Bread offers nourishment. Bread comes in many varieties: muffins, buns, pita, rolls, biscuits, leavened and unleavened loaves. With bread we are nourished; without bread we go hungry. Bread gives us strength for living. It is filled with the necessary nutrients for life. "Bread builds strong bodies twelve ways." Bread is a complement to every meal. Bread and water are all that is needed for life.

Questions: Have you ever had an experience of bread that spoke to you of something other than simply food? What did it mean to you?

Biblical Signs

Bread in the Bible was considered a general term for food.[75] "Bread" is referred to 234 times in the Old and New Testaments. When God judged the people for their sins, it was understood that he withheld the "staff of life" (Lev 26:26). Bread is used to name certain human conditions: "bread of tears," "bread of wickedness," "daily bread," etc.

In the Hebrew scriptures, bread was a sign of hospitality. Melchizedek offered bread to Abraham and Abraham offered bread to strangers as a sign of hospitality. Shared bread suggested a relationship. The meal covenant bond was so strong that it was considered very serious to turn against someone with whom one had eaten. David tricked the enemies of his son, Absolom, into eating a meal with him so they would not carry out their plot to kill him. Contractual agreements between parties were ratified through the ritual of breaking bread. Israel commits itself to the Lord through the communal meal of Passover (Ex 24: 9–11).

The bread of exodus was unleavened bread (Ex 23:18, 34:25). Only unleavened bread was allowed in Israel's ritual worship. Anything but unleavened wheat bread was deemed impure. Bread was a sign of trust and a sign of God's providential care. God provided manna in the desert for the sojourners. Israel's part of the agreement with Yahweh was to trust him implicitly to care for them. Because God's part was to provide, God provided manna.

---

[75]John F. Craghan, "Bread," in *CPDBT*, 109.

On every sabbath, twelve cakes of flour were placed on a table in the holy of holies as a sign of the covenant God had made with the twelve tribes of Israel (Lv 24: 5–9). The book of the prophet Isaiah used the image of banquet to refer to the eschatological day of the Lord, the end of the world. Jesus also referred to the banquet as a metaphor for the end of his earthly reign. Bread is an important symbol for Jesus, a sign of covenant and community (Lk 14:15).

Jesus multiplies the loaves and in doing so demonstrates, in action, the univerality of his messianic mission. Jesus came to save all people.

The Jews celebrated a ritual blessing to accompany every human endeavor throughout the day. Blessings sanctified all of life and were understood to make the recipients and the actions holy. So, too, the early Christians gathered to give thanks and praise to God (to bless God) for the wonders of creation and for God's action in salvation history. They gathered for the breaking of the bread, and in so doing they gathered to worship God. Those first Christians translated the Hebrew word *blessing* into the Greek word *eucharist*. It is clear that the eucharist was understood as ritual celebration.

The eucharist they celebrated has its origins in the Jewish table blessing. Jewish families gathered at mealtime to give thanks and praise to their Creator. "Here the prayer of blessing took the form of a ritual, celebrated in bread as grace before meals, and in wine as grace after meals."[76] The father of the household led the prayer and the rest of the family responded to the prayers. In official gatherings the rabbi assumed the role of father. "These then were the rituals out of which the Lord formed his eucharist."[77] Raymond Maloney makes the interesting observation that Jesus used the rituals of the Jewish family meal, not the elaborate rituals of the Temple, to form his new community's worship.

The biblical genesis of the eucharistic meal is found in the institution narratives of the Last Supper as related in the gospels. However, those texts are more liturgical than historical accounts. The Last Supper account resembles the Jewish retelling of the exodus event at Passover—a liturgical celebration. The evangelists were not concerned with providing an historical sketch of the events on Holy Thursday. The biblical texts reflect the eucharistic faith of the first Christian community. So we must look to faith, rather than to the recorded words and actions of Jesus, in order to understand our eucharistic theology. "Our theology of the eucharist has to take its stand on the faith of the church, indwelt by the Holy Spirit, as we find it in those early texts, rather than in any historical reconstruction of the institution event, for about the latter, little agreement is possible."[78]

While not intentionally historical, the gospel traditions do provide the basis for what is generally considered historical about the narratives. Of this we can be sure: the institution of the eucharist originated at the Last Supper. There was a celebration with bread and wine that was integrally connected to the death and resurrection of Christ. "The setting [of the Last Supper] was significant—the lamb had served year after year to prefigure the great expectation."[79] Jesus was the new paschal lamb. Bread and wine eucharist would sustain and nourish until Christ's return. The final age had arrived. All would feast on the Lamb of God who takes away the sins of the world.

The biblical-liturgical tradition of first century Israel helps us to understand the implications of Jesus' actions at that first eucharistic supper. Luke and Paul both refer to corporate memory in the liturgical action: "Do this in memory of me." It is important to understand what that meant for the participants of the meal and what we inherited as a result. When Jews gathered to remember the action of God in salvation history, their recollections actualized the benefits of grace for each generation. For example, when they gathered for Passover and ate ritual foods, when they drank from the ritual cups of wine and recalled how their ancestors were delivered from slavery in Egypt, they believed that the liberation won for their ancestors was a grace actualized (made present and real) for every community of people—

[76]Ibid.

[77]Raymond Maloney, S.J., "Eucharist," in *NDT*, 343.

[78]Ibid.

[79]*MRR*, 7.

past, present and future. It is called *anamnesis*, a remembering that makes present and real what is remembered. When Jesus said "Do this in memory of me," he was, in effect, saying: "Every time you gather to remember this story and do the ritual actions that accompany it, it will become real and present to you. I will become present. You will participate in the new exodus, my liberating and salvific life, death and resurrection." According to Joseph Jungman: "If the whole celebration is not only the sign of Christ's death and resurrection but its living memorial..., [then] these gifts are not only the signs of Christ's body and blood but... in some mysterious way, they are indeed what Christ says they are: his very body and his very blood.... In the new Law the offerings of bread, wine, incense, beasts [Old Testament sacrifices] have all been replaced and fulfilled by the body and blood of Christ offered on the cross."[80] This is the context in which the eucharist of the first church was celebrated and understood—as a living memorial (see 1 Cor 10:16–17; 11:27–32 and Jn 6:51–58).

Paul details our Christian theology of eucharist in his letter to the Corinthians proclaimed at the Holy Thursday liturgy. Even though we are diverse, with many and varied gifts, eucharist unites us and makes us one body in Christ. Eucharist is a sign of unity. It is also a sign of sharing. Eucharist demands that we share with those who are in need. (See also "Feast of Corpus Christi.")

The synoptic traditions equate the broken bread of eucharist with Jesus, the suffering messiah (Mt 26:28). Bread becomes a sign of Christ's paschal mystery. The covenant meal of eucharist replaces the old covenant meal of Passover. Jesus is the New Passover; his meal is the new covenant meal. Jesus is the Bread of Presence. No one who eats Jesus' bread will ever know hunger again.

Blood in the synoptics is interpreted as a sign that Christ shed his blood for the sins of the world. Blood is associated with the forgiveness of sins (Mt 24:27–28, Mk 14:24, Lk 22:20). The Old Testament concept of blood as expiation is carried over in the sacrifice of the cup. John equates blood with the giving of eternal life (6:53–56).

[80]Maloney, *NDT*, 345.

Questions: What do the uses of bread and wine in scripture have to do with the life of your community? What does it mean that bread represents the universality of Jesus' mission? How does it speak to the life of your community? How is the eucharist a sign of unity? What does it mean to you in practical terms? How does the broken bread of the eucharist reveal the suffering Messiah? What do the biblical signs of bread and wine teach you about God, Christ, Spirit, church, or yourself?

Ecclesial Signs

The meal of the Last Supper was unleavened bread. However, Christians of the early centuries did not assign special significance to the unleavened nature of the bread. They no doubt used leavened bread brought from home and presented along with their offerings for the needy. The ritual action of breaking bread was the eucharistic worship of the early church. There is a detailed description of the ritual in a second-century document, the *Didache*. Early Christians understood eucharist to be a corporate sharing in the risen Christ as experienced in the breaking of the bread. This sharing unified them into one people. Raymond Maloney offers this definition of eucharist: "The eucharist is a celebration of Christian community as people commemorate in the rituals of bread and cup the key events from which their community draws its life, namely the death and resurrection of the Lord."[81]

Eucharist means *thanksgiving* in Greek. The early Christians gathered for thanks and praise and the breaking of bread. That early eucharistic liturgy evolved from Jewish table prayers of praise and thanks at festive meals. The early Christians gathered in their house churches for the breaking of the bread while still maintaining their ties to the synagogue. Around 100 C.E., there was a break from the synagogue and the ritual meal continued in the house churches. This meal was eschatological. The eucharist was believed to be the final means of bringing members to belief in Christ before his final coming. Thus, baptism was a requisite for eucharist.

Joseph A. Jungman transports us back to the primitive church and its understanding of that first eucharistic meal.

[81]Ibid., 343.

> From the start the basic motif was to observe the memorial of the Lord, the remembrance of his redemptive Passion, in the form of a meal. Therefore, at first, the framework of supper remained in the foreground. The faithful sat at table; under cover of simple nourishment they feasted upon the Body and Blood of him who had laid down his life for us all and who should someday come again to gather his own into his kingdom. The spoken word would slip easily from the recital of the words of institution and the command therein contained into such thoughts of memory and expectation. Union with our Lord in his glory came as strongly into the consciousness as union amongst themselves came visibly to the eye by means of the meal.... The meal was not an ordinary meal but a sacred banquet, not only hallowed and inspired by the memory which gave it value and which in its course was sacramentalized, but also borne Godwards by the word of the prayer that was added to it. For if, in primitive Christian culture, every meal imported not only various blessings but the prayer of thanks as well, it was never truer of this meal.
>
> The mind of man not blinded by pride will be turned toward God by even a natural meal. Nowhere is it more plainly and visibly seen that man is a receiver, than when he takes nourishment to keep his life powers together. Therefore a meal has always been the incentive to acknowledge one's own creation by means of [a] prayer of thanks which is bound up with the meal.[82]

The early liturgy consisted of two parts. The word of God was proclaimed: this consisted of the Hebrew scriptures and memoirs of the apostles. A homily was given based on the readings, and prayers of intercession were offered. The second part of the liturgy included the prayers of thanks and praise over the elements of bread and wine. The Body and Blood of Christ were then shared in communion. Very early (ca. 115), Ignatius of Antioch wrote of eucharist as recalling the passion and death of Jesus; it was offered as strength in times of persecution.

By the third century the liturgy had become more formalized with the established orders of bishop, priest, and deacon. The *Apostolic Tradition,* by Hippolytus of Rome, describes the liturgy in detail. The Tradition's prayer of thanks is the origin of the Second Eucharistic Prayer in today's Roman Missal. The *anaphora* (eucharistic prayer) remembers God's saving deeds since the creation of the world, culminating in the death and resurrection of Christ (*anamnesis*) and the calling down of the Holy Spirit to transform the gifts of bread and wine into the Body and Blood of Christ (*epiclesis*). This action is performed for the unity of the church because of its participation in sharing the Body and Blood of Jesus.

Later in the patristic period, there emerged a more sacrificial understanding of eucharistic bread and wine. The prayers over the elements were referred to as offerings rather than as thanksgiving prayers. The bread was still leavened, and beautifully adorned loaves (such as a braided loaf in the shape of a crown of thorns) were baked by skilled bakers. The Arian heresy was plaguing the church at the time and scholars believe that the special breads emerged at around the same time that theology was stressing the divinity of Christ.

During this same period (fourth to seventh centuries), beginning with Constantine's edict of Milan (315) legalizing Christianity, the liturgy changed to reflect the situation at hand. Christianity became the religion of the Empire. Worship moved from house churches to basilicas, the civic auditoriums large enough to hold the influx of people. It was now advantageous to become a Christian. The catechumenate declined and quality control for converts was minimal. Motivation was questionable. One had to be Christian in order to secure the best employment. The liturgy became more formalized. The hierarchy assumed religious and civic roles of leadership (stoles, miters, and special vestments derived from these roles). The liturgy still maintained the two parts of word and sacrament, but embellishments were added for greater participation of the assembly: processions, litanies, chants, incense, etc.

[82] *MRR,* 21.

The churches of the East and the West were established, each adopting its own style of worship. The metaphors of previous times became literalisms of this time. Eucharist was sacralized to such an extent that the meal aspect was difficult to detect. However, the eucharistic action of offering thanks and praise was understood as the "sacrifical action of the priestly community by virtue of their baptism."[83] Augustine asserted that eucharist was the offering of the church to the Father.

During the Middle Ages, the people received communion very infrequently. In order to further distinguish eucharistic bread from real bread, the church mandated that eucharistic bread be unleavened and then reduced it to a coin-shaped size, normally consumed by the priest (smaller varieties were used for the people). The Council of Florence in 1439 acknowledged the right of the Eastern church to use leavened bread while the Roman Church maintained its previous mandate.

In the next period (eighth to sixteenth centuries), the laity became less involved and were reduced to being spectators. Latin was established as the language of liturgy (only the clergy understood Latin). The Eastern church translated the prayers of the liturgy into the vernacular, but Rome maintained Latin as its official liturgical language. The mass was explained as an allegory on the life of Christ. The eucharist was defined as the real Body and Blood of Christ in which the priest broke the body and the people crushed it with their teeth. The Fourth Lateran Council (1215) and Thomas Aquinas refined that theology with terms such as "transubstantiation."

The sacrifical aspect of the mass increased and centered on the re-creation of the sacrifice of Christ on the cross. Because of the penitential overtones and the people's sense of unworthiness, the reception of communion severely declined. Receiving from the cup was reserved for the clergy only. Leaders of the Reformation spoke out against such abuses.

The Council of Trent sought to reestablish the teaching authority of the church and thus affirmed most practices while abolishing the more obvious abuses. The next four hundred years would see little change.

The Second Vatican Council retrieved the church's earlier biblical and patristic heritage. The meal aspect of eucharist was recovered and the role of the church was strengthened. The primary signs of God's presence in the liturgy were set forth in priest, sacrament, word, and church. "Christ is present in the sacrifice of the Mass, not only in the person of his minister... but especially in the eucharistic elements... in the sacraments. ... He is present in his word.... He is present when the Church prays and sings" (CSL, 7).

The church teaches that eucharist completes initiation. The goal of initation is not baptism; it is eucharist. Augustine called eucharist the repeatable sacrament of initiation because it has the power to forgive sins, just as baptism forgives sins. Eucharist is our participation in the paschal mystery of Christ. We are incorporated into his death and resurrection. It is a sign of unity and of charity. We are to share what we have received. We are to become that which we have shared. Eucharist calls us to be bread for the world: the hungry, the suffering, the oppressed. Eucharist strengthens us to take up the cross and live the gospel. In the eucharist, we offer our praise and thanks to God for all his great saving acts since the creation of the world. Eucharist is the way we are church; it is our ongoing participation in Jesus' life. We come together as God's people to offer praise and thanks, to share the story of salvation and Christ's covenant meal. Eucharist commits us to the poor.

Questions: How does the church's teaching on the eucharist impact the life of your community? In what way is the eucharist "the repeatable sacrament of initiation"? How does it commit us to the poor? Does it have anything to do with your everyday life? What does it teach you about God, Christ, Holy Spirit, church, or yourself?

Liturgical Sign

The *Constitution on the Sacred Liturgy* (CSL) asserted that the eucharist is the action of the entire

[83]Mark R. Francis, C.S.V., "Eucharist," in *CPDBT*, 277.

church and that "the liturgy is the summit toward which the activity of Church is directed; at the same time it is the fount from which all the Church's power flows..." (#10). "The Church earnestly desires that all the faithful be led to full, conscious, and active participation in liturgical celebrations called for by the very nature of the liturgy. Such participation by the Christian people as a 'chosen priesthood, a holy nation, God's own people' (1 Pet. 2:9; see 2:4–5) is their right and duty by reason of their baptism" (#14). "Every liturgical celebration is a sacred action... surpassing all others; no action of the Church can equal its effectiveness by the same title and to the same degree" (CSL, #7).

From all this, it can be concluded that the celebration of the eucharist is the greatest endeavor of the church. Its celebration deserves our greatest attention. The symbols of the liturgy must be robust and reflect the reality they effect. Real bread, quality wine, full water immersion, abundantly slathered oil, a worthy book, a cross, a real garment, a huge fire and a large Easter candle: these are our primary symbols. We must give them the opportunity to speak to us. Most have heard the quip that it takes more faith to believe that the wafer-like hosts are bread than it does to believe in the real presence of Jesus Christ in the elements.

> The bread must be made from wheat and must have been baked recently, according to the long standing tradition of the Latin Church, it must be unleavened. The nature of the sign demands that the material for the eucharistic celebration truly have the appearance of food. Accordingly, even though unleavened and baked in the traditional shape, the eucharistic bread should be made in such a way that in a Mass with a congregation the priest is able actually to break the host into parts and distribute them at least to some of the faithful.... The action of the breaking the bread, the simple term for the eucharist in apostolic times, will more clearly bring out the force and meaning of the sign of the unity of all in the one bread and of their charity, since the one bread is being distributed among the members of one family. ("General Instruction of the Roman Missal" [GIRM], 282, 283)

"Holy Communion has a more complete form as a sign when it is received under both kinds. For in this manner of reception a fuller light shines on the sign of the eucharistic banquet. Moreover, there is clearer expression of that will by which the new and everlasting covenant is ratified in the blood of the Lord and of the relationship of the eucharistic banquet to the eschatological banquet in the Father's kingdom" (GIRM, #240). "The act of drinking the consecrated wine, the Blood of Christ, strengthens the faith of communicants in the sacrificial nature of the Mass. Communion under both kinds can therefore manifest more fully the nature of the Mass both as a sacrifice and as a sacred banquet, ritually expressing that 'the sacrifice and the sacred Meal belong to the same mystery, to such an extent that they are linked to one another by a very close theological and sacramental bond'"[84] ("Directory for the Celebration of Communion under Both Kinds," #19).

On this night of new fire, water, oil, and bread, we encounter the risen Christ anew. We are renewed as we go forth with Easter joy. The liturgy calls us to be world changers, to offer our lives for the sake of the world. There is an ancient symbol of eucharist that speaks of the mystery we just celebrated. A mother pelican is pictured with droplets of blood dripping from her breast. It was believed that in time of famine, the mother pelican would scratch her breast until droplets of blood dripped into her starving babies' anxiously waiting beaks. Her babies fed off of her freely offered blood. We go forth this Easter night willing and strengthened to offer our droplets of love in the service of God's people.

Questions: Have you had a memorable experience of Christ in the eucharist? Describe your communal experience of eucharist. Does it reflect the theology just expressed? Where is there need for growth? What is the challenge of the church's teaching on the eucharist? How are you and your community called to respond?

---

[84]Congregation for Divine Worship, *Actio Pastoralis,* "Instruction on Masses for Special Gatherings" (May 15, 1969), 5.

Conversation with the Liturgy and the Scriptures

Test your original understanding in dialogue with the text.

Were there any new insights, anything you had not considered before in relation to the entire celebration of the Easter Vigil? How does your original understanding of this liturgy compare with what we just shared? How does this liturgy speak to your life?

Sharing Life Experience

Participants share an experience from their lives that connects with the biblical interpretation just shared.

> *Thank God for the Easter Vigil. It is a sign of hope. When parishes struggle in the process of dying and rising through the year, we are offered the opportunity to cast off the old and become a new community in Christ. One year, the pastor stood before us and asked us to stand during his homily and repeatedly sing the refrain: "And God saw that it was good!" He asked us if we really believed the power in those words. He repeatedly affirmed that if we truly believed in our own goodness we could transform the world. We know our sinful natures. It is very difficult to see our own goodness. But tonight's liturgy is a testament to the creative ongoing infusion of goodness in our lives.*
>
> *It is the annual commitment to stay in the struggle to live the call of our baptism. It is a reminder that we are called to die and to rise. We are to eliminate injustice and become the eucharist. Our parish has had many opportunities over the years to die and rise. Sometimes we stay in death by our own choosing and other times we rise triumphant to new life. When we continue to reach out to the lonely, the sick, the sorrowing, and the poor, we die to our own selfish concerns and live in the resurrection of Jesus Christ. We should rejoice when people get angry that we feed the hungry, offer shelter to the homeless, give blankets to those on the streets, and preach the seamless garment of life. When Jesus made similar choices, he was sent straight to the cross. We are told that we should rejoice when we are persecuted for the sake of the gospel. That is what it means to live the paschal mystery, to be a resurrection people. We have a long way to go, but the Spirit of God continues to lead us in the struggle of death and resurrection. This is the night we take our annual pledge. We recommit ourselves to our covenant with God. The Easter Vigil brings us to our senses, shakes the dust off our feet and the sleep out of our eyes, and tells us to wake up and get on with the business of being God's people, created in the image and likeness of none other than God alone. Washed, anointed, and filled, we are fortified for another year of allowing the spiritually and physically hungry to feed from the satiated Body of Christ. Next year we will return, depleted, ready to be filled again.*

All share their life experience.

In what way has this liturgy expressed creation, covenant, church, death, and resurrection? How are those images relevant to our community's life today? In what way is our community challenged by this liturgy? What is our collective and personal response to all of the above questions? Do we still feel the same way about this liturgy and these scriptures as we did when we began?

The gospel demands a response.

What am I /we/community/parish called to do in response to the Easter Vigil?

DOCTRINAL ISSUES

What church truth/teaching/doctrinal issue could be drawn from the gospel for the Easter Vigil?

Participants suggest possible doctrinal themes that flow from the readings.

Possible Doctrinal Themes

Resurrection, paschal mystery, baptism/confirmation, eucharist; symbols: community, fire/light, water, oil, garment, bread and wine, cross

Present the doctrinal material at this time.

1. The facilitator gives input on a particular doctrinal issue of his/her prior choosing. OR
2. The group chooses a doctrinal issue from the list they created. They read together from the Doctrinal Appendix.

(The doctrinal issues are found in the Doctrinal Appendix in the back of this workbook. If you are choosing an issue from this resource, please refer to it now.)

Reflection questions centered around the chosen doctrinal theme can be found at the end of each topic in the Doctrinal Appendix. The questions are based on the five-step reflection process. If you choose a topic not included in the Doctrinal Appendix, craft your own questions according to the same five-step process.

Following the reflection questions you will be reminded to return to chapter 7, "Preparing the Catechetical Session," to assist you in crafting your own session.

Closing Prayer

God, the all-powerful Father of our Lord Jesus
Christ,
has given us a new birth by water and the Holy
Spirit,
and forgiven all our sins.
May he also keep us faithful to our Lord Jesus
Christ
for ever and ever.[85]

[85]Service of Baptism: "Concluding Prayer," *RCIA*.

Easter Sunday

Environment

The dark days of purple give way to festive joy as Easter days of white adorn our environments. Your catechetical space might include the draping of cross and book in an elegant, well-chosen, white material. As a reminder of the paschal candle, you might want to replenish your formerly consumed candle with a new (perhaps decorated) candle. An Easter lily or other spring flowers could adorn your space. The ancient icon of the resurrection called *Anastasis* would be a wonderful addition to your Easter environment.[1] The icon is a representation of Christ standing on top of the cross that crushes the evil of hell. Christ takes our first parents by the hand and escorts them out of their graves. "Amazing! Here the departure from the tomb is not that of Jesus but of all humanity."[2]

INTRODUCTORY RITES

Opening Song (or Entrance Antiphon)

Song: Jesus Christ Is Risen Today

The Lord has indeed risen, alleluia. Glory and kingship be his for ever and ever. (Lk 24:34; see Rev 1:6)[3]

Opening Prayer

The facilitator of the session may lead the prayer. Others in the group may be asked to proclaim the readings.

Let us pray
[on this Easter morning for the life
that never again shall see darkness]

Pause for silent prayer.

God our Father, creator of all,
today is the day of Easter joy.
This is the morning on which the Lord appeared
to men
who had begun to lose hope
and opened their eyes to what the scriptures
foretold:
that first he must die, and then he would rise
and ascend into his Father's glorious presence.
May the risen Lord
breathe on our minds and open our eyes
that we may know him in the breaking of the
bread,
and follow him in his risen life.
Grant this through Christ our Lord.[4]

LITURGY OF THE WORD

Let us listen to God's word.

The readings are proclaimed.

First Reading
Acts 10:34, 37–43

Overview of the Acts of the Apostles: The Acts of the Apostles was the second volume written by Luke, the evangelist (the gospel of Luke was the first). The original Greek title was "Acts of Apostles, not Acts of the Apostles; the meaning is somewhat indefinite, but it is not limited to the Twelve."[5] The book is intended not as a history, but rather as a record of the church's growth through the power of the Holy Spirit. Luke wrote two gospels: the gospel of the Son and the gospel of the Spirit. The gospel of Luke was the former and the Acts of the Apostles the latter. Luke portrays the spread of the church to the gentile world and considers it complete once the mission extends to Rome. It is believed that Luke wrote his book from oral, rather than written, tradition.

[1]Icons are symbols that draw us into the sacred presence. They help make present what they portray. There are companies that produce icons for purchase by catalogue. One such company is Monastery Icons, Rt. 1, Box 75, Geneva, NE 68361.

[2]*TCY,* 130.

[3]Easter Sunday: "Entrance Antiphon," *The Sacramentary.*

[4]Easter Sunday: "Alternative Opening Prayer," *The Sacramentary.*

[5]*DB,* 9.

Irenaeus named Luke the author of Acts and further asserted that it was written in Rome sometime after the death of Paul. Eusebius claimed that it was written during Paul's Roman imprisonment. There is similarity in the structure of Luke and Acts. In Luke, there is movement from Galilee to Jerusalem. In Acts, there is movement from Jerusalem to Rome. The Acts of the Apostles places Rome at the center of the known world. It ends in Rome because the incredible has happened and the "gospel has become a world gospel."[6] It was believed to have been composed between 70–90 C.E.

The Old Testament writers did not record their salvation history in order to chronicle the events that took place. Their primary concern was to interpret that history. Luke inherited that same tradition. Acts is considered the second volume of a two-part work by Luke the evangelist. Rather than writing a detailed history of the growth of the early church, Luke has another agenda in mind. He writes to interpret three major events that caused tension in the missionary communities. The first key event was the destruction of Jerusalem. According to Luke, the destruction of Jerusalem did not signal God's abandonment of his promises to the people. Salvation history proves his point. God did not abandon Israel during the Babylonian exile. God's fidelity is constant. Luke stresses the faithfulness of God as evidenced in the resurrection of Jesus. God did not abandon Jesus but raised him to new life.

Luke's purpose is also to demonstrate that community life is in the hands of God. All things happen according to the will of God. It is God's will that the mission of Jesus go forth to the gentiles. It is God's will that Paul, the scoundrel persecutor that had wreaked so much havoc in their lives, be converted to Christ and chosen to take the word of God out to the nations.

A second event plaguing the early church was the "difficulty of mission."[7] Even though some Jews were converted to Jesus, many were not. For them, Jesus was not the fulfillment of Old Testament prophecy. This was very hard on the missionaries. There was a strong temptation to believe that Jesus abandoned them—that he was no longer with them. A primary issue for Luke was to assure the church that the Spirit of Jesus was alive and well in the community and that the church would spread according to God's plan.

Luke provides the church with the apologetics needed for dealing with the Jews. The apostles appointed by Jesus continue to be in solidarity with him. They are representative of the patriarchs who led the twelve tribes of Israel. The apostles continue in the same tradition for the restoration of Israel. They will win converts to Jesus Christ.

Paul preaches to pagan and Jew alike and not without considerable difficulty. Both Jesus and Paul fulfill the prophetic destiny [see gospel exegesis—Third Sunday of Easter] and do not abandon their mission in the face of difficulties. They serve as models for the burgeoning church.

The third event that concerns Luke is the persecution of the church by the pagans and the Jews. The Acts of the Apostles is a word of consolation for the persecuted church. The way of the church is the way of the cross. Luke assures his readers that persecution is transitory. God will rescue God's people from the clutches of such persecution. Many will be led to Jesus because of the persecution they are willing to endure.

Luke writes to interpret the past history of the people. Only then will they understand what is going on in their present. Only then will Christians know how to face what is ahead for them.

The Acts of the Apostles also depicts the lives of the early saints—Peter, Paul, Barnabas, Stephen, etc. Such a chronicle is called hagiography. Hagiography honors the saints by extolling their wondrous deeds while on earth. Acts demonstrates how Paul and the others patterned their lives after Jesus, the martyred Son of God. In solidarity with the living Christ, they are Spirit-filled as they go forth spreading his mission. Those first saints are models for other Christians to emulate and follow.

Luke insists that the Spirit-filled church could only advance through the life and example of Spirit-filled Christians. The church needs missionaries.

[6]Ibid., 12.

[7]*IA*, 12.

They are empowered by the Spirit of Christ that is present in the church. Missionary life was not a "Jesus and me" affair. The Spirit was not given for the edification of one individual, but to build up the church. The church, in turn, is to use the gifts of the Spirit to reach out and help others. This is one of Luke's primary and essential themes.

While the church can expect persecution, it will be strengthened through the Spirit and through prayer. Prayer is essential; it is through prayer that the church will know and respond to the will of God. The missionary church experienced difficulty maintaining continuity with the past and at the same time remaining open to the movement of the Spirit in the present. What about adherence to the Law? Should pagan converts be subject to Jewish law? These questions caused great tension in a church that was adding gentile converts to its membership. The first converts were Jewish. What does it mean to be Jewish now? How were they to respond to the movement of the church into metropolitan centers such as Antioch? Should they still preach the gospel of the poor to a culture that cares not a fig for the poor? These were difficult questions midst difficult circumstances.

Luke seeks to uphold a vision of church—an ideal. He challenges those first communities to strive for the ideal. Luke's ideal community is one in which all things are shared in common, the poor are cared for, and bread is broken in worship of the God of infinite love and mercy.

Luke upholds the same image of God as he portrayed in his first gospel. God is all-loving, all-merciful, and all-forgiving. God is constant. God is faithful to God's promises. God is in covenant relationship with God's people. God will not disappoint. God walks with us into our future.

Luke employed a common literary tool used by Greco-Roman historians in which the characters enacted and spoke the historical commentary and analysis they wished to convey. In the Acts of the Apostles, the speeches of the characters interpret and analyze the events of Luke's first volume, the gospel according to Luke.

Peter's speech is a primary piece of the Christian kerygma (proclamation). The Acts of the Apostles was a catechetical tool for early believers. The characters in the text set forth the Christian creed. Peter's speech today is considered the earliest formulation of that creed. Peter and his apostles were the first witnesses. They were the first to confess their faith and were charged with passing on the faith to the world. Every believer was and is to witness to that faith. Today's speech by Peter follows very early christological patterns. Reginald Fuller notes three: 1. Salvation was offered through the scandalous death and subsequent resurrection of Jesus and Israel rejected that salvation. 2. Jesus was vindicated through the resurrection while his religious peers rejected him. 3. The apostles are the first witnesses from his earthly ministry through the post-resurrection appearances.[8]

Peter's Credo is the living faith of the first Christian community passed on to succeeding generations of the church through its living tradition. The roots of Peter's confession can be found in the Apostles' Creed.[9]

On this Easter Sunday, Peter's speech in the Acts of the Apostles contains within it not only the Christian kerygma, but a challenge to the Jewish Christian community. Peter's confession about Christ would have upset long-held religious views. God was demanding the unthinkable of good, law-abiding Jews. This whole section of chapter ten is about God removing obstacles to the gentile mission. Not only was Peter's confession for all people, including the gentiles, but it paved the way for Jewish Christians to consider their gentile counterparts worthy of association.

In order to understand this, it is important to consider the reading within the context of its setting. An angel appeared to Cornelius and told him that God favored him because he was an upright man. He was then instructed to go and seek out Peter in Joppa. Cornelius was a pagan, a God-fearing centurion. He was a holy man as is evidenced by his constant prayer and almsgiving. Meanwhile, Peter had a vision of his own. He was hungry. God dropped four-legged animals and reptiles from the sky and declared them no longer unclean. Cornelius's baptism by Peter and Peter's vision are

[8]*PNL*, 23.

[9]*DL* (III), 68.

the catalyst for a significant turning point in the early church.

Cornelius went to Peter's house and was invited to stay. Peter was still reeling from his vision and what it meant. Peter already knew of the universality of Jesus' mission. Jesus had commissioned the apostles to go and baptize *all nations.* However, prior to this time, the mission to the gentiles had not advanced much in the Jerusalem church. There were missionary successes, but not much was happening in Jerusalem.

Jesus' plan for the gentile mission had not taken root in Jerusalem. Why? The apostles did not have to go "to all nations" to find gentiles. They lived in their own backyards. Evangelization to the gentiles had not yet begun.

This reading is not about affirming the gentile mission. It is about clearing away the obstacles to it. Up to this point, the obstacle had been so great that it would have taken nothing less than a vision from God to overcome it. By law, gentiles were unclean pagans. A committed, communal relationship assumed reciprocal hospitality. If gentiles were converted, they would be initiated into the New Covenant. Thus, Jewish Christians and gentile Christians would have in common a covenantal relationship in which both parties shared reciprocal hospitality. In other words, there would necessarily be shared *agape,* communal meals. The obstacle for Jewish Christians was: How could they share meals with the unclean? It was forbidden by God. "Nevertheless he [Peter] is the one who takes the new step that requires the Jerusalem church to reexamine its relation to Gentiles. It is not enough that Peter takes the new step. The Jerusalem church must be convinced of its rightness."[10] God was lifting the status of *unclean* off of the backs of the gentiles, thus paving the way for a Jewish/gentile Christianity. Communal relationship between Jews and Christians was now possible.

In today's pericope, Peter confesses the Jesus story to Cornelius and friends to affirm that "God sent good news to the people of Israel about the peace now available through their Messiah, and this Messiah is Lord of all, offering peace to all. Peter reviews the Jesus story as told in Luke in order to say to Cornelius that this story is a word of salvation for him also."[11]

Peter's address to the new converts is indicative of the method used for evangelizing gentiles. Methods used for evangelizing Jews would include blaming the Jewish leaders for Jesus' death and using the Hebrew scriptures as a proof text for Jesus' life. Methods of evangelization for gentiles involved the proclamation of Jesus' life and work and the witness of the apostles to back up his claims.

In today's text, Peter confesses the Christians' story (the agenda of every Easter Christian) and asserts the universal message of God's salvation.[12] In other words, Peter demonstrates the inclusivity of God, and paves the way for disciples to move beyond religious fundamentalism and centuries-old prejudices. Only the Spirit could accomplish such a major shift.

Questions for mystagogical reflection: *What does this reading have to do with Easter? How is this a word for our community? What are the implications for our community during this season that immerses us in the paschal mystery and Christian witness? What does this reading teach us about God, Christ, Spirit, church, ourselves? How might our community be called to respond? How does this reading challenge us to live the paschal mystery?*

Responsorial Psalm
Psalm 118:1–2, 16–17, 22–23

Of all the psalms, Psalm 118 was one of the first that was used to refer to the death and resurrection of Christ. Psalm 118 is an individual song of thanks. "The stone which the builders rejected" (v. 22) was probably an ancient proverb. "A piece of stone judged unworthy of a position of prominence in the structure by the 'experts' has become the most prominent."[13] This line was a metaphor that the early church used to help explain Israel's rejection of its own people. "This is

[10] *NULA* (II), 143.

[11] Ibid., 142.

[12] *LY,* 83.

[13] John S. Kselman, S.S. and Michael L. Barre, S.S., "Psalms," in *NJBC,* 547.

the day the Lord has made" (v. 24) referred to the day in which Yahweh acted to save his people. The resurrection was just such a day.

Second Reading
Alternative 1: Colossians 3:1–4

Paul's letter to the Colossians is written in the midst of turmoil. Gnosticism is threatening the church. According to gnosticism, spirit is good and matter is evil. Thus, the only way to attain God is through special knowledge (knowledge that only the elite can obtain); those without this knowledge are trapped in their human, evil bodies. There were two extreme responses to gnosticism: excessive spiritual exercises and extreme attempts to wear down the evil body. Both point to the denigration of Christian redemption through Christ. "If you have been raised in Christ" is a literary phrase. "It means if (and of course you are)."[14] The word, *raised,* is literally translated *co-raised.* We were raised with Christ and given a share in his life. Because we have been given a share in Christ's divine life, we are called to live the redemption that was won for us. Thus, we are called to a higher moral standard.

Reginald Fuller suggests that the letter to the Colossians takes the Romans exhortation from last night's vigil one step further. Romans tells us "that we died with Christ." Colossians is more optimistic and is cause for Easter rejoicing. In this letter Paul maintains that we die *and rise* with Christ. However, this death and resurrection carries with it the responsibility to live the moral life and be aware of the "hidden reality which is not fully revealed until Christ's second coming."[15]

Questions for mystagogical reflection: *How is our community dying and rising with Christ (living the paschal mystery)? Do we live the challenge of the gospel? Do we respond in love to our brothers and sisters around the world? Do we live the moral responsibility to care for one another, especially those who cannot care for themselves? Where is there death? Where is there resurrection? What are we called to do about it as a community? How are we called to respond?*

[14] *PNL,* 24
[15] Ibid.

Second Reading
Alternative 2: 1 Corinthians 5:6–8

Prior to Passover, Jewish women spent many hours removing every particle of leaven from their homes. Leaven was used in a figurative sense in the early church. Leaven was considered an impurity and was a metaphor for sin. A very little leaven impacted the entire batch of dough. Unleavened bread was a sign of purity.

"Do you not know that a little yeast has its effects all through the dough?" (v. 5). The opening line of today's pericope is actually a proverb. "Jesus used it to teach that if the kingdom had modest beginnings, it contains the seeds of great growth."[16] Leaven was also used to symbolize corruption. It is this last reference that Paul uses here. Paul exhorts the reader to get rid of all the old yeast so a new batch can grow. Last night at the Easter Vigil, the neophytes put on the new person of Christ. The old yeast was washed away in the waters of baptism, a new batch was begun, and new life began.

Paul speaks this word to the Corinthians in response to the case of a man who was guilty of incest. He had had relations with his father's wife, which was considered an abomination. Paul was more disconcerted over the community's lack of response than he was about the sin of the man. Paul exhorts the community to rid itself of the sinful leaven. He challenges the community to rid itself of such sin. Easter people are to cast off the darkness of sin and live in the light of the resurrection. Like the Jewish women of old, who swept their houses before Passover looking for the tiniest morsel of leaven, we too are to sweep the houses of our heart to rid them of the leaven of corruption. In so doing, we will then live as unleavened bread, in the resurrection of purity and holiness. Christians are to live and preach the truth and to call one another to holiness. This call to holiness has its basis in living the moral life. "These passages resound to the great Pauline intuition that we are not saved because of our works but neither are we saved without our works. . . . Moral and ascetic commitment is not the *cause* of salvation; it does, however, have to be the *effect* of

[16] *DL* (III), 71.

it."[17] The Christian community and individual are to seek out the leaven of sin through purification from the old yeast in order to live in the resurrection of new, Easter life.

This is the first time that Christian Passover is mentioned and it refers to two different Passovers. One Passover is that already accomplished through Christ's sacrifice of his life on Calvary. The other is the Christian Passover: the passage of the person from death to life, sin to purity. The verb used in reference to Jesus' Passover is in the past tense. Jesus' Passover is already a reality. The Christian need only accept it, "believe it and celebrate it."[18] The verbs that refer to the Christian Passover, on the other hand, infer that the action is still in process. "The verbs in this case are in the imperative: 'purify yourselves, let us celebrate.'"[19]

Questions for mystagogical reflection: *Christians are called to be a eucharistic people. In what way is your community like the leavened bread of the Pharisees? How have you grown in the image of unleavened bread—the eucharist? How has your community grown in holiness through the lenten season? What are you called to do in response to this reading?*

Gospel
John 20:1–9

Mary Magdalene finds Jesus' tomb empty and runs to tell Peter and the others.

Sequence

> To the Paschal Victim let Christians offer a sacrifice of praise.
>
> The lamb redeemed the sheep. Christ, sinless, reconciled sinners to the Father.
>
> Death and life were locked together in a unique struggle. Life's captain died; now he reigns, never more to die.
>
> Tell us, Mary, What did you see on the way?
>
> "I saw the tomb of the now living Christ. I saw the glory of Christ, now risen.
>
> "I saw angels who gave witness; the cloths too which once had covered head and limbs.
>
> "Christ my hope has arisen. He will go before his own into Galilee."
>
> We know that Christ has indeed risen from the dead. Do you, conqueror and king, have mercy on us. Amen. Alleluia.

[17] *ME*, 85.
[18] Ibid., 92.
[19] Ibid.

STEP 1
NAMING ONE'S EXPERIENCE

What were your first impressions? What was your first response? What grabbed your attention? How did you feel?

Each person names his or her initial impression. Statements should be brief. No reasons should be given at this time. All simply listen without agreeing or disagreeing.

STEP 2
UNDERSTANDING

In a brief statement, what do you think the readings are trying to convey?

STEP 3
INPUT FROM VISION/STORY/TRADITION

Liturgical Context

The Beginning of the Easter Season

The Easter Vigil is the primary ritual celebration of the Easter event. Easter Sunday is considered the first Sunday of Easter, and the next Sunday the Second Sunday of Easter. There are no special rituals for Easter Sunday other than to revisit the rituals initiated at the Easter Vigil the night before. On Easter Sunday we renew our baptismal promises, sprinkle the community with the newly blessed water of baptism, and continue the jubilant celebration in word, symbol, ritual, and song.

Penitence is over and now begin the seven weeks of meditation on the awesome implications of the paschal mystery.

He has made us pass:
from slavery to freedom,
from sadness to joy,
from mourning to the feast,
from darkness to the light,
from slavery to redemption.
Therefore we say before him: Alleluia![20]

The Easter season is not a time for giving an historical representation of the chronology of events in Jesus' post-resurrection life. It is, rather, intended to give sufficient time to uncover, unpack, and reflect on the paschal mystery in order to allow all of its dimensions to impact and affect the Christian life. It is a time for the entire church, neophyte and faithful, to reflect upon the Easter gospels, to live their paschal commitment with renewed vigor, and to process in joy to the Easter table. Eucharist, as the living presence of the risen Christ, is our prime focus. The eucharists of the Easter season help us remember and bring into the present the Christ who appeared on the road to Emmaus in the breaking of the bread, the Christ who appeared to believers to dispel the doubts of Thomas, and the Shepherd Christ who lays down his life for the church. Jesus appears to the apostles in the Easter season in the form of a meal. "The roots of the Christian Eucharist lie not only in the last supper, but in the meals which the Risen One celebrated with his disciples in the Easter season."[21]

Through the eucharist, we fully live the paschal mystery. St. Augustine asserted that we are to become that which we eat: the Body of Christ. During the Easter season we enter the mystery unfolding in our lives. (One meaning of the word mystery is "that which is unfolding in our midst.") We are challenged from the opening moments of the liturgy (Opening Prayer) to reflect on the mystery we celebrate with enthusiastic joy:

God our Father, creator of all,
today is the day of Easter joy.
This is the morning on which the Lord appeared to men
who had begun to lose hope
and opened their eyes to what the scriptures foretold:
that first he must die, and then he would rise
and ascend into his Father's glorious presence.
May the risen Lord
breathe on our minds and open our eyes
that we may know him in the breaking of bread....[22]

The liturgies of Easter demand mystagogical reflection (*breathe on our minds and open our eyes*) not only for the neophytes, but for the faithful as well. They ask: What does it mean to live the *unfolding mysteries* of our sacramental life? What does it mean to be people of the water, light, word, cross, garment, oil, bread, and wine? This is not just the task of the newly baptized Catholic Christian. It is the task of the entire church. Just as the lenten church entered the womb of penitence, so too the Easter church enters into the new birth of mystagogical reflection.

The neophytes are a sign of the new life of Easter. As they begin the period of mystagogia, they are a symbol of Easter life. They sit in our midst, perhaps vested in their baptismal garments, and are a living sign of the unfolding mystery of Christ's death and resurrection. These new Christians, who died to the old leaven and rose again to the new leaven of Christ in the eucharist (alternative second reading), remind us that we are to continue in the struggle between life and death. Eucharist strengthens us for the struggle.

The neophytes spend the weeks of Easter growing in the paschal mystery through meditation on the gospel (RCIA, #244).

> How do these Easter scriptures help me experience the risen Christ in my daily effort to die and rise with Christ?

Through sharing in the eucharist and doing works of charity, neophytes grow in the newness of the life they have just received.

> How am I growing through my participation in the eucharist and the giving of myself in the spiritual and corporal works of

[20] *Pesachim* 10.5; and Melito of Sardis, *On Pascha* 68 (Sources Chretiennes 123, p. 96, Paris: 1942), in *ME*, 91, #2.

[21] *PNL*, 23.

[22] Easter Sunday: "Opening Prayer," *The Sacramentary*.

mercy? How does the eucharist enlighten my understanding of the Scriptures? (RCIA, #246)

Are these not questions we should all be asking if we wish to grow in the Christian life? Is this not the agenda of the Easter Vigil and the entire Easter season?

For the neophyte, the period of mystagogia is a time for unpacking the sacramental mysteries experienced in baptism, confirmation, and eucharist at the Easter Vigil and eucharist during the masses of the Easter season. It is a time to delve deeply into the symbols of the Vigil, to name the experience, and to discover the meaning and the challenge for the Christian life. Easter, then, is a time to lavishly feast and crack open the symbols of bread, wine, oil, water, garment, cross, and light.

The season is a single period of celebration, culminating with the feast of the Holy Spirit given to the church on Pentecost. The *Great Fifty Days of Easter* give ample time and expression to the mystery of Christ's death, ascension, and resurrection. We meditate on what it means to be Easter people. During these fifty days the church commemorates the fruits of Jesus' death and resurrection just as Israel celebrated the first fruit of the harvest during its fifty-day Pentecost feast. Today begins a fifty-day meditation on the wonders of Jesus' saving event and the life and witness of the early church.[23]

The Easter Sunday Liturgy

The readings today are the same for all three cycles. The mass is filled with the joy of the resurrection. It begins in exultation with the words: "The Lord has risen indeed, Alleluia!" Today's opening prayer is an adaptation from the old Gelasian Sacramentary. "*Deus, qui hodierna die,*" the original Latin beginning words, highlight the understanding of *day* in the liturgical sense. The concept of *this day* (also in the responsorial psalm) is important to all liturgical celebration, as it is truly on this Easter day (Easter Vigil and entire season) that we especially remember the saving event of Jesus' *pasch.* After our forty days of prayer, fasting, and almsgiving, we rise to new life with Christ. The prayers of the liturgy (Opening Prayer—"may we rise again"—and the second reading from Colossians 3: "You have been raised in company with Christ") remind us that through the liturgy we commemorate and share in Jesus' death and resurrection. The responsorial psalm, Psalm 118, is a fitting song of praise to ring in this feast of victory. The second song devoted to the joy of Easter faith is the Easter Sequence: *Victimae Paschali Laudes* ("Praises to the Paschal Victim").[24]

This is the only time of the year when the church experiences the life of the early church through the readings of the Acts of the Apostles. The Acts of the Apostles reads like an adventure-filled novel and is enacted in every community that strives to live the Easter kerygma. In the first reading from Acts, Peter confesses faith in the death and resurrection of Christ. Both choices for the second reading take us to the next step: our moral response. How will we behave, act, and live as people who are incorporated into Jesus' death and resurrection? The gospel from John is the story of the first Christian witness of the resurrection. The Beloved Disciple witnessed to the resurrection without seeing the event himself. Easter is a call for all people to believe without seeing and to go and witness it to the world.

The first Easter preface also refers to "this day" and stresses the victory of Jesus through the sacrifice of his death. The passover images from the Easter Vigil are strong in the preface and remind us that it is "the true Lamb who took away the sins of the world," who offered us redemption and forgiveness of sins.

The church is so insistent on the primacy of the Easter Vigil that it instructs its priests to preach on the unity of the redemptive paschal mystery and on the primacy of the Easter Vigil in the liturgical

[23]Please refer to the Easter season overview for a brief history of the Easter Sunday celebration. The gospel from the Easter Vigil is also an option for Easter Sunday morning. Afternoon masses on Easter Sunday may use Luke 13–35.

[24]On Easter Sunday the sequence is sung after the second reading and before the gospel. There are presently only four assigned sequences for the liturgy: Easter Sunday—*Victimae Paschali Laudes* ("Praises to the Paschal Victim"), Pentecost—*Veni Sancte Spiritus* ("Come, Holy Spirit"), Corpus Christi—*Lauda Sion* ("Praise Zion"), Feast of Our Lady of Sorrows—*Stabat Mater* ("The Mother Stood").

year on Easter Sunday.[25] Since many people do not attend the Easter Vigil, the church wishes that we be brought into the annual remembrance of Christ's saving event so explicitly encountered in the Vigil liturgy.

The Easter Vigil and Easter Sunday end with the solemn blessing. This solemn blessing asserts an important sacramental reality. The last part of the blessing reminds us of what it is we are to keep in mind at every liturgy. We feast at this banquet, while awaiting the final, glorious banquet with Christ in the hereafter.

The Triduum is brought to a close with the celebration of vespers on Easter Sunday night.

Gospel Exegesis

The facilitator gives input regarding what critical biblical scholarship has to say about this text. The input includes insights as to how people would have heard the gospel in Jesus' time.

Mary Magdalene enters the tomb, finds it empty, and runs to tell Peter that the Lord's body has been stolen. There is not a hint that she suspects Jesus was raised from the dead. Peter and the Beloved Disciple come to the tomb. The Beloved Disciple enters, sees the burial cloths, and believes. Peter does not believe, but his lack of faith is explained away as lack of understanding: he does not yet understand the scripture in relation to this event.

The two men are needed at the tomb because two witnesses are required to authenticate an event. Women were not acceptable witnesses. Thus, John "places the discovery of the empty tomb by men alongside its discovery by a woman or women. The one confirms the testimony of the other."[26] The cloths were perceived as proof of the resurrection. No one would steal a body by first unwrapping it. Even though grave robbing was a common problem, and even if the disciples had stolen the body (as they were accused of doing), no one would have unwrapped the body. The wrappings left on the floor seemed to suggest a new reality. The person inside those cloths had simply dematerialized, leaving the cloths in place as if his body had simply vanished. "His corpse has not been resuscitated; he has been transformed from mortal to immortal."[27]

Raymond Brown offers a different perspective regarding Jesus' burial wrappings. He suggests that they reflect typical Johannine symbolism. Lazarus came forth from the tomb bound from head to foot. Jesus also was bound from head to foot—just as Lazarus was bound. Lazarus was merely resuscitated, however. He would die again—a natural death in which he would be wrapped for burial a second and final time. The wrappings left by Jesus served as a reminder to the disciples that Jesus would never die again; he rose to eternal life. The disciples did not understand the meaning and implications of the resurrection. They would only come to understand when the scriptures were explained to them.[28]

This story does not set out to prove the resurrection. The New Testament had no need to prove it. This is more a story of faith. There was nothing that could be proved from the evidence of the empty tomb and the left-behind burial cloths. None of it made any sense until Jesus began to appear to the disciples after the resurrection.

The Beloved Disciple enters the tomb and believes without seeing. The Disciple is both an authentic witness of the resurrection event and a model believer for all those generations of people who will also believe without seeing Jesus.

The tomb is no proof of the resurrection. Mary Magdalene did not run off to tell Peter that Jesus was raised from the dead. She thought someone had stolen his body! The entire resurrection account is intended to prove that this man Jesus, whom they knew well, died on a cross and was raised from the dead. Without the cross there was no resurrection. Without the resurrection there was no gospel, no two-thousand year history. The resurrection was understood in the New Testament as the "climactic achievement in the saving deeds of God."[29] Yet John's gospel does not place

[25] *LY,* 83–84.
[26] *RJ,* 249.
[27] Ibid., 250.
[28] *RCE,* 69.
[29] *DOB,* 733.

the full meaning of Easter at the tomb. Jesus' mission is completed only when he returns to his Father in glory and the Spirit is sent upon the earth. Thus we must look at Easter Sunday with an eye toward Ascension and Pentecost.

Jesus' life and death were redemptive because they were a sign of victory over death. It takes great faith to believe in the resurrection. The disciples did not believe in the resurrection until the risen Lord himself appeared to them. They would not understand the scriptures in regard to his resurrection until Jesus' glorification. The resurrection had to be accepted on faith and on the word of Christian witnesses. The same is true today. During the Easter season the church enters into Jesus' dying and rising, the paschal mystery. We are to give Christian witness to the saving deeds of the Lord. Are we unbelieving, yet chosen for God's mission, like Peter? Or are we like the Beloved Disciple, who believes without seeing for himself and yet cannot contain the power of what he did not see?

Proclaim the gospel again.

Sometimes we gain new insights when we hear the text after the interpretation has been given. Someone from the group proclaims the gospel a second time.

STEP 4
TESTING

Conversation with the Liturgy and the Scriptures

Test your original understanding in dialogue with the text.

(You might consider breaking into smaller groups.)

Are there any new or renewed insights in today's readings or liturgy? How does your original understanding of Easter, the gospel, readings and themes, compare with what was just shared? How does this story speak to your life?

Sharing Life Experience

Participants share an experience from their lives that connects with the biblical interpretation just shared.

I am reminded of so many stories of death and resurrection, not only in my own life, but in the life of our friends (who are like family), and in the life of our parish community. I am reminded of our dearest friend who, at age forty-five, was involved in a life-and-death struggle because his five-year-old's mumps had ended up in the lungs. I remember our prayerful vigil as we stood the death watch in the early morning hours, praying that God would heal him. Like Lazarus, Dan was resuscitated. I also remember the time four months later when my husband's ruptured appendix put him at that same door. There was the same vigil, prayer, and death watch. And again, like Lazarus and Dan, Bob was resuscitated. But I also remember nineteen-year-old Adam, my son's best friend, who was killed in a car accident. I remember Jackie, a forty-year-old friend in the parish who died unexpectedly. I also remember the mother who never recovered from the death of her young daughter fifteen years ago. In addition, this past summer she lost her husband and almost lost her will to live. I remember the pain we felt when a young man took his own life. God did not, like Lazarus, resuscitate them. Our hope sustains us, however, as we envision them ushered to the exalted throne of the Savior, where weeping and tears are no more. We know the power of the resurrection when we see our community being the loving presence of Christ to those who suffer.

Death and resurrection—resurrection and death. In the midst of our joy and sorrow the Spirit of God is present. Jesus reigns from his throne, but not like some lofty, aloof, disinterested ruler. He resides in glory so that his resurrected presence, the Holy Spirit, might stand with us at our vigils and death watches, lament with us in our grief, and sing with us in our joy.

When a baby in our midst suffers from a rare disease that threatens his year-old life and our catechumens ask why God permits such suffering, we are brought to this day, this Easter day. It is this special day that gives us hope in the worst of circumstances and allows us to celebrate in the most graced of circumstances. Suffering and death are mysteries, the depths of which we will never fully plumb. Yet, this day is the day that gives us hope. Death is never final—no matter how hopeless things appear to be, death will not *have the last word. This is why Jesus reigns triumphant. He paid the price and today we reap the benefits. This is our Easter faith. We are called to be the weeping, consoling Christ with those who mourn. We are to stand the vigils and keep the watches, and in so doing offer Easter joy to a suffering world. Easter calls us to live the paschal mystery—to embrace death and resurrection. When we lay down our lives for the world's suffering, the poor, and the lost and alienated, this is the day that reminds us that we will take them up again—we will be raised! It is our hope; it is our common calling!*

All share their life experience.

What was John's message to the early Christian community in the first reading? What was he trying to tell his community? What does he have to say to our community and to me today? How are we challenged to be re-created (*biblical theme of creation*), to enter more fully into relationship with God (*covenant*), to live in Christian community (*community*), and to die and rise (*exodus*)? In what way have I/we known death/resurrection in my/our experience and understanding of this gospel? How is God speaking to us as a community and how are we challenged? What is our collective and personal response to all of the above questions?

Step 5
Decision

The gospel demands a response.

In what concrete way does this liturgy call our parish to action in the church, parish, neighborhood, or world? Has this conversation with the exegesis of this Easter liturgy changed or stretched my personal attitudes? What is one specific action I/we will take this week as a response to what was learned and shared today?

DOCTRINAL ISSUES

What church truth/teaching/doctrinal issue could be drawn from the gospel for Easter Sunday?

Participants suggest possible doctrinal themes that flow from the readings.

Possible Doctrinal Themes

Paschal mystery, resurrection, eucharist, baptism, confirmation, symbols: bread, water, oil, Christian witness

Present the doctrinal material at this time.

1. The facilitator gives input on a particular doctrinal issue of his/her prior choosing. OR
2. The group chooses a doctrinal issue from the list they created. They read together from the Doctrinal Appendix.

(The doctrinal issues are found in the Doctrinal Appendix in the back of this workbook. If you are choosing an issue from this resource, please refer to it now.)

Reflection questions centered around the chosen doctrinal theme can be found at the end of each topic in the Doctrinal Appendix. The questions are based on the five-step reflection process. If you choose a topic not included in the Doctrinal Appendix, craft your own questions according to the same five-step process.

Following the reflection questions you will be reminded to return to chapter 7, "Preparing the Catechetical Session," to assist you in crafting your own session.

Closing Prayer

May almighty God bless you on this solemn feast of Easter, and may he protect you against all sin.
Response: Amen.

Through the resurrection of his Son,
God has granted us healing.
May he fulfill his promises,
and bless you with eternal life.
Response: Amen.

You have mourned for Christ's sufferings;
now you celebrate the joy of his resurrection.
May you come with joy to the feast which
lasts forever.
Response: Amen.[30]

[30]Easter Sunday, "Solemn Blessing," *The Sacramentary.*

Second Sunday of Easter

Environment

Refer to Easter Sunday.

INTRODUCTORY RITES

Opening Song (or Entrance Antiphon)

Like newborn children you should thirst for milk, on which your spirit can grow to strength, alleluia. (1 Pt 2:2)[1]

Opening Prayer

The facilitator of the session may lead the prayer. Others in the group may be asked to proclaim the readings.

Rite of Sprinkling

Dear friends,
this water will be used
to remind us of our baptism.
Let us ask God to bless it
and keep us faithful
to the Spirit he has given us.
Lord God almighty,
hear the prayers of your people:
we celebrate our creation and redemption.
Hear our prayers and bless + this water
which gives fruitfulness to the fields,
and refreshment and cleansing to man.
You chose water to show your goodness
when you led your people to freedom
through the Red Sea
and satisfied their thirst in the desert
with water from the rock.
Water was the symbol used by the prophets
to foretell your new covenant with man.
You made the water of baptism holy
by Christ's baptism in the Jordan:
by it you give us a new birth
and renew us in holiness.
May this water remind us of our baptism,
and let us share the joy
of all who have been baptized at Easter.
We ask this through Christ our Lord.
(When salt is mixed with the holy water:)
Almighty God,
we ask you to bless + this salt
as once you blessed the salt scattered over the water
by the prophet Elisha.
Wherever this salt and water are sprinkled,
drive away the power of evil,
and protect us always
by the presence of your Holy Spirit.
Grant this through Christ our Lord.
(After the sprinkling:)
May almighty God cleanse us of our sins,
and through the eucharist we celebrate
make us worthy to sit at his table
in his heavenly kingdom.[2]

LITURGY OF THE WORD

Let us listen to God's word.

The readings are proclaimed.

First Reading[3]
Acts 2:42–47

(Refer to the Overview of the Acts of the Apostles, Easter Sunday.) Luke's main agenda in the Acts of the Apostles was to teach the early community how to live, grow, and thrive as a church. In the Acts of the Apostles, Luke followed literary techniques commonly found in ancient literature. One such technique was to tell the stories of a group's founder so new followers would emulate his actions. These stories, called cultic biographies, also related the actions and movements of the

[1]Second Sunday of Easter: "Entrance Antiphon," *The Sacramentary.*

[2]"Rite of Blessing and Sprinkling Holy Water," *The Sacramentary.*

[3]The exegesis for the first and second readings may or may not be the focus of your group's reflection as there may only be time to give adequate attention to the gospel, your primary concern. However, all of the readings during the Easter season fully express and reveal the richness of our Easter theology.

founder's newly formed disciples. The greater purpose of cultic biography was to authenticate the mission of the leader and his followers.

One literary technique used by the author of Acts is the summary. Today's reading is a summary. The summary was used to demonstrate the growth of the church. The summaries portrayed the developing life of the community as it lived in the resurrected presence of Christ. The community shared all things in common, and community members gathered for common worship and instruction. Signs and wonders not only prove the presence and power of the risen Christ, but they are also reminders of the messianic, eschatological age. The church furthers the reign of God in the here and now as it awaits God's reign in the age to come—the final age.

Today's pericope emphasizes the community's unity and sharing. Future events in Acts serve to underscore these two themes (for example, confrontation with Annanias and Sappira and the tension between the Hellenists and the Hebrews). Confrontation stories highlight the threat to unity and the sharing of goods that expressed that unity.

The Christian community was doing what it was commissioned to do. Peter offered freedom from sin and the gift of the Spirit at Pentecost.[4] Today's pastoral scene provides evidence of that freedom and outpouring. The Spirit empowers Christian witness, preaching, and teaching. The Spirit prompts an uncommon sharing of life and possessions. As a result of this communal life, converts were added to their number.

Luke continued the themes that were woven throughout his gospel. Jesus exhorted the disciples to sell their possessions and to care for the poor. In Luke's gospel the disciples were vying for the best seats at the Lord's table. Contrast that with the disciples in the Acts of the Apostles. They were known by their unity and their care for one another. They obeyed Jesus' command. The church was unified—united in mind and soul. Evidence of this unity was observed by the way they shared their possessions with one another.

[4]*NULA* (II), 44.

Robert Tannehill asserts that the early church sought to uphold the ideal church described above (by being united in the care for one another and in the sharing of all things in common), but the more likely reality was that while the ideal was certainly something to strive for, it was not necessarily always achieved. In practice they did not always match the ideal. The ideal was nevertheless emphasized. Jesus called the church to respond in faith. Acts exhorts and encourages Christians to embrace the ideal and to live in its fullness. Care for the poor was understood as a moral response to the gospel.

Questions for mystagogical reflection: *In what way does this reading from the Acts of the Apostles invite participation in the paschal mystery of Jesus? In what way does the ideal church described by Luke challenge our contemporary communities today? Is it just pie-in-the-sky Christian piety or is it relevant for our parish today? How might our parish be called to respond? In what ways is our community striving for the ideal set forth in today's reading? Where is growth needed? How does this reading speak to me personally? In what ways am I living up to the ideal? Where is growth needed? How might I respond in a concrete way to today's reading?*

Responsorial Psalm
Psalm 118:2–4, 13–15, 22–24

Second Reading
1 Peter 1:3–9

Overview of 1 Peter: The letters of Peter are part of a group of letters known as "general" or "catholic" because "they are not addressed to a specific church."[5] Even though 1 Peter is written as a letter, including an opening thanksgiving, the body of the letter does not have the personal elements that are usually found in a letter. The letter was written to the church in Asia Minor and some scholars believe that it was written in the Roman church by an associate of Paul's named Silvanus (5:12). Some scholars doubt Peter's authorship of the letter for a variety of reasons, one of which was the fact that the church during Peter's time did not experience the persecution referred to throughout the letter. Those that opt for Petrine authorship, however, cite the primitive theology based on eschatology, servant christology, and

[5]*RNT*, 293.

church order inherent in the letter. If Peter did not write the letter and it was written at a later time, William Dalton, S.J. maintains that in light of the persecutions mentioned in the letter, it would have been unlikely that there was no mention of the persecutions by Nero shortly after Peter's death (c. 64 C.E.).[6]

Scholars suggest a parallel between 1 Peter and Paul's letter to the Romans, not only thematically but regionally as well. The region addressed in the letter parallels Paul's missionary tour. Thematically both letters address relationship to civil governments and to brotherly love, and both express liturgical language common in the early Christian community.

One of the primary concerns of 1 Peter is the life of the community in the face of growing persecution. It tries to answer the question: "What does it mean to be a Christian in a persecuted church?" 1 Peter's concern was to exhort Christians to faithfulness in Christ midst persecution and pagan animosities. "By recalling the greatness of their vocation and by showing that persecution is a sign of their calling, the writer encourages and exhorts his readers to stand firm (5:12)."[7] The letter also addresses the duties of Christians in the midst of such persecution. Slaves and women might find themselves in abusive situations by antagonistic non-Christian masters and husbands. "In each instance exemplary behavior may also be a strategy for alleviating the tension in the situation."[8]

The letter refers to the Christian as a resident in an alien land. This was understood not only in an eschatological, metaphorical way, referring to the Christian's eventual heavenly destination, but also in a geo-political way. They did not see themselves as citizens of the cities in which they lived. "The 'resident alien' at least had some status as a 'registered' member of the city."[9] Christians were particularly susceptible to suspicion not only because of their Christianity, but their legal status was also questionable. The letter asserted that the Christian's new life is evident to outsiders and thus their persecution was a reaction to this new way of life, changed patterns of living, and their newly formed relationships. "Conversion has meant breaking off past ties and associations (1:3–5, 10–12, 18, 21; 2:4–10) to enter the new familial community of mutual love which is God's holy people (1:17; 2:5, 10; 5:9). Abuse was not isolated to one specific cause. Christians were harassed due to ignorance, the suspicion of wrong-doing, and curiosity that prompted a test of their new-found faith. Christians were to turn to the crucified Christ as an example in the midst of suffering. They were to turn their faces with hope to the resurrected Christ and the promise of eternal glory."[10]

1 Peter is known as a pastoral letter. "By emphasizing the dignity of the Christian vocation, which provides a God-given 'home' (*oikos,* 2:5, 4:17) for the 'homeless' (*paroikoi,* 2:11; cf. 1:17), and the positive value of sharing the passion of Christ through persecution, the writer reminds his readers to remain faithful."[11]

Today's Pericope: 1 Peter is not a lofty theological treatise or sterile creedal formula. Today's pericope expresses the foundational hope of all Christians. The promises made to Israel are fulfilled in the life and resurrection of Jesus and subsequently in the church. Israel was promised the land; the new Israel was promised an "imperishable inheritance"—heaven.[12] It is only through the cross and resurrection of Jesus that people find meaning in their own destiny. Jesus Christ, God's very own Son, endured the most degrading death human beings can suffer. He was raised from the dead to reign as our Lord. Jesus did not endure the cross simply to ease the pain and suffering in this world. He died and rose again in order to share his life with us beyond the hopelessness of the grave.

Eternal life is not only our hope, it is our assurance. God will not disappoint. God will accomplish his plan for humanity. It is for this reason that we can praise God in the midst of whatever travail this earthly sojourn conjures up for its unwilling victims.

---

[6]William J. Dalton, S.J. "The First Epistle of Peter," *NJBC,* 903.

[7]Ibid., 904.

[8]*RNT,* 295.

[9]Ibid.

[10]Ibid.

[11]*NJBC,* 904.

[12]Ibid., 905.

Human beings are tested like gold in the fire, not to be consumed but refined. 1 Peter affirms and encourages his readers by reminding them that even though they did not see the Lord, they believed in him. It is because of their faith that Christians look forward in hope to their eternal reward. The "salvation of souls" in verse nine does not refer to the immortality of the soul, but rather employs the common biblical understanding of soul—the self or person.

Questions for mystagogical reflection: *How does this reading reflect the paschal mystery? How does this reading invite participation in Jesus' life, death, and resurrection? In what way is this a word for your community? How might this reading speak to situations in your parish? How does this reading reflect the biblical themes of covenant, exodus, community, and creation? In what way are those themes relevant for you and your community? In what way can you and your community relate to the teaching about hardships and trials in today's reading? What are the implications for your life?*

Gospel[13]
John 20:19–31

Jesus appears to the Twelve and eight days later, with Thomas present, he appears again.

STEP 1
NAMING ONE'S EXPERIENCE

What were your first impressions? What was your first response to the gospel or the other readings? What captured your attention?

Each person names his or her initial impression. Statements should be brief. No reasons should be given at this time. All simply listen without agreeing or disagreeing.

STEP 2
UNDERSTANDING

In a brief statement, what do you think this gospel is trying to convey?

STEP 3
INPUT FROM VISION/STORY/TRADITION

Liturgical Context[14]

The liturgies of the Sundays of Easter are centered around the unity of the paschal mystery: the death, resurrection, and ascension of Jesus and sending of the Spirit. This four-fold reality is the focus of mystagogical reflection during the Easter season.

The readings of the Easter liturgies are chosen to reflect the spirit and heart of the season.

> The first reading is from the Acts of the Apostles, arranged in a three-year cycle of parallel and progressive selections. Thus the life, growth, and witness of the early Church are presented every year.
>
> The selections from the writings of the apostles are year A, First Letter of Peter; year B, First Letter of John; year C, the Book of Revelation. These texts seem most appropriate to the spirit of the Easter season, a spirit of joyful faith and confident hope.[15]

John's intention in the final chapters of his gospel is to define paschal faith. He wants his readers to understand that even if seeing is believing, not seeing and believing opens a person to a myriad of hidden truths. Those of us left to live the paschal faith in the messianic age are called to be-

[13]The gospel exegesis is provided later in this session so that it may be presented in the proper sequence where it occurs in the adult five-step reflection process. The exegesis is provided for the first and second readings for your information and edification, and for you to use at your discretion. Once again, the gospel is the primary source of reflection. If there is time for reflection on the other readings, all the better.

[14]The scriptures in the Lectionary, the seasons of the year, and the ritual prayers of the mass are interrelated and form the basis for liturgical catechesis. The *liturgical context* attempts to explore and clarify the themes and this interrelatedness.

[15]Lectionary: Introduction, Ch. 2, IV, 14, #1, p. 13.

lieve with new eyes. The early disciples had to move from their actual experience of the human Jesus to radical faith in the resurrected, glorified Jesus who now lives in the presence of the Spirit in the church.

During Easter we are reminded that we have died with Christ and rise again to new life with him through our baptism. We are sprinkled with the waters of baptism in order to remember and call forward our own baptism. We are reminded that through baptism we participate in Jesus' paschal mystery.

In the opening prayer of today's liturgy, we ask to share God's mercy and life. Christians wash away sins in the water of baptism, are given new birth in the Holy Spirit, and are redeemed by the blood of Christ. Our primary focus during the Easter season is to immerse ourselves in the paschal mystery. The opening prayer reflects this paschal faith and life.

> Let us pray
> [for a deeper awareness of our Christian baptism].
> God of mercy,
> you wash away our sins in water,
> you give us new birth in the Spirit,
> and redeem us in the blood of Christ.
> As we celebrate Christ's resurrection
> increase our awareness of these blessings,
> and renew your gift of life within us.[16]

We are called to be Easter people—people of the Word and people of the eucharist. The disciples in today's reading from the Acts of the Apostles are the epitome of Easter faith. They gathered to pray and to worship, to listen to the apostles' instruction, and to break the bread of life. They lived their Easter faith. They were a new creation in Christ and many were added to their number through the example of their lives. They were living their baptismal faith. We too are those people.

> Lord,
> through faith and baptism
> we have become a new creation.
> Accept the offerings of your people
> (and of those born again in baptism)
> and bring us to eternal happiness.[17]

During Easter we meditate on what it means to be that new creation—to live paschal faith. Through baptism we died to sin and have been resurrected to new life. There are implications. Christian living brings hardships and trials. Today's reading from the first letter to Peter alludes to it. Paschal faith requires that we believe in Christ simply on his word and invitation. Paschal faith demands that we confess that faith, even if it leads to the cross—*especially* if it leads to the cross. Paschal faith also demands that we lay down our lives for one another. Neophytes (as well as the faithful) are to be strengthened by the eucharist they celebrate and they, in turn, are to become the eucharist they receive.

Thus, the period of mystagogy necessarily includes meditation on the Easter gospels and living the charity demanded by the gospel. Easter is the time for the neophyte and the faithful to celebrate the saving deeds of God in the midst of the Christian community. How has God called our community to transformative faith and life? Easter is the time to witness to God's marvelous deeds. How are we telling our corporate and personal stories of death and resurrection?

The Easter sacraments, especially the eucharist, are the way in which we fully participate in Jesus' paschal mystery. Jesus appears to his disciples on the first day of the week. It is the day on which Christians gather to experience Jesus in the eucharist—both his real presence and his concealed presence. John's community was struggling with what it meant to live as Easter people in the reality of Christ's non-imminent return. They, too, celebrated the presence of Jesus in the eucharist: not only bread eucharist, but the eucharist of service (foot washing). Just as Christ beckoned Thomas to embrace a committed faith, eucharist is our similar invitation. "May the Easter sacraments we have received live forever in our minds and hearts" (Prayer After Communion). Jesus is both hidden and present in the eucharist. Like Thomas, we are called to choose. When we fully commit, we are

[16]Second Sunday of Easter: "Opening Prayer," *The Sacramentary.*

[17]Second Sunday of Easter: "Prayer Over the Gifts," *The Sacramentary.*

able to come before Christ in the eucharist and profess, "My Lord and My God!" Eucharist strengthens our doubting faith and helps us believe without seeing.

Gospel Exegesis

The facilitator gives input regarding what critical biblical scholarship has to say about this text. The input includes insights as to how people would have heard the gospel in Jesus' time.

Today's two post-resurrection appearances of Jesus are read every year throughout all three cycles. Jesus offers his peace, faith, the gift of the Holy Spirit, and a lasting legacy of his merciful forgiveness. He appears first on Easter night, and then a week later. Luke did not relate Jesus' resurrection, ascension, and Pentecost as a one-time event. He extended it over a period of time in order to lead and guide his community to a deeper faith. John's portrayal is probably more accurate: Jesus bestowed the Spirit and commissioned his disciples on the same day. According to Charles Talbert, one purpose of this resurrection account is to show that Jesus is alive and to offer further instructions to the disciples.[18]

A few verses before this pericope, Jesus encountered Mary Magdalene standing beside the tomb. She did not recognize him at first glance. We are led to understand that something has changed; Jesus is different. "In his new identity, Jesus is no longer subject to the constraints of space and time."[19] Today's gospel continues to portray Jesus in his new, altered state. He appears in the midst of the Twelve. There is no question that it is Jesus; he identifies himself by showing his hands and his side. His body is still real, though changed. Mary Magdalene in earlier verses was told not to touch him. Jesus passed through his shroud and through doors, but he could still be seen with the human eye. Talbert asserts that Jesus continues in his incarnation even after the resurrection, albeit in a different corporeal form.[20] "The incarnation did not cease with the cross and the tomb; it continues even now in transcendental glory."[21]

[18]*RJ*, 253.
[19]*JGNP*, 71.
[20]*RJ*, 253.
[21]*TI*, 382.

Jesus first greets the disciples with peace (he offers it twice). He then offers them the gift of his Spirit; he commissions them and sends them out to forgive sins. The commission to forgive sins has its implications in the Christian community. Charles Talbert suggests that the forgiveness of sins implies that if disciples forgive the sins of other disciples against them, the community will remain intact. If those sins are not forgiven, then community peace and harmony will be disrupted.[22] The Holy Spirit is therefore given in order to help Christians live the peace Christ bestowed upon them and to empower them for their mission to the world. (Later theologians used the forgiveness text as the primary source for the church's understanding of the sacrament of penance or reconciliation.) The power to forgive one another will be given by the Holy Spirit.

In the same gospel, Jesus appears again, eight days later. This time Thomas is present. Jesus miraculously materializes through the doors. Thomas was given the opportunity to touch Jesus' wounds so he would believe. Thomas needed to be assured that the appearance was indeed the human Jesus he knew.

Thomas's scene is regarded by some scholars as the culminating scene of John's entire gospel. It brings closure and satisfaction. John began his gospel by stating the purpose for its writing: to proclaim Jesus, the incarnate Word of God. All the events of the gospel lead to this point. Thomas, upon seeing Jesus' wounds, acclaims him Lord and God. "Jesus is described as being of the essence of God at the outset of the Gospel, and then, fully twenty chapters later, one of his disciples comes to believe in him fully and affirms him loftily as 'my Lord and my God.'"[23] The last phrase of this gospel is the summary of the purpose of the work: 1. that people may believe in him, and 2. that they may have life.

John strongly connects belief with eternal life. "Yet the consequence of believing is itself of extreme importance for John; this consequence is that his readers have eternal life. The one purpose thus involves the other, for to have eternal life cannot be separated from believing."[24]

[22]*RJ*, 255.
[23]*JGNP*, 72.
[24]Ibid.

Jesus' greeting of peace is significant. Israel believed that the advent of the messianic era would be accompanied by the reign of peace, evidenced by people living in reciprocal covenant relationship with God and one another. Jesus manifested his messianic reign by offering the Holy Spirit to accomplish and realize harmony and peace among God's people. Thus, Jesus' salutation—"Peace!"—functioned as realized eschatology. That is, the promised, future reign of God was at hand in the presence of the Holy Spirit of God. The Spirit who was manifest, dynamic, and active in all of God's acts of salvation is the Spirit offered to the disciples on the day of this gospel event. The same Spirit who presided over the stirring waters at creation is the same Spirit who goes with the disciples in their work of healing the sick, forgiving sins, and announcing the messianic reign of God.

John's agenda was to connect the human Jesus with the divine Jesus. He wanted his readers to fully realize that the Jesus who walked the earth was the Jesus who reigned prior to his earthly life in union with his Father and the Spirit. Plagued by the influence of gnosticism, some in the Johannine church preferred to center on Jesus, the divine-man, wonder-worker, to the exclusion of Jesus, the crucified Lord who was raised and glorified. John's Jesus shows his wounds to Thomas in order to remind the community that Jesus' exalted status has its roots in his humiliating death.

The post-resurrection appearances also serve to strengthen the community in the Lord's absence until he returns in glory for a second time. Jesus' healing and forgiving mission will continue until he comes again.

Today's gospel also stresses the journey of faith. Thomas reminds us that doubt sometimes is a precursor of committed faith. Thomas struggled, and in his struggle he embraced a deeper, lasting faith. He did not come to belief because he touched the Lord's wounds. Faith was prompted by Jesus' invitation.

Easter reminds us to persevere in our faith in the Risen One, even though we have not put our hands into his wounds. Today's gospel is a challenge to live in the presence of the abiding Spirit, to forgive one another and to promote the reign of God.

Proclaim the gospel again.

Sometimes we gain new insights when we hear the text after the interpretation has been given. Someone from the group proclaims the gospel a second time.

Step 4
Testing

Conversation with the Liturgy and the Scriptures

Test your original understanding in dialogue with the text.

(You might consider breaking into smaller groups.)

Now that you've heard what the scholars have to say about this passage, how do you feel about it? How does your original understanding of this gospel compare with what we just shared? Were there any new insights for you? How does this story speak to your life?

Sharing Life Experience

Participants share an experience from their lives that connects with the biblical interpretation just shared.

> *Today's Easter readings shout to us about life in the community. We are to forgive one another. We are to preserve unity. The greatest disgrace in the early Christian community as far as Paul and Luke were concerned was disharmony. Luke insisted that living the paschal life in the midst of the community is witness to the world. Radical Christian behavior calls attention to itself. The world notices when people behave as if they are gathered in Jesus' name. I often dream of a church in which unity is the charism most observed and admired by the outside world. Lack of unity in the church is scandalous.*
>
> *I recently received a call from an out-of-state friend who was very depressed because of the tremendous discord in her parish. The community is divided by animosities, stubborn pride, and the lack of respect for one another. When I hear stories like that I thank God for my parish community. We are not perfect. We have had our days of struggle in the past, but there is an incredible sense of love and respect for*

each other in our faith community. The first thing people notice when they come to the parish is the warmth and hospitality of our members. We are as diverse as any parish, yet there seems to be a place for everyone. One of my pastor's greatest gifts is his ability to meet people where they are and to encourage honest, forthright communication and dialogue. He has fostered an atmosphere of common ground; consequently we do not seem to be pulled apart by destroying factions within the community.

Jesus asked his father that we might all be one. When I invite discord through gossip; when I approach everything that happens in our parish with a suspicious eye (much like the doubting Thomas); and when I shut myself off to the movement of the Spirit in my community (in often the most surprising places), I tear down rather than build up the people of God. Jesus extended peace and forgiveness. When I let the sun go down on my anger, hurts, and jealousies, I give fertile ground to the destructive forces that divide us.

The Easter paschal life demands that we die and rise. It insists that we profess our faith like the Easter women of the gospels and pray that our doubting, contrary spirits be challenged. Jesus extended peace and forgiveness. I must extend it not only to my parish community, but to my family community as well. When I am in right relationship with my God and living the peace envisioned at the creation of the world, then I will love God with my whole heart. I am to love my neighbor as much as I love myself. There will be evidence of that love by the way I live and minister to the world community. Do I build up or tear down? Do I reach out to the poor, the oppressed, and the marginalized? Today's liturgy demands that I offer shalom peace not only to the communities in which I live, but to the global community as well. It is because of the cross and resurrection that I am so empowered.

All share their life experience.

What was John's message to his community? How does it relate to your community and to you today? Whom do you relate to the most in today's gospel? What are the times in your life when you are most like Thomas—Mary Magdalene—the women of the gospels—the apostles—Jesus? How might today's liturgy invite re-creation within yourself and your community (biblical theme of creation)? In what way does today's liturgy express our covenant with God? What are the implications of that covenant? In what way does today's liturgy speak to your community specifically? How does today's liturgy speak to the wider world community? In what way do today's readings invite us to embrace the paschal mystery? What new insight do you take with you as a result of your sharing?

Step 5
Decision

The gospel demands a response.

In what way do today's scriptures invite transformation in your life? How might your parish be invited to respond to today's liturgy? Have any of your attitudes or your thinking been challenged as a result of your reflection on the exegesis for today's readings? How are you specifically and personally invited to respond to today's readings?

Pastoral Considerations: In many parishes the Easter season unfortunately ends on the second Sunday of Easter. There are fifty days of feasting in the Easter season. How is your parish feasting? We need to remind ourselves that the *entire season is Easter.* That is why the Sundays of the season are called the Sundays of Easter—not the Sundays after Easter. Are there opportunities offered in your parish for sharing Easter faith? What are the stories of death and resurrection in your community in the past year? Is there any forum for sharing those stories? Have your outreach efforts subsided simply because the season of prayer, fasting, and almsgiving has ended? What are the ongoing structures in your community that promote the *peace* Jesus demands in today's gospel?

Christian Initiation: The liturgy of mystagogia is the Sunday eucharist. The purpose of the Easter season homilies is to crack open the mystery of Easter and the paschal mystery for the entire community. We are *all* to be engaged in mystagogical reflection—not just the neophytes. The neophytes meet weekly until Pentecost to break open the symbols of the vigil. Thereafter they meet monthly until the anniversary of their initiation. Neophytes continue to be a symbol of Easter life in our midst. Are they included in the prayers of the faithful? Perhaps throughout the Easter season they might wear their baptismal gown and carry their baptismal candle in procession. A special place could be reserved for them in the assembly. What opportunities do you offer them to witness to their faith? Perhaps they might dress the altar and process with the bread and wine, the offering, and the gifts for the poor. Also, all who celebrated a sacrament of initiation this year (first communion, confirmation, baptism) might carry their baptismal candle or wear their baptismal garment during mass. (The white communion dress has its roots in the baptismal garment. First communicants are of course not "brides of Christ.")

DOCTRINAL ISSUES

What church truth/teaching/doctrinal issue could be drawn from the gospel for the Second Sunday of Easter?

Participants suggest possible doctrinal themes that flow from the readings.

Possible Doctrinal Themes

Paschal mystery, baptism, confirmation, eucharist, sacraments, reconciliation, ecclesiology, symbols: water, light, oil, garment, bread, wine, cross, community.

Present the doctrinal material at this time.

1. The facilitator gives input on a particular doctrinal issue of his/her prior choosing. OR
2. The group chooses a doctrinal issue from the list they created. They read together from the Doctrinal Appendix.

(The doctrinal issues are found in the Doctrinal Appendix in the back of this workbook. If you are choosing an issue from this resource, please refer to it now.)

Reflection questions centered around the chosen doctrinal theme can be found at the end of each topic in the Doctrinal Appendix. The questions are based on the five-step reflection process. If you choose a topic not included in the Doctrinal Appendix, craft your own questions according to the same five-step process.

Following the reflection questions you will be reminded to return to chapter 7, "Preparing the Catechetical Session," to assist you in crafting your own session.

Closing Prayer

Let us pray
[as Christians thirsting for the risen life]
Heavenly Father and God of mercy,
we no longer look for Jesus among the dead,
for he is alive and has become the Lord of life.
From the waters of death you raise us with him
and renew your gift of life within us.
Increase in our minds and hearts
the risen life we share with Christ
and help us to grow as your people
toward the fullness of eternal life with you.
Grant this through Christ our Lord.[25]

[25]Second Sunday of Easter: "Alternative Opening Prayer," *The Sacramentary.*

Third Sunday of Easter

Environment

Refer to Easter Sunday.

INTRODUCTORY RITES

Opening Song (or Entrance Antiphon)

Let all the earth cry out to God with joy; praise the glory of his name; proclaim his glorious praise, alleluia. (Ps 66:1–2)[1]

Opening Prayer

The facilitator of the session may lead the prayer. Others in the group may be asked to proclaim the readings.

Let us pray
[in confident peace and Easter hope]

Father in heaven, author of all truth,
a people once in darkness has listened to your Word
and followed your Son as he rose from the tomb.
Hear the prayer of this newborn people
and strengthen your church to answer your call.
May we rise and come forth into the light of day
to stand in your presence until eternity dawns.
We ask this through Christ our Lord.[2]

LITURGY OF THE WORD

The readings are proclaimed.

First Reading
Acts 2:14, 22–28

(Refer to Easter Sunday for an overview of the Acts of the Apostles.) It is Pentecost and, with the boldness of the Spirit, Peter proclaimed the first missionary discourse (the good news of Christ's death and resurrection) to the gathered crowd. Peter, the Lord's appointed, stood before the crowds in Jerusalem; he preached Christ's salvific passover from death to life and heralded Jesus' life and mission. He quoted the great David,[3] the one whose dynasty would last forever, to help prove that Jesus *was* who they said he was—the *Faithful One* referred to in the psalm text. Jesus, he told them, was the long-awaited Messiah. Peter did in that Pentecost sermon what Jesus did with the disciples on the road to Emmaus. He used the scriptures to shed light on God's saving plan that was unfolding in their midst.

Peter lays blame at the feet of Israel for the death of Jesus. He held the Jews responsible. "The declaration of Jewish guilt is the mainstay of the missionary sermons to the Jews."[4] It is used to motivate the hearers of the Christian kerygma [message] to repentance and conversion.

Jesus conquered death; that is our faith—it is what we celebrate in every liturgy. But what does that really mean? In the New Testament, death was understood as the end of a person's relationship to others as well as to God. Understood in a theological sense, death was the definitive separation from God "as a result of rebellion and consequent alienation."[5] Jesus submitted to death's reality in obedience to God's will, thereby overcoming his separation from God.

Death could not hold Jesus because of his divinity and his oneness with God. Jesus, though divine, did not possess an "unfair advantage over us."[6] He conquered death, but certainly not in the biological sense. Like every human being he was subject to the same fate. But for Jesus his death did not end in death. Christ suffered, died, and rose from the dead. He was triumphant over the power of death [sin and the end of relationships]. Through

---

[1]Third Sunday of Easter: "Entrance Antiphon," *The Sacramentary.*

[2]Third Sunday of Easter: "Opening Prayer," *The Sacramentary.*

[3]Jewish tradition believed that David was the author of the psalms.

[4]Richard J. Dillon, "Acts of the Apostles," *NJBC,* 733.

[5]*PL,* 77.

[6]Ibid., 76.

the cross Jesus overcame death. Jesus' death was victory over human alienation and separation from God.

Questions for mystagogical reflection: *How is Peter's message to the crowds relevant for your life today? What does it mean to you that Jesus was triumphant over death? How do you reconcile that when you face the death of a loved one? If death was understood as the end of one's relationship with others and with God, what are the implications of that for your life, since Jesus has conquered death?*

Responsorial Psalm
Psalm 16:1–2, 5, 7–8, 9–10, 11

It is no wonder that the psalm chosen for today's liturgy is the psalm that is quoted in Peter's sermon. In the Old Testament this psalm was probably used as prayer of thanks for being rescued from the jaws of death and did not express hope in life after death. Christians appropriated the psalm as a reference to the Jesus event and plumbed its depths in light of the paschal mystery.

Second Reading
1 Peter 1:17–21

(Refer to Overview of 1 Peter, Second Sunday of Easter.)
1 Peter draws close parallels and connections between baptism and the paschal mystery. We were ransomed by the blood of Christ. Baptism is immersion in that reality. We are baptized into his death. 1 Peter clearly connects the death and resurrection of Jesus with the Passover. Through the death of Jesus we are liberated. Jesus ransomed us with his blood; he completely gave his life and his will over to God. It is the surrender of Jesus that made us heirs to the salvation he won through his death.

The human response of faith to such a gratuitous gift is to live the moral life. We conform our lives to Christ and our behavior reflects our relationship with him. Prior to our relationship with Christ we were without purpose and hope. Christ now strengthens us through his death and resurrection. He offers us eternal life as his legacy. Christ the new Passover Lamb freed us from the power and slavery of sin. We too pass over into a new creation of God. Isaiah prophesied that humanity would be redeemed by the sacrifice of the Servant who, like a lamb, was led to the slaughter. Peter affirms that the prophecies in regard to Jesus have been fulfilled now—not in some future time. Christians are heirs to the benefits of Christ's sacrifice. Now is the acceptable time, now is the day of salvation. It was prophesied that the Messiah would come to gather all the nations to himself in the final age. Christ's death inaugurated the final age. Christians then and now live in the tension of the reign of God *now* and *yet to come.* Thus our Christian response is to be attentive to our relationship with Christ as we await the final glory. Our lives will reflect that relationship.

Questions for mystagogical reflection: *How does the liberation won by the death of Christ speak to your everyday life? What is your response as a Christian to this liberation? What would it cost you to surrender to God as Jesus surrendered to God? In what way have you been made a new creation in Christ? What is the evidence in your life? What are the implications of your baptism in light of this reading?*

Gospel
Luke 24:13–35

STEP 1
NAMING ONE'S EXPERIENCE

What were your first impressions? What was your first response to the gospel and/or other readings? What captured your attention?

Each person names his or her initial impression. Statements should be brief. No reasons should be given at this time. All simply listen without agreeing or disagreeing.

STEP 2
UNDERSTANDING

In a brief statement, what do you think this gospel is trying to convey?

STEP 3
INPUT FROM VISION/STORY/TRADITION

Liturgical Context[7]

It is worthy of note that Luke uses the entire twenty-fourth chapter to uncover, break open, and shed light on the mystery of Jesus' passion, death, and resurrection. Luke's agenda is the agenda of the entire church during the Easter season. Each year the church takes time out during the Easter season to reflect on the paschal mystery—to engage in mystagogical reflection. The homilies of the Easter season are intended to crack open that mystery and help the faithful to reflect on their own experiences of death and resurrection in light of the Jesus event.

By sharing the story of Christ and interpreting it in light of the scriptures, by inviting the stranger into their home and sharing their meals, the disciples' eyes were opened. They were transformed. Luke sets forth a pattern of conversion for all of us. We experience the Emmaus mystery every time we gather for eucharist.

The episode on the road to Emmaus provides the church with a model for what takes place in the catechumenate and in many small Christian communities. Questions are asked, hospitality is extended, stories are told, scripture and tradition are shared and interpreted. Discussion and dialogue invite conversion and transformation. The life of Christ as it is celebrated and proclaimed throughout the liturgical year is the basis for the primary formation of catechumens. The lesson of Emmaus is important in their formation, for it is through dialogue and reflection on that word, and making it operative in their lives, that the catechumens' hearts are opened to recognize and encounter Christ in the breaking of the bread at Easter.

Luke presented the church with a foundational understanding of the eucharist. The eucharist is intimately connected with the paschal mystery of Christ. Eucharist is a remembering, an anamnesis, that brings the passion event into the present and makes it real. "It [the liturgy] is concerned with past events, the saving work of Christ, but it is not concerned with them *as past.* It seeks to bring about an encounter between the worshipers and the saving mystery. If an event is to be experienced, it has to be experienced *as present.*"[8] When preaching an Ascension homily, St. Leo the Great avowed that Christ's visible suffering and death have become manifest in the sacraments. Our sacraments remember and make present Jesus' life, mission, death, resurrection, ascension into glory, and the sending of the Spirit to the church. Why? So the church of every generation might meet and encounter the Risen Christ as they worship. "By the liturgical mystery we are actualizing the past event, making it present so that the saving power of Christ can be made available to the worshiper in the here and now."[9]

Today's pericope cleverly shows us the intimate connection between the liturgy of the word and the liturgy of the eucharist. On the road to Emmaus the word prepared the hearts of the disciples to recognize Jesus in the breaking of the bread. "Word and sacrament are not only not mutually exclusive, they are in fact complementary. Augustine's adage still holds: *accedit verbum ad elementum et fit sacramentum* (the word is spoken upon the human reality and it becomes a sacrament)" (*In Joann. Ev.* Tr. 80, 3).[10] The word proclaimed in liturgy is Christ himself who speaks to us (*Constitution on the Sacred Liturgy,* #10). His self-gift opens our hearts and our eyes to encounter him in the eucharist.

Jesus opened the eyes of his disciples when he shared the scriptures with them. They were no longer blind but recognized the light. The Alternative Opening Prayer for today's liturgy affirms those who were once in darkness, but because they listened to the Word they followed Christ as

[7]The scriptures in the Lectionary, the seasons of the year, and the ritual prayers of the mass are interrelated and form the basis for liturgical catechesis. The *liturgical context* attempts to explore and clarify the themes and this interrelatedness.

[8]J. D. Chrighton, "A Theology of Worship," *SL,* 14.

[9]Ibid., 15.

[10]Kathleen Cannon, O.P., "Theology of the Word," *NDSW,* 1330.

he rose from the tomb. The *Word* [Christ] strengthens and empowers Christians to stand firm in the faith and be faithful to God's call. We will then share in the joy of the resurrection that is ours because God has made us his sons and daughters (Opening Prayer). It is our Easter faith.

The center of today's liturgy is the paschal mystery. It is the central reality of every liturgy, every sacrament—particularly of the Easter season. The gospel portrays disciples who lost all hope in the mission of Christ. Jesus appeared to them in his risen state but they were unable to recognize him until he took the bread, blessed it, broke it, and gave it to them. Those ritual actions took them back in time and transported their remembering into the present. They bore the imprint of their Master. The sacrifice of Calvary was an integral part of the remembering. We participate in the mystery of Easter every time we take, bless, break, and share the Body of Christ. We then are taken, blessed, broken, shared, and poured out for the world, just as Jesus was and continues to be in his living memorial. Today's liturgy offers consolation to those who have lost all hope, who have forgotten the touch of the Master's hand, and have given up on life. It is often difficult to believe in the promises of God when our lives are besieged by pain, sorrow, and disappointment. The disciples on the road to Emmaus are a sign of hope for us. When all seems lost and our dreams are dashed, the Good Shepherd is there to give us the gift of himself and to offer us Easter joy.

This is the *One* of whom we speak today:

> Let me tell you how I came to know him.
> I had heard many speak of him, but had paid no attention.
> Each day he sent me presents, and I never thanked him.
> Often he seemed to want my friendship, but I ignored him.
> I was homeless and miserable and hungry;
> every moment I was in peril:
> he offered me shelter, comfort, food; he guarded me from all danger:
> but I was always ungrateful.
> Finally he met me on the road, and with tears in his eyes,
> he entreated me, saying, "Come and dwell with me."
> Let me tell you how he treats me now:
> He provides all my needs,
> He gives me more than I dare ask;
> He anticipates all my desires,
> He urges me to ask for more;
> He never reminds me of my past ingratitude.
> Never does he reproach me for my past foolishness...
> Let me tell you what I think of him:
> He is as good as he is great,
> He loves me with a love both ardent and true,
> He is as bounteous with promises as faithful to keeping them;
> He is as jealous of my affection as worthy of retaining it.
> In everything, I am his debtor, but he wants me to call him "My Friend."[11]

Today's liturgy invites us to see Christ as "Friend"—the One who loved us *unto death*. He is the One who gives us the precious gift of his life. We are to see Jesus with Easter eyes of faith and conform our lives to his as we become immersed in his paschal life. "May we rise and come forth into the light of day to stand in your presence until eternity dawns (Alternative Opening Prayer)."

Gospel Exegesis

The facilitator gives input regarding what critical biblical scholarship has to say about this text. The input includes insights as to how people would have heard the gospel in Jesus' time.

Imagine the scene. The two disciples are on their way from Jerusalem to Emmaus. Depressed, disappointed, and almost to the point of despair they meet a stranger on the way. We know it is Jesus, but they do not. Luke artfully leads us into the mystery of Jesus' new mode of presence after the resurrection. He is changed. He can carry on a conversation with his most intimate friends and yet they do not recognize him. "He can really appear in the guise of a stranger on the road in the midst of human dialogue; he can be recognized in

[11] R.H. Benson, *L'Amité de Je'sus Christ* (Paris: Perrin, 1923), XI–XII, in *DL* (III), 137.

the ritual gestures of the community fellowship meal."[12]

Luke's intention in the twenty-fourth chapter is to smoothly transition the reader from the Jesus story to the story of his witnesses.[13] This simple straightforward story serves one of Luke's broader purposes. When Jesus explained the scriptures to the disciples, he was showing the church how to interpret the prophecies of the Hebrew scriptures. When people tell the story to others, they also interpret the events. The promised messiah of the scriptures was none other than Jesus Christ. Like the prophets of old, Jesus was sent by God and then rejected.

There are four scenes in the chapter: the empty tomb, today' story of the disciples on the road to Emmaus, Jesus' appearance in Jerusalem, and Jesus' departure. A common thread weaving all the scenes together is the recalling of Jesus' recent death and resurrection. The chapter functions as a commentary on the significance of Jesus' paschal mystery.

The following commentary[14] helps us crack open the riches of Luke's twenty-fourth chapter. Luke emphasizes the same themes stressed by Jesus—themes that the disciples simply failed to understand. They could not comprehend when Jesus spoke of the passion and death he would endure. Luke recalls the prophecies made by Jesus to his disciples while he was on earth; Jesus had foretold his death and resurrection. Even when the disciples were told about Jesus' resurrection, they still did not understand the implications of it. There were no flashing beams of insight; they remained bewildered. "The solution requires more than the appearance of the risen Jesus. Changing the disciples' perceptions involves a rather lengthy process which covers the whole of Luke 24. Only an issue of urgency and importance deserves the amount of attention given in Luke 24 to the revelation to the disciples of the necessity of Jesus' suffering and resurrection."[15]

[12]Luke T. Johnson, *GL*, 398.

[13]*NULA* (I), 277.

[14]The primary source for the commentary on the gospel is based on the work of Robert Tannehill in *NULA* (I).

[15]Ibid., 278.

The women were chastised by the angel: Why did you look for the living among the dead? When Jesus was with them in Galilee he told them that he would die and then rise again from the dead. How could they have forgotten? The empty tomb should not have come as a surprise. Jesus' prophecy came to pass. Yet in spite of the messenger's revelation, the disciples still did not believe the women who came bearing news of their encounter with the angel. In the scripture verses prior to today's pericope, Peter ran to the tomb to check out the situation for himself. Luke tells his readers that Peter was astonished. His *astonishment,* however, was not to be confused with faith. The word used for *astonished* was often used in the scriptures when referring to persons who were amazed at the unfolding events before them but did not understand, and who sometimes opposed Jesus and his mission.[16]

The same word [astonished] is used in today's gospel when the disciples on the road to Emmaus told Jesus what the women had related to them. They still did not understand what had taken place. Jesus led the disciples into the light of faith and taught them the meaning of the paschal mystery.

A pivotal piece of the conversation on the road centered around scripture's messianic prophecy. Scripture foretold a suffering messiah.[17] It was imperative that the disciples understand the implications of Jesus' death. What did it mean? What was God doing in Christ?

Jesus seized the "teachable moment." He entered into mystagogical reflection with his disciples. They expressed (named) their understanding of the events of recent days and Jesus shed light on their understanding by explaining the scriptures to them. Jesus taught them the meaning behind his death and resurrection.

In their conversation with Jesus, the disciples bemoaned their dashed hopes and what they believed to be the hope of Israel. The disciples had lost hope in the mission Jesus proclaimed; those hopes had ended with his death. They were blinded by tunnel vision. They could not see the

[16]Ibid., 279.

[17]Ibid.

victory of the cross on the other side. They were blind to the reason for Jesus' suffering and death. Even though Jesus tried to prepare them while on earth, they did not expect his death. God's plan through Christ was a far cry from what they had envisioned. The disciples' plans for the *new kingdom* were dashed. The cross was an absurdity. "God's power resides in weakness?" "What kind of a king reigns from a throne of lowliness, rather than might?" Today's story invites the reader to explore those questions.

The disciples continued to tell Jesus about the events in Jerusalem. They still did not recognize him. Seeing the risen Christ was crucial, but seeing alone was not enough. It was imperative that they understand, God's prophesied plan of salvation through the spurned and glorified Messiah. "It was their inability to accept the passion that prevented their eyes from recognizing Jesus."[18] The empty tomb and the appearance of the angel did nothing to alleviate their despair. Only the appearance of the risen Christ and his explanation of the paschal experience would make the difference.

Luke's brilliant use of irony serves to punctuate the theme of this chapter. There is a giant chasm between human understanding and what God was doing in the passion, death, and resurrection of Jesus. Luke uses irony to emphasize human blindness. The disciples do not recognize that they are trying to inform Jesus about Jesus. They rebuke Jesus for his ignorance (v. 18), when *they* are the ones who do not understand! They try to explain to Jesus at some length what he knows better than they. We as readers know that the stranger is Jesus. We watch the disciples making their mistake and thereby come to know how human blindness appears, viewed from beyond it.

The ultimate purpose of Luke 24 is to announce that Jesus' suffering, death, and resurrection were necessary for Jesus to *enter into glory with his Father.* It was also God's plan for the salvation of the world as revealed in the scriptures. *Entrance into glory with the Father* required that Jesus *pass over* into his new, exalted state. In order for Jesus to *pass over,* he had to endure the cross. It is important to note that while Jesus was the fulfillment of God's plan as foretold through the prophets, nowhere in Luke/Acts are we told that it is for the atonement for sin. Readers are left with the question: "Why is the death of Jesus an integral and necessary part of God's saving purpose?"[19]

There are two possible ways to respond to the above question. First, Jesus had to suffer and die; his death was foretold in the scriptures. If it was in scripture, then so be it. It was not up to the disciples to question. They were simply to accept it. It did not have to make sense to human reasoning. God's purposes are not subject to human approval or control. The disciples thought they knew the mind of God. They were on his side and thought they were "privy to the script." Although they were thrown off their proverbial horses, the scales did not drop quickly from their eyes; blindness remained for a while longer. They thought their savior was a failure. Luke uses the exchange between Jesus and the disciples to invite a transformed understanding of who God is and how God acts. It was not his intent to give the disciples a theological explanation of Jesus' death. If scripture proclaimed it, that was enough.

A second answer to the question as to why Jesus' death was necessary has its roots in scripture and human history. Human beings are capable of insight into the way God works in human history. Humanity is capable of plumbing the depths of Jesus' life and mission. God was always active in human history. In today's story, Jesus referred to Moses and all the prophets. He recalled the history of a people and of their biblical giants. The prophets who went before Jesus preached God's saving action in human history. Moses, the liberator of his people, was rejected, but God nevertheless made him the deliverer of the people. However, the fate of prophets in scripture was to endure misunderstanding, rejection, and death, always with the assurance of God's favor. (This is particularly evident in the Moses/Elijah tradition in which both were taken up into heaven.) In Luke's gospel Jesus was understood as Prophet and Messiah (13:33–34). The disciples in today's story referred to him as prophet. Jesus, the long-awaited Messiah and Mosaic prophet, like the

[18]Eugene LaVerdiere, *DKG,* 166.

[19]Ibid., 285.

prophets of old, was vindicated by God and raised to glory. This makes the appearance of Moses and Elijah at Jesus' transfiguration quite appropriate. They "prepare Jesus for his 'exodus.'"[20]

We are to glean important insight from Luke's masterful use of irony. The disciples understood Jesus' death to be a result of God's rejection of him, as well as a rejection of God's plan that was to be accomplished through him. The irony? The death of Christ is the very means by which God's plan was accomplished. It is the great parable of God. Human expectations and assumptions were overturned; there is an invitation to embrace a new reality.

In the gospel we are told that "it is necessary" that Jesus suffer. Why was it necessary? "... God's purpose must be realized in a recalcitrant world. By not annihilating the world or robbing it of its power of decision and action, God lays upon God's servants the harsh destiny of suffering."[21] The world will not easily submit to the will of God. As a result, Jesus must follow in the pattern of all the prophets (such as Moses) who went before him. He must fulfill his prophetic destiny. Prophets proclaimed the word of God. They denounced sin and evil in the world. Their prophetic ministry ultimately led to rejection and death. It was the destiny of prophets, and Jesus was a prophet. Luke portrays Jesus as a martyr, and in so doing places his death in the context of his prophetic mission. Those who were to follow in his footsteps and proclaim the gospel would endure a similar fate. Luke seems to suggest that Jesus opened the eyes of his disciples by helping them comprehend the sacred pattern of prophetic destiny. Comprehending prophetic destiny, in turn, was the key to understanding Jesus and the scriptures that revealed him.

The dialogue over, the day drawing to a close, Jesus acts as if he is going to leave the disciples and be on his way. But we know that he will not leave them. He is the Good Shepherd that does not abandon his flock.

The disciples invited the stranger to eat with them. They offered him hospitality, so Jesus stayed with them. In Luke's gospel, the word *stay* refers to "making one's home with others and dwelling with them."[22] Hospitality was very important to Luke. He believed that the hallmark of the Christian community was hospitality. Christians were to extend gracious hospitality and make their homes with one another. Hospitality throughout scripture was always connected to sharing a meal—breaking bread together.

The disciples may have invited the stranger to dinner, but Jesus ends up as the host. It is Jesus who takes the bread, blesses it, breaks it, and gives it to his friends. The guest became the host. We are led to understand that the meal was not a typical one, but that it was special because they reclined at the table. Reclining at table was a position assumed at formal meals.

Jesus' exegesis of scripture prepared the disciples' hearts to recognize him. It was in the liturgical action of taking, blessing, breaking, and sharing the bread that the disciples recognized Jesus. He assumed a role that was familiar to them. There were two previous meals that were shared in similar fashion—the Last Supper, and the feeding of the multitudes. Jesus' four-fold ritual action was significant; it was intended to recall to them similar actions on previous occasions. The ritual action prompted their remembering. Remembering was very important for the Christian community. Remembering the past effectively brought it into the present and applied it to the future. It is the kind of remembering that we do at every liturgy. We remember the story of what Jesus did; we pray the same blessing and perform the same ritual gestures. In our active remembering we make present the reality of what Jesus did with his disciples.

With new eyes to see and understand Jesus' passion, with the experience of remembering their Master and recognizing him in the breaking of the bread, the disciples returned to Jerusalem to report to their friends what they had experienced. No longer depressed, they returned rejoicing. They returned to news of a similar visitation Jesus made to Peter.

Proclaim the gospel again.

[20]Ibid., 287.

[21]Ibid., 288.

[22]Ibid., 168.

Sometimes we gain new insights when we hear the text after the interpretation has been given. Someone from the group proclaims the gospel a second time.

Step 4
Testing

Conversation with the Liturgy and the Scriptures

Test your original understanding in dialogue with the text.

(You might consider breaking into smaller groups.)

Were there any new insights in the readings from today's liturgy? What are the central themes of this gospel? How do they relate to your life? What does it mean that Jesus fulfilled his prophetic destiny? What does that have to do with your life today? What does today's gospel teach us about liturgy and its implications? What are the implications of Jesus' meal with his disciples? What is Luke trying to teach his readers about the Christ event? Have you ever experienced depression and disappointment similar to that of the disciples? How does the paschal mystery speak to that experience? Has your original understanding of these readings been stretched in any way? How does this story speak to your life?

Sharing Life Experience

Participants share an experience from their lives that connects with the biblical interpretation just shared.

> *I know I have spoken of this situation often, but right now our community is immersed in its sorrow. There is a young family in our parish that is experiencing the affliction of a lifetime. We all want to scream to the heavens, "Where are you God?" "Why don't you do something, God?" We ask ourselves: How can this be? How could a God of love permit the suffering of this innocent baby? Could this be God's will? How could God will the death of this infant? Is that what is meant in the Holy Thursday psalm (116): "Precious in the eyes of the Lord is the death of his faithful ones"? Why is our death precious? Jesus healed people and restored them to life. He hated sickness and death.*

This young couple is losing their infant, their only child, to a rare genetic disease. There are only a handful of known cases in this country. When today's scripture reminds us that Jesus conquered death we want to scream, "Well, then, please conquer this one!" There are so many unanswered questions when it comes to suffering like this. Why does God permit this suffering? If God can heal, why are some healed and others are not? The disciples were asking similar questions on that road to Emmaus.

Perhaps our answer lies in the story itself. The disciples followed Jesus and thought they understood his mission. They believed in the God of their limited capacity. They could not understand what Jesus meant when he told them about the suffering he would endure. Of one thing we can be sure—Jesus was not spared from suffering and death. If this suffering young family were the only family on earth, he still would have gone to the cross, just for them.

Our community was recently reflecting on the depths of this tragedy. Whether accurate or not (we can never begin to know or control the mind of God), our reflection led us to some conclusions (albeit tentative). Suffering is a part of life. God is not a puppeteer who stands on the world stage and pulls our strings, saying, "Your turn now." God hates human suffering and death—the gospels attest to that. Someone used the image that suffering is like a hammer suspended in midair. God does not drop the hammer. It is not his will that the hammer come crashing to the ground. But once the hammer drops, God's will becomes manifest and God is present in the midst of the experience.

Even though it is so difficult to see (perhaps only in hindsight will it be possible), there are many ways that God is present and offering his love and consolation to this beautiful young family. They do recognize Jesus in the breaking of the bread; they do recognize his hand in the incredible outpouring of love and support of the community. They are touched by the sorrow and powerlessness we all feel. They have allowed the community to be the love of Christ for them. They acknowledge that Jesus has graced them in so many ways. Their faith and their strength in the midst of this horror stand as a beacon in the darkest night. Yet they still face the anguish of saying goodbye to their dying infant. The hope to which they cling is best expressed in the introduction to the fu-

neral liturgy which says, in effect, that the bonds of love forged in life do not end in death, but continue beyond the grave. Perhaps if we could see the joy that awaits this child of God there would be no more questions. But we cannot. We have the hope of Jesus who was and is present in the breaking of the bread and in the love of the community. Suffering is our lot in life. Jesus died so we would have an advocate who walked in our shoes. We will look back in the years to come and see much good and resurrection out of this tragedy, but for the present, we lament. We are powerless and words fail. What we can *offer is love, a shoulder to cry on, and the laying down of our lives. We cling to the hope that the resurrected Jesus of the Emmaus road is with this young family and loves them from death into life.*

Jesus never promised that we would not suffer mortal death. Lazarus is a sign of that reality for us. He was raised from the dead once—he was resuscitated as a reminder that we will all share in the life Jesus would win for us. But Lazarus would once again be subject to the bitter pangs of biological death. Jesus wept over Lazarus. He weeps with us as we pour out our tears.

All share their life experience.

What was Luke trying to teach his community? What does the Emmaus story have to teach your community and you today? How are the biblical themes of covenant, exodus, creation, and community expressed in the readings today? How has God's promise been made manifest? Where are the themes of liberation to freedom evident? Where is the creative power of God best expressed in the readings and what does it have to teach us? What do the readings teach us about community? Do you still feel the same way about these readings as when you began? Has your original understanding been stretched, challenged, or affirmed?

Step 5
Decision

The gospel demands a response.

How does today's liturgy invite transformation? In what way does your community need to grow in the fullness of today's scriptures? In what concrete ways is your parish called to respond? Have you experienced a change in attitude, outlook, or behavior as a result of today's word? What does this gospel challenge you to do or to become? What one concrete action will you take this week as a response to today's liturgy?

Pastoral Considerations: Hospitality is a key issue in today's gospel. Perhaps this would be a good time to look at that issue in your parish community. In what ways are you an hospitable people? Is everyone in your community invited to the meal? Who are invited but ignored? Who are the outsiders? Who would not get invited? How do you welcome newcomers? Does your Sunday worship reflect a welcoming community? How are children welcomed in your parish? Are they a nuisance to endure, or do they have an honored place at the table? How are the handicapped welcomed? The poor? The marginalized? Is cultural diversity recognized and celebrated or is it something to be endured? Where is transformation needed in your parish? What needs to happen to change that?

Christian Initiation: Mystagogia continues. The neophytes have a visible place in the assembly. They break open the riches of the Easter symbols. They, along with all the faithful, explore the paschal mystery in light of their experience of the sacraments. They put their sacramental life into practice. Catechumens who are still in process continue to be dismissed to reflect on the word of God. Perhaps there are people in the inquiry ready to celebrate a rite of acceptance/welcome and move to the catechumenate. Perhaps there are candidates for full communion ready to be received. The Easter season is a wonderful time to celebrate the initiation sacraments.

DOCTRINAL ISSUES

What church truth/teaching/doctrinal issue could be drawn from the gospel for the Third Sunday of Easter?

Participants suggest possible doctrinal themes that flow from the readings.

Possible Doctrinal Themes
Paschal mystery, eucharist, symbol of bread, word, baptism, hospitality, christology, confirmation, sacraments

Present the doctrinal material at this time.

1. The facilitator gives input on a particular doctrinal issue of his/her prior choosing. OR
2. The group chooses a doctrinal issue from the list they created. They read together from the Doctrinal Appendix.

(The doctrinal issues are found in the Doctrinal Appendix in the back of this workbook. If you are choosing an issue from this resource, please refer to it now.)

Reflection questions centered around the chosen doctrinal theme can be found at the end of each topic in the Doctrinal Appendix. The questions are based on the five-step reflection process. If you choose a topic not included in the Doctrinal Appendix, craft your own questions according to the same five-step process.

Following the reflection questions you will be reminded to return to Chapter 7, "Preparing the Catechetical Session," to assist you in crafting your own session.

Closing Prayer

Deacon: Bow your heads and pray for God's blessing.

Priest: Through the resurrection of his Son,
God has redeemed you and made you his children.
May he bless you with joy.
Response: Amen.

The Redeemer has given you lasting freedom.
May you inherit his everlasting life.
Response: Amen.

By faith you rose with him in baptism.
May your lives be holy,
so that you will be united with him for ever.
Response: Amen.

May almighty God bless you,
the Father, and the Son, and the Holy Spirit.
Response: Amen.[23]

[23]Third Sunday of Easter, "Solemn Blessing or Prayer Over the People," *The Sacramentary.*

Fourth Sunday of Easter

Environment

Perhaps an icon of Christ, the Good Shepherd, might be added to your catechetical space.

INTRODUCTORY RITES

Opening Song (or Entrance Antiphon)

The earth is full of the goodness of the Lord; by the word of the Lord the heavens were made, alleluia. (Ps 32:5–6)[1]

Opening Prayer

The facilitator of the session may lead the prayer. Others in the group may be asked to proclaim the readings.

Let us pray
[to God our helper in time of distress]

God and Father of our Lord Jesus Christ,
though your people walk in the valley of
darkness,
no evil should they fear;
for they follow in faith the call of the shepherd
whom you have sent for their hope and strength.
Attune our minds to the sound of his voice,
lead our steps in the path he has shown,
that we may know the strength of his outstretched
arm
and enjoy the light of your presence for ever.
We ask this in the name of Jesus the Lord.[2]

LITURGY OF THE WORD

The readings are proclaimed.

First Reading
Acts 2:14, 36–41

(Refer to Easter Sunday for an overview of the Acts of the Apostles.) It is still Pentecost. The scene from last week continues with Peter exhorting all of Israel to conversion in Jesus Christ. Peter proclaims the Christian kerygma. The mission of Jesus Christ, now fully inaugurated, must go forward. With full command of the authority given to him by Jesus, Peter professed the living Christ—crucified, risen, and glorified. The Messiah, who was once crucified, rose from the dead and now lives and reigns from his Father's throne. Like many of the crowds in the gospels, the people asked: "What are we to do?"

The first step in conversion is to acknowledge humanity's need for God through repentance and sorrow for sin. Peter was inviting his Jewish audience to understand who Jesus was: the long-awaited One. Jesus Christ, the Messiah and Savior of the world, had indeed arrived. The messianic age had begun. Those who worshiped false gods must reject them and turn to the living Christ. It was the dawn of a new day!

Peter's message was urgent: "Reform your lives and turn to the living Christ." Repentance was not understood just as the turning away from a laundry list of sins. For Peter's crowd it meant a radical reassessment of who Jesus really was—what his significance was. Many of Jesus' contemporaries turned away from him at the crucifixion. He was certainly not God's *Anointed One,* they reasoned. He must have been either crazy or an imposter. They now had to decide—was he who he said he was? Those who accept the kerygma must "reassess him: he is the emissary of God and the bringer of salvation."[3]

Baptism is the gateway for converts to enter into this salvation. Through baptism their sins are forgiven, "which again has a far richer meaning than the remission of individual peccadilloes—it means God's eschatological salvation in its wholeness. And they receive the gift of the Spirit, for baptism 'adds' them to the Spirit-bearing community. . . ."[4]

[1]Fourth Sunday of Easter: "Entrance Antiphon," *The Sacramentary.*

[2]Fourth Sunday of Easter: "Opening Prayer," *The Sacramentary.*

[3]*PL,* 79.

[4]Ibid., 80.

Baptism incorporates us into Christ's life, but we must continually repent, turn our lives to God, and become active participants in the eschatological mission that is our inheritance. Conversion is not a one-time event. It is an ongoing process, a daily struggle. Our responsibility as baptized Christians is to conform our lives to Christ, to seek his will for our lives, and to lay down our lives as Christ laid down his. We must seek the strength to live in the power of the Holy Spirit. We are to claim our identity as forgiven and forgiving people.

Luke reminds his readers of the universality of Jesus' mission: "... to those still far off whom the Lord our God calls" (v. 39). Baptism empowers us to "go out and baptize all nations." Inherent in our baptism is the mandate to proclaim the word of God to distant and far-off lands, which sometimes can mean to us the office down the hall. We are baptized priest, prophet, and king. As priest we are to serve God's people; as prophet we are to proclaim his message; and as king we are to lead others to Jesus Christ. Baptism challenges us to reach out to those the world rejects—whomever that might be and wherever we find them. Luke reminds his readers that the increase of converts to Christ is the work of the Spirit of Christ, alive and active in the church.

Questions for mystagogical reflection: *How is Peter's message to the Pentecost crowd relevant in your life today? In what way are you invited to participate in the challenge he offers? In what way do you resist the invitation to ongoing conversion? What are the greatest obstacles to conversion in your life right now? What would it take to overcome those obstacles? Can you identify ways in which your community lives in the power of the Spirit given at Pentecost? How are you so empowered? What is your parish's response to "those who are still far off"?*

Responsorial Psalm
Psalm 23:1–6

At one time this was the psalm used on the Second Sunday of Easter, which used to be the day the church reflected upon Christ, the Good Shepherd. Probably the most familiar of the psalms, psalm 23 is appropriately chosen today to point to the shepherd images of today's second reading and gospel.

The shepherd of Old Testament understanding was Yahweh. When the Greek-speaking Christians espoused the term *kyrios* for the exalted Christ, many of the Old Testament images of *Yahweh-Kyrios* were transferred to *Christ/Kyrios*.[5] This was not an attempt to deny Jewish monotheism. "It meant that henceforth the exalted Christ is that aspect of the being of God that is turned toward us in saving action."[6] This would eventually lead to the formulation of the doctrine of the Trinity. Through Jesus Christ, God accomplishes his saving action in our lives. Through the Good Shepherd, who cares for his people and leads them to life-giving waters, God is revealed and glorified.

Second Reading
1 Peter 2:20b–25

(Please refer to the Second Sunday of Easter for an overview of 1 Peter.) Reginald Fuller reminds us that today's second reading is the traditional epistle for Good Shepherd Sunday. It is an exhortation to be patient in the midst of suffering, trials, and persecution. The author exalts Jesus Christ crucified as a model of patience, quoting from Isaiah's hymn of the suffering servant (Is 53).

Jesus' death on the cross is not only a model of patience, but it also is redemptive. By his death we are saved. His wounds made us whole and are the source of our healing. By his wounds we are empowered to live the Christian life.

The author of 1 Peter addresses the forms of leadership that were developing near the turn of the first century. The gentile converts were like sheep returning to their shepherd and guardian. The Greek word *episcopos* was translated *overseer* or *guardian*, and eventually was the term used for leaders of the early Christian communities. Ministerial titles of leadership such as shepherd, overseer, and guardian were intimately connected with the divine action of Christ, the Good Shepherd. It was understood that through the ministerial leadership of the local *episcopos*, the risen Christ himself was guiding and leading the flock. Christ the Good Shepherd, then, is the model for all those who lead the people of God.

Questions for mystagogical reflection: *We will never know the persecution endured by that first community. How, then, can 1 Peter be a relevant word for us today?*

---

[5]Ibid.

[6]Ibid.

How does the exhortation to be patient in this reading connect with your own life experience? Have you ever experienced a time in which you were able to look to Christ crucified as a model for your own suffering? What did you learn from the experience? What is the ongoing challenge in this reading?

Gospel
John 10:1–10

Jesus is the Good Shepherd whose sheep know the sound of his voice.

STEP 1
NAMING ONE'S EXPERIENCE

What were your first impressions? What was your first response to the gospel (or the other readings)?[7] What captured your attention?

Each person names his or her initial impression. Statements should be brief. No reasons should be given at this time. All simply listen without agreeing or disagreeing.

STEP 2
UNDERSTANDING

In a brief statement, what do you think this gospel is trying to convey?

STEP 3
INPUT FROM VISION/STORY/TRADITION

Liturgical Context[8]

Good Shepherd Sunday helps us focus our attention on our Shepherd, Jesus, and his sheep, the church. We ask for the strength to follow the Shepherd to the end and our glorification in Christ: "give us new strength from the courage of Christ our shepherd, and lead us to join the saints in heaven" (Opening Prayer). The shepherd motif is carried throughout the liturgy. It appears again in an adapted form in the Prayer After Communion: "Father, eternal shepherd, watch over the flock redeemed by the blood of Christ. . . ." Note that, in this instance, the title of "shepherd" is used in reference to the Father. Chapter 10 of John's gospel contains Jesus' series of parables of the Good Shepherd. The whole section is read over the three year cycle, beginning in Cycle A. While not stated in today's section of the chapter (it is directly stated in years B and C), Jesus strongly asserts that he and his Father are one. When Christ protects, it is with the power and protection of the Father because they are one. John asserts that there is "one flock, one shepherd."

We who gather for eucharist, are in communion with one another. We are all a part of the same flock. We, the church, a sacrament of Christ,[9] have been redeemed by his blood. We are in the process of transformation. We are to persevere in our response to God's redeeming work within us: "may the continuing work of our redeemer bring us eternal joy" (Prayer Over the Gifts).

The image of Jesus as shepherd and the church as lamb offers hope to the suffering of the world. "Because Jesus was victorious in his death, by the sacrifice of his own body and blood, so will his faithful followers share in that ultimate victory over evil and death."[10]

In this paschal season we are reminded that there is another gate to enter. Jesus is the gate for us, but he himself passed through a gate—death to glory. It is to this gate he leads us.

> Jesus has passed the gate of death to enter into glory: "God has made him Lord and Messiah." To proclaim his res-

[7]The primary focus of reflection is the gospel. However, very often the other readings demand attention and must be brought into the dialogue.

[8]The scriptures in the Lectionary, the seasons of the year, and the ritual prayers of the mass are interrelated and form the basis for liturgical catechesis. The *liturgical context* attempts to explore and clarify the themes and this interrelatedness.

[9]"By her relationship with Christ, the Church is a kind of sacrament or sign of intimate union with God, and of the unity of all mankind." (*Dogmatic Constitution on the Church [Lumen Gentium]*, #1).

[10]Carol Osiek, R.S.C.J. and Ronald D. Witherup, S.S., "Shepherd," in *CPDBT,* 907–909.

urrection is to recognize that he is the guide in whose footsteps we must follow in order to have life, and to have it more fully. He marches at the head of the ransomed people, leading them on the road of their paschal exodus.[11]

The custom of focusing on the Good Shepherd during the Easter season is a very ancient practice. During the seventh century, the passage, "I am the good shepherd..." (Jn 10:14–16) was read on the Second Sunday of Easter. There is evidence that proclamation of the Good Shepherd scriptures dates as far back as Pope Gregory (590–603 C.E.), and perhaps even as far back as the fifth century with Pope Leo the Great (440–461 C.E.). Pope Leo intimately connected the sheep to the Good Shepherd as he proclaimed the reading on the Wednesday before Easter. What happened to the sheep, happened to the shepherd, and vice versa. Christ and his people shared a mutual life. When people enter the waters of baptism, die to the old self, and are born again to the new, true conversion and transformation take place and they are incorporated into Jesus' paschal mystery. "For these newly baptized creatures are filled and fed by their Shepherd—since to participate in Christ's body and blood is to become, in fact, what we consume (St. Leo)."[12]

Later in the patristic period, the image of Christ as the Good Shepherd was appropriated as an image to describe leadership in the church. Christ who nourished and safeguarded his flock became a metaphor for those who would shepherd the people in his church. The word *pastor* was derived from this image. Gregory the Great formulated a working pastoral theology. Gregory, like those before him, connected the shepherd to Christ's passion and cross. Gregory insisted that pastors must not please people at the expense of the truth; they must bear the pain of those they serve in self-sacrificing love.

The Second Vatican Council drew on the patristic formulations as it developed a theology of pastoral ministry.

In the Constitution on the Church, no. 6, the Johannine images of flock and Shepherd are invoked to support the view that the Church is a communion born of Christ's sacrifice on the cross, enlivened by the Spirit, and nourished by the paschal sacraments. Similarly, the council's documents on the Bishop's Pastoral Office in the Church, nos. 2, 16, and on the Life and Ministry of Priests, no. 3, interpret ordained ministry by reference to Christ the shepherd, who freely surrendered his own life that others might live.[13]

Gospel Exegesis

The facilitator gives input regarding what critical biblical scholarship has to say about this text. The input includes insights as to how people would have heard the gospel in Jesus' time.

Scholars surmise that the discourse of the Good Shepherd is the combining of two separate parables. It is believed that they became intertwined in the process of oral transmission. The two original parables are probably authentic parables of Jesus. The two parables center around the same images and pastoral setting: shepherd, sheep, sheep gate, thieves, and marauders. There are two distinct focuses, however. The first parable centers around a sheepfold in which two people try to enter—a shepherd and a thief. The second parable is concerned with the relationship between the shepherd and his sheep and between the shepherd and the stranger. In putting the two parables together John allegorically interprets Jesus as the gate and the shepherd.

Like many of Jesus' parables, today's gospel is a challenge to Israel's religious leadership. Will they recognize the shepherd's voice, or not? Jesus cannot prove his authority, but those who hear his voice and accept it know that it is the voice of God. Jesus used parables to challenge the Pharisees, the religious authorities of his day. John no doubt had his own circumstances in mind when he combined the parables of Jesus into an allegory of his own weaving. Jesus struggled with the Pharisees; John's community struggled with the Jewish

[11]*DL* (III), 139.

[12]Nathan D. Mitchell, "Shepherd," in *CPDBT,* 909–911.

[13]Ibid., 911.

leaders of their day. "The first parable then (v. 1–3) and its teaching can be seen as a challenge to religious leaders of the 30s, 90s and 1990s."[14]

In the preceding chapter of John's gospel, Jesus confronted the Pharisees in the story of the man born blind. He challenged *their* blindness. In the parable of the Good Shepherd, the reader is aware that the Pharisees still lurk in the shadows and stand in sharp contrast to the Shepherd of the flock. Jesus, the Good Shepherd, cares for his flock while the Pharisees care only for themselves.

John draws from the shepherd figure found in the Old Testament and in the Synoptic tradition. By the time John was writing, other New Testament writers were using "shepherd" as a term for human pastors of the church (see second reading). John uses the shepherd motif in relation to Jesus and Jesus alone. Jesus is the model shepherd. Like the blind man in the previous chapter, the flock recognizes Jesus for who he is—the Son of Man, guardian of the flock. One need only look back to a pastoral scene from first century Palestine to appreciate how this parable was heard and understood by Jesus' contemporaries.

Each day the shepherd would take his flock out into the desert for the day's grazing and then return to the sheepfold, a common enclosure with a low stone wall and a gated entrance. At day's end, the shepherds would bring their sheep to the fold to keep them safe from the dangers of the night—wolves and thieves. Each night a shepherd was designated to lie down in front of the sheep gate so no one could enter. He was the protector of the flock—with his very life, if need be. After all the sheep were safely inside the yard, the shepherds would return to their nomadic tents. In the morning they would return to the fold, each whistling or calling out the names of his sheep. The sheep instinctively knew the sound of their shepherd's voice. They would not respond when anyone other than their shepherd called them. One would assume that the scene would be all chaos and confusion. Not so. The sheep knew the sound of their shepherd's voice and instinctively followed him. This is the pastoral reality that helped frame Jesus' parable, and also framed the hearing of it.

[14] *WWC*, 39.

A common theme in the Synoptic gospels is the failure of onlookers to understand Jesus' message. He usually applied several variations on the point he was trying to make: 1) Jesus is the shepherd who guards the gate to the enclosure. He will designate who enters and who does not. "The only authentic pastors are those admitted by Jesus (of whom Peter will be a chief example for the redactor in ch. 21)."[15] The Pharisees who cannot accept Jesus, and seek to come in some other way, are the thieves. 2) Only through Jesus, the gate, will the sheep *go out to* or *come in from* the pasture. "Those who come through this gate will have life (Jesus is the water of life, the bread of life, the gate of life)."[16]

Jesus is the model Good Shepherd. He cares for his sheep; they know his voice and respond to his voice. There is ownership. Contrast that with the Pharisees who are merely hired workers who come in to sheer the sheep and care nothing for their welfare. Jesus knows his sheep. He is in loving relationship with them, which is why he is willing to lay down his life for them. "In the last analysis, both identifications of Jesus—gate and shepherd—make the same point. The risen Christ is the One who nourishes his people in his word and sacraments, giving them life and enabling them to have it abundantly."[17]

Through baptism we are incorporated into Christ Jesus. Jesus knows each of us by name and invites us in through the gate. He loves us so intimately that he is willing to lay down his life to keep us from becoming prey to wolves and marauders.

Jesus also offers a model of authentic Christian leadership. Rather than indulging in self-serving interests, we are to take the time to learn the names of our sheep and to become the guardian of the gate that keeps them safe from the dangers of the night.

Proclaim the gospel again.

Sometimes we gain new insights when we hear the text after the interpretation is given. Someone from the group proclaims the gospel a second time.

[15] *GEJ*, 58.
[16] Ibid., 59.
[17] *PL*, 81.

STEP 4
TESTING

Conversation with the Liturgy and the Scriptures

Test your original understanding in dialogue with the text.

(You might consider breaking into smaller groups.)

How does the interpretation of the scholars shed light on your original understanding of this parable? Were there any new insights for you? How does this story speak to your life?

Sharing Life Experience

Participants share an experience from their lives that connects with the biblical interpretation just shared.

> A *coworker of mine is such a good example of one who follows the voice of the Shepherd. Though not a stranger to sorrow and pain, she knows that she can rely on the Shepherd to take care of her. She* had *to rely on him— she raised eleven children! (The thought of eleven teenagers sends me screaming in frenzied anxiety!)*
>
> *Eleanor never wavers. I envy her absolute confidence and optimism, no matter what the circumstances. It is not a pie-in-the-sky piety, either. She is solidly rooted in the paschal life. I have the potential to be more like the disciples of last week—depressed and dejected. Not Eleanor. Her steadfast faithfulness comes from hearing the voice of the Shepherd, knowing and responding to his voice, and confident that she will be led each night back to the safety of the sheepfold. When the wolf is lurking at my door, I sometimes forget that the Shepherd is standing guard on the other side, carefully watching out for me.*
>
> *I relate more to the sheep in Luke's gospel that wandered off, got lost in the wilderness, and ended up in a panic. The Shepherd always finds me, but I put myself through such unnecessary turmoil while I wait. There is a radical message in today's gospel. The Good Shepherd is not the shepherd of pious art. He is the shepherd who lies down in front of the gate, refusing to let anyone come near us or snatch us away. He is the shepherd who guards the gate with his bloodied body. So many times in my life his bloodied body stood guard at my door—in the death of my parents, and through the myriad of family experiences and personal crises that rendered me, like the lost sheep, unable to move. Jesus, my Shepherd, was there, guarding me and leading me through the darkest hours of my journey, toward the light of healing.*
>
> *The Good Shepherd is a model for all of us who are baptized. By virtue of our baptism we are to pattern our lives after Jesus—not only Jesus Christ crucified and risen, but Jesus Christ, the Good Shepherd. We are to go out of our way to bring the sheep home, to protect and care for them as Jesus would care for them—and not just the pretty sheep, either. If our parishes do not resemble the sheepfold in today's gospel, then serious transformation is in order. Today's liturgy demands that we be attentive to the people in our communities and in the world. Like the protected sheepfold, my own parish strives to be a similar safe haven. One of our graces is the gift of hospitality. No doubt there are numerous occasions when we fall short, when people fall through the cracks, and when we are less than welcoming to the marginalized. But in our conscious efforts, we work toward becoming the church Jesus intended, albeit imperfectly. It is sometimes difficult to see the areas where healing is needed.*
>
> *A friend of mine went to mass in another city. As she was preparing for the liturgy, there were people sitting near her who were hurling intermittent obscenities. At first she was afraid to look around her, fearing that if her eyes met theirs there might be an unwanted display of raucous emotion. She restrained herself. As she sat there for a few more minutes, she realized that the people sitting near her were suffering from a rare disease named Tourette's syndrome. There was a hospital nearby that specialized in treating the disease. Like the Good Shepherd, that parish had gathered up this small band of worshipers, sent a van for them, and welcomed them with open arms. Not an eyebrow was raised or a glance of disgust directed at them. They were welcomed, loved members of that parish.*
>
> *That is the kind of pastoral leadership that is invited in today's gospel. I am confident that my community would do the same thing, yet I realize we don't know until faced with a situation how we will respond. Will we hear, or will we be deaf, to the sound of the Shepherd's voice?*

All share their life experience.

In what way have you experienced Jesus, the Good Shepherd, in your life and in the life of your community? How has Jesus been shepherd for you? Whom do you relate to the most in today's gospel: the shepherd, the thief, or the sheep? In what ways have you been all three? How would your community respond to that question? What was John's intention in redacting the two parables of Jesus? How do the readings today express the biblical themes of covenant, exodus, creation, and community? Do you still feel the same way about this text as when you began? Is there any renewed meaning for you?

Step 5
Decision

The gospel demands a response.

In what way does today's liturgy invite a change in attitude or behavior? What are the implications of this gospel for your life? Where are areas in your life, or in your community, where transformation is needed the most? In what way are you called to respond? How should your parish respond? What one concrete action are you willing to take this week in response to today's liturgy?

Pastoral Considerations: How is your parish a welcoming place for those sheep who seek a safe haven? How does your parish reflect Jesus, the Good Shepherd, and in what way is it perhaps more like the thief?

Christian Initiation: Neophytes continue to be a symbol of new life in our assemblies. When they don their baptismal garment and carry their baptismal candle in procession, they are a reminder to all of us that we are all baptized into the death and resurrection of Jesus Christ.

DOCTRINAL ISSUES

What church truth/teaching/doctrinal issue could be drawn from the gospel for the Fourth Sunday of Easter?

Participants suggest possible doctrinal themes that flow from the readings.

Possible Doctrinal Themes

Jesus the Good Shepherd, paschal mystery, christology, baptism, conversion, church, symbols: cross, community, light/fire/water, oil, garment, bread, wine, sacraments

Present the doctrinal material at this time.

1. The facilitator gives input on a particular doctrinal issue of his/her prior choosing. OR
2. The group chooses a doctrinal issue from the list they created. They read together from the Doctrinal Appendix.

(The doctrinal issues are found in the Doctrinal Appendix in the back of this workbook. If you are choosing an issue from this resource, please refer to it now.)

Reflection questions centered around the chosen doctrinal theme can be found at the end of each topic in the Doctrinal Appendix. The questions are based on the five-step reflection process. If you choose a topic not included in the Doctrinal Appendix, craft your own questions according to the same five-step process.

Following the reflection questions you will be reminded to return to chapter 7, "Preparing the Catechetical Session," to assist you in crafting your own session.

Closing Prayer

Let us pray.
Father, eternal shepherd,
watch over the flock redeemed by the blood of
 Christ
and lead us to the promised land.
Grant this through Christ our Lord.[18]

---

[18]Fourth Sunday of Easter, "Prayer after Communion," *The Sacramentary.*

Fifth Sunday of Easter

INTRODUCTORY RITES

Opening Song (or Entrance Antiphon)

Sing to the Lord a new song, for he has done marvelous deeds; he has revealed to the nations his saving power, alleluia. (Ps 97:1–2)[1]

Opening Prayer

The facilitator of the session may lead the prayer. Others in the group may be asked to proclaim the readings.

Let us pray...
[in the freedom of the sons of God]

Pause for silent prayer.

Father of our Lord Jesus Christ,
you have revealed to the nations your saving power
and filled all ages with the words of a new song.
Hear the echo of this hymn.
Give us voice to sing your praise
throughout this season of joy.
We ask this through Christ our Lord.[2]

LITURGY OF THE WORD

The readings are proclaimed.

First Reading
Acts 6:1–7

(Refer to Easter Sunday for an overview of the Acts of the Apostles.) Diversity was the hallmark of first century Palestine. Hellenization was rapid. Greek immigrants were converted to Judaism. There was tension between the Greeks and the Jews. There was also tension among the Greeks themselves, because of the varying philosophies, as well as among those who ascribed to the various schools of thought of Judaism (Pharisees, Sadducees, etc.).

[1]Fifth Sunday of Easter: "Entrance Antiphon," *The Sacramentary.*

[2]Fifth Sunday of Easter: "Alternative Opening Prayer," *The Sacramentary.*

As the Christian church grew, there was a need to adapt community mores to meet the needs of the newly-formed community. Old structures would no longer suffice. Converts with diverse backgrounds were added to the membership of the developing church. There were Greek-speaking converts, Greek-speaking Jewish converts, and Jewish Hebrew-speaking converts—all of them Christian. The church had to adapt and adjust to the influx of new people.

It was difficult to maintain autonomy in the midst of the fast-growing empire. Many people were absorbed into the Greek culture. Enculturation was a problem for the Jews as well as the Christians. Many of the Greeks were converted to Judaism, then to Christianity.

The Greeks attended synagogues where the Bible was proclaimed in Greek. Other synagogues read an Aramean translation of the Targum. The language barrier created tension between the two groups. Mistrust existed between the new immigrants and the natives. Participation in separate synagogues helped ease the tension. However, when conversion to Christianity merged both groups into one church, difficulties erupted. One area in which this tension was particularly troublesome was in the daily distribution of alms. The Greek-speaking Christians felt that their widows were given less than their Jewish counterparts. The apostles concurred with their accusations. However, they could not spend all their time settling such matters or the word of God would be neglected. To solve the problem the apostles invited the Hellenists to appoint seven of their own men to take on the task of waiting on the tables of the entire community.[3] The seven Hebrew-speaking men, already in charge of alms for the poor, retained their position in the community, however. Thus, the seven Greek-speaking appointees were charged with taking care of the needs of Greek-speaking people. The apostles prayed and laid hands on them (reminiscent of investiture in an office).

[3]*DL* (III), 153–154.

Thus the apostles adapted to the needs of the growing community. A new "service" structure was implemented in the community. Soon the seven men would be included in the preaching and missionary activity of the apostles. "They imparted to their group, more outward-looking by language and culture than the Hebrews, a remarkable missionary zeal."[4]

The "laying on of hands," while not an ordination (as that was a later development in the church), was a sign that the community appointed them for a specific task. Some scholars suggest that the Seven had already been active in the ministry of the word and that the gesture was a sign that the Hellenistic Jewish Christians were accepted in the community.

If they ignored the brewing tensions, the apostles feared a split in the community. The unity of the community was in jeopardy. Thus, they responded to the needs of the community and gave them a voice in the decision. Unity was preserved and the ministry flourished.

Questions for mystagogical reflection: *In what way does this reading speak to your community? Where is unity threatened? Is unity in your community a value? How does this reading challenge your community to deal with its divisive issues? Are there any present issues that need the creative wisdom offered in today's reading? What does this reading have to teach us about ministry in the church? If there are multicultural issues in your parish, do you address them openly, or are they hidden in hopes they will disappear? What needs to happen to deal with these issues? If not multi-cultural issues, what are the areas that cause the most tension? How can you be an agent for change?*

Responsorial Psalm
Psalm 33:1–2, 4–5, 18–19

This is a psalm of thanksgiving for the mighty deeds of God in salvation history. It is especially fitting during the Easter season. The last stanza referring to the deliverance from death was originally understood as deliverance from tragedy. Christians appropriated it to mean the liberation won by Christ through his passion, death, and resurrection.

[4]Ibid., 154.

Second Reading
1 Peter 2:4–9

It is suggested that today's reading is taken from a section of an early baptismal homily, probably at an Easter celebration. It is likely that it was given as instruction for candidates for baptism. The homily was divided into three parts. The first part provided a Christian understanding of Exodus, connecting Israel's history with Christianity. The second section addressed what it meant to be people who were baptized into Jesus' death and resurrection. The third section [today's] dealt with the implications of that paschal life for the community.

The reading describes the community as a temple, the place where God dwells. It is made up of living stones. The church is a royal priesthood, a people set apart, much like the people of the old covenant. Using quotations from the Old Testament, the author posits a "vision for the *new* Israel (church) and of the *new* temple of living stones (believers in Jesus)."[5] The letter was intended to provide the people with a sense that they belonged to a "new people." They too would be heirs to the covenant made with Israel.

Christians, the living stones, are joined by Christ himself who is the cornerstone—the foundation that supports the living stones. In the Old Testament no one was to approach the rock of Sinai, under penalty of death. Contrast that with Jesus, the cornerstone, who invites his people to come close to him. He has created something new and wonderful. He has gathered his living stones and formed them into a new people, a new religion.

The church has a priestly function as it offers a spiritual sacrifice made acceptable to God through Jesus. This sacrifice proclaims the wondrous deeds of God. "Instead of an elitist priesthood, the entire new people of God is a royal priesthood" (v. 9). "Instead of animal and grain offerings, the new liturgy of God's people will be celebrated with 'spiritual sacrifices'" (v. 5).

God was not pleased with Israel's sacrifices. The new spiritual sacrifice would be pleasing to God. The new sacrifice is the death and resurrection of Jesus Christ.

[5]*WWC,* 40.

Questions for mystagogical reflection: *What does it mean to you that Jesus is the cornerstone and we are like living stones? In what way are we living stones? In what way do we fall short? How does the author's vision of church compare with your experience of church? What is the challenge inherent in this reading? How might this reading speak to the church of today?*

Gospel

John 14:1–12

Jesus said, "I am going to prepare a place for you, and then I will come back and take you with me."

STEP 1

NAMING ONE'S EXPERIENCE

What were your first impressions, your first response to the gospel [or the other readings]?[6] What captured your attention?

Each person names his or her initial impression. Statements should be brief. No reasons should be given at this time. All simply listen without agreeing or disagreeing.

STEP 2

UNDERSTANDING

In a brief statement, what do you think this gospel is trying to convey?

STEP 3

INPUT FROM VISION/STORY/TRADITION

Liturgical Context[7]

Today's liturgy has far-reaching implications for the life of ministry within any parish. The readings are rooted in self-sacrificing love. All of our work is to flow from the example of Christ. We are to lay down our lives for one another. We are to persevere in promoting the gospel of Christ and we are to be agents of Christ's love to all of God's people.

The alternative opening prayer calls for the joy necessary to sing praise to Christ, in other words, to proclaim his mighty deeds to all people.

The liturgy today is a celebration of church. It is an exhortation to examine our ecclesiology. How do we understand church? Like the Christians in the first reading, are we stuck in models that are no longer our reality? One of the metaphors used by the church to express the *meaning* of *church* is drawn from today's first letter from Peter.

> The Church is also a human reality, a community of believers, the People of God. Jesus called men and women to become free from the slavery of sin, to pass through the saving waters of Baptism, to believe, to worship, and witness to all He said and did. The first letter of Peter calls this new people "a chosen race, a royal priesthood, a holy nation, a people he claims for his own to proclaim the glorious words of the One who called you from darkness into his marvelous light" (1 Peter 2:9).[8]

Both the first and second reading today demand that we seriously examine our communities. Are they places that enter into the death and resurrection of Jesus, places where self-sacrificing love is the rule rather than the exception? Can outsiders look in and say, "See how much they love one another?" And even more importantly, "See how much they love us?" Are our communities comprised of living stones, or unmovable slabs of granite?

John's gospel today is the most profound expression of love. Jesus is the only way home to the loving, forgiving arms of God. Jesus reveals God; the church reveals Jesus. Jesus desires nothing more than that we be united in him as he is one with the Father. We experience that unity in the liturgy,

[6]The primary focus of reflection is the gospel. However, very often the other readings demand attention and must be brought into the dialogue.

[7]The scriptures in the Lectionary, the seasons of the year, and the ritual prayers of the mass are interrelated and form the basis for liturgical catechesis. The *liturgical context* attempts to explore and clarify the themes and this interrelatedness.

[8]*NCD*, #64.

in the sacraments, and ultimately in the eucharist. Love forgives a multitude of sins. We need to examine where love is lacking in our parishes. If Jesus went home to prepare a place for us, and if the church is where we live, encounter, and celebrate his presence until we go there, perhaps we had better go to extraordinary lengths to make this place reflect his love until he returns.

The first reading offers us a model. Diversity was recognized and honored in the community. Do our parishes value unity as much as the apostles valued it in today's first reading? Is diversity celebrated, or something to be endured? Do factions and disunity threaten the very core of the parish? Today's first two readings are a serious challenge for the church of all generations.

The gospel brings us back to reality. Jesus is the sacrament of God. He is the real, tangible, touchable expression of God's love for us. Only through Jesus can we begin to imagine how deeply we are loved. Jesus went home to prepare a place for his beloved children. If we lose our way, we need only look to him, for "he is the way, the truth, and the life." The opening prayer says: "You redeem us and make us your children in Christ. Give us true freedom and bring us to the inheritance you promised." The church is where we celebrate and live his presence until we join him in glory. We cannot afford to allow disunity to distract us from our purpose. The early church went to extravagant lengths to insure that harmony existed in the community. They entered into Easter faith. As Easter people they stayed in the struggle. They did not walk away from it; they walked into it. There are times when we need to be like the Hellenists who demanded that the community listen to the needs of their poor widows. There are other times when we need to be like the apostles who listened, concurred, and sought to remedy the situation. If we as church, as People of God, truly believed what we profess in the Prayer Over the Gifts, the ideal posed in today's liturgy would be the norm rather than the ideal. "... [B]y this holy exchange you share with us your divine life. Grant that everything we do may be directed by the knowledge of your truth."[9] (For further reflection see the Easter Vigil: Symbol of Church and Doctrinal Appendix, Mystery of the Church.)

[9]Fifth Sunday of Easter: "Prayer Over the Gifts," *The Sacramentary.*

Gospel Exegesis

The facilitator gives input regarding what critical biblical scholarship has to say about this text. The input includes insights as to how people would have heard the gospel in Jesus' time.

Toward the end of chapter eleven Jesus begins the journey to Jerusalem. It is there that death awaits him. His disciples are understandably troubled. In today's gospel, Jesus asked them to deepen their faith as they stood in the hour of his fulfillment. Chapters 14 through 17 of John's gospel are comprised of a series of Jesus' teachings, referred to as the farewell address or discourse. A farewell address in the Bible is usually given before the person giving the address is about to die. Jacob, Moses, and Paul also bid farewell to their communities in similar fashion. The discourses generally included prophecies about the future, or a word of caution for the leaders who would take their place.

In today's pericope, Jesus exhorts his disciples that he is about to leave. He is going to prepare a place where they will one day join him. It will be a place of intimate union with God. Jesus encourages his disciples by telling them that they already know the way to this place. Thomas, of course, doubts that he knows the way. Jesus then tells them, in essence, that he—the Jesus they know and love—is the way, the truth, and the life.

The discourses of chapter fourteen are closely related to Jesus' last meal with his disciples. At the end of chapter thirteen, Jesus warns his disciples that he will soon die. He promises them, however, that he will not leave them alone but will return to take them home with him. This is one of the few places in John's gospel where there is reference to the parousia.

Thomas has no idea what Jesus was talking about. He did not understand; like the Jews, Thomas was clueless. He did not sense that Jesus was returning to his Father. It is at this juncture that Jesus speaks one of the most quoted lines in scripture: "I am the way, the truth, and the life." As the way, Jesus is the incarnate reality of "I Am." He is the only way that people in this earthly reality can know and experience the Creator of all. They know God because Jesus is one with God. If they know Jesus, they know God. Jesus is the revelation of God. Within the person of Jesus is the essence of the Father. Only Jesus reveals who God truly is. Jesus is *the life* because God is the author of all life. Life comes from God and Jesus is the truth of God. To know Jesus is to know God.

Jesus' discourses simply exude the unconditional, extravagant, lavish love that Jesus has for his disciples. He provides his followers a way and the means to live to their fullest potential. Only through self-giving love can human beings become their most authentic selves. We were created to love. Jesus shows us what that means. If we live the love that Jesus lived, we will know God, Who *Is Love.*

Whenever disciples, then and now, are tempted to question that love in the face of the wretchedness of the human condition, we have Jesus, the revelation of God, to remind us of the gift of creation. Karl Rahner says it eloquently:

> Because he did not begin to save and transfigure the world with the superficial symptoms but started with its innermost root, we creatures of the surface think that nothing has happened. Because the waters of suffering and guilt are still flowing where *we* are standing, we think the deep sources from which they spring have not yet dried up. Because wickedness is still inscribing its runes of the face of the earth, we conclude that in the deepest heart of reality love is extinct. But all that is mere appearance, the appearance which we take to be the reality of life. He has risen because in death he conquered and redeemed forever the innermost center of all earthly reality. And having risen, he has held fast to it. And so he has remained. When we confess him as having ascended to God' s heaven, that is only another expression for the fact that he withdraws from us for awhile the tangible manifestation of his glorified humanity and above all that there is no longer any abyss between God and the world.[10]

Jesus' self-gift of love had to mean so much to his gathered disciples, and no doubt to John's community many years later. Surely the former and the latter were extraordinarily bolstered by Jesus' unconditional outpouring. Christians of John's community were beginning to feel the sting of religious prejudice. They were expelled from the synagogue. The synagogue had been heart and hearth to them. For Yahweh's chosen people, it was the place of encounter with God. How would they now encounter God? Jesus encouraged them and us: "If you know me, you know God."

Appearing next on the scene is Philip. He must have broken Jesus' heart. Here is Philip, the one whom Jesus invited to be a part of his motley band of disciples; the one who introduced Jesus to Nathaniel; the one Jesus turned to when there was no food to feed the multitudes to ask him how they should be fed; the one who ran interference for the Greeks who inquired about Jesus. All one and the same Philip. After walking so far and so long with his Master, how could he possibly ask Jesus to show him the Father? Didn't he understand who Jesus was? Philip's question must have cut to the very marrow of Jesus' bones.

Jesus reiterates that he and the Father are one. The Father is revealed in and through Jesus. He is in complete unity with God. God's words and actions are Jesus' words and actions. Jesus also proclaims that future disciples will do even greater works than he himself had done. "The works of Jesus are the works of God: to give life, and to restore meaning to life or enrich life's meaning. Already at creation God called us to take dominion over evolution ('to till the garden and keep it,' Gn 1:26–28)."[11]

Proclaim the gospel again.

Sometimes we gain new insights when we hear the text after the interpretation is given. Someone from the group proclaims the gospel a second time.

[10] *GCY,* 196.

[11] *CWJ,* 81.

this is a big deal

Step 4
Testing

Conversation with the Liturgy and the Scriptures

Test your original understanding in dialogue with the text.

(You might consider breaking into smaller groups.)

Were there any new insights for you? Can you name an experience in your life when the Jesus of today's gospel was most present in your life? What about your community? How does this story speak to your life?

Sharing Life Experience

Participants share an experience from their lives that connects with the biblical interpretation just shared.

> *Speaking on a personal level, today's liturgy reminds me how much I am loved. It is a message of hope. It was my only anchor when I lost my parents. I found great consolation knowing that Jesus went before us to prepare a place. My parents were already in that place, and someday I would join them.*
>
> *So often I am like Thomas and Philip—I fail to see the obvious. There are times when I question God's action (or non-action) in my life. When God does not live up to my expectations, follow my script, or do what I tell him he should, I become like Thomas. I don't have a clue where I am going; I am in the dark. Or on the other hand, when I complain to God of his absence only to find his presence in the midst of it, I am awed and humbled. Then I feel like Philip, the one who broke the Master's heart. I am thankful there was a Thomas and a Philip who went before me. I don't have to get stuck in my guilt. Jesus forgives it all. He invites me more deeply into the sacrament of his presence.*
>
> *On a communal level, today is a day to celebrate. Yes, my community, like every community, has warts. No doubt there are many times that we do not reflect the presence of Christ in our midst. There have been numerous times over the years that we have fallen short. However, today is a day to reflect on the priesthood of our community: the way it serves God's people, the way it is the presence of Christ in the world—the face of God.*
>
> *This* Royal People *gives conscious, active praise of God week after week. This* Holy Nation *gathers every week to celebrate community, to encounter Christ in word and sacrament, to break the bread of life together so that it can go out and be bread in the world. Ministry abounds. The grieving, the dying, the lonely, the aging, the sick, the homebound, the hospitalbound, the widowed, the separated, the divorced, the seekers, the poor, the hungry, the lost—they are a concern to this* Pilgrim Church, *which tries (however imperfectly) to make them its business.*
>
> *In the past ten years, this* People Set Apart *has tithed over one million dollars to the world's poor. It has built a school in Haiti and supplied it with teachers, desks, and books. It is building a church in the Dominican Republic and a clinic in Peru. This* Community of Love *has supported a water purification system for Third World countries. This* Servant Church *has built homes for Habitat and for the poor in Appalachia. Thirty percent of its school children are on scholarship. This* People of God *care for the aged, built a home for elderly women, and open up their facilities to the homeless in cold weather. This* One Body in Christ *is building a school for the future of its own children. It collected over two-million dollars over one weekend, as a result of hard work, excellent preparation, and a great deal of good will.*
>
> *Yes, it falls short, and often fails to reveal the face of Christ. Very often it acts like Thomas or Philip, and sometimes even like the denying Peter. But there are times when it shines like the brightest beacon. I thank God every day for my community. It truly is the Church of Our Saviour!*

All share their life experience.

In what way do you relate to Thomas and Philip? When have you or your parish extended the message of Jesus in today's gospel to others? In what way is this gospel relevant today? In what way does this gospel reflect God's promise to be with us (biblical themes of covenant)? How does this gospel invite transformation—the liberation from one state of being or place to the promised land of freedom, hope, and life with God (exodus)?

How is this gospel reflective of God's power of re-creation? What is the word to communities of all generations? Is there anything you would like to change about the way you originally understood this gospel? Is there a renewed insight?

STEP 5
DECISION

The gospel demands a response.

How does your understanding of these scriptures and today's liturgy invite transformation? In what way does your community need to grow in the fullness of today's scriptures? How might your parish respond? In what way have you grown as a result of today's liturgy? What are the implications of these readings (liturgy) in your life? What is one concrete action you will take this week as a response?

Pastoral considerations.

The pastoral considerations have been addressed throughout this session. You will need to make application for your own parish situation.

Doctrinal Issues

What church truth/teaching/doctrinal issue could be drawn from the gospel for the Fifth Sunday of Easter?

Participants suggest possible doctrinal themes that flow from the readings.

Possible Doctrinal Themes

Symbol of church, Christology, paschal mystery, baptism, mystery of church, service and servanthood.

Present the doctrinal material at this time.

1. The facilitator gives input on a particular doctrinal issue of his/her prior choosing. OR
2. The group chooses a doctrinal issue from the list they created. They read together from the Doctrinal Appendix, or other appropriate official church documents, and the works of respected theologians.

(The doctrinal issues are found in the Doctrinal Appendix in the back of this workbook. If you are choosing an issue from this resource, please refer to it now.)

Reflection questions centered around the chosen doctrinal theme can be found at the end of each topic in the Doctrinal Appendix. The questions are based on the five-step reflection process. If you choose a topic not included in the Doctrinal Appendix, craft your own questions according to the same five-step process.

Following the reflection questions you will be reminded to return to chapter 7, "Preparing the Catechetical Session," to assist you in crafting your own session.

Closing Prayer

God our Father,
look upon us with love.
You redeem us and make us your children in
Christ.
Give us true freedom
and bring us to the inheritance you promised.
We ask this through our Lord Jesus Christ, your
Son,
who lives and reigns with you and the Holy Spirit,
one God, for ever and ever.[12]

[12]Fifth Sunday of Easter: "Closing Prayer," *The Sacramentary.*

Sixth Sunday of Easter

INTRODUCTORY RITES

Opening Song (or Entrance Antiphon)

Speak out with a voice of joy: let it be heard to the ends of the earth: The Lord has set his people free, alleluia. (See Is 48:20)[1]

Opening Prayer

The facilitator of the session may lead the prayer. Others in the group may be asked to proclaim the readings.

Let us pray
[that we may practice in our lives
the faith we profess]

Pause for silent prayer.

Ever-living God,
help us to celebrate our joy
in the resurrection of the Lord
and to express in our lives
the love we celebrate.
Grant this through our Lord Jesus Christ, your Son,
who lives and reigns with you and the Holy Spirit,
one God, for ever and ever.[2]

LITURGY OF THE WORD

The readings are proclaimed.

First Reading

Acts 8:5–8, 14–17

(For an overview of Acts, refer to Easter Sunday.) Following the death of Stephen, the Greek- speaking Christians were forced to leave Jerusalem as they became the first targets of persecution. Rather than deterring the missionary activity of the church, Luke purports that persecution advanced it. One of those who fled was Philip, one of the Greek disciples (one of the Seven) chosen in last week's reading to serve the Greek community.

Philip went to Samaria where he preached the good news and performed the signs and wonders of the Risen Christ. Unlike the chilly response of the Jews, those in the "far corners of the earth" greeted Philip's message with enthusiasm and fervor.

The apostles, still in Jerusalem, managed to avoid the persecution. Peter and John, the elders of the church, went to confer the Holy Spirit on those Philip had baptized. Jesus promised that the apostles would receive the Holy Spirit and would in turn baptize and confer the Spirit on all nations, from Samaria throughout Judea to the ends of the earth. Those whom Philip evangelized were the first of those converts. Jesus' promise continues in the sacramental life of the church through baptism, the laying on of hands, and the seal of the Holy Spirit.

The Acts of the Apostles chronicles the church's expansion from Jerusalem, Judea, and Samaria to the far corners of the earth. The missionary tour undertaken by Philip was understood as a decisive stage in the implementation of this expansion. One of Luke's primary themes is the continuity and unity between the missionary communities and the mother church in Jerusalem. Throughout Acts, Luke's purpose is to show that the missionary expansion is fully supported and endorsed by the apostles and the Jerusalem community.

The ministry to the Samaritans is significant when one considers the situation of the Samaritans in first century Palestine. When the northern kingdom was conquered (around 800 B.C.E.), Samaria was subsumed into the foreign culture of the oppressor. They maintained their worship of Yahweh and continued the practice of circumcision, but they intermarried and succumbed to worship of many of the pagan gods introduced by the conquering power. However, they still worshiped Yahweh on Mount Gerizim, which was their religious center (rather than Jerusalem). They believed

[1]Sixth Sunday of Easter: "Entrance Antiphon," *The Sacramentary.*

[2]Sixth Sunday of Easter: "Opening Prayer," *The Sacramentary.*

that the advent of the messiah would take place on Gerizim, whereas Judeans believed it would happen in Jerusalem.

There was bitter enmity between Judeans and Samaritans. The Jews treated the Samaritans like lepers. There was mutual distrust and hate. Contact with a Samaritan rendered a Jew unclean. Jesus, however, broke the chains of religious prejudice and reached out to the Samaritans, as did his followers in the post-resurrection ministry activity of the church.

Reginald Fuller finds it curious that the baptism by Philip did not confer the Spirit (as was believed then and today), and that the converts had to wait for Peter and John for the laying on of hands. According to Fuller, we are not to take this text as a proof text for the sacrament of confirmation. "The author of Luke-Acts knows nothing of 'confirmation' as a separate rite, distinct from baptism, performed by the apostles or their successors. . . ."[3] That was a later liturgical development. "The text does, however, hint at the later liturgical distinctions between baptism and confirmation."[4]

Questions for mystagogical reflection: *In what way might contemporary Christians experience or understand the cost of discipleship as experienced by our ancestors in faith, such as Stephen and Philip? Many of the Jews in Jerusalem turned a deaf ear to the good news, while the Samaritans enthusiastically embraced it. How does that speak to us today? What does this reading have to teach us about evangelization? How do you witness to your faith? In what way is your parish an evangelizing community? In what way does today's reading challenge the contemporary church? What are the implications of the laying on of hands? What does it mean that the Spirit was conferred?*

Responsorial Psalm

Psalm 66:1–3, 4–5, 6–7, 16, 20

Originally this psalm celebrated some act of liberation of the nation. The language recalls the Exodus event. For Christians this exodus is realized in the paschal mystery, the passage from death to life of the risen Savior, and our immersion in that reality through baptism.

[3] *PL*, 86.

[4] *WWC*, 42.

Second Reading

1 Peter 3:15–18

The readers of 1 Peter were a church scattered in the midst of a culture that not only did not share their faith, but was antagonistic toward it. Peter speaks of Jesus in a manner reminiscent of the way ancient biblical authors referred to Yahweh. Jesus is the one in whom we must place our complete trust and confidence. Thus fear is the opposite of trust in the power and glory of the risen Lord.

This early baptismal catechism reminds the neophytes that although there is joy in their new baptismal life, there will also be hardships. Persecution will come. Jesus Christ suffered, died, and rose again for the world. Through baptism, Christians participate in the sacrifice of Calvary; they can expect to suffer as Jesus suffered. Christians are to be prepared, and are not to be surprised or shaken when persecution and suffering come.

The reading ends with a hymn about the passion, death, and resurrection of Christ. It is believed that verses 14 and 16 were added to the original hymn in order to make it more relevant to their present circumstances. 1 Peter upholds Jesus as an example of one who, although innocent, had to suffer persecution.

The author maintains that such persecution is the result of an active faith. In following Christ's lead, the persecuted church is to love their enemies and treat them with respect. Only then will such enemies be dishonored by their behavior.

Questions for mystagogical reflection: *How does this reading from 1 Peter have relevance to contemporary society? In what way might you relate to the message in this reading? What does it teach you about faith? About suffering? What are the implications for the life of the church? For you? What is the challenge? How does this reading invite a change in attitude on your part? Is there any situation in your life that might benefit from the message in this reading?*

Gospel

John 14:15–21

I shall ask the Father and he will give you another advocate.

Step 1
Naming One's Experience

What were your first impressions? What was your first response to the gospel (or the other readings)?[5] What captured your attention?

Each person names his or her initial impression. Statements should be brief. No reasons should be given at this time. All simply listen without agreeing or disagreeing.

Step 2
Understanding

In a brief statement, what do you think this gospel is trying to convey?

Step 3
Input from Vision/Story/Tradition

Liturgical Context[6]

Today's liturgy is a blending of Easter themes—baptism, paschal mystery, Spirit. Baptismal gestures, conferral of the Spirit, and the laying on of hands place this liturgy squarely in the midst of the initiatory life of the church. In today's gospel, Jesus promised to send his Holy Spirit as his living presence in the world. Through the laying on of hands, John and Peter confer the Spirit on the new converts. We are not to miss the obvious. Through the sacrament of baptism, we are given the gift of the Spirit. When the early Christians gathered and the bishop prayed the prayer of blessing over the Easter waters, they believed that the Trinity became present in the water. Through the calling down of the Holy Spirit upon the sacred chrism, it transcends from mere ointment to "Jesus' grace which through the presence of the Holy Spirit instills his divinity into us."[7] Through baptism, the Father calls us, we die with Jesus, and we are sealed with the Holy Spirit.[8] "Theodore saw the font as womb into which the candidate descended to receive second birth from the Holy Spirit, whose presence impregnates the water."[9] Jesus' promise to send the Holy Spirit is made real through baptism and the sacraments. All of the readings today punctuate the fulfillment of Jesus' promise to his disciples. We see the effects of his word in the ministry of the apostles and in those first early communities.

In today's second reading, the community is reminded to hold firm in the midst of persecution. God will use it to further the reign of God. Persecution will not deter the Spirit. Through baptism we are plunged into Jesus' death. We will share in the suffering of Jesus and our sharing will have redemptive effects. We are called to martyrdom. The tombs of martyrs shout to a world lost in the abyss of meaningless pursuits.

View from a Martyr's Grave

He gave them food, they called him Saint Francis.
When he asked, "Why are they hungry?"
. . . then he was Marxist.
He was the Pied Piper of children; they called him a lover
Till he empowered their parents . . .
He was the worst kind of traitor.
A man in good standing, he was polite and political,
Till he discovered the poor; they branded him radical.
He spoke without fear from the streets and the pulpit,
"Justice, not charity, our God demands it!"
The Kingdom of God belongs to just such as these. . . .
The poor, the oppressed, those brought to their knees.
So listen, you rich, you powerful,
you hidden evil powers,
We stand in the midst of the God of this hour.
You may pierce my hands, put a crown on my head,
You can send flying bullets with blood flowing red.
But God will be heard in the cries of the poor.
You may run, you may hide, you may feel quite secure.
All who will listen, I give my command, Now is the time,
You, be my hand . . .
That will summon the poets, give sweat to the plow,
Suck blood from the martyrs,

---

[5]The primary focus of reflection is the gospel. However, very often the other readings demand attention and must be brought into the dialogue.

[6]The scriptures in the Lectionary, the seasons of the year, and the ritual prayers of the mass are interrelated and form the basis for liturgical catechesis. The *liturgical context* attempts to explore and clarify the themes and this interrelatedness.

[7]*AIRI*, 23–24.

[8]Ibid.

[9]Ibid., 24.

Who cry, "Listen to us now.
We spoke with our lives, we shout from our graves...
Listen people, hear us,
You're not free... you are slaves
To the riches that bind,
the greed that rots the soul,
To death-dealing power,
To lives heartless and cold."
Turn not a deaf ear when rumors start to roam
About a God who is angry, is weeping, who moans...
For a people in silent pain, for a world in grave danger,
For the weak, the powerless, the lost, and the stranger.
Take heart, O Hopeful, for all is not lost,
There is time, it is now,
But great is the cost.
You must work, you must build,
You must fight and demand more,
For now it is their *banquet,*
You must stand with the poor!

—Mary Birmingham

We are baptized priest, prophet, and king. By virtue of our baptism we are mandated to go and do what Philip (first reading) showed us how to do—proclaim the good news. Philip showed us the effects of enthusiastic evangelization on a hungry world.

John's gospel exhorts us to follow the great commandment of love. Our Easter faith empowers us to experience what the Opening Prayer asks of God: "... help us to celebrate our joy in the resurrection of the Lord and to express in our lives the love we celebrate." Through the eucharist we actualize and make tangible the indwelling Spirit. We are thus empowered to go out and live the law of love, to evangelize and give witness to the saving power of God. "Strengthen us by this Easter sacrament; may we feel its saving power in our lives" (Prayer After Communion).

The Lord asks us to be with his brothers and sisters in the world. When we receive the Spirit of God, we too become defenders of the people. We become God's advocate for those who cannot defend themselves in a hostile world. "In his surrender, Jesus gave us life. This gift from the Lord should make us respect and welcome our neighbors with their needs, their suffering, and their life projects. All of this makes up the 'good conduct in Christ' to which Peter is calling us (3:16). We cannot, therefore, allow people to set themselves up as masters of the lives of others. The right to life is the primary right of the human person."[10]

We are given a glimpse of where that love will lead, in today's second reading: to the cross. Love ultimately means the sacrifice of self. Dietrich Bonhoeffer, the German theologian who was killed in the Nazi concentration camps, expressed it with his life. His legacy and wisdom live on.

> When a man really gives up trying to make something out of himself—a saint or a converted sinner or a churchman (a so-called clerical somebody), a righteous or unrighteous man . . . When in the fullness of tasks, questions, successes or ill-haps, experiences and perplexities, a man throws himself into the arms of God . . . Then he awakes with Christ in Gethsemane. That is faith, that is metanoia and it is thus that he becomes a man and a Christian. How can a man wax arrogant if in *a this-sided life* he shares in the suffering of God?[11]

G. Leibholz, when writing about Bonhoeffer, wrote of him: "To Bonhoeffer Christianity was not the concern of the believing pious soul who shuts himself up and keeps himself within the bounds of the sacramental sphere. No, according to him Christianity has its place in this world and the Church as the Body of Christ and the fellowship in him can only be the visible church. Man must follow him who has passed through this world as the living, dying and the risen Lord. Therefore, wherever it pleases God to put man in this world, the Christian must be ready for martyrdom and death. It is only this way that man learns faith."[12]

The season of Easter is an extended meditation on the paschal mystery. It is the time in which the entire church is to engage in mystagogical reflection. Today's liturgy takes us right into the heart of Easter's purpose.

---

[10] *SWTLY,* 104.

[11] Dietrich Bonhoeffer, *Das Zeugnis eines Boten,* Geneva, 1945, pp. 46–47.

[12] G. Leibholz in *The Cost of Discipleship* by Dietrich Bonhoeffer, New York: Collier Books, Macmillan Publishers, 1963.

Gospel Exegesis

The facilitator gives input regarding what critical biblical scholarship has to say about this text. The input includes insights as to how people would have heard the gospel in Jesus' time.

In a continuation of Jesus' farewell address to his disciples at the Last Supper, Jesus describes to them the way in which he will continue to offer his self-gift to the world—his unconditional, unmerited, gratuitous love and presence after his death, resurrection, and ascension. Jesus tells them that he will send his Spirit to continue his mission in the world. This section of chapter fourteen explains the special way in which Jesus will continue his presence in the community of believers. We hear of the love that Jesus has for his disciples, how the disciples will be rewarded for such love, and how they will experience opposition in the world.[13]

In the face of such love, Christians are to keep the commandments given by Christ. Jesus exhorted his followers to keep the two great commandments. Disciples must love the Lord their God with their entire, body, soul, and spirit—with the totality of themselves. They are to love one another, as Jesus himself loved—unto death. This love will be evident by the way in which it is poured out to God's anawim (the poor, marginalized, and oppressed), and to all people in the world—even to enemies. (Today's first reading from Acts demonstrates that such love knows no bounds.) It is a tall order, but through Jesus and the Spirit, Christians will be so empowered. Love will win. The poor will be cared for, animosity will cease, and where two or more are gathered in his name, the reign of God will be realized.

Jesus' compassion and love for his disciples capture our hearts and take residence there. He knows the disciples will feel lost and abandoned. He knows they will long for his comforting presence and to return to the way things used to be. He knows they will be lonely and bewildered. Jesus prepares the disciples for his absence by assuring them of his indwelling in the midst of absence. "The permanence of the Paraclete is contrasted with Jesus' departure."[14] He promises to return, this time not at his Second Coming, but spiritually, in the hearts of all believers. He promises to send his Spirit to dwell within. Then they will fully appreciate and know that Jesus and the Father are one.[15] His return hinges on their fidelity to the commandments—Jesus' commandments—the great commandments.

The Paraclete (Advocate) referred to in this pericope means a counselor, or one who supports a defendant at a trial. It is juridical language. Jesus would be found guilty, sentenced, and crucified. After his death the Paraclete would turn the tables and reverse the sentence. The world would be convicted and Jesus would be vindicated. "He will show that Jesus did not sin; rather the world sinned by not believing in him."[16]

The Spirit will also protect and defend the disciples. The Spirit will plead their case. The Spirit is referred to as *another* Paraclete. Jesus, however, is the first Paraclete—the first defender, protector, and advocate of the disciples. Jesus, like Moses of the Hebrew Scriptures, will plead for the sinful people before God.[17] In chapter five of John's gospel, Jesus' opponents are warned that Moses himself will turn an accusing finger at those who do not believe in him. Jesus' role as Paraclete did not end upon his death but continues as he sits upon his throne at the right hand of God.

It is the role of the "Spirit of truth" to impart the truth about Jesus Christ to the world. In last week's readings, Jesus revealed the truth of God to the disciples. Today Jesus reminds them that in order to know the truth of the Spirit, Jesus must be acknowledged and accepted. To know the Spirit one must know Jesus; similarly, to know the Father demands knowledge of and relationship with the Son. Ultimately, Jesus promises a relationship with God similar to his own.

Proclaim the gospel again.

Sometimes we gain new insights when we hear the text after the interpretation has been given. Someone from the group proclaims the gospel a second time.

---

[13]Pheme Perkins, "The Gospel According to John," *NJBC*, 975.

[14]Ibid.

[15]*GEJ*, 77.

[16]*OCSP*, 72.

[17]*GEJ*, 77.

STEP 4
TESTING

Conversation with the Liturgy and the Scriptures

Test your original understanding in dialogue with the text.

(You might consider breaking into smaller groups.)

How does this gospel speak to you now? Were there any new insights? How does this liturgy speak to your life?

Sharing Life Experience

Participants share an experience from their lives that connects with the biblical interpretation just shared.

> *Today's gospel reminds me again of what I know to be true. I know it to the core of my being. The promise of Jesus in today's gospel is truth. The Spirit truly dwells within me and within the church. I can do no less than share that truth with others. I am often surprised to awaken to the depths of my unconscious only to find the Spirit of God praying with and for me. The Spirit is with me to guide and lead. The Spirit has empowered me for ministry and gives me the boldness that I need to proclaim the year of liberty for the captives and favor from our God. I have always believed that ministry is as effective as the willingness to embrace the paschal mystery. How can I preach Jesus Christ, crucified and risen, if I have not experienced his suffering, liberation, and healing myself? How can I experience that and not share it—even when it leaves me vulnerable and laid bare, as Christ was vulnerable and laid bare? I have known that vulnerability. It takes courage to be willing to embrace it. There were a few times in my life when I was willing to become vulnerable for Christ and the gospel. There were other times when courage failed me. I have never had to lay down my life or suffer in any real way because I defended the cross of Christ. I marvel at the martyrs of then and those of today who are and were so strengthened for their great gift to the church. Today's gospel demands that I look within and ask the question: How am I living the law of love? The answer? When I do more than give lip service to it. A few weeks ago our catechumens and candidates served dinner at a local soup kitchen. The people we served had been beaten down by life. I wanted to go to each of them individually—hug them and tell them that I loved them. I experienced such incredible feelings of compassion. It was so easy to feel those feelings—quite another to act on them. One man who appeared to be mentally ill took me by the hand and wouldn't let go. He was disheveled and dirty, and had a strong body odor. This man wanted someone to listen to him. He clung tightly to my hand. I became repulsed by his presence and his odor. I wanted to run away. I resisted the temptation to feign an excuse so I could leave him. But I sat down and listened to him.*
>
> *Michael had fallen on his head in a work-related accident. He was wheelchair bound and attended the soup kitchen because he had to choose between eating at the soup kitchen or keeping his apartment. His compensation was only enough to cover his apartment.*
>
> *I was embarrassed at my repulsion. My meager, minuscule moments with him were more for my benefit than his. If I cannot see Jesus in the face of the world's forgotten and wretched, then I cannot see him anywhere. I had failed the test once more. Michael asked me for my phone number so he could call and talk to me. I was afraid to give it to him, lest I become too involved.*
>
> *Perhaps in a cautious world I did the right thing. Yet I was so taken with the innocent suffering of this young man, what could giving him my phone number hurt? The longer I stayed, the more I was able to see the face of Christ in his wretchedness. The joy of Easter demands that I remember not only the resurrected Christ, but also the suffering Christ that still resides in the world. Easter is a blending of joy and sober realism. The Body of Christ continues to suffer for the sake of the world. How willing am I to join in the suffering? Easter faith demands that I lay down my life, especially for the Michaels of this world.*
>
> *I wonder what would happen if I were to invite him to my parish, or any parish, and escort him up front to a place of honor in the assembly? Truthfully, do we (do I) see Michael as part of the same Body as the rest of us? Are we (am I) ready to make him part of our family? The Spirit of God dwells in Michael too—most especially in Michael. I obviously was not ready. Maybe I will be the next time.*

All share their life experience.

What specifically was Jesus' message to his disciples? How does that have any relevance for your life today? Do you really believe that you will not be abandoned or left orphaned by God? In what ways have you experienced the presence of the Spirit in your life? How do you know that the Spirit dwells in you? What evidence is there in your life? How is this gospel an Easter story of faith? What implications are there for your community? How are the themes of covenant, exodus, creation, and community expressed in today's liturgy? How do those themes speak to you? How would you express your understanding of this gospel now? Has your original understanding been challenged or affirmed?

STEP 5
DECISION

The gospel demands a response.

How do the scriptures and today's liturgy call us to transformation? In what way does today's liturgy invite change in the community? How might your parish be invited to respond? Has this conversation with the exegesis of the Sixth Sunday of Easter invited a change in outlook, attitude, or behavior in you? What are the implications for your life? What is one concrete action you will take this week in response?

Christian Initiation: This would be an appropriate day to celebrate a rite of full communion for Christians who were baptized in another ecclesial tradition. This would also be a marvelous day to celebrate infant baptisms. The initiation themes are very strong in today's liturgy. It might also be fitting to celebrate a rite of acceptance or a rite of welcome. Neophytes remain a visible presence in the Sunday assembly, and continue to meet to break open the symbols of the Vigil. Catechumens and candidates continue to be dismissed to further reflect on word and tradition.

DOCTRINAL ISSUES

What church truth/teaching/doctrinal issue could be drawn from the gospel for the Sixth Sunday of Easter?

Participants suggest possible doctrinal themes that flow from the readings.

Possible Doctrinal Themes

Holy Spirit, Christian witness, evangelization, baptism, paschal mystery, symbols: cross, water, oil, laying on of hands

Present the doctrinal material at this time.

1. The facilitator gives input on a particular doctrinal issue of his/her prior choosing. OR
2. The group chooses a doctrinal issue from the list they created. They read together from the Doctrinal Appendix or other appropriate official church documents and the works of respected theologians.

(The doctrinal issues are found in the Doctrinal Appendix in the back of this workbook. If you are choosing an issue from this resource, please refer to it now.)

Reflection questions centered around the chosen doctrinal theme can be found in the Doctrinal Appendix. The questions are based on the five-step reflection process. If you choose a topic not included in the Doctrinal Appendix, craft your own questions according to the same five-step process.

Following the reflection questions you will be reminded to return to chapter 7, "Preparing the Catechetical Session," to assist you in crafting your own session.

Closing Prayer

Through the resurrection of his Son,
God has redeemed you and made you his children.
May he bless you with joy.
Response: Amen.

The Redeemer has given you lasting freedom.
May you inherit his everlasting life.
Response: Amen.

By faith you rose with him in baptism.
May your lives be holy,
so that you will be united with him for ever.
Response: Amen.[18]

[18]Sixth Sunday of Easter: "Solemn Blessing," *The Sacramentary.*

Ascension

Environment

The Easter environment continues. Perhaps an icon of the ascension may be added.

INTRODUCTORY RITES

Opening Song (or Entrance Antiphon)

Men of Galilee, why do you stand looking in the sky? The Lord will return, just as you have seen him ascend, alleluia. (Acts 1:11)[1]

Opening Prayer

The facilitator of the session may lead the prayer. Others in the group may be asked to proclaim the readings.

Let us pray
[that the risen Christ
will lead us to eternal life]

Pause for silent prayer.

God our Father,
make us joyful in the ascension of your Son Jesus Christ.
May we follow him into the new creation,
for his ascension is our glory and hope.
We ask this through our Lord Jesus Christ, your Son,
who lives and reigns with you and the Holy Spirit,
one God, for ever and ever.[2]

LITURGY OF THE WORD

Let us listen to God's word.

The readings are proclaimed.

First Reading

Acts 1:1–11

The narrative of Christ's ascension in the Acts of the Apostles is concerned with the mission of the church and the future coming of Christ. Both the end of Luke's gospel and the beginning of the Acts of the Apostles deal with the commissioning of new members to promote the new reign of God. The commissioning of the chief characters highlights the central purpose of the entire narrative, which is concerned with rooting the events of the story in the divine purpose of God and Jesus' command.[3]

In this pericope Jesus reminds his hearers that not only did he promise the Spirit, but so did his Father. John the Baptist also prophesied regarding the sending of the Spirit. Jesus thus relates the prophetic utterances of two prophets: himself and the Baptist.

The Pentecost event is foreshadowed in verses 4 and 5. Even though the power of the Spirit is poured out at Pentecost, these early verses attest that the Spirit's role is more than just one of extending power. The Spirit has something to do with the essence of God. The connection of the Spirit with the essence of God as Father suggests that the Spirit's presence is a powerful experience of God's grace.[4] Even though Pentecost is anticipated, there is a sense throughout Acts that the conferral of the Spirit is not just a one-time event, but is the active movement of the Spirit in the ongoing life of the church.

The forty-day resurrection period is a time to teach the disciples about the reign of God (v. 3) that finds complete fulfillment in Jesus Christ. The number forty is symbolic and represents a sufficient period of time to prepare those who witnessed the Easter event for the mission of the church. This pericope sets the stage for the entire missionary thrust of the volume. God's reign is synonymous with the reign of Christ.

There is concern in verse 6 over God's intention for the salvation of Israel. Where was Israel's place in what God was doing in Christ? There is hope

[1]Ascension: "Entrance Antiphon," *The Sacramentary.*
[2]Ascension: "Opening Prayer," *The Sacramentary.*

[3]*NULA* (II), 12.
[4]Ibid., 13.

that Christ will deliver Israel, but there is also concern and question. Hope is not dead in spite of Israel's rejection of Jesus. Acts highlights the drama of a people turning away from the messianic fulfillment that was theirs for the taking. However, this rejection is still fraught with the future hope of restoration. All is not lost for Israel.

The evangelists are commissioned to further the mission of Christ and to go out to the ends of the earth with the Good News, again proving that God's mission is to the whole world.

The scene ends with the Galileans being chided for looking upward, when their gaze should be toward the missionary activities they have been commissioned to pursue. The chastisement of the angels is a call to action. Servants of the master are called to go out and gather in new members. They will one day be held accountable for their successes and failures.

The reader is made aware that the action of God throughout Acts is prompted by God's direction, not by human desires. Jesus' exalted reign has a future dimension. He will one day return as divine judge. Thus, the church waits in hope for the future day when Christ will return in his exalted state to judge and to bring the faithful home to share his heavenly reality.

Responsorial Psalm
Psalm 47:1–2, 5–8

This psalm is an enthronement psalm. It celebrates the hypothetical annual feast that enthroned an earthly king as a sign of Yahweh's reign over his people. The church appropriated this psalm to its celebration of the ascension of Christ. Jesus is enthroned in heaven with Yahweh, the supreme ruler over all creation.

Second Reading
Ephesians 1:17–23

Most scholars believe that the letter to the Ephesians was written by a devotee of Paul's. It begins with a hymn that is reminiscent of an ancient liturgy's opening prayer of thanksgiving. The first section of this reading is a prayer for the church to grow in wisdom and knowledge through the power of the risen and ascended Christ. Knowledge of God fills us with God's illumination. We can scarcely take in the brilliance of God's light within us. The rest of the pericope highlights the exalted, glorified Christ. Christ is Lord over his own faithful as well as over the world, which does not yet recognize him. We, like the small child who recognizes the voice of his or her parents, recognize the voice and the light of our heavenly Father. The missionary thrust of the church is to bring the world to knowledge of Christ and his saving works. It is up to the church, the Body of Christ, to help others recognize the voice and the light of God.

Gospel
Matthew 28:16–20

Jesus sends his disciples forth to "make disciples of all nations."

STEP 1
NAMING ONE'S EXPERIENCE

What were your first impressions? What was your first response? What grabbed your attention? How did you feel?

Each person names his or her initial impression. Statements should be brief. No reasons should be given at this time. All simply listen without agreeing or disagreeing.

STEP 2
UNDERSTANDING

In a brief statement, what do you think this gospel is trying to convey?

STEP 3
INPUT FROM VISION/STORY/TRADITION

Liturgical Context

"Let us remind ourselves once more that if we are to be true to the perspective of the New Testament and the early liturgy we should not think of the Ascension Day as a historical commemoration."[5] The ascension of Jesus is an integral piece of the resurrection. The feast of the Ascension is not the commemoration of the historical ascending of Jesus into heaven, but rather it celebrates the glorification of Christ as a result of the resurrection. Jesus rose from the dead on the third day. He went immediately to the Father. His post-resurrection appearances flowed from his heavenly, glorious existence. Even though Luke and John seem to posit the ascension and resurrection separately, they are not regarded as two successive events. They are regarded separately in order to appropriately contemplate the dimension of each reality. Luke places the ascension on Easter Sunday night or the next day. John places the event after the appearance to Mary Magdalene. The Acts of the Apostles places the event forty days after the resurrection. (However, "forty" is "symbolic of the time of revelation, and there may be no intention to suggest the ascension actually 'occurred' on the fortieth day."[6]) It is obvious in the post-resurrection Emmaus account that Jesus was understood to have come from his realm of glory before the final ascension.

The New Testament gives us three different narratives of the ascension of Christ that describe Jesus' final withdrawal of his physical presence from his disciples. The ascension is an expression of Jesus' risen state that celebrates his victory and points toward Pentecost and the second coming.[7]

The passion, death, resurrection, and ascension were always considered a single entity. This reality is the fullness of the paschal mystery. In the first Christian centuries, ascension was not celebrated as a separate feast. By the end of the fourth century, there is evidence of a separate feast. The Apostolic Constitution (380 C.E.) describes a celebration that took place forty days after Easter. The pilgrim Egeria (384 C.E.) reported a celebration of the ascension and the sending of the Spirit on the fiftieth day after Easter. St. John Chrysostom asserted that even though there were two separate celebrations (Pentecost and Ascension), they nevertheless were "two facets of the same reality."[8]

[5]*PNL*, 33.

[6]Ibid., 34.

[7]M. Dennis Hamm, S.J., "Ascension," in *CPDBT*, 52.

[8]Edward Foley, O.F.M.Cap., "Ascension," in *CPDBT*, 52.

By 388 C.E., St. Gregory Nyssa preached a sermon on the feast of the Ascension that did not look toward Pentecost. The fifth century entertained a celebration of ascension forty days after Easter, followed by a fast, thus the term, "the great forty day pascha." As a result of these shifts, the celebration of Easter as a fifty-day feast diminished and was replaced by historicization of the Easter event.

The "General Norms for the Liturgical Year and the Calendar" (#7) restored a non-literal understanding to the feast, stressing the connection between the passion, resurrection, ascension, and sending of the Spirit. The feast is a solemnity and in places where it is not designated as a holy day of obligation, it is to be moved to the next Sunday. The feast still is celebrated forty days after Easter in order to give it the proper focus for contemplation. There is no intention of making an historical connection.

The ascension was understood as symbolizing Christ's exaltation as well as the exaltation of those who believe in Christ. One scholar refers to the ascension as a metaphor that reflects an ancient belief in the divine destiny of Jesus. The theology of ascension includes Jesus' relationship to his church, his supremacy over the created universe, the sending of his Holy Spirit, his role as revealer, his heavenly priesthood, and the expectation of his return.[9]

No human being dares presume the right to live in heaven's exalted glory. Only unique chosen ones such as Enoch and Elijah were "taken up" to God. By affirming that Jesus is exalted and sits at his Father's right hand, the New Testament asserts that Jesus' death and resurrection transported him to an entirely new mode of existence with God. The resurrection symbolizes Jesus' victory over death. The ascension symbolizes Jesus' divinely controlled destiny.

The ascension narratives explain why the post-resurrection appearances of the risen Christ ended. Jesus entered into a new kind of existence in heaven. Scripture understood heaven as symbolic of God's mysterious inaccessibility as well as God's abiding presence. In his absence, Jesus is

[9]Lionel Swain, "Ascension of Christ," in *NDT*, 63.

profoundly present. Jesus, now with God, is present to the world as God is present to the world.

Jesus is understood as the Lord of the universe. The ascension reveals Jesus' status as Lord and Christ. Since he ascended into heaven, he demonstrated control over the created order of the universe. Thus, Jesus is its master.

Jesus' ascension served as prelude to the sending of his Spirit. In the Acts of the Apostles, Jesus was reported to have ascended the mountain (symbol of heaven) where he "poured out his Spirit." The Spirit would be the *One* who would continue the work of Christ's new Covenant.

Jesus, now in heaven, is able to reveal the things of God as well as exercise his role as intercessor and high priest (letter to the Hebrews). The ascension of Jesus guarantees that Jesus will return again. It is because Jesus ascended to his Father that he became the Son of Man who will accomplish the completion of God's ultimate plan of salvation for the world. Jesus' ascension reminds us that we will one day share his heavenly home. We are on a journey to our ultimate destiny.

The entrance antiphon of this liturgy emphasizes Jesus' return. The communion antiphon highlights his presence within the community: "Father, in this eucharist we touch the divine life you give to the world. Help us to follow Christ with love to eternal life where he is Lord for ever and ever." The opening prayer reminds us that Christ is indeed exalted and, as his followers, we share in his exaltation.

Gospel Exegesis

The facilitator gives input regarding what critical biblical scholarship has to say about this text. The input includes insights as to how people would have heard the gospel in Jesus' time.

Once in Galilee, the twelve were summoned to the mountain by Jesus. A treasure house of meaning is implied and assumed by this alpine manifestation. In the Old Testament, mountains were significant places of revelation and encounter with God. It is no accident that the Great Commission should take place on a mountain summit.

Mountains were the sight of Jesus' foundational events—"the call of the twelve, prayer, and the transfiguration."[10] Mountains were places of revelation and eschatological authority. The mountain is an intentional motif in Matthew's gospel, "employed to develop his theological purpose."[11] For Matthew, mountains were used "as eschatological sites where Jesus enters into the full authority of his Sonship, where the eschatological community is gathered, and where the age of fulfillment is inaugurated."[12] Such is the setting of today's gospel for the feast of the Ascension.

Consider the picture. The reader is taken from Jerusalem to Galilee where Jesus inaugurated his mission to the world. Before he died, Jesus predicted that he would return to the disciples in Galilee. The angel at the tomb and Jesus himself reiterated the promise. And so he met them on the mountain. It is the mountain of the Sermon and the Transfiguration. Moses was given the Law on Mount Sinai. Jesus was transfigured in glory in the presence of his awestruck disciples on this mountain. Jesus interpreted the Law on this mountain. Matthew's cyclical purpose comes full circle. Jesus, who was worshiped by the magi at his birth, now is worshiped by his disciples after his death, in his resurrected glory, on this mountain of holy events.

Raymond Brown reminds us that the disciples were plagued by doubt throughout Jesus' earthly and post-resurrection life. Yet, such doubt did not deter Jesus from coming close to his disciples to speak to them. They worshiped him; Jesus responded.

Not only did the appearance stories serve an apologetic function to prove that Jesus died and rose again, they also laid the groundwork for the future mission of the church. Disciples were to go and tell what they had seen—they were to proclaim Christ crucified and risen from the dead. Jesus appeared to the apostles to commission them to carry on his work. "The sending is based on Jesus' own status, showing that as Jesus carried on God's work, the apostles carry on Jesus'

[10]Benedict T. Viviano, O.P., "Mountains," in *CPDBT,* 650.

[11]Ibid., 652.

[12]T.L. Donaldson, "Jesus on the Mountain," in *CPDBT,* 652.

work. . . . The authority of the church is delegated from Jesus who has been elevated and has authority in heaven and on earth; the mission that flows from it will touch all nations."[13]

With full authority Jesus commissioned the twelve to go out and continue his mission. Earlier in Matthew's gospel, the apostles were instructed to stay away from some people (Samaritans and gentiles). They were to gather the lost sheep of Israel. In Matthew's gospel, Jesus ministered only to Jews. So did the apostles at first. It was not until a few decades later that God's wider plan for the development of the church was understood as outreach beyond their borders—to the gentiles.

Now, with the full authority of his Sonship and Lordship, Jesus commissioned the twelve to go to *all* nations. Israel is still welcome, but there are no boundaries when it comes to those who are included in the new kingdom. It is from his exalted throne that Jesus will reign until all his enemies have been defeated.

The mission of Jesus is to be accomplished through baptism. By the time Matthew's gospel was written, baptism was in the name of the Father, and of the Son, and of the Holy Spirit, whereas in the Acts of the Apostles and Paul's letter to the Corinthians, baptism was in the name of Jesus. The Trinitarian formula found in Matthew's gospel signals the church's inauguration of the baptismal profession of faith in the triune God.

The apostles are now commissioned to go forth and teach all that Jesus commanded. Jesus' authority has now been passed on to the church. The final verse of today's gospel echoes the first words ever spoken about Jesus. He is Emmanuel—*God is with us*. Now in fulfillment, Jesus remains with the church. God is with God's people.

The ruling powers of the earth tried to stop *God is with us* at the birth of Jesus, and then again at his crucifixion. God's plan is not to be deterred; it will go forward until the end of time.

[13] *RCE*, 35.

Proclaim the gospel again.

Sometimes we gain new insights when we hear the text after the interpretation is given. Someone from the group proclaims the gospel a second time.

STEP 4
TESTING

Conversation with the Liturgy and the Scriptures

Test your original understanding in dialogue with the text.

(You might consider breaking into smaller groups.)

Were there any new insights? Was there anything you had not considered before in regard to the feast of the Ascension? How does your original understanding of this feast compare with what we just shared? How does this story speak to your life?

Sharing Life Experience

Participants share an experience from their lives that connects with the biblical interpretation just shared.

> *Abraham Heschel once said, "There are no proofs for the existence of God, there are only witnesses." Today's liturgy reminds us that thanks to those first witnesses who walked with Jesus and were able to pass on what they witnessed, we too are able to witness to the marvels of God in our lives.*
>
> *At a recent retreat, the participants began to create the expectation of God's action in their lives. We told one another to expect miracles, to expect God to act powerfully. The greatest experience of God's presence during the week was in the shared stories of our lives. We were awed by the way God had been present to each of us throughout our life experiences. Whether our story was one of an estranged marriage, troubled family relationships, parenting problems and disappointments, or problems of health or doubting faith, our shared pain gave us a sense of solidarity with all who suffer. Once we gave each other permission to break open the stories of our lives with one another, God was with us in our vulnerability. The Spirit of God was with us, prompting us,*

teaching and challenging us to new growth. We were all witnesses to the incredible power of God's love and action.

The first witnesses of Jesus life, death, resurrection, and ascension were together in their fear and their doubts. They needed the reminder of the scriptures and Jesus' words and actions to keep them grounded in what God was doing. They were able to go out and witness because of what he had done in their midst and because they were able to connect it to God's greater plan of salvation.

We did not stand with Jesus on the mount of his ascension, but we knew we shared its promise. As we shared our stories and connected them to the larger story we share in the gospel, we became more certain of our common destiny and our common hope. As we shared our joys, our struggles, and the incredible pain of our lives, we were able to unite our dying and rising to Jesus' own paschal mystery. The power of the Spirit was unleashed in our midst through the witness of God's action in our lives. Jesus gave permission for the church to witness to that same power.

All share their life experience.

What was Matthew's concern in today's gospel? How does Matthew's challenge impact the contemporary church? What does it mean to you that we are baptized in the name of the Trinity? What is your experience of Emmanuel—*God is with us*? Would you be able to share that experience with others? What is the significance of the feast of the Ascension for your life? The life of the community? In what way do today's readings reflect the four biblical themes of covenant, creation, community, and exodus? In what way does this liturgy invite transformation in your life?

STEP 5
DECISION

The gospel demands a response.

In what concrete way does this liturgy call our parish to action in the church, parish, neighborhood, or world? What am I/we/our community/our parish called to do in response? What is one concrete action we will take this week as a response to what we have learned and shared today?

DOCTRINAL ISSUES

What church truth/teaching/doctrinal issue could be drawn from the liturgy for the feast of the Ascension?

Participants suggest possible doctrinal themes that flow from the readings.

Possible Doctrinal Themes

Ascension, paschal mystery, christology, Trinity, Holy Spirit, Christian witness, sacraments, baptism, confirmation, eucharist, penance, orders, marriage, symbols: light, water, cross, oil, bread, wine, laying on of hands, white garment, assembly

Present the doctrinal material at this time.

1. The facilitator gives input on a particular doctrinal issue of his/her prior choosing. OR
2. The group chooses a doctrinal issue from the list they created. They read together from the Doctrinal Appendix.

(The doctrinal issues are found in the Doctrinal Appendix in the back of this workbook. If you are choosing an issue from this resource, please refer to it now.)

Reflection questions centered around the chosen doctrinal theme can be found at the end of each topic in the Doctrinal Appendix. The questions are based on the five-step reflection process. If you choose a topic not included in the Doctrinal Appendix, craft your own questions according to the same five-step process.

Following the reflection questions you will be reminded to return to chapter 7, "Preparing the Catechetical Session," to assist you in crafting your own session.

Closing Prayer

May almighty God bless you on this day
when his only Son ascended into heaven

to prepare a place for you.

Response: Amen.

After his resurrection,
Christ was seen by his disciples.
When he appears as judge
may you be pleasing forever in his sight.

Response: Amen.

You believe that Jesus has taken his seat in majesty
at the right hand of the Father.
May you have the joy of experiencing
that he is also with you to the end of time,
according to his promise.

Response: Amen.[14]

[14]Ascension: "Solemn Blessing," *The Sacramentary.*

SEVENTH SUNDAY OF EASTER

INTRODUCTORY RITES

Opening Song (or Entrance Antiphon)

Lord, hear my voice when I call to you. My heart has prompted me to seek your face. I seek it, Lord; do not hide from me, alleluia. (Ps 27:7–9)[1]

Opening Prayer

The facilitator of the session may lead the prayer. Others in the group may be asked to proclaim the readings.

Let us pray
[to our Father who has raised us to life in Christ]

Pause for silent prayer.

Eternal Father,
reaching from end to end of the universe,
and ordering all things with your mighty arm:
for you, time is the unfolding of truth that already is,
the unveiling of beauty that is yet to be.
Your Son has saved us in history
by rising from the dead,
so that transcending time he might free us from death.
May his presence among us
lead to the vision of unlimited truth
and unfold the beauty of your love.
We ask this in the name of Jesus the Lord.[2]

LITURGY OF THE WORD

The readings are proclaimed.

First Reading
Acts 1:12–14

Luke's purpose in this section is to paint the Easter event as a triptych—three distinct events: the resurrection, the ascension forty days later, and the sending of the Spirit fifty days after the resurrection. Luke's canvas in today's reading includes Jesus' ascension into heaven and the subsequent gathering of the first church in the upper room. The disciples assembled in prayer as they awaited the Spirit's arrival at Pentecost. Luke does not portray the apostles as being in a state of chaotic fear or as unable to function following the crucifixion. They still had the presence of mind to come together for prayer.

The reader is given a glimpse of the beginnings of the first church under the structured leadership of the apostles. We are not to miss Luke's point as we consider who was present in the upper room—the apostles, some other disciples, Mary, and the other women. The women were the first to bear the good news of the resurrection. Throughout Luke's gospel the women were the first to hear and respond to revelation. Their faithfulness was not to go unnoticed!

Mary is the only woman Luke mentions by name, however. Mary would continue to be significant in God's unfolding plan of salvation. Mary, whose womb was home to the Savior of the world, is present now with the apostles as the Holy Spirit descends upon the church. Even though this would be the last time we were to hear about Mary in the scriptures, she would continue to have a role in the continuing mission of her Son.

Last on Luke's list of those present were Jesus' relatives. During Jesus' earthly life they were slow to accept him or his message. They wanted Jesus to impress Jerusalem with a flashy show of divine power. Jesus chastised them for missing the point of his mission. They eventually melded into the throng of Jesus' followers. James would be the only one who would have a leadership position in the later Jerusalem community.

Questions for mystagogical reflection: *Has there ever been a circumstance in your life when all you could do was sit in silent retreat and wait for God to act, or*

[1]Seventh Sunday of Easter: "Entrance Antiphon," *The Sacramentary.*

[2]Seventh Sunday of Easter: "Opening Prayer," *The Sacramentary.*

for life's events to unfold? What did it teach you about life? About God? What is the primary message for the church in today's pericope? What is the primary message for you? In what way might this reading invite transformation in your life? In the life of the community?

Responsorial Psalm
Psalm 27:1–4, 7–8

The theme of *waiting for God to act,* evident in today's psalm refrain, is appropriate in this period of pause as the church silently prays and waits for Pentecost.

Second Reading
1 Peter 4:13–16

Today's pericope is taken from the section of 1 Peter that serves as a warning for the persecution that the community is about to endure. The letter was written in the early days of Christianity's status as an illegal religion. Judaism was legal and thus guaranteed the right to exist under Roman law. Christianity was considered separate from Judaism. As a consequence, Christians faced state-sponsored persecution.

Peter reminds his community that their glory is the cross of Christ. Christ was triumphant in the face of the horror of the cross. The cross is the heritage, destiny, and honor of all believers. Suffering in this life is transitory and is as nothing in comparison to the glory that awaits God's faithful. Martyrs for the faith offer praise to God with the sacrifice of their lives.

When we align our suffering with the suffering of Jesus on the cross, we participate in his death and resurrection, and in his saving action. Peter reminds his suffering church that their suffering is a cause for joy, an opportunity to share more fully in the paschal mystery.

Questions for mystagogical reflection: *In what way can you relate to Peter's message to his community? What is your experience of suffering? Have you ever experienced redemptive suffering? What does that mean to you? How are you called to participate in the suffering of Christ in your everyday life? In what way might your parish respond to Peter's message to his community? What is your response?*

Gospel[3]
John 17:1–11

Jesus looked heavenward and asked his Father to glorify him.

STEP 1
NAMING ONE'S EXPERIENCE

What were your first impressions? What was your first response to the gospel (or the other readings)?[3] What captured your attention?

Each person names his or her initial impression. Statements should be brief. No reasons should be given at this time. All simply listen without agreeing or disagreeing.

STEP 2
UNDERSTANDING

In a brief statement, what do you think this gospel is trying to convey?

STEP 3
INPUT FROM VISION/STORY/TRADITION

Liturgical Context[4]

In today's first reading the church is gathered in the upper room to wait and pray for the Spirit to descend upon the church. Karl Barth once referred to the period between the ascension and Pentecost as a "significant pause." "It is a pause between the actions of God, a pause in which all the community can do is wait and pray. It may seem paradoxical, but although the Spirit came, in Johannine language, 'to abide with you [the com-

[3]The primary focus of reflection is the gospel. However, very often the other readings demand attention and must be brought into the dialogue.

[4]The scriptures in the Lectionary, the seasons of the year, and the ritual prayers of the mass are interrelated and form the basis for liturgical catechesis. The *liturgical context* attempts to explore and clarify the themes and this interrelatedness.

munity] for ever,' the Church nevertheless has to pray constantly, *Veni, Creator Spiritus.* The gift of the Spirit is never an assured possession but has to be constantly sought anew in prayer."[5]

The Seventh Sunday continues the theme of Ascension: the glorification and enthronement of the risen Christ. Jesus speaks today as if he is already at God's right side. Today's Opening Prayer reminds us that Christ now lives in glory and promises to be with the church until the end of time. That promise is fulfilled at Pentecost.

John gives us a glimpse of Jesus in his ascended glory and invites us to enter into the mystery of his resurrection and ascension—the mystery of intimate union with God in heaven. From that intimate union flows the unity of the church. The Communion Antiphon reminds us of Jesus' prayer that his believers may become one, as he is one with the Father (Jn 17:22). Jesus prayed for the unity of the church. The Spirit is the tangible presence of Christ, who strengthens the church to work for the unity that Christ envisioned.

While we wait for the Spirit's action in our lives, we are to pray without ceasing. The Spirit is not God's agent to answer our every manipulative request. The Holy Spirit is the gratuitous, unmerited gift of God's love and action in our lives. In response, we are called to constant prayer and to self-sacrificing discipleship. We are given the bold reminder that to be a follower of Christ we must be willing to lay down our lives (1 Peter). Incorporation in the Body of Christ is also incorporation into the paschal mystery. We wait in awe for the coming of the Spirit at Pentecost, and every day of our lives.

Gospel Exegesis

The facilitator gives input regarding what critical biblical scholarship has to say about this text. The input includes insights as to how people would have heard the gospel in Jesus' time.

The first twenty-six chapters of John's gospel constitute a unit by themselves. They contain the conclusion to Jesus' Last Discourse, which is his "Priestly Prayer." We are led into a panoramic view of the eternal. It is as if Jesus has already bid farewell to his earthly ministry. The prayer of Jesus before his passion functions like a eucharistic prayer. He raised his eyes and blessed God for all God's works of salvation and for the work he would accomplish through the Son and through the sending of the Spirit. The Trinitarian prayer is constructed like all eucharistic prayers. The prayer transitions from thanks and blessing to intercession as the Trinity is remembered and invoked. "With no parallels in the other Gospels, this text is extremely important: by placing before our eyes the mystery of salvation in its totality and by presenting it in its internal dynamic, it is the perfect model for all Christian prayer and liturgy."[6] Some scholars refer to Jesus' prayer as his prayer of consecration. He consecrates himself for his redemptive death.[7] His priestly action is to offer the obedient sacrifice of his life to his Father.

Jesus the high priest is taking his place at God's right hand where he once reigned before the creation of the world. Jesus, our advocate and representative before God, prays for unity on our behalf. His farewell serves as a prelude to his final and eternal sacrifice of the cross.

Jesus' "hour" transcends earthly time. It is *kairos* time—time that has one foot in the past, walks purposefully in the present, and has arrived triumphantly in the future. It is the moment the world audience has been anxiously awaiting. The curtain goes up on the fulfillment of God's plan. Amoeba and beast alike hold their breath as all creation gasps in awe at the fulfilling event that marks the reason for their entrance onto the world stage in the first place. The Word who witnessed and caused their genesis returns to God in glory.

As Lord of Life, Jesus offers eternal life to his chosen. Through Jesus we are God's own. Only through Jesus is it possible to know the author of all life. The purpose of Jesus' life is accomplished now, at the hour of our vindication. The Semitic understanding of "knowing" meant intimacy and union with the one known.[8] Human beings are capable of intimate union with God because we

[5] *PL,* 93.

[6] *DL,* (III), 230.

[7] *PL,* 92.

[8] *GEJ,* 84.

"know" the Son. On earth our knowledge is imperfect; in heaven we will know intimate, perfect union with God.

Now that Jesus' mission is accomplished, he is returning to God. Jesus never really left God's side, as they were in perfect union throughout his earthly life. Jesus' glorified human nature is now ready to return to the throne of heaven to sit at God's right hand. Jesus prays for the disciples he is leaving behind. Even though they are no longer *of the world,* they still have to live in it. He prays that God will protect and keep them firm in their commitment as they struggle to carry out his mission in the world. Jesus' life will continue in them. But first he must leave.

Karl Rhaner reminds us that Jesus was not raised from the dead to demonstrate that he was leaving the tomb of the earth once and for all, "but in order to demonstrate that precisely that tomb of the dead—the body and the earth—has finally changed into the glorious, immeasurable house of the living God and of the God-filled soul of the Son. . . . He rose again to reveal that through his death the life of freedom and beatitude remains established forever within the narrow limits and sorrow of the earth, in the depths of its heart."[9]

Proclaim the gospel again.

Sometimes we gain new insights when we hear the text after the interpretation has been given. Someone from the group proclaims the gospel a second time.

STEP 4
TESTING

Conversation with the Liturgy and the Scriptures

Test your original understanding in dialogue with the text.

(You might consider breaking into smaller groups.)

Was there anything in this gospel that had never occurred to you before—any new insights? How does this story speak to your life?

[9]*GCY,* 195.

Sharing Life Experience

Participants share an experience from their lives that connects with the biblical interpretation just shared.

> *Waiting for the Spirit in prayer, redemptive suffering, Jesus' consolation and compassion, Jesus' presence in absence—the themes of today's liturgy jump off the page and leave me breathless and in awe. My lower lip quivers in utter amazement at the extraordinary action of God's Spirit in the lives of his children.*
>
> *For the past few months we have prayed, waited, and begged for healing. We have stood watch and stormed the heavens for the young family whose year-old child is suffering from an extremely rare and fatal disease. I am not writing this in awe of a miraculous healing for their only child; he is still fighting and hanging on to his little life. So far he has crossed every hurdle, and through every hurdle we have held our breath and thanked God for his continued gift of life—each precious moment of it. The struggle and the hope continue. But today we received the miraculous news that the couple is expecting another baby. It is an unplanned surprise—a gift from God. The baby boy in utero, who had a one-in-four chance of sharing the same disease as his brother, has been tested free of the disease. In the midst of this family's sorrow and grief, they pause to ponder the precious joy of new life growing within. Who, but they, can speak to us of the paschal mystery? Life is such a mystery—joy and sorrow balanced delicately together on a tightrope.*
>
> *We cannot look at this gift as a holy exchange—one life for another life. One child does not wait in the wings to take the place of another child who lies perilously close to death. God's ways are simply not our ways. We are to continue in our prayer and wait for God's glory (often only to be found in the most unexpected places). Jesus lamented with his disciples over his coming absence but, at the same time, he hinted at the glory they would one day share. Agony and ecstasy—together they reveal the amazing mystery of God.*
>
> *Easter draws to a close. We have walked the paschal walk, pondered the gift of death and life, and now we await the powerful wind of Spirit to fall afresh on us—to renew and strengthen us to spend another year living the Easter mystery we have professed and*

celebrated. Our good news today is a gentle reminder of the Spirit of Life who dwells in our midst, who walks with us when we grieve, and who sings with us when our happiness spills over the brim of our hearts. We still await the Spirit; we still ponder in awe!

All share their life experience.

What was Jesus trying to tell his disciples? How might his word be relevant for the contemporary world? In what way does this gospel reflect God's promise to the world? What does it have to do with your life? In what way does this liturgy invite liberation and new life—transformation? Does your conversation with this liturgy invite you to change the way you look at life?

STEP 5
DECISION

The gospel demands a response.

What is the challenge for your community? What are the implications of this gospel for your life? What is one concrete action you will take this week as a response to today's liturgy?

Christian Initiation: Next week is Pentecost. Perhaps all those who celebrated a sacrament of initiation (baptism, confirmation, or eucharist) last year might be recognized and blessed at the Sunday liturgies. Today would be an appropriate day to celebrate a rite of full communion into the Catholic Church, provided that you have candidates ready and prepared. This would also be an appropriate time to celebrate a rite of welcome or acceptance. The neophytes continue to be a visible presence in your assembly.

DOCTRINAL ISSUES

What church truth/teaching/doctrinal issue could be drawn from the gospel for the Seventh Sunday of Easter?

Participants suggest possible doctrinal themes that flow from the readings.

Possible Doctrinal Themes

Paschal mystery, christology, Holy Spirit, church, ecclesiology, baptism, confirmation, eucharist, cost of discipleship
Present the doctrinal material at this time.

1. The facilitator gives input on a particular doctrinal issue of his/her prior choosing. OR
2. The group chooses a doctrinal issue from the list they created. They read together from the Doctrinal Appendix or other appropriate, official church documents and the works of respected theologians.

(The doctrinal issues are found in the Doctrinal Appendix in the back of this workbook. If you are choosing an issue from this resource, please refer to it now.)

Reflection questions centered around the chosen doctrinal theme can be found at the end of each topic in the Doctrinal Appendix. The questions are based on the five-step reflection process. If you choose a topic not included in the Doctrinal Appendix, craft your own questions according to the same five-step process.

Following the reflection questions you will be reminded to return to chapter 7, "Preparing the Catechetical Session," to assist you in crafting your own session.

Closing Prayer

Father,
help your people to rejoice in the mystery of
 redemption
and to win its reward.
We ask this in the name of Jesus the Lord.
 Response: Amen.

May almighty God bless you,
the Father, and the Son, and the Holy Spirit.
 Response: Amen.[10]

---

[10]Seventh Sunday of Easter: "Solemn Blessing," *The Sacramentary.*

Pentecost Sunday

Environment

The feast of Pentecost has always been associated with the first gathering of the harvest. The fifty days of spring were an anxious time of waiting for the fruits to ripen. The Jewish feast of Pentecost, "The Feast of Weeks—Shavuot," was a time of gathering the grain harvest.

Strawberries, cherries, and apricots are associated with the feast as these are usually the first ripened fruits of summer. Easter pastels should turn to vibrant shades of reds. Since the liturgical color of Pentecost is red, the catechetical environment should be draped in abundant shades of red. One is hampered only by a limited imagination. The image of the dove, while not directly associated with Pentecost, is associated with the coming of the Spirit upon Christ at his baptism. Icons have used the image of a firebird with vibrant feathers as a symbol of Pentecost. The symbol of the phoenix rising up out of the ashes has been a traditional symbol of the resurrection. Perhaps one of these images might be incorporated into a Pentecost environment.

INTRODUCTORY RITES

Opening Song (or Entrance Antiphon)

Song: Veni Creator Spiritus

The Spirit of the Lord fills the whole world. It holds all things together and knows every word spoken by man, alleluia. (Wis 1:7)[1]

Opening Prayer

The facilitator of the session may lead the prayer. Others in the group may be asked to proclaim the readings.

Let us pray
[in the Spirit who dwells within us]

Pause for silent prayer.

Father of light, from whom every good gift
comes,
send your Spirit into our lives
with the power of a mighty wind
and by the flame of your wisdom
open the horizons of our minds.
Loosen our tongues to sing your praise
in words beyond the power of speech,
for without your Spirit
man could never raise his voice in words of
peace
or announce the truth that Jesus is Lord,
who lives and reigns with you and the Holy
Spirit,
one God, for ever and ever.[2]

LITURGY OF THE WORD

There are two liturgies of Pentecost: the vigil mass and the mass during the day. The vigil mass is not widely celebrated since the mass during the day is usually chosen for the Saturday evening liturgy prior to Pentecost Sunday. However, exegesis is provided for both the vigil and the mass during the day. Readings from both liturgies together form the fullness of truth inherent in the feast of Pentecost.[3]

Let us listen to God's word.

The readings are proclaimed.

Readings from the Vigil of Pentecost

Vigil First Readings
Genesis 11:1–9, Tower of Babel, or
Exodus 19:3–8, 16–20, Giving of the law and the manifestation at Mount Sinai, or

[1]Pentecost Sunday: "Entrance Antiphon," *The Sacramentary.*

[2]Pentecost, Mass During the Day: "Alternative Opening Prayer," *The Sacramentary.*

[3]The second reading and the gospel for the vigil mass are always the same: Romans 8:22–27 and John 7:37–39. The first reading is chosen from among four possibilities: Genesis 11:1–9; Exodus 19:3–8, 16–20; Ezekiel 37:1–14; Joel 3:1–5.

Ezekiel 37:1–14, Ezekiel and his vision of the dry bones, or

Joel 3:1–5, prophecy about the outpouring of the Holy Spirit

The Tower of Babel

The author of Luke-Acts no doubt made a connection between the sending of the Spirit and the story of the Tower of Babel. At Babel the people were following their own whimsical designs. They wanted to establish a permanent settlement, achieve their own prestige. Their human designs were thwarted and they were dispersed as a people. They were in disarray and they no longer understood one another's language. Pentecost answers the tragedy of Babel. Pentecost gathers and unites God's dispersed people. The preaching in tongues at the Pentecost event was understood as the restoration of the human race. People were able to understand one another in their own languages. Unity was again possible. People would be able to understand the gospel in their own language. The ravages of sin had been broken through the power of the Spirit.

Manifestation at Sinai

In the manifestation of God at Mount Sinai, God was present and spoke in majesty, in mystery, and in great Cecil B. DeMille fashion, midst thunder, lightning, and clouds. God is both accessible and inaccessible. Sinai was connected to Pentecost in the symbolism of the tongues of fire and the rushing wind. God is still both present and absent; we are still in relationship as Creator and creature. Yet, Christ is the ongoing presence of God in the community of his new covenant.

Ezekiel's Dry Bones

Israel had sinned. They were dispersed. They saw their captivity as a result of their sin. All was lost. There was no hope. They could do nothing on their own power. Ezekiel rose up as prophet in their midst and offered encouragement in their desperate situation.

God, through his prophet, sends down the Holy Spirit (an epiclesis) and breathes new life into the dry, dead bones. The Spirit breathes new life and gives new hope. The dry bones of Ezekiel summarize the entire drama of salvation history. When we lose our way (as we have and we will), God has been and will be there to breathe new life into what is dead, lost, and forgotten. Pentecost is the restoration and ongoing life of that same Spirit in the life of the community.

Prophecy of Joel

Peter quotes Joel in his speech at Pentecost. Joel was referring to the outpouring of the Spirit upon Israel. Usually it was understood that the Spirit was poured down upon a charismatic leader, a prophet, or particularly the messiah. However, Joel's vision extended beyond that narrow understanding. It was inclusive of the entire community. The community was to be empowered by the Spirit and would know the law in their hearts. Knowing the law would give them knowledge of God. In the community of the messianic age, the Spirit would come upon not just the leaders, but the entire community.

Responsorial Psalm

Psalm 104:1–2, 24, 27–28, 29, 30, 35

This is a psalm in praise of the God of creation. The understanding of Spirit throughout the Wisdom tradition is that the Spirit of God participated in the creation of the world. The New Testament tradition centers on the work of the Spirit in the messianic age. In the Hebrew Scriptures, says Reginald Fuller, "'renewal' by the Spirit probably refers to the renewal of nature at springtime."[4] However, Christianity expanded the notion of renewal to mean the renewal of creation in the messianic age, beginning first with the church, the people of God.

Vigil Second Reading

Romans 8:22–27

Paul's letter to the Romans picks up the theme of the Spirit at work in the universe. It is not just the Christian community that is renewed by the Spirit; the entire cosmos is renewed. Paul is concerned about the bondage of sin that traps people and keeps them enslaved to sin. On their own power, people can do nothing. Paul knows this principle from personal experience. He understands that we are still in the flesh and, as long as we are, the battle will continue and we will not achieve our destiny.

---

[4] *PNL*, 38.

However, in spite of our innermost groaning, we do have the Spirit of God to renew and lead us to this ultimate destiny. The Spirit will help us withstand the suffering in our lives and persevere courageously. The Spirit uplifts all creation as we strive to live in accord with the will of God.

Vigil Gospel

The Jewish feast of Booths was a feast of great rejoicing over the end of the harvest. During the feast, the people erected and spent seven days living in tents (*sukkoth*). Later, this celebration was combined with a memorial of certain aspects of the Passover. The priests would go to the pool of Siloam ("the one who has been sent"); they would draw water in a golden pitcher, ceremoniously process into the temple, and then pour out the water at the corner of the altar. The water was reminiscent of the water that Moses caused to spring up from the desert and the water of Ezekiel's vision that flowed from under the temple. These were purifying waters that watered the whole country and purified the waters of the Dead Sea. "I will sprinkle clean water upon you to cleanse you from all your impurities, and from all your idols I will cleanse you. I will give you a new heart and place a new spirit within you, taking from your bodies your stony hearts and giving you natural hearts. I will put my spirit within you and make you live by my statutes, careful to observe my decrees. You shall live in the land I gave your fathers; you shall be my people and I will be your God" (Ez 36:25–28).

The feast of Booths was a celebration of all the mighty things God has accomplished, the new "Exodus of joy and glory, the definitive purification of the people, the coming of the Messiah, the effusion of God's Spirit and its manifestation on the last day."[5] This was a great feast of rejoicing that ended on the eighth day. It was on this eighth day that Jesus pronounced what was in this gospel.

"Let any one who thirsts come to me and drink." It is Jesus who now offers the life-giving waters of refreshment. All the hopes and dreams embodied in the great feast are now to be found in Jesus. The life-giving water was a sign of the Spirit who came in the sign of water at the Red Sea, the water from the rock in the desert, Ezekiel's spring, the water promised to the Samaritan woman by Jesus, and water flowing from the side of Christ. The Spirit is given at baptism and confirmation and continues to be poured out on the church as it gathers to offer perfect worship in spirit and truth in the sacred liturgy.

A constant theme in the farewell discourses is that Jesus suffered, died, and rose again in order to send his Spirit to those who believe. In John's gospel, the water and blood that poured from Jesus' side at the crucifixion was a sign of the coming of the Holy Spirit upon the church. Blood and water, then, became the symbolic sign of Christ's fulfilled promise to those who believe. The coming of the Spirit to the gathered twelve at Pentecost was the actual event: the conferral of the Holy Spirit upon the church.

Readings from the Mass During the Day on Pentecost Sunday

First Reading
Acts 2:1–11

The actual historical event of the sending of the Spirit is not what is at issue in today's readings. In this reading, the Spirit comes at Pentecost; in the gospel it happens on Easter Sunday. The *when* is not important. This appearance denotes the establishment of the church as larger than just the twelve. It is also the beginning of the church's mission: the Christian kerygma.

The Pentecost account is told in a way that reminds the reader of the giving of the law on Mount Sinai. The new *Twelve*, like the twelve tribes of Israel, gather together for the event. There is a sound from heaven that fills the *whole* house, just as there was a thunderous noise from God on Mount Sinai that shook the *whole* mountain. The fire of Pentecost is reminiscent of the fire at Sinai—both evoking the manifestation or theophany of God. The tongues of fire are symbolic of the presence of God that will manifest itself in human language, the "prophetic ministry of the disciples (tongues)."[6] Jesus mediates God's

[5] *DL* (III), 265.

[6] M. Dennis Hamm, S.J., "Pentecost-New Testament," in *CPDBT*, 715.

word to his people. The Holy Spirit will empower God's people with a new evangelical strength. The apostles will go out and spread the word among the nations.

By naming all the places of origin of those present, the Acts of the Apostles is positing a very powerful eschatology. Pentecost is the fulfillment of the promises made to Israel. All are now living in the eschatological age. This is the final gathering of Israel. The gift of Pentecost is first intended for the Jews and then for all the nations on earth. As said earlier, this pericope is understood as an answer to Babel. The people of Babel, filled with self-importance and sin, are scattered in confusion. They do not understand one another. In contrast, this reading highlights the gathering of a people, who now, under the power of the Spirit, are able to communicate. Formed as a repentant and reconciled new community, they now are able to understand one another, each in their own native language—under God's initiative, not their own.

Questions for mystagogical reflection: *Has your community ever had an experience in which the Spirit of God brought understanding out of confusion? How are you personally challenged by the reading from Acts? Does your baptismal commitment have anything to do with today's liturgy? What might be going on in the world, in the church, or in your life that is in need of the Spirit today?*

Responsorial Psalm
(same as vigil)

Second Reading
1 Corinthians 12:3–7, 12–13

One of the effects of gnosticism on Paul's community was that they treated those who did not have all the special gifts of the Spirit as somehow *less than.* Glossalalia (speaking in tongues) was just one such instance. Those who did not speak in tongues were considered inferior. This caused division within the community.

Paul puts priorities in the right place. He definitively asserts that to be in the Spirit means one confesses Jesus as Lord. He is referring here to the earthly, crucified Lord. The gnostic Corinthians regarded the death of Jesus as a past, forgotten reality and were more interested in an ethereal, intangible Jesus. Paul grounds them in the reality of the cross. All the gifts of the spirit are for the uplifting of the Body. One gift is not to be stressed over another. All are to be used with prudence and balance for the good of the community, not for self-edification. Through baptism, the church is one Body. Through eucharist, all are "to drink of the one Spirit." There is to be no divisiveness. All gifts are to be used for the common good, to uplift and nourish the entire Body. Reginald Fuller notes that this letter was possibly written for the paschal feast.

Questions for mystagogical reflection: *How does this reading challenge our community today? Is there any evidence of using gifts for personal gain rather than for the common good? How are we personally challenged by this reading? What does this reading have to say about our status as baptized, fully initiated people in the Body of Christ?*

Sequence

> Come, Holy Spirit, and from heaven direct on man the rays of your light. Come, Father of the poor; come, giver of God's gifts; come, light of men's hearts.
>
> Kindly Paraclete, in your gracious visits to man's soul, you bring relief and consolation. If it is weary with toil, you bring it ease; in the heat of temptation, your grace cools it; if sorrowful, your words console it.
>
> Light most blessed, shine on the hearts of your faithful—even into their darkest corners; for without your aid man can do nothing good, and everything is sinful.
>
> Wash clean the sinful soul, rain down your grace on the parched soul and heal the injured soul. Soften the hard heart, cherish and warm the ice-cold heart, and give direction to the wayward.
>
> Give your seven holy gifts to your faithful, for their trust is in you. Give them reward for their virtuous acts; give them a death that ensures salvation; give them unending bliss. Amen. Alleluia.[7]

Today and on Easter Sunday the sequence is sung. The sequence is a hymn that is sung after the sec-

[7]Pentecost Sunday: "Sequence," *The Lectionary.*

ond reading and before the gospel. The Alleluia is prefaced by the sequence. The Veni Creator was written by Stephen Langton, the Archbishop of Canterbury (d. 1228), says Joseph A. Jungman, S.J. All of the attributes of the Spirit's presence, such as light, comfort, consolation, guidance, healing, refreshment, forgiveness, warmth, and joy are poetically set forth in the sequence assigned to Pentecost Sunday. There are presently only four assigned sequences for the liturgy: Easter Sunday–*Victimae Paschali Laudes* ("Praises to the Paschal Victim"), Pentecost–*Veni Sancte Spiritus* ("Come, Holy Spirit"), Corpus Christi–*Lauda Sion* ("Praise Zion"), Feast of Our Lady of Sorrows–*Stabat Mater* ("The Mother Stood").

Gospel
John 20:19–23

Jesus passed through the locked doors, stood in the presence of his disciples, and offered his peace and the Holy Spirit.

STEP 1
NAMING ONE'S EXPERIENCE

What were your first impressions? What was your first response? What grabbed your attention? How did you feel?

Each person names his or her initial impression. Statements should be brief. No reasons should be given at this time. All simply listen without agreeing or disagreeing.

STEP 2
UNDERSTANDING

In a brief statement, what do you think this gospel is trying to convey?

STEP 3
INPUT FROM VISION/STORY/TRADITION

Liturgical Context

Pentecost is the grand finale to the extended celebration of the Lord's resurrection that takes place during the seven weeks of Easter. It is the day the church celebrates the gift of the Holy Spirit. By the first century, the feast also had "an historical association with the law given on Mount Sinai as well as the covenant with Noah and Abraham."[8] Pentecost ushers in the new covenant, the Good News that was foretold by the prophets. Pentecost is the final manifestation of God that gave birth to the church. "It appears on the fiftieth day, when the Spirit was poured out on the first Christian community, giving it the strength and confidence to testify publicly to the resurrection."[9] The paschal celebration of redemption through Christ took place over the fifty days of Easter and was understood to include the "victorious passion and death, his resurrection and ascension, and the sending of the Spirit upon the Church."[10] Thus, Easter was not just a celebration of the resurrection of Christ, but it was an extension of his ministry through the Spirit to the Church: "... Pascha was a total celebration of our redemption...."[11]

When the Easter Vigil became the prime locus for initiation, Pentecost also was used as an occasion for the celebration of baptism. This is the source of the term "Whit Sunday," which referred to the white garments worn by the newly baptized neophytes.

Refer to the overview of the Easter season for further historical background regarding the feast. Its origins, briefly, lie in the connection to the Jewish feast of gathering in the grain harvest that was inaugurated at Passover. In later Jewish history, the feast was associated with Israel's salvation history including the giving of the law at Sinai and the forming of Israel into a people. The Christian appropriation of the feast included the gift of the Spirit in place of the grain harvest and the law. The forming of Israel as a people was adapted in the Christian understanding to refer to the forming of a people in the new covenant.

In the early church there was no sense that the celebration of the Easter season included three

[8]John F. Baldovin, S.J., "Pentecost," in *NDT,* 755.
[9]*DL* (III), 293–294.
[10]*OLY,* 57.
[11]Ibid.

separate feasts within the season. Resurrection, Ascension, and Pentecost were considered one great joyful feast that celebrated Christ's victory over death. "The early community did not share the tendency of later periods to divide this fifty-day feast into three feasts, each with its own season. Until the end of the second century, notices about Christians celebrating Pentecost refer to their keeping of the Jewish agricultural festival (e.g., *Epistula Apostolorum* 17)."[12]

Tertullian is the first to give evidence of a Christian rendering of the feast. It is noted as a fifty-day period of festival and as a "feast day appropriate to baptism."[13] As the feast evolved and in places where it was celebrated on Sunday, the feast of Pentecost was counted from Easter day itself, thus making Pentecost the eighth Sunday after Easter Sunday.

Edward Foley maintains that it was Origen (254) who asserted: "If a man is able to say truthfully 'we are risen with Christ,' and also that 'he raised us up and made us sit with him in the heavenly places of Christ,' he is always living in the days of Pentecost... [and] he becomes worthy also of some share in the fiery tongue given by God" (*Contra Celsum*).

The first four centuries understood Ascension and Pentecost to be intimately connected: "Ascension is the triumphant completion of Christ's earthly ministry, with the missionary outpouring of the Holy Spirit as the unavoidable result. Thus they were celebrated on the same day."[14] This tradition comes from John 20 where the resurrection, the sending of the Spirit, and the end of Jesus' earthly mission all took place on the same day.

By the fourth century, the unitive dimension to the fifty days of Easter waned in the Roman church as Ascension and Pentecost were regarded as distinct festivals. Adolf Adam reminds us that the East always regarded Pentecost as the close of the Easter season. The Roman liturgy, on the other hand, "made this day an independent entity and thus a more or less isolated feast of the sending of the Holy Spirit."[15] Foley suggests that the reason for this might be due to the Council of Constantinople that occurred around the same time. The Council definitively asserted the divinity of the Holy Spirit. This shift may have resulted in taking a primarily christological feast and turning it into a feast celebrating the Holy Spirit.

Liturgical renewal restored Pentecost to its unity with Easter and reaffirmed the close connection between the Resurrection, Ascension, and the sending of the Spirit. The "General Norms for the Liturgical Year and the Calendar" states: "The fifty days from Easter Sunday to Pentecost are celebrated in joyful exultation as one feast day, or better as one 'great Sunday'" (#22). Even though the unity was restored, there is nevertheless still a tendency to focus primarily on the Holy Spirit rather than on the Easter mystery. However, today's preface strongly adheres to the proper connection between Resurrection, Ascension, and Pentecost.

> Today you sent the Holy Spirit
> on those marked out to be your children
> by sharing the life of your only Son,
> and so you brought the paschal mystery to its completion.
> Today we celebrate the great beginning of your church
> when the Holy Spirit made known to all peoples the one true God,
> and created from the many languages of man
> one voice to profess one faith.
> The joy of the resurrection renews the whole world,
> while the choirs of heaven sing for ever to your glory....[16]

Pentecost brings the great Fifty Days of Easter to a close. The paschal candle is removed and placed by the font and there is great rejoicing and merriment. Perhaps parishes might consider gathering in a place where the entire parish could assemble for one large annual liturgy that celebrates their identity as church.

[12]Edward Foley, O.F.M.Cap., "Pentecost-Pastoral Liturgical Tradition," in *CPDBT*, 717.

[13]Ibid.

[14]Ibid.

[15]*LY*, 89–90.

[16]Pentecost Sunday: "Preface," *The Sacramentary*.

Christian Initiation: This is, perhaps, a day in which those who were not baptized at the Easter Vigil could be baptized.

During the seven weeks of Easter, the newly baptized gathered with the assembly for the masses of the Easter season. They entered into mystagogical reflection on the mysteries of the Easter season and the sacraments. They were fed at the table, they took their place with the people of God at the banquet table, and they continued to ask their questions. Their questions flowed from their experience as fully initiated members of the Roman Catholic Church.

The Rite of Christian Initiation calls the seven weeks of Easter the period of mystagogia or postbaptismal catechesis. During the seven weeks, the neophytes engage in an intense time of post-baptismal reflection. It culminates today on the feast of Pentecost. Paragraph #249 of the RCIA suggests that "some sort of celebration should be held at the end of the Easter season near Pentecost Sunday; festivities keeping with local custom may accompany the occasion." The formation of the neophyte continues to take place in the midst of the celebrating assembly with monthly gatherings for the first full year following baptism at the vigil. At the end of the year, on the anniversary of their baptism, "the neophytes should be brought together in order to give thanks to God, to share with one another their spiritual experiences, and to renew their commitment."

Pentecost was inaugurated in the first Christian community, but its power is ongoing for all generations. Pentecost celebrates the perpetual gift of the Spirit to build the Body of Christ. Pentecost celebrates within the community that which takes place in the individual through baptism and eucharist. The Spirit who breathes transforming life into the church is given at baptism and continues to be manifest through the ongoing celebration of eucharist. It is the same Spirit who challenges, teaches, seals us permanently to Christ, and leads us forward in holiness to the new Jerusalem, the holy, eternal city. Pentecost celebrates the reign of God *now and not yet;* it is a present and future reality. The Spirit of Pentecost continues the work of Christ on earth as we are formed and prepared for the great day of his return. Pentecost is the ongoing renewal of our participation in Christ's new covenant. The liturgy of Pentecost calls us to worship in spirit and in truth. We are strengthened for mission to the world's poor, oppressed, and spiritually hungry.

Perhaps Pentecost is a day on which all those who have celebrated an initiation sacrament during the year, such as infants, neophytes, first communicants, those who were confirmed or received into full communion could gather to be a visible sign in the assembly. Perhaps all those mentioned might don their baptismal garments and gather in the midst of the community as a visible sign of Christ's resurrection and the new life of the church as we bring this season to a close.

Gospel Exegesis

The facilitator gives input regarding what critical biblical scholarship has to say about this text. The input includes insights as to how people would have heard the gospel in Jesus' time.

John uses the event of Jesus' appearance to his disciples in Jerusalem to demonstrate that Jesus was fulfilling his promise to return in the hour of his exaltation/glorification. In John's gospel, Jesus gives the Holy Spirit on Easter Sunday. Reginald Fuller suggests that perhaps all of Jesus' post-resurrection appearances were associated with the gift of the Holy Spirit. Today is the day that the church is empowered for mission. It is given the Spirit to live out the Christian story.

The mission in today's story, however, has more to do with the forgiveness of sins. Catholic and high Anglican tradition traditionally associated this with the conferral of the sacrament of penance. However, in the New Testament understanding, the forgiveness of sin is always associated with baptism. It is not surprising that the command to forgive sins is associated with a missionary emphasis. Baptism was withheld for those who did not believe after hearing the Good News. Pentecost was a day for baptisms in the early church. It is fitting that this gospel's baptismal mandate be given on a day that was often devoted to the celebration of baptism.

Pheme Perkins suggests that since John uses "only the general expression, 'disciples,' the commissioning in these verses may be intended to apply to the believing community as a whole, not to some specific group within that community such as the 'Twelve.' This 'power' of forgiveness is probably expressed in the bestowing of the Spirit on those who believe as a result of the disciples' 'mission' and who join the community, rather than in a process of dealing with Christians who have committed sins (as in Mt 18:19)."[17] Jesus insists that this is possible because of the gift of the Spirit. If people forgive each others' sins, then there will be no "obstacles to community oneness. If they continue to hold on to the sins against them . . . the sins remain as obstacles to community harmony."[18] The Holy Spirit, thus, is not only given to empower them for mission, but to enable them to live in harmony with one another. Jesus gives the Spirit to fulfill the promise that all would be one in him. This oneness is accomplished through the forgiving of one another. The sins that are to be forgiven are post-baptismal sins of Christians committed against one another. Many though we are, through the power of the Holy Spirit we are called to be one in Christ.

John posits this event on Easter Sunday as a foundational document. Through it he hopes to remind his progressive community that the Christian life is lived only through the cross and resurrection of Christ. John believes that it is essential to identify the Christ who appeared after Easter as the earthly one who suffered and who promised to return. Today's gospel is a reminder that Jesus' journey to Jerusalem took him eventually to Golgotha before the subsequent resurrection of Easter morn. We, too, are to walk the same journey to Jerusalem, strengthened and supported by the risen presence of Christ in the Holy Spirit.

Proclaim the gospel again.

Sometimes we gain new insights when we hear the text after the interpretation has been given. Someone from the group proclaims the gospel a second time.

---

[17]Pheme Perkins, "The Gospel According to John," in *NJBC*, 984.

[18]*RJ*, 255.

STEP 4
TESTING

Conversation with the Liturgy and the Scriptures

Test your original understanding in dialogue with the text.

(You might consider breaking into smaller groups.)

Were there any new insights? Was there anything you had not considered before? How does your original understanding of this story compare with what was just shared? How does this story speak to your life?

Sharing Life Experience

Participants share an experience from their lives that connects with the biblical interpretation just shared.

> *There are so many things going on in today's liturgy. There is celebration of the many gifts, though one Body. There is celebration of being in community, of being church, the people of God. There is a call to mission and to forgiveness. There is a singleness of purpose in those who were empowered to understand the word of God though they each spoke a different language. There is the ultimate celebration of Christ's passion, death, resurrection, ascension, and the sending of the Spirit culminating in the Pentecost event. One experience does not quite express the many dimensions of this liturgy.*
>
> *I am reminded of the power of the Spirit at work in a community that suffered terribly over the death and destruction caused by the explosion of the space shuttle Challenger so many years ago. The Space Center is the number-one employer in our area. Our schoolchildren watched as the shuttle their parents had worked on blew up before their eyes. In addition to the loss of lives of those on board, the event caused great suffering in the lives of many. Lots of folks lost their jobs. Our school lost a third of its population immediately due to transfers and loss of jobs. Our community strongly felt the impact. There was great depression and desolation over the tragedy. Those who remained working did so under very stressful circumstances.*

This time of intense suffering in our community bound us together. It was several years before the shuttle would be allowed to fly again. Many jobs depended on its success. The day of the first launch was approaching. Finally it was time for the launch. We celebrated an outdoor liturgy in prayer for a safe launch. Parents who could join their children in the school parking lot to view the launch did so. Many people in our community gathered together to look to the skies for our long-awaited resurrection after so much devastation. Future hopes were riding on the shuttle. We gathered for this moment of reckoning as one community that had shared a common disaster and pain. Those of us who were not directly affected were touched by the tension and worries of those who were. As the shuttle lifted off successfully, cheers, loud prayers, and vocal sobs broke out on the playground. There were people huddled in embraces and people on their knees in prayers of thanks. We looked to the heavens for the mighty evidence of God's awesome power. That day was an Easter event for our community. We had been sustained through the difficult interim years by the power of the Spirit. The community was bound together in a common concern. Prayer and thanksgiving were the order of the day before and after the launch. Lives would be maintained, futures secured. Balloons lifted into the skies, celebration was everywhere. Joy echoed amidst the deafening explosion of the propellant that lifted the shuttle bird carrying its special cargo of the hopes of so many people. We were a community that shared a common joy. Our witness extended to the wider world as the TV crews were there to televise our prayers and experience our joy. Every interview expressed hope in our God who promised to sustain us through the power of the Spirit.

One other event that comes to mind on this day of church is that of a difficult time in our communal history. There was an event that caused serious division. Factions were formed and those involved on both sides stuck to their strongly held, self-righteous positions. After much pain, prayer, time, and eventual forgiveness, we experienced a paschal dying and rising. It was only through the power of the Holy Spirit that we are able to stand together so many years later and still call one another brother and sister. Forgiveness and healing took time, but they were accomplished. The experience was more than anything a growth experience. Rather than have the feelings go underground and end in despair and resentment, most folks were able to forgive and heal. We were thus able to stand united and corporately bonded at the eucharistic table.

Evidence of this strong Spirit-filled community can be found in the multitudes of ministries that are performed each day by the community and by individuals within the community. It would take volumes to include them all (from building a school in Haiti to ministry to the sick).

One of the strongest challenges for any community and for our community can be found in the second reading from the mass of the day. No one person's gift is valued over another's. There are to be no marginalized members of our communities. Each person is gifted by baptism and has something to contribute. If we could remember that one thing, our communal living would be so much easier and less fraught with the temptation of self-righteous self-importance.

All share their life experience.

What was John's intention in his telling of this event in the post-resurrection appearance of Jesus? What might the Spirit be creating or re-creating in us through this liturgy (creation)? In what way does this liturgy point to God's promise to be with us (covenant)? In what way does this gospel invite us to die and rise (exodus)? How does this liturgy speak to our community? In what way is our community challenged? Do we still feel the same way about these scriptures and this feast as we did when we began? Has our original understanding been stretched, challenged, or affirmed?

STEP 5
DECISION

The gospel demands a response.

What are the contemporary implications of the scriptures in today's liturgy? In what concrete way does this gospel call our parish to action in the church, parish, neighborhood, or world? Has our conversation with these scriptures and this liturgy changed or stretched my/our personal attitudes?

What am I/we/our community/our parish called to do in response? What is one concrete action we will take this week as a response to what we have learned and shared today?

DOCTRINAL ISSUES

What church truth/teaching/doctrinal issue could be drawn from the gospel for the feast of Pentecost?

Participants suggest possible doctrinal themes that flow from the readings.

Possible Doctrinal Themes

Mystery of the church, resurrection/ascension/ Pentecost, paschal mystery, ministry in the church, sacraments, symbols of the church, evangelization

Present the doctrinal material at this time.

1. The facilitator gives input on a particular doctrinal issue of his/her prior choosing. OR
2. The group chooses a doctrinal issue from the list they created. They read together from the Doctrinal Appendix.

(The doctrinal issues are found in the Doctrinal Appendix in the back of this workbook. If you are choosing an issue from this resource, please refer to it now.)

Reflection questions centered around the chosen doctrinal theme can be found at the end of each topic in the Doctrinal Appendix. The questions are based on the five-step reflection process. If you choose a topic not included in the Doctrinal Appendix, craft your own questions according to the same five-step process.

Following the reflection questions you will be reminded to return to chapter 7, "Preparing the Catechetical Session," to assist you in crafting your own session.

Closing Prayer

This day the Father of light
has enlightened the minds of the disciples
by the outpouring of the Holy Spirit.
May he bless you
and give you the gifts of the Spirit for ever.
Response: Amen.

May that fire which hovered over the disciples
as tongues of flame
burn out all evil from your hearts
and make them glow with pure light.
Response: Amen.

God inspired speech in different tongues
to proclaim one faith.
May he strengthen your faith
and fulfill your hope of seeing him face to face.
Response: Amen.[19]

[19]Pentecost: "Solemn Blessing," *The Sacramentary.*

Ordinary Time

Ordinary Time: An Overview

The word *ordinary* in Ordinary Time is not to be confused with *ordinary* as in lackluster, boring, or routine. *Ordinary* in this instance refers to ordinal (counted time). Each Sunday is designated a number that is counted from Sunday to Sunday. The liturgical color of Ordinary Time is green.

Ordinary Time's primary focus is the feast of Sunday.[1] Each Sunday is an Easter celebration of sorts. We remember and celebrate the life, death, and resurrection of Jesus. Each Sunday the paschal mystery is revealed in its fullness. During Ordinary Time there is no highlighted, singular aspect to the remembered story of Christ as in the other seasons. Rather, all the many facets of Christ's mystery are unfolded on these thirty-three to thirty-four Sundays of the year.[2]

> Ordinary Time begins on Monday after the Sunday following 6 January and continues until Tuesday before Ash Wednesday inclusive. It begins again on Monday after Pentecost and ends before evening prayer I of the First Sunday of Advent. (GNLY, #44)

The Ordinary Time cycle is often delineated in bite-sized chunks corresponding to the time of the year. Thus, winter Ordinary Time covers the block of time immediately following Christmas. The Second Sunday in Ordinary Time begins Ordinary Time and it falls after the feast of the Baptism of the Lord. Winter Ordinary Time extends to the lenten season. Summer Ordinary Time begins after the feast of Pentecost on the feast of the Trinity. Following Trinity and Corpus Christi, the counted Sundays begin again where they ended before Lent began. Autumn Ordinary Time begins around the 23rd or 24th Sunday and continues until the season of Advent.

[1]See Chapter 8 regarding liturgical time and the liturgical calendar. The understanding and celebration of Sunday are covered extensively.

[2]*GNLY*, #43, in *TLD*.

SUNDAYS OF CYCLE A

Much of Matthew's gospel is proclaimed on the Sundays and weekdays of Ordinary Time. (Refer to chapter 9, Overview of Matthew's Gospel.) The *Introduction to the Lectionary* explains: "On the Second Sunday of Ordinary Time the gospel continues to center on the manifestation of the Lord.... Beginning with the Third Sunday, there is a semicontinuous reading of the Synoptic Gospels. This reading is arranged in such a way that as the Lord's life and preaching unfold the teaching proper to each of these gospels is presented."[3]

The meaning of each gospel for a given Sunday corresponds to the flow and the movement of the liturgical cycle. For example, after the feast of Epiphany, at the transition between the Christmas season and the beginnings of Ordinary Time, the church centers on the *beginnings* of Christ's preaching ministry. This connects well to the First Sunday of Ordinary time, the solemnity of the Baptism of the Lord, with its stories of "the first events in which he manifests himself."[4] By the same token, the theme of "last things, *eschatology*" naturally coincides with the readings and liturgies of the end of the liturgical cycle. The beginning of the year reflects beginnings and the end of the year reflects endings.

The first readings are chosen to bring unity to the Old and the New Testaments by their connection to the gospel. There is no logical order given for the readings from the Hebrew scriptures (Old Testament) other than their connection with the gospel.

[3]"Introduction to the Lectionary," #105, in *TLD*.

[4]Ibid.

Paul's and James's letters are read semicontinuously. Peter and John are read during the Easter and Christmas season. The letters are distributed over the three-year cycle.

On the solemnities of the Lord during Ordinary Time (Holy Trinity, Corpus Christi, and Sacred Heart), the readings are chosen to highlight the central theme of the solemnity. Some call these feasts "idea feasts," as they do not celebrate an event of Jesus' life, but rather a creed in regard to the mystery of Christ.

All of the Sundays, feasts, and solemnities of the sacred liturgy celebrate the mystery of redemption through Jesus Christ. In his encyclical, *Mediator Dei,* Pius XII asserted:

> In the sacred Liturgy, the whole of Christ is proposed to us in all the circumstances of His life, as the Word of Eternal Father, as born of the Virgin Mother of God, as He Who teaches us truth, heals the sick, consoles the afflicted, Who endures suffering and Who dies; finally, as He Who rose triumphantly from the dead and Who, reigning in the glory of heaven sends us the Holy Paraclete and Who abides in His Church forever: "Jesus Christ, yesterday and today; and the same forever." (#163)

WEEKDAYS OF THE LITURGICAL YEAR

The first nine weeks of weekday readings proclaim the first twelve chapters of Mark's gospel.[5] The readings from Matthew and Luke consist of all material not contained in Mark. The first readings of the weekday masses rotate between sections from the Old and New Testament. During a period of weeks the first reading is taken from the Old Testament; another block of weeks will center on the New Testament. The number of weeks depends on the length of the specific book being read. There are large sections of the New Testament readings proclaimed so that the fullness of the apostles' teaching may be provided. The Old Testament readings are limited and very select. The passage chosen reflects the character of the book from which it was taken.[6]

Just as Matthew redacted the story of Jesus according to his community's needs, so too the church, through the chosen texts of the Lectionary, determines the scriptural texts that best reflect our Christian faith as celebrated in the context of the liturgical cycle. There is no attempt made to render an historical, chronological depiction of the life of Christ from his birth to his death and resurrection. Rather, the intent is to reveal the entire mystery of Christ. In the last analysis, every liturgical feast celebrates the paschal mystery of Christ, who empties himself, sacrifices himself in obedience, and is present and active in his community of believers. Herein lies the beauty, depth and intensity of this extended season we call Ordinary Time. Far from being *ordinary,* it is imbued with passion—the passion of a people in covenant, radical relationship with the Christ of the gospels, the Christ of the eternal universe! No Sunday is routine, humdrum, or subservient and antithetical to the major seasons of the year. Each Sunday, solemnity, and feast is *manifestation* in itself!

CHRISTIAN INITIATION

A thorough explanation of the ongoing process of Christian initiation is placed in the overview of Ordinary Time since initiation is the normative way a parish lives as *church.* It is part of the ongoing life of a parish. Since Ordinary Time is where the church spends thirty-four weeks of the year, this is an appropriate place to digress and include an examination of an initiation process that is fluid and continually celebrated in the midst of the Christian community throughout the weeks of the liturgical cycle. With the exception of the initiation rituals of Lent and Easter, most of the rites of initiation are celebrated on the Sundays of Ordinary Time. There is a comprehensive explanation of the rites of Lent and Easter such as election, scrutinies, and Christian initiation in the chapters that deal with Lent and Easter.

[5]There is one exception. Two passages from the sixth chapter of Mark are read in other cycles and thus are not read in those first nine weeks.

[6]"Introduction to the Lectionary," #105–110, in *TLD.*

THE YEAR-ROUND CATECHUMENATE

Operating Assumptions

The Spirit is not a respecter of time. The Spirit moves where the Spirit wills. How do we welcome people who inquire at inopportune times, times that do not fit our neatly packaged school calendar models? Each journey is unique.

Formation for the catechumen consists of living and experiencing the life, death, and resurrection of Jesus as it unfolds in one complete liturgical cycle. Thus, a candidate who enters the precatechumenate in September, celebrates the Rite of Acceptance in December, and is initiated at the Easter Vigil in April, is in the catechumenate stage for only four or five months. Such a person is formed by less than half of Christ's complete story of redemption!

In an ongoing model, the process is suited to the needs of each individual. The process takes into account the movement of God's grace and the circumstances of time and place of each person's faith journey (RCIA, #5). Realizing that God deals with us as individuals, an ongoing model is crafted in such a way that each person moves through the process when he or she is ready, not when it is convenient to the parish structure.

Thus, there is no official beginning or "start-up" time in an ongoing process. It is continuous. Once the four periods of the catechumenate are in progress, each period continues forever. There is no beginning or ending.

> The catechumenate is an extended period during which the candidates are given suitable pastoral formation and guidance, aimed at training them in the Christian life.... A suitable catechesis is provided, planned to be gradual and complete in its coverage, accommodated to the liturgical year.... (RCIA, #74)

> The duration of the catechumenate will depend on the grace of God and on various circumstances.... The time spent in the catechumenate should be long enough, several years—if necessary—for the conversion and faith of the catechumens to become strong. By their formation in the entire Christian life and a sufficiently prolonged probation the catechumens are properly initiated into the mysteries of salvation and the practice of an evangelical way of life. (RCIA, #76)

> The period of the catechumenate, beginning at acceptance into the order of catechumens and including both the catechumenate proper and the period of purification and enlightenment after election or the enrollment of names, should extend for at least one year of formation, instruction, and probation. Ordinarily this period should go from at least the Easter season of one year until the next; preferably it should begin before Lent in one year and extend until Easter of the following year. (National Statutes of the RCIA, #6)

> ...It [the catechumenate] should extend over a substantial and appropriate period of time. The rites prior to sacramental initiation should not be unduly compressed, much less celebrated on a single occasion. (National Statutes of the RCIA, #20)

It is clearly the vision of the Rite that the catechumenate proper extend for one full year in order for the catechumens to experience the paschal mystery as it unfolds in one complete liturgical cycle.

FINAL REFLECTIONS

When do inquirers enter the precatechumenate?

Whenever they come seeking.

How long does the precatechumenate last?

As long as it needs to.

How do we know when people are ready to move to the catechumenate?

When they demonstrate initial stirring of faith, a spirit of repentance, the *beginnings* of the spiritual life, including calling on God in prayer, initial conversion, the intention to change their lives and a sense of church. (RCIA, #42)

When is the Rite of Acceptance celebrated?

The Rite of Acceptance is celebrated whenever there are people ready to move to the catechumentate, the next stage. This works out to be approximately four times a year, but preferably not during Lent and Advent.

Entry into the catechumenate is marked by the Rite of Acceptance.

The Rite of Acceptance celebrates what people experienced in the inquiry and foreshadows what they will experience in the catechumenate.

When are baptized Christians received into full communion with the Catholic Church?

Whenever they are ready.

For an illustration of how this might be implemented in a parish setting, see *Word & Worship Workbook for Year C,* pages 331–338.

LITURGICAL PRAYER

Liturgical prayer is the official, communal, public prayer of the church. It is the primary way we should begin all our Catholic/Christian gatherings and mark all major life experiences and transitions. Liturgical prayer is different from other prayer forms such as private prayers, devotions, spontaneous prayer, or prayer services crafted in a catechetical resource. Our church enjoys a vast repertoire of liturgical prayer. As stated in the introductory section of this book, catechesis has the responsibility of forming children and adults in the liturgical life of the church. This does not simply mean the eucharistic liturgy of the church.

Since liturgy forms children and adults in their Catholic Christian faith, we must be attentive to all the church's liturgical prayer. This prayer constitutes the way we live our Catholic life on a routine, day-to-day, week-to-week basis. Thus, this section on liturgical prayer is placed in the overview of Ordinary Time as liturgical prayer is the normative way we are to pray as community throughout the year, not only seasonally, but throughout the days and weeks of the year. Suggestions for use of this vast repertoire will be included in the weekly sessions.

The treasury that comprises the church's liturgical prayer includes:

Eucharistic liturgy

Liturgy of the hours

Liturgy of the word

Rite of Penance:

Sacramental celebrations of the sacrament of reconciliation, including three revised liturgical celebrations:

a) Rite of Reconciliation of Individual Penitents
b) Rite of Reconciliation of Several Penitents with Individual Confession and Absolution
c) Rite of Reconciliation of Several Penitents with General Absolution

Non-sacramental Celebrations

Penitential celebrations are gatherings of the people of God to hear the proclamation of God's word. This invites them to conversion and renewal of life and announces our freedom from sin through the death and resurrection of Christ. (Rite of Penance, #36)

It is desirable to arrange such services especially for these purposes:

– to foster the spirit of penance within the community;
– to help the faithful to prepare for confession that can be made individually later at a convenient time;
– to help children gradually form their conscience about sin in human life and about freedom from sin through Christ;
– to help catechumens during their conversion. (Rite of Penance, #37)

Within the Rite of Penance there are various models for these non-sacramental liturgical celebrations that should be adapted to the specific conditions and needs of each community.

I Penitential Celebrations during Lent
II. Penitential Celebrations during Advent
III. Common Penitential Celebrations
IV. For Children
V. For Youth

We are a people in need of continuous reconciliation and healing. The rite provides a fount of grace to heal and reconcile as we struggle with abuse, sin, pain, and broken relationships. We should celebrate reconciliation on a continuing basis in sacramental and non-sacramental celebrations. Non-sacramental celebrations do not require a priest and may be presided over by a lay minister.

Book of Blessings

The following is a sample list of blessings from the *Book of Blessings* that might be appropriately celebrated throughout the liturgical cycle.

Order for the Blessing of Children
Order of Blessing of the Sick
Order for the Blessing of a Person Suffering from Addiction
Order for Blessing of a Victim of Crime or Oppression
Orders for Blessings that Pertain to Catechesis and to Communal Prayer
Order for the Blessing of Animals
Order for the Blessing of Students and Teachers
Order for the Blessing of Seeds at Planting Time
Order for the Blessing on the Occasion of Thanksgiving for the Harvest
Order for the Blessing before or after Meals
Order for the Blessing of an Advent Wreath
Order for the Blessing of a Christmas Manger or Nativity Scene
Order for the Blessing of a Christmas Tree
Order for the Blessing of Throats on the Feast of Saint Blase
Order for the Blessing and Distribution of Ashes
Order for the Blessing of Food for Thanksgiving Day
Order for the Blessing of Readers
Order for the Blessing of Altar Servers, Sacristans, Musicians, and Ushers
Order for a Blessing in Thanksgiving
Order for a Blessing to be Used in Various Circumstances

Other Liturgical Celebrations

Celebration of the Triduum

Holy Communion and Worship of the Eucharist outside Mass
- Rite of Eucharistic Exposition and Benediction
- Eucharistic Processions

Rite of Baptism for Children—celebrated in the parish
Rite of Confirmation—celebrated in the parish
Rite of Marriage—celebrated in the parish
Rite of Ordination
Pastoral Care of the Sick: Rites of Anointing and Viaticum
- Visits to a sick child
- Anointing of the Sick
- Celebration of Viaticum

Order of Christian Funerals

Catholic Household Blessings and Prayers—a vast repertoire of liturgical prayers for use in the home—for every occasion.[7]

Feasts and Events of Note Throughout the Year

The following is a compilation of some of the events and feasts of note that occur throughout the year. While they will not be addressed in full in this resource, they are nevertheless part of our Christian/Catholic/social life and are worthy of mention in our catechetical ministry.

January. January 1—New Year's Day. (Mary, Mother of God and Epiphany, Baptism of the Lord are covered during the Christmas season.) January 4—Memorial of St. Elizabeth Ann Seton (religious founder from the U.S.A., 1774–1821). January 5—Memorial of St. John Neuman (bishop, religious, missionary—U.S.A., 1811–1860). January 18-25 is the Christian Unity Octave in which eight days are set aside for special prayer for the unity of Christians. There are prayers in the *Book of Blessings* for use at ecumenical gatherings. The church prays for the unity of Christians throughout the year, but sets aside the octave for special remembrance and prayers. January 25—Conversion of Paul. Third Monday in January—Martin Luther King, Jr. Day. January 26—Sts. Timothy and Titus. January 28—Thomas Aquinas.

February. February 25—Feast of the Presentation of the Lord (Candlemas, the day on which enough candles for the entire year are blessed).

---

[7]This section on liturgical prayer was taken from Sister Linda Gaupin's course, "Catechesis and Liturgy 106," Diocese of Orlando, Orlando, Florida, 1996.

February 3—St. Blase (Order for Blessing Throats, *Book of Blessings*); February 12—birth of Abraham Lincoln. February 22—The Feast of the Chair of Peter, birth of George Washington. President's Day—third Monday in February.

March. First Friday in March—World Day of Prayer. March 8—International Women's Day. March 19—Solemnity of St. Joseph. March 24—Anniversary of the death of Oscar Arnulfo Romero. March 25—Solemnity of the Annunciation of the Lord.

April. April 1—April Fools' Day. April 22—Earth Day. April 25—Feast of St. Mark the evangelist.

May. Second Sunday in May—Mother's Day. Last Monday in May—Memorial Day (U.S.A.). Monday on or before May 24—Victoria Day (Canada). May 3—Feast of Sts. Philip and James, apostles. May 14—St. Matthias, apostle. May 15—St. Isidore the Farmer (a good day to bless gardens and fields—check Catholic Household Blessings and *Book of Blessings* for an appropriate blessing). May 31—Feast of the Visit of the Virgin Mary to Elizabeth.

June. Third Sunday in June—Father's Day. June 3—Anniversary of the death of Pope John XXIII. June 24—Solemnity of the Birth of John the Baptist. June 29—Solemnity of Sts. Peter and Paul.

July. July 1—Canada Day. July 3—St. Thomas, apostle. July 4—Independence Day (U.S.A.). July 16—Our Lady of Mount Carmel. July 22—St. Mary Magdalene. July 25—Feast of St. James, apostle.

August. August 6—Feast of the Transfiguration of the Lord. August 10—Feast of St. Lawrence, deacon, martyr. August 15—Solemnity of the Assumption of the Virgin Mary into Heaven. August 22—The Queenship of the Virgin Mary (octave[8] of Assumption).

September. First Monday in September—Labor Day. September 8—Feast of the Birth of the Virgin Mary. September 14—Feast of the Holy Cross. September 15—Our Lady of Sorrows. September 21—Feast of St. Matthew, apostle and evangelist. September 29—Sts. Michael, Gabriel, and Raphael, archangels.

October. Second Monday in October—Thanksgiving Day (Canada). October 4—St. Francis of Assisi, patron saint of ecologists and all environmentalists. October 18—Feast of St. Luke the evangelist. October 28—Feast of Sts. Simon and Jude.

November. First Tuesday after the first Monday in November—Election Day (U.S.A.). Fourth Thursday in November—Thanksgiving Day (U.S.A.). November 1—All Saints, solemnity. November 2—All Souls. November 9—Feast of Dedication of the Lateran Basilica in Rome (reminds us of our history as a people; this church thinks of itself as the parish for the entire world as it is the cathedral of Rome, home to the bishop of Rome—the pope). November 11—Veterans Day (U.S.A.); Remembrance Day (Canada). November 21—Memorial of the Presentation of Mary. November 29—Anniversary of the death of Dorothy Day. November 30—Feast of St. Andrew the apostle.

December. December 1—Anniversary of the day Rosa Parks kept her bus seat. December 8—Solemnity of the Immaculate Conception of the Virgin Mary. December 10—International Human Rights Day. December 12—Feast of Our Lady of Guadalupe. December 25—Solemnity of the Birth of our Lord. Octave of Christmas begins. December 26—Feast of St. Stephen, first martyr. December 27—Feast of St. John the apostle, evangelist. December 28—Feast of the Holy Innocents.

[8] "In church tradition, an octave represents eternity.... Seven days make a normal, run of the mill week. But add an eighth day and you've got something special. You've got a week that ends and begins on the same day. In the early church, they thought that eight days was a symbol of perfection and of heaven." Mary Ellyn Hynes, *Companion to the Calendar* (Chicago: Liturgy Training Publications, 1993), 126.

Second Sunday in Ordinary Time

Environment

The season of Ordinary Time is thirty-three to thirty-four weeks long, interrupted by the Lent/Easter season. The liturgical color of the season is green. The catechetical environment may simply include a candle, green cloth, and plants. The early days of Ordinary Time center on the beginning of Jesus' ministry. Perhaps an icon reflecting one of those early scenes could be incorporated into the catechetical environment. Ordinary Time spans thirty-four weeks and might naturally be divided into segments by the natural rhythm of the winter, spring, summer, and fall seasons. Thus, in order to provide variation in the environment, images from the seasons (or recurrent themes that occur in those seasons) might be incorporated into the catechetical setting.

INTRODUCTORY RITES

Opening Song (or Entrance Antiphon)

May all the earth give you worship and praise and break into song to your name, O God, Most High. (Ps 65:4)[1]

Opening Prayer

The facilitator of the session may lead the prayer. Others in the group may be asked to proclaim the readings.

Let us pray... to our Father for the gift of peace.

Pause for silent prayer.

Father of heaven and earth,
hear our prayers,
and show us the way to peace in the world.
Grant this through our Lord Jesus Christ, your Son,
who lives and reigns with you and the Holy Spirit,
one God for ever and ever.[2]

[1]Second Sunday in Ordinary Time: "Entrance Antiphon," *The Sacramentary.*

[2]Second Sunday of Ordinary Time: "Opening Prayer," *The Sacramentary.*

LITURGY OF THE WORD

The readings are proclaimed.

First Reading[3]
Isaiah 49:3, 5–6

Overview of Second Isaiah: It was generally accepted that Isaiah of Jerusalem wrote all sixty-six chapters of Isaiah. Scholars now maintain that there were three separate authors and that Second Isaiah was written after the Babylonian exile. What led to the conclusion of separate authorship is the fact that the intended audience of Second Isaiah no longer lived in Jerusalem. Jerusalem had been destroyed by Babylon. Second Isaiah was written as encouragement to a people in bondage. Third Isaiah, on the other hand, was written to the people after they were returned to their homeland. First Isaiah includes chapters 1–39; Second Isaiah chapters 40–55; Third Isaiah chapters 56–66. There is a distinct change in tone between the three segments. Isaiah is threatening and condemning; Second Isaiah is consoling and encouraging; Third Isaiah moves from consolation to hope for the future.

First Isaiah was written during prosperous times in Israel. The people were too self-assured and materialistic. In Deutero-Isaiah, things changed. The prophets considered the deportation of the nation's elite into Babylon following the takeover of Judah to be the result of divine retribution for Israel's Godlessness. Israel was unworthy of Yahweh's election. The people were depressed, in shock at their circumstances, and in the throes of poverty. Consequently, they were in danger of leaving the faith. They were in exile and needed encouragement. In spite of the despair of the situa-

[3]The exegesis for the first and second readings may or may not be the focus of your group's reflection as there may only be time to give adequate attention to the gospel, your primary concern. However, the exegesis is included here in order to provide a thorough investigation of the entire liturgy of the word as there may be parts (or all) that would be necessary to the direction you wish to take with your particular ministry group.

tion, the prophets were certain that God would not completely abandon Israel. They needed to be prepared for the emergence of a new world religion opened to all the nations once they returned from exile. The focus of all three books was Jerusalem. With the destruction of the Temple, people could no longer put their trust in the things of this world. The new Temple of post-exilic Israel was plagued by unworthy leaders, thus opening it to inclusion of the Gentiles. The editor displays a sympathetic attitude toward Gentiles.[4]

The prophet of Deutero-Isaiah was compassionate and optimistic and was firmly rooted in the God of salvation history. The language of his poetry reads like a solemn liturgy. He draws on the themes of salvation and the reconstruction of Israel: the fulfillment of God's promises; Yahweh who is doing something new for Israel; the justice of God; the power of God's living word (the word is understood as divine action); and Jerusalem who announces the return of Israel. Deutero-Isaiah takes place in the latter part of the Babylonian exile c. 550.

When King Cyrus of Persia defeated the Babylonians he allowed all deported peoples to return to their homeland. Isaiah understood this action as divine intervention and reconciliation. It was a sign that the people had reformed their errant ways and returned to the Lord.

The Servant Songs: There are four poems that comprise what is known as the Servant Songs. The identity of the Servant is still debated. In the second song it seems as if Israel looks upon itself as servant. Initially Yahweh is the speaker (42:1–4) who describes the mission of one who would bring judgment upon the world. In later verses the Servant is the speaker (49:1–6) who describes his status as the chosen one, his ability to speak, and his mission to gather the chosen together and bring salvation to all the nations. In verses 4–9 of chapter 50, the Servant speaks again to describe his mission, the opposition to it, and the subsequent success of it with Yahweh's help.

In later chapters, Yahweh and others are the speakers. They relate the suffering and death of the innocent Servant who died in shame. His dying is understood for "the vicarious atoning merit of his death, vindicated by his resurrection."[5] Christians obviously connected the Suffering Servant with the Suffering Christ of Calvary. Even though the Servant's identity is greatly disputed, it can be said that the Servant is a person greater than any previous prophet, such as Moses. The Servant offers himself as a sin offering. People are healed because of his innocent suffering. The Servant liberates the people through his death.

In early Christian understanding, the Suffering Servant poems served as proof text that Jesus was indeed the Chosen Servant of Second Isaiah. Jesus associated himself with the Servant. He was understood as the fulfillment of the mission of the Servant. The Suffering Servant provided the biblical basis for Jesus' atoning death and for the meaning of suffering.[6] The return from Babylon and subsequent reconciliation of the nation was understood in Christian times to be a prefiguration of the ministry of reconciliation inaugurated by the messianic reign of Christ.

Today's Pericope: Today's reading from Isaiah is taken from the second poem of the "Servant Songs." Isaiah speaks of an unknown mysterious Servant who would one day unite the people of God. This Servant would restore Israel. He would be a light to the nations and bring God's salvation to all the world. Christians have always understood Jesus and his mission to be the fulfillment of that messianic prophecy. Jesus was Israel's restoration; Jesus brought salvation to all the world; Jesus is the Light to all the nations. Through his death he gathered all the lost into his kingdom. The mission of the Servant is to be universal; it is to extend beyond Israel to all the nations.

Responsorial Psalm
Psalm 40:2, 4, 7–8, 8–9, 10

This is a psalm of thanks for deliverance from trials. The author intends to thank God with his entire person. Rather than sacrifice, the psalmist offers his complete will to God. In Christian terms

[4] Carroll Stuhlmueller, CP., "Deutero-Isaiah and Trito-Isaiah," *NJBC,* 329–331.

[5] *DOB,* 791.

[6] Ibid., 794.

this psalm is understood as the self-offering of Christ in his baptism. Jesus offers his complete will to his Father's will. This offering of self will lead to his ministry of reconciliation to the poor, the downtrodden, and the marginalized.

Second Reading
1 Corinthians 1:1–3

Overview of 1 and 2 Corinthians: Corinth was a Greek city that was demolished in 146 B.C.E. and restored a century later. The diversity of Corinth was most apparent in the disparity between the very wealthy and the very poor. Most of those on the lower end of society's ladder were slaves. Corinth was an intellectual center that played host to many aberrant religious philosophies and doctrines. Paul preached and ministered in Corinth for about eighteen months on his second journey, beginning in the fall of 51 A.D. His third missionary journey to Corinth occurred in the spring of 54 A.D.

Paul became aware of troubles in Corinth. 1 and 2 Corinthians is a response to those concerns. This letter did not produce the desired result, so Paul sent Timothy to Corinth. Timothy also was unsuccessful. Paul followed up with a visit of his own, but to no avail. Second Corinthians was written as a response to Paul's visit. Both letters were probably written in 57 A.D, 1 Corinthians in the spring; 2 Corinthians in the fall.

The letters were written as a response to Hellenism. "All we know about Corinth leads us to believe that there was scarcely a more unlikely place in the entire Roman world for the gospel to find a favorable reception."[7] Paul's letters not only reflect that the Corinthian community did indeed accept the gospel, but they also demonstrate his affection for the community in spite of their faults.

The moral problems inherent in the Corinthian community have to do with their recent conversion from paganism. Paul's community was under a great deal of pressure because of the temptations and lures of the culture's religious and intellectual oddities. People were succumbing to pagan influences. The concerns of morality center around the community's attitude toward sex, toward the eating of meat sacrificed to idols, and around the appropriate celebration of the eucharist. There was also a problem distinguishing spiritual gifts from the phenomena associated with certain cults and their practices. The Greek-influenced Corinth experienced difficulty in accepting the teaching of the resurrection of the body. Gnosticism was also a concern, which was addressed and refuted by Paul. Gnosticism claimed a special knowledge of God that only a privileged few could experience, and was a serious problem in the Corinthian community. One of the effects gnosticism had on Paul's community was manifested by the way they treated those whom they considered as not having all the special gifts of the Spirit. Glossolalia (speaking in tongues) was just one such special gift. Those who did not speak in tongues were considered inferior. This caused division within the community. Second Corinthians addresses the community's difficulty in accepting the apostleship of Paul.

The Corinthians, like their ancient counterparts, were beginning to take God's gifts and the promise of salvation for granted. Paul put priorities in the right place. He definitively asserts that to be in the Spirit means one confesses Jesus as Lord—the earthly, crucified Lord. The gnostic Corinthians regarded the death of Jesus as a past, forgotten reality and were more intent on centering in on the ethereal, intangible Jesus. Paul grounds them in the reality of the cross.

All the gifts of the Spirit are for the uplifting of the Body. One gift is not to be stressed over another. All are to be used with prudence and balance for the good of the community, not for self-edification. Through baptism, the church is one Body. Through eucharist, all are "to drink of the one Spirit." There is to be no divisiveness. All gifts are to be used for the common good—to uplift and nourish the entire Body. Reginald Fuller notes that 1 Corinthians was possibly written for the paschal feast.

Scholars maintain that the brilliance of Paul in these letters shines forth in his synthesis and application of belief and doctrine. Paul cleverly uses doctrine to address the immediate needs of the everyday life and problems of Christians.

[7] *DOB,* 150.

Today's Pericope: Today's passage begins the letter to the Corinthians. Paul refers to himself as the one who was called by the will of God to be an apostle. He addresses the Corinthians as those who have been sanctified by Christ and who are called to be saints. He begins with the Christian blessing of grace and peace.

Paul reminds the Corinthians that they belong to a more universal reality. They are the Church of God "at Corinth."[8] They are not separate or set apart from the entire people of God. The people of Corinth spent much of their energy being concerned with their own problems. They failed to see themselves as part of the wider church, called and formed by Jesus himself. Paul understood the problems of Corinth to be rooted in the fact that they had cut themselves off from the wider church: "[H]e will trace back their faults to the supreme mistake of identifying [only] their own congregation with the Church catholic, of isolating themselves from the whole body."[9]

Gospel[10]
John 1:29–34

STEP 1
NAMING ONE'S EXPERIENCE

What were your first impressions? What was your first response to the gospel (or the other readings)?[11] What captured your attention?

Each person names his or her initial impression. Statements should be brief. No reasons should be given at this time. All simply listen without agreeing or disagreeing.

STEP 2
UNDERSTANDING

In a brief statement, what do you think this gospel is trying to convey?

STEP 3
INPUT FROM VISION/STORY/TRADITION

Liturgical Context[12]

Today begins the season of Ordinary Time. At the end of each liturgical season the readings are eschatological in nature and the gospels focus on the end of Jesus' life and ministry. Similarly, at the beginning of the new liturgical cycle the focus is on the beginning of Jesus' ministry. Thus, today's gospel tells of John the Baptist who, upon seeing Jesus approaching, gives witness to Jesus and professes him as the Chosen One of Israel.

On the Second Sunday of Ordinary Time each year the gospel is from John rather than from one of the evangelists—Matthew (Cycle A), Mark (Cycle B), or Luke (Cycle C). Matthew will be read on the following consecutive Sundays in a semi-continuous reading. Matthew's gospel will begin with Jesus' learning of John the Baptist's arrest. The reason John's gospel is used each year is to place the first Sunday of Ordinary time in continuity with the feasts of manifestation—Epiphany and Baptism of the Lord.[13]

Scholars divide Matthew's gospel in thematic units or sequences. The themes of the gospels for the Second Sunday (from John) and Third Sunday (from Matthew) of Ordinary Time deal with themes that are included in the first sequence of Matthew's gospel: the infancy narrative and the preparation for Jesus' ministry. Thus, these two Sundays share an internal unity. The Sermon on

[8] *PL*, 110.

[9] Ibid.

[10] The gospel exegesis is provided later in this session so that it may be presented in the proper sequence where it occurs in the adult five-step reflection process. The exegesis is provided for the first and second readings for your information and edification, and for you to use at your discretion. Once again, the gospel is the primary source of reflection. If there is time for reflection on the other readings, all the better.

[11] The primary focus of reflection is the gospel. However, very often the other readings demand attention and must be brought into the dialogue.

[12] The scriptures in the Lectionary, the seasons of the year, and the ritual prayers of the mass are interrelated and form the basis for liturgical catechesis. The *liturgical context* attempts to explore and clarify the themes and this interrelatedness.

[13] *DL* (IV), 21.

the Mount is part of the second sequence of Matthew, so the Fourth Sunday begins a new sequence.

The reading from Isaiah is taken from the oracles of the Servant of the Lord. The verses chosen are those verses that refer to the mission of the Servant who is proclaimed by John the Baptist in today's gospel.

The manner in which John comes to belief in Jesus Christ demonstrates the way of conversion for most believers. John shows how the faith journey often is developmental and occurs in stages. There are obvious implications and connections that can be made with Christian initiation. The wisdom of acknowledging the stages of faith development that are inherent in the RCIA has its roots in the journey of John the Baptist himself. The encounter with Jesus in the gospels as they are proclaimed in the liturgical year assists in this gradual conversion and serves as the basis of formation for the initiation of Christians. "This progressive knowledge of Jesus is the fruit of the unceasingly renewed reading of the Gospels—this year, that of Matthew—as it is done, above all, in the framework of the liturgy, within a group, or in one's 'inner room' (Mt 6:6), by the light of the Spirit and in a prayerful climate. This reading must be coupled with a conscious, full, and complete participation in the sacraments of the faith, which celebrate and unveil the mystery. Let us not forget, besides, that we become Christians in proportion to how much we live according to Christ."[14]

The symbolism surrounding John's title for Jesus, "Lamb of God," should be remembered in every eucharistic liturgy in which we profess in the breaking of the bread that the bread we break is Jesus, "the Lamb of God who takes away the sins of the world."

The Spirit of God made it possible for John to recognize Jesus as Messiah. That same Spirit makes it possible for us to recognize Jesus in the assembly of believers, in the breaking of the bread, and in all of our sacramental signs and symbols.

[14]Ibid., 26.

Gospel Exegesis

The facilitator gives input regarding what critical biblical scholarship has to say about this text. The input includes insights as to how people would have heard the gospel in Jesus' time.

This gospel is read on the Second Sunday in Ordinary Time in order to place the baptism of Jesus in the context of Epiphany and manifestation. John does not directly recount the baptism of Jesus, possibly because of the "baptist sect" who believed that John was the promised one. John probably did not wish to make Jesus appear subordinate to the Baptist by having him baptize Jesus. A primary agenda of John the evangelist is to correct any notion that Jesus is in any way inferior to John the Baptist. The Baptist himself definitively asserts that Jesus ranks ahead of him.

Prior to this moment, John had not recognized Jesus as the Messiah that he had come to profess and preach. Through divine revelation, John was promised that the Messiah would be made known to him. When the Spirit, in the form of a dove, came to rest upon Jesus, John knew that Jesus was indeed the *Promised One.* Awareness now flooded John's consciousness. He had been sent by God to testify to the Light. That Light had just illumined John's darkness. In testifying, John fulfilled his God-given mission.

John's slow awareness of Christ as Messiah demonstrates the way one normally comes to full, rooted, and conscious belief in Jesus Christ. It is through a slow process of awakening (unlike Paul's unusual experience at Damascus). The journey of faith is carried out in steps and stages of "knowing," but never comes to full completion in this earthly realm.

John refers to Jesus as *coming* toward him. There is significance in his coming. Jesus is the *One Who Is To Come.* Jesus is the Messiah, the One who existed before John. "It is he" is reminiscent of the name God used in reference to himself when he answered Moses that his name was: "I Am." Thus, the heart of Christian theology about Jesus can be found in this text. Jesus is the One who was foretold in the scriptures. Jesus is the Son of God. Jesus is the "I Am" of burning-bush fame. Jesus is God. The christological implications of John's testimony are the axis upon which the entire Christian life turns. The witness, John, now fades into the background because the *One* he points to has arrived and is manifest to the world.

John somehow understands that his own baptism in water is merely a preparation for what God is doing through Jesus. The dove descending upon Jesus is reminiscent of the power of God's Spirit hovering over the Genesis waters of creation. It is one and the same Spirit who empowers Isaiah's Servant for the mission designated by God in which he would become a light to the nations. It is the same Spirit who opens the eyes of John to recognize Jesus as the one who will baptize with the Holy Spirit. Jesus is the one who will send his own Spirit to continue his life and work through the power of the resurrection. The primary agenda of the gospels is to show that Jesus is the fulfillment of all that was foretold by the prophets about the *Messiah to come.*

The title, "Lamb of God" possesses many layers of meaning, and all have a bearing on the symbolism of the name as it appears in this text. The nomads on hearing John might have had images of the ram going before the ewes in protection of the flock. Or there might have been association with an ancient tradition in which it was believed that in the great apocalyptic day of the Lord there would emerge the "ram of God," the warrior Messiah, who would liberate the people. "At that time, in the circles influenced by apocalyptic ideas and in Qumran, there was a belief in a warrior lamb, taken from the flock and defending its brothers by attacking and dispersing their enemies."[15] In the Book of Revelation, John refers to Jesus as the Lamb that was slain, who was victorious over his enemies, and whose blood redeemed all people and all nations. The image of "lamb" also has roots in the sacrificial lamb of Passover, in the ram substituted for Isaac on the altar of sacrifice, in the Suffering Servant's allusion to the "lamb led to the slaughter," and in the just man who will bear the guilt and the sins of the multitudes. The lamb of Passover reminds us not only of the sacrificial lamb, but also of the liberation of the people out of slavery. From the very outset of his ministry, we are reminded of Jesus' redemptive mission.

John the evangelist puts the meaning and theology behind Jesus' baptism in the mouth of the Baptist himself. In naming Jesus the Lamb of God, John professes that Jesus is truly the servant of God who takes away the sins of the world. He is the Christ who reconciles the world to God. He is the Christ who invites sinners into relationship with God, who shows mercy to the sinner, and who will lay down his life in order to gather his flock. The manifestation of Jesus at his baptism leads the reader to look forward to his passion, death, and resurrection, even in the earliest moments of his mission.

Proclaim the gospel again.

Sometimes we gain new insights when we hear the text after the interpretation has been given. Someone from the group proclaims the gospel a second time.

Step 4
Testing

Conversation with the Liturgy and the Scriptures

Test your original understanding in dialogue with the text.

(You might consider breaking into smaller groups.)

Now that you've heard what the scholars have to say about this passage, how do you feel about it? How does your original understanding of this gospel compare with what we just shared? Were there any new insights for you? How does this story speak to your life?

Sharing Life Experience

Participants share an experience from their lives that connects with the biblical interpretation just shared.

> *I am particularly touched at this moment of my life by the incredible power of the Spirit to reveal God to God's people. Last night I spent an evening of retreat with our candidates for baptism. I was touched by the faith of one young man who shared how God has*

[15] *DL* (III), 27.

walked with him throughout his life—through the knowing of the people in his life, and through the gradual unveiling of God's presence in his life. There were no thunderbolts, but gradual recognition. He watched his life change. Peace and joy crept into his life like the slow emergence of spring's first buds. He began to recognize the presence of God not only in his own life, but also in the lives of his loved ones and his community. His beautiful, virgin faith, yet to be worn ragged by life's hurts and disappointments, reflects an innocence we are all called to have in our relationship with God. This young man shared how his relationship with God has truly led him to extend love in ways he never could have imagined. He harbors no resentment toward anyone in his life. If there ever were such resentments, he has forgiven them all. He is so overwhelmed by God's love for him, that he sees resentment as a waste of God's love. His faith is a living testimony to the God who desires intimate relationship with all of us. He touches my own faith, challenges it, and as a result, I have grown.

I was also touched by the story of another young man whose own life typifies that of the Suffering Servant. He knows what it means to be misunderstood and rejected, and to find hope, promise, and joy in the midst of it. For these two young men there was no sudden revelation, but rather a gradual manifestation of Jesus, the Lamb of God who takes away our sins and "loves us unto death."

It is humbling to minister in the face of such intimate, trusting faith. Rather than "teach" catechumens and candidates, I am often knocked off my horse of pious righteousness by the way they reveal the face, the heart, and the hope of God to me. There is nothing like the innocent faith of neophytes to remind me of what is most important in life. Things are not really as complex as I have a tendency to make them. Jesus is the Lamb of God who laid down his life for us, for me. He desires nothing less than my heart. All I have to do in return is to love as he loved. It is not difficult, but it is also not easy. If it were easy the cross would have no meaning.

Today's liturgy reminds me that I do not have to "get it" all at once. I am constantly in process. I have an entire lifetime to encounter Jesus in the liturgy, in the gospels, in the people of God, and in those whom God sends into my life to show me the way.

What was John's primary message in this gospel? What might be the most important message of this gospel for your community? How does this liturgy reflect the biblical themes of covenant, creation, exodus, and community? All three readings have a strong impact, and shed light on this liturgy. What relevance do they have for your life? How does Isaiah's Suffering Servant speak to you? How does Paul's word to the Corinthians speak to you? What difference do these readings make as you attempt to live the Christian life? How does this liturgy reveal Jesus? Who is the Jesus of this liturgy and what does he have to say to you and to your life at this time? Do you still feel the same way about this gospel as when you began? Has your original understanding been stretched, challenged, or affirmed?

Step 5
Decision

The gospel demands a response.

How does today's liturgy invite transformation of your life? What is the challenge? In what way does your community need to grow in the fullness of today's scriptures? In what way is your parish called to respond? What are the implications of this gospel for your life? What one concrete action will you take this week as a response to today's liturgy?

Pastoral Considerations: With the themes of Christian witness, conversion, and baptism, today might be a wonderful time to highlight the ministries of evangelization, outreach, and initiation in your parish community and to invite people to participate. It would also be a good time for reminding ourselves that we are baptized priest, prophet, and ruler, and as such are called into Jesus' ministry of reconciliation and evangelization. Since January is usually the time we pray for Christian unity, issues of ecumenism might occupy a place of priority in your concerns.

Christian Initiation: With such strong baptismal themes, today might be an appropriate time to celebrate a rite of full communion, infant baptisms, or a rite of acceptance or welcome.

DOCTRINAL ISSUES

What church truth/teaching/doctrinal issue could be drawn from the gospel for the Second Sunday of Ordinary Time?

Participants suggest possible doctrinal themes that flow from the readings.

Possible Doctrinal Themes

Jesus Christ, conversion, Christian witness, grace, baptism, paschal mystery, christology, evangelization

Present the doctrinal material at this time.

1. The facilitator gives input on a particular doctrinal issue of his or her prior choosing. OR

2. The group chooses a doctrinal issue from the list they created. They read together from the Doctrinal Appendix.

(The doctrinal issues are found in the Doctrinal Appendix in the back of this workbook. If you are choosing an issue from this resource, please refer to it now.)

Reflection questions centered around the chosen doctrinal theme can be found at the end of each topic in the Doctrinal Appendix. The questions are based on the five-step reflection process. If you choose a topic not included in the Doctrinal Appendix, craft your own questions according to the same five-step process.

Following the reflection questions you will be reminded to return to chapter 7, "Preparing the Catechetical Session," to assist you in crafting your own session.

Closing Prayer

Almighty and ever present Father,
your watchful care reaches from end to end
and orders all things in such power
that even the tensions and the tragedies of sin
cannot frustrate your loving plans.
Help us to embrace your will,
give us the strength to follow your call,
so that your truth may live in our hearts
and reflect peace to those who believe in your love.
We ask this in the name of Jesus the Lord.[16]

[16]Second Sunday in Ordinary Time: "Alternative Opening Prayer," *The Sacramentary.*

THIRD SUNDAY IN ORDINARY TIME

Environment

Refer to Second Sunday in Ordinary Time.

INTRODUCTORY RITES

Opening Song (or Entrance Antiphon)

Sing a new song to the Lord! Sing to the Lord, all the earth. Truth and beauty surround him, he lives in holiness and glory. (Ps 95:1, 6)[1]

Opening Prayer

The facilitator of the session may lead the prayer. Others in the group may be asked to proclaim the readings.

Let us pray . . .

Pause for silent prayer.

All powerful and ever living God,
direct your love that is within us,
that our efforts in the name of your Son
may bring mankind to unity and peace.
We ask this through our Lord
Jesus Christ, your Son,
who lives and reigns with you and the Holy Spirit,
one God, for ever and ever.[2]

LITURGY OF THE WORD

The readings are proclaimed.

First Reading[3]
Isaiah 8:23–9:3

(See the First Sunday of Advent for an Overview of First Isaiah.)

Today's Pericope: The northern kingdom was on the edge of annihilation and defeat at the hands of their oppressors. Gloom and doom abounded. Spirits were low. Today's pericope reveals the fall of two northern provinces at the hands of Tiglath Pileser III. Many were fearful that the same fate would befall the southern kingdom. Isaiah offers them hope, consolation, and the prospects of a new harvest. He promises that light, not darkness, will prevail; that abundance, not famine, will be the order of the day.

Isaiah blamed the defeat of the two provinces of Zebulum and Naphtali on the people of Israel. He considered it to be God's punishment for their unfaithfulness. Isaiah promises that if the people in the southern kingdom will remain faithful to Yahweh, they need not fear political ruin, disaster, and defeat.

Isaiah makes an allusion to the defeat of the Midianites by Gideon (Jgs 7:16–25). He remembers the victory of the people as they joyfully celebrated Yahweh's great deeds. He cast off the signs of their oppression—the pole, the taskmaster's rod, and the entire yoke that burdened them as a people.

The early days of Ordinary Time still carry forward the memory of manifestation, light, and the joy of Christmas days. Today's reading is reminiscent of the reading from Isaiah for Midnight Mass. Jesus is understood as that light; he is understood as the one who delivered the people from the yoke of oppression. He is the one who delivers up the suffering, sorrowful people of the world, and offers them hope and a new reality. Throughout the scriptures, biblical authors have used the images of light and darkness, harvest and famine, as symbols of life and death, good and evil, salvation and destruction. Isaiah heralds

[1]Third Sunday in Ordinary Time: "Entrance Antiphon," *The Sacramentary.*

[2]Third Sunday in Ordinary Time: "Opening Prayer," *The Sacramentary.*

[3]The exegesis for the first and second readings may or may not be the focus of your group's reflection as there may only be time to give adequate attention to the gospel, your primary concern. However, the exegesis is included here in order to provide a thorough investigation of the entire liturgy of the word as there may be parts (or all) that would be necessary to the direction you wish to take with your particular ministry group.

the great work of Yahweh in salvation history with such metaphors. Christianity understands Jesus as the fulfillment of Isaiah's prophecy of the dawn of new light. Jesus is the one who brings life and conquers death. He is the one who squashes evil and upholds the goodness of God. Jesus is the one who, by his very life, offers salvation and destroys the evil that would stand in the way of humanity's salvation. Matthew uses today's passage from Isaiah to announce the beginning of Jesus' Galilean ministry. Jesus is the light who has come into the world. Jesus is the one whose mission was heralded by the great prophet. Isaiah's prophecy is fulfilled in the person, nativity, life, and mission of Jesus, the Christ.

Responsorial Psalm
Psalm 27:1, 4, 13–14

Today's psalm is expressive of the themes of manifestation and Epiphany. We might very easily read into the psalm the great work of God in Christ, who is the light and salvation of all, the one who takes away all fear.

Second Reading
1 Corinthians 1:10–13, 17

(Refer to Second Sunday in Ordinary Time for an Overview of 1 and 2 Corinthians.)

Today's Pericope: Paul's first letter to the Corinthians allows the reader to get an insider's view of what life was like in this early Christian community. We learn about the community, its organization and endeavors. We learn of the struggles to live in and become a Christian community.

Paul understood his response to the Corinthian community to demonstrate and flow from his apostolic authority. He was responding to reports passed on to him by messengers of Chloe ("... one is tempted to speculate that she was a wealthy Christian woman in whose house the Corinthian Christians used to meet"[4]). Hers was not the only message given to Paul, however, as the community also wrote to him to keep him informed.

[4]*PL*, 113.

Paul expressed his wish that the community be united in heart, mind and judgment, and to share a common purpose. This is the theme of the entire letter. The heart of Paul's letter to the Corinthians is best expressed in the first verse of today's reading.

Paul was concerned with those who reduced Christianity to an intellectual exercise. He railed against gnosticism and its attention to hidden knowledge and wisdom. Paul mixes severity and tenderness in regard to the divisiveness present in the community. He is insistent that the cross of Christ not be diluted through misdirected attention to philosophical speculation. The only knowledge worthy of the Christian is the knowledge of Jesus Christ crucified. The cross was not to be reduced to a philosophical, intellectual reflection. Paul insisted that to do so would rob the cross of its power in the lives of Christians.

Ultimately, the divisiveness in the community was of paramount concern. Paul considered it to be scandalous. The divisions were not due to theological differences but to the formation of cliques within the community, "each claiming the patronage of one of the great leaders of the Church."[5] Paul insisted that those who claimed to follow human leaders were going against the reality of their baptism. When one is baptized, he or she is baptized into Jesus Christ. No one is baptized into the life of any human leader, no matter how great that person is imagined to be. Unity in the community was of critical importance. "Here is what is at stake: Any assault on the unity of an ecclesial community undermines the indivisible unity of Christ."[6]

Gospel[7]
Matthew 4:12–23

[5]Ibid.

[6]*DL* (IV), 31.

[7]The gospel exegesis is provided later in this session so that it may be presented in the proper sequence where it occurs in the adult five-step reflection process. The exegesis is provided for the first and second readings for your information and edification, and for you to use at your discretion. Once again, the gospel is the primary source of reflection. If there is time for reflection on the other readings, all the better.

Step 1
Naming One's Experience

What were your first impressions? What was your first response to the gospel (or the other readings)?[8] What captured your attention?

Each person names his or her initial impression. Statements should be brief. No reasons should be given at this time. All simply listen without agreeing or disagreeing.

Step 2
Understanding

In a brief statement, what do you think this gospel is trying to convey?

Step 3
Input from Vision/Story/Tradition

Liturgical Context[9]

Refer to the Second Sunday in Ordinary Time for the connection that exists between the Second and Third Sundays of the year. The Third Sunday in Ordinary Time celebrates the beginning of Jesus' Galilean ministry. Today's gospel from Matthew serves as the beginning to the chapters from Matthew that will be read during the thirty-three Sundays of the year. Today we are called to conversion and repentance, and to become fishers of people. Every liturgical celebration has those exhortations as its goal. We are not to go away from liturgy the same as when we began. We are to enter into the mystery of Christ's life, death, and resurrection. We are to become transformed by the power of the Spirit. We are to become the eucharist we have received as we go forth to be the fishermen called by Jesus in today's gospel.

[8]The primary focus of reflection is the gospel. However, very often the other readings demand attention and must be brought into the dialogue.

[9]The scriptures in the Lectionary, the seasons of the year, and the ritual prayers of the mass are interrelated and form the basis for liturgical catechesis. The *liturgical context* attempts to explore and clarify the themes and this interrelatedness.

The letters of Paul, read between the Second and Eighth Sundays of the year, are concerned with unity in the community. The divisiveness Paul addresses is a very real concern in contemporary communities. We need only look at the controversies between the various factions within our own ecclesial community. Add to that the divisiveness between traditions and we still must confess to a scandalous lack of harmony. Paul exhorts us today in his word to the Corinthians. He "gives us a timely reminder: no one possesses the gospel; no one should presume to selfishly monopolize Christ's name. To divide the Church into rival, jealous cliques would be to break apart the Body of him who came to unite all in his person. To follow a leader in a particular way, to ban expressions of faith differing from our own would be to ignore the salvation that comes to us from the one cross of Christ."[10] R. Marle eloquently sums up the heart of Paul's challenge to communities of all ages.

> [Ecclesial communities], being structured in a hierarchical manner, always have a shape of their own, recognizable among all other human communities. This singular stamp that each one owes to both its origin and its end signifies that the gathering taking place in the Church, the communion realized there, oversteps the boundaries that would exist in an assembly ruled by purely human decisions. The Church is the result of a "convocation" of God, according to the first sense of the biblical term. It cannot seek a kind of unity more restricted than that of God himself, that is to say, one including the entire human family. This stamp of divine origin, marking her and demanding, so to speak, an unceasing extension, forbids her to yield to the temptation of partisanship or sectarianism. Moreover, this stamp widens to infinity—God's very infinity—the space allowed for the blossoming of each believer's spiritual life.[11]

[10]*DL* (IV), 32.

[11]R. Marle, *La singularite chretienne*, Paris: Casterman, 1950, 151, in *DL* (IV), 33.

Today's Opening Prayer asks God to accomplish in us the unity and peace Paul wanted so much for his community. We must not forget that unity and peace imply the biblical understanding of peace. We are to live in right relationship and harmony with God, with one another, and with all creation. Right relationship with God, one another, and creation is evidenced by humanity's response to the world's poor and disadvantaged. Such peace can only be achieved through the grace of God. Today's Opening Prayer is particularly fitting.

The following prayer for Christian Unity expresses it best:

> Almighty and eternal God,
> you gather the scattered sheep
> and watch over those you have gathered.
> Look kindly on all who follow Jesus, your Son.
> You have marked them with the seal of one
> baptism,
> now make them one in the fullness of faith
> and unite them in the bond of love.
> We ask this through Christ, our Lord.[12]

Gospel Exegesis

The facilitator gives input regarding what critical biblical scholarship has to say about this text. The input includes insights as to how people would have heard the gospel in Jesus' time.

John the Baptist's imprisonment was used by Matthew to announce and inaugurate Jesus' divinely ordained ministry. After John's imprisonment Jesus moved from Nazareth to Capernaum. Matthew is the only evangelist who relates that Jesus changed his residency to Capernaum. Jesus' Galilean ministry emerged from that seaport village. Galilee was a suspect region, despised by Jews from Jerusalem. It was an area where many pagans lived and thus, as a mixed culture, was regarded with contempt by those wishing to maintain ritual purity.

In today's gospel, Matthew sets the stage for Jesus' messianic mission by showing that there was biblical prophecy supporting the Messiah's emergence from this Galilean point of embarkation. Matthew's use of Isaiah's quote also hints at the mission to the Gentiles that would begin with Jesus. Matthew responds to a community in profound transition. The imprisonment of John and the inauguration of Jesus' ministry initiate the movement of the community from one age, that of Palestinian Judaism, to a new cultural, religious, and social world. Today's gospel heralds the movement of the Spirit to new and unexpected worlds—the movement that is already taking place. Jesus, the light, will shine his radiance on those who reside in spiritual darkness. He will heal the lost and bind up the wounds of brokenness.

Today's gospel depicts a constant thread running through Matthew's gospel—continuity with the past and propulsion into the future. Faith in Jesus reclaims what it means to be a member of the people of God, a true Israelite. The life and mission of Christ fulfills the Hebrew scriptures. Jesus is the fulfillment of Judaism.[13]

In the first section of this gospel, Matthew heralds Christ as the Messiah of Israel. Jesus is empowered by the Spirit of God to live in accordance with the will of God. We are given a subtle look into the future inclusion of Gentiles into the mission of God. Jesus is sent to bring the lost sheep of Israel back into the Father's fold. Jesus himself heralds the coming of God's reign.

Matthew has Jesus echoing John the Baptist's earlier cry for the reformation of lives. Jesus, however, is not preparing his audience for the *one who is to come.* Rather, his message and his mission center around the kingdom of heaven *already at hand.* Matthew is the only evangelist to use the term *kingdom of heaven.* David Garland maintains that this is not due to a pious aversion to the use of God's name. It is rather, he says, a way to refer to God's mighty work and lordship that comes down from the heavenly realm. It is a term that denotes God's sovereign authority and rule over the earth as master and Lord of the universe who will bring all things under his authority. This kingdom of heaven is described as *on the way.* It is to be shared with the entire world. It is to be proclaimed and understood as a gift from God.

[12]"Third Week in January: Week of Prayer for Christian Unity," *CHBP,* 160.

[13]Donald Senior, Workshop, "Gospel of Matthew" (Church of Our Saviour, Cocoa Beach, Florida, October, 1995).

The language, *reign of heaven,* was understood by the hearers of Matthew's gospel in the context of Israel's religious and political history. Yahweh was their King. The term immediately conjured the understanding that God's rule is happening *now.* Jesus did not create the term, *reign of heaven.* It was born out of earlier Jewish thought. Early formulations, liturgical texts, acclamations, and psalms referred to Yahweh as king and sovereign. God rules. The earliest organization of Israel as a people or as a nation was in the form of tribes or a federation of clans. The people of Israel were very suspicious of a central government. It only worked once in their history, under David and Solomon. Israel's history with kings was tarnished, and their experience of rule under a king was brief.

One hundred years before Christ, Pompeii was invited by the people into the region due to the tyranny of the Maccabees. Subsequently, the Roman legions never left. Rome provided its own brand of tyranny, however. It is this reality that undergirds the understanding of kingdom of God. The people prayed earnestly that God would come and bring peace to them on earth. When political control floundered, the people hoped that God would do what they could not do for themselves. They longed for God to establish God's own kingdom here on earth. The reign of God was understood as social and political. The reign was not understood as going to heaven to be with God; rather, Israel longed for the kingdom *here*—and *now.*

There were four characteristics to the metaphor *reign of God.* First, the term was understood to be soteriological (*soter* = rescuing, salvation). The kingdom was to bring about a change in the intolerable situations plaguing the people. The reign of God was understood as a means of salvation. Second, the term revealed Israel's theology of God. God cared about the conditions of God's people. For Christ to bring about the reign of God meant that when he delivered people from demonic influences, healed them of illness, offered liberation, then indeed they experienced the reign of God. Third, the kingdom was understood in eschatological terms. The reign of God ushered in the final stage, the culmination of history. Jesus was proclaiming the world's final history. At the end of the age there would be be no more tears, no more death, the old would pass away. The destiny of the human race was being fulfilled within their hearing. Fourth, the reign of God was understood in terms of community. The reign could not be experienced in isolation. Israel was a community. The transformation of the world promised with the advent of Christ is not an individual experience. The purpose of the reign is for the transformation of the world. Christianity, for the first century Palestinian and for the Christian today, is future oriented. The reign of God is now and not yet. What we are going to be needs to drive the Christian. Nowhere in the gospel does Jesus define the reign of God. It is defined by what Jesus says and does. The reign of God is understood as a many-sided prism. There are many meanings to the metaphor. Unlike a steno symbol that conveys only one meaning, such as the stop sign, the metaphor *reign of God* is a tensive symbol. It possesses many meanings. There are many hopes for Israel.[14]

Before there was any recorded response to Jesus' exhortation to repentance in Matthew's gospel, he called four fishermen, two sets of brothers. "Jesus finds them in their family and work environment."[15] It is a misconception to think of Peter and the others as poor fishermen. The fishing industry was a profitable industry. Families formed partnerships. The four brothers called in today's gospel were no doubt in such a partnership. Some scholars and archaeologists today believe that Peter and the other fishermen were probably considered middle to upper middle class by the standards of the day. It is known that Capernaum was their home port. Leaving everything and following the Lord probably meant that they went out across the Sea of Galilee and the surrounding areas during the day and returned to their families by night or after short intervals. The *leaving all to follow Jesus* was understood first in terms of an interior disposition that is the prerequisite of all Christian disciples. The fishermen's response is instant and serves as a model for all believers. Christians are to drop everything and respond immediately to God's call in their lives. It is an issue of priorities.

---

[14]Ibid.

[15]*SWTLY,* 130.

The repentance called for by Jesus involves complete conversion and *metanoia.* It involves a turning away from *what was* to enter into *what is now* and *what is to come.* Repentance is an immediate response to the love of God. The repentance demanded in the gospel is nothing less than responding to God's call—the turning from all of life's attractions to follow the call and mission of God. "It requires a total reordering of priorities in life and unreserved commitment to Jesus."[16]

Something new is happening in this master/disciple relationship we see emerging in today's gospel. Rabbinic literature reveals that it was common practice for disciples to seek the master of their choice. The number one priority in Rabbinic literature is commitment to the law. Consequently, in order to learn more about the law, disciples might change masters frequently. What we see happening in today's gospel upsets the common pattern in such relationships. Jesus sought his own disciples. Jesus chose them; they did not choose him. Jesus made demands of his would-be disciples. He insisted that they give him complete loyalty and that, instead of pursuing the intellectual demands of the Torah, they would now turn their priorities to gathering people into the reign of God.

The symbol of the net immediately connects fishing with the mission of Jesus, and subsequently to the mission of the disciples. The mission of the disciples is announced as soon as they are chosen. There is to be no mistake. The disciples were chosen for a purpose—*to go and catch fish.* However, a new and different species is to fill their nets. Their catch is to be humans. Their nets are to bulge with the suffering sea of humanity. Their prized catch is to include those whose life breath is slowly being sucked out of them by poverty, oppression, illness, and sorrow, and those who long for meaning and purpose in their lives. They are the ones, whether they realize it or not, who desperately yearn for the reign of God. These new fishermen are to be an example of what all disciples are to do. Disciples are to place Christ at the center of their lives. They are to detach from all that stands in the way of a radical relationship with the Master. They are to go out and, through the contagious gift of enthusiasm and joy, net other such disciples in the service of God's reign. This is the new catch heralded by the proclamation given in today's gospel. It is not just *good* news—it is *great* news.

[16] *RM,* 48.

Proclaim the gospel again.

Sometimes we gain new insights when we hear the text after the interpretation has been given. Someone from the group proclaims the gospel a second time.

Step 4
Testing

Conversation with the Liturgy and the Scriptures

Test your original understanding in dialogue with the text.

(You might consider breaking into smaller groups.)

In light of the exegesis, were there any new insights for you? Are there any adjustments you would like to make in your original understanding of these texts? How does this story speak to your life?

Sharing Life Experience

Participants share an experience from their lives that connects with the biblical interpretation just shared.

> *There are many themes that emerge out of today's liturgy—conversion, discipleship, the call of God, Christian unity. Many of them are connected. Conversion and the call of God merge into one theme that speaks particularly to an event in the life of my family—a time when we responded to what we thought could be the call of God. There were no flashing lights, no bells, and the Lord did not sit on his lofty throne and call out to us to do this or that, or to go here or there. Life simply offered us some options. We prayed and acted in the best way we knew how about a circumstance that was presented to us on our life's journey. Very early in our married life we both felt committed to the Christian life and ex-*

pressed our willingness to follow the call of God wherever it would lead us. The question was always, "How do we know if it is God's call or our own inclinations?" We were not sure, and very often it was only in looking back on our lives that we realized the hand of God in our important decisions.

About twenty years ago we bought a lovely home and were happy there. Shortly after that my husband was offered another job in a different city. It required a major move, but it was a good offer. We prayed about it and felt confident that we should accept it. We put our house on the market and sold it immediately. My husband started his new job while the children and I remained behind to close the house. We were just days away from moving to our new city when my husband lost his brand new job. The company was small and decided they were not in a position to expand after all. When we got the news, the people who bought our house were to move in the next day. We had to leave. Where would we go? Two adults, four kids, a dog, and a cat needed a place to live. The only place we could find on such short notice was an apartment complex in a different part of town. I was angry. I thought we had listened to God's call and that God blew it!

However, it turned out to be the most life-changing, direction-turning event of our lives. We ended up in a parish that needed a music director. They hired me instantly and the rest is history. That lost job of my husband's changed the course of our lives in profound ways. It would lead eventually to full-time ministry for both of us.

God had used that circumstance, and the choice we had made, to help us both grow in the gifts we had been given. We were not asked to make an instant decision, like Peter and the other fishermen, but we were asked to place God at the top of our list of priorities. Always when we were able to put God first, marvels abounded.

Conversion and the call of God are intimately connected. Jesus invited a radical change in life and perspective. He was calling for a complete reordering of our life and priorities. He was asking that we be open to hear his invitation to enter into intimate relationship with him and to act on it. The call of Jesus demands that we put him first and then invite others into the abundant life that awaits.

Jesus was leading and guiding us as we attempted to follow his call and enter into a closer relationship with him. Alone it would have been impossible. It has only been possible through living, praying, and ministering with other Christians in community, where together we seek to be the fishermen we were intended to be.

A word about the second reading's concern with Christian unity. *I have had many opportunities over the years of parish and diocesan ministry to observe firsthand the devastating effects of disunity on a community. When there is peace the Spirit flourishes in a community. When there is discord and lack of harmony it is very difficult to find life. Paul cannot speak strongly enough on the topic in today's second reading. Whatever it takes to work through destructive discord in a parish community is worth the effort.*

I am in a community that has had its share of ups and downs. We have known times of struggle, but we also know what it means to journey to the other side of struggles, and now there is incredible peace and joy. It is the love and unity in our communities that invites people to enter our nets. I thank God every day for my community and ask him to continue to bless us with his abundant life.

What was Matthew's agenda? What was he trying to convey to his community in today's gospel? How does Jesus' and his contemporaries' understanding of the metaphor of the reign of God fit in with what many people today understand it to mean? What are the implications for today's communities? How do today's readings reflect the biblical theme of covenant, in which God promises to be actively engaged in human history? Where are the themes of exodus and liberation evident? How might the biblical theme of creation be expressed in today's readings? The theme of community jumps off the pages. What are the implications for communities then and now? How might these texts be a challenge to your community today? Do you still feel the same way about this text as when you began? In what way, if any, do these readings invite transformation of your life? Be specific. Has your original understanding been stretched, challenged, or affirmed?

Step 5
Decision

The gospel demands a response.

In what ways might your parish be invited to respond to today's gospel and/or readings? What are the implications of this gospel for your life? What is the challenge of today's liturgy? What is one concrete action you will take this week as a response to today's liturgy?

Pastoral Considerations: Since unity is addressed in today's liturgy, perhaps it would be a good time for your parish to discover ways to grow in that unity. Is there an active ministry of hospitality in your parish? How are people who have lost a loved one, who are lonely, who are sick and depressed, ministered to in your community? In what ways does your parish foster communication between the various groups and ministries? In what ways is your parish unity something to be celebrated? What activities or attitudes foster disunity and harmony? What needs to change? How does your parish respond to our church's mandate to support and promote ecumenism? What specific action might you suggest to foster ecumenism?

Evangelization is another key issue in today's liturgy. In what way does your parish reach out beyond its borders to welcome others into the loving embrace of God and God's people? Is your parish primarily concerned with in-house realities rather than mission-oriented goals? What can be affirmed? What needs to change?

Christian Initiation: If you have waited until after the Advent/Christmas season before scheduling a rite of acceptance, this would be an especially suitable Sunday for celebrating a rite of acceptance or rite of welcome. The call of the fishermen is most appropriate to the rite. The gospel and the cross invite and demand that we go out and become such fishermen.

DOCTRINAL ISSUES

What church truth/teaching/doctrinal issue could be drawn from the gospel for the Third Sunday of Ordinary Time?

Participants suggest possible doctrinal themes that flow from the readings.

Possible Doctrinal Themes

Kingdom of God, evangelization, Christian witness, Christian unity, conversion, discipleship, Christology

Present the doctrinal material at this time.

1. The facilitator gives input on a particular doctrinal issue of his or her prior choosing. OR

2. The group chooses a doctrinal issue from the list they created. They read together from the Doctrinal Appendix.

(The doctrinal issues are found in the Doctrinal Appendix in the back of this workbook. If you are choosing an issue from this resource, please refer to it now.)

Reflection questions centered around the chosen doctrinal theme can be found at the end of each topic in the Doctrinal Appendix. The questions are based on the five-step reflection process. If you choose a topic not included in the Doctrinal Appendix, craft your own questions according to the same five-step process.

Following the reflection questions you will be reminded to return to chapter 7, "Preparing the Catechetical Session," to assist you in crafting your own session.

Closing Prayer

Let us end with the words of Origen.

> Blessed assembly whom Scripture attests all had their eyes fixed on Jesus! How I wish this assembly might receive similar testimony that all catechumens and faithful, women, men, and children have their eyes, not of the body, but of the soul, filled with the sight of Jesus! When you look at him, his light and his contemplation will lighten your faces, and you will be able to say: "The light of your face has left its imprint on us, O Lord!"

Therefore we humbly ask, imprint on us,
O Lord, the Light of your Spirit that we
may boldly proclaim your good news![17]

[17]Origen (3rd c.), *Homelies sur saint Luc* XXXII, 6, in *Sources chretiennes* 87 (Paris: Cerf, 1962), 391–393, in *DL* (VI), 26.

FOURTH SUNDAY IN ORDINARY TIME

INTRODUCTORY RITES

Opening Song (or Entrance Antiphon)

Save us, Lord our God, and gather us together from the nations, that we may proclaim your holy name and glory in your praise. (Ps 105:47)[1]

Opening Prayer

The facilitator of the session may lead the prayer. Others in the group may be asked to proclaim the readings.

Let us pray . . .

Pause for silent prayer.

Father in heaven,
from the days of Abraham and Moses
until this gathering of your Church in prayer,
you have formed a people in the image of your Son.
Bless this people with the gift of your kingdom.
May we serve you with our every desire
and show love for one another
even as you have loved us.
Grant this through Christ, our Lord.[2]

LITURGY OF THE WORD

The readings are proclaimed.

First Reading
Zephaniah 2:3; 3:12–13

Overview of Zephaniah: Zephaniah is read on only two Sundays of the liturgical cycles: The Third Sunday of Advent, Cycle C, and The Fourth Sunday of Ordinary Time, Cycle A. Zephaniah was written in response to the idolatry practiced during Manasseh's time. Zephaniah was a devoted prophet and preacher who prophesied during the "reign of the reforming King Josiah"[3] around the sixth century B.C.E. He had a sense of coming destruction. He was not caught up in the reforms of Josiah. Instead he saw the day of the Lord coming in which God's judgment would come to bear on Israel. He railed against Assyria's aggression and against idolatry. He loved Yahweh deeply. It is conjectured that Zephaniah's oracles span a very short time—perhaps weeks or months. It is possible that Zephaniah was one of the prophets who were assigned to the temple and its liturgical rites.

All of the oracles share a common theme—the coming of the day of the Lord. He exhorted the people to repentance and warned that if they did not listen, death and destruction would result. Zephaniah believed that Israel was in the throes of a precreation state of chaos. He denounced the foreign powers, especially Assyria, for their arrogance before God.

While Zephaniah speaks of coming death and destruction, he holds out the promise of hope that God will restore a remnant from out of the rubble and that those who were exiled will be returned to their land midst abundant rejoicing. It is suggested that the oracles were written during a festival time of celebrating the kingship of Yahweh.[4]

Today's Pericope: In today's text Zephaniah urges the people to seek righteousness and humility as a protection from the day of wrath. Zephaniah's major contribution to Old Testament thinking is his concern for God's *anawim,* the poor. We see this concern echoed in today's beatitudes. Humility is upheld as a safeguard against the coming day of the Lord.

Responsorial Psalm
Psalm 146:6c–10

The refrain for today's psalm is the first beatitude from Matthew's gospel in today's liturgy. This

[1]Fourth Sunday in Ordinary Time: "Entrance Antiphon," *The Sacramentary.*

[2]Fourth Sunday in Ordinary Time: "Alternative Opening Prayer," *The Sacramentary.*

[3]*PL,* 114.

[4]*ROT,* 340–363.

psalm stresses the theme of Yahweh's concern for the poor, and by extension, the church's concern.

Second Reading
1 Corinthians 1:26–31

(Refer to the Second Sunday in Ordinary Time for an Overview of 1 and 2 Corinthians.)

Last week Paul responded to reports from Chloe about the problems of division in Corinth. The schisms that were occurring in the Corinthian community were an insult to the cross of Christ. The Corinthians were arrogant. They relied too heavily on their own wisdom and on their gnostic tendencies. Their gnosticism made the Corinthians feel superior to others who they believed did not possess the same heavenly wisdom that they enjoyed.

In today's reading, Paul gives them a dose of reality. He assures them that while they think of themselves as superior, the rest of the world looks at them as being very low on the totem pole of life. The community was comprised of slaves, insignificant merchants, and uneducated men and women—people with absolutely no influence in the world of their day. God chose those of society's lowest rung—the simple—to confound the wise. In and of themselves, there was absolutely nothing for the Corinthians to boast of. They could dare to boast only in their Lord and Master, Jesus Christ. Their spiritual achievements were nothing more than grace and gift from God, merited through the saving act of Jesus, not through their own powers. They were to be humbled in the face of such gratuitous greatness. Before God, all disciples stand in abject poverty. Human talents and achievements were given by God to enrich humankind. However, God is not concerned with our giftedness; it is our hearts God desires. God loves us in our nothingness.

Christians must cast off their arrogance and recognize all they have as gift from God. Alone they possess nothing; in Christ, they possess eternal life. Paul exhorted against the false worship of self [see the scriptural interpretation for the third beatitude]. Only God is to be on the throne of our hearts—not ourselves! All people are tempted to boast about their own greatness. Paul saw this as nothing more than human sinfulness. In reality, we have nothing to brag about. We can only find security and contentment through Jesus. "The communities today that resemble Corinth yesterday teach us to take pride in the Lord by giving thanks for the only valuable riches, given equally to all."[5]

Gospel
Matthew 5:1–12a

STEP 1
NAMING ONE'S EXPERIENCE

What were your first impressions? What was your first response to the gospel (or the other readings)?[6] What captured your attention?

Each person names his or her initial impression. Statements should be brief. No reasons should be given at this time. All simply listen without agreeing or disagreeing.

STEP 2
UNDERSTANDING

In a brief statement, what do you think this gospel is trying to convey?

STEP 3
INPUT FROM VISION/STORY/TRADITION

Liturgical Context[7]

Today begins Jesus' inaugural and evangelical discourse on the Mount. It spans three chapters. The first chapter contains forty-eight verses and is read

[5]*DL* (IV), 40.

[6]The primary focus of reflection is the gospel. However, very often the other readings demand attention and must be brought into the dialogue.

[7]The scriptures in the Lectionary, the seasons of the year, and the ritual prayers of the mass are interrelated and form the basis for liturgical catechesis. The *liturgical context* attempts to explore and clarify the themes and this interrelatedness.

from the Fourth to the Seventh Sundays. There is a certain unity between the Fourth and Fifth Sundays, as the verses in the gospel serve very much like an introduction to the Sermon on the Mount.

Matthew's gospel cuts to the heart of our relationship with God. We are to order our mind, heart, and soul to God, and to no other gods. When Matthew refers to "giving yourself" (*douleuein*), there are liturgical implications. The emptying of self required by Matthew has consequences in worship. We will worship a god. It will either be the living God, or something else. The beatitudes today ask us to discern which we will serve. "'Giving yourself,' for Matthew, refers to a servant who is committed to a god. Nobody, Matthew is saying, easily gives up his or her worship, be it true worship or idolatrous worship. It is not easy to be a wealthy disciple of Jesus."[8]

In his lenten message to the world on February 17, 1998, Pope John Paul II echoed the sentiments of today's readings. He encouraged people to enter the desert of solitude in order to acknowledge their inadequacy before God, thereby becoming more sensitive to the presence of the poor.

> This year I wish to propose for reflection by the faithful words inspired by the Gospel of Matthew: "Come, O blessed of my Father, for I was poor, marginalized, and you welcomed me!" [Cf. Mt 25:34–36]
>
> Poverty has different meanings. The first which comes to mind is the absence of sufficient material means. This poverty, which for many of our brothers and sisters crosses the line to misery, is a scandal. It assumes a multiplicity of forms and is found linked to various painful phenomena: the lack of necessary means of survival and primary health care; the absence of home, or its inadequacy, and the consequent abnormal situations; the marginalization of the weakest from society, and the unemployed from the productive sector; the loneliness of those having no one to count on; the condition of international refugees and those who suffer war and its cruelties; the inequality of salaries; the absence of a family and the grave consequences which derive from this, such as drugs and violence. The individual is humiliated by the lack of these necessities of life. It is a tragedy before which those who have the possibility to intervene cannot in conscience remain indifferent. . . . The church continually combats all forms of poverty because, as mother, she is concerned that each and every person be able to live fully in dignity as a child of God.[9]

The Alternative Opening Prayer for today's liturgy reminds us that we have been gathered as God's people since the time of Abraham and Moses. The prayer asks that God bless the people with the gift of his reign. The gospel today shows us what the reign of God involves. The prayer asks for the strength to serve God with our entire being, just as the beatitudes assume, and that we extend that love to everyone, just as the beatitudes demand.

The Entrance Antiphon reminds us that it is our prayer and praise of God at God's own initiative that empowers us to carry out Jesus' commands. The church reminds us of our responsibility to live the beatitudes by the very function of the dismissal rite of the mass. We are to go out to love and serve the Lord. Serving with a love that extends to one another and to the poor. Every Sunday we are mandated to live the just life.

There are also votive masses set aside for remembering such concerns with special attention: For Persecuted Christians, For Peace and Justice, For the Progress of Peoples, In Time of Famine or For Those Who Suffer from Famine, For Refugees and Exiles, For Those Unjustly Deprived of Liberty, For Prisoners, For the Sick, For the Dying, For Charity, For Promoting Harmony, For Our Oppressors. Included in this list are the masses from the proper of the saints. Many saints were so named as a result of their service to the demands of a just society.

---

[8] *SB*, 51.

[9] Pope John Paul II, 1998 Lenten Message, "Welcoming the Poor: Reuniting Hope," February 17, 1998, in *Origins*, April 1998, 604–605.

The words of the Opening Prayer for the Mass for the Progress of Peoples sums up the heart of the beatitudes:

> Father,
> you have given all peoples one common origin,
> and your will is to gather all men with the fire of your love
> and the desire to ensure justice for all their brothers and sisters.
> By sharing the good things you give us
> may we secure justice and equality for every human being,
> an end to all division,
> and a human society based on love and peace.
> We ask this through our Lord Jesus Christ, your Son,
> who lives and reigns with you and the Holy Spirit,
> one God for ever and ever.[10]

Gospel Exegesis

The facilitator gives input regarding what critical biblical scholarship has to say about this text. The input includes insights as to how people would have heard the gospel in Jesus' time.

The beatitudes inaugurate the great Sermon on the Mount. They introduce it. What is being revealed to us on the Mount is the destiny to which we are called. What are the many possibilities that move me closer to who I really am, or away from it? What are my many choices? Do I act with violence? Human communities have the responsibility to act morally. The Sermon places an obligation on Christians to seek the truth, to become authentic witnesses of Christ, to live the gospel.

We are called to be like God. If we love like God loves, we will be perfect like God is perfect. We are to love our enemy because God loves and is love. Jesus understood well the graciousness of God. God is the ultimate lover. When we reach the end of our journey, when we go as far as we can go, we will be complete if we love everyone, especially our enemies. Perfect love resides in unreserved reconciliation.

[10]"Mass for the Progress of Peoples," *The Sacramentary.*

We act morally and love to the limits because that is what God does—he is the lover of all lovers. God's love exists and is prior to any human initiative. God's love is prior to the human being who follows the law. Human action does not prompt God's love. God is unconditionally gracious. We are to journey toward the perfection of God, and perfection resides in love. When we have gone as far as we can go with acts of love, compassion, mercy, and reconciliation, in the end we will be like God.

Mercy is the order of the day. The Sermon demands that, when faced with violence, the Christian will understand that he or she is faced with an array of responses to the violence. The beatitudes answer what happens when grace captures a child of God, as someone has put it.

The vision of Christ's morality is future-based—a vision of what will be. There will be justice, not oppression, peace, not war. The future is more real than the present, because the future motivates what our actions will be today. "What drives the New Testament ethics is the urgency to live now by the future you most desire to see."[11]

In Matthew, the Sermon is on the mount; in Luke, it was on the plain. The reason Matthew chooses the mountain is that he wants everyone to understand that the teaching given there is the new law that coincides with the old law given to Moses on Mount Sinai. Jesus is the new Moses.

Each beatitude has two sections. The first section deals with the shame of the present condition, and the second deals with the future reward and glory. It is important to remember that the beatitudes are intended for Jesus' disciples—*not for all people indiscriminately.* The beatitudes are presented to those who refocused their priorities and gave up everything to follow Jesus.

The beatitudes epitomize the life of Christ. He embodied in word and action what the beatitudes demand. His life of faithfulness to the beatitudes led him to the cross, and ultimately to his resurrection, a destiny we share.

[11]Donald Senior, Workshop, "Gospel of Matthew" (October 1995).

1. ***Blessed are the poor in spirit; theirs is the kingdom of God.*** This beatitude is not a divine sanction of poverty. The biblical understanding of justice in the Hebrew Scriptures is that God entered into relationship with the human race at the creation of the world. He struck a deal, a covenant, with men and women. It was an offer we could not refuse. God promised to be our benefactor, to provide for our needs, to love and care for us. In this covenant with the human race, God intended that people be in right relationship with God, with one another, and with all of creation. As a sign of that relationship and of the covenant, human beings would love and care for one another, especially for those who could not care for themselves. The response God expected to the covenant he forged with humanity was that men and women would feel a responsibility to work to alleviate poverty and human suffering. Thus, where there is poverty, people are not fulfilling their covenant relationship with God. God's perfection is perfect love. Human beings strive for and grow in that perfection when they love as God loves—when they care for the poor.

In the new reign of God, people are to sell their possessions and relinquish their power. Such poverty and powerlessness brings freedom—freedom to work to relieve the suffering of God's *anawim.* It is not just an interior disposition that Jesus demands, but external action as well. We are to honestly ask the question: How can I enjoy the wealth I enjoy when there are those without the basics of life? Matthew's community struggled with such questions, as his was not exactly a poor community. Christians were to love the Lord their God with their whole mind, heart, and soul and evidence of that love would be observed in their response to the poor. How could they carry out this covenant in the midst of unshared wealth? It was a sobering issue for the hearers of Jesus' new law. How could they justify their riches when so many were hungry? It is a question Christians must ask themselves today.

In no way does this beatitude uphold poverty as a pious virtue. "Poverty never glorifies those who suffer its misery. Yet today we get saturated with simplistic cliches (often coming from those who have not directly experienced poverty and the poor): 'Isn't that beautiful—the uncluttered life of the poor!'"[12] Poverty denies God's goodness. God's goodness is revealed when such conditions are eliminated. Jesus identified with those who suffer poverty's ugliness. To be poor in spirit means to willingly embrace poverty. "Poverty can be sanctioned only if it is freely embraced as a way to promote that reign of God more concretely in our world. Otherwise it contradicts the blessedness and goodness of God; it is a curse that violates God's plan. It signifies that the reign of God has not yet arrived. To experience that reign more fully, to experience its authority and power, it is necessary to reorder our possessions on behalf of the poor (19:21). Jesus offers no other way to experience the treasure of heaven except in solidarity with the poor (see 19:29). Give to the poor; then you will have treasure in heaven."[13]

Last week the fishermen left all to follow Christ—their priorities were ordered toward God. We can only be poor in spirit and follow the commands of the new law of Jesus by investing in a deeper relationship with him. Our spirit resides in poverty when we love God with our whole mind, heart, soul, and being, when we turn to God in prayer and contemplation, and when we decide to order our lives with a preferential option for the poor. (To learn more about a preferential option for the poor, read "Communities of Salt and Light," published by the National Council of Catholic Bishops.)

Pope John Paul II speaks to us about spiritual poverty in his 1998 lenten address: "Every Christian feels called to share the pain and difficulty of the 'other' in whom God himself is hidden. However, this opening to the needs of others implies a truly warm welcoming which is only possible in a personal commitment of poverty in spirit. Poverty, in fact, does not only exist in the negative sense. There is also a poverty which is blessed by God. This the Gospel calls 'blessed' (Mt 5:3). Thanks to this poverty in spirit, the Christian recognizes that salvation comes exclusively from God and makes him ready to serve his brother, considering him 'better than yourself' (Phil 2:3). Spiritual poverty entails the fruit of the new heart which God gives us.... [S]uch fruit must mature through concrete

[12]*SB,* 53.

[13]Ibid., 56.

behavior such as the spirit of service, the openness to look for the good of the other, the willingness to share with our brother, the commitment of combating that pride which isolates us from our neighbor."[14]

2. ***Blessed are those who mourn; they shall be comforted.*** People are born into the human condition fraught with pain, suffering, evil, sickness, oppression, and unimaginable suffering. Often those who have known such suffering have been able to embrace their suffering, mourn, and in turn offer consolation to others who similarly suffer. Jesus is the fulfillment of this beatitude. He went to Calvary for those who mourn. He took upon himself the sins that caused the need for much of the mourning in our world. Matthew's Jesus intends that those who mourn be comforted. It is the hallmark of his ministry. He comforted the grieving, the sick, the possessed, the depressed. He desired wholeness for the broken.

3. ***Blessed are the meek for they shall inherit the land.*** Most of the Jews and Christians who approached Jesus responded to his authority with a certain meekness. The religious authorities, the scribes and Pharisees, and political leaders responded defensively to his authority. They acted with suspicion and violence. Those in authority, whether religious, political, or wealthy, enjoyed control of the land or the world's resources. Israel maintained strong convictions about its relationship to God and to the world.

The word *land* was synonymous with *world* and the *world's goods and resources.* Israel was in relationship not only with God, but also with the land. The land was an integral part of its identity. Israel's love and relationship with the land was not to overshadow its relationship with Yahweh. Israel was under the sovereignty of Yahweh, and was not to be controlled by an obsession with the land. The Torah understood the inclination for people to make the land (world) the primary focus in their lives (thus the law against coveting resources). Israel was mandated to take a Sabbath rest one day a week, and one year every fifty years, in order to reflect on whether or not they had been influenced or tainted by the desire for power and prestige that often accompanies an excess of goods and resources.

In Israel's belief system there was to be a balance between Yahweh and the land/world. When obsession with the world and its resources became a primal focus, then idolatry was a logical consequence. People (then and now), however, needed some assurance that they would continue to be blessed with some of the riches the world had to offer. "God's blessing is equated with 'making it on the land.'"[15] On the other end of the imbalance, Israel understood that its spirituality could become so oriented to Yahweh that it ignored its responsibility to the world. An example of that might be seen in praying that God alleviate a condition that causes suffering in the lives of others, when the cause of that suffering in the first place might be humanity's misuse, abuse, misappropriation, or perhaps the lack of stewardship, of resources. A contemporary example of this imbalance can be seen in the following situation: In the Dominican Republic much of the available land has been taken by the government to plant crops for export to reduce the country's lingering massive debt to various world banking organizations. As a result, the poor, by law, are not allowed to plant crops for their own survival. An imbalanced relationship between Yahweh and the land would be reflected in people simply praying that God alleviate that condition rather than doing something to work toward elimination of its cause. The balance between Yahweh and the land was a principle deeply rooted in Israel's biblical understanding. When we simply ask God to alleviate a condition other human beings have caused, without doing a thing to change the situation, we support the attitude that says, "If there is something wrong in God's world, then it is up to God to fix it." As created beings made in the image and likeness of God, we are called to use all the resources at our disposal to insure that all of God's creatures have the benefit of the world's riches. Once again, the biblical principle of justice applies: when one is in right relationship with Yahweh, he or she will also be in right relationship with one another, with the land (world), and with the world's poor. Our spirituality is intertwined with

[14]Pope John Paul II, "Welcoming the Poor: Reuniting Hope," *Origins,* 605.

[15]Ibid., 100.

our responsibility to the poor. The third beatitude calls for a balance between prayer and action. When disciples are in right relationship with God, each other, and the world, then the land and everything in it will be theirs because they no longer covet it. They are free to enjoy its fruits and rewards, because they know they have passed around its goods for *all* to enjoy, not just a select few.

It was difficult for Israel not to get caught up in the land of milk and honey; it was difficult for them to always rely on God as the ultimate provider, rather than on themselves. This is why Moses insisted that there be symbolic reminders of who God is and what God did. Once they inherited and were caught up in the daily concerns of the promised land, it would be so easy to forget. They (we) might again be tempted to fashion yet another molten calf of their (our) own desires and passions. Israel was mandated to remember. The acquisition of land usually is won only for a great price and often results in a staggering loss of life. We are not to forget what it means to subdue the land. Many times it costs us our life. It is worth the sacrifice when it insures the future well-being of God's people. It is a frivolous waste when it is intended to serve only a select few.

The need to control our world often keeps us from encountering the God who cares for us. God will not intervene if we have no need for him to do so. That is why it is often only in the face of our own poverty that we can understand our absolute reliance on God for our very life's breath. This is the heart of conversion.

Meekness means that we dedicate our lives to live in right relationship (*hesed*) with God, with all its inherent implications. Meekness means that our *metanoia* includes a change in attitude toward the world, the world's resources, and how those resources are shared. Meekness means a commitment to avoid the lure of power, prestige, and possessions.

> In taking on the yoke of God's plan for the world, meekness reflects a nonviolent way of dealing with wealth in all its forms. A meek person has an entirely new way of dealing with power through service (20:20–28), with possessions by using them on behalf of the poor (6:19ff.; 19:16–22), and with prestige by avoidance of any show or titles.[16]

The opposite of meekness is violence. The meek person carries out God's plan for the world. The violent person controls the world by power, possessions, and prestige. When we meekly submit to the will of God, and covet nothing, we inherit the land by virtue of our status as adopted children of God.

4. ***Blessed are those who hunger and thirst for justice; they shall be satisfied.*** Hunger and thirst are the two basic instincts for survival. They represent life and death to us. Hunger left unsatisfied leads to starvation. Thirst unquenched leads to death. Thus, the demand of this beatitude is clear. We are to make the demands of justice as necessary to our life as food and water. As mentioned above, the biblical notion of justice assumes that all creatures are to be in right relationship with the Creator. Human beings are to love God with an insatiable hunger and thirst. They are to yield totally to the will, power, and providence of God in their lives. As a result of God's promise to love and care for them (God's covenant), they will live in harmony with one another, with all creation, and with the poor. We are to love with a love that God bestows on us. This is the justice God demands. Every human being is created in God's image. Justice insists that all be treated with basic human dignity. Thus, after loving the Lord our God with our whole heart and soul, and after loving our neighbor as ourselves, we are to hunger and thirst after loving and caring for the poor, the suffering, and the oppressed of the world. God demands it; so shall it be. When we hunger and thirst for justice we will be satiated, filled, cup running over, baskets filled to overflowing. But there can be no satisfaction when the demands of biblical justice are ignored.

5. ***Blessed are those who show mercy; they shall receive mercy.*** Mercy is the outpouring of God's love, concern, and care to human beings by the very recipients of that mercy. Mercy demands that we as Christians offer to every living creature the same

[16]Ibid., 115.

compassion and love that Jesus offers. One need only turn to Jesus' teaching, preaching, and healing ministry to experience his mercy.

Mercy begets mercy. When we are treated mercifully, we experience the reconciling love of God. When we experience forgiveness, we are thereby freed to offer reconciliation to others. Mercy resides in relationship. God forgives our failings. God enters into relationship with us and, in so doing, heals our wounds and forgives our sins. When we forgive those who have hurt us, we extend similar mercy to them. The reign of God goes hand in hand with mercy. Where mercy is absent, so is God.

Our spirituality depends on our having a forgiving heart. Mercy demands that we move beyond the boundaries of our own expectations and norms and respond to people where they are. For Matthew, mercy is intimately connected with a person's character. Someone who is merciful is dedicated to living according to God's will. Jesus moved beyond the norms of the day, as well as the constraints of the law, in order to show mercy to those in need. There were no barriers to his limitless mercy. We are to extend that same limitless mercy to others. Such mercy is the heart of the scriptures and it is the heart of our worship. We cannot come before God in thanks and praise and refuse to extend God's love and mercy to those in need of it. The scriptures tell us that before presenting our gifts at the altar, we should take care of any unfinished business that would keep us from God's forgiveness, reconciliation, and presence. God demands that our relationship with him be characterized by a heart willing to extend itself in love, mercy, and forgiveness to all of God's children—the lowest as well as the highest. Mercy ultimately takes us all to the cross of Christ. We are invited to offer our lives as Christ offered his. This is the greatest act of mercy the world has ever known. It continues in our celebration of eucharist.

6. ***Blessed are the pure of heart; they shall see God.*** There is very little exegetical background regarding the meaning and origin of "purity of heart." However, *to see God* in the biblical sense means to dwell in God's presence. To be pure of heart means one is committed to God's will and plan for his or her life. This covenant relationship, as stated many times before, carries an ethical responsibility. Those who are pure of heart, and live in an ordered relationship with God, are also in right relationship with one another, with the world, and with the world's poor.

Jesus lived according to the will of God and thus God showed him favor. Jesus insisted that the righteous person should act in similar manner. To be pure in heart means to have a singular purpose and focus—to dwell in the light and love of the *Transcendent Other.* A person who is living in perfect harmony with God will sacrifice all for the love and will of God that flow from that relationship. Thus, to live by this beatitude requires a self-emptying, a *kenosis*—a total submission to God's embracing, all-consuming love. To live according to this beatitude, we must relax and fall into the arms of the *all-knowing, all-caring God,* with the assurance that we will be caught gently in God's embrace before plummeting to the floor with our worries and concerns. It implies trust. When we focus on God, trust in his plan for our lives, and act according to his ethical, loving, and moral imperatives, our gaze never leaves God's beckoning and summoning presence.

7. ***Blessed are the peacemakers; they shall be called children of God.*** Matthew insisted that the community would enjoy the restoration, promised by Isaiah, only to the extent that they lived the "new law" of Jesus—the beatitudes. Jesus is the promised one, the one anointed of God to bring peace and to gather all together into the house of Yahweh. Jesus was the one to inaugurate the year of favor from the Lord. Jesus lived his life by the beatitudes. We are to imitate his life. Jesus lived according to the perfect will of God. He epitomized one who was faithful to the covenant. He communed with God with his whole mind, heart, soul, and spirit. He lived a life of love and extended that love to the culture's unlovable. He extended *shalom* peace. He reached out to the unclean, the prostitutes, the tax collectors, those who were ignored and passed over—those who never enjoyed the benefits awarded to their more fortunate brothers and sisters.

Jesus was shown favor by God. In biblical terms, "God's favor is identified with messianic restoration."[17] As Messiah, Jesus' mission was to restore the shalom peace that was lost when humanity stepped into sin at the beginning of the world.

The offering of peace in biblical times was a prayer that God's blessing be granted to the recipient of the blessing. It recalled the peace of Genesis when order was brought out of chaos and all was right with the world. It was reminiscent of a world in which there was no discord and all things were in harmony with the created order. Shalom peace longed for the return of such a world, a world in which mourning and tears were replaced with harmony, joy, and everlasting peace. Such peace was evidenced by the moral imperatives of the covenant. When the world's marginalized, powerless, and poor lose their advocates among the children of God, it is a sign of a rupture in the covenant between God and the human race. Shalom demands reciprocal covenant relationship. Jesus was perfectly obedient and faithful to God's will. His messianic mission was the antithesis of what the known world expected the messianic reign to be. In the mind of those waiting, there was the expectation of a mighty, powerful, and political control. Jesus came riding on the back of a donkey. His was a reign of complete submission to God's will in his life. His was a reign of love and service, not domination. His was a reign of shalom peace and biblical justice, not violence, oppression, and excessive control of peoples and nations. His was a reign that invited people to live for and with one another in harmony, and for a common purpose—to further the reign of the peace established at the creation of the world. Jesus was God's Son, as evidenced by his perfect faithfulness to the will of God. We are God's children, as evidenced by the way we further the reign of God by working earnestly for the establishment of the shalom that Jesus inaugurated.

8. ***Blessed are those persecuted for justice' sake; the reign of God is theirs.*** This beatitude is a natural consequence, if one lives the other seven. Matthew's community was a church in transition. Persecution was inevitable as Christians began to live the moral imperative demanded by gospel living. Governments maintain the status quo and religious authorities oftentimes maintain religious superiority. When those delicate balances are upset, the ones in control are threatened. Persecution is then inevitable. Faithfulness to the will of God leads to the cross. We know this well; there is One who went before us who taught us this. Persecution, for Christians, was proof positive that they were living the gospel. Matthew's Jesus presents the last beatitude as an offer of blessing and consolation midst the persecution and rejection. The reign of heaven is *now* for those so persecuted. They live in the eschatological glory of everlasting life.

Matthew's community was experiencing tension and misunderstanding. There is a sense throughout the gospel of an "us versus them" mentality. The Christians were being evicted from the synagogues. Matthew maintained that the persecution his community was experiencing was a direct result of living up to the ethical demands of biblical justice. Jesus knows well the consequences of such living. His life and work provided the perfect example. Rejection is inevitable when anyone challenges deeply-ingrained ideologies. The social and hierarchical order of the day, both culturally and religiously, are the result of centuries-old established structures. When the gods of self-aggrandizement, power, prestige, control, and the need to dominate are challenged, they rebel, and persecution and rejection follow.

To change the condition of the poor and oppressed might mean that we relinquish all that keeps us in a posture of superiority. That might just be too much for an unsuspecting subconscious to endure.

> Rejection can be expected by anyone preaching Jesus' word to a world that refuses to change its idealogy and be converted. As Matthew showed in the thirteenth chapter, a society that has legitimated its accumulation of "more," even at the expense of "what little" others have (13:12), will refuse to convert to a new ethic that promotes "just enough" in order to be more.[18]

[17] *SB*, 178.

[18] Ibid., 203.

Matthew's gospel is mindful of the two poles of response to Jesus' life and work: prayer and justice. Justice can only be accomplished through attention to prayer and a reciprocal covenant relationship with God. Without prayer, the works of justice are empty and void of meaning. Without prayer, justice runs the risk of promoting idolatry. "I am your benefactor and provider, thus you may now bow down and worship at my feet." On the other hand, prayer without justice runs the risk of empty self-righteousness before God. Balance between the two is essential.

This last beatitude serves as an exclamation point to the other seven. "If you live these commands, this is what you can expect. But take heart, it is a sure sign that you are living in God's presence and have found favor with God. You are living in the reign of God."

Proclaim the gospel again.

Sometimes we gain new insights when we hear the text after the interpretation has been given.

STEP 4
TESTING

Conversation with the Liturgy and the Scriptures

Test your original understanding in dialogue with the text.

(You might consider breaking into smaller groups.)

Now that you've heard what the scholars have to say about this passage, how do you feel about it? How does your original understanding of this gospel compare with what we just shared? Were there any new insights for you?

How does this story speak to your life?

Sharing Life Experience

Participants share an experience from their lives that connects with the biblical interpretation just shared.

The words of today's gospel ring in my ear. They are not only words spoken by the Master, but they are words, images, and passions that seem to me to be expressed by a young person I know. It seems as if the imperatives of this gospel were etched on his heart at a very young age. He tries to live for God and to love the world's poor. He believes in living in a spiritual and self-embracing poverty to the best of his ability. He trusts that God is in charge of his life and is leading him. He believes that God has invited him to a life of prayer, contemplation, and ministry to the poor.

He questions the excessive attention given to material concerns in people's lives. He is an impatient and impetuous young person—certainly not perfect. Yet he is often a voice of conscience in the midst of a world that desperately needs modern-day prophets.

Ultimately the beatitudes invite us to find the appropriate balance between prayer and action. This young man finds strength and direction through prayer. He believes that God is charting his course and he follows it the best way he knows how (which can often be frustrating for those whom he loves). He feels called to live his most authentic self and follow his destiny. Jesus' relatives were often frustrated with his activities, too. There were times they probably told him to forget what he was doing and go home and be a good carpenter. Jesus had to be faithful to his mission and he calls each one of us to do the same.

The eighth beatitude is a reminder that we are all baptized to be priest, prophet, and ruler. We are all called to live the prophetic life—some in more dramatic ways than others. Without prophets, the beatitudes would have run the risk of becoming just a nice story about the day Jesus went up the mountain to teach his friends. The Sermon is radical. It will always be radical. Adherence to it will elicit persecution and rejection. It is very easy to reduce it to fit our own controlling understanding of God and God's expectations of us. It takes no less than the faithfulness of prophets, ancient and contemporary, to remind us that the beatitudes are not pious fervorinos, but rather a serious call to justice, prayer, and discipleship. Hopefully the voices of our contemporary prophets will not be stilled.

In this world of certainties and the need to maximize our options, there are still people in the world who are willing to cast certainty to the wind and discover the chaotic opportunities of living the Sermon on the Mount. This young man seeks to follow Jesus' example. He listens and acts. Like other prophetic people, his passion is like that of Moses, his frustration is like Jeremiah's, his impetuosity is like Peter's, and his anger over the plight of the poor and oppressed is like that which Jesus had. We all share those same characteristics to a greater or lesser degree.

The beatitudes insist that I take seriously my life of discipleship. If I love the Lord my God with my whole heart, my whole being, and with all my strength, then I can do no less than love others as God loves me. One must follow the other. When I love perfectly as God loves perfectly, then the demands of justice will flow naturally. There is a delicate balance. Faith without works is dead; works without prayer are empty and futile.

What for you was the most striking insight in the beatitudes? What was Matthew's Jesus trying to say to his community? How might the challenges inherent in the beatitudes impact your community? Where would the stumbling blocks be? Discuss the biblical themes of covenant, exodus, creation, and community inherent in today's readings, and how those themes invite you to enter more deeply into relationship with God. What are the two tensions in the beatitudes, and how do these tensions speak to your life? Was there anything about the exegesis that made you uncomfortable? What, and why? How does this gospel challenge you to a new way of thinking or behaving?

STEP 5
DECISION

The gospel demands a response.

In what way do you see the Sermon on the Mount in a new light? In light of this sharing, where is transformation still needed? In what way does your community need to grow in the fullness of today's scriptures? In what ways is your parish called to respond? What are the implications of this gospel in your life? What is one concrete action you will take this week as a response to the liturgy today?

Pastoral Considerations: What is your parish's response to the poor and suffering of your parish, your civic community, your nation, the world? Do you share your resources with the world's poor? If not, why not? Perhaps the question needs to be asked. How might you invite your parish community into a greater awareness of their responsibility to care for God's *anawim?*

Christian Initiation: Perhaps today would be a good day to invite people, who minister in some way to the concerns addressed in the beatitudes, to come and share their story and ministry with the catechumens. How are catechumens mentored in the life of service and justice in your community?

DOCTRINAL ISSUES

What church truth/teaching/doctrinal issue could be drawn from the gospel for the Fourth Sunday of Ordinary Time?

Participants suggest possible doctrinal themes that flow from the readings.

Possible Doctrinal Themes

The Sermon on the Mount (as the basis for the moral life), justice, conversion, discipleship, prayer and action

Present the doctrinal material at this time.

1. The facilitator gives input on a particular doctrinal issue of his or her prior choosing. OR

2. The group chooses a doctrinal issue from the list they created. They read together from the Doctrinal Appendix.

(The doctrinal issues are found in the Doctrinal Appendix in the back of this workbook. If you are choosing an issue from this resource, please refer to it now.)

Reflection questions centered around the chosen doctrinal theme can be found at the end of each topic in the Doctrinal Appendix. The questions are based on the five-step reflection process. If you choose a topic not included in the Doctrinal Appendix, craft your own questions according to the same five-step process.

Following the reflection questions you will be reminded to return to chapter 7, "Preparing the Catechetical Session," to assist you in crafting your own session.

Closing Prayer

Almighty and eternal God,
you gather the scattered sheep
and watch over those you have gathered.
Look kindly on all who follow Jesus, your Son.
You have marked them with the seal of one baptism,
now make them one in the fullness of faith
and unite them in the bond of love.
We ask this through Christ, our Lord.[19]

[19] "Third Week in January: Week of Christian Unity," *CHBP*, 160.

FIFTH SUNDAY IN ORDINARY TIME

Environment

Perhaps the catechetical environment might be simply adorned with a beautiful candle, a bowl of salt, and the color green.

INTRODUCTORY RITES

Opening Song (or Entrance Antiphon)

Come, let us worship the Lord. Let us bow down in the presence of our maker, for he is the Lord our God. (Ps 94:6–7)[1]

Opening Prayer

The facilitator of the session may lead the prayer. Others in the group may be asked to proclaim the readings.

Let us pray . . .

Pause for silent prayer.

In faith and love we ask you, Father,
to watch over your family gathered here.
In your mercy and loving kindness
no thought of ours is left unguarded,
no tear unheeded, no joy unnoticed.
Through the prayer of Jesus
may the blessings promised to the poor in spirit
lead us to the treasures of your heavenly kingdom.
We ask this in the name of Jesus the Lord.[2]

LITURGY OF THE WORD

The readings are proclaimed.

First Reading
Isaiah 58:7–10

(Refer to the Second Sunday in Ordinary Time for an Overview of Second Isaiah.)

Today's Pericope: The verses prior to this reading deal with the issue of true fasting. Today's reading is a response to people in the community who used fasting as a means of showy self-aggrandizement. Many believed that fasting was a means of invoking God's favor. Isaiah reminded such people that their focus was misdirected, that it should turn instead to those in need, to the homeless, the naked, and the hungry.

The hunger that comes from abstinence invites the penitent to encounter the divine presence within. Fasting empties the body so that the soul might be filled. The soul is filled so that love might be poured out. Fasting fosters communion with *Infinite Love.* In the face of such love, one can do no less than love in return. Fasting that turns inward with no outward manifestation runs the risk of becoming an empty exercise at the very least, and a form of self-idolatry at the worst. Spirituality that is other-centered shines like a beacon in the midst of the darkness. Isaiah insists that the fasting God desires is poured out in the care and feeding of those in need.

Sheltering, clothing, and feeding God's *anawim* has its genesis in Yahweh's covenant with Israel. He freed Israel from bondage. In response to God's gratuitous covenant love, the people were to share their bread with the hungry, clothe the naked, and shelter the homeless (Ex 4:22, Dt 5:6, Jn 8:33). The condition of freedom depended on just action. The community envisioned by God excludes no one, and treats all people with dignity and respect. God's community is to be a light to the nations. God's glory is revealed through such a community. It bears witness to God's love and reveals who God is and how God acts. Thus, a community that lives the ethical demands of biblical justice is a prophetic community. The life, prayer, and action of the community is a sign of God's presence in the world. A community that lives in right relationship with God is a shining light that dispels darkness, a theme that resounds in today's gospel.

---

[1]Fifth Sunday in Ordinary Time: "Entrance Antiphon," *The Sacramentary.*

[2]Fifth Sunday in Ordinary Time, "Alternative Opening Prayer," *The Sacramentary.*

Responsorial Psalm
Psalm 112:4–5, 6–7, 8–9

Today's psalm describes the characteristics of a righteous person. The light metaphor refers to compensation a person receives for doing well. It is understood as a general sense of well-being. Darkness, on the other hand, is understood as affliction.

Second Reading
1 Corinthians 2:1–5

For the last few weeks we have been given an insider's view of the issues concerning Paul's Corinthian community. Like a Shakespearean audience, we are made privy to the inner workings and the human motives that drive the behaviors Paul was challenging. The brilliance of Paul's letters is that they are timeless. We are not to be lulled into the false sense that such issues were problematic only for Paul's ancient, far-away community. Paul was speaking to every community of every generation.

What contemporary community has not experienced the ravages of bitterness, jealousies, rivalries, and unbridled self-righteousness? Many communities know well the sting of factions, cliques, and groups who insist they are the ones with all the answers, or that their way is the only way. Communities that lack introspection run the risk of falling prey to their own ideologies. True human wisdom is pure gift from God, and would never consist of petty backbiting, noninclusiveness, or arrogant self-righteousness.

In three different places in today's reading God's wisdom is contrasted with human wisdom (verses 1, 4, and 5). Paul makes it clear that the power and wisdom of God and God's word are not to be judged by human standards. Who would ever look for God's wisdom and power within an instrument of capital punishment and torture? Yet that was exactly what Paul was demanding that followers of Christ do if they wished to know true, divine wisdom. Paul was reticent to proclaim the power of the cross. It was such a horrific means of execution that it was a stumbling block for those who were asked to embrace its rewards. So barbaric was it, that the Romans would not even use it for their own citizenry. Yet indeed that was the wisdom Paul preached—that in and through the crucified Christ God's wisdom is revealed.

Paul asserts that the proclamation of the gospel includes two very real components: *mysterion* and testimony. In other parts of the letter the gospel is associated with the Greek word *mysterion.* This suggests that inherent in the gospel lies the hidden dimension of God's ways—ways that we can understand only within the confines of our human limitations, the depths of which we will never fully plumb. Testimony (Greek: *martyrion*), on the other hand, depicts the element of public witness. By his life, actions, death, and resurrection Jesus gave witness to the mystery of God in our midst. Only through the gift of faith can such wisdom be understood, and such mysteries explored.

Gospel
Matthew 5:13–16

STEP 1
NAMING ONE'S EXPERIENCE

What were your first impressions? What was your first response to the gospel (or the other readings)?[3] What captured your attention?

Each person names his or her initial impression. Statements should be brief. No reasons should be given at this time. All simply listen without agreeing or disagreeing.

STEP 2
UNDERSTANDING

In a brief statement, what do you think this gospel is trying to convey?

STEP 3
INPUT FROM VISION/STORY/TRADITION

Liturgical Context

Matthew uses the metaphor of salt to illustrate what happens when a disciple's fervor and enthu-

[3]The primary focus of reflection is the gospel. However, very often the other readings demand attention and must be brought into the dialogue.

siasm for the word of God goes flat. The metaphors of salt and light are intended to show the disciples what they are to become: the "salt of the covenant," and the light of Christ in the world. Inherent in the metaphor is the symbolic meaning of salt as it was understood in Jesus' own Jewish tradition (refer to Gospel Exegesis).

The ancient symbol of salt has been carried through the centuries and is still in use today. In the early church, salt was used as symbol of a preservative against the influences of evil for those preparing for baptism. The rigors of discipleship demand that persons be preserved and remain steadfast in their covenant relationship with God. The symbol of salt was used in the ancient rite of acceptance. St. Augustine referred to it in his *Confessions*: "I was signed with the sign of His Cross and seasoned with His salt straight from the womb of my mother, who had great hope in You."[4] Mark Francis recounts a letter written by John the Deacon around the year 500: "The catechumen received blessed salt... to signify that just as all flesh is kept healthy by salt, so the mind that is drenched and weakened by the waves of the world is held steady by the salt of wisdom and of the preaching of the word of God: so that it may come to stability and permanence, after the distemper of corruption is thoroughly settled by the gentle action of divine salt" (John the Deacon, *Letter to Senarius 3*).[5] Edward Yarnold states that there "is some evidence for the use of salt as an anti-demonic rite in pre-Christian Rome. The salt continued to be given throughout the catechumenate, and was regarded as in some sense the catechumen's substitute for Eucharist. The rite survived in the Roman liturgy as part of the baptismal service until 1969, but does not appear in eastern liturgies."[6]

In the prereform rite of baptism the "salt of wisdom" was given to the infant to invoke God's mercy, forgiveness, and everlasting life. While no longer used in the rite of baptism, salt is still used in the blessing of holy water. In the "Rite of Blessing and Sprinkling Holy Water" in the "Order of Mass" (*The Sacramentary*), we remember the story of Elisha throwing salt into the spring:

> Almighty God,
> we ask you to bless + this salt
> as once you blessed the salt scattered over the water
> by the prophet Elisha.
> Wherever this salt and water are sprinkled,
> drive away the power of evil,
> and protect us always by the presence of your Holy Spirit.
> Grant this through Christ our Lord.[7]

Both salt and light, as referred to in today's gospel, are symbols preserved through the centuries that reveal the many dimensions of God's relationship with the human race. (For material concerning the symbol of light, refer to: "Easter Vigil: Symbol of Light.")

The purpose of every liturgy is to strengthen us and nourish us so that we can live the ethical demands of the gospel. Today we are called to be salt and light. The eucharist empowers us to be just that. Today's Prayer After Communion reminds us that we are made one in Christ through the eucharist. We ask God to help us bring salvation and joy to the entire world—in a word, to be the light Jesus asks us to be in today's gospel.

> God our Father,
> you give us a share in the one bread and the one cup
> and make us one in Christ.
> Help us to bring your salvation and joy to all the world.
> We ask this through Christ our Lord.[8]

The challenge of today's gospel is to grow in the fullness of what we were created to be. We are able to fulfill the demands of today's gospel by the power of God. One of the prefaces for Ordinary Time explains why: we are made in God's image. Today's gospel invites us to fulfill our destiny: to be a steward of creation made in God's image, to praise God for his wisdom and power, to reveal God to the world, to be salt and light.

> All things are of your making,
> all times and seasons obey your laws,

---

[4] St. Augustine, *Confessions*, quoted in *AIRI*, 3.

[5] Mark Francis, "Salt," *CPDBT*, 866.

[6] *AIRI*, 5.

[7] "Rite of Sprinkling," *The Sacramentary*.

[8] Fifth Sunday in Ordinary Time, "Prayer After Communion," *The Sacramentary*.

but you chose to create man in your own image,
setting him over the whole world in its wonder.
You made man the steward of creation,
to praise you day by day for the marvels of your wisdom and power,
through Jesus Christ our Lord.[9]

Gospel Exegesis

The facilitator gives input regarding what critical biblical scholarship has to say about this text. The input includes insights as to how people would have heard the gospel in Jesus' time.

The first metaphor used in Matthew's account of the Sermon on the Mount is the metaphor of salt. In the ancient world salt was used as a means to preserve foods. Thus it was logical for salt to be used as a symbol of preservation and permanence. Salt was also used for purification of people, conquered lands, and sacrifices. Elisha used salt to purify a spring near Jericho for the inhabitants of the town.

> "Bring me a new bowl," Elisha said, "and put salt into it." When they had brought it to him, he went out to the spring and threw salt into it, saying, "Thus says the Lord, 'I have purified this water. Never again shall death or miscarriage spring from it.'" And the water has stayed pure even to this day, just as Elisha prophesied (2 Kgs 2:20–22).

Salt was also a sign of hospitality. People who supped together were united in a sacred bond of friendship through the shared sign of salt. In the Book of Numbers (18:19) salt is understood as a sign of the covenant bond that existed between Yahweh and the people. It was referred to as a "covenant made in salt" (2 Chr 13:5); this relationship with Yahweh is permanent and not to be broken.

Jesus no doubt brings the Hebrew understanding of salt to bear on his use of the word in today's gospel. "It is likely that Jesus used the metaphor of salt as a way of speaking about the need for steadfast faith before the judgment of God."[10] Salt reminds disciples of their own relationship with God—a relationship of permanence, friendship, solidarity, and an unbreakable covenant with God.

Even though salt cannot technically lose its flavor (salt is salt), in Jesus' time it could become ritually impure and subsequently had to be thrown out. In this context, salt becomes a sign of God's judgment and is a reminder that no one is to take his or her relationship with God for granted.

If disciples become "flat," that is, if they take God for granted and stray from their covenant with God (and all its inherent moral imperatives), they will know divine judgment and will be useless in the service of God's reign. Disciples are to go out, proclaiming the good news of salvation and extending God's love to the world. Disciples are to become the salt of the covenant, the salt of permanence, and the salt of hospitality as they set out on their mission to the world.

The second metaphor Matthew uses is light. Light is a primary symbol in our church today (see Easter Vigil: Symbol of Light). Disciples are called to be a light to the nations. By their life and example they are to reveal God to the multitudes, just as Jesus did by the sacrifice of his life. The reference to the city is probably an allusion to the lights of a city at night. Scholars suggest that Isaiah 2:2–5 serves as a backdrop for this image. Jerusalem, the city built on the mountain of Zion, was to be the place where the light of the Lord would be revealed to the world. Disciples are to become the beacon on the hill, the city that lights up the world. They are salt and light because Jesus called them and they responded. They are therefore expected to reveal what they are. They are to let their light shine for all to see, and to show by their behavior that they are salt and light in the midst of darkness. "'You are salt, yes, but for the earth, not for yourselves. You are light, but for the whole world, not for a closed fellowship.' These verses are an anticipation of the missionary imperative with which the gospel [of Matthew] will close (28:18–20)."[11]

---

[9]Sundays in Ordinary Time V, "Preface 33," *The Sacramentary.*

[10]Mark R. Francis, C.S.V., "Salt," *CPDBT,* 866.

[11]*MI,* 44.

This is not an exhortation to an individual. The "you" is plural. Today's gospel is a challenge to the community as a whole. Matthew's exhortation emphasizes the universal and corporate mission of the church. We are all in this together. *To be light* is the job of everyone as a unified body. The church is called to be visible. "The wish to be seen is all too human, however; it is fed by our insatiable vanity. Here the motive derives rather from a vivid awareness of the greatness of God. The church's good works are to function in the secular world as indelibly etched pictures of the Father's love."[12]

Proclaim the gospel again.

Sometimes we gain new insights when we hear the text after the interpretation has been given. Someone from the group proclaims the gospel a second time.

STEP 4
TESTING

Conversation with the Liturgy and the Scriptures

Test your original understanding in dialogue with the text.

(You might consider breaking into smaller groups.)

Were there any new insights for you? Is there anything you would like to add to your original understanding of this gospel?

How does this story speak to your life?

Sharing Life Experience

Participants share an experience from their lives that connects with the biblical interpretation just shared.

> *Jesus was exhorting the entire community. It was a challenge for the church. Yet individuals belong to the church and I am an individual that is part of a community. Today's gospel is an opportunity for us to reflect upon the ways our communities are called to be a light to the nation. Where is there light and salt and where has the light burned out and the salt gone flat? I constantly thank God for the many ways my community lives today's gospel. We have given hundreds of thousands of dollars to the world's poor over the past ten years; we have built schools, clinics, and homes in the Third World and in Appalachia. We tithe as a community and support most missionary activities that come our way.*
>
> *There is always, however, the challenge to give God the glory instead of ourselves. We do not tell our "good news " enough as a church. It is always the bad news that makes the headlines. There is risk in telling the good news, but maybe we don't even need to tell it; maybe we just need to live it, and when we do the world will see. It is easy to stand on a soapbox and say, "See how great we are." Hopefully the real truth is that the church does not need to tell of its goodness because people don't see that goodness as out of the ordinary—they see it as normal Christian living. Recently, when a woman was making sandwiches for the homeless in our area, someone commented about her ministry. The woman responded, "Is that what it is? I am just doing what I* should *be doing."*
>
> *It is only through the power and love of God shining through people in our community that we are able to respond to the gospel in the way we do. Today's gospel also invites us to look at the ways in which we have gone flat. I often wonder how we would respond as a community to politically unpopular issues that demand a gospel response. I believe the ethical imperatives of the gospel would triumph, but one never knows until faced with the situation. The social mission of the parish and its hospitality are two of the charisms I cherish most. People who come to our parish speak of the wonderful warmth and hospitality of the people. Hospitality has become our parish's most identified charism. Yet, there are people who have not experienced that love and warmth. At a recent parish function I observed that someone, whom the world would consider as marginalized, was ignored by all present. Not* one *person reached out to or spoke to this individual. So no matter how hard we try, or how well we think we are doing, there is room for growth and room to be challenged. Because we are human beings, we are imperfect.*
>
> *Recently the state in which I live has put seven men to death in the electric chair with nary a word from*

[12]Ibid., 45.

churches; or, for that matter, from me. One night I listened while the nightly news anchor interviewed people in Italy who regard our death penalty as barbaric and against the spirit of human dignity. I listened as the Italians pointed out how very few civilized countries still practice capital punishment. I was embarrassed when our country's record on capital punishment was compared unfavorably to that of other countries. While recognizing the heinous nature of some crimes and the need to insure that perpetrators of such crimes never go free, I cannot in conscience reconcile capital punishment with the gospel. In my opinion, it is institutionalized revenge. (I hope that I will never be asked to put my conviction to the test.) Yet, what did I do about it? Nothing. It is very easy to talk, but talk is cheap. I did nothing and I said nothing.

The liturgy today reminds me that I must be an agent of God's peace; that I must work for unity and harmony instead of being a source of dis-unity and dis-harmony. That does not mean, however, "peace at any price." Sometimes the Christian life demands that we rattle the cage and upset the proverbial apple cart. Jesus overturned many a cart in his earthly sojourn. I do not know if I would have the courage to upset the wrong cart, or even the ultimate cart. Would I be willing to risk my job or even my life for the sake of the gospel? There have been times in my Christian life when I have responded to the gospel appropriately and times when I have not. Being salt and light requires that I take my relationship with God seriously and work toward living the gospel I profess, in any and all situations. The Sermon on the Mount lays out for us what it means to be a Christian. My job is to discover the appropriate balance for my life between faith and action. It is my responsibility to discern the will of God in my life and become the salt and light that today's gospel challenges me to become. When I engage in gossip, when my actions are more exclusive than inclusive, when I participate in factions, cliques, or destructive, hateful talk, and when I am too concerned with self-serving interests—I bring darkness, not light. I can certainly confess that I have known such darkness. However, when I am able to empty myself and give God the glory for all I do; when my actions point to God, rather than to myself; and when I strive to maintain my "salty" self and become other-centered, only then am I able to become an authentic light for the world.

What was the Hebrew understanding of salt and how are you challenged by it? What was Matthew's primary concern in today's gospel? What is the bottom line? How is today's liturgy a relevant word for our communities? How do contemporary communities live the command to be salt and light? Where do they fall short? To whom are they not salt and light? How are the themes of creation, covenant, exodus, and community evident in today's readings and how do they speak to you and to your community? Do you still feel the same way about this text as when you began? Were there any new insights? Has your original understanding been stretched, challenged, or affirmed?

Step 5
Decision

The gospel demands a response.

How does your understanding of these scriptures and today's liturgy invite transformation or change in your life? In what way does your community need to grow in the fullness of today's scriptures? In what concrete way is your parish called to respond? What is one concrete action you will take this week as a response to the liturgy today?

Pastoral Considerations: There is no better Sunday to affirm the ministries in your parish and to invite people to consider the ways they are (or *are not*) salt and light in their world—their families, the marketplace, and the secular world. Perhaps it is time for an honest dialogue about the community's call to be a light in the world. Perhaps the community might explore ways that the parish could do more to be a light "in the world," not just be concerned with in-house concerns. How does your parish respond to the world's poor? How is your parish a voice for the voiceless in your community? How is your parish an example of the gospel in your surrounding community? Are there people in your midst that do not have the benefit of your community's salt and light bestowed on them? Who are they? Are there multi-cultural issues that need your community's attention?

Christian Initiation: It might be appropriate to celebrate the rite of acceptance or welcome; a rite of full communion in the Catholic Church, if there are baptized candidates ready for confirmation and eucharist[13]; or a rite of anointing of catechumens. A reminder: the minor rites are intended for use on an ongoing basis throughout the initiation process. They may be used to open or close the catechetical session.

DOCTRINAL ISSUES

What church truth/teaching/doctrinal issue could be drawn from the gospel for the Fifth Sunday in Ordinary Time?

Participants suggest possible doctrinal themes that flow from the readings.

Possible Doctrinal Themes

Discipleship, morality, mission of church, kingdom of God, symbol of light, conversion, justice/social teaching of the church, evangelization

Present the doctrinal material at this time.

1. The facilitator gives input on a particular doctrinal issue of his or her prior choosing. OR

2. The group chooses a doctrinal issue from the list they created. They read together from the Doctrinal Appendix.

(The doctrinal issues are found in the Doctrinal Appendix in the back of this workbook. If you are choosing an issue from this resource, please refer to it now.)

[13]However, should a rite of full communion into the Catholic Church be celebrated today, it would be important to avoid any sense of triumphalism that might be from the gospel. Many people come to us having spent a lifetime living as a disciple of Christ and are simply seeking entry into full communion with the Catholic Church. The challenge for them would be the same as it is for every member of the gathered community—to grow in their life of Christ and to constantly strive to be a better disciple in the context of their new Catholic Christian identity.

Reflection questions centered around the chosen doctrinal theme can be found at the end of each topic in the Doctrinal Appendix. The questions are based on the five-step reflection process. If you choose a topic not included in the Doctrinal Appendix, craft your own questions according to the same five-step process.

Following the reflection questions you will be reminded to return to chapter 7, "Preparing the Catechetical Session," to assist you in crafting your own session.

Closing Prayer

Lord,
bless your people and fill them with zeal.
Strengthen them by your love to do your will.
We ask this through Christ our Lord.[14]

[14]"Prayers Over the People," #22, *The Sacramentary.*

Sixth Sunday in Ordinary Time

INTRODUCTORY RITES

Opening Song (or Entrance Antiphon)

Lord, be my rock of safety, the stronghold that saves me. For the honor of your name, lead me and guide me. (Ps 30:34)[1]

Opening Prayer

The facilitator of the session may lead the prayer. Others in the group may be asked to proclaim the readings.

Let us pray . . .

Pause for silent prayer.

God, our Father,
you have promised to remain
for ever
with those who do what is just and right.
Help us to live in your presence.
We ask this through our Lord
Jesus Christ, your Son,
who lives and reigns with you and
the Holy Spirit,
one God, for ever and ever.[2]

LITURGY OF THE WORD

The readings are proclaimed.

First Reading
Sirach 15:15–20

(Refer to the Feast of the Holy Family for an Overview of Sirach.)

Today's Pericope: Today's reading is the most explicit treatise on human free will in canonical and deuterocanonical Old Testament literature. The author is explicit—God is not the source of human sin. For Ben Sira, free will has its genesis at the creation of the world. Free will is part of human nature. Evil choices and good choices are just that—choices. They cannot be forced upon anyone. The rabbis translate the Hebrew for "free will" as inclination—a person has an *inclination* either to good or evil.

Keeping God's commands is an exercise of faith. In scripture faith means accepting God's word as authentic and normative, and also acting on it. Sirach is calling for action. The contrasting choices are clear—choices between life and death, fire and water. Ben Sira's exhortation is reminiscent of Moses as he admonished the people on the day of covenant renewal in the Book of Deuteronomy: "I have set before you life and death, the blessing and the curse. Choose life, then, that you and your descendants may live, by loving the Lord your God, heeding his voice, and holding fast to him. For that will mean life for you" (Dt 30:19–20). When one is faithful to God's law, there is life. When one chooses against God, there is death and destruction.

Today's pericope ends by affirming God's wisdom and power. While all wise and powerful, God does not cause or command that a person sin: ". . . nor does God ever give power to sin (v. 20)."[3] Ben Sira is emphatic. God is not responsible for our sin; that falls solely on human shoulders.

Responsorial Psalm
Psalm 119:1–2, 4–5, 17–18, 33–34

It is most appropriate that today's psalm asks for guidance and discernment in keeping the law of God. Since the responsibility for sin rests with human beings, the power and wisdom of God are needed to make the appropriate choices. Psalm 119 is the longest psalm in the psalter. It is a poem in praise of the Torah. The psalm exalts the Torah as the manifestation of God in the midst of the people. It praises God's action in human history,

---

[1]Sixth Sunday in Ordinary Time: "Entrance Antiphon," *The Sacramentary.*

[2]Sixth Sunday in Ordinary Time: "Opening Prayer," *The Sacramentary.*

[3]*CBC,* 36.

especially in his relationship with humanity through the Torah.

Second Reading
1 Corinthians 2:6–10

(Refer to the Second Sunday in Ordinary Time for an Overview of 1 and 2 Corinthians.)

Last week Paul challenged those who thought they were wise of their own accord. He preached to them instead about the wisdom of Jesus Christ crucified. Today Paul sets forth the appropriate understanding of wisdom, as opposed to the gnostic understanding. He even uses the language of the gnostics to punctuate his point: mystery, wisdom, etc. Paul's use of such words and his understanding of wisdom is entirely different than that of the Corinthians.

The gnostic Corinthians believed that they had been initiated into a special spiritual revelation that automatically made them mature in the faith. Paul challenged their thinking. He preached that wisdom is only to be found in the cross of Christ; that the mystery of Christ is not in some secret knowledge, but in plumbing the depths of his suffering and death; that it is the crucified One who sits with the Father in glory. According to Reginald Fuller, the cross is God's eschatological action.

But the Corinthians disagreed with Paul. They saw the cross as an unfortunate past event. Their only concern was that Jesus had risen, and was showering them with a special gnosis, knowledge, and wisdom. They felt this knowledge afforded them special status. With this knowledge they were "in," but those without it were "out." They thought they possessed a spiritual and intellectual spirituality that surpassed that of other Christians. But their failure to see the power of the cross betrayed their immaturity.

Paul refers to the rulers of his time who put the Lord of Glory to death. According to Fuller, Paul may have believed that the political authorities were acting out of their own blindness, that they were under the influence of an unseen evil power. Thus, they blindly crucified the Lord, thinking him to be a messianic imposter. In a sense, they had been duped by powers greater than themselves. If this was Paul's thinking, there is a touch of irony in his challenge of the Corinthians. Like the blind political rulers, they too did not recognize the Messiah as the crucified One. By not accepting Jesus Christ crucified, they may have inadvertently been aligning themselves with Herod, Pilate, and the powers of evil.

Gospel
Matthew 5:17–37

STEP 1
NAMING ONE'S EXPERIENCE

What were your first impressions? What was your first response to the gospel (or the other readings)?[4] What captured your attention?

Each person names his or her initial impression. Statements should be brief. No reasons should be given at this time. All simply listen without agreeing or disagreeing.

STEP 2
UNDERSTANDING

In a brief statement, what do you think this gospel is trying to convey?

STEP 3
INPUT FROM VISION/STORY/TRADITION

Liturgical Context

The gospels of the last two Sundays served as an introduction to the Sermon on the Mount that begins today and continues for the next three Sundays. Thus the Sixth, Seventh, and Eighth Sundays of Ordinary Time form an internal unity of their own. Some have called this an early catechism. However, that is misleading. The Sermon as it is recorded is not a complete entity, nor is it a dry

---

[4]The primary focus of reflection is the gospel. However, very often the other readings demand attention and must be brought into the dialogue.

and abstract rendering of principles to be followed, as most catechisms are intended to be. Rather, the Sermon is a powerful exhortation intended to convince every person who hears it to take heed and follow its practical imperatives and principles. The purpose is to form the listener in a renewed understanding of the law. "But we should not make any mistake; this teaching with its unending demands '... is not rigorous and intransigent; it is not an observance to maintain at all costs, but a call which urges us on farther and farther and which is increasingly identified with the deepest part of our personality. The most compelling demand ends up being that of freedom.'"[5]

The Sermon is divided into recognizable sections. The first section (read on the Sixth and Seventh Sundays) demonstrates how Jesus' teaching renewed and fulfilled the ethical demands of justice in the law. The second section deals with the interior disposition we are to possess as we perform the good works we are exhorted to perform. The gospel for the Eighth Sunday brings closure to the section by telling the reader that he or she must choose between God and money. Trust is to be their constant attitude. The third and last section of the Sermon relates the three admonitions of Jesus. The liturgy for the Ninth Sunday remembers and celebrates his last admonition: diligent adherence to the teachings of the Master is the only way to be fruitful in establishing the reign of Christ.

Today's journey into the heart of the law is echoed by the Opening Prayer for today's liturgy: "Let us pray that everything we do will be guided by God's law of love."[6] The wisdom necessary to live the commands of Jesus are requested in the Alternative Opening Prayer and echo the wisdom of Jesus Christ crucified, preached by Paul in today's second reading: "... the loving plan of your wisdom took flesh in Jesus Christ, and changed mankind's history by his command of perfect love. May our fulfillment of his command reflect your wisdom and bring salvation to the ends of the earth...."[7]

[5]J. Guillet, *Jesus devant sa vie et devant sa mort* (Paris: Aubier, 1971), 101, in *DL* (IV), 53.

[6]Sixth Sunday in Ordinary Time, "Opening Prayer," *The Sacramentary.*

[7]Sixth Sunday in Ordinary Time, "Alternative Opening Prayer," *The Sacramentary.*

Gospel Exegesis

The facilitator gives input regarding what critical biblical scholarship has to say about this text. The input includes insights as to how people would have heard the gospel in Jesus' time.

Today Jesus teaches his disciples about the proper understanding of the law. There are three divisions of the Hebrew Bible: the law, the prophets, and the writings. The law is known as the Pentateuch, the first five books of the Bible originally attributed to Moses. Jesus emphasized that he did not come to abolish the law. Rather, he came to fulfill it. Jesus was asking for greater fidelity of heart, mind, and soul to the spirit of the law. In terms of the law, more is expected of disciples than mere observance. "The difference must be *qualitative.* Their obedience must be to the spirit of Torah as revealed to them by Jesus, not merely to the letter as strictly construed by their opponents. Not bad theology (v. 19) but bad behavior (including sins of omission) will result in exclusion from the kingdom."[8]

What follows in the Sermon are six "antitheses," four of which occur in today's gospel. Jesus' purpose in this section is to restore God's intention in the law. He asks us to look at reasons for law in the first place—the motivation for human sin. The principal issues in today's gospel are anger, lust, divorce, and oaths.

Anger. The first two "antitheses" in today's gospel refer to the Ten Commandments. In no way was Jesus suggesting that the Ten Commandments were no longer relevant. He was admonishing his listeners to go deeper into their hearts and their intentions. God intended for all people to be in right relationship with God and with one another. Thus, it is God's plan that all people love one another. Murder is the extreme sin against this law of love. Outbursts of anger and insults are serious sins, but the remedy is found in God's grace and through reconciliation. When there is strife, discord, misunderstanding, and injury, reconciliation between injured parties is to be the disciples' primary concern.

[8]*MI,* 49.

Reconciliation precedes worship. When one is out of sorts with a brother or sister, then one is also out of sorts with God. It would have been obviously next to impossible to leave a goat, a pigeon, or a cereal offering on the steps of the altar area in order to go reconcile with a brother or sister. The point is clear. Do not let your anger go that far; reconcile before you bring your gifts to the altar. "Whatever our gift to God, its acceptance is conditional upon honest repentance concerning the ways in which we have injured our neighbors."[9]

Jesus' teaching was not so much novel as it was a fresh and renewed perspective. Jesus was more concerned with relationships than he was with the legal formulas and rituals that so many of his contemporaries (the scribes and Pharisees) were concerned about.

Lust. The command not to lust is based on the command not to covet in the Ten Commandments. Covet means more than envy in the biblical sense. It means to plan and conspire to take the coveted property of another. A man's wife was first on the list of his property and assets. *Not to covet someone's wife* meant not to conspire to take his most prized possession. One was not to even think about it. Throughout biblical literature there is a warning against sinning in one's thoughts. The thought always precedes the action: no thought, no sin. Again, Jesus' exhortation *not to lust* was not novel to first-century listeners. Earlier biblical literature would have supported a similar directive. What was novel, however, was the way in which Jesus and the subsequent Christian communities welcomed and respected women as sisters. Women enjoyed a new dignity never before enjoyed. The implication of Jesus' command was that while it is not sinful to look at a woman, it *is* sinful to covet or lust after her. To do so was tantamount to adultery. In Jesus' kingdom men would be required to exert more self-discipline and harness their urges.

Divorce. The Old Testament did not forbid divorce; it regulated it. Again Jesus invited a closer look into the heart of the law. The basis for his teaching was his concern for the welfare of women. There is no question that Jesus upheld monogamy rather than polygamy. It was a popular notion held by the Jewish men of Jesus' day that they possessed an inalienable right to divorce their wives at will. Jesus insisted that a man who divorced his faithful wife was guilty of grave sin. There was a cultural and economic assumption undergirding this situation. When a man divorced his wife, she was forced to remarry (or worse, forced into prostitution) in order to survive. The second marriage rendered her an adulteress. Jesus insisted that the man had no right to divorce his wife in the first place. Even though the law allowed a man to divorce his wife, it was immoral in the eyes of God. The divorce was legally valid, but morally invalid. If the man's wife remarried, her second marriage was an adulterous union "... since in God's eyes she belongs not to him but to her first husband."[10]

The exception clause ("unless the marriage is unlawful") (5:32) has been a source of great debate by scholars. The simplest hypothesis suggests that since ancient printing did not enjoy such conventions as italics, footnotes, brackets, and parentheses for clarification, Matthew might simply have been stressing what was automatically assumed by Jesus. If a woman had already been unfaithful, the husband could hardly be held responsible for making her an adulteress if she married again—she already was an adulteress.[11] Jewish law insisted that adultery automatically severed the marriage bond. "The wife had already violated the marriage; she cannot be made an adulteress if she is divorced and remarries."[12]

What is integral to this teaching and the basis for the law regarding divorce is the *intention of God.* What was God's intention for marriage? At the creation of the world God created men and women. In Genesis 1:27 an unbreakable relationship is implied. And Jesus said, in response to the Pharisees' questions concerning the lawfulness of divorce: "Therefore what God has joined together,

[9]Ibid., 52.

[10]Ibid., 221.

[11]It is interesting to note that a serious double standard existed. There is no consequence in the law if a man was adulterous. However, Jesus turned the tables somewhat by charging a man guilty of adultery simply by lusting after a woman.

[12]*RM,* 68.

no human being must separate" (Mk 10:9). Sin was certainly not God's plan for men and women, as the first reading so clearly points out.

Jesus' teaching on divorce stresses God's will for marriage. It is God's will that men and women enter into a loving, unbreakable bond of marriage. Disciples must go the extra mile to repair fractured relationships and live according to God's will. Disciples must spurn all that leads to divorce, beginning with lust and unbridled evil desires. As a final comment regarding Jesus' teaching on divorce in today's gospel, Douglas Hare leaves us with the following caution:

> While it [the teaching on divorce] points to God's ultimate will for men and women, there are numerous instances in which marriage is no longer real, whether because of infidelity, neglect, abuse, failure to communicate, or simply unresolved tensions regarding reciprocal expectations. While every effort should be made to redeem fractured marriages, some must be acknowledged as beyond repair. In such cases, divorce may be not only the lesser of two evils from the point of view of God's ultimate will, but also a positive step.[13]

Oaths. This antithesis is concerned about behavior in the marketplace. According to John Pilch, the context is selling. There were no regulatory bodies to control honest practices in commerce. A seller would indirectly call on God to testify on his behalf concerning the quality of his goods. He would swear by his head, his beard, his life, and by Jerusalem. Underneath these indirect oaths lie the supposition that God himself was testifying to the trustworthiness of the individual or the product he was selling. "When he refused to make God explicit, conflict erupted. Jesus advised his followers to be honest and direct with one another at the market: yes or no."[14] An oath is "implicitly a profession of faith in God . . . who will not fail to react in case of untruthfulness."[15]

[13]*MI*, 54.
[14]*CWJ*, 36.
[15]*DL*, 61.

Jesus insists that disciples be honest with themselves, with one another, and with God. "Disciples are to speak the truth as a matter of course because they are inwardly pure in heart, not because it has been imposed upon them by the use of an oath. Jesus' demand assumes that humans are bound to God in all of life, not just when they call upon God as a witness; and they will be accountable for every idle word (12:34–37)."[16] Jesus requires that his followers mean what they say and say what they mean. Jesus forbids the pledging of oaths. They are unnecessary in the new reign of God. Words are for building up the reign of God.

The heart of today's gospel is attitude and interior disposition. Jesus looks into the human heart of his would-be followers. He did not abolish the law; he demanded that his disciples go directly to the law's intent. Jesus expects more than mere adherence to the law. If today's exhortations were nothing more than a new set of laws, a new laundry list of do and don't, then it was more strangling than the legalism of the Pharisees. The behavior demanded in today's gospel is a free response to the love of God. One can do no less than respond in faith. That response is made possible by the grace of God. The behavior Jesus expects from his followers is a natural consequence of being in right relationship with God; it is the Christian response to the reciprocal covenant relationship.

Proclaim the gospel again.

Sometimes we gain new insights when we hear the text after the interpretation has been given. Someone from the group proclaims the gospel a second time.

STEP 4
TESTING

Conversation with the Liturgy and the Scriptures

Test your original understanding in dialogue with the text.

[16]*RM*, 72.

(You might consider breaking into smaller groups.)

Were there any new insights for you?

How does this story speak to your life?

Sharing Life Experience

Participants share an experience from their lives that connects with the biblical interpretation just shared.

Today's gospel is a powerful word for communities today that are torn by internal discord over issues of orthodoxy. Friends of a relative of mine invited me to their parish a few years ago. It was so torn by strife that they were on the verge of breaking apart. Two camps were formed—both certain that only they held the truth. Both camps perched atop their self-righteous soapbox. Suspicion, fear, and animosity reigned. Insults and threats were commonplace. In today's gospel, Jesus invites his disciples into a deeper covenant relationship with him—a relationship that demands a loving response. Such a response can only come from freedom—not from coercion or bullying into submission. When we treat each other with anger and insults, even if we think we are the only guardians of truth, we are, by our very actions, defying what Jesus was asking of us today. My heart ached for this community, and I left feeling that only God could heal the division.

We are to go beyond the rules; more is required of Christians. What Jesus was inviting in today's gospel was a proper understanding of the law, and the motivations behind human sin. Very often people approach the law with a legalistic perspective because they do not know or understand it. It is our responsibility to be formed in the faith of Jesus Christ and in the teaching of the church. Jesus knew and understood the law. The scribes and Pharisees also knew and understood the law, but they forgot what the law signified. Living the law is the human response, in freedom, to God's love.

Anger gone amok was denounced by Jesus in today's gospel, yet so many communities are torn asunder by bitter words and hurtful accusations that can lead to extreme and sinful behavior. An acquaintance of mine was giving a presentation in another city. She received threats from a couple of people who believed that her presentation was not official church teaching. Not only was it official church teaching, but it was a well-documented presentation. The people were not just uncharitable, they were uninformed as well.

I was recently touched by an address given by Cardinal Roger Mahoney of Los Angeles to the Pontifical Council on Social Communications, in which he asked: Who speaks for the church? He asked that structures be created for the lay faithful to grow in discernment. He suggested that discerning Catholics would be able to discover whether a voice speaking for the church is authentic or not, and that a discerning Catholic would know that a person is speaking for the church by the way he or she speaks. "Are the gifts, fruits, and harvest of the Spirit present in their message," he asked, "or is the message one of fear and divisiveness?" Today Jesus rails against divisiveness, anger, and fear. If we go beyond mere observance of the law into its heart, we will act in love. Cardinal Mahoney reminded his listeners that the Holy Spirit dwells within the whole body of Christ. "No one individual or grouping within the church has a monopoly on the Spirit," he said. "The presence of the Spirit is recognized by the flourishing of gifts and fruits in an abundant harvest" (cf. Gal 5:22).

Because there are many different voices today which insist that they speak with the authority of the church, Cardinal Mahoney continued by instructing his audience how to listen for the authentic, Spirit-filled voices: "Some of the voices speaking in the church are clearly from the church and for the good of the church—sound and Spirit-guided theologians in service of Christ and his church, contemporary martyrs and holy women and men who speak through personal witness to the cross of Christ—prophetic voices."[17] *It behooves each of us, then, to know what the church really teaches; to love God with our whole mind, heart, and soul; and thus be empowered to love as Jesus loved. Jesus' love led him to the cross. We are destined to follow him there if we are faithful to the rigors of today's gospel. The world cannot handle love like that.*

[17] *Origins,* April 2, 1998, Vol. 27, No. 41, 686.

On a personal level, today's gospel reminds me of an incident in my life where I felt I just had to be right. Technically speaking, I was *right. However, the legalism with which I approached the situation was far afield from the attitude Jesus demanded in today's gospel. Anger and self-righteous indignation was the order of the day. Only after a great deal of prodding and coercion was I able to let go of my need to be right and allow the Spirit to work in the situation. Only then was it resolved. Today's gospel reminds me that I have to do more than the law requires. I have to look at the motives for my actions. I must remember that God is my all in all. If I love as I am commanded to love, then all my relationships will be in right order. Jesus forbade divorce because it was God's intention for the bond between a husband and wife not be broken. If both parties would enter into such a covenant of love, there would obviously be no need for divorce. (Wouldn't it be wonderful if that were the real world we live in?)*

It is God's intention that we love God with our whole mind, heart, and soul; that we respond to that love by the way we love in return. When I display a stubborn need to be right, I am much like the Pharisees who touted the law, but were not living the intention of the law in their own hearts. Jesus' exhortation does not mean that we cannot disagree with one another. We can and we do. Because we are human, we will disagree often. However, although we sometimes disagree, if love and respect are missing, so is the Spirit.

What was the underlying message behind this section of the Sermon on the Mount? What implications were there for Matthew's community? What implications are there for your community today? What part of this liturgy (readings and/or gospel) is most needed in your community at this time? How do today's readings reflect the biblical theme of covenant, exodus, creation, and community? What touched you the most? What word or idea relates to your life right now? What attitudes are challenged in today's gospel? Where are those attitudes prevalent in your community or in your life (family, workplace, world)? Do you still feel the same way about this text as when you began? How would you articulate an understanding of today's gospel now? Is there anything you would like to add to your original understanding?

Step 5
Decision

The gospel demands a response.

How might today's liturgy invite your community to take a look at its attitudes and behaviors? How does it challenge you to look at your own attitudes and behaviors? Where is transformation needed the most in your community? In your own life? How have you already changed as a result of today's conversation with the liturgy of the Sixth Sunday in Ordinary Time? What is one concrete action you will take this week as a response to the liturgy today?

Pastoral Considerations: There is sometimes a temptation to focus solely on divorce as a result of today's gospel. Divorce is a very painful subject in the lives of people. To focus solely on that one issue, however, robs the gospel of its primary focus and power—the intent and heart of the law and our relationship with God and one another. Today speaks to all of our relationships. All Christian behavior is bound by the reading of today's gospel. Since the heart of today's gospel is the right ordering of *all relationships,* perhaps the parish might begin to consider ways to celebrate all the various life's vocations represented in your community. Perhaps married couples might gather for a meal, a liturgy of the word, and a blessing of marriage. Sunday liturgy may not be the best place for such a blessing as there are too many who suffer with fresh wounds of separation. A gathering outside the Sunday liturgy is a way for people to voluntarily come together in solidarity with one another and to thank God for blessings received. A similar event might be planned for singles, for separated, widowed and divorced, for the elderly, etc.... the list is endless. The *Book of Blessings* offers many liturgical celebrations for just such occasions.

DOCTRINAL ISSUES

What church truth/teaching/doctrinal issue could be drawn from the gospel for the Sixth Sunday of Ordinary Time?

Participants suggest possible doctrinal themes that flow from the readings.

Possible Doctrinal Themes

The moral life, the Ten Commandments, hierarchy of truths, sacrament of marriage: community of love, conversion, biblical justice, God, Jesus Christ, discipleship

Present the doctrinal material at this time.

1. The facilitator gives input on a particular doctrinal issue of his or her prior choosing. OR

2. The group chooses a doctrinal issue from the list they created. They read together from the Doctrinal Appendix.

(The doctrinal issues are found in the Doctrinal Appendix in the back of this workbook. If you are choosing an issue from this resource, please refer to it now.)

Reflection questions centered around the chosen doctrinal theme can be found at the end of each topic in the Doctrinal Appendix. The questions are based on the five-step reflection process. If you choose a topic not included in the Doctrinal Appendix, craft your own questions according to the same five-step process.

Following the reflection questions you will be reminded to return to chapter 7, "Preparing the Catechetical Session," to assist you in crafting your own session.

Closing Prayer

Lord, we make this offering in obedience to your word.
May it cleanse and renew us,
and lead us to our eternal reward.
We ask this in the name of Jesus the Lord . . .[18]

or

Lord,
you give us food from heaven.
May we always hunger
for the bread of life.
Grant this through Christ, our Lord.[19]

[18]Sixth Sunday in Ordinary Time: "Prayer Over the Gifts," *The Sacramentary.*

[19]Sixth Sunday in Ordinary Time: "Prayer After Communion," *The Sacramentary.*

Seventh Sunday in Ordinary Time

INTRODUCTORY RITES

Opening Prayer (or Entrance Antiphon)

The Lord has been my strength; he has led me into freedom. He saved me because he loved me. (Ps 17:19–20)[1]

Opening Prayer

The facilitator of the session may lead the prayer. Others in the group may be asked to proclaim the readings.

Let us pray . . .

Pause for silent prayer.

Father in heaven,
form in us the likeness of your Son
and deepen his life within us.
Send us as witnesses of gospel joy
into a world of fragile peace and
touch the hearts of all men with your love
that they in turn may love one another.
We ask this through Christ, our Lord.[2]

LITURGY OF THE WORD

The readings are proclaimed.

First Reading
Leviticus 19:1–2, 17–18

Overview of Leviticus: The Book of Leviticus, a compilation of Israel's priestly regulations, provides a glimpse into the religious life and practices of ancient Israel. This is a legal code for priests who served at the Temple in Jerusalem. It is believed that a large agricultural community supplied the necessary sacrifices and offerings used for festivals and feasts. Leviticus was compiled by the Priestly authors around the sixth century B.C.E. Much of the material in the book centers around appropriate behavior for worship. Included in the book is a listing of ritual sacrifices and foods to abstain from, as well as the narrative story explaining how Moses was the originator of the liturgical practices.

The first part of Leviticus includes the ordination of priests (ch. 1–7), the sacrifices (ch. 8–10), foods that were taboo (ch. 11–15), and the liturgy of atonement (ch. 16). The final liturgy of atonement is the climax of the first part of the book. Once a year the high priest placed the sins of Israel on the head of a goat[3] and then sent the goat out into the desert to die as a sign of God's forgiving nature, and as a sign that God is always eager to wipe out human sin.

The taboo laws demonstrated that worship of God extended into everyday life. The restrictions on certain foods were probably a result of medical concerns of contamination. Some scholars suggest that perhaps the fear of trichinosis is responsible for the prohibition against pork. Similarly, the law demanding quarantine of those with skin disorders is probably the result of the highly contagious nature of skin rashes.

In addition to the concerns about contamination, there seems to have been an inherent order that regulated the prohibition of foods, based on Genesis 1 and the general order in which God created living things: plants are in the ground, birds are in the air; fish swim and animals graze. Foods that were taboo were those that did not fall into the natural order of creation: birds that did not fly, fish without fins and scales, and animals that did not graze. "It teaches us that the basic outlook of Israel toward food was not just to gain nourishment but to reflect God's goodness in creation."[4]

The last part of Leviticus contains the "holiness code." The holiness code is a set of laws that high-

[1]Seventh Sunday in Ordinary Time: "Entrance Antiphon," *The Sacramentary.*

[2]Seventh Sunday in Ordinary Time: "Opening Prayer," *The Sacramentary.*

[3]The word *scapegoat* originates from this ritual practice.

[4]*ROT,* 189.

light the holiness of God. The laws demand that Levites act holy as God is holy and refrain from "profane behavior unworthy of their special calling."[5] The code highlights Israel's relationship with Yahweh and contains regulations concerning sex, marriage, touching blood, violating moral commandments, upholding justice, and observing feast days. The concluding chapter in Leviticus concerns the repayment of vows.[6]

The Holiness Code is concerned with the meaning, implications, and foundation of worship and daily conduct, and how both are connected. Laws are observed because God is holy. "The deep reason why we must conform to the Lord's commands is best expressed with the utmost clarity."[7] God's transcendence is emphatically heralded throughout the scriptures. However, God's transcendence does not mean that he was uninvolved in human history. On the contrary, God was and is intimately involved in human history. While expressing God's other-ness and God's transcendence, the Bible uniquely extols God's nearness. God does not direct human events as a "sidewalk supervisor," but is intimately involved in human affairs. God entered into a covenant relationship with human beings and is partner with them in their unfolding history. God is not completely hidden in a cloud of unknowing, but allows himself to be known and to be seen. Human beings can know God because God has revealed God's name—people may call God "You." God allows human beings to share in his holiness. God is not stingy; God does not keep his holiness to himself.

God is near at God's own initiative—because God desires to be in relationship with humanity. The Code of Holiness reveals the face of God: who God is, how God acts, and how God expects those in relationship with him to act. Human beings are to love because God is holy and God loves.

Today's Pericope: People are to be holy as God is holy. The people of God will be recognized and distinguished because of their behavior. This behavior is best observed by responding to the great commandment of love. The commandment to love one's neighbor in Israel meant to love a fellow Israelite. Jesus in his expansive love extended neighbor to include one's enemies.

[5]Ibid., 190.

[6]Ibid., 188–190.

[7]*DL* (IV), 63.

Responsorial Psalm

Psalm 103:1–2, 3–4, 8, 10, 12–13

This is the best known thanksgiving psalm in the psalter. The psalmist praises God in light of his own understanding of God's purpose. God is praised for God's mercy and kindness.

Second Reading

1 Corinthians 3:16–23

(Refer to the Overview of 1 and 2 Corinthians on the Second Sunday in Ordinary Time.)

Paul used the term "temple" for the first time in today's reading. He used the term to refer to the church. The temple is where the Spirit of God is present—in the church, the people of God. Later in Corinthians Paul likened the individual and the Corinthian community to the temple, telling them that they were the temple of God. The word he used is *naos,* which in Judaism referred to the holy of holies, the sacred space believed to be the dwelling place of the Lord. Thus, according to Paul, the Spirit dwelling within a Christian makes him or her a *naos*—the sacred temple of God.

Paul continued his angst over the divisions and cliques within the Corinthian community. Disunity defiles the holiness of God's temple. Paul insisted that their special "gnosis" was simply human wisdom—not God's wisdom. Again, the message resounds as it has in the past weeks. ***God's wisdom resides in the cross of Christ!*** Christ alone saved the human race through his death on the cross. No other human being can lay claim to such distinction. The community belongs to Christ. Jesus is the only foundation upon which the church is built. Human leaders are sent as servants. Boasting about human leaders is the result of human wisdom, not God's wisdom. Those who would defile the temple by introducing the wisdom of the world, damage and shake the very foundation of the church in which the Spirit dwells. It is a most grievous offense. Only through Jesus is one's future secure.

Gospel
Matthew 5:38–48

STEP 1
NAMING ONE'S EXPERIENCE

What were your first impressions? What was your first response to the gospel (or the other readings)?[8] What captured your attention?

Each person names his or her initial impression. Statements should be brief. No reasons should be given at this time. All simply listen without agreeing or disagreeing.

STEP 2
UNDERSTANDING

In a brief statement, what do you think this gospel is trying to convey?

STEP 3
INPUT FROM VISION/STORY/TRADITION

Liturgical Context

Refer to the Sixth Sunday in Ordinary Time for the context and continuity between the Sixth through the Ninth Sundays in Ordinary Time. The Opening Prayer for today's liturgy (the closing prayer used for this session) echoes Paul's words to the Corinthians. We are reminded that it is only through Jesus that we possess the wisdom of God: "[K]eep before us the wisdom and love you have revealed in your Son. Help us to be like him in word and deed."[9]

Jesus shows us what it means to be like him in word and deed in today's gospel. Jesus' challenge is radical. To be like Jesus means that disciples accept their God-given status and dignity as a child of God. Disciples are to choose the path of non-violence and respond to their life situations with the dignity befitting a child of God. Disciples are to go the extra mile, love their enemies without the expectation of reciprocation, and welcome outsiders at their table. Such perfection is only possible by the grace and love of God.

The eucharist empowers disciples to live the ethical imperatives of today's gospel. The challenge of every eucharist is to become eucharist in the world and to live the gospel of Christ. The demands of the gospel are challenging. Jesus invites the Christian into a deep intimacy. The human response in the face of such love is to love in return, just as Jesus loved—unto death. This is what eucharist celebrates—Jesus' self-sacrifice and our participation in that mystery. Today's liturgy helps us to remember that it is our eucharistic life that leads us to limitless love. Pope Paul VI eloquently reminds us that response to today's gospel is nourished and strengthened at the Lord's table:

> The eucharist is the most direct, the most powerful invitation to friendship, to the following of Christ. The eucharist is, as well, the sustenance that gives the energy and joy to respond to love. The eucharist thus puts the problem of our life as a supreme challenge of love, of choice, of fidelity; if we accept the challenge, the issue from being simply religious becomes social. . . . Love received from Christ in the eucharist is communion with him and is therefore transformed into and expressed by our communion with our brothers and sisters—that is with all human beings, who actually or potentially are our brothers and sisters. Nourished by the real and sacramental body of Christ, we become ever more fully the Mystical Body of Christ: "Is not the cup of blessing that we bless the communion of the body of Christ? . . . For we who are many are one bread and one body, for we are all partakers of that one bread" (1 Cor 10:16–17).

Gospel Exegesis

The facilitator gives input regarding what critical biblical scholarship has to say about this text. The input in-

[8] The primary focus of reflection is the gospel. However, very often the other readings demand attention and must be brought into the dialogue.

[9] Seventh Sunday in Ordinary Time: "Opening Prayer," *The Sacramentary.*

cludes insights as to how people would have heard the gospel in Jesus' time.

Today's gospel continues where last week's gospel left off. Last week there were four antitheses from the Sermon on the Mount proclaimed in the gospel. Jesus was inviting a response of radical proportions to the reign of God. The perfection he invited was rooted in going beyond the righteousness demanded by the law of Moses and strictly observed by the scribes and Pharisees. Jesus had no intention to abolish the law or to create his own law. His desire was to restore God's original intention of the law.

The Rabbis reinterpreted many of the ancient laws by allowing less stringent adherence to many of them. One such reinterpretation involved allowing a person to seek redress and monetary punitive damages in court instead of the former *eye for an eye and tooth for a tooth.* No one, however, accused the Rabbis of trying to abolish the law. Yet when Jesus suggested a more stringent observance of the law, based on God's intention in the law, he was accused of trying to abolish or circumvent it. Jesus was positing a bold new way to respond to life's hurts. He was suggesting that Christians choose positive, creative, non-violent means to settle their disputes and deal with injury and humiliation. Jesus was not suggesting a nearly unattainable emotional feeling of love toward one's enemies; he was suggesting that Christians act in a positive manner toward them—that they choose a response other than retaliation. Where the law of the talion (*lex talionis*) used to be the order of the day (so that no more than what had been exacted could be asked in return), Jesus was suggesting that a new approach to old problems must now be sought. He gave three examples in today's gospel. The challenge for the reader is to follow Jesus' lead, and use the imagination to seek positive responses to other, often similar situations in life.

One must enter the extremely shame-based cultural world of ancient Palestine in order to appreciate the implications of this text. A strike on the right cheek involved either a backhanded slap from a right-handed person, or an open slap from a left-handed person. The left hand was used for bodily hygiene. It was a serious affront to use the left hand for such things as eating, placing it on the table, or offering it to others. Whether the slap was left-handed or right-handed made no difference—both were considered an insult.

To be backhanded is an extreme, calculated indignity, considered four times more injurious and requiring a much higher award for injuries:

> If a man cuffed his fellow he must pay him a *sel* [four *zuz*; a *zuz* was approximately a day's wage]. R. Judah says in the name of R. Jose the Galilean: One hundred *zuz.* If he slapped him he must pay 200 *zuz.* If he [struck him] with the back of his hand he must pay him 400 *zuz.*[10]

Today's gospel builds on the law of exact retaliation. The law of the talion (*eye for an eye*), also called the "law of the tooth," served to restrict and limit unrestricted blood vengeance against another for wrongdoing. A person who loses an eye may not ask for two eyes from the accused perpetrator in retaliation. The law "mandates responsibility for damages, equality of justice, and a just proportion between the crime and the punishment. Jesus, however, prohibits even measured retaliation. . . ."[11]

Secular literature of Jesus' day encouraged humble submission in the face of humiliating violence. Jesus offered another alternative: *turning the other cheek.* It was neither submission nor surrender. When the victim turned the other cheek, he demonstrated his own personal freedom—he was in control, not the oppressor. "The oppressor must decide whether or not to slap the person again, but this time not as one would slap a slave with the back of the hand but as one would an equal. [Walter] Wink contends that turning the cheek 'seizes the initiative from the oppressor, overcomes fear, and reclaims the power of choice, all the while maintaining the humanity of the oppressor' [*Sojourners* 15, no. 11, 1986]."[12]

Oppressors and those in power have a vested interest in translating these verses to mean that people should humbly take anything and everything that is meted out to them. However, there is obvi-

---

[10]*RM,* 73.

[11]Ibid., 72.

[12]Ibid., 74.

ously more to these verses than the literal interpretation suggests. Jesus was making a point and punctuating it in bold letters. He was condemning violence. His point? One violent act must not beget another act of violence. Jesus was proposing an alternative response to violence—a response that respected the dignity of victim and oppressor. No follower of Christ was to become another person's unwitting doormat.

Another possible intention of this passage might be to address and challenge the human urge for revenge. "It is possible, however, that the principle of talion is here attacked in its more common, nonlegal sense of 'tit for tat' (as reflected in the bumper sticker, 'I don't get mad, I get even')."[13] Jesus insisted that "getting even" is not the way Christians are to live in the reign of God he had come to establish.

The next antithesis involved a court situation in which a man was being sued for his tunic. It seems as if Jesus was encouraging passivity in such litigation. If a man was sued for his tunic, he was to give his cloak as well. The result? The poor man would be without tunic or cloak—he would be naked. Whose problem would it be? In the shamed-based culture, nakedness was an unspeakable, unimaginable condition. Shame would be forced on the one who was responsible for the nakedness—the plaintiff. He would be the embarrassed one. He would be forced to insist that the man put his clothes back on. Some scholars suggest that this was an indirect indictment against Roman taxation. It is possible that Jesus was advising contemporary revolutionaries to let the authorities have their way and leave vengeance to God.

Roman soldiers were allowed by law to commandeer civilians' pack animals and grain boats to carry their military supplies. The civilians themselves could also be forced to carry a soldier's gear for one mile. The soldiers often abused their right to press civilians into service, which caused bitter resentment among the citizenry. "In first century occupied Palestine, [the] soldier frequently was a fellow Israelite who turned mercenary. Carrying the gear was humiliating enough; being forced to do so by a traitorous fellow citizen was even more humiliating (v. 41)."[14] Resistance to Rome was absurd, and bitter hatred against the enemy was self-defeating and destructive. Jesus suggested an alternative approach. In going the extra mile, disciples were exercising their own internal freedom.

The antithesis that follows involves giving without asking for something in return. Giving was often a means of exerting power and control over another person. The giver became the patron and benefactor of the recipient; there were strings attached. The recipient was expected to reciprocate in kind. The motive was self-serving and a form of self-aggrandizement. Jesus maintained that a person was to give while expecting nothing in return.

The rich in Galilee wanted to invest their wealth in the land. However, the land was not for sale because it was part of a person's ancestral heritage. The only way to add to one's land was to lie in wait for the poor peasant farmers to default on their land and then, like vultures, snatch it from under them. During the revolt against Rome, the first action of the revolutionaries was to seize the debt records of wealthy landowners. Jesus was suggesting that poor peasants band together and help each other so they would not fall prey to the greedy creditors. They were to take care of one another and loan each other what was needed in order to prevent the loss of land.

Jesus upheld a consistent principle of non-violence. He creatively offered other-than-violent means to empower the rural peasants to solve their own problems with dignity in the face of indignation and intimidation. The exhortations against non-violence were not intended as a means to convert the oppressors or force them to alter their behavior. Nor were they intended as a spiritual exercise for the Christian (even though that might naturally be the case). Jesus' intention was to help believers comprehend God's will for the human family. Although not to be taken in the exact literal sense, the situations posed by Jesus were not to be reduced to simple figures of speech either: "They are meant to shock the imagination and instill a profounder insight into God's inten-

[13] *MI*, 56.

[14] *CWJ*, 37.

tion. The old ways of retaliation and self-protection must give way to a gentler, more magnanimous approach to those we deem enemies."[15] Non-violent action responses do, however, stand as stark reminders to oppressors that their actions are evil and unacceptable.

Since retaliation was no longer an option in dealing with enemies, Jesus provided the rationale, in the last antithesis, to love one's enemies. To love your neighbor was a command of the Hebrew Bible. Neighbor was understood as a fellow Israelite and resident aliens. The Bible does not enjoin people to hate their enemies. "To love means 'to favor, prefer, or select'; to hate means to 'disfavor or neglect.' Simply put, loving the neighbor and hating the enemy is to place the neighbor first and the enemy second. . . ."[16] Jesus invalidated the common principle that the one closest to you (the poor over the rich, relatives over non-relatives, residents over aliens, etc.) is to be given precedence. In the reign of God everyone is to be treated equally. To treat enemies with love does not necessarily mean that their hearts will soften and they will reconcile. Sometimes the opposite happens and the enemy showers down more wrath than before.

Jesus was teaching his disciples a lesson about God. God showers his love on those who are good and those who are not. God's love is inclusive. When disciples love their enemies, they love as God loves. When disciples extend God's all-embracing love to others, they demonstrate to the world that they are a child of God. The perfection expected of Christians is not moral perfection. True perfection exists when our love touches God's love and it spills out upon the lovable and the unlovable alike.

"Anger, adultery, divorce, false statements, retaliation, and hatred are destructive behaviors that fragment individuals and society. God's redemptive purpose as expressed in Jesus' interpretation of the law is to restore harmony, create community, and elevate humanity."[17]

---

[15] *MI*, 58.

[16] Ibid., 76.

[17] Ibid., 77.

Proclaim the gospel again.

Sometimes we gain new insights when we hear the text after the interpretation has been given. Someone from the group proclaims the gospel a second time.

Step 4
Testing

Conversation with the Liturgy and the Scriptures

Test your original understanding in dialogue with the text.

(You might consider breaking into smaller groups.)

Are there any insights in this gospel that are new for you? How does your original understanding of this gospel compare with what we just shared?

How does this story speak to your life?

Sharing Life Experience

Participants share an experience from their lives that connects with the biblical interpretation just shared.

> *I remember a time in my life when I was embroiled, along with several others, in a serious controversy. It was the first time I was ever aware that I might have a real enemy. This was simply unconscionable to me; it went against every Christian principle I believed in. But here I was, right in the thick of a situation I hated. The question was always: what should be my/our Christian response? The temptation to retaliate was almost overpowering. Yet, the response we chose was silence. We did not openly engage in hostility (even though I dare say hostility was seeping into my pores). We made a serious attempt to be kind and to refrain from destructive, open gossip. We regularly vented our anger and frustration within our own small group of five or six people, however, which no doubt perpetuated the intensity of feelings. In looking back on the situation in light of today's gospel, it's conceivable that silence was not the best response. Perhaps an alternative approach—a more proactive stance—would have been more in keeping with today's gospel. Perhaps aggressive hostility could have been met with open acts of kindness and*

attempts at reconciliation. Hindsight is 20-20, as they say; but it is also a great teacher. The situation eventually was resolved, healing ensued, and harmony was restored after a considerable length of time. Yet inner, self-destructive animosity toward those I perceived to be the antagonists remained for a longer time than necessary.

Jesus invites us to choose a non-violent approach to our conflicts. We cannot live in the human family without conflict, but today's gospel offers us the possibility to grow through it. Jesus invites us to look at God's intention for our lives and for the life of our community. God expects us to work through our difficulties and to approach one another as children of God. Every real or imagined enemy is also a child of God. Would that we could remember that when confronted with hatred and discord. Today's gospel reminds me that I have other options. Hopefully I will always take my past experience and contrast it to today's gospel, so that in the future I will choose a more life-giving response.

What was Matthew trying to tell his community? What does today's gospel have to teach your community? What part of today's gospel is most relevant to your parish right now? What part is most relevant in your life right now? Are the biblical themes of covenant, exodus, creation, and community evident in today's readings? How do they speak to your life and the life of your community? In what way does the *turn the other cheek* imperative speak to your life right now? If not now, what are the implications for the future? Who do you perceive as enemies? How does this gospel address your response to them? Do you still feel the same way about this text as when you began? Has your original understanding been stretched, challenged, or affirmed? How would you articulate an understanding of this gospel now?

STEP 5
DECISION

The gospel demands a response.

How does today's gospel/liturgy invite you and your community to change? In what concrete way does today's gospel challenge your community to respond? Has this conversation with the exegesis changed or stretched any of your personal attitudes? What are the implications of this gospel for your life? What is one concrete action you will take this week as a response to the liturgy today?

Pastoral Considerations: Are there presently any factions, animosities, or controversies in your community (parish, neighborhood, or civic) that call for and demand the wisdom of Jesus' Sermon on the Mount? What strategies might be implemented to address them?

Christian Initiation: As today's gospel stresses the implications of the Christian life, it might be an appropriate time to celebrate a rite of acceptance. Jesus shows in concrete terms what it means to live the gospel and embrace the cross in everyday life.

DOCTRINAL ISSUES

What church truth/teaching/doctrinal issue could be drawn from the gospel for the Seventh Sunday in Ordinary Time?

Participants suggest possible doctrinal themes that flow from the readings.

Possible Doctrinal Themes

Moral life, foundations of morality, beatitudes, love of God, mystery of the church, discipleship, paschal mystery, christology, reconciliation, sacrament of penance

Present the doctrinal material at this time.

1. The facilitator gives input on a particular doctrinal issue of his or her prior choosing. OR

2. The group chooses a doctrinal issue from the list they created. They read together from the Doctrinal Appendix.

(The doctrinal issues are found in the Doctrinal Appendix in the back of this workbook. If you are choosing an issue from this resource, please refer to it now.)

Reflection questions centered around the chosen doctrinal theme can be found at the end of each topic in the Doctrinal Appendix. The questions are based on the five-step reflection process. If you choose a topic not included in the Doctrinal Appendix, craft your own questions according to the same five-step process.

Following the reflection questions you will be reminded to return to chapter 7, "Preparing the Catechetical Session," to assist you in crafting your own session.

Closing Prayer

Father,
keep before us the wisdom and love
you have revealed in your Son.
Help us to be like him
in word and deed,
for he lives and reigns with you
and the Holy Spirit,
one God for ever and ever.[18]

[18]Seventh Sunday in Ordinary Time: "Opening Prayer," *The Sacramentary.*

Eighth Sunday in Ordinary Time

INTRODUCTORY RITES

Opening Song (or Entrance Antiphon)

The Lord has been my strength; he has led me into freedom. He saved me because he loves me. (Ps 17:19–20)[1]

Opening Prayer

The facilitator of the session may lead the prayer. Others in the group may be asked to proclaim the readings.

Let us pray
[that the peace of Christ may find welcome in the world]

Pause for silent prayer.

Father in heaven,
form in us the likeness of your Son
and deepen his life within us.
Send us as witnesses of gospel joy
into a world of fragile peace and broken promises.
Touch the hearts of all men with your love
that they in turn may love one another.
We ask this through Christ, our Lord.[2]

LITURGY OF THE WORD

The readings are proclaimed.

First Reading
Isaiah 49:14–15

(Refer to Second Sunday in Ordinary Time for an Overview of Second Isaiah.)

Today's Pericope: The situation: Israel is in Babylonian captivity and is discouraged. It has been seventy years! Zion wonders when and if God will ever hear them again. Have they been forsaken? The answer: Today's reading is emphatic—God will never forsake God's children. How could we ever think it possible? A mother could forget the child at her breast before God could ever forget God's own.

One can only imagine Israel's hopelessness. There is nothing harder to bear than to have the one you counted on the most desert you in the midst of despair. Because of what Israel perceived to be God's non-action, they felt they had been completely abandoned by their God. But today's word of the Lord has spoken. There is no need for interpretation; it stands on its own. God could not be more succinct. The human person is a child of God's womb—God's very own creation. God's children will never, ever be forgotten. God's children reflect God's innermost self. To forget one's own infant is to forget a part of oneself. God could no more forget his children than God could forget God's self. Human beings are a part of God—the womb of God—never to be forsaken or abandoned.[3]

God's tenderness and compassion make no sense in light of the human condition. No human person deserves the love lavished upon him or her by the expansive love of God. Yet God always forgives, invites, and tenderly caresses those who are God's children, God's own. A greater word of consolation could not be found in all of literature since the creation of the world.

Responsorial Psalm
Psalm 62:2–3, 6–7, 8–9

In the face of such tender love, the psalmist can do no less than express, in humble sincerity, utter trust and abandonment to Yahweh who loves so completely. Today's psalm is an expression of this complete trust in God, in contrast to the impassioned, frantic pleas for God's immediate atten-

[1] Eighth Sunday in Ordinary Time: "Entrance Antiphon," *The Sacramentary.*

[2] Eighth Sunday in Ordinary Time: "Alternative Opening Prayer," *The Sacramentary.*

[3] "This is one of the few examples in the Bible of female imagery used for God—today a welcome corrective to the predominant use of male imagery." *PL,* 126.

tion, often found in the psalms of lament. This psalm reflects the theme of trust found in today's gospel.

Second Reading
1 Corinthians 4:1–5

(Refer to Second Sunday in Ordinary Time for an Overview of 1 and 2 Corinthians.)

Today's Pericope: Paul had a difficult time being accepted. He was not an apostle who walked with the Lord as the others had. He had a difficult time rising above the fact that he had been a major persecutor of the Christian church. In order to validate his apostleship and thus, his authority, Paul was often impelled to recount the circumstances of his conversion. Added to Paul's difficulties in being accepted as an authentic apostle was the fact that there were also leaders in the community who enjoyed an elevated, exalted status. These leaders were believed to possess a special "gnosis" (knowledge) that they imparted to all the people they initiated into the Christian faith. Paul paled in comparison to these "charismatic leaders."

He thus was forced to defend the role of a trustworthy and true apostle. He insisted that an apostle was a servant, very much like a "secretary of a religious society."[4] However, the servant's service was to Jesus, not to any human organization. According to Reginald Fuller, Paul referred to apostles as stewards who were entrusted with the care of someone else's property—God's property. Patricia Sanchez offers further insight: "The Greek word *hyperetes* was originally used to designate the oarsman on the lower level of the galleys of a ship. According to this metaphor, Paul envisioned Christ as the captain of the ship, and himself as one who received and carried out Christ's orders."[5]

Paul also maintained that apostles were administrators of God's mysteries. While the word *mysteries* is very often interpreted to mean sacraments, the New Testament authors understood it to mean the hidden truths revealed by God (in which sacraments are certainly included).

[4] *PL*, 126.
[5] *WWC*, 59.

Paul teaches that good stewardship requires faithfulness. The Corinthians were disillusioned with Paul. They expected more of him. They expected him to exercise more personal authority. He did not measure up to the showy false apostles who were on the circuit in Corinth. (One can only be reminded of the flashy televangelists of today.) Paul, however, refused to be caught up in the Corinthians' expectations of him. Nor would he succumb to emulating the much admired Corinthian preachers. He chose, instead, to wait for God's evaluation of him, rather than to rely on the Corinthian critique. His role as servant and administrator would be judged on its own merit by Jesus himself.

Gospel
Matthew 6:24–34

STEP 1
NAMING ONE'S EXPERIENCE

What were your first impressions? What was your first response to the gospel (or the other readings)?[6] What captured your attention?

Each person names his or her initial impression. Statements should be brief. No reasons should be given at this time. All simply listen without agreeing or disagreeing.

STEP 2
UNDERSTANDING

In a brief statement, what do you think this gospel is trying to convey?

STEP 3
INPUT FROM VISION/STORY/TRADITION

Liturgical Context

Refer to the Sixth Sunday in Ordinary Time for the context and continuity between the Sixth through

[6] The primary focus of reflection is the gospel. However, very often the other readings demand attention and must be brought into the dialogue.

the Ninth Sundays in Ordinary Time. If any one "theme" were to emerge from today's liturgy, it would be God's incredible love for humanity and the human response of absolute faith and trust in God. The Entrance Antiphon begins the liturgy with an expression of that trust and the reason for it. We are to place our trust in God because God has strengthened, liberated, and saved us. Why? Because he loves us. It is because of that love that we are empowered to love one another, as expressed in the Alternative Opening Prayer. We can do no less than respond with complete abandonment.

God is to direct our lives. There is to be no room in our hearts for idols of our own making. Our treasure must be the treasure of God's love. One message resounds throughout the liturgy and could not be more explicit: God will never abandon us. We hear it in the first reading, the psalm, the gospel, and expressed emphatically in the text for the Communion Rite: "I, the Lord, am with you always, until the end of the world" (Mt 28:20). It is almost as if God is saying to us: "Do you get it yet? Is there any other way I could possibly say it?"

A wonderful prayer that summarizes the heart and the implications of this liturgy can be found in the closing prayer for this session (the Preface in Ordinary Time V, Creation). God, as Creator of heaven and earth, created men and women to be stewards of that creation. God made human beings in his image—God loves us that much. So we can do no less than sing God's praises with all the angels in heaven in their song of joy.

St. John Chrysostom preached a lasting word to the church on this gospel. Let it continue to be a relevant word for us today:

> I say now again to you, what I am always saying: that Christ urges his hearers to obedience to his words, both by means of what is profitable to them, and by what is painful; like a good physician, pointing out the disease that comes through neglect, and the good health that will come through obedience to his directions.
>
> See here then how he again points out what gain there is for us in this life; how he prepares for us things that are useful, and takes from us what is a danger to us. It is not for this only that wealth is harmful to you, he says: because it arms robbers against you, or because it can wholly darken your mind; but also because it drives you from the service of God, and makes you slaves of soulless riches; harming you as much by making you slaves of what you should rule, as by driving you from the service of God, whom before all others you must serve. Here he shows us that our loss is twofold: to be turned away from serving God, and to be made slaves of mammon.
>
> We shudder to think of what we have compelled Christ to say, to place God side by side with mammon. And if this is a horrifying thing, it is still more horrifying to do this by our own acts: to prefer the tyranny of gold to the fear and love of God. But why not? Did not this happen among the ancients? Far from it. How then, you may say, was Abraham, was Jacob so honored? I am not speaking of riches; I am speaking of those who are a slave of riches. Job was indeed rich. But he was no slave of mammon. He possessed riches and ruled them, as a master, not as a slave. He held all he had as though he were the steward of another man's riches. And not only did he not rob others of what belonged to them, he gave what was his to those in need. And what was greater, he took no delight in present things. And so he did not grieve when he lost them. But the rich now are not like this, but rather in a state worse than any slave, and as though paying tribute to some tyrant. For such minds become a sort of stronghold, held by money; and from there each day money sends out its commands, commands that are fulfilled [illegible] and decency; [illegible] does not obey. [illegible] philosophize.
>
> [illegible] has declared that it is not possible for the service of mammon to accord with the service of God. Therefore do not say it possible. For when

the one master commands you to plunder, the other to give away what is yours; the one commands you to be chaste, the other to commit fornication; the one invites you to drunke[illegible] restrain ou[illegible] one couns[illegible] things, the[illegible] one tells yo[illegible] gilded walls and paneled ceilings, the other not to esteem them, but to honor virtue only; how can there be concord between them? (John Chrysostom, c. 347–407, bishop of Constantinople and preacher)[7]

Gospel Exegesis

The facilitator gives input regarding what critical biblical scholarship has to say about this text. The input includes insights as to how people would have heard the gospel in Jesus' time.

This section of the Ser[illegible] with material possessio[illegible] toward them. The ultim[illegible] section is to exhort disciples to have absolute trust in and abandonment to the care of God. Which will you trust—God or mammon? To which will you give allegiance? This part of Jesus' Sermon could be titled: "What does it mean to have faith in God?" Jesus provides the test by which to answer that question. If your faith is in money and material possessions, it is obviously misdirected and misplaced.

Faith in God is not a question of faith in the existence of a Supre[illegible] epochs ago, but [illegible] the God who is [illegible] ings—now—an[illegible] lives. Every breath is a gift from God. Every breath is imbued with God's presence. When trust is lacking, human beings deny that all-encompassing presence.

Most people did not consider a life in search of material security to be in conflict with their relationship with God. The meaning of the word *mammon* in Jewish literature was a neutral reference to property or anything of value.[8] It was not the name of a false god. However, it does have the characteristics of a god. The word was translated in the gospel in order to give it the appropriate punch it deserves. As "mammon" it is presented more forcefully as a false idol.[9] It has the similar impact as the English colloquialism "the Almighty Dollar." Jesus understood mammon to be a dangerous and potential obstacle to an intimate relationship with God. The lure of mammon is great. It would be difficult to resist the temptation to become indifferent to the commands of the Lord. When people are engrossed with the acquisition of money and goods, they are possessed by it. Jesus exhorts disciples to be possessed by God instead. There is not enough room in one's heart to be possessed by both God and mammon. It is far better to be possessed by God.

In verses 24 and following, Jesus warns against an incessant worry about the future and about material concerns. When a person worries to the point of distraction and inability to function, he or she has lost trust in the God who cares for even the birds of the air and the flowers in the field.

Jesus praises the grandeur of the birds and the flowers although they had absolutely nothing to do with their own splendor. Not even Solomon was bedecked with such glory. Jesus' words fill our imaginations with fragrant, flower-filled meadows; then he brings us back to sober reality. We are barely able to shake the sight and scent from our minds when Jesus changes direction and refers to the flowers as "the grass of the field." A listener in ancient times would have been startled by the contrast. The "grass of the field" was a common phrase that meant something was worthless. Jesus metaphorically is reminding us that although for a while something might possess breathtaking beauty and seemingly limitless worth, it is only transitory. In the end, it is insignificant—thrown into the fire and used for fuel.

Again Jesus paints the Father's love in such brilliant tones that the beholder cannot miss the beauty or the clarity. If God so lavishly clothes the

---

[7] John Chrysostom, *Sunday Sermons of the Great Fathers,* IV, 102–103, tr. and ed. M.F. Toal. Copyright © 1958 by Henry Regnery, Regnery Gateway, Inc., Chicago, IL.

[8] *RM,* 83.

[9] *MI,* 73.

flowers who will in the end be used for nothing more than fuel, how much more will he lavish his treasures on human beings? If God's birds and flowers are so well cared for, would it not be logical for humans to expect as least as much? Our worry is not only unnecessary, but is a lack of trust in One who is so benevolent. Pagans worry about such things, but the children of God need not worry, for they know the Source of all life.

Worry plagued the ancient world: What would tomorrow bring? Would there be enough to eat? Would there be work? Would they be sold as slaves? Jesus taught us to live in God's reign which meant that worries are unfounded because the concerns of this world are transitory. To live in God's reign means to thirst and hunger after the things of heaven. Nothing else matters. But when one's concerns are centered around the self, then concern for others becomes less and the demands of biblical justice become nothing more than pious proselytizing—all talk and no action.

We are all aware that birds and flowers are not always so richly bedecked. Drought, fires, and floods certainly impact nature and often lead to the destruction of the birds and flowers. We also are aware that many people are not so well cared for: there is famine, poverty, and unequal distribution of this world's resources. We know, too, that it is imprudent not to plan for tomorrow's drought. Douglas Hare suggests that this text was possibly a consolation for those disciples who left everything to follow Jesus and were left totally dependent upon the graciousness and hospitality of others. It is also a commentary on what Paul (who himself experienced hunger, deprivation, and homelessness) knew to be true. There is nothing that can compare with the blessings and love that God has for his children. Famine, poverty, homelessness, the lack of material possessions—all these are nothing when we think of the abundant, overflowing love God has for us.

Where there is famine and poverty, those of us who have known God's love are to respond by becoming his providential hands. The imperative inherent for us in this gospel and in every gospel is to work toward providing what is needed to alleviate the suffering of those who do not enjoy the world's abundant resources. Today's gospel stresses God's intention for the world. A portrait is painted for us of creation in perfect harmony. When we remember the moral imperatives associated with God's covenant with creation at the beginning of the world, we must also remember that the human response to the established order and harmony is biblical justice. Are we living as worthy stewards of God's ship (second reading)? Do we help feed and care for all those aboard God's vessel, or do we enclose ourselves in our own luxurious, isolated staterooms? Inherent in today's gospel is that question and the subsequent challenge.

We cannot look at this gospel, or get caught up in the images it brings of nature's incredible beauty, without reflecting upon the creation in which we live today. How are we exercising our own role as steward of God's earth? Do we contribute to the beauty of the birds and the lilies, or do we consciously or unconsciously contribute to their demise by the destructive tendencies human beings display toward Mother Earth?

Another perspective with which to view this gospel is the celebratory nature of the text. Even the lilies and the birds give God glory. All creation sings God's praise.

Proclaim the gospel again.

Sometimes we gain new insights when we hear the text after the interpretation has been given. Someone from the group proclaims the gospel a second time.

STEP 4
TESTING

Conversation with the Liturgy and the Scriptures

Test your original understanding in dialogue with the text.

(You might consider breaking into smaller groups.)

Are there any new insights? Is there anything you had not considered before? How does your original understanding of this gospel compare with what we just shared?

How does this story speak to your life?

Sharing Life Experience

Participants share an experience from their lives that connects with the biblical interpretation just shared.

> *This gospel continues to speak to our community to remind us that it is God who is the source of all we have, and who we are. We have a responsibility therefore to share with the world. I have many times expressed my joy at the way in which my community responds to the needs of the world's poor. I see that response as an act of faith in God. Tithing poses no hardship for our parish, so it is very easy for me to extol its virtues. I am not living in a parish that struggles for every penny just to keep its doors open. I would hope, however, that if hard times were to fall on our community, we would continue to remember our Source and respond accordingly. I often reflect on what an impact the church could have on the world if every parish would respond in faith to God's incredible bounty and tithe, either from their surplus or from their need, in order to share with the world's poor, hurting, and disadvantaged. Imagine how the world might change! If one very insignificant parish was able to build a school, a church, two clinics, and homes for the poor, think of what all the parishes in this country might accomplish. What a witness to the world!*
>
> *On a personal level, today's gospel is a major command to let go and let God manage my life. It is very difficult not to get caught up in the concerns of "mammon" when there are mortgages and college tuition to pay. Yet I am challenged not to be distracted by those concerns. I remember a time in the early years of my marriage when there was more month left at the end of the money. Our oil furnace (with its insatiable eight-hundred-dollar-a-month addiction), and my hungry babies, simply could not understand such an absurdity. With a great deal of God's providential care, human benevolence, and ingenuity there was an eleventh-hour reprieve and my furnace and my babies were fed.*
>
> *There were several such experiences of God's help in those early years. But there were also times when it appeared as if God was deaf. I remember more than once when I beseeched God like a despondent child. Thus, it is not universally true that God necessarily provides for every material need we have. There are starving people in the world today who can attest to that reality. However, what is true is God's incredible love, steadfast presence, and encouragement to abandon my life to God's care and to seek God above all else. Without that, in the midst of life's most pressing difficulties I would not today be playing the ivories in praise of his name or clicking away at the word-processor extolling his greatness.*
>
> *It is only because of God's awesome presence in my life that I continue to be a disciple. If God did not constantly extend his hand to me in invitation, I wonder if I would not have long ago succumbed to the pressures of mammon. I know well what it means to forget and lose focus—to center on so many things that mean nothing. I know what it means to worry, obsess, and to place blockades over my heart's door. I make many mistakes. I will continue to put up barriers. But I will also continue to place great hope that love (albeit imperfect love) covers a multitude of sins.*
>
> *And I continue to be challenged to respond to God's love by my response to the poor. I must put my money where my mouth is and work toward becoming the hands and the feet of God wherever I encounter hungry, starving, and hurting people. It cannot be just pious talk, but must be grounded in determined, focused action.*

How does today's gospel speak to your community? What was the relevance of this gospel for Matthew's community? In what way does today's gospel reflect God's promise to be in relationship with the human race (covenant)? How does this gospel invite change and liberation (exodus)? How is this a word about God's relationship with *a people*? How does this gospel speak to the biblical theme of creation? How does this gospel invite a relationship with God's creation? What might be your response to such an invitation? In what ways have you experienced the love of God that is expressed and celebrated in this liturgy? Do you still feel the same way about this text as when you began? Has your original understanding been stretched, challenged, or affirmed?

STEP 5
DECISION

The gospel demands a response.

How might your community be invited to respond to today's liturgy? In what way have you changed or grown as a result of your conversation with this liturgy? In what concrete way might your parish be called to respond? Has this conversation with the exegesis changed or stretched your personal attitudes? What are the implications of this gospel for your life? What is one concrete action you will take this week as a response to the liturgy today?

Pastoral Considerations: How does your community respond to the needs of the poor locally and globally? Is care for the poor a part of your mission and vision? In what way does your parish promote good stewardship of the earth?

DOCTRINAL ISSUES

What church truth/teaching/doctrinal issue could be drawn from the gospel for the Eighth Sunday in Ordinary Time?

Participants suggest possible doctrinal themes that flow from the readings.

Possible Doctrinal Themes

Creation, faith, trust, stewardship, Trinity, christology, conversion, living the moral life, social teaching, biblical justice

Present the doctrinal material at this time.

1. The facilitator gives input on a particular doctrinal issue of his or her prior choosing. OR

2. The group chooses a doctrinal issue from the list they created. They read together from the Doctrinal Appendix.

(The doctrinal issues are found in the Doctrinal Appendix in the back of this workbook. If you are choosing an issue from this resource, please refer to it now.)

Reflection questions centered around the chosen doctrinal theme can be found at the end of each topic in the Doctrinal Appendix. The questions are based on the five-step reflection process. If you choose a topic not included in the Doctrinal Appendix, craft your own questions according to the same five-step process.

Following the reflection questions you will be reminded to return to chapter 7, "Preparing the Catechetical Session," to assist you in crafting your own session.

Closing Prayer

Father, all-powerful and ever-living God,
we do well always and everywhere to give you thanks.
All things are of your making,
all times and seasons obey your laws,
but you chose to create man in your own image,
setting him over the whole world in all its wonder.
You made man the steward of creation,
to praise you day by day for the marvels of your wisdom and power,
through Jesus Christ our Lord.
We praise you, Lord, with all the angels
in their song of joy:
Holy, holy, holy Lord, God of power and might,
heaven and earth are full of your glory.
Hosanna in the highest.
Blessed is he who comes in the name of the Lord.
Hosanna in the highest.[10]

[10]Sundays in Ordinary Time V: "Preface 33," *The Sacramentary.*

Ninth Sunday in Ordinary Time

INTRODUCTORY RITES

Opening Song (or Entrance Antiphon)

O look at me and be merciful, for I am wretched and alone. See my hardship and my poverty, and pardon all my sins. (Ps 24:16, 18)[1]

Opening Prayer

The facilitator of the session may lead the prayer. Others in the group may be asked to proclaim the readings.

Let us pray
[for God's care and protection]

Pause for silent prayer.

Father,
your love never fails.
Hear our call.
Keep us from danger
and provide for all our needs.
Grant this through our Lord
Jesus Christ, your Son,
who lives and reigns with you and the Holy
Spirit,
one God for ever and ever.[2]

LITURGY OF THE WORD

The readings are proclaimed.

First Reading
Deuteronomy 11:18, 26–28.

Overview of Deuteronomy: The Book of Deuteronomy is in the form of an address. It is written as Moses' last speech to the people before they cross over the Jordan into the promised land. It is his farewell address to the Israel he led out of bondage of Egypt through the Sinai desert. Moses delivered God's covenant to them. He also saved them from God's wrath due to their infidelity on numerous occasions.

Deuteronomy is different from the other four books of the Pentateuch. It contains long speeches and sermons, unlike Genesis and Exodus which contain short stories and incidents. Deuteronomy was not written at the same time as the other books, but was a much later reflection of the ancient history of Moses and the people of Israel. The book demands that the people return to their covenant relationship with God. It places the exhortations in the mouth of Moses himself. (A common ancient practice involved placing words and exhortations in the mouth of an ancient respected leader in order to bring that leader's authority to bear on the writer's material.) The purpose of the book was to exhort the people to return to the covenant living experienced under the leadership of Moses.

The book is divided into sections: a long preface, a restatement of the old covenant laws, a final section containing the teaching of Moses and his final blessing and death scene. The heart of Deuteronomy is the section containing the law code. It is similar to the law code of Exodus and is therefore referred to as the second law (deutero).

The second law code was written at a much later date, however. The situations in Deuteronomy reflect a nation that had grown since the days of exodus. A nation of small farmers had developed into a land of populated cities (evident during the later reign of the kings). There is also evidence in the book that a long time had passed since the liberation from Egypt. The book looks back and remembers the exodus and the covenant as completed events in the history of Israel.

One of the primary focuses of Deuteronomy is to look back on the covenant with a mind and heart to return to it in faithfulness. The book exhorts the people to become more faithful than their ancestors had been in following the law. There is a constant call to reform, to return to the covenant

[1]Ninth Sunday in Ordinary Time: "Entrance Antiphon," *The Sacramentary.*

[2]Ninth Sunday in Ordinary Time: "Opening Prayer," *The Sacramentary.*

made with God. The election of Israel by God is an example of the special relationship that existed between God and the people of Israel. The book used language reminiscent of language used in treaties between nations to describe the covenant between God and the people.

The central theme of the law was true worship of the one God, creator of heaven and earth. The people were to reject all pagan idols. The relationship between God and Israel was summed up in the Shema—Israel's prayer—the heart and the creed of Judaism. "Hear, O Israel, the Lord our God is one Lord, and you shall love the Lord your God with all your heart and with all your soul and with all your strength" (Dt 6:4–5). Those words were to be handed on to their children, talked about in the house, bound on the hands and the forehead, and written on the doorpost. In other words, never to be forgotten!

The theology of Deuteronomy also extols a single sanctuary in a place appointed by God (Jerusalem was the implied place). In addition, it upholds the importance of the right use of the land. Faithfulness and obedience to God would insure a prosperous land. Disobedience and unfaithfulness would result in loss of the land, exile, and destruction. Sin leads to a curse. A curse insures failure in war, failed crops, and failure in preserving the one nation. If Israel fails to live the imperatives of justice, they will lose their right to the land. Their society will fail. Deuteronomy looks back at the history of Israel and explains it in terms of fidelity and infidelity to the covenant.

Today's Pericope: Today's reading refers to the covenants of old that were often accompanied by either a blessing or a curse. A person following the covenant would be blessed; those who did not follow the covenant would be sanctioned with a curse. In today's gospel those who choose the appropriate path for their lives are blessed—their house will stand. Those who choose the wrong way are cursed and their house will fall.

Responsorial Psalm
Psalm 31:2–3, 3–4, 17, 25

Psalm 31 is an individual's thanks for healing from sickness and trouble. We are to read these verses as sinners who have been redeemed from the bondage of sin through the saving action of Christ.

Second Reading
Romans 3:21–25, 28

(Refer to First Sunday of Advent for an Overview of St. Paul's Letter to the Romans.)

Today's Pericope: Paul maintains that all humanity sinned—both Jew and Greek. For Paul, "now" is the operative word. It is the turning point for humanity. Paul repeats an assertion made in an earlier part of the letter. The gospel is the revelation of God's righteousness and both Jew and Gentile alike have sinned before God.

Paul posits the role that *faith* and *works* play in the process of a person's justification, and asserts that a person is saved by faith, not by the works of the law. Paul's primary issue is the death and resurrection of Jesus. It is through the death of Christ, not by one's works, that a person is saved. Through faith humanity shares in that event.

For Paul, "righteousness" does not refer to moral living. Righteousness refers to God's saving action. Ancient prophets of the Old Testament foretold this salvation. Jesus Christ is the fulfillment of it. Paul insists that salvation (righteousness) is not "won" by strict adherence to the law. It was a commonly held belief that a person could secure God's favor, and subsequently his or her salvation, by following the law. Paul contends that sinful human beings are incapable of achieving their own salvation. Salvation comes only through acceptance of God's gratuitous gift of faith. A person is justified through faith, and for Paul, justification assumed that an individual was in right relationship with God.

The word *redemption,* according to Reginald Fuller, is a word that has roots in the Old Testament. It referred to the exodus event in which God delivered Israel out of bondage in Egypt. In later biblical history and literature it was a term used to designate the final saving act of God at the end of the world. Christianity borrowed the Hebrew word and understanding and associated it with the mission of Christ. Redemption, in the Christian sense, referred to the saving act of Christ on the cross. Through his death on the cross the human race was delivered from the bondage and death caused by sin. Paul's use of the term *blood* refers to the sacrificial saving action of Christ accomplished through his death.

Paul upheld that expiation of sin was accomplished for all believers through the blood of Jesus. There are three common definitions of the term *expiation*: (1) The traditional meaning (propitiation) holds that human beings sin and consequently must do something in order to appease God's wrath. Since human beings are incapable of doing this on their own merit, God accomplished it through his Son Jesus. Thus, Jesus propitiated the Father. (2) A modern explanation (expiation) holds that God, through his Son Jesus, desired to obliterate human sin. (3) The third meaning has its roots in a linguistic interpretation of the word. Expiation is the mercy seat where atonement takes place.

It is most likely that Paul's use of expiation is closer to the second definition. God desired to rid the world of sin through the sacrifice of his Son. However, the first meaning (propitiation) is nevertheless accomplished through Jesus' saving action: "[S]in that might justly have excited God's wrath is expiated (at God's will), and therefore no longer does so."[3]

Gospel
Matthew 7:21–27

Step 1
Naming One's Experience

What were your first impressions? What was your first response to the gospel (or the other readings)?[4] What captured your attention?

Each person names his or her initial impression. Statements should be brief. No reasons should be given at this time. All simply listen without agreeing or disagreeing.

[3]C. K. Barret in *PL*, 130.

[4]The primary focus of reflection is the gospel. However, very often the other readings demand attention and must be brought into the dialogue.

Step 2
Understanding

In a brief statement, what do you think this gospel is trying to convey? What original understanding did you bring with you to this conversation?

Step 3
Input from Vision/Story/Tradition

Liturgical Context

Today's gospel includes the parable that concludes the Sermon on the Mount. For the past weeks the Sermon has been consecutively proclaimed in the liturgy, thus forming an internal unity between the weeks. Every liturgy invites transformation. The gospel echoes that invitation and reminds the disciples that choices are placed before the believer. When one chooses appropriately, there will be evidence. We will know the false prophets from the true prophets by the fruit of their efforts.

The second reading from Romans is a brilliant proclamation of the paschal mystery, the heart of the Christian faith. The paschal mystery is proclaimed, remembered, made present, and celebrated at every liturgy and sacramental celebration.

Gospel Exegesis

The facilitator gives input regarding what critical biblical scholarship has to say about this text. The input includes insights as to how people would have heard the gospel in Jesus' time.

Today's pericope is part of the closing address of the Sermon on the Mount. It is one of three sayings that serve as warnings that balance the blessings found in the first part of the address. The sayings are intended to evoke a decision on the part of the listeners. The first saying (both the first and second saying are not included in this pericope) expresses the difficult choices one must make and ultimately how those choices will impact the future path a disciple will take in following Christ. The second saying reminds disciples that simple lip service is not enough when it comes to the mission of Christ. Disciples will be known and false prophets will be discerned through their actions and the way in which they live the gospel. Good gospel living produces fruit. Adherence to the law, mighty works, or the mere pronouncement of faith is not enough to enter the reign of God. Disciples must bear fruit. A person must be obedient to God's word. One's life must reflect *metanoia*—a changed heart—conversion.

Today's third saying asserts that a person must also be obedient to Jesus' words and his interpretation of the law. That is, a law emanating from the living God. Jesus' words and the Father's will are one. Jesus was speaking with an authority that amazed the crowds. Yet the response that Jesus was demanding was complete obedience to God's will. Moses read the covenant to the people and they responded that they would do all that he commanded. Similarly the people followed Jesus down the mountain with the intention to follow him. The ensuing chapters in Matthew lay out the blueprint for what following Jesus really entails.

Matthew, after the tradition of Q and Luke, ends the Sermon with a parable. Luke tells of a house that is built so well that it withstands rising flood waters. Matthew uses the same house imagery, but instead of centering on the quality of the construction of the house, chooses instead to comment on the suitability of the site chosen for construction. The foolish man builds on sand, "the dry bed of a seasonal river."[5] The stupid man gave no serious thought to the consequences of his choice.

The parable contrasts the two ways to respond to Jesus' teaching. The prominent church leaders referred to in earlier verses (21–23) heard Jesus' words repeatedly but did not incorporate them into their lives. Their reputation as good Christians is built on nothing more than sand. There are humble Christians, on the other hand, who possess no great gifts but have incorporated Jesus' words into their daily lives. They are the ones who have built their foundation in Christ on sturdy ground. They will withstand the storms of life and be faithful to the end.

[5] *MI*, 86.

The final judgment will not be concerned with charismatic achievements but rather with obedience to the righteousness demanded by Jesus, defined in the Sermon, and laid out in following chapters. Matthew was addressing two poles. On the one hand there were those who believed that strict orthodox Pharisaic Jewish practice was necessary to unite Jerusalem after the fall. On the other hand there were the charismatic enthusiasts. Matthew addressed both groups by insisting that life in Christ demands and will be evidenced by their actions, not by flashy achievements or rigid adherence to the law. The actions Jesus demanded were works of mercy, love, and compassion.

It was common in the ancient Mediterranean world to prefer words over action. Jesus constantly challenged the temptation toward passivity over decisive action. It is simply not enough to honor God. One must take decisive, loving action and do God's will.

Proclaim the gospel again.

Sometimes we gain new insights when we hear the text after the interpretation has been given. Someone from the group proclaims the gospel a second time.

STEP 4
TESTING

Conversation with the Liturgy and the Scriptures

Test your original understanding in dialogue with the text.

(You might consider breaking into smaller groups.)

In light of the exegesis, were there any new insights? How does your original understanding of this gospel compare with what we just shared?

How does this story speak to your life?

Sharing Life Experience

Participants share an experience from their lives that connects with the biblical interpretation just shared.

I am always touched by the people in my parish who quietly and faithfully live the message of the gospel. They reach out to those in need day after day. They live the gospel of love and are an example of that love. Over and over we hear of people who are attracted to our community because of the love they have experienced from someone in the parish. I am humbled by those in our initiation process who go out of their way to feed the poor, to take care of the sorrowing, and to live this life with passion in their everyday lives. They are a challenge to me. I constantly ask myself: "Am I simply talking the talk, or am I walking the walk to the best of my ability?" It is a delicate balance to discern. The bottom line answer lies in love. How do I treat the marginalized? Do I regard the least among us with the dignity due them? Do I respond with just love when challenged? Do I feed the hungry—not just talk about it? It is very easy to think that because I talk about it a lot, I am doing what the gospel demands. If I am faithful to the daily, small invitations to love in my everyday life, I will then have practice in fidelity to the large challenges. It is very easy to ignore the daily procession of needy people that come to our office in search of food and money. It is easy to regard them anonymously instead of taking the time to speak to them and offer them a few minutes of my time and attention. Today's gospel invites me to take the time.

What was Matthew trying to tell his community? What does *obedience to God's will* mean in today's gospel? How do you know you are living according to God's will? Is there enough evidence to convince you that you are living the gospel? How does this liturgy speak to your community? To you? In what way does today's gospel address the biblical themes of covenant, exodus, creation, and community? How is God's promise to be in relationship with us expressed? How does this gospel invite passage from death to life? In what way does this gospel invite new life and re-creation? How does this gospel challenge the people of God? Do you still feel the same way about this text as when you began? In what way has your original understanding been stretched, challenged, or affirmed?

Step 5
Decision

The gospel demands a response.

How does today's liturgy invite transformation? How does this gospel specifically invite change in your community? In what concrete way is your parish called to respond? What are the implications of this gospel for your life? What is one concrete action you will take this week as a response to the liturgy today?

Pastoral Considerations: Perhaps today would be a good time to reflect on the apostolic life of your community. It is so easy to center in on those concerns only during Advent and Lent and ignore the imperative to live the just life all the time. How does your community welcome the marginalized? How does your community reach out to your community's poor as well as the global poor? How does your community embrace the cross for the world's suffering?

Christian Initiation: Today's gospel is particularly appropriate for celebrating a rite of acceptance and/or welcome. The implication of living the paschal mystery and the gospel of Christ is broken open in this liturgy. Do not forget to celebrate the minor rites in your gatherings with catechumens. This would be a great week to spend time doing apostolic works and then gathering to reflect on the experience.

DOCTRINAL ISSUES

What church truth/teaching/doctrinal issue could be drawn from the gospel for the Ninth Sunday in Ordinary Time?

Participants suggest possible doctrinal themes that flow from the readings.

Possible Doctrinal Themes

Living the moral life, morality, justice, paschal mystery, Sermon on the Mount, conversion, faith/works, discipleship, reign of God

Present the doctrinal material at this time.

1. The facilitator gives input on a particular doctrinal issue of his or her prior choosing. OR

2. The group chooses a doctrinal issue from the list they created. They read together from the Doctrinal Appendix.

(The doctrinal issues are found in the Doctrinal Appendix in the back of this workbook. If you are choosing an issue from this resource, please refer to it now.)

Reflection questions centered around the chosen doctrinal theme can be found at the end of each topic in the Doctrinal Appendix. The questions are based on the five-step reflection process. If you choose a topic not included in the Doctrinal Appendix, craft your own questions according to the same five-step process.

Following the reflection questions you will be reminded to return to chapter 7, "Preparing the Catechetical Session," to assist you in crafting your own session.

Closing Prayer

God our Father,
teach us to cherish the gifts that surround us.
Increase our faith in you
and bring our trust to its promised fulfillment
in the joy of your kingdom.
Grant this through Christ our Lord.[6]

[6]Ninth Sunday in Ordinary Time, "Alternative Opening Prayer," *The Sacramentary.*

TENTH SUNDAY IN ORDINARY TIME

INTRODUCTORY RITES

Opening Song (or Entrance Antiphon)

The Lord is my light and my salvation. Who shall frighten me? The Lord is the defender of my life. Who shall make me tremble? (Ps 26:1–2)[1]

Opening Prayer

Let us pray
[to our Father who calls us to freedom in Jesus his Son]

Pause for silent prayer.

Father in heaven,
words cannot measure the boundaries of love
for those born to new life in Christ Jesus.
Raise us beyond the limits this world imposes,
so that we may be free to love as Christ teaches
and find joy in your glory.
We ask this through Christ our Lord.[2]

LITURGY OF THE WORD

The readings are proclaimed.

First Reading
Hosea 6:3–6

Overview of Hosea: Hosea was a prophet who preached in the northern kingdom of Israel. His prophetic ministry extended from about 786 to 746 B.C.E (around the time of the fall of the northern kingdom). Hosea possessed a passion for the precepts of the covenant. The early chapters of the book seem to suggest that Hosea was in a marriage that caused him great grief. His wife was unfaithful. He used the painful situation to highlight how the covenant and the unconditional love of God for Israel were impacted by Israel's infidelity and sinfulness.

The book is divided into three sections. Section one (ch. 1–3), the prelude to the book, describes the broken marriage covenant between God and God's people. Section two (ch. 4–13) is a compilation of Hosea's oracles. Section three (ch. 14) proclaims a post-judgment vision of hope.

Hosea's message is one of justice and judgment. He denounced oppression to the poor and infidelity to the commandments. He demanded a return to a faithful covenant relationship with God. Hosea portrays a God who is sorrowful over the sins of the people and who mourns over their need for correction and discipline. The prophet upholds fidelity, love, compassion, and a personal relationship with God. He denounces the pious churchgoer who worships God while continuing to live a vain, sinful life. Hosea insists that corporate amnesia and rebellion are the causes of the broken covenant. People forgot God's benevolent action in their history and chose instead to live reckless, materialistic, idol-worshiping lives. Hosea regards their rebellion as stupid. He continues to hold out the promise of hope and God's compassion. God's love is radical, personal, and unending. Israel's wanton hubris in the days prior to the fall stands in stark contrast to the God who is welcoming and forgiving. It is never too late to turn away from sin and toward God's love.

Today's Pericope: What God wants from us more than anything is our hearts. God wants nothing less than total commitment to God and the covenant. The oracles of the prophets denouncing sacrifice over steadfast love did nothing to diminish the practice of ritual sacrifice, however. Sacrifice even increased after the exile. Word and sacrifice continued to go hand in hand in Israel's cultic life. What did emerge from the prophets' warning against sacrifice was the understanding that God was asking for a personal relationship with human beings. God desires our hearts—not our sacrifices. Sacrifices are empty, meaningless

[1]Tenth Sunday in Ordinary Time: "Entrance Antiphon," *The Sacramentary.*

[2]Tenth Sunday in Ordinary Time, "Opening Prayer," *The Sacramentary.*

rituals when conversion of heart is absent. The denouncing of sacrifices by the prophets was not intended to abolish sacrifice. The denouncement was instead used as a Hebrew figure of speech. What the prophets were railing against was sacrifice offered with expectation of God's favors. God wants our thanksgiving and our love, not our selfish, manipulative maneuvering.

Responsorial Psalm
Psalm 50:1, 8, 12–13, 14–15

Like the reading from Hosea, today's psalm is a prophetic pronouncement against sacrifices that are void of relationship with God and the assumed moral imperatives associated with that relationship.

Second Reading
Romans 4:18–25

(Refer to First Sunday of Advent for an Overview of St. Paul's Letter to the Romans.)

Paul uses the story from Abraham as support for his position that human beings are justified by faith ("... shorthand for justification by the grace of God manifested in Jesus Christ and apprehended by faith ..."[3]). Abraham believed God when God told him that he would be the father of many nations. Abraham was one hundred years old and his wife Sarah was ninety. Yet, what seemed to be ridiculous by human standards was not impossible for God. Abraham trusted God's word. Like Abraham, we are to believe in the power of God to accomplish in us what we cannot accomplish ourselves. We cannot become justified before God by ourselves. We do not have the power to make things right with God. Only God can do that. God accomplished our justification through the death and resurrection of God's Son, Jesus Christ. Jesus did for us what we are incapable of doing for ourselves. He saved us by the power of his death and resurrection.

Gospel
Matthew 9:9–13

[3]*PL*, 132.

STEP 1
NAMING ONE'S EXPERIENCE

What were your first impressions? What was your first response to the gospel (or the other readings)?[4] What captured your attention?

Each person names his or her initial impression. Statements should be brief. No reasons should be given at this time. All simply listen without agreeing or disagreeing.

STEP 2
UNDERSTANDING

In a brief statement, what do you think this gospel is trying to convey? What assumptions did you bring with you to this conversation with the gospel?

STEP 3
INPUT FROM VISION/STORY/TRADITION

Liturgical Context

There is an internal unity between the Tenth and Eleventh Sundays of Ordinary Time. The unity exists in the celebration of God's mercy and the actions of Jesus to demonstrate that mercy. The gospel for each Sunday centers around the call for mission at the initiative of God. Matthew is called this Sunday; the Twelve are called next Sunday. Mercy is the impetus for Jesus' action.

It is rare that all of the readings for the Sundays in Ordinary Time would share a common theme. However, one common thread can be found in all three readings today. God gives to human beings incredible, completely gratuitous, mercy.

Today would be an excellent time to remind ourselves of liturgy's (sacrifice, ritual, etc.) purpose: to give thanks and praise to God; to listen and respond to God's word; to take, bless, break, and

[4]The primary focus of reflection is the gospel. However, very often the other readings demand attention and must be brought into the dialogue.

share the Body of Christ, so that we in turn may be taken, blessed, broken, shared, and poured out in the world. Liturgy transforms and invites continuous transformation and conversion. The same caution found in the first reading and in the gospel still holds today. God does not wish empty ritual; rather, he wants converted, transformed hearts that are recognized by changed behavior and attitudes.

Today's Prayer After Communion reminds us that we are completely dependent on God's merciful love in order to follow the call of Jesus: "Lord, may your healing love turn us from sin and keep us on the way that leads to you."[5]

Both Opening Prayers reflect our hope that God will show us the way of love, and tell us that without God's help we are powerless to live the imperatives of the gospel: "[G]uide our actions in the way of peace...."[6] "Raise us beyond the limits this world imposes, so that we may be free to love as Christ teaches...."[7]

Gospel Exegesis

The facilitator gives input regarding what critical biblical scholarship has to say about this text. The input includes insights as to how people would have heard the gospel in Jesus' time.

The gospel of Matthew is considered by scholars to be a later gospel than Mark's gospel. It is a collection of earlier documents and an oral tradition. In Mark's version the person in this story is called Levi. In this version, the same person is called Matthew. It is suggested that Matthew has a theological reason for changing Levi's name. In chapter three of Mark's gospel Matthew is named as one of the Twelve Apostles. According to Reginald Fuller, Matthew wants to interpret Mark's story as "the call of one who would subsequently became a member of the Twelve, and one of the Twelve was a social outcast."[8] Thus, Matthew is clear: to be an apostle is a matter of God's grace—not human achievement.

[5]Tenth Sunday in Ordinary Time: "Prayer After Communion," *The Sacramentary.*

[6]Tenth Sunday in Ordinary Time: "Opening Prayer," *The Sacramentary.*

[7]Tenth Sunday in Ordinary Time: "Alternative Opening Prayer," *The Sacramentary.*

[8]*PL*, 133.

Matthew differed from Mark in another instance. He included the quotation from Hosea 6:6 (first reading). This has often been assumed to mean that God cares about following the moral law to the exclusion of ritual. This is a complete misreading of this text and of Hosea. Sacrifice, in the appropriate Jewish sense, was understood as the human recognition of powerlessness before God. When used for self-serving, manipulative purposes, however, it was an abomination before God. Matthew was simply reiterating the true purpose of sacrifice. True sacrifice recognizes that human beings cannot save themselves. They are totally dependent upon God's mercy.

Matthew was making another point in telling the story of Jesus' eating with sinners. When Jesus ate with outcasts he was making God's mercy real, active, and present. It was further example of God's forgiveness and mercy. "Jesus embodies God's mercy and purpose to take away the diseases, infirmities, and sins of all the people; and the meal was a concrete expression of the acceptance of sinners."[9] Jesus' acceptance of the outcasts and sinners was abhorrent to the Pharisees. They would not have had a problem with sinners repenting. Repenting was expected and demanded. The Pharisees' problem existed in the fact that Jesus did nothing to insist that sinners follow the traditional Jewish rituals of repentance required of sinners. All these sinners were required to do was *follow Jesus.*

Matthew, a tax collector and sinner, followed the Lord immediately when the Lord called him. He did not hesitate. There was no demand for a sign of his sincerity or repentance. Christians are also to follow Christ when called. All people are sinners, but Jesus dines with everyone. He calls, invites, and challenges. As part of that call, he also heals and forgives. The only response is loving submission, without hesitation, to the call.

Proclaim the gospel again.

Sometimes we gain new insights when we hear the text after the interpretation has been given. Someone from the group proclaims the gospel a second time.

[9]*RM*, 103.

STEP 4
TESTING

Conversation with the Liturgy and the Scriptures

Test your original understanding in dialogue with the text.

(You might consider breaking into smaller groups.)

Were there any new insights for you?

How does this story speak to your life?

Sharing Life Experience

Participants share an experience from their lives that connects with the biblical interpretation just shared.

There have been some significant moments of healing and reconciliation in my life. All of them were moments of grace. I remember a time when two friends drifted apart over two different perspectives of the same situation. Quiet, unspoken enmity developed. It was only by the directive of God that the friendship was healed. The call came to me to respond to God's initiative. I resisted. The invitation continued to be offered. I continued to resist. Yet God would have God's way. But instead of exhibiting Matthean-like resolve, with much hesitation I reluctantly responded to the call. God's mercy and love were manifest in so many ways, and continue to be manifest. God's call usually invites submission to God's will, and it is always an invitation to accept God's mercy and forgiveness. We cannot accept that forgiveness if we hold others bound. Usually God's most profound movements in my life center around invitations to let go of stubborn pride and allow healing and reconciliation to take place. The only thing that gets in the way is me. Today's gospel reminds me that I must work toward responding quickly and without hesitation to God's call. I can be very slow to respond.

It is so much a part of human nature to be upset over what appears to be "cheap grace" offered to the sinners in today's gospel. How many times am I like the Pharisees who resent Jesus' mercy and forgiveness? It is easy to fall into that trap. Sins of judgment are difficult to overcome. Self-righteousness seems to be synonymous with the human condition. Instead of being happy that the same grace is offered to everyone, we often feel resentful that some people seem to steal heaven with an eleventh-hour save. Some seem to "get it" much easier than others. Some seem to be easily tuned in to the mind and heart of God, while others have to struggle. Yet the same invitation is offered to all. Matthew points the way of responding to Jesus' call without hesitation.

One particular time our community was invited to respond to God's call for forgiveness. It was a very difficult time. People held strong positions, with each faction believing theirs was the correct one. Healing and reconciliation was a slow process. If we would just respond like Matthew (without hesitation) and realize that without God we are powerless; if we would just allow God to act and let our self-righteous egos take a back seat, then perhaps learning the lessons that are so hard won would not be so laborious and painstaking.

All share their life experience.

What was the underlying message behind this gospel? What implications were there for Matthew's community? What implications are there for your community today? What part of this liturgy (readings and/or gospel) is most needed in your community at this time? How do today's readings reflect the biblical theme of covenant, exodus, creation, and community? What touched you the most in this exegesis? What word or idea related to your life right now? What attitudes are challenged in today's gospel? Where are those attitudes prevalent in your community or in your life (family, workplace, world)? Do you still feel the same way about this text as when you began? How would you articulate an understanding of today's gospel now? Is there anything you would like to add to your original understanding?

STEP 5
DECISION

The gospel demands a response.

How might today's liturgy invite your community to take a look at its attitudes and behaviors? How does it challenge you to look at your own attitudes and behaviors? Where is transformation needed the most in your community? In your own life? How have you already changed as a result of today's conversation with the liturgy of the Tenth Sunday in Ordinary Time? What is one concrete action you will take this week as a response to the liturgy today?

Pastoral Considerations: How might God be calling your community to action at this time? If Jesus were to come to your community, whom do you think he would invite to be his dinner guests? Who are the outcasts in your community? What needs to happen to foster healing and reconciliation? When was the last time your parish celebrated the sacrament of reconciliation?

Christian Initiation: Perhaps since the focus on God's mercy is inherent in today's liturgy, this would be a good time to celebrate a non-sacramental penitential celebration with catechumens as the Rite of Penance suggests, or an exorcism from the RCIA.

DOCTRINAL ISSUES

What church truth/teaching/doctrinal issue could be drawn from the gospel for the Tenth Sunday of Ordinary Time?

Participants suggest possible doctrinal themes that flow from the readings.

Possible Doctrinal Themes

God's mercy, salvation/soteriology, faith/works, Christology, forgiveness, repentance, morality, goal of liturgy, conversion, social justice, sacrament of reconciliation, sacrament of the sick

Present the doctrinal material at this time.

1. The facilitator gives input on a particular doctrinal issue of his or her prior choosing. OR

2. The group chooses a doctrinal issue from the list they created. They read together from the Doctrinal Appendix.

(The doctrinal issues are found in the Doctrinal Appendix in the back of this workbook. If you are choosing an issue from this resource, please refer to it now.)

Reflection questions centered around the chosen doctrinal theme can be found at the end of each topic in the Doctrinal Appendix. The questions are based on the five-step reflection process. If you choose a topic not included in the Doctrinal Appendix, craft your own questions according to the same five-step process.

Following the reflection questions you will be reminded to return to chapter 7, "Preparing the Catechetical Session," to assist you in crafting your own session.

Closing Prayer

I can rely on the Lord; I can always turn to him for shelter.
It was he who gave me my freedom.
My God, you are always there to help me.[10]

[10]Tenth Sunday in Ordinary Time, "Communion Rite (Psalm 17:3)," *The Sacramentary.*

ELEVENTH SUNDAY IN ORDINARY TIME

INTRODUCTORY RITES

Opening Song (or Entrance Antiphon)

Lord, hear my voice when I call to you. You are my help; do not cast me off, do not desert me, my Savior God (Ps 26:7, 9)[1]

Opening Prayer

The facilitator of the session may lead the prayer. Others in the group may be asked to proclaim the readings.

Let us pray
[for the grace to follow Christ more closely]

Pause for silent prayer.

Almighty God,
our hope and our strength,
without you we falter.
Help us to follow Christ
and to live according to your will.
We ask this through our Lord
Jesus Christ, your Son,
who lives with you and the Holy Spirit,
one God for ever and ever.[2]

LITURGY OF THE WORD

Let us listen to God's word.

The readings are proclaimed.

First Reading[3]
Exodus 19:2–6a

Overview of Exodus: The Exodus event is at the heart of Israel's identity. God was not a disinterested, aloof deity, but a God who was involved in the history and the lives of the people. God delivered Israel from bondage. Yahweh and the Exodus were inseparable realities for the people of Israel. It was the Exodus experience that inaugurated Israel's role as God's people. Upon receiving the covenant at Sinai, they entered into an unbreakable bond with Yahweh. Thus, the Exodus not only identified Yahweh as their involved God, but it identified Israel as the people of their involved God. The Book of Exodus is a chronicle of that twofold reality. It captures and records Israel's roots. It is not intended as a biographical sketch and history of the people (although much of their history is indeed included in the book). It is the story of a people in relationship with their God. It is a story of sin and grace and bondage and deliverance. The Exodus event, then and now, was the axis upon which Israel's salvation history spun, just as the cross is the axis upon which Christianity revolves. While there is no certain date for the book, most scholars place it around the thirteenth century B.C.E.

The Book of Exodus contains a myriad of biblical literary styles, from legendary embellishment to liturgical formulas, covenant codes, and songwriting. The multiple styles are a testament to the creativity used by the biblical authors to record and remember their central event. The book is influenced by the authorship of three different theologians at work in the creation of the text. The Yahwist, the Elohist, and the Priestly writers, each writing at a different time, posited their own perspective of events. Very often they do not mesh and at times they even conflict with each other. As readers we are not to attempt to harmonize the accounts, but simply to acknowledge that all three contributed their interpretation of events. They remembered and judged the past from the per-

[1]Eleventh Sunday in Ordinary Time: "Entrance Antiphon," *The Sacramentary.*

[2]Eleventh Sunday in Ordinary Time: "Entrance Antiphon," *The Sacramentary.*

[3]The exegesis for the first and second readings may or may not be the focus of your group's reflection as there may only be time to give adequate attention to the gospel, your primary concern. However, the exegesis is included here in order to provide a thorough investigation of the entire liturgy of the word as there may be parts (or all) that would be necessary to the direction you wish to take with your particular ministry group.

spective of their present, while looking ahead to the future. Each writer possessed his own bias. The story of the Exodus is Israel's premier story of deliverance from bondage. Christians believe that Exodus prefigures the liberation won by Christ, and his passover from death on the cross to new life in the resurrection.

Today's Pericope: The first reading is usually connected with the gospel. The connection today is very difficult to ascertain, however. Reginald Fuller suggests that the only discernible common theme is that the people of God are depicted by means of various images in all of the readings. The image found in the first reading is that of a kingdom of priests and a holy nation. The image portrayed in the psalm is that of sheep in the flock of God. The second reading depicts a reconciled people—reconciled by the death of Jesus. The gospel illustrates the people established by the mission of the Apostles.

Today's reading from Exodus is a hymn that extols the mission of God's people. The exodus signaled a unique covenant between God and Israel. From this covenant flowed Israel's theology and its national identity. Israel was to be faithful to the covenant. In return God would bless them. This blessing meant that Israel would enjoy status as a holy nation, a kingdom of priests. Israel's special relationship with and closeness to God meant that it would represent God to all the world. Christianity understood the Sinai covenant to prefigure the relationship between God and humanity due to the saving mission of Jesus Christ.

Israel passed over from slavery into freedom in the promised land. Christians pass from death to life through the waters and are baptized into the royal priesthood of Jesus Christ.

Responsorial Psalm
Psalm 100:1–2, 3, 5

This psalm is a song of thanksgiving and praise that was sung upon entering the sanctuary. According to Reginald Fuller this psalm was sung at the entrance to the temple when the king was enthroned. God is not mentioned as king; there is allusion to the image of God as shepherd with the reference to the people as sheep. This connects with the gospel in which Jesus sends out the Apostles on their mission to the sheep without a shepherd.

Second Reading
Romans 5:6–11

(Refer to the First Sunday of Advent for an Overview of St. Paul's Letter to the Romans.)

Those who are justified by faith are heirs to salvation and glory. They can be assured of this salvation through the paschal mystery of Jesus Christ. Paul believed this to be self-evident—that it only needed to be stated and people would believe it. If we offer our life for another, it is the ultimate proof of our love. Jesus' love was not just pious lip service, but love in action.

Christ died for us and in so doing made us right with God—he justified us before God. "God sent his Son to die for the ungodly, while we were yet sinners."[4] Through the death of his Son, Jesus, God demonstrated to the world that his love for us is stronger than his justifiable anger over our sinfulness. God raised his Son, Just Servant that he was, from the snares of death, and in so doing saved and reconciled all people. Thus reconciled, people are delivered from final judgment and the wrath of God. The wrath of God does not mean impulsive anger; it refers to humanity's alienation and isolation from the living, loving, holy God as a result of sin and evil. Since Christ already redeemed us by his blood, we can be confident that we will not be cut off from God's love at the last judgment. We can rejoice as we await the final judgment. We have already been given proof of God's love and it stands before us in stark reality in the cross of Christ.

Gospel[5]
Matthew 9:36–10:8

---

[4] *PL*, 134.

[5] The gospel exegesis is provided later in this session so that it may be presented in the proper sequence where it occurs in the adult five-step reflection process. The exegesis is provided for the first and second readings for your information, edification, and for you to use at your discretion. Once again, the gospel is the primary source of reflection. If there is time for reflection on the other readings, all the better.

Step 1
Naming One's Experience

What were your first impressions? What was your first response to the gospel (or the other readings)?[6] What captured your attention?

Each person names his or her initial impression. Statements should be brief. No reasons should be given at this time. All simply listen without agreeing or disagreeing.

Step 2
Understanding

In a brief statement, what do you think this gospel is trying to convey? What meaning of this gospel did you bring with you to this conversation?

Step 3
Input from Vision/Story/Tradition

Liturgical Context[7]

Last week and this week form an internal unity. The unity exists in the celebration of God's mercy. The gospels for both weeks center around God's call. Matthew was called last Sunday, the Twelve are called this Sunday. Jesus sends the Twelve out to extend his ministry of compassion to the world.

The Alternative Opening Prayer asks that we be given strength to follow Jesus and that we be "one in the love that sealed our lives." We also ask God to help us to "live as one family the gospel we profess." Today's liturgy reminds us that the goal of our celebration is always to live the gospel we profess—to go and proclaim Christ to all the world. The catechism tells us that eucharist commits us to the poor. Liturgy demands that we become what we have received and take Christ to the world. Today's gospel requests that we heed the call and proclaim Christ's mission of mercy to the world. When we live our lives in accord with today's gospel, we further the reign of God in our midst and in our time.

The Prayer After Communion asks that unity and peace be accomplished in the church by the eucharist we received during today's liturgy. The eucharist itself signifies this unity and peace. It is this same unity and peace that we take with us into our everyday lives. Christ himself goes with us.

It will not always be easy. Discipleship never is easy. Ignatius of Antioch's advice is still relevant for us today as we set out on the mission of Christ:

> Pray constantly for others also, for in their case there is a hope of repentance, that they may find God. Permit them to be instructed by you, at least through your deeds. To their anger, be meek; to their boasts, be humble; to their abuse, utter your prayers; to their error, be steadfast in faith; to their savagery, be gentle; not jealous to imitate them. Let us be zealous to imitate the Lord, . . . so that no plant of the devil may be found in you, but with all purity and sobriety you may remain in union with Jesus Christ, in both flesh and spirit.[8]

Gospel Exegesis

The facilitator gives input regarding what critical biblical scholarship has to say about this text. The input includes insights as to how people would have heard the gospel in Jesus' time.

Today's gospel begins the next important section of Matthew's gospel following the Sermon on the Mount and Jesus' ministry of healing. This section recounts the *mission* of the gospel and it is here that Jesus sets the stage for the mission of the church. Jesus insists that his own ministry of love and compassion be extended to others—to the

[6]The primary focus of reflection is the gospel. However, very often the other readings demand attention and must be brought into the dialogue.

[7]The scriptures in the Lectionary, the seasons of the year, and the ritual prayers of the mass are interrelated and form the basis for liturgical catechesis. The *liturgical context* attempts to explore and clarify the themes and this interrelatedness.

[8]*RF*, 49.

sheep who have no shepherd. Underneath this shepherd motif is the allusion to Jesus as the Shepherd who replaces David, Israel's shepherd—Jesus, the promised Messiah.

Douglas Hare reminds us that up to this point in the gospel Jesus has been the only missionary. Today he expands the mission. He commissions others to go out and do his ministry of preaching, teaching, and healing. Matthew wants his readers and listeners to pray for the mission as it goes out to the world. We are reminded that to evangelize is often more difficult among those who know us than it is among those in faraway places.

Jesus makes it clear that he gives authority to the Twelve to carry on his ministry of healing and to preach Jesus' message that the reign of God is at hand. Even though the New Testament accounts do not agree when it comes to the names of the Twelve Apostles, it is nevertheless clear that Jesus intended to choose twelve appointees, as a symbol of Israel's twelve tribes, to go out and continue his mission to restore God's people.

Matthew believed in the inclusive mission to all the world—to the gentile world as well as to Israel. The reference to the lost sheep of Israel is therefore confusing. Douglas Hare suggests that Matthew's intention might be regarded on two levels: the historical, actual earthly mission of the Twelve, and the post-Easter mission that moved out into the gentile world. Jesus' actual mission was to Israel alone, and extended to the gentiles after the resurrection. "Matthew thus gives expression to the principle enunciated so firmly by Paul: 'To the Jew first and also to the Greek' (Rom 1:16). To Matthew the priority of Israel is important both historically and theologically."[9]

Matthew's Jesus was commenting on the condition of the "house of Israel." They were a people without a shepherd. They were without good pastoral leadership. He was also commenting on the condition and quality of leadership by the religious leaders. They failed to give the people the appropriate spiritual leadership and direction that they deserved. Their incompetence is evident by the fact that they failed to see God in the midst of Jesus' healing mission. They indicted themselves by their refusal to see the action of God right under their noses. They, above all, should have recognized the work of God in the compassion and mercy shown to broken, hurting people.

Matthew's first concern of the kingdom is elucidated in the imperative to preach and heal. The kingdom of God will be evidenced by signs. Yet the spectacular miracles are not to be overshadowed by the reason for the miracles in the first place: God's incredible love and compassion for those who are suffering and in distress. The expectation to believe in God's reign and accept God's rule lies in the recognizable sign of God's compassion and care for human beings—his healing love. The contemporary church understands this imperative when it sends out missionaries to hurting communities, along with medical personnel and technical support. Communities that concern themselves with the care of peoples' bodies, along with care for their souls, demonstrate in sign, symbol, and service the compassion of God. Preaching and healing go hand in hand.

Matthew's Jesus chose the Twelve and empowered them for mission to the lost house of Israel. Their mission was clearly defined. They would be given authority to heal as Jesus healed. Only God has the power to heal and cast out demons. Human beings are given a share in God's power with the clear understanding that it is God who gives the power—God who is the healer.

At the end of this section Jesus exhorts his missionaries to take nothing with them. They are to rely on the hospitality of others. When no hospitality is offered, they are to move on and evangelize elsewhere. They are to ask for no more than the Mediterranean understanding of hospitality would demand. They were not to expect riches for their efforts—but they could expect to make a network of trustworthy friends.

The compassion Jesus exhorts his disciples to extend to the world is not just a casual feeling of concern. It is love in action. It is solidarity. "Compassion is not pity, and it entails more than interest. It signifies sharing and making the sufferings and anticipations of others our own. Being com-

[9] *MI,* 111.

passionate is practicing solidarity."[10] The ministry of evangelization demands that we offer life where life is lacking. Where people do not enjoy what is necessary to uphold a decent standard of life, then life is lacking, and Christians have a responsibility to be in solidarity with such people. It is the mandate of the mission. This is not a lip-service crusade. Words without action are empty. Thus, the scale is always balanced with the ministry of the word in one hand and the ministry of justice in the other. Gustavo Gutierrez eloquently admonishes us:

> In the face of enormous shortages and sufferings afflicting and burdening the people in our society, the meaning of the mission, its urgency, and its vastness continue: proclaiming the kingdom and giving life. We have to discover the specific and effective ways to do that through discernment and our committed search, starting with the communities and the lucid analysis of concrete circumstances. For that search to be authentically pastoral, we must bear in mind two evangelical attitudes indicated by Jesus: trusting prayer to the Father, the "Lord of the harvest," and gratuitous surrender: "You have received without payment; give without payment" (v. 8).[11]

Proclaim the gospel again.

Sometimes we gain new insights when we hear the text after the interpretation has been given. Someone from the group proclaims the gospel a second time.

STEP 4
TESTING

Conversation with the Liturgy and the Scriptures

Test your original understanding in dialogue with the text.

(You might consider breaking into smaller groups.)

How does the exegesis compare with your original understanding of this gospel? Were there any new insights for you?

How does this story speak to your life?

Sharing Life Experience

Participants share an experience from their lives that connects with the biblical interpretation just shared.

> *I am reminded of a pilgrimage my son made with other teens of our diocese to the Dominican Republic to live with the poor a few summers ago. In living with the poor, the teens encountered the loving face of God. The purpose of the trip was not to "go and do," but rather to "go and live." In the living, however, the teens were the ones who received. The beautiful people of the Dominican Republic taught them many powerful lessons about life. They were taught what it means to have nothing, to rely on God for life itself. They learned what it means to give to others, and to look at every opportunity as an opportunity to share the love of God. Every time they left their village they took extra food with them to share with strangers along the way, believing that it was their responsibility to share out of their poverty with those who might have even less than they had. They lived the mission of Jesus, extending hospitality to all. My son was accepted as family by everyone in the community. They taught him how to experience joy in suffering and how to live with an eye to the joy they would know in their future life.*
>
> *The poor of this Third World village lit a fire in the teens of our diocese as they experienced the sober reality and challenge that living the mission of Christ entails. They learned that furthering the mission of God goes hand in hand with caring for the needs of hurting people in the world. My son's experience deeply touched and empowered him. He left with the resolve to tell their story to the world and to commit his energies to working with the poor.*
>
> *Such experiences are certainly ways in which the imperatives of today's gospel are realized in our contemporary world. We do not have to go to the Dominican Republic to live the mission, however. There are always people in our midst—in our own communities and families—who are hurting. When I reach out in love to the sick, lonely, grieving, homeless,*

[10] *SWTLY*, 164.
[11] Ibid.

and depressed people I meet in my everyday life, I am living today's gospel. When I witness to Christ by the example of my own life, I am living today's gospel.

All share their life experience.

What was Matthew trying to tell his community? What does he have to say to your community and to you today? How does today's gospel reflect God's promise to be with us (covenant)? How does today's liturgy invite passage from bondage to freedom (exodus)? How does today's gospel invite re-creation in our lives? What does today's liturgy have to teach us about the people of God (community)? How are you living the mission described in today's gospel? Where is growth needed? What are the obstacles in your path? Do you still feel the same way about this gospel as when you began? Has your original understanding been stretched, challenged, or affirmed?

STEP 5
DECISION

The gospel demands a response.

In what way does this liturgy invite you to change? In what way might your community be invited to respond to today's liturgy? What are the implications of this gospel for your life? What is one concrete action you will take this week as a response to the liturgy today?

Pastoral Considerations: How is your parish furthering the mission of Christ in your local and global community? In what concrete ways is your parish extending Christ's ministry of compassion? Perhaps it is time to celebrate the ministry you are doing, and empower the ministry that has yet to take place. How are the hungry in your community being fed? How are the grieving being ministered to? Who in your midst is without shelter? naked? thirsty? sick? dying? lonely? oppressed?

Christian Initiation: With such an emphasis on evangelization in today's gospel, it might be a good opportunity to remind the people of your community that it is their role to go out and spread the good news. Initiation is the responsibility of all the baptized (RCIA #9). Perhaps your community might go out and invite those friends and neighbors who do not have a church home to come and inquire.

DOCTRINAL ISSUES

What church truth/teaching/doctrinal issue could be drawn from the gospel for the Eleventh Sunday in Ordinary Time?

Participants suggest possible doctrinal themes that flow from the readings.

Possible Doctrinal Themes

Kingdom of God, mystery of the church, mission, evangelization, discipleship, social teaching of the church, ministry of the laity, Jesus Christ

Present the doctrinal material at this time.

1. The facilitator gives input on a particular doctrinal issue of his or her prior choosing. OR

2. The group chooses a doctrinal issue from the list they created. They read together from the Doctrinal Appendix.

(The doctrinal issues are found in the Doctrinal Appendix in the back of this workbook. If you are choosing an issue from this resource, please refer to it now.)

Reflection questions centered around the chosen doctrinal theme can be found at the end of each topic in the Doctrinal Appendix. The questions are based on the five-step reflection process. If you choose a topic not included in the Doctrinal Appendix, craft your own questions according to the same five-step process.

Following the reflection questions you will be reminded to return to chapter 7, "Preparing the Catechetical Session," to assist you in crafting your own session.

Closing Prayer

God our Father,
we rejoice in the faith that draws us together,
aware that selfishness can drive us apart.
Let your encouragement be our constant
strength.
Keep us one in the love that has sealed our lives,
help us to live as one family
the gospel we profess.
We ask this through Christ our Lord.[12]

[12]Eleventh Sunday of Ordinary Time, "Alternative Opening Prayer," *The Sacramentary.*

Twelfth Sunday in Ordinary Time

Environment

Most likely it is summertime. The catechetical environment needs to change from the Easter whites and spring flowers to the bright greens and yellows of the late spring and early summer. A candle, a book, and splashes here and there of the liturgical color of green are always appropriate in the environment. The addition of summer hues and images is limited only by the imagination.

INTRODUCTORY RITES

Opening Song (or Entrance Antiphon)

God is the strength of his people. In him, we his chosen live in safety. Save us, Lord, who share in your life, and give us your blessing; be our shepherd for ever. (Ps 27:8–9)[1]

Opening Prayer

The facilitator of the session may lead the prayer. Others in the group may be asked to proclaim the readings.

Let us pray
[that we may grow in the love of God]

Pause for silent prayer.

Father,
guide and protector of your people,
grant us an unfailing respect for your name,
and keep us always in your love.
Grant this through our Lord
Jesus Christ, your Son,
who lives and reigns with you and the Holy Spirit,
one God, for ever and ever.[2]

[1]Twelfth Sunday in Ordinary Time: "Entrance Antiphon," *The Sacramentary.*

[2]Twelfth Sunday in Ordinary Time: "Opening Prayer," *The Sacramentary.*

LITURGY OF THE WORD

Let us listen to God's word.

The readings are proclaimed.

First Reading
Jeremiah 20:10–13

Overview of Jeremiah. During a period in which Jeremiah was in hiding (c. 604 B.C.E.), he dictated to his secretary Baruch a summary of what he had preached during his prophetic ministry. Jeremiah preached in the southern kingdom under the rule of King Jehoiakim. The king burned Jeremiah's first manuscript. Jeremiah had Baruch compile a second manuscript. Scholars suggest that chapters 1–20 and 25 of the Book of Jeremiah are the bulk of that second manuscript.

There is very little chronological order in the book. This is often confusing. The siege of Jerusalem, which occurred around 588–587 B.C.E., is mentioned in chapter 21, and events that took place in 604 B.C.E. are mentioned in chapter 25. The reason for this, scholars suggest, is that rather than try to put the vast collection of different types of prophetic material in some kind of reasonable chronological order, they chose instead to arrange it thematically.

Jeremiah speaks out against the kings of Israel. He puts Israel on trial and charges Israel with crimes against God. He pronounces God's judgment against Israel. Jeremiah claims to speak as one sent by God—God's messenger. The prophet understood his role as one of messenger sent by God to announce judgment on Israel for infidelity to the covenant. Israel failed to live up to moral imperatives of the covenant.

Others could claim to be God's messenger, but only one truly sent by God could speak God's word. A prophet who asserted that he was God's messenger, but in reality was not sent by God, was considered a false prophet. Prophets therefore had to make a strong case and authenticate that they were truly sent by God. Jeremiah, Isaiah, and Ezekiel all testified that their prophetic mission was directly commissioned and sanctioned by God. There is no doubt about their divine commission when one considers how their extremely unpopular message has withstood the test of time.

When Israel failed to live the commandments—the love of God and love of neighbor—they failed to live up to the covenant. It is usually sins against the two great commandments that make up the primary agenda of the prophets. When the people worshiped false idols and failed to take care of the poor and oppressed, a prophet was sent to speak God's word of judgment. Prophets behaved like a prosecuting attorney when speaking about God's anguish over Israel's failure to be faithful to the covenant. When speaking for the people, they took the role of a defense attorney. The prophets' concern was to reconcile and help Israel understand and appreciate their unique, special relationship with God. Jeremiah had a burning passion for God, and an abiding love for God's people.

Today's Pericope: Today's reading from Jeremiah is chosen for its connection to the gospel in which the disciples are warned about the persecution and rejection they will encounter as they proclaim the mission of Christ. Jeremiah's fate highly influenced the Jewish belief that persecution, martyrdom, and rejection were to be expected when one lived an authentic prophetic ministry. All those who bring the word of God to others can expect suffering.

The "Confession of Jeremiah" reflects the interior dialogue of a prophet who gave his life as an authentic witness to God. Jeremiah suffered at the hands of his own colleagues. He was in great turmoil because he believed God ill-equipped him for his mission. He felt inadequate—that he was not up to the impossible task at hand. He felt duped and angry. Yet he knew that God had called him to the prophetic life. He was confident that the Lord remains faithful to those who are faithful to him.

Jeremiah does not want to speak, but is compelled to speak. He cannot keep quiet. God's word burns within him and must come forth from him. He knows what it will cost him—perhaps even his life. His enemies plot against him. He takes little solace in the fact that such things happen to just prophets of the Lord. He wishes he had never been born.

Yet after his turmoil, faith wins out and Jeremiah returns to his steady course, praising the God who protects and defends him. Jeremiah affirmed his total dependence on God. Trust is triumphant in the face of tyranny. Jeremiah turns to the God who saves in a song of thanks and praise. We are all invited into Jeremiah's trusting hymn of grateful praise.

Responsorial Psalm
Psalm 69:8–10, 14, 17, 33–35

Today's psalm was frequently associated with Christ's passion. In like manner, it is easily connected to the plight of Jeremiah in today's first reading.

Second Reading
Romans 5:12–15

In today's pericope Paul describes the effects of Christ's death and resurrection. Jesus freed human beings from sin and death. The law does not save. Paul made his point by comparing Jesus with Adam. Adam sinned. He was disobedient and as a result of his disobedience lived in sin and suffered the consequences of death. His sin spread to others. Jesus, on the other hand, was obedient to God, was not a sinner, and broke the chains of death forever. The effects of his death and resurrection spread to the many. He offered the free gift of life through his death.

God's grace transcends our sin. Human beings are born into the sinful human condition. It is quite easy to succumb to its snare. It is difficult, however, to get rid of sin after it has a foothold in a person's life.

The people who came after Adam sinned just as he sinned. Adam may have taken the first plunge into the murky waters, but generations to follow willingly jumped into the muck right behind him. Adam created an environment of sin. All who followed him were thus subject to the same environment and the same subsequent spiritual death.

Death is understood as separation from God, not as a punishment for sin. Reginald Fuller refers to it as a "theological consequence of sin."[3] Separation is the result of sin. Biological death is part of the human condition. It will happen to all who live. Theological death is total alienation from God by people who have turned away from God due to the sin in their lives.

"Not only does Christ repair the catastrophic state that had its origin in Adam, he initiates a new, an incomparably better state."[4] Christ is our hope. Through his paschal mystery we are heirs to the new life he inaugurated by his saving action.

Gospel
Matthew 10:26–33

Step 1
Naming One's Experience

What were your first impressions? What was your first response to the gospel (or the other readings)?[5] What captured your attention?

Each person names his or her initial impression. Statements should be brief. No reasons should be given at this time. All simply listen without agreeing or disagreeing.

Step 2
Understanding

In a brief statement, what do you think this gospel is trying to convey? What pre-understanding did you bring to this session?

[3] *PL,* 138.

[4] *DL* (IV), 103.

[5] The primary focus of reflection is the gospel. However, very often the other readings demand attention and must be brought into the dialogue.

Step 3
Input from Vision/Story/Tradition

Liturgical Context

The gospels for Sundays Twelve through Fourteen in Ordinary Time possess an internal unity. The gospels for the Twelfth and Thirteenth Sundays are part of what is known as the "Apostolic Discourse," or the "Discourse on the Mission." The Fourteenth Sunday deals with the mystery of the reign of God, but it also includes the prayer of Jesus in which he thanks God for protecting those he sent out on the mission. This third gospel serves as an appropriate conclusion to the previous two gospels.

The Communion Rite antiphon reminds us of the implications of today's gospel: "I am the Good Shepherd; I give my life for my sheep" (Jn 10:11, 15). Like the Good Shepherd, we are all called to offer our lives for the sheep of God's flock. Hints of the gospel's exhortation "not to fear" can be found in the Alternative Opening Prayer: "From this world's uncertainty we look to your covenant. Keep us one in your peace, secure in your love."[6] Jesus' peace and love are certainly antidotes to fear.

Let us remember that the eucharist nourishes us for the difficult challenge posed by today's liturgy. "Lord, you give us the body and blood of your Son to renew your life within us. In your mercy, assure our redemption and bring us to the eternal life we celebrate in this eucharist."[7] We can count on the strength needed to live the mission and see it through to the end through our nourishment at the Lord's table.

Gospel Exegesis

The facilitator gives input regarding what critical biblical scholarship has to say about this text. The input includes insights as to how people would have heard the gospel in Jesus' time.

[6] Twelfth Sunday in Ordinary Time: "Alternative Opening Prayer," *The Sacramentary.*

[7] Twelfth Sunday in Ordinary Time: "Prayer After Communion," *The Sacramentary.*

Today's gospel is part of Jesus' discourse on the mission. Jesus reminds his disciples that they will experience persecution and rejection by their own people as they go forth preaching the gospel. He encourages them not to be afraid of those who oppose the mission of Christ—and to proclaim the gospel with boldness. Through the power of God, the gospel will triumph—no power will prevail against it; God, through Christ, will be revealed. Those who "have ears to hear" and accept the good news of Jesus Christ are to go out and preach what was first revealed to them by Jesus himself.

Before the disciples heard Jesus' preaching they were in darkness, but now that they have heard the word and have accepted it, they have come into the light. Having come into the light, they *are* light. Disciples are the light of Christ.

Matthew's Jesus uses Greek images when he speaks of the body being deprived of life but not the soul. The Greeks believed that people were made up of body, which will eventually decay, and soul, which will live forever. Matthew's Jesus makes the point that living the life of prophet and promoting the gospel of Christ in the world may be quite costly—perhaps even costing a person his or her earthly life. Missionaries may end up giving their bodily lives for the mission, but their souls will live on forever. Enemies can kill the body, but in and through God, the soul lives on. Inherent in this dialogue about body and soul are hints of the belief in the future resurrection of the body promised to the righteous. Disciples are not to fear death of the body, but rather, they are to fear Gehenna, the post-life place where body and soul reside in constant torment for the sin of alienation. There is nothing to fear in death except to be lost and cut off from God. What does it matter if the body is dead? Life in Christ offers eternal life. Jesus admonishes his disciples not to fear death, but to remain steadfast and maintain their faith under pressure. Matthew exhorts the fainthearted among his listeners to stand their ground and be strong.

The sparrows were useless, yet not one fell from the sky without God's awareness and consent. God ordains all life and activity. Jesus asserted that every hair on our head has been counted and reminds us that we are worth more than the sparrows. The reference to numbered hairs in the gospel was alluding to *something that people have no way of knowing—something only God knows.* God knows everything about us—things we do not even know ourselves.

We might be tempted to associate this numbered-hairs image with other biblical references promising that no harm will come to a hair on a disciple's head (1 Sm 14:45; 2 Sm 14:11; 1 Kgs 1:52; Lk 21:18; Acts 27:34). Jesus, however, makes no such promise in Matthew's gospel. He only promises that our hairs have been counted. The implication? God is fully aware that we are subject to harm. Not only is God aware of it, but it does not happen without God's knowledge or consent. Jesus implies the following question: "How can you, who do not even begin to know how many hairs are on your head, think you can understand God's purpose in suffering?" It is part of God's plan. But the disciple is to trust that God knows what God is doing and will make things right. "They are therefore not to allow their message to be muted by external pressures or internal fears."[8]

Proclaiming the gospel is not an easy undertaking. The proclaimer is vulnerable to hostility and suspicion. Boldness and fervor are required. The message of the gospel is love. When lack of love is exposed, those guilty of the failure to love often feel resentment and refuse to be confronted. Their failure to love is often the result of selfish pride, power, and prestige—difficult sins to overcome. The evangelical mission demands that the gospel of love be preached—even when it is difficult to hear. "This is why disciples have to be both frank and clear. The light of the evangelical message does not allow us to take refuge in dark corners to hide our fears and infidelities."[9] Where the poor and the defenseless are mistreated, the gospel of love is not lived. It may be preached, but not heeded. The result? The messenger who delivers the unwanted message is often killed. Today's gospel reminds us to be bold in the face of such a challenge. "No doubt the gospel is good news, but

[8] *RM,* 118.

[9] *SWTLY,* 168.

it also radically calls into question a world built without recognition of God and upon values foreign or even contrary to his law. Confrontation is unavoidable. A gospel that bothers no one and questions nothing is no longer the gospel."[10]

Proclaim the gospel again.

Sometimes we gain new insights when we hear the text after the interpretation has been given. Someone from the group proclaims the gospel a second time.

STEP 4
TESTING

Conversation with the Liturgy and the Scriptures

Test your original understanding in dialogue with the text.

(You might consider breaking into smaller groups.)

How does your original understanding of this gospel compare with the exegesis? Were there any new insights for you? How does this story speak to your life?

Sharing Life Experience

Participants share an experience from their lives that connects with the biblical interpretation just shared.

> *I am reminded of the Jesuits who recently gave their lives preaching a just word in Latin America. Would I have had similar courage? Someone close to me knows well the kind of rejection Jesus speaks of today. He has not been beaten or his body burned, but he has lost friends and has been ridiculed for trying to be a voice for Christ and for those who cannot speak for themselves. Yet in spite of the rejection, his resolve seemed to grow. His proclamation became stronger and louder. As I ponder today's gospel, I wonder if it is really humanly possible to "fear not." In the face of abuse and torture I do not know if I could "fear not." Yet we have the example of martyrs such as Maximilian Kolbe to encourage and offer hope. Where did their courage come from? In observing the person I mentioned earlier, I have seen him grow stronger and face each new rejection with more boldness than before. If God knows how many curly hairs reside on the top of my head, then God certainly knows what I need in order to withstand persecution, rejection, and suffering; God knows what I need to be strong. My job is to trust that God will provide what I need.*
>
> *In a few months it is possible that I will be in a situation in which I will have the opportunity to test this gospel. It is my inclination to say, "Thanks God, but no thanks." If fear would have its way, that is exactly what I would do. My prayer is to remain steadfast and to keep focused on Christ's mission of healing and compassion. There is no place for fear in that mission. It must be possible to let it go, or Jesus would not have demanded it. Perhaps letting go of fear simply means doing the will of God in spite of the feelings or the consequences. Perhaps in the act of doing the feeling of trust will follow. If I believe that God is with me, I have nothing to fear. "Fear not" is an exhortation to trust. Alone I will not have the courage, but with God's help, I will.*
>
> *I am reminded of times in our church communities when unwelcomed messages were preached that were greeted with scorn and derision. I have noted that some who preach a just word are accused of being too political. Often our communities are influenced by nationalistic rather than gospel concerns. Many good people in our church today suffer great rejection for taking a gospel stance. I once met a priest who told me that people in his parish sought his transfer for preaching about issues of justice such as poverty and capital punishment. It made them uncomfortable. Today's gospel is a reminder that we have to be faithful to the gospel even when it is unpopular to do so. Today's gospel is a word to our communities to preach with boldness and forget about the consequences.*

What was Matthew trying to tell his community? How is Matthew's message to his community relevant for your community today? Have you ever had to suffer because of your convictions? What did you learn from the experience? How does it feel to you when Jesus asks you "not to fear" impending persecution and suffering? Is it a reasonable expectation? Have you ever known anyone who was courageous in the face of tribulation? Did

[10] *DL* (IV), 103.

you learn anything from them? How are the biblical themes of covenant, exodus, creation, and community evident in today's readings? Do you still feel the same way about this text as when you began? What are the implications of this gospel for your life? Has your original understanding been stretched, challenged, or affirmed?

STEP 5
DECISION

The gospel demands a response.

In what way does today's liturgy invite change? What might your community be called to do in response to today's liturgy? What is one concrete action you could take this week as a response to today's liturgy?

Christian Initiation: The scriptures today would be most appropriate in the context of a rite of acceptance. The readings certainly speak to what it means to be signed with the cross of Christ. Catechumens very often experience difficulty when trying to live the imperatives of the gospel in the marketplace. This would be an excellent time to reflect on the challenges of living the gospel, and perhaps to celebrate an exorcism with them.

DOCTRINAL ISSUES

What church truth/teaching/doctrinal issue could be drawn from the gospel for the Twelfth Sunday of Ordinary Time?

Participants suggest possible doctrinal themes that flow from the readings.

Possible Doctrinal Themes

Paschal mystery, mystery of suffering, kingdom of God, cross, trust, faith, hope, eschatology, soteriology/salvation, prophetic life, discipleship, sin and grace

Present the doctrinal material at this time.

1. The facilitator gives input on a particular doctrinal issue of his or her prior choosing. OR

2. The group chooses a doctrinal issue from the list they created. They read together from the Doctrinal Appendix.

(The doctrinal issues are found in the Doctrinal Appendix in the back of this workbook. If you are choosing an issue from this resource, please refer to it now.)

Reflection questions centered around the chosen doctrinal theme can be found at the end of each topic in the Doctrinal Appendix. The questions are based on the five-step reflection process. If you choose a topic not included in the Doctrinal Appendix, craft your own questions according to the same five-step process.

Following the reflection questions you will be reminded to return to chapter 7, "Preparing the Catechetical Session," to assist you in crafting your own session.

Closing Prayer

May God, who in Christ has shown us his truth and love, make you messengers of the Gospel and witnesses to the divine love before all the world. Amen.

May the Lord Jesus Christ, who promised that he would be with his Church until the end of time, guide your steps and fill your words with power. Amen.

May the Spirit of the Lord be upon you, enabling you as you go through the world to bring the Good News to the lowly and to heal the brokenhearted. Amen.[11]

---

[11]Blessing of Missionaries within a Celebration of the Word: "Concluding Rite," *Book of Blessings*, 200.

Thirteenth Sunday in Ordinary Time

Environment

The summer Ordinary Time environment continues. See the Twelfth Sunday in Ordinary Time. With the gospel's reference to taking up your cross to follow Christ, it would be important to place a cross in a prominent place in your catechetical environment.

INTRODUCTORY RITES

Opening Song (or Entrance Antiphon)

All nations clap your hands. Shout with a voice of joy to God. (Ps 46:2)[1]

Opening Prayer

The facilitator of the session may lead the prayer. Others in the group may be asked to proclaim the readings.

Let us pray
[that Christ may be our light]

Pause for silent prayer.

Father,
you call your children
to walk in the light of Christ.
Free us from darkness
and keep us in the radiance of your truth.
We ask this through our Lord Jesus Christ, your Son,
who lives and reigns with you and the Holy Spirit,
one God, for ever and ever.[2]

LITURGY OF THE WORD

Let us listen to God's word.

[1]Thirteenth Sunday in Ordinary Time: "Entrance Antiphon," *The Sacramentary.*

[2]Thirteenth Sunday in Ordinary Time: "Opening Prayer," *The Sacramentary.*

The readings are proclaimed.

First Reading
2 Kings 4:8–11, 14–16a

Overview of First and Second Kings, Joshua, Judges, Samuel: The two Books of Kings, Deuteronomy, Joshua, Judges, and 1 and 2 Samuel are part of a section in the Hebrew Scriptures known as Deuteronomic History. Deuteronomy is the code of law. God entered into covenant relationship with Israel. As a response to the unconditional love and care of Yahweh, Israel promised to live the moral imperatives of the law. Deuteronomy sets forth the code of conduct expected of the people once they are in the promised land. The Book of Joshua is a chronicle of Israel's conquest of the land after they arrived in the promised land. It is a rosy embellishment of the crusade that marched across into Canaan. It depicted a faithful people who were successful in all their endeavors because they were obedient to the will of Yahweh. The Book of Judges is not so glossy, however. It is a more realistic account of events. It portrayed the campaign as slow and tedious and sometimes less than successful. The people were not always faithful. They succumbed to Canaanite idol worship and thus were forced by God to live alongside the Canaanites. They were ruled during this two-hundred-year-plus period by military leaders who were called judges. The Book of Samuel is an account of Israel's last judge, Samuel. He was the judge who would appoint Israel's first king, Saul. Saul's infidelity to God led to his removal and David was appointed king. David was the Lord's own appointee. The spirit of God found favor with David and with David's reign would begin the golden age of Israel. The Second Book of Samuel continues with the saga of David's monarchy. David quickly rose in stature as a king. He was loved by the people. He entered into a holy covenant with God and as a result was promised a unique, enduring dynasty. First and Second Kings recount the events of David's dynasty. David is succeeded by his son Solomon, who built a temple in honor of Yahweh. With the appointment of Solomon and the building of the Temple, the dynasty of David was initiated and God's promise to David was fulfilled.

The First Book of Kings chronicles the building of the Temple. We are given a front-row seat to the debacle in which Solomon's arrogant infidelity leads to the disintegration of the one nation and the division of the country into the northern kingdom, Israel, and the southern kingdom, Judah. Most of this first book centers around conditions in the northern kingdom. Israel's leaders were so depraved that the prospect of a lasting dynasty was out of the question. The Second Book deals with the leadership of both kingdoms. The northern kingdom is lost. It is afflicted with evil rulers and is punished by the Lord. Assyria invades its borders and the exile begins. Judah receives mixed reviews. Bad and good kings dot its historical landscape. Eventually Judah does not fare much better than the north. Evil King Manasseh led the south down the primrose path into the Babylonian exile. The Temple was destroyed in the process. The Second Book ends with a word of encouragement and hope that God will restore Israel.

Scholars believe that the above-named books were originally scattered fragments written by multiple authors that were eventually woven together into a thematic whole by an editor or editors. The historical accounting of Israel's salvation history spans centuries, from as early as the tenth century B.C.E. until the sixth century B.C.E.

The Deuteronomist theologians share one consistent agenda. God is portrayed as being in relationship with a people. Israel sins and God punishes. Israel repents and God forgives. Israel prays and God restores. It is a pattern that is repeated throughout Deuteronomic History. Another common motif in the Book of Kings is blessings for fidelity and curses for infidelity. The kings and the people are blessed for being faithful to the covenant, and ruin occurs when they are unfaithful.

Today's Pericope: Today's reading is the hospitality scripture *par excellence.* The woman in today's reading is incredible. She is "independent and maternal, powerful and pious. She brings to mind a number of other female characters yet surpasses them all. She is observant in both practical and spiritual ways: she notices not only Elisha's regular passing through Shunem but also the aura that marks him as a man of God."[3]

The woman was not poor or she would have been unable to provide a permanent lodging for Elijah. Since she was able to offer the hospitality of meals, a bed, a lamp, and a chair, we are to assume that she was a woman of means, and probably an influential woman in her own right. Last week we learned that prophets needed to authenticate their mission. The story of the Shunemite woman and other stories that follow in the Book of Kings are intended to authenticate God's initiative in sending the prophet Elijah, and his successor Elisha. Not only were they sent by God, but the results of the mission were effective. God's word was realized. Another agenda of the Deuteronomist was to prove that God's word once spoken was fulfilled. There are over forty-five different stories in 1 and 2 Kings that depict the fulfillment of prophecy.

The woman today testifies that Elijah is a *man of God.* She knows this because he resuscitated a mother's dead son in an earlier story. God's word was fulfilled, proving that Elijah was God's messenger. In the Hebrew tradition, holy men of God were people who spoke the word of God and the word came to pass. The word could be authenticated historically.

Hospitality in the scriptures was not an option. It was part and parcel of the people's biblical faith. Not to offer hospitality was an abomination before God. It was a sacred duty. The patriarchs were exemplary in their exercise of hospitality. In the Book of Genesis, Abraham and Sarah's hospitality to the strangers was rewarded by the promise of a son.

For the people of Israel, the traveling stranger was a reminder of their sojourn through the desert and of their role as traveling pilgrims on earth. Hospitality was a way to offer God's mercy to others and to witness to God's love. Hospitality was an imperative of the two great commandments. How could there be love if hospitality was

[3] *WBC,* 122.

lacking? Visitors were welcomed with no expectation of recompense. There was no such thing as intrusion or inopportune moments. To the Mideastern way of thinking, there was nothing more important than to welcome a stranger in the name of the Lord.

Responsorial Psalm
Psalm 89:2–3, 16–17, 18–19

The verses in today's psalm have their origin in the messianic psalms that foretell the coming of the ideal Davidic monarch. The last verse reflects the promise of the future messiah. The rest of the psalm, however, is a hymn of praise because of God's steadfast love and fidelity.

Second Reading
Romans 6:3–4, 8–11

(Refer to the First Sunday of Advent for an Overview of Paul's Letter to the Romans.)

Paul's letter to the Romans is read at every Easter Vigil. It is our premier catechism on baptism. This is the moment during the Easter Vigil when a transition occurs. We move from being immersed in the stories of creation and the fall, the sacrifice in faith of Abraham, Israel's passage from slavery to freedom, the proclamation of prophets promising God's forgiveness and vindication (all of which stories prefigure God's action in Christ), to the fulfillment of that action in the Easter event—the death and resurrection of Jesus. Believers participate in Christ's passover from death to new life through baptism. This is the moment during the Easter Vigil in which we turn from darkness to light. The Sacramentary instructs us to light our altar lights. Baptism assures us that we no longer live in the darkness, but are children of the Light.

We are no longer dead. Paul reminds us that through baptism we die to sin and become a new creation in Christ. The neophyte plunges deeply into the waters of death, suffocated by the crushing weight of water and sin, only to come up gasping for the air of invigorating new life and freedom.

"The rite of Christian initiation introduces a human being into union with Christ's suffering and dying."[4] The newly baptized are initiated into Christ's resurrected life. Baptism gives the Christian the power to live the Christian life. Paul asserts that through baptism we are dead to sin; it no longer lives in us. "The destruction of the sinful 'self' through baptism and incorporation into Christ means liberation from enslavement to sin. Hence one's outlook can no longer be focused on sin."[5]

Reginald Fuller tells us that the verbs used in Paul's address remind us of the effects of baptism. When speaking of "dying to ourselves," Paul used past-tense verbs. He used future-tense verbs in relation to the resurrection. Through baptism we *died* (past tense) with Christ.[6] However, our resurrection is our future goal as we live out our baptismal commitment and moral response. We continue to renew our commitment to die to sin each day.

Gospel
Matthew 10:37–42

STEP 1
NAMING ONE'S EXPERIENCE

What were your first impressions? What was your first response to the gospel (or the other readings)?[7] What captured your attention?

Each person names his or her initial impression. Statements should be brief. No reasons should be given at this time. All simply listen without agreeing or disagreeing.

STEP 2
UNDERSTANDING

In a brief statement, what do you think this gospel is trying to convey? What pre-understanding did you bring to this gospel?

---

[4]Fitzmyer, "The Letter to the Romans," *NJBC,* 847–848.
[5]Ibid., 848–849.
[6]*PNL,* 21–22.
[7]The primary focus of reflection is the gospel. However, very often the other readings demand attention and must be brought into the dialogue.

STEP 3
INPUT FROM VISION/STORY/TRADITION

Liturgical Context

Today's gospel continues the sequence comprised of the Twelfth through Fourteenth Sundays in Ordinary Time (see Twelfth Sunday, Liturgical Context). It is part of what is known as the Apostolic Discourse. "In this discourse Matthew insists that the authority of Jesus to preach (chs. 5–7) and to act (chs. 8–9) has been transmitted by him to his disciples—and also to their successors in the time of Matthew himself."[8] Jesus reminds disciples what it means to take up their cross and follow him. It is a proclamation of our immersion in the paschal mystery that we celebrate and live at every liturgy, every sacramental celebration, and throughout our daily living.

Today's second reading, from Romans, resonates with the same theme. We are baptized into Jesus' death in order to become new creations in Christ. The way we continue to live that baptismal reality is by embracing the cross in our life and by living the gospel of Jesus.

Today's Prayer Over the Gifts asks that we be given God's grace and that the eucharist empower us to serve God faithfully. To serve God faithfully assumes that one is willing to embrace the cross and to participate in Jesus' ministry of healing and reconciliation in the world. The "Prayer After Communion" asks that the eucharist give us a share in God's life so that we can go out and share God's love in the world. We carry the cross of Christ when we offer God's love to all we encounter in our everyday lives.

Gospel Exegesis

The facilitator gives input regarding what critical biblical scholarship has to say about this text. The input includes insights as to how people would have heard the gospel in Jesus' time.

This chapter in Matthew reveals evidence of two different time spans. It reflects the actual time, experience, and sayings of Jesus as he exhorts and empowers his disciples. It also contains reflections of the post-Easter Matthean church. It is suggested by Neal Flanagan, O.S.M. that verses 5–15 (of chapter 10) refer to the time of Jesus, his mission to the lost sheep of Israel, the commissioning of the apostles, the passing on of the authority to preach and heal, and the brief span of Jesus' mission. The remaining verses (16 and following) are probably the reflection of the post-resurrection church that tries to connect their situation to that of the Master and to find meaning in the midst of their suffering and persecution. It probably reflects the conditions in Matthew's community, as they struggle to live the mission and deal with Roman and Jewish opposition to Christianity indicative of the post-70 C.E. period.

In antiquity it was not unusual for people to kill the bearer of an unpopular message. Matthew's community was experiencing persecution for proclaiming the gospel. By the time the oral gospel was recorded, around the middle of 80 C.E., the Jewish Christians were beginning to be expelled from the synagogue. They were considered heretics by their Jewish neighbors. Judaism was allowed to exist under Roman law. Christian Jews enjoyed protection as long as they were connected to a synagogue. When Christians were expelled from the synagogue they were forced to be part of an illegal religion and were thus subject to persecution. The Edict of Jamnia disallowed the Christian religion. It is probable that Matthew's community understood their persecution to be a sharing in the cross of Jesus.

The cost of discipleship was experienced in ways other than persecution by the ruling powers. Families and relationships were often under stress as a result of the serious commitment gospel living demanded. Lest we expect too quickly to have the lion and the lamb feast at the same table, Jesus warns us against false expectations. In verse 34 (which is not in today's pericope), Matthew's Jesus reminds us that it is not peace he brings, but the sword. "The sword is not the sword of judgment that will mow down the oppressors (1 Enoch 91:12). It is the sword of decision, and the call to decision will bring division."[9] Families will be torn

[8] *MML*, 56–57.

[9] *RM*, 118.

apart, especially if they believed that the disciple was proselytized by a false prophet. Jesus did not set out to destroy families. However, as people's priorities, commitments, and decisions shifted to conform to the ethical imperatives of the kingdom, disruption in families was inevitable as some still preferred darkness over the light.

The lives of the early saints provide a glimpse of this disruption. Perpetua was a Christian woman from a good family. She was also a nursing mother. When arrested for her faith, her father begged her to deny the faith, but she refused. She could not deny her faith; it was her identity. Her father was so enraged when he heard the word *Christian* that he wanted to gouge out her eyes. He pleaded with his daughter to let go of her foolish pride for the sake of her mother and family members.

In antiquity it was understood that life was closely connected with the family. Jesus taught that life was intimately connected to God's family—the reign of God. Jesus invited complete abandonment to the reign of God. Those who seek their fulfillment in Christ, rather than in self-fulfilling pursuits, will find wholeness and authentic self-realization.

Christians were to extend hospitality to apostles, prophets, holy people, and the lowly. In the last couple of weeks we have examined the role of the prophet. The prophet was a messenger sent by God. When truly sent by God to bear God's word, he was considered righteous and holy. Jesus sent the disciples out into the kingdom. They, too, were messengers of God. It was a grave matter to reject God's messenger. It was understood that even the smallest act of kindness and hospitality to one of God's messengers would be richly rewarded. The poor, marginalized, and disenfranchised were to be recipients of the special care, concern, and compassion that Jesus himself extended to them. Hospitality is rooted deeply in our Judeo-Christian heritage (see first reading). Hospitality is a sign of God's reign. It is a witness to the love of God. Hospitality is not an option. It overflows out of Jesus' friendship and communion with us. "In this way discipleship, which involves taking up the cross of contradiction, is translated into surrender and unconditional service to the poor. For the disciple it means finding life in an absolute and definitive way."[10]

The situation of Matthew's community was the lens through which the story of Jesus' surrender and self-sacrifice is told. The sacrifice of the cross is the model for all who are persecuted for a just cause. Those who serve the mission will ultimately share the death of Christ, but they will also share his resurrection. To embrace one's cross is a parable in action. A parable turns the expected order upside down and, in an "aha!" moment, reveals the presence and action of God. The cross was an instrument of torture. The culture of Jesus' day considered it an absurdity to even remotely suggest that the cross was a means of redemption. A modern-day corollary would be for us to say, "The electric chair is our strength and our salvation." However, we boldly assert that "there is no salvation except through the cross, no savior except Christ dead on the cross and risen."[11] The primary focus of all the gospels is the call to carry the cross. Thus, when disciples promote the ministry of the word, they bear the cross of Christ to the world. Disciples also carry the cross when they embrace the trials and tribulations associated with life and the mission of Christ. This is what it means to live the paschal mystery.

Today's gospel affirms the appropriate attitude disciples should assume as they proclaim the gospel and mission of Christ. They are to put their relationship with Christ above all human concerns. Christians are not to be surprised when they experience persecution and family alienation. When it comes, they are to face it and embrace it. Their example is Jesus Christ crucified. The gospel also affirms the attitude that should be shown toward the disciples themselves. Christians are to offer hospitality to Christ's ambassadors.

Disciples are asked to make a choice. Jesus' life and work created a dilemma. People had to choose. They were either for or against Jesus. The right choice often created havoc in their lives. Yet the gospel is clear: the bond of love between Jesus and his disciples and between disciples and their Creator is deeper than any forged in this life.

---

[10] *SWTLY*, 173.

[11] *DL* (IV), 110.

Proclaim the gospel again.

Sometimes we gain new insights when we hear the text after the interpretation has been given. Someone from the group proclaims the gospel a second time.

STEP 4

TESTING

Conversation with the Liturgy and the Scriptures

Test your original understanding in dialogue with the text.

(You might consider breaking into smaller groups.)

Is there anything in today's gospel or readings that you had not considered before? How does your original understanding of this gospel compare with what we just shared? Were there any new insights for you?

How does this story speak to your life?

Sharing Life Experience

Participants share an experience from their lives that connects with the biblical interpretation just shared.

> *Hospitality is an exalted virtue in today's readings. It has many faces. I have been the recipient of this overflowing virtue and in the process encountered God's presence. Some people are the personification of hospitality. I am reminded of the Irish Sisters of Mercy who opened their doors, their hearts, and their lives to me, my family, and the people of our parish community. Even today, six years after they returned to Ireland, their absence is still mourned and the loss of their hospitality is still grieved. Their charism was so powerful that we had described them as the heartbeat of our community. When my very young children first arrived in the community, they were filled with awe by the loving hospitality of the sisters. They were made to feel special, loved, and unique. The sisters were the face of God to my family, and to the community. They taught me the power of hospitality and why so much value is placed on it in the scriptures. True hospitality welcomes strangers and outcasts, as well as friends. The sisters reached out to the poor and marginalized in our community. They were advocates in quiet, powerful ways. When there was need, the sisters responded. When someone was hurting, the sisters were there. They were ministers of healing and reconciliation. They brought peace where there was rancor. Families in crisis were their special concern. They lived the compassionate mission of Christ. Everyone was treated with love and respect, and transgressions were given the benefit of the doubt. Their home was a place of welcome and refuge. I thought I understood the meaning of hospitality until they expanded my consciousness. They opened their lives and hearts to God's people.*
>
> *The Sisters of Mercy epitomized their name. They were Christ-bearers to our community, bringing life in the midst of bleakness, humor in the midst of stress, and a warm hearth in the midst of loneliness.*
>
> *About twenty-five years ago my faith, and the faith of my husband, was awakened. Those early days were marked by passion, impetuosity, and immaturity. Following Christ was our zealous concern. However, we often made impulsive decisions that were greeted by a less-than-enthusiastic response, and understandably so, from some folks who were very close to us. Our exuberance may have looked like going overboard. Having made that confession, we nevertheless learned a powerful lesson that is rooted in today's gospel. There were many times when we told ourselves that living out the gospel, and its subsequent challenges, simply had to take priority over familial concerns. In hindsight, many of their concerns were valid. The experience did give us the opportunity, however, to appreciate the implications of today's gospel, and to resonate with the plight of those who have to pay the price to live the gospel they profess. The gospel's challenge is never soft or easy. It's unpopular to be a voice for the poor, especially the so-called "undeserving poor." My husband and our friend Dan minister in our parish shelter. They have encountered people in our city (religious leaders among them) who believe that alcoholics and drug addicts do not deserve to have food in their stomachs or a blanket to keep them warm. The gospel is often a word of contradiction and discomfort, and takes us places we would rather not go. Herein lies the cross. Jesus invites us to embrace it. It is the mandate of our baptism. We die so we can rise to new life.*

All share their life experience.

What was Matthew's agenda in this gospel? What was he trying to tell his community? How is this a relevant word for your community today? How does today's liturgy reflect God's promise to be in relationship with us (covenant)? In what way is there an invitation to move from slavery to freedom (exodus)? What are the implications for your life? How does today's liturgy invite us to become a new creation (creation)? In what way is the biblical theme of community expressed in today's readings? What one important insight do you wish to take with you as a result of this sharing today? Do you still feel the same way about this text as when you began? Have you in any way been invited to change an attitude or behavior?

Step 5
Decision

The gospel demands a response.

How might today's liturgy call your community to an explicit action? What is one specific action you will take this week as a response to the liturgy today?

Pastoral Considerations: Perhaps this would be a good time to reflect on the ways in which your parish is a hospitable, initiating community. How do you offer hospitality to one another? To strangers? Do people feel welcome when they come to worship at your parish church? Is your parish inclusive or exclusive? Is everyone equally welcome? How are newcomers welcomed into your parish? The *Book of Blessings* provides blessings for multiple occasions in the life of a community and the people in that community. Do you use it? How do you address the special needs of those in your community who are hearing-impaired or physically challenged? How does your community respond to its cultural diversity? Does your liturgy reflect the multicultural dimension of your parish? Is everyone welcome at your Sunday liturgies, including children? Is child care provided for parish functions? How does your community respond to the needs of their poor? How does your parish address the needs of the elderly, the grieving, the infirm, the lonely, the widowed, the divorced, the families, the children, the teens, the singles? Does your physical plant support the ministry of hospitality? Is there truly *life* in your parish life?

Christian Initiation: Perhaps this would be a good time to do apostolic works with the catechumens. What better way to reflect on today's gospel than to go out and bear the cross through performing acts of mercy and hospitality? Are there sick people who need visiting? Is there a soup kitchen where you can help serve dinner? Perhaps in lieu of a catechetical session this week, you might let the catechumens go with you as apprentices in apostolic ministry, then gather to reflect on the experience.

It would certainly be an appropriate occasion to celebrate a rite of acceptance/welcome, or reception into the full communion of the Catholic Church.

DOCTRINAL ISSUES

What church truth/teaching/doctrinal issue could be drawn from the gospel for the Thirteenth Sunday in Ordinary Time?

Participants suggest possible doctrinal themes that flow from the readings.

Possible Doctrinal Themes

Paschal mystery, cross, baptism, discipleship, evangelization, mystery of suffering, death and resurrection, kingdom of God, social teaching of the church, mystery of the church, eucharist

Present the doctrinal material at this time.

1. The facilitator gives input on a particular doctrinal issue of his or her prior choosing. OR

2. The group chooses a doctrinal issue from the list they created. They read together from the Doctrinal Appendix.

(The doctrinal issues are found in the Doctrinal Appendix in the back of this workbook. If you are choosing an issue from this resource, please refer to it now.)

Reflection questions centered around the chosen doctrinal theme can be found at the end of each topic in the Doctrinal Appendix. The questions are based on the five-step reflection process. If you choose a topic not included in the Doctrinal Appendix, craft your own questions according to the same five-step process.

Following the reflection questions you will be reminded to return to chapter 7, "Preparing the Catechetical Session," to assist you in crafting your own session.

Closing Prayer

Lord,
may this sacrifice and communion
give us a share in your life
and help us bring your love to the world.
Grant this through Christ, our Lord.[12]

[12]Thirteenth Sunday in Ordinary Time: "Prayer After Communion," *The Sacramentary*.

Fourteenth Sunday in Ordinary Time

INTRODUCTORY RITES

Opening Song (or Entrance Antiphon)

Within your temple, we ponder your loving kindness O God. As your name, so also your praise reaches to the ends of the earth; your right hand is filled with justice. (Ps 47:10–11)[1]

Opening Prayer

The facilitator of the session may lead the prayer. Others in the group may be asked to proclaim the readings.

Let us pray
[for greater willingness
to serve God and our fellow man]

Pause for silent prayer.

Father,
in the rising of your Son
death gives birth to new life.
The sufferings he endured restored hope
to a fallen world.
Let sin never ensnare us
with empty promises of passing joy.
Make us one with you always,
so that our joy may be holy,
and our love may give life.
We ask this through Christ, our Lord.[2]

LITURGY OF THE WORD

Let us listen to God's word.

The readings are proclaimed.

First Reading
Zechariah 9:9–10

[1]Fourteenth Sunday in Ordinary Time: "Entrance Antiphon," *The Sacramentary.*

[2]Fourteenth Sunday in Ordinary Time: "Alternative Opening Prayer," *The Sacramentary.*

Overview of Zechariah: Scholars suggest that the book of the prophet Zechariah was written over a period of a few centuries by at least two or more authors. Chapters one through eight were probably written following the Babylonian exile. The prophet of this section of the book worked with Haggai in the reconstruction of the southern kingdom, Judah, after the exile around 520 B.C.E. The first section is a word of hope and reassurance to the returning exiles.

It is believed that chapters 9–14 were written by disciples of Zechariah. Thus, the latter portion of the book, often referred to as Deutero-Zechariah, was probably written during the time of Alexander the Great, according to some scholars. The conquest of Alexander brought Persian control of the land to a screeching halt. People were tired of foreign control. Israel was hopeful that their national identity would be restored. Hopes for a messiah had all but vanished. Zechariah took it upon himself to restore that lost vision.

Zechariah preached about the great battle that would take place between the forces of God and the forces of evil. His writing was eschatological and messianic. He urged repentance in order that the broken covenant between God and Israel could be restored.

Today's Pericope: Zechariah promised that a king would come to bring peace and would reign over the whole earth. This king would come riding on the back of a donkey. He would restore peace. Hopes for restoration of the promised Davidic dynasty persisted throughout the years of oppression and destruction. This promised, hoped-for king would be righteous in the eyes of God. He would follow the covenant and live by its precepts. This king-to-come would rule justly and uphold the law of God, and would be meek and humble.

The etymology of the word *meek* comes from the Greek and means "not easily provoked." The Greeks understood meekness to be a balance between extreme anger and the total absence of anger. A meek person is in full control, not acting out of weakness, but out of controlled power. A meek person is receptive to knowledge and to God, whereas those who are arrogant are incapable of learning. Discipleship requires the virtue of meekness. How can someone who does not recognize the need for healing ask God for healing and forgiveness? Jesus' meekness was a sign that he was obedient and open to God's will.

In the preceding verses of Chapter 9, the image of God is that of a warrior who defends the people against enemies. In today's reading, Zechariah announces the coming reign of a peace-bearing king. Rather than the machines of war (chariots and horses), this king of peace will come riding on a donkey, a sign of the reign of peace. This king-to-come is to be meek, just as Moses, the meekest man ever to live, was meek. This king will rely on God's power, not his own. This king of peace will reunite the north and the south. Israel and Judah are to once again be one nation. The rule of this just king is to extend to all nations, including that of the gentiles.

Responsorial Psalm
Psalm 145:1–2, 8–9, 10–11, 13–14

This psalm was probably chosen for the connection between the exhortation to rejoice, in the first reading, and the fulfillment of that rejoicing in the prayer of the psalmist, who promised to extol his God and king.

Second Reading
Romans 8:9, 11–13

(Refer to the First Sunday of Advent for an Overview of Paul's Letter to the Romans.)

It is important to understand Paul's use of the words *flesh* and *spirit.* A common misconception has been to translate "flesh" to mean the body, or carnal nature. However, the word *flesh* (*sarx*) means human nature that is self-centered rather than God-centered. Flesh is human nature born into the human condition and thereby into weakness, a weakness human beings share with Adam. *Flesh* means the innate proclivity toward sin and death.

For Paul, the word *body* means the whole person. The body is subject to sin and death, but it is also subject to redemption in Christ. Paul uses the term *spirit,* on the other hand, to mean human nature that is God-centered rather than self-centered. Even though humanity shares Adam's proclivity toward sin, they are freed from the permanent chains that bind them to Adam's sin. Through faith in the power of Jesus' death and resurrection, we can rise above this natural inclination to sin. We are free to live a new life in the Spirit of God. Since God's Spirit dwells in the heart of believers, they are changed—a new creation. They are empowered for love, service, and mission by the Spirit. We will find our true, authentic selves only if we turn our hearts and faces toward the living, loving God.

Gospel
Matthew 11:25–30

STEP 1
NAMING ONE'S EXPERIENCE

What were your first impressions? What was your first response to the gospel (or the other readings)?[3] What captured your attention?

Each person names his or her initial impression. Statements should be brief. No reasons should be given at this time. All simply listen without agreeing or disagreeing.

STEP 2
UNDERSTANDING

In a brief statement, what do you think this gospel is trying to convey?

STEP 3
INPUT FROM VISION/STORY/TRADITION

Liturgical Context

All the readings today are an exhortation to center our lives in Christ. Today's gospel serves as a

[3]The primary focus of reflection is the gospel. However, very often the other readings demand attention and must be brought into the dialogue.

conclusion to the Apostolic Discourse of the past two Sundays. Enduring the cross and the challenges of the mission is only possible if we anchor our lives in Christ, become like children, and turn our lives completely over to his care.

Our only hope is in Christ. Today's Alternative Opening Prayer asks that we be one with God, so that our joy may be holy and the love we share with others truly life-giving. The gospel tells us how this is possible. We are to be meek as Christ was meek. We are to learn the ways of God and *ponder God's loving kindness* as the Entrance Antiphon exhorts us to do. We are to be humble and rejoice that we are children of God. The entire liturgy is set in a spirit of rejoicing. The Entrance Antiphon is a call to praise, and the Prayer After Communion asks that we never fail to praise God for the salvation that is ours through the eucharist.

Jesus tells the *childlike* that his burden is light and that he will give us rest. We must conclude that living in the reign of God is not as difficult as it might sometimes appear. The ultimate command is to love, and love casts out all fear. Our hope is that God will be with us, strengthen us, and give us what we need. Our responsibility is to love God and extend that love to others. The conclusion to the sequence of the last three weeks ends in a spirit of joy. The disciples' hearts must have burst with joy and trust as they listened to the good news from the mouth of the Master himself.

We strengthen and nourish our childlike trust through our participation in the sacraments, especially the eucharist. Liturgy is the place where we bring the concerns of life. We give thanks and praise to God; we take, bless, break, and share the Body of Christ. Before we come to the table we ask to be delivered from worry and, like the bread and wine, we also are taken, blessed, broken, shared, and poured out for others. The eucharist transforms us and empowers us to be the meek and humble servants that Jesus is speaking of in today's liturgy.

The words of a fourth-century theologian, Ephraem, still echo today:

> Come to me, all of you, and I will refresh you, where there are wondrous gifts, and joy without compare, rest unchanging, happiness without end, unceasing melody, perpetual glory, unwearied giving of thanks, loving absorption in divine things, infinite riches, a kingdom without end, through all ages and ages, deeps of compassion, an ocean of mercy and kindness, which the human tongue cannot describe but makes known only through figures. . . .
>
> Come to me, all you who labor, and shake off and cast from you the burden of your sins. For no one who comes to me remains burdened but casts off the evil way of life and learns of me a new way of life. . . .
>
> Come therefore to me; for whoever comes to me I shall not cast forth. You have heard the perfect hope, the sweet promises, the words of the Savior of our souls. Glory to his goodness! Glory to his loving kindness! Glory to his longanimity! Glory to his care for us, to his tenderness! Glory to his words of pity! Glory to his kingdom! Glory, honor, adoration to his holy name for ever and ever! (*Ephraem, c. 306–373, Syrian theologian and poet*)[4]

Gospel Exegesis

The facilitator gives input regarding what critical biblical scholarship has to say about this text. The input includes insights as to how people would have heard the gospel in Jesus' time.

It is important to situate this gospel in the context out of which it comes. In previous verses, Jesus chided those who refused to believe in him and accused them of lacking meekness. Proud, arrogant, and too self-absorbed, they were unable to recognize the action of God in Jesus' ministry. Jesus commended the childlike who, through their meekness, were able to absorb the mystery of his identity. They were the good and faithful servants, the ones who would make the best disciples.

Both Luke and Matthew relate this gospel. Reginald Fuller refers to it as "the synoptic thunder-

[4] *RF*, 52.

bolt from the Johannine sky."[5] It sounds so unlike the synoptic gospels and so much like John that upon reading it one is immediately compelled to authenticate the source. Is it really a text from Matthew, or is it from the Fourth Gospel? (The discourse about the mutual knowledge of the Father and Son sounds so Johannine.) Reginald Fuller suggests that it is a surviving liturgical fragment that celebrated Jesus Christ as the source of our knowledge about God. "But it is deeply rooted in our Lord's self-understanding, as registered by the word *Abba* for his Father. This betokens a unique relationship, which he invites others to share through his word."[6]

The second portion of this pericope, also a liturgical fragment, is reminiscent of the wisdom literature found in Sirach. In this piece, Jesus speaks the wisdom of God. This reflects the church's earliest theology of Jesus. It also reflects Jesus' own understanding of who he was.

Chapters 11 and 12 of Matthew seek to answer the question: Just who is this man? Matthew's answer? Jesus is the "WISDOM of God, hidden from the proud, but revealed to the little ones."[7] Who accepted Jesus' identity? Verses 25–27 of Chapter 11 remind us that it is the little ones who believe that Jesus is the revelation of the Father. Jesus is the WORD that GOD speaks so believers will come to know who GOD is. Jesus is the mirror of GOD. Jesus is the personification of GOD'S Wisdom.

Matthew's intention is to associate Jesus with the divine wisdom of the Old Testament. It serves an apologetic purpose. Jesus is greater than the Torah, the Prophets, and Wisdom—the major divisions of the Hebrew Scriptures. Jesus is the divine WORD who is greater than the Law and even the Jerusalem Temple. One can only accept in faith the reality of Jesus' identity. It is a mystery, the depths of which take a lifetime to explore. Our faith is to be a childlike faith.

The last section of this gospel concludes with an invitation from Jesus. His invitation is directed to the people who were mocked and negatively referred to as *'am-ha aretz* (the "people of the land") by the Pharisees. They were certainly not the spiritual elite; that title belonged to the Pharisees. Pharisees regarded the spirituality of the *people of the land* as inferior. They were thought to be incapable of following the strict demands of the *halakah*, the oral interpretation of the law. It was a heavy burden for the ordinary folks of Jesus' day to assume, thus they were derided, hated, and cursed.

The rabbis of the day referred to the Torah as a yoke. Jesus invites the people to put down the burden of that yoke (the Pharisaic interpretation of the Torah) and take instead the yoke that Jesus offered. Jesus' interpretation of the law was not burdensome. Jesus himself is the heart of the law. To know Jesus, study about him, and learn from him is to know the law. To know Jesus is to know what it means to be meek. Jesus promised peace and tranquility to those who cast away their burdensome yoke for his easy yoke. Peace, harmony, and rest were believed to be the result of being in right covenant relationship with God. Jesus promised this rest to people who joined their spirit to his.

Proclaim the gospel again.

Sometimes we gain new insights when we hear the text after the interpretation has been given. Someone from the group proclaims the gospel a second time.

STEP 4
TESTING

Conversation with the Liturgy and the Scriptures

Test your original understanding in dialogue with the text.

(You might consider breaking into smaller groups.)

Is there anything in today's gospel or readings that you had not considered before? How does your original understanding of this gospel compare with what we just shared? Were there any new insights for you?

How does this story speak to your life?

[5] *PL*, 142.
[6] Ibid., 143.
[7] *MML*, 57.

Sharing Life Experience

Participants share an experience from their lives that connects with the biblical interpretation just shared.

> *Last week we celebrated a rite of acceptance in which four children stood before our community and committed to embrace the cross of Christ in their life and to live the gospel. One of them, a ninth grader, chose not to go to a state sports final because his Christian journey is just too important to him—he did not want to miss the rite. One might think that middle-schoolers would not possess wisdom enough to realize the implications of the ritual. However, when questioned what they asked of God and God's church, their answers totally removed any liturgical lethargy that might have been present, and prodded even the most sleepy-eyed adult to come to full attention. Their answers revealed more wisdom and meekness than many adults possess in a lifetime. One child asked that God be with him as he faced a lifetime of difficult choices. He reminded our community that growing up is difficult at best, and that he will have to learn to make choices. He asked God to help him discern his choices and make appropriate decisions for his life. He acknowledged that making such choices is a learning process and that he is bound to make mistakes. He asked our community to give him the space to make those mistakes in freedom, to challenge him, but not to judge him too harshly when he does make mistakes. He asked the community to be there for him, to strengthen and support him, and to offer him the same unconditional love that he knows God has for him.*
>
> *I was astounded. Did this child know the Father? Maybe better than most. Did this child understand Jesus' role in his life? I believe so. Did this child challenge our community to be the people of God, thereby the presence of God, in a way it had never been asked to before? Most assuredly. Did this child show me the wisdom of God? Absolutely.*
>
> *Children often are regarded as second-class citizens. They are to be seen and not heard. Glaring eyes often burn holes through frustrated parents who are trying to keep a restless toddler quiet during community worship. Yet we have much to learn from their spirituality. Recently one little four-year-old asked his mommy after a liturgy of the word, "Mommy, what does it mean that Jesus emptied himself? What did he empty himself into?" Seizing the moment, his mother said, "It means he has so much love for you and daddy and mommy, for everyone, that he pours that love right into our hearts."*
>
> *Sometimes we make things more difficult than need be. Sometimes we take ourselves too seriously. Jesus' message is not difficult. His yoke is easy. We are simply to keep our eyes focused on him and prepare ourselves to encounter him in the most unsuspecting ways.*

All share their life experience.

Why did Jesus tell us that mere children will understand the ways of God easier than the wise and learned? What was he trying to tell his community? How does that relate to your community? Was Jesus telling people that they did not have to follow the law? What was behind his exhortation? What are the implications of that for your community today? How does today's liturgy reflect God's promise to be in relationship with us (covenant)? In what way is there an invitation to move from slavery to freedom (exodus)? How does today's liturgy invite us to become a new creation (creation)? In what way is the biblical theme of community expressed in today's readings? What one important insight do you wish to take with you as a result of this sharing today? Do you still feel the same way about this text as when you began? Have you in any way been invited to change an attitude or behavior?

Step 5
Decision

The gospel demands a response.

How might today's liturgy call your community to a particular, concrete action? What is one specific action you will take this week as a response to the liturgy today?

Pastoral Considerations: How are the children in your parish treated, as a general rule? Are they celebrated as equal members of your community? Perhaps today would be a good time to read and reflect upon the document, *Directory of Masses With*

Children, to see ways in which your parish can honor their presence in your community's worship.

Christian Initiation: Just a reminder. There is no such thing as RCIC. There is no separate rite for children; The Rite of Christian Initiation of Adults is for them also. Children of catechetical age are included in the designation *adult.* Thus, in the RCIA, whatever we do with adults, we also do with children (taking age and development into consideration, of course).

DOCTRINAL ISSUES

What church truth/teaching/doctrinal issue could be drawn from the gospel for the Fourteenth Sunday in Ordinary Time?

Participants suggest possible doctrinal themes that flow from the readings.

Possible Doctrinal Themes

Word of God, Trinity, God, Jesus Christ, Holy Spirit, image of God, ministry of the word, prophets, conversion, sin and grace, spirituality, prayer, paschal mystery, discipleship

Present the doctrinal material at this time.

1. The facilitator gives input on a particular doctrinal issue of his or her prior choosing. OR

2. The group chooses a doctrinal issue from the list they created. They read together from the Doctrinal Appendix.

(The doctrinal issues are found in the Doctrinal Appendix in the back of this workbook. If you are choosing an issue from this resource, please refer to it now.)

Reflection questions centered around the chosen doctrinal theme can be found at the end of each topic in the Doctrinal Appendix. The questions are based on the five-step reflection process. If you choose a topic not included in the Doctrinal Appendix, craft your own questions according to the same five-step process.

Following the reflection questions you will be reminded to return to chapter 7, "Preparing the Catechetical Session," to assist you in crafting your own session.

Closing Prayer

Lord,
may we never fail to praise you
for the fullness of life and salvation
you give us in the eucharist.
We ask this through Christ, our Lord.[8]

[8]Fourteenth Sunday in Ordinary Time: "Prayer After Communion," *The Sacramentary.*

Fifteenth Sunday in Ordinary Time

INTRODUCTORY RITES

Opening Song (or Entrance Antiphon)

In my justice I shall see your face, O Lord; when your glory appears, my joy will be full. (Ps 16:15)[1]

Opening Prayer

The facilitator of the session may lead the prayer. Others in the group may be asked to proclaim the readings.

Let us pray
[to be faithful to the light we have received,
to the name we bear]

Pause for silent prayer.

Father,
let the light of your truth
guide us to your kingdom
through a world filled with lights
contrary to your own.
Christian is the name and the gospel we glory in.
May your love make us what you have called us to be.
We ask this through Christ, our Lord.[2]

LITURGY OF THE WORD

Let us listen to God's word.

The readings are proclaimed.

First Reading
Isaiah 55:10–11

(Refer to the First Sunday of Advent for an Overview of the Book of the Prophet Isaiah.)

[1]Fifteenth Sunday in Ordinary Time: "Entrance Antiphon," *The Sacramentary.*

[2]Fifteenth Sunday in Ordinary Time: "Alternative Opening Prayer," *The Sacramentary.*

Isaiah's conclusion to the "Book of Consolations" speaks of that day in which rich fare and flowing water will be lavishly poured on God's people. The word of God again plays a very important sacramental role in this reading. "God's word is the initiator: from it comes salvation."[3] In Isaiah, God's word is not so much a message as it is an event in the mystery of salvation history. God's word is not static, but living; it causes action. God's word will accomplish what God intends. God's word will restore Israel. The world rejoices as God brings Israel home. Sin will be no more in the new Jerusalem. Sin and death will not be invited guests at the eternal banquet; they will be gone forever. The shalom peace of God will reside eternally in God's restored Paradise.

The Hebrew word *dabar* is translated *word,* as well as *deed.* Prophets have spoken the word of God and God has acted in human history. Throughout salvation history both word and deed reveal the heart and the mind of God. The word and actions of God are like the rain and snow that water the earth and provide the necessary moisture for life to continue. Seeds sprout and grain is grown for bread. Water, therefore, causes an effect. God's *dabar* also causes an effect. There is a purpose to God's word going forth on the earth.

Throughout all of chapter 55 of Isaiah, Israel's need for God is depicted by the image of thirst for water and hunger for food. Israel is invited to come, drink, and have their thirst quenched. God is addressing the exiled Israelites. The exiles are the earth and God's word is the water and snow. The thirst of the Israelites will be quenched by God's word. God's word, like water, causes life, is effective, and achieves its purpose. God's word invites a return to covenant living.

Responsorial Psalm
Psalm 65:10, 11, 12–13, 14

Psalm 65, a psalm of thanksgiving, is chosen for its obvious connection to the first reading—water that

[3]*DL* (III), 52.

gives life and seed that bears fruit. The rain in this psalm falls on the hardened soil, causing the seeds to sprout and bear fruit for the harvest. The repeated antiphon is taken from Luke's parable of the sower.

Second Reading
Romans 8:18–23

(Refer to the First Sunday of Advent for an Overview of Paul's Letter to the Romans.)

Paul also hints of harvest when he refers to the first fruit of the Spirit. The Spirit effects the harvest of faith in believers. The Spirit dwells within God's children and intercedes on their behalf when they do not know how to pray, even though they are unaware of it.

Paul reminds us that the suffering of this life is nothing when compared to the joy of the resurrection. Our suffering is joined to the cross of Christ. We share in his suffering, death, and resurrection throughout our life's journey. Since the Spirit of God dwells within us, sin no longer has a hold on us. Conversion to Christ results in the indwelling of the Spirit, the first fruit harvested in our lives. This indwelling is only the beginning. There is so much more that awaits the believer. That is why the present suffering pales when we consider the incredible joy that awaits us when our bodies are resurrected with Christ and we share in his glory in the next age. All creation will share in this glory. Paul, prophet of hope, encourages the eager expectation of the glory that is to come, and will not fail to come.

Gospel
Matthew 13:1–23

STEP 1
NAMING ONE'S EXPERIENCE

What were your first impressions? What was your first response to the gospel (or the other readings)?[4] What captured your attention?

Each person names his or her initial impression. Statements should be brief. No reasons should be given at this time. All simply listen without agreeing or disagreeing.

STEP 2
UNDERSTANDING

In a brief statement, what do you think this gospel is trying to convey? What understanding of this parable did you bring with you to this conversation?

STEP 3
INPUT FROM VISION/STORY/TRADITION

Liturgical Context

The Fifteenth through the Seventeenth Sundays form a definitive, recognizable unity. The parables of chapter 13 are known as the "Discourse Parables." All of chapter 13 is read on these three Sundays. The first reading of each of the three Sundays prepares us for the gospel. Today's first reading proclaims the effectiveness of God's word. The gospel describes the conditions necessary for the word to take root in those who want to be disciples.

Both of the opening prayers for today's liturgy proclaim the efficacy of the gospel in our lives. The Opening Prayer reflects the heart of today's gospel. We ask that the gospel guide us to truth and lead us to Christ. We also ask for the light of truth so we might reject all that is opposed to the teaching of the gospel. The Alternative Opening Prayer asks that the light of God's truth will lead us all to God's reign in our lives, especially in the midst of a world that is so contrary to what the gospel teaches. The word of God is our stronghold and we are to glory in it.

Christ's word is powerful and effective. It continues to be effective in the church through the living of, and the proclamation of, the gospel of Christ. The church asserts the effectiveness of God's word in the life of the community. The *Constitution on the Sacred Liturgy* reminds us that Jesus

[4]The primary focus of reflection is the gospel. However, very often the other readings demand attention and must be brought into the dialogue.

is truly present in the proclamation of the word in the liturgy (CS, #7). "The Church loves sacred scripture and is anxious to deepen its understanding of the truth and to nourish its own life by studying these sacred writings. The Second Vatican Council likened the bible to a fountain of renewal within the community of God's people. . . ."[5] Through the liturgy of the word, "God speaks to his people, revealing the mystery of their redemption and salvation and offering them spiritual nourishment. Through his word, Christ himself is present in the assembly of his people."[6] Pope Paul VI reflects the hopes for the efficacy of God's word in the lives of worshipers in the following exhortation:

> The revision of the Lectionary is indeed a wise directive, aimed at developing among the faithful an ever-increasing hunger for God's word, the word which leads the people of the new covenant to the perfect unity of the Church under the guidance of the Holy Spirit. We are fully confident that priests and the faithful alike will prepare their hearts together more earnestly for the Lord's Supper, meditating more thoughtfully on sacred scripture, nourishing themselves daily with the words of the Lord. The fulfillment of the wishes of the Second Vatican Council will be the inevitable consequence of this experience of God's word: sacred scripture will become a perpetual source of spiritual life, an important instrument for, and the center of all theological formation.[7]

Gospel Exegesis

The facilitator gives input regarding what critical biblical scholarship has to say about this text. The input includes insights as to how people would have heard the gospel in Jesus' time.

Jesus sat in the boat to teach the disciples. In Matthew's gospel Jesus frequently taught sitting down. Sitting was the official teaching posture for rabbinic Judaism. Matthew's intention was to announce to Israel the teaching authority of Jesus.

The parable of the sower is the first of Jesus' parables in Matthew's gospel. It is a simple parable, drawn from the agricultural milieu of the ordinary people of Jesus' early Galilean community. Many of the people in his audience were probably Galilean farmers. As in all parables, there is a hook intended to catch the attention of the listener. The hook is found in the ridiculous way the farmer planted his seeds. No one, of course, would plant seeds on rocky soil or amidst the weeds if they expected the seeds to sprout.

As the parable develops, the sower is a minor player. The star of this one-act play is the seed and its ability to do what it was intended to do. Jesus describes the path of the seed after it was thrown by the sower. The listener's attention is drawn to the condition of the soil. Obviously the seed planted in the thorny and rocky soil did not bear fruit—no surprise there. The surprise comes when the farmers hear how *large* the harvest was for the seed that fell on the good soil. They would have been pleased with a tenfold harvest, but *this* seed produced three to ten times as much as the farmers would have expected a good crop to produce.

The seed is the good news of God's reign. This is the heart of Jesus' preaching mission—God's reign has finally arrived. Matthew's repeated reference to Jesus' word is intended to stress his teaching mission and its extension to the disciples. The soil represents the interior receptivity of those who hear the message. They will either hear and accept or hear and reject. Many who heard Jesus did not accept his message or his mission. The tension between the Christians of Matthew's community and the Jewish community is clear evidence of the rejection of Jesus' teaching.

Later the disciples approach Jesus and ask him why he teaches in parables. Jesus interprets the parable for them because they believe in him and thus have the ears to hear and the eyes to see—they are able to understand, and will be further enlightened. Parables are not difficult unless the heart is already stony and unreceptive. Jesus does not speak in parables to trick people or to keep

[5] *Lectionary for Mass:* "Introduction," #1.

[6] *GIRM,* #33.

[7] Pope Paul VI, Apostolic Constitution on the Roman Missal, April 3, 1969: *AAS* 61 (1969), 220–221.

them from understanding—those who reject his word *already do not understand.* "The separation between those who do and do not understand has therefore occurred before Jesus speaks in parables.... Obduracy is therefore assumed to be a prior condition in the people, and they are culpable for it (13:13–15). They have closed their eyes, shut their ears, and refused to repent (11:20–24; 12:41); as a consequence, they get only parables, which reinforce their blindness and deafness."[8]

Jesus' works were not hidden; yet Israel did not believe. Even Jesus' family and friends were embarrassed. The parables of this chapter seek to shed light on the reason for this failure of the people to understand. Partly at fault are the Pharisees, who thwart the Spirit's work. Other reasons for the failure of the seed of God's word to take root are the lack of spiritual insight, Satan's interference, lack of endurance in the midst of persecution, the everyday worries of life, and the enticement of wealth. "In other words, the reason for the failure of the seed is the lamentable spiritual state of the hearer's heart."[9]

Today's gospel describes the purpose of the parables and the various responses of those who hear Jesus' message. According to David Garland, in Jewish literature sowing was a metaphor for God's work. The renewal of Israel will begin when God begins sowing. Sowing in this parable alerts the listener that the new Israel has been planted and the final age inaugurated. "The sower is the Lord of the harvest."[10]

When Matthew's Jesus cites the passage from Isaiah, he assures the reader that rejection of his mission is part of God's plan. Last Sunday's gospel seems to imply that God purposefully keeps the mysteries of the kingdom hidden from some people. Scholars suggest that this is intended to stress God's election—the intention of God to choose who God wills to choose.

The disciples, then, are truly blessed to see, hear, and believe what has been revealed to them.

[8]*RM*, 147.

[9]Ibid.

[10]Ibid., 146.

Those who accept Jesus and his teaching are greater than all the prophets before them. They will go out and bring others into the reign of God. They will be the new harvesters.

Proclaim the gospel again.

Sometimes we gain new insights when we hear the text after the interpretation has been given. Someone from the group proclaims the gospel a second time.

Step 4
Testing

Conversation with the Liturgy and the Scriptures

Test your original understanding in dialogue with the text.

(You might consider breaking into smaller groups.)

How does your original understanding of this gospel compare with what we just shared? Were there any new insights for you?

How does this story speak to your life?

Sharing Life Experience

Participants share an experience from their lives that connects with the biblical interpretation just shared.

> *Today's gospel reminds me how easy it is to be closed to the mind and heart of God, and to miss the action of God that is right under my nose. I can sit in aloof arrogance and think I know what God is doing, when in fact, I don't. Someone I know was in the midst of a very difficult time. It was plain to me that one definite course of action was indicated, yet this person was convinced that God was doing something altogether different from that, and remained steadfast. In my stupidity, I believed that to be ill-advised. I was wrong. Patient endurance and yielding to God brought about a surprising harvest that is still being reaped today. This person had ears that could hear and eyes that could see what God was doing, in spite of what seemed to be evidence to the contrary.*

On a more communal level, this gospel is a strong word to communities today that are torn by strife and polarized by ideologies (no matter how noble or truth-filled they appear to be). Those on both sides of a dispute sometimes believe they have the mind and heart of God neatly wrapped, sewed up, and stored in a box to be carefully guarded as their exclusive possession. The message in today's gospel is to look into our hearts. Where there is hatred, animosity, rancor, and divisive bitterness, the Spirit cannot work. Where there is an openness to come together in a spirit of mutuality, there is fertile soil for the planting of seed so that eventually benefits will be reaped from allowing the Spirit to reveal the mind, heart, and purpose of God. For me personally, and for communities at large, I believe that today's gospel is a call to fertilize the soil of our hearts. How receptive are our hearts to receiving the good seed?

All share their life experience.

What was Jesus' primary concern in today's gospel? How is it still a relevant word for your community today? Where do you see evidence of rocky, thorny soil in your community, and where do you see good soil? Is there a time in your parish life when you were aware that seed fell on poor ground? On good ground? How are the biblical themes of covenant, exodus, creation, and community expressed in today's liturgy? In what way does this gospel invite transformation in your community? In you? What difference does it make? Do you still feel the same way about this text as when you began? Has your original understanding been stretched, challenged, or affirmed?

Step 5
Decision

The gospel demands a response.

What one specific action might your community take in response to today's liturgy? Has this conversation with the exegesis changed or stretched your personal attitudes or behaviors? What is one concrete action you will take this week as a response to the liturgy today?

Pastoral Considerations: Reflection on the condition of the soil in your community would be a worthwhile endeavor. Where are there areas of rocky soil? Where is there blindness and deafness that keeps your community from recognizing the action of God?

DOCTRINAL ISSUES

What church truth/teaching/doctrinal issue could be drawn from the gospel for the Fifteenth Sunday in Ordinary Time?

Participants suggest possible doctrinal themes that flow from the readings.

Possible Doctrinal Themes

Word of God/scripture, discernment, prayer, reign of God, conversion, discipleship, Holy Spirit, Jesus Christ, paschal mystery, evangelization, will of God

Present the doctrinal material at this time.

1. The facilitator gives input on a particular doctrinal issue of his or her prior choosing. OR

2. The group chooses a doctrinal issue from the list they created. They read together from the Doctrinal Appendix.

(The doctrinal issues are found in the Doctrinal Appendix in the back of this workbook. If you are choosing an issue from this resource, please refer to it now.)

Reflection questions centered around the chosen doctrinal theme can be found at the end of each topic in the Doctrinal Appendix. The questions are based on the five-step reflection process. If you choose a topic not included in the Doctrinal Appendix, craft your own questions according to the same five-step process.

Following the reflection questions you will be reminded to return to chapter 7, "Preparing the Catechetical Session," to assist you in crafting your own session.

Closing Prayer

God our Father,
your light of truth
guides us to the way of Christ.
May all who follow him
reject what is contrary to the gospel.
We ask this through our Lord
Jesus Christ, your Son,
who lives and reigns with you and the Holy Spirit,
one God for ever and ever.[11]

[11]Fifteenth Sunday in Ordinary Time: "Opening Prayer," *The Sacramentary.*

7/20/14

Sixteenth Sunday in Ordinary Time

INTRODUCTORY RITES

Opening Song (or Entrance Antiphon)

God himself is my help. The Lord upholds my life. I will offer you a willing sacrifice; I will praise your name, O Lord, for its goodness. (Ps 53:6, 8)[1]

Opening Prayer

The facilitator of the session may lead the prayer. Others in the group may be asked to proclaim the readings.

Let us pray
[to be kept faithful in the service of God]

Pause for silent prayer.

Lord,
be merciful to your people.
Fill us with your gifts
and make us always eager to serve you
in faith, hope, and love.
Grant this through our Lord,
Jesus Christ, your Son,
who lives and reigns with you and
the Holy Spirit,
one God, for ever and ever.[2]

LITURGY OF THE WORD

Let us listen to God's word.

The readings are proclaimed.

First Reading
Wisdom 12:13, 16–19

Overview of the Book of Wisdom: "The book of Wisdom is known only in Greek and may be the last book of the Old Testament to be written."[3] The book draws upon philosophical material of Philo of Alexandria and other Jewish authors living in the Hellenized city of Alexandria in the first century before Jesus was born. It employs the oratorical techniques of the period. The following overview is based on the work of Lawrence Boadt in his book *Reading the Old Testament.* He divides the book into four sections. First, chapter 1:1 through chapter 6:21, in which the wisdom and justice of God afford victory and immortality to the righteous. Second, chapter 6:22 through chapter 11:1, which includes Solomon's praise of wisdom as something that is beyond compare. Third, chapter 11:2 through chapter 19:5, which reviews salvation history up to the exodus to show that God was always merciful to Israel. Fourth, chapters 19:6 and remaining conclude with a psalm praising wisdom.[4]

The first ten chapters extol the wisdom in creation as coming from God. God gifted Israel with God's revelation. God punishes sinners and rewards the righteous. The book is intended to encourage believers living in Egypt that they are to hold fast to their faith in spite of the pressures and temptations inherent in living in a pagan land. The book reminds the reader of God's benevolence during the exodus and stresses the idiocy of choosing pagan idols over the law.

There are two prominent themes in the Book of Wisdom that are noteworthy: salvation history is the lens through which one learns wisdom, and the immortality of the soul is the just reward for those who live the righteous life. The Book of Wisdom reveals the struggle of people who try to preserve the values of their tradition in the midst of competing philosophical and contemporary pressures.

Even though the law and prophets were given more attention than the books of wisdom, the wisdom tradition endured far longer and was the heart of Jewish life. The prophets Amos, Hosea,

[1]Sixteenth Sunday in Ordinary Time: "Entrance Antiphon," *The Sacramentary.*

[2]Sixteenth Sunday in Ordinary Time: "Opening Prayer," *The Sacramentary.*

[3]*ROT,* 488.

[4]Ibid.

Isaiah, and Jeremiah, drew heavily on the wisdom tradition in their preaching. The wisdom tradition borrowed insight from other cultural and philosophical systems and applied it to Jewish teaching.

Roland Murphy asserts that the wisdom sages were "relentless in pressing home their insights into life: the rewards of justice, the value of diligence and self-control, and so forth. It is said that they were in pursuit of the order that governed the world, but it can be equally maintained that they pressed against the mysteries of creation."[5]

Today's Pericope: Today's reading is a proclamation praising God's mercy that is based on God's love and God's power. The setting for the discussion is the second plague sent upon Egypt during the Exodus. The Egyptians themselves are named beneficiaries of God's mercy, even though they are the oppressors of Israel. God's mercy rains down on all. Egypt certainly deserved God's wrath, but God chose instead to offer mercy and a chance to repent and relent.

God is just and righteous, and because God is all powerful, God is in a position to offer leniency toward all people. God's power is multi-dimensional. It is compassionate, fair, lenient, patient, as well as wrath-filled. God's wrath is shown when people doubt God's power. God does not tolerate arrogance in the face of God's benevolent might.

Therefore, God was fair when God punished Egypt for its aggression, idolatry, and inhumanity. Israel was to learn that righteousness and covenant living demand the extension of love and compassion to others. If God was patient with Egypt, how much more will God be patient with the transgressions of Israel.

Responsorial Psalm
Psalm 86:5–6, 9–10, 15–16

This is a psalm of individual lament. It nevertheless portrays incredible trust in God's benevolence and fidelity. Trials and tribulations do not seem to have shaken the confidence of the psalmist. This psalm continues the theme of God's mercy and patient forbearance found in the first reading.

[5]*CPDBT,* 1085.

Second Reading
Romans 8:26–27

(Refer to the First Sunday of Advent for an Overview of Paul's Letter to the Romans.)

Today's reading from Romans is a continuation of Paul's message from last week. Today Paul tells us that the indwelling Spirit, the first fruit of the redemption won for us by Jesus Christ, now groans within each of us to bring us to the fullness of life in God. The Spirit helps us in our powerlessness before God. In the midst of suffering and pain, the Spirit upholds us. The Spirit prays for us, supports and helps us through this life's travails. The Spirit of God joins with the human spirit to do what the human person cannot do on his or her own power. When we are powerless even to pray, the Spirit prays for us. The Spirit intercedes on our behalf.

The Spirit knows our hearts better than we know them. The Spirit searches our depths and sighs and groans deep within our spirits. Paul reminds the Romans that God's love and fidelity are not to be discounted or surpassed. God has gifted each of us with Godself—the Holy Spirit who lives within us and beckons us to encounter the living, loving God.

Gospel
Matthew 13:24–43

Step 1
Naming One's Experience

What were your first impressions? What was your first response to the gospel (or the other readings)?[6] What captured your attention?

Each person names his or her initial impression. Statements should be brief. No reasons should be given at this time. All simply listen without agreeing or disagreeing.

[6]The primary focus of reflection is the gospel. However, very often the other readings demand attention and must be brought into the dialogue.

Step 2
Understanding

In a brief statement, what do you think this gospel is trying to convey?

Step 3
Input from Vision/Story/Tradition

Liturgical Context

Today's gospel is the second in a unified series called the "Discourse Parables," found in chapter 13 of Matthew's gospel and proclaimed on the Fifteenth, Sixteenth, and Seventeenth Sundays in Ordinary Time. The intention of the parables is to proclaim the reign of God. Scholars suggest that rather than refer to the *kingdom of God,* we call it instead the *reign of God.* Kingdom refers to a place where someone lives. Reign as it is described in the parables suggests *a way to live.*

Today's parable follows upon last week's parable of the sower. Good seed was sown by the farmer, but when everyone in the house was asleep and unaware, someone came and put weeds in the midst of the good seed. The farmer knew that judging the good wheat from the weeds was a task that could only be accomplished at the end of the harvest.

Both secular and religious history remind us how the validity of a person's (or a people's) convictions and beliefs can be wrongly judged, or condemned. The Jewish people have repeatedly been recipients of such judgment, beginning with their exile from Rome in 49–50 C.E. up to and including their genocide in twentieth-century Nazi Germany. The Inquisition is testimony to the cruelty that can be imposed when human beings attempt to do the work of God in judging others. Religious intolerance is rampant, even in today's culture.

Intolerance, like bad leaven that destroys an entire batch of dough, is a culprit that can lead to oppression, persecution, slavery, genocide, torture, and war. It is the window through which humanity's propensity for cruelty can observe its origin.

Today's liturgy is a word for the contemporary church. Intolerance is no less rampant today than in centuries past. Breaking the cycle of intolerance begins in our own homes, parishes, and civic communities. From there it extends globally. Intolerance begins with elitism—the arrogance of some people to assume that they are better than others. While not the only message in today's gospel, it is an important one, one that is worthy of our reflection.

Jesus reached out to the outcasts and untouchables of his day. The arrogant Pharisees judged the sinfulness of the outcasts to be worse than their own self-righteous lack of charity. Jesus was reminding them that such judgment is the prerogative of God.

If we wonder why God allows the weeds to continue to flourish in the midst of the good seed, we must turn our attention to God's incredible patience. The same patience God offers evildoers is available to everyone. We will all be judged, but we are also all beneficiaries of God's marvelous mercy and patience. St. Augustine offers us a sober reflection:

> If we ask that the criminal go unpunished, it is not because crime pleases us, but because, considering the person, we detest in him the crime or the vice. The more vice displeases us, the more we desire the guilty one may not die before mending his ways. It is easy—and it is even a natural tendency—to hate evil persons because they are evil. But it is good—although rare—to love them because they are human, so that we at once blame the sin and show compassion for human nature in the same person. Without any doubt, many, to their loss, take advantage of this divine indulgence and kindness. . . . Because the evildoers persevere in their misdeeds, will God not persevere in his patience?[7]

Every liturgy acknowledges our powerlessness before God and our need for God's mercy. Today's

[7]St. Augustine (354–430), *Lettres,* 153 (1:3–2:4), in Migne, ed. *Patrologie latine* 33, cols. 654–655, *DL* (IV), 134–135.

reign of God

Opening Prayer asks that we be kept faithful to God's service and that God continue to show us his mercy. If we live the virtues of faith, hope, and love that we seek in the Opening Prayer, we will not be judged harshly when the separation of the good seed from the weeds occurs at the last judgment. The designated psalm for the Communion Antiphon extols the love and compassion of God and reminds us that God takes care of the faithful. Today's liturgy is a call to keep our eyes on God, to trust, and to live our lives according to God's plan for the world. In the Prayer After Communion we ask to be given a new purpose and new life in Christ. Even though we cannot always see what God is accomplishing in and through us, the eucharist sustains our hope and strengthens us to live the life Jesus exhorts us to live in today's gospel.

Gospel Exegesis

The facilitator gives input regarding what critical biblical scholarship has to say about this text. The input includes insights as to how people would have heard the gospel in Jesus' time.

Matthew provides seven parables in the third discourse. Today's gospel presents three of them. Jesus tells the disciples that the parables are intended to announce the arrival of God's reign. The parables of Jesus were based on the lived experience of his particular listener. He used what was familiar to them to teach them something new about God and about God's reign. Parables are stories. We all know how stories have the power to captivate and transport us into the situation and reality of the story. Jesus uses a story to catch his audience and invite them to see things in a new, transformed light. Jesus invited his listeners to learn for themselves. He did not impose his teaching. He offered them the opportunity to hear the message, struggle with it, and then embrace it as their own. Those who are unwilling to be challenged and enlightened fail to see the point of his parables.

The parable of the wheat and the weeds is told in the context of Jesus' trouble with the Pharisees. They were criticizing him for his ministry to and association with sinners. Pharisees would never have had contact with lowly characters they considered to be unclean and unsaved. Jesus reaches out to sinners and reveals God's loving reign. Today's parables challenge those who would consider themselves elite or better than others. They remind us that the world is made up of saints and sinners and that we all reside at the same banquet table. Judgment at the end of the world belongs only to God. There is time in the interim to mend one's ways, to repent, and to live as a child of God. Jesus is quite clear that in God's reign no one is better than anyone else and self-righteous behavior will not be tolerated. God will decide who is worthy of eternal life at the last judgment.

The parable of the weeds also served to remind Matthew's community that it was not their responsibility to play God and thereby pick and choose who would be in and who would be out. The community was to be diligent in preaching the word and to bear patiently with one another until Christ's return in glory.

In the parable, the sower of the good seed is the Son of Man and the field is the world. The good seed are those who live in God's reign; the weeds are those who reject God; and the enemy is Satan who works while everyone is sleeping. The weeds are all those who cause others to fall and stumble. They will be judged by God at the end and God will separate those who are evil from those who are good. Those who reject God obviously will not respond to Jesus. The evil ones still have a chance to repent, however, as their judgment will come only at the end. It is not the job of the just to weed out the unjust.

The point of the parable of the mustard seed has to do with insignificant beginnings. The mustard seed grows into an immense, eight-to-ten-foot shrub. The humble beginnings of the establishment of Jesus' kingdom will grow. The small seed will grow into a mighty shrub. God will transform Jesus' ministry. It will grow to immense proportions from its insignificant beginnings. Great things grow from small, insignificant origins. No one can see into the future or possibly imagine the ramifications of Jesus' ministry. Its beginnings may have been small, but wait and see what God can and will do!

There is also an inherent exaggeration in this parable that is worthy of our interest. The mustard shrub, while not small, certainly does not tower to heaven as the birds perch in its branches. There is more going on here. The mustard plant is a fast-growing annual that is beneficial for one's health, but it can also quickly grow out of control like a weed. The Jewish listeners of this parable would have instantly been reminded of the great cedars whose branches do tower to heaven and serve as the nesting place for birds. Scripture and tradition would have conditioned them to think in terms of pagans who were brought into the refuge and protection of a triumphant Israel.[8] They would have considered the tree image to be like the cedars of the Hebrew Scriptures. The cedar was symbolic of the dominion comprising all the nations of the world, and symbolic of the hope that Israel would one day return to the status of powerful nation. The mustard tree certainly does not suggest such a grand image. What, then, is Jesus saying?

The reign of God is crashing into the world—but not in the way Israel expected. According to David Garland, the reign Jesus proclaimed was disarming and disenchanting. "We do not sing, 'A mighty mustard bush is our God.'"[9] The kingdom is not an ostentatious realm of imperial power; it is a small venture of committed, faith-filled people living the word and promoting the gospel by word and deed. "The incongruity between glorious expectations about what the kingdom should be like and its unassuming manifestation before the end is a cause of stumbling for many in Israel."[10]

The parable about the yeast was a shocking image for the listeners of Jesus' day. The leaven was considered a symbol of corruption in the scriptures. Leaven, if not properly handled in making dough, not only poisons the batch, but affects future batches as well. Thus, leaven was understood as a symbol of evil's ability to infect and spread.

To the naysayers, Jesus' ministry to sinners was a corrupting force. The religious leaders could not abide him upsetting the religious status quo. Jesus' ministry of preaching and healing had the power within itself to affect whatever it touched. Like leaven, the reign he came to establish grew into something brand new, while not losing its ties with the old.

The amount of dough mentioned in the parable is also significant. The dough is plentiful enough to provide for the needs of a large banquet. The reign of God is like a festive banquet. The leaven may be "hidden" to those who refuse to believe, but its effects are not hidden. In due time they will become obvious.

Proclaim the gospel again.

Sometimes we gain new insights when we hear the text after the interpretation has been given. Someone from the group proclaims the gospel a second time.

STEP 4
TESTING

Conversation with the Liturgy and the Scriptures

Test your original understanding in dialogue with the text.

(You might consider breaking into smaller groups.)

Was there anything in these parables you had not considered before? How does your original understanding of this gospel compare with what we just shared? Were there any new insights for you? How does this story speak to your life?

Sharing Life Experience

Participants share an experience from their lives that connects with the biblical interpretation just shared.

> *Today's gospel invites me not to get discouraged when things seem to be not what I expected. I am also reminded that God can multiply our very small efforts. One need only look at the spread of Christianity to see that God will accomplish what God intends. The gospel also reminds me that I am not to judge others. I must allow God to do God's work. My job, our job, is to love and offer Jesus' compassion.*
>
> *There is so much judging going on in our communities today. The "unworthy poor" are judged, those who are inactive in our parishes are judged, those*

[8] *RM,* 149.
[9] Ibid., 150
[10] Ibid.

who are very active are judged, those with minimal faith are judged, those with over-zealous faith are judged, those who question the church are judged, those who stand by the church are judged. I was once accused of "not being spiritual enough" because I did not participate in a certain group in a parish where I was working. Intolerance of one another kills our unity. It was the unity of those early communities that made the very small beginnings of the church blossom. "See how they love one another." We are a diverse church. Only God knows where the weeds really are. Our job is to keep our eyes on Christ and offer his ministry of compassion even to those we think are "sinners"—to the outcasts, the untouchables, and those we find it difficult to tolerate.

All share their life experience.

What was Jesus trying to teach his community? How is it relevant for your community today? In what way does today's liturgy reflect God's promise to be in relationship with us (covenant)? How does this liturgy invite transformation, movement from bondage to freedom (exodus)? How does this liturgy express our need for re-creation? How does the gospel reflect the biblical image of the people of God (community)? How do these images speak to your life? Do you still feel the same way about this text as when you began? Has your original understanding been stretched, challenged, or affirmed? Have you experienced any transformation in your attitudes or behavior as a result of this liturgy?

STEP 5
DECISION

The gospel demands a response.

In what specific ways is your parish invited to respond to today's liturgy? What one concrete action will you take this week as a response to the liturgy today?

DOCTRINAL ISSUES

What church truth/teaching/doctrinal issue could be drawn from the gospel for the Sixteenth Sunday in Ordinary Time?

Participants suggest possible doctrinal themes that flow from the readings.

Possible Doctrinal Themes

Reign of God, mystery of the church, repentance, social justice, Holy Spirit, evangelization, ecumenism, social sin, parables, conversion

Present the doctrinal material at this time.

1. The facilitator gives input on a particular doctrinal issue of his or her prior choosing. OR

2. The group chooses a doctrinal issue from the list they created. They read together from the Doctrinal Appendix.

(The doctrinal issues are found in the Doctrinal Appendix in the back of this workbook. If you are choosing an issue from this resource, please refer to it now.)

Reflection questions centered around the chosen doctrinal theme can be found at the end of each topic in the Doctrinal Appendix. The questions are based on the five-step reflection process. If you choose a topic not included in the Doctrinal Appendix, craft your own questions according to the same five-step process.

Following the reflection questions you will be reminded to return to chapter 7, "Preparing the Catechetical Session," to assist you in crafting your own session.

Closing Prayer

Father,
let the gift of your life
continue to grow in us,
drawing us from death to faith, hope and love.
Keep us alive in Christ Jesus.
Keep us watchful in prayer
and true to his teaching
till your glory is revealed in us.
Grant this through Christ, our Lord.[11]

---

[11]Sixteenth Sunday in Ordinary Time: "Alternative Opening Prayer," *The Sacramentary.*

Seventeenth Sunday in Ordinary Time

INTRODUCTORY RITES

Opening Song (or Entrance Antiphon)

God is in his holy dwelling; he will give a home to the lonely, he gives power and strength to his people. (Ps 67:6–7, 36)[1]

Opening Prayer

The facilitator of the session may lead the prayer. Others in the group may be asked to proclaim the readings.

Let us pray
[that we will make good use of the gifts that God has given us]

Pause for silent prayer.

God our Father and protector,
without you nothing is holy,
nothing has value.
Guide us to everlasting life
by helping us to use wisely
the blessings you have given to the world.
We ask this through our Lord
Jesus Christ, your Son,
who lives and reigns with you and the Holy
Spirit,
one God for ever and ever.[2]

LITURGY OF THE WORD

Let us listen to God's word.

The readings are proclaimed.

First Reading
1 Kings 3:5, 7–12

(Refer to the Thirteenth Sunday in Ordinary Time for an Overview of the Book of Kings.)

Today's Pericope: Today's reading is taken from a section of Kings in which Solomon's wisdom is described and praised. In the Bible, Solomon was considered an ideal king. He was a leader, a builder, and a merchant. Today's reading shows us how he acquired wisdom, the gift for which he was most noted. When God appeared to Solomon in a dream, he asked God for wisdom above any other gift. He sought wisdom before riches, and even before a long life. We are to conclude that wisdom is the greatest treasure to be pursued—above any other gift. A wise, attentive heart is the result of meditation on God's law, and on the mind, heart, and will of God. Such meditation brings confidence and the security that comes from living according to God's revelation. Solomon asked for divine wisdom because he was aware of his own weakness before God. Such humility is pleasing to God.

Responsorial Psalm
Psalm 119:57, 72, 76–77, 127–128, 129–130

Second Reading
Romans 8:28–30

(Refer to the First Sunday of Advent for an Overview of Paul's Letter to the Romans.)

Today's Pericope: In the past Sundays we have been listening to Paul's teachings about the mystery of suffering and about the transitory nature of earthly matters. Paul continues to remind us that the hope we share is that our suffering will not end in defeat, but in transformation and vindication.

Today we move from the dark portrait of the human condition and concentrate instead on a hymn that exalts the glory and redemption that await the just in Christ. It is not simply a figure of speech or a pious platitude to say that all will be well in the end. Christians can be confident in the election of God and the knowledge that God called them and justified them through the saving

[1]Seventeenth Sunday in Ordinary Time: "Entrance Antiphon," *The Sacramentary.*

[2]Seventeenth Sunday in Ordinary Time: "Opening Prayer," *The Sacramentary.*

death of Jesus. Christians are to be glorified not only in the next life, but share in that glory in the here and now. They are already living the life of Christ.

Paul reminds us that we are made in God's image. God created men and women in God's image. God saw that it was good. Human beings are elevated to divine status because they are conformed to Christ. They are "in the image of the image." Human beings are brothers and sisters of Christ, which makes them heir to glory—not only in the next life, but even in the midst of the troubles of this life.

Gospel
Matthew 13:44–52

STEP 1
NAMING ONE'S EXPERIENCE

What were your first impressions? What was your first response to the gospel (or the other readings)?[3] What captured your attention?

Each person names his or her initial impression. Statements should be brief. No reasons should be given at this time. All simply listen without agreeing or disagreeing.

STEP 2
UNDERSTANDING

In a brief statement, what do you think this gospel is trying to convey?

STEP 3
INPUT FROM VISION/STORY/TRADITION

Liturgical Context

Today's gospel wraps up the proclamation of the Parable Discourse, in chapter 13 of Matthew's gospel, that we have celebrated for the past three weeks. Today's liturgy reminds us that seeking, living, and working in the reign of God are the most important treasures we can seek. The truly wise person will seek the reign of God above all else, realizing its inestimable value. Jesus reminds us that whether it accidentally comes our way, or we go after it with a vengeance, once we have it we are to move heaven and earth to keep it.

The ritual prayers of the liturgy support Jesus' exhortation today. The Opening Prayer asks that we be good stewards of the gifts that God has given us. We are to remember that without God nothing has any value for our lives. We ask God to guide us to our ultimate destination and to help us (as he helped Solomon) wisely use the gifts that have been given to us in service of God's reign. The Alternative Opening Prayer picks up a consonant theme in that it asks God to help us cherish the gifts (kingdom) that have been given to us. We ask to be given the wisdom to see the reign of God as a pearl of great price. The prayer takes it a step further, however, and asks for the strength and the grace to extend what we have been given to others. Always the liturgy reminds us of the ethical imperatives of the gospel. It is not a "Jesus and me" affair. Our faith is rooted in living in community and responding to the needs of a broken world. The Entrance Antiphon sets the tone and reminds us of all we need to know. God is in his holy dwelling. That dwelling is the reign of God, here and now, and not yet. God always reaches out to the lonely—to anyone in need of compassion. God strengthens us so that we may also comfort the lonely. The reign of God, the pearl of great price, cannot be hoarded. It must be shared. This is the bottom line of today's liturgy, the response in faith to every liturgy.

"Eucharist commits us to the poor," affirms the Catholic Catechism (1397). Eucharist empowers us to live in God's reign as God would have us live. Thus, there is always a commitment and a responsibility.

> Is the way of justice and love so smooth? Certainly the image of the reign of God as a banquet is often tried and tested, purified even, when we see hatred and injustice living side by side with those who cele-

[3]The primary focus of reflection is the gospel. However, very often the other readings demand attention and must be brought into the dialogue.

brate liturgy every Sunday and claim to be disciples of Jesus Christ. Perceptive people grow disillusioned by institutional violence and benign indifference. At that moment one must be just with one's own consciousness and one's own conscience. It is then that one learns the meaning of honesty and truth, that one learns how to respond to the presence of God's Spirit in the human heart calling for a deeper entry into the paschal mystery of Jesus Christ in order to share in the transformation of the world. The meaning of the banquet is transposed to a level where hope for the future becomes the great source of nourishment that one offers to others.[4]

Gospel Exegesis

The facilitator gives input regarding what critical biblical scholarship has to say about this text. The input includes insights as to how people would have heard the gospel in Jesus' time.

Today's gospel picks up last week's theme. We are reminded that the reign of God is a treasured possession and that when we find it we should do everything to keep it. Matthew takes the gospel tradition as it was handed down to him ("what is old") and applies it to the situation in his community. He interpreted Jesus' life and work for the needs of his church. The church today continues this tradition of interpretation in its preaching ministry. The old tradition, the gospel, is made relevant for a contemporary listening audience. This is done by expressing the centuries-old text in a way that is more applicable to current life situations. The evangelist in Matthew did the same thing. He redacted the text to fit the needs of his community.

While interesting to note, the evangelical needs of Matthew's community are not our only concern. Our task is also to discover the gospel's intention. The first reading reminds us that today's liturgy is an exhortation to seek after what is really important in this life. For Solomon it was wisdom. If we possessed the wisdom of Solomon, we would realize that Christians must seek the reign of God above all else. It is the pearl of great price. It is the object of our hope. Jesus tells us that because this treasure is so valuable, some will cheat to get it and keep it. Jesus makes his point in ways we will remember. It is easy to say that the reign of God is so great that a person should do whatever is possible to pursue it, but that doesn't get our attention. But, were we to say, "The kingdom of God is such an incredible treasure that, even if it was stored in a vault in the basement of the heavily-guarded Federal Reserve, we should do whatever it takes to go after it,"—then our point would be made. Such is the function of Jesus' parables. He uses human behavior, sometimes outlandish human behavior, to teach us the truths of the kingdom.

The pearl of great price does not highlight unethical behavior in its illustration, but it does demonstrate how someone might be willing to take great pains to secure the object of his or her desire. Matthew used the parables to make a point in his own community. Reginald Fuller points out that Matthew's church was suffering from a disregard of the moral law (antinomianism), from the teaching of false prophets, and from persecution. Midst such pressures, drastic action must be taken by the Christian if he or she is to withstand the temptations and pressures of the day and live a life that will secure a good seat at the final banquet table. Both the parable of the treasure and the parable of the pearl of great price stress the human response to the action of God. The stress is not on the finding. A person might stumble upon the reign of God or diligently seek after it, but what is important is the response once it has been acquired. We are not to indulge in the temptation to assume a literal meaning in the parables. Jesus is not suggesting that we can "buy" or earn the kingdom by renouncing our worldly possessions. One constant theme in the gospel is that God's action is an unmerited, gratuitous gift. The reign of God is not our personal possession to acquire. We are to enter into it, live in it, and commit our lives to furthering it here on earth.

The parable of the dragnet is a sober reminder of our ultimate destination. We will all be judged at the end. Where we end up depends on how we lived our lives. When a fisherman goes out to haul

[4]R. Kevin Seasoltz, O.S.B., "Liturgy and Social Consciousness," *TDJ*, 47.

in his catch, he must wait until arriving on the shore before he separates the good fish from the trash that also gets picked up in the nets. The dragnet is a reminder that everyone will be gathered together at the end and judged.

Today's parables demonstrate the attitude Christians are to have toward the reign of God. They are to be resourceful, decisive, and willing to risk everything. When one first encounters the kingdom it is an unexpected "find,"—a surprise and a treasure. No one went out seeking the treasure in today's parable. The finding was not the result of human initiative. The unsuspecting field hand stumbled upon it. All he was seeking was a day's paycheck. The parables suggest that "the kingdom comes as a chance of a lifetime. Its presence elicits joy, but decisiveness is required if one is to capitalize on the opportunity."[5] A commitment is required once the object is in one's possession. The investment is high. In the story, everything had to be sold in order to acquire the find. "Neither gets something for nothing. They get something for everything."[6] What is sold is valueless in comparison, however. Those who leave everything, and sell all they have to follow Jesus, gain everything.

The disciples are asked if they understand what Jesus was trying to convey. There is more involved here than Jesus' testing the disciples' knowledge or intellectual comprehension. Jesus invites no less than total submission to the word in the believer's heart. Evidence of this will be observable by one's actions.

The scribes in the story are a reference to the biblical understanding of scribe—those trained in the law, an ideal teacher of the law. Jesus' scribe is given divinely-appointed understanding. Jesus' scribe understands the mystery of the reign of God. The scribe in the gospel serves as an illustration to would-be disciples. They are to be ideal teachers in the community. They are to teach the new law while drawing from the old. Inherent in the text is a proclamation of the new order in the kingdom, an order not expected by the listeners. The new teaching is not superimposed on the old teaching. The old teaching now focuses on the new teaching and thereby is itself a new teaching. The Hebrew Scriptures are not to be cast aside. They are to be understood now in light of the death and resurrection of Jesus. The disciples of Jesus will replace the Pharisees as the new teachers of the law. The Pharisees may hold proper title to the chair of Moses, but their teaching is now preempted by the new law, the new covenant in Jesus Christ. "Matthew's scribe, however, is ever mindful of the importance of the Old Testament. The crypto-Marcionites in our midst, who treat the Old Testament as superfluous, need to be reminded that what God was doing in Jesus was merely a continuation of the grand story that began with the creation. To ignore the Old Testament is to truncate the gospel."[7]

If we are to sell everything we have, giving up all to acquire this new gift of kingdom, then it follows that we are to live according to its principles. Kingdom living that does not result in care and concern for others, especially those who have no one to care for them or be concerned for them, is not kingdom living at all. Evidence of the reign of Christ, evidence of living the new covenant, will be observed by the way one lives the ethical imperatives of the gospel. "Being Christian, having a responsibility in the church, cannot be a pretext for presumption. No part of it is private property: it is a gift from the Lord to be at the service of others."[8]

Proclaim the gospel again.

Sometimes we gain new insights when we hear the text after the interpretation has been given. Someone from the group proclaims the gospel a second time.

STEP 4
TESTING

Conversation with the Liturgy and the Scriptures

Test your original understanding in dialogue with the text.

[5] *RM,* 151.

[6] Ibid.

[7] *IM,* 159.

[8] *SWTLY,* 190.

(You might consider breaking into smaller groups.)

Is there anything in this gospel that you had not considered before? How does your original understanding of this gospel compare with what we just shared? Were there any new insights for you? How does this story speak to your life?

Sharing Life Experience

Participants share an experience from their lives that connects with the biblical interpretation just shared.

> *Many years ago, when the faith that lay dormant just beneath the surface of our consciousness was awakened, my husband and I, in our early zealous fervor, made the commitment to go wherever God would ask us to go and do whatever God would ask us to do. We certainly did not realize what that would mean for our lives. It has been a wonderful, terrible, exciting, dull, event-filled, sometimes doubt-filled, story of faith. It is a very human story filled with times of joy, sorrow, disappointment, and success. At the beginning of our commitment, our primary focus was to make living the reign of God the only priority in our lives. I long for those early days of passionate intensity. It is now twenty-five years later and the gospel has not changed. Today's parable still invites that same fervor and asks us to do whatever we need to do in order to live the gospel. Perhaps there is another reason that Jesus shared this parable with us. It is a reminder. Think about it for a minute. Who would not be thrilled at finding a huge treasure? The early days of the find no doubt would be exciting. Yet, the newness and the excitement of the treasure naturally would wane after years of managing the investment, giving some of it to charities, and making sure it grew. There would be a constant sense of well-being if the treasure was doing well, but would there always be that early passion and fervor? It takes work and constant diligence to maintain such enthusiasm.*
>
> *Today's gospel reminds me that I cannot become complacent with the great gift I have been given. Outward appearances may suggest that all is going well, but often it seems that the ordinary concerns of life take precedence over everything else and the reign of God is taken for granted. Jesus reminds us that we can never lapse into complacency. We do not know the hour or the day of the Lord's return. One way to test my fervor in light of today's gospel would be to ask myself: "Do I still reach out in love to others with the same commitment as always? Do I still value living the moral imperatives of the gospel? Is there still an urgency to preach and teach the gospel of Jesus Christ in the world?*

What was Jesus' intent in the parables and how did Matthew interpret them and why? What do today's parables have to teach your community today? How are the biblical themes of covenant, exodus, creation, and community expressed in today's liturgy? What do they mean for your life? Do you still feel the same way about this text as when you began? Has your original understanding been stretched, challenged, or affirmed? In what way has the conversation with this liturgy invited change with an attitude or behavior?

STEP 5
DECISION

The gospel demands a response.

In what specific ways is your parish called to respond to today's liturgy? What are the implications of this liturgy for your life? What is one concrete action you will take this week as a response to the liturgy today?

Christian Initiation: This might be a good time for candidates to reflect on their journey in light of today's gospel. How is it going? Are they still seeking the pearl of great price (living in Christ's reign) above all else? It is very important to celebrate the minor rites with the catechumens as they are intended for strengthening and encouraging them on their journey to the table. With the emphasis on the reign of God, this would be an appropriate time to celebrate a rite of acceptance or welcome, or even a rite of reception into the Catholic Church. However, it would be important not to convey the triumphalistic attitude (in fact, the church insists that we strictly avoid it) that says: "Now you have really found the real pearl of great price—the Catholic Church." The reign of God might be best lived for some people in a tradition other than the Catholic Church, and we are to respect that.

DOCTRINAL ISSUES

What church truth/teaching/doctrinal issue could be drawn from the gospel for the Seventeenth Sunday in Ordinary Time?

Participants suggest possible doctrinal themes that flow from the readings.

Possible Doctrinal Themes

Reign of God (now and not yet), living the mission of Christ, evangelization, conversion, discipleship, eschatology, heaven/hell, justice, moral imperatives of the reign of God, church's social teaching

Present the doctrinal material at this time.

1. The facilitator gives input on a particular doctrinal issue of his or her prior choosing. OR

2. The group chooses a doctrinal issue from the list they created. They read together from the Doctrinal Appendix.

(The doctrinal issues are found in the Doctrinal Appendix in the back of this workbook. If you are choosing an issue from this resource, please refer to it now.)

Reflection questions centered around the chosen doctrinal theme can be found at the end of each topic in the Doctrinal Appendix. The questions are based on the five-step reflection process. If you choose a topic not included in the Doctrinal Appendix, craft your own questions according to the same five-step process.

Following the reflection questions you will be reminded to return to chapter 7, "Preparing the Catechetical Session," to assist you in crafting your own session.

Closing Prayer

God our Father,
open our eyes to see your hand at work
in the splendor of creation,
in the beauty of human life.
Touched by your hand our world is holy.
Help us to cherish the gifts that surround us,
to share your blessings with our brothers and sisters,
and to experience the joy of life in your presence.
We ask this through Christ our Lord.[9]

[9]Seventeenth Sunday in Ordinary Time: "Alternative Opening Prayer," *The Sacramentary.*

Eighteenth Sunday in Ordinary Time

INTRODUCTORY RITES

Opening Song (or Entrance Antiphon)

God, come to my help. Lord, quickly give me assistance. You are the one who helps me and sets me free: Lord, do not be long in coming. (Ps 69:2, 6)[1]

Opening Prayer

The facilitator of the session may lead the prayer. Others in the group may be asked to proclaim the readings.

Let us pray
[to the Father whose kindness never fails]

Pause for silent prayer.

God our Father,
gifts without measure flow from your goodness
to bring us your peace.
Our life is your gift.
Guide our life's journey,
for only your love makes us whole.
Keep us strong in your love.
We ask this through Christ our Lord.[2]

LITURGY OF THE WORD

Let us listen to God's word.

The readings are proclaimed.

First Reading
Isaiah 55:1–3

(Refer to the First Sunday of Advent for an Overview of Isaiah.)

Today's Pericope: In today's reading God invites the hungry to come and be lavishly fed at God's banquet table. In both the first reading and the gospel the Lord satisfies both the physical and spiritual hungers of those who respond to the invitation.

There is more meaning to the Lord's offer of rich food than the satiation of hunger. The covenant between God and human beings was understood to be sealed and ratified by the celebration of a meal. In the Old Testament the meal, while a very simple event, was nonetheless considered highly symbolic. There were social, personal, and religious implications. The Israelites were bound to God by a covenant. They were forbidden to share in or replicate the ritual meals of other religions. The meals celebrated during the feast of Passover are as a memorial of the Lord's saving action in the history of Israel. The sharing of a meal also designated a strong bond of friendship that made disloyalty and treachery an unspeakable offense.

Sharing bread in the Wisdom tradition of the scriptures sheds light on the relationship between the teacher and the disciple. When a disciple ate the bread of the teacher it was said that he or she shared the wisdom of the teacher.

The Lord's rich fare brings with it images of God's relationship with people, and people's relationship with one another. The image of banquet was also used to describe the messianic age. The messiah's reign was described in terms of a copious banquet. Jesus himself used that motif throughout his preaching ministry to describe the reign of God.

God tends to the physical needs of the returning exiles in today's reading. They are poor, beaten down by their sojourn, and in need of their provident, compassionate, and understanding God. God hears them and provides for their needs. He sees to their hunger and satiates their empty spirits. At the feast the Lord prepares, all hunger and thirst is satisfied. God hears the cry of the poor; all who come humbly seeking their God, encounter God's mercy. All who come, recognizing their

[1]Eighteenth Sunday in Ordinary Time: "Entrance Antiphon," *The Sacramentary.*

[2]Eighteenth Sunday in Ordinary Time: "Alternative Opening Prayer," *The Sacramentary.*

powerlessness before God, know well the incredible grace of the Lord's banquet.

There is no need to state the connection between today's first reading and gospel. It is obvious. Jesus echoes the same invitation to come and eat. The early Christians understood today's reading from Isaiah to be fulfilled in the eucharistic feast established by Jesus' new covenant.

Responsorial Psalm
Psalm 145:8–9, 15–16, 17–18

Today's psalm resonates with both the first reading and the gospel. The Lord feeds us and satisfies our needs. The image of being filled and satisfied is a common theme throughout scriptures and often refers to the eschatological banquet.

Second Reading
Romans 8:35, 37–39

(Refer to the First Sunday of Advent for an Overview of Paul's Letter to the Romans.)

Paul's concluding words in his letter to the Romans sound like a song of triumph. Paul names the cosmic powers that cannot separate believers from the love of God in Christ. The love of God and the love of Christ are one and the same thing according to Paul.

Paul reminds the Romans that the cross is a physical manifestation of the love of God. It is not an intangible idea. We can be certain of God's love because of the witness and example of the cross of Christ. Jesus' obedience and faithfulness led him to the cross. The cross, in turn, is God's action of redemption for human beings. Like Abraham, God offered his firstborn for all the world. If God was willing to sacrifice God's own Son out of love for us, who are we not to trust that God will take care of us? We are to have no fear because, no matter what comes our way, we are children of a God who cares for us.

Thus, Jesus' death was a victory over cosmic evil forces, which were rendered ultimately powerless over the faithful. Reginald Fuller reminds us that Paul does not suggest that we are immune from their onslaught. Paul simply believes that in the end, believers will not be conquered by them.

Gospel
Matthew 14:13–21

STEP 1
NAMING ONE'S EXPERIENCE

What were your first impressions? What was your first response to the gospel (or the other readings)?[3] What captured your attention?

Each person names his or her initial impression. Statements should be brief. No reasons should be given at this time. All simply listen without agreeing or disagreeing.

STEP 2
UNDERSTANDING

In a brief statement, what do you think this gospel is trying to convey?

STEP 3
INPUT FROM VISION/STORY/TRADITION

Liturgical Context

We are alerted by Matthew himself that we are at a transition point and are entering a new section in his gospel when, at the end of chapter 13, he tells us that Jesus left after finishing telling his parables to the people (13:53). Just prior to this we spent considerable time reflecting on the kingdom of God. This section moves now into the kingdom of the church and the mission of the disciples that will be built after the resurrection. The Lectionary has five of these mission sequences together, in groups of two. The first group begins today with the Eighteenth Sunday in Ordinary Time and continues through the Twentieth Sunday. The central focus of these three Sundays is *faith in Christ.* Disciples are to have faith in the Jesus who feeds the multitudes,

[3]The primary focus of reflection is the gospel. However, very often the other readings demand attention and must be brought into the dialogue.

saves those tossed around in the storms of life, and answers the prayers of foreigners.[4]

The Opening Prayer fills us with confidence in the God who hears the prayers of all who praise him, the God who forgives and restores us to life. To confidently make that prayer, one needs faith. The Alternative Opening Prayer echoes the same plea. We are aware that it is God who gifts us with peace, and with life itself. We ask to be guided on the journey through life. This prayer presupposes faith. The Prayer After Communion reminds us of what the gospel expresses so succinctly. It is the eucharist that gives us the strength of new life and leads us to our final redemption in Christ.

The stories of shared meals in the gospels are eucharistic in nature and come out of the earliest understanding of ritual meal. Examining them gives us a greater appreciation for the evolution of the eucharistic liturgy we celebrate today, as well as the rich heritage and tradition that have come down to us through the ages.

Ancient cultures were acutely aware that something had to die in order for human beings to eat. They knew that a living being, an animal or a plant, was destroyed in order to provide sustenance for their bodies. Thus, most ancient religions gave thanks to their deities in prayer for the living thing that was sacrificed so that they could live. Part of this ritual of thanks included offering some of the animal in sacrifice to the gods. It was also customary to offer a portion of the first produce of the harvest and the livestock in sacrifice to the gods. Leftover portions were then eaten in a meal believed to be shared by the gods themselves. In the ancient mind, there was not a great deal of distinction between meal and sacrifice.

Mark Francis provides an insightful historical perspective regarding the meal aspect of eucharist, pointing out that eucharist evolved out of the ancient setting mentioned above. In both the Hebrew and Jewish Scriptures heaven is described in terms of a joyful banquet. The meal has always had implications of God's presence and God's relationship with people, and people's relationship to one another and to the earth. Within the Jewish experience, the meal was a place to encounter the sacred. After the destruction of the Temple around 70 C.E., there was no longer a place to offer animal and cereal sacrifice to God for the forgiveness of sins. Sacrificial worship was then moved to the family table. It was a logical progression to assign actions at the table for the sacrifice that once occurred in the Temple. "Rabbi Yohanan (+279) and Rabbi Eleazar (+ca. 270) note that 'As long as the sanctuary existed, the altar expiated the sins of Israel, but now it is the human table of hospitality that expiates sin' (Tractate Berakhot, IX, f. 55a, i *Der Babylonischer Talmud*)."[5]

One cannot ignore the similarity between the Jewish thanksgiving prayer after meals and our own eucharistic prayers. The liturgy we celebrate is rooted in the sacred meal of the Jewish family table. The primary ritual activity of the Christian Church was the reinterpretation of the Jewish Passover meal that Jesus gave to his disciples at the Last Supper when he offered them his Body and Blood. Passover was understood in terms of the sacrifice of the paschal lamb, the life-giving blood of the lamb, liberation from slavery (exodus), and the future liberation of Israel through the promised Messiah. When Jesus referred to himself as bread and wine, the action of eucharist was very logically appropriated to the Jewish understanding of Passover. The reinterpretation of Passover, the old covenant meal, resulted in the new covenant meal of Christ Jesus. It was the means to remember and make effective the sacrifice of Jesus, the promised Messiah, through the life-giving action of shedding his blood and the liberation he won for us by his death and resurrection.

> The Mass is the sacred banquet in which, through the communion of the body and blood of the Lord, the people of God share the benefits of the paschal sacrifice, renew the new Covenant with us made once and for all by God in Christ's blood, and in faith and hope foreshadow and anticipate the eschatological banquet in the Father's kingdom as they proclaim the death of the

[4] *DL* (IV), 142.

[5] Mark R. Francis, C.S.V., "Meal," *CPDBT,* 602.

> Lord "until he comes" (Paul VI's Instruction *Eucharisticum mysterium 3 a.*).

The very earliest celebration of eucharist was in the context of a meal. The meal was probably separated from reception of the eucharist very early in the history of the church because of abuses that were taking place—such as the ones Paul described in his first letter to the Corinthians—and because of the eventual growth of the church. Celebrating eucharist at a meal became impractical with large numbers of people.

When Christianity became the official religion of the empire, other influences detracted as well from the meal aspect of eucharist. There was greater emphasis on the awe-inspiring nature of Christian worship, and a near de-emphasis on the symbols used in worship that come from everyday life, such as water, bread, wine, and oil. During the Middle Ages the numbers of communicants began to dwindle, due to an overemphasis on sinfulness and unworthiness. Thus the mass was interpreted as an allegory on the life of Christ. The liturgy of the eucharist was understood as a reenactment of the sacrifice on Calvary. The earlier meal aspect to the liturgy was obscured, even though never completely lost.

The Second Vatican Council set out to restore the understanding of eucharist that is found in today's gospel—the human activity of sharing nourishment.

> Many of the liturgical changes revolve around accentuating the Mass as a sacred meal of the community gathered around the "table of God's word" and the "table of the Eucharist." Far from rejecting the understanding of the Mass as sacrament of the sacrifice of Christ, the liturgy of Vatican II seeks to balance the richness of this later medieval understanding with the earlier Eucharistic traditions of the Church which, based on the Jewish-Christian matrix of sacred meal, emphasize that it is in the action of sharing in the Eucharistic bread and wine that we become one in Christ Jesus.[6]

[6]Ibid., 603.

Gospel Exegesis

The facilitator gives input regarding what critical biblical scholarship has to say about this text. The input includes insights as to how people would have heard the gospel in Jesus' time.

Matthew's penchant for connecting Jesus' mission with that of Moses is very evident in today's gospel. Matthew sought to help his community see themselves as a church forged by the new covenant and rooted in, but distinct from, the old covenant. Moses went up the mountain to receive the law. Jesus went up the mountain to teach the new law. Moses led the people through the Red Sea and then through the desert. By the power of God he fed them manna. Jesus fed the multitudes in a deserted place by the sea. By the power of God Jesus also fed the multitudes.

The feeding of the multitudes in Matthew's gospel must also be observed from the perspective of the audience Matthew was addressing. He was speaking to a Jewish Christian audience after the destruction of Jerusalem in 70 C.E. He was also speaking to a community that was finding it difficult to be shunned and ostracized by Pharisaic Judaism. Jewish Christians were also trying to maintain their identity in a church in which they were fast becoming a minority in the midst of so many gentile converts to Christianity. Many Jewish Christians felt out of place in the new Christian communities. The new gentile converts did not share the same passion for the Jewish traditions and customs that were such an integral part of Jewish life. Some Jewish Christians formed their own communities and others returned to Judaism. Others longed to return to the security of the law and the authoritative teaching of the Pharisees. Matthew, therefore, emphatically stressed the new covenant and the teaching authority of Jesus.

Whereas Mark kept Jesus' identity a secret, Matthew, on the other hand, proclaimed that Jesus was the Son of God from his birth. Bread played an important role in Matthew's gospel because one thing that distinguished Christians from Jews was the fact that Christians gathered for the breaking of the bread.

Today's scene opens with Jesus being told by the disciples about John the Baptist's death and Jesus subsequently retreating to a deserted place. And when we read how the crowds followed Jesus to the place where he had fled, and how he took pity on them, we are immediately, and soberly, reminded of the implications of Jesus' ministry of healing, feeding, and nourishing. The murder of John the Baptist by Herod is a stark reminder of what happens to prophets of the Lord. What happened to John will also happen to Jesus. "The slaying of John, the greatest of the prophets (11:11), therefore prepares the reader for Jesus' death."[7]

The special news report about John has a specific function in the story. We hear the story of the loaves and fishes from the perspective of where this feeding of the crowd ultimately leads. Hovering over this scene is Jesus' future passion and death. Hovering over the Last Supper was the awareness of Jesus' impending passion and death. The feeding of others that God asks us to do involves the laying down of our lives for one another. (It is interesting to note that missionaries in Third World countries are often executed for simply helping the poor feed themselves and provide for their families.)

Matthew makes an obvious connection between the Last Supper and this feeding of the multitudes that took place in the evening, as did the Last Supper. Matthew tells us the hour is *already late*; Jesus' *hour* had arrived at the Last Supper. Clearly Matthew intends to redact the Markan version of the parable through the lens of eucharistic teaching. In Mark's version of the story the focus is on food. In Matthew's it is on Jesus. "The Greek phrase, literally 'You give them to eat,' exactly corresponds to the last words of Jesus in the Judgment scene, '[I was hungry and] you gave me to eat' (25:35), except for the change in person. It seems that Jesus' words to feed the hungry are a command to the Church at any time, a command for which they are responsible at Judgment. Hence the necessity of the daily prayer in Matthew: 'Give us this day our daily bread' (6:11)."[8]

In Mark's gospel there are elements that suggest that the feeding of the crowds was more a communal sharing of resources than it was a miracle. This is not so in Matthew's gospel, however. "Jesus alone is the source of bread and the complete master of the situation."[9]

There is an irrefutable link between Jesus' action in this feeding and the feeding of the Twelve at the Lord's Supper. Jesus *took* the loaves and fish in this story and *blessed* them. At the Last Supper Jesus *took* the bread and *blessed* it. Jesus *broke* the loaves and *gave* them to his *disciples* in this story. At the Last Supper Jesus *broke* the bread and *gave* it to his *disciples*. Matthew takes the story a step further in order to stress the implications for discipleship. After Jesus gave the bread to his disciples, the disciples in turn gave the bread to the crowd. The implication is clear. This is what the church is to continue to do—give the bread of life to others. "Jesus' action is to continue in the Church through the disciples."[10]

There is a very strong emphasis on the mission of the church in chapters fourteen through eighteen of Matthew's gospel, evidenced by Matthew's use of the word *church*. It is the only time the Greek word *ekklesia* is used in all four gospels. Yet Paul used the word repeatedly in his writings that preceded the gospels. Matthew's intention in his use of the word here is to stress his constant theme: the role, mission, and faith of the church.

The faith of the church is a critical issue for Matthew. In chapter 13 we read that Jesus could not perform his miracles because of the people's lack of faith. Now Jesus performs a miracle *because* of their faith. "For Matthew, faith is confidence in Jesus' power."[11] The faith of the people is demonstrated by the fact that they brought the sick to him to be healed. Their faith contrasts with that of the disciples whose faith was less than exemplary in chapter 14:17, 31. The disciples had said to Jesus that someone should go and secure food for the crowds from the neighboring villages. When Jesus told the disciples to give them something to eat, they responded that they only had meager supplies on hand, so how in the world could they possibly feed so many with so little. They doubted Jesus' power to provide for the needs of the peo-

---

[7]*RM*, 155.

[8]*LF*, 55.

[9]Ibid., 56.

[10]Ibid.

[11]*RM*, 155.

ple. Moses also doubted God's power to provide for the people in the desert.[12]

Matthew emphasizes the presence of women and children, which is unusual for such a gathering in that day. In the first two chapters of his gospel Matthew frequently refers to the holy family by name. Joseph Grassi suggests that this family-centered orientation of Matthew might be reason for the mention of the women and children. It is probably a significant inclusion, no matter what the reason.

The feeding of the multitude possesses many layers of meaning for our reflection. We are reminded of exodus and the provisions made for the multitudes in the desert. The abundance of the leftover food is a reminder that the messianic age had indeed arrived. The obvious connection with the Last Supper reminds us that Jesus is the true source of our nourishment. The abundant leftover fragments were gathered in twelve baskets, reminiscent of the twelve tribes of Israel. Thus, there was plenty to supply the needs of Israel. "The Eucharist, however, will offer bread for humankind."[13] This story also reminds us of Jesus' abundant love, mercy, and compassion for the needy, the poor, and the sick.

But we cannot ignore the fact that there are among us this day millions of undernourished people. The scriptures tell us that on the day of the Lord we will lack for nothing. Isaiah reminds us that on that day we will not even have to pay to eat. "In satisfying this need, money is useless, and it even perverts the process. Utopia? Maybe, though not in the sense of something illusory and deceitful but rather as a project in history which upsets the present order. What is abnormal is having to pay—and still worse, not have the money to pay for it—for something to which we are entitled. . . . As John Paul II said to a million hungry people in Villa El Salvador (Lima), every person is entitled to having bread on the table, including 'you that have no money' (v. 1)."[14] We cannot, we may not, reflect on this gospel without considering those who are still hungry.

[12]Ibid.

[13]Ibid.

[14]*SWTLY*, 195.

Proclaim the gospel again.

Sometimes we gain new insights when we hear the text after the interpretation has been given. Someone from the group proclaims the gospel a second time.

Step 4
Testing

Conversation with the Liturgy and the Scriptures

Test your original understanding in dialogue with the text.

(You might consider breaking into smaller groups.)

Was there anything in this exegesis that you had not considered before? How does your original understanding of this gospel compare with what we just shared? Were there any new insights for you? How does this story speak to your life?

Sharing Life Experience

Participants share an experience from their lives that connects with the biblical interpretation just shared.

> *Today's gospel is a reaffirmation of the power of the eucharist. Eucharist nourishes us, strengthens us, and empowers us. I feed off of Christ's body and blood so I can go out and allow others to feed off of me. I am reminded of the many ways we are invited to feed others. Whenever I give to the poor, help feed the poor, share my life with others, lay down my life so others can live, speak out in the face of injustice, I am living the mission that Jesus gave to his disciples today. Just as the disciples did, I often ask where I am going to find the necessary provisions, and I am always amazed at the resourcefulness of our God.*
>
> *I remember a time when I felt that God was inviting me to share a painful experience in my life with someone. I was amazed at what God accomplished through this sharing. It was an opportunity for healing for that person and for me—an opportunity to break free from the bondage of past hurts and to be nourished by the body of Christ, present in the eucharist and also in each other.*

As we received the body and blood of Christ together, I was particularly moved by our sharing of the cup. My friend's pain, my pain, and the pain of the whole world are poured out of that cup every time we sip from it. God nourishes us and heals our wounded spirits. Today's liturgy reminds me that God cares about what happens to us. God cares about the wounds that leave their imprint on our spirit. God cares about the spiritual and physical nourishment we need in order to thrive. Jesus gives us himself in the eucharist and provides what we need to be broken bread for each other.

Today's gospel is a reminder that eucharist commits us to care for and minister to the poor. Jesus cared about what happened to people. I cannot come to the table and ignore the needs of those people around me. If our community did not care for the poor, build schools, hospitals, and homes, and offer Jesus' ministry of healing and reconciliation, I would wonder if we perhaps thought ourselves to be fat on eucharistic grace, while in fact we were starving ourselves of it without realizing it. Christ feeds us and we in turn must feed others. There is no way to get around it.

All share their life experience.

What was Matthew's primary concern in today's gospel? How is that relevant for your community today? What does the feeding of the multitudes have to teach the contemporary church? What are the implications of this story for us today? How are the biblical themes of covenant, exodus, creation, and community expressed in today's liturgy? How do they have anything to do with your life and the life of your community? How might this gospel speak to the modern world? How do you feel about the implications of the mention of what happened to John the Baptist at the beginning of this gospel? How are you challenged by this gospel? Has your original understanding been stretched, challenged, or affirmed? How have you been challenged to change as a result of your conversation with this liturgy?

STEP 5
DECISION

The gospel demands a response.

In what concrete ways is your parish invited to respond to today's liturgy? What is one specific action you will take this week as a response to the liturgy today?

Pastoral Considerations: How is your parish community living the mandate of eucharist that commits us to the poor? Does your parish community respond to Jesus in faith and trust? How are those who are broken, hurting, lonely, sick, grieving, alienated, abused, thirsty, and hungry in your parish community (and civic community) fed?

Christian Initiation: With the eucharistic themes of today's liturgy, today would be a most appropriate time to celebrate a rite of full reception in the Catholic Church. Perhaps this would also be an opportune time to make the special effort to "be bread" in your parish or wider community—realizing the implications of eucharist in very concrete terms. Rather than only teaching catechumens *about* eucharist, their formation must include living the effects of eucharist. Who are the people in need of your bread?

DOCTRINAL ISSUES

What church truth/teaching/doctrinal issue could be drawn from the gospel for the Eighteenth Sunday in Ordinary Time?

Participants suggest possible doctrinal themes that flow from the readings.

Possible Doctrinal Themes

Eucharist, faith, discipleship, mystery of the church, eucharist and mission, eucharist as meal and as sacrifice, eucharist committing us to the poor (CCC 1397), justice, paschal mystery, Jesus Christ.

Present the doctrinal material at this time.

1. The facilitator gives input on a particular doctrinal issue of his or her prior choosing. OR

2. The group chooses a doctrinal issue from the list they created. They read together from the Doctrinal Appendix.

(The doctrinal issues are found in the Doctrinal Appendix in the back of this workbook. If you are choosing an issue from this resource, please refer to it now.)

Reflection questions centered around the chosen doctrinal theme can be found at the end of each topic in the Doctrinal Appendix. The questions are based on the five-step reflection process. If you choose a topic not included in the Doctrinal Appendix, craft your own questions according to the same five-step process.

Following the reflection questions you will be reminded to return to chapter 7, "Preparing the Catechetical Session," to assist you in crafting your own session.

Closing Prayer

Lord,
you give us the strength of new life
by the gift of the eucharist.
Protect us with your love
and prepare us for eternal redemption.
We ask this through Christ our Lord.[15]

[15]Eighteenth Sunday in Ordinary Time: "Prayer After Communion," *The Sacramentary*.

Nineteenth Sunday in Ordinary Time

INTRODUCTORY RITES

Opening Song (or Entrance Antiphon)

Lord, be true to your covenant, forget not the life of your poor ones for ever. Rise up, O God, and defend your cause; do not ignore the shouts of your enemies. (Ps 73:20, 19, 22, 23)[1]

Opening Prayer

Let us pray
[that through us others may find the way to life in Christ]

Pause for silent prayer.

Father,
we come, reborn in the Spirit,
to celebrate our sonship in the Lord Jesus Christ.
Touch our hearts,
help them grow toward the life you have
promised.
Touch our lives,
make them signs of your love for all men.
Grant this through Christ, our Lord.[2]

LITURGY OF THE WORD

The readings are proclaimed.

First Reading
1 Kings 19:9a, 11–13a

(Refer to the Thirteenth Sunday in Ordinary Time for an Overview of the Books of Kings.)

Today's Pericope: Today's reading takes place on Horeb (Sinai), the Lord's mountain. Elijah had killed the prophets of Baal (the god of Queen Jezebel). She set out to avenge their death. Elijah fled the scene in fear of his life. In verse four of this chapter (not in today's pericope), Elijah prayed for death, but the Lord's angel came to him and instructed him to eat the food that God would give him. After eating it he left on his journey to Mount Horeb, arriving there after forty days and forty nights in the desert. He sought safe haven there in a cave. Like the Israelites, Elijah was fed by the providential hand of God throughout his ordeal in the desert. Throughout scripture God is manifested to the people in grand Cecil B. DeMille fashion: fire, light, earthquakes, clouds, wind. As Israel developed into a sedentary, agrarian culture, the divine presence became associated with the temple, while acknowledging that no human-made structure could ever hold or contain the presence of God.

Yet in today's reading God comes to Elijah in a quiet, small voice—in the sound of silence. Contrasted with Baal, the storm god, Yahweh needs no flashy loud demonstration of power. Yahweh is Lord of all creation, and as such is a far different kind of God than the deity in the story. Yahweh is a God we encounter in all of creation, but which we also encounter in the silent recesses of our being.

Moses mediated the presence of God for Israel. Elijah also experienced the face of God on Horeb and was thus commissioned to go out and preach the word of God to the people. Moses fled Pharaoh and Elijah fled Jezebel. Elijah was ready to give up his prophetic ministry. He lost all faith in the people. He complained to God about the state of affairs. He reminded God that the people broke their covenant with God and killed all the prophets. Elijah was the only one left, and he was reminded by God that the plan of salvation would go forward.

Elijah hid his face from God, for as we know from Exodus 33:18–23, no one can look upon the face of God and live. Following this manifestation of God's presence, Elijah went out and followed the Lord's instruction to continue his ministry and to appoint Elisha as his successor. God's

[1]Nineteenth Sunday in Ordinary Time: "Entrance Antiphon," *The Sacramentary.*

[2]Nineteenth Sunday in Ordinary Time: "Alternative Opening Prayer," *The Sacramentary.*

saving mission would thus be accomplished and the faithful remnant would listen to the prophets.

Responsorial Psalm
Psalm 85:9, 10, 11–12, 13–14

This psalm was probably chosen for its allusion to listening to the Lord. Elijah listened to the Lord on Mount Horeb. Like Elijah, the psalmist also listens: "I will hear what God proclaims." The psalm likely refers to the returning exiles in Deutero-Isaiah.

Second Reading
Romans 9:1–5

(Refer to the First Sunday of Advent for an Overview of Paul's Letter to the Romans.)

Paul's sadness that so many of his fellow Israelites rejected Christ is evident in chapters nine through eleven of his letter to the Romans. They were the chosen ones—the ones who should have been first in line to receive the blessings of the new covenant. In these chapters also, Paul contrasts the acceptance of Christ by the Gentiles with the Jews' rejection of him. Paul did not have an accusatory attitude toward the Israelites, however, and he was not speaking to them as if they were outsiders. Rather, he wanted to teach his brother and sister Israelites the truth of what God was doing in Christ. They were, after all, the first heirs to the promise.

Paul expressed his anguish over the fact that his Jewish brothers and sisters have failed to acknowledge Jesus. He was even willing to sacrifice his own salvation if only it would only help bring the Israelites to faith in Christ. Paul names all the reasons why the Israelites should have recognized Jesus. They had long ago been prepared for this day. They were chosen of God, after all. They were God's adopted children. They were the ones privy to the manifestation of God throughout history. They were the ones in covenant relationship with God. Through the law, Israel was an active participant in God's plan of salvation for the world. They, above all, should have been able to see what God was doing in Christ. They were the ones who were promised the Messiah. How could they not have recognized him?

Gospel
Matthew 14:22–33

STEP 1
NAMING ONE'S EXPERIENCE

What were your first impressions? What was your first response to the gospel (or the other readings)?[3] What captured your attention?

Each person names his or her initial impression. Statements should be brief. No reasons should be given at this time. All simply listen without agreeing or disagreeing.

STEP 2
UNDERSTANDING

In a brief statement, what do you think this gospel is trying to convey?

STEP 3
INPUT FROM VISION/STORY/TRADITION

Liturgical Context

In the storm-tossed sea of life, the church is promised that Jesus will continue to be a presence that guides, leads, sustains, and offers compassion. Today's liturgy is a word of encouragement for the church. It reminds us that no matter what seems to threaten our safety, we can rely on the presence of Christ to uphold us. We are reminded as well that our response is an act of faith.

All of the prayers of the liturgy are an affirmation of our faith in the God who sustains us and who gives us the grace to live the life of faith. We ask to be given an increase of Christ's Spirit so we can share our eternal destiny with Christ in glory. The Entrance Antiphon asks that God may defend our

[3]The primary focus of reflection is the gospel. However, very often the other readings demand attention and must be brought into the dialogue.

cause and protect his poor defenseless ones. It is an acclamation of praise and trust in the God who is present and who cares for his people. The Alternative Opening Prayer asks that others may find Christ through the example of our lives of faith. We ask that God may touch our lives and make us signs of the love God has for all people. Today's gospel heralds that love and reminds us that God is present to the church throughout the storms of life.

The prayer of Umilta of Faenza, a Vallombrosan preacher and abbess in Tuscany (c. 1129) reflects the heart of today's liturgy:

> O Jesus, gentle love, you who are the true and complete peace in every discord, bring peace and concord to every conflict. When you are with me and I feel your power, my heart is merry and leaps with joy, my mind adorns itself with flowers of great beauty, and my soul dreams in the sweetness of blessed love. Let my enemies come, who in the world are so numerous, but if I feel myself to be with you, I overthrow them all, and the world itself I overthrow, along with all its speeches. I am like a fish that rests in the sea; when the waves sweep over it and the great tempests assail it, the fish enjoys swimming, because it cannot be captured, and it leaps more nimbly. Thus do I in this world that is a troubled sea: the great currents arrive, and I sail below them, and I take shelter in your bosom, and let them pass by. Then my soul arms itself with two wings so noble and flying so high that no one can see me: I rush then into your arms, O Jesus, up into your heavenly realms. Still I offer invocations to you, so that you may be always near me. Feeling myself with you I have no fear of the currents. I even conquer them in navigating, and I come forth from them unharmed. But if I do not possess you, I am like the whale that when the tide goes out sits on the sand and is condemned to death, because without the tide it no longer has the chance to escape.[4]

[4]Umilta of Faenza, tr. Richard J. Pioli, in *Medieval Women's Visionary Literature,* 251, in *RF,* 57.

Gospel Exegesis

The facilitator gives input regarding what critical biblical scholarship has to say about this text. The input includes insights as to how people would have heard the gospel in Jesus' time.

Matthew borrowed Mark's story of walking on water and retold it with his own community's needs in mind. He added the dialogue between Peter and Jesus. He also added the piece about Peter walking on the water. Mark's disciples misunderstand the event; Matthew's disciples make a confession of faith. Matthew's telling of this event is influenced by the theme of this section of his gospel. Last week we learned that Matthew's concentration on the reign of God was shifting to concentration on the church and the post-resurrection mission of the disciples. This is the lens through which Matthew tells this story. Matthew is concerned with discipleship. The boat is an image of the church. The storm represents the persecution facing the Matthean community. Jesus is exalted as the "church's champion, who is strong to save those who call on him in faith."[5] Jesus challenged Peter to trust him. Peter was afraid and begged Jesus to save him. Jesus rebuked him for his fear, saved the lot of them, whereupon everyone confessed him as Lord.

The Sea of Galilee is known for its violent storms. It is 696 feet below the Mediterranean Sea. It is about thirteen miles long and eight miles wide and its maximum depth is about 200 feet. The weather of the area is subtropical and the surrounding towering hills promote rapid changing wind currents.[6] In the summer months when the sun warms the lake, the wind, mixed with the warm water of the lake, can cause extreme sudden and severe storms.

Matthew tells us that the disciples are in the boat at Jesus' own bidding. We do not know why Jesus told them to go out in the boat. The fact that there was a storm is not noteworthy; but the way the storm ended is indeed noteworthy. In chapter eight the disciples had already experienced Jesus' awesome power over storm waters. In today's story

[5]*IM,* 169.

[6]*JHT,* 39–40.

Jesus walked on the water. Scriptures such as Job 9:8, Psalm 77:17–20, and Isaiah 43:16 attest that only God has such power. Matthew thus reveals Jesus' divine power and Jesus affirms the revelation. Scholars suggest that Jesus' reference to himself as "It is I" (*ego eimi*) is reminiscent of the divine name told to Moses on Mount Sinai. Also, most theophanies in scripture are accompanied by the divine exhortation found in today's gospel: "*fear not.*" Matthew does not want his listeners to miss the point. In the theophany taking place here, Jesus is manifesting the power of God to his disciples. Douglas Hare suggests that more than stressing Jesus' divine nature, the gospel stresses his function. "As Messiah he is the one charged and empowered by God to shepherd and care for God's people."[7]

Today's story, and the earlier story in chapter eight in which the sleeping Jesus was frantically asked to save the storm-tossed disciples, are indicative of the "first-century Mediterranean belief in spirits, including wind spirits that play havoc with human life."[8] The only way for human beings to protect themselves is to find a more powerful spirit to challenge the chaos-creating spirit. This more powerful spirit is God, and God's agent, Jesus, who is known for his ability to challenge evil and mischievous spirits throughout the gospel.

We are told that Jesus went off to pray. This time he went alone and he prayed most of the night. In the Mediterranean cultural context, prayer was intended to get results. It was a "message communicated to someone who is ultimately in charge of one's existence."[9] When Jesus is called upon to save the disciples from the storm later that evening, we see the results of his prayer. Jesus did not doubt the power of God to still the storms of the sea; we likewise are never to doubt our source of power.

Peter is known in all of the gospels for his fervor and his impetuosity. There is no doubt that he holds a position of distinction and authority in relation to the other apostles. Yet Peter is like all those "people of little faith." He wants proof—a sign—that it is really Jesus.

[7]*IM,* 169.

[8]*CWJ,* 122.

[9]Ibid., 123.

Jesus gave Peter a command and an invitation. By obediently following the Lord's command, Peter was able to do what he could not do on his own power. As long as he remained focused on Jesus, he was secure. When he became too self-absorbed, fear set in and he began to sink. His plea, "Save me, Lord," sounds very much like the cry of all those who came to Jesus begging for healing. Peter, in spite of evidence of Jesus' divine power, still doubted him. It is a powerful message for Matthew's community. If Peter, who personally walked with the Lord and observed his miracles firsthand, could still doubt the Lord, then is it any wonder that Matthew's community struggled with doubt as well? "It graphically depicts what it means to be a Christian caught midway between faith and doubt. Peter represents all who dare to believe that Jesus is Savior, take their first step in confidence that he is able to sustain them, and then forget to keep their gaze fixed on him instead of on the towering waves that threaten to engulf them. In the depth of crisis, when all seems lost, they remember to call on the Savior, and find his grace sufficient for their needs, whose power is made perfect in weakness (2 Cor 12:9)."[10]

Peter also reminds us of the implications of living a life of faith. There is risk involved; there are no certainties when it comes to living a faith-filled life. A constant theme for Matthew is faith and the lack thereof. Matthew does not admonish unbelievers for their lack of faith. He admonishes believers. He chides people for not drawing upon the faith they have been given when things go awry. Faith is an action word. It is not static. It is always active. Even a little faith can go a long way. Matthew's is the only gospel that uses the word *doubt.* Faith and doubt sit side by side at the same table in the lives of Christians. It is a curious mix, but the Christian can expect both realities in the journey of life. Doubt is held in check only through grace.

The message of today's gospel for Matthew's community is to remain calm and committed to Christ in the midst of difficulties. Believers are to keep focused on Christ and remain confident of his care, concern, and presence in the church as they strive to live his mission in the world.

[10]*IM,* 170.

Proclaim the gospel again.

Sometimes we gain new insights when we hear the text after the interpretation has been given. Someone from the group proclaims the gospel a second time.

Step 4
Testing

Conversation with the Liturgy and the Scriptures

Test your original understanding in dialogue with the text.

(You might consider breaking into smaller groups.)

Was there anything in this exegesis that you had not considered before? How does your original understanding of this gospel compare with what we just shared? Were there any new insights for you? How does this story speak to your life?

Sharing Life Experience

Participants share an experience from their lives that connects with the biblical interpretation just shared.

> *Today's liturgy immediately calls to mind the cherished young couple in our parish who is suffering because of the incurable illness of their infant son. Like Peter, every day they face another day of climbing out of the boat, trusting that the Lord's hand will be there to hold them up lest they sink. Their faith is a shining light to the entire community. They give thanks for each extra day of life they have with their son. Repeatedly he drifts into unconsciousness, and repeatedly they lovingly revive him, for how many more days or months they do not know. But they celebrate each moment of his life. In the meantime, they struggle through a problem pregnancy as they await the birth of another child. Hope still reigns in their hearts. It is not a Pollyanna hope based on denial, but a hope based on the trust that God will see them through no matter what. There have been periods of doubt, but they have heeded Matthew's exhortation to draw on their reserves of faith in the midst of their hell. They trust that God is with them in their sorrow.*
>
> *As this young family continues to be tossed about in the sea of life, we, of Our Savior's Catholic Community, are all acutely aware of God's presence and action in their lives. They have been an example to the entire parish that God does sustain us in the difficult times of our lives. The community's response has been an example to them, and to us all, that Christ is truly present in the midst of God's people. I often wonder how folks survive the tragedies of life without the support of a faith-filled community.*
>
> *The witness of faith by this family, and the witness of love by the community, are truly a testimony to the power of God and the compassion of God. God cares about what happens to his people. In today's gospel Jesus did not promise to keep us out of harm's way; nor did he promise that we would never again encounter another storm. Jesus does promise us God's presence, care, and concern. He shows us the power that is in prayer and in a loving community. Our prayers may not effect the physical healing of this baby, but the family has experienced God's wondrous healing and peace in other ways. And our community has been strengthened by the witness of God's action in the life of this family and the life of our community.*

All share their life experience.

What was Matthew's primary theme in today's gospel? How is that theme relevant for your community today? How are the biblical themes of covenant, exodus, creation, and community expressed in today's liturgy? How do they have anything to do with your life and the life of the church? How might this gospel speak to the modern world? How does Peter speak to your experience as a committed Christian? In what way might you relate to Peter? What is the most hopeful message in today's gospel? How are you challenged by this gospel? Has your original understanding been stretched, challenged, or affirmed? How have you been challenged to change as a result of your conversation with this liturgy?

Step 5
Decision

The gospel demands a response.

In what specific ways is your parish invited to respond to today's liturgy? What is one concrete action you will take this week as a response to the liturgy today?

DOCTRINAL ISSUES

What church truth/teaching/doctrinal issue could be drawn from the gospel for the Nineteenth Sunday in Ordinary Time?

Participants suggest possible doctrinal themes that flow from the readings.

Possible Doctrinal Themes

Faith, prayer, mystery of the church, Christology, Jesus fully human, Jesus fully divine, discipleship, paschal mystery, mystery of suffering, God's love, sacraments of the sick and holy orders, conversion

Present the doctrinal material at this time.

1. The facilitator gives input on a particular doctrinal issue of his/her prior choosing. OR
2. The group chooses a doctrinal issue from the list they created. They read together from the Doctrinal Appendix.

(The doctrinal issues are found in the Doctrinal Appendix in the back of this workbook. If you are choosing an issue from this resource, please refer to it now.)

Reflection questions centered around the chosen doctrinal theme can be found at the end of each topic in the Doctrinal Appendix. The questions are based on the five-step reflection process. If you choose a topic not included in the Doctrinal Appendix, craft your own questions according to the same five-step process.

Following the reflection questions you will be reminded to return to chapter 7, "Preparing the Catechetical Session," to assist you in crafting your own session.

Closing Prayer

Lord,
may the Eucharist you give us
bring us to salvation
and keep us faithful to the light of your truth.
We ask this in the name of Jesus the Lord.[11]

[11]Nineteenth Sunday in Ordinary Time: "Prayer After Communion," *The Sacramentary*.

Twentieth Sunday in Ordinary Time

INTRODUCTORY RITES

Opening Song (or Entrance Antiphon)

God, our protector, keep us in mind; always give strength to your people. For if we can be with you even one day, it is better than a thousand without you. Ps 83:10-11.[1]

Opening Prayer

The facilitator of the session may lead the prayer. Others in the group may be asked to proclaim the readings.

Let us pray
[with humility and persistence]

Pause for silent prayer.

Almighty God, ever loving Father,
your care extends beyond the boundaries of race and nation
to the hearts of all who live.
May the walls, which prejudice raises between us,
crumble beneath the shadow of your outstretched arm.
We ask this through Christ, our Lord.[2]

LITURGY OF THE WORD

Let us listen to God's word.

The readings are proclaimed.

First Reading
Isaiah 56:1, 6–7

Today's reading comes from the third section of the Book of Isaiah, often referred to as Trito-Isaiah. It is the section of Isaiah written after the exile. It reflects the teaching of Second Isaiah. In Second Isaiah the mighty saving deeds of God who delivered the people out of bondage were referred to as justice and righteousness. In Trito-Isaiah, those same words not only apply to the action of God, but also to expected and required human ethical behavior. There is a moral imperative inherent in the third book of Isaiah.

The cultural and religious situation of the day centered around the experience of those who returned from exile. King Cyrus gave the people permission to return to Jerusalem and to begin building a new temple. They were even given the sacred vessels stolen by the Babylonians nearly sixty years earlier. Some who began the project of restoration were thrilled at the prospects of building a new temple. For some reason the building of the temple was stalled and not resumed again for another fifteen years. This third book of Isaiah begins after construction of the temple had begun and before Ezra and Nehemiah began the reforms to restore their Jewish identity.

Even though the prophets of the exile promised that the restoration would be joyful and a cause for merriment and dancing, things were not at all as they hoped they would be. Poverty was vast and there was an immense task of reconstructing the religious and secular infrastructure. The political scene was not stable either.

Added to those tensions was the influx of foreigners who practiced foreign religions. Intermarriage was common. This was not too great an obstacle, however, as the husband was responsible for the religious life of the family. It therefore mattered little what religion the woman professed. Yet when Nehemiah and Ezra arrived on the scene, they blamed the ills of the religious culture on the intermarriage between "outlandish" foreign women and Jewish men. Today's hymn-like reading is a prayer seeking the conversion of foreigners to the worship of Yahweh, promising that their sacrifice would be acceptable.

The situation today centers around foreigners and what is expected of them in and around the

---

[1]Twentieth Sunday in Ordinary Time: "Entrance Antiphon," *The Sacramentary.*

[2]Twentieth Sunday in Ordinary Time, "Alternative Opening Prayer, " *The Sacramentary.*

temple precincts. Previously, Ezekiel wanted uncircumcised foreigners to be forbidden such activity. Third Isaiah set forth the conditions under which foreigners may serve at the temple. They were to observe the Sabbath and "keep the covenant, as far as it is applicable to non-Israelites."[3]

During the exile the people experienced the presence of God in their sojourn in a far-off land. This experience helped them understand a God who was not tied to the land—a God who was much larger than they once thought. It thus followed that God's mission also extends to foreigners. However, Ezra and Nehemiah's conservative reforms put that idea on hold for a few centuries before it resurfaced again. Judaism, prior to the time of Christ, had a particularly strong evangelical focus and sought converts to the faith.

The stance of inclusivity in today's reading foreshadowed the eventual universal mission of the gospel and the day when the temple would be a house of prayer for everyone. This is the Markan interpretation of Jesus' action of cleansing the temple. This reading was chosen for the theme of universality found also in the story of the Canaanite woman in the gospel.

Responsorial Psalm
Psalm 67:2–3, 5, 6, 8

Today's psalm is a song of thanks for the harvest and a prayer that God will continue to bestow blessings. It is appropriate thanksgiving for the way in which God showers his love upon all people, giving blessings to all nations. This is a theme consonant with that of both the first reading and the gospel.

Second Reading
Romans 11:13–15, 29–32

Today's second reading also speaks of the universal mission of the gospel; it is an inclusive word to the foreigners who were converts to faith in Jesus Christ. Even though the Jewish people were called first, it was non-Israelites who responded to the call. The invitation to the messianic reign of God was offered first to Jews, but they rejected it. They chose instead to continue in the way of salvation God had given them earlier, which in their understanding could not be disavowed.

Paul believed himself to be an apostle to the Gentiles. Paul was a good Jew who was called to bring the good news to non-Jews. Everywhere Paul went he preached first to the Jews. When and if they rejected his message, he moved on to the Gentiles. Paul yearned for the day when other Jews would join him in his love for Christ. A primary concern for Paul was to raise the consciousness of the people regarding God's establishment of the mission to the Gentiles. In so doing, Paul authenticated his own vocation. Even though his primary mission was to the Gentiles, Paul hoped that his ministry would have an effect on Jews.

Paul asserts in today's reading that all people are sinners, and that pagans who turned to the gospel of Christ did so because of God's grace and mercy. All people will be heirs to this same grace and mercy in the end. That is why Paul is confident that his Jewish brothers and sisters will be eventual recipients of the same mercy shown to faithful believers. God's love and mercy are gratuitous. We can do nothing to earn them. We are all recipients of the benefits of Christ's life, death, and resurrection.

Gospel
Matthew 15:21–28

STEP 1
NAMING ONE'S EXPERIENCE

What were your first impressions? What was your first response to the gospel (or the other readings)?[4] What captured your attention ?

Each person names his or her initial impression. Statements should be brief. No reasons should be given at this time. All simply listen without agreeing or disagreeing.

[3]*PL*, 158.

[4]The primary focus of reflection is the gospel. However, very often the other readings demand attention and must be brought into the dialogue.

Step 2
Understanding

In a brief statement, what do you think this gospel is trying to convey?

Step 3
Input from Vision/Story/Tradition

Liturgical Context

The Twentieth Sunday in Ordinary Time brings the sequence of the Eighteenth, Nineteenth, and Twentieth Sundays to a close. This three-part unity was the first of a two-part series that explores the mission of the disciples in Matthew's gospel.

The message of universality that resonates throughout today's liturgy is most succinctly expressed in today's Alternative Opening Prayer. We pray to the Father whose "care extends beyond the borders of race and nation to the hearts of all who live." We ask that the walls of prejudice come crashing down midst the shadow of God's outstretched arms.

Our liturgy demands that we extend the love we share in the celebration of eucharist to all the world. Christian faith without tolerance is not faith at all; it is self-righteous arrogance. Eugene LaVerdiere reminds us of the ethical imperatives demanded by worship in the scriptures.

> The Bible is clear on the ethical responsibility demanded by worship, in both the Old and New Testaments. It is also clear regarding the difficulty of fulfilling those demands. But it never backs down from them. Its story tellers and prophets do not allow their hearers and readers to forget what is at stake is the value of their worship. Apart from ethical responsibility, their worship becomes worthless.
>
> It took nearly the whole of biblical history to recognize that the entire human race was our neighbor. That recognition came through successive manifestations of grace in the long biblical journey. There was the Mosaic covenant and the formation of a special people of God, when the neighbor included only those who belonged to that people. This covenant had special concern for the alien residing among the people of God. Then there was the new covenant in the blood and life of Christ the Lord. The neighbor now included all human beings. Jesus Christ is not only our Lord. He is the Lord of all.
>
> The Lord's Supper represented a challenge for the early Christian community. The New Testament provides clear witness to their failures in living up to that challenge. The Lord's Supper remains a tremendous challenge for us as well, in that it contains the essential agenda for our Christian life and mission.[5]

Today's liturgy is a time for us to reflect on the universal mission of the church. Such a reflection is rooted not only in our experience of God's people, in the witness of the gospel, and in the celebration of the liturgy, but also in the teachings of the church. The Pontifical Council for Promoting Christian Unity's document regarding the Catholic perspective on ecumenism is worthy of note and serious deliberation. It sets forth the mission of the church in the context of God's plan of salvation for the whole world.

> The Council situates the mystery of the Church within the mystery of God's wisdom and goodness which draws the whole human family and indeed the whole of creation into unity with himself. To this end God sent into the world His only Son, who was raised up on the cross, entered into glory and poured out the Holy Spirit through whom he calls and draws into unity of faith, hope and charity the people of the New Covenant which is the Church....
>
> The Council presents the Church as the New People of God, uniting within itself, in all the richness of their diversity, men

[5]Eugene LaVerdiere, S.S.S., "Worship and Ethical Responsibility in the Bible," in *TDJR,* 31–32.

and women from all nations, all cultures, endowed with manifold gifts of nature and grace, ministering to one another and recognizing that they are sent into the world for its salvation . . . (#11).

. . . The unity of the Church is realized in the midst of a rich diversity. This diversity in the Church is a dimension of its catholicity. At times the very richness of this diversity can engender tension within the communion. Yet, despite such tensions, the Spirit continues to work in the Church calling Christians in their diversity to ever deeper unity... (#16).

The ecumenical movement is a grace of God, given by the Father in answer to the prayer of Jesus and the supplication of the Church inspired by the Holy Spirit. While it is carried out within the general mission of the Church to unite humanity in Christ, its own specific field is the restoration of unity among Christians. Those who are baptized in the name of Christ are, by that very fact, called to commit themselves to search for unity. . . (#22).

. . . Those who identify deeply with Christ must identify with his prayer, and especially with his prayer for unity; those who live in the Spirit must let themselves be transformed by the love that, for the sake of unity, "bears all things, believes all things, hopes all things, endures all things" (1 Cor 13:7); those whose lives are marked by repentance will be especially sensitive to the sinfulness of divisions and will pray for forgiveness and conversion. Those who seek holiness [will] be able to recognize its fruits also outside the visible boundaries of their own Church. . . .

They will be led to know, truly, God as the one who alone is able to gather all into unity because he is the Father of all (#25).[6]

[6]Pontificium Consilium Ad Christianorum Unitatem Fovendam, *Directory for the Application of Principles and Norms on Ecumenism,* Vatican City, March 25, 1993.

Gospel Exegesis

The facilitator gives input regarding what critical biblical scholarship has to say about this text. The input includes insights as to how people would have heard the gospel in Jesus' time.

After a bout with the Pharisees, Jesus withdrew to the region of Tyre and Sidon. Earlier, in Matthew's gospel, Jesus referred to these two cities as godless cities that would have repented in sackcloth and ashes if they had witnessed his miracles. Yet he nearly rebuffed one of its citizens in today's gospel. Jesus' abrupt response to the woman catches us off guard and offends our sensibilities. We would expect him to show the same compassion to her as to others who cried out for his mercy.

When the woman cries out for help, Jesus does not respond—he is silent. The disciples are annoyed with the woman and ask Jesus to get rid of her. Jesus replies that his mission is only to the lost house of Israel. The woman, with more fervor than before, approaches Jesus again. She worships him. Jesus responds with an insult. In Mark's version of this story, Jesus held out a ray of hope for the Gentiles by suggesting that they would be allowed to eat after the children (Israel) were fed. Matthew's version offers no such hope.

The woman was referred to as "Canaanite," a term that was probably used infrequently, if at all. Mark referred to the woman as Phoenician or Syrophoenician. The designation "Canaanite" probably was intended as an allusion to the people of the Old Testament called by that same name. The prophets called them *enemies* of the Lord because they worshiped Baal and other false gods. Matthew drives home the point that this woman is a pagan. There is a question lying just beneath the surface in this story. What will happen when a pagan seeks to reap the same benefits as those who have been living the covenant throughout salvation history? Will pagans be allowed to circumvent the law and go directly to Christ?

Jesus tells the woman that "it is not right to take the food of sons and daughters and throw it to the dogs." She quite cleverly responds that even the dogs eat the crumbs that fall from their master's table. In other words, dogs eat only what falls from the table in the course of the meal, so the children do not go hungry because of what the dogs ate. The woman knows that Israel's election entitles it to an honored, rightful place at the table—and the status of child. She is not asking for that. She is simply and humbly asking that the blessings reserved for Israel can overflow to her. Jesus granted her request and marveled at her great faith.

The emphasis here is not on Jesus' miracle; it is on the faith of the woman. She displayed an extraordinary confidence that Jesus would hear and answer her. She possessed an undaunted and persistent faith in the Christ, the Messiah, Israel's promised one. Her faith was like the faith of the centurion, in contrast with those in Matthew's gospel who demonstrated "little faith" (such as Peter and the disciples).

In her desperation, human pride no longer served her. She acknowledged the difference between Jew and Greek, but insisted that no matter what obstacles were in her path, they could be overcome: "[S]he acts on her own conviction that the barriers that separate her, a gentile, from Israel are not impregnable."[7]

It appears as if Jesus is saying that no one except Israelites can expect compassion and healing from him. The sons and daughters in the story are obviously the Jews, the dogs are the Gentiles, and the food is salvation and life offered by Jesus Christ. Our modern perceptions are scandalized by Jesus' treatment of the woman. The term "dogs" was a contemptuous slur used against the Gentiles. Dogs foraged for and ate food wherever they could find it. They were considered unclean. So were all those who were not members of the Israelite community. It would seem that Jesus shared the bigotry of his day. Yet in verse eleven of this chapter Jesus clarifies the meaning of unclean: "It is not what enters one's mouth that defiles that person, but what comes out of the mouth is what defiles one."

Another possibility has been suggested by G. Theissen. It is possible that Jesus shared the anger of the Galileans toward the rich city of Tyre. Tyre was taking bread away from Galilee. Jesus may have been speaking as an underprivileged against the privileged. His response might have been a statement asserting that the poor should have their fill first. The rich always take what they want first, and then leave the crumbs for the poor.[8]

As contemporary readers we expect Jesus to respond to every request for healing. We tend to forget that Jesus was Jewish and are "offended by the particularity of God's election. During the ministry of Jesus, the boundary between Jews and Gentiles is very real. On the one hand, this incident affirms the priority of Israel's children."[9] We know the rest of the story; Matthew's community did not. We know that the Gentiles were the ones who accepted Jesus in large numbers. We also know that Israel ultimately rejected him. We read our historical bias into this text. In the long run, the Gentiles have a more important role than Israel when it comes to the mission of Christ in the world. Matthew's point, however, is for the benefit of his Jewish Christian audience. God did not impulsively reject the chosen people. Jesus affirmed that his mission was to Israel. The Gentile woman professed the faith of Israel. She attested that Jesus was the son of David and that the house of Israel was God's elect. Matthew's stories about God feeding his people—before and after this story—remind us that even though God provides for Israel, there is an abundance left over for everyone. Matthew also affirmed that Israelites are not guaranteed salvation—that faith is required. But for now, Jesus' mission is limited to Israel. It does not extend to the whole world until after his death and resurrection. The woman's strong faith allowed her to overcome the obstacle standing in the way of her encounter with Christ.

"The story reminds us that members of despised or oppressed groups must be bold in seeking relief of their misery. The woman is not content to be ignored, because she is convinced that her daughter deserves to be given a chance at living a normal, productive life. Her persistence, based on her faith in a God who can change things for the better, is rewarded."[10]

---

[7] *RM*, 164.

[8] Ibid., 165.

[9] Ibid.

[10] *IM*, 179.

Proclaim the gospel again.

Sometimes we gain new insights when we hear the text after the interpretation is given. Someone from the group proclaims the gospel a second time.

STEP 4
TESTING

Conversation with the Liturgy and the Scriptures

Test your original understanding in dialogue with the text.

(You might consider breaking into smaller groups.)

Was there anything in this exegesis that you had not considered before? How does your original understanding of this gospel compare with what we just shared? Were there any new insights for you? How does this story speak to your life?

Sharing Life Experience

Participants share an experience from their lives that connects with the biblical interpretation just shared.

> *Today's liturgy is a sign of the universal nature of God's mission. It is a command to cast off our triumphalistic attitudes about who possesses the "real truth" and realize that God calls who God wills. God will not be placed in any religious box we choose to craft, no matter how elegant. Perhaps today's word reminds us that at any given time we may either be like the Canaanite woman or like Israel. Sometimes we are like the pagan woman and humbly recognize our powerlessness; we do whatever we have to do to encounter Jesus in our lives. Sometimes we relate more to Israel and, as a cradle-churchgoer, have a difficult time seeing God in the midst of change or in the midst of the unexpected. Today's liturgy invites me to be tolerant and to realize that my religious beliefs and practices are not somehow better than those of other people.*
>
> *One of my children recently observed that he believes Catholics need to have more tolerance for people who express their faith more passionately and emotionally than we do. Whether we are or are not tolerant of such people, I do not know. But I do know that one of the attributes most lacking in all of our churches today is tolerance. However, in my opinion, there is enough intolerance lurking within our own tradition that we need to clean up our own house first.*
>
> *The other day someone showed me a media communication written by a prominent religious personality. This article was not only untruthful, but was extremely divisive. It invited people to chastise their priests for an action this writer likened to heresy. He then quoted one of the official church documents to support his position. The document he quoted not only* did not support *his position, but completely* refuted *it. Not only was his position misleading, it was false. All I could assume from this communiqué was that there was deliberate ill will and a deliberate intention to cause division. The poor unsuspecting people who elected to follow his directive would be doing so believing they were defending the faith. This kind of behavior is the antithesis of the gospel. It exalts the ideology of a small group of people and upholds it as the only narrowly defined truth.*
>
> *Today's gospel is an invitation to seek Christ even when there seems to be insurmountable obstacles. It is also a call to inclusiveness, tolerance, and a spirit of mutual respect and dignity.*

All share their life experience.

What was Matthew's primary goal in today's gospel? How does that speak to the contemporary church? What does the Canaanite woman have to teach you today? How are the biblical themes of covenant, exodus, creation, and community expressed in today's liturgy? How do they have anything to do with your life and the life of the church? Do you see yourself more in the image of the woman or in the image of Israel? How do you feel about Jesus' response to the woman? How does that speak to your life as a Christian? What is the most hopeful message in today's gospel? How are you challenged by this gospel? Has your original understanding been stretched, challenged, or affirmed? How have you been challenged to change as a result of your conversation with this liturgy?

Step 5
Decision

The gospel demands a response.

In what specific ways is your parish invited to respond to today's liturgy? What is one concrete action you will take this week as a response to the liturgy today?

Pastoral Considerations: Where is there division present in your parish? Is it underground? Is there anything you can do to foster unity and reconciliation? In what ways is your community inclusive of those who are different? How does your community reach out to people of other traditions? Is ecumenism a priority in your parish? How does your parish engage in the ministry of evangelization?

Christian Initiation: When was the last time your parish engaged in evangelization efforts? When was the last time your community reminded itself that initiation is the responsibility of all the baptized (RCIA #9)? Perhaps there might be an effort to invite people (neighbors and co-workers) who do not have a parish home to come and visit your community. Perhaps this would be a good time to remind parishioners to invite inquirers to their homes for dinner, and to pray for people in the initiation process.

DOCTRINAL ISSUES

What church truth/teaching/doctrinal issue could be drawn from the gospel for the Twentieth Sunday in Ordinary Time?

Participants suggest possible doctrinal themes that flow from the readings.

Possible Doctrinal Themes

Faith, ecumenism, mystery of the church, prayer, conversion, evangelization, discipleship, justice, social sin, unity

Present the doctrinal material at this time.

1. The facilitator gives input on a particular doctrinal issue of his/her prior choosing. OR
2. The group chooses a doctrinal issue from the list they created. They read together from the Doctrinal Appendix.

(The doctrinal issues are found in the Doctrinal Appendix in the back of this workbook. If you are choosing an issue from this resource, please refer to it now.)

Reflection questions centered around the chosen doctrinal theme can be found at the end of each topic in the Doctrinal Appendix. The questions are based on the five-step reflection process. If you choose a topic not included in the Doctrinal Appendix, craft your own questions according to the same five-step process.

Following the reflection questions you will be reminded to return to chapter 7, "Preparing the Catechetical Session," to assist you in crafting your own session.

Closing Prayer

Save us, Lord our God,
and gather us together from the nations,
that we may proclaim your holy name and glory in
your praise.[11]

[11]Psalm 105:47, *NAB.*

TWENTY-FIRST SUNDAY IN ORDINARY TIME

INTRODUCTORY RITES

Opening Song (or Entrance Antiphon)

Listen, Lord and answer me. Save your servant who trusts in you. I call to you all day long, have mercy on me. (Ps 85:1–3)[1]

Opening Prayer

Let us pray
[with minds fixed on eternal truth]

Pause for silent prayer.

Lord our God,
all truth is from you,
and you alone bring oneness of heart.
Give your people the joy
of hearing your word in every sound
and of longing for your presence more than life itself.
May all the attractions of a changing world
serve only to bring us
the peace of your kingdom which this world does not give.
Grant this through Christ our Lord.[2]

LITURGY OF THE WORD

The readings are proclaimed.

First Reading
Isaiah 22:15, 19–23

Shebna, the master of the palace, was a principal official of King Hezekiah's court. As far as Isaiah was concerned, he was a rogue. Anyone who wished to see the king had to go through Shebna first. He wore the great key of the palace looped over his shoulder as a sign that he was the keeper of the keys of the House of David.

In verses 15–18 of this chapter, Isaiah revealed the reason Shebna was deposed. He feathered his own self-interests rather than the interests of the king and the people. He used his office for his own purposes. He ordered the construction of a lavish tomb for himself on the top of a hillside. Usually only the wealthy built such tombs as a perpetual sign of their greatness and nobility.

Scholars believe that Isaiah's disdain for Shebna was far greater than his stated offenses warranted, however. Shebna's grandiose tomb and a fascination with chariots were hardly causes for Isaiah to be so upset. Isaiah probably held Shebna responsible for being the mastermind behind Hezekiah's alliance with Egypt against Syria.

Shebna was removed and Eliakim was appointed in his place. As a sign of Eliakim's court authority, he was vested with a robe, sash, and key. The image of the peg in a sure spot was presented as a sign of the permanence of his investiture. However, later in Isaiah we learn the rest of the story. Eliakim ended up no better than Shebna. Eliakim also abused his power and betrayed those he served. Both officials are an example of how not to use one's authority.

The keeper of the keys of David's House was an image the early church appropriated to apply to Jesus. Jesus passed his authority subsequently to the apostles.

Responsorial Psalm
Psalm 138:1–3, 6, 8

Today's psalm reflects the first reading in that we are reminded that God's plan will not be thwarted by unfaithful human beings.

Second Reading
Romans 11:33–36

(Refer to the First Sunday of Advent for an Overview of Paul's Letter to the Romans.)

Today's Pericope: Today's pericope from Romans draws the doctrinal section of his letter to a close.

[1]Twenty-First Sunday in Ordinary Time: "Entrance Antiphon," *The Sacramentary.*

[2]Twenty-First Sunday in Ordinary Time: "Alternative Opening Prayer," *The Sacramentary.*

Paul, sadly and with resignation, speaks about Israel's place in God's plan for the salvation of the world. It frustrated this apostle to the Gentiles to know that his own beloved people refused to see what was so clear to Paul and to the throng of Gentile converts. He could not understand why Israel could not accept Jesus as messiah and savior of the world. He tried to understand, but there was no explanation. He finally decided to accept and trust God's will.

Paul set forth his theology of salvation, concluding, as do most theologians, that God cannot and will not be confined or defined.

> But the theologian must always confess the inadequacies of his or her work. The riches and wisdom of God are always too deep to penetrate, his judgements and his ways are unsearchable. No theologian has ever known the mind of the Lord. No theology, however venerable, can claim to be absolute. There comes a time when the theologian must lay down the pen and confess the relativity of all his or her formulations. Theology is therefore always subject to change. And theology is best done in the context of liturgy. It must be doxological. . . . True theology emerges from liturgy and returns to it.[3]

Gospel
Matthew 16:13–20

Step 1
Naming One's Experience

What were your first impressions? What was your first response to the gospel (or the other readings)?[4] What captured your attention?

Each person names his or her initial impression. Statements should be brief. No reasons should be given at this time. All simply listen without agreeing or disagreeing.

[3] *PL*, 160, 161.

[4] The primary focus of reflection is the gospel. However, very often the other readings demand attention and must be brought into the dialogue.

Step 2
Understanding

In a brief statement, what do you think this gospel is trying to convey?

Step 3
Input from Vision/Story/Tradition

Liturgical Context

There is an internal unity between the Twenty-First and the Twenty-Second Sundays of Ordinary Time. For the first time in Matthew's gospel, Peter emerges today as a leading figure, a person who occupies a special place within the ranks of the disciples. Peter confesses Jesus as Son of the living God and Jesus confers on him special leadership responsibilities in the community. In next Sunday's gospel reading, Peter finds it difficult to accept that Jesus must suffer and die to bring about the kingdom.

The first reading is chosen for today's liturgy to introduce us to a shadowy character who possessed a place of authority in the House of David. A contrast is thus set up between the two models of authority. It also foreshadows the day of the Lord in which a new and trustworthy leader will come to rule the people. Jesus was that trustworthy steward and today is the day of the Lord. Jesus is the long-awaited One. Today he passes the torch and establishes authority in the new covenant he came to establish.

We are reminded in today's Alternative Opening Prayer that all truth comes from God alone. God gives us the power and the authority to confess Jesus as Lord. It is in this confession that we become his agents and work toward establishing peace in the world. The authority Jesus established in his church continues in the celebration of the eucharist. The Prayer After Communion asks that our eucharist "guide and direct our efforts to please God." We are reminded in the Prayer Over the Gifts that it was Jesus' death and resurrection that established us as church. The paschal mystery is the foundation for the authority Jesus bestows on Peter today.

In today's liturgy there is a reflection centered around the understanding of "authority." Sometimes the words *authority* and *power* are interchanged, as it is often difficult to separate them. Power generally refers to the strength, skill, resources, or energy a person has to carry out a task or to achieve a certain goal. It does not necessarily imply that force needs to accompany the action to achieve results. Sometimes power refers to the conferral of God-given authority (John 19:11). People can possess such authority, yet act contrary to God's will. Power can refer to military, economic, political, human, and spiritual strength.

Authority usually accompanies the power to back up the command imposed.

> Perhaps the best distinction is between the authority one has to issue a command and the external power one can bring to bear, if necessary, to ensure that the command is carried out. Authority can be said to do what one wills in a given instance. It refers especially to the right one has, by virtue of office, position, or relationship, to command obedience.[5]

When power is coercive, domineering, and controlling, it is ineffectual. Since there is no consensus for that type of power, it must be maintained by force. There is an inherent responsibility in the way human beings structure power, both in the social milieu and in institutions. Theologians are looking at power as "empowerment of people to become fully human within social systems that work to sustain justice for all.... Thus power wears the face of enabling, love, voice, vision, community, and transformative action...."[6]

Gospel Exegesis

The facilitator gives input regarding what critical biblical scholarship has to say about this text. The input includes insights as to how people would have heard the gospel in Jesus' time.

[5]D. Sweetland, "Power," *CPDBT,* 746.

[6]A. Graff, "Power in Relation to Human Beings," *CPDBT,* 751.

Two verses in this chapter of Matthew deal with the issue of Jesus as messiah. Verse 13 is included in today's pericope and deals with the identity of the Son of Man. Verse 21 (not included in today's pericope) is a reminder that the messiah will endure suffering. Peter breaks into the scene in verse 16 and again in verse 22. In verse 16, Peter asserts that Jesus is the messiah. In verse 22, Peter suggests to Jesus that he [Jesus] should not have to undergo suffering. Although Jesus affirms Peter for understanding his identity and calls him the rock upon which the church will be built, when Peter refuses to accept that Jesus must suffer, Jesus rebukes him and calls him an obstacle.

There is a powerful lesson in today's gospel. Leadership bears an awesome responsibility in the church. It depends on the action and grace of God. In order for Peter to be the rock of faith rather than a stumbling block, he had to pattern his life after the example of Jesus who died out of love for a sinful world. Thus, those who exercise God-given authority can expect to suffer. Jesus, shepherd and servant, is the model to follow.

Matthew changed Mark's version of this scene. In Mark's gospel, Peter acknowledges Jesus as the Son of the living God. Upon Peter's confession, the disciples are warned to keep silent. Jesus then informs them of the necessity of his passion, whereupon Peter remonstrates and Jesus rebukes him saying, "Get behind me, Satan." Matthew, on the other hand, places Jesus' prediction of his passion, Peter's objection, and Jesus' subsequent rebuke in a later scene, after Peter's confession of faith in Jesus as Son of God.

Jesus then praises and blesses Peter and calls him "Rock," the foundation upon which Jesus will build his church. Peter was not praised for making a good educated guess. Peter's acknowledgment of Jesus was praised as being divinely inspired. The Pharisees demanded signs. Peter asked for nothing and was given everything: God's spoken revelation of the Son. Jesus promises that nothing will prevail against the church he has come to establish. Then Jesus follows with the promise of the keys and the authority to bind and loose.

According to Reginald Fuller, some scholars maintain that this portion of the text was written from a post-resurrection perspective by an early Aramaic-speaking community who was asserting that Peter himself, not Peter's faith, is the Rock upon which to build the church.[7] David Garland posits that it was Peter's confession of faith that was the foundation of the church. When Christians stand on the confession of Jesus Christ, Son of the living God, messiah and savior of the world, there is no power that can stand against the name and the person of the risen Christ. "This confession alone provides the church a secure, defensive position from which it can repel attacks from the powers of the abyss. It is the foundation for strong faith as opposed to little faith."[8]

Scriptural scholarship regarding the continuation of Peter's authority in the church is divided according to denominational lines. Protestant scholars understand this saying about the "Rock" to mean a "once-and-for-all role that played such a large part in the foundation of the Church after the first Easter and resurrection appearances (Cullman), and sees the power of the keys and of binding and loosing as continued in the Church as a whole, though capable of being entrusted to particular officers by the community (Marxsen)."[9] Anglican and Orthodox understand the authority to be shared by the entire episcopate, while giving Rome a special place in that collegial office. Catholic scholarship, of course, understands Peter's authority to be vested in the papacy.

There is a growing tendency by all scholars to attest to this section as an affirmation of Peter's authority as rooted in the witness to the resurrection. God's fidelity to the human race continues to be operative in the authority given through the keys and in the power to bind and loose.

Three things emerge in this text as primary: the church is built on solid rock—a sure foundation, its strength will stand against the powers of evil, and Peter is given authority for the church. Peter's position in the church cannot be questioned. He is mentioned in all four gospels. Peter was the first disciple to be called and is placed first in any listing of the disciples. He was the first witness of the resurrection and John's gospel names Peter as the one who will feed Jesus' sheep.[10] The revelation of Jesus to Peter and Peter's subsequent confession is the foundation upon which the church will stand. Peter, weak and confused though he sometimes was, is the established leader of faith.

The foundation of this church will not be toppled by the power of evil or the power of death. Trouble will come, the boat will be tossed about by the torrents of life, but nothing will permanently destroy the church. Jesus' resurrection protects the church from destruction.

As observed in the first reading today, for someone to be given the keys was a sign of vested authority. "The keys are an image for God's stewardship of God's affairs on earth."[11] The keys afford Peter the authority to interpret and teach the pearls of God's reign so others may be drawn in. Later on, Jesus accused the scribes and Pharisees of shutting people out of God's reign. Their teaching dissuaded people from embracing the good news of the gospel. When Jesus spewed his "woes" against them, they were woes against their role as interpreters of God's word. When Jesus conferred the keys upon Peter, he was also taking away the teaching office from the Pharisees. Jesus legitimated the teaching authority of the new covenant.

The authority to bind and loose will allow the church to determine what is permitted and what is forbidden. Peter was given the authority to establish rules, to grant exemption to the rules, and to make decisions based on the gospel of Jesus. One example of this authority was Peter's decision to allow the entry of uncircumcised Gentiles into the church. Matthew makes the point that integral to binding and loosing is the interpretation of the law of Moses and the gospel of Jesus. This authority to interpret, according to David Garland, includes the task of governing, discipline, condemnation, and acquittal. Since the revelation of Jesus given to Peter was also given to others (14:33), and since the blessing given to Peter was also shared by others (13:16), it holds that the authority to bind and loose was given also to the entire church.[12]

[7]*PL,* 161.

[8]*RM,* 171.

[9]Ibid.

[10]Ibid., 170.

[11]Ibid., 171.

[12]Ibid., 173.

Another critical element in the authority Jesus came to establish was the imperative to serve. The authority Jesus passed on to Peter in today's gospel was rooted in his passion and death, and his mission to lay down his life for others. "It is not a power to dominate but to serve."[13] The authority he passed on to Peter and the church is the authority we are all given as a royal, priestly people. At our baptism we were anointed priest, prophet, and ruler. As priest, we were commissioned to serve one another; as prophet, we were commissioned to proclaim the word of God; and as ruler, we were baptized to lead all people to Jesus Christ. Any leadership that is not rooted in the biblical imperative to love is not authority at all—it is abusive power. The biblical imperative to love is rooted in justice. Thus, wherever there are starving, marginalized, and oppressed peoples, the authority we have been given through the ministry Christ passed on to the church is to address those needs and to respond in love.

Proclaim the gospel again.

Sometimes we gain new insights when we hear the text after the interpretation has been given. Someone from the group proclaims the gospel a second time.

STEP 4
TESTING

Conversation with the Liturgy and the Scriptures

Test your original understanding in dialogue with the text.

(You might consider breaking into smaller groups.)

Were there any new insights for you in light of the exegesis? How does your original understanding of this gospel compare with what we just shared? How does this story speak to your life?

Sharing Life Experience

Participants share an experience from their lives that connects with the biblical interpretation just shared.

Those who truly witness to Jesus Christ and have the most credibility (authority) are those who put their lives on the line and live the paschal mystery. Mother Teresa comes immediately to mind. She spoke with authority because of the witness of her life, not because she was a nun, or a great orator, or a woman of stature. There is a woman in our parish who speaks with authority, and when she speaks people listen. She offers her life in service of others. She does not complain or boast about all she does in the Lord's service. She commands the respect of the entire parish. When she speaks in the community, she speaks with authority—she has earned the right. Whenever we want to get a sense of the pulse of the community, we seek her advice. She will not hesitate to tell us—bluntly, if need be. She supports change, but is pastorally concerned about how change occurs. She does not give in to petty gossip and always goes out on a limb in the service of truth. No one has conferred this authority upon her. She has received it because of her baptism and the way in which she has lived her baptismal call as priest, prophet, and ruler. She has been given the keys of the kingdom and she opens many doors with those keys.

All share their life experience.

How was today's gospel an important message for Matthew's community? How is it an important word for your community today? How does this word invite transformation in us as church? How are biblical themes of covenant, exodus, creation, and community evident in today's liturgy, and what do they mean in the life of the church? How does today's message about Peter's (and subsequently our) confession of faith, community, and authority speak to the situation in the church today? Does our understanding of those issues invite reflection, dialogue, and transformation—or divisive entrenchment? Do you still feel the same way about this text as when you began? Has your original understanding been stretched, challenged, or affirmed?

STEP 5
DECISION

The gospel demands a response.

[13] *SWTLY,* 209.

How does today's liturgy invite transformation? In what specific ways might your parish be invited to respond? How have you changed or been invited to change as a result of this conversation? What is one concrete action you will take this week as a response to the liturgy today?

Pastoral Considerations: Today's liturgy might prompt discussion in small groups regarding the proper exercise of power and authority in our lives, in the church, and in the world. This might also be a good time to discern the ways in which we are invited to make the same confession of faith that Peter made in today's gospel. Perhaps this is a good time to reflect on the profession of faith we make at every eucharistic liturgy and what that means as we live our lives. Today's liturgy would also be an excellent springboard for us to name the ways in which the church models Jesus' authority and the way in which his authority was rooted in service and in the offering of his life. How do we as church exemplify that authority? How do we fall short?

Christian Initiation: Today's liturgy naturally lends itself to the celebration of a rite of acceptance. Peter's confession of faith, and the conferral of Jesus' authority to Peter, are given to us all as we willingly embrace the cross of Christ and live the gospel in our everyday lives.

DOCTRINAL ISSUES

What church truth/teaching/doctrinal issue could be drawn from the gospel for the Twenty-First Sunday in Ordinary Time?

Participants suggest possible doctrinal themes that flow from the readings.

Possible Doctrinal Themes

Confession of faith, teaching authority of the church, royal priesthood rooted in baptism, conversion, service, mystery of the church, reign of God, hierarchy of truths, church structure, leadership, discipleship, magisterium, *sensus fidelium* (sense of the faithful), papacy

Present the doctrinal material at this time.

1. The facilitator gives input on a particular doctrinal issue of his/her prior choosing. OR
2. The group chooses a doctrinal issue from the list they created. They read together from the Doctrinal Appendix.

(The doctrinal issues are found in the Doctrinal Appendix in the back of this workbook. If you are choosing an issue from this resource, please refer to it now.)

Reflection questions centered around the chosen doctrinal theme can be found at the end of each topic in the Doctrinal Appendix. The questions are based on the five-step reflection process. If you choose a topic not included in the Doctrinal Appendix, craft your own questions according to the same five-step process.

Following the reflection questions you will be reminded to return to chapter 7, "Preparing the Catechetical Session," to assist you in crafting your own session.

Closing Prayer

Merciful God,
the perfect sacrifice of Jesus Christ
made us your people.
In your love,
grant peace and unity to your Church.
We ask this through Christ our Lord.[14]

[14]Twenty-First Sunday in Ordinary Time: "Prayer Over the Gifts," *The Sacramentary.*

Twenty-Second Sunday in Ordinary Time

Environment

Fall is the time of harvest. Since we are tuned in to our culture's natural rhythm of the seasons, fall is also a time for new beginnings that coincide with the beginning of the academic year.

> For the church the harvest is an intense spiritual image of the paschal mystery. . . . The liturgist Pius Parsch wrote: "The autumn of the church year is devoted to preparation for the end of life and the second coming of Christ. Now we more readily see the truth: Advent is really a continuation of the church's autumn season, her preparation for the Savior's return." Without overemphasizing the imagery, we might say that the weeks between Pentecost and Advent are a gradually intensifying ingathering, a process that echoes the harvest and that is completed in the liturgy (and in the agricultural cycle) at Christmas and Epiphany, at the turning of the year.[1]

Some natural harvest symbols of autumn that are easily incorporated into the catechetical environment are: squash, gourds, pumpkins, cornucopias, grapevines, bundled grains and grasses, corn shocks, dried flowers, vegetables, cattails, leaves, acorns, fall flowers, fruits and vegetables, honeycombs and honey. The green of ordinary time might be laced with the deep tones of red, purple, yellow, gold, and brown. Tasteful art and icons of the prominent saints and fall feasts that appear during this season might be incorporated throughout autumn, such as the feasts of the Blessed Virgin Mary (August 15) and John the Baptist (August 29), Holy Cross (September 14), the Archangels Michael, Gabriel, and Raphael (September 29), All Saints, All Souls (November 1, 2).

The challenge of taking up our cross and following Christ is a strong message in today's liturgy. It would be most important to display and enthrone a "worthy" cross in your catechetical environment.

[1] *CY*, 176.

INTRODUCTORY RITES

Opening Song (or Entrance Antiphon)

I call to you all day long, have mercy on me, O Lord. You are good and forgiving, full of love for all who call to you. (Ps 85:3, 5)[2]

Opening Prayer

Let us pray
[to God who forgives all who call upon him]

Pause for silent prayer.

Lord God of power and might,
nothing is good which is against your will,
and all is of value which comes from your hand.
Place in our hearts a desire to please you
and fill our minds with insight into love,
so that every thought may grow in wisdom
and all our efforts may be filled with your peace.
We ask this through Christ our Lord.[3]

LITURGY OF THE WORD

The readings are proclaimed.

First Reading
Jeremiah 20:7–9

(See the Twelfth Sunday in Ordinary Time for an Overview of the Book of the Prophet Jeremiah.)

Of all the Old Testament prophets, Jeremiah looked and acted the most like a new covenant prophet. He preached that witness to God means

[2] Twenty-Second Sunday in Ordinary Time: "Entrance Antiphon," *The Sacramentary*.

[3] Twenty-Second Sunday in Ordinary Time: "Opening Prayer," *The Sacramentary*.

suffering. This is the hallmark of Christian belief. Paul preached Jesus Christ crucified, and that through our suffering we share in Jesus' suffering. The word goes forth through the witness of the servant's faithful life of suffering. Jeremiah was scorned for preaching God's word. Yet he could do no less than respond to God's invitation in his life. Jeremiah was not prepared for the rebuffs he received. The word that came forth from Jeremiah was a word of judgment on his own people. It was a word that promised ruin. How could he deliver such a message to those he loved?

Jeremiah denounced the temple liturgy and promised destruction upon Jerusalem during the reign of King Jehoiakim. He was beaten and imprisoned for his efforts. Yet Jeremiah never relented. In today's reading, however, his depression has led him to self-doubt and pity. He feels he was not cut out for this mission and questions why God chose him. God ultimately assures him that not only was he cut out for it, he was chosen for it even before he was born. Jeremiah felt that he was tricked by God. No matter how he tried, he could not escape the compulsion to preach God's word, regardless of what happened to him. In spite of his limitations, Jeremiah had been empowered by God and the fire within his heart could not be squelched.

Responsorial Psalm
Psalm 63:2, 3–4, 5–6, 8–9

The psalmist's cries, while deeply personal, were appropriated for the temple liturgy to have a corporate meaning. The "I" of the psalm is read through the eyes of the people of God. On their journey to the kingdom, the people of God pass through a dry and weary land. But as they assemble for worship, they encounter God's rich banquet. They are blessed. For Christians, the "name" they will call on in worship and the "you" they will honor is Christ. Thus, in the midst of any desert sojourn, God's people have the confidence to gather in praise of God and call on his name.

Second Reading
Romans 12:1–2

(Refer to the First Sunday of Advent for an Overview of Paul's Letter to the Romans.)

Today's Pericope: Paul's exhortation today "... begins by regarding the Christian moral life as worship of God...."[4] Living the Christian ethic has been called true Christian worship. As far as Paul is concerned, true Christian worship exists in the way in which the Christian lives his or her life.

In the scriptures there was a constant exhortation that people's ethical life should correspond to their life of worship. In other words, how could someone be so arrogant as to come before God in worship while living in a way that does not honor God? It was inconceivable. Liturgy that does not speak to the living of one's life is empty and meaningless. Jesus worshiped God through the way he lived a life of obedience.

True metanoia is evidenced by behavior. Converted Christians live the ethical imperatives inherent in the gospel. The decisions of Christians are naturally rooted in the gospel, if true conversion has taken place. Conversion results in a transformed mind that is able to discern the will of God and live it in love. A transformed mind is the result of living the paschal mystery of Jesus. When one opts to embrace the cross and listen and respond to the word of God they are a new creation in Christ. Evidence of this new life is to be observed through their ethical behavior. This is also the function and the reality of the liturgy. We gather to listen to the word of God, to remember and make present the sacrifice of Jesus and to conform our lives to that sacrifice. As a result we are converted more deeply to God and pledge to go out and live in a transformed manner.

Gospel
Matthew 16:21–27

STEP 1
NAMING ONE'S EXPERIENCE

What were your first impressions? What was your first response to the gospel (or the other readings)?[5] What captured your attention?

[4] *DL* (IV), 172.

[5] The primary focus of reflection is the gospel. However, very often the other readings demand attention and must be brought into the dialogue.

Each person names his or her initial impression. Statements should be brief. No reasons should be given at this time. All simply listen without agreeing or disagreeing.

STEP 2
UNDERSTANDING

In a brief statement, what do you think this gospel is trying to convey?

STEP 3
INPUT FROM VISION/STORY/TRADITION

Liturgical Context

Today's gospel is the second in a two-part sequence. Last week we celebrated Peter's confession of faith. Today Jesus reminds us that unless we lose our lives for his sake we cannot be saved. Taking up one's cross is the way of the true disciple.

The antiphon for the Communion Rite best reflects the heart of today's liturgy—that we are called to be suffering servants for the gospel of Christ. It reminds us that the reign of God is ours when we suffer persecution for the sake of the gospel.

In addition to carrying our cross, our eyes and our hearts must be turned toward God in love. It is from this love that the power to carry the cross flows. Without love the cross means nothing. Today's Alternative Opening Prayer asks that our minds be filled with "insight into love." This insight into love leads us to please God, which ultimately leads us to live the example of Christ and offer our lives for others. The Prayer After Communion asks that the communion we have just shared will strengthen us to love and serve God in one another. We cannot love God and treat our brothers and sisters with contempt, scorn, or indifference.

We begin every celebration with the sign of the cross. In that gesture we affirm that we are baptized into Jesus' death and resurrection and that we will live the cross in our everyday lives. We will suffer for the sake of the gospel. (See the Easter Vigil for further development on the symbol of the cross.)

Gospel Exegesis

The facilitator gives input regarding what critical biblical scholarship has to say about this text. The input includes insights as to how people would have heard the gospel in Jesus' time.

There are two predictions of Jesus' impending suffering and death. The first one takes place in verse 21 in today's pericope; the second one takes place in chapter 17, verses 22–23. The two predictions frame the conversation between Jesus and his disciples regarding the implications of his ministry. Included in this section is Peter's refusal to accept Jesus as the suffering servant of Isaiah, rather than the triumphant liberator of Israel. Also included is Jesus' teaching regarding the implications of suffering for discipleship and salvation, and a warning about the coming judgment of God. Jesus assures the disciples that they will be vindicated. We also hear the story of Jesus' transfiguration, an explanation about the coming of Elijah and the resurrection of the dead, and a scene that stresses the importance of faith during Jesus' earthly absence.[6]

Jesus gives his disciples a dose of reality in today's gospel. He wants to make sure they understand the implications of his mission. There is to be no confusion. They have accepted and confessed Jesus as messiah. Now they must understand the will of God. They must understand Jesus' mission. As the promised One, he will suffer. At this point in the story we are not given a reason for Jesus' suffering. It is sufficient for now to know that Jesus' mission involves suffering and that there is no other way. Preconceived notions of Israel's messiah are to be laid to rest. This messiah is a suffering servant. He is ready to fulfill his mission.

Peter's reaction to Jesus' suffering was rooted in Israel's hopes for a messiah that would unite the nation and lead the people in an earthly kingdom. "The Messiah was expected to inflict suffering and death on Israel's enemies and on the wicked within Israel, not to experience it himself."[7] Since Jesus promised that the gates of hell would not prevail against the kingdom, then surely the king

[6] *RM*, 179.
[7] *MI*, 194.

of that kingdom should be immune from suffering and death. Peter may have even unconsciously hoped that, as Jesus' chief minister, he too might forego suffering and move right to glory.

Jesus rebuked Peter and said, "Get behind me, Satan." His rebuke of Peter is reminiscent of the temptation scene with Satan in the desert. Peter's way was contrary to God's will. Like Satan, Peter attempted to lead Jesus away from the cross and entice him with visions of a triumphant earthly kingdom. Jesus exhorted Peter to get out of the way. There is a touch of irony in this scene: "Simon the Stone has placed himself in front of Jesus and become a rock to stumble over."[8] Jesus' mission simply would not be thwarted by the machinations of human desire. Even though Jesus rebuked Peter, there is an inherent invitation in his rebuke. He did not say to Peter, "Get lost and never return." He told him to get behind him, to get out of the way, but to follow him. Jesus' rebuke of Peter includes forgiveness for his mistake and the confidence in him that he will continue to walk the way of the cross.

Jesus then seized the moment and taught the disciples about the rigors of discipleship. It is not enough for disciples to make a confession of faith. They must become like the Master. They must denounce self and live for others. Disciples are to center their entire lives on Jesus. They are to take up their cross.

To deny oneself has Semitic origins and is an idiom that means "love less" or "give lower priority to" oneself. It means to submit to the will of another and to avoid the security promised by the temptations of this world. Self-denial involves total commitment to God. Self-denial involves the ordering of one's passions, appetites, and will to God's will. Douglas Hare cited modern studies which show that verse 24 "has had a negative influence, because it reinforces a cultural pressure to subordinate oneself to others in a way that is not self-affirming."[9] This is especially true for women. Hare affirms that when properly understood, this saying in Matthew's gospel is a celebration of oneself as a child of God. It is not a call for self-effacement. When we follow Jesus, we are subordinate only to God. Christians are only reciprocally subordinate to one another.

[8]Ibid., 195.

[9]Ibid.

Following Jesus involves more than a confession of faith. It means following him even if it leads to persecution, misunderstanding, and suffering. Following Jesus means that we embrace his life—all of it. It means that we are willing to lay down our lives for others. Jesus' teaching about the cross does not demand that we become martyrs. Rather, it extols "fearlessness in following the crucified Lord."[10]

There is a temptation in this text to reduce it to simply offering our daily troubles and annoyances to Jesus. While this is a laudable endeavor, it nevertheless trivializes the implications of taking up the cross. It was not just death that Jesus endured; it was a shameful death. Embracing one's cross means to endure ridicule and hostility from those who reject God. Disciples must be prepared to endure persecution because of the gospel. The cross is the source of humanity's redemption. This instrument of torture was transformed into our hope. As absurd as this seems, it is the foundation of our faith. Disciples are to find meaning midst the sufferings of life. When believers embrace the cross and offer their lives, when they lose their life for others, they gain everlasting life. Those who are willing to pay the price will be vindicated at the final judgment. The lives of human beings will be judged according to the way in which they lived or did not live for others.

Proclaim the gospel again.

Sometimes we gain new insights when we hear the text after the interpretation has been given. Someone from the group proclaims the gospel a second time.

STEP 4
TESTING

Conversation with the Liturgy and the Scriptures

Test your original understanding in dialogue with the text.

(You might consider breaking into smaller groups.)

[10]Ibid.

How do you feel about this gospel? Were there any new insights for you? How does this story speak to your life?

Sharing Life Experience

Participants share an experience from their lives that connects with the biblical interpretation just shared.

So often in the midst of the liturgical year we are asked to reflect on the implications of the cross for our lives. Very seldom do I have an opportunity to suffer in the way Jesus tells us we will have to suffer in today's gospel. I do not have to suffer persecution for the sake of the gospel. There have been times where I have been misunderstood and wrongly judged, but the kind suffering Jesus is speaking of here is very seldom asked of us in contemporary America. We are not tortured and put to death for our belief in Christ. There are places in the world that know such suffering and persecution. We are blessed to live in freedom.

However, we are invited to endure situations in which living the gospel results in ridicule and abuse. A friend of mine who entered the church at the Easter Vigil shared how he had to draw on all his reserves in order to keep from responding in hatred and violence to a coworker who attacked him both physically and verbally. The world would have suggested that he meet violence with violence. My friend offered the hand of reconciliation and was rebuffed. He denied his need for revenge and accepted a solution that was contrary to the way of the world. He picked up his cross. He found it incredibly difficult to carry, but was aware that he would be given the strength to respond in faith. It was a very painful experience, but for him it gave new meaning to the Christian imperative in today's gospel to carry our cross.

Communities embrace the cross when they choose to be a voice for justice. Our community is extremely generous. There is an overall sense that we have a responsibility to the world's poor. The parish has built a school in Haiti, plus two clinics and a church in Latin America, to name just some of their outreach activities. However, there was a little controversy over those endeavors. The attitude of a very few people was, "I support the church with my donations. If I wanted to donate to those things I would have donated to them myself. I expect my donations to this parish to go for the upkeep of the parish. It is not the responsibility of this parish to tithe." At one time, they made their loud complaints sound as if they were speaking for "everyone." "Everyone" turned out to be less than what you could count on one hand. The experience reminded us that communities as a whole will meet rejection and are invited to carry the cross and to suffer hostility when trying to live the paschal mystery.

On a personal level, I can connect Jesus' interpretation of carrying the cross to the challenge of raising teenagers in today's world. My teenagers are my joy. They offer excitement and challenge and never a dull moment in our home. We have tried and often failed to be a voice of unconditional, yet challenging love and acceptance in a world of alienation and permissiveness. We have also tried to be a voice of morality in a world that tells them that casual sex is a normative cultural experience and care for the poor is not their business. The culture tells our kids that upholding Christian virtue is "not cool," irrelevant, and a thing of the past. The kingdom of self is preached to the kids by the culture. Trying to uphold gospel values in a culture that holds them in disdain is extremely difficult. Kids that try to live moral and just lives are ridiculed by their peers. Those who try to live the mission of Christ are often humiliated. It is a challenge to be a parent, or a teenager, in today's complicated world. Trying to live a just, moral life is tantamount to carrying the cross midst the struggles of contemporary living.

All share their life experience.

What was Matthew's concern in his interpretation of Jesus' prediction of the Passion? How does today's gospel speak to your community and to you? How are the biblical themes of covenant, exodus, creation, and community expressed in today's liturgy? What do they mean for your life? What does today's liturgy have to say to you as a disciple of the Lord? How has conversation with this liturgy invited transformation of your attitudes or behavior? What are the areas in your life that need to be conformed more with today's gospel? In what way do you relate to Peter in this gospel? Is there any resistance in you (or your community) to the challenge of today's gospel? Do you still feel the same way about this text as when you began?

Step 5
Decision

The gospel demands a response.

In what specific ways is your parish called to respond? What one concrete action will you take this week as a response to the liturgy today?

Pastoral Considerations: It is always a challenge to discern the ways in which a community is or is not living the command to carry the cross of Christ. Does your community address unpopular issues? Does your parish afflict the comfortable and comfort the afflicted? Does your parish's actions reflect its preaching? If you preach about justice, do you reach out in concrete ways to the needs of the poor and suffering? If you are not preaching and living a just word, why aren't you? Does your parish respond to community and civic issues that affect the least among us in a vocal way, or does it ignore such issues? Does your parish address issues of division that occur in the parish or do they go underground? Does your parish treat the poor and lowly with the same respect with which it treats the greatest among you?

Christian Initiation: With Jesus' emphasis on carrying the cross and the implications of discipleship, all of the rites of initiation would be appropriately celebrated today. Perhaps the catechumens would benefit from anointing of catechumens. If there are baptized candidates ready for a rite of reception into full communion, today would be a fitting day to celebrate the completion of their initiation in the paschal mystery of Christ. It would also be most apt to celebrate a rite of acceptance or welcome.

DOCTRINAL ISSUES

What church truth/teaching/doctrinal issue could be drawn from the gospel for the Twenty-Second Sunday in Ordinary Time?

Participants suggest possible doctrinal themes that flow from the readings.

Possible Doctrinal Themes

Cross, paschal mystery, mystery of suffering, cost of discipleship, final judgment, reign of God, Jesus the Suffering Servant of Isaiah, martyrdom, Christian witness, eschatology

Present the doctrinal material at this time.

1. The facilitator gives input on a particular doctrinal issue of his/her prior choosing. OR
2. The group chooses a doctrinal issue from the list they created. They read together from the Doctrinal Appendix.

(The doctrinal issues are found in the Doctrinal Appendix in the back of this workbook. If you are choosing an issue from this resource, please refer to it now.)

Reflection questions centered around the chosen doctrinal theme can be found at the end of each topic in the Doctrinal Appendix. The questions are based on the five-step reflection process. If you choose a topic not included in the Doctrinal Appendix, craft your own questions according to the same five-step process.

Following the reflection questions you will be reminded to return to chapter 7, "Preparing the Catechetical Session," to assist you in crafting your own session.

Closing Prayer

Happy are the peacemakers: they shall be called sons of God.
Happy are those who suffer persecution for justice' sake;
the kingdom of heaven is theirs. (Mt 5:9–10)[11]

[11]Twenty-Second Sunday in Ordinary Time, "Communion Rite," *The Sacramentary.*

Twenty-Third Sunday in Ordinary Time

Environment

See the Twenty-Second Sunday in Ordinary Time.

INTRODUCTORY RITES

Opening Song (or Entrance Antiphon)

Lord, you are just, and the judgments you make are right. Show mercy when you judge me, your servant. (Ps 118:137, 124)[1]

Opening Prayer

Let us pray
[to our just and merciful God]

Pause for silent prayer.

Lord our God,
in you justice and mercy meet.
With unparalleled love you have saved us from death
and drawn us into the circle of your life.
Open our eyes to the wonders this life sets before us,
that we may serve you free from fear
and address you as God our Father.
We ask this in the name of Jesus the Lord.[2]

LITURGY OF THE WORD

The readings are proclaimed.

First Reading
Ezekiel 33:7–9

(Refer to the Fifth Sunday of Lent for an Overview of Ezekiel.)

[1]Twenty-Third Sunday in Ordinary Time: "Entrance Antiphon," *The Sacramentary.*

[2]Twenty-Third Sunday in Ordinary Time: "Opening Prayer," *The Sacramentary.*

Today's Pericope: Ezekiel understood his role as prophet to be that of watchman who discerns the moral pulse of the culture, and who also watches for and announces to the people any impending disasters. He was to warn the house of Israel so they might take notice and mend their ways. The job of the watchman stationed at an outpost was to warn the nation of imposing threat. The people entrusted their security to the sentinel.

Scholars suggest that Ezekiel's oracle was written in response to the invasion by Nebuchadnezzar and the subsequent destruction of Jerusalem. It is believed that Ezekiel was one of the first to be deported to Babylon before the final destruction of Jerusalem ten years earlier. His oracle was thus a warning to those left in Judah and a word of consolation to those who had been deported to Babylon.

Ezekiel preached that war was the least of their troubles. They had no one to blame but their own wicked ways and their failure to live the covenant. War was symptomatic of the decadence of the society. Breaking the covenant with God was a far more grave event than being pillaged by Babylon. Ezekiel placed the blame of this rupture on individuals within the nation. One reason he spoke to individuals rather than to the nation was because of the "destruction of the nation as a corporate entity."[3] The Lord had appointed Ezekiel to watch over the house of Israel, and he realized full well that he would be held personally responsible if he failed to prophesy to his brothers and sisters as the Lord had instructed. His obligation would be fulfilled, however, once he exhorted them to repent, turn away from their sinful ways, and return to their covenant with God. It was also Ezekiel's job to assure the people of God's goodness. The responsibility for responding to Ezekiel's admonitions, however, was on the individual; it was no longer Ezekiel's problem. "Ezekiel's picture of the prophet as watchman has been selected to go with the gospel which speaks of mutual concern in the

[3]*PL*, 164.

eschatological community in which we all share the gift of the Spirit."[4]

Responsorial Psalm
Psalm 95:1–2, 6–9

Today's psalm is comprised of two sections. One is a call to worship and the other is a warning against the neglect of God's word. The stern warning associated with the second part of this psalm was used by the author of the letter to the Hebrews. It was considered relevant to his church. Just like Israel, who grew weary in the desert, Paul's Hebrew community was also growing lackluster in their practice of Christianity.

Second Reading
Romans 13:8–10

(Refer to the First Sunday of Advent for an Overview of Paul's Letter to the Romans.)

Today's Pericope: Last Sunday Paul exhorted his Roman community regarding their ethical responsibilities. Paul enumerates portions of the Ten Commandments and then summarizes it all with the commandment of love from the Book of Leviticus: "You shall love your neighbor as yourself" (19:18). The bottom line for Paul is that all the commandments can be reduced to one—the law of love. The individual commandments themselves are merely an expression of how love is lived in the context of certain situations.

Paul was acting in the tradition of the rabbis. It was a common practice for the students to quiz the rabbis about which law was the greatest. Paul was not only quoting the essence of Jesus' message but also the heart of the best of Jewish thought. "Rabbi Akiba is quoted as saying, 'You shall love your neighbor as yourself—this is the greatest general principle in the law.'"[5]

Jewish understanding of *neighbor*, however, meant their own citizens. Jesus extended *neighbor* to mean everyone. Paul's message to the Romans is that the law of love was to extend to *all* people. A consistent theme for Paul is that all the actions of Christians should be motivated by the love of God and by God's incredible gratuitous gifts.

Gospel
Matthew 18:15–20

STEP 1
NAMING ONE'S EXPERIENCE

What were your first impressions? What was your first response to the gospel (or the other readings)?[6] What captured your attention?

Each person names his or her initial impression. Statements should be brief. No reasons should be given at this time. All simply listen without agreeing or disagreeing.

STEP 2
UNDERSTANDING

In a brief statement, what do you think this gospel is trying to convey?

STEP 3
INPUT FROM VISION/STORY/TRADITION

Liturgical Context

The eighteenth chapter of Matthew's gospel has been referred to as the "Discourse on the Church." Matthew compiled a corpus of Jesus' teachings that directly refer to ecclesial issues. This is the second section of the discourse. In the first section Jesus addressed who will be first in the kingdom, the issue of scandal, and the behavior the shepherd is to display toward his sheep. Today's pericope begins a sequence that includes the Twenty-Third through the Twenty-Fifth Sundays. This new sequence is a reminder to all the gathered faithful that we are gathered into one community of reconciled believers. The liturgy is a commentary on what it means to be a disciple of

[4] Ibid., 165.
[5] *WWC*, 86.

[6] The primary focus of reflection is the gospel. However, very often the other readings demand attention and must be brought into the dialogue.

the Lord. The old way of violence, hatred, and conflict is not the way of Christians. There is a Christian approach to conflict resolution between Christians.

The Alternative Opening Prayer reminds us that God is the author of justice and mercy and that through the death of Christ we are forgiven and reconciled. The Entrance Antiphon reminds us that God is our judge and we pray that God is merciful in judging us. That same prayer is extended to the church as it relies on God's presence in the judgment it is exhorted to make in the name of Christ (today's gospel).

Gospel Exegesis

The facilitator gives input regarding what critical biblical scholarship has to say about this text. The input includes insights as to how people would have heard the gospel in Jesus' time.

Matthew was writing for a community that was living midst the tension and struggle of enculturation. The intermixing of the races through conversion to Christ was a challenge and often a burden when it came to living the realities of the communal life.

This section of Matthew's gospel is a compilation of Jesus' teaching regarding community life. We are dealing with a community struggling to respond to very real situations in the life of their community. It seeks to answer the question: "What do we do when one of our members fails in his or her responsibility as a disciple of Christ?" After the destruction of the temple in 70 C.E., and the expulsion from the synagogues c. 85 C.E., the Christian church was forced to forge a new identity for itself. The well-defined authority structures of Judaism no longer worked for the emerging Christian church. Matthew tried to fashion the moral and ecclesial life of the community based on the teachings of Jesus. Matthew tells us of Jesus' promise to be present when two or more are gathered in his name. This is the heart of Matthew's ecclesiology: because Jesus is present in the church, the church is to act morally. This motivates the community's response to God and one another.

In today's gospel, Matthew lays out the plan for correction of the brothers and sisters of God's family. It behooves the community to bring those who stray back into the fold. Those who have "missed the mark" (Hebrew—*hattat*, Greek—*hamartia*) are to be reconciled to the community. The "law of the tooth" (law of retaliation) no longer holds in this new community of believers.

The process of reconciliation described in this gospel was to be driven by a spirit of forgiveness. Only when the sinner refused to accept the judgment of the church was the church to impose censures on the sinner. The exhortation to treat the sinner like a Gentile or tax collector is probably not from the mouth of Jesus, but was the early community's way to make a point. It is unlikely that Jesus would have used such terminology when he took such pains to reach out to the Gentiles and the tax collectors.

The power to bind and loose that was conferred on Peter in chapter 16 is now given to the entire church in today's pericope and is a reflection of "an administrative discipline."[7] Matthew reminds his readers that prayer is the unifying force that will reconcile the community. They are gathered in the first place because of Christ. They are church because of Jesus Christ crucified. Christ is present in their midst. They can do no less than behave in love and reconciliation toward one another.

John Pilch provides an interesting perspective on today's gospel. In the ancient Mediterranean world, conflict between people was common. Such conflict could lead to violence and ultimately to blood feuds and the eventual death of all parties involved. People developed strategies for diffusing the conflict before it became unmanageable and then out of control. One technique was to rant and rave loudly, but to avoid carrying out threats. Jesus ranted and raved against Bethsaida, Chorazin, and Capernaum, but left it to God to mete out consequences. It was believed that words, in such cases, spoke louder than actions.

Another strategy was to turn the other cheek rather than to retaliate. Since the text employed the word *brother* in the scenario presented in today's pericope, it was referring to the way of governance within the church itself. Matthew was establishing the way to resolve conflicts within the

[7] *WWC*, 87.

community—not in the world at large. "The word 'brother' (New American Bible translation) in Matthew's gospel always means 'another member of the church' (New Revised Standard Version). The advice is intended to head off conflicts between insiders; it is not intended to govern relationships with outsiders."[8]

Conflict was understood as a result of sin between people. The ancient world was a shame/honor-based culture. To bring shame to someone was a grave offense. A three-step process of conflict resolution is presented in today's gospel: confrontation, negotiation, and adjudication. *Confrontation.* Those who felt they had been dishonored were to go to the offender in private. If there was no intention to bring shame, or if the offense was nothing but a misunderstanding, things were to be worked out in private and everyone would save face; they need not go public with it. *Negotiation.* When confrontation failed, two or three witnesses or negotiators were to go with the victim to settle the dispute. This scenario was semi-private and a legal matter, requiring more than one witness. The witnesses were well aware of the serious nature of their deliberations and of the consequences of bringing false witness. The decision of the witnesses was legally binding. This step of the negotiation was expected to restore honor between the parties so as to avoid this last step of the negotiation. *Adjudication.* All else having failed, the matter was to go before the entire church. All the cultural implications of shame and honor are brought to bear publicly. The community acts as judge and jury. If offenders refuse to accept the decision of the community, they are excommunicated—considered an outsider and expelled from the community. (Tax collectors and Gentiles were considered outsiders.) It was, in essence, a death sentence. Without community there were no roots, no home, no family, no support—no life.

Jesus was understood to be present in the gathered assembly in such matters. Jesus' authority to settle such disputes was given to the community. When the community agrees, God affirms the community's decision. Such conflict in the community of believers is shameful.[9]

[8]*CWJ*, 133.

[9]Ibid., 134, 135.

Gustavo Gutierrez reminds us of the serious implications inherent in today's gospel. It is a gospel that calls the church and its members to accountability as disciples of the Lord. While this is a delicate matter to address in practical terms today, we are challenged to belong to "the ecclesial assembly in an authentic and responsible way."[10] Gutierrez reminds us that when Christians are involved in structures and policies that dehumanize and bring poverty and death, the Christian community has the responsibility to challenge them and bring them to task. Such challenge, however, is to be done in the spirit of prayer and loving correction. The only motivation for correction of this sort is love.

Proclaim the gospel again.

Sometimes we gain new insights when we hear the text after the interpretation has been given. Someone from the group proclaims the gospel a second time.

Step 4
Testing

Conversation with the Liturgy and the Scriptures

Test your original understanding in dialogue with the text.

(You might consider breaking into smaller groups.)

Now that you've heard the exegesis, how do you feel about this gospel? How does your original understanding compare with what we just shared? Were there any new insights for you? How does this story speak to your life?

Sharing Life Experience

Participants share an experience from their lives that connects with the biblical interpretation just shared.

> *If we could only follow the imperatives of this gospel instead of living codependent lives, our parish conflicts would be sources of community building rather than destruction. I remember a situation many years*

[10]*SWTLY*, 217.

ago in a parish where I once worked. There was one person who was extremely divisive. No matter what direction the parish tried to take, this person was a negative voice and force who became enraged with the community and promised to "bring the parish down"—and was nearly successful. If we had been wise enough to follow the imperatives of this gospel, so much pain could have been averted. The situation was allowed to go unchecked for a long period of time. Too much water had gone under the bridge by the time the problem was addressed, so division had gained a foothold and the entire community was impacted.

If unity and love are the hallmarks of our Christian experience, why are they so difficult to maintain? Why do we find it so hard to reach out and confront conflict in a loving way? Very often we think we are taking a stance of humility: "Where do I get off thinking I should confront this person?" While this is sometimes a noble emotion, this attitude more often than not accomplishes nothing so that anger and resentment are given a chance to ferment.

I was struck by the confrontation portion of John Pilch's exegesis of today's gospel. The confrontation was intended to sort out the misunderstanding. Very often the offense was a case of unintentional action or a misunderstanding. We often never get to the point to test those options. We make assumptions about the intentions and the guilt of the offender. In the process we become equally guilty because it puts us in a position of smug self-righteousness. Today's gospel invites us to confront with loving firmness and not to jump to conclusions and solutions without approaching one another in charity and trust.

If we could consistently live today's gospel in this contemporary milieu, people would flock to our parishes, because they would not be able to resist the magnetism of communities that so clearly communicate to the world the message: "See how they love one another."

All share their life experience.

What was Matthew trying to tell his community? How is today's word a relevant word for your community? Is there any situation in your parish that needs the light of today's gospel to speak to it? How does this gospel speak to your life? Does it challenge any situations in your life? How does this gospel invite transformation in your life? Are the biblical themes of covenant, exodus, creation, and community evident in today's scriptures? Do you still feel the same way about this text as when you began? Has your original understanding been stretched, challenged, or affirmed?

STEP 5
DECISION

The gospel demands a response.

In what specific way might your parish be called to respond? What one concrete action will you take this week as a response to the liturgy today?

Pastoral Considerations: Are there presently any situations in your parish that could benefit from the wisdom of today's gospel? Are there unresolved disputes that have the potential to cause serious division in your community? What would it take to address those situations? At a recent workshop, a gentleman was commenting on the practice of many employers in his small town to purposefully hire people for thirty-two hours instead of forty so they would not have to provide benefits—a practice that was wreaking havoc in the lives of single mothers. He was exhorting those present to challenge the members of their parish communities who are employers to look at their own practices in light of the gospel. His suggestion to his listeners was exactly in the spirit of today's gospel. Are there similar situations that you might address in your own community?

DOCTRINAL ISSUES

What church truth/teaching/doctrinal issue could be drawn from the gospel for the Twenty-Third Sunday in Ordinary Time?

Participants suggest possible doctrinal themes that flow from the readings.

Possible Doctrinal Themes

Reconciliation, conflict resolution, non-violence, forgiveness, discipleship, sacrament of reconciliation, prophecy, ethical imperatives of the gospel, foundations of morality

Present the doctrinal material at this time.

1. The facilitator gives input on a particular doctrinal issue of his/her prior choosing. OR
2. The group chooses a doctrinal issue from the list they created. They read together from the Doctrinal Appendix.

(The doctrinal issues are found in the Doctrinal Appendix in the back of this workbook. If you are choosing an issue from this resource, please refer to it now.)

Reflection questions centered around the chosen doctrinal theme can be found at the end of each topic in the Doctrinal Appendix. The questions are based on the five-step reflection process. If you choose a topic not included in the Doctrinal Appendix, craft your own questions according to the same five-step process.

Following the reflection questions you will be reminded to return to chapter 7, "Preparing the Catechetical Session," to assist you in crafting your own session.

Closing Prayer

Lord,
your word and your sacrament
give us food and life.
May this gift of your Son
lead us to share his life for ever.
We ask this through Christ our Lord.[11]

[11]Twenty-Third Sunday in Ordinary Time: "Prayer After Communion," *The Sacramentary*.

Twenty-Fourth Sunday in Ordinary Time

Environment

See the Twenty-Second Sunday in Ordinary Time.

INTRODUCTORY RITES

Opening Song (or Entrance Antiphon)

Give peace, Lord, to those who wait for you and your prophets will proclaim you as you deserve. Hear the prayers of your servant and of your people Israel. (See Sirach 36:18)[1]

Opening Prayer

Let us pray
[that God will keep us faithful in his service]

Pause for silent prayer.

Almighty God,
our creator and guide,
may we serve you with all our heart
and know your forgiveness in our lives.
We ask this through our Lord Jesus Christ, your Son,
who lives and reigns with you and the Holy Spirit,
one God, for ever and ever.[2]

LITURGY OF THE WORD

The readings are proclaimed.

First Reading
Sirach 27:30, 28:7

(Refer to the Feast of the Holy Family for an Overview of the Book of Sirach.)

Since the time of Cyprian (d. 258), the Book of Sirach was also known as the "Church Book" (*Liber Ecclesiasticus*), as it was used to instruct the catechumens. The book is one of the last books of the Old Testament, written very close to the time of the New Testament period.[3] Its central themes are still pertinent today. Today's pericope deals with relationships. Relationship is at the heart of what it means to be human. Healthy, life-giving relationships make the difference between depression, anxiety, and violence versus a vibrant, happy, peace-filled, and meaningful journey through this earthly sojourn. Relationships are what distinguish human beings from the lower levels of creation. Good relationships require effort and discipline.

Pride, egotism, jealousy, power, and control are the driving forces behind the human tendency to destroy rather than to uplift. Unchecked and unbridled anger and resentment are what prompt human beings to kill one another. This is not new. It is part of the human story since Cain killed Abel. Scripture is filled with exhortations and admonishments to restrain these powerful emotions. Sirach emphatically names wrath and anger as "hateful things." He minces no words. Most people know where wrath and anger can lead. Many people have experienced firsthand the internal ravage left by a lost temper. It does not take a biblical sage to know that anger and resentment left unchecked can destroy the human spirit. It is simply good psychology to avoid such things.

Sirach takes the argument a step further, however. He appeals directly to our relationship with God. Those who know God and are in relationship with God must avoid anger and resentment because they are cognizant "of their own need for divine mercy."[4] Only God has the authority to judge. It is arrogance for human beings to assume God's role. To do so leads to vengeance. People can seek God's mercy and forgiveness. God is magnanimous in his love and eager to grant forgiveness. God does not keep a divine score card but wipes clean the slate of sinners. Sinners in turn are to extend the same mercy to others.

[1]Twenty-Fourth Sunday in Ordinary Time: "Entrance Antiphon," *The Sacramentary.*

[2]Twenty-Fourth Sunday in Ordinary Time: "Opening Prayer," *The Sacramentary.*

[3]*PL,* 167.

[4]*DL* (IV), 186.

God is in covenant relationship with human beings. At the beginning of the world God promised to care for his children. In response, God's children are to love God utterly and completely. They are also to love, care for, and behave morally toward one another and toward the earth. The entire saga of God's relationship with people is based on divine mercy and grace. When men and women do not extend the same forgiveness and mercy to others, they simply cannot expect to be recipients of God's merciful bounty.

Responsorial Psalm
Psalm 103:1–4, 9–12

Today's psalm is chosen for its theme of forgiveness. Human forgiveness is to be patterned after the forgiveness and mercy shown by God, a theme that resonates both with the first reading and the gospel.

Second Reading
Romans 14:7–9

(Refer to the First Sunday of Advent for an Overview of Paul's Letter to the Romans.)

Today's Pericope: The context of this reading is set in the dispute between the Gentile Christians and the Jewish Christians regarding legal observance of the law. The Gentiles were liberal in their observance and the Jews were scrupulous. In Paul's mind the Gentiles were strong and the Jews were weak. Paul entreats mutual toleration. He insists that the strong Gentiles should not look too harshly upon the scruples of their weaker Jewish brothers and sisters, but rather should respect the religious observances of the Jews.

Paul theologizes the reason for his assertion by teaching that no one lives for himself or herself. Christ suffered, died, and rose again for the liberation of human beings. Christ's act of liberation freed people from "bondage to law, sin and death . . . and enabled them to live for God."[5] All live completely and solely for the risen Christ and are to acknowledge their relationship to Christ as Lord. Since Christians are joined to Christ, they are also joined to other church members who also live for Christ. Thus, everyone belongs to Christ and is ultimately required to serve God in all things. This service is the basis of Christian life.

At his resurrection Jesus became the exalted ruler over both the living and the dead. "It is a universal dominion proper to the *Kyrios* of all."[6] Through faith and baptism Christians will ultimately share in Christ's redemption. They will share Christ's glory in heaven.

Reginald Fuller asserts that this Pauline text was probably a baptismal hymn because of the use of "we" common in hymns and because of the way in which it goes beyond the immediate point at hand (the issue of the weak and the strong) to speak of the living and the dead. "As Lord of the living, Christ is the Lord of both groups within the Church."[7]

Gospel
Matthew 18:21–35

STEP 1
NAMING ONE'S EXPERIENCE

What were your first impressions? What was your first response to the gospel (or the other readings)?[8] What captured your attention?

Each person names his or her initial impression. Statements should be brief. No reasons should be given at this time. All simply listen without agreeing or disagreeing.

STEP 2
UNDERSTANDING

In a brief statement, what do you think this gospel is trying to convey?

[5]Joseph A. Fitzmyer, S.J., "The Letter to the Romans," *NJBC,* 865.

[6]Ibid.

[7]*PL,* 167.

[8]The primary focus of reflection is the gospel. However, very often the other readings demand attention and must be brought into the dialogue.

Step 3
Input from Vision/Story/Tradition

Liturgical Context

This section of Matthew's gospel deals with Jesus' sermon on the church. It is a simple, concise, profound, and very direct portrait of what church life is intended to be. Church life is relational. Members of the church are first in relationship with Christ and then with one another. The foundation for these relationships will be built upon the fortress of humility, love, mutual care and concern, unity, and the forgiveness and correction of one another. The church of Christ is a church comprised of people who are fully aware of their identity. They know that they belong to God, that they are God's children.

The first place we encounter Christ present in the Sunday liturgy is in the assembly of believers (Constitution on the Sacred Liturgy, #7). This acknowledges what is at the heart of Jesus' sermon on the church. We are in relationship, not only with Christ, but with each other. How can we appreciate Christ present in the eucharist if we cannot or will not accept Christ present in one another, the gathered assembly?

Matthew's gospel characterizes the relationships that are to exist within the church. It is a great year to reflect on what it means to be church. What is the gathered assembly? What does it mean? Jesus sheds light on that reality in these weeks of Ordinary Time.

Matthew's gospel, proclaimed last week and this week, is taken from chapter 18, the sermon on the church. It highlights for us the relationship that is to exist between church members, one to another, and between church authorities and church members. [In chapter 18], Matthew presents us with a "series of seven 'church counsels': (1) counsel to childlike humility (vv. 1–4); (2) counsel to special care of the weak (v. 5); (3) counsel against scandal: scandal of the weak, in the world, of self (6–9); (4) counsel to apostolic spirit concerning the lost sheep (10–14); (5) counsel to fraternal correction (15–18) [23rd Sunday]; (6) counsel to common prayer and unity (19–20), concluding with 'there am I in the midst of them,' reminding us of Emmanuel, God with us, with whom the Gospel began [23rd Sunday]; (7) counsel to complete, unfailing forgiveness.... This forgiveness is illustrated by the uniquely Matthean parable of the unjust steward who failed to forgive his brother from his heart (21–35)" [24th Sunday—today's gospel].[9] Matthew counsels the church on the way to live in the reign of God. It is a relevant word for a contemporary world.

Today's parable is an extended meditation on the many dimensions of the mystery of forgiveness. Today's liturgy echoes that meditation in the Opening Prayer in which we ask God that we might serve him and might know God's forgiveness in our lives. We are reminded in the Alternative Opening Prayer that God alone is our source of peace. We ask God to make us poor in spirit and to show us how privileged we are to be called into God's service. When we serve God as God intends (by laying down our lives for others), we will share in God's peace. It follows that we will live and behave morally in the reign of God. We will also forgive as Christ forgave us, ultimately, as the Alternative Opening Prayer reminds us, through his death on the cross. The Prayer After Communion asks that the eucharist we share will influence the way we think and the way we behave: "Lord, may the eucharist you have given us influence our thoughts and actions. May your Spirit guide and direct us in your way."[10]

We have been reading the bulk of Paul's letter to the Romans in these past several weeks. Today is the last time we read from Romans. Paul's theme today is consonant with the gospel's theme of forgiveness. Ultimately, today's pericope is an exhortation to the community to be tolerant and accepting of others.

Let us recall these words from St. John Chrysostom's homily on today's parable:

> The evil of remembering past offenses is twofold: it is inexcusable before God, and it serves to recall past sins already forgiven

[9] *MML*, 62.

[10] Twenty-Fourth Sunday in Ordinary Time: "Prayer After Communion," *The Sacramentary*.

> and places them against us. And this is what happened here [in today's parable]. For nothing, nothing whatsoever does God hate, and turn away from, as cherishing remembrance of past offenses, and fostering our anger against another. Instructed therefore in all these things, and with this parable inscribed in our hearts, let us, when the thought comes of what our fellow servants have done to us, think also of what we have done against our Lord and then through remembrance of our own sins, we shall be able at once to banish the anger we feel at others' sins against us.... Therefore I shall make bold to say, that this sin is more grievous than any sin. Let us therefore be zealous in nothing so much as in keeping ourselves free from anger, and from not seeking to be reconciled with those who are opposed to us; since we know that neither prayer nor alms nor fasting nor partaking of the sacraments nor any of these will profit us, if on that last day we are found remembering our past offenses. But should we triumph over this fault, though stained with a thousand other crimes, we shall be enabled to obtain forgiveness. And neither is this my word only, but the word of that God who shall come to judge us....[11]

Gospel Exegesis

The facilitator gives input regarding what critical biblical scholarship has to say about this text. The input includes insights as to how people would have heard the gospel in Jesus' time.

Today's parable is found only in Matthew's gospel. Peter sets the context for today's parable of the king who decided to settle accounts when he asks the Lord, "Lord, when my brother wrongs me, how often must I forgive him?" We know we are about to hear a story on forgiveness and the magnanimity of God's mercy. While it was most common in the culture to expect a tit for tat form of justice, this parable demonstrates that God's mercy is unlike their previous expectations of justice and mercy.

[11]As quoted in *RF*, 63.

As the story develops the Jewish listener *does not* sympathize with the first servant. The story is automatically placed in a Gentile context. First, the king would have been a Gentile. The excessive amount of money owed to the king by the servant would have indicated that the first servant was a Gentile tax farmer. "The servant of the king owes his master ten thousand talents, a deliberate exaggeration. Ten thousand was the highest figure in arithmetic...."[12] A Jew would not have been trusted to manage an account that large. Right away the listener of the parable views the first servant as a member of the rich class who are rich at the expense of the poor. Thus, they eagerly await the punishment that will befall this undeserving farmer. The listener places himself or herself in a position of superiority very early in the story.

The servant ridiculously believed that he could repay his debt in small restructured payments. He refused to accept that he was permanently impoverished. The servant asked for time and patience and the king gave him unparalleled compassion.

The listener would have expected the usual Gentile punishment for failure to pay such taxes. Jewish listeners would have considered the punishment rash cruelty. Jewish law forbade the sale of wife and children into slavery to pay off debts. Also, no Jew would ever grovel and "worship" at the feet of another human being. The listener is disposed to continue his or her stance of smugness and superiority to the events unfolding in the narrative, perhaps musing, "Those scoundrel Gentiles certainly treat each other abominably!"

The first surprise in the story appears when the king shows compassion. The listener would have expected some form of punishment for so huge a debt and such failure by the servant. So the listener is faced with a new dilemma. No longer can he or she maintain the posture of superiority. The king has taken center stage due to his unexpected reaction of forgiveness and has upset the listener's applecart of superiority. The first event in the parable is now complete. The offense of the servant results in the unexpected behavior of the king—non-punishment and forgiveness.

[12]*RM*, 194.

The listener, caught off guard, has no idea where the story is leading. In the first event we are told that the servant was "brought in." The servant in this second scene is violently "seized by the throat." We are immediately aware that there is a contrast between this scene and the first scene. "There are two significant differences: the staggering amount of the debt—a hundred million denarii as opposed to one hundred—and the opposite responses—mercy versus ruthlessness."[13] The second servant's debt is small in contrast to the debt of the first servant. The listener is tempted to sympathize with the second servant and look with disdain upon the first servant. The second servant asks the original servant for the same mercy that was shown to him earlier in the parable. The difference between the two supplication scenes is that the first servant knelt down and worshiped the king, whereas the second servant does not give similar homage to his master. This would have been inappropriate behavior between two people who shared a common bond as servants.

A new expectation is created in this second scene. Since the second servant's debt is small, and there is, or should be, a common bond between servants, and since the king had forgiven the first servant's debt, surely then the king's forgiven servant will forgive the small debt of his fellow servant? But the listener isn't quite sure what to expect. Tension mounts. What will the first servant do?

We know that he failed to forgive and threw his debtor into prison. The probable response of Matthew's listeners would have been righteous indignation, followed by judgment. One can almost hear them saying: "Just like those unloving, unforgiving Gentiles!"

The king's extravagant mercy is contrasted with the servant's unmitigated mercilessness. It appears as if the servant misinterpreted the king's mercy as a claim to special favoritism. His miscalculation fed his arrogance and stupidity and led to his ultimate lack of charity. The listener is automatically propelled to identify with the second servant.

A third plot emerges in the story. The onlooking fellow servants report their comrade to the king.

[13]Ibid., 195.

Everyone—the king, the onlookers, and the listeners—all share the same viewpoint: the servant is a rogue. He must be punished for his unjust response to the second servant. The king must make things right. Immediately the listener and the fellow servants are allies. Everyone becomes quickly and acutely aware that the king has already passed judgment. His rage is obvious. What will he do? The king punishes him terribly, far worse than expected. He is sentenced to be tortured until he pays the original sum which, of course, will never happen. The punishment is as exaggerated as the size of the original debt. Both are intended to shock the listener to attention, to move them beyond the normal, everyday, expected and mundane and move them to expect the unexpected, astonishing, often shocking possibilities inherent in living in the reign of God.

Bernard Brandon Scott asserts that the greatest shock for all involved lies in the fact that an oriental king went back on his word. They were shaken to their core. The unthinkable happened. "*He has taken back his forgiveness* and reinstated the original debt."[14] Everyone was now at risk. The ordered Hellenistic world was shaken. No one was safe if a king could go back on his original sentence. Chaos reigned. Because the listener internally cheered the fellow servants into action, he or she bears equal responsibility with those servants who reported the incident to the king, which had resulted in the excessive punishment. "By bringing vengeance on the servant, the fellow servants (and the hearer) have left their own situation in jeopardy. The demand for 'like-for-like' for apparent justice, has left them exposed. If a king can take back his forgiveness, then who is safe?"[15] No one is innocent here. The fellow servants demanded vengeance for the servant's insensitive lack of forgiveness, yet they were no better than the one they reported. They too failed to forgive.

David Garland, on the other hand, insists that the exaggerated punishment is meant as a warning to disciples that forgiveness can be forfeited.[16] Disciples are to remember that they are forgiven by God and that they, in turn, are to extend that

[14]*HTP*, 276.

[15]Ibid., 278.

[16]*RM*, 195.

same forgiveness to others. Score cards that tabulate the offenses of others are not to be tolerated in the reign of God.

A common character in rabbinic stories was the king. The king was often used as a metaphor for the way God deals with Israel. The king, while a leading character in today's parable, is not used as a metaphor. This king shows the listener that the kingdom of God is unlike anything this world knows or understands. God's kingdom does not depend on human justice, but rather on mercy. The fellow servants, who asked that the king settle the account, wanted the king to justly punish the servant. There is a conflict between what the listener expects in the story and the story itself. This is a parable about the reign of God. The fellow servants and the listener (by his or her identification with the fellow servants) want to control the natural logic of the story, which is that "failure leads to punishment."[17] However, instead of logical results, there was chaos—a world out of balance, a world in which no one is safe. There is great irony in the parable. The fellow servants believed that when they asked the king to settle the account, it would automatically make everything right. Instead, it upset the created order in a way they could have never conceived. "By appealing to the hierarchical structure to bring right order, the servants have instead brought chaos."[18] Scott maintains that the story means the same thing as "the final petition of the Lord's Prayer: 'Let us not succumb to the test.'"[19]

The listener of this story is trapped in secret complicity with the servants who sought to bring about what they thought was justice. The parable catches them unaware and reminds them that unlimited mercy, not legalistic justice, is the hallmark of God's reign. Both the fellow servants and listener failed the test of forgiveness—just like the first servant. "The narrative leads to a parabolic experience of evil, not intentional evil, but implicit, unanticipated, systemic evil. The ability to acknowledge one's entanglement in evil is part of the experience of the kingdom."[20]

[17]*HTP,* 279.
[18]Ibid.
[19]Ibid.
[20]Ibid., 280.

Ultimately, then, the parable asserts that no one is free from sin. All are caught up in it. Everyone is a sinner and every sinner is called to God's reign. The only requirement is that the sinner acknowledge his or her sinfulness and repent in earnest. Matthew does not paint the community through rose-colored glasses. He knows full well that it is comprised of sinners capable of gross arrogance, obstinacy, and ruthlessness. The antidote for such evil is love. "Matthew emphasizes the need for the church to be infused with a spirit of care, tolerance, and kindheartedness as well as regulated by high standards of conduct. All are to be treated as equals (23:8) regardless of past history, race, or social station; and all should regard themselves humbly as 'little ones.'"[21] Christians will not be able to take the message of Christ's unconditional love and forgiveness to a waiting world if they are not first reconciled with one another. Forgiveness is to be extended "seventy-times seven,"—in other words, forever.

Another result of this parable was that it unraveled for the Jewish listeners their stance of moral superiority over the Gentiles. Christians must resist religious elitism. No one is better than others—all are sinners. The reign of God is for everyone. The listener is left with determining the rest of the story. Where will I go from here? What will I do about it?

Proclaim the gospel again.

Sometimes we gain new insights when we hear the text after the interpretation has been given. Someone from the group proclaims the gospel a second time.

STEP 4
TESTING

Conversation with the Liturgy and the Scriptures

Test your original understanding in dialogue with the text.

(You might consider breaking into smaller groups.)

[21]*RM,* 196.

Now that you've heard the exegesis, how do you feel about it? How does your original understanding of this gospel compare with what we just shared? Were there any new insights for you? How does this story speak to your life?

Sharing Life Experience

Participants share an experience from their lives that connects with the biblical interpretation just shared.

> *I am particularly struck by the emphasis on the role and responsibility of the listener in today's parable. The story is replete with protagonist and antagonist. As an onlooker, I do not have to do anything but listen and react. I might even believe that I am neutral. However, it is in the reacting and responding to the parable that the listener is caught unaware and helped to see his or her own self-righteousness. I can look with indignation on any situation without having to look within myself to see where I contribute to the problem, either through indifference, inappropriate attitudes, or unconscious support for actions that are contrary to the gospel. This is a common corporate problem in church life. It is very easy to listen to the misdeeds of others, form an opinion, make a judgment and, by our judgment alone, make matters worse than they were before.*
>
> *I remember an incident many years ago in which someone brought to the attention of a small group of people that a member of the community was engaged in inappropriate behavior. Judgment was fierce and swift. This group wanted to take action to stop the behavior. What seemed to be a demand that justice be served and that this person be forced to assume some form of accountability, was actually intended as a cause for confrontation. After considerable discernment and prayer they ultimately decided that it was not in the best interest of all involved to do anything. They reasoned that they could not possibly know all the facts and that a rush to judgment would hurt more people than it would help. They chose instead to remain quiet and let God take care of the problem. Had they taken action as they originally planned, it would have destroyed some very good people, including innocent children. While the action of God in this situation is not fully known, from what could be observed it seems as if peace was restored to the situation.*
>
> *In looking back on the situation in light of today's parable, I can see how the self-righteous fervor of the group took hold, and how the concern became not really for the injured parties as much as it was for making sure the guilty one suffered as a result of his or her transgression. The group eventually was as sinfully motivated as was the offense they set out to chastise. It was a great lesson for me not to rush to judgment but to weigh all matters, and to turn to God in prayer for the discernment to know when we are called to action and when we are called to remain silent and let God do what God does best. The social dimension of sin is insidiously sinister. It often is cloaked in veiled virtue. We can think we are pursuing justice and the "American way" by leading the pack of accusers. Today's parable is an ominous warning that none of us is innocent. We are all sinners who have been saved through the blood of Christ. Only when I am truly living the paschal mystery can I be strengthened enough to resist the temptation to follow the herd and ask for the hangman's noose.*

All share their life experience.

What was Matthew trying to tell his community? How would you describe the theme of this parable? How does this parable speak to your community today? In what way is it pertinent for your own life? How are the biblical themes of covenant, exodus, creation, and community evident in today's liturgy? In what way do you relate to the king, the servant, the second servant, the fellow servants, and the listener? Can you remember a time in your life when you fit one or all of those roles? Do you still feel the same way about this gospel as when you began? Has your original understanding been stretched, challenged, or affirmed? How has this gospel challenged you to transformation? How have you changed as a result of this conversation?

Step 5
Decision

The gospel demands a response.

In what specific way might your parish be called to respond to today's liturgy? What one concrete action will you take as a response to the liturgy?

Pastoral Considerations: In what way is there lack of forgiveness evident in your parish? There is an obvious communal dimension to the lack of forgiveness found in today's parable. When was the last time your community gathered for a celebration of the sacrament of reconciliation? If that is not possible, it might be a good time for groups to celebrate a non-sacramental penitential service found in the *Rites of the Catholic Church.* It might also be an appropriate time to invite folks to meditate on the multiple ways they have experienced God's forgiving mercy in their lives.

Christian Initiation: This might be an appropriate occasion to celebrate an anointing of catechumens. The anointing is intended to strengthen the catechumens on their journey to the table. Everyone certainly needs God's strength and grace to withstand the temptation inherent in today's gospel. Fully initiated Catholics receive that strength at the Lord's table. The anointing provides that strength for the catechumen. It is fall Ordinary Time. There might be a greater interest in the catechumenate at this time of the year simply because it is our culture's natural rhythm to begin new ventures and new directions in the fall. Even though the RCIA suggests a different approach, following the liturgical year rather than the school year, it takes a long time to break old patterns. Thus, many folks come to us in the fall expecting that it is the time to begin their inquiry. According to the RCIA, *anytime* is the right time to begin the inquiry. Therefore, it might be a good time to invite people to come and inquire (while reminding the community that people continue to knock on our doors all year long). If there are inquirers ready to move into the catechumenate, today would also be an appropriate time to celebrate a rite of acceptance. When we are signed with the cross of Christ, we are signed into his life. That means we too are willing to embrace the cross for the sins of others. Jesus died for the forgiveness of our sins. Today is a sober reminder of the call and the challenge of the gospel that the rite so powerfully celebrates.

DOCTRINAL ISSUES

What church truth/teaching/doctrinal issue could be drawn from the gospel for the Twenty-Fourth Sunday in Ordinary Time?

Participants suggest possible doctrinal themes that flow from the readings.

Possible Doctrinal Themes

Forgiveness, sacrament of reconciliation, God's mercy, sin (personal, social, and systemic), grace of baptism, repentance and reconciliation, mystery of the church, reign of God, judgment, foundations of morality

Present the doctrinal material at this time.

1. The facilitator gives input on a particular doctrinal issue of his/her prior choosing. OR
2. The group chooses a doctrinal issue from the list they created. They read together from the Doctrinal Appendix.

(The doctrinal issues are found in the Doctrinal Appendix in the back of this workbook. If you are choosing an issue from this resource, please refer to it now.)

Reflection questions centered around the chosen doctrinal theme can be found at the end of each topic in the Doctrinal Appendix. The questions are based on the five-step reflection process. If you choose a topic not included in the Doctrinal Appendix, craft your own questions according to the same five-step process.

Following the reflection questions you will be reminded to return to chapter 7, "Preparing the Catechetical Session," to assist you in crafting your own session.

Closing Prayer

Let us pray
[for the peace which is born of faith and hope]

Pause for silent prayer.

Father in heaven, creator of all,
look down upon your people in their moments of need,
for you alone are the source of our peace.
Bring us to the dignity which distinguishes the poor in spirit

and show us how great is the call to serve,
that we may share in the peace of Christ
who offered his life in the service of all.
We ask this through Christ our Lord.[22]

[22]Twenty-Fourth Sunday in Ordinary Time: "Alternative Opening Prayer," *The Sacramentary*.

Twenty-Fifth Sunday in Ordinary Time

Environment

See the Twenty-Second Sunday in Ordinary Time.

INTRODUCTORY RITES

Opening Song (or Entrance Antiphon)

I am the Savior of all people, says the Lord. Whatever their troubles, I will answer their cry, and I will always be their Lord.[1]

Opening Prayer

Let us pray
[that we will grow in the love of God and of one another]

Pause for silent prayer.

Father, guide us, as you guide creation
according to your law of love.
May we love one another
and come to perfection
in the eternal life prepared for us.
Grant this through our Lord, Jesus Christ, your Son,
who lives and reigns with you and the holy Spirit,
one God for ever and ever.[2]

LITURGY OF THE WORD

The readings are proclaimed.

First Reading
Isaiah 55:6–9

(Refer to the Overview of the Book of the Prophet Isaiah on the First Sunday of Advent, and to the fifth reading of the Easter Vigil.)

[1]Twenty-Fifth Sunday in Ordinary Time: "Entrance Antiphon," *The Sacramentary.*

[2]Twenty-Fifth Sunday in Ordinary Time: "Opening Prayer," *The Sacramentary.*

Today's reading from Isaiah plummets us into the mysterious ways of God and invites us to live, think, and behave with the renewed mind and heart of God. Isaiah invites the people to turn away from their wicked, sinful, and false ways and turn with heart, mind, and soul to the ways of God. Only God can satisfy the hunger of Israel and deliver the exiles from their oppressors. On two other Sundays in Ordinary Time, the 15th and the 18th Sundays of the year, we also read from Isaiah's 55th chapter, which emphasizes God's nearness. God invites Israel to come and listen, to turn to God and away from sin and infidelity that they understood to be the cause of the exile. Turning to God involves listening to the word of the Lord and seeking God's will. Seeking and calling in the context of Isaiah's 55th chapter is synonymous with repentance. When Israel turns to the Lord it encounters a merciful and forgiving God. The ways of Israel are contrasted with the ways of God. Israel's ways were rooted in infidelity while God's ways are rooted in faithfulness and mercy. God's ways lead to abundance and a return to covenant living and, ultimately, to being close to God.

Responsorial Psalm
Psalm 145:2–3, 8–9, 17–18

Today's psalm picks up the theme of God's nearness to all who call on God. Psalm 145 is a psalm of praise that extols the compassion of God and the justice of God's actions.

Second Reading
Philippians 1:20–24, 27

Overview of Paul's Letter to the Philippians. Philippi was a city nestled on a plain and surrounded by mountains, located in Northeast Macedonia on the Gulf of Neapolis. The city's namesake was Phillip II of Macedon. Rome conquered Macedon in 167 B.C.E. Philippi became a Roman colony, subject to Roman law, and was home to many Roman veterans.

Paul visited Philippi on his second missionary tour, the first known missionary effort on the European continent. A woman Paul converted, by the name of Lydia, offered him lodging. She was a traveling merchant from Thyatira who traded in purple cloth. She was obviously good at her trade as she was wealthy enough to own her own home in Philippi. The early Philippian church gathered in her home. This first experience of "house churches" was the means by which Christianity was nurtured, grew, and spread out to the Hellenized world. "Lydia is probably a typical and early example of a constant pattern whereby wealthy and prominent women act as patrons and protectors of the early Christian movement."[3]

Paul's first speaking engagement took place in the Jewish place of prayer.[4] After Paul and Silas exorcised a spirit from a possessed girl, her parents brought charges and they were convicted of practicing an illegal religion. Both were beaten and thrown into prison. When an earthquake struck the prison gates, the prison guard was so impressed by the fact that Paul and Silas did not escape that he was converted to Christ and subsequently baptized. After Paul declared that he was a Roman citizen, the authorities nervously and fearfully released them since they had illegally flogged a Roman citizen. They asked the apostles to leave the city.

The authorship of the letter to the Philippians is not disputed by scholars. However, because of periodic lack of continuity in the text, a few scholars suggest that the letter is a combination of several letters. This theory does not enjoy widespread acceptance. The lack of unity in the letter remains an unsolved mystery. The eloquent Christological hymn found in chapter 2:6–11 contains differences in vocabulary not found in other passages. The differences do not necessarily suggest that the hymn was not written by Paul, but simply that he inserted a familiar hymn used in the Christian liturgy into the corpus of the letter. The letters to the Philippians, Ephesians, Colossians, and Philemon are known as the captivity epistles, written during one of Paul's imprisonments.

Today's Pericope: Paul's intention in today's letter was to encourage believers not to be impeded by hostile non-Christians. The letter begins with a formal greeting, blessing, and thanksgiving. He relates his present situation to his readers. Paul believes his death is immanent, but he is not afraid. His belief in the resurrection sustains him. Death is the doorway to Christ's eternal presence, but life offers continuous opportunities to take the message of Christ to the world. Paul does not know which option he prefers.

Paul resolved to forge ahead no matter what was in store for his future, and to continue to work for Christ and for the church. He wished to dwell in abiding peace, regardless of what destiny might lie in wait for him. Paul's readers were invited to embrace the same attitude.

Gospel
Matthew 20:1–16

STEP 1
NAMING ONE'S EXPERIENCE

What were your first impressions? What was your first response to the gospel (or the other readings)? What captured your attention?

Each person names his or her initial impression. Statements should be brief. No reasons should be given at this time. All simply listen without agreeing or disagreeing.

STEP 2
UNDERSTANDING

In a brief statement, what do you think this gospel is trying to convey?

STEP 3
INPUT FROM VISION/STORY/TRADITION

Liturgical Context

There are incredible implications for church life inherent in today's parable. Is our church ordered in such a way that we truly believe that the

[3] *PCW,* 67.
[4] *DB,* 670–671.

first and the last are equal at the Lord's banquet table? We sometimes pay lip service to that truth, but our actions reveal something different. We cannot self-righteously lay blame at the feet of our hierarchical structure, either. It is a very human tendency to regard later converts to anything as immature, uninformed, and less enlightened. Starting at the presumed top, there is no doubt a temptation for cardinals to regard new bishops as lower on the food chain, thus less important. Bishops could be tempted to regard the ministry of clergy as insignificant in comparison to the important work of bishops. Clergy might view the laity as Johnny-come-latelies with an axe to grind and their place to find. Laity in upper level church work could be enticed to regard those in parish work as inferior and their work as trivial. Those in parish work might be seduced into judging their parishioners as ignorant and uninformed. Active parishioners might tend to dismiss inactive parishioners as inconsequential. Groups within the parish might be tempted to think that new groups are a threat to their established stature and tenure. Churchgoers might be beguiled into thinking that somehow God loves them the most and knows them better.

Like a merry-go-round on a frenzied, unstoppable track, the very human temptation to think we know how God will act, how God should respond, and who God should choose, persists ad nauseam on the human continuum.

Today's liturgy is a clear call to continued, determined conversion of mind, soul, and spirit. There is only one God and, as the saying goes, it is not us. Yet we sometimes plop ourselves squarely upon the one and only throne, wave our magic wands, and think we can control the events of the ordered universe. "She's in; he's out; I haven't decided about these people yet; etc., etc., etc." Today's liturgy is a reminder that there *is* a place for us, but God's throne is not it. Our place for now is at the Lord's table, humbly, yet with dignity, acknowledging our sinfulness before the God we worship and the God who loves everyone as equal heirs to the throne of glory. The Prayer After Communion asks that with the help of God's kindness put into action, we live the mystery of the eucharist in our everyday lives. Alone we can do nothing. With God all things are possible.

For the last three weeks we have celebrated the fact that God gathers us into one flock of forgiven children. God forms us as one people who are responsible to God, to one another, and to all of creation. Discipleship is a serious matter. Christian living in the context of community is also a serious matter. We need all the insight and grace we can muster in order to "love one another and come to perfection in the eternal life prepared for us" (Opening Prayer). The Alternative Opening Prayer echoes the heart of today's parable—that justice is only possible through love. Humanity needs God's law, but it is not a juridical, legalistic observance that God asks of us. It is law based on the love of God and love of others.

No one is immune from the implications set forth in today's parable. The liturgy of these days calls us to examine our ecclesial structures and the way we live as church. So much of the gospel boils down to attitude. The parables of the kingdom challenge our attitudes and our everyday conventions and invite us to think as transformed, Spirit-filled Christians. The liturgy is a constant call to conversion.

Gospel Exegesis

The facilitator gives input regarding what critical biblical scholarship has to say about this text. The input includes insights as to how people would have heard the gospel in Jesus' time.

Chapters 19–23 of Matthew are nearly identical to the corresponding elements in Mark (10–12) with the exception of Mark's story of the widow's mite. Matthew copied nearly all of Mark's material while adding a few stories of his own: the parable of the laborers in the vineyard, the two sons, the marriage feast, and the lament over Jerusalem. This section of Matthew's gospel serves as a preparation for the grave part of the story yet to come—the entry into Jerusalem and Jesus' subsequent passion and death. One of the features of these chapters in Matthew's gospel is "Jesus' sacrificial pilgrimage to Jerusalem."[5] One way today's gospel points to Jerusalem is in the final warning that appears at the end of the parable: the first will be last and the last will be first. Matthew alerts the reader

[5] *MML*, 62.

that a reversal of God's election is immanent. Neal Flanagan reminds us that Matthew's gospel includes a number of passages that point to the welcome and the inclusion of unanticipated members into the reign of God. Israel's expectations are shattered as God's plan for the salvation of the world is not what they anticipated. Thus, these preparatory chapters help the listeners to be attentive to the God of surprises and to prepare their minds and hearts to walk with the Master on the ominous road ahead.

The parable of the owner of the estate who went out early (related only by Matthew) presents us with its own clues for interpreting the parable. The owner was looking for hirelings to work in his vineyard. Vineyards traditionally and biblically were understood as a metaphor for Israel. The listener would immediately have made that connection. The workers were given a denarius. In no way was this considered a generous wage. A denarius a day would provide for the needs of a worker and his family only at the basic level of existence.

The owner of the estate contracted day laborers to work in the vineyard for the going rate. Later in the day, he came upon another group that was just standing around because no one had hired them. They too were told to go into the vineyard. The first group bargained for their wage and we are informed of the amount. The second group is told that they will be given what is *right* and the amount is not mentioned. The word *right* (*dikaios*) has religious overtones. In Judaism it described someone who was righteous before God—a virtuous, holy person. Right not only meant just, but charitable as well.

The listener wonders where the story is going. How much will these latecomers receive? Will they receive appropriate pay for their work, or will the owner cheat them out of the pay they have coming? The latter scenario was all too common.

The story progresses. We have no clue as to whether it is harvest time or not. We do not know why the owner is in such urgent need of help. We simply know that throughout the day new workers are hired to work in his vineyard, and we do not know how much they will be paid. Again, there is no bargaining. The story repeats itself until we are at the eleventh hour. Workers are hired with very little time left to work.

Now it is evening. The blanks in the story are filled in and the listener's burning question is finally answered. The Johnny-come-latelies will receive the same pay as those who worked a full day. The listener now is compelled to reflect on the generosity of the patron/owner, yet this reflection must lead to more questions. The owner/patron may appear generous to the last hired worker, but the wage could hardly be considered generous in the first place. And if generous is the term one could use in relation to the last hired workers, what word would be used to describe the situation of the first hired workers? If generosity is the theme of the story, then it follows that the first workers should have received more pay than the last workers. The listener expects the owner to pay the agreed-upon wage to the first hirelings, but perhaps less to those hired last. The first workers echo that sentiment. It is interesting at this time to note the owner's dialogue with the first hirelings. No longer is the bargained-for denarius referred to. Now the story refers to their wage in terms of *what is right and just.*

The listener is moved to sympathize with the first workers. Paying all the workers the same seems most unjust. "How could such *lazy* workers be entitled to the same pay as those of us who worked our fingers to the bone all day long?" The owner remonstrated with one of the workers whom he now addressed as "friend." This is particularly noteworthy in light of the fact that this worker failed to address the owner with the customary title of respect. We are aware of a rift in the relationship.

The owner entered into a contractual agreement for an agreed-upon wage with the first workers, which set up a structured order and a hierarchy. Those on the top of the pyramid were those who were hired first. Even though the wage of the later hirelings was not mentioned, an expectation was set up based on the hierarchy that was already established at the beginning of the story. The latter wage would be judged according to the bargained-for wages of the first workers. This scenario was typical of the patron/client relationship of the time.

The scene in which the last workers are paid the same as the first workers alerts the listener that the parable is moving in an unexpected direction. The parable communicates the idea that wages are relative and have nothing to do with the relationships in the story (and by extension, in the reign of God). There is an expectation of generosity throughout the parable. Expectation would dictate that the owner might possibly be generous to the last workers, but it would also insist that he "do right" by those he hired first.

However, the owner shattered all normal conventions. He addressed the worker as "friend," and in so doing broke through the barrier of patron/client relationship and invited a more intimate association. The parable asserts that wages do not determine the worth of the individual. All are equal and are equally needed in the vineyard, at every hour of the day.

The parable intentionally moves listeners through an everyday, routine plane of understanding in which normal cultural and religious patterns bring about expected consequences. Expected consequences would assume that the first workers should receive *more money* for the *more work* accomplished. That is not only customary, but by all standards of justice is expected. Just as listeners of the parable reach the precipice of the story, they are caught, almost in mid-air, and invited to turn their expectations upside down before they fall off the edge. The expected is no longer a reality and a new possibility emerges. The listener is now primed and invited to consider a new world view. Herein lies the catch: the first workers did not do *more* work. They did the work *they agreed to do.* One can only think in terms of *more* work if the *work they did* is judged solely by comparing the *work they did* with the *work done* by those hired later in the day. There would have been no grounds for complaint at all had the first group not been privy to the wages paid to the later groups. As this is another parable about the reign of God, the listener is invited to delve deeper into the mystery of the kingdom. The advent of God's reign is not what most people expect it to be. It is filled with surprises. In order not to miss what God is doing, everyone has to be alert and pay attention. Status quo has no place in God's reign. Grace, not justice, will be the way in which this new city will be ordered.

The parable accents the values associated with the reign of God. Wages customarily determined order and a person's place and status. Wages are associated with justice. The parable demonstrates that our understanding of justice is relative. The parable plays on the natural cultural and religious expectations of justice. The listener "opts for a world in which justice is defined by a hierarchical relation between individuals.... To treat all the same is not just, because all are not alike, all have not earned the same." The parable seeks to demonstrate that justice cannot be the way that the kingdom is structured. We are told at the end of the parable that everyone received what was *right*—what was just. "The householder has paid what was just, yet the parable's clever strategy still maneuvers him into the appearance of injustice."[6] Obviously, justice does not always work or apply equally in every situation. What is just to one may not be just to another.

Human beings simply cannot control the reign of God. In God's reign, worth is determined simply by God's acceptance. Brandon Scott maintains that the owner's need for many laborers (the call) is the parable's metaphor for grace. The only thing that matters is that one is called. There are no other distinctions that qualify the workers of the Lord's vineyard.

Some scholars suggest that the parable also justifies Jesus' ministry to outcasts and sinners. That conclusion is certainly appropriate when we acknowledge the basic premise of the parable: the only requirement needed to work in God's reign is that the person is invited. No one is better qualified, enjoys more privilege, or is of higher status than anyone else. Invitation is by grace and cannot be earned. "The problem with justice is that it misses the invitation."[7] Jesus no doubt addressed this parable to those who would question the respectability of those who seek membership in the reign of God. Religious people of Jesus' day believed that tax collectors and prostitutes were not heirs to the salvation offered to Israel. They, after all, were trying to live righteous lives. They were part of groups (Pharisees and Sadducees) dedicated to living the law and acting justly. A little

[6] *HTP,* 297.

[7] Ibid., 298.

righteous indignation is understandable when one considers all their spiritual efforts in contrast to the perceived lack of effort by newcomers. Then, to add insult to injury, the newcomers included a cast of unseemly characters who not only were welcomed, but were considered on the same par as themselves. Quite a blow to their egos. It would have the same impact today if we were to go out on the street, bring a homeless drug addict into our church, stand him up before the "respectable" members of the parish, and announce that God looks upon him in the same way that he looks upon the rest of us. Our religious acrobatics do not guarantee a more privileged seat at the eschatological banquet table. Jesus affirmed that such folks not only are invited into the kingdom, but they enjoy a special outpouring of God's love, mercy, and forgiveness.

Disciples must seriously discern and be careful about what they really expect and want from their God. While it appears as if justice is what they want (a God who will set things right and order the world juridically), are they really ready for all that justice implies? If justice were the standard by which all people are judged, how many would pass the litmus test? Heaven would be attaching "for rent" signs on its front gate.

Some scholars translate the latecomers in the parable as Matthew's way of exhorting the community to remember that inclusion of the Gentiles in the mission of Christ is not only authentic, but part of God's plan for the salvation of the world. The first workers were the Jews who were the first to hear the message of God. The Gentiles were those who arrived on the scene later, but with no less devotion and passion for the God of Israel. They too were rightful beneficiaries of God's grace and redemption. As the first reading suggests, God's ways are not our ways and God's thoughts are not our thoughts. We cannot arrogantly presume to know the mind and heart of God. We can be sure that God is near, but we dare not assign to God our human designs and machinations.

The last line of the parable serves as a warning to all disciples. Those who were hired last, even though they came in at the eleventh hour, accomplished what they were charged to do. They were no worse or better than any of the others. The first hirelings, however, were jealous and complained about the grace that was extended to the last hired. The warning is clear. Those who behave like the workers who were hired early in the morning, even though they put in a full day's work and carried the lion's share of the load, will nevertheless be the last ones to enter the reign of God. Attitude! Attitude! Attitude! Everyone is a servant of God. What is the quality of our servanthood?

Proclaim the gospel again.

Sometimes we gain new insights when we hear the text after the interpretation has been given. Someone from the group proclaims the gospel a second time.

Step 4
Testing

Conversation with the Liturgy and the Scriptures

Test your original understanding in dialogue with the text.

(You might consider breaking into smaller groups.)

Now that you've heard the exegesis, were there any new insights for you? How does your original understanding of this gospel compare with what we just shared? How does this story speak to your life?

Sharing Life Experience

Participants share an experience from their lives that connects with the biblical interpretation just shared.

> *God has never dealt with me in conventional, expected ways. Throughout this Christian trek of mine God has had to keep me on my toes. If I had followed expected conventions, I never would have known the opportunities to serve in God's reign that I have experienced over the past twenty years. Lest I am ever tempted to take credit for those opportunities, I am reminded all too quickly that only God could have managed to put the puzzle pieces together so neatly.*
>
> *Twenty years ago, I ended up ministering in liturgy and music because my husband's job fell through.*

We sold our house and were forced to move to a different part of town where we joined a parish that was looking for someone to do that particular job. The newly-assigned pastor was a friend of ours and he asked if I would be interested in the position. I was at that time a Montessori teacher who ministered in music on weekends. Training followed the call. That is one of many absurd, unexpected, irrational, marvelous, crazy, exciting, and wonderful ways God has worked in my life. My story has always been painted with crooked lines. Whenever I am tempted to question my ministry, or the experience of people who emerge from other-than-ordinary sequences of events, I have to take two steps back and seriously ask the question: "What is God doing *here?" God's grace is not bound to our limited conventions.*

I am privileged to know a woman who is incredibly talented and gifted in ministry. She never dreamed a year ago that she would be in professional ministry. I have watched God take her and gift her with wisdom beyond her experience, and compassion beyond her own imaginings. Very often we respond to such people with suspicion and jealousy, believing they have not paid their dues, come up through the ranks, taken hard knocks, or put in their required years of elbow grease, and that somehow they simply cannot measure up to our standards of excellence. Those feelings simply mask our own feelings of inferiority and bespeak a threatened, wounded psyche.

Today's gospel invites us as church and as members of the human family to be open to new possibilities, to expect God to often act in improbable ways, and to be flexible enough to celebrate and empower the burgeoning gifts and ministry of all the "new kids on the block." Human nature often entices us to be suspicious and threatened by the gifts others have. How many people in our churches today are held down and squelched due to someone's jealousy and animosity? When that happens the church becomes impoverished. There is room for everyone and for all their gifts. We simply cannot afford to exclude anyone. The warning at the end of today's parable stands as a clear and present danger for all disciples who would grumble when recipients of God's eleventh-hour grace are given the same gold watch reserved for "old-timers." If we are all to be given the watch, what difference does it make when it is given? Who am I to question the giver?

All share their life experience.

What was Matthew trying to tell his community? In what way does this gospel invite the listener to change? What needs to change as a result of reflection on this parable? What does Matthew have to teach your community today? How is this a relevant word? How does it challenge you personally? In what way are the biblical themes of covenant, exodus, creation, and community evident in today's liturgy? Do you still feel the same way about this text as when you began? What, if anything, has changed? Has your original understanding been stretched, challenged, or affirmed?

Step 5
Decision

The gospel demands a response.

In what specific ways might your parish be invited to respond to today's liturgy? What one concrete action are you willing to take as a result of this conversation?

Doctrinal Issues

What church truth/teaching/doctrinal issue could be drawn from the gospel for the Twenty-Fifth Sunday in Ordinary Time?

Participants suggest possible doctrinal themes that flow from the readings.

Possible Doctrinal Themes

Grace, reconciliation, forgiveness, morality, Law of God, images of God, Christology, sacrament of baptism, sacrament of reconciliation, conversion, discipleship, reign of God, mystery of the church, social teaching of the church, service, vocation

Present the doctrinal material at this time.

1. The facilitator gives input on a particular doctrinal issue of his/her prior choosing. OR
2. The group chooses a doctrinal issue from the list they created. They read together from the Doctrinal Appendix.

(The doctrinal issues are found in the Doctrinal Appendix in the back of this workbook. If you are choosing an issue from this resource, please refer to it now.)

Reflection questions centered around the chosen doctrinal theme can be found at the end of each topic in the Doctrinal Appendix. The questions are based on the five-step reflection process. If you choose a topic not included in the Doctrinal Appendix, craft your own questions according to the same five-step process.

Following the reflection questions you will be reminded to return to chapter 7, "Preparing the Catechetical Session," to assist you in crafting your own session.

Closing Prayer

Let us pray
[to the Lord who is a God of love to all peoples]

Pause for silent prayer.

Father in heaven,
the perfection of justice is found in your love
and all humanity is in need of your law.
Help us to find this love in each other
that justice may be attained
through obedience to your law.
We ask this through Christ, our Lord.[8]

[8]Twenty-Fifth Sunday in Ordinary Time: "Alternative Opening Prayer," *The Sacramentary.*

TWENTY-SIXTH SUNDAY IN ORDINARY TIME

Environment

See the Twenty-Second Sunday in Ordinary Time.

INTRODUCTORY RITES

Opening Song (or Entrance Antiphon)

O Lord, you had just cause to judge men as you did: because we sinned against you and disobeyed your will. But now show us your greatness of heart, and treat us with your unbounded kindness. (Dn 3:31, 29, 30, 43, 42)[1]

Opening Prayer

Let us pray
[for God's forgiveness and for the happiness it brings]

Pause for silent prayer.

Father,
you show your almighty power
in your mercy and forgiveness.
Continue to fill us with your gifts of love.
Help us to hurry toward the eternal life you promise
and come to share in the joys of your kingdom.
Grant this through our Lord Jesus Christ, your Son,
who lives and reigns with you and the Holy Spirit,
one God, for ever and ever.[2]

LITURGY OF THE WORD

The readings are proclaimed.

First Reading
Ezekiel 18:25–28

[1]Twenty-Sixth Sunday in Ordinary Time: "Entrance Antiphon," *The Sacramentary.*

[2]Twenty-Sixth Sunday in Ordinary Time: "Opening Prayer," *The Sacramentary.*

(Refer to the Fifth Sunday of Lent for an Overview of Ezekiel.)

Today's Pericope: The prophet's responsibility is to reveal the mind, heart, and will of God. The believers' responsibility is to respond, change their course of action, and bring their behavior in line with the mind, heart, and will of God. The bottom line for Ezekiel is that it is never too late to change the course of one's life, or to change one's mind, one's life, and one's orientation toward evil, into propensity for God and for good. Today's pericope is part of a longer section in which Ezekiel was weighing the question of corporate versus individual responsibility for sin.

Israel's self-understanding was based on its membership in the community. The behavior of one impacted everyone. This notion was so ingrained in Israel's psyche that it was believed that future generations would be held accountable for the individual and communal sins of previous generations.[3] The Babylonian exile and the subsequent destruction of Israel's institutional life resulted in a new concentration on the individual. Ezekiel made sure that his exiled comrades were aware that even though the community was an important entity, the responsibility for sin still rested with the individual. Each person would be held accountable for his or her sins and would suffer the consequences individually. The tension between corporate sin and individual sin must always be held in delicate balance.

Ezekiel would not allow the people the luxury of placing blame only on the past generations, or simply on the sins of the community, for the oppression, sorrow, and suffering they were forced to endure. He wanted them to understand that their own sins played a part as well. They were not the innocents they professed to be. Yet Ezekiel offered a ray of hope and a promise that all was not lost. They could be freed from the permanent

[3]An example of that theology can be observed in the Book of Kings (24:3–4). The fall of Jerusalem was believed to be chastisement for the transgressions of Manasseh.

bondage of ancestral, communal, and individual sin—it was not too late. The answer was metanoia. If people would only rely on God's mercy, turn from their wicked ways, and live in and through God, God would ultimately spare them. The key belonged to them. They need only turn it by changing their minds and returning to the God of the covenant.

Responsorial Psalm
Psalm 125:4–5, 6–7, 8–9

Today's psalm is an individual lament. The psalmist bemoans his oppression at the hands of his enemies, but he is acutely aware of his own sinfulness. He calls on God to forget his sins, to deliver him from his enemies, to extend divine mercy, and to keep him on the straight and narrow following his deliverance. It is a most appropriate choice to complement the first reading from Ezekiel.

Second Reading
Philippians 2:1–11

(Refer to the Twenty-Fifth Sunday in Ordinary Time for an Overview of St. Paul's Letter to the Philippians.)

Today's Pericope: Paul's letter to the Philippians is not one of Paul's most eloquent doctrinal treatises. The hymn of 2:6–11, however, continues to be "one of the most remarkable monuments of primitive Christian faith."[4] The hymn professes the divine preexistence of Jesus and the abasement he endured because of his incarnation and death. It also extols his glorification and the worship due him by all creation. Christ's incarnation is referred to in the hymn as an emptying, a kenosis that required Jesus to renounce the glory that was due him as equal Son of the Father.

The hymn is set in the context of the encouragement Paul was sending to the Philippian house communities and to all his readers. He reminded them that all communal relationships must be rooted and based in Christ. The attitude of all believers must be that of their Lord and Master, Jesus Christ. They literally were instructed to assume Jesus' attitude, to take on the mind of Christ. Only then would Christians have the necessary grace to love one another as Christ loved them. To illustrate the attitude they were to assume, Paul included the Christological hymn. This same hymn is professed every Passion Sunday. Christ did not seek glory, but glory and suffering were the cornerstones of his redemption. Jesus did not demand that his rightful place as God's equal be recognized. He was content to assume the role that was given him. He was willing to give up his honor, pride, and his life to accomplish so difficult a plan. Through Jesus' self-emptying (kenosis) he willingly became powerless. He gave up all his rights and his influence.

Paul exhorts his readers, ancient and contemporary, to put on the mind of Christ, to empty and divest themselves of power, and to live and act for others, just as Christ lived and acted for others. Such self-sacrifice is the only way we will enter into the glory of Christ, even though we will have to walk through suffering to get there.

Gospel
Matthew 21:28–32

STEP 1
NAMING ONE'S EXPERIENCE

What were your first impressions? What was your first response to the gospel (or the other readings)?[5] What captured your attention?

Each person names his or her initial impression. Statements should be brief. No reasons should be given at this time. All simply listen without agreeing or disagreeing.

STEP 2
UNDERSTANDING

In a brief statement, what do you think this gospel is trying to convey?

[4] *NJBC*, 672.

[5] The primary focus of reflection is the gospel. However, very often the other readings demand attention and must be brought into the dialogue.

Step 3
Input from Vision/Story/Tradition

Liturgical Context[6]

Today's liturgy begins a new series of exhortations for disciples. The situation in the gospel is becoming ever more tense. The movement toward Jesus' destiny is fast approaching. His preaching gains momentum and intensity. Matthew insists that actions speak louder than words and seeks to seriously impress that truth on the minds and hearts of his readers. For the next three weeks the parables of the two sons, the wicked vinedressers, and the wedding feast will invite us to delve more deeply into the seriousness of Matthew's contention that faithfulness to the Lord requires more than a pretentious nod of the head. It requires serious attention and action. We must do as Jesus did. It is the only way to gain our lives—by losing them. Our proclamation must be backed up by the way we live our lives. The greatest witness to Christ is a well-lived life. Words are wonderful, but if the life does not match the words, then the words are meaningless and hypocritical.

The liturgy's exhortation to "go and serve the Lord" serves as an exclamation point to today's gospel. In essence it demands that we take what we have received in the liturgy and do it in our lives. Jesus did not say, "*Pray* this in remembrance of me," or "*Preach* this in remembrance of me." He said, "*Do* this in remembrance of me." It is the heart of eucharist. Eucharist is a verb, an action word. "Every liturgical celebration, because it is an action of Christ the Priest and of his Body, which is the Church, is a sacred action surpassing all others. No other action of the Church can equal its efficacy by the same title and to the same degree" (Constitution on the Sacred Liturgy #7). Eucharist implies a response. It empowers and strengthens us to grow more fully into the chosen, royal, and holy priesthood we were baptized to be, but it still requires a response. "But in order that the liturgy may be able to produce its full effects, it is necessary that the faithful come to it with proper dispositions, that their minds be attuned to their voices, and that they cooperate with heavenly grace lest they receive it in vain" (CSL, #11).

The ritual prayers of the liturgy constantly exhort us to action—to make our lives speak the truth we proclaim. "May the power of this love be in our hearts to bring your pardon and your kingdom to all we meet" (Alterative Opening Prayer).

Today's liturgy also stresses our need for forgiveness and mercy. The gospels of the past Sundays have been an extended meditation on our need to repent our sinfulness. The liturgy affirms that need and calls it forth in our lives. We are challenged to go and make it effective by forgiving others. "Father, you show your almighty power in your mercy and forgiveness. . . ." (Opening Prayer); "You have revealed the beauty of your power through your constant forgiveness of our sins" (Alternative Opening Prayer). "This is how we know what love is: Christ gave up his life for us; and we too must give up our lives for our brothers." [1 Jn 3:16] (Communion Rite Antiphon).

The refrain assigned for today's responsorial psalm, "Remember your mercies, O Lord," conjures up the biblical understanding of remembrance. Another word for the type of remembering referred to in this psalm is the Greek word *anamnesis.* In this type of biblical remembering, God recalls a past event and makes it effective in the present. The mercies extended by God throughout salvation history, when recalled, become present and effective for each generation.

> When we come to the Eucharist we are confronted with a liturgical action which, perhaps it is not too much to say, is defined by anamnesis. It is the sacrament of anamnesis, and because it is, it is the supreme celebration of the mystery of Christ. . . . It [anamnesis] is a term (and a reality) that is found in both the Old and New Testaments, and in its first movement it is a recalling before God by men of the past events of his saving mercy. Through making the memorial of the events we are asking that their saving power may be

[6]The scriptures in the Lectionary, the seasons of the year, and the ritual prayers of the mass are interrelated and form the basis for liturgical catechesis. The *liturgical context* attempts to explore and clarify the themes and this interrelatedness.

> made present to us here and now. In the Eucharist we are recalling before the Father the saving deeds of his Son; and because we do so according to the command of Christ and because he and his Father are faithful to their covenanted promises, Christ makes himself present in all his redeeming activity. . . . Through the celebration of the Eucharist, the Christian is able to make a living encounter with the Lord who died and rose again, to join the offering of himself and his life (Rom 12, 1) to that of Christ, who enfolds it in his own and presents it to the Father. Through this encounter and through his reception of Christ in Holy Communion, he is able to enter into and share in the paschal mystery of Christ. He makes or begins to make the passover of the Lord the passover of his own life.[7]

This type of remembering is the basis of eucharist. When every generation gathers to tell the stories of salvation, pray the blessing and thanksgiving, remember and recall the life and the deeds of Jesus, and perform the ritual action of the Master, then his life, action, death, and resurrection become effective and present. We remember that Jesus took bread and wine, blessed it, broke the bread, and gave thanks to God. He offered the bread to his friends and proclaimed that it was his Body and Blood shed for the sins of the world. Every time we remember that event, therefore, Christ's paschal mystery becomes present and effective in our midst. In the remembering, it becomes real for every generation. "'Do this in remembrance of me' means not only that we recall in our minds the messianic sacrifice, the supreme act of God's mercy, but that in response to the Church's action, God will make present that sacrifice."[8] Today's psalm refrain is not only the assigned psalm for today's liturgy, but it is a most fitting eucharistic acclamation.

Gospel Exegesis

The facilitator gives input regarding what critical biblical scholarship has to say about this text. The input includes insights as to how people would have heard the gospel in Jesus' time.

Today's liturgy provides us with another parable about the kingdom of God. Today's parable centers around a dispute between Jesus and the Pharisees. Jesus followed the Pharisees' challenge with a question concerning the origin of John the Baptist's baptism. Jesus trapped them in their own dishonesty and insincerity. If they affirmed that John's authority was divinely commissioned, then they were acknowledging their own failure to accept his call to repentance and conversion and his revelation about Jesus. On the other hand, if they denounced John as a fraud, they would lose the respect of the multitudes who revered him as a prophet. It was a lose/lose situation for them. Because they feared the people, they chose to remain non-committal.

The parables that follow Jesus' exchange with the Pharisees set out to condemn them for their refusal to listen to the prophetic voice of John and for their participation in the violence that will be done to Jesus.

The parable of the two sons serves either as a warning or as a consolation, depending on the listener's attitude. Parables lay bare stark truth in ways that nothing can match. No one can argue with a parable. There is no coercion to accept a certain perspective. We either accept, reject, or write the conclusion to the story ourselves. The listener is forced to form an opinion, albeit a sometimes silent one. Parables sometimes shock us so that it is difficult to remain neutral. Parables invite listeners to either convict or acquit themselves of attitudinal maliciousness.

The context of this parable is set for us in the opening scene. Jesus is addressing the priests and elders, the religious leaders. The parable contains an apologetic motive in defense of Jesus' questionable new associates—the outcasts and the sinners. His audience was not ignorant, nor were they naive. They were instructed in the school of midrash and parabolic literature. They knew what Jesus was implying and certainly recognized themselves in his parables. They were no doubt bitterly provoked; that kind of self-revelation is hard to swallow when no one is in the

---

[7] J.D. Chrichton, "A Theology of Worship," *SL*, 26.
[8] *PL*, 172.

mood to taste. It is no wonder they plotted against him.

Jesus' intended audience (the Pharisees) was represented in the parable by the son who said "yes" to his father, but did nothing. They paid lip service to obedience, but their inaction rendered them ineffective and empty. They talked the talk, but refused to walk the walk. Words without action mean absolutely nothing. Anyone can talk holiness; it is quite another thing to live it authentically. David Garland maintains that one of Matthew's primary themes, his leitmotif, is that the test of a person's convictions is recognizable by the evidence of his or her actions.

The son who refused to go out in the field, but later relented and obeyed his father, represents the sinners whose lives were once the antithesis of righteousness. After heeding the message of John the Baptist, they changed their minds and turned their lives toward God. These reformed sinners were thus offered an honored place in the reign of God.

John Pilch suggests that a not uncommon response of the extremely public Middle Eastern village (then and today) would have been to favor the response of the disobedient son, since honor was a greater value than obedience. To publicly dishonor their father would have been unthinkable. In Western cultures, making the ideal the reality is extremely important. In some Middle Eastern cultures there is a preference to blur the line between the ideal and reality. It might have simply been enough for the second son to respond respectfully to his father in order to comply with the imperative to honor one's father or mother. In this very public confrontation the second son's response might have been valued over the first son's public insolence. Jesus did not ask which son behaved more honorably. The response of the crowd would have been much different. Jesus asked which son did the will of the father. Obedience was important, but honor was more important.

Neither son would win the prize as poster child for the "Would Those Who Are Sinless Please Cast the First Stone Society." Both sons were sinners. But at least the son who initially refused to obey his father, and then changed his mind, displayed substantive transformation by his actions. He remembered the mercies and the love of his father and chose to do the right thing. He did not say one thing and do something entirely different. Matthew's primary accusation against the Pharisees was that they *said* the right things but failed *to do* the right things.

Jesus trapped them into pointing the accusing finger at themselves. He asked them which son was obedient to the will of his father. His question demanded a response. There was only one answer. Lest they not *get it*, Jesus was explicit. Those sinners and outcasts who are scorned by everyone are the very ones who do the will of God. They will also be the very ones who are first to enter God's reign. All who make a showy display of piety, yet change nothing and do nothing, are really the non-repentant sinners. In pointing the one finger at the sinners, the Pharisees pointed four at themselves. They will be usurped in the kingdom by none other than the despised harlots and tax collectors they castigated.

John the Baptist questioned whether or not the Pharisees could even call themselves God's children if they failed to repent. Jesus says they could not. Only those who do the will of God can be called God's children.

Proclaim the gospel again.

Sometimes we gain new insights when we hear the text after the interpretation has been given. Someone from the group proclaims the gospel a second time.

STEP 4
TESTING

Conversation with the Liturgy and the Scriptures

Test your original understanding in dialogue with the text.

(You might consider breaking into smaller groups.)

Now that you've heard the exegesis, were there any new insights for you? How do you feel about it? How does your original understanding of this gospel compare with what we just shared? How does this story speak to your life?

Sharing Life Experience

Participants share an experience from their lives that connects with the biblical interpretation just shared.

> *Today's parable invites reflection on our lives. I am reminded of the witness of my husband. Sometimes he complains about the ministry he does with the homeless. He often wants to wring the guys up by their toes. He gets tired of sleeping on the gym floor when it is consistently cold. He might even say that he just isn't going to go anymore, that someone else can do it. But then, when the time comes, Bob is up there again with the homeless, cooking their dinner and listening to their drunken stories. It gets very old. He's sometimes reluctant, but he ultimately goes when he's asked.*
>
> *I have a feeling that when I get to heaven Jesus will not ask me how many beautiful liturgies I crafted, or how many prayer meetings I attended, or how many times I lost myself in contemplation. While all worthy endeavors, I assume that he will be far more interested in the way in which I have loved those around me, and those nobody wants around as well.*
>
> *Living in the reign of God demands that I acknowledge my sinfulness, my reluctance to serve God, and forge ahead anyway. When I behave like the son who said yes but did nothing, or like the Pharisees in Jesus' life, then I risk being spat out of the mouth of God for my lackadaisical refusal to do what God intends that I should do.*
>
> *Long ago one of my Montessori instructors shared a pious platitude with me that I pull out of my memory's closet when I feel it is time to ponder it anew. While shocking to our American work ethic, I believe there is profound wisdom in the proverb and that it reflects the heart of today's gospel. He would say, "Anything worth doing, is worth doing poorly." It is in the action itself that we give glory to God, not in the results of the action. Today's parable did not tell us how much work the second son accomplished. We are simply told that he responded in obedience. I am a sinner. We are all sinners. That is a fact. The greatest sin is to be blind to my/our sinfulness.*
>
> *People, like my husband, whose ministries are authentic, do not profess to be something they are not. You can always count on them to get the job done—sometimes later than sooner, but the job will get done. But their care and compassion for others is what really motivates them, not some false sense of piety. Is he a sinner? Absolutely! Could he pray better? Of course! Am I a sinner? Most assuredly. Could I pray better? Without a doubt. My hope for us lies in the fact that God loves us just as we are, while inviting us to be more than we think we can be. God even accepts my last minute responses to him. Today's parable promises me that much.*

All share their life experience.

What was Matthew trying to tell his community? In what way does this gospel challenge your community today? In what way has this conversation with the scriptures for today's liturgy invited change in your life? Has your community ever resembled the older son? The younger son? When and how? In what way have you responded to God like the older son? The younger son? Have you ever had an experience in which a story invited you to rethink an attitude or behavior? What did you learn from it? In what way are the biblical themes of covenant, exodus, creation, and community evident in today's readings? Do you still feel the same way about this text as when you began? Has your original understanding been stretched, challenged, or affirmed?

Step 5
Decision

The gospel demands a response.

In what specific way might your parish be invited to respond? Are there any attitudes or behaviors you would like to change as a result of today's conversation? What one concrete action will you take this week as a response to the liturgy today?

Pastoral Considerations: Perhaps this would be a good time for groups and for the parish to reflect on the biblical understanding of remembrance and on the mandate of the liturgy to "go and serve the Lord." In what way is the parish like the son who said yes but did nothing, and the one who said no but changed his mind and obeyed?

Christian Initiation: Is there anyone ready to celebrate a rite of acceptance or a rite of welcome? Are there catechumens who are ready to be received into full communion of the Catholic Church? Perhaps it would also be an appropriate time to celebrate a non-sacramental penitential celebration with catechumens. Some time might be spent reflecting on how the catechumens are living the gospel in their respective worlds.

DOCTRINAL ISSUES

What church truth/teaching/doctrinal issue could be drawn from the gospel for the Twenty-Sixth Sunday in Ordinary Time?

Participants suggest possible doctrinal themes that flow from the readings.

Possible Doctrinal Themes

Repentance, forgiveness, conversion, self-righteous legalism, eucharist, sin (personal, social, and systemic), sacrament of reconciliation, grace, the reign of God, the mystery of the church, dignity of human persons, Christology, faith and works, prayer, contemplation and action, social teaching of the church, morality

Present the doctrinal material at this time.

1. The facilitator gives input on a particular doctrinal issue of his/her prior choosing. OR
2. The group chooses a doctrinal issue from the list they created. They read together from the Doctrinal Appendix.

(The doctrinal issues are found in the Doctrinal Appendix in the back of this workbook. If you are choosing an issue from this resource, please refer to it now.)

Reflection questions centered around the chosen doctrinal theme can be found at the end of each topic in the Doctrinal Appendix. The questions are based on the five-step reflection process. If you choose a topic not included in the Doctrinal Appendix, craft your own questions according to the same five-step process.

Following the reflection questions you will be reminded to return to chapter 7, "Preparing the Catechetical Session," to assist you in crafting your own session.

Closing Prayer

Lord, may this eucharist
in which we proclaim the death of Christ
bring us salvation
and make us one with him in glory,
for he is Lord for ever and ever.[9]

[9]Twenty-Sixth Sunday in Ordinary Time, "Prayer After Communion," *The Sacramentary.*

Twenty-Seventh Sunday in Ordinary Time

Environment

See the Twenty-Second Sunday in Ordinary Time.

INTRODUCTORY RITES

Opening Song (or Entrance Antiphon)

O Lord, you have given everything its place in the world, and no one can make it otherwise. For it is your creation, the heavens and the earth and the stars: you are the Lord of all. (Est 13:9, 10–11)[1]

Opening Prayer

Let us pray
[before the face of God in trusting faith]

Pause for silent prayer.

Almighty and eternal God,
Father of the world to come,
your goodness is beyond what our spirit can touch
and your strength is more than the mind can bear.
Lead us to seek beyond our reach
and give us the courage to stand before your truth.
We ask this through Christ our Lord.[2]

LITURGY OF THE WORD

The readings are proclaimed.

First Reading
Isaiah 5:1–7

(Refer to the first Sunday of Advent for an Overview of the Book of the Prophet Isaiah.)

Today's Pericope: The image of Israel as vine is a common metaphor used throughout the Hebrew scriptures. Today's reading takes place before the destruction of the northern kingdom, Israel. Spoken in parabolic or song form, the oracle is about the owner of the vineyard who sings about his vineyard. Isaiah drew from the lived experience of the people in composing his ballad. Vineyards dotted the landscape of Judah. They required a lot of nurturing in order to produce a good yield. The soil demanded constant attention—watering, clipping, hoeing, cultivating, and the removal of debris. The vinedresser had to make sure that the protective wall of stone or thorn bushes that surrounded the vineyard was maintained. A conscientious vinedresser did nothing else in a day but tend his vineyard with exacting precision and care.

In antiquity each vineyard had its own winepress. The owner of the vineyard could not manage the vineyard alone. People would be needed as winepressers—to get into the vats and press the grapes with their feet. Watchtowers were erected at the perimeter of the vineyard to keep watch and guard against animals and thieves during harvest season. The owner of the field expected a bountiful harvest as he had planted nothing but the choicest grapes.

Isaiah's love ballad depicts a God who loved Israel throughout its salvation history. God's mercy and love had always been showered on his fertile vineyard. He cultivated the people, cared for them, pruned them, nurtured them, watered them, and removed the stones from their hearts. He expected a good harvest, but what the Almighty Harvester received instead was a field of wild sour grapes. There was nothing more God could have done. Israel condemned itself. Isaiah ends his ballad and summons the people of Judah to judgment.

God had named Israel as the vineyard, but Israel produced a sour harvest. They broke their covenant with God. As beneficiaries of God's promise, the people had promised in return to love God with heart, mind, and soul, and to love one another. Evidence of that love would be manifested by the way they treated one another, and es-

[1]Twenty-Seventh Sunday in Ordinary Time: "Entrance Antiphon," *The Sacramentary.*

[2]Twenty-Seventh Sunday in Ordinary Time: "Alternative Opening Prayer," *The Sacramentary.*

pecially the oppressed and disenfranchised. Isaiah accused the people of murder, infidelity, and oppression. They are responsible for their own sentence. The vineyard would no longer enjoy the protective hedges they once enjoyed. God would no longer protect Israel.

Responsorial Psalm
Psalm 80:9, 12, 13–14, 15–16, 19–20

Echoing the vineyard image of the first reading, today's psalm refers to Israel as the vine that was transplanted out of Egypt. It is not a psalm of judgment, but a prayer for deliverance.

Second Reading
Philippians 4:6–9

(Refer to the Twenty-Fifth Sunday in Ordinary Time for an Overview of St. Paul's Letter to the Philippians.)

Today's Pericope: Paul counsels the house churches of Philippi on how to live together in community. Paul exhorts the Philippians not to worry. Worry drains the energy and hope of believers. Worry and anxiety are exercises in futility. He was not suggesting a Pollyannaish approach to life. He was very much aware of the difficulties of living the gospel in a secular and hostile world.

It was stressful and frightening to live in a city with such a large military presence. The Roman leadership was suspicious of Christians. They were considered a threat because of their loyalty to their religious leader who, they believed, was threatening to establish a new kingdom. It was also difficult for Gentile Christians to deal with the religious taunts of the Judaizers, the extremely conservative Jewish Christians who tried to force circumcision and strict Jewish observance of the law on the new converts. There was plenty to be anxious about in the Philippian community.

Paul encouraged his Philippian brothers and sisters and urged tenacity in prayer. He promised a peace that only God can bestow, a peace beyond human understanding. The Philippians were urged to hold fast to the teaching that had been handed down to them, and to fill their minds and hearts with the truths of the tradition and live by those truths. Then there would be no need for anxiety.

Gospel
Matthew 21:33–43

STEP 1
NAMING ONE'S EXPERIENCE

What were your first impressions? What was your first response to the gospel (or the other readings)?[3] What captured your attention?

Each person names his or her initial impression. Statements should be brief. No reasons should be given at this time. All simply listen without agreeing or disagreeing.

STEP 2
UNDERSTANDING

In a brief statement, what do you think this gospel is trying to convey?

STEP 3
INPUT FROM VISION/STORY/TRADITION

Liturgical Context

Last week, this week, and next week we proclaim parables about God's judgment. Mark, Luke, and the Gospel of Thomas relate this same parable. Matthew's version differs from Mark's in that Mark has Jesus teaching in the temple over a period of three days, while Matthew's Jesus teaches for just one day. Matthew's interpretation of the parable is similar to Mark's. The distinctions, and his unique rendering, further Matthew's theological position and agenda.

If the liturgy were to have one main theme (which it does not), today it could be summed up in the Entrance Antiphon. God orders all creation. We can try to control our world, but ultimately God is in charge. Salvation history is a chronicle of God's

[3]The primary focus of reflection is the gospel. However, very often the other readings demand attention and must be brought into the dialogue.

giving, caring, nurturing, punishing, restoring, pruning, chastising, and loving providence. People have always forgotten and continue to forget that there is a God and *they are not it.* Jesus understood our propensity toward infidelity, cruelty, violence, and self righteousness, and our blindness to sin. He cleverly used stories to open the eyes of his listeners. The Antiphon reminds us that God is Lord of everything. If we lived according to that reality there would be no need for parables like the one we proclaim today. The Opening Prayer tells us that God's love for us knows no boundaries, so we humbly ask that God "forgive our failings and bring us peace." Peace conjures images of the peace (shalom) Jesus inaugurated when he established the messianic reign. The last age or messianic kingdom was always understood in the Hebrew scriptures as a return to the perfect harmony of Eden. In that new paradise, people would live in perfect harmony with the God of the covenant. Peace and harmony would reign. The lion would lie down beside the lamb. Violence would be no more. People would love the Lord their God with all their heart, mind, body, and soul; they would love one another as they loved themselves. That love would be evident by the way in which they cared for the least of the Lord's children, God's anawim. Whenever we live the love that Christ established in this new kingdom, we are living in the peace of Eden.

Eucharist strengthens and empowers us to realize the reign of God here on earth. It also strengthens us to live in peace, not violence, and to conform our lives to the life of Christ. In the Prayer After Communion we state: "May the love of Christ which we celebrate here touch our lives and lead us to you."

Gospel Exegesis

The facilitator gives input regarding what critical biblical scholarship has to say about this text. The input includes insights as to how people would have heard the gospel in Jesus' time.

Some scholars believe that the original source of this parable was prior even to Mark's version. Matthew's version of the parable is his own interpretation of it. Israel is the Lord's vineyard. The vineyard is cared for by tenants who prove to be untrustworthy rogues. The owner's servants are sent to collect the rent (harvest). The tenants kill the owner's messengers. Matthew wants his listeners to make a connection between the servants and the fate of the prophets who were also sent to the Lord's vineyard but were "stoned and killed." The owner then sends his own son, the heir to the land, to collect what the servants before him could not collect. The son is thrown off the property and he too is murdered like those before him. Tension mounts in the story. What will happen to the murderous scoundrels? Donald Senior suggests that Matthew answers the question by using a favorite early Christian text. Jesus was referred to as the cornerstone of the kingdom in the early church. When the tenants of the land (Israel's religious leaders) rejected Jesus, they rejected the foundation of the kingdom. Jesus, the present stumbling block for so many, would turn out to be the stone who will return in glory "to crush all opposition."[4] What will happen to the tenants? Since Israel refused to accept the message of Jesus and his messianic reign, the vineyard will be taken away from them and given to the Gentiles who will produce good fruit. Senior maintains that rather than a preoccupation with the past infidelity of Israel, the parable serves as a warning to Matthew's community. If Israel missed it, so could they. Those who fail to live the gospel of Christ are warned of the consequences.

The parable is set in the context of Jesus' final days and his confrontations with the temple leadership. There is a question of authority. Jesus enters Jerusalem as the authentic bearer of God's will for the people. He challenges the temple authorities on their own turf. The tenant farmers in the parable represent the religious leaders of Israel who, "despite their alleged loyalty to the Torah, fail to give God his due by believing in God's present activity in the ministries of John and Jesus. Although they have been charged with the responsibility of leading Israel in the way of righteousness, they have in fact rebelled against God and will be replaced."[5] The parables of the man with two sons, the man with the vineyard, and the wedding feast support Matthew's ongoing doctrine. The Christian church is the true Israel over

---

[4] *IM,* 250.

[5] Ibid., 248.

and above Judaism. The parables support and speak to that assertion and claim.

Bernard Brandon Scott gives further insights into the parable: the parable condemns the religious leaders for keeping the rightful owners of the vineyard (Christians, the new Israel) from taking over the land. The issue was raised, the controversy out in the open. Just who has authentic authority here, Jesus or the temple leaders?

Matthew produces his evidence, pleads his case, and primes the jury. The son who was killed outside the parameters of the vineyard by the tenants is all the evidence needed to prove his contentions. Judaism is unfit and no longer qualified to be the true Israel. Israel's guilt is evident. Matthew then sets out to confirm that the Christian church *is qualified* because it will produce the necessary harvest. The owner of the vineyard will rent his vineyard to other nations[6] who will produce good fruit. Jesus makes sure that his listeners understand that the kingdom of God is the vineyard and the "true Israel" is the kingdom.[7] Jesus avows that the kingdom "will be taken away from you" (the religious leaders, as well as anyone who rejects Jesus and John) and given to a nation which will produce the desired fruit.

Scott asserts that there is an interesting use of the word *nation* in the parable. Usually when the word *nation* was used, it referred to Israel and the translation was *laos*. The word used in this parable, however, was not *laos*, but *ethnos*, an interpretation that referred to the Gentiles. The vineyard will be leased to other nations, the Gentiles.[8] Douglas Hare, however, refutes the designation of *ethnos* as exclusively meaning Gentiles. "The church, for Matthew, is neither Jewish nor Gentile but a 'third race' that transcends the old distinction."[9]

Scott postulates a fascinating, yet sobering interpretation of this parable drawing on all the traditions, including the Gospel of Thomas. Thomas "filled in many of the blanks" created by some of the unanswered questions in the various accounts of the parable. Scott suggests that the parable also implies another commonly used metaphor—the master/servant motif. The master went on a journey and left a servant in charge. Such a scenario usually signals a test and includes an eventual accounting by the servant. The object of the test is stewardship. This story adds a different twist, however, and uses the occasion as a test for the master.

The master does seem a bit like a fool. He desperately tries to take control of his land and fails. The tenants get the better of him; he is ashamed. Listeners almost always identified with the tenants in a story because usually the tenant was oppressed, not the master. This scenario no doubt troubled many a listener. These were not tenants with whom they could either sympathize or identify. These were violent people who plotted to kill the owner's son for his inheritance.

Scott insists that we do not, at this point in the story, know for sure that the vineyard represents Israel. Usually when the image of a vineyard is used as a reference for Israel, the story also includes discussion of the vineyard's fruit. Who or what the vineyard represents is not clear. All the listener really knows is that the owner entrusted his vineyard to someone else. The stars of this tragedy are the tenants and the owner.

Scott suggests that we are faced with two possible representations for both the owner and the tenants. The owner could be either God or Israel and the tenants could be either Rome or Israel. If God is the owner, then, like the owner in the story, God fails to take back his own vineyard. If Israel is the owner, then Israel fails to be restored. Similarly, if Roman occupiers are the tenants, they still remain in control of the land. If Israel is the tenant, then Israel is usurping and stealing the land from its rightful title holder. Listeners would find none of the above scenarios acceptable. The parable at this point moves into the arena of "gotcha!" Nothing makes sense; there is annoyance at the possibilities. Everyone is at attention. All the normal expectations have been overturned. Perhaps there are clues yet to be discovered that will shed light on all this absurdity. There is only one thing left to consider—the inheritance.

---

[6]"Nation" is translated as "people" in the New American Bible.

[7]*HTP*, 242.

[8]Ibid.

[9]*IM*, 249.

What makes the tenants think that killing the son will make them heirs to his inheritance? Something lies beneath the text that is worth exploring—the dialogue. The tenants say to one another, "Come, let us kill him. . . ." The listener's biblically-tuned ears should have perked up. The language is reminiscent of language used long ago by some very famous biblical characters who, like the tenants in this story, tried to steal an inheritance through the use of violence. Those same words, "Come, let us kill him," were used by the brothers of Joseph in the Old Testament as they plotted their jealous, violent actions against Joseph. This literary tool is called intertextuality; that is, the words echo a well-known story. The snatching of one's inheritance is a common theme in the scriptures. Jacob tried to trick his father into giving him his brother Esau's inheritance. Allusion to the scriptural inheritance theme sets up a new question in the parable: *Will the land go to the promised heirs?*

In the story line of the parable, the vineyard's ownership is questionable. The owner does not have control, but the tenants' claim to the inheritance is shaky at best. The parable gives no clues as to how it will end up. We are left with the question: Who is the rightful owner of the land? Who really should inherit it? Who has the necessary power to claim it?

The parable does not tell us the rest of the story. We cannot predict whether a "good" person or the "right" person will ultimately win the inheritance. Rightful heirs do not always triumph. The owner is still alive and the inheritance has yet to be awarded, so the parable gives us no indication how things are going to turn out in the end. The owner could be killed, or he could take back the vineyard. Nothing up to this point has turned out as expected, so guessing is useless.

This interpretation of the parable moves the listener from "a kingdom will triumph" story to "a kingdom might live in affliction" story. "The owner is a fool, the tenants are bandits, and the messengers are beaten or murdered."[10] The parable now resembles the parable of the man left for dead who was saved by his mortal enemy, the Samaritan. The one who should have been the hero (the expected one, the priest) who would have inherited the kingdom, lost it. The one not expected to be the hero (the Samaritan), or inherit the kingdom, inherited it. Similarly, Jesus' association with outcasts removes the predictability of who will inherit the kingdom. Popular opinion would never have approved inclusion of Jesus' friends. This parable might serve to remind the listener that those who think they are "in" might be "out," and those who think they are "out" might be "in." We may think we know who is deserving, but that is human arrogance. Only God knows. Since the story still does not have an ending, perhaps we are invited to write it ourselves. We can repent and live as good and faithful stewards of the life we have been given, or we can be thieves who try to steal what is not ours.

There are many layers of meaning for consideration and reflection in the parable: (1) The agenda of Matthew regarding the authenticity of the Christian and Gentile mission, the heirs of the true Israel and the messianic kingdom; (2) Israel's rejection of it;[11] (3) rigid, legalistic, self-

[10] *HTP*, 253.

[11] Douglas Hare cautions us in regard to this parable. He contends that misinterpretation of parables like this have caused pain and prejudice against the Jews over the centuries. This parable and other passages like it have been used as proof texts that the Jews killed Christ. Hitler made "Christ-killers" his clarion call as he herded the Jews into the gas and death-filled cattle cars. Hare insists that there are two ways to interpret this text so as not to promote anti-Semitism. The first approach is to understand the exhortation hurled against the Jews to be from one Jew to other fellow Jews. Matthew might be wallowing in his own disappointment and pessimism. It had to be frustrating to watch his own people reject what was so clear and life-giving to all the Christians who accepted it. Matthew's frustration and pessimism must be considered in tandem with Paul's optimism and hope for Israel's future. A second approach, according to Hare, is to center not on the condemnation of the Jewish leaders, but rather on the challenge to the Christians who were charged with being good stewards of the vineyard and who would ultimately be held accountable. The chastisement of others is a warning to us all. To Hare's exhortation I would like to add a perspective posited by the Jewish historian Ellis Rivkin:

> What crucified Jesus was the destruction of human rights, Roman imperialism, selfish collaboration. . . . If these were among the Jews who abetted such a regime, then they too shared the

righteous religious superiority, leadership, attitudes, and posturing; (4) the need to continue to work toward restoration of the reign of God; (5) the fact that salvation is unmerited, gratuitous grace, but that it can be lost through arrogance, presumption, inattention, idolatry, sin, and violence; (6) that God's messengers and prophets face rejection and death; (7) the need to repent while there is still time; (8) that living the gospel in the kingdom of God often invites rejection, suffering, sorrow, pain, and disappointment; (9) that power, greed, and control lead to violence; (10) that God's ways are not our ways and God does not judge by human standards; (11) that God welcomes the sinner and chastises the self-righteous.

Proclaim the gospel again.

Sometimes we gain new insights when we hear the text after the interpretation has been given. Someone from the group proclaims the gospel a second time.

STEP 4
TESTING

Conversation with the Liturgy and the Scriptures

Test your original understanding in dialogue with the text.

(You might consider breaking into smaller groups.)

Now that you've heard the exegesis, were there any new insights for you? How do you feel about it? How does your original understanding of this gospel compare with what we just shared? How does this story speak to your life?

Sharing Life Experience

Participants share an experience from their lives that connects with the biblical interpretation just shared.

> *A friend of mine told me about a parish in which people are removed from the membership roster if they have not given monetary support to the parish in over a year. No calls are made to see if there is a reason for their lack of financial support (such as financial hardship); their names are simply removed. It appears as if this community has set itself up as judge and jury as to who belongs and who does not belong. Human standards are used, not God's standards. The fruit of that vineyard is exclusion. Perhaps the messengers have yet to be sent. I do not know if there are dead messengers lurking in their skeleton closet or not. Perhaps they would respond and yield the harvest they are expected to yield when presented with the challenge. Isn't that just what this parable invites?*
>
> *In my own life, this parable demands that I continue to keep my eyes and my heart focused on God, and on what God is doing. It is so easy to fall back on legalistic approaches to things and fail to see that God is inviting something altogether new. Not too long ago we were discerning over an issue regarding some folks in our initiation community. I held up the vision of the rite, as I believe that is my role and my responsibility. I still believe that. However, I was challenged by some very wise, pastoral people to reconsider the situation of a certain person. For specific reasons this individual simply did not fit into the vision and we needed to do a different thing for that person. It was very difficult for me to yield. I believe so strongly in the vision of pastoral formation inherent in the RCIA. God is doing a mighty work in and through it. However, Jesus was always going outside the tradition he knew and loved when it meant inviting people into his reign.*
>
> *It remains to be seen whether or not our decision was the right one. However, it was a powerful lesson for me and one that was affirmed through serious reflection on this parable. Israel thought they had the vision—all the right answers. And in many ways they did. But "having all the right answers" and "safe-*

---

responsibility. The mass of Jews, however, who were so bitterly suffering under Roman domination that they were to revolt in but a few years against the tyranny, can hardly be said to have crucified Jesus. In the crucifixion, their own plight of helplessness, humiliation and subjection were clearly written on the cross itself. By nailing to the cross the one who claimed to be the Messiah to free human beings, Rome and its collaborators indicated their attitude towards human freedom. (John T. Pawlikowski, O.S.M., in *Chicago Studies,* 24 (1986): pp. 88–97, 88f.; in John P. Kealy, C.S.Sp., *JP,* 65.)

guarding the tradition" became more important than the heart of the tradition itself. It could not see the new thing God was doing because it was not what they knew or expected. A vision is good; it is necessary. But it must always be open to the action of God. It is so human to want to make idols out of our laws. Then the law, not God, becomes the instrument of grace. If anything elevated St. Paul's blood pressure—that was it. Jesus Christ is the source of our grace and salvation, not the law. I must be vigilant and watch for God's action in unexpected places.

All share their life experience.

What was Matthew trying to tell his community? In what way does this gospel challenge your community today? With whom in the story do you most identify right now? Have there been moments in your life when you could identify more with the owner? The servants? The son? The tenants? What have you learned about yourself? What does it teach you about God? In what way has this conversation with the scriptures for today's liturgy invited change in your life? Has your original understanding of this parable been stretched, challenged, or affirmed?

STEP 5
DECISION

The gospel demands a response.

In what specific way might your parish be invited to respond? Are there any attitudes or behaviors you would like to change as a result of today's conversation? What one concrete action will you take this week as a response to the liturgy today?

Pastoral Considerations: The liturgies of these weeks have been a minicourse in ecclesiology. They so powerfully challenge the church. They scream to us to take notice and respond: "Hello, is anyone listening?" Response must begin in our parish communities. To the church as community the liturgies of these weeks question our exclusionary attitudes and policies. It questions the way in which we judge people's relationship with God according to human standards. It judges our feelings of triumphalism in which we think we "have it all." It challenges the Christian church's belief that we are the only game in town, that somehow we are better than others, that most assuredly we have a direct pipeline to God and that God is confined to the action we observe within our church walls. Sometimes we, as universal church, diocesan church, local church, and small community churches resemble the Israel of the first reading and the parable. We fail to see the new thing God is doing or worse, we are guilty of the lack of any harvest to gather, as mentioned in both readings. We exclude others and we fail to love.

We are living in a time when God is doing a mighty action in the church and in the world. It is an exciting time to be alive and to live and work in the church. I sincerely believe that the truth of our Catholic tradition is the best kept secret in town. Yet, on the other side of the coin, there is also pain, struggle, animosity, suspicion, entrenchment, lack of unity, and lack of charity toward one another. Today's parable is a powerful word for our church communities. Do we resemble the true Israel that Matthew was talking about? Imagine the possibilities if church communities would commit themselves to serious, ongoing reflection and examination of the ways in which they refuse to yield a good harvest. Who is still excluded—actually or attitudinally—in our church communities? Where is there division, rigidity, and legalistic behavior displayed toward other members of God's family? Perhaps efforts to raise consciousness is the first place to start. Are we hearing a just word preached in our assemblies? All one needs to do to judge a parish's harvest is to look at the ways in which it (or a good many of its members) are reaching out to the needs of the "least of God's children." Care and concern for our own people are good, noble, and worthy, but that almost goes without saying. Who in a family would not take care of one of its own sick members? The big questions are: How are we reaching out to the undesirables? What are we doing about the politically incorrect issues of the day? Are there "undeserving" poor in our midst? How might our parishes engage in serious dialogue and attention to these critical invitations posed by Christ of the parables?

DOCTRINAL ISSUES

What church truth/teaching/doctrinal issue could be drawn from the gospel for the Twenty-Seventh Sunday in Ordinary Time?

Participants suggest possible doctrinal themes that flow from the readings.

Possible Doctrinal Themes

Repentance, evangelization, ministry, social teaching, ecumenism, reign of God, mystery of the church, conversion, discipleship, paschal mystery, parables, Christology, God's mercy, sacrament of reconciliation, images of God

Present the doctrinal material at this time.

1. The facilitator gives input on a particular doctrinal issue of his/her prior choosing. OR
2. The group chooses a doctrinal issue from the list they created. They read together from the Doctrinal Appendix.

(The doctrinal issues are found in the Doctrinal Appendix in the back of this workbook. If you are choosing an issue from this resource, please refer to it now.)

Reflection questions centered around the chosen doctrinal theme can be found at the end of each topic in the Doctrinal Appendix. The questions are based on the five-step reflection process. If you choose a topic not included in the Doctrinal Appendix, craft your own questions according to the same five-step process.

Following the reflection questions you will be reminded to return to chapter 7, "Preparing the Catechetical Session," to assist you in crafting your own session.

Closing Prayer

Lord,
we thank you for the harvest the earth has produced
for the good of man.
These gifts witness to your infinite love;
may the seeds of charity and justice also bear fruit in our hearts.
Grant this through our Lord Jesus Christ, your Son,
who lives and reigns with you and the Holy Spirit,
one God for ever and ever.[12]

[12]Masses for Various Public Needs: "After the Harvest," *The Sacramentary.*

Twenty-Eighth Sunday in Ordinary Time

Environment

See the Twenty-Second Sunday in Ordinary Time.

INTRODUCTORY RITES

Opening Song (or Entrance Antiphon)

If you, O Lord, laid bare our guilt, who could endure it? But you are forgiving, God of Israel. (Ps 129:3–4)[1]

Opening Prayer

Let us pray
[in quiet for the grace of sincerity]

Pause for silent prayer.

Father in heaven,
the hand of your loving kindness
powerfully yet gently guides all the moments of
our day.
Go before us in our pilgrimage of life,
anticipate our needs and prevent our falling.
Send your Spirit to unite us in faith,
that sharing in your service,
we may rejoice in your presence.
We ask this through Christ our Lord.[2]

LITURGY OF THE WORD

The readings are proclaimed.

First Reading
Isaiah 25:6–10

(See the First Sunday of Advent for an Overview of the Book of Isaiah.)

Today's Pericope: Today's pericope comes from a section within a section (chapters 24–27) in the Book of Isaiah known as the "Isaiah Apocalypse."[3] Isaiah looks ahead to the last age and the end of all time. He tries to verbalize it so the people will have a sense of what to expect. This piece, written after the exile, describes the reconstruction that will take place after the destruction of the earth and all its people. This destruction is a result of the sin of the people. Everything will die because of the sin of the people, and the earth will be ravaged.

But all is not lost. God can turn the tables, change his course, and refrain from striking the mighty blow. The feast is a sign that he will do it. He will restore the city on the mountain (Jerusalem). He will restore all people. This restoration will be signified by great rejoicing. The time of tribulation will be over. There will be feasting on good food and rich wine. The last tear will have been shed and all will have seen the end of death. This passage is particularly noteworthy as it is the earliest expression in the scriptures that God intends to conquer death.

The feast or banquet is a metaphor used commonly throughout scriptures. The feast had many functions and possessed various levels of meaning. To eat with someone meant that you entered into a special covenant of hospitality and community with that person. There were different types of banquets. Ritual banquets celebrated profound change, such as the reconciliation between friends or nations. Ceremonial banquets celebrated the common covenant bond and relationship between the peoples in attendance. The feast in today's reading contains both elements. It celebrates the covenant between God and the people of God. It also celebrates the profound change in people's lives from sorrow to joy and death to life.

Isaiah paints the picture of the restoration of Israel in grand strokes. He wants the people to

[1]Twenty-Eighth Sunday in Ordinary Time: "Entrance Antiphon," *The Sacramentary.*

[2]Twenty-Eighth Sunday in Ordinary Time: "Alternative Opening Prayer," *The Sacramentary.*

[3]Scholars believe that this section was not written by Isaiah himself, but by later prophets who were trained in Isaiah's style.

know in no uncertain terms that it is a result of God's intervention and mercy. God's action and grace in the restoration of the people prompted them to look to that future day when even death would be wiped away by the powerful hand of the Almighty. The banquet is a sign that joy (the wine) will reign triumphant over anguish (the veil over the people). "Just as the vineyard became, since the song in Isaiah 5, an accepted symbol for Israel as the people of God in salvation history, so our present reading made the great banquet a classic symbol of the consummation of God's saving purpose in history."[4]

This passage from Isaiah was understood in eucharistic terms by the early church. They believed the eucharist to be the eschatological banquet here on earth while they were awaiting the glorious banquet in heaven.

Responsorial Psalm
Psalm 23:1–3, 3–4, 5–6

The emphasis in today's psalm is on the place of the great banquet, the house of the Lord or the temple. The Lord's house is where the great banquet is prepared and the people will be invited to share in the blessings.[5] God is depicted first as shepherd, then as host, in the third stanza.

Second Reading
Philippians 4:12–14, 19–20

Paul is accused by some scholars of being too embarrassed to accept offers of help, while others insist that in order for Paul to lay claim to the title of apostle, he had to demonstrate a willingness to bear the cross of Christ. An apostle must forge readily into affliction and hunger as well as into glory and plenty.

Paul was contented with whatever situation that lay before him. If there was hunger, he praised God; if there was plenty, he gave thanks to God. Paul lived in peace and believed that everything in this world except the love of Christ is insignificant. He was willing to do anything, endure all things, for a share of Christ's life. The word Paul used to describe his tranquility was a well-known word from the Greek philosophical system that meant *satisfaction and self-sufficiency resulting from the elimination of all desire.* The Greeks believed that desire could be completely mastered through a sheer act of will. Paul eliminated his desire for earthly concerns, but he could never eliminate his desire for Christ. He was consumed with it. There was room for nothing more. Only God could have imbued him with that kind of passion. This kind of serenity, kenosis, or self-emptying is the grace of God in Christ.

Paul was grateful for the Philippians' care and concern, however. He accepted their generous gift and promised that God would abundantly bless them with his glory and provide for all their needs.

Gospel
Matthew 22:1–14

STEP 1
NAMING ONE'S EXPERIENCE

What were your first impressions? What was your first response to the gospel (or the other readings)?[6] What captured your attention?

Each person names his or her initial impression. Statements should be brief. No reasons should be given at this time. All simply listen without agreeing or disagreeing.

STEP 2
UNDERSTANDING

In a brief statement, what do you think this gospel is trying to convey?

STEP 3
INPUT FROM VISION/STORY/TRADITION

Liturgical Context

The last three Sundays have been an extended meditation on one of Matthew's principal themes.

[4] *PL,* 178.

[5] Ibid.

[6] The primary focus of reflection is the gospel. However, very often the other readings demand attention and must be brought into the dialogue.

Following Christ involves more than words. It must be backed up by action. Christians must follow the will of God. Pious rhetoric is nothing more than that—rhetoric. The test of a person's convictions will be borne out by the way he or she lives in response to the will of God. Matthew writes his message to the church with three parables: the two sons, the vinedressers and, today, the parable of the wedding feast. He knows well the temptations lurking in every Christian community. So that we do not lose sight of what is really important, he wants us to know without question that God's reign is a reign of surprises and that there is absolutely no room for complacency. Diligent watchfulness is necessary if we are not to fall prey to the illusion that we know what God will do, how God will act, and whom God will choose. God chooses whom we least expect. The Communion Rite Antiphon reminds us of that.

God expects us to be humble, faithful, and repentant servants. The liturgy of these past weeks resounds with the theme of God's forgiveness and reconciliation. Today's Entrance Antiphon sings the very familiar song again. If God were to show us the magnitude of our sinfulness we could hardly endure it. But the good news is that the God of Israel forgives us anyway. In the Alternative Opening Prayer we ask God to go before us in this life and to assist us on our journey through the kingdom. We hope and pray that we do not fall, and that the presence of God's Spirit will unite us as we journey. Today's parable is a sober reminder that the choice is ours. There is responsibility inherent in living the demands of the gospel. We are confident, however, that with God's help we will remain steadfast.

Let us recall the words of St. Augustine:

> Let no one delay in coming to the supper. Let us put aside all ideal, wicked excuses, and come to the supper in which our souls are fed. Let no swelling of pride keep us back, or lift us above ourselves; and neither let unlawful superstition frighten us, or turn us away from God. Let not the delights of the senses keep us from the delights of the soul. Let us come, and let us be feasted. And who have come but the poor and the feeble and the lame and the blind? But the rich have not come there, nor the healthy, who as it were could walk well and see clearly, sure of themselves, and the more arrogant were they, the more endangered.
>
> Let the poor come, for he who invites us, though rich, became poor for our sakes, that by his poverty we might be made rich.
>
> Let the feeble come, for they who are in health need not the physician, but they that are ill. Let the lame come. Let the blind come. Compel them to come in. I have prepared a great supper, a great house. I shall suffer no place there to remain empty.
>
> The Gentiles came from the streets and the lanes. Let the heretics come from the hedges; here they will find peace. For they who make hedges are seeking to bring about divisions. Let them be drawn from the hedges; let them be plucked free of the thorns. They refuse to be compelled, and they cling to their hedges. Let us, they say, come in our own will. But this is not what the Lord commanded. Compel them, he says, to come in.[7]

Gospel Exegesis

The facilitator gives input regarding what critical biblical scholarship has to say about this text. The input includes insights as to how people would have heard the gospel in Jesus' time.

The parable of the wedding feast is known to have three distinct sources: Luke, Matthew, and the non-canonical Gospel of Thomas (discovered first in fragments in 1900, then in complete form in the Coptic language in 1945, both in Egypt). Scholars believe that the latter is probably the most authentic version of the parable. The host invites guests who decline for business reasons. The parable ends by saying, "Buyers and merchants will not enter the places of my Father." The theme is one of Jesus' favorites: the reign of God is not what you expect it to be.

---

[7]St. Augustine in *RF*, 67.

Luke's parable picks up the same logic, insisting that the poor and the outcasts will be the ones included. Matthew, on the other hand, continues to promote his doctrinal agenda (refer to last week's gospel).

The cultural backdrop of this parable helps shed light on its meaning. Meals were a replica of the larger society's social order, according to John Pilch. In antiquity, if the king hosted a party for his son, common folk would not have been invited. Only the rich, the prominent, the elite, would have been invited. We are told that the king's original guest list included such people—a landowner and a business person.

The king sent his slaves out to call the people who had already been invited. It was a common practice for people to wait until the last minute before deciding whether or not they would attend such a gala. People would wait to see how plans for the party were developing and who was planning to attend. If key people stayed away, others would be prompted to do likewise. In our story today, it is obvious that the guests were voicing their disapproval of the king's party plans by staying home. By so doing, they shamed the king. To add insult to injury, they gave lame excuses. Attending to business concerns, it seemed, was more important than celebrating the wedding of the king's son.

The next group to be summoned by the king behaved worse than the first. They seized, throttled, and murdered the king's slaves, shaming the king even further. An honor and shame-based culture is based on reciprocity. Such an action deserved a swift response. The king destroyed their city in retribution, and by the process restoring his honor.

The king then went against all known cultural mores. He invited commoners to the palace. He sent his messengers to the highways and byways to get them. Pilch asserts that verse 9 is translated as *main roads, main streets, or thoroughfares,* but that it actually refers to the town square or the plaza. The king sent his servants out to the place where folks congregate—the only place where the commoners and the elite might ever have occasion to mingle. It was a very public invitation.

His guest list now resembling the "who's who" of the rank and file, the king's action was not without risk. He risked being shunned by the elite upper class. Not only did *he* take a risk, but the elite who chose to attend the king's party were taking a risk also. "Since all of life and survival in itself in the Mediterranean world depends on one's social network, for an elite to eat with a non-elite would be the equivalent of suicide."[8] But among this new group of guests, there was someone who refused to wear the garment the king had provided for the occasion. Once again the king is shamed, and expells the man from the banquet.

Pilch contends that Jesus' target audience was the chief priests and elders. The parable was a commentary on their elitism. He contrasted their exclusiveness with the welcoming inclusiveness of God. In the reign of God everyone is welcome; no one is excluded.

Other scholars suggest that Matthew used the parable as a commentary on the history of salvation. In Matthew's allegory, the king who prepares the wedding feast for his son is God. The banquet is the kingdom of God, and the son is Jesus. Those who refused the invitation were intended to represent Israel (last week the tenants and the vineyard repeated the same theme). The servants probably represented the prophets and the apostles.

There is an interesting insertion in the parable. The city of the invited guests is destroyed by fire. The implication is not to be missed. This is what happens when God's messengers are rejected. "One cannot trifle with God and get away with it."[9] Scholars believe that the destruction of the city is a reference to the destruction of Jerusalem that occurred in 70 C.E. It was put back in the text to update the events of salvation history to the time of the gospel's writing (c. 80 C.E.).

If this is a commentary on salvation history, then what is Matthew's perspective of it? God elected Israel. God entered into a covenant relationship with Israel. God formed Israel into a people—God's people (banquet). God led the people through bondage to freedom and into the

[8] *CWJ,* 149.
[9] *RM,* 222.

promised land. God provided rich food for God's people who dwelt on the land that God gave them. Then God's people sinned. God sent the prophets (servants) to invite the people and to prepare them for the new banquet his Son (Jesus) would prepare. The Son was rejected and God sent more servants (apostles) to repeat the invitation. Again the people declined. Thus, the guests who had been invited from the very beginning (Israel) refused the invitation to the banquet (reign of God). The king then told the servants to go out and get both bad and good people (reign of God is comprised of all people—all are invited) from the highways and byways (Gentiles) and invite them to the feast (reign of God). The original guests (Israel) may have declined the Lord's feast, but the Gentiles would accept. "The banquet hall [the reign of God] was filled with guests" (v. 10, *NAB*).

Always the reader is left with a challenge and a warning. In spite of the festivity, there was not perfect harmony at the banquet. Good and bad people were invited, yet not all were allowed to remain. The fellow who was improperly clad for a wedding feast was expelled. We are soberly reminded at the end of the parable that everyone is invited, but only the elect remain. The message is clear. Everyone is invited but those who accept the invitation have a responsibility to respond appropriately to it. "The Gospel makes the same demand on all, Jew and gentile alike: a life that is 'turned around' and given to good deeds. Anything less—an Israel without its harvest, a church without its wedding garment—will be cast into darkness."[10]

Matthew reminded us in chapter 13 that the final judgment will not come until the end of time. Until that time, however, the good and the bad must sit at the same table. It hardly seems fair to our modern sense of justice that this poor fellow, who was pulled off the streets at the last minute, was expelled from the banquet for his inappropriate dress. The reaction of the king seems too severe. David Garland insists, however, that the guest's silence is an admission of guilt. Readers are to interpret the garment allegorically. There was an implied expectation that the man would come appropriately attired.

> Clothing is frequently used as a metaphor in the New Testament (Rom 13:12, 14; Gal 3:27; Eph 4:22; Col 3:9–11) and particularly as an apocalyptic image for moral worthiness (Rev 3:4–5, 18; 6:11; 7:13–14; 22:14–15). In Revelation 19:8 the fine linen represents the righteous deeds of the saints. This meaning fits an emphasis found throughout Matthew: grace does not cancel the reality of the judgment; each one will be judged according to their works (16:27; see 7:15–17 and the three parables in chapter 25). God's summons requires a changed life that results in fruit (3:8), and a righteousness that surpasses conventional norms of behavior.[11]

Matthew's version of the parable was not intended as a running diatribe against Israel for its refusal to accept Christ and the gospel. On the contrary, according to Donald Senior, it was intended to remind the Christian community what can happen to those who refuse to be faithful to the gospel. Matthew's favorite theme continues to be: actions speak louder than words. "This parable makes clear that one need not possess the garment to be invited to the party—both good and bad are brought in—but one needs it to stay. God's grace may not be taken for granted. God requires obedience, which does not merit salvation but is evidence of it."[12]

Proclaim the gospel again.

Sometimes we gain new insights when we hear the text after the interpretation has been given. Someone from the group proclaims the gospel a second time.

STEP 4
TESTING

Conversation with the Liturgy and the Scriptures

Test your original understanding in dialogue with the text.

(You might consider breaking into smaller groups.)

[10]*ITM,* 211.

[11]*RM,* 221–222.

[12]Ibid., 223.

Now that you've heard the exegesis, were there any new insights for you? How do you feel about it? How does your original understanding of this gospel compare with what we just shared? How does this story speak to your life?

Sharing Life Experience

Participants share an experience from their lives that connects with the biblical interpretation just shared.

There has been so much emphasis on who is in and who is out during these past weeks that I think Matthew knows us only too well. He has to say it over and over again like a broken record. Maybe the reason for the repetition is that our arrogant propensity for self-righteous elitism is very difficult to uncover. How many of us would not feel just a bit of smug self-righteousness standing next to a homeless person on the street? I know it lurks deep within my own psyche. Just when I think I have rooted it out, I am tested again and again.

My husband stops on the street to talk to homeless people, no matter where we are or what we are doing. I find myself bored, distracted, and antsy to move on. Last week, when we pulled up in front of the grocery store, John, one of our community's homeless people, was sitting on a bench outside the door. My husband was just going to run in quickly to pick up something. He invited me to go and talk to John while he was in the store. I talked to him for about five minutes. I became very uncomfortable, apologized, and offered a lame excuse that I needed to go shopping in one of the nearby shops.

Here was an invitation to a banquet staring me in the face and I had refused it. I could have extended the gift of time and presence to someone who very seldom has anyone take an interest in his life. I could have shown him that I regard him as I do other human beings, with full dignity. My husband shows him that all the time. I am forced to admit that doing is a lot more difficult than just talking. It is one thing to write about justice and to preach about justice; it is quite another thing to do *something about it.*

The king risked a lot when he reached out to the highways and byways. I wonder what would happen in our community if we were to take John up to the front row and give him a place of honor at the eucharistic banquet? How would we, as community, respond? Would we reach out? Would we be afraid to shake his dirty hand? Would we ignore him as I ignored him? What Jesus was saying in today's parable is that John just might be the first one to stand with the king to welcome all the new guests to the heavenly banquet. If I am to be included in the guest list, I must be diligent in uncovering all those hidden and sinister areas of elitism, self-righteousness, and hypocritical superiority. Then I must do something about it, since I am certain that Matthew is speaking the mind of God when he asserts that actions speak louder than words.

All share their life experience.

What was Matthew trying to tell his community? Can you think of anything in our modern culture that might resemble the scene in the parable? Have things changed much over the centuries? How might this parable challenge your church community? In what way have you ever identified with the king, the first guests, the last guests, the guest that was expelled, the messengers? What did your experience teach you about God? About yourself? Does this parable challenge any of your own attitudes or behaviors? In what way has this conversation with the scriptures for today's liturgy invited change in your life? In what way are the biblical themes of covenant, exodus, creation, and community evident in today's readings? Do you still feel the same way about this text as when you began? Has your original understanding been stretched, challenged, or affirmed?

STEP 5
DECISION

The gospel demands a response.

In what specific way might your parish be invited to respond? Are there any attitudes or behaviors you would like to change as a result of today's conversation? What one concrete action will you take this week as a response to the liturgy today?

Pastoral Considerations: There are some major questions that demand attention as a result of the proclamation of this parable. Our parishes could change the world if we were to attempt to answer them. "Who is not welcomed at our table?" "How do we still resemble the guests who refused the king's invitation?" "What can we do about it?" Dare we take those questions seriously?

Christian Initiation: These weeks would be an excellent time to go with your catechumens to reach out to the highways and byways. Perhaps this would be a good week to skip a session of extended catechesis and instead go out in your community on some sort of apostolic mission. Are there soup kitchens in your area? See if they would allow you to come and serve a meal for them. Are there efforts in your wider community to help the homeless? Drug addicts? Alcoholics? AIDS patients? Is there a St. Vincent de Paul society in your parish? Perhaps your catechumens could go on a call with the ministers. If actions speak louder than words, then it behooves us to provide opportunities for our catechumens to go out as Jesus' messengers went out to extend his invitation to the banquet.

If you do go out on such a mission, you might begin by gathering first for prayer. There are blessings in the *Book of Blessings* provided for such occasions. Also, do not forget to reflect on the experience when you meet afterward.

Is there anyone ready to be received into full communion of the Catholic Church, or celebrate a rite of acceptance or welcome? Are you remembering to use the minor rites in the catechumenate?

DOCTRINAL ISSUES

What church truth/teaching/doctrinal issue could be drawn from the gospel for the Twenty-Eighth Sunday in Ordinary Time?

Participants suggest possible doctrinal themes that flow from the readings.

Possible Doctrinal Themes

Reign of God, ecumenism, social teaching of the church, creation (dignity of all creation), cost of discipleship, paschal mystery, mystery of suffering, eschatology, last judgment, social sin, foundations of morality, conversion, evangelization

Present the doctrinal material at this time.

1. The facilitator gives input on a particular doctrinal issue of his/her prior choosing. OR
2. The group chooses a doctrinal issue from the list they created. They read together from the Doctrinal Appendix.

(The doctrinal issues are found in the Doctrinal Appendix in the back of this workbook. If you are choosing an issue from this resource, please refer to it now.)

Reflection questions centered around the chosen doctrinal theme can be found at the end of each topic in the Doctrinal Appendix. The questions are based on the five-step reflection process. If you choose a topic not included in the Doctrinal Appendix, craft your own questions according to the same five-step process.

Following the reflection questions you will be reminded to return to chapter 7, "Preparing the Catechetical Session," to assist you in crafting your own session.

Closing Prayer

God our Father,
you send the power of the gospel into the world
as a life-giving leaven.
Fill with the Spirit of Christ
those whom you call to live in the midst of the world
and its concerns;
help them by their work on earth
to build up your eternal kingdom.
We ask this through our Lord Jesus Christ, your Son,
who lives and reigns with you and the Holy Spirit,
one God for ever and ever.[13]

[13]Masses for Special Occasions: For the Laity, "Opening Prayer," *The Sacramentary*.

Twenty-Ninth Sunday in Ordinary Time

INTRODUCTORY RITES

Opening Song (or Entrance Antiphon)

I call upon you, God, for you will answer me; bend your ear and hear my prayer. Guard me as the pupil of your eye; hide me in the shade of your wings. (Ps 16:6, 8)[1]

Opening Prayer

Let us pray
[to the Lord who bends close to hear our prayer]

Pause for silent prayer.

Lord our God, Father of all,
you guard us under the shadow of your wings
and search into the depths of our hearts.
Remove the blindness that cannot know you
and relieve the fear that would hide us from your sight.
We ask this through Christ our Lord.[2]

LITURGY OF THE WORD

The readings are proclaimed.

First Reading
Isaiah 45:1, 4–6

Salvation history reveals an evolution in religious thought. God entered into a covenant with Israel. He delivered them out of slavery in Egypt through the desert to the promised land of Canaan. The people were surprised to find that God went with them into the promised land. The ancients believed that gods ruled over exclusive territories. Each geographical area was believed to be presided over by its own god. Thus, when the people entered their new land, they were tempted to worship the Canaanite god, Baal. It took a long time before they grew in awareness of the sovereignty of the one God. This awareness developed into the belief that there were no other gods, that Yahweh alone ruled the universe. Today's pericope demonstrates the awesome power of God in the history of salvation. God is Lord of all, even of Cyrus the pagan Persian king.

Cyrus was regarded favorably by Israel's historians. They referred to him as anointed, a title reserved only for Hebrew kings. Even though he was pagan, Cyrus allowed the exiles the freedom to return home and to practice their religion, once he overthrew the throne of Babylon and took control. Isaiah understood this to be the result of God's faithfulness to the covenant.

Isaiah proclaims that Cyrus carried out the will of God, thus attesting to the omnipotent universality of God. Israel's notion of government was that of theocracy. There were no distinctions between church and state. God ruled over both. There could be no other way because God is supreme, the ruler of all the nations of the earth.

Responsorial Psalm
Psalm 96:1, 3, 4–5, 7–8, 9–10

It is believed that this was an enthronement song sung at a (hypothetical) annual feast in which the king was enthroned symbolically as a sign of God's rule over the people. The people would have sung this psalm as the king took his place on the throne. It attests to the sovereignty of God over all the nations, thus its connection with the first reading.

Second Reading
1 Thessalonians 1:1–5

Overview of St. Paul's Letters to the Thessalonians: The letters to the Thessalonians are probably the beginning of Christian literature. Thessalonica was a city in northern Greece. Paul had attempted to evangelize the Jews of the city, but

[1] Twenty-Ninth Sunday in Ordinary Time: "Entrance Antiphon," *The Sacramentary.*

[2] Twenty-Ninth Sunday in Ordinary Time: "Alternative Opening Prayer," *The Sacramentary.*

when his attempts failed, he turned his efforts to the Greeks. This enraged the Jews and they expelled Paul and his disciples from the city. The Pauline letters are evidence of Paul's mission. Paul was concerned about the identity of the Christian community. Paul sent messengers to Thessalonica to relay his concern that the Thessalonians' church might be tempted to turn away from God in the face of persecution. There was no immediate crisis; Paul simply wanted to affirm the work already accomplished by Timothy and challenge the community to continued diligence. His letter[3] is an admonition against future temptations while affirming community members in their present adherence to gospel living. Paul sought to offer strength and consolation to the communities as they awaited the fulfillment of Christ's promise to return. While encouraging them in their progress, Paul nevertheless exhorted them to an even greater commitment to the Christian life.

Today's Pericope: The report Timothy brought back to Paul about the Thessalonian church was positive. Thus, the tone of the opening part of this letter is warm and affectionate. Today's pericope opens with Paul's giving thanks for the Thessalonians. Paul affirms the young community for their faith, hope, and love. He reminds them that he owes the success of his preaching ministry to God's grace, not to his own efforts. He affirms their hard work, their love, and their steadfast trust in God's saving power, which has been the testing ground of their faith. They have proved themselves trustworthy. Paul confirms Jesus' equality with the Father. His words of encouragement and affirmation are intended to strengthen this fledgling church as they continue to persevere in the midst of growing persecution.

Gospel
Matthew 22:15–21

[3]Paul wrote both letters and epistles. A letter was a personal communication between two parties who were separated. The letter was usually occasioned by a particular situation. An epistle was a form of literature that resembled a letter only in style and form. There was little else about it that resembled a letter. The epistle was a written essay for the purpose of public instruction or discussion of a disputed subject.

STEP 1
NAMING ONE'S EXPERIENCE

What were your first impressions? What was your first response to the gospel (or the other readings)? What captured your attention?

Each person names his or her initial impression. Statements should be brief. No reasons should be given at this time. All simply listen without agreeing or disagreeing.

STEP 2
UNDERSTANDING

In a brief statement, what do you think this gospel is trying to convey?

STEP 3
INPUT FROM VISION/STORY/TRADITION

Liturgical Context

Today begins a new sequence that spans the next three weeks. Rather than posit the teaching of Jesus through the proclamation of parables, the gospels of the next three weeks continue to profess his teaching in the context of confrontations with the religious authorities. These gospels continue to stress what it means to live according to gospel values in the reign of God. It comes down to a matter of the heart—not the law. When the law is examined from the perspective of how to find the necessary loopholes to circumvent it, then the law serves no purpose. The gospel teaches that what is important comes from the person's heart. The Pharisees were not interested in Jesus' answer to their question. They simply asked it in order to trap him. Jesus, however, would not be trapped. He affirmed that we are to give our allegiance and our entire being to God because we belong to God.

The Entrance Antiphon asks that we be guarded in the shadow of God's wings. It is a prayer that seeks what Jesus demands we must do to live in the kingdom—lose ourselves in the shadow of God's wings.

We are to abandon ourselves completely to God. The Alternative Opening Prayer echoes that same plea. It also asks that the blindness (similar to that of the Pharisees) be removed so we might fully know God and not hide ourselves from him out of fear. All the prayers of the liturgy echo Jesus' exhortation in the gospel to abandon ourselves to God. "See how the eyes of the Lord are on those who fear him, on those who hope in his love, that he may rescue them from death and feed them in time of famine" (Communion Rite). The Opening Prayer reminds us that God is our only source of power and inspiration. Our strength and joy come from God. We are to pray that God will accomplish in us what we cannot accomplish in ourselves.

Gospel Exegesis

The facilitator gives input regarding what critical biblical scholarship has to say about this text. The input includes insights as to how people would have heard the gospel in Jesus' time.

The Pharisees, bristling from being revealed in an unfavorable light in Jesus' parables, are now lying in wait, ready to entrap him the first chance they get. They tried three times, and three times he cleverly turned the tables on them. Now the Pharisees and some supporters of King Herod join to ask Jesus a politically-sensitive question. It was a dangerous question, as imposition of the tax they were questioning was cause for the revolt in 6 C.E. by Judas of Galilee. Judas was revolting against the placing of "God's own land at the service of pagans. . . ."[4] The Pharisees asked Jesus about the Roman tax. Is Caesar entitled to it? The tax they were referring to was the poll tax paid by every man, woman, child, and slave between the ages of twelve and sixty-five. The amount of the tax equaled a day's wages. Jesus asked them for one of their own coins and responded to them with his own teaching. Give to Caesar what is rightfully Caesar's and to God what is rightfully God's.[5] Give to God no less than your entire being.

John Pilch sets up the ancient Mediterranean context for today's gospel. He maintains that there was no such thing as a neutral question. Every question posed had the potential to challenge a person's honor. Jesus cleverly turned the tables on their plotting.

The Pharisees began by flattering Jesus. They called him honest and truthful—someone who authentically teaches the will of God and who does not care about honor or a person's status or opinion. Pilch offers: "Jesus was very sensitive to honor. He did care about the opinion of others (Mt 16:13). Eagerness to trap Jesus causes the Pharisees to exaggerate. Jesus is not taken in."[6] Pilch also maintains that the question they asked of Jesus was flattery as well. The question implied that Jesus could interpret the Torah.

Jesus asked them for a coin. On the coin was an image of Caesar with the inscription, "Tiberius Caesar, son of the divine Augustus, high priest."[7] Jews were aghast that Caesar labeled himself divine. They believed that possession of a graven image was a form of idolatry. They crafted ways to pay the tax so they would not have to touch the coin. Yet, these Pharisees were able to produce the coin when Jesus asked for it. Shame on them! Even if the Herodians produced the coin, it would be a source of shame. It would mean that the Pharisees aligned themselves with unsavory allies. Jesus did not have to say a word and the Pharisees exposed themselves.

Jesus asked the Pharisees whose head was on the coin? Everyone knew whose head was on the coin. Jesus just wanted them to say it out loud. If Caesar's head is on the coin, it obviously belongs to Caesar, so give it to him. "Jesus reminds them that they already acknowledge Caesar's authority by having in possession Caesar's money."[8] Jesus and the Pharisees probably felt the same way about paying the tax. If people wanted to live in peace, they paid the tax. It was obvious that the Pharisees' ploy was nothing more than that—a plot to trap Jesus. But they were caught in their own trap.

When Jesus said, "Give to God what belongs to God," he was implying that his accusers were not doing that. It was a powerful affront. The Phar-

[4] *RM*, 223.
[5] *ITM*, 215.

[6] *CWJ*, 151.
[7] Ibid., 152.
[8] *RM*, 223.

isees were fastidious in following the law. They followed more of the law than was necessary just so they could please God a little bit more. Jesus' main issue with the Pharisees was the "rendering to God" part of his response to them. The word "render" meant to pay a debt. Jesus insisted that for a person to belong to God's reign they must render to God what is God's. They must repay the debt to God. Caesar is owed money—that which bears his name and image. God is owed what bears his image—our very selves.

Pilch tells us that Americans have used this text in support of the separation of church and state. He reminds us that this concept would have been ludicrous to ancient Israel. "Religion and economics both are embedded in politics and kinship. There was state religion (Temple; empire) and family economics (gifts and sharing). Our modern Western situation and its challenges are very different. For us as for our ancestors what matters most is to please God."[9]

Gustavo Gutierrez proposes another interpretation. He suggests that Jesus was also telling us that we are not to have an unnecessary attachment for money. The coin is the symbol of the Roman oppressor. The Pharisees insinuate that maybe they will not pay the tax but keep it for themselves. The Pharisees, nationalistic Jews, align themselves with Herodians, followers of the despised despot ruler who oppressed the people. Together they confront Jesus because of Jesus' claim to establish a kingdom in which the poor have a prominent place. That was certainly not acceptable to the Pharisees. They set out to trip him up.

Jesus insists that Christians are to forego their dependence on money. Give to Caesar what is Caesar's. To live in the kingdom means to liberate oneself from the obsessive "attachment of money and its possibilities of exploiting others."[10]

Proclaim the gospel again.

Sometimes we gain new insights when we hear the text after the interpretation has been given. Someone from the group proclaims the gospel a second time.

[9] *CWJ*, 153.

[10] *SWTLY*, 245.

Step 4
Testing

Conversation with the Liturgy and the Scriptures

Test your original understanding in dialogue with the text.

(You might consider breaking into smaller groups.)

Now that you've heard the exegesis, were there any new insights for you? How do you feel about it? How does your original understanding of this gospel compare with what we just shared? How does this story speak to your life?

Sharing Life Experience

Participants share an experience from their lives that connects with the biblical interpretation just shared.

> *Manipulation of people, such as the attempted manipulation of Jesus in today's parable, has gone on since the beginning of time. The Pharisees' manipulations were no match for Jesus. There have been times when I was aware that flattery was being used to help win me over to an issue or to gain an ally. It is so very human. The Pharisees used it hoping that Jesus would fall for it and allow his ego to get the better of him, thus trapping himself in the process. It is so easy to do. Many times I have said yes to things I should have said no to, simply because flattering words were spoken. I was obviously not listening to the will of God, but instead was allowing flattery to bolster my ego and prompt me to do what later discernment taught me I should have declined to do.*
>
> *Jesus invites us all to become single-minded. If we keep our eyes on Christ and allow ourselves to be guided by his Spirit, we will be able to withstand those pressures when they come our way.*
>
> *I remember a time when I was invited to go somewhere and do something I believed would be very exciting and rewarding. I was extremely busy and family pressures were cautioning me to decline. But the invitation was strongly tugging at my heart. It was very affirming to be asked. My initial excitement stirred me to answer yes immediately. For once in my life I decided to prayerfully discern my deci-*

sion. It was not long before it was very clear what my decision should be. I yielded to God and gave over my will to God and God's plan for my life. I said those very difficult words: No thank you.

We will not often encounter the clever manipulations of people like the Pharisees. Some of us, however, unfortunately will. The primary message in today's gospel is to turn our lives completely over to God and not allow anything to keep us from God's love and will for our lives. If we free ourselves from any attachments, whether they be money or relationships, we will be free to allow Christ to take up full residence in our heart. A friend of mine once said, "The less you have the freer you are." If I am encumbered by all of life's junk, I become so blind and cluttered that there is no room left in my heart for God—the space is already taken. If I free myself as Christ enjoins me to do, I needn't worry when folks like the Pharisees come wielding their sinister plots.

All share their life experience.

What was Matthew trying to tell his community? In what way does this gospel challenge your community today? Have you ever had an experience similar to that of Jesus in which you felt you were being manipulated or trapped? Where someone was trying to harm you? How did it feel? How did you respond? How would you respond today? What did the experience teach you about God? About yourself? What does it mean to you to abandon yourself completely to God? Are you presently doing that? In what way has this conversation with the scriptures for today's liturgy invited change in your life? In what way are the biblical themes of covenant, exodus, creation, and community evident in today's readings? Do you still feel the same way about this text as when you began? Has your original understanding been stretched, challenged, or affirmed?

STEP 5
DECISION

The gospel demands a response.

In what specific way might your parish be invited to respond? Are there any attitudes or behaviors you would like to change as a result of today's conversation? What one concrete action will you take this week as a response to the liturgy today?

DOCTRINAL ISSUES

What church truth/teaching/doctrinal issue could be drawn from the gospel for the Twenty-Ninth Sunday in Ordinary Time?

Participants suggest possible doctrinal themes that flow from the readings.

Possible Doctrinal Themes

Christology, prayer, discipleship, conversion, paschal mystery, images of God, spiritual poverty, option for the poor, reign of God, mystery of the church

Present the doctrinal material at this time.

1. The facilitator gives input on a particular doctrinal issue of his/her prior choosing. OR
2. The group chooses a doctrinal issue from the list they created. They read together from the Doctrinal Appendix.

(The doctrinal issues are found in the Doctrinal Appendix in the back of this workbook. If you are choosing an issue from this resource, please refer to it now.)

Reflection questions centered around the chosen doctrinal theme can be found at the end of each topic in the Doctrinal Appendix. The questions are based on the five-step reflection process. If you choose a topic not included in the Doctrinal Appendix, craft your own questions according to the same five-step process.

Following the reflection questions you will be reminded to return to chapter 7, "Preparing the Catechetical Session," to assist you in crafting your own session.

Closing Prayer

Almighty and ever-living God,
our source of power and inspiration,
give us strength and joy

in serving you as followers of Christ,
who lives and reigns with you and the Holy Spirit,
one God, for ever and ever.[11]

[11]Twenty-Ninth Sunday in Ordinary Time: "Opening Prayer," *The Sacramentary*.

Thirtieth Sunday in Ordinary Time

INTRODUCTORY RITES

Opening Song (or Entrance Antiphon)

Let hearts rejoice who search for the Lord. Seek the Lord and his strength, seek always the face of the Lord. (Ps 104:3–4)[1]

Opening Prayer

Let us pray
[in humble hope for salvation]

Pause for silent prayer.

Praised be you, God and Father of our
Lord Jesus Christ.
There is no power for good
which does not come from your covenant,
and no promise to hope in,
that your love has not offered.
Strengthen our faith to accept your covenant
and give us the love to carry out your command.
We ask this through Christ our Lord.[2]

LITURGY OF THE WORD

The readings are proclaimed.

First Reading[3]
Exodus 22:20–26

The Book of Exodus contains the code of the covenant. It is very similar to other codes of the ancient world, such as the Code of Hammurabi (12th century B.C.E). The code of the covenant was probably established around the ninth century B.C.E. Today's section of the code deals with social behavior. Inherent in the code is the perspective that actions speak louder than words. It was not enough to be a voice for the lowly and oppressed, there was an expectation of action and response. One's behavior must accompany one's words.

Today's reading spelled out for the Israelites some of the demands of the covenant. In this covenant, God demanded that orphans, widows, and the lowly and oppressed be cared for as a sign of God's providential relationship with Israel. Foreigners were to be respected and treated with dignity. The author of Exodus reminds the people that they too were once foreigners in an alien land.

Today's reading serves as a sober reminder of the differences in the human family. Some people are poor, others are rich. Some people are foreigners, others are citizens. This exhortation enjoins the listener to extend God's compassion to everyone in the human family. Covenant relationship with God demanded responsibility. To be in covenant relationship with God meant that God's love and compassion must be extended to the vulnerable members of society—because this is what God wants from us.

Widows, orphans, and aliens were considered vulnerable members of society. Aliens, being in a foreign land, did not enjoy the protection of family and friends. Widows were entirely dependent on men for their care and support. The law (Dt 25:5–10) provided for the care of widows, but very often the law was ignored. Children were considered orphans if their father was dead. Both widows and orphans were powerless, without rights, and often subject to abuse. There was to be no mistake: if Israel was to remain in covenant relationship with God, it had to extend God's own love and compassion to the widow and the orphan. It was not a suggestion; it was a command.

---

[1]Thirtieth Sunday in Ordinary Time: "Entrance Antiphon," *The Sacramentary.*

[2]Thirtieth Sunday in Ordinary Time: "Alternative Opening Prayer," *The Sacramentary.*

[3]The exegesis for the first and second readings may or may not be the focus of your group's reflection, as there may only be time to give adequate attention to the gospel, your primary concern. However, the exegesis is included here in order to provide a thorough investigation of the entire liturgy of the word since there may be parts (or all) that would be necessary to the direction you wish to take with your particular ministry group.

Also inherent in today's reading is the issue of lending money to the poor. It was a common practice to exact huge interest on loans given to the poor. The law allowed collateral to be exacted from the person requesting the loan. Very often the only thing a poor person might offer as collateral was his cloak that was used as clothing during the day, and as a blanket at night. By insisting that the cloak be returned by evening, there was at least a guarantee that the poor person would be protected from the cold during the night. Also, if the cloak had to be returned each evening, the inconvenience of it all might discourage the lenders from securing such collateral in the first place.

The hallmark of covenant living was to be compassion, mercy, and God's abiding love extended to one another, and especially to the most vulnerable among them. The extent to which the Israelites lived today's exhortation was the extent to which there was evidence of their fidelity to God and the covenant. That same command to love was to be the Christian response to Jesus' new covenant. This pericope was chosen to accompany the gospel in which Jesus summarized the law.

Responsorial Psalm
Psalm 18:2–3, 3–4, 47, 51

Today's psalm was probably written by David. It is a royal psalm of thanks for victory in battle. Reginald Fuller maintains that the only discernible connections in today's readings can be found in the refrain in which the love of God is extolled. Love is the summary of the law, according to the perspective of Exodus and today's gospel.

Second Reading
1 Thessalonians 1:5–10

Paul continues the theme from last week. He affirms the good reputation of the Thessalonian church and reviews the history of its origin. He reminds the Thessalonians that he and his coworkers were not dishonest with them and did not lead them astray, but rather were upright and trustworthy in their dealings with them (unlike other greedy and pretentious evangelists).

Paul, Silvanus, and Timothy did not expect the Thessalonian church to support them financially. They worked to support and provide for themselves, thus proving no self-serving motivation in their missionary efforts. They had the right to ask for support, as apostles of the Lord, but chose instead to provide for their own needs.

Paul reminded the Thessalonians how news had spread far and wide about the way in which they had turned away from false idols in order to serve the Lord and await his return in glory. Jesus' return was probably the reason for the letter in the first place (which will be emphasized in more detail next week).

Gospel[4]
Matthew 22:34–40

STEP 1
NAMING ONE'S EXPERIENCE

What were your first impressions? What was your first response to the gospel (or the other readings)?[5] What captured your attention?

Each person names his or her initial impression. Statements should be brief. No reasons should be given at this time. All simply listen without agreeing or disagreeing.

STEP 2
UNDERSTANDING

In a brief statement, what do you think this gospel is trying to convey?

[4]The gospel exegesis is provided later in this session so that it may be presented in the proper sequence where it occurs in the adult five-step reflection process. The exegesis is provided for the first and second readings for your information and edification, and for you to use at your discretion. The gospel is the primary source of reflection. If there is time for reflection on the other readings, all the better.

[5]The primary focus of reflection is the gospel. However, very often the other readings demand attention and must be brought into the dialogue.

Step 3
Input from Vision/Story/Tradition

Liturgical Context[6]

Today is the second in a series of three gospels (of the 29th through the 31st Sundays) that reflect upon the teachings of Jesus set in the context of his confrontations with the scribes and Pharisees. His teaching focuses on, and is in direct response to, their attempts to trap him. He seizes upon the situation as an opportunity to herald the reign of God and enlarge our understanding, and hence our capacity for love—that is, the biblical understanding of love.

Today's gospel is a reminder of the two dimensions of Christ's gospel: love of God and love of neighbor. There is often a tension in the church between these two imperatives. When there is imbalance, both suffer. Some people love and worship God with little or no concern for others; concern for others is secondary and "added to what is really important. From that perspective, it is difficult to understand the relevance of the historical commitment of Christians or the demands of the poor, what the Bible calls orphans, widows and aliens. . . . "[7]

There are still others who insist that to be Christian is exclusively to have a commitment and a solidarity with others. Gustavo Gutierrez insists that there is an inherent risk to this narrow way of thinking. "We are running the risk that prayer, celebration, knowing and savoring the word of God, vital expressions of the gratuitous world in which our relationship with the Lord is situated, lose their full meaning and reduce their outreach."[8]

Thus, balance between love of God and love of neighbor means that from our prayer flows the desire to put love into action and to be in solidarity with and provide for the needs of others. This is what it means to live in covenant relationship with God.

The prayers of the liturgy herald that covenant love and demand its realization. The Opening Prayer asks that we be strengthened in the virtues of faith, hope, and love. We ask that our hearts mirror the love God has for us and that we be given the grace to act in love. The Alternative Opening Prayer echoes that same request. We are reminded that all our power for good and all our hope are empowered by the covenant expressed in today's readings and flow from the love of God. We ask that our faith be strengthened enough to carry out the ethical command to love inherent in our covenant with God. We are soberly reminded of love's implications in the Communion Antiphon. We are to love as Christ loves us; Christ loved us to his death. We are to go and do the same. Today's Communion Rite quotes from Ephesians: "Christ loved us and gave himself up for us as a fragrant offering to God" (5:2).

Gospel Exegesis

The facilitator gives input regarding what critical biblical scholarship has to say about this text. The input includes insights as to how people would have heard the gospel in Jesus' time.

Once again the Pharisees try to trip Jesus. Today they come back for "round two." Their questions are full of insincerity. They care little for Jesus' opinion. The Pharisee who addresses Jesus in today's gospel is referred to in some manuscripts as *nomikos*, a teacher of the law. He has no intention to learn from Jesus—he thinks he knows it all already. He simply wants to test him. The Pharisee questions Jesus about the greatest commandment of the law. Jesus' response is a summary of his entire teaching in Matthew's Gospel.[9] The greatest commandment is to love. It is the heart of the old and the new covenant. The law of love is a summary of God's plan of salvation for the world since the beginning of time. If one is to live in right relationship with God, in obedience to God's will, then one will live the law of love. Our fidelity will be judged according to the way in which we live the imperative of biblical justice.

[6]The scriptures in the Lectionary, the seasons of the year, and the ritual prayers of the mass are interrelated and form the basis for liturgical catechesis. The *liturgical context* attempts to explore and clarify the themes and this interrelatedness.

[7]*SWTLY,* 248.

[8]Ibid.

[9]*IM,* 216.

Jesus summarized the law in Deuteronomy. Verse 5 of chapter 6 stated that believers were to love God with their entire being—heart, soul, and strength. The heart was considered the center of a person's entire being—the life, emotion, and totality of the person. The soul was considered the life force or physical life itself. Matthew used the term *mind* rather than *strength* in order to stress the element of understanding and decision that is required to turn one's heart over completely to God.

Jesus responded to the Pharisees' question by reducing the law to the two great commandments. This was not a new concept in Judaism. The Pharisees cataloged 613 laws in the first five books of the Bible (Torah): 248 "*thou shalts*," and 365 "*thou shalt nots*." Some were of greater value than others and were distinguished as "heavy" or "light." The Ten Commandments were considered "heavy"—they carried more weight. There was also a common practice of summing up the laws into smaller summary statements. One rabbi suggested that David reduced the 613 precepts to 11 in Psalm 15. Isaiah reduced them to six (33:15); Micah to three (6:8); Amos to one (5:4). Words nearly identical to Jesus' words can be found in other Jewish literature of the day. Where Jesus' response was atypical, however, was because of the fact that Jesus understood both laws (love of God and love of neighbor) to possess equal importance. The law's command to love God was based on the law of love in Deuteronomy—a heavily weighted law. The command to love neighbor as self was based on the law found in Leviticus—a less weighted law. When Jesus placed equal importance on both laws, he signaled a breakthrough, a shift in moral teaching, over and above the teaching of the rabbis. Love of God and love of neighbor were of equal importance.

A radical element of Jesus' teaching consisted in the imperative to love one's neighbor. The Israelite understanding of *neighbor* was a brother or sister Israelite. Neighbor did not include outsiders; it only referred to those who shared the covenant. *Compassion* was to be extended to the outsider, but not necessarily *love*. Jesus turned that understanding on its end and included the entire human family in the designation. When Jesus exhorted the people to love one's *neighbor* as oneself, he meant that they were to love brothers, sisters, insiders, outsiders, Jews, and Gentiles, just as they loved themselves. This was a radically new concept for ancient Israelites.

Jesus did not discard the other commandments; he simply stated that all the commandments flow from the law of love. What did Jesus mean by love? Israel's self-understanding was based on the community. A person was a member of a family, a neighborhood, a clan, a village, or a group, such as the Pharisees. The group gave a sense of belonging and membership. The group determined how a person should feel or believe. "The group was an external conscience exerting enormous pressure on its individual members."[10] The emotions of love and hate were synonymous with belonging and not belonging. To love God meant that a person belonged completely and totally to God. To love one's neighbor as one's self was to have a sense of belonging to that person or persons as if they were a member of one's own family. John Pilch asserts that when Jesus exhorted his disciples to hate one's father and mother (Luke 14:26), he was insisting that in order to follow him, disciples must first detach themselves from the family (hate) and then become a member (love) of Jesus' group. "Paul says the greatest among the virtues faith, hope, and charity is charity, that is, love or attachment to the group. The group-attachment aspect of love poses a challenge to individualistically oriented, emotional American believers."[11]

The theology that underpins Jesus' response to the Pharisees is best described in a presentation given by Walter Burghardt in Orlando, Florida, in which he outlined the biblical dimensions of love.

> Love is rooted in biblical justice. Biblical justice is fidelity to relationships. . . . The biblical focus of love/justice is faithfulness to the demands of relationships, to responsibilities that stem from our covenant with God.
>
> In the Old Testament, Israelites were united by bonds of family or covenant.

[10]*CWJ*, 155–156.

[11]Ibid., 156.

God's love/justice was rooted in the way God acted. God acted as God should; God was always faithful to God's promise, thus God provided, God punished violations, God was always faithful. We are just when we are in right relationship with our brothers and sisters, and with the earth.

In the Genesis creation story, everything was in right relationship with everything else. The covenant with God was based on love. God welcomed the stranger, fed the hungry, gave a home to the alien, not because they deserved it, but because this is how God acted toward Israel. Deuteronomy insisted that the stranger was to be loved because God loved him or her first. Thus, the justice of God, fidelity to relationships, and the expression of love were synonymous. Not to execute justice/love was not to worship God.

Contemporary Christian thinking suggests that Christianity is concerned only with the relationship of the soul to eternity. That attitude does violence to scripture. A stance of individuality does not revere God's word. God was incredibly imaginative; God did not envision isolated independent groups. God had in mind a people—the human family. Israel, the people of God, was a symbol of the proper ordering of relationships: love of God and love of one another and reverential care for the earth. We were told to subdue the earth—not to exploit it, but to subdue it. In Greek, *subdue* means reverential care.

. . . Israel was considered a single family when God brought them out of bondage. Why did God deliver them? God delivered them because of the promise made to their ancestors. Before, they had not been a people—God made them a people. God liberated them and offered them the freedom to live in intimate covenant with their God, with all its inherent responsibilities.

The prophets taught that the law was not to be obeyed for the law's sake. The promise of the covenant was behind the law. God's people were to respond to God's love for them by living according to the demands of the law. The rights of the oppressed, the marginalized, and the lowly were expressed in the law. This, in itself, was a sign of God's covenant. Through God's concern for such people, God proclaimed to Israel: I reject those things that you think I want from you, such as sacrifices and burnt offerings. The prophets Micah and Hosea were constantly reminding the people that God did not like their sacrifices. God wanted steadfast love and justice—not sacrifices.

The New Testament's perspective of justice/love/*hesed* is based on the ministry of Jesus. "The Spirit is upon me to preach good news to the poor." The downtrodden go away relieved. Christians were not to give people just what they deserved; rather, they were to give more because of the command of love. Loving one another, one's neighbor, is synonymous with loving God. The Christian is to assume the mind-set that says: I am my neighbor; my neighbor is an extension of myself. Jesus said, "Love as I have loved you." In the New testament perspective, to love as Jesus loved is over and above the demands of human ethics. It is the kind of love that compelled God's Son to totally give of himself for the downtrodden and the beleaguered.

Love places demands on the community. "If anyone is hungry," Jesus says in Matthew 25, "then *feed* them! Go help them!" John's gospel insists that if anyone is rich in worldly goods, but has a closed heart towards others, that God's love cannot abide in him or her. We cannot say to anyone "I have no need of you." We are to be one with others as Christ is one with the Father.

Ethical justice demands that we give people what is their right. A Catholic in good standing has a right to the eucharist. All races, creeds, and nationalities have a right to equal protection under the law.

Charity is another matter. Charity has to do with what cannot be demanded. Charity goes beyond obligation. Charity begins and is rooted in biblical justice. God loves us, not because we can demand it, or have a right to it. God gives to us out of love; not because we deserve it. This is charity. God does not have to do anything.

God's justice is tempered by God's mercy. In the parable of the prodigal son, the father does not give to the son because the son deserves it; rather, he gives out of love. He freely offers his mercy.

Biblical justice, then, is based not on what we deserve. We exercise biblical justice because that is what God wants us to do. Biblical justice and charity merge and demand that we love everyone.

Biblical justice impacts our teaching ministry in the church: what we teach and how we love. Ethical justice is a value, but it is not enough. People come to hear God's word, echoed from the past, alive in the present. It is enshrined in God's book. There is ethical justice throughout all of scripture. However, over and above ethical justice is the *law of love.* The Lord gave it to Moses centuries before Christ proclaimed it: the two great commandments, love of God and love of neighbor as much as love of self.

Justice is not equal treatment, but appropriate treatment. It is an attempt to equalize relationships between the *haves* and the *have nots.* Scripture exhorts the farmer to leave the droppings of the harvest in the field by not sending workers back to pick up the missed harvest. This is so that the poor workers may gather them up to feed their own families. It is not a call for abundance; it is a call for enough.

We must stress biblical justice in our ministry of evangelization. If we do not, there is little that separates us from the secular humanist or the pagan who performs good actions for the sake of doing them.

The Christian response of love insists that we take care of the poor because of our covenant relationship with God, because God wants it. We do not take care of them simply because they are deserving as children of God (which they are), but because everyone's being taken care of is part of God's promise. We, too, are in the covenant. Thus, we must help God's people because God would want us to.

Preaching a just word is not simply one more category in scripture. Rather, it is the lens through which we are to see all of life. All homilies should have a component of justice and emphasize the relationship between God, God's people, and the earth.

Our spirituality links what we are on the inside with what we do on the outside. Thus, biblical justice is an important element in our spirituality. We are gradually shaped to Christ for the sake of others. If we are just in the biblical sense, we will see each person as the crucified image of Christ. We will touch everything with reverence. ("The earth is the Lord's." Although creation bears the trace of the God who gives life—all things are traces of God's divinity.) There is presently a crisis of communication. How are we to be an effective medium to preach God's word? God's concern is that we do it face to face, person to person.

Finally, justice stemming from our covenant says that if we live it, if we teach it, we are shaped to Christ. Then the church will be transformed. Thus, in your most precious apostolate,

May God lead you,
may God feed you,
and may God speed you![12]

Proclaim the gospel again.

---

[12]Walter J. Burghardt, S.J. (Orlando Catechetical Conference), Sept. 7, 1996.

Sometimes we gain new insights when we hear the text after the interpretation has been given. Someone from the group proclaims the gospel a second time.

Step 4
Testing

Conversation with the Liturgy and the Scriptures

Test your original understanding in dialogue with the text.

(You might consider breaking into smaller groups.)

Now that you've heard the exegesis, were there any new insights for you? How do you feel about it? How does your original understanding of this gospel compare with what we just shared? How does this story speak to your life?

Sharing Life Experience

Participants share an experience from their lives that connects with the biblical interpretation just shared.

> *It is very easy to love the lovable. It is hard to love the unlovable. Jesus' radical word is a call to be one with the lovable and the unlovable—rich, poor, clean, dirty, righteous, criminal, insiders, outsiders, friends, enemies—all are members of God's family. There is no such thing as "undeserving poor." No one is truly deserving. The only thing that makes us deserving is that we were all created in the image and likeness of God. My worship of God empowers me to love as Jesus loved. I feel compassion for the poor. It is one thing to feel it and another thing to act on it, however.*
>
> *Last year a homeless woman with two small children came to our parish door one evening. She was looking for a place to stay. We sent her to the agency responsible for helping in such instances. They refused to help her as they had a long history of dealing with this woman. She was using her children to "scam" money for drugs. When I looked at her, all I could see were the faces of her homeless children, so I wanted to help her anyway. She asked me if I would get her a bus ticket so she could take her children up north to be with family and to start a new life. I went to a great deal of trouble to help her. We bought her a ticket and took her to the bus station. When she left my side for a moment, the man at the ticket counter told me to wait with her until she got on the bus because she told him that she wanted to change the ticket for cash as soon as I left. I waited with her until the bus arrived. I could tell that she was getting more nervous with each passing moment. She boarded the bus with her two small children and was thus unable to cash in the ticket. I felt taken advantage of and I was angry. How do I reconcile today's gospel with that all-too-common scenario? Who is my neighbor? Will the help I offer enable further dependency and dysfunction?*
>
> *People who work with the poor face this dilemma every day. The poor are human and sinful just like everyone else. They can be controlled by greed, fear, and addiction, just like anyone else. However, someone who works with the poor reminded me not too long ago that when a rich person is ill-tempered we shrug it off as eccentric; when a poor person behaves similarly we dub them as ungrateful, ill-mannered, and undeserving. Not everyone will respond to our acts of kindness accordingly. When the brothers would chide St. Francis for giving his cloak to the beggars who would turn around and sell it on the next street corner, St. Francis replied that he did what he was supposed to do—he responded to the poor. What the beggars did was not his problem—it was God's. Whether or not this woman got off at the next stop and turned in her ticket for cash was not my problem—it was God's. Who knows, maybe that was precisely the hundredth second chance this woman needed to change things in her life.*
>
> *In this case, I was called to respond to this woman. I could not control her response to the love I extended. Sometimes we idealize the poor. We think that because we help them they should be indebted to us. We are given a grand sense of superiority. But if charity is a responsibility, then we cannot indulge in such self-seeking motivations. I was to respond to that woman because God wanted me to respond to her. Whether it was a right or wrong decision remains to be seen. I have never seen her again. Perhaps she stayed on the bus and went home to family. Like all things, what was important for me in this situation was attitude. Do I consider this woman a part of my family, or do I feel superior to her? Am I in solidarity with her, even if she cheats those who try to help*

her? Today's gospel demands that my actions back up my words, but it also demands that my attitudes back up my actions.

All share their life experience.

What was Matthew trying to tell his community? How is today's gospel a relevant word for your life today? Where is the love, as described in today's gospel, lacking in your community? In your own life? Where is it evident? In what way has this conversation with the scriptures for today's liturgy invited change in your life? In what way are the biblical themes of covenant, exodus, creation, and community evident in today's readings? Do you still feel the same way about this text as when you began? Has your original understanding been stretched, challenged, or affirmed?

STEP 5
DECISION

The gospel demands a response.

In what specific way might your parish be invited to respond? Are there any attitudes or behaviors you would like to change as a result of today's conversation? What one concrete action will you take this week as a response to the liturgy today?

Pastoral Considerations: Who are the people in your community who are in most need of the love described in today's gospel? What needs to happen in order to respond to their needs?

DOCTRINAL ISSUES

What church truth/teaching/doctrinal issue could be drawn from the gospel for the Thirtieth Sunday in Ordinary Time?

Participants suggest possible doctrinal themes that flow from the readings.

Possible Doctrinal Themes

Conversion, social teaching, charity, biblical justice, discipleship, service, mission, morality, law of God

Present the doctrinal material at this time.

1. The facilitator gives input on a particular doctrinal issue of his/her prior choosing. OR
2. The group chooses a doctrinal issue from the list they created. They read together from the Doctrinal Appendix.

(The doctrinal issues are found in the Doctrinal Appendix in the back of this workbook. If you are choosing an issue from this resource, please refer to it now.)

Reflection questions centered around the chosen doctrinal theme can be found at the end of each topic in the Doctrinal Appendix. The questions are based on the five-step reflection process. If you choose a topic not included in the Doctrinal Appendix, craft your own questions according to the same five-step process.

Following the reflection questions you will be reminded to return to chapter 7, "Preparing the Catechetical Session," to assist you in crafting your own session.

Closing Prayer

It is truly right to give you thanks,
it is fitting that we offer you praise,
Father of mercy, faithful God.
You sent Jesus Christ your Son among us
as redeemer and Lord.
He was moved with compassion
for the poor and the powerless,
for the sick and the sinner;
he made himself neighbor to the oppressed.
By his words and actions
he proclaimed to the world
that you care for us
as a father cares for his children.
And so, with all the angels and saints
we sing the joyful hymn of praise.[13]

[13]Eucharistic Prayer for Masses for Various Needs and Occasions: "Preface—Jesus the Compassion of God," *The Sacramentary.*

Thirty-First Sunday in Ordinary Time

INTRODUCTORY RITES

Opening Song (or Entrance Antiphon)

Do not abandon me, Lord. My God, do not go away from me! Hurry to help me, Lord, my savior. (Ps 37:22–23)[1]

Opening Prayer

The facilitator of the session may lead the prayer. Others in the group may be asked to proclaim the readings.

Let us pray
[that our lives will reflect our faith]

Pause for silent prayer.

God of power and mercy,
only with your help can we offer you fitting service
and praise.
May we live the faith we profess
and trust your promise of eternal life.
Grant this through our Lord
Jesus Christ, your Son,
who lives and reigns with you and the Holy Spirit,
one God, for ever and ever.[2]

LITURGY OF THE WORD

Let us listen to God's word.

The readings are proclaimed.

First Reading
Malachi 1:14—2:2, 8–10

Overview of the Book of the Prophet Malachi: Virtually nothing is known about the anonymous author of the Book of Malachi. It was probably written around 460–450 B.C.E., after the exile. It is believed that the name of the book comes from a reference in 1:1 and 3:1—*mal'akki,* my messenger. Although the exile was over and the people had been allowed to return home, they were disheartened. With the assistance of the Syrian government the people had been given the necessary aid to rebuild the temple. Even though the temple was built, it did not guarantee communal, liturgical, or spiritual cohesiveness. The people were in disarray. The clergy were negligent, the ritual sloppy, and there was an indifference to the needs of the poor. The rich became richer and the poor became poorer.

It seemed to Malachi as if those who turned their backs on God prospered, while the God-fearing faithful poor were barely surviving. Malachi was incensed, and through his prophetic word promised that the situation would one day be overturned.

Three centuries earlier, the prophet Amos had prophesied that the "Day of the Lord" would come upon the people. The people had fantasized that it would be a day marked by great joy. God's people would reign victorious over their enemies. Amos, however, shattered their illusions. The "Day of the Lord" was to be a day of judgment for Israel, and rather than joy, there would be terror.

After the exile, fervor for the "Day of the Lord" again came to the fore, heralded as a day of fire and brimstone when the righteous would be saved, and the evil would be destroyed by the sun's fiery blaze. The fiery sun that was to destroy the evil would, however, be the healing agent of the righteous. Sun of justice (3:20) literally means "sun which is justice." In ancient Persia and Egypt, the sun was depicted as a winged solar disk. This sun god was believed to be the source of light and warmth, and thus the source of all life. Biblical authors embraced the symbol of the sun god and applied it to Yahweh—Yahweh who is light and life, source of all that is good, and the one who will send the wicked to be consumed in the blazing fire.

When the Christians applied the term "Sun of Justice" to Jesus, they were signifying Christ, the light and the judge, who came into the world as the incarnate presence of God, and who will come again as judge of the world.

[1]Thirty-First Sunday in Ordinary Time: "Entrance Antiphon," *The Sacramentary.*

[2]Thirty-First Sunday in Ordinary Time: "Opening Prayer," *The Sacramentary.*

Today's Pericope: Today's reading is taken from a section dealing with priests. The priests of Jerusalem considered themselves an elite class and assigned all the other priests the role of Levite. The author of Malachi was an unpopular prophet. He made no distinction between the Levites and the priests. He considered himself the guardian of the people's religious traditions. He had little patience for the religious leaders who refused to set a good example for the people.

When the people were taken into exile, they became enmeshed in the religious and cultural ways of their place of exile. Malachi was insistent that the people forsake all vestiges of foreign religious and cultural practices. It was the responsibility of the priests to lead the people in a return to cultic purity. If they failed in their role, there would be stern repercussions. All the blessings (stipends and privileges) they enjoyed because of their priestly status would become a curse instead of a blessing.

In the last verse of today's pericope, the author of the Book of Malachi speaks of his disapproval of marriages between Israelites and foreigners. He feared the effects of religious dilution that occurs when people of differing faiths and cultures come together. The prophet was apprehensive of the way in which intermarriage might taint Judaism. When people married outside the tradition, the author of Malachi considered it tantamount to breaking the covenant. In the covenant agreement, not only were the people bound to Yahweh, they were united with one another as family in a close unbreakable bond. Mixed marriages implied a break with the family. Preservation of Israel's religious tradition was extremely important in a rapidly changing world.

In today's reading, in the final paragraph, the question is asked: Have we not all one father? Jesus echoes this sentiment in the gospel.

Responsorial Psalm
Psalm 131:1, 2, 3

Today's psalm is a prayer of trust in God by the "poor" of Israel who place all their hope and confidence in God.

Second Reading
1 Thessalonians 2:7–9, 13

(Refer to the Twenty-Ninth Sunday in Ordinary Time for an Overview of St. Paul's Letters to the Thessalonians.)

Today's Pericope: Paul once again affirms the faith and life of the Thessalonian community, as well as their response to his preaching. Paul did not impose his preaching on this fledgling community. He was very pastoral. He did not wish to impose economic hardship on the community, so he worked night and day to support himself and take care of his own needs. We know from the Acts of the Apostles that Paul earned a living as a tentmaker. When he was not preaching, he probably continued to make tents. Paul was content to do whatever needed to be done to serve the gospel of Christ.

The Thessalonians were open to receive the word of God preached by Paul and his associates. It was not a word of human origin, but a word from God spoken through human beings. Preaching required a response in faith not only on the part of the listener, but also on the part of the preacher. Preachers were to exemplify the word they preached. They were to live a wholesome gospel life of prayer and apostolic service. The listeners were to discern God's word, then take that word and make it bear fruit in their lives. All was possible through the power, presence, and gift of the Holy Spirit. Thus, they were to pray continually for the gift of the Spirit.

Gospel
Matthew 23:1–12

STEP 1
NAMING ONE'S EXPERIENCE

What were your first impressions? What was your first response to the gospel (or the other readings)?[3] What captured your attention?

Each person names his or her initial impression. Statements should be brief. No reasons should be given at this time. All simply listen without agreeing or disagreeing.

[3]The primary focus of reflection is the gospel. However, very often the other readings demand attention and must be brought into the dialogue.

Step 2
Understanding

In a brief statement, what do you think this gospel is trying to convey?

Step 3
Input from Vision/Story/Tradition

Liturgical Context

Today's liturgy is the last in a three-part sequence that proclaims the teaching of Christ in the context of his confrontation with the scribes and Pharisees. Today's gospel extols the appropriate attitude Christian leaders are to possess. Christian leaders are not to behave like the Pharisees, who place heavy burdens on the people and consider themselves better than those they serve. They are to be humble servants and regard all people as brothers and sisters.

Today's Opening Prayer acknowledges that only through God's help can we offer our service. The tone of the prayer reflects the humility that servants of God are to possess. It is only through God's grace that we are able to serve God and to profess our faith in God. The Alternative Opening Prayer reminds us that we are sinful people, and that only when we keep our eyes focused on God will we be able to remain steadfast and live the demands of love. When we live according to the gospel of Christ, we will exalt God instead of ourselves.

We are strengthened to live the imperative in today's gospel through the power of the eucharist. The Prayer Over the Gifts and the Prayer After Communion reflect its power and strength in our lives:

God of mercy,
may we offer a pure sacrifice
for the forgiveness of sins.[4]

Lord,
you give us new hope in this eucharist.
May the power of your love
continue its saving work among us
and bring us the joy you promise.[5]

Gospel Exegesis

The facilitator gives input regarding what critical biblical scholarship has to say about this text. The input includes insights as to how people would have heard the gospel in Jesus' time.

Today's gospel reflects Jesus' great respect for the law. Matthew's Jesus revered the institutions of Judaism.[6] John Pilch asserts that there are three things going on in today's gospel: Jesus objects to the way in which the Pharisaic scribes do not practice what they preach. He challenges the narrow interpretation of the Torah that the people find burdensome. He speaks against their ostentatious need for status and public recognition.

The scribes and Pharisees were commissioned to preach the law. They figuratively sat on Moses' seat, thereby possessing the authority to interpret the Mosaic tradition. This scene in Matthew's gospel is filled with examples of hypocrisy. Jesus railed against those religious leaders who enjoyed their exalted status, but did little to embody the law by the example of their own lives. They definitely did not practice what they preached. They placed burdens on others, while failing to live the precepts themselves. The Pharisees established precise and arduous rules that made the law increasingly difficult to follow, thus creating hardship on the people trying to live righteously. What was missing in the Pharisees' interpretation of the law were love and mercy.

Even worse was the behavior of the Pharisees when they acted in an ostentatious show of piety in order to gain the notice and approval of others. They were more interested in their rank and social status than they were in the heart of the law they preached. They wanted to be exalted by those they served. Humility was not one of their

[4]Thirty-First Sunday in Ordinary Time: "Prayer Over the Gifts," *The Sacramentary.*

[5]Thirty-First Sunday in Ordinary Time: "Prayer After Communion," *The Sacramentary.*

[6]*ITM,* 221.

virtues. Titles and places of honor were more important to them than the flock they shepherded.

Followers of Jesus were not to follow the example of these religious leaders. They were to follow the example of Jesus. Status, title, fame, notoriety—none of it had a place in the kingdom of God. Jesus offered a radical new way to think, act, and live. He humbly submitted to the will of God. He lifted everyone in God's family to the status of brother and sister. No one was to seek after rank and status. All would be equal in the reign of God. "Equality, not elitism, is its mark of distinction."[7] True authority is observed in those who serve the least of those among them.

The gospels were not written as an historical biography. We know very little about the religious society of the day. What is known about the scribes and Pharisees is consonant with what is known from other ancient sources. However, it would be a mistake to assume that all scribes and Pharisees were cut out of the same cloth as those who were in confrontation with Jesus in the gospels. When Matthew wrote his gospel, the Pharisees were already a people who lived in the past. However, there were people like the Pharisees in Matthew's community (albeit in every community). Matthew recalled the teaching of Jesus in order to speak to hypocritical attitudes within his own community. He tries to answer the question: How do we treat people who behave like the Pharisees and how do we avoid similar behavior and attitudes ourselves?

Today's reading is an exhortation to all leaders in the Christian community. No one is called to simply teach the gospel; everyone is called to live it. All Christians are called to the ministry of preaching through the example of their lives. Without such example, preaching is empty and void.

The language used against the Pharisees in this chapter of Matthew is extremely disparaging. It seems to go against the very spirit of the gospel itself and the command to love one's enemies ("hypocrites," "brood of vipers," "blind fools"). Today's pericope does not contain such references directly, but the tone is certainly in the same spirit and thus deserves some serious reflection. Very often texts such as these have been used throughout history as a polemic to promote and support anti-Semitism. David Garland reminds us that the style of the text is very common in ancient Greek philosophical and Jewish literature. Dialogue and arguments between opposing sides of an issue were customarily caustic and insulting. There is evidence that the Christians were being similarly attacked. We are to consider the vitriolic language leveled against the Pharisees as a commentary against recognized authority. It was not meant to be anti-Semitic or anti-Judaism. The epithets leveled against the Pharisees were more in the spirit of the ancient prophets who railed against the abuses of the false stewards of their day. Matthew was speaking to a Jewish Christian community, steeped in its Jewish tradition. He was certainly not promoting anti-Jewish sentiments. Matthew's community was just as capable of hypocrisy as were the Pharisees.

The tone of this dialogue was not intended, either, as an apologetic means to win converts over to Christianity's way of thinking. The language of this section is prophetic, similar to that used by prophets as they challenged recalcitrant sinners. Jesus was named a prophet; his actions were those of a prophet, and he was recognized by everyone except the temple authorities as a prophet. Matthew's Jesus now speaks out like a prophet. His language resembles the prophets of old who preached about their displeasure with a stubborn, deaf, and resistant people. Jesus' language reflects the age-old prophetic angst over greed and injustice.

Proclaim the gospel again.

Sometimes we gain new insights when we hear the text after the interpretation has been given. Someone from the group proclaims the gospel a second time.

Step 4
Testing

Conversation with the Liturgy and the Scriptures

Test your original understanding in dialogue with the text.

[7] *RM*, 230.

(You might consider breaking into smaller groups.)

Now that you've heard the exegesis, were there any new insights for you? How do you feel about it? How does your original understanding of this gospel compare with what we just shared? How does this story speak to your life?

Sharing Life Experience

Participants share an experience from their lives that connects with the biblical interpretation just shared.

> *The readings for today's liturgy are an extended meditation on what it means to be a Christian leader. I am reminded immediately of my pastor. Contrary to the Pharisees, he is a model of Christian leadership. If the gospel calls us to model our own Christian service after the witness of good and sound example, I feel very confident in modeling my own ministry after the example he provides. He is not perfect, and I do not place him on a pedestal. However, I admire him because he is a man of prayer and action. He is objective, fair, and honest in his dealings with people. He is quick to forgive and every person receives equal treatment from him. He, like Paul, is extremely pastoral and allows love to guide his counsel, rather than rigid adherence to the law. He is approachable and very understanding. He challenges people when necessary and is quick to offer compassion. He is not threatened by the giftedness of those around him—he empowers and celebrates it. He acknowledges his own mistakes and has an uncanny ability to put himself in other people's shoes—even people who disagree with him and cause him annoyance. He is not showy or pretentious. I feel honored to work for him and to call him pastor and friend.*
>
> *I am also reminded of the natural leaders in our parish who live the word of God in their everyday lives. No one ever named them leaders; they simply* are *leaders. They have earned the title through the witness of their lives. When certain ones of them speak, everyone listens, including the pastor. They speak with authority and authenticity. Their credentials are their humility and their self-sacrificing love. There are at least five people who come to mind. I have learned more from them about Christian leadership than I have from all my experiences of church. They put the imperatives of today's gospel into recognizable action. The best Christian witness is a well-lived life.*

All share their life experience.

What was Matthew trying to tell his community? Have you ever been called to exercise a role of leadership? How do today's readings speak to your experience? Have you ever experienced leadership like that displayed by the Pharisees in today's gospel? How did you respond? What did you learn from the experience? In what way does this gospel challenge your community today? In what way has this conversation with the scriptures for today's liturgy invited change in your life? In what way are the biblical themes of covenant, exodus, creation, and community evident in today's readings? Do you still feel the same way about this text as when you began? Has your original understanding been stretched, challenged, or affirmed?

Step 5
Decision

The gospel demands a response.

In what specific way might your parish be invited to respond? Are there any attitudes or behaviors you would like to change as a result of today's conversation? What one concrete action will you take this week as a response to the liturgy today?

Pastoral Considerations: Perhaps the impetus of today's readings might lead parishes to reflect upon what it means to be a good Christian leader. Every person, through baptism, is called to lead people to Christ because of their role as priest, prophet, and ruler. Are we all exercising good leadership skills? Is our parish leadership exercised in the spirit of today's gospel? If not, what can we do to improve our leadership? Do our programs place unnecessary burdens on people by fulfilling our own agendas rather than the needs of the people? Is love the motivating force behind all our decisions? Do the people we elect to our pastoral councils reflect the spirit of leadership described in today's liturgy? How might we make the appropriate connections for leadership in the marketplace?

Christian Initiation: Are there any people ready to celebrate the rite of acceptance or welcome as this liturgical year begins to draw to a close? What is taking place in your catechumenate that might warrant the celebration of the anointing of catechumens?

DOCTRINAL ISSUES

What church truth/teaching/doctrinal issue could be drawn from the gospel for the Thirty-First Sunday in Ordinary Time?

Participants suggest possible doctrinal themes that flow from the readings.

Possible Doctrinal Themes

Christian leadership; sacrament of orders; role of baptized as priest, prophet and ruler; conversion; discipleship; service; stewardship; evangelization; ministry; priesthood; role of the laity; church authority

Present the doctrinal material at this time.

1. The facilitator gives input on a particular doctrinal issue of his/her prior choosing. OR
2. The group chooses a doctrinal issue from the list they created. They read together from the Doctrinal Appendix.

(The doctrinal issues are found in the Doctrinal Appendix in the back of this workbook. If you are choosing an issue from this resource, please refer to it now.)

Reflection questions centered around the chosen doctrinal theme can be found at the end of each topic in the Doctrinal Appendix. The questions are based on the five-step reflection process. If you choose a topic not included in the Doctrinal Appendix, craft your own questions according to the same five-step process.

Following the reflection questions you will be reminded to return to chapter 7, "Preparing the Catechetical Session," to assist you in crafting your own session.

Closing Prayer

Let us pray
[in the presence of God, the source of every good]

Pause for silent prayer.

Father in heaven, God of power and Lord of mercy,
from whose fullness we have received,
direct our steps in our everyday efforts.
May the changing moods of the human heart
and the limits which our failings impose on hope
never blind us to you, source of every good.
Faith gives us the promise of peace
and makes known the demands of love.
Remove the selfishness that blurs the vision of faith.[8]

[8]Thirty-First Sunday in Ordinary Time: "Alternative Opening Prayer," *The Sacramentary.*

Thirty-Second Sunday in Ordinary Time

Environment

This Sunday falls in or around the month of November. During November we remember the dead. Some parishes display a special book of the dead in which the names of the deceased are written and displayed near the baptismal font. The church remembers its deceased members in prayer especially during this month. While not wishing to duplicate the book of the dead used in the worship space, it still might be worthwhile to find a way to imaginatively and creatively remember the deceased relatives of those in the catechetical group. Perhaps the names could be written in calligraphy on parchment paper, or pictures of the deceased might be gathered into an album of sorts and then placed in the late autumn catechetical environment. Small votive candles in dark red, green, or amber holders might be placed throughout the environment. Perhaps the catechetical environment might include late fall flowers (fresh or dried), a cornucopia filled with the late fall harvest of corn, squash, dried grasses, and gourds.

Icons that reflect an eschatological theme might also be used during these last days. Another possibility is to place a grape vine wreath, adorned with produce, wheat stalks, or dried grasses, in the environment. It may then be used later to craft an Advent wreath. There are multiple sizes available. "A wreath is more than a decoration. It is an emblem of royalty, of victory, of God's reign, of the wedding band we wear to remember our fidelity to Christ."[1]

INTRODUCTORY RITES

Opening Song (or Entrance Antiphon)

Let my prayer come before you, Lord; listen and answer me. (Ps 87:3)[2]

[1] *TCY,* 191.

[2] Thirty-Second Sunday in Ordinary Time: "Entrance Antiphon," *The Sacramentary.*

Opening Prayer

The facilitator of the session may lead the prayer. Others in the group may be asked to proclaim the readings.

Let us pray
[for health of mind and body]

Pause for silent prayer.

God of power and mercy,
protect us from all harm.
Give us freedom of spirit
and health in mind and body
to do your work on earth.
We ask this through our Lord Jesus Christ, your Son,
who lives and reigns with you and the Holy Spirit,
one God for ever and ever.[3]

LITURGY OF THE WORD

Let us listen to God's word.

The readings are proclaimed.

First Reading
Wisdom 6:12–16

(Refer to the Sixteenth Sunday in Ordinary Time for an Overview of the Book of Wisdom.)

Today's Pericope: The Book of Wisdom, written shortly before the time of Christ, was written to show the superiority of Jewish teaching over Greek philosophy. It may have also been intended as a polemic to demonstrate how leadership such as Solomon's wise leadership is far superior to the leadership of the Roman Caesars. The purpose of the work is also to exhort readers to allow their own knowledge, and their encounter with the wisdom of God, to impact their thoughts, behavior, and daily living.

[3] Thirty-Second Sunday in Ordinary Time: "Opening Prayer," *The Sacramentary.*

Today's reading personifies wisdom as a woman who tenaciously stands as sentinel at the city gates to await those who rise early (the favored time for prayer) to search for her. The city gates were bustling places of activity and commerce. The elders gathered for consultations, passing judgment, discussions, and decision-making. Wisdom was certainly needed in the administration of their daily dealings regarding the everyday life of the people.

The feminine image of wisdom is a common motif in the Hebrew scriptures. The words *sophia* in Greek and *hokmah* in Hebrew are feminine nouns that mean wisdom. In the Greek philosophical tradition, wisdom was understood as a human endeavor—something to be conquered by sheer human will and mastery. The Hebrew understanding describes wisdom as a readily attainable gift from God, just waiting to be embraced by the receiver. The attributes of Lady Wisdom are also attributes of the living, loving, pursuing God. Today's reading describes wisdom as resplendent and unfading.

Solomon, believed to have possessed great wisdom, is listed as author of the Book of Wisdom (even though he lived about 900 years earlier). In this section of Wisdom, he reminds other rulers how easily wisdom may be obtained and how important it is to obtain her. Earthly rulers receive their authority from God and will be judged by God and held accountable to a higher degree than other people. They carry far more responsibility and thus need wisdom's power, knowledge, and strength. The Romans certainly did not live by this creed, but it was the heart of Jewish theology.

Lady Wisdom is to be sought after, while we keep in mind that she is readily found by those who love and seek her. The reader is led into an odyssey of passion and urgency through the language of the text. Wisdom does not just look for the seeker, she "hastens to make herself known"; she desires to be "perceived." She is eager to find a place in the human heart. Ultimately, *Wisdom* is none other than God the Pursuer, who eagerly searches for the hungering human spirit. It is deep within the recesses of those spirits that Lady Wisdom takes up her residence.

Responsorial Psalm
Psalm 63:2, 3–4, 5–6, 7–8

Today's psalm picks up the theme of longing and thirsting for God. Psalm 63 reflects the deepest hunger of the heart to encounter the living God.

Second Reading
1 Thessalonians 4:13–18

(Refer to the Twenty-Ninth Sunday in Ordinary Time for an Overview of St. Paul's Letter to the Thessalonians.)

Today's Pericope: Today Paul writes to a community that is concerned over the fate of those who died before Christ's return. Paul responded to their concerns by assuring them of his faith in eternal life. The early Christians believed in the return of Christ in glory—in their lifetime. They were anxious to enter into complete and final union with the Christ who suffered, died, and rose again for their salvation. Where was he? Why had he not returned as quickly as expected? What did it all mean? What about those who had died already—especially their loved ones? Would they too be entitled to the same final glory? Had they been duped?

The prevalent cultural belief regarding death was that it was final and would consist of nothingness, that all was over with the last breath. But Paul taught the Christians of Thessalonica that they should console one another with hope and belief in eternal life. The foundation of their faith was the resurrection, not a foundation built on shaky ground. It was based on the hope of what they knew to be true: the sacrifice of Christ's life for them, his death and subsequent resurrection. Jesus' resurrection assures his people of a place in the realm of glory—even those who die before his return.

The Christian hope possesses two dimensions—Christological and communal. We wait in hope to take up residence with Christ in glory, and we wait to be united with all the faithful who have been restored in Christ and who already share in his glory.

Gospel
Matthew 25:1–13

STEP 1
NAMING ONE'S EXPERIENCE

What were your first impressions? What was your first response to the gospel (or the other readings)?[4] What captured your attention?

Each person names his or her initial impression. Statements should be brief. No reasons should be given at this time. All simply listen without agreeing or disagreeing.

STEP 2
UNDERSTANDING

In a brief statement, what do you think this gospel is trying to convey?

STEP 3
INPUT FROM VISION/STORY/TRADITION

Liturgical Context

The last sequence before the Feast of Christ the King (Thirty-Second and Thirty-Third Sundays) is concerned with the theme of the end of time and the Lord's coming. The gospels for this Sunday and next Sunday are taken from the discourse in Matthew regarding Jesus' return. This section comes before the account of the passion, death, and resurrection. The focus of these last Sundays is diligent watchfulness. The parables chosen for the Thirty-Second and the Thirty-Fourth Sundays center around the assumption that *no one knows when the Son of Man will return.* We must therefore be ready and watchful at all times. We should never be found asleep or off guard. This discourse of Matthew's gospel is addressed to all Christians in order to prepare them for the great and final day—the last day, the day of the Lord's return. Since no one can know when that day will be, Christians are to be prepared every day and live their lives accordingly. The Lectionary has chosen two out of the three parables in Matthew that reflect this theme.

The pericopes from Thessalonians for this week and next also center around the theme of the end times. This week's letter professes hope in Christ's return in glory. Next week's centers around the watchfulness that the church and all the faithful are to assume as they wait in joyful hope for the Lord's second coming.

The ritual prayers of today's liturgy ask that God will provide the necessary gifts for us to live in the kingdom of God and to realize God's reign here on earth as we await Christ's return. Without God's grace we will never be prepared. Every liturgy strengthens, nourishes, and reminds us to be alert and ready to receive Christ when he comes again. Every liturgy looks forward to that great and terrible day. The Opening Prayer asks that God will protect us from harm and free us in body and spirit to do God's work on earth. The Alternative Opening Prayer asks that we will be shielded from the distortions of pride and become more aware of God's loving plan, so that we can give our lives completely to God's service.

The end of the liturgical year brings focused attention on the end of time, while the beginning of the year dovetails our reflection on ending things with new beginnings. Both the ending and the beginning express our constant hope—the hope we celebrate at every liturgical gathering: Lord Jesus, come again in glory!

Today's liturgy is a reminder that the church is like the five wise young women who have their torches ready in anticipation of the Lord's final return. "Every liturgical celebration is like the dress rehearsal of the great procession to the wedding hall. In any event, the Lord is already here; he comes for his own to whom he manifests himself under the veil of signs. Those who have preceded us in death also prepare themselves. With us and like us, they wait in hope for the signal, given by the archangel's voice, which will cause the great portals of the wedding hall to open wide."[5]

[4]The primary focus of reflection is the gospel. However, very often the other readings demand attention and must be brought into the dialogue.

[5]*DL* (IV), 248–249.

Gospel Exegesis

The facilitator gives input regarding what critical biblical scholarship has to say about this text. The input includes insights as to how people would have heard the gospel in Jesus' time.

Jesus used parables to describe the reign of God. Today is no exception. However, there are other things going on in this parable as well. At first glance the parable tells us that the reign of God is somewhat like a first-century Mediterranean wedding feast. It is up to us to discover its meaning. John Pilch provides the lens with which to see and understand this parable. At the time of the gospel the cultural Jewish wedding practice was known as a *patrilocal* marriage.[6] The bride moved to the groom's home, located near his father's home. Everyone lived in a family cluster of homes, very close to one another, a family compound of sorts.

A first cousin (ideally the father's brother's son or daughter) was considered an ideal marriage partner. Ancient cultures were not bound by cultural taboos regarding marriage between cousins.[7] The uniting of families through the arrangement of marriages between cousins is one reason ancient Middle Eastern families were so close-knit.

Fathers, as patriarchs of the clan, arranged the legal matters surrounding the wedding. Mothers exerted powerful influence over the decisions, but the father was ultimately responsible for ratifying any contractual agreements. The purpose of the marriage was the joining of two families.

When the intended partners were old enough to marry, a celebration was planned. Central to the ceremony was the moment in which the groom went to the bride's family home to get her and bring her to his home. The ceremony resumed from the couple's new home—the groom's home.

Pilch believes that this is the setting where today's parable begins. The bridesmaids (most likely teenagers) are probably relatives of the bride and groom. They are waiting for the return of the groom with his new bride. Five bright teenage girls, and five who are not so bright, are anxiously waiting for the groom to return home. They are eager for the celebration to continue and to await the consummation of the marriage by observing the blood-stained sheets, insuring the physical integrity of the bride demanded by law (Dt 22:13–21).[8]

All are excited for the feast to continue. The not-so-bright teenagers did not adequately prepare and found themselves unable to participate in the celebration. They could not observe anything, as they did not have enough oil to light their lanterns so they could see. Thus, they were left out of the ritual festivities. The well-prepared teens planned ahead and were ready for the celebration to begin as soon as the bridegroom arrived. The ill-prepared teens had not even taken advantage of the groom's delay; they simply stood around and did nothing. The obvious meaning of this parable is simple: do not be caught without oil in your lamps when Jesus returns. You will not be ready or able to participate in the wedding feast (a common eschatological metaphor for the return of Christ in glory). Be ready.

Matthew's community understood this parable on another level. It reflected God's continuing unfolding plan of salvation. The Jews failed to be ready for Jesus, the bridegroom. The Jews were compared to the foolish virgins. Others, including Gentiles, were prepared to receive the bridegroom and participate in the reign of God in Christ. These were the Christians, who were compared to the five wise virgins.

The parable has yet another meaning for disciples of Jesus. Those who are prepared to meet the bridegroom must possess the necessary wisdom. The five wise virgins possessed such wisdom. Wisdom is attained by listening to God's word and living it in everyday life. The wise virgins practiced what they preached and acted upon what they had learned. Contrast that with the foolish virgins who did not act, possessed no wisdom, and were thus unprepared.

---

[6] *CWJ*, 160–162.

[7] Today, fear of birth defects and mental retardation disallows such marriages. Research has proven no higher incidence of retardation in that culture than in our culture, however.

[8] *CWJ*, 161.

The parable ends with a stiff warning. Since no one knows the day of the bridegroom's return, all must be ready at any time. Wise persons will make all the necessary preparations; they will not be caught asleep. They will not be left out of the feast because they will possess the necessary wisdom to do what needs to be done in order to secure a place at the great celebration.

We might be tempted to ask why the five prepared virgins would not share their oil. This parable is about being spiritually prepared. We cannot do the spiritual preparation for anyone else. We can only do it for ourselves. "Spiritual readiness is not something that can be transferred from one to another. The point is that one must take steps to furnish oneself with oil *before* going to sleep while one has the chance."[9]

Some scholars suggest that the oil and the wedding garment in this parable stand for works of righteousness—good deeds. It is not enough that we come to the feast, we must be lathered in and clothed in the actions and living that conform us to Christ. "Those who respond to the invitation . . . must have something more to bring to the judgment other than having said, 'Yes, Lord.' They must be properly clothed with the deeds of Christian discipleship."[10]

Douglas Hare questions that proposal. He asks if that means that our oil of good deeds can burn out before final judgment. Can we buy them somewhere? He insists that the oil is not an allegory but is simply part of the parable; that it goes without saying that Matthew expects good deeds, which are the hallmark of the Christian's life. But other things are also expected, such as loving one's enemies, refraining from bad behavior, forgiving others, having faith and love and loyalty for Christ and for God. Good deeds alone are simply not enough. He insists that the main point of the story is that the five *not-so-bright* virgins are simply not prepared for the great moment when it finally arrives. The underpinning question for us all is: Will we be ready?

Proclaim the gospel again.

[9] *RM,* 240.

[10] J.R. Donahue, *The Gospel in Parable,* in *RM,* 241.

Sometimes we gain new insights when we hear the text after the interpretation has been given. Someone from the group proclaims the gospel a second time.

Step 4
Testing

Conversation with the Liturgy and the Scriptures

Test your original understanding in dialogue with the text.

(You might consider breaking into smaller groups.)

Now that you've heard the exegesis, were there any new insights for you? How do you feel about it? How does your original understanding of this gospel compare with what we just shared? How does this story speak to your life?

Sharing Life Experience

Participants share an experience from their lives that connects with the biblical interpretation just shared.

> *Today's gospel reminds me of the challenge of raising teenagers and how it can be a metaphor for the very point Matthew was trying to make. How many times has a concerned mother harangued and cajoled her teens to get ready for some future event only to be assured, "I'll do it, Mom, stop worrying about it. Trust me. Everything is under control. Chill out. I know what I am doing." I can remember preparing my teens for college. Preparations were always last minute affairs—from initial registration to the packing of bags. I often marveled how they ever got out the door in the first place. Yet the impetuosity of the teen years reminds me of my own inattention to the task of being prepared. It is sometimes easy to procrastinate and put things off. I know what it is like to have the best intentions, with little action to back them up. As they say, "The road to hell is paved with good intentions."*
>
> *Today's parable reminds me of all those mothers of teens who gently (or not so gently), but persistently, keep reminding them to be prepared. That is the function of today's parable. It reaches out to the teen in me who waits and drags my heels, thinking I can put*

off until tomorrow what needs to be attended to today. When there is reconciliation in relationships that still needs to happen; when there is behavior that still needs the grip of discipline's strong arm; when there are attitudes in need of overhauling, it means that my oil gauge is low and is in need of filling.

Today's gospel gently reminds me that I have today, but I may not necessarily have tomorrow. I must be attentive to matters of the spirit today so I will be ready to meet Jesus when he comes for us tomorrow.

This is not only a word for me personally, but a word for the entire community. Are we, as church, prepared to meet Christ? Have we been a safe haven for those who need help in their preparation efforts? Today's parable is a serious challenge for our church communities. I thank God for the ways in which our parish ministers to those who seek, those who grieve, those who are dying, and those who doubt the presence of God in the midst of a suffering world. This gospel invites us to take another look, however, and not to be complacent. We are not to rest in a false sense of security. Where are the areas where we are not prepared? This gospel is a serious call to look at the ways in which we personally and corporately are or are not ready to meet Christ when he comes again.

All share their life experience.

What was Matthew trying to tell his community? In what way does this gospel challenge your community today? In what way has this conversation with the scriptures for today's liturgy invited change in your life? If the Lord was going to return tomorrow, what would you want to do about it today? What does your parish need to change before the Lord returns? What would you change in your life? What would you not change? In what way are the biblical themes of covenant, exodus, creation, and community evident in today's readings? Do you still feel the same way about this text as when you began? Has your original understanding been stretched, challenged, or affirmed?

STEP 5
DECISION

The gospel demands a response.

In what specific way might your parish be invited to respond? Are there any attitudes or behaviors you would like to change as a result of today's conversation? What one concrete action will you take this week as a response to the liturgy today?

DOCTRINAL ISSUES

What church truth/teaching/doctrinal issue could be drawn from the gospel for the Thirty-Second Sunday in Ordinary Time?

Participants suggest possible doctrinal themes that flow from the readings.

Possible Doctrinal Themes

Eschatology, parousia, final judgment, conversion, discipleship, service, heaven, hell, purgatory, reign of God, pilgrim church, communion of saints, soteriology

Present the doctrinal material at this time.

1. The facilitator gives input on a particular doctrinal issue of his/her prior choosing. OR
2. The group chooses a doctrinal issue from the list they created. They read together from the Doctrinal Appendix.

(The doctrinal issues are found in the Doctrinal Appendix in the back of this workbook. If you are choosing an issue from this resource, please refer to it now.)

Reflection questions centered around the chosen doctrinal theme can be found at the end of each topic in the Doctrinal Appendix. The questions are based on the five-step reflection process. If you choose a topic not included in the Doctrinal Appendix, craft your own questions according to the same five-step process.

Following the reflection questions you will be reminded to return to chapter 7, "Preparing the Catechetical Session," to assist you in crafting your own session.

Closing Prayer

Let us pray
[that our prayer rise like incense
in the presence of God]

Pause for silent prayer.

Almighty Father,
strong is your justice and great is your mercy.
Protect us in the burdens and challenges of life.
Shield our minds from the distortion of pride
and enfold our desire with the beauty of truth.
Help us to become more aware of your loving design
so that we may more willingly give our lives in service to all.
We ask this through Christ our Lord.[11]

[11]Thirty-Second Sunday in Ordinary Time: "Alternative Opening Prayer," *The Sacramentary.*

Thirty-Third Sunday in Ordinary Time

Environment

Refer to the Thirty-Second Sunday in Ordinary Time.

INTRODUCTORY RITES

Opening Song (or Entrance Antiphon)

The Lord says: my plans for you are peace and not disaster; when you call to me, I will listen to you, and I will bring you back to the place from which I exiled you. (Jer 29:11, 12, 14)[1]

Opening Prayer

Let us pray
[that God will help us to be faithful]

Pause for silent prayer.

Father of all that is good,
keep us faithful in serving you,
for to serve you is our lasting joy.
We ask this through our Lord
Jesus Christ, your Son,
who lives and reigns with you and
the Holy Spirit,
one God, for ever and ever.[2]

LITURGY OF THE WORD

The readings are proclaimed.

First Reading
Proverbs 31:10–13, 19–20, 30–31

Overview of the Book of Proverbs: The Book of Proverbs was written around the ninth or tenth century B.C.E. It was a compilation of wise sayings and poetry. Solomon was remembered for his unparalleled wisdom; he was therefore considered the founder of the wisdom tradition. He was believed to have written the Book of Proverbs, The Song of Songs and Ecclesiastes, and the Book of Wisdom (the last book written of the Old Testament).

The themes inherent in the collection of sayings in the Book of Proverbs date back to the Sumerians in 3,000 B.C.E., so it is possible that the sayings could have been gathered together during Solomon's time and put in one collection. However, chapters 25–29 were not written until two centuries after Solomon's death in the reign of King Hezekiah.

The only organized section of the book is chapters 1–9 in which there is a planned section of short proverbs mixed in with long instructions. Those first chapters serve as a prologue to the entire collection and they describe wisdom as a way of life. The Book of Proverbs was a treasured source of practical wisdom to assist people in finding meaning for their lives.[3] The purpose of the proverbs was to guide people as they struggled to live a well-ordered life. Overall, the book exalts Yahweh, the living God and Master who orders the universe and everything in it and has complete power over it.

The proverbs are concerned with the issues of relationships—parents, children, husbands, wives, and friends. They are concerned with the difference between the righteous and the unrighteous. They uphold the virtues of honesty, generosity, justice, and integrity. The proverbs extol the need to discipline one's passions and sexual appetites. They encourage the appropriate use of speech—when to speak and when to be silent. They insist upon good stewardship of resources, such as wealth and the land. They describe the proper attitude one is to display toward one's superiors, and they exalt the "value of wisdom over foolish and careless behavior."[4]

---

[1]Thirty-Third Sunday in Ordinary Time: "Entrance Antiphon," *The Sacramentary.*

[2]Thirty-Third Sunday in Ordinary Time: "Opening Prayer," *The Sacramentary.*

[3]*ROT,* 480.

[4]Ibid., 481.

Today's Pericope: The Book of Proverbs begins with the personification of Wisdom, the one who promises wealth, prosperity, happiness, and a long life to those who would follow her counsel. It ends by depicting a woman who faithfully followed Lady Wisdom's counsel. The image of the woman is drawn with broad, artistic strokes. This woman of worth is the personification of the Lady Wisdom of the first nine chapters. Like Lady Wisdom, the lady of worth ministers in her home to the needs of those who come seeking. The lady of worth is not an exceptional or extraordinary woman, yet her tasks she performs with skill, tenacity, and commitment. As she lives her day-to-day life with wisdom, she brings joy to her family. She finds peace and happiness in the midst of the mundane and the ordinary. No chore is routine when performed within the shadow of Wisdom's wings; every event of life is an opportunity to encounter the living God.

Responsorial Psalm
Psalm 128:1–2, 3, 4–5

This psalm was chosen because its theme is consonant with the first reading. The God-fearing husband in the psalm balances the theme of the God-fearing wife in the first reading. The psalm reflects Israel's concern for the community in which "the welfare of the family enriches the life of the whole community."[5] When the community cares for the poor, the same blessings bestowed on the good wife are bestowed to the wider community.[6]

Second Reading
1 Thessalonians 5:1–6

When Paul speaks of Jesus' second coming, he is speaking from the perspective of biblical tradition and Israel's understanding of the "Day of the Lord." At one time, scripture understood the "Day of the Lord" as a time when Israel would be victorious over its enemies. The prophets eventually tore that meaning asunder in light of the people's idol worship, hypocritical worship, and social injustice. Rather than a day of light, it would be a day of darkness and a day of retribution for their sins.

[5]*PL,* 193.

[6]Ibid.

Isaiah understood it to be a time when God would reign victorious over the sins of an arrogant people. After the exile, the "Day of the Lord" was understood eschatologically. It would be a day when the unjust would be reproved and the righteous would be recompensed. Jesus' second coming was also understood in this context. Jesus would come to judge the living and the dead. Judgment would be severe for those who were not prepared for his coming.

Paul's intention in Thessalonians is to comfort the fears of those who were dreading this great and terrible day. What if they were not ready? Paul offered them hope. Paul referred to that future day, but reminded them that they were also living in its reality; they were at present living in the last age—the age of the Lord's return. They were already living out the salvation granted to them through Christ's paschal mystery. It was an ongoing, day-to-day process. Their hope was Jesus Christ crucified.

The Thessalonians lived under Roman rule. Life was tenuous and fragile. It was easy to make a wrong move and have the strong arm of government come crashing down upon them at any minute. People could not afford to make any false steps or do anything that might be interpreted as civil unrest. They needed to live cautiously and be prepared for any eventuality. Paul was reminding his community that this same sense of caution and preparedness should be the stance of Christians as they awaited the coming of the Lord. They were to be spiritually vigilant, and live each day fully prepared to meet Christ. They were to live out their baptismal commitment—to die and rise each day, and live their lives according to the gospel. They were to live as children of the light. Through this light others would be led out of the darkness and into the brilliance of the resurrected presence of Jesus Christ. This was their hope. They need not fear.

Gospel
Matthew 25:14–30

Step 1
Naming One's Experience

What were your first impressions? What was your first response to the gospel (or the other readings)? What captured your attention?

Each person names his or her initial impression. Statements should be brief. No reasons should be given at this time. All simply listen without agreeing or disagreeing.

STEP 2
UNDERSTANDING

In a brief statement, what do you think this gospel is trying to convey?

STEP 3
INPUT FROM VISION/STORY/TRADITION

Liturgical Context

Today is the last Sunday before the Feast of Christ the King, which ends the liturgical cycle. After next week, Cycle A ends and we begin the new liturgical year with Cycle B (Gospel of Mark). Today's gospel is the second in a two-part sequence that reflects upon the end times. As stated previously, the last Sundays of the liturgical year are thematically eschatological. They reflect on the end of time, final judgment, and Christ's second coming. Every liturgical celebration is eschatological. Every liturgy remembers and makes present the death and resurrection of Jesus. Every liturgy remembers the Christ who will come again and exhorts us to wait with unflagging diligence for his return at the consummation of the world.

In the years closest to a new millennium there is always talk about the end of the world. Such times invariably spark apocalyptic fervor. Even Hollywood gets swept up in the enthusiasm. Movies depicting asteroids bearing down on earth to bring it to its fiery end burst upon our cinema screens with apocalyptic anticipation. It is usual for such fervor to accompany the end of a century or a millennium.

The church takes time each year, however, to reflect on the finite nature of things. The liturgical calendar presents us with the opportunity to seriously reflect on the end of the world, and on the Lord's second coming. We do not have to wait for a millennium celebration to reflect on such things. It is built into our psyche and our identity. We are alerted that the liturgical year is winding to a close when, on the last Sundays of the cycle, the church begins its yearly meditation on end times, the last things, and the parousia. We are given ample opportunity to reflect on our lives, our deaths, and on our prospects for the hereafter. We are, after all, a pilgrim church on its journey toward the world's final consummation.

The new millennium presents us with the occasion to meditate on our history—past, present, and future—with perhaps more intensity, urgency, and honesty. As our future, it demands discernment, discipline, and decision, and asks the question, "Before time goes on to the next one thousand years, just how have you people lived as children of the light for the past one thousand years?" We can only row into the future with our backs turned so that our eyes are looking back to our past. Only then can we name our mistakes, learn from them, and avoid them in the future.

Today's Opening Prayer echoes the intent of today's parable when it asks that God keep us faithful in serving him. We are reminded that such service is tantamount to perfect joy. The same theme is resounded in the Alternative Opening Prayer. Again, we ask that God fill us with God's truth so that our hearts might be filled with the fullness of truth needed to carry out the life of service to which we are called. The Entrance Antiphon reminds us that God's plans for us do not bring disaster, but peace. We are to cast aside all fear when reflecting upon such things as the Lord's return and the end of the age. If we live each day as if it were our last, if we boldly serve the Lord each day, we have nothing to fear.

Gospel Exegesis

The facilitator gives input regarding what critical biblical scholarship has to say about this text. The input includes insights as to how people would have heard the gospel in Jesus' time.

Donald Senior reminds us that today's parable of the talents is another exhortation to fidelity. "The 'good and faithful' servants are those who are willing to risk their own security in using their gifts well."[7] Everyone is given a gift, an enormous gift, and everyone is faced with the responsibility of putting it to good use. The servant who was given only one talent was paralyzed into inaction by his fear. Fear cripples effective discipleship. Both Peter and the disciples were rendered immobilized by fear earlier in Matthew's gospel (8:26; 14:30–31).

This parable was handed down orally to Matthew and Luke. Their retelling of the parable was influenced by their own interpretation of the story they heard, as well as by their own biases and agendas. Matthew places the parable midst Jesus' eschatological exhortations to be diligent while waiting for his return. From Matthew's perspective, the parable is a transition into the final judgment scene. Bernard Brandon Scott asserts that the parable of the talents is a prelude to the "either-or" context of the last judgment—people are either saved or not saved. In today's parable, there is an exhortation to diligently wait and a mandate to grow in faith or face the consequences of judgment.

The talent was the largest sum of money in the Hellenized world. In silver coinage it weighed between fifty-seven and seventy-four pounds.[8] It was a huge amount of money for the average peasant, yet the master in the parable insisted that the servant was faithful over a "little." Why? Scott maintains that Matthew's parable is an allegory of faithfulness for the reign of God. Thus, it falls in the category of a "how much more" parable. The "little" that the faithful servant is faithful over is money. The "larger affairs" he will be put in charge of (how much more), is the kingdom. If the faithful servant was industrious and creative with something as insignificant as money, *then how much more* will he be industrious and creative when it comes to the reign of God. Matthew restates the common axiom ("the rich get richer and the poor get poorer") and applies it to spiritual matters. The spiritually richer person's reward is heaven. It is an eschatological promise.

Another interpretation of this parable suggests that it is about the proper use of gifts. The parable of the talents is considered one of the judgment parables. The other judgment parables exhort and challenge church leaders and ordinary Christians. This parable, insists Douglas Hare, addresses anyone who is blessed with special gifts (probably the gift of Christian service). The third slave in the story does not love his master, and his only concern is self-interest: "security, not service, is his goal."[9] He failed to put even his small and limited gift of service to worthwhile use in the kingdom of God. Everyone in the community is gifted. Some more than others. Whether our gift is meager or abundant, it is to be shared and multiplied.

The parable demands that love of God (not fear), as well as good stewardship, be demonstrated in the exercise of service for the community. The delay of the master's return was (and is) an opportunity to risk, to grow, and to imaginatively and creatively increase one's service in the reign of God.

John Pilch suggests a unique and fascinating perspective of this parable. In what seems to be a tongue-in-cheek observation, he asserts that this parable is loved by both capitalists and fundamentalist counselors. Capitalists would love the assumption that the rich steward ended up much richer than when he started. The fundamentalist counselor would translate the word *talent* literally—personal giftedness. "Jesus' listeners, of course, were neither capitalists nor committed to self-improvement."[10]

Pilch invites us to consider how first century peasants might have understood this parable. He questions whether Matthew's version of the parable would have been considered "good news" to them. In antiquity it was understood that all "goods" were already distributed. There were no "extra goods" lurking around for others to devour. If a person wanted more, he or she would have to defraud someone else to get it. Anyone who suddenly turned up with "more" would be under suspicion of being a thief. As a result, wealthy people were always distrusted and would enlist the services of slaves (who already had a reputation for dishonesty) to do their bidding. No one would be

[7] *IM*, 239.

[8] *HTP*, 224.

[9] *MI*, 287.

[10] *CWJ*, 163.

surprised if slaves were thieves or if they defrauded someone.

In the beginning of the story the listener is led to believe that the rich man is an honorable man. However, it is later learned from the third servant that he is a "'hard man,' reaping what he did not sow and gathering where he did not scatter seed (v. 24)."[11] Today in America the rich master would be called a "good businessman" or a "clever entrepreneur." To others, especially ancient listeners, he would have been considered arrogant, opportunistic, and greedy. In verse 26, the master does not deny the servant's perception of him as a "hard man." We can only assume that he must agree with it. Thus, the master's point to the slave is: "Since you already knew that I am a 'hard man,' then you should have had enough sense to put the money in the bank so it could have at least earned interest." Pilch asserts that the first two slaves not only *served* the master, they *acted just like him.* They too were arrogant, dishonest, and greedy.

Ancient peasants would have been disheartened by this parable as Matthew related it. It would have confirmed what they had already experienced—that the rich continue to get richer, and since there was only so much to go around in the first place, they did so on the backs of the poor. If God was like the rich master, then who in the world would ever want God? Pilch solves the incongruence in the parable by referring to the church historian Eusebius who also noticed the problem with Matthew's version of the story. Eusebius related a different account of this parable from the now lost Gospel of the Nazoreans. In that version of the story, the first slave was thrown in prison, the second slave was scolded, and the third slave was happily welcomed and honored. Pilch wonders if this might not have been the original version told by Jesus.[12] Matthew may have reworked it for the sake of what was happening in his community at the time.

However, we do not proclaim the Gospel of the Nazoreans today, we proclaim the Gospel of Matthew. It is certainly the Lectionary's intention that our primary concern in today's gospel is with the parable's eschatology. As noted previously, Matthew's interpretation of the oral tradition fulfilled his purpose. His account of the gospel was written in about 80 C.E., fifty years after Jesus' death and resurrection. Jesus had not yet returned as anticipated. Matthew was faced with ministering to a waiting community. He wanted to shed light on what it means to be a community that continues to wait for Jesus' return and for the last judgment. Matthew's position was that it is better to creatively risk everything for the kingdom while waiting for Christ's return than to play it safe and rest in the security of the status quo. Jesus was a risk-taker. Disciples were to follow his example. The window of opportunity was still wide open. The choice belonged to the community. They could either make the most of their wait or do nothing and face the consequences.

We might do well to reflect on Eusebius' version of the parable *along with* the eschatological interpretation Matthew presented to the community. There is much food for thought in this parable.

---

[11]Ibid.

[12]My imagination invites me to listen to this parable with the ears of the ancient peasant and develop Eusebius' version of the story to its seemingly logical conclusion. Obviously the wealthy master (who probably defrauded in order to have more of the world's goods than everyone else in the first place) was greedy, opportunistic, and arrogant. When the two slaves increased what they had been given, they acted just like the master. They too must have defrauded someone. Remember, it was understood that all the goods (talents) there were had already been distributed; thus one had to defraud or steal from someone else to get more. The first two servants must have stolen the talents in order to increase their original amount. The first one was thrown in prison because he took more than the second one, who was only reprimanded. Thus, the first one's sin was greater than the second one's sin. The third servant was faithful to what he had been given. He defrauded no one, he took from no one, nor did anyone take from him. He protected and safeguarded the goods (talents) that were entrusted to him. He was a good steward. He did not covet or steal more than what was originally entrusted to him. The third slave ended up the good and faithful servant. This is simply conjecture, but it does provide grist for reflection in relation to the world's distribution of goods and resources. Understood in this context, the parable challenges the greed of human beings that promote the unequal distribution of the world's resources. This is one way the rich get richer. They take more of what there is, leaving less for the poor.

Proclaim the gospel again.

Sometimes we gain new insights when we hear the text after the interpretation has been given. Someone from the group proclaims the gospel a second time.

STEP 4
TESTING

Conversation with the Liturgy and the Scriptures

Test your original understanding in dialogue with the text.

(You might consider breaking into smaller groups.)

Now that you've heard the exegesis, were there any new insights for you? How do you feel about it? How does your original understanding of this gospel compare with what we just shared? How does this story speak to your life?

Sharing Life Experience

Participants share an experience from their lives that connects with the biblical interpretation just shared.

> *Matthew invites us to be creative with our gifts and resources in order to promote the reign of God until Jesus comes again. This entails risk. It invites us to "step out in faith" and listen to the promptings of the Holy Spirit to go where we never thought we could go in the service of God's reign. In this interim time of waiting we are not to pack our bags and go to the hills and wait for the parousia to whisk us into the clouds of heaven. We are to wait, to be diligent, and to risk everything. That is scary stuff for families. Many years ago our family was invited to risk the security of deeply planted roots and move across the country to a new place. It was scary then and would be scary now. But the grace we received was beyond what we could ever have imagined or anticipated.*
>
> *How does today's parable play out in all our lives? The first way it plays out is through faithfulness. When we are constantly attentive to living the gospel in this materialistic world, then we are always ready to meet Christ when he comes. That is no simple undertaking. What does it mean? It often means living counter-culturally. When the culture says get more, more, more, the gospel invites us to live with what is enough, enough, enough. There is an incredible temptation to believe that good parenting means providing the best of all this world's goods in order to raise happy, well-adjusted children. I remember times over the years when I struggled with feelings of anger and frustration when we could not afford the latest computer game, tennis lessons, or super-vacations. We wanted the best for our children, as does everyone, even the world's poor. But the "best" is not always what the world tells us is the "best." Maybe what was the best for us was really struggling to live with "enough." Perhaps the way we lived (or failed to live) the imperative of this gospel is to be seen in the way in which we instilled (or did not instill) proper gospel values in the life of our family.*
>
> *Today's gospel invites me to discern the ways in which I am unwilling to boldly live the gospel. When my children were young, the first place for that discernment was our home and from there it extended out into the world. Perhaps now that our children have moved into young adulthood, discernment will invite us to use our gifts in new arenas. The parable invites a willingness to make mistakes (which we have and will continue to do) and a readiness (which we hope to maintain) to use our gifts to the fullest. The only thing to stand in our way is fear.*

All share their life experience.

What if Matthew's Gospel had portrayed the master and the first two slaves as greedy and opportunistic and the third slave as the faithful servant? What are the implications and how would that speak to the church today? In what way would that be relevant? How does Matthew's version of the parable speak to the church today? How does the theme of diligent waiting and taking bold risks for the reign of God speak to your life? The life of your community? In what way are you living the imperatives of this gospel? In what way do you need to grow? In what way does today's liturgy challenge you to change? In what way does this gospel challenge your community? In what way are the biblical themes of covenant, exodus, creation, and community evident in today's readings? Do you still feel the same way about this text as when you began? Has your original understanding been stretched, challenged, or affirmed?

STEP 5
DECISION

The gospel demands a response.

In what specific way might your parish be invited to respond? Are there any attitudes or behaviors you would like to change as a result of today's conversation? What one concrete action will you take this week as a response to the liturgy today?

Pastoral Considerations: Would there be enough evidence to convict your parish if it was charged with boldly promoting the reign of God while waiting for Christ to come again? How would your parish respond to that question? In what way does your parish step out in faith and take risks to further the reign of God on earth? In what way is your parish stuck in maintaining the status quo? Before beginning a new liturgical cycle, are there any New Year's resolutions your parish might consider?

Christian Initiation: Are there people ready to celebrate a rite of acceptance or welcome? Since this is prior to the beginning of the new liturgical cycle and the season of Advent, it might be a good Sunday to celebrate one of the rites. It would also be an appropriate time to celebrate a non-sacramental penitential celebration (found in the appendix of the Rite of Penance). Baptized Christians preparing for full communion should be prepared for the celebration of the sacrament of reconciliation and then participate in the parish celebration of the sacrament during their formation. In what way have you lately apprenticed catechumens in the apostolic life? Today's gospel exhorts the bold use of our resources. How have you helped the catechumens in the exercise of their apostolic gifts?

DOCTRINAL ISSUES

What church truth/teaching/doctrinal issue could be drawn from the gospel for the Thirty-Third Sunday in Ordinary Time?

Participants suggest possible doctrinal themes that flow from the readings.

Possible Doctrinal Themes

Eschatology, last judgment, parousia, end of the world, heaven, evangelization, Christian service, discipleship, ministry, social mission of the church, preferential option for the poor, pilgrim church, virtues of faith, hope, and trust

Present the doctrinal material at this time.

1. The facilitator gives input on a particular doctrinal issue of his or her prior choosing. OR
2. The group chooses a doctrinal issue from the list they created. They read together from the Doctrinal Appendix.

(The doctrinal issues are found in the Doctrinal Appendix in the back of this workbook. If you are choosing an issue from this resource, please refer to it now.)

Reflection questions centered around the chosen doctrinal theme can be found at the end of each topic in the Doctrinal Appendix. The questions are based on the five-step reflection process. If you choose a topic not included in the Doctrinal Appendix, craft your own questions according to the same five-step process.

Following the reflection questions you will be reminded to return to chapter 7, "Preparing the Catechetical Session," to assist you in crafting your own session.

Closing Prayer

Let us pray
[with hearts that long for peace]

Father in heaven,
ever-living source of all that is good,
from the beginning of time you promised man salvation
through the future coming of your Son,
our Lord Jesus Christ.
Help us to drink of his truth

and expand our hearts with the joy of his
promises,
so that we may serve you in faith and in love
and know for ever the joy of your presence.
We ask this through Christ our Lord.[13]

[13]Thirty-Third Sunday in Ordinary Time: "Alternative Opening Prayer," *The Sacramentary.*

Christ the King—Last Sunday in Ordinary Time

Environment

There need not be a special catechetical environment just for this feast. The space should reflect the overall eschatological tone of the past weeks. The liturgical color for this feast is white.

INTRODUCTORY RITES

Opening Song (or Entrance Antiphon)

The Lamb who was slain is worthy to receive strength and divinity, wisdom and power and honor: to him be glory and power for ever. (Rev 5:12; 1:6)[1]

Opening Prayer

Let us pray
[that all men will acclaim Jesus as Lord]

Pause for silent prayer.

Almighty and merciful God,
you break the power of evil
and make all things new
in your Son Jesus Christ, the King
of the universe.
May all in heaven and earth
acclaim your glory
and never cease to praise you.
We ask this through our Lord
Jesus Christ, your Son,
who lives and reigns with you and
the Holy Spirit,
one God, for ever and ever.[2]

OR:

Let us pray
[that the kingdom of Christ
may live in our hearts and come
to our world]

Pause for silent prayer.

Father all-powerful, God of love,
you have raised our Lord Jesus Christ
from death to life,
resplendent in glory as King of creation.
Open our hearts,
free all the world to rejoice in his peace,
to glory in his justice, to live in his love.
Bring all mankind together in
Jesus Christ your Son,
whose kingdom is with you and
the Holy Spirit,
one God, for ever and ever.[3]

LITURGY OF THE WORD

The readings are proclaimed.

First Reading
Ezekiel 34:11–12, 15–17

Overview of the Book of Ezekiel: Ezekiel was called to the prophetic ministry during the fifth year of the exile (593 B.C.E.). Ezekiel and Jeremiah possessed similar characteristics as they both exercised the role of prophet and priest. Ezekiel was influenced by Jeremiah, but even more than Jeremiah, he drew upon his priestly background in the exercise of his prophetic mission. He knew the affairs of the city of Jerusalem and of the temple and he spoke about them as if he were present to the events that took place in both.[4] Some scholars suggest that perhaps travelers passing through filled him in on events of Jerusalem and the temple. However, others maintain that the accounts are so explicit that he simply had to have been present to events of the last days of Judah.

While some commentators insist that Ezekiel was in need of serious psychoanalysis because of his highly provocative prophetic actions, such as lying on his side for three hundred and ninety days or

[1] Christ the King: "Entrance Antiphon," *The Sacramentary.*
[2] Christ the King: "Opening Prayer," *The Sacramentary.*
[3] Christ the King: "Alternative Opening Prayer," *The Sacramentary.*
[4] *ROT,* 386.

being silent for long periods of time, others maintain that he was drawing on a previous prophetic tradition from centuries earlier. Much of his material is reminiscent of the old curses that used to be attached to covenant ceremonies and treaties. Ezekiel was simply trying to assure the people with exclamation points that God was as faithful as God had always been.

God appointed Ezekiel watchman over Israel. His message was no more popular or well received than Jeremiah's, but he understood that his duty was to speak the word of God and prophesy to the people. It was the people's duty to listen.

The Book of Ezekiel is a very structured work. It is divided into three segments. Chapters 1–24 contain the oracles against Judah and Jerusalem before 586 B.C.E. The second section, chapters 25–32, contains the oracles against the foreign nations, and the third section, chapters 33–48, contains the oracles of hope and future restoration for Judah. The oracles so reflect the historical situation of the time that there is little doubt that many of them came directly from the prophet's own mouth.

Ezekiel uses dramatic images, stories, visions, and symbolic actions to drive home his point and proclaim his message with power and emphasis. He is certainly not lacking in imagination. His people are to know with certainty that his message is serious and that God is in control of their destiny.

Ezekiel heralds the theme of God's judgment. Pagan idolatry, lack of justice toward the poor, and false worship are a few of the issues that Ezekiel prophesies against. God is in covenant relationship with Israel. When Israel sins, God punishes. But God is also merciful and will restore repentant sinners. Israel gave up on their love relationship with God. Ezekiel calls for a return to holiness and to their faithfulness to the covenant. Ezekiel also tackles the issue of personal responsibility. One generation is not responsible for the sins of another. Each person is responsible for his or her own conduct and relationship with God. Ezekiel understood the exile as a tool used by God to bring about conversion in the lives of the people.

Hope was not lost. After the destruction of the exile God would restore Israel. Ezekiel insisted that God would restore the people with a two-part plan. First, God would bring the exiles out of captivity, purify them, and return them to the covenant. This restoration would involve conversion and transformation. "There will be a new David to shepherd the people; God will abolish idols and abominations; old hearts will be removed so that new hearts and a new obedience can be given to the people and God will drive all the arrogant pagans from the land and make his people secure in peace."[5]

The second part of the plan would involve the construction of a new temple where the new, restored, and renewed Israel would worship Yahweh. Religion was a matter of the heart—a renewed heart called to worship God through the demands of the moral life and the devotional practices of worship in the temple.[6]

Today's Pericope: The metaphor of *shepherd* is used primarily in cultures with predominantly pastoral settings. The shepherd ruled over his flock of sheep with strength and discipline, but he was also very close to them. He knew them by name and they knew the sound of his voice. Sheep and goats were used for food (meat and milk) and for clothing and sacrifices. The horns and hides were used in the making of tents and the making of writing materials. Sheep usually grazed in unfenced rough terrains in the wilderness. It was therefore necessary that the flock be guided by a shepherd and his dog in order to protect it from predators and from the elements. Thus, the shepherd and shepherding are commonly used metaphors in the Bible for kings, leaders, for ministry, and for God. Today's reading from Ezekiel is part of that pastoral tradition.

God does not allow others to take care of his flock—God alone is personally responsible. God will tend to them, rescue them, pasture them, and give them rest. God will find the sheep that are lost and bring them back. However, God will destroy the sheep who are sleek and strong (the judgment between the rams and the goats in

[5]Ibid., 396.

[6]Ibid.

today's gospel). God will bring order to God's flock. The strong will not overpower the weak. The vulnerable ones will be protected.[7]

Ezekiel railed against the former kings of Judah who were false shepherds. Ezekiel insists that Yahweh will take over for them. Yahweh will assume the role the former kings should have taken. God will shepherd the people, restore them, and bring them home. God, not the monarchy, will rule Israel. God will establish another David over the people (early vestiges of the messianic hope).

Rather than the pious, saccharine Shepherd of popular folk art, the Good Shepherd is a strong, athletic, weather-beaten protector of his sheep. God is a Shepherd who protects his sheep with his life. The Good Shepherd protects his sheep with strength, compassion, discipline, and love. The Good Shepherd is the God in whom we place our trust.

Responsorial Psalm
Psalm 23:1–2, 2–3, 5–6

Today's psalm is an appropriate response to Ezekiel's prophetic word in the first reading.

Second Reading
1 Corinthians 15:20–26, 28

Today's text has often been used by millenarians to give credence to their eschatological beliefs. People who believe in millenarianism have used this text and Revelation 20 to prove their fundamentalist understanding of Christ's second coming and the end of time. Those who ascribe to millenarianism believe that when Christ comes again the righteous will rule the earth for one thousand years. Prior to that time, there will be a brutal war between Gog and Magog. These apocalyptic beliefs have been around since the early centuries. Those who ascribe to them today are fundamentalists who take the eschatological and apocalyptic literature of scripture literally and therefore limit their meaning.

The theme of today's liturgy suggests that our concentration on today's second reading should center on verse 24: "[T]hen comes the end, when he delivers the kingdom to God the Father after destroying every rule and every authority and power." Paul insists that Christ's reign will last a limited time. When it comes to an end, God alone will take over—Christ will deliver his rule into the hands of God. The reign of Christ will last from the resurrection and ascension of Christ until his return in glory. Thus, the period of Christ's reign will coincide with the period of the church. The period of Christ's reign and the reign of the church is a time in which peace will not reign. There will be war: Christ and the church will engage in war with Christ's enemies. During this time, God will deal with the church directly through Christ. God's action in the church is an extension of God's redeeming action through Christ on the cross. However, after the consummation of the world, Christ's return, and the completion of his action of redemption, God will deal with the world directly.

Another aspect of Paul's eschatology centered around his theology regarding Christ, the new Adam. Paul compared Adam, the first human being, to the new Adam—Christ and his redeeming activity. Adam sinned, resulting in ongoing sin and death; Christ, on the other hand, brought salvation and life. Freedom from sin and the salvation won by Jesus is not only an after-life reality. Its fruits are also enjoyed here on earth by people who live the paschal mystery of Christ.

Jesus is the "firstfruits" referred to in the reading. "Firstfruits," in the language of Jewish worship, referred to the consecration of the entire harvest to the Lord. The resurrection of Christ is our "firstfruits," the promise of abundance and the fullness of life through Christ's death and resurrection. We share in those firstfruits both now and in the future realm of glory. We experience the saving joy of eternity in the here and now, in the life of the church and the Spirit's continued work in and through the church. When we celebrate the sacraments and encounter Christ in the word and in the community of believers, we, as pilgrim people, experience the future glory of heaven here on earth as we journey to our final glory.

Gospel
Matthew 25:31–46

[7] *DL* (IV), 264–265.

Step 1
Naming One's Experience

What were your first impressions? What was your first response to the gospel (or the other readings)?[8] What captured your attention?

Each person names his or her initial impression. Statements should be brief. No reasons should be given at this time. All simply listen without agreeing or disagreeing.

Step 2
Understanding

In a brief statement, what do you think this gospel is trying to convey?

Step 3
Input from Vision/Story/Tradition

Liturgical Context

This is the final Sunday of the liturgical cycle. It is the last time we encounter Jesus Christ through the lens of Matthew for another two years. One of the so-called "idea feasts," the feast of Christ the King serves as a climactic celebration and finely-tuned blending of the major themes of the gospel. There are three texts chosen for this feast. "As opposed to the other Sundays in Ordinary Time, the Liturgy of the Word here takes the form of a triptych. The center, chief panel is the Gospel; the other panels, of the Old Testament and the epistle, are not quite on the same level as the first, but turned slightly toward it."[9]

Today's solemnity is reminiscent of the solemnity of the Ascension, Epiphany, and Palm Sunday. All celebrate the reign of Christ. Pope Pius XI instituted this feast in his Encyclical Letter *Quas primas,* December 11, 1925, in response to the destructive forces of the age. He insisted that the only weapon against such forces and chaos is the acknowledgment of the sovereignty of Christ.

> ...It is necessary that the royal dignity of Our Lord be recognized and accepted as widely as possible. To this end it seems to Us that nothing else would help so effectively as the institution of a special feast dedicated to Christ our King. The annual celebration of the sacred mysteries is more effective in informing people about the Faith and in bringing them the joys of the spiritual life than the solemn pronouncements of the teaching Church. Documents are often read only by a few learned men; feasts move and teach all the faithful. The former speaks but once; the latter every year and forever. The former bring a saving touch to the intellect; the latter influence not only the mind but the heart and man's whole nature.[10]

At the time when the encyclical was written, the world had experienced the Bolshevik Revolution in 1917, the spread of fascism, the loss of the church's political power, and the decadence of the 1920s. However, as cultural conditions changed, so did the focus of this feast. The moving of this feast to the last Sunday of the liturgical cycle placed it center stage in our unfolding eschatological agenda. Thus, today the feast of Christ the King serves as an appropriate way to remember the Second Coming of Christ. "It is now clearer that the exalted Lord and King is the goal not only of the liturgical year but of our entire earthly pilgrimage.... At the end of the liturgical year, then, stands the Lord of Glory. "[11]

Adolph Adam suggests that Epiphany is the feast par excellence that remembers the kingship of Christ in the liturgy as expressed in Epiphany's entrance antiphon: "The Lord and ruler is coming; kingship is his, and government and power." He quotes W. Durig on the matter:

> Only an obscuring of the content of the liturgical feast of Epiphany and an intel-

[8]The primary focus of reflection is the gospel. However, very often the other readings demand attention and must be brought into the dialogue.

[9]*DL* (VI), 314.

[10]As quoted in *LY,* 177.

[11]*LY,* 178.

lectualization of liturgical theology could have led Pius XI in 1925 to introduce a second Feast of Christ the King on the last Sunday of October. This move is typical of the development that modern piety has undergone; this development becomes clear from a comparison of the two feasts. The feast of Christ the King *celebrates the general idea of Christ's kingship; it celebrates a title of honor, a name, a concept* [italics mine]. On the other hand, it is essential to the liturgical feast of Epiphany that it brings before us, in a concrete way, a royal action of Christ, an event that is an essential part of the process of salvation. On the one hand, then, an idea; on the other, the reality of the mystery of Epiphany which contains in itself the entire mystery of redemption.[12]

Reginald Fuller asserts that the feast duplicates the themes of Ascension Day and provides a distinctive emphasis on social action. According to Fuller, this feast provides the liturgical support for the social teaching of the great papal encyclicals since Leo XIII.

When it was first established as a feast assigned to the last Sunday in October, there was danger of removing the kingship of Christ from its eschatological context. Jesus' enthronement at the Ascension is the inauguration of his eschatological reign, his rule over all until he comes again in glory, and his ongoing defeat of the power of evil. By moving the feast to the last Sunday of the year, this eschatological emphasis was retained.

The events that prompted establishment of the feast had to do with the sixteen-century anniversary of the Council of Nicea's pronouncement that Christ and the Father are one and the same (consubstantiality), thus providing the basis for his kingly rule. "He [Pius XI] chose this day chiefly in view of the coming feast of all Saints; the feast of Christ the King would exalt 'before all men the glory of Him who triumphs in His saints and His elect.'"[13] On this feast there was to be a consecration to the heart of Christ, the Redeemer.

[12]Ibid., 147.

[13]Ibid., 177.

In a decree promulgating the *editio typica* of the General Roman Calendar on March 21, 1969—*Anni liturgici ordinatione, #3760*—the feast of Christ the King was moved to a new day: "The feasts of the Baptism of the Lord and Christ the King are to be celebrated on the days newly assigned to them."[14] The revised liturgical calendar reflected the change away from the last Sunday in October.

> Because of its special importance, the Sunday celebration gives way only to solemnities or feasts of the Lord. The Sundays of the seasons of Advent, Lent, and Easter, however, take precedence over all solemnities and feasts of the Lord. Solemnities occurring on these Sundays are observed on the Saturday preceding.
>
> By its nature, Sunday excludes any other celebration's being permanently assigned to that day, with these exceptions: a. Sunday within the octave of Christmas is the feast of the Holy Family; b. Sunday following 6 January is the feast of the Baptism of the Lord; c. Sunday after Pentecost is the solemnity of the Holy Trinity; d. The last Sunday in Ordinary Time is the solemnity of Christ the King.[15]

The liturgy exalts the universal reign of Christ, not just today, but in every celebration of liturgy. Today's Entrance Antiphon asserts Christ's divinely instituted power. Christ, the slain Lamb, is worthy to receive strength and divinity and to him be "glory and power for ever." The Opening Prayer expresses our confidence in Christ's exaltation and his power to reign over all creation: "You break the power of evil and make all things new. . . ." The Prayer Over the Gifts acknowledges the sacrifice of Christ's life on the cross that reconciled the world to the Father and inaugurated Christ's kingship. The Preface for today's liturgy makes repeated references to the kingdom established by Christ:

Father, all-powerful and ever-living God,
we do well always and everywhere to give you
thanks.

[14]*DOL*, 1156.

[15]*GNLY*, #5 and #6.

You anointed Jesus Christ, your only Son, with the oil of gladness,
as the eternal priest and universal king.
As priest he offered his life on the altar of the cross
and redeemed the human race
by this one perfect sacrifice of peace.
As king he claims dominion over all creation,
that he may present you, his almighty Father,
an eternal and universal kingdom:
a kingdom of truth and life,
a kingdom of holiness and grace,
a kingdom of justice, love, and peace.[16]

The third form of the penitential rite picks up the same theme: "Lord Jesus, you rule over the kingdom of truth and life."

As Ordinary Time comes to a close and Advent begins, they dovetail in their focus. Both exalt Christ, who reigns triumphant over the world and will come again in glory. Thus, Advent's "Solemn Blessing Over the People" is included in this session's closing prayer. It echoes today's contemplation on the reign of Christ.

Gospel Exegesis

The facilitator gives input regarding what critical biblical scholarship has to say about this text. The input includes insights as to how people would have heard the gospel in Jesus' time.

There are several different lenses through which to examine today's gospel. Scholars approach this gospel from varying perspectives which, in and of itself, is an indication of the apparent richness contained within the verses of the text. This exegesis attempts to set a table of diverse perspectives before us in order to broaden our vision and invite serious reflection and digestion.

One interpretation centers around the biblical theme of justice. Matthew insists that the reign and the kingship of Christ is realized in the hearts of the hungry who have been fed, in the oppressed who have been delivered from bondage, in the imprisoned who have been released, in the stranger who has been welcomed, and in the lost who have been found, loved, and accepted. Not only is Christ's reign and authority realized in such instances, but it continues.

Today's gospel is a combination of other literary genres used by Matthew to stress God's eschatological judgment. The judgment parables highlight the criteria that will be used when it comes time for God's ultimate judgment. Apocalyptic literature was not new to Matthew. There was evidence of apocalyptic fervor in other contemporary Jewish and Egyptian works of Jesus' time. The criterion found only in Christian literature is the criterion of love. Love will be the measure by which people are judged. This love will be measured by behavior. Love will result in acts of kindness, mercy, and justice. Christians who feed the hungry, give drink to the thirsty, and clothe the naked are living in God's reign—they are realizing it in their midst. The action of selfless love is a sign of Christ's reign in the here and now. No act of love is insignificant. We will be judged according to the small and large ways we respond to God's gratuitous love for us by offering selfless love to others.

The pastoral setting of ancient Palestine provides the context for understanding the metaphors and similes used by Matthew's Jesus to unveil the eschatological reign of God. Shepherds tended to the sheep and goats each day. They grazed side by side in a common pasture. At the end of the day, however, the shepherd separated the goats from the sheep. The sheep were stronger than the goats and were better able to thrive and to survive the cold nights. The goats needed to be sheltered. The story stresses the separation of the two by the shepherd. One school of thought suggests that this parable is not intended to compare the sheep and the goats, but is simply laying out the facts—judgment will occur at the end of the world by the Judge of the universe. The criterion for favorable judgment is acceptance of Jesus Christ and his mission. Jesus addressed the parable to his disciples and his point is unmistakable. There will be judgment, and those who have rejected Jesus will be rejected.

This is the only place in the gospel where Jesus acknowledges and uses the royal title assigned to him. Scholars suggest that this might be a later development of Christology by the church and by

[16]Christ the King: "Preface," *The Sacramentary.*

Matthew, and placed back into the story. However, this gospel exalts the Son of God who sits at God's right hand and who is the judge of the world. Christ the Savior, who is one with his Father, is brought front and center onto the human stage of salvation history.

Some scholars question the justice-oriented interpretation just presented. They maintain that while living the ethical life is certainly a value, there is nothing particularly Christian about it. Other pagan cultures also believed that they would gain reward for similar behavior, but faith played no part in the equation. Also, previous chapters in Matthew laid out other criteria for judgment. Jews will be judged for their rejection of the Messiah. Christians will be judged for their lack of faithfulness to Christ, for their failure to complete their assigned tasks, for bad behavior, and for their lack of good deeds. There is more involved than just taking care of the poor. There is more to this parable, according to this school of thought, than simply pointing out that a lack of love, compassion, and care for the poor will result in an unfavorable final report card.

Examining today's gospel from the standpoint of the ancient shame- and honor-based culture helps provide another perspective for our reflection. The Son of Man comes in glory (honor) and sits on the throne of glory (honor). He is accompanied by the angels (honor) and all nations will witness this marvelous event (honor). The king will separate the sheep (honorable) from the goats (the shame-filled).[17]

Our ancestors were very much influenced by the pastoral life of the times. As mentioned earlier, such a way of life provided the similes and metaphors for speaking about God's relationship with Israel. Ancient peoples were impressed by the way sheep suffer in silence. Thus, the sign of a real man in antiquity was judged by the way he was able to suffer in silence. "Sheep came to symbolize honor, virility, and strength."[18] Goats were not looked upon as favorably as were sheep. They were considered lascivious as they allowed other males access to their females. A man who allowed another man access to his wife (then and today) in an Eastern Mediterranean context was considered to be like a goat. Goats were a symbol of shame and shameful behavior. Goats were associated with the shameful Greek gods, women, and the devil.[19]

[17]*CWJ*, 166.

[18]Ibid.

John J. Pilch proposes that the basis for the final separation of the sheep and the goats—the determining factor for who will be in and who will be out in the end—is hospitality. The gospel is a treatise on hospitality. In the Middle East, hospitality is extended to strangers.[20] Kindness shown to one's relatives is considered steadfast love—not hospitality. In the end, the sheep (Christians, pagans, or Israelites) are the ones who offer hospitality to strangers: "Lord, when did we see you hungry?" The honorable and expected thing to do is to extend hospitality to the stranger. In so doing, one is extending hospitality to Jesus himself. The goats were those who refused to extend such hospitality.

An extension of this interpretation can be found by asking whom the different groups in the gospel represent. Who are the sheep? Who are the goats? Who are "all the nations?" Does "all the nations" represent Christians, non-Christians, or *all* people—Gentiles, Jews, Christians? Who are the "least of my brothers?" Are they the poor and oppressed, only Christians, or simply the Christian poor?

David Garland reminds us that Matthew always uses the term "all the nations" in reference to the "nations that Christian disciples are sent to evangelize (24:9, 28:19)."[21] The parable reminds us that judgment will be upon those to whom the gospel has been proclaimed—"all the nations." All those who hear the gospel and reject it will be judged accordingly. Garland recalls that earlier in Matthew's gospel the disciples were sent to Israel with the message of salvation. Now they are sent to "all the nations." The same instructions apply to this mission today as they did to the former mission. The "nations" are no different than Israel. They too will either accept Christ or reject him.

[19]Ibid.

[20]Refer to Appendix II, "Hospitality," for further elaboration on this subject.

[21]*RM*, 243.

Their kindness to the missionaries will be an indication of their acceptance of Jesus' message.

Douglas Hare, on the other hand, insists that "all the nations" refers simply to the Gentiles in the Galilean neighborhoods. Thus, he believes "all the nations" is not intended to mean other national entities; it simply refers to pagans.[22] Good Jews and Christians in antiquity worried about the fate of their good pagan neighbors. Today's gospel answers their question: "What will happen to good pagans who live a good life?" They, too, will be judged according to certain criteria. Both Jewish and Christian sources commonly referred to two different judgments—one judgment for Israel and another judgment for the Gentiles. Paul does the same in Romans 2:1–11. Thus, the judgment in this scene does not refer to Jews, Jewish Christians, or any other Christians. They will be judged according to the criteria established by Jesus in the Sermon on the Mount. Pagans will be judged by other criteria and hospitality is at the heart of it.

Garland reminds us that "brothers" is a term used in Matthew's gospel that refers exclusively to Jesus' disciples, and the "little ones" are all those who believe in his message. Douglas Hare, however, asserts that "brothers" in this case does not mean what it usually means. It was a broader interpretation than merely "Jesus' disciples." He maintains that it is a little self-serving to think that only those actions that help Christians are worthy of eternal reward. Hare believes that "brothers" is a term that is, in this case, more encompassing than its usual interpretation in Matthew's gospel. He insists that "brothers" is everyone, "whoever they may be, . . ."[23] who is poor and distressed; they should "be regarded as Jesus' brothers and sisters."[24]

The "least of these" are not placed in the same judgment predicament as others in the text. They will stand with Christ. The "least" are Jesus' followers. Douglas Hare infers that perhaps "the least" is even a reference to poor Christians—a reminder that we are all to possess a certain poverty. "In the case of missionaries it is a voluntary poverty; they have abandoned their usual vocations and 'travel light,' as prescribed by Jesus in 10:8–9, and are, thus, totally dependent on the hospitality of those among whom they proclaim the gospel."[25]

David Garland suggests that this parable does not intend to promote a "humanitarian ethics" of good works (salvation based on kindness to all in need) with no specific Christian content. Rather, "the nations are judged according to the way they treated Jesus' humble brethren who represented Christ to them."[26]

Garland also highlights Matthew's view of the church's mission in the world with four points drawn from today's parable: "(a) The world meets Christ through his disciples. (b) The primary function of the disciples is to represent Christ to the world. (c) The solidarity between Christ, as God with us, and his disciples will be revealed to one and all only at the parousia. (d) The humbleness of the son of man's presence in his oppressed disciples contrasts sharply with the glory of his future coming with all the authority of God."[27]

It was no surprise to the sheep that they won eternal reward. What was a surprise, however, was the reality that when they welcomed Christ's ambassadors they were welcoming Christ. When "sheep" reached out with love and compassion to the disciples, they were reaching out to the *One Who Sits on the Throne of the Father.* "Goats" disregarded the messengers and failed to see the living Christ in them. Thus, by their own actions, the goats sealed their own fate: they were cast aside in the final gathering.

Garland explains that the parable here is a word of encouragement to a persecuted church sent on the mission to spread the gospel of Christ. The mission and the locus for its spread—the world—is fraught with danger and uncertainties. Disciples are sent out into a hostile environment. Matthew describes the hardships that disciples will encounter on the mission. They closely parallel the sufferings that Paul endured on the same mission (1 Cor 4:9–13). Such suffering will end and vindication will be achieved at the final judgment.

[22] *MI,* 289.
[23] Ibid., 290.
[24] Ibid.
[25] Ibid.
[26] *RM,* 243.
[27] Ibid., 244.

Garland questions other interpretations of this parable that insist that this gospel is really a pronouncement of our obligation to the poor and marginalized of society. While Matthew does indeed assert just such an obligation throughout the gospel, this parable has an entirely different purpose. Today's parable is not a demand that the "haves" reach out and take care of the "have-nots" (even though that imperative is a *given*). This parable speaks to the Christian community that puts its life on the line in order to live and promote the gospel, and is often rejected for its efforts. It is a sobering reminder that such rejection is in truth a rejection of Christ and his mission.

Douglas Hare, however, states that there is nothing uniquely Christian about the imperative to treat the messenger as if he [or she] were the one sent. It is based on the Jewish principle of *shaliach*: "A man's representative is the man himself."[28] Hare emphasizes that the uniquely Christian principle in this case is the fact that even children, the poor, the "least of these," are also considered Christ's messengers, Christ's representatives, and thus Christ himself. Thus, the powerless and the needy also share the status of messenger. They have something to teach us about Christ and his mission. That is revolutionary!

Pagans who perform good deeds do not do so because they imitate God, or because they are atoning for their sins. Rather, such deeds indicate "a *relationship with Jesus*."[29] Thus, pagans who offer kindness to "such as these" are unconsciously in Christ's service. "They are anonymous Christians."[30] Pagans who offer hospitality to strangers, who receive all of Christ's ambassadors (missionaries, children, the poor, the marginalized and oppressed) with kindness, are already part of the reign of God and will be judged as sheep.

Proclaim the gospel again.

Sometimes we gain new insights when we hear the text after the interpretation has been given. Someone from the group proclaims the gospel a second time.

[28] *MI*, 290.

[29] Ibid., 291.

[30] Ibid.

Step 4
Testing

Conversation with the Liturgy and the Scriptures

Test your original understanding in dialogue with the text.

(You might consider breaking into smaller groups.)

Now that you've heard the exegesis, were there any new insights for you? How do you feel about it? How does your original understanding of this gospel compare with what we just shared? How does this story speak to your life?

Sharing Life Experience

Participants share an experience from their lives that connects with the biblical interpretation just shared.

> *Who are Christ's ambassadors in my life? Who are the obvious ones and who are not so obvious? Those who proclaim Christ crucified and risen are the obvious ones, but there are so many opposing voices in the church today. How do I know which ones are the authentic ambassadors of Christ? Today's gospel helps me discern the answer: those who come in humility and in poverty; those who have no axe to grind, but simply profess the Christ they know and love; those who are child-like in their faith; those who know the ravages of poverty in body, soul, and spirit; and those who not only preach the gospel, but live it. These are the ambassadors I am to recognize and the ones to whom I am to extend hospitality. I am to question those whose first fruits are hate-filled and divisive. How can that be the word of the living God?*
>
> *Today's liturgy invites me to find Christ in the most unexpected people and places. Even though Catholic truths find a place on many people's agendas on both sides of the religiously political spectrum, today's gospel is an invitation to break down the agendas and experience such truths in the lived reality of Christ present and active in the lives of faith-filled Christian men and women. When someone offers hospitality even to the world's "undeserving poor," and that same person extends hospitality to all, no matter what their religious politics, and*

treats everyone with human dignity, I know I am in the presence of Christ's ambassador. I know that Christ the King reigns. Today's gospel reminds me that when I encounter the poor and the oppressed in my midst, I see the face of Christ. I am also reminded of his unconditional love for all of us. The poor and the oppressed are Christ's ambassadors to me. I can do no less than to be responsive to them if I want to be part of the reign of Christ the King.

When Christ's messengers are treated with scorn, mistrust, and suspicion because they do not follow a particular way of thinking and believing, they are the ones spoken of in today's gospel as deserving the word of encouragement. A friend of mine belongs to a parish in a large city that invited a nationally-known speaker to come and do a parish mission. His was a strong message of justice based on the biblical imperative to love. He was judged by some before he ever arrived as not being "orthodox." He bent over backward to extend love and an understanding spirit to those who had been maligning him. He understood that their ill feeling was a result of a great deal of misinformation and lack of communication. He reached out to them and tried to offer reconciliation but they would have none of it. Their minds were set. They were sure they were right—he was a heretic!

There was nothing in this man's presentation that was unorthodox. He was, in fact, a powerful, honest, prophetic ambassador of Christ's love and mission. Yet he was rejected by some who were certain that they had indeed already been separated from the goats and appropriately were standing in the line of honor—the line marked "sheep." It is a powerful warning to us all. Perhaps we think we are sheep when in truth we have "goat" written all over us.

There is a caution in today's gospel. It behooves us to discern carefully. Very often the word of God comes to us from people and places from which we would least expect it to come. The challenge of the gospel is to be ready to accept it, even when it comes from one of the "least of these."

I remember, when I was presenting a workshop in another city, I shared a story of the healing power of Christ in an event in my life. One man had been purportedly teasing me all week long. It was not until later in the week that I realized that his teasing remarks were intended, though veiled, to be demeaning and sarcastic editorial comments. I was angry with myself for being so naive! I felt hurt and vulnerable. Today's gospel always brings me back to that experience. Sometimes when we share the good news of Christ in our lives we are treated with anything but hospitality.

The gospel challenges me to be strong when I am rejected, but also to be very careful lest I falsely reject others. I may be rejecting an ambassador of Christ. I must pay close attention when I feel uncomfortable, however. It could very well mean that Christ is trying to shout a word of truth to me that I am unwilling to hear. If I am to live and promote the reign of Christ I must become empty in order to recognize him in the circumstances of my life and ministry.

All share their life experience.

What interpretation touched you the most? In what way are you most challenged by that interpretation? What was Matthew's primary concern in this gospel? In what way does this gospel challenge your community today? How does today's liturgy/readings invite you to change? Can you name several ways to understand or interpret this gospel and how they might apply to you or your community? In what way are the biblical themes of covenant, exodus, creation, and community evident in today's readings? Do you still feel the same way about this text as when you began? Has your original understanding been stretched, challenged, or affirmed?

STEP 5
DECISION

The gospel demands a response.

In what specific way might your parish be invited to respond? Are there any attitudes or behaviors you would like to change as a result of today's conversation? What one concrete action will you take this week as a response to the liturgy today?

Pastoral Considerations: What is the most pressing need in your community at this time in terms of furthering the reign of Christ in your midst? How are you falling short? Who are the ambassadors of Christ in your midst that you fail to recognize? What needs to happen in order to address these issues?

Christian Initiation: The Feast of Christ the King strongly echoes the fullness of the Easter Vigil. Christ's sovereignty over all creation through his life, death, resurrection, and ascension into heaven, and the coming of his Spirit, finds concrete expression in the passage of the elect through the waters of new birth from death to new life in baptism. The newly baptized died to the old self to rise again with Christ, the Lord and Ruler of their lives. Thus, the feast of Christ the King might be an appropriate time to baptize infants and those unable to be baptized at the Easter Vigil.[31] It might also be an occasion to celebrate a Rite of Acceptance/Welcome, or a Rite of Reception into Full Communion of the Catholic Church, where needed.

DOCTRINAL ISSUES

What church truth/teaching/doctrinal issue could be drawn from the gospel for the Feast of Christ the King?

Participants suggest possible doctrinal themes that flow from the readings.

Possible Doctrinal Themes

Eschatology, final judgment, heaven, hell, cost of discipleship, evangelization, mission, human dignity of all persons, the Body of Christ, apostles, paschal mystery

Present the doctrinal material at this time.

1. The facilitator gives input on a particular doctrinal issue of his or her prior choosing. OR
2. The group chooses a doctrinal issue from the list they created. They read together from the Doctrinal Appendix.

(The doctrinal issues are found in the Doctrinal Appendix in the back of this workbook. If you are choosing an issue from this resource, please refer to it now.)

Reflection questions centered around the chosen doctrinal theme can be found at the end of each topic in the Doctrinal Appendix. The questions are based on the five-step reflection process. If you choose a topic not included in the Doctrinal Appendix, craft your own questions according to the same five-step process.

Following the reflection questions you will be reminded to return to chapter 7, "Preparing the Catechetical Session," to assist you in crafting your own session.

Closing Prayer

You believe that the Son of God once came to us;
you look for him to come again.
May his coming bring you the light of his holiness
and free you with his blessing.
(Amen.)

May God make you steadfast in faith,
joyful in hope, and untiring in love
all the days of your life.
(Amen.)

You rejoice that our Redeemer came to live with us as man.
When he comes again in glory,
may he reward you with endless life.
(Amen.)[32]

[31]For example, fully catechized unbaptized persons (such as spouses who have attended weekly liturgy for years) might fall into this category. Since there would be no need to delay their initiation any longer, they could be initiated on this feast. The Easter Vigil remains the church's premier time for adults to celebrate baptism, confirmation, and eucharist, however. (See *RCIA,* Part II: "Christian Initiation of Adults in Exceptional Circumstances.")

[32]"Advent Solemn Blessing," *The Sacramentary.*

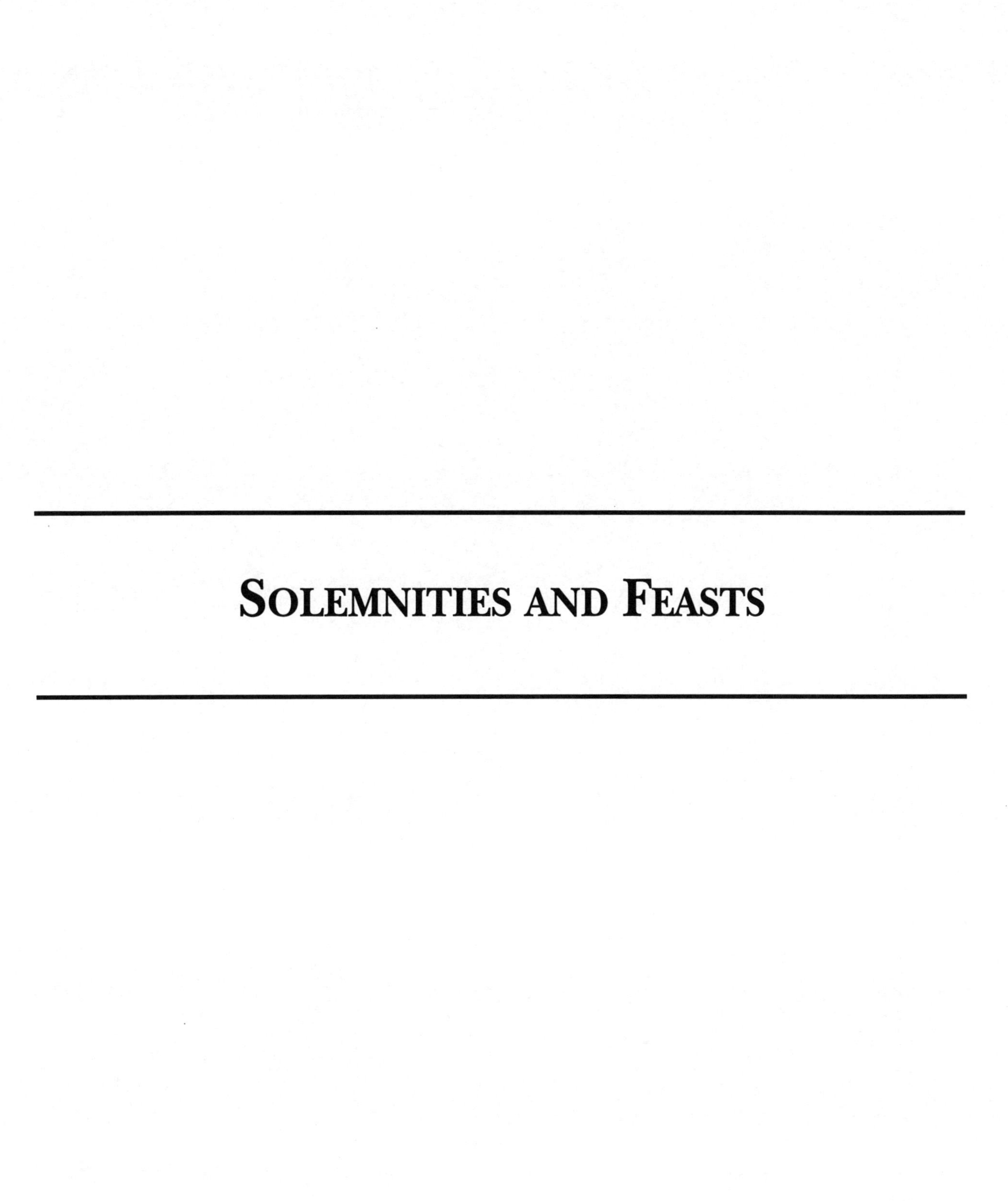

SOLEMNITIES AND FEASTS

Environment

We have just left the pinnacle season of the church year. One almost needs time to catch one's breath. It almost seems anticlimactic to go from the festive whites and golds of Easter, the red of Pentecost, to the simplicity of green with instant abruptness. But move we must. Trinity Sunday and Corpus Christi give us two opportunities to slowly ease into the ripened green of summer Ordinary Time. We are not, however, to assume that the Easter season is extended for two more weeks. Ordinary Time has definitely begun. The liturgical color of these two solemnities is white, even though Ordinary Time has returned. The profound nature of the two feasts, God's sacramental expression of love, calls for highlighted attention.

Perhaps one way to return to the longest season of the year is to replace any remaining festal flowers of the Easter season with the simple green plants. What better plant to begin with on this feast than the shamrock, natures own hint of the Triune God? Without verbiage, its placement in the catechetical environment is a simple reminder that all creation praises the Creator. Perhaps the stark simplicity of a white cloth adorned with nothing but the shamrock and the nearby enthronement of the scriptures would be all that is needed to capture a sense of the feast and movement into a new season.

INTRODUCTORY RITES

Opening Song (or Entrance Antiphon)

Blessed be God the Father and his only begotten Son and the Holy Spirit: for he has shown that he loves us.[1]

Opening Prayer

The facilitator of the session may lead the prayer. Others in the group may be asked to proclaim the readings.

[1]Trinity Sunday: "Entrance Antiphon," *The Sacramentary.*

Let us pray
[to the one God, Father, Son, and Spirit,
that our lives may bear witness to our faith]

Pause for silent prayer.

Father,
you sent your Word to bring us truth
and your Spirit to make us holy.
Through them we come to know the mystery of your life.
Help us to worship you, One God in three Persons,
by proclaiming and living our faith in you.
We ask this through our Lord Jesus Christ, your Son,
who lives and reigns with you and the Holy Spirit,
one God, for ever and ever.[2]

LITURGY OF THE WORD

Let us listen to God's word.

The readings are proclaimed.

First Reading[3]
Exodus 34:4–6, 8–9

God was known to Israel by the way in which God acted in its history. God was the God of salvation history. God was not a disinterested deity who ruled from a lofty perch. God was involved in human affairs and desired an intimate relationship with human beings. Thus, God is known through what God does. This is one reason why God was always referred to by his actions: "The

[2]Trinity Sunday: "Opening Prayer," *The Sacramentary.*

[3]The exegesis for the first and second readings may or may not be the focus of your group's reflection as there may only be time to give adequate attention to the gospel, your primary concern. However, the exegesis is included here in order to provide a thorough investigation of the entire liturgy of the word, as there may be parts (or all) that would be necessary to the direction you wish to take with your particular ministry group.

One who parted the waters and delivered the people out of bondage . . . ," etc.

The Exodus was the premier action in the life and history of Israel. God was in covenant relationship with Israel. God promised to be with the people and to care for them, providing for their needs. In response, the people were to love the Lord their God with their heart, mind, and soul and to love and care for one another. God kept God's part of the bargain when he delivered Israel out of bondage and led the people through the desert to the promised land. Moses was the spokesman for God in this covenant arrangement.

God revealed to Moses the depths and the limits of humanity's perception and understanding of God. Full knowledge of God is beyond human capacity. Only God can reveal God. Similarly, only God can reveal the depths of the mystery of the Trinity. Thus, today's reading from Exodus is most appropriate for our reflection on Trinity Sunday.

God took the initiative to speak to Moses. God speaks to whomever God chooses to speak. God cannot be manipulated or controlled by human machinations. God is known as the *One who delivered the people out of bondage.* God is slow to anger and rich in mercy. It is of God's essence to love and care for God's people. God is the transcendent Other—the Unknowable. God's mystery can never be fully known. In order to keep Yahweh's name from profanation, Israel forbade the use of the name "God." "Lord," "Holy," "Most High," "Father in Heaven," "Presence," "Power," "the Word"—all are names ascribed to God. "God" was not to be uttered; it was too sacred.

God is invoked by calling to mind God's attributes or God's grace. God is powerful, almighty, merciful, forgiving, just, and loving. God desires the salvation of all people. At the beginning of Yom Kippur, after confessing their sins, every Jewish assembly "implores God's grace: 'Our Father, our King, forgive us and listen to us. We do few good works, so give us your love, your kindness, and save us.'"[4] The Christian community asks the same thing at the beginning of each eucharistic liturgy. It is the faith and hope of all believers.

[4] *DL* (VII), 9.

God manifests God's power by the continual process of transforming humanity. Moses' prayer of humble submission is the prayer of all believers for all time. The unutterable name of God resounds in our hearts. God is ineffable and God's mystery is never to be fully plumbed. There are no words that capture God's imposing reality. Everything that seeks to capture God's essence is limited. One must spend a lifetime tasting and experiencing the fruit of God's essence. Such is the mystery of God; such is the mystery of the Trinity.

The Trinitarian doctrine is not explicitly expressed in the Old Testament. However, scholars do admit to a "triadic character in the manner in which humanity experienced God."[5] God is always in the process of self-revelation to the world. God reveals godself and human beings respond to God's revelation. The pattern of *revelation followed by human response* is common throughout scriptures. God gifts human beings with the ability to know him and thereby respond to his gift with faith. Reginald Fuller defines the triadic pattern thus: 1. Yahweh in his own essential being; 2. Yahweh going out of himself in self-communication; 3. Yahweh creating within the heart of Moses the response to this self-revelation.[6]

God appeared to Moses on Mount Sinai in a cloud. God proclaimed God's mercy and faithfulness and renewed his covenant relationship with a sinful Israel. God continues that same relationship with humanity through the Christ event.

Responsorial Psalm
Daniel 3:52, 53, 54, 55, 56

Today's psalm is taken from the canticle in the Book of Daniel of the three young men who endured the fiery flames in Nebuchadnezzar's furnace. The second part of the psalm is taken from a different canticle. The canticle is in the same style of the liturgical language used in the Old Testament psalms. It is chosen for its connection with the "name of God" in the first reading. When we sing of God's name we are to remember that for Christians it is the Triune God of whom we sing—Father, Son, and Spirit.

[5] *WWC*, 110.
[6] *PL*, 101.

Second Reading
2 Corinthians 13:11–13

The letters from Paul were intended to be read at the gathering of the Christian assembly. This reading makes that intention obvious as it is an evident lead-in to the celebration of the eucharist. The community is exhorted to be at peace with one another and, as a sign, to exchange a holy kiss (which at one time took place before the canon, not after it).

Paul deliberately used the triadic formula in this portion of his letter to the Corinthians. However, he does not simply make a statement of belief or theology of Trinity. He is liturgically expressing the lived, graced experience of the risen Christ within the Christian community: "The grace of Christ, the love of God, and the *fellowship* (*koinonia*) of the Holy Spirit. It speaks of grace, love and fellowship. The order—Son, Father, and Spirit—is striking and again reflects the order of Christian experience."[7] We experience the love of God through the paschal mystery of Christ that leads to our incorporation in his Spirit-led, redeemed community.

Gospel[8]
John 3:16–18

STEP 1
NAMING ONE'S EXPERIENCE

What were your first impressions? What was your first response to the gospel (or the other readings)?[9] What captured your attention?

[7]Ibid., 103.

[8]The gospel exegesis is provided later in this session so that it may be presented in the proper sequence where it occurs in the adult five-step reflection process. The exegesis is provided for the first and second readings for your information and edification, and for you to use at your discretion. Once again, the gospel is the primary source of reflection. If there is time for reflection on the other readings, all the better.

[9]The primary focus of reflection is the gospel. However, very often the other readings demand attention and must be brought into the dialogue.

Each person names his or her initial impression. Statements should be brief. No reasons should be given at this time. All simply listen without agreeing or disagreeing.

STEP 2
UNDERSTANDING

In a brief statement, what do you think this gospel is trying to convey?

STEP 3
INPUT FROM VISION/STORY/TRADITION

Liturgical Context[10]

Trinity Sunday is one of the four solemnities of the Lord during Ordinary Time. Since these feasts are dependent upon the celebration of Easter, they are called moveable solemnities of Ordinary Time. The solemnities are Trinity Sunday, Corpus Christi, Sacred Heart, and Christ the King.

Adolf Adam calls them feasts of devotion and feasts of ideas. As feasts of devotion they are expressions of piety born in response to an internal or external trial. As idea feasts, each one extols a particular truth or specific aspect of the mystery of Christ. By stressing these truths or mysteries, the church hoped to renew and strengthen the faith of God's people.

The Arian controversies of the fourth and fifth centuries gave rise to a strong emphasis on and devotion to the Trinity in Spain and Gaul. Arius, a priest in Alexandria who died in 336, denied the divinity of Christ. As a result, faith in God, the Father, Son, and Holy Spirit, and the equality of the Three Divine Persons was threatened. The Councils of Nicea and Constantinople (381) condemned the heresy and formulated the Nicene Creed, the profession of faith recited at every Sunday Mass.

[10]The scriptures in the Lectionary, the seasons of the year, and the ritual prayers of the mass are interrelated and form the basis for liturgical catechesis. The *liturgical context* attempts to explore and clarify the themes and this interrelatedness.

The heresy had an impact on Catholic faith and life. Preaching sought to strengthen faith in the church's doctrine regarding the Trinity. The first preface of the Trinity found its way into the liturgy in the 400s as this feast was born out of controversy. The modern preface of the Trinity appeared during the eighth century. By 800 the Mass of the Trinity was celebrated as a votive Mass for Sundays. All Sunday liturgies became more trinitarian in focus. By the year 1000 the feast of the Trinity was celebrated on the Sunday after Pentecost in Frankish and Gallic monasteries. The feast reminds the faithful of what it means when we refer to the Father, Son, and Spirit: We believe in three divine persons in one God.

In the year 1077 Pope Alexander challenged a special feast devoted to just the Trinity. The Pope's contention was that Trinity is remembered and celebrated every Sunday, even every day. One hundred years later Alexander III said the same thing. However, the feast continued to exist. John XXII made it an official feast during the exile in Avignon in 1334. Adam suggests that the placement of this feast on the Sunday after Pentecost served as a mirror to reflect back on the mystery of salvation just culminated with the celebration of Pentecost.

The feast celebrates a lofty abstract dogma that seems unrelated to our everyday lives. The overall context for approaching this feast, then, is best found in the following exhortation: "The feast is only a feast if we follow the lead of the assigned scriptures and acclaim a God of love, not dissect an arcane theological treatise."[11]

The liturgy for Trinity Sunday has assigned to it three different readings and responsorial psalms for the three-year cycle. The gospel for cycle A is taken from John's gospel. God willed the salvation of the world by sending his only Son. The Hebrew scriptures herald the God who has revealed godself to us personally through God's divine action in the world. The human race knows God through the ways in which God has acted in history. One of those actions is proclaimed in today's reading from Exodus. God revealed godself to Moses. Paul's letter to the Corinthians expresses a very early liturgical formula in which the Trinity is proclaimed and professed. The heart of today's liturgy resides in the statement: "God does not prove himself; he shows himself."[12] There is no proof for the existence of the Trinity. We know the Trinity through the action of God in Christ continued in and through the Spirit.

The alleluia verse is one grand summation and doxology in praise of the One, Triune God: "Glory to the Father, the Son and the Holy Spirit: to God who has been given to us." The Opening Prayer asks that the Father help us pray to the One God in Three Persons by living and proclaiming our faith. "One hears criticism about this feast because it commemorates not an event but a Christian doctrine. However, the opening prayer blends both event and doctrine: Belief in the Trinity leads us to the life of the Father by experiencing the truth revealed by Jesus and the holiness of the Spirit."[13]

All liturgy professes belief in the Triune God. Never is there a liturgical celebration in which the power of the Trinity is not invoked. The Sunday assembly professes faith in the Triune God when it begins every gathering with "The grace of our Lord Jesus Christ and the love of God and the fellowship of the Holy Spirit be with you all."[14] "Celebrated on the Sunday after Pentecost, it [the feast of the Trinity] is a great doxology to the Father who raised his Son and brought him into the glory where he reigns with the Holy Spirit he has sent to us. When the sequence of the Sundays in Ordinary Time is about to begin again, this feast sheds light on the face and true nature of Jesus, the Son of God, who, by his teaching and his acts, reveals the Father and leads humankind to himself in the Spirit."[15]

If we were to say that there is a bottom line in this liturgy, it can be summed up in these words from the entrance antiphon: Blessed be God the Father

[11]Bishops Committee on the Liturgy Secretariat, National Conference of Catholic Bishops, *Study Text 9: The Liturgical Year Celebrating the Mystery of Christ and His Saints* (Washington: USCC, 1984), 60.

[12]*DL* (VII), 10.

[13]Stephen T. Jarrell, *Guide to the Sacramentary* (Chicago: Liturgical Training Publications, 1983), 74.

[14]"Greeting-Order of Mass," *The Sacramentary.*

[15]*DL* (VII), 7.

and his only begotten Son and the Holy Spirit: *for he has shown that he loves us.*

Gospel Exegesis

The facilitator gives input regarding what critical biblical scholarship has to say about this text. The input includes insights as to how people would have heard the gospel in Jesus' time.

The scene: a courtroom. The players: John, Jesus, disciples and entourage. Such is the stage of John's gospel. It reads like a first-century Perry Mason episode. Skillfully the protagonists and antagonists weave their respective cases. An overarching question starts the first scene. John is asked: "Who are you?" John answers the question by attesting to *who he is not*! The question serves as the focus for the rest of the unfolding drama that attempts to answer it—not in relation to John, however, but in relation to Jesus. "Just who are you?" Today's pericope not only answers the question but also serves as the summation and closing argument for the entire gospel: This is who Jesus is, and this is the evidence by which we can make that assertion. Today's pericope is a concise summary of John's entire gospel.

It comes from a three-part section which asserts that Jesus' death and resurrection prompted a new birth in the Holy Spirit. This portion of the gospel follows dialogue that obviously questioned Jesus' legitimate authority and his miracles. John's abundant use of legal terminology betrays the polemic stance of the gospel. "The fourth evangelist's use of the language of the courtroom sharply distinguishes his story from those of the earlier evangelists, Matthew, Mark and Luke."[16]

In order to appreciate the context for this gospel it is necessary to understand the locus for its proclamation. It was written around 90 C.E. Judaism had already suffered the destruction of the Temple around 70 C.E. By the time this gospel was written, the cultic practice of the Temple had extended to the synagogue and the home. "What remained as a symbol of their ethnic and religious identity was their tradition, embodied in the Scriptures and the synagogue service, which focused on the reading of the Law."[17] After the destruction of the Temple, Pharisaic Jews gathered at Jabneh to address and safeguard their ethnic and ritual purity. The Jewish canon of scriptures was established as well as the ritual demand to pray eighteen benedictions each day (one of which was believed to be a curse directed against the Christians). The benediction denounced heretics and slanderers. If Christians refused to pray the benediction, thus cursing themselves, they would be suspected of heresy and expelled from the synagogue. Because of their confession of faith in Jesus Christ, they were subjected to rejection, suspicion, and expulsion from the Jewish community. In a country in which Judaism was acknowledged as a religion with a legal right to exist and Christianity was not, such expulsion had serious ramifications. In addition to the troubles between Christians and the leadership of the Jewish community, the gospel also addresses the errors of other quasi-Christian sects that broke away, forming their own hybrid theology. The juridical stance of the gospel, then, comes out of those religious tensions experienced by the first-century Johannine community. "Similarly, the existence of local controversies with the proponents of Jewish orthodoxy probably explains why the Fourth Gospel fairly breathes the atmosphere of the courtroom."[18]

Examination of today's gospel must begin by referring to earlier scenes. When Jesus overturned the Temple money-changers he prophetically and profoundly repudiated a foundational religious observance in Judaism. The money-changers were present in the temple area to provide the necessary change for people to pay their pledge to the Temple so that "public offerings might be made that atone for Israel's sins—after analogy with practice in the wilderness (Exod 30:16)."[19] The money-changers were an integral part of that system. Jesus' action called the actual practice (atonement for sins), and thus the entire system, into question. Jesus' act denounced the primary ritual experience of Judaism: "The overturning of the money-changers' tables represents an act of rejection of the most important rite of the Israelite

[16]*JHW*, 15.

[17]Ibid., 16.

[18]Ibid., 18.

[19]*RJ*, 96.

cult, the daily whole offering."[20] Jesus' action signaled the rejection of prior Temple worship and the replacement of that Temple system with something new. One can imagine why this was a cause for great consternation among Jews and even Jewish Christians. The obvious question hung like a pall over the air: "By what authority do you have the right to render our sacrifices impossible?" A modern-day corollary would be if someone were to come to the fore today and repudiate our celebration of the eucharist and take steps to thwart its observance!

Jesus responded to the Jewish leaders by appealing to his future resurrection. His resurrection from the dead is all the authority he needs. It was only after the resurrection that the disciples would remember and understand what Jesus had said. However, in the next section of the gospel, Jesus provides further clarity.

In chapter two of John (vs. 18), the Jews asked for a sign to legitimate Jesus' mission. Jesus does not regard this request favorably even though many did believe in him because of his signs. Jesus could read their hearts. What would it take for people to accept and know Jesus' true identity? In the verses directly preceding this pericope, Nicodemus asserts that Jesus performed such signs because God was with him. Nicodemus was part of the crowd who believed *because of* Jesus' signs. Such people were often of the ilk who believed that miracles, signs, and wonders were an automatic divine legitimation of an individual. That assertion, however, selectively forgets the story of how the Egyptians were able to perform signs and wonders (similar to those of Moses) at Pharaoh's court. Signs and wonders in and of themselves do not insure God's presence or activity. John's vision of the first and second beasts drives home a similar point in the Book of Revelation. The first beast made the people worship the second beast because of the deceptive signs and wonders he performed. Signs can deceive.[21]

Thus, Jesus presented the Jews with his resurrection—not his miracles—as his legitimization. Jesus suggests to Nicodemus a different source of authority—a new birth. It is only through new birth in the Spirit that a person is able to recognize God in and through Jesus. Jesus based his argument to Nicodemus on a commonly known Greco-Roman philosophical assertion that "like is known by like."[22] Only when one is born again by the Spirit and *thus elevated to divine status* is one able to know, see, and understand the divine (Christian belief asserts that through his ascension, and once glorified, Christ elevated human nature to the status of divine). The reason for our new birth into God's divine life is so we might encounter God: because *like can only be known by like.* Our newly-acquired divine status makes it possible for us to know the divine. Nicodemus is confused and asks how someone can enter a mother's womb a second time to be reborn. Jesus asserts that it is not a physical rebirth, but a rebirth through water and the Spirit (translated: *water that is the Spirit*), that one is born anew. A person must be born of the Spirit *before* it

[20] Ibid.

[21] ***John's perspective on miracles/signs.*** A momentary diversion is in order at this juncture in the dialogue. Much of John's gospel is intent on authenticating Jesus' identity. His miracles play a key role in that discussion. The scriptures provide us with various perspectives regarding Jesus' miracles. Luke/Acts proposes a positive view of Jesus' miracles. In Luke's gospel and in the Acts of the Apostles, Jesus' miracles are the impetus for faith (Lk 4:31–5:11). The disciples' miracles proclaim and promote the growth of the faith (Acts 3:1–4, 4, 5:12–14, 8:6–8, 13:4–12). Mark's view is not as positive as Luke/Acts. He reflects a negative perspective. Mark reminds us that Jesus' miracles are not accepted by everyone. He reminds us that our faith is not to be completely based on Christ's miracles, but also on the power of the cross (Mk 8:14–21, 22–26, 27–31). John's gospel posits a complex multivalent understanding of Jesus' miracles, called signs. They sometimes elicit faith (4:53, 10:41–42, 11:45, 47–48, 14:11). Not everyone believes in Jesus because of his miracles. Signs are often ambiguous (10:25–26, 11:45–48). Some people are interested in Jesus' miracles or signs simply for their own self interest (physical benefits, 6:26). Some see them as a threat to Israel's security (11:46–48). Some believe that Jesus' signs are not from God because his regular behavior does not conform to certain standards (9:16, 30, 34). Scripture anticipated the rejection of Jesus' signs (12:37–40). People who accept Jesus' signs often possess some initial faith (2:11; 4:46–54; 20:30–31; 21:6–7). Sometimes the contrary is true, however (2:23; 3:2; chap. 9; 11:45). If faith already exists, Jesus' miracles strengthen and deepen it (2:11; 4:46–54; 20:30–31). The early Christian community believed that they shared Jesus' power and thus were agents of his miracles-working activity. John's community believed that they were agents of Jesus' signs continued in the life of the community. However, the miracles, in and of themselves, do not authenticate Jesus' mission. (*RJ*, 103–104)

[22] Ibid., 98.

is possible to enter into the reign of God. Thus, Jesus establishes two criteria for determining his legitimate authority: his resurrection and his followers' rebirth in the Spirit.

How then, does this new birth take place? This questions leads us into today's actual pericope, which can only be understood in the context of all the verses that came before it. The new birth does not transpire by human design. Human beings are not transported into heaven to encounter the divine by their own mystical power.[23] New birth in the Spirit occurs because "heaven was wedded to earth" and Jesus, Son of Man, came down to earth and revealed the face of God. Only through the Christ-event is it possible for human beings to be reborn in the Spirit.

Verses 14–15 of this chapter center on Jesus' ascent into heaven—his resurrection—as the ultimate saving event. "Being lifted up" refers to Jesus' being "lifted up on the cross and being lifted up into heaven. In Jesus' return to his Father, the cross is the first step on the ladder of the ascension."[24] Verse 16 and following (today's gospel) center on Jesus' descent to earth and the salvation that was wrought because of it. Ultimately, then, God sent Jesus, his Son, to earth because God loves human beings. Those who continue to believe in the Son are assured of eternal life. The phrase "God *gave* his Son" is a reference to the Incarnation in its entirety—the entire paschal mystery. Jesus lived, suffered, died, rose from the dead, sent his Spirit to continue his saving mission, and will return again—all for the salvation of the world. It is for this purpose that God *gave* his Son. Jesus represents, embodies, and accomplishes God's ultimate plan—to save the world, not to condemn it.

However, not all will believe, so there is judgment (separation) involved. Human beings are given free will and thus have the power to choose. They will choose either to accept or reject God. Those who reject God will be judged accordingly.

> Evil is darkness; with Jesus, the light has come into the darkness. But the darkness will not receive it, and this very refusal constitutes judgment (theology, too, tells us that in condemning to hell God is simply accepting people's state of will at their death; they have turned away from God and God leaves them to their fate).[25]

Jesus has the power to suspend Temple sacrifices because he offers a new worship—a worship in the Spirit. John drives home the point in seven different episodes that Christian worship is the new worship in the Spirit and is rooted in what Jesus said and did through the paschal mystery. Also, "...we should notice that Jesus, in stressing the necessity of spiritual rebirth, has negated the importance of natural birth into the Chosen People; another pillar of Judaism has been replaced."[26]

The bottom line for John is that only through the Incarnation—Christ's becoming human and dying, rising, and ascending to the throne of glory—are we able to be born anew in the Spirit. It is a free gift—we have no mystical powers that can attain it on our own. We must only accept it and live our lives accordingly.

Proclaim the gospel again.

Sometimes we gain new insights when we hear the text after the interpretation has been given. Someone from the group proclaims the gospel a second time.

Step 4
Testing

Conversation with the Liturgy and the Scriptures

Test your original understanding in dialogue with the text.

(You might consider breaking into smaller groups.)

[23] During the time of the Johannine community, there was a fringe group that insisted that they received direct revelation from the Spirit without the intervention of Christ. This chapter in John's gospel also addresses that error and insists that no one on his or her own merit can ascend into heaven to encounter God. Jesus became a human being and walked the earth with human beings. Through his incarnation God became truly known and experienced by humanity.

[24] *GEJ*, 33.

[25] Ibid., 34.

[26] Ibid.

Now that you've heard the exegesis, were there any new insights for you? How do you feel about it? How does your original understanding of this gospel compare with what we just shared? How does this story speak to your life?

Sharing Life Experience

Participants share an experience from their lives that connects with the biblical interpretation just shared.

> *It is somewhat easy to accept Jesus Christ midst the flashy show of signs and wonders. Who would not marvel at God's awesome power at the sight of a loved one, popping up from eternity's permanent slumber, to unbind the death wrappings and take to the streets in raptured joy? It is easy to become addicted to such signs. Without the consolation of signs we often lose heart, lose our way, and ultimately our primary goal—abundant life in Christ. We thirst for the signs instead of that which the signs reveal. We are a people who hunger for miracles. Often our search for them leads us to membership in the exclusive "1000 Club" (Those Who have Witnessed Over a Thousand Miracles). It is easy to look for the miracle and miss the truth. Jesus invited conversion—complete metanoia. He invited us to embrace the "God-Who-Christ-Was-and-Is." The miracle that changed the world forever was the miracle of the cross, resurrection, ascension, and sending of the Spirit. Through that miracle which comes down to us from the realm of glory, we share a piece of God's divinity. Christ–God–Spirit lives within us. We, in turn, are empowered to live, die, rise, ascend, and live in the Spirit for others, just as Jesus did for us.*
>
> *On this feast of the Trinity, the feast that celebrates our life in the fullness of God, I am reminded of the precious baby in our community who lingers at eternity's portal. To the baby, the entrance beckons in eager anticipation. To its mommy, daddy, family, and friends, it remains in shadows that provide momentary glimpses of the grief that awaits, once that threshold has been crossed.*
>
> *We have summoned the hounds of heaven begging for a Lazarus sign (not today's gospel, but one of the "signs" in John's gospel). And that is precisely what we were supposed to do. The real miracle in this story, however, is that it is exactly what we received. This baby will die—Lazarus died a second time—but today's gospel proclaims the hope this family clings to. Jesus came to earth, walked in our shoes, and knows well the pain of death. It is not forever. Jesus came down so we could go up. The divine life that has been given to this mother and father shows itself in their trust and acceptance of God's love, and in their gratitude for the gift of this baby's life—short though it may be. They do not see God as destroyer. Yes, they would give their lives for their child to be restored to health. But the Christ-Spirit within them has given them the power to see other miracles sprouting like a seed in the womb of their present moment. They are expecting another child. Life and Death reside at the same altar in this family's home.*
>
> *Another miracle for them resides in their own faith. The separation they will know by their baby's death will never break the bonds of love they have forged. Only with eyes of faith are they able to see that miracle. Death will not have the final word. Hope reigns eternal in their hearts—not despair. Herein lies the sign, the miracle, of their story.*
>
> *Our community has been privileged to witness the power, the face, and the revelation of a merciful Father who welcomes this tiny child into joy no mortal can comprehend; the merciful Son whose tears flow with ours into one river of hope; and the life-giving Spirit who sustains us until that final day of jubilant reunion. The life, faith, doubts, grief, anxiety, prayers, and hope of this young family have gifted all of us with a taste of the feast that awaits us. I know the baby's parents would cross the Sahara on foot without water if only they could receive the sign they first stormed the heavens to receive. Yet, God's face—the self-revelation of Father, Son, and Spirit, has transported them and us to new depths that will continue to reveal joy in sorrow, power in weakness, and Love Incarnate's life-giving legacy. There are no words that adequately express such an ineffable mystery.*

All share their life experience.

What was John trying to tell his community? How is it a relevant word for your community today? Are there any circumstances that might benefit from the proclamation of today's gospel? In what way does this gospel challenge your community? Have you ever been in a position of "proving" the existence of God (or even the Trinity) to others? What did you say? What do you believe and why? In what way does this liturgy invite change in your life? How might this feast have any relevance for your everyday life? In what way are the biblical themes of covenant, exodus, creation, and community evident in today's readings? Do you still feel the same way about this text as when you began? Has your original understanding been stretched, challenged, or affirmed?

STEP 5
DECISION

The gospel demands a response.

In what specific way might your parish be invited to respond? Are there any attitudes or behaviors you would like to change as a result of today's conversation? What one concrete action will you take this week as a response to the liturgy today?

DOCTRINAL ISSUES

What church truth/teaching/doctrinal issue could be drawn from the gospel for Trinity Sunday?

Participants suggest possible doctrinal themes that flow from the readings.

Possible Doctrinal Themes

Trinity—Father, Son, and Holy Spirit, Christology, faith, creed, images of God, paschal mystery, conversion, miracles, grace, revelation

Present the doctrinal material at this time.

1. The facilitator gives input on a particular doctrinal issue of his or her prior choosing. OR
2. The group chooses a doctrinal issue from the list they created. They read together from the Doctrinal Appendix.

(The doctrinal issues are found in the Doctrinal Appendix in the back of this workbook. If you are choosing an issue from this resource, please refer to it now.)

Reflection questions centered around the chosen doctrinal theme can be found at the end of each topic in the Doctrinal Appendix. The questions are based on the five-step reflection process. If you choose a topic not included in the Doctrinal Appendix, craft your own questions according to the same five-step process.

Following the reflection questions you will be reminded to return to chapter 7, "Preparing the Catechetical Session," to assist you in crafting your own session.

Closing Prayer

The Lord be with you.
(And also with you.)
Lift up your hearts.
(We lift them up to the Lord.)
Let us give thanks to the Lord our God.
(It is right to give him thanks and praise.)
Father, all-powerful and ever-living God,
we do well always and everywhere to give you
thanks.
We joyfully proclaim our faith
in the mystery of your Godhead.
You have revealed your glory
as the glory also of your Son
and of the Holy Spirit:
three Persons equal in majesty,
undivided in splendor,
yet one Lord, one God,
ever to be adored in your everlasting glory.
And so, with all the choirs of angels in heaven
we proclaim your glory
and join in their unending hymn of praise:
Holy, holy, holy Lord, God of power and might,
heaven and earth are full of your glory.
Hosanna in the highest.
Blessed is he who comes in the name of the Lord.
Hosanna in the highest.[27]

[27]Trinity Sunday: "Preface," *The Sacramentary.*

Solemnity of the Body and Blood of Christ (Corpus Christi)

INTRODUCTORY RITES

Opening Song (or Entrance Antiphon)

The Lord fed his people with the finest wheat and honey; their hunger was satisfied. (Ps 80:17)[1]

Opening Prayer

The facilitator of the session may lead the prayer. Others in the group may be asked to proclaim the readings.

Let us pray
[to the Lord who gives himself in the Eucharist
that this sacrament may bring us salvation and
peace]

Lord Jesus Christ,
you gave us the Eucharist
as the memorial of your suffering and death.
May our worship of this sacrament of your body
and blood
help us to experience the salvation you won for us
and the peace of the kingdom
where you live with the Father and
the Holy Spirit,
one God, for ever and ever.[2]

Alternative Opening Prayer

Let us pray
[for the willingness to make present in our world
the love of Christ shown to us in the Eucharist]

Lord Jesus Christ,
we worship you living among us
in the sacrament of your body and blood.
May we offer to our Father in heaven
a solemn pledge of undivided love.
May we offer to our brothers and sisters
a life poured out in loving service of that kingdom
where you live with the Father and the Holy Spirit,
one God, for ever and ever.[3]

[1]Corpus Christi: "Entrance Antiphon," *The Sacramentary.*

[2]Corpus Christi: "Opening Prayer," *The Sacramentary.*

[3]Corpus Christi: "Alternative Opening Prayer," *The Sacramentary.*

LITURGY OF THE WORD

Let us listen to God's word.

The readings are proclaimed.

First Reading
Deuteronomy 8:2–3, 14–16

Today's pericope from Deuteronomy tells of a people lost in the wilderness and chronicles their difficulties, suffering, and trials as they sojourn through the desert. They were exposed to the elements and all the ravages of a harsh environment. They experienced hunger and thirst, poisonous insects, and fiery serpents. But God heard them and took care of them. God provided for their needs. God gave them water from the rock and manna from heaven. Paul connected the water and manna to the sacraments of baptism and eucharist in 1 Corinthians 10:1–4. John also picks up the same theme in the discourse on the bread of life proclaimed in today's gospel. The manna is understood in terms of eucharistic bread.

Responsorial Psalm
Psalm 147:12–13, 14–15, 19–20

This psalm is chosen for its connection with the first reading—the line of verse 14 which proclaims that God "fills us with finest wheat."

Second Reading
1 Corinthians 10:16–17

Some people wonder why the above-mentioned verses from 1 Corinthians that refer to the first reading were not chosen for today's second reading. In the first verse of today's pericope, Paul is believed to be quoting a traditional eucharistic formula.[4] He uses the Hebrew expression "we bless" (*berakah*), rather than his favored Greek expression meaning "to give thanks" (*eucharistein*). The words "participation in the body and blood" (*koinonia*) reflect a probable exegesis of the words

[4]*PL,* 105.

spoken over the bread and wine. Fuller asserts that *koinonia* refers to the saving event of Jesus' self–offering through his death. Through such *koinonia* we are able to partake of Christ's death, thereby participating in his paschal mystery. Paul's words reveal an explanation and interpretation of the ritual actions and words of the Last Supper.

Today's pericope is part of a longer section in which Paul addresses the issue of meat offered to pagan idols. The strong Christians are convinced that they can eat anything they want without being affected by it, unlike their scrupulous, weaker counterparts. Paul begins chapter 10 (1–4) with this issue in mind and exhorts the entire community to remember the Exodus and use it as an analogy for their own situation. The Israelites were baptized *into Moses* through the water of the sea and the cloud, and they were provided with food and drink. Paul warns the Corinthians that the Israelites were not immune from sin and temptation, rejection or death.[5] The reference in 1–4 to both sacraments is the only time in the New Testament that they are referred to together. The special food and drink that God provided was understood by Paul to be "God–given, divinely or supernaturally provided."[6]

Initially Paul agrees with those who say they are immune from the dangers of the food of the idols. He shifts, however, and refers to the Old Testament tradition that idols represent pagan gods and pagan demons and should not be taken lightly. Sharing from the one cup forms a bond—a *koinonia*—between Jesus and the community, just as Jewish (and pagan) sacrifices establish a bond between deity and humans. Thus, a person cannot be divided. He or she cannot eat or drink from the Lord's banquet, and the banquet of demons. God is jealous and desires our complete selves. Paul invokes the Corinthians' intelligence and calls attention to their eucharistic practice: the bread and cup they share is a sharing in Christ's body and blood. It is more explicitly stated: the spiritual food we eat is the body and blood of Jesus. The sharing of the bread from one loaf is not only a sharing in Christ's life—his body and blood—but also a communion with one another. "The eucharistic body creates the ecclesial body (cf. *Did. 9–4*)."[7] When we partake of the one cup, we partake in Christ's blood, thus making present Jesus' sacrifice on Calvary—the new covenant.

[5]C.P.M. Jones, "The Eucharist—The New Testament," *SL*, 190.

[6]Ibid.

Gospel
John 6:51–58

STEP 1
NAMING ONE'S EXPERIENCE

What were your first impressions? What was your first response to the gospel (or the other readings)?[8] What captured your attention?

Each person names his or her initial impression. Statements should be brief. No reasons should be given at this time. All simply listen without agreeing or disagreeing.

STEP 2
UNDERSTANDING

In a brief statement, what do you think this gospel is trying to convey?

STEP 3
INPUT FROM VISION/STORY/TRADITION

Liturgical Context

Prior to the ninth century there was no true worship of the eucharist outside of mass. Such worship began in about the eleventh century. It grew in accord with controversies regarding the "real presence" of Jesus in the sacrament. The controversies helped define eucharistic theology: "the Eucharist is really the Body and Blood of Christ, but under the sign—the sacrament—of bread and

[7]Ibid., 191.

[8]The primary focus of reflection is the gospel. However, very often the other readings demand attention and must be brought into the dialogue.

wine."[9] Controversies over the eucharist gave birth to eucharistic devotion.

The origin of this feast dates back to the twelfth century. During that time there was an "intense cult of the Blessed Sacrament that placed particular emphasis on the real presence of 'Christ whole and entire' in the consecrated bread."[10] This strong emphasis led to the desire *to see.* Thus, in 1220 in Paris, the practice of elevating the host began.

The feast originated largely due to the vision received by an Augustinian nun who saw a shining disk with a dark spot on it. She was told that the spot was there because there was no feast to commemorate the eucharist. Consequently the Bishop of Liege introduced the feast into his diocese in 1246. In 1264 Pope Urban IV established the feast for the entire church. In his presentation intended to explain the reasons for establishing the feast (*Bull Transiturus*—the document establishing the feast), the pope put forth a balanced theology of eucharist as sacrifice and meal. Some believe that Thomas Aquinas wrote the text for the mass and office. The feast did not spread very rapidly. However, Pope Clement V reintroduced it at the Council of Vienne in 1311–12.

Traditionally the feast was called "Feast of the Most Holy Body of Christ." The new Roman missal expanded the title to include the fullest understanding of the sacrament and to include the mystery of the "precious blood": "Solemnity of the Most Holy Body and Blood of Christ." However, popular usage has retained the Latin title, "Corpus Christi."

Corpus Christi is a duplication of the feast that already commemorates the sacrament of the eucharist: the day of its institution—Holy Thursday. Both feasts emphasize the redemptive effects of Jesus Christ. However, Adolph Adam insists that it is a defensible duplication, as Holy Thursday cannot quite enter into the fullness of festal joy as it is explicitly connected to Good Friday. Thus, a feast dedicated to the expression of joy in the eucharist as the "precious fruit and operative presence of the paschal mystery"[11] is certainly a laudable practice. Every Sunday celebrates the paschal mystery in its entirety in the celebration of eucharist. Notwithstanding, Adam asserts that "the objection of duplication has no place." [12]

St. Thomas Aquinas's influence is evident in the eucharistic theology woven through the presidential prayers of the proper of the mass. In his *Summa,* Thomas examines the importance of the eucharist in terms of past, present, and future. As a past reality it commemorates Jesus' sacrifice of passion, death, and resurrection. As a present reality it unites us with Christ and one another. As a future reality it anticipates "enjoyment of the divinity."

The liturgy reflects this past, present, and future understanding. The opening prayer touches the past remembrance: "You gave us the eucharist as the memorial of your suffering and death." The prayer over the gifts touches on the present reality: "Lord, may the bread and wine we offer bring your Church the unity and peace they signify." The concluding prayer connects us to the future hope: "May we come to possess it fully in the kingdom."

The Sequence, *Lauda, Sion, Salvatorem (Zion, praise your Savior)*, expresses classical eucharistic theology.

> Zion, praise your Savior. Praise your leader and shepherd in hymns and canticles. Praise him as much as you can, for he is beyond all praising and you will never be able to praise him as he merits.
>
> But today a theme worthy of particular praise is put before us—the living and life-giving bread that, without any doubt, was given to the Twelve at table during the holy supper.
>
> Therefore let our praise be full and resounding and our soul's rejoicing full of delight and beauty, for this is the festival day to commemorate the first institution of this table.

[9] *DL* (VII), 38.

[10] *LY,* 169.

[11] Ibid., 171.

[12] Ibid.

At this table of the new King, the new law's new Pasch puts an end to the old Pasch. The new displaces the old, reality the shadow and light the darkness. Christ wanted what he did at the supper to be repeated in his memory.

And so we, in accordance with his holy directions, consecrate bread and wine to be salvation's Victim. Christ's followers know by faith that bread is changed into his flesh and wine into his blood.

Man cannot understand this, cannot perceive it; but a lively faith affirms that the change, which is outside the natural course of things, takes place. Under the different species, which are now signs only and not their own reality, there lie hid wonderful realities. His body is our food, his blood our drink.

And yet Christ remains entire under each species. The communicant receives the complete Christ—uncut, unbroken and undivided. Whether one receives or a thousand, the one receives as much as the thousand. Nor is Christ diminished by being received.

The good and the wicked alike receive him, but with the unlike destiny of life or death. To the wicked it is death, but life to the good. See how different is the result, though each receives the same.

Last of all, if the sacrament is broken, have no doubt. Remember there is as much in a fragment as in an unbroken host. There is no division of the reality, but only a breaking of the sign; nor does the breaking diminish the condition or size of the One hidden under the sign.

Behold, the bread of angels is become the pilgrim's food; truly it is bread for the sons, and is not to be cast to dogs. It was prefigured in type when Isaac was brought as an offering, when a lamb was appointed for the Pasch and when manna was given to the Jews of old.

Jesus, good shepherd and true bread, have mercy on us; feed us and guard us. Grant that we find happiness in the land of the living. You know all things, can do all things, and feed us here on earth. Make us your guests in heaven, co-heirs with you and companions of heaven's citizens. Amen. Alleluia.[13]

The Earliest Celebration of the Eucharist: Weaving together all the elements of chapters ten and eleven in 1 Corinthians, we are able to "sketch the rite of the Lord's Supper as Paul had introduced it at Corinth and as he wished it to be maintained."[14] The Supper should not begin until all are gathered. "It is a real meal, to which the well-off contribute food and drink. It opens with the customary Jewish blessing of God over the bread, which is then broken in pieces and distributed to all, probably with the words of interpretation of distribution identifying the bread as the Body of Christ (11:24). By this gathering it is constituted as the ecclesial Body of Christ (10:17). The meal continues, and at the end 'the cup of blessing' is produced and the thanksgiving is said before all drink of it. It would seem that during the thanksgiving the death of the Lord, the risen, victorious, ever-present Lord of the community, is *proclaimed* 'until he come' (11:26). The action is not an acted parable that needs no explanation. It needs a verbal proclamation, for which there is no satisfactory antecedent in Jewish tradition other than the extended thanksgiving after the meal, the *birkat ha-mazon.* The content of this thanksgiving and proclamation might have been the recalling of the wonderful words of God in creation, election, and providence, and now in his Son and all he has done though his death and resurrection. In this way the whole eucharistic action is performed 'for my memorial *(anamnesis), because*... you proclaim....' Thus the memorial is raised to God through the thanksgiving of those who are mindful and grateful; and yet men are enjoined to 'do this,' that they may remember. '... Until (that goal is reached that) he may come.' This phrase seems to be a paraphrase of the Aramaic *Maranatha,* still preserved in the Corinthian liturgy.... The death of the risen Lord is so pro-

[13]Corpus Christi: "Sequence" (prose text), *The Lectionary.*

[14]Jones, "The Eucharist—The New Testament," *SL,* 192.

claimed that his return is invoked and anticipated; his *parousia* is both his expected arrival and also in some sense his presence."[15]

In Corinth, the meal came before the celebration of the word. The father of the house presided over the blessing of the bread and may have allowed a guest to pray the thanks over the cup. It appears as if Paul was passing on a tradition that was already established even before his conversion; "it is the earliest surviving account of the Last Supper, and there is a *prima facie* case for its authenticity."[16]

The prayer over the cup is based on Jeremiah 31:31–34, in which he authorized the establishment of a new covenant, yet provided no way to initiate it. Jesus provided the way—he offered his own blood, just as the first covenant had been inaugurated with a blood sacrifice (Ex 24:4–8). However, the thanksgiving over the cup refers specifically to the "cup" (with only implicit allusion to its contents) in order to respect the Jewish prohibition and abhorrence for drinking blood.

The Ritual Prayers for the Feast of Corpus Christi: In the liturgical prayers for this Sunday, two images of eucharist emerge. The first is eucharist as Jesus at table with his disciples, feeding the people with the gift of himself (Preface II of the Holy Eucharist). The second image is eucharist as a gift of adoration and worship ("...we worship you living among us in the sacrament of your body and blood"—Alternative Opening Prayer). The first is more communal in nature; the second reflects a posture of private devotion. Both are valid and helpful reflections on the eucharist, but coming from the context of Sunday worship, the communal image best reflects our Sunday experience and theology of the eucharist. The opening prayer, prayer after communion, and first preface reflect a theme of personal worship, strengthening, and cleansing. The alternative opening prayer begins with our worship of Christ in the sacrament of his Body and Blood, and ends with the prayer that we offer our lives poured out in service of our brothers and sisters. The second preface refers to the feeding of God's people with the gift of Christ in the eucharist. The prayer over the gifts asks that the bread and cup, signs of peace and unity, bring unity and peace to the church. The second invocation of form C of the penitential rite expresses the fullness of eucharist. "Lord Jesus, you came to gather the nations into the peace of God's kingdom: Lord have mercy. You came in word and sacrament to strengthen us in holiness: Christ have mercy, You will come in glory with salvation for your people: Lord have mercy." Eucharist gathers us as a people in unity and peace. Eucharist strengthens us and makes us holy as we await the day we will feast at the heavenly banquet.

This feast has moved from a feast of devotion to the blessed sacrament reserved in the tabernacle and presented to the people for adoration, to a celebration of eucharist. Observe the preface for Holy Thursday which reflects that focus:

> Father, all-powerful and ever-living God,
> we do well always and everywhere to give
> you thanks
> through Jesus Christ our Lord.
> He is the true and eternal priest
> who established this unending sacrifice.
> He offered himself as a victim for our deliverance
> and taught us to make this offering in his
> memory.
> As we eat his body which he gave for us,
> we grow in strength.
> As we drink his blood which he poured
> out for us,
> we are washed clean.
> Now, with angels and archangels,
> and the whole company of heaven,
> we sing the unending hymn of your
> praise.[17]

One distinguishing feature of this feast is the eucharistic procession. During the Middle Ages the procession included tableaus of the passion and Old Testament figures. During the baroque era, the procession became far more elaborate. It evolved into a public, triumphant procession of thanksgiving. Floats and scenes that had little or nothing to do with the eucharist became part of

[15]Ibid., 192–193.

[16]Ibid., 195.

[17]Holy Thursday—Mass of the Lord's Supper: "Preface of Holy Eucharist I" (P47), *The Sacramentary.*

the procession. During the Enlightenment, this all but disappeared.

The procession is considered an exercise of devotion (*pia exercitia*) under the direction of the local ordinary. There is a recent call for a return to the practice of eucharistic processions, perhaps sparked by a renewed vision of the Vatican Council. The Council affirmed the image of God's people as a pilgrim people who could withstand the dangers of the journey only with the help and assistance of Christ.

> Our contemporaries so often suffer from the randomness of existence. If the Corpus Christi procession were properly conducted in the spirit of the liturgy, it could, more than any other procession, be or become a way of making them aware, by means of a real symbol, that they are not alone as they make their way along the difficult mountain path of life on earth, but rather that in the communion of the Church, which has the eucharistic Lord with her, going before, beside and behind her, they are on the way to eternal union with the Christ of the parousia, when "he comes on that day to be glorified in his saints, and to be marveled at in all who have believed." (2 Thes 1:10)[18]

Ultimately, then, "Corpus Christi retains its theological significance as a celebration of God's gift of Christ in the Spirit to the church and the world as its food and drink of everlasting life. Moreover, in the celebration of this feast the church as the body of Christ experiences itself is called to let the Spirit fashion it more into bread and drink for the world."[19]

Gospel Exegesis

The facilitator gives input regarding what critical biblical scholarship has to say about this text. The input includes insights as to how people would have heard the gospel in Jesus' time.

[18]W. Durig, "Zur Liturgie des Fronleichnamsfeier," in *Am Tisch des Wortes,* Neue Reihe 113 (Stuttgart, 1971), p. 17; in *LY,* 169, 170.

[19]McDermott, "Feasts of Christ," in *NDSW,* 204.

C.P.M. Jones suggests a liturgical setting for today's gospel. He speculates that perhaps today's section of John's gospel reflects the celebration of a eucharistic liturgy. Jesus begins by referring to himself as bread. He is the bread of life; he is manna; he is nourishment. Jesus is the Father's gift to the world. Jesus too must give freely of himself. A transition takes place in verse 52, however. Whereas Jesus previously referred to himself as bread, now he uses the term *flesh and blood.* There is movement from the vague symbolism of manna to the specific symbolism inherent in the sacrament of eucharist—flesh and blood. Jones suggests that perhaps there is more going on than just the discourse on the bread of life. Perhaps chapter 6 reflects a eucharistic order of service in the Johannine community—a eucharistic liturgy: proclamation of the word, sermon, commemoration of the passion and communion under both kinds (vv. 53–56). This order also is reflected in the future order of liturgy established by Justin Martyr in the mid-second century. While John does not provide us with a specific institution narrative, perhaps he left us the liturgy as it was celebrated by his community in word and action.

In antiquity, *flesh* was understood to mean the totality of the person. The *flesh* is powerless to do anything unless the Spirit empowers it. The actions of the liturgy similarly are lifeless without the power and invocation (*epiclesis*) of the Spirit to transform them into a new sacramental reality. On Calvary the water and blood that flow from Jesus' side are quickened, enlivened, and empowered by the Spirit to inaugurate the sacraments of baptism and eucharist and thus give birth to the church.[20]

Raymond Brown asserts that this passage is a profound proclamation of sacramental and eucharistic theology. The living bread given by Christ is his own flesh. John uses a paraphrase of the institution narrative at the Last Supper: "The bread that I will give is my flesh for the life of the world." Compare that to: "This is my body given up for you." According to Paul's understanding of it, the eucharist is Jesus' death remembered and made present until he comes again at the consummation of the world. John's focus is on Jesus Christ, the *Word made flesh.* Jesus' flesh—the totality of his

[20]Jones, "The Eucharist—The New Testament," *SL,* 210.

person, his complete life-force (blood), is the only food that gives life. The coming of Christ into the world is the supreme act of redemption. "The sacramental theology here is truly profound; namely, if baptism gives us that life which the Father shares with the Son, the eucharist is food nourishing it."[21]

John's Jesus promises to dwell within the hearts of believers—to abide within. There is a mutual indwelling between Jesus and his disciples. Jesus abides in them and they abide in Jesus. Eucharist continues that holy indwelling. "Elsewhere, the evangelist informs his readers that the ultimate significance of the Eucharist is that it is the means of this mutual and life-giving indwelling."[22] This indwelling is understood on an even deeper level. It presupposes and invites intimacy with Christ. It means "intermingling"—personal intimacy. This incredible act of intimacy with Jesus opens the door to life.

There are three biblical understandings of the Lord's Supper: 1) It is a memorial of Jesus' death and resurrection—a covenant sacrifice; 2) it is a continuation of Jesus' earthly and post-resurrection meals in which the messianic banquet is anticipated; 3) it is a ritual extension of Jesus' Incarnation. The bread and wine become the living body and blood of Christ. John's theology fits the third understanding. It is only through his death that his ongoing presence and life continue in the community. The eucharistic meal is an ingesting of *Love Incarnate, Word Become Flesh,* and *Christ, the Living Bread.*

The emphasis in this section of John's gospel deals with the consumption of the bread given by God. People must eat the bread before they can understand its meaning and its value. People eat real food and still die—manna does not guarantee life. This bread, however, offers eternal life. Both come from heaven, but only one offers life.[23] Charles H. Talbert reminds us that the language of today's gospel "is understandable in light of a saying of R. Hillel, son of Gamaliel III: 'There shall be no Messiah for Israel, because they have already eaten him in the days of Hezekiah' (b. Sanhedrin 99a). Just as one may devour books, drink in a lecture, swallow a story, stomach a lie, and eat one's own words, so one may eat the living bread, Jesus the incarnate Word."[24]

Proclaim the gospel again.

Sometimes we gain new insights when we hear the text after the interpretation has been given. Someone from the group proclaims the gospel a second time.

Step 4
Testing

Conversation with the Liturgy and the Scriptures

Test your original understanding in dialogue with the text.

(You might consider breaking into smaller groups.)

Now that you've heard the exegesis, were there any new insights for you? How do you feel about it? How does your original understanding of this gospel compare with what we just shared? How does this story speak to your life?

Sharing Life Experience

Participants share an experience from their lives that connects with the biblical interpretation just shared.

> *Today's gospel seems to stress the individual personal benefits of the eucharist more than it does the communal and ecclesial aspects. Yet taken to its logical conclusion, eucharist is ultimately communal. It can be no less. John gives us a vision of eucharist as the most personal, intrinsic act of intimacy a person can participate in. We are intermingled with Christ himself. His breath is our breath. When we celebrate eucharist we remember and make present the saving life, death, and resurrection of Jesus, but we actually take that reality into our own person—we ingest, consume, and devour that truth and make it effective.*

[21] *GEJ,* 47.
[22] *JHW,* 44.
[23] *RJ,* 138.
[24] Ibid.

Conscious awareness of this intimacy has powerful, transformative implications. If I take Jesus into my being, I must become him. If I become him, then I must act like him. If I act like him I will love unconditionally—those who are lovable as well as those who are unlovable. I too will offer my life. While personally intimate, eucharist is ostensibly public.

I remember a time when I believed God was asking me to become vulnerable, to risk and share a private part of my life with some folks. I stubbornly resisted. Yet the invitation was persistent. I relented and reluctantly became willing to "be eucharist" in a way I had never been before. The fruit of that experience was beyond my imagination; grace abounded. It was not until we celebrated eucharist, however, that the depths of that experience came crashing in upon me. As I drank from the cup I became acutely aware that Jesus' blood was poured out and continues to be poured out for me and for everyone. That blood, poured out on the sand of human sorrow, gives life in the midst of hopelessness. But that same blood, burning on its descent to my soul's inner depth, infiltrated my being with Holy Presence and I thought I would burst from love too large to be contained in such a limited vessel. It simply had to spill over.

Eucharist can never just be a personal act of devotion. Such intimacy demands to be shared—it is too precious to keep to oneself. Every eucharist I celebrate certainly does not illicit the same awareness or intensity of experience. It was no doubt a result of my raw vulnerability. While personally intimate, it was at the same time expansive, enlarging, and profoundly communal. John's gospel offers me a profoundly contemplative and communal reflection on Jesus—Bread of Life and Nourisher of Souls—on this feast of Corpus Christi.

All share their life experience.

What was John trying to tell his community? How do you understand this liturgy and this gospel? What does it mean to you? How has your understanding of eucharist grown as a result of this liturgy? How might this gospel challenge growth and transformation in your life—in the life of your community? In what way are the biblical themes of covenant, exodus, creation, and community evident in today's readings? Do you still feel the same way about this text as when you began? Has your original understanding been stretched, challenged, or affirmed?

Step 5
Decision

The gospel demands a response.

In what specific way might your parish be invited to respond? Are there any attitudes or behaviors you would like to change as a result of today's conversation? What one concrete action will you take this week as a response to the liturgy today?

DOCTRINAL ISSUES

What church truth/teaching/doctrinal issue could be drawn from the gospel for the Solemnity of the Body and Blood of Christ (Corpus Christi)?

Participants suggest possible doctrinal themes that flow from the readings.

Possible Doctrinal Themes

Corpus Christi, eucharist, symbol of bread and wine, Christology, sacramentality, eucharistic prayer, providence of God, Incarnation, paschal mystery, Body of Christ

Present the doctrinal material at this time.

1. The facilitator gives input on a particular doctrinal issue of his or her prior choosing. OR
2. The group chooses a doctrinal issue from the list they created. They read together from the Doctrinal Appendix.

(The doctrinal issues are found in the Doctrinal Appendix in the back of this workbook. If you are choosing an issue from this resource, please refer to it now.)

Reflection questions centered around the chosen doctrinal theme can be found at the end of each topic in the Doctrinal Appendix. The questions are based on the five-step reflection process. If you choose a topic not included in the Doctrinal Appendix, craft your own questions according to the same five-step process.

Following the reflection questions you will be reminded to return to chapter 7, "Preparing the Catechetical Session," to assist you in crafting your own session.

Closing Prayer

Father,
you have brought to fulfillment the work of our
redemption
through the Easter mystery of Christ your Son.
May we who faithfully proclaim his death and resurrection in these sacramental signs
experience the constant growth of your salvation
in our lives.
We ask this through our Lord Jesus Christ, your
Son, who lives and reigns with you and the
Holy Spirit, one God for ever and ever.[25]

OR

Lord, hear our prayer for your mercy
as we celebrate this memorial of our salvation.
May this sacrament of love be for us
the sign of unity and the bond of charity.[26]

OR

Lord,
may our sharing at this holy table make us holy.
By the body and blood of Christ
join all your people in brotherly love.
Grant this through Christ our Lord.[27]

[25]Votive Masses, Holy Eucharist: "Opening Prayer," *The Sacramentary.*

[26]Votive Masses, Holy Eucharist: "Prayer Over the Gifts," *The Sacramentary.*

[27]Votive Masses, Holy Eucharist: "Prayer After Communion," *The Sacramentary.*

Solemnity of the Sacred Heart of Jesus

INTRODUCTORY RITES

Opening Song (or Entrance Antiphon)

The thoughts of his heart last through every generation, that he will rescue them from death and feed them in time of trouble. (Ps 32:11, 19)[1]

Opening Prayer

The facilitator of the session may lead the prayer. Others in the group may be asked to proclaim the readings.

Let us pray
[that we will respond to the love of Christ]

Pause for silent prayer.

Father,
we rejoice in the gifts of love
we have received from the heart of Jesus your Son.
Open our hearts to share his life
and continue to bless us with his love.
We ask this through our Lord Jesus Christ, your Son,
who lives and reigns with you and the Holy Spirit,
one God, for ever and ever.

OR

Father,
we have wounded the heart of Jesus your Son,
but he brings us forgiveness and grace.
Help us prove our grateful love
and make amends for our sins.
We ask this through our Lord Jesus Christ, your Son,
who lives and reigns with you and the Holy Spirit,
one God for ever and ever.[2]

LITURGY OF THE WORD

Let us listen to God's word.

[1]Sacred Heart: "Entrance Antiphon," *The Sacramentary.*
[2]Sacred Heart: "Opening Prayer," *The Sacramentary.*

The readings are proclaimed.

First Reading
Deuteronomy 7:6–11

The Deuteronomist is concerned with answering the question: Why did God act on behalf of humanity when establishing the covenant and what should be the human response? What was obvious to the author of this book is that "everything comes from God's initiative."[3] Moses proclaimed that God's people were holy because they were chosen by God. Because they were chosen by God, they are sacred and thus belong to God. God acted on behalf of human beings because of God's incredible unmerited love. Israel had no reason to boast about their greatness. They did nothing on their own to warrant God's action. They were not chosen for their great nation status—they were instead chosen because of God's love for them. They were also chosen because of God's faithfulness to the oath God made with their ancestors. Thus, God's love and faithfulness are the reasons God acted. The only acceptable human response is the response of love and fidelity in return.

The language that suggests that God metes out punishment and terror to those who do not keep God's commands is a reminder to us that God takes our response very seriously. "It is a way of stressing the seriousness, the depth of God's love by comparing him to a jealous lover who cannot tolerate seeing his or her immense love despised."[4]

By following God's decrees, people commit their entire being to the God who is Lord and Master of their lives. The Deuteronomist shouts the Shema to the rooftops of heavenly spires when in earlier chapters he proclaims, "The Lord God is one—love the Lord God with your heart, your entire mind and your entire soul—thus, your entire being."

[3]*DL* (VII), 69
[4]Ibid., 70.

Responsorial Psalm
Psalm 103:1–4, 6–8, 11

This psalm praises God for leading Moses and for showing him the face of God. It also praises God for the acts of salvation on behalf of God's people, Israel. This song was sung by Israel in remembrance of the Exodus. Christianity appropriated it to reflect the paschal mystery of Christ.

Second Reading
1 John 4:7–16

No one is more concerned with love than this New Testament author. The word *love,* both the verb and noun, is used in reference to humanity's relationship with God, with Jesus, with the Spirit, and the Trinity's relationship with humanity. What is this *love* that so captures John's imagination? Love that is charity (*agape*) is love of divine origin—supernatural love. "The economy of salvation is marked by a law whose operation we can still verify in our own lives: the 'theophanies,' or manifestations of the mystery, are measured by the kenosis of love; the more our God gives himself, the more he reveals himself."[5] The love that John preaches is the hallmark of his theology and spirituality, and its locus is Christianity.

Christians can do no less than love one another because love is the essence of God. God may be the essence of love, but no one can be reduced to his or her essence. God embodies love, but no name can adequately describe or define the Author of all Life. The scriptures use many names to try to capture the essence of God, yet they are all limited and can only attempt to describe the ineffable reality of who God is.

However, if anything even remotely comes close to God's essence it would be love. The tender mercies of God can be experienced in life's moment-by-moment theophanies. God acts in human history. That alone is proof of God's love and mercy. "It is the Father who has thus 'drawn' us (Jn 6:44) and, in our impoverished but loving faith, his passionate love for his beloved Son has to some extent become ours."[6] The premier action of love is the Incarnation of the Son. Christ, in turn, loved humanity unto death—a self-sacrificing kenosis—an outpouring of gratuitous love. "In the kenosis of the incarnation grace dawned; in the kenosis of the cross it shines forth where the darkness is thickest."[7]

Human beings on their own can do nothing to earn such love. It is freely offered. We are sinners, and as such hardly lovable. But through the action of God, the transforming power of love, we are rendered lovable and ultimately divine. Those who know the love of God, according to John's perspective, are in intimate union with God. They have been born into the new life of love. "Birth into this divine life confers on believers the power to love God and to love like him."[8]

The love that John insists is the hallmark of intimate union with God can do no less than pour out on others. The acid test of a person's relationship with God is by the way in which he or she loves others. We will be judged by the quality of our love for God and for one another.

Gospel
Matthew 11:25–30

STEP 1
NAMING ONE'S EXPERIENCE

What were your first impressions? What was your first response? What grabbed your attention? How did you feel?

Each person names his or her initial impression. Statements should be brief. No reasons should be given at this time. All simply listen without agreeing or disagreeing.

STEP 2
UNDERSTANDING

In a brief statement, what do you think this gospel is trying to convey?

[5] *TWOW,* 22.
[6] Ibid., 65.
[7] Ibid., 29.
[8] *DL* (VII), 72.

STEP 3
INPUT FROM VISION/STORY/TRADITION

Liturgical Context

This feast is celebrated on the third Friday after the feast of Pentecost. Since this feast takes place on a Friday, it is seldom thoroughly treated in catechetical groups. However, it is an important solemnity of the Lord and, as such, is part of the deposit of faith as it is revealed in the unfolding liturgical cycle. While most parishes will not have the luxury of meeting on this day, it would nevertheless be important that this liturgy be addressed in catechetical groups whose formation is centered on breaking open the riches of the liturgical cycle.

The feast of the Sacred Heart is a devotional feast that honors Christ for the love he showers upon humanity. That love is symbolized by his heart. The earliest origins of such a devotion can be traced back to the church Fathers who stressed certain passages in John (7:37, 19:34). Anselm and Bernard of Clairvaux also cited similar passages in the twelfth century, only to be followed by others such as Albert the Great and Bonaventure in the thirteenth century.

According to Adolf Adam, later mystics increased their devotion to the Sacred Heart and by the sixteenth century Jesuits and other groups also promoted the devotion. French Oratorians Pierre Berulle and John Eudes helped move the devotion to official levels. After receiving permission from his bishop, Eudes celebrated the first feast in honor of the Sacred Heart in his community.

Visitation nun Margaret Mary Alacoque had a series of visions encouraging her to work toward establishment of the feast on the Friday after Corpus Christi. She also promoted the observance of Fridays in honor of the Sacred Heart.

Rome did not allow the feast to be officially celebrated for another hundred years. In 1856 Pius IX established the feast as obligatory for the universal church. Pope Leo XIII raised the feast to a higher rank and consecrated the world to the Sacred Heart of Jesus. Pius XI in 1927 elevated it again and, without making it a holy day of obligation, raised it to the same status as Christmas.

In this century, Karl Rahner addressed some objections to the feast when he explained the word "heart" as a primordial concept. Rahner maintained that the word "heart" in scripture and tradition refers to the body and soul, the totality of a person. Thus, the heart of Christ refers to the complete essence of his being.

The text for this mass was compiled by Pius XI in 1928 in collaboration with Benedictine Abbot H. Quentin. An earlier focus for this feast was the passion of Christ and the mysticism of the Song of Solomon. Pius XI emphasized expiation, humanity's need for the love of Christ to redeem sin.

There are two opening prayers—one old, the other new. The new prayer, the first, acknowledges the love we have received through Christ and asks that we continue to be blessed with that love. The second acknowledges human guilt and asks that we worship Christ through the service we offer to our brothers and sisters. Love, then, is not just an internal state of being between Creator and created, but rather is demonstrated and evidenced in love extended to others.

The old concluding prayer, "we have tasted the sweetness of your loving heart," was replaced with "May this sacrament fill us with love. Draw us closer to Christ your Son and help us to recognize him in others." A new preface was assigned to the feast that centers more closely on the scriptures and the theology of the Fathers: "Lifted high on the cross, Christ gave his life for us, so much did he love us. From his wounded side flowed blood and water, and the fountain of sacramental life in the Church. To his open heart the Savior invites all men, to draw water in joy from the springs of salvation."

There are other forms of devotion to the Sacred Heart: the first Fridays of each month and the eve of first Friday. There is also a votive mass for First Fridays approved at the end of the nineteenth century by Leo XIII. When properly explained within its scriptural and historical context, this feast has great pastoral value.

Gospel Exegesis

The facilitator gives input regarding what critical biblical scholarship has to say about this text. The input in-

cludes insights as to how people would have heard the gospel in Jesus' time.

(Refer to the Gospel Exegesis for the Fourteenth Sunday in Ordinary Time.)

Today's gospel is a hymn of joy addressed to Jesus' heavenly Father and an invitation to everyone to become a disciple of Jesus. God's love is manifest and his power shown by the way in which he cares for those who do not have the intellectual ability to grasp the theologies of the wise and learned. Those with the humility to hear the truth of God's word, accessible to all, will stand with the childlike who "see themselves fulfilled beyond all expectations. Paradoxically, their poverty puts them in a privileged situation. . . ."[9]

Jesus was able to give comfort to such little ones because he alone knew the heart of God and the love God has for God's children. Jesus' wisdom was borne out in the self-sacrificing love he offered to humanity through the sacrifice of the cross. An invitation to radical love is at the nexus of today's liturgy. Jesus reminds us that the love he is talking about is not saccharine piety, but love that demands radical choices and sacrifices. Such love is liberating and initiates growth.

Proclaim the gospel again.

Sometimes we gain new insights when we hear the text after the interpretation has been given. Someone from the group proclaims the gospel a second time.

STEP 4
TESTING

Conversation with the Liturgy and the Scriptures

Test your original understanding in dialogue with the text.

(You might consider breaking into smaller groups.)

Now that you've heard the exegesis of this liturgy, were there any new insights? Was there anything you had not considered before? How does your original understanding of this story compare with what was just shared? How does this story speak to your life?

Sharing Life Experience

Participants share an experience from their lives that connects with the biblical interpretation just shared.

> *I cannot reflect on the love of God and the love that pours out from his Sacred Heart for me and for the world without thinking about two people who are the personification of love in our parish. They are beacons of God's light and love. There is never a time of encounter with them in which the words "I love you" are not spoken. Their words are always words of encouragement and positive reinforcement. Never do we meet them when they do not ask about our families, our concerns, and our general well-being. If they even remotely reflect the love God has for us, then God's love for us is beyond mere words. They exude God's presence and their love pours out and impacts the parish in powerful ways. If they promise to pray for someone, that person can be assured that the hound of heaven is persistently storming the gates of the eternal city. The judge (of the "judge and widow" fame of the gospel) would run in fear at the sight of these two faithful servants on their knees. My children know that they have prayer advocates in this holy couple.*
>
> *When asked whom they know that reminds them of God's love, our school children always point to this incredible couple. They know they are loved and cherished—even if not personally known by them. As I write this reflection, these two special people are living with life-threatening illnesses. I sit with tears as I think of the possibility of losing them, and how our parish would suffer an unspeakable loss. We have been blessed with the breath of God through the self-gift of these two committed disciples of the Lord. On this feast of God's gracious gift of love for humanity, I thank him for the Sacred Heart of his Son, and I also thank him for the sacred hearts of these two faithful children of the covenant. Our parish family is blessed by their lives.*

All share their life experience.

What does this liturgy have to say to our community and to me today? In what way is our commu-

[9] Ibid., 74.

nity challenged? Do we still feel the same way about this liturgy as we did when we began? Has our original understanding been stretched, challenged, or affirmed?

STEP 5
DECISION

The gospel demands a response.

How does our sharing and this biblical interpretation challenge our community and how does it challenge me? In what way does this gospel call our parish to action in the church, parish, neighborhood, or world? What is one concrete action we will take this week as a response to what was learned and shared today?

DOCTRINAL ISSUES

What church truth/teaching/doctrinal issue could be drawn from the liturgy for the feast of the Sacred Heart?

Participants suggest possible doctrinal themes that flow from the readings.

Possible Doctrinal Themes

Sacred Heart of Jesus, Trinity, Christology, charity-agape, paschal mystery

Present the doctrinal material at this time.

1. The facilitator gives input on a particular doctrinal issue of his/her prior choosing. OR
2. The group chooses a doctrinal issue from the list they created. They read together from the Doctrinal Appendix.

(The doctrinal issues are found in the Doctrinal Appendix in the back of this workbook. If you are choosing an issue from this resource, please refer to it now.)

Reflection questions centered around the chosen doctrinal theme can be found at the end of each topic in the Doctrinal Appendix. The questions are based on the five-step reflection process. If you choose a topic not included in the Doctrinal Appendix, craft your own questions according to the same five-step process.

Following the reflection questions you will be reminded to return to chapter 7, "Preparing the Catechetical Session," to assist you in crafting your own session.

Closing Prayer

Father,
we honor the heart of your Son
broken by man's cruelty,
yet symbol of love's triumph,
pledge of all that man is called to be.
Teach us to see Christ in the lives we touch,
to offer him living worship
by love-filled service to our brothers and sisters.
We ask this through Christ our Lord.[10]

[10]Sacred Heart: "Alternative Opening Prayer," *The Sacramentary.*

Presentation of the Lord (February 2)

INTRODUCTORY RITES

Opening Song (or Entrance Antiphon)

Within your temple, we ponder your loving kindness, O God. As your name, so also your praise reaches to the ends of the earth; your right hand is filled with justice. (Ps 47:10–11)[1]

Blessing of Candles and Procession

The Lord will come with mighty power,
and give light to the eyes of all who serve him,
alleluia.

Forty days ago we celebrated the joyful feast of the birth of our Lord Jesus Christ. Today we recall the holy day on which he was presented in the temple, fulfilling the law of Moses and at the same time going to meet his faithful people. Led by the Spirit, Simeon and Anna came to the temple, recognized Christ as their Lord, and proclaimed him with joy.

United by the Spirit, may we now go to the house of God to welcome Christ the Lord. There we shall recognize him in the breaking of the bread until he comes again in glory.

Then the priest joins his hands and blesses the candles.

Let us pray.
God, our Father, source of all light,
today you revealed to Simeon
your Light of revelation to the nations.
Bless + these candles and make them holy.
May we who carry them to praise your glory
walk in the path of goodness
and come to the light that shines for ever.
Grant this through Christ, our Lord.[2]

Opening Prayer

The facilitator of the session may lead the prayer. Others in the group may be asked to proclaim the readings.

All powerful Father,
Christ your Son became man for us
and was presented in the temple.
May he free our hearts from sin
and bring us into your presence.
We ask this through our Lord Jesus Christ, your Son,
who lives and reigns with you and the Holy Spirit,
one God, for ever and ever.[3]

LITURGY OF THE WORD

Let us listen to God's word.

The readings are proclaimed.

First Reading
Malachi 3:1–4

The reading from Malachi heralds the coming of the "messenger of the covenant." This messenger comes for judgment. The coming "Day of the Lord" will accomplish the purification of the people. We are to prepare by living the covenant.

The people had returned from exile and the temple had been rebuilt, but the people's response was lackluster. Those who turned away from God would be punished in the coming "Day of the Lord." Those who suffered while the wicked prospered would enjoy vindication on the "Day of the Lord." Placing this reading within this feast makes it clear how the church understands Malachi's prophecy. The presentation of Jesus in the temple is understood as the fulfillment of Malachi's prophecy.

Responsorial Psalm
Psalm 24:7–10

Second Reading
Hebrews 2:14–18

Jesus came to be the new high priest in the new covenant. He offered his life as a perfect sacri-

---

[1] Presentation of the Lord: "Entrance Antiphon," *The Sacramentary.*

[2] Presentation of the Lord: "Blessing of Candles and Procession," *The Sacramentary.*

[3] Presentation of the Lord: "Opening Prayer," *The Sacramentary.*

fice. By doing this, Jesus reconciled humanity with God. Jesus freely surrendered to death for the salvation of the world. He did this because of his faithfulness to Yahweh. Jesus' death was a passage to his glory, not to darkness. Because of Jesus' sacrifice, we are heirs to his resurrected life. We will die, but we will live with Jesus forever. Jesus' death was real. His suffering was real. He was a human being (with both a human and divine nature) and suffered as other human beings do. Like us in every way except sin, Jesus knows our suffering and is our advocate. He strengthens us and intercedes for us as we endure the trials of this life.

Gospel
Luke 2:22–40

Mary and Joseph take Jesus and present him in the temple.

STEP 1
NAMING ONE'S EXPERIENCE

What were your first impressions? What was your first response? What grabbed your attention? How did you feel?

Each person names his or her initial impression. Statements should be brief. No reasons should be given at this time. All simply listen without agreeing or disagreeing.

STEP 2
UNDERSTANDING

In a brief statement, what do you think this gospel is trying to convey?

STEP 3
INPUT FROM VISION/STORY/TRADITION

Liturgical Context

Jesus is the center of attention in today's gospel. The feast takes place forty days after Christmas and is centered around events that took place in the Jerusalem temple.

In antiquity, a woman was considered unclean for forty days after delivering a male child (eighty days after a female). She was to go to the temple and offer the priest a lamb and a young pigeon or turtledove or, if poor, two turtledoves. This was to be her sin offering, to make her ritually clean again.

Mary was dutifully following the law when she presented her son Jesus to the temple. Firstborn male children belonged to the Lord (Ex 13:2) and were to be taken to the temple so the parents could ransom them back with money. "In keeping with these regulations Mary and Joseph brought Jesus to the temple, and Mary offered the sacrifice that 'purified' her and at the same time ransomed her firstborn."[4]

It is possible that this feast was celebrated as early as the fifth century. The feast was a continuation of the Christmas event and its focus was clearly driven by today's gospel. While it is a feast strongly connected to the Nativity, it also has a paschal orientation.

The celebration included a procession. It began as a replacement for the pagan procession of expiation that took place every five years in February. To capture the original penitential flavor of the feast, purple vestments were worn (up to 1960).

The procession with candles reminds us that Simeon called Jesus "a revealing light to the gentiles" (Lk 2:32). This feast has also been referred to as Candlemas. In the middle of the eighth century the feast was designated the "Purification of Blessed Virgin Mary." The new calendar made clear that the feast was a feast of the Lord, not of Mary, and the change of name in 1969 captured the original intent of the feast. The blessing of candles dates back to around 1000 C.E. in Gaul.

There are two forms of procession and blessing that may be used. In the first form, people gather outside and process into church with blessed candles (perhaps singing the Canticle of Simeon, the *Nunc dimittis*: "Now Master, you may let your servant go in peace according to your word."). The simpler form has a representative group enter the church carrying candles in procession with the priest.

---

[4] *LY*, 150.

The temple events are the lens through which all the ritual prayers of the mass are viewed. The prayers of the mass reflect the biblical understanding of the feast. We are to be joyful and praise God forever, because we have seen the light of the Lord (Preface). His light has gone out to all the world. We share that light as we await the day he will return and bring us into everlasting life (Prayer After Communion).

Gospel Exegesis

The facilitator gives input regarding what critical biblical scholarship has to say about this text. The input includes insights as to how people would have heard the gospel in Jesus' time.

Today's episode with Simeon during the presentation of Jesus in the temple accomplishes far more than the actual event described. The Lord's mission and destiny are heralded and the law and the Old Testament's importance are underscored. This gospel pronounces of the mystery of Christ: "Jesus, by submitting to the prescriptions of the Law imposed on first-born sons, manifested as soon as he entered the world his obedience to God, his Father (Luke 2:49)."[5]

Simeon, representative of the just of Israel, understood salvation to be the dawning of light to all the nations. Simeon echoed the words of the prophets who attested to the universal mission of the messiah. Yet, even though this mission is inclusive of all people, it will not be easy. Those who accept Christ will be rejected, just as Christ will be rejected. Simeon prophesies about the division that will be brought about as a result of faith in Christ. Mary, as representative of all believers, is an example of a faithful servant who listens to God's word and acts upon it. We are to do the same.

The Eastern Church calls this the Feast of the Encounter. Through celebration of the liturgy and the biblical texts, we encounter the mystery of the *Living One Who Came to Bring Light to the Nations* and we are challenged to live in a radical new way because of it. God promised to send a messenger to purify the temple, the priesthood, and the people. He sent his Son to be the light for the entire world.

Proclaim the gospel again.

Sometimes we gain new insights when we hear the text after the interpretation has been given. Someone from the group proclaims the gospel a second time.

Step 4
Testing

Conversation with the Liturgy and the Scriptures

Test your original understanding in dialogue with the text.

(You might consider breaking into smaller groups.)

How does your original understanding of this story compare with what was just shared? How does this story speak to your life?

Participants share an experience from their lives that connects with the biblical interpretation just shared.

What does this liturgy have to say to our community and to me today? Has our original understanding been stretched, challenged, or affirmed?

Step 5
Decision

The gospel demands a response.

In what way does this gospel call our parish to action in the church, parish, neighborhood, or world? Has this conversation with the exegesis of this liturgy changed or stretched my personal attitudes? What is one concrete action we will take this week as a response to what was learned and shared today?

DOCTRINAL ISSUES

What church truth/teaching/doctrinal issue

[5] *DL* (VII), 112.

could be drawn from the gospel for the Presentation of the Lord?

Participants suggest possible doctrinal themes that flow from the readings.

Possible Doctrinal Themes

Mystery of Christ, incarnation, evangelization, ecumenism

Present the doctrinal material at this time.

1. The facilitator gives input on a particular doctrinal issue of his/her prior choosing. OR
2. The group chooses a doctrinal issue from the list they created. They read together from the Doctrinal Appendix.

(The doctrinal issues are found in the Doctrinal Appendix in the back of this workbook. If you are choosing an issue from this resource, please refer to it now.)

Reflection questions centered around the chosen doctrinal theme can be found at the end of each topic in the Doctrinal Appendix. The questions are based on the five-step reflection process. If you choose a topic not included in the Doctrinal Appendix, craft your own questions according to the same five-step process.

Following the reflection questions you will be reminded to return to chapter 7, "Preparing the Catechetical Session," to assist you in crafting your own session.

Closing Prayer

Lord,
you fulfilled the hope of Simeon,
who did not die
until he had been privileged to welcome the Messiah.
May this communion perfect your grace in us
and prepare us to meet Christ
when he comes to bring us into everlasting life,
for he is Lord for ever and ever.[6]

---

[6]Presentation of the Lord: "Prayer After Communion," *The Sacramentary*.

SOLEMNITY OF JOSEPH, HUSBAND OF MARY (MARCH 19)

INTRODUCTORY RITES

Opening Song (or Entrance Antiphon)

The Lord has put his faithful servant in charge of his household. (Lk 12:42)[1]

Opening Prayer

The facilitator of the session may lead the prayer. Others in the group may be asked to proclaim the readings.

Let us pray
[that the Church will continue
the saving work of Christ]

Pause for silent prayer.

Father,
you entrusted our Savior to the care of St. Joseph.
By the help of his prayers
may your Church continue to serve its Lord, Jesus Christ,
who lives and reigns with you and the Holy Spirit,
one God, for ever and ever.[2]

LITURGY OF THE WORD

Let us listen to God's word.

The readings are proclaimed.

First Reading
2 Samuel 7:4–5, 12–14, 16

Today's reading from Samuel reminds us of Yahweh's promise that David's reign would endure forever. This promise is considered typological of the promise that would be fulfilled in the messianic reign of Jesus Christ. Jesus fulfilled the promise made to David, since Joseph was a descendant of David.

[1]Solemnity of Joseph, Husband of Mary: "Entrance Antiphon," *The Sacramentary.*

[2]Solemnity of Joseph, Husband of Mary: "Opening Prayer," *The Sacramentary.*

Responsorial Psalm
Psalm 89:2–3, 4–5, 27, 29

This psalm is a reflection on the promise made to David: David's house would endure forever and his reign would extend for all time.

Second Reading
Romans 4:13, 16–18, 22

Joseph is called "Just in the eyes of God" *(tzaddik).* It is the greatest accolade paid to anyone in biblical tradition. Anyone who played a role in the history of salvation was considered a model to follow and was thus entitled to be called "just." Paul's letter to the Romans seeks to teach the disciple how to become "just" like the *tzaddik.* Paul used Abraham as an example.

Abraham was righteous ("just") because of his faith in God. God did not grace Abraham because of his observance of the law. Abraham was elected completely through the grace of God and trusted that God would multiply his descendants even though the aged Sarah was childless. Abraham even stood firm in his trust of Yahweh when asked to sacrifice his son, Isaac.

Paul's letter to the Romans invites the reader to share Abraham's faith. We, too, are heirs of the promise made to Abraham. Our response is complete trust.

Gospel
Matthew 1:16, 18–21, 24

Joseph obeyed the angel and took Mary as his wife.

Or Luke 2:41–51

Jesus is left behind in the temple in Jerusalem as Mary and Joseph search for him.

STEP 1
NAMING ONE'S EXPERIENCE

What were your first impressions? What was your first response? What grabbed your attention? How did you feel?

Each person names his or her initial impression. Statements should be brief. No reasons should be given at this time. All simply listen without agreeing or disagreeing.

STEP 2
UNDERSTANDING

In a brief statement, what do you think this gospel is trying to convey?

STEP 3
INPUT FROM VISION/STORY/TRADITION

Liturgical Context

The earliest evidence of observance of a devotion to Joseph, husband of Mary, can be traced back to the eighth century in Coptic calendars. A celebration taking place on March 19 occurred in the twelfth century. Bernadine of Sienna, a Franciscan, fostered the celebration of the feast in honor of St. Joseph. A church was built in honor of Joseph in Nazareth during the crusades.

By the end of the sixteenth century Pope Sixtus IV established the feast for the church universal. Pope Gregory XV made it a holy day of obligation in 1621. Pius IX named Joseph the patron and protector of the universal church in 1870.

A preface in honor of St. Joseph was introduced in 1920 and was retained in the New Missal of 1970. Pope John XXIII added St. Joseph's name to the Roman canon in 1962. Since the feast falls in Lent, permission is granted to episcopal conferences to transfer it to another time.

In 1847 Pius IX established another feast in honor of St. Joseph and placed it on the third Sunday after Easter. This feast had been celebrated by the Carmelites of Italy and France since 1860. Pius X made it a first-class feast and moved it to the third Wednesday after Easter. Since this was a duplication of the present solemnity, it was abolished by the Congregation of Rites in 1956.[3]

[3] *LY*, 230.

In the secular contemporary world, May 1 has been observed as a day in honor of the rights of the working person. Pius XII established a feast on May 1 in order to give the secular observance a Christian dimension. The pope also wished to highlight the rights of workers. The "Solemnity of St. Joseph the Worker, Husband of the Blessed Virgin Mary, Confessor and Patron of Working People" was retained in the new calendar as an optional memorial. The reason for reducing the rank of the feast is evidence of Rome's attempt to lessen the number of *idea feasts*.

The preface for this solemnity speaks of Joseph, the "just man" who served as protector in the infancy stages of the Incarnation event, protector of Mary, the Mother of God, and protector of Jesus, God's Son. Joseph served as earthly father in place of Jesus' natural father.

By being faithful to his mission of serving God, Joseph took his place in the annals of salvation history. Joseph is named as a wise, loyal, selfless servant. The liturgy opens by illuminating the character of Joseph: "The Lord has put his faithful servant in charge of his household" (Entrance Antiphon). We are exhorted to follow the example of Joseph in his ministry of service and care: "Father, with unselfish love St. Joseph cared for your Son, born of the Virgin Mary. May we also serve you at your altar with pure hearts" (Prayer Over the Gifts).

Flowers are allowed in church on this lenten weekday and are therefore an appropriate adornment for the St. Joseph shrine. An Italian tradition, the St. Joseph's table originated as a meal for the poor. It was offered in thanksgiving and in honor of St. Joseph for answered prayer. The meal is comprised of meatless dishes. It is a wholesome combination of the lenten disciplines of prayer, fasting, and almsgiving. *Catholic Household Blessings and Prayers* provides a litany and domestic prayer for the day. The *Book of Blessings* provides an "Order of Blessing of St. Joseph's Table." "Joseph is the patron saint of Mexico, Canada, Bohemia (in the Czech Republic) and Belgium, too. He has become known as the patron saint of the church, of fathers, of a happy death and of prayer."[4]

[4] *CC*, 60.

Gospel Exegesis

The facilitator gives input regarding what critical biblical scholarship has to say about this text. The input includes insights as to how people would have heard the gospel in Jesus' time.

Matthew 1:16, 18–21, 24

The genealogy of Matthew ends with Joseph, who was to play a role in God's messianic plan of salvation. Through the mediation of an angel, God revealed to Joseph the role he was to play in the lives of Mary and Jesus. It is through Joseph's genealogy that Jesus would be an heir to the promise made to David. When Jesus assumed Joseph's name, Jesus was legitimated as a descendant of David. When Joseph accepted Jesus as his son, he acknowledged Jesus' role as messiah. Joseph, as a righteous man, lived according to the law and was faithful to the will of God. All who follow Joseph's example are also righteous in the eyes of God.

Scripture does not credit Joseph with speaking a single word. Joseph's silence is the silence of one who lets God do the talking and simply and humbly follows God's commands. After the first two chapters in Matthew, Joseph is not heard from again. His role, according to Matthew, was assigned to the early life of Christ. He passed on his lineage to Jesus, he saved Jesus from Herod, and he brought his small family back to Galilee after the sojourn in Egypt. Joseph acted always at God's initiative, thus making him the personal representative of the Father at the side of the Son on earth. Joseph was a trustworthy guardian because he was faithful to God's word.

Joseph was not a wild-eyed dreamer. He was a man of action. But God revealed his intentions to Joseph through dreams, a common biblical medium of divine revelation. Joseph listened and followed God's leading. Joseph is a model for all who seek to do God's will.

Luke 2:41–51

Today's gospel from Luke serves as a transition from the infancy narratives to the adult manifestation of Christ. The event in today's story is more about Jesus than it is about his parents. It reflects and illuminates the mystery of the Incarnation and how the believer is to understand it. Jesus, Mary, and Joseph's pilgrimage to Jerusalem for the annual feast of Passover is of particular importance in the context of this passage. We are told that Jesus was twelve years old. This is Luke's way of telling the reader that Jesus was no longer a child and was now subject to the law.

The fact that Jesus remained in the temple after his parents left demonstrates Jesus' close connection to the sacred place. It was in this very same place that Jesus' future destiny would play itself out and lead to the cross on Calvary. However, in this scene, the learned teachers marvel at the wisdom of this budding would-be rabbi. We are not to sentimentalize this scene as that of a child prodigy amazing the scholars. We must look at this event through the lens of the crucifixion.

When Jesus responded to his anxious parents that he must be about his Father's business, we are told that they did not understand. They who lived with Jesus, his own parents, had to grow in understanding of his mission. As the words and experiences of Jesus' life unfolded, they would be able to reflect back on them and grow in understanding. Believers are thus encouraged in the face of their own doubts and lack of understanding.

Proclaim the gospel again.

Sometimes we gain new insights when we hear the text after the interpretation has been given. Someone from the group proclaims the gospel a second time.

Step 4
Testing

Conversation with the Liturgy and the Scriptures

Test your original understanding in dialogue with the text.

(You might consider breaking into smaller groups.)

How does your original understanding of this story compare with what was just shared? How does this story speak to your life?

Participants share an experience from their lives that connects with the biblical interpretation just shared.

What does this liturgy have to say to our community and to me today? Has our original understanding been stretched, challenged, or affirmed?

STEP 5
DECISION

The gospel demands a response.

In what way does this gospel call our parish to action in the church, parish, neighborhood, or world? Has this conversation with the exegesis of this liturgy changed or stretched our personal attitudes? What is one concrete action we will take this week as a response to what was learned and shared today?

DOCTRINAL ISSUES

What church truth/teaching/doctrinal issue could be drawn from the gospel for the Solemnity of Joseph, Husband of Mary?

Participants suggest possible doctrinal themes that flow from the readings.

Possible Doctrinal Themes

Incarnation, faith, mystery of Christ, St. Joseph, protector of the Universal Church

Present the doctrinal material at this time.

1. The facilitator gives input on a particular doctrinal issue of his/her prior choosing. OR
2. The group chooses a doctrinal issue from the list they created. They read together from the Doctrinal Appendix.

(The doctrinal issues are found in the Doctrinal Appendix in the back of this workbook. If you are choosing an issue from this resource, please refer to it now.)

Reflection questions centered around the chosen doctrinal theme can be found at the end of each topic in the Doctrinal Appendix. The questions are based on the five-step reflection process. If you choose a topic not included in the Doctrinal Appendix, craft your own questions according to the same five-step process.

Following the reflection questions you will be reminded to return to chapter 7, "Preparing the Catechetical Session," to assist you in crafting your own session.

Closing Prayer

Lord,
you nourish us at this altar
as we celebrate the feast of St. Joseph.
Protect your Church always,
and in your love watch over the gifts you have
given us.
Grant this through Christ, our Lord.[5]

[5]Solemnity of Joseph, Husband of Mary: "Prayer After Communion," *The Sacramentary.*

SOLEMNITY OF THE ANNUNCIATION OF THE LORD (MARCH 25)

INTRODUCTORY RITES

Opening Song (or Entrance Antiphon)

As Christ came into the world, he said: Behold! I have come to do your will, O God. (Heb 10:5, 7)[1]

Opening Prayer

The facilitator of the session may lead the prayer. Others in the group may be asked to proclaim the readings.

Let us pray
[that Christ, the Word made flesh,
will make us more like him]

Pause for silent prayer.

God, our Father,
your Word became man and was born of the Virgin Mary.
May we become more like Jesus Christ,
whom we acknowledge as our redeemer, God and man.
We ask this through our Lord Jesus Christ, your Son,
who lives and reigns with you and the Holy Spirit,
one God, for ever and ever.[2]

LITURGY OF THE WORD

Let us listen to God's word.

The readings are proclaimed.

First Reading
Isaiah 7:10–14

King Ahaz was undecided on his course of action in the face of military conflict. Like other arrogant monarchs, Ahaz believed in his own self-sufficiency. He did not need the intervention of Yahweh in the affairs of state. The prophet was urging one course of action and Ahaz's advisers another. Isaiah offered a sign. Ahaz was encouraged to seek confirmation of Isaiah's promise, but his mind was already closed. It seemed to him that the obvious course of action was to make an alliance with a powerful nation and rise up against a weaker one. What could go wrong? He did not listen to the Lord's warning. Without a firm faith he would not stand.

God would keep his promise to David and the sign would remain—not to convince Ahaz, but rather to prove the truth of the prophet's word. The word referring to the *woman* with child was not the technical term for virgin. Scholars suggest that the woman, though a hazy character, is probably one of Ahaz's wives. The promised child was a sign himself. This woman would give birth to a child who would be a sign. The child would possess a unique destiny in salvation history. Isaiah's prophecy served as the foundation for Israel's messianic hope.

Christ is the obvious fulfillment of this messianic hope. Christ, Immanuel, is with us as his salvation plan unfolds before the world.

Responsorial Psalm
Psalm 40:7–8, 8–9, 10, 11

Second Reading
Hebrews 10:4–10

The letter to the Hebrews is primarily concerned with reflection upon the Jewish scriptures. The Lectionary omits a very important piece of Hebrews in which the humanity of Jesus is addressed at great length. It is perhaps the "New Testament's most profound and systematic discussion of what it means for Jesus to have been human."[3] This reading is particularly appropriate on this feast that celebrates the announcement of Jesus' birth. The reason for Christ's Incarnation is reparation

[1]Annunciation of the Lord: "Entrance Antiphon," *The Sacramentary.*

[2]Annunciation of the Lord: "Opening Prayer," *The Sacramentary.*

[3]*PTE,* 120–121.

for the sins of the world. With the coming of Jesus, the sacrifices of old are rendered meaningless. Jesus replaced the burnt offerings and sacrifices of the old covenant.

The Pauline community asserts that Jesus definitively assumed unto himself such oblations once and for all. One cannot meditate on the Incarnation without reflection upon the reason for it in the first place: the cross and resurrection.

Gospel
Luke 1:26–38

The angel Gabriel announces the birth of Jesus to Mary.

STEP 1
NAMING ONE'S EXPERIENCE

What were your first impressions? What was your first response? What grabbed your attention? How did you feel?

Each person names his or her initial impression. Statements should be brief. No reasons should be given at this time. All simply listen without agreeing or disagreeing.

STEP 2
UNDERSTANDING

In a brief statement, what do you think this gospel is trying to convey?

STEP 3
INPUT FROM VISION/STORY/TRADITION

Liturgical Context

The first hint of a celebration honoring the Annunciation of the Lord can be traced to the Council of Toledo in 656. Thirty years later the feast was celebrated in Rome. The March 25 date has had a dubious background. There is evidence that the feast was celebrated on December 18, a week prior to Christmas, in Spain around the year 1000. The feast is understood in the context of the Nativity event. The reform of the Vatican Council appropriately named it a feast of the Lord.

The feast strongly resonates with a sound Mariology. Mary is the Mother of God's Son who came to save the world through the paschal mystery—death, resurrection, and glorification. She is a venerated person in the history of salvation because God chose her and graced her to be the mother of Christ. The scriptural texts, the announcement of Jesus' birth, the promised Immanuel of Isaiah, and Paul's letter to the Hebrews regarding the self-gift of Christ to the world, give us the absolute lens through which we are to view and celebrate this event. It is a Christ event—it calls us to fix our gaze on Jesus Christ, Son of God, born of the Virgin Mary.

The introductory rites open the liturgy with a proclamation of Jesus' mission: He came to do his Father's will. This liturgy celebrates the God who sent his Son to become bone and flesh, to be born of a human, virgin mother, to experience life as all human beings experience it (except for the experience of sin) and to one day allow his human body to suffer, die, and rise again for the salvation of all. The Virgin Mary gave completely of herself. She gave her very womb to bear the will of the Father in the flesh.

The liturgy knows well the longing of the human heart and that only Jesus' presence will satisfy it. Mary intercedes for the waiting world (Alternative Opening Prayer) and asks that Jesus fill the void of incompleteness. The opening prayer asks that we become more like Jesus, our redeemer, who is both human and divine. The prayer over the gifts reminds us that the Incarnation of Christ was the beginning of the church. This feast is about Christ. It is a feast of the Lord. It is the cornerstone of our faith and celebrates the primary truths of the Christian faith: Jesus, the Father's only Son, our Lord, became a man and dwelt among us. "...By the power of the Holy Spirit he was born of the Virgin Mary, and became man. For our sake he was crucified under Pontius Pilate; he suffered, died and was buried. On the third day he rose again in fulfillment of the Scriptures; he ascended into heaven and is seated at the right hand of the Father. He will come again in glory to judge the living and the dead, and his kingdom will have no end. We believe in the Holy

Spirit, the Lord, the giver of life, who proceeds from the Father and the Son. With the Father and the Son he is worshiped and glorified. . . ."[4]

Gospel Exegesis

The facilitator gives input regarding what critical biblical scholarship has to say about this text. The input includes insights as to how people would have heard the gospel in Jesus' time.

Luke's announcement story is patterned after other biblical birth announcements of extraordinary persons. The similarities are so strong that they place the contrasts in stark focus. Only twice in biblical tradition does an angel appear to a woman: Hagar (Gen 16:7–16) and Samson's mother (Judg 13: 1–25). The appearance of the angel is to announce to the reader that the events being foretold are part of God's plan of salvation for the world.

The angel's words are similar in the birth announcements of John and Jesus; there are differences, however, in the description of each child's role and identity. John is to be "great before the Lord," but Jesus will be "great and Son of the Most High." John will prepare the people, but Jesus will rule over them. John's role is temporary, Jesus' is endless. John is a prophet, Jesus is more than a prophet: he is the Son of God. Luke's readers are alerted to the graphic differences between John and Jesus and that Jesus is something far greater than a Davidic king.[5]

It is quite remarkable that Luke gave Mary such an important focus. The patriarchal biblical and secular world would have given little credence to the exalted role of a woman. Even more remarkable is the fact that it was Joseph who gave Jesus his legitimacy as heir to the Davidic dynasty. Luke Timothy Johnson maintains that Luke's intention remains unclear. It is possible that his treatment of Mary is a "historical reminiscence, special tradition, or Luke's predilection for presenting positive women figures (evident throughout his narrative)."[6]

[4]Nicene Creed, *The Sacramentary.*

[5]*GL,* 38–39.

[6]Ibid., 39.

In Matthew's account the emphasis is placed on the role of Joseph. Luke gives Mary center stage. Mary's name, a Semitic name (*Mariam* in Greek; *Miryam* in Hebrew), is derived from the Hebrew word for *height* or *summit.* In a feminine context it probably meant "excellence." It is not without significance that Mary's name is the same as that of the mother of Moses. Both are significant characters in God's salvation plan and both have similar stories. Luke tells us very little about Mary in the infancy narratives. The other characters are well introduced. Elizabeth, Joseph, Zechariah, Simeon, and Anna are all identified by their genealogy or their piety. Mary is not heralded as possessing any special characteristics. She is not called righteous, or an astute observer of the law. She is one of society's powerless: she is young in a culture that values age, a female in a man's world, and poor in an unequal economy. A woman's identity is validated through her husband and child—yet she has neither. The great paradox of this passage is that Luke understands God to be a God of surprise, "always reversing human expectations."[7]

We have to wait until the angel's proclamation before we are given a glimpse of how God considers Mary. "Hail, rejoice, Mary!" gives us a clue to her exalted status with God. We are told of her virginity and of her high standing with God. There is no question: Mary is a decent person, in spite of outward appearances. There is no hint of impropriety in Luke's gospel.

Mary is fearful at the angel's announcement. In biblical tradition, fear is a common reaction to angelic messengers. Mary is troubled that the angel said she "had found favor." She was a "favored one." That was an uncommon salutation in the New Testament. The Hebrew scriptures attest to people who were "favored": Noah, Moses, Gideon, Samuel. Perhaps Mary is troubled because a woman was being called "favored by God." A woman was named a key player in God's salvation plan. Perhaps Mary is troubled at the thought of the heavy burden usually placed on "those favored by God." The "favored of God" usually end up paying the ultimate price in their service of God.

[7]Ibid.

Gabriel's declaration to Mary that the Lord is with her is a reminder that she will participate in "God's action to save."[8] The angel announces to Mary that she is to bear a Son and tells her what she is to name him and what his role will be. Mary is incredulous. So was Zechariah. However, there is a difference. Mary's question asks how it could be possible in light of her virginity. Hers is a practical question. Zechariah's question is one of basic disbelief.

Mary's question keeps the story line in a suspenseful forward motion. Gabriel proceeds to tell her how all this will happen. The Holy Spirit will accomplish it. The Holy Spirit will overshadow and come upon her. These are not sexual metaphors for divine-human intercourse. Rather, they are simply statements that God will intervene and do what God intends.

Mary's assent, "be it done unto me according to your will," places her in the role of disciple. Disciples hear the word of God and act on it. All Mary needed to hear was the angel's assurance that it was by divine intervention, not by human design that she should be so blessed. "She prefigures her son's acceptance of God's will, despite the high price that it demands."[9]

The Incarnation is shrouded in obedience. The Son was obedient to the Father, Mary and Joseph were obedient to the word of God through the mediation of an angel. Faithful obedience to God's will is demanded of all faithful disciples. The ancient martyrologies referred to this feast as "The announcement of the divine incarnation to the Blessed Virgin Mary." Today it is less explicitly named "Annunciation of the Lord." "Today is the announcement of the first day of the new era of creation."[10]

Proclaim the gospel again.

Sometimes we gain new insights when we hear the text after the interpretation has been given. Someone from the group proclaims the gospel a second time.

[8] *CBP*, 67.
[9] Ibid., 69.
[10] *DL* (VII), 142.

Step 4
Testing

Conversation with the Liturgy and the Scriptures

Test your original understanding in dialogue with the text.

(You might consider breaking into smaller groups.)

How does your original understanding of this story compare with what was just shared? How does this story speak to your life?

Participants share an experience from their lives that connects with the biblical interpretation just shared.

What does this liturgy have to say to our community and to me today? Has our original understanding been stretched, challenged, or affirmed?

Step 5
Decision

The gospel demands a response.

In what concrete way does this gospel call our parish to action in the church, parish, neighborhood, or world? Has this conversation with the exegesis of this liturgy changed or stretched our personal attitudes? What is one specific action we will take this week as a response to what was learned and shared today?

DOCTRINAL ISSUES

What church truth/teaching/doctrinal issue could be drawn from the gospel for the Solemnity of the Annunciation of the Lord?

Participants suggest possible doctrinal themes that flow from the readings.

Possible Doctrinal Themes

Incarnation, Holy Spirit, role of Mary: mother of God, disciple, Christology

Present the doctrinal material at this time.

1. The facilitator gives input on a particular doctrinal issue of his/her prior choosing. OR
2. The group chooses a doctrinal issue from the list they created. They read together from the Doctrinal Appendix.

(The doctrinal issues are found in the Doctrinal Appendix in the back of this workbook. If you are choosing an issue from this resource, please refer to it now.)

Reflection questions centered around the chosen doctrinal theme can be found at the end of each topic in the Doctrinal Appendix. The questions are based on the five-step reflection process. If you choose a topic not included in the Doctrinal Appendix, craft your own questions according to the same five-step process.

Following the reflection questions you will be reminded to return to chapter 7, "Preparing the Catechetical Session," to assist you in crafting your own session.

Closing Prayer

Father, all powerful and ever-living God,
we do well always and everywhere
to give you thanks through Jesus Christ our Lord.
He came to save mankind by becoming a man
himself.
The Virgin Mary, receiving the angel's message in
faith,
conceived by the power of the Holy Spirit
and bore your son in purest love.
In Christ, the eternal truth,
your promise to Israel was realized beyond all expectations.
Through Christ the angels of heaven
offer their prayer of adoration
as they rejoice in your presence for ever.
May our voices be one with theirs
in their triumphant hymn of praise:
Holy, Holy, Holy Lord, God of power and might,
heaven and earth are full of your glory.
Hosanna in the highest.
Blessed is he who comes in the name of the Lord.
Hosanna in the highest.[11]

[11]Annunciation: "Preface," *The Sacramentary.*

SOLEMNITY OF THE BIRTH OF JOHN THE BAPTIST (JUNE 24)

INTRODUCTORY RITES

Opening Song (or Entrance Antiphon)

There was a man sent from God whose name was John. He came to bear witness to the light, to prepare an upright people for the Lord. (Lk 1:6–7; 17)[1]

Opening Prayer

The facilitator of the session may lead the prayer. Others in the group may be asked to proclaim the readings.

Let us pray
[that God will give us joy and peace]

Pause for silent prayer.

God, our Father,
you raised up John the Baptist,
to prepare a perfect people for Christ the Lord.
Give your Church joy in spirit
and guide those who believe in you
into the way of salvation and peace.
We ask this through our Lord Jesus Christ, your Son,
who lives and reigns with you and the Holy Spirit,
one God, for ever and ever.[2]

LITURGY OF THE WORD

Let us listen to God's word.

The readings are proclaimed.

First Reading
Isaiah 49:1–6

Isaiah foretold a *Suffering Servant,* especially chosen by God, who would suffer and in the end would lead people to salvation. In biblical history this figure eventually became associated with the messiah. Christianity easily saw the Suffering Servant to be a prefigure of Christ who suffered, died, was buried, and rose again for the salvation of the world.

[1]Birth of John the Baptist: "Entrance Antiphon," *The Sacramentary.*

[2]Birth of John the Baptist: "Opening Prayer," *The Sacramentary.*

The Suffering Servant figure was also reminiscent of other prophets who suffered so that others might come to recognize the Holy One upon his arrival. John the Baptist was understood as such a prophet.

His mission was difficult and discouraging. It was easy to lose heart. Prophets were acutely aware that they were driven and propelled by the power of Yahweh. The Servant in today's pericope was assured of God's confidence in the mission God had appointed him to accomplish. The prophetic message is to have everlasting consequences, reaching to the ends of the earth by the power of God. John's mission was to prepare the way for the *Anointed One of God.* His message was one of conversion and repentance. John would be misunderstood and in the end give his life for the *Word* he was sent to herald. But his message not only would reach to the ends of the earth, it would do so for all time. Today's prophetic message would extend to the end of the ages.

Responsorial Psalm
Psalm 139:1–3, 13–14, 14–15

Second Reading
Acts 13:22–26

On Paul's first missionary journey he preached in the synagogue at Pisidia. Paul addressed the people with a foundational truth that both the speaker and the audience shared: Israel was elected by God and David, also elected, was regarded as the king who found favor with God and to whom God made a promise. Unlike the political leaders of today, there were no "spin-doctors" to whitewash David's character. All of his faults were laid bare for biblical history to examine. However, David was memorialized as a larger-than-life character who repented, loved, and was loyal to his God. "Idealized by the biblical tradition in chronicles that are apologies David became the figure of the Messiah himself."[3] Thus, the messiah would come from David's dynasty and emerge

[3]*DL* (VII), 156.

from David's throne. All in Paul's audience could agree on that premise. There was nothing new until Paul spoke of the messiah in past tense terms. By implying that the messiah had already come, Paul threw them a curve. "Paul speaks in the past tense of the Messiah who has already come to Israel and identifies the Messiah with Jesus."[4]

Here is where Paul sparks controversy. This Jewish audience would not be coming with any such presupposition. Paul built on the foundation they knew and understood in order to help them see that within their cherished history lay the seeds of what God had already accomplished through Jesus. Paul's speech is an announcement that the promised messiah has indeed arrived and today sits on the Davidic throne by the power of his death and resurrection.

John heralded the advent of the Savior by preaching a baptism of repentance. He specifically gave testimony to Christ by attesting that a greater one than he was still to come. John was not the expected messiah: of this he was emphatic! He reminds us that we are to prepare our hearts for the reign of Christ in our lives. We are to turn from sin, change our lives and live the good news.

Gospel
Luke 1:57–66, 80

The birth of the Baptist is announced and he is named John.

STEP 1
NAMING ONE'S EXPERIENCE

What were your first impressions? What was your first response? What grabbed your attention? How did you feel?

Each person names his or her initial impression. Statements should be brief. No reasons should be given at this time. All simply listen without agreeing or disagreeing.

[4] *NULA* (II), 166.

STEP 2
UNDERSTANDING

In a brief statement, what do you think this gospel is trying to convey?

STEP 3
INPUT FROM VISION/STORY/TRADITION

Liturgical Context

Jesus himself proclaimed to the world that John was more than a prophet: "the greatest of human beings." The fact that Jesus attested to his greatness and the fact that he was a martyr won him a venerated place among the saints of the early church. He was on a par with the apostles and Stephen.

Celebration of a feast in honor of John the Baptist dates back to the fourth century. The Greeks celebrated it on January 7, the day after Epiphany, the day that commemorated the baptism of the Lord. Since John baptized Jesus in the Jordan, the celebration of his feast was placed on the day following Epiphany. The West celebrated his feast on June 24, thus placing it six months prior to the Nativity of the Lord according to the scripture attesting to this time frame (Lk 1:36a).

Six churches were built in Rome in honor of John. By the sixth century a vigil was attached to the celebration and there were three assigned masses for the day. One of the masses was to be celebrated at the baptistry *(ad fontem)*.

The East established two other feasts in his honor, but the West maintained only one of them: the Beheading of John the Baptist on August 29. His birth is still commemorated in the Byzantine Church on September 24.

The solemnity has a vigil attached to it that includes most of the prayers from the old vigil mass in addition to the inclusion of a second reading, an alleluia verse, and the special preface.[5] This chapter will deal only with the mass of the day, however.

[5] *LY*, 234.

The preface for this feast depicts God's favor bestowed on John. It describes his mission, his martyrdom, and his role in salvation through Christ. The opening prayer asks that we be guided to walk the path of salvation and peace. John, we are told, prepares us to become a perfect people (notice the present tense). The teaching of John will lead us to Christ. We ask for help to live, by the action of our lives, the mystery we celebrate (Vigil Prayer Over the Gifts). This is done in the shadow of John's message of repentance and gospel living.

"In the liturgy of the Church, a 'nativity' is not a birthday. Birthdays are anniversaries of a birth. Instead, a nativity is the birth itself. Today is not John the Baptist's birthday. Today John is born. That is what we sing in the liturgy today!"[6] We remember and make present the effects, implications, and mission of John the Baptist as we celebrate this feast. He is born anew to herald the same message of repentance and conversion.

Places around the world honor the feast day in various ways. People in Europe mark the feast by staying up all night and burning "St. John's fires." In Poland candles are placed on wreaths and floated downriver. In Morocco the Muslims also light fires in his honor. In Sweden people decorate cars, buses, doors, and a Maypole with green birch twigs. The pole is hoisted in the afternoon amid shouts of joy. In Lithuania people sweeten a cheese with honey, which is reminiscent of the food eaten by John. The cheese is prepared to look like the sun.

Gospel Exegesis

The facilitator gives input regarding what critical biblical scholarship has to say about this text. The input includes insights as to how people would have heard the gospel in Jesus' time.

Today's story is less about the announcement of John's birth and more about the naming of John. When John was named, his special identity and role in salvation history were announced. John was given his name on the day of his circumcision. It was a day of celebration and all expected John to be named after his father, Zechariah. Elizabeth, however, proclaimed that his name would be John (in obedience to the command given earlier by Gabriel). The gathered crowd was taken aback and approached Zechariah expecting him to rectify this breach of tradition. Zechariah, unable to speak, confirmed in writing that indeed the child's name was "John." The crowd was astonished!

In antiquity, people's names expressed their role, their character, and very often their mission in life. "Transcending all classifications, it is a person's proper word, speaking his unique identity and singular contribution to history."[7] However, it is not the meaning of John's name ("The Lord has been gracious") that sparks attention in this case; it is the fact that he was named by divine intervention. The fact that God intervened in John's conception and now intervened in his naming called attention to John's significant destiny. A child was born who enjoyed great favor with God. This was great news not only for his parents, but for all in their region.

Because Zechariah did not believe the angel's word that God would send them a child, he was subsequently struck dumb. His speech was restored when he responded to God's earlier directive and named his son *John*, blessing God as he did so. Everyone who heard or witnessed the event was afraid. Zechariah's ability to speak was understood by all as a sign from God that focused attention not on Zechariah's miracle, but on the person of John. All were alerted to the fact that this child was indeed favored by God and great things could be expected as a result. John's mission, however, remained cloaked in mystery.

The story ends with a fast-forward into John's adult life. We are taken to the edge of the desert to await his adult mission. The desert image alerts the reader that John is about to enter a time of preparation for his mission. In the scriptures, the desert signifies a barren area with low rainfall. Sometimes it is called the wilderness. In the bibli-

[6] *CC*, 94.

[7] *LK*, 26, 27.

cal perspective barren places are places where humans encounter God. In the Christian perspective, the desert is a symbol of inner pilgrimage leading to the experience of God.

Many of the salvific acts of the Old Testament occurred in the desert. *It was a place of death.* If people lost their way in the desert, they would surely die. *It was a place of protection and a place of testing.* In the story of Exodus, God led Israel through the desert for forty years. He fed them, provided water for their thirst, and showed them the way through the desert. God entered into a covenant with Israel and it became a people. God tested Israel through its forty-year sojourn. Many of God's dealings with Israel occurred in the desert. "Clearly the desert and God's plan for Israel were intimately bound together."[8] The desert is a place where God tests, forms, and prepares his chosen for their mission, just as God tested, formed, and prepared Israel for its mission in the promised land.

We are told that the child John grew up and matured in spirit. Such an announcement was a biblical formula used to depict the "harmonious development of a child marked before birth by divine grace and one whom 'the hand of the Lord' reposed."[9] John was destined to preach the good news of salvation from his very conception. God's favor rested on him; he could do no less.

John's mission is intimately bound to the mission of Christ. John preached conversion and repentance, thus preparing people to hear and accept Jesus' message. Today the church continues John's preaching mission. John preached a word that cost him his life. It was not a soft word, but a word that demanded *metanoia,* a complete turning of one's heart and life to God. Such preachers usually pay the ultimate price for their work. John paid with his head.

John reminds us that we must prepare the way for Christ to come into our hearts and to the hearts of all people everywhere. He invites us to become evangelists. John reminds us that we are to preach the good news and repent. He invites us to share the gospel and to change our lives.

[8]Craghan, "Desert," in *CPBDT,* 216.

[9]*DL* (VII), 159.

John reminds us that we are to give of our lifeblood in pursuit of the gospel way of life. He invites us to become martyrs. John is our model who reaches out his hand and invites us to follow him, if we dare!

Proclaim the gospel again.

Sometimes we gain new insights when we hear the text after the interpretation has been given. Someone from the group proclaims the gospel a second time.

Step 4
Testing

Conversation with the Liturgy and the Scriptures

Test your original understanding in dialogue with the text.

(You might consider breaking into smaller groups.)

How does your original understanding of this story compare with what was just shared? How does this story speak to your life?

Participants share an experience from their lives that connects with the biblical interpretation just shared.

How does this liturgy challenge our community? How does it challenge me? Has our original understanding been stretched, challenged, or affirmed?

Step 5
Decision

The gospel demands a response.

In what way does this gospel call your parish to action in the church, parish, neighborhood, or world? Be concrete. Has this conversation with the exegesis of this liturgy changed or stretched your personal attitudes? Name one concrete action you will take this week as a response to what was learned and shared today.

DOCTRINAL ISSUES

What church truth/teaching/doctrinal issue could be drawn from the gospel for the Solemnity of the Birth of John the Baptist?

Participants suggest possible doctrinal themes that flow from the readings.

Possible Doctrinal Themes

Conversion, Christology, repentance

Present the doctrinal material at this time.

1. The facilitator gives input on a particular doctrinal issue of his/her prior choosing. OR
2. The group chooses a doctrinal issue from the list they created. They read together from the Doctrinal Appendix.

(The doctrinal issues are found in the Doctrinal Appendix in the back of this workbook. If you are choosing an issue from this resource, please refer to it now.)

Reflection questions centered around the chosen doctrinal theme can be found at the end of each topic in the Doctrinal Appendix. The questions are based on the five-step reflection process. If you choose a topic not included in the Doctrinal Appendix, craft your own questions according to the same five-step process.

Following the reflection questions you will be reminded to return to chapter 7, "Preparing the Catechetical Session," to assist you in crafting your own session.

Closing Prayer

God our Father,
the voice of John the Baptist challenges us to repentance
and points the way to Christ the Lord.
Open our ears to hear his message,
and free our hearts
to turn from our sins and receive the life of the gospel.
We ask this through Christ our Lord.[10]

[10]Birth of John the Baptist: "Alternative Opening Prayer," *The Sacramentary.*

SOLEMNITY OF PETER AND PAUL, APOSTLES (JUNE 29)

INTRODUCTORY RITES

Opening Song (or Entrance Antiphon)

These men, conquering all human frailty, shed their blood and helped the Church to grow. By sharing the cup of the Lord's suffering, they became the friends of God.[1]

Opening Prayer

The facilitator of the session may lead the prayer. Others in the group may be asked to proclaim the readings.

Let us pray
[that we may remain true to the faith of the apostles]

Pause for silent prayer.

God our Father,
today you give us the joy
of celebrating the feast of the apostles Peter and Paul.
Through them your Church first received the faith.
Keep us true to their teaching.
Grant this through our Lord Jesus Christ, your Son,
who lives and reigns with you and the Holy Spirit,
one God for ever and ever.[2]

LITURGY OF THE WORD

Let us listen to God's word.

The readings are proclaimed.

First Reading
Acts 12:1–11

Today's story of Peter's rescue from prison has a deeper significance than that which appears at first glance. It is a story that is reminiscent of other biblical stories of divine rescue. As such, it has a higher purpose than just relating the events of this particular story. "It [the story] recalls the power of God to rescue those chosen for God's mission, a power repeatedly demonstrated in the past."[3]

We are reminded of past events in which there is rescue from evil rulers. Peter's arrest is similar to Jesus' arrest in Luke 22:54. The reference to Passover is intentional. The reader is to make a parallel connection between Jesus' passion story and the story at hand. Jesus' disciples are experiencing the fate he assured them they would endure.

The Passover allusion also serves as a reminder of another past event, the exodus out of bondage in Egypt. The reader is asked to look below the surface for another type of exodus rescue, suggests Robert Tannehill. Peter's language in the later telling of his rescue is laced with exodus language: the Lord "rescued me from the hand of Herod." The command of the angel for Peter to rise and gird himself is reminiscent of the command to the Israelites to eat the Passover with their loins girded and sandals on their feet (Ex 12:11). The rescue of Peter serves as an exodus parable. "For the Church, it is still the time of the Exodus. During the night of this world, it prays with confidence, remembering the pasch of Christ and giving thanks for the marvels God has accomplished, including thanksgiving ahead of time for the crowning marvel: when Christ himself, and no longer an angel, will come back to 'snatch her finally and forever from the hands of all her enemies.'"[4]

Responsorial Psalm
Psalm 34:2–3, 4–5, 6–7, 8–9

Second Reading
2 Timothy 4:6–8, 17–18

---

[1]Peter and Paul, Apostles: "Entrance Antiphon," *The Sacramentary.*

[2]Peter and Paul, Apostles: "Opening Prayer," *The Sacramentary.*

[3]*NULA* (II), 151.

[4]*DL* (VII), 176.

Paul's second letter to Timothy is in the genre of a farewell discourse and exhortation. It is generally believed that Paul was not the author of this letter and that it was written somewhere near the second century. It is further believed that the letter contains fragments of Paul's original words. Those authentic fragments are believed to be the words of today's second reading. Paul is awaiting death from his prison cell as he writes to Timothy. (Please refer to Twenty-Seventh Sunday in Ordinary Time for further background information on 2 Timothy.) "Although he feels close to death (4:6–8), he writes to encourage and admonish his favorite delegate in *his* struggles."[5] *Life poured out like a libation* is language indicative of Greek thought. Libations of wine and oil were often associated with the Jewish liturgy of offering sacrifice. They were also used by the Greeks and the Romans. Wine was poured on the ground in homage to gods at banquets and festive occasions. Paul adapted the pagan notion as an image of his own life, being poured out in sacrifice for the sake of others.

When Paul mentioned that he had kept the faith (v. 7), he meant that through the witness of his life and adherence to the doctrine of Christ crucified, he endured in spite of persecution.

There is no new word for Timothy in this letter; it is simply a reiteration of what Timothy already knows and holds to be true. Paul challenges Timothy to remain steadfast to what he already knows.

In this fourth chapter of second Timothy, Paul presents himself as the model of suffering in hope. In spite of being opposed, Paul had remained strong in his ministry. Timothy is thus exhorted to remain steadfast through suffering and adherence to the gospel, just like Paul. Hope resonates through Paul's encouragement to Timothy. Paul is assured of God's love, God's reign, and God's protection until such time as he is taken safely to the heavenly reign. Paul would win the crown (an olive, laurel, or pine branch wreath was awarded to athletes at the end of a great feat of endurance) through his participation in Jesus' suffering, death, resurrection, and subsequent victory over evil.

[5] *WNT,* 391.

In the second part of today's pericope, Paul speaks of a *first hearing* that no doubt functioned like an arraignment to determine if charges would be leveled. It appears that no one came to Paul's defense at this first hearing. Some scholars suggest that the absence of support by Paul's Christian brothers and sisters might have been due in part to the Roman church's concerns about his orthodoxy. Paul assures Timothy that, with or without their support, Jesus was with him to strengthen and uphold, *to stand by his side and give him strength* (v. 17)

Gospel
Matthew 16:13–19

Peter confesses faith at Caesarea Philippi.

STEP 1
NAMING ONE'S EXPERIENCE

What were your first impressions? What was your first response? What grabbed your attention? How did you feel?

Each person names his or her initial impression. Statements should be brief. No reasons should be given at this time. All simply listen without agreeing or disagreeing.

STEP 2
UNDERSTANDING

In a brief statement, what do you think this gospel is trying to convey?

STEP 3
INPUT FROM VISION/STORY/TRADITION

Liturgical Context

The apostles, those first eyewitnesses to the Jesus event, were paid great homage by the early Christian church. Christ hand-picked them to carry out his mission of salvation to the world. He empowered the first apostles, particularly Peter, to form, strengthen, and build the church. They were the foundation upon which the future church would be built. The early community venerated these noble saints as evidenced by the devotion of Constantine who built a church in their honor.

Origins of a feast commemorating the apostles can be traced to the East where all twelve apostles were remembered in a single feast. Individual feasts were primarily celebrated in places where the tomb of each apostle was located or in places connected with memories of certain apostles.

The two great apostles, Peter and Paul, were martyred in Rome by Nero (54–68). Paul was beheaded and Peter was crucified. Even though there is nothing to suggest that these two martyrdoms occurred simultaneously, both apostles have been remembered on the same day since the mid-third century.

Three liturgies were celebrated in Rome on this feast. Peter was commemorated at a special liturgy celebrated on Vatican Hill in the church that was named after him. Paul was honored in a liturgy on the road to Ostia at St. Paul Outside the Walls. A liturgy commemorating both apostles was celebrated at the "catacombs" (near the present-day St. Sebastian's. It is believed that this is where their bodies or their heads were kept during the persecution of Valerian). Observance of three liturgies posed a hardship for the church of the eighth century, so St. Paul's feast was moved to the next day, even though he was still remembered on June 29. However, the revised Roman calendar removed Paul's feast from the calendar (June 30) except in the place that honors his name: The Roman Basilica of St. Paul.

By the third century, a feast commemorating both apostles extended to the church in Italy and North Africa. By the fifth century most Eastern and Western countries held similar observances. St. Ambrose attested to a vigil observance as early as 397.

The revised Roman calendar maintained the vigil as a mass for the evening preceding the solemnity. Some ritual texts such as the entrance antiphon, the second reading, the presidential prayers, and the preface are new. The opening prayer reminds us that it was through the apostles that the church received its initial faith. We ask for the strength to remain faithful to their teaching. The preface reminds us that each apostle was chosen to gather the church in unity, Peter as its fearless leader and Paul as its gifted preacher. We are reminded of the price each paid for his call to ministry. We too are called to lead and to preach the word of God by the action of our lives. Paul and Peter serve as models of faithful service.

> Father, all-powerful and ever-living God,
> we do well always and everywhere to give you thanks.
> You fill our hearts with joy
> as we honor your great apostles:
> Peter, our leader in faith,
> and Paul, its fearless preacher.
> Peter raised up the Church
> from the faithful flock of Israel.
> Paul brought your call to the nations,
> and became the teacher of the world.
> Each in his chosen way gathered into unity
> the one family of Christ.
> Both shared a martyr's death
> and are praised throughout the world.
> Now, with the apostles and all the angels and saints,
> we praise you for ever:
> Holy, holy, holy Lord, God of power might,
> heaven and earth are full of your glory.
> Hosanna in the highest.
> Blessed is he who comes in the name of the Lord.
> Hosanna in the highest.[6]

We continue to ask for their prayers in the ongoing ministry of word and sacrament in today's church reflected in the prayer over the gifts: "Lord, may your apostles join their prayers to our offering and help us to celebrate this sacrifice in love and unity."[7] We further ask that we be united in love through the breaking of bread in the sacrament of eucharist and through the teaching of the apostles. We are confident that the church will be renewed through our participation in the eucharist and through listening and responding to the teaching of the apostles:

---

[6]Peter and Paul, Apostles: "Preface," *The Sacramentary.*

[7]Peter and Paul, Apostles: "Prayer Over the Gifts," *The Sacramentary.*

Lord,
renew the life of your Church
with the power of this sacrament.
May the breaking of bread
and the teaching of the apostles
keep us united in your love.
We ask this through Christ our Lord.[8]

The celebration of this solemnity reminds us of the church's two-fold dimension: one and universal. Peter and Paul represent the diversity of ministries to further the mission of Christ on earth. "Peter and Paul are the two pillars of the Church, the one the shepherd of Christ's flock who governs from his 'chair' at Rome, the other the missionary, the 'Apostle of Nations' who went all over the world to found ecclesial communities everywhere and to strengthen, in the course of his apostolic journeys, those he had already established."[9]

Gospel Exegesis

The facilitator gives input regarding what critical biblical scholarship has to say about this text. The input includes insights as to how people would have heard the gospel in Jesus' time.

Peter's confession of faith, Jesus' pronouncement of the rigors of discipleship, and the envisioning of the transfiguration are turning points in Jesus' ministry in all three synoptic gospels. Matthew, however, adds the investiture of Peter by Jesus as leader and rock of the church.

Jesus asked the ultimate question of his disciples: "Who do you say that I am?" In answering they would profess faith in him. Peter's insight was astounding as he answered for the whole church. Jesus was overwhelmed at Peter's insight and praised his Father for revealing this truth to one with such childlike faith. Peter professed the faith of the church and was given the keys of the kingdom of God. Until the master's return, the keys will safeguard and protect the Master's property. When Jesus gave Peter the keys, it was a symbol of confidence. He was handing over his property for Peter. As new master of the house, Peter was to lead as a servant and steward. The apostles were fully aware that they would be held accountable for their management of the property in the master's absence. "They were given their authority only for the service of their brethren (John 13:13-17)."[10]

Jesus, as head of the kingdom, or household, exercises authority in God's name. Jesus passes authority on to the church to "mediate salvation in the time between the earthly ministry of Jesus and the future coming of the kingdom."[11]

Enormous authority is given to Peter. Citing R. H. Hiers and J. Jeremias, Benedict Viviano maintains that according to rabbinic legislation, binding and loosing may refer to exorcism of the devil, "to the juridical acts of excommunication and of definitive decision-making (a form of teaching through legislation, policy setting)."[12] The disciples are given the authority to bind and loose in verse 18, but only Peter is the foundation and only Peter is given the keys.

In the gospel of Thomas, James, the leader of the Jewish Christians, was afforded a special role of leadership. The Gentile Christians would have preferred to have had Paul named as their foundational leader. Thus, the ecumenically sensitive Matthew named Peter as the rock, thus holding both communities together in peaceful, delicate balance. It was, after all, Peter who served as spokesman for Jesus in his earthly ministry. Peter may be the keeper of the keys, but in Matthew's ecclesiology, Christ is always present in the whole church and through the power of the Holy Spirit continues to guide the church as it waits for Jesus' return.

The apostles were stewards of Christ's salvation and servants of God's servants. Even though their ministries and their personalities were different, Peter and Paul had similarities. Peter denied Jesus; Paul persecuted him through his disciples. Peter was generous, presumptuous, often hesitant but steadfastly loyal. Paul was a proud Roman citizen who demanded his rightful title of apostle and

[8]Peter and Paul, Apostles: "Prayer After Communion," *The Sacramentary.*

[9]*DL* (VII), 162.

[10]Ibid., 181.

[11]Benedict T. Viviano, O.P., "The Gospel of Matthew," in *NJBC,* 659.

[12]Ibid.

owned his own fragility. Peter was loyal to the institution, but was not afraid to be challenged by the Spirit. Paul evangelized to the nations, but was resisted by his own people. Both were martyrs and gave their lives for the Christ they adored and served with ardent passion. We are to do no less.

Proclaim the gospel again.

Sometimes we gain new insights when we hear the text after the interpretation has been given. Someone from the group proclaims the gospel a second time.

Step 4
Testing

Conversation with the Liturgy and the Scriptures

Test your original understanding in dialogue with the text.

(You might consider breaking into smaller groups.)

How does your original understanding of this story compare with what was just shared? How does this story speak to your life?

Participants share an experience from their lives that connects with the biblical interpretation just shared.

How does this liturgy challenge your community? How does it challenge you? Has your original understanding been stretched, challenged, or affirmed?

Step 5
Decision

The gospel demands a response.

In what way does this gospel call your parish to action in the church, parish, neighborhood, or world? Be concrete. Has this conversation with the exegesis of this liturgy changed or stretched your personal attitudes? Name one concrete action you will take this week as a response to what was learned and shared today.

DOCTRINAL ISSUES

What church truth/teaching/doctrinal issue could be drawn from the gospel for the Solemnity of Peter and Paul, Apostles?

Participants suggest possible doctrinal themes that flow from the readings.

Possible Doctrinal Themes

Discipleship, apostleship, reign of God, martyrdom, the mystery of the church

Present the doctrinal material at this time.

1. The facilitator gives input on a particular doctrinal issue of his/her prior choosing. OR
2. The group chooses a doctrinal issue from the list they created. They read together from the Doctrinal Appendix.

(The doctrinal issues are found in the Doctrinal Appendix in the back of this workbook. If you are choosing an issue from this resource, please refer to it now.)

Reflection questions centered around the chosen doctrinal theme can be found at the end of each topic in the Doctrinal Appendix. The questions are based on the five-step reflection process. If you choose a topic not included in the Doctrinal Appendix, craft your own questions according to the same five-step process.

Following the reflection questions you will be reminded to return to chapter 7, "Preparing the Catechetical Session," to assist you in crafting your own session.

Closing Prayer

Let us pray
[one with Peter and Paul in our faith in
Christ the Son of the living God]

Pause for silent prayer.

Praise to you, the God and Father of our Lord
Jesus Christ,
who in your great mercy
have given us new birth and hope

through the power of Christ's resurrection.
Through the prayers of the apostles Peter and Paul
may we who received this faith through their
preaching
share their joy in following the Lord
to the unfading inheritance
reserved for us in heaven.
We ask this in the name of Jesus the Lord.[13]

OR

The Lord has set you firm within his Church,
which he built upon the rock of Peter's faith.
May he bless you with a faith that never falters.
(Amen.)

The Lord has given you knowledge of the faith
through the labors and preaching of St. Paul.
May his example inspire you to lead others to
Christ
by the manner of your life. (Amen.)

May the keys of Peter, and the words of Paul,
their undying witness and their prayers,
lead you to the joy of that eternal home
which Peter gained by his cross, and Paul by the
sword. (Amen.)[14]

---

[13]Peter and Paul, Apostles: "Alternative Opening Prayer," *The Sacramentary.*

[14]Peter and Paul, Apostles: "Solemn Blessing," *The Sacramentary.*

Feast of the Transfiguration (August 6)

INTRODUCTORY RITES

Opening Song (or Entrance Antiphon)

In the shining cloud the Spirit is seen; from it the voice of the Father is heard: This is my Son, my beloved, in whom is all my delight. Listen to him. (See Mt 17:5)[1] (Or sung psalm or song)

Opening Prayer

The facilitator of the session may lead the prayer. Others in the group may be asked to proclaim the readings.

Let us pray
[that we may hear the Lord Jesus
and share his everlasting life]

Pause for silent prayer.

God our Father,
in the transfigured glory of Christ your Son,
you strengthen our faith
by confirming the witness of your prophets,
and show us the splendor of your beloved sons
and daughters.
As we listen to the voice of your Son,
help us to become heirs to eternal life with him
who lives and reigns with you and the Holy
Spirit,
one God, for ever and ever.[2]

LITURGY OF THE WORD

Let us listen to God's word.

The readings are proclaimed.

First Reading
Daniel 7:9–10, 13–14

The prophet is not a fortune teller. He proclaims what he hears, but even he does not fully understand all there is to know about the word he has been given. With time and the passage of events, the meaning becomes clearer. The prophet and his contemporaries do not necessarily see the prophetic word as foretelling specific future events.

Often it is only hindsight that gives meaning to the biblical prophecy. The New Testament uses much of Hebrew prophecy in that way. A past prophecy helps explain the meaning of present events. Daniel's vision helps explain the full implications of what the disciples witnessed on Mount Tabor.

The church often chooses scripture in its liturgy to shed light on specific mysteries. It does not give new meaning to the texts, but it uses them to further reveal the meaning of an event, feast, or specific celebration. Jesus, the Son of Man, is the *One* Daniel heralds in his vision.

In Daniel's vision the people of God are living in the midst of persecution and oppression. To all appearances, God appears to be powerless. An ageless, ancient personage takes his place on the throne. His white hair and garment give him a radiant brilliance. All attend to this magnificent person as he passes judgment on the good and the evil. Then another person appears, one like a son of man, who has been given authority over all the earth. The Ancient One gives this person everlasting authority. The term "son of man" originally referred to every member of the human race. It eventually came to refer to a perfect man, who was an image of God and was representative of the entire human race. This new man, unlike Adam, originates from heaven. Jesus is understood in the New Testament as this Son of Man. Jesus, the Son of Man, will establish the reign Daniel proclaims in this first reading. Jesus, Son of Man, does have dominion over all the earth. Jesus' reign is everlasting and the entire world bows before him.

Responsorial Psalm
Psalm 97:1–2, 5–6, 9

The Lord is king, the most high over all the earth.

[1]Feast of the Transfiguration: "Entrance Antiphon," *The Sacramentary.*

[2]Feast of the Transfiguration: "Opening Prayer," *The Sacramentary.*

Second Reading
2 Peter 1:16–19

Peter is exhorting his believers to embrace the message they have been given about Christ as an authentic and true word. It is a not a myth. Peter and the other disciples witnessed Jesus' glory themselves on top of Mount Tabor. The apostles experienced the presence of the risen Christ after his death. Their testimony is true and trustworthy. The church can count on their eyewitness account. The church's faith rests on the testimony of the apostles. The Christian professes belief in the resurrection and ascension into glory of Christ and understands it as an act of prophetic fulfillment. The gospel opens to us the meaning of past prophecy, but always points us to the future. Through his life, passion, death, and resurrection, Jesus fulfilled scripture and revealed to us its deepest meaning. Even though Christ was revealed in his glory on Tabor, we still await the final glory when all will stand with him in the light of heaven. We continue to wait for his final return but are sustained and nourished by the sacrament of Christ's word in the scripture and eucharist.

Gospel
Matthew 17:1–9

Jesus is transfigured before their eyes.

STEP 1
NAMING ONE'S EXPERIENCE

What were your first impressions? What was your first response? What grabbed your attention? How did you feel?

Each person names his or her initial impression. Statements should be brief. No reasons should be given at this time. All simply listen without agreeing or disagreeing.

STEP 2
UNDERSTANDING

In a brief statement, what do you think this gospel is trying to convey?

STEP 3
INPUT FROM VISION/STORY/TRADITION

Liturgical Context

The foundation for this feast rests with the fact that all three versions of the event in the synoptic gospels agree on what happened. Early in Lent our eyes are turned toward Mount Tabor in order to prepare us to encounter the glory of Christ crucified during the Triduum. Now, forty days before the feast of the Triumph of the Cross, we are once again asked to reflect in similar fashion. We are reminded that through Christ's passion and death he entered into glory. Once again, on August 6, we are invited into the glory and brilliance of Easter that reminds us of our ultimate destiny and eschatological hope—a share in the glory of Christ.

This feast dates back to the fourth century in the East. The monks of the desert were the first to pay particular attention to the transfiguration event. They reflected upon the transfigured glory of Christ as part of their mystic spirituality.

An official feast was observed in Spain around the tenth century and rapidly spread due (it is believed) to a heightened interest in the sacred sites of the Holy Land. Abbot Peter the Venerable established the feast and wrote an office for it at Cluny. Calistus III instituted it in Rome before he became pope (1455–1458). It was placed in the calendar in 1457 in thanksgiving for the victory over the Turks the previous year by John of Capistrano and John Hunyadi.

We are reminded in the opening prayer that the transfigured glory of Christ was foretold by the prophets of old. We ask that as we listen to and grow in Christ we may become heirs to his promise. The prayer over the gifts reminds us that through the power of the resurrected, glorified Christ, the gifts of bread and wine are made holy, transformed and become his body and blood.

> Lord, by the transfiguration of your Son,
> make our gifts holy,
> and by his radiant glory free us from our sins.[3]

---

[3]Feast of the Transfiguration: "Prayer Over the Gifts," *The Sacramentary.*

The celebration of this liturgy serves as a further reminder that every eucharistic liturgy is participation in the passion, death, resurrection, and ascension into the glory of Christ. Thus, through the power of Christ in the eucharist we are changed to become more like him.

> Lord,
> you revealed the true radiance of Christ
> in the glory of his transfiguration.
> May the food we receive from heaven
> change us into his image.[4]

Gospel Exegesis

The facilitator gives input regarding what critical biblical scholarship has to say about this text. The input includes insights as to how people would have heard the gospel in Jesus' time.

All three synoptic gospels report the story of the transfiguration of Jesus on Mount Tabor. The accounts are very similar, yet distinct. As is customarily the case, each of the evangelists interpreted the events from his own unique perspective and for his own purposes.

Matthew and Mark both tell us that the event on Mount Tabor took place six days after Jesus announced that he would suffer and die. Luke insists that it was eight days later. This puts the event in close proximity to the death and resurrection and thus with the Passover of the Lord.

In order to interpret the mystery of the transfiguration, in itself inexpressible and indescribable, the evangelists employed a double literary structure.[5] They called upon two very well-known biblical characters of old who themselves had experienced God's manifestation. Both Elijah and Moses came face to face with God on a mountain in the Old Testament. The evangelists also draw on the apocalypses in the Book of Daniel.

All three gospels give approximately the same details. Jesus went up the mountain with Peter, James, and John. Suddenly Jesus changed in appearance; he was transfigured by a brilliant light as Moses and Elijah appeared with him. Peter is dumbfounded, but speaks first. He does not understand what is happening. A voice from heaven thunders the same message that was announced at Jesus' baptism: "This is my beloved Son." The voice addresses the apostles and then the vision vanishes.

Jesus and the apostles are alone again and make their way down the mountain together. The apostles do not understand what they just experienced and therefore do not say anything to anyone. They do not, however, forget. They speak of it again after the resurrection when they interpret it in light of the resurrection, and they interpret the resurrection in light of their experience on Tabor.

The apostles, though the only privileged ones to witness the event, were given the experience for the sake of the entire church. The transfiguration was understood as a preview of Christ's resurrected glory. The transfiguration reminds the church and the people of God of the hope and the glory of the resurrection as we experience Jesus Christ crucified, and his persecution, trials, tribulations, suffering, doubts, and lack of hope. The transfiguration bolsters our spirit during those times that try our souls and our patience. When in the depths of hell, the transfiguration transports us to the heights of heaven.

Matthew's version of the transfiguration presents Christ as the one who will return to the world in glory at the end of time. Matthew's common theme of God's reign and the Old Testament tradition weaves its way into his account of the transfiguration. The kingdom was proclaimed by the prophets and established by Christ himself. Jesus will come again—when we do not know, but come he will. And the church will be waiting for his return. In the meantime, we are to put into action the words, life, and commands of our Master. We can be confident that Jesus will return because, even though none of us has seen him, the three apostles *did* see him in his resurrected glory. This is the hope to which we cling.

Jesus entered into God's glory. He sits at God's throne and from that throne he will judge both the living and the dead. We know him to be God's Son, the beloved one. We are to spend our lives preparing to meet him when he comes again.

---

[4]Feast of the Transfiguration: "Prayer After Communion," *The Sacramentary.*

[5]*DL* (VII), 193.

Great and significant events in Jesus' life take place on a mountain. It is a place of manifestation for Matthew. In Matthew's gospel the temptation of Jesus (4:8), his inaugural sermon (5:1), the sending of the apostles on the mission of the church, were all mountain-top events. The Lord will usher those who are his own into the light of glory on a high mountain at the end of time; Tabor evokes that image.

When the people of God are taken to the light of glory they will know the same transfiguration that Jesus experienced on Mount Tabor. They will shine with the light of God.

Moses and Elijah represent the law and the prophets—the entire scripture—the revealed word of God now fulfilled in the Christ event. We have seen his glory. Now we can go back down the mountain and share that glory with others until the day when it will be fully revealed to all the nations.

The language Matthew uses is reminiscent of the Easter language of the passion, death, and post-resurrection stories. The apostles are told "not to be afraid." Jesus "touched" them like he touched those he healed. They were told to "rise" just as Christ would rise. Jesus also tells the church not to be afraid, to rise, and to continue to march to the light of the glory that awaits us. We cannot just give lip service to our march, but we must back it up with our service in the kingdom of God. On that great and wonderful day we will joyfully go with Christ into the light of his glory.

Proclaim the gospel again.

Sometimes we gain new insights when we hear the text after the interpretation has been given. Someone from the group proclaims the gospel a second time.

STEP 4
TESTING

Conversation with the Liturgy and the Scriptures

Test your original understanding in dialogue with the text.

(You might consider breaking into smaller groups.)

How does your original understanding of this story compare with what was just shared? How does this story speak to your life?

Participants share an experience from their lives that connects with the biblical interpretation just shared.

How does this liturgy challenge your community? How does it challenge you? Has your original understanding been stretched, challenged, or affirmed?

STEP 5
DECISION

The gospel demands a response.

In what way does this gospel call your parish to action in the church, parish, neighborhood, or world? Be concrete. Has this conversation with the exegesis of this liturgy changed or stretched your personal attitudes? Name one concrete action you will take this week as a response to what was learned and shared today.

DOCTRINAL ISSUES

What church truth/teaching/doctrinal issue could be drawn from the gospel for feast of the Transfiguration?

Participants suggest possible doctrinal themes that flow from the readings.

Possible Doctrinal Themes

Christology, Spirit of God, transfiguration, ascension, paschal mystery, resurrection, parousia, eschatology, mission of the church, evangelization, sacrament of baptism

Present the doctrinal material at this time.

1. The facilitator gives input on a particular doctrinal issue of his/her prior choosing. OR
2. The group chooses a doctrinal issue from the list they created. They read together from the Doctrinal Appendix.

(The doctrinal issues are found in the Doctrinal Appendix in the back of this workbook. If you are choosing an issue from this resource, please refer to it now.)

Reflection questions centered around the chosen doctrinal theme can be found at the end of each topic in the Doctrinal Appendix. The questions are based on the five-step reflection process. If you choose a topic not included in the Doctrinal Appendix, craft your own questions according to the same five-step process.

Following the reflection questions you will be reminded to return to chapter 7, "Preparing the Catechetical Session," to assist you in crafting your own session.

Closing Prayer

Lord,
you revealed the true radiance of Christ
in the glory of his transfiguration.
May the food we receive from heaven
change us into his image.
We ask this in the name of Jesus.[6]

---

[6]Feast of the Transfiguration: "Prayer After Communion," *The Sacramentary.*

Solemnity of the Assumption (August 15)

INTRODUCTORY RITES

Opening Song (or Entrance Antiphon)

All honor to you, Mary! Today you were raised above the choirs of angels to lasting glory with Christ.[1]

Opening Prayer

The facilitator of the session may lead the prayer. Others in the group may be asked to proclaim the readings.

Let us pray
[that the Virgin Mary will help us with her prayers]

Pause for silent prayer.

Almighty God,
you gave a humble virgin
the privilege of being the mother of your Son,
and crowned her with the glory of heaven.
May the prayers of the Virgin Mary
bring us to the salvation of Christ
and raise us up to eternal life.
We ask this through our Lord Jesus Christ, your Son,
who lives and reigns with you and the Holy Spirit,
one God for ever and ever.[2]

LITURGY OF THE WORD

Let us listen to God's word.

The readings are proclaimed.

First Reading
Revelation 11:19; 12:1–6, 10

[1]Vigil of the Assumption: "Entrance Antiphon," *The Sacramentary.*

[2]Vigil of the Assumption: "Opening Prayer," *The Sacramentary.*

This eschatological reading reminds us of previous prophets who spoke of Jerusalem's and the people's promised glory in the last days. The image of a woman in the pangs of childbirth emerges as a symbol of new life that can come to pass only in the fullness of time and only after enduring unavoidable pain.

It is tempting to think that Mary is the mother about to give birth to Christ, the child about to be born. However, the author was not thinking of Mary. Christ is about to come to birth in the lives of people. It is painful because it is accompanied by sorrow, persecution, and the daily struggle to persevere. The woman is a symbol of the church who exists in the midst of God's glory, yet nevertheless is bound to the struggles of this earthly sojourn. Christ protects and strengthens her as she passes from death to life.

Even though the author of Revelation was not referring to Mary in his vision, Christian tradition has always understood the woman as an image of Mary. The meaning is not changed, however. Mary is a symbol of the church who still gives birth to Christ in the lives of the faithful. "God willed this unique and marvelous divine motherhood to be the figure and exemplar of the fecundity of the virgin Church that also becomes a mother... the Church in the sacrament of baptism somehow continues Mary's virginal motherhood. We may offer one example of this teaching from our predecessor St. Leo the Great; in one of his Christmas sermons he says: '[Christ] placed in the baptismal font the source of his own origin in the womb of the Virgin: the power of the most high and the overshadowing of the water to give rebirth to the believer.'[3] And if we want to find the same idea in liturgical

[3]Leo the Great, *Tractatus* (In Nativitate Domini) 5: CCL 138, 123: SC 22 bis, 132; see also *Tractatus* (In Nativitate Domini) 1: CCL 138, 147; SC 22 bis, 178; *Tractatus* 63 (De Passione Domini) 6: CCL 138, 386; SC 74, 82. In *DOL, 1963–1979: Conciliar, Papal and Curial Texts,* Section 4: Sanctoral Cycle: A. Mary, 1213.

sources, we can cite the very beautiful *Illatio* [preface] of the Mozarabic liturgy: '[Mary] carried life in her womb; the Church, in the baptismal font. In the body of Mary Christ put on flesh; in the waters of the Church the baptized put on Christ.'"[4, 5]

Responsorial Psalm
Psalm 45:10, 11, 12, 16

The queen stands at your right hand, arrayed in gold.

Second Reading
1 Corinthians 15:20–26

There is no denying that Jesus rose from the dead. This is the core of our faith: Christ conquered death once and for all. Our salvation depends on it. All will live because of Christ, the "first fruit." When the first fruits of the harvest were offered, it was considered a sample of the entire harvest. Symbolically it was a rendering of the entire harvest to God. Thus, Christ offered himself completely for the human race. In that offering the entire human race was offered with him. Christ freed Adam's heirs from the stain of his sin. Christ's act of self surrender was definitive. His death and resurrection accomplished salvation for the entire world—once and for all. We still await the final day when he will return and establish his heavenly rule forever. We continue to remain vigilant until that last and final victory over death. When Jesus comes again, death will be no longer. In one last grand act, the human race will be resurrected into everlasting glory. Mary is a sign of the hope we all share as we await that great and glorious day.

Gospel
Luke 1:39–56

Mary sets out to see Elizabeth, the baby leaps in Mary's womb, and Mary proclaims the glory of God.

[4]M. Ferotin, *Le Liber Mozarabicus Sacramentorum* col. 56. In *DOL 1963–1979: Conciliar, Papal and Curial Texts*, Section 4: Sanctoral Cycle: A. Mary, 1213.

[5]*DOL 1963–1979: Conciliar, Papal and Curial Texts*, Section 4: Sanctoral Cycle: A. Mary, #19, #3917, p. 1213.

Step 1
Naming One's Experience

What were your first impressions? What was your first response? What grabbed your attention? How did you feel?

Each person names his or her initial impression. Statements should be brief. No reasons should be given at this time. All simply listen without agreeing or disagreeing.

Step 2
Understanding

In a brief statement, what do you think this gospel is trying to convey?

Step 3
Input from Vision/Story/Tradition

Liturgical Context

Even after they had converted to Christianity, people who had formerly been pagans continued the practice of honoring their dead. They purged the paganism from their commemoration of dead ancestors by placing their memorial celebrations within the context of their faith in Christ and his resurrection. They sang hymns to Christ and eventually began the practice of gathering near the tombs of their ancestors on anniversaries of their death. If a person had been martyred, all gathered around his or her tomb to commemorate the anniversary of that person's death. These celebrations were eventually moved into the church. Commemoration of the most famous martyrs spread to the church at large.

Veneration of martyrs continued. Added to the list were those "confessors of faith," who had not spilt their blood, but had suffered prison, exile, or forced labor for the cause of Christianity. Virgins and mystics who had given their lives to the Lord's service of prayer and solitude were also included as persons to be venerated and remembered. A life of dedication and consecration was understood as a type of martyrdom. This is how the church's practice of venerating the saints evolved.

Mary's role in scripture seemed to end with the Pentecost event. We do not hear of her again. However, in 431 the third ecumenical council at Ephesus took action that resulted in the beginning of the cult of the Virgin Mary. The council declared that Christ was both God and man, refuting the teaching of Nestorius. Mary became the "Mother of God—Theotokos." Afterward, Pope Sixtus III (432–440) built a basilica in honor of the Mother of God—"St. Mary Major." The first liturgical observance centered around the feast of the Nativity both in the East and in the West.

There is evidence of apocryphal writings dating from the fourth century telling of Jesus' appearance to Mary two years after his ascension to tell her that she would soon be assumed into heaven. There were other apocryphal writings that spoke of Mary's death and of her being carried up to heaven.

The origin of this feast occurred in Jerusalem with a celebration that took place near the location where it is believed that Mary *rested* (*koimesis,* which in Greek means either rest of sleep or sleep of death) before entering Bethlehem. By the end of the fifth century the feast (Dormition of Mary) was celebrated at Gethsemane where Mary's tomb was venerated. The feast commemorated her death and entrance into heaven.

By the end of the sixth century this was made an obligatory feast in the East. The West celebrated a similar obligatory feast remembering her motherhood on January 1 in Rome. The August 15 date was established around the year 650 and the celebration centered around the glorification of the Virgin Mary. The term *dormition* was used until 770 when the word *assumption* appeared.

Since there were no authentic witnesses to the Marian events, the reticent church of the ninth century did not insist upon adherence to the doctrine of Mary's glorification. "For a long time the magisterium remains silent: It silently observes the dialogue between the intuitions of the 'lovers' of Mary and the reticence of the theologians, who respect above all the witness of the word of God, including its silences."[6] There were, however, nearly twenty feasts devoted to Mary in the Roman Calendar.

The church took a stronger position with regard to Mary in 1854 when Pius IX defined the Dogma of the Immaculate Conception and in 1950 when Pius XII defined the Assumption. The new calendar promulgated by Paul VI arranged the Marian feasts according to their importance; the feasts were "integrated in a clear way into the mystery of salvation through Christ, the true object of Christian faith and worship."[7]

> On August 15 we celebrate the glorious Assumption of Mary into heaven. It is the festival honoring the fullness of blessedness that was her destiny, the glorification of her immaculate soul and virginal body that completely conformed her to the risen Christ. This is a celebration that offers to the Church and to all humanity an exemplar and a consoling message, teaching us the fulfillment of our highest hopes: their own future glorification is happily in store for all those whom Christ has made his own brothers and sisters by taking on their "flesh and blood" (Heb. 2:14, see Gal. 4:4). The solemnity of the Assumption is continued on into the celebration of the Queenship of Mary on the octave day. She who is enthroned next to the King of Ages is contemplated as the radiant Queen and interceding Mother. These then are the four solemnities [Immaculate Conception, Mary Mother of God, the Annunciation, and the Assumption of Mary] that in their high rank as liturgical celebrations bring out the main truths related to the simple handmaid of the Lord.[8]

---

[6]M. Bobichon, *Marie dans la nouvelle Liturgie de la Parole,* tome 1, Pâque nouvelle (Lyon: Chalet, 1971), 110, in *DL* (VII), 202.

[7]Ibid.

[8]Paul VI, Apostolic Exhortation *Marialis cultus,* on rightly grounding and increasing Marian devotion, 2 February 1974: AAS 66 (1974) 113–168; Not 10 (1974) 153–197, in *DOL 1963–1979: Conciliar, Papal and Curial Texts,* Section 4: Sanctoral Cycle: A. Mary, #3904, p. 1208.

There are two masses for this solemnity: the vigil and the day of the feast. The vigil celebration focuses on "Mary's glory and her significance in the history of salvation. The Mother of our Savior, the Son of God, is already elevated to the glory of the elect, where she bears witness to the victory over death that will shine for all those who follow Christ, who hear the word of God and observe it."[9] The mass during the day reminds us of the self-offering of Mary and the foreshadowing of that same pasche in the church. Mary's joy at the birth of her Son is intimately connected to her sorrow at his death. The mass of the day celebrates Mary as the symbol of the church and a sign for all believers who journey toward their heavenly glory with Christ. Mary is a sign of hope for us all.

Gospel Exegesis

The facilitator gives input regarding what critical biblical scholarship has to say about this text. The input includes insights as to how people would have heard the gospel in Jesus' time.

Luke is not concerned with telling us a story about two pregnant relatives who meet one last time before their babies' birth. Nor is it a story that denotes Mary's concern and care for Elizabeth in her time of need. If that were the case, Luke would not have Mary departing when Elizabeth's need is obviously the greatest. Rather, through the literary devices inherent in storytelling, Luke provides a theology of God's plan of salvation through Jesus. The two mothers-to-be are gathered in praise of God for the work God is doing in and through them. In their gathering, the theological reality that John is the precursor of Jesus and that Jesus is the Savior who is superior to John is proclaimed. This is the point of the story.

There are four literary devices commonly used in Luke/Acts to illustrate God's plan. They are: previews and reviews, repeated or highlighted scriptural references, commission statements, and interpretive statements by reliable characters. Robert Tannehill suggests that there may be details in the story that review what God has already done in the past and preview what God is about to do, "in a way that interprets these events."[10] Through the birth stories of both John and Jesus, Luke previews what God intends for humanity's redemption. Through various images and words, the reader knows that reference is being made to God's plan revealed throughout the scriptures.

Through allusions to scriptural passages and traditions, the reader is shown that "the law and the prophets are fulfilled in Jesus."[11] These same passages also express a particular understanding of God's purpose and are programs for action.[12] For example, when Elizabeth tells us that the baby leapt in her womb, the reader is reminded of the leaping of Rebekah's twin children, Jacob and Esau. According to biblical tradition, leaping in-utero foreshadowed a future relationship and "symbolized destinies that would be lived out by the children."[13] In John's leaping we are previewing a future relationship between Jesus and John.[14] Through the power of the Holy Spirit, Elizabeth is able to interpret John's leaping. John leapt in Elizabeth's womb because the destiny of the world was being fulfilled in the baby within Mary's womb.

The third literary device is the agent, the chosen instrument, "reliable persons commissioned by God to carry out God's purpose."[15] In this story both Elizabeth and Mary are those instruments. Both have been obedient to the will of God and, as a result, both bring God's intended plan of redemption to birth in the world. In biblical tradition, Mary leaving in haste refers to an "interior disposition that makes one act with fervor and zeal."[16] Mary is understood as great because of the child she will bear and is praised because of her relationship to Christ. Mary's role is christological. She has a role in God's liberating plan for the human race.

The fourth literary technique is the commission, the call and mission of the individual in question. When Elizabeth says, "... blessed is the fruit of

[9]*DL* (VII), 203–204.

[10]*NULA* (II), 20–38.

[11]Ibid., 21.

[12]Ibid., 22.

[13]*WWC*, 272.

[14]Karris, "The Gospel According to Luke," in *NJBC*, 681.

[15]*NULA* (II), 21.

[16]*DL* (I), 158.

your womb. Who am I that the mother of my Lord should come to me?" she prophesies about the mission of the child in Mary's womb. This child will bring salvation. He will be the fulfillment of God's plan. Luke wants to make it clear that both John and Jesus have a unique role to play. John will prepare the way and will be the bridge between the old covenant and the new covenant. John will help prepare hearts for giving birth to the advent of the Messiah. Jesus, however, is that messiah. Jesus is the One who will fulfill Israel's hopes. Luke insists that his community have no illusions about "who's who" in the eschatological events about to take place.

Mary and Elizabeth, two great women of scripture, listen to God and become the ultimate paradigm of disciple. In this scriptural text Mary becomes the great gift and model for the church. She listens, she responds, she obeys with fervor and zeal the voice of God and she acts on that Word. We, too, are exhorted to "go in haste," to go with zeal and fervor to live the call of the gospel and to share the mighty news it contains. Mary models for us the perfect liturgy. She listens, she gives thanks and praise, she responds in faith to the Word of God, and then she goes in haste.

Proclaim the gospel again.

Sometimes we gain new insights when we hear the text after the interpretation has been given. Someone from the group proclaims the gospel a second time.

Step 4
Testing

Conversation with the Liturgy and the Scriptures

Test your original understanding in dialogue with the text.

(You might consider breaking into smaller groups.)

How does your original understanding of this story compare with what was just shared? How does this story speak to your life?

Participants share an experience from their lives that connects with the biblical interpretation just shared.

How does this liturgy challenge our community? How does it challenge me? Has our original understanding been stretched, challenged, or affirmed?

Step 5
Decision

The gospel demands a response.

In what way does this gospel call your parish to action in the church, parish, neighborhood, or world? Be concrete. Has this conversation with the exegesis of this liturgy changed or stretched your personal attitudes? Name one concrete action you will take this week as a response to what was learned and shared today.

DOCTRINAL ISSUES

What church truth/teaching/doctrinal issue could be drawn from the gospel for the Solemnity of the Assumption of Mary?

Participants suggest possible doctrinal themes that flow from the readings.

Possible Doctrinal Themes

Mary, Mother of God, the Assumption of Mary, Mary, symbol of the church

Present the doctrinal material at this time.

1. The facilitator gives input on a particular doctrinal issue of his/her prior choosing. OR
2. The group chooses a doctrinal issue from the list they created. They read together from the Doctrinal Appendix.

(The doctrinal issues are found in the Doctrinal Appendix in the back of this workbook. If you are choosing an issue from this resource, please refer to it now.)

Reflection questions centered around the chosen doctrinal theme can be found at the end of each topic in the Doctrinal Appendix. The questions are based on the five-step reflection process. If you choose a topic not included in the Doctrinal Appendix, craft your own questions according to the same five-step process.

Following the reflection questions you will be reminded to return to chapter 7, "Preparing the Catechetical Session," to assist you in crafting your own session.

Closing Prayer

Lord,
may we who receive this sacrament of salvation
be led to the glory of heaven
by the prayers of the Virgin Mary.
We ask this in the name of Jesus the Lord.[17]

[17]Solemnity of the Assumption: "Prayer After Communion," *The Sacramentary.*

FEAST OF THE TRIUMPH OF THE CROSS (SEPTEMBER 14)

INTRODUCTORY RITES

Opening Song (or Entrance Antiphon)

We should glory in the cross of our Lord Jesus Christ, for he is our salvation, our life and our resurrection; through him we are saved and made free. (See Gal 6:14)[1]

Opening Prayer

The facilitator of the session may lead the prayer. Others in the group may be asked to proclaim the readings.

Let us pray
[that the death of Christ on the cross
will bring us to the glory of the
resurrection]

Pause for silent prayer.

God our Father,
in obedience to you
your only Son accepted death on the cross
for the salvation of mankind.
We acknowledge the mystery of the cross on earth.
May we receive the gift of redemption in heaven.
We ask this through our Lord Jesus Christ, your
Son,
who lives and reigns with you and the Holy Spirit,
one God, for ever and ever.[2]

LITURGY OF THE WORD

Let us listen to God's word.

The readings are proclaimed.

First Reading
Numbers 21:4–9

The snake was a sign of danger, confusion, and even wisdom. In mythology the snake was a sign of fertility and rebirth. If a person was bitten by a snake and remained unharmed, it was a sign of some sort of divine protection. All these images creep into the telling of today's story.

The scene is the desert following Israel's escape from Egypt. The cast includes Moses and the people of Israel. The situation centers around the amnesia of Israel. The people had forgotten all that God had done for them. They obnoxiously believed that God took them to the desert to let them die. God was angered by their lack of faith and sent serpents among them. Many people died from the sting of these serpents. The people understood this tragedy to be a result of and punishment for their sin.[3] They prayed to be delivered. God told them to take a pole and fashion a serpent on the top of it. All who looked at the pole would be healed.

The serpent episode is typical of God's relationship with Israel. Israel sinned. God punished. The people repented and were converted wholeheartedly to the Lord who was ready to forgive their sins. The Christian tradition connected this reading and the image of the bronze serpent with the cross of Christ. Christ, elevated on the cross, was a sign of healing, salvation, and forgiveness.

Responsorial Psalm
Psalm 78:1–2, 34–35, 36–37, 38

Do not forget the works of the Lord!

Second Reading
Philippians 2:6–11

It is believed that Paul inserted this beautiful, previously crafted hymn into his letter to the Philippians. Some consider it a perfect expression of Pauline theology regarding the passion and death of Jesus. This hymn was probably used in ancient Christian liturgies and profoundly captures the essence and the paradox of Christian redemption. Jesus, through abject humiliation (see Fourth Sun-

[1]Feast of the Triumph of the Cross: "Entrance Antiphon," *The Sacramentary.*

[2]Feast of the Triumph of the Cross: "Opening Prayer," *The Sacramentary.*

[3]Israel understood all life to be ordered by God. They understood all blessings to be a result of God's benevolence and all tragedy to be a result of God's anger.

day of Lent, Cycle C, parable of prodigal son), offered the free gift of himself. Through such humiliation, salvation was won. Jesus left his rightful throne with Yahweh, descended into the midst of humanity and took the form of a slave, subject to the suffering and limitations of the human person. He allowed himself to be rejected, misunderstood, and treated like a slave and a criminal. Because of this free gift of self, this abasement, Jesus ascended back to the throne victorious. Because of the resurrection, humanity was and is offered freedom from the ravages of sin and death, and the promise of eternal life. Jesus, the perfect servant, model of all perfect servants, earned the rightful title, Lord, *Kyrios* (Greek), *Adonai* (Hebrew).

Paul was addressing the dissensions and factions in the Philippian community. He pleaded that all assume the posture of Jesus. If they would only assume the model of Christ's self-abasement, then harmony and peace would be restored to the community. Jesus could have claimed all the rights and privileges of royalty. But he did not. "He became sin"; he entered the human condition with all its defects and in the process emptied himself. The Philippian community was exhorted to embrace *kenosis,* a voluntary emptying of oneself in the manner of Jesus. Paul challenged his community to assume the humble stance of self-giver rather than give in to the lure of power and control. Jesus, emptied and poured-out, went willingly to his passion and death. We are to follow in his footsteps.

Gospel
John 3:13–17

Jesus tells Nicodemus that the Son of Man must be lifted up.

Step 1
Naming One's Experience

What were your first impressions? What was your first response? What grabbed your attention? How did you feel?

Each person names his or her initial impression. Statements should be brief. No reasons should be given at this time. All simply listen without agreeing or disagreeing.

Step 2
Understanding

In a brief statement, what do you think this gospel is trying to convey?

Step 3
Input from Vision/Story/Tradition

Liturgical Context

In the early days of the church the cross was simply considered Jesus' instrument of execution. As Christianity evolved it became a multivalent symbol. It came to symbolize Christ's sacrificial death as well as Christ himself. It was also understood as a sign of Christianity.

Veneration of the cross is evidenced by the fourth century. The cross of Christ was found by Empress Helena on September 14, 320. Five years later, on September 13, two churches were consecrated in honor of the cross—Martyrium (the Church of the Cross), and the Resurrection (the Church of the Anastasis). Helena's discovered cross was displayed and venerated by the faithful on the next day, September 14, 325. The solemn observance became an annual event. Constantinople observed a similar feast by the fifth century and Rome by the seventh century. Those churches that had major relics of the cross showed the relics to the faithful in a solemn celebration called the *Exaltatio* (lifting-up).

During the eighth century, the people of Gaul celebrated a feast honoring the cross on May 3. A relic of the cross was captured by the Persians. It was subsequently recovered and carried in triumphant procession into Jerusalem. Rome placed this observance in the calendar and erroneously called it "Discovery of the Holy Cross." The September 14 feast was called "The Exaltation of the Holy Cross." The September feast was incorrectly designated as the feast to honor the restoration of the cross. Pope John XXIII rectified the situation and removed the May 3 observance from the calendar. The original meaning was restored to the September 14 feast.

The entrance antiphon gives us the theme for today's liturgy: we are to glory in the cross, for it is our salvation. The liturgy celebrates the salvation won for humanity by the sacrifice of Christ on the cross. The preface makes the comparison between the cross of Christ and the tree of paradise that was ultimately the sign of sin and death.

The cross is a sign of our identity as Christians. We sign ourselves with the cross. Catechumens are traced with the cross as a sign of God's strength and incorporation into the life of Christ. We sign ourselves with the cross when we enter and leave church; when we begin every liturgical celebration; when we eat a meal; and when we go to bed and wake up in the morning. The cross is the sign of Christ and the sign of the Christian life.

There are forty days from the feast of the Transfiguration on August 6 to the feast of the Holy Cross on September 14. This was once a period of pilgrimage to welcome the autumn season.

Gospel Exegesis

The facilitator gives input regarding what critical biblical scholarship has to say about this text. The input includes insights as to how people would have heard the gospel in Jesus' time.

Jesus was to be lifted up, like the serpent of Moses, as a sign of healing and salvation. Through the sign of the cross all who believe in Jesus will inherit eternal life. The cross, then, becomes the throne of glory, not the tool of an executioner. John insists that Jesus was "lifted up" on the cross. He uses coronation language rather than execution language. John's gospel reads like a royal liturgy. The language of crucifixion sounds like the installation of royalty upon a throne. The king is lifted up and crowned triumphant upon the throne of the cross.

Jesus willingly and knowingly went to his death. He was in control. It was a horrible death, but the torturous details are not the point of the story. Jesus, Son of Man, God-Man, saved the world from his throne of the cross. Those who looked upon Moses' serpent were saved. Those who look to the cross of Christ, believe in its power to save, and conform their lives to its power are also saved.

We are not to forget the gravity of sin, its lure and its death-dealing consequences. But today's liturgy is a joyful reminder that the cross is our hope in the midst of our sinfulness. This feast, situated halfway between the Triduum's celebration of the passion, death, and resurrection of Christ and the end of the liturgical year, serves as a midyear reality check. Every day is an opportunity to join in the sacrifice of Christ on the cross. Every liturgy remembers and makes present its saving power. Today's liturgy is an invitation to model Christ's saving action in our everyday lives. Do we love to the point of self-sacrifice, to the point of dying on the cross of our own selfishness?

Proclaim the gospel again.

Sometimes we gain new insights when we hear the text after the interpretation has been given. Someone from the group proclaims the gospel a second time.

STEP 4
TESTING

Conversation with the Liturgy and the Scriptures

Test your original understanding in dialogue with the text.

(You might consider breaking into smaller groups.)

How does your original understanding of this story compare with what was just shared? How does this story speak to your life?

Participants share an experience from their lives that connects with the biblical interpretation just shared.

How does this liturgy challenge our community? How does it challenge me? Has our original understanding been stretched, challenged, or affirmed?

STEP 5
DECISION

The gospel demands a response.

In what way does this gospel call your parish to action in the church, parish, neighborhood, or world? Be concrete. Has this conversation with the exegesis of this liturgy changed or stretched your personal attitudes? Name one concrete action you will take this week as a response to what was learned and shared today.

DOCTRINAL ISSUES

What church truth/teaching/doctrinal issue could be drawn from the gospel for Triumph of the Cross?

Participants suggest possible doctrinal themes that flow from the readings.

Possible Doctrinal Themes

Cross, redemptive suffering, paschal mystery

Present the doctrinal material at this time.

1. The facilitator gives input on a particular doctrinal issue of his/her prior choosing. OR
2. The group chooses a doctrinal issue from the list they created. They read together from the Doctrinal Appendix.

(The doctrinal issues are found in the Doctrinal Appendix in the back of this workbook. If you are choosing an issue from this resource, please refer to it now.)

Reflection questions centered around the chosen doctrinal theme can be found at the end of each topic in the Doctrinal Appendix. The questions are based on the five-step reflection process. If you choose a topic not included in the Doctrinal Appendix, craft your own questions according to the same five-step process.

Following the reflection questions you will be reminded to return to chapter 7, "Preparing the Catechetical Session," to assist you in crafting your own session.

Closing Prayer

Lord,
may this sacrifice once offered on the cross
to take away the sins of the world
now free us from our sins.
We ask this through Christ our Lord.[4]

[4]Feast of the Triumph of the Cross: "Prayer Over the Gifts," *The Sacramentary.*

Solemnity of All Saints (November 1)

INTRODUCTORY RITES

Opening Song (or Entrance Antiphon)

Let us all rejoice in the Lord and keep a festival in honor of all the saints. Let us join with the angels in joyful praise to the Son of God.[1]

Opening Prayer

The facilitator of the session may lead the prayer. Others in the group may be asked to proclaim the readings.

Let us pray
[that the prayers of all the saints
will bring us forgiveness for our sins]

Pause for silent prayer.

Father, all powerful and ever-living God,
today we rejoice in the holy men and women
of every time and place.
May their prayers bring us your forgiveness and love.
We ask this through our Lord Jesus Christ, your Son,
who lives and reigns with you and the Holy Spirit,
one God for ever and ever. [2]

LITURGY OF THE WORD

Let us listen to God's word.

The readings are proclaimed.

First Reading
Revelation 7:2–4, 9–14

Christ, who is risen, exalted, and appears in glory, is the primary theme of the book of Revelation. After giving a word of encouragement to the seven churches, Christ reveals the turmoil that will take place in the great battle between good and evil at the end of time.

[1]Solemnity of All Saints: "Entrance Antiphon," *The Sacramentary.*

[2]Solemnity of All Saints: "Opening Prayer," *The Sacramentary.*

Today's liturgy celebrates the joy of martyrs who share Christ's glorification. They shared in Christ's passion through their martyrdom. This is John's second vision in which there is a large gathering of people. In this vision, the number of people is beyond counting. The first vision was in reference to Israel. This vision refers to everyone—all nations. The palm fronds that are held by the assembled are a sign of victory.

The great trial referred to in this pericope is the tribulation that will come at the end of the age. During these latter days of tribulation, God's faithful will experience persecution. The robes represent the interior, spiritual disposition of the individual. The soiled robes represent sin and the clean robes represent holiness. This cleanliness is associated with the sacrificial death of Jesus. Through Jesus' death and resurrection, the robes (interior lives) are washed clean.

Baptism is the means through which the person is transformed, washed clean by the blood of the Lamb, and made holy. "The fundamental allusion here seems to be repentance, conversion, and baptism taken together as a transformation of the person."[3]

The image of the last tribulation or the trial is an exhortation to persevere in conversion and *metanoia.* Perseverance will give people the necessary means to endure and share in the salvation offered through Jesus' paschal mystery. Some of those who persevere will be called to martyrdom.

Responsorial Psalm
Psalm 24:1–6

Lord, this is the people that longs to see your face.

Second Reading
1 John 3:1–3

[3]Adela Yarbro Collins, "The Apocalypse (Revelation)," in *NJBC,* 1006.

John's favorite message is the love of God for his people. If we would only keep God's love in our consciousness, then we would convert our entire lives to God. The world will not understand. We are not to provoke persecution, but persecution will be ours. Without the eyes of faith, Jesus' identity is incomprehensible to the world. Through God's love we are made his children. As God's children we share his divine nature. Because we are God's children we will share his glory at the end of time.

Gospel
Matthew 5:1–12

Jesus gives us the blueprint for living in his reign: the beatitudes.

Step 1
Naming One's Experience

What were your first impressions? What was your first response? What grabbed your attention? How did you feel?

Each person names his or her initial impression. Statements should be brief. No reasons should be given at this time. All simply listen without agreeing or disagreeing.

Step 2
Understanding

In a brief statement, what do you think this gospel is trying to convey?

Step 3
Input from Vision/Story/Tradition

Liturgical Context

During the fourth century, martyrs were remembered at a celebration. The day of the celebration was different in each of the churches. In Syria it was celebrated on May 13. In Antioch it was celebrated on the day after Pentecost. The Greek Orthodox still observe this day and call it "All Saints Sunday." The Eastern Syrian liturgy observes the feast on the Friday after Easter.[4]

There is evidence that in Rome all three dates were observed. Pope Boniface IV accepted the Pantheon, a pagan temple, as a gift from Emperor Phocas. It was consecrated in honor of the Virgin Mary and martyrs on May 13, 609. Twenty-eight wagon loads of martyrs' bones were brought to the church from the catacombs. The pope named the feast assigned to May 13 the feast of All Saints.

In the eighth century in England and Ireland a feast in honor of All the Saints was celebrated on November 1. Pope Gregory IV gave permission to Louis the Pius, emperor of the West, to promulgate November 1 as the feast of "All Saints" for his entire kingdom. That date spread to the entire church and May 13 eventually disappeared. From the beginning the feast was assigned a vigil and by the fifteenth century an octave was also included. However, both vigil and octave were eliminated in the liturgical reform of 1955.

The feast remembers deceased friends, relatives, and ancestors who upon their death entered into heavenly glory. It also remembers the canonized saints. The liturgy seeks the intercessions of the saints who went before us. We ask that their prayers bring us forgiveness and love.

The feast also celebrates the Triune God who gathers the elect together in the courts of the heavenly Jerusalem to worship him. Every liturgy foreshadows our future participation in the heavenly banquet. This, however, is an extended meditation on the hope we celebrate. The praise and worship of God are at the center of this celebration.

Gospel Exegesis

The facilitator gives input regarding what critical biblical scholarship has to say about this text. The input includes insights as to how people would have heard the gospel in Jesus' time.

---

[4] *LY*, 228.

When Jesus returned from his ordeal in the desert, he went to Capernaum to announce the arrival of the messianic reign. He exhorted the people to repent. Jesus went up to a mountain and began to teach them. For Matthew, the mountain location was significant. It was a high place where human beings encounter divine authority. Moses went up the mountain to encounter God. Jesus, too, went up the mountain, the place of divine authority, and he sat down to teach the people. Matthew paints this picture with an exclamation point: he wants his audience to know that Jesus was speaking with the highest authority. He sat down to teach them as one who would rule from a royal throne.

Jesus began to exhort and encourage the people. In Jesus' reign, this is how it is to be. Jesus gives a blueprint for holiness. In a workshop given in 1995, Donald Senior noted that "The key to Matthew's gospel is that it is a call to doing things, not saying things." The sermon on the mount was a response to a crowd in need of healing. Matthew portrays Jesus as Teacher and Healer. Matthew's Jesus teaches for the transformation of people through the reign of God. Jesus' reign was not a future event, but a present reality.

There are four characteristics to the kingdom of God motif, says Senior.

1. soteriological: the kingdom is intended to rescue people from an intolerable situation.
2. theological: the kingdom reveals Israel's image of God. God cares enough to come and save Israel. God cares about the lives of the people.
3. eschatological: the final history is at hand.
4. community: the kingdom is a community effort. Individuals cannot experience the reign of God in isolation. Israel was a community. The transformation of our world was not an individual experience.[5]

Those who were listening to Jesus' message were experiencing the reign. The kingdom of God is now! Jesus gives the Christian the blueprint for sainthood. As we await the future heavenly glory of the heavenly Jerusalem, we live in this earthly reality. Thus, we are to be meek and clean of heart. We are to thirst after justice and hunger for righteousness. All these things lead the saints of God on their way to their final resting place where they will join all those saints who went before them. Joachim Jeremias asserts that good gospel living is sign and symptom of what happens when grace seizes a child of God. Donald Senior takes it another step. "The Beatitudes are what happens when grace seizes a child of God."

Proclaim the gospel again.

Sometimes we gain new insights when we hear the text after the interpretation has been given. Someone from the group proclaims the gospel a second time.

STEP 4
TESTING

Conversation with the Liturgy and the Scriptures

Test your original understanding in dialogue with the text.

(You might consider breaking into smaller groups.)

How does your original understanding of this story compare with what was just shared? How does this story speak to your life?

Participants share an experience from their lives that connects with the biblical interpretation just shared.

How does this liturgy challenge our community? How does it challenge me? Has our original understanding been stretched, challenged, or affirmed?

STEP 5
DECISION

The gospel demands a response.

[5]Donald Senior, "Gospel of Matthew," Workshop, Church of Our Savior, Oct. 1995.

In what way does this gospel call your parish to action in the church, parish, neighborhood, or world? Be concrete. Has this conversation with the exegesis of this liturgy changed or stretched your personal attitudes? Name one concrete action you will take this week as a response to what was learned and shared today.

DOCTRINAL ISSUES

What church truth/teaching/doctrinal issue could be drawn from the gospel for the feast of All Saints?

Participants suggest possible doctrinal themes that flow from the readings.

Possible Doctrinal Themes

Saints, eschatology, kingdom of God, soteriology

Present the doctrinal material at this time.

1. The facilitator gives input on a particular doctrinal issue of his/her prior choosing. OR
2. The group chooses a doctrinal issue from the list they created. They read together from the Doctrinal Appendix.

(The doctrinal issues are found in the Doctrinal Appendix in the back of this workbook. If you are choosing an issue from this resource, please refer to it now.)

Reflection questions centered around the chosen doctrinal theme can be found at the end of each topic in the Doctrinal Appendix. The questions are based on the five-step reflection process. If you choose a topic not included in the Doctrinal Appendix, craft your own questions according to the same five-step process.

Following the reflection questions you will be reminded to return to chapter 7, "Preparing the Catechetical Session," to assist you in crafting your own session.

Closing Prayer

Father, holy one,
we praise your glory reflected in the saints.
May we who share at this table
be filled with your love
and prepared for the joy of your kingdom,
where Jesus is Lord for ever and ever.[6]

[6]Solemnity of All Saints: "Prayer After Communion," *The Sacramentary.*

FEAST OF ALL SOULS (NOVEMBER 2)

INTRODUCTORY RITES

Opening Song (or Entrance Antiphon)

Just as Jesus died and rose again, so will the Father bring with him those who have died in Jesus. Just as in Adam all men die, so in Christ all will be made alive. (1 Thess 4:14; 1 Cor 15:22)[1]

Opening Prayer

The facilitator of the session may lead the prayer. Others in the group may be asked to proclaim the readings.

Let us pray
[for all our departed brothers and sisters]

Pause for silent prayer.

Merciful Father,
hear our prayers and console us.
As we renew our faith in your Son,
whom you raised from the dead,
strengthen our hope that all our departed brothers and sisters
will share in his resurrection,
who lives and reigns with you and the Holy Spirit,
one God, for ever and ever.[2]

LITURGY OF THE WORD

The Readings

There are no set readings for today's liturgy. The Lectionary refers us to the readings for the masses for the dead. Any of the readings from the vast repertoire may be chosen. The large number of readings shed light on and reflect the inexhaustible meaning of death. The scriptures tell the story of past communities who struggled with the pain of death and thereby appropriated meaning for their lives. The word of God is a living word that has relevance today as similar communities struggle with similar issues. Scriptures "demonstrate how revelation can and must be constantly read in light of everyday life and the thought of people of all races and cultures. In this way, Scripture appears as a powerful and sure contribution to progress of thought, offering always new perspectives and lighting up its way."[3]

With nearly fifty different scripture passages included in masses for the dead, there is not sufficient space to provide an exegesis for all of them. It is important, however, to be aware of their purpose.

The Old Testament readings reveal the mystery of death as understood by believers five centuries before the birth of Jesus. These readings reflect the yearnings, questions, and queries of believers of those ancient times, the answers they received, and the meaning they were able to appropriate from their searching inquiries. The same questions are still asked today. Reflection on the Old Testament readings helps us understand how our ancestors grappled with the same questions about death that we ask today.

The psalms provide us with a timeless prayer book. Centuries of previous generations have been strengthened, consoled, encouraged, and exhorted by their use. Jewish and Christian faith have been nourished by the psalms. The psalms are always relevant. They reflect the longing, aching, and supplication of the human heart. They speak in honest, direct, and frank terms. They are so filled with faith and trust that they hold us up when we are tempted to despair in the midst of sorrow and pain. The healing words of the psalms console us and give us the courage to speak to God in words that we might be afraid to utter. The psalms connect us with others who have cried the same tears and suffered the same anguish. They also give us the means of direct dialogue with a God who is with us in the struggles of our everyday life.

---

[1]All Souls Day: "Entrance Antiphon," *The Sacramentary.*
[2]All Souls Day: "Opening Prayer," *The Sacramentary.*

[3]*DL* (VII), 260.

The New Testament writings include the Acts of the Apostles, the apostolic letters, and the book of Revelation. The Acts of the Apostles reflects the good news, the Christian kerygma, as proclaimed by the first Christian community. The apostolic letters are letters of encouragement written to early Christian communities who struggled with living the gospel in light of the Christ event. The letters were written to guide the faith of those first communities. The book of Revelation is a prophetic book that gives us a look at the last days and the fulfillment of the reign of Jesus Christ, the messiah. The New Testament readings in the masses for the dead are from these three literary genres. "Each one of these twenty-four texts takes up the central message of the preaching of the apostles while emphasizing one or more particular points, sometimes giving more concrete consequences of the basics of faith as proclaimed by the apostles."[4]

The gospels, beginning with Mark (ca. 64–69 C.E.) and ending with John (end of the first century), are witnesses to the life and mystery of Jesus Christ. They tell the story of his life, his teaching, and his saving actions. The evangelists were not seeking to produce historically accurate biographies, but rather to express the living faith of communities who experienced Christ and were brought to faith as a result of their experience. The gospel proclaims the good news of his life and mission. The one central message of the gospel is the paschal mystery: the life, passion, death, resurrection, ascension into glory and coming of the Spirit of Jesus Christ.

Jesus is the source of happiness. In the midst of despair, he is reason for hope. Jesus offers the human soul joy in the midst of suffering. Jesus came to save us all. He is the good shepherd who knows his sheep by name and gathers them all together to be with him. Jesus died and went to prepare a place for all of us who will one day join him and his Father in eternity.

Jesus broke the chains of death once and for all when he died on the cross. He understood death. Jesus knew that he had to die and that his death would bring about his glorification; yet he still suffered untold anguish. The human Christ gives the human race the hope to endure. Jesus suffered and cried out. In our anguish we are consoled by the suffering Christ who conquered death in order for us to live eternally with him. The gospels for the masses for the dead express essential truths revealed either through Jesus' teaching or his actions. The mystery of death is laid before us and hope is placed in its path through reflection on the gospels for this day.

[4]Ibid., 273.

Liturgical Context

The pagans of antiquity kept memorials of dead relatives. Christians retained the practice of remembering their dead as long as it was consonant with their Christian faith. There is evidence of a celebration commemorating deceased relatives as early as the second century. The dead were prayed for and a mass was celebrated. The custom of the early church was to celebrate a remembrance of the deceased person three days after burial and on the one-year anniversary of the person's death. A later practice included an observance seven days following burial and then thirty and forty days after that.

In the seventh century, Bishop Isodore of Seville began a yearly commemoration of the souls of the dead. He ordered his monks to celebrate mass for this purpose on the day after Pentecost. By the ninth century the practice had spread and an office of the dead was added to the liturgy of the hours on the feast of All Saints.

In 998 "All Souls Day" was established when Abbot Odo of Cluny ordered that all monasteries celebrate a festal memorial of all the faithful departed. The practice spread but was not accepted in Rome until the thirteenth century.

Previously, if All Souls Day occurred on Sunday, the readings for the Sunday were given precedence. However, in the revised Roman Missal of 1970, the All Souls Day readings are given precedence. The missal provides three sets of prayers for this day. Each set contains an entrance antiphon, an opening prayer, a prayer over the gifts and a post-communion prayer. There are also five prefaces from which to choose.

This liturgy is intended to highlight the paschal nature of Christian death. The paschal mystery (the life, death, resurrection and ascension) of

Christ is the ultimate source of our hope. Previously used texts that hinted at the fear of God's judgment were replaced with texts that express Christian faith in the resurrection. The Easter pasch is at the heart of this celebration. All Souls Day celebrates the Christian's participation in the death and resurrection of Jesus. The entrance antiphon expresses this well: "Just as Jesus died and rose again, so will the Father bring with him all those who have died in Jesus. Just as in Adam all men die, so in Christ all will be made alive." We ask in the opening prayer that our hope be strengthened that our departed brothers and sisters will share in Christ's resurrection.

The ritual prayers reveal for us the church's perspective in relation to death, dying, and life after death. Any reflection on All Souls Day would necessarily require that the ritual texts from the liturgy of this day be prayed and reflected upon.

DOCTRINAL ISSUES

What church truth/teaching/doctrinal issue could be drawn from the celebration of All Souls Day?

Possible Doctrinal Themes

Death, eschatology, resurrection of the dead, heaven

Closing Prayer

Lord God,
may the death and resurrection of Christ
which we celebrate in this eucharist
bring the departed faithful to the peace of your
    eternal home.
We ask this in the name of Jesus.[5]

---

[5]All Souls Day: "Prayer After Communion," *The Sacramentary.*

Feast of the Dedication of the Basilica of St. John Lateran (November 9)

INTRODUCTORY RITES

Opening Song (or Entrance Antiphon)

Greatly to be feared is God in his sanctuary; he, the God of Israel, gives power and strength to his people. Blessed be God! (Ps 67:36)[1]

Opening Prayer

The facilitator of the session may lead the prayer. Others in the group may be asked to proclaim the readings.

God our Father,
from living stones, your chosen people,
you built an eternal temple to your glory.
Increase the spiritual gifts you have given to your Church,
so that your faithful people may continue to grow
into the new and eternal Jerusalem.
We ask this through our Lord Jesus Christ, your Son,
who lives and reigns with you and the Holy Spirit,
one God, for ever and ever.[2]

The Readings

The readings for today's liturgy are taken from the Commons of the Dedication of a Church.

Liturgical Context

The Basilica of St. John Lateran is the cathedral of the diocese of Rome. The pope is the bishop of this church. The name Lateran is derived from the reign of the Laterani family. The edict of Milan brought an end to persecution and Christianity became the official state religion. Older churches were refurbished and new ones were built. Emperor Constantine gave the Lateran palace and the surrounding property to the Church of Rome. He had a church built on the grounds in 324. On November 9 Pope Sylvester I dedicated the new basilica built on the site that had once housed the imperial guard. He dedicated the basilica to the Holy Redeemer. It was damaged by earthquakes in the fourth and especially the tenth centuries and was rebuilt by Sergius III (904–911).

Since the twelfth century the second titular patron of the basilica has been St. John the Baptist. Later, St. John the Evangelist was also associated with the basilica. This is why it is referred to as St. John Lateran.

The palace was the home of the bishop up until 1304 when Pope Benedict XI was forced to leave Rome because of political uprisings. His successors made Avignon their residence until 1377. During this time the Lateran palace was unused. During Nicholas V's term as pope, the church offices were moved to the Vatican. However, the Basilica of the Lateran has always been the cathedral church of the bishop of Rome, the pope. The basilica of the Lateran was damaged by fire in 1308 and again in 1361. Pope Benedict XIII consecrated it in 1726. It has since been under constant reconstruction and renovation. Clement XII (1730–1740) had an inscription placed on the basilica: this church is "Mother and Head of all the churches of the City and the world." The annual commemoration of the dedication spread throughout the church as a result of the efforts of the Augustinian hermits.

This feast holds great importance because the Basilica of St. John Lateran is the cathedral of the universal church. The cathedral is a symbol of the unity of the church gathered around its bishop. The bishop of Rome is responsible for the unity of his own diocese and the entire church. Thus, the cathedral of Rome has great significance for the entire church. "Celebrating the anniversary of the cathedral that is the mother of all others founded

[1]Common of the Dedication of a Church (A. In the Dedicated Church): "Entrance Antiphon," *The Sacramentary.*

[2]Common of the Dedication of a Church (B. Outside the Dedicated Church): "Opening Prayer A," *The Sacramentary.*

down through the ages is to celebrate the Lord, who founded his Church in order to gather together in unity, under the crozier of Peter and his successors, all the children of God, wherever they may live."[3]

The celebration of the anniversary of the dedication of the Lateran Basilica expresses the unity of all local parish churches with the universal Church of Rome, founded by Peter and Paul. The pope, as head of the college of bishops "presides over the charity of all the Churches throughout the world."[4]

Churches elegant and churches humble are living testament to the presence of God and the faith of those who built them. We are to remember that the people are the living stones upon which the church is built. It is the only church that will live on at the end of time—the church as people of God.

DOCTRINAL ISSUES

What church truth/teaching/doctrinal issue could be drawn from the gospel for feast of the Dedication of St. John Lateran?

Possible Doctrinal Themes

Mystery of the church

Closing Prayer

Father,
you called your people to be your Church.
As we gather together in your name,
may we love, honor, and follow you
to eternal life in the kingdom you promise.
Grant this through our Lord Jesus Christ, your
Son
who lives and reigns with you and the Holy Spirit,
one God, for ever and ever.[5]

---

[3]*DL* (VII), 280.

[4]Ibid., 290.

[5]Common of the Dedication of a Church (B. Outside the Dedicated Church): "Opening Prayer B," *The Sacramentary.*

INTRODUCTORY RITES

Opening Song (or Entrance Antiphon)

I exult for joy in the Lord, my soul rejoices in my God; for he has clothed me in the garment of salvation and robed me in the cloak of justice, like a bride adorned with her jewels. (Is 61:10)[1]

Opening Prayer

The facilitator of the session may lead the prayer. Others in the group may be asked to proclaim the readings.

Let us pray
[that through the prayers of the sinless
Virgin Mary, God will free us from our sins]

Pause for silent prayer.

Father,
you prepared the Virgin Mary
to be worthy mother of your Son.
You let her share beforehand
in the salvation Christ would bring
by his death,
and kept her sinless from the first
moment of her conception.
Help us by her prayers
to live in your presence without sin.
We ask this through our Lord Jesus Christ, your
Son,
who lives and reigns with you and the Holy
Spirit,
one God, for ever and ever.[2]

LITURGY OF THE WORD

Let us listen to God's word.

The readings are proclaimed.

[1]Solemnity of the Immaculate Conception: "Entrance Antiphon," *The Sacramentary.*

[2]Solemnity of the Immaculate Conception: "Opening Prayer," *The Sacramentary.*

First Reading

Genesis 3:9–15, 20

The sages of Israel meditated on the relationship between God and the sinner and the nature of sin. Their reflection was based on their historical experience of God and God's people. Israel understood misfortune to be punishment for sin. When they lived outside the law, tragedy befell them. However, even when God punished them, he loved them, offered forgiveness, and promised them future blessing. The very first telling of this story of grace and sin takes place in today's story of Adam and Eve in the garden. This is the first fall from grace into sin.

Sin is an act of rebellion on the part of the created person who believes he or she can survive without God. Sin cuts the person off from God. Today's story depicts two human beings who enjoyed trusted freedom with their Creator. They chose to rebel and thus became afraid of their Creator. Awareness of nudity was a sign of their poverty and lack of protection against destruction. Sin caused a lack of communion with God. This lack of communion caused dissension between Adam and Eve.

We are given no information about the serpent who tempted Eve. The serpent was sentenced to a life of crawling on his belly because of his evil action. The serpent will continue to do battle with the human race, but he will not be victorious. He will be destroyed by the offspring of the woman. "St. Jerome's (ca. 342–420) Latin translates the Hebrew neuter with a feminine pronoun.... It is a daughter of the woman, a new Eve, who will crush the head of the serpent."[3] This interpretation probably was not the original intent of the author of Genesis, but Christian tradition has interpreted the story in light of the Christ event.

Christian tradition understands Jesus as the new Adam who conquered sin and brought salvation.

[3]*DL* (VII), 300.

Mary is the new Eve, the mother of the Savior, whose victory was foretold after the fall. The Genesis reading sheds light on the mystery celebrated in this solemnity.

Responsorial Psalm
Psalm 98:1, 2–3, 3–4

Sing to the Lord a new song, for he has done marvelous deeds.

Second Reading
Ephesians 1:3–6, 11–12

The letter to the Ephesians begins with a liturgical prayer of thanksgiving. Its subject is God's plan of salvation, hidden throughout time, fulfilled in the person of Christ and revealed to all believers. Today's pericope refers especially to the Virgin Mary who was chosen beforetime to bear the Christ and to be holy in the sight of God. The apostle celebrates the work of salvation already accomplished by God through Jesus and in the Spirit. Ephesians asserts that we are chosen by God to be holy and without blemish. We are his adopted children and salvation is initiated solely through the love of God. Jesus was also part of the decision. With the Father, Jesus chose the human race for salvation just as he chose Israel as his own.

If we are so chosen, how much more, then, is Mary, the mother of Christ, chosen and blameless in the eyes of God. She is the perfect model of holiness for us.

Gospel
Luke 1:26–38

The angel appeared to Mary to tell her that she would conceive and bear a son.

Step 1
Naming One's Experience

What were your first impressions? What was your first response? What grabbed your attention? How did you feel?

Each person names his or her initial impression. Statements should be brief. No reasons should be given at this time. All simply listen without agreeing or disagreeing.

Step 2
Understanding

In a brief statement, what do you think this gospel is trying to convey?

Step 3
Input from Vision/Story/Tradition

Liturgical Context

This feast celebrates the dogma that Mary was free from original sin from the first moment of her existence. Pope Pius XII promulgated the papal bull *Ineffabilis Deus* on December 8, 1854. The feast is still celebrated on this date. The doctrine of the Immaculate Conception holds that through the grace of God and the saving action of Christ, Mary was free from sin from the moment of her conception. Mary was born free of original sin.

While the Immaculate Conception is not found explicitly in scripture, there are texts that support it, such as today's Lectionary readings: victory over the serpent (Gen 3:15) and the angel's salutation to Mary as full of grace (Lk 1:28).

Special devotion to Mary that included a recognition of the uniqueness of her conception began around the seventh century in the East. In the twelfth century a feast in honor of the Immaculate Conception was celebrated in England.

However, controversy over the doctrine grew. Theologians such as Anselm, Bernard, Aquinas, and Bonaventure attested to Mary's sanctification in the womb, but they argued that she had to be affected by original sin even if for only a moment in order to be a recipient of Christ's redeeming grace. These objections were resolved by Duns Scotus (d. 1308) who asserted that Christ saves in two ways. "In one, he rescues from sin those already fallen. In the other, he preserves someone from being touched by sin even for an instant."[4] The Council of Trent (1545–1563) purposely

[4]Richard P. McBrien, "The Immaculate Conception," in *HCEC*, 655.

eliminated Mary from the doctrine on original sin. It asserted that she was sin-free her entire life. In 1846 the United States bishops named Mary in her Immaculate Conception as patroness of the country.

This feast is christological in that it centers on the salvation offered for sinful humanity. Jesus suffered, died, and was buried for the sins of the world. The doctrine of the Immaculate Conception celebrates Christ's victory over the evil powers of the world at Mary's conception. "In her very being, through the mercy of God, the grip of evil is broken. To the Catholic imagination it is fitting that grace be freely given to her from the first moment of her existence because of her role in being the faith-filled mother of Jesus. Her yes to God brought Christ into the world, through whom the ancient sin of Adam and Eve is overturned."[5] This feast reminds us that grace is freely given and is more powerful than sin.

We are not to lose sight of the season in which this celebration is situated. "During Advent the liturgy frequently brings Mary to mind. On 8 December the solemnity of the Immaculate Conception recalls the preparation for the Savior's coming at its origins (See Is 11:1 and 10) and also the happy beginning of the Church in its beauty without spot or wrinkle."[6]

Gospel Exegesis

The facilitator gives input regarding what critical biblical scholarship has to say about this text. The input includes insights as to how people would have heard the gospel in Jesus' time.

Luke's concern in this pericope is the unusual circumstance surrounding Jesus' conception. Verse 35 asserts that Jesus would be the promised Davidic Messiah, thus the meaning of Jesus' name: "Yahweh saves." Jesus was conceived through the power of the Holy Spirit in the womb of Mary and thus is the Son of God. Jesus' birth of the virgin Mary is evidence of his humanity.

St. Augustine developed this theology when he asserted that all people are sinful because of original sin. All people need Christ's salvation. We are all heirs of original sin because of sexual generation. Christ as Savior was sinless and did not inherit original sin. Thus, Jesus could not have become human through sexual procreation. When Christ was conceived by the Holy Spirit he avoided the stain of original sin and was sinless Savior of the world.

In Greco-Roman literature the hero's greatness was often explained by a story of the hero's miraculous conception. "Jesus was what he was because he was divinely begotten."[7]

One emphasis in Luke/Acts is that Jesus descended from the Davidic monarchy and is the fulfillment of messianic Jewish prophecy. Through the paschal mystery Jesus is the glorified, exalted Son of God who sits at the right hand of his Father. Christ rules from his Father's right hand and intercedes for the people. Through the power of divine intervention (miraculous conception) Jesus was Savior of the world: he lived, suffered, died, rose again, and ascended to sit at the right hand of his Father's throne.

Proclaim the gospel again.

Sometimes we gain new insights when we hear the text after the interpretation has been given. Someone from the group proclaims the gospel a second time.

Step 4
Testing

Conversation with the Liturgy and the Scriptures

Test your original understanding in dialogue with the text.

(You might consider breaking into smaller groups.)

Were there any new insights? Was there anything you had not considered before? How does your original understanding of this story compare with

[5]Ibid., 656.

[6]*DOL*, #467, Section 4, Sanctoral Cycle: A. Mary, #3901, #3, 1207.

[7]*RL*, 20.

what was just shared? How does this story speak to your life?

Participants share an experience from their lives that connects with the biblical interpretation just shared.

What was Luke trying to tell his community? What does he have to say to our community and to me today? Do we still feel the same way about this text as we did when we began? Has our original understanding been stretched, challenged, or affirmed?

STEP 5
DECISION

The gospel demands a response.

In what way does this gospel call your parish to action in the church, parish, neighborhood, or world? Be concrete. What are you called to do in response? Name one concrete action you will take this week as a response to what was learned and shared today.

DOCTRINAL ISSUES

What church truth/teaching/doctrinal issue could be drawn from the gospel for the feast of the Immaculate Conception?

Participants suggest possible doctrinal themes that flow from the readings.

Possible Doctrinal Themes

Immaculate Conception of Mary

Present the doctrinal material at this time.

1. The facilitator gives input on a particular doctrinal issue of his/her prior choosing. OR
2. The group chooses a doctrinal issue from the list they created. They read together from the Doctrinal Appendix.

(The doctrinal issues are found in the Doctrinal Appendix in the back of this workbook. If you are choosing an issue from this resource, please refer to it now.)

Reflection questions centered around the chosen doctrinal theme can be found at the end of each topic in the Doctrinal Appendix. The questions are based on the five-step reflection process. If you choose a topic not included in the Doctrinal Appendix, craft your own questions according to the same five-step process.

Following the reflection questions you will be reminded to return to chapter 7, "Preparing the Catechetical Session," to assist you in crafting your own session.

Closing Prayer

Born of the Blessed Virgin Mary,
the Son of God redeemed mankind.
May he enrich you with his blessings.
    Response: Amen.

You received the author of life through Mary.
May you always rejoice in her loving care.
    Response: Amen.

You have come to rejoice at Mary's feast.
May you be filled with the joys of the Spirit
and the gifts of your eternal home.
    Response: Amen.

May almighty God bless you,
the Father, and the Son + and the Holy Spirit.
    Response: Amen.[8]

---

[8]Solemnity of the Immaculate Conception: "Solemn Blessing Over the People," *The Sacramentary.*

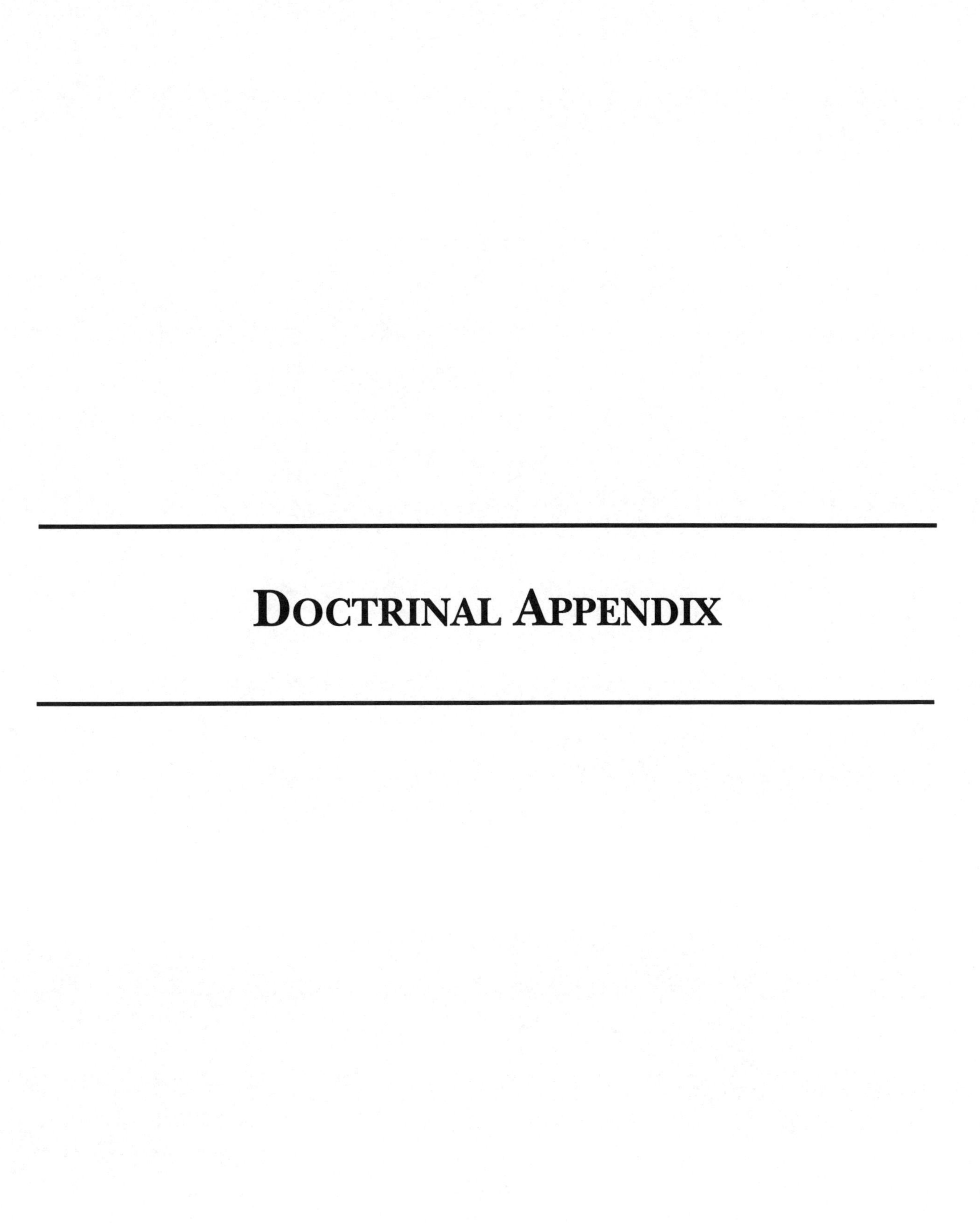

DOCTRINAL APPENDIX

DOCTRINE AND THE LITURGICAL YEAR

This appendix contains doctrinal material that flows from and surfaces out of the experience of word and worship on Sunday. The church has always revered the scriptures in much the same way as it reveres the Body of Christ. The people of God are offered the bread of life at both the table of God's word and the table of the eucharist.[1]

The Second Vatican Council's document, *The Dogmatic Constitution on Divine Revelation,* asserts that sacred scripture and tradition are intimately connected. They flow from and through one another. They have the same purpose. Scripture is God communicating with human beings through human writers by the power of the Holy Spirit. Tradition provides us with the full message of God's word given to the apostles by Jesus and the Holy Spirit. Thus, all future generations are enlightened by what was handed on to us by the apostles. Through that inheritance the Spirit strengthens us to live a gospel life and spread the good news of salvation. "Therefore both sacred Tradition and sacred Scripture are to be accepted and venerated with the same sense of devotion and reverence"[2]

The church has always considered scripture and tradition to be the primary rule of faith. Theology's foundational roots hinge on the written word of God and sacred tradition. Through both, the mystery of Christ is encountered, bringing light and life to the believer. "Therefore, the 'study of the sacred page' should be very soul of sacred theology."[3]

As an introduction to this Doctrinal Appendix, basic principles regarding the core issues of tradition will be articulated once again for review. This appendix will address the central core of the church's teaching, the hierarchy of truths that comes to us from scripture and tradition that began with the apostles and has continued through the ages. All other teachings of our faith are rooted and find meaning in those essential, primary truths. The church has many teachings that are not included in the "hierarchy of truths." This section will focus only on those that form the basis of our faith. This in no way diminishes the fact that we are to believe all that the church holds to be true. However, some truths hold more importance than others as they are foundational to all we believe.

The General Catechetical Directory asserts that "the message of salvation has a certain hierarchy of truths which the Church has always recognized when it composed creeds or summaries of the truths of the faith. Some truths of the faith are based on others as of a higher priority and are illumined by them."[4]

The hierarchy of truths is listed in both the General and National Catechetical Directory. These truths are grouped under four headings. Once again they are:

1. The mystery of God the Father, the Son, and the Holy Spirit, Creator of all things.

2. The mystery of Christ, the incarnate Word, who was born of the Virgin Mary and who suffered, died, and rose for our salvation.

3. The mystery of the Holy Spirit, who is present in the church, sanctifying it and guiding it until the glorious coming of Christ, our Savior and Judge.

4. The mystery of the church, which is Christ's Mystical Body, in which the Virgin Mary holds a preeminent place.

All other truths are informed by and in direct relation to the hierarchy of truths. These truths

[1] *The Dogmatic Constitution on Divine Revelation (Dei Verbum),* in *The Documents of Vatican II,* ed. Walter M. Abbott, S.J. (New York: America Press, 1966), 125, #21.

[2] Ibid., #9.

[3] Ibid., #21, 24.

[4] General Catechetical Directory (GCD), in *The Catechetical Documents* (Chicago: Liturgy Training Publications, 1996), 33, #34.

are encountered and remembered ritually throughout the liturgical year through the Lectionary scriptures and in the feasts and seasons we celebrate.

The doctrinal issues in this appendix are thematic overviews. This chapter is not an attempt to provide a comprehensive rendering of all the articles of Catholic belief and practices. The primary sources used in this appendix are the documents of the church. All other resources provide supplemental background. We encourage you to study church documents, the rites of the church, the *Catechism of the Catholic Church,* historical context, and the related works of theologians in order to broaden your understanding.

This is not "everything you ever wanted to know about a topic." Rather, it provides a brief overview of post-biblical teaching or practice as it relates to the lived experience of past communities, flows from the gospel exegesis, and connects to the lived experience of people today. What is provided in this appendix is but a taste and is intended to provide a model that may be used to assist others in crafting doctrinal sessions not included in this workbook.

The facilitator may prepare material on a doctrinal issue or the group may choose and read together a doctrine from this appendix. The suggested themes may or may not be appropriate for each parish. It is not our intention to suggest that every parish should teach the same doctrine on a particular Sunday. Each community should decide for itself what issues of tradition are pertinent and best flow from the Sunday's readings and from the needs of the community.

This appendix will not include every doctrinal issue listed under the following list of core issues. Some of the topics are addressed within the body of the workbook, however. For example, the dominant symbols of the church are examined in the Easter Vigil section. One need only use that material in conjunction with the learning model used in these structured sessions.

The following list is a compilation of doctrinal themes that are inherent in and flow from the liturgical year.

CORE ISSUES OF FAITH IN THE LITURGICAL YEAR

Advent
Eschatology, Christ's Coming: Future, Present, Past, Son of Man, Parousia, Kingdom of God

Christmas
Incarnation, Epiphany/Manifestation, Holy Family, Christology

Lent
Renewal, Preparation, Penitence, Fasting, Conversion, Almsgiving, Practices of Prayer, Sin, Transfiguration, Grace, Providence, Soteriology

Easter Triduum
Paschal Mystery, Redemption, Vigil, Eucharist, Priesthood, Service, Justice; Dominant Symbols of the Church: Assembly, Light, Cross, Water, Oil, Laying on of Hands, Garment, Bread/Wine

Easter Season
Fifty Days, Ascension, Pentecost, Resurrection, Holy Spirit, Charisms, Ecclesiology, Discipleship, Hope

Ordinary Time
Trinity, Body and Blood of Jesus, Christian Witness, Sacraments, Death/Dying, Suffering, Beatitudes, Vocation, Moral Decision Making, Non-violence, Christian Stewardship, All Saints, All Souls, Sacred Heart, Solemnity Mary Mother of God, Assumption, Immaculate Conception, Saints, Kingdom of God

DOCTRINAL TOPICS

ADVENT

See Advent Overview.

ALL SAINTS

See Feast of All Saints.

ALL SOULS

See Feast of All Souls.

ALMSGIVING

See Lenten Overview.

ASCENSION

See Easter Overview and Feast of the Ascension.

ASSUMPTION

See Feast of the Assumption.

BAPTISM

See CHRISTIAN INITIATION: Part I—Baptism (Appendix). See Easter Vigil, Symbols of Water, Light, and Garment.

BODY AND BLOOD

See CHRISTIAN INITIATION: Eucharist (Appendix). See Easter Vigil, Symbol of Bread. See Feast of Corpus Christi.

BREAD

See Easter Vigil.

CHRISTIAN INITIATION

Through the sacrament of initiation people are freed from the power of sin and evil. They die and are buried with Christ and are raised again to new life. They receive the Spirit of adoption, making them children of God. With the entire church they celebrate the memorial of Christ's death and resurrection.

Through baptism people are incorporated in the life of Christ. They are formed as God's people and are forgiven their sins. They are elevated to the dignity of adopted children. They are a new creation in Christ through water and the Spirit, and thus are called children of God.

Christians more perfectly become the image of Christ when they are signed with the gift of the Holy Spirit in confirmation. They bear witness to Christ and strive to bring others to him.

They come to the Lord's table to eat and drink his Body and Blood so they may have eternal life and show the unity of God's people. They offer themselves with Christ, thereby sharing in his paschal mystery. They pray for an outpouring of the Holy Spirit so the human race may be brought together in unity as God's people. The three sacraments bring the faithful to full stature in Christ and empower them to carry out the mission of Christ in the church and the world.[1]

I. Baptism

Natural Sign
What is your experience of water in everyday life? How might water express something about the mystery of God? What is your present understanding of baptism? How would you articulate a definition? Complete this sentence: "Baptism is. . . ."

Tradition: Biblical, Ecclesial, and Liturgical Signs
The sacraments of initiation (baptism, confirmation, and eucharist) free us from the power of darkness and evil. We are united to Christ and his paschal mystery, his death, burial and resurrection. We are adopted children of God by the power of the Holy Spirit and are incorporated

[1]Christian Initiation, *The Rites of the Catholic Church,* English translation prepared by the International Commission on English in the Liturgy (New York: Pueblo Publishing Co., 1976), p. 3, #s 1, 2.

into the Body of Christ in the celebration of the memorial of the paschal mystery—the eucharist.

"Baptism incorporates us into Christ and forms us into God's people. This first sacrament pardons all our sins, rescues us from the power of darkness, and brings us to the dignity of adopted children, a new creation through water and the Holy Spirit. Hence we are called and indeed are the children of God."[2] (See Colossians 1:13; Romans 8:15; Galatians 4:5.) The three sacraments of initiation allow us to carry out the mission of Christ in the world.

Baptism initiates us into God's reign and is the gateway to eternal life. It is the first sacrament offered by Christ who later entrusted it and his gospel to the church when he exhorted his disciples to "Go and make disciples of all the nations, and baptize them in the name of the Father, and of the Son, and of the Holy Spirit" (Mt 28:19). Through baptism, we are enlightened by the Spirit of God to live the gospel.

Baptism incorporates us into the church and into the house of God (Eph 2:22). We are made a royal priesthood. We are all united through the sacramental bond of baptism. We have been signed into this unchangeable effect through the anointing with chrism in the presence of God's people. Baptism, validly celebrated even by Christians with whom we are not in full communion, may never be repeated.[3]

Through the sign of water, baptism cleanses away every stain of sin, original and personal, and offers us a share in the life of Christ. We become his adopted children. Through the water of baptism we are reborn into Christ. The Blessed Trinity is invoked over the person who is baptized. The baptized enter into communion with the Father, the Son, and the Holy Spirit. The baptized are prepared for and led to this communion through biblical readings, the prayer of the community, and their own profession of faith in the Father, Son, and Spirit.[4]

[2]RCIA, #2.
[3]Ibid., #4.
[4]Ibid., #5.

This is all accomplished through the death and resurrection of Jesus Christ. We who are baptized are united to him in his death. We are buried with Christ and then are born again to new life in Christ. Baptism remembers and makes present the death and resurrection of Jesus, his paschal mystery. Through baptism we die to sin and are born to new life.[5] (See Ephesians 5:26, 2:5–6, 2:22; 1 Peter 2:9; 2 Peter 1:4; Romans 6:4–5, 8:15; Galatians 4–5; Titus 3:5; John 3:1, 5, 6:55; Matthew 28:19.)

Through the ritual of baptism we are anointed priest, prophet, and king. As priest we are called to serve, as prophet we are called to proclaim the good news, and as royalty we are called to lead.

Water used in baptism is to be true water, pure and clean. Immersion, a more suitable symbol denoting the death and resurrection of Christ (we go down into the waters and are buried in Christ and rise out of the waters to new life), or pouring can be used to lawfully administer the sacrament. The words for the conferral of baptism are: "I baptize you in the name of the Father, and of the Son and of the Holy Spirit."[6]

Refer to the symbol of water in the Easter Vigil chapter. A similar, separate reflection process centered around the symbol of water would be recommended and would include: natural sign of water in everyday life; biblical uses of water throughout the scriptures; ecclesial understanding of water throughout the history of the church; liturgical use of water.

Testing
Were there any new insights or clarifications? What might this doctrine have to do with my everyday life or the life of the community? What are the implications for living the Christian life?

Decision
What concrete action will I take as a result of this teaching?

Refer to chapter 7, "Preparing the Catechetical Session," if you intend to plan your catechetical session at this time.

[5]Ibid., #6.
[6]Ibid., #23.

II. Confirmation

Natural Sign

What is your experience of oil in everyday life? How does it speak to you about God? How would you explain the sacrament of confirmation?

Tradition: Biblical, Ecclesial, and Liturgical Signs

Confirmation is an initiation sacrament. The Rite of Confirmation #1 states that the baptized continue on the path of Christian initiation through the sacrament of confirmation. The joining of both baptism and confirmation signifies the unity of the paschal mystery, and the close connection between the work of the Son and the outpouring of the Holy Spirit. The Father, Son, and Spirit come to those who are baptized. Adults and children of catechetical age are to receive the sacraments of baptism, confirmation, and eucharist in a simple celebration.[7] The priest receives authority to confer confirmation at these celebrations from canon law itself.

The conferral of the Spirit at confirmation is the second stage of initiation, not a rite of passage into adulthood. Confirmation leads us more fully into our baptismal identity. Confirmation is not about ratifying an adult faith. It is the gift of the Spirit.

The initiatory character of confirmation and its connection with baptism and eucharist are based on the life, death, and resurrection of Christ. Confirmation is a sign of the paschal mystery. "This makes clear the specific importance of confirmation for sacramental initiation, by which the faithful members of the living Christ are incorporated into him and *configured* to him through baptism and through confirmation and the eucharist."[8]

One significant aspect of confirmation reform as set forth in the Apostolic Constitution or the Rite of Confirmation places the coming of the Spirit at Pentecost in center stage. The anointing with chrism is understood as having its basis in Jesus' baptism and the outpouring of the Spirit on the disciples at Pentecost. "The descent of the Spirit at Jesus' baptism reflects a new and extraordinary vision of the pneumatic quality of baptism itself, and the intrinsic unity of the baptismal event: baptism and the outpouring of the Spirit are one mystery and sacrament."[9]

Those who are born anew in baptism receive the inexpressible Gift, the Holy Spirit himself who imparts a special strength. Confirmation, then, is closely related to eucharist. After being signed by baptism and confirmation, the faithful are then fully incorporated into the Body of Christ through participation in the eucharist. This is signified more fully in the new sacramental formula: "Be sealed with the Gift of the Holy Spirit." The Gift *is* the Spirit, not the gifts *of* the Spirit. Thus, confirmation makes us:

1. more completely the image of Christ and fills us with his Spirit so we may bear witness to him;
2. configured to Christ and strengthened by the Holy Spirit;
3. witnesses to Christ in order to build the Body of Christ in faith and love.

Confirmation so marks the recipient with the character of Christ that, like baptism, it also cannot be repeated. The seal of the Spirit marks our total being for Christ. We are forever in the service of Christ's mission and we are promised divine protection until the final day.

Confirmation completes baptism; eucharist completes initiation. It is eucharist that fully incorporates a person into the Body of Christ. Eucharist is the repeatable sacrament of initiation [Augustine]. We grow into our identity as fully initiated members of the Body of Christ through our sharing in the eucharist. Confirmation takes place within mass in order to stress the fundamental connection between confirmation and Christian initiation that culminates in the communion of Christ's Body and Blood. "Thus, even when confirmation is celebrated after first communion, the initiatory identity of Eucharist as the sacrament

---

[7]National Statutes of the RCIA, #14.

[8]"Rite of Confirmation—Apostolic Constitution," *The Rites of the Catholic Church,* English translation prepared by the International Commission on English in the Liturgy (New York: Pueblo Publishing Co., 1976), 290–297.

[9]Linda Gaupin, CDP, Ph.D., Specialized Certification for Sacramental Catechesis (Diocese of Orlando, Fla., 1996–1997), unpublished course text, 7.

which completes initiation should be maintained."[10]

Confirmation, therefore, is not an occasion of personal commitment to an adult faith. It is not a rite of adult passage, nor is it a sacrament of maturity. "Although Confirmation is sometimes called the 'sacrament of Christian maturity,' we must not confuse adult faith with the adult age of natural growth, nor forget that the baptismal grace is a grace of free, unmerited election and does not need 'ratification' to become effective."[11]

"Some are teaching that the main reason for the Rite of Baptism for Children is that infants be allowed at some point to accept for themselves the faith. That is where confirmation comes in. Response: This is pure fantasy. The rite says no such thing. Some are teaching that confirmation 'assists the transition into adult faith... it develops experiences of faith based upon both the individual and the community.' Response: This is the purpose of the eucharist."[12]

The sacrament of confirmation is conferred by anointing the candidates with chrism on the forehead and saying the words: "Receive the Gift of the Holy Spirit." *The anointing with chrism represents the apostolic laying on of hands and the anointing with the Holy Spirit.* The laying on of hands and accompanying prayer prior to the anointing with chrism does not belong to the substance of the rite yet it is to be held in high regard.

Refer to the Rite of Confirmation (chapter 5, III) for the scriptural passages that taken together shed light on the celebration of this sacrament.

Refer to the symbol of oil in the Easter Vigil chapter. A similar, separate reflection process centered around the symbol of oil would be recommended and would include: natural sign of oil in everyday life; biblical uses of oil throughout the scriptures; ecclesial understanding of oil throughout the history of the church; liturgical use of oil.

Testing
Were there any new insights? How would you articulate a definition of confirmation now? Have your original assumptions been stretched in any way? How does this doctrine of confirmation have anything to do with living everyday life?

Decision
What action will I take as a result of today's sharing?

Refer to chapter 7, "Preparing the Catechetical Session," if you intend to plan your catechetical session at this time.

III. Eucharist

Natural Sign
What is your experience of bread and wine in everyday life? How do they speak to you about the nature of God? What is your present understanding of the sacrament of eucharist?

Tradition: Biblical, Ecclesial, and Liturgical Signs
Eucharist completes initiation. Those who have been elevated to the status of royal priesthood through baptism and configured to Christ through confirmation share with the entire community in the Lord's sacrifice of Calvary through the eucharist. The eucharist ["liturgy," *Constitution on the Sacred Liturgy*, #10] is the source and summit of all we do. All catechesis, all our efforts as Christian people lead us to full and active participation in the eucharistic banquet. Eucharist is a sacrament of unity and it strengthens the Body of Christ. The eucharistic celebration is carried out in response to the mandate of Christ to "Do this in memory of me."

In the liturgy the priest prays the words of eucharistic consecration and the bread and wine are changed into the Body and Blood of Christ. Under the appearance of bread and wine, Jesus, true God and true Man, "is substantially present, in a mysterious way, under the appearance of bread and wine."[13]

It is called *eucharist* (Greek: *eucharistein, eulogein*—recollection of the Jewish blessing in praise of God's work or redemption and sanctification) as it is a ritual action of praise and thanks to God.

The paschal mystery (passion, death, and resurrection of Christ) is celebrated anew in an un-

[10]Ibid., 9.

[11]*CCC*, 1308.

[12]Gaupin, 9.

[13]"Basic Teachings for Catholic Religious Education," in *CD*, #12.

bloody manner through the ministry of the priests. This holy meal recalls and makes present the Last Supper and it celebrates the unity we share in Christ. It also looks toward our participation in the heavenly banquet.

Bread and wine, the two symbols of eucharist, are changed into Christ's Body and Blood through the invocation of the Holy Spirit. We are nourished by the Body and Blood of Christ so that we may become a people more acceptable to God and that we may be capable of greater love for God and one another.

In the celebration of the eucharist the church gathers to celebrate the presence of Christ in the Body of Christ, the eucharistic assembly, in the proclamation of the word, in the presiding celebrant, and in the eucharistic elements. "To accomplish so great a work, Christ is always present in his Church.... He is present in the sacrifice of the Mass, not only in the person of his minister... but especially under the eucharistic elements.... He is present in his word since it is Christ himself who speaks when the holy scriptures are read in the Church. He is present lastly, when the Church prays and sings, for he promised: 'Where two or more are gathered together in my name, there am I in the midst of them' (Mt. 18:20)."[14]

The eucharist is foreshadowed in the Hebrew scriptures in the gesture of the king-priest Melchizedek who offered bread and wine (Gen 14:18). Bread and wine were offered under the old covenant as a sign of grateful thanks for the harvest and the Creator's benevolence. Bread and wine were significant symbols in the Passover meal that remembered the liberation out of Egypt's bondage into the promised land (Deut 8:3). The miracle of the loaves and fishes foreshadowed the eucharist in the multiplication, breaking, and distribution of the loaves to the crowd, prefiguring "the superabundance of this unique bread of his Eucharist."[15]

Jesus left a pledge of his love by leaving a memorial of his death and resurrection and commanding his followers to repeat the ritual action of this memorial until his return. "The three synoptic Gospels and St. Paul have handed on to us the account of the institution of the Eucharist; St. John, for his part, reports the words of Jesus in the synagogue of Capernaum that prepare for the institution of the Eucharist: Christ calls himself the bread of life, come down from heaven."[16] Jesus instituted this memorial on the night before he would die and in the process gave new and definitive meaning to the Passover event: Jesus passed from this life to his Father through his death and resurrection. This new Passover is anticipated in the eucharist that fulfilled the Passover of the old covenant and anticipates the last Passover of the entire church at the end of the age.[17]

The eucharist, center of the church's life, proclaims the paschal mystery of Christ and makes it present. The eucharist strengthens the community of believers as they embrace the cross and move forward to their final destination in heaven, where all the "elect will be seated at the table of the kingdom."[18]

Eucharist initiates conversion again and again. It invites and causes transformation. The bread is taken, blessed, broken, and shared; we too are taken, blessed, broken, and shared and in that way participate in the paschal mystery of Jesus. Eucharist strengthens our union in Christ, forgives our sins, makes us church, and empowers us to do good, promote the gospel, and serve the needs of the world. "Eucharist commits us to the poor."[19]

Refer to the symbols of bread and wine in the Easter Vigil chapter. A similar, separate reflection process centered around the symbols of bread and wine would be recommended and would include: natural signs of bread and wine in everyday life; biblical uses of bread and wine throughout the scriptures; ecclesial understanding of symbols of bread and wine throughout the history of the church; liturgical use of bread and wine.

Testing

Were there any new insights? How would you now finish this sentence: "Eucharist is..."?
What are the implications for living Christian life?
What is the challenge of eucharist?

---

[14]*CSL,* in *TLD,* #7.

[15]*CCC,* #1335.

[16]Ibid., #1338.

[17]Ibid., #1339–1340.

[18]Ibid., #1344.

[19]Ibid., #1397.

Decision
What am I/we going to do about it? What response am I going to make?

Refer to chapter 7, "Preparing the Catechetical Session," if you intend to plan your catechetical session at this time.

CHRISTMAS

See Overview of Christmas and the Sundays of the Christmas Season.

CHRISTOLOGY

See JESUS (Appendix).

CHURCH, MYSTERY OF

Natural Sign
Have you ever had an experience of being part of a community other than your church community? What were the things that attracted you to this community? Did you ever have the sense that a community you were part of possessed corporate power?

One of the first symbols of God's presence in the world is the church. There are many interchangeable terms for church—community, church, people of God, assembly—but they are all the same reality. God is present to the world through the visible, tangible sign of God's love, the church. "As a divine reality inserted into human history, the Church is a kind of sacrament. Its unique relationship with Christ makes it both sign and instrument of God's unfathomable union with humanity and of the unity of human beings among themselves. Part of the Church's mission is to lead people to a deeper understanding of human nature and destiny and to provide them with more profound experiences of God's presence in human affairs."[20]

Tradition: Biblical, Ecclesial, and Liturgical Signs
Please refer to Easter Vigil: Symbol of Church (p. 232), for information regarding the biblical understanding of church/community and for further historical elaboration.

The Second Vatican Council redefined our understanding of church. The following principles are a summary of our theology as articulated in *Sharing the Light of Faith: The National Catechetical Directory.* "The Church is a mystery. It is a reality imbued with the hidden presence of God (From Pope Paul VI's opening allocution at the second session [September 19, 1963]." The Church is a gift coming from the love of God, Christ's redeeming action and the power of the Holy Spirit (National Catechetical Directory [NCD], #63). "As a divine reality inserted into human history, the Church is a kind of sacrament. Its unique relationship with Christ makes it both a sign and instrument of God's unfathomable union with humanity and of the unity of human beings among themselves" (NCD, #63)."...As a mystery, the Church cannot be totally understood or fully defined. Its nature and mission are best captured in scriptural parables and images, taken from ordinary life, which not only express truth about its nature but challenge the Church: for example, to become more a People of God, a better servant, more faithful and holy, more united around the teaching authority of the hierarchy" (NCD, #63).

The church is a community of believers, the people of God. We are called to become a new people, a royal priesthood, a people claimed by God to proclaim the greatness of God (1 Pet 2:9). Jesus freed us from sin and because of the saving waters of baptism we are called to believe, worship, and witness to his saving works.

We are one body in Christ (Rom 12:5). Through Jesus' death, resurrection, and glorification, he remains a living presence and head of his church, of which we are all members. *We celebrate this identity most especially in the eucharist.* Through the eucharist, we become the Body and Blood of Christ.

The church is servant and has a mission to heal and reconcile as Jesus did. The church is to live the gospel through the works of mercy, assisting the needy or anyone who is in need of our help. The church as servant acts out of love and concern, not for personal glory. One way the church is servant is through its teaching ministry in which it witnesses to the gospel and the power of God in the world.

The church is a sign of the reign of God. The church is evidence that God is alive in our midst.

[20] *NCD*, #63.

In order to be that sign, the church "must be committed to justice, love and peace, to grace and holiness, truth and life, for these are the hallmarks of the kingdom of God" (NCD, #67).

The church is a pilgrim church. Aware of its sins, the church journeys to its final destination as it repents and overcomes patiently the trials and tribulations that come its way. In this way it demonstrates its steadfast faithfulness to the world.

"As mystery, people, one body in Christ, servant, sign of the kingdom, and pilgrim, the Church is conceived as God's family, whose members are united to Christ and led by the Spirit in their journey to the Father. The Church merits our prayerful reflection and wholehearted response" (NCD, # 68).

The church is one, holy catholic and apostolic. Unity is the substance of the church and is based on the unity of the Trinity. While unified, the church is diverse; this is expressed by the various liturgical rites within the church such as Catholic Coptic Rite, Ethiopian Rite, etc.

We express our unity through a profession of faith, apostolic succession, and the communal celebration of worship, especially the sacraments. Heresy, apostasy, and schism wound the unity of the church. The Catholic Church shares baptism, scripture, belief in the Trinity, and some sacraments with some ecclesial communities; it shares devotion to Mary, Mother of God, and some common liturgical texts with other ecclesial communities.

The symbol of church as people of God is a primary symbol in the liturgy. The gathered community is a sign of God's presence in our midst. Before the book is opened or the bread shared, God is experienced in the community. "For these people are the people of God, purchased by Christ's blood, gathered together by the Lord, nourished by the word. They are a people called to offer God the prayers of the entire human family, a people giving thanks in Christ for the mystery of salvation by offering his sacrifice. Finally, they are a people growing together into unity by sharing Christ's Body and Blood. These people are holy by their origin, but becoming ever more holy by conscious, active and fruitful participation in the mystery of the eucharist."[21] In every liturgical celebration the community is a primary experience of God's presence. We profess the mystery of the church in our ritual prayers and the creed, and through the eucharist we live its reality. Through all the ministries of the church, Christ is present. Thus, when the people participate and celebrate, the lector proclaims, the priest presides, the eucharistic minister serves, the cantor sings, the hospitality people welcome, etc., Christ is made manifest in our midst.

The church is a priestly, prophetic, and royal people. Through baptism and faith in God the church shares Christ's priestly role as leader. The church is consecrated a holy priesthood and a spiritual house. The church shares the prophetic ministry as it witnesses to God's reign in the world. The church is royal in its ministry of service to the poor and the needs of the world.

Testing
Are there any new insights? Have any of your original assumptions about church been stretched or affirmed? Does this teaching about church resonate with your experience of church in your own community? What are the areas of death/resurrection? What are some specific areas that are in need of growth?

Decision
What is the challenge and what action will I take as a result of this teaching on the mystery of the church?

Refer to chapter 7, "Preparing the Catechetical Session," if you intend to plan your catechetical session at this time.

CONFIRMATION

See CHRISTIAN INITIATION: Part II—Confirmation (Appendix). See Easter Vigil, Symbol of Oil.

CONVERSION

Natural Sign
Have you ever experienced making a change in direction in the course of your life? Have you ever changed your thinking or pattern of behavior?

[21] *GIRM,* in *TLD,* #5.

What prompted these changes? What did you learn from these experiences?

Tradition: Biblical, Ecclesial, and Liturgical Signs
The Sundays of Lent, in fact the entire liturgical year, invite us to embark on a journey of deep conversion. Since *conversion* is a word that is bounced around a great deal in evangelical parlance, it might be a beneficial exercise to explore the biblical understanding of conversion as we embark on the journey into its heart and spirit. In modern usage, conversion often refers to an event—a "born-again" experience of faith in Jesus Christ. "It boils down to a singular experience of being born again in Jesus Christ on a given occasion. It entails becoming a Christian and being saved on a given occasion."[22] This narrow vision helps the recipients of this one-time event to distance themselves from conversion's ongoing imperative. "It is usually 'other people' who need to heed the message. It is seldom directed inwardly to ourselves and even less to a call to societal or ecclesial change."[23] Ronald Wintherop cites a study by Beverly Roberts Gaventa (1986) in which she notes "three categories of personal change which are found in the NT: alternation, conversion, and transformation. She notes that the distinctions are not mutually exclusive, yet are distinctive enough for the following separate descriptions: 'Alternation is a relatively limited form of change that develops from one's previous behavior; conversion is a radical change in which past affiliations are rejected for some new commitment and identity; transformation is also a radical change, but one in which an altered perception reinterprets both past and present' (1986:12)."[24]

Conversion involves some form of change. Conversion is fluid, moving, and dynamic. When the Hebrew Scriptures refer to the human person they bespeak a united wholeness. The human being is not separated into body and spirit as in later Greek anthropology. The perspective of conversion in the scriptures involves the action of the whole person—body, mind, and spirit. Someone in need of conversion is a person who is in dire need of a change in direction for the course of his or her life. So great is their need that they are to stop dead in their tracks, make an about-face, and turn in the opposite direction from their original course. A big change—a monumental change!

Another interesting concept of conversion in the Hebrew Scriptures (OT) is the conversion of God. How presumptuous can we get? God in need of conversion? Not at all. Yet God repeatedly made changes in his course. God changed his plans and his direction as an act of love. God repented. "If you remain quietly in this land I will build you up, and not tear you down; I will plant you, not uproot you; for I regret the evil I have done you (Jer 42:10)." "From the OT perspective, then, God is a God of change and of integrity, one who can set limits on relating to the world and yet who can also have a change of heart when deemed appropriate."[25] God gives us the perfect model of conversion and repentance. If God can change his heart, then we in turn can do no less.

According to scriptural perspective, true repentance can only be accomplished through the grace of God. Human beings, in and of themselves, are incapable of true repentance. God will accomplish the repentance of his people by divine initiative; it will not be accomplished by human design.

Conversion in the Old Testament is often accompanied by "symbolic gestures and rituals."[26] The most observable ritual is the use of ritual cleansing, also prominent in the NT. Ezekiel's proclamation of God's sprinkling clean water upon Israel while offering a new heart, in place of Israel's stony heart, is indicative of Israel's ritual celebration of God's covenant and the ongoing journey of conversion with the People of God.

The New Testament understands conversion in terms of *metanoia* (change in one's mind and direction) and *epistrepho* (change in direction—a turning away from or toward). Conversion presupposes remorse for one's actions and is an act of repentance. As in the Old Testament, *conversion* involves a change in one's life and a turning toward God. "Whenever the nominal form of the word is used (twenty-two times in the NT), it is always in

[22] *CNT*, 4.

[23] Ibid., 5.

[24] Ibid., 6.

[25] Ibid., 14.

[26] Ibid., 15.

the singular rather than the plural form. This usage emphasizes conversion as a process rather than a once-for-all-time action."[27]

Both Testaments have spoken definitively on the issue of conversion. It is not a one-time event. It is always a movement either toward something or away from something. The primary perspective of the NT is turning away from sin and a turning toward God and Jesus.

Conversion in the Gospel of Matthew picks up the same theme that Mark develops: conversion goes hand-in-hand with faith and discipleship. However, Matthew nuances it even further. Matthew connects conversion with "bearing good fruit." True conversion will be evidenced in the fruit that it bears. From Matthew's perspective, "people reap exactly what they sow.... Matthew has a great concern that interior motivation be matched by exterior reality."[28]

Matthew insists that conversion involves an ethical response. It involves a personal choice with attached consequences. Conversion leads to salvation. Matthew ultimately embraces scripture's common understanding of conversion—a turning away from sin and foolishness and a turning toward God and new life.

Luke personalizes conversion. Rather than simply a call to the people or a nation, as in the OT, Luke insists on individual conversion. Luke's understanding of conversion has its basis in the mercy of God. Luke believed that conversion, repentance, forgiveness, and reconciliation pour forth from the free-flowing fountain of God's mercy. Luke's understanding of conversion, reconciliation, and the mercy of God is the cornerstone upon which our contemporary theology of the sacrament of reconciliation is built. Rather than an extended meditation on sin, the sacrament celebrates the fount of grace at the hands of our merciful God.

The *Constitution on the Sacred Liturgy* understands conversion as a call to faith in Jesus Christ. In the *Decree on the Church's Missionary Activity*, the Second Vatican Council asserted that conversion involves awareness of being delivered from sin and led into the mystery of God's love (#13) and a personal relationship with him. The decree describes conversion as a spiritual journey, a process in which a person is gradually and progressively changed. Following the lead of scripture, the church understands conversion as a process, a journey, a change in outlook, behavior, and life. "When man accepts the Spirit of Christ, he establishes *a way of life* that is totally new and gratuitous."[29] Conversion is a turning toward or a return to God with our whole being. Conversion desires an end to sin and is a turning away from evil, "with repugnance toward the evil actions we have committed."[30] Conversion involves the commitment to change one's life, while trusting in the grace and mercy of God to accomplish the task.[31]

The liturgy invites conversion. Every liturgy—every sacrament—is a call to continued growth in Christ and participation in his life, death, and resurrection. Sacraments "not only presuppose faith, but by words and objects they also nourish, strengthen and express it...."[32] "They do indeed impart grace but, in addition, the very act of celebrating them disposes the faithful most effectively to receive this grace in a *fruitful manner, to worship God duly and to practice charity* [italics mine]."[33] The liturgy assumes change and transformation. Every celebration is a call to action and ongoing growth in a person's relationship with God, one another, and the world.

Decision

How is our community in need of conversion at this time? How might I/we be challenged to be an agent of change within my/our community? In what way have I been cooperating with the grace of conversion in my life right now? What are the areas most in need of conversion and transformation at this time in my life? In what concrete way am I prompted to respond to the implications of this teaching in my family life, my work life, my parish life, or my civic and world communities?

[27] Ibid., 19.

[28] Ibid., 32.

[29] *GCD*, #60.

[30] *CCC*, 1431.

[31] Ibid.

[32] *CSL*, 59.

[33] Ibid.

Refer to chapter 7, "Preparing the Catechetical Session," if you intend to plan your catechetical session at this time.

CREATION

Natural Sign

Have you ever reflected upon the mystery of creation when gazing at a starlit sky, beholding the grandeur of a spring day, or gazing across the horizon at the beach's edge? How do such experiences speak to you about God?

Tradition: Biblical, Ecclesial, and Liturgical Signs

The creation of the world has been a fascination for peoples since the beginning of time. Ancient myths, as well as biblical themes and stories, have attempted to capture the mystery of the creation of the universe.

The Old Testament considers creation to be a primary motif or theme. God is the Creator and human beings and the world are the created. However, God is mostly described in the action of creating—not as Creator. "This creative activity is often referred to as stretching out the heavens (Is 40:22; 44:24; 45:12; 51:13), firmly establishing the earth (Ps 75:4; 93:1; 96:10; 104:5), or conquering the mythological beasts (Ps 74:13–15; 89:10f.; Is 51:9f.; Job 9:13)."[34]

Creation in the Old Testament was understood as an ordering of chaos rather than the creation of something out of nothing. This is best expressed in the creation account read at the Easter Vigil: "the world was a formless wasteland...." (Gen 1:2) God ordered creation by establishing all things in their rightful place—the water, the sky, the land, and the things contained within. The writers of Genesis probably drew upon the contemporary mythological account of creation known as *Enuma Elish.* In that account two gods were engaged in battle. One god represented chaos, the other order. Order won and chaos was defeated. The biblical authors drew upon this mythology as it shaped its own story of creation to fit Israel's monotheistic religion. God was thus understood as the warrior who restored order and took up residence in the new city, the Temple, and the promised land where God reigns triumphant. The beginning of the world reflected the establishment of order and harmony. History and creation are intimately connected by the biblical authors. Thus, the goal of history is understood as the restoration of the perfect harmony and order that were established at the creation of the world.

Israel understood God to be the author of all creation. Israel believed that the world possessed an inherent order. To discover and live within this order resulted in peace and harmony. Those who were deemed capable of grasping this order were said to possess wisdom. If human beings were able to perceive this order through wisdom, then there must be a divine source of this order as well. Thus, wisdom and creation are intimately connected throughout scriptures. This is particularly evident in the Genesis story about the tree of knowledge of good and evil (Gen 2:9).

The creation of men and women is considered God's crowning creative achievement. "The creation of the human person is the climax of God's creative activity in this world. Made in God's likeness each person possesses a capacity for knowledge that is transcendent, love that is unselfish, and freedom for self-direction. Inherent in each unique human person called into existence by God, these qualities reflect the essential immortality of the human spirit."[35]

Biblical texts reveal nothing but praise in the face of God's grandeur in creation. All creation is called upon to worship God for the magnificence of his handiwork. The Old Testament embodies a portrait of the warrior God who, as benefactor and benevolent master of creation, chose man and woman to rule over the created order. They were chosen to live in harmony with all creation. They were in covenant relationship with God and with God's creation. They would subdue the earth and rule it. Thus, God would enter into reciprocal covenant relationship with the human race. God would provide and care for human beings. In return, human beings would love the Lord with their whole heart, body, soul, mind, and spirit. They would love one another, love themselves, and love and care for God's little ones—those who

---

[34]Dianne Bergant, C.S.A., "Creation," in *CPDBT,* 187.

[35]*NCD,* #85.

could not care for themselves. Humanity would respect and care for all of God's creation. This was understood as biblical justice.

The New Testament reflects the same images and themes inherent in the Old Testament. However, creation is understood in light of the Christ event. The New Testament perspective understands history as moving toward the culminating creation event: the paschal mystery of Jesus Christ. "Creation should be presented as directly related to the salvation accomplished by Jesus Christ. In reflecting on the doctrine of creation, one should be mindful not only of God's first action creating the heavens and the earth, but of His continuing activity in sustaining creation and working out human salvation."[36]

In the gospels, Jesus proclaims God's creative power and providence in the world. He insisted that all creation is good when he declared all foods clean (Mk 7:19). In the gospels creation is understood in terms of God's overall plan for the world. From the very beginning God's plan included the salvation of all the world.

Paul asserted Christ's role in creation, assigning to him the mediatory role of wisdom found in the Book of Proverbs. The pre-existence of Christ is hinted at throughout the scriptures. Creation comes to fullness and fulfillment through Jesus Christ. We were chosen in Christ from the very beginning of the world.

Jesus' sacrifice does not do away with the effects of sin, but humanity is heir to the final glory that awaits us. That is why all creation is said to groan in anticipation for the consummation of the created order.

St. Paul speaks of the new life of baptism in terms of "new creation." God's creative work continues in the life of Christians as they enter the waters of new birth to new life in Christ. It is the generative, creative work of God that continues in the life of baptized Christians. The old self dies and the new person puts on the new life in Christ—behavior is thus transformed. Human beings participate in the creative work of God when they enter into Jesus' ministry of reconciliation. This "new creation" through baptism assumes that the harmony established at the creation of the world is once again realized and human beings live in harmony with God, one another, and with the universe.

[36]Ibid.

The fulfillment of creation will be complete at the consummation of the world when the old order will pass away and a new heaven and a new earth will be established. At that time all creation will live in glory with Christ at the right hand of God. Victory over evil will be final and complete and all creation will be eternally renewed.

Three principles have guided the church's theology of creation. First, creation is the handiwork of God. The world was created out of nothing. God alone is responsible. Evil will not win over God's creative power. Secondly, God's world is good. The litany professed in the Genesis account of creation is ultimate truth. "God saw that the world was good." The point is not to be missed. Even though sin and evil exist, the world is created good, and evil will not have the final say. In and of itself the world was not created evil. Evil entered the world after creation. Thus, creation is a gift from God and creation is good. Thirdly, God can be experienced through creation. Creation itself reveals God. Creation reveals God even before God is revealed to Israel and before God is revealed through Jesus. Creation mirrors God. Catholic Christianity affirms the sacramentality of creation.

Late in the nineteenth century, the literal account of creation was questioned due to the scientific data concerning evolution. Science and faith seemed to be at odds with each other. Science suggested that the world was epochs older than the Bible maintained. Science suggested that plants and animals inhabited the earth long before the appearance of humans. The literal account of creation was brought into serious question. Fundamentalists today still strictly adhere to the literalist view. Fundamentalism insists that the world was created four thousand years ago and took place over the span of six days. This theory is known as "creationism."[37] Creationism maintains that evolution is merely a scientific theory that cannot be proven.

[37]Robert J. Schreiter, C.PP.S., "Grace: Pastoral Liturgical Tradition," in *CPDBT*, 191.

Most Christians, however, believe in the probability of evolution and hold that the creation story in Genesis is a theological rather than a historical account. The Genesis narrative is intended to show the ultimate power and authority of God, the Creator of all. The six days of creation are intended to manifest the God who brings order out of chaos and does it in orderly fashion. The theological reading serves the story without requiring one to explain all its contradictions, such as how light existed before the sun was created. Creation continues to be understood as the ongoing, dynamic action of God in creating and re-creating the world. We are in constant process. God continues to create anew. God continues to do a new thing in the lives of people.

"God manifests Himself through creation. 'Since the creation of the world, invisible realities, God's external power and divinity, have become visible, recognized through the things he has made' (Romans 1:20). The first chapter of Genesis tells us that God spoke and created all things."[38] The world was *spoken* into creation. Since the world came into being through the *Word*, "creation is a great symbol of Him."[39]

Every liturgy proclaims and heralds God's creative and generative work. Easter is understood in light of the re-creation of the world. "The joy of the resurrection renews the whole world, while the choirs of angels sing forever to your glory": (Easter Preface IV). "All things are of your making, all times and seasons obey your laws, but you chose to create man in your own image . . ." (Sundays in Ordinary Time V: Preface). The ongoing re-creative power of God elevates human nature to divine likeness. "Through your beloved Son you created our human family. Through him you restored us to your likeness" (Weekdays III: Preface). Every profession of faith is an odyssey of remembrance into the creative, generative power of God. It recalls the mystery of the Trinity and the genesis of salvation history. Every Rite of Sprinkling acknowledges the wonders of creation, particularly in the symbol of water. All the dominant symbols of the church have their genesis in the sacramentality of creation itself. Our sacramental symbols come to us from the "stuff" of everyday life. Things of the earth remind us of God, reflect his image, and bring into the present his saving presence.

[38] *NCD*, #51.

[39] Ibid.

When the gifts of bread and wine are brought forward, those things, made of human hands that will become transformed by the power of the Spirit, we are transported into the mystery of Divine creation, and in the process we too are re-created. We become a new creation along with the transformed bread and wine. We, too, become the Body and Blood of Christ. Creation theology is the thread that underpins our understanding of sacraments.

> Blessed are you, Lord, God of all creation.
> Through your goodness we have this bread
> to offer,
> which earth has given and human hands
> have made.
> It will become for us the bread of life.
> By the mystery of this water and wine may
> we come
> to share in the divinity of Christ, who humbled himself
> to share in our humanity.
> Blessed are you, Lord, God of all creation.
> Through your goodness we have this wine
> to offer,
> fruit of the vine and work of human hands.
> It will become our spiritual drink.
> (Preparation of the Altar and Gifts, *The Sacramentary*)

In our liturgy we honor God's creation, the work of God's hands. All creation is understood as bowing in humble adoration of God, the Creator. "Therefore it is right to receive *the obedience of all creation*, the praise of the Church on earth, the thanksgiving of the saints in heaven . . ." (Preface: Weekdays III, P39, *The Sacramentary*).

Everything in creation is sanctified and made holy by the hand of our Creator God. We are made holy; the symbols of our faith are made holy and reveal the transcendence of God, and the earth is made holy. Our church cares for human activity, human life, what affects human life, and all human endeavor. Our church has a deep respect for things of the earth and for our world and its concerns. Evidence of such care is to be found in the Masses and the Prayers For Various Needs and Occasions, such as Masses For the Laity, For the Unity of Christians, For the Nations, For Those

Who Serve in Public Office, For Congress, For the President, For the Progress of Peoples, For Peace and Justice, In Time of War or Civil Disturbance, For the Blessings of Human Labor, For Productive Land, After the Harvest, In Time of Famine or For Those Who Suffer from Famine, For Refugees and Exiles, For Those Unjustly Deprived of Liberty, For Prisoners, For the Sick, For the Dying, In Time of Earthquake, For Rain, For Fine Weather, To Avert Storms, For Any Need, In Thanksgiving, For Charity, For Forgiveness of Sins, For Promoting Harmony, For the Family, For Relatives and Friends, For Our Oppressors, and For a Happy Death.

The *Book of Blessings* is given to the church to sanctify all of life's activities, from the work of our hands to the seeds that die in the earth to be born into new buds of life. Included in the *Book of Blessings* are blessings that reflect our great respect for the world, for life, for human labor, and for all human situations and activity such as: Order for the Blessing of Families and Members of Families, for Children, Blessing of Sons and Daughters, Blessing for Parents before Childbirth, for Mothers before Childbirth, for Mothers after Childbirth, Blessing of Parents after a Miscarriage, Blessing of Parents and an Adopted Child, on the Occasion of a Birthday, Orders for the Blessing of Elderly People Confined to Their Homes, Orders for the Blessing of the Sick, Order for the Blessing of Students and Teachers, Blessing of a Person Suffering from Addiction or from Substance Abuse, for the Victim of Crime or Oppression, Blessing of Seeds at Planting Time, Order for the Blessing of an Athletic Event, Order for the Blessing of a New Hospital, or other Facility for the Care of the Sick, Order for the Blessing of an Office, Shop, or Factory, Orders for the Blessing of Those Gathered at a Meeting, Order for the Blessing of Organizations Concerned with Public Need, Order for the Blessing of Travelers, Order for the Blessing of a New Building Site, a New Home, a New Religious House, a New School or University, a New Library, a Parish Hall or Catechetical Center, Centers of Social Communication, Gymnasium or a Field for Athletics, Blessing of Boats and Fishing Gear, Order for the Blessing of Various Means of Transportation, Order for the Blessing of Technical Installations or Equipment and the Blessing of Tools or Other Equipment for Work. The Masses for Various Needs and Occasions and the myriad of Blessings provided in the *Book of Blessings* prove in triplicate that the church regards all life and human experience as sacred, holy, and worthy of honor.

Testing
How does the church's teaching on creation have any relevance for your life? In what way does the dynamic ongoing creative power of God impact your life? What are the implications of creation theology for the life of believers? What are the implications of creation in relation to baptism? How does the understanding of creation in terms of God's bringing order out of chaos speak to you? Is there any experience in your life that you might connect to this teaching? Have you ever experienced the creative power of God in your life? How does this teaching speak to your community?

Decision
What is the challenge inherent in this teaching? What is the invitation to change? In what way does this teaching invite a response? What one concrete action might you take as a result of this teaching?

Refer to chapter 7, "Preparing the Catechetical Session," if you intend to plan your catechetical session at this time.

CROSS

See Easter Vigil.

EASTER SEASON

See Overview of Easter Season, Easter Vigil, and the Sundays of Easter.

EASTER VIGIL

See Easter Vigil.

EPIPHANY

See Overview of Christmas and Feast of Epiphany.

ESCHATOLOGY

The Collegeville Pastoral Dictionary of Biblical Theology defines eschatology, from the Greek *eschatos,* last, as that which has to do with beliefs and ideas about the end time, and with the valuation of time and history in this perspective. "Most religious traditions have some set of beliefs about an ultimate future of the individual and of the earth, whether that future is envisioned as eternal, cyclic, or limited."[40]

Natural Sign

When we speak about the end of the world, what does it evoke in you? How do you feel when we speak about the end of your own world through death? If you were to articulate an understanding of what happens to us after we die, what would you say? How would you articulate an understanding of your faith tradition's belief in the afterlife and the end of time?

Tradition: Biblical, Ecclesial, and Biblical Signs

Eschatology is the area of theology that studies the last things. The last things refer to the final manifestation of God's loving relationship to humanity. Issues that fall under the umbrella of eschatology's concerns are "death, particular judgement, heaven, hell, purgatory, Second Coming of Christ, resurrection of the body, general judgment, consummation of all things in the perfection of the Kingdom of God."[41] Richard McBrien asserts that even though future oriented, these realities have already been accomplished in the present through people who live the life awarded to them by the death and resurrection of Jesus. "Our *judgment* will be the visible manifestation of the judgment of acquittal already rendered in Jesus Christ."[42]

All of time is sanctified by God. In the Christian perspective, eschatology refers to the sanctification of future time and hinges upon the life, death, and resurrection of Jesus. Eschatology's springboard is the reality of Jesus' first entrance into human history through his Incarnation, the resulting effects, and the future promise of eternal life at the end of time.

One type of eschatology found in the New Testament is apocalyptical. That is, it alludes to the end of the world with preceding signs and wonders. The end time is seen as a time in which evil is conquered and Jesus will come again on a cloud, summoning all the faithful to their final destination: life with all the saints in the heavenly kingdom. Apocalyptic literature is often rich in symbolic language and speaks powerfully of a present reality, not just some future expectation. Berard Marthaler states: "Apocalyptic literature is purported to be a revelation of the future, whereas in actuality it was most often a commentary on the times in which it was composed."[43] The book of Revelation is an example of apocalyptic literature. Often the purpose of such literature was to offer consolation to persecuted people in present crisis situations.

Another type of eschatology in the scriptures can be found in the synoptic gospels of Matthew, Mark, and Luke. This type of eschatology heralds the reign of God both now and in the future. God is celebrated as the ONE who reigns in our midst. God's presence demands nothing but the total giving of self in response: complete conversion and *metanoia.* The kingdom of God is present when people are gathered in the name of Jesus.

Another scriptural image for eschatology is that of banquet. In the Old Testament the image of feasting was used in reference to "heavenly happiness."[44] The Last Supper was also seen as eschatological. It signaled the beginning of the last days. That which Christ was sent to do was coming to completion, beginning with the Lord's Supper. Thus, every eucharistic celebration has remembrances and reminders of our eschatological center.

Another biblical principle of eschatology appears in the gospel of John and is referred to as *realized eschatology.* The term refers to the fulfillment of that which is awaited and hoped for. Thus, those who believe in Jesus are already living in the promise and imbued with the Spirit of his very presence.

The history of eschatology in the church developed over time. It moved through stages in which there were notions that after a thousand year reign the end would come. This understanding came from a literalist view of Revelation 20. It was

[40]Carolyn Osiek, R.S.C.J., "Eschatology," in *CPDBT,* 264.

[41]*CSM,* 1101-1105.

[42]Ibid., 1103.

[43]*CR,* 206.

[44]John J. Collins, "Eschatology," in *CPDBT,* 261–264.

an understanding easily reputed in the year 1001. The end, of course, did not arrive.

Later there was great debate concerning where people would go upon their death. Questions of location came to the fore. Where would the individual soul go? Were there interim places before the final beatific vision? It is out of such debate that our understandings of purgatory and the resurrected body come.

These understandings remained intact until the advent of biblical scholarship in recent times. There was a shift away from the concept of the individual and the locale of his or her final resting place toward a broader, more inclusive understanding of eschatology. Contemporary theology thinks more in terms of humanity's final collective relationship to the Creator as a people.

More recently, Marxism criticized the *future only oriented* Christian stance as an excuse to avoid engaging in the concerns of the world. From such critique emerged the perception that indeed God and humanity were to be coworkers in the work of transforming the world. Disciples are called to be actors in the ongoing theater of life. They are to be history makers.

Lest we negate the creed of the kingdom of God *yet to come* in favor of a narrower interpretation as only meaning the kingdom of God *here and now,* the Second Vatican Council redefined the church's theology in regard to eschatology. The church defined the reign of God as a transcendent future, yet acknowledged humanity's role to be active participants in changing the present world while awaiting the coming of the next *(Dogmatic Constitution on the Church)*.

Thus, we are to face death with courage and joy. We should be counseled about our belief in death, judgment, and eternity, but always with "consoling hope, as well as salutory fear."[45] The Lord's death has conquered death. In our funeral liturgy we proclaim that through the resurrection of Jesus we share in his life; we live, we die, and we shall live again. We are to look forward with hope as we realize our responsibility toward our own eternal destiny and the destiny of the world. Evangelization, spreading the reconciling good news of Jesus, is no light matter when one considers the stakes.

The following citations are a few that reflect the eschatology of Israel, the gospels, and the early church:

Hebrew Scriptures

National Eschatology: Prophet Amos—professed the fall of the Northern Kingdom (9:8); Prophet Isaiah—insisted Southern Kingdom would stand (6:13); he also foretold the messianic reign (11:1–9).

Cosmic Eschatology: Prophet Isaiah—envisioned the new heaven and new earth (65:1); Prophet Jeremiah—spoke of the void earth (4:23); Prophet Ezra spoke about the end of the world (4 Ez 7:30).

Personal Eschatology: resurrection of the dead (Dn 12:2; 2 Mac 7).

New Testament

Christ's future return (Jn 21:22–23; Acts 1:11); parousia (Mt 24:29–31; Mk 13:24–27); eschatological reign of God (Mt 13:31–32, Mk 4:30–32); eschatological banquet (Mt 26:29; Mk 14:25; Lk 22:15–16); realized eschatology (Jn 14:6; 17:3); final judgment (Rev 13:1–8; Mt 19:28; Lk 22:30; 1 Cor 6:2–3).

Testing

In what way, if any, has your original understanding regarding the end times been stretched, challenged, or affirmed? Was there any new information for you? If so, what was it? In light of the material just presented, is there any implication for living the Christian life? Are there any implications for the wider church? In what way can we as church participate in helping people live in *realized eschatology*? How are the biblical themes of covenant, exodus, creation, and community evident in the post-biblical teachings about the end times, final judgment, eternal life, and resurrection of the body? In what way are these post-biblical teachings related to the scriptures of this Sunday's liturgy? In light of this sharing, how would you articulate a theology or an understanding of eschatology? Is it the same as your first understanding, or has it changed?

[45] "Basic Teaching for Catholic Religious Education," #25, p. 142.

Decision
How does this understanding of eschatology challenge me personally? How am I living the message? In what way do I need to grow? What is one concrete action I can take this week as a response to our sharing? Prepare to share the experience next week.

Refer to chapter 7, "Preparing the Catechetical Session," if you intend to plan your catechetical session at this time.

EUCHARIST

See Christian Initiation, Part III: Eucharist (Appendix).

FASTING

See Lenten Overview.

GARMENT

See Easter Vigil, Symbol of Garment.

GRACE

Natural Sign
What is the most precious gift you have ever been given? Why? What did the gift express to you? What was the meaning behind the gift? Did the gift bear any significance for your life? What does the word *grace* mean to you?

Tradition: Biblical, Ecclesial, and Liturgical Signs
The word *grace* conjures up a wide range of meaning both in theological as well as secular terms. Theologically the word can imply favor or kindnesses given by God to the human race, or gifts given by God to individuals, or the gift of thanks offered by human beings to God for God's many kindnesses. In everyday parlance the word implies a salutation of high honor, such as "Your Grace." The usage of the word *grace* in everyday speech, such as "There but for the grace of God go I," or "I hope that I have the grace to . . . ," is derived from theological origins. The genesis of both secular and theological forms is found in the concept of favor. Theologically the word suggests a relationship between God and God's children. It is a relationship in which God bestows on the human race God's complete, gratuitous, unmerited love. Grace is not an event, an object, a person, or an act of God, but rather the gratuitous self-gift of God to the human race. Grace is also the action of God in human history. Grace is union with God. Grace is not a holy bank account in the sky in which one deposits favor from God, only to have it withdrawn by some infraction of law. Throughout the ages the church has spent volumes exploring and meditating on the usage, implication, and meaning of the word *grace.*

The word grace in the Hebrew Scriptures means to "incline oneself favorably to another."[46] It is best understood in terms of the client-patron relationship of ancient Mediterranean cultures. When governments could not provide for the needs of their citizenry, the wealthy landowners entered into a relationship of favor with their less fortunate lower-class clients. The higher-class patron cared for the basic needs of the lower-class client. When a patron did not share his surplus, he was considered greedy. The patron enjoyed honorable acclaim and the client enjoyed benefits that could be obtained in no other way.

God was understood in similar terms. God was the patron of Israel. The election of Israel meant that God, the patron, took care of the needs of Israel, the client. Israel was totally dependent upon God. The client-patron relationship was not without strings attached. The patron would provide, but the client owed the patron allegiance. There was an intended response. The client would be grateful for the gifts rendered. When Israel was not grateful, when Israel sinned, they severed the client-patron relationship. God was an extraordinary patron, however, as he continually restored the client-patron relationship following a rupture on the part of Israel, the client. God bestows *grace* (favor) without end to God's client, Israel.

In the New Testament, Jesus Christ epitomizes the favor shown by God. No longer does Israel act like the client of the Patron, God, but now Christians enjoy a status not enjoyed before. Followers of Christ are true members of God's family. They are no longer clients, but enjoy status as children of the Patron's family.

[46]John J. Pilch, "Grace," in *CPDBT*, 397.

The word grace as used in the New Testament infers a refined theology of gratitude for the saving action of God accomplished through Jesus Christ. The biblical authors use the language of their Hebrew tradition to reflect their gratitude for God's election of Israel, and the subsequent inclusion of Gentiles in that election. The early Christians reflect their gratitude for the forgiveness of sins offered by Christ's sacrifice on Calvary. They are grateful for the new life of Christ in the Spirit, for the peace and shalom offered by this new life, for the love and transformation that are possible because of Christ's self-sacrifice. Christians are thankful for the anticipation they share in waiting for the final consummation of the world and Christ's return in glory. They did not, however, attempt to narrow this gratitude into one single concept called grace. The word *grace* is used, but in reference to a favor or blessing, to forgiveness, or to specific gifts called charisms. Grace is not used as the singular expression of the gift of God's self. Wherever the word is used, one can readily substitute the word gift or favor in its place. Only later in church history will the concept of *grace* take on a theology of its own.

The early Christians spoke of grace (*charis*) when describing the effects of the gift of Christ. The etymology (origin) of the word from both Latin and Greek can mean "(1) graciousness, attractiveness, charm, or (2) a favor granted to someone, or (3) the gratitude due to someone in response to a gift. Moreover, in both Greek and Latin the term can designate either the source of a gift in the giver or the effect of the gift in the recipient."[47]

The early church also connected the term grace (*charis*) to reflect a connection with the eucharist and Christ's presence in the assembly through the eucharist. Grace was that present and future gift of God's presence. The grace of Christ's presence is a foretaste of the eschatological pledge of eternal life.

Justin Martyr, an early Father of the Church (c. 100–165), understood God's grace as the universal gift of *God's Love* active in salvation history. According to Justin, all who lived according to Christ, God's incarnate *Word* (who was active in human history since the beginning of time), would be beneficiaries of God's everlasting grace/life/love. They need not necessarily accept the God of Israel or Christianity. Those who opposed God, or lived against the principles of Christ, would not be saved. Thus, pagans who lived an exemplary life would be heir to God's saving grace.

Later however, Cyprian of Carthage (c. 200–258) limited the beneficiaries. Only those who were in union with the Catholic Church could be saved. Cyprian's theology dominated much of Catholic theology until the Second Vatican Council. *The Pastoral Constitution on the Church in the Modern World* reaffirmed God's universal gift of love and salvation to all humanity.

A further defining event for Western theology in regard to grace was a result of the debate between St. Augustine of Hippo, and Pelagius, an English spiritual guide. Pelagius taught that people were created good by God, and because human beings were created good by God, they had the instinctive power, in and of themselves, to do good without God's help. Pelagius did acknowledge the need for grace, but understood grace as merely a necessary support, or aid, very much like a moral code, or the example of Christ or his teaching. Pelagius understood grace as an external support. Augustine, on the other hand, refuted the Pelagian heresy, and used St. Paul to prove his position. In Paul's letter to the Romans, Paul insists that human beings are saved through the power of Christ's death and resurrection, not by their own good works. For Augustine, grace was a gift from God that empowers the human will to do good—a completely gratuitous gift. He believed that human beings can do nothing to earn the necessary grace for salvation—that it is a free gift that empowers people to change their lives and live according to the law of love. "The mystery of grace is at the heart of Augustine's writings which include a sacramental view of reality that sees the 'vestiges of the Trinity' present throughout creation, an inner desire for God at the core of every human heart, and the Baptism as a share in the inner divine life of love."[48] Augustine asserted a "strong emphasis on grace as a divine force liberating the

[47]Leo D. Lefebure, "Grace: Pastoral Liturgical Tradition," in *CPDBT*, 400.

[48]Richard P. McBrien, "Grace," in *HCEC*, 578.

human will from the bondage of sin."[49] He believed that people are justified and made righteous through faith and God's grace. Pelagius insisted that if we were created good, that we must have the capacity to choose good, which is itself a gift from God, or God's grace, whereas Augustine taught that human beings are so tainted by the effects of original sin that only by grace are we able to live righteously. Grace is the "internal assistance of the Holy Spirit" needed to become a healed and transformed mind, body, soul, and spirit.

The Eastern Church developed an understanding of grace as empowerment to live righteously but also as participation in God's divine nature. Grace is a share of the divine life of God, our life as adopted children of God. Grace is the gift of God's self to humanity. Grace is participation in God's divine life. Grace is the new life of God's *created grace* within every human being. St. Athanasias draws upon this notion of grace in his teaching concerning the Incarnation of Christ. The Incarnation represents God's offer of divine self to humanity, whereby human beings are offered a share in God's divine life. "For Athanasias of Alexandria (c. 295–373), this is the central meaning of the incarnation: God became human so that humans could share in God's own life and become divine. Similarly, Cyril of Alexandria (d. 444) viewed grace as a state of communion with God, a state in which we become partakers of the divine nature."[50] (See the preface for Christmas.)

St. Thomas Aquinas of the Middle Ages posits an understanding of grace as everything that comes from God and similarly returns to God. Aquinas drew upon Augustine's healing notion of grace, but he also drew upon the Eastern tradition of grace as divinization—participation in the divine life of love. Aquinas made the distinction between created and uncreated grace. Uncreated grace is synonymous with the gift of love present in the Trinity—it is God's self. Created grace is the effect that God's love has on human beings who are captured by God's uncreated grace. Not only is human nature healed by this love, but human beings are elevated to divine status; they share and participate in the divine life; they share God's life and love. It is beyond human capacity to attain this divine life. God elevates human nature through the gift of God's indwelling Spirit in the human soul. Grace allows human beings to enter into intimate relationship and friendship with the Trinity. Human beings become adopted heirs to what is natural and inherent to the Trinity—perfect love. This divinization was referred to as the "habit" of grace by Aquinas.

Later debates about faith and justification during the Reformation led to the Council of Trent's formulation of the theology of grace. Justification is the forgiveness of sins as well as the radical transformation of the baptized. The transformed person's new habit of grace allows that person to move from enmity with God to friendship with God. This habit of grace that leads to radical transformation empowers the person to act and live righteously by God's initiative, and by human participation in God's initiative. This did not stop the debate on the nature and effects of grace. It would continue over the centuries. Twentieth-century theologians attempted to recapture the notion of grace as the gratuitous gift of God's self and God's love to human beings. Theologians such as Karl Rahner (1984), Henri de Lubac (1991), Pierre Teilhard de Chardin (1955), and Edward Schillebeeckx reaffirmed the understanding of grace as God's self-offer of *Ultimate Love*. They also posited the belief in the human will as naturally directed and oriented to seek and encounter the living God. God desires relationship with human beings. Human beings are naturally predisposed and created to love and seek God, whether they are conscious of that fact or not. Rahner insisted that human beings are created with this natural predisposition to love God. It is God's gift of self-love to human beings. He called it the "supernatural existential," implying that such orientation for the love and seeking of God is the result of the unmerited, gratuitous action of God. This is eloquently expressed in the Weekdays IV Preface: "You have no need of our praise, yet our desire to thank you is itself gift. Our prayer of thanksgiving adds nothing to your greatness, but makes us grow in your grace, through Jesus Christ our Lord."

Rahner affirmed God's universal salvific will that all people be saved, while still maintaining salvation through the life, death, and resurrection of

[49] Ibid.

[50] Lefebure, "Grace: Pastoral Liturgical Tradition," in *CPDBT*, 401.

Jesus Christ. He insisted that people who live in fidelity to God's love found deep within their own hearts, whether consciously Christian or not, are living in the reality of God's love and God's salvation. He called such people "anonymous Christians."

Edward Schillebeeckx asserts that grace flourishes in the human heart when people stand in solidarity with those who suffer, and when human beings make the effort to resist the evil that permeates our world. Liberation theologians such as Leonardo Boff and Gustavo Gutierrez understand grace as the liberating power of God present in the midst of oppressed peoples and societies. Liberation theologians propose that grace is both gift and responsibility. We are gifted and empowered for action, and that action resides in solidarity with the whole human race—and especially the oppressed and exploited.

God's gift of self is manifest through divine revelation. The Spirit of God manifests God's self to human beings through natural, biblical, ecclesial, and liturgical signs. God's divine revelation calls for a response from human beings. This response is the grace of God's self within each human heart. This habit of grace within each person allows them to respond with mind, will, heart, and emotions—the total self. The inner dwelling of the Spirit disposes human beings to turn the heart and the will to God. This Spirit-presence is grace. "One believes in response to grace."[51] "Grace is God's generous and free gift to His people. It is union with God, a sharing in his life, the state of having been forgiven one's sins, of being adopted as God's own child and sustained by God's unfailing love. Grace is possible for us because of Christ's redemptive sacrifice."[52]

The sacraments are an effective means to experience God's grace. The sacraments are the gift of God's self to the church. "The sacraments are important means for bringing about the Christian's union with God in grace. They are sources of grace for individuals and communities, as well as remedies for sin and its effects."[53]

[51] *NCD*, #57.

[52] Ibid., #98.

[53] Ibid.

Grace is also understood to be present in creation itself. God's presence is mediated through the gift of this world, its resources, its art, its music, its treasures, its science and technology, its healing arts, and all things that enhance human life and dignity.

Testing

Were there any new insights for you, or anything you had not considered before? How would you articulate an understanding of grace? What is a habit of grace? How does one get it? What do you think it means that grace is participation in God's divine life? What does that mean for your everyday life? How does this teaching on grace invite transformation in your life? In what way can you relate to the liberation theologians' understanding of grace? How does it invite a response? How do you experience grace in creation? If grace is the gift of God's self to humanity, what is the human response in the face of such unmerited love? Do you know any anonymous Christians? What do they teach you about grace? How does the church celebrate grace in its liturgy? How might this teaching on grace speak to your community?

Decision

What is the challenge of the church's teaching on grace? How does this teaching concretely invite transformed behavior? What one specific thing might you do in response to this teaching?

Refer to chapter 7, "Preparing the Catechetical Session," if you intend to plan your catechetical session at this time.

HOLY FAMILY

See Feast of the Holy Family.

HOLY SPIRIT

See Trinity: God as Spirit (Appendix). See Feast of Pentecost. See Easter Season Overview. See Feast of the Baptism of the Lord.

INCARNATION

The Incarnation (from the Latin, *caro,* "flesh," "enfleshing") refers to God assuming human nature. It specifically refers to God becoming a human being when Jesus was conceived by the Holy Spirit in his mother, Mary. It also refers to the mystery of Christ, as one divine person, possessing a fully human and a fully divine nature.

Natural Sign

When we speak about the Incarnation, what does it evoke in you? How do you feel about the idea of God coming to earth in the person of Jesus? If you were to articulate an understanding of Incarnation, first, do you have such an understanding, and second, what is it? How would you [or could you] articulate an understanding of your faith tradition's belief in the Incarnation?

Tradition: Biblical, Ecclesial, and Liturgical Signs

Belief in the incarnation is a foundational truth. It is among the *hierarchy of truths*. The essence of being Christian is to accept the reality and the mystery of the Incarnation. Jesus, who was one with God, entered human history and took on a human nature. We are taught that Jesus became a human being to save us from our sins, to reconcile us with God (1 Jn 4:10; 4:14). We proclaim that truth every time we pray the Nicene Creed together in liturgy.

Another reason God took human form through Jesus is so that we all could experience God's unfathomable love. We humans are very stubborn sometimes. God understands us all too well. God knew that if he did not come to us in the flesh, we would never really believe the love God has for us. Unless someone could walk with us in our struggles, suffer with us in our pain, laugh with us in our joys, we would never really own the love that God has for us. Thus, Yahweh sent his Son to endure what all human beings have to endure, the struggles of life.

Jesus, the Son of God, also came to us to show us the way to God, to show us what it means to be a holy people. Jesus is the perfect model. As our brother, he showed us how to live by the example of his own life. Through his teaching we are shown what it means to be a holy people, a royal priesthood, a people set apart. Jesus came to offer us the law of love. He gave us the great commandment of love: we are to love God and one another. We are to lay down our lives for one another, just as Jesus laid down his life for us.

God became human in order for us to share in his divine nature. "For this is why the Word became man, and the Son of God became the Son of man: so that man, by entering into communion with the Word and thus receiving divine sonship, might become a son of God."[54] Sometimes this is the most difficult reality for people. We are so sure of our wretchedness that we find it difficult to accept that we share the divine nature of God through our incorporation into Jesus' Mystical Body. We *are* holy people. To echo the words of Genesis: God created male and female and God saw that it was good. By taking human form God elevated human nature and restored human dignity.

Jesus is not a divided self, part God and part human. The mystery we celebrate is that Jesus was fully human and fully divine at the same time. The first heresies denied that Jesus was fully human (Gnostic Docetism). According to the Arian heresy, Jesus was not from the same substance as the Father. In response, the Nicean Council stated that Jesus was begotten, not made. There never was a time when Jesus was not.

Jesus, as true God and true human being, possessed a human will and intellect. This will and intellect were subject to his divine will and intellect, the same will and intellect of Father and Son. The mystery of the Incarnation "sheds light both on the mystery of God and the mystery of human life."[55] Through the mystery of the Incarnation God is so dedicated to humanity and to creation (God's handiwork) that he exploded into human history to be one with us in all things. God desired to experience our humanity in its completeness: the joys and the struggles.

The Incarnation shows us what it means to be human and gives meaning and purpose to the human life. To live is to hunger for intimate relationship with God. For this we were created. Consequently, the Incarnation is good news for the human race. It expresses the potential goodness of every human life. How could human life be anything but potentially worthy if God was willing to take its form? While there is propensity for sin

[54]St. Irenaeus, Adv. Haeres. 3, 19, 1:PG7/1, 939, in *CCC*, p. 116, #460.

[55]*EC*, 659.

in human nature, the Incarnation gives us the hope and the means to enter deeply into relationship with God. It is the kind of relationship that God envisioned and desired at the creation of the world.

The messiah came to restore the perfect harmony created by God in the genesis event. Creation's perfect harmony consisted in right ordered relationships: God's perfect justice. Perfect justice is an ordering of relationships that places human beings in reciprocal covenant relationship with God, with one another, and with creation. God and humanity were to share an unbreakable bond and as a result were to enter into a similar union with one another. They were to offer God's justice and love to the powerless and to those difficult to love by the world's standards. This love was to be extended not necessarily because such persons deserved to be loved, but because God would do as much and wished that we do no less. Humanity's response was a sign of their love for God (or lack thereof).

However, people interrupted God's plan through sin. They turned from God and lost God's just and perfect kingdom. The *Word Made Flesh* was to restore creation's justly ordered design. The peace that accompanied Jesus' birth was nothing less than the restoration of God's first grand design. Through Jesus the relationships envisioned by God are possible.

The Advent/Christmas season highlights the Incarnation in the liturgical texts and scriptures celebrated throughout the season. Every eucharistic liturgy celebrates the Incarnation and professes it in ritual and prayer, Gloria, Creed, eucharistic prayers, etc.

Testing
In what way, if any, has your original understanding regarding the Incarnation been informed, stretched, challenged, or affirmed? Was there any new information for you? If so, what was it? In light of the material just presented, is there any implication for living the Christian life? What does this teaching have to say about the community's and your role in God's plan for the redemption of the human race? In what way is this post-biblical teaching related to the scriptures of this Sunday's liturgy? In light of this sharing, how would you articulate an understanding of the Incarnation? Is it the same as your first understanding, or has it changed?

Decision
How does this teaching about the Incarnation challenge our community? In what way is our community living the message we just shared? In what specific way is our community in need of transformation? Is there any concrete action I can take to be an agent of change in my community? How does this reflection concerning the Incarnation of Jesus challenge me personally? How am I living the message? In what way do I need to grow? What one concrete action can I take this week as a response to what we have shared?

Refer to chapter 7, "Preparing the Catechetical Session," if you intend to plan your catechetical session at this time.

JESUS

Natural Sign
Have you ever had a personal experience of Jesus in your life? Define what you believe about Jesus. What do you think the church teaches about Jesus Christ?

Tradition: Biblical, Ecclesial, and Liturgical Signs
Non-Christian sources do give testimony to the existence of Jesus. However, they give little or no historical information.

The New Testament answers the question of "Who is Jesus?" through the use of a multitude of titles that reflect his multi-faceted personhood and mission such as: Jesus the Prophet, Jesus the Suffering Servant of God, Jesus the High Priest, Jesus the Messiah, Jesus the Son of Man, Jesus the Lord, Jesus the Savior, Jesus the Word, Jesus the Son of God.

The gospels are the final, edited, redacted version of the oral and written remembrance of Christ proclaimed in the early church. The resurrection of Christ is the central pivot upon which the Christian kerygma hinges. It is the event that prompts the early church's faith in Christ as the promised messiah and Savior of the world. No one saw the resurrection, but many experienced Christ after the resurrection. Jesus' central message was the arrival of the reign of God that he proclaimed through parables, proverbial sayings, and the Lord's Prayer.

The church's understanding of Jesus grew gradually in the apostolic age especially between 100 and 700 with the primary focus centered on his nature. Doctrine in relation to Christ developed as a result of curiosity, controversies, and heresies.

The main question or problem centered around the divinity and the humanity of Christ. Belief in Jesus, the God-Man, was the cause of controversy. Jesus was both human and divine. To stress the divinity over the humanity undermines belief in Jesus' humanity. When Jesus' humanity is too greatly stressed his divinity is diminished. Balance is critical.

Heresies centered around belief in Christ's humanity and divinity prompted an articulation of the church's creed in relationship to Christ. The Council of Nicea definitively asserted the divinity of Christ and rejected the Arian heresy that stated that Jesus was made at a certain point in time. The Council attested to Jesus' oneness with the Father. The Council of Constantinople was concerned with upholding the humanity of Christ so that the effect of Christ's redemption not be minimized. The Council of Ephesus maintained that Jesus is both God and human at the same time and that Mary, his mother, is the mother of Jesus and the Mother of God (Theotokos). The Council attested to the two natures of Jesus: human and divine at the same time. The Council of Chaldeon affirmed Jesus' two distinct natures. He is fully human and fully divine and like us in all things except sin.

Doctrine in relation to Christ was firmly established in the historical period of 100–700 and forms the basis of our christology today. The church teaches that Jesus is the Word made flesh. God took on human form in order to accomplish his plan of salvation. He became human for us that we might be reconciled with God and saved for all eternity. He became human so that we would know God's love for us and so we would have an example of holiness. Jesus taught us what it means to be fully human and fully alive.

Jesus is truly God and truly human. He became man while remaining fully divine. Belief in the passion, death, and resurrection is at the heart of the Christian kerygma. Christ loved us to death. He died and rose again for the sins of the world. The blood ritual of the old covenant was replaced by the Christ's blood, the blood of the new covenant. Christ's sacrifice surpasses all other sacrifices. None is greater. Through Christ's death we are freed from sin; through his resurrection we are raised to new and eternal life. Jesus is the second person of the Blessed Trinity.

Jesus is the centerpiece of all liturgical celebrations, blessings, sacraments, private prayer, and devotions. He is the object and purpose of our gathering and the source of our prayer.

Testing
Were there any new insights? Have any of your original assumptions been stretched? How would you articulate an understanding about the church's belief in Christ in light of this presentation? What does belief in Christ have to do with everyday life?

Decision
How does this teaching about Christ challenge me personally? How am I living the message? In what way do I need to grow? What one concrete action can I take this week as a response to what was shared?

Refer to chapter 7, "Preparing the Catechetical Session," if you intend to plan your catechetical session at this time.

JUSTICE

Natural Sign
What does the word *justice* mean to you? What does justice mean in the secular world? How might you connect the secular understanding of justice with the spiritual understanding of justice?

Tradition: Biblical, Ecclesial, and Liturgical Signs
The command to care for the world's less fortunate, for the oppressed, and for the downtrodden is an ancient one. It begins with our understanding of creation and biblical justice. At the 1996 Orlando Catechetical Conference, the noted scripture scholar Walter Burghardt asserted that

biblical justice is fidelity to the demands of relationships, and to responsibilities that stem from our covenant with God.

> The Old Testament asked: what did it mean for an Israelite to live? They were united by bonds of family or covenant. In that framework or context, how is God just? God acts as God should: always faithful to his promise. God provides and God punishes violations. *God is always faithful.* When are we just? When we are in right relationship to our God, to our brothers and sisters, and to the earth. In the Genesis creation story everything was in right relationship to everything else. All were in covenant relationship with God. Because of this covenant the people of God were to welcome the stranger, feed the hungry, give a home to the alien—not because they deserved it, but because this is how God acted toward Israel. Deuteronomy said to love the stranger because God did. Justice of God, then, is fidelity to relationships, expressions of love. Not to execute justice was not to worship God.

God was Israel's caretaker (Ex 19:3–6; 20:2). Israel's response was to be faithful to the Law and the commandments (Ex 19:5; 20:1–17). This treaty between God and humanity demanded that Israel respond in obedience and trust. Deuteronomy insists that the love and mercy God shows to Israel is to be extended to everyone in their community and to foreigners. "... (J)ustice lives on in the world both by divine action and through those who fulfill the obligations of their covenant relationship with God."[56]

The prophets railed against Israel's inattention to the covenant. They professed God's mercy, compassion, and incredible patience in the face of Israel's injustice. The prophets clamored for a return to right relationship (*hesed*) with God. This meant a return to righteousness, justice, compassion, and steadfast kindness. Israel would be re-created and the harmony of paradise would be restored. This harmony meant that humanity was in right relationship with God. God would provide for human beings. God would love human beings and in return humanity would love as God loves. This love would be evident in behavior. Wherever and whenever God's children are not cared for, this is evidence of a ruptured covenant. The absence of justice is understood as complete darkness. Living in justice is living in the light. The practice of justice was synonymous with salvation.

Jesus demanded biblical justice for all people. He strongly challenged those who did not live according to the biblical command to live in right relationship. A primary motif in Luke/Acts is care and concern for the lowly, the marginalized, the sinner, and those on the fringe of society. Jesus insisted that the hallmark of his mission was that the poor have the good news preached to them. The main thread running through the garment of New Testament teaching is care and concern for all of God's people: the lowest of the low and the poorest of the poor. "The NT authors—especially Luke—are optimistic about the ability of the Church to ameliorate social injustice while awaiting the coming reign of God."[57]

The church's teaching on social justice is rooted in creation. God's creation is good. All humanity is created in the image and likeness of God, thereby possessing a divine status and dignity as God's children. As a result of this divine status, all people are entitled to live to their fullest human potential. In order to live according to their fullest potential, every human person is entitled to health, well-being, happiness, and the best possible opportunities to achieve the potential for which they were created. Biblical justice, therefore, is the right of every person on earth. The liturgy affirms the equal status of all people before God:

> Lord,
> you guide all creation with fatherly care,
> As you have given all men one common origin,
> bring them together peacefully into one family
> and keep them united in brotherly love.
> (Mass for Peace and Justice, "Alternative Opening Prayer," *The Sacramentary*)

[56] Gregory J. Polan, O.S.B., "Justice," in *CPDBT*, 511.

[57] J. Albert Harrill, "Justice," in *CPDBT*, 515.

The covenant forged with God at the creation of the world demands a moral response. The moral response of human beings involves living in right relationship with God and one another. Thus, every Christian has a moral responsibility to act justly toward all of God's people. Every person is called to an eternal destiny. Every person is redeemed by the blood of the cross. We are therefore to recognize Christ in all people and treat them accordingly. "We must be concerned for the spiritual condition of others and for their temporal condition. Our concern will therefore extend to their authentic freedom, their spiritual and moral well-being, their intellectual and cultural welfare, their material and physical needs (e.g. housing, food, health, employment, etc.). Such concern will be expressed in action, including efforts to build a cultural, social, and political order based on peace and justice—locally, nationally, and internationally."[58]

Any action that is contrary to the life, health, and well-being of others is an action contrary to the gospel. Any action or omission that fails to enhance human dignity violates biblical justice and the human responsibility to fulfill the covenant treaty and relationship with God.

Every liturgical celebration places us in harmony and solidarity with all of God's creation. The celebration of eucharist demands that we become the Body of Christ in the world, that we lay down our lives for all people. The *Catechism of the Catholic Church* asserts that eucharist commits us to the poor (1397). In the General Intercessions we exert our priestly role and intercede on behalf of the world's poor and suffering. The church heralds concern for peace and for lasting harmony in the world.

> God our Father,
> you reveal that those who work for peace
> will be called your sons.
> Help us to work without ceasing for that
> justice
> which brings true and lasting peace.
> (Mass for Peace and Justice: Opening
> Prayer, *The Sacramentary*)

[58]*NCD*, #105.

The liturgy reflects the church's concern for justice in the wide selection of masses set aside for various needs and occasions: For Persecuted Christians, For the Progress of Peoples, For Peace and Justice, In Time of War or Civil Disturbance, In Time of Famine or For Those Who Suffer from Famine, For Refugees and Exiles, For Those Unjustly Deprived of Liberty, For Prisoners, For the Sick, For the Dying, In Time of Earthquake, For Charity, For Forgiveness of Sins, For Promoting Harmony, For the Family, For Relatives and Friends, For Our Oppressors (*The Sacramentary*). The *Book of Blessings* also shows concern for issues of justice as evidenced by blessings for: Elderly People Confined to Their Homes, Blessing of the Sick, Blessing of a Person Suffering from Addiction or from Substance Abuse, Blessing of a Victim of Crime or Oppression, and the Blessing of Organizations Concerned with Public Need.

Testing

What are the implications of biblical justice for living the Christian life? What does this teaching have to do with your everyday life? Is there anyone that you know who does not enjoy the benefits demanded in this teaching? Where is there need for an attitude adjustment in relation to this teaching? How does this teaching invite transformation of your attitudes and behavior? Your community's attitudes and behavior? How do you feel about the concept that justice is a right and not simply charity? What are the implications?

Decision

What concrete action are you willing to take in response to this teaching? What does this teaching invite your community to do in response? What attitudes are in need of healing and transformation? What are the obstacles to changing your perspective and behavior in relation to this teaching?

Refer to chapter 7, "Preparing the Catechetical Session," if you intend to plan your catechetical session at this time.

KINGDOM OF GOD

Natural Sign

What does the term "kingdom of God" evoke in you? What does it call to mind? Have you ever had a personal experience of God's kingdom in your life? If you were to give a definition of "the kingdom of God," what would it be? What do you think is meant by the term?

Tradition: Biblical, Ecclesial, and Liturgical Signs
The kingdom of God is now. There is evidence in scripture to make such an assertion. Jesus said that "the kingdom of God is at hand" (Mk 1:14-15). In obedience to his Father's will, Jesus initiates the kingdom of heaven in our midst, here and now, on earth.

As members of this kingdom we share in God's divine life. We call this gathering of God's people the church, the family of God. Jesus is the head of that family through his word, through signs that reveal God's reign, and through the sending of disciples to spread the good news. "The Word of the Lord is compared to a seed which is sown in a field; those who hear the Word with faith and become part of the little flock of Christ, have received the Kingdom itself" (*Lumen Gentium,* #5).

Jesus established his kingdom on earth. We are invited to be part of that kingdom by living Christ's paschal mystery. When we accept the daily dyings and risings of life, we share in Jesus' suffering, death, and resurrection.

Everyone is called to God's kingdom. It belongs to the poor and the lowly. Jesus identifies with the poor and those humble enough to hear his word. The condition for membership in God's kingdom is that we respond in love to the poor and less fortunate.

Sinners are welcome and are part of God's kingdom. They are invited to deep conversion and transformation.

We learn a great deal about God's kingdom through Jesus' parables. They challenge us to give all that we are to build God's kingdom—in word and action. "The parables highlight the social character of the kingdom. Jesus never presents the kingdom as a private affair between God and an individual. Rather, it is an active force in the world, a reconciling presence creating a sense of solidarity among people."[59]

[59] *CR,* 223–227.

We know the kingdom is at hand through the signs Jesus performed. Miracles strengthen faith. "The miracles of Jesus also confirm that the Kingdom has already arrived on earth" (*Lumen Gentium,* #5). We are not, however, to view them in a magical, manipulative way.

Jesus empowers the apostles to carry on his work in establishing the kingdom. That authority continues through the pope, bishops, priests, deacons, religious, and all God's people.

We live in God's kingdom now with hope in the kingdom yet to come. Through the story of the Transfiguration we are given a glimpse of God's heavenly kingdom. We will one day share in Jesus' transfigured glory when we join him in the eternal city.

We must not lose sight of that hope. Yet we live in the present. Our reality is that the kingdom of God is *now.* Jesus envisions a kingdom of peace where the lame walk, where the blind see, where people lay down their lives for one another and the poor and oppressed are cared for. When one looks at present day society it is often difficult to imagine such a kingdom. However, the kingdom of God *is at hand* when Christians gather in truth, hope, and love; when they live a gospel life, repent, change their lives, and spread the good news.[60]

The following gospel citations address the reign of God. The kingdom of God in Mark's gospel: "is at hand..." (1:15); purpose of the parables (4:11, 26, 30). The kingdom of God in Matthew's gospel: on earth, in heaven (6:10); parables—"kingdom is like..." (13:24, 31, 33–34, 44–45, 47; 18:23; 20:1; 22:2; 25:1). Kingdom of God in Luke's gospel: now and not yet (4:43; 8:1; 9:2, 11, 60, 62; 16:16). Kingdom of God in John's gospel: who is admitted? (3:1–5).

The kingdom of God is proclaimed at every liturgy when the gospel is proclaimed and the eucharist and the sacraments are celebrated. Every liturgy is a proclamation of the reign of God. The kingdom of God is definitely announced in the Lord's Prayer.

[60] Ibid.

Testing
In what way, if any, has your original understanding regarding the kingdom of God been stretched, challenged, or affirmed? Was there any new information for you? If so, what was it? In light of the material just presented, is there any implication for living the Christian life? What does this teaching have to say about the community's and your role in God's kingdom? Who is invited? What are the signs of God's kingdom? The biblical themes of the presence of God through his covenant, the exodus, creation, and community are evident in this teaching. How are those themes connected to this understanding of the kingdom of God?

In what way is this church teaching related to the scriptures of this Sunday's liturgy? In light of this sharing, how would you articulate an understanding of the kingdom of God now? Is it the same as your first understanding, or has it changed?

Decision
How does this teaching about the kingdom of God challenge our community? In what way is our community living the message we just shared? In what specific way is our community in need of transformation? Is there any concrete action you can take to be an agent of change in your community? How does this understanding of the kingdom of God challenge you personally? How are you living the message? In what way do you need to grow? What one concrete action can you take this week as a response to this sharing?

Refer to chapter 7, "Preparing the Catechetical Session," if you intend to plan your catechetical session at this time.

LAYING ON OF HANDS

See Trinity: God as Spirit (Appendix). See Easter Vigil: Symbol of Laying on of Hands.

LENT

See Lenten Overview and the Sundays of Lent.

LIGHT

See Easter Vigil: Symbol of Light.

MARY, MODEL FOR THE CHURCH

Natural Sign
What role, if any, does Mary play in your life? What does the image of mother evoke in you? What is your understanding of the church's teaching on Mary?

Tradition: Biblical, Ecclesial, and Liturgical Signs
The basis of the church's teaching regarding Mary is belief in Jesus Christ. As the first Christian, Mary is a model for how to reveal Christ to the world and how to live the Christian kerygma.

The *Catechism of the Catholic Church* calls Mary the "Eschatological Icon of the Church" (972). Through her we reflect upon what the church already is as it makes its journey of faith toward the final resting place in heaven.

Christ is the focus of Marian devotion. Church teaching about Mary is best summed up in the liturgical feasts of the year. Mary, Mother of God (Jan. 1) stresses the true nature of Christ—his humanity and divinity, and honors Mary as the Mother of God. The Annunciation honors the virginal conception of Christ by the power of the Spirit. The Immaculate Conception (Dec. 8) celebrates the utter graciousness of God toward humanity in that Mary was conceived without original sin due to grace, not merit. The Visitation (May 31) celebrates the working of the Spirit as Mary was inspired to visit her cousin Elizabeth. The Assumption of Mary (Aug. 15) into heaven was intended to strengthen our belief in the resurrection of the body. The feast also honors Mary who shares a unique union with God in Christ from the very beginning through the end of her life. The Queenship of Mary (Aug. 22) honors Mary as queen and mother of the human race. Our Lady of Sorrows (Sept. 15) remembers the suffering of Mary and reminds us that the church is united with Christ through suffering and death so that we may live eternally with him.[61]

Commentary in this workbook on the liturgical feasts honoring Mary offers a more elaborate and detailed analysis of various facets of Marian devo-

[61]Linda Gaupin, CDP, Ph.D., *Catholic Faith and Life: Catechist Training* (Diocese of Orlando, Fla., 1996). Unpublished course text, 81.

tion. Please refer to those feasts for further insights.

Testing
Were there any new insights? Is your understanding of the role of Mary expanded or affirmed? How might the role of Mary have anything to do with your everyday life? What are the implications for living the Christian kerygma?

Decision
In what way does this teaching call me to action in my life, in the church, or in the world? What action will I take as a result?

Refer to chapter 7, "Preparing the Catechetical Session," if you intend to plan your catechetical session at this time.

MORALITY: FOUNDATIONS

Natural Sign
If you were asked what it means to live a moral life, how would you respond? Complete this sentence: "Morality is. . . ."

Tradition: Biblical, Ecclesial, and Liturgical Signs
Morality refers to behaviors that flow from an individual's principled assumptions. Both the Hebrew scriptures (Old Testament) and the Christian scriptures (New Testament) view the totality of life, secular and the spiritual, as one. The Hellenistic world (Greek) and its philosophical constructions introduced to us a sense that we are divided between matters spiritual and temporal. This is called dualism. The scriptures paint an entirely different picture, however. All life is sacred and consecrated to God's saving presence. God wishes us to be happy and whole, not divided. The Hebrew understanding of wholeness is the right ordering of relationships (*hesed*), that is, right relationship to God, to one another, to the earth, and to oneself.

The Christian scriptures uphold a standard that speaks of moral behavior in terms of *just actions,* such as feeding the hungry and giving drink to the thirsty. In contrast with a fundamentalist approach to morality in which morality is founded on direct biblical revelation and directives,[62] Catholic morality is based primarily on the biblical themes of creation, exodus, covenant, and cross. From a biblical and early church perspective, when one's morality was weighed, it was judged in light of discipleship. For example, before one was admitted for baptism, that person's readiness was discerned. The criteria for this discernment were based on the person's moral behavior. Was *metanoia* visible in the person's life? Was there a change, a turning from one thing toward another, a turn from one way of living to a new way of living in Christ? Early documents, such as the Didache, directed that catechumens be given clear instruction regarding the type of life they were to live after baptism. Baptism empowered them for incorporation into the life and mission of Christ.

Christian morality is based on the understanding posited by Thomas Aquinas that nature and supernature are graced by God. As human beings we possess dignity. God is infinitely present to all of life, thus all of life is graced by God. We have been told in the story of our human genesis that we are made in God's image. We are sacred because *we are,* not because of anything we have done. Jesus lives within us and teaches us what it means to be fully human. "All people seek happiness: life, peace, joy, wholeness and wholesomeness of being. The happiness human beings seek and for which they are fashioned is given in Jesus, God's supreme gift of love. He comes in the Father's name to bring the fulfillment promised to the Hebrew people and, through them, to all people everywhere. He is Himself our happiness and peace, our joy and beatitude."[63]

Through our union with God, who is communal by nature (Father, Son, and Spirit), we are *social beings.* We are intended to live in relationship. As human beings we live in the community of family, church, and world. We are destined for happiness insofar as we live in right ordered relationships

[62]It is interesting to note that fundamentalists often ignore the biblical directive to sell all you have and give to the poor. "We don't take the bible that literally," is often the reply. In essence, they become their own redactors of biblical ethics. The result is a canon within the canon: a biblically interpreted moral code, delicatessen style. Biblical interpretation insists that the historical, cultural, and literary milieu of the text be considered when appropriating meaning for our contemporary culture.

[63]*Sharing the Light of Faith, NCD,* #100.

(*hesed*). When we respond in love to uphold the dignity of the human person we become fully human and fully alive. There is no room for an individualistic faith. We are ecclesial by nature and by design.

Our moral life is communal by nature and by design. Even our personal sins impact others in some way. Thus, our pursuit of happiness must be grounded in care and concern for others. Living a moral life demands that we uphold the ethical teaching of Christ in the gospel.

God created us with a free will. We have the power to choose the path for our lives. We are free to pattern our lives in conformity to God's will, to say yes or no to God. Human beings are free to choose between good and evil; thus we are called to responsibility. As a mature person of faith I am called to behave in a moral way because God desires it.

The church teaches that the moral law is expressed in different ways, all of which are connected. The moral law is expressed through eternal law, given by God who is the source of all law, through natural law, through revealed law (Old Covenant and New Covenant) and civil and ecclesiastical law. Moral law, then, hinges on more than the Ten Commandments. All forms of moral law find meaning in the life of Jesus.

For example, as a Christian, my choice to obey the civil law regarding the speed limit brings my Christian perspective into the choice. On a very practical level I do not disobey the civil law against speeding because I do not want to get a ticket. On a moral level, however, my choice to obey the law is illumined by my relationship with Christ. I am in covenant relationship with Jesus. Jesus loves me unconditionally. I, in turn, love Jesus and wish to act according to his design. We are all God's children and are graced by God. As a child of God, I have a responsibility to care for those around me. If I choose to place anyone in danger because of my actions, my relationships are not in right order. My relationship with Christ is strained because I have violated the law of love—care and concern for others. My relationship with my neighbor has been strained because I have placed others in harm's way. My relationship to myself is strained because in order to live in *shalom*-peace[64] my life has to be ordered to the will of God. As I reflect upon the life of Jesus in the gospel, I am invited into relationship. That relationship demands a response. The response made in love helps give meaning to my life.

Testing

Were there any new insights? How would I answer the question, "Morality is..." in light of the tradition presented? What is the challenge of this doctrine?

Decision

What action will I take as a response to this presentation? How am I called to transformation? Be specific.

Refer to chapter 7, "Preparing the Catechetical Session," if you intend to plan your catechetical session at this time.

ORDINARY TIME

See Overview of Ordinary Time. See chapter 8, "Time and the Liturgical Cycle."

PAROUSIA

The term *parousia* (pronounced pahr-*oo*-see'-uh) is a Greek word meaning "presence" or "arrival." In the ancient Greek world, cities awaiting the arrival of dignitaries to their region would be awaiting their *parousia.* Paul uses the term in reference to himself when visiting the various communities. The term later was transferred to the belief in Jesus' second coming.

Natural Sign

What are your feelings in regard to the second coming of Jesus? Is it completely foreign to your experience or understanding or are you comfortable with the concept? Have you ever considered it before? What possible connection might there

[64]When the heavenly hosts came announcing good news and peace to people of good will, *shalom*/peace was understood to mean wholeness. *Shalom* is a wholeness achieved only through the right ordering of relationships with God, one another, self, and the natural world.

be to your own personal life? What might you say if asked to explain what the parousia or second coming of Jesus is about? What do you think is meant by the term?

Tradition: Biblical, Ecclesial, and Liturgical Signs
Parousia is referred to as the glorious coming of Christ a second time, but is also related to the completion of God's plan of salvation for the human race, the final arrival of God's reign, the resurrection of the body on the last day, and final judgment. The coming of Jesus is the fulfillment of all God has been doing throughout salvation history. From the very beginning, at the creation of the world, God's master plan of salvation was intended to be accomplished through the life, death, and resurrection of Jesus Christ, the Son of God. Jesus is God's spoken Word that entered the lives of human beings. "The entire economy of salvation receives its meaning from the Incarnate Word. It prepared his coming; it manifests and extends his kingdom on earth from the time of his death and resurrection up to his second glorious coming, which *will complete the work of God.*"[65] Thus, when Jesus comes again, God's plan of salvation for the human race will be completed.

Our understanding of the parousia is expressed in our core truth, "the mystery of God the Father, the Son, and the Holy Spirit, Creator of all things; the mystery of Christ, the Incarnate Word, who was born of the Virgin Mary, and who suffered, died, and rose for our salvation, the mystery of the Holy Spirit, who is present in the Church, sanctifying it and guiding it until *the glorious coming of Christ,* our Savior and Judge; and the mystery of the Church, which is Christ's Mystical Body, in which the Virgin Mary holds a preeminent place."[66] We proclaim this truth every time we gather for liturgy when we pray the Nicene Creed, "... he will come again in glory to judge the living and the dead...." The parousia underscores the presence of Christ throughout all of salvation history, and the completion of the ultimate plan or process of salvation that began with the Incarnation, death, and resurrection of Jesus.[67]

[65]*GCD,* #41.

[66]Ibid., #43.

[67]Zachary Hayes, O.F.M., "Parousia," in *NDT,* 743.

The early church struggled with the reality that Jesus' second coming was not as imminent as they first had thought. In response, the evangelists formulated an understanding of God that put him beyond human time limitations. Believers were exhorted to view God's delay as a sign of "merciful opportunity for repentance."[68]

It is important not to consider the parousia as the return of Christ who has been absent all these long generations. "It is a breaking through of a presence that has been continuous throughout history."[69]

Jesus promised us that we would be judged at the end of time. Our hearts will be laid bare and all will be given a personal accounting of how they have or have not lived the law of love in their lives. Each person will be held accountable for the actions of his or her life and judged accordingly.

Jesus reigns today in the church through the Holy Spirit. However, the entire world has yet to recognize his reign. At the end of time Jesus will prevail victorious over the evil that permeates the world. Evil will be definitively squashed.

The church embraces the basic biblical understanding that human history has a purpose and that Jesus will win out over evil. Our doctrine is essentially a message of hope and consolation in the face of what often seems to be the ultimate victory of evil over good. We will one day experience a reversal and thus live in the eternal Presence where evil reigns no more.

The implication of the parousia is to be constantly on guard, to have our houses in order, to live in right relationship, and to assist in God's work of establishing justice in our temporal world.

Biblical passages that address the parousia (Jesus' second coming in glory and the final coming of God's reign, resurrection from the dead and final judgement) are the following:

Foreshadowed in the Old Testament:
Genesis 49:8. Numbers 23:21. Isaiah 2:2–5; 9:2;

[68]Sean P. Kealy, "Parousia," in *CPDBT,* 692–694.

[69]Hayes, "Parousia," in *NDT,* 743–744.

11:6–16. Jeremiah 23:6. Daniel 7:13–14. Hosea 2:21–25. Zechariah 11:10.

New Testament:

Acts 1:11. 1 Corinthians 15:23. 1 Thessalonians 2:19; 3:13; 4:15; 5:23. 2 Thessalonians 1:7. 2 Timothy 4:1. Titus 2:13. Peter 1:7. 1 John 2:28; 3:2, 5, 8.

Gospels:

Matthew 10:23; 14:62; 16:27–28; 24:3, 27, 30, 36–37, 39. Mark 13:24. Luke 9:26; 12:40, 46; 17:20–37; 18:8; 21:27.

The parousia is addressed at every liturgical celebration that exhorts us to hope for the day when Christ will come again. ("Christ has died, Christ is risen; Christ will come again.") The season of Advent particularly looks toward that future day.

Testing

In what way, if any, has your original understanding regarding the second coming of Jesus been informed, stretched, challenged, or affirmed? Was there any new information for you? If so, what was it? In light of the material just presented, is there any implication for living the Christian life? What does this teaching have to say about the community's and your role in preparing for the parousia? In what way is this teaching related to the scriptures of this Sunday's liturgy? In light of this sharing, how would you articulate an understanding of the parousia? Is it the same as your first understanding, or has it changed?

Decision

How does this teaching about Jesus' second coming challenge our community? In what way is our community living the message we just shared? In what specific way is our community in need of transformation? Is there any concrete action I can take to be an agent of change in my community? How does this understanding of the parousia challenge me personally? How am I living the message? In what way do I need to grow? What one concrete action can I take this week as a response to what we have shared?

Refer to chapter 7, "Preparing the Catechetical Session," if you intend to plan your catechetical session at this time.

PASCHAL MYSTERY

Natural Sign

What images from everyday life might evoke the sense of dying and rising? If you were asked what it meant to die and rise again, how would you respond? Finish this sentence: "The paschal mystery is. . . ."

Tradition: Biblical, Ecclesial, and Liturgical Signs

The paschal mystery refers to the essential elements of Christian redemption. It encompasses the passion, death, resurrection, and ascension of Jesus Christ that we celebrate every time we gather and especially at the church's premier celebration during Holy Week and Easter. God's plan for the salvation of the world was accomplished once and for all by the death and resurrection of Christ.

Jesus did not come to abolish the covenant, but rather to fulfill it (Mt 5:17–19). He revealed the deepest meaning of the law and reformed the sins against it (Heb 9:15). Jesus honored the temple and the Jewish feasts. Jesus used the temple to prefigure his own death as he announced the destruction of the temple and the entrance into the messianic age in which his body would become the new temple.

Jesus suffered at the hands of the chief priests and the scribes who handed him over to the authorities to be tortured and crucified (Mk 8:31; Mt 20:19). They sought his death because of his acts of forgiving sins, expelling demons, and healing people on the sabbath as well as his unusual stance regarding the ritual laws of purity. It did not sit well with the religious authorities that he ate with sinners and tax collectors. Some people even believed that Jesus was possessed and others accused him of blasphemy, false prophecy, and religious crimes punishable by the death penalty—stoning (Mk 2:7, 14–17; 3:1–6, 22; 7:14–23; 14:1. Mt 12:24. Jn 8:48; 10:20; 7:12, 52; 8:59; 10:31, 33).

God sent his only Son to demonstrate his love for us and Jesus freely died for our sins. He gave us a lasting memorial of his death and resurrection when he gave us his Body and Blood at the Last Supper. Jesus atoned for the sins of the world through his death and resurrection, thereby fulfilling the atoning mission of the Suffering Servant (CCC, #623). Jesus went down to the domain of the dead to release those who had died before him and were held captive by the power of death. He opened the doors to the heavenly kingdom.

The resurrection was attested to by the disciples who encountered Christ in his risen state. Through the resurrection Christ entered into his glory. The empty tomb and cloths are reminders that Christ escaped the power of death. Christ entered into heavenly glory in his full humanity at his ascension into heaven. Jesus went ahead of us to prepare a place for us to dwell with him for all eternity. The paschal mystery also includes the sending of the Spirit to be with the church until such time as Christ will return to judge the living and the dead according to their righteousness before God.

The paschal mystery includes salvation as foretold in the Hebrew scriptures, incorporation into Jesus' life, and the origins of the church and its sacramental life. We especially are united into the paschal mystery through the sacraments of initiation—baptism, confirmation, and eucharist.

Through the sacraments of initiation and especially through what Augustine referred to as the repeatable sacrament of initiation, eucharist, Christians are united with Christ's suffering, death, and resurrection; his passover from death to life. That is, Christians reenact and make present the paschal mystery when they take up their cross and unite their joys and sorrows with those of Jesus in the daily experience of their lives.

The paschal mystery is celebrated at every liturgy. This is why the Sunday celebration of eucharist is often referred to as an Easter event and why Easter is considered the Great Feast of Sunday. All the sacraments express incorporation into the paschal mystery of Christ.

In the sacrament of baptism an individual plunges into the life-giving waters and in so doing dies to sin and passes over into new life in Christ. Through the sacramental anointing of confirmation the Spirit is given and the person is configured to Christ, which seals him or her permanently with the life, death, and resurrection of Jesus. Through eucharist the faithful participate in the death and resurrection of Christ in the taking, blessing, breaking, and sharing of the eucharist at each eucharistic liturgy. The suffering, death, resurrection, and ascension of Christ and the sending of the Spirit are remembered and actualized at every celebration of eucharist.

Testing
Has your original understanding of the paschal mystery been affirmed, stretched, or challenged? Were there any new insights? Was there anything just shared that had not occurred to you before? What are the implications for everyday life? In what way have you experienced death and resurrection in your life? What are the implications for the church? In what way does the post-biblical teaching on paschal mystery have to do with this Sunday's readings? In light of this sharing, how would you articulate an understanding of the paschal mystery? Is it the same as your first understanding, or has it changed?

Decision
In what way do we as community live the message we just shared? Are there ways we need to grow in our understanding of what was shared? Where are the specific places where transformation is needed? How does the paschal mystery challenge me personally? How am I living it? In what way do I need to grow? What one concrete action can I take this week as a response to our sharing?

Refer to chapter 7, "Preparing the Catechetical Session," if you intend to plan your catechetical session at this time.

RECONCILIATION

Natural Sign
Have you ever experienced the forgiveness of someone close to you? Please explain. What did it teach you about reconciliation? How would you complete this sentence: "Reconciliation is..."?

Tradition: Biblical, Ecclesial, and Liturgical Signs
Please refer to the Rite of Penance (#386–394) for the scripture citations that are suggested in the Rite of Penance. These scriptural texts shed light on God's mercy experienced through his healing love and reconciliation.

The church exhorts men and women to repentance so that they may turn away from sin and be converted completely to the Lord (Rite of

Penance [RP], #1). We are called to reconciliation with God and the church. Every sin is an offense against God that disrupts our friendship with him. "The ultimate purpose of penance is that we should love God deeply and commit ourselves deeply to him"[70] Sinners who embrace the way of penance come back to the Father who loved us first, to Christ who gave himself up for us, and to the Spirit who has been abundantly poured upon us.

By the mystery of God's love we are joined in the bond of solidarity. The sin of one harms others and the holiness of one benefits others.[71] Penance always involves reconciliation with brothers and sisters who are harmed by our sins (RP, #5). Through the grace of Christ we are all to work for justice and peace in the world (RP, #6). Hence, we are to be cognizant of the social dimension of sin. "Men frequently join together to commit injustice (RP, #6)."

> Sin and its effects are visible everywhere: in exploitative relationships, loveless families, unjust social structures and policies, crimes by and against individuals and against creation, the oppression of the weak and the manipulation of the vulnerable, explosive tensions among nations and among ideological, racial and religious groups, and social classes, the scandalous gulf between those who waste goods and resources, and those who live and die amid deprivation and underdevelopment, wars and preparations for war. Sin is a reality in the world.[72]

Thus, we are to help each other do penance by working with others to realize justice and peace for all.

There are observable effects of reconciliation. We are converted to God with our whole heart. This conversion leads to sorrow for sin and the intention to live a new life. The intent to lead a new life is expressed through confession made to the church, through due satisfaction for sin and the promise to amend one's life. Pardon is granted through the church, which works by the ministry of priests (RP, #6).

Reconciliation occurs through the four components of the sacrament of penance. 1. Contrition: we are sorry for our sins and intend to sin no more. We are completely converted to Christ and turn our lives to the holiness and love of God in order to render ourselves more like Christ. 2. Confession: we examine our sin in light of God's mercy before God; we are sorry for our sins, and our heart is to be opened to God's minister, the priest. 3. Act of penance: True conversion is completed and evidenced by satisfaction for sins committed, amendment of conduct, and reparation of injury (suited to personal condition of each penitent). 4. Absolution is given through the sign of laying on of hands. God grants pardon to the sinner in sacramental confession and penance is completed.

> In the sacrament of penance the Father receives the repentant Son who comes back to him, Christ places the lost sheep on his shoulders and brings it back to the sheepfold, and the Holy Spirit sanctifies this temple of God again or lives more fully within it. This is finally expressed in a renewed and more fervent sharing of the Lord's table, and there is great joy at the banquet of God's church over the Son who has returned from afar.[73]

The church celebrates reconciliation through liturgical signs in the following manner: Rite of Reconciliation of individual penitents, Rite of Reconciliation of Several Penitents with Individual Confession and Absolution, Rite of Reconciliation of Several Penitents with General Confession and Absolution and Various Texts Used in the Celebration of Reconciliation, including sample nonsacramental penitential celebration. "Penitential celebrations, mentioned in the Rite of Penance (#36–37), are beneficial in fostering a spirit and

[70]Paul VI, Apostolic Constitution *Paenitenini,* February 17, 1966. AAS 57 (1965), 15–16. In Rite of Penance: *The Rites of the Catholic Church,* #5.

[71]Paul VI, Apostolic Constitution *Indulgentiarum doctrina,* Jan. 1, 1967, no. 4: AAS 59 (1967), 9; see Pius XII, encyclical *Mystici Corporis,* June 29, 1943. AAS 35 (1943), 213.

[72]*NCD,* #98.

[73]Rite of Penance, #6d.

virtue of penance among individuals and communities; they also help in preparing for a more fruitful celebration of the sacrament of penance. However, the faithful must be reminded of the difference between these celebrations and sacramental confession and absolution."[74]

Testing
Were there any new insights? How would you answer the following question now? "Reconciliation is. . . ."? What is the challenge? How are you called to live in a new way as a result of this doctrine?

Decision
What concrete action will I take as a result of this sharing?

Refer to chapter 7, "Preparing the Catechetical Session," if you intend to plan your catechetical session at this time.

SACRAMENTALITY

Sacramentality refers to the presence and encounter of God in all spheres of relationships and human endeavors.

Natural Sign
Do you remember a time when you experienced a sense of God's presence? How do you remember it? Describe it. What happened? How do you understand the meaning of the encounter you just described?

Tradition: Biblical, Ecclesial, and Liturgical Signs
In order to better understand sacraments it would be helpful to understand the concept of sacramentality on a purely human or anthropological level. Sacramentality is an activity that all human beings engage in by virtue of being in relationship. It is a process of discovery. People perform the rituals of life and in the process seek to appropriate meaning for their lives. Through sacramentality we give deeper meaning to the observable events around us. Moments of significant encounter, relational moments, form us and cause us to reflect on the meaning for our lives.

[74]Rite of Penance, Appendix II, #1.

In the scriptures the word sacrament is translated "mystery." It has a broad meaning and refers to God's plan and activity, revealed in Christ, for our salvation. The word sacramentality encompasses all the ways that God reaches out to us in the world. Any object, person, or thing that somehow brings God and people into contact, that reveals God's saving love, is understood as sacrament.

Sacramentality occurs whenever there is a precious encounter, a presence of God in any situation. Sacramentality embodies everyday moments of grace that have meaning for our lives. Wherever human beings are fully alive, God is present.

By our very nature, we Catholics are a sacramental people. We regard all creation as holy. We see God's life and energy in all created things, and we particularly set aside specific symbols from our natural world to speak and celebrate that reality.

The National Catechetical Directory states that there are four signs of God's presence: natural signs, biblical signs, ecclesial signs, and liturgical signs. Sacramentality is the essence of these signs. God is present throughout all human experience, through the natural signs in everyday life. God is sacramentally present in human experiences and relationships, in art, in music, in technology. God is sacramentally present in biblical signs, in the word of God spoken through the generations. God is revealed to us sacramentally (real presence) in the scriptures. God is truly (sacramentally) present to us in the church, through the living of our faith, through our beliefs and practices and through the service we perform in his name. God is sacramentally present to us in the rites of identity, passage, and celebration that we perform in the gathering and worship of God's people, the liturgy.

Even before Christ became human, there were rituals, blessings, signs, prayers, and gestures that spoke to the people about their identity and about a sacramental presence of God. The Spirit-guided church determined seven signs to be the most important and the most authentic because within them there appeared to be the very essence and life energy of Christ. Thus, there are seven unique signs that are especially determined to be sources of God's life and grace for the uplifting of the church. They are called the seven sacraments.

Testing

Had you ever considered the concept of sacramentality before? Were there any new insights? Was there anything just shared that had not occurred to you before? What are the implications for everyday life? In what way does sacramentality have anything to do with this Sunday's readings? How would you articulate an understanding of sacramentality?

Decision

How does sacramentality impact my life? How should I respond? How does this understanding of sacramentality challenge me personally? In what way do I need to grow? What one concrete action can I take this week as a response?

Refer to chapter 7, "Preparing the Catechetical Session," if you intend to plan your catechetical session at this time.

SACRAMENTS

Sacraments are the seven designated "liturgical rites of the church through which participants experience the love and power of God (grace) that flows from Christ's Passion, death and Resurrection."[75]

Natural Sign

Call to mind a particularly meaningful sacramental rite you have experienced. (Remember that people in the initiation process may or may not have had any church rituals. Thus, they instead might be asked: "Do you have a conscious memory of celebrating any church ritual or any other type of family or organization's ritual?") Please describe the experience. What happened? Based on your experience, how would you define *sacrament?* (Or, for a person in initiation, one might ask: "How would you explain the meaning of the word *ritual* in light of the experience you just shared?")

Tradition: Biblical, Ecclesial, and Liturgical Signs

The seven sacraments were not presented to us by Christ in specific formula and intent. One cannot go to the scriptures and find the as-is liturgical rituals of sacraments. Their origins are reminiscent of the so-called Jewish sacraments. However, the spirit and meaning of the sacraments can be found in scripture through the life, ministry, and paschal mystery of Christ. We celebrate the mystery of salvation through the sacraments. They point us toward our eventual participation in the great banquet of heaven.

The term sacrament (from the Latin *sacramentum,* "oath," "pledge") refers to the seven liturgical rites of the church. Through the celebration of these rites people experience the love and grace of God and share in the paschal mystery of Christ, his life, passion, death, and resurrection. The seven sacraments are baptism, confirmation, eucharist, penance, anointing of the sick, holy orders, and matrimony.

The original word, *mysterion* (Greek "mystery"), was translated into the Latin word *sacramentum.* "A sacrament was an oath of allegiance made by a soldier in the military. Sometimes the soldier was branded on the arm with a sign of the general he was to serve."[76] An early church Father, Tertullian, used this image to refer to baptism. We are permanently consigned to the mission of God "through word 'oath' and visible 'sign' (brand) made possible through sharing in the Paschal Mystery of Christ."[77]

During the Middle Ages the church designated a list of seven sacraments. Prior to that time there had been a broader understanding of sacrament. It was understood to mean the power, love, and manifestation of God in any and all circumstances. Sacraments were also referred to as mysteries. The hidden nature of sacrament reflected God's hidden plan of salvation for all the world. God's plan was realized through the paschal mystery of Christ.

The theology of sacrament was developed during the scholastic period of the church (1100–1300). God offers salvation and strengthens the church through the sacraments that are instruments of God's grace. Sacraments unify the church and make holy its people. God's action is inherent in

[75]Richard McBrien, "Sacrament," in *HCEC,* 1146.

[76]Ibid.

[77]Ibid., 1147.

the sacramental signs. The familiar definition was "Sacraments are an outward sign, instituted by Christ, to give grace."

To expand the scholastic understanding of sacramental theology, modern sacramental catechesis "has emphasized that *Jesus Christ is the first sacrament.*"[78] Since the power of the sacraments flows from the life, passion, death, and resurrection of Jesus, he is our first sacrament. *The Church has also been referred to as sacrament since it is the living presence of Christ on earth until he comes again in glory.* The church as the Body of Christ is the instrument that "proclaims God's powerful love for humanity in and through the Paschal mystery."[79]

Christ himself, through the Holy Spirit, offers the grace and power that each sacrament expresses. Through the Holy Spirit the sacraments have the power of healing and transformation. Through the sacraments we are made more into the image of Christ. Thomas Aquinas stated: "Therefore a sacrament is a sign that commemorates what precedes it—Christ's Passion; demonstrates what is accomplished in us through Christ's Passion—grace; and prefigures what that Passion pledges to us—future glory."[80] In other words, through the sacraments, the passion of Jesus is remembered and made present. We are graced, given a share in his life, and are promised eternal life. Sacraments strengthen and empower us to cooperate with the life we have been given.

Sacraments have their genesis out of the signs and symbols of everyday life. Humanity experiences the spiritual world through symbols. Language, gestures, and actions express and communicate meaning on a very basic level. The elements of creation speak to us of the power and nature of God. Fire, water, light speak to us of God's presence and God's power. Actions of everyday life, washing, anointing, breaking bread, sharing a cup, can express for us the way God graces us and the way we offer praise and thanks for all of God's saving work. God takes the gifts made from human hands and through the power of the Holy Spirit makes them holy. The elements (bread, wine, water, oil, light, laying on of hands, cross, fire) are transformed into a new reality and in the process we are changed and transformed as well. It is not magic, but it is mystery. It is mystery when the church is able by the grace of the Holy Spirit to remember past events and actions, bring those events and actions into the present through story telling and symbolic ritual, and know that the same effect of the original event is a present, experienced reality.

Sacraments are celebrations of conversion and are related to life and human experience. They possess meaning on two levels, theoretical and practical. We understand conceptually what a sacrament means and we *experience* the meaning given to it through its celebration in the community.

The sacraments are not private. They are communal by nature and by intent. The Constitution on the Sacred Liturgy states: "Liturgical services are not private functions but are celebrations of the entire Church which is 'the sacrament of unity,' namely, the holy people united and organized under the authority of the bishops. Therefore, liturgical services pertain to the whole Body of the Church. They manifest it, and have effects upon it."[81] Thus, sacraments are celebrated through active participation of all the faithful. By virtue of our baptism we are consecrated a holy people. We are anointed priest, prophet, and king and therefore "may offer spiritual sacrifices."[82] "Rites that are meant to be celebrated in common, with the faithful present and actively participating, should as far as possible be celebrated in that way rather than by an individual and quasi-privately."[83] Sacramental celebration, therefore, is a communal response of word, song, prayer, and gesture to the God who calls us to life through Christ Jesus.

Sacraments assume celebration in faith. It is said that sacraments effect what they signify. When the celebration of a sacrament expresses a specific grace, for example, membership, cleansing, and empowerment for mission, it is not only bestowed on the person, but it is also operative in the life of the one who celebrates. However, since faith is assumed, the effects are dependent on the disposi-

[78]Ibid.

[79]Ibid.

[80]St. Thomas Aquinas, *Summa theologiae,* III, 60, 3.

[81]*CSL,* #26.

[82]*Lumen Gentium* 10; cf. 1 Pet 2:45.

[83]*CSL,* #27.

tion (faith, conversion) of the individual. One either cooperates with the grace or one does not. I used to be an excellent guitar player. Over the years I have had to use my keyboard talents more than my guitar playing skills. I no longer can play as I used to play. However, if I were to invest the time and energy into the practice of the guitar, my playing would rapidly improve. Sacraments operate in somewhat similar fashion. Grace (the presence of Christ) is there for the asking, but without faith it is not necessarily evident and operative in the life of the individual.

Sacraments call us to action. They are not simply gifts for our own spiritual benefit. They are intended to build up the entire church. That can happen only when its members live and act as children of God, when they live the paschal mystery and take what they have received into the world in order to transform it.

Testing

Was there anything just shared that had not occurred to you before? Were there any new insights? What are the implications of sacraments for living your everyday life? What difference do sacraments make to the wider church? In what way have sacraments made a difference in your life? What do sacraments have to do with this Sunday's readings? How would you explain sacraments to a stranger? Has your original understanding been changed, affirmed, or challenged in any way?

Decision

How do sacraments call for a response by the community? What are the implications of sacraments for the church? How do sacraments as described in this session challenge me personally? What one concrete action can I take this week as a response to our sharing?

Refer to chapter 7, "Preparing the Catechetical Session," if you intend to plan your catechetical session at this time.

SIN

Natural Sign

When we speak about sin, what does it mean to you? Have you ever given any thought to your own sinfulness? In what way? How would you articulate an understanding of your faith tradition's belief about sin?

Tradition: Biblical, Ecclesial, and Liturgical Signs

The etymology of the word sin means to "miss the mark" or, in a religious sense, "to fall short of God's will for us."[84] Human beings were created in the image and likeness of God. As such, we are holy in God's sight. However, since the beginning of time human beings have abused the freedom given to them by God. Men and women have turned away from God and attempted to be fulfilled apart from God.[85]

Sin wreaks havoc in the lives of people. It causes great sorrow and upheaval. People sin when their actions "knowingly and deliberately violate the moral law and in a serious matter also seriously offend God."[86] Most of us have experienced a time in our lives when our actions affected another person in a negative, hurtful, or destructive way. This is sin.

Throughout the history of salvation God has intervened in the lives of men and women in order to help them in their struggle against the forces of sin and evil. Sin was, is, and always will be a part of our lives. In the Old Testament sin was usually personified in terms of a character (e.g., the serpent in the garden). For the ancients, sin resulted in humanity's foolish belief that they could get along without God, or that they could be like God. The primary motif of the Old Testament scriptures is God in relationship to a people. God entered into covenant with Israel. Israel sinned; God invited it to repent; Israel repented, and God rescued and liberated it.

In both the Old and the New Testaments there is very little understanding of sin in personal terms. It is most commonly understood to be communal. Serious sins such as rebellion, infidelity, and sexual misconduct were seen as disturbances to community and family order and would be reprimanded accordingly. When people revolted by turning away from God completely, the punish-

[84]Robert J. Schreiter, C.PP.S., "Sin," in *CPDBT,* 921–922.
[85]*Dogmatic Constitution on the Church,* #13, in *DVII.*
[86]*GCD,* #62.

ment was either banishment from the community or death. It was believed that sinners brought such judgment down upon themselves.[87]

Jesus' primary role through his passion, death, and resurrection, was to free the human race of the effects of sin. God is alive for us in the person of his Son. The grace given to us by Jesus is far more abundant than the sins we commit. Through repentance for our sins we can share in the love and salvation offered by Jesus.[88]

Sin is the greatest obstacle men and women face in their efforts to love God and one another. There are different types of sin. Humanity is born into original sin, the first obstacle to a life of love. We are born into the human condition, a fallen state: "human nature . . . fallen, stripped of the grace that clothed it, injured in its own natural powers and subjected to the dominion of death, that is transmitted to all."[89]

Human beings as individuals commit personal sins. "It is willful rejection, either partial or total, of one's role as a child of God and a member of His people. By it sinners knowingly and deliberately disobey God's command to love Him, other people, and themselves in a morally right way."[90] By sins of omission (failing to do what one should do) or commission (willfully doing what one should not do) men and women turn from God's will. Personal sin begins within the heart of an individual and extends to behavior that defies God's greatest commandment to love God, neighbor, and self.

Grave sin, called mortal, seriously disrupts one's relationship with God. Mortal sin is committed with malice of intent, by deliberately choosing evil over good. Mortal sin assumes full consent and knowledge of the offense. Lesser sins, called venial, also impair that same relationship and can accumulate to the point of leading to more serious sin.[91]

Because God loves us, the entire human race is formed in an eternal bond of "supernatural solidarity, so much so that the sin of one harms the others just as the holiness of one benefits the others."[92] Penance calls us to reconcile with our brothers and sisters who are always harmed by our sins.[93] God calls us away from sin. This conversion constitutes a "profound change of the whole person by which one begins to consider, judge, and arrange his life according to the holiness and love of God."[94]

We are forgiven our sins and reconciled with God and one another through the sacraments of penance and eucharist. Through baptism our fallen nature is crucified with Christ so that the body of sin may be destroyed and we may no longer be slaves to sin, but rise with Christ and live for God (Rom 6:4–10). The sacrament of penance is like a second baptism. Rather than the water of baptism, there are tears of penance.[95]

The eucharist is also for the forgiveness of sins. In the liturgy we recall and make present Jesus' words, "Take and eat. This is my Body given up for you for the forgiveness of sins." We are forgiven by the death and resurrection of Jesus. We, in turn, take up our cross and offer our lives for the sins of others, just as Christ offered his life for us.

Sometimes we unconsciously trivialize the actual atrocity of sin. We reduce it to a laundry list of do's and don't's and fail to get inside the permeating and devastating aspects of another dimension of sin called *social sin.* It is very easy to relegate social sin to be out of our control, unrelated to us or our lives and, in essence, not our problem. We often fail to see that we are part of a global human village.

Sin occurs in both personal and social forms. Social sin is a concept that most of us have not had the occasion to consider. What is it? "Social sin represents, as it were, the accumulation of sinful acts that cre-

[87]James A. Fischer, "Sin—Old Testament," in *CPDBT,* 916–919.

[88]*GCD,* #62.

[89]Pope Paul VI, *Credo of the People of God* (June 30, 1968).

[90]*NCD,* #98.

[91]Ibid.

[92]Paul VI, Apostolic Constitution *Indulgentiarum doctrina,* January 1, 1967, no. 4: AAS 59 (1967), 9; see Pius XII, encyclical *Mystici Corporis,* June 29, 1943. AAS 35 (1943), 213.

[93]Rite of Penance, #5.

[94]Pope Paul VI, Apostolic Constitution *Paenitemini,* February 17, 1966.

[95]St. Ambrose, Letter 41:12: PL 16, 1116.

ate environments of oppression, racism, and sexism, environments of sinfulness so powerful and so pervasive that no one can escape them."[96]

How do we commit social sin? Social sin has seriously impacted the lives of innocent people around the world. This sinister reality was confronted in 1983 by a group of bishops gathered at the Synod of Reconciliation. As a result of this meeting, Pope John Paul II addressed the topic of social sin in an apostolic letter resulting from this Synod, "Reconciliation and Penance," Dec. 2, 1984.

The highlight of the letter's main points are as follows:

I: The presence of social sin exists in laws, policies, and social practices that result in the failure to respect or enhance the human dignity of certain groups within society.

II: Social sin is the accumulation of personal sins. Human beings contribute to social sin in a number of ways.

a. Actions or omissions that cause or support the evil condition, that fail to enhance human dignity. ("*The School of the Americas is training guerrillas in the art of torture and warfare to use in Third World countries. That's the government's business, not mine.*")
b. Actions or omissions that exploit the evil condition, that take advantage of people or situations for self-interest or gain. *("I think I might hire an illegal immigrant. I can get a lady to clean my house for $2.00 an hour because she is desperate.")*
c. Failure to avoid, eliminate, or at least limit the evil condition due to laziness, fear, indifference, the conspiracy of silence, or through secret complicity. *("I know that my boss is knowingly discriminating against the minorities in my company and is falsifying records in order to get away with it. But I'll never tell anyone; it's none of my business.")*
d. Another way personal sin contributes to social sin is when I take refuge in the impossibility of changing the evil condition with the attitude that there is nothing I can do. *(Henry Thoreau was imprisoned during the Mexican War. He thought the war was an attempt to gain control of other regions for the purpose of building their slave labor pool. He would not support the war and refused to pay taxes. When his friend, Ralph Waldo Emerson visited him in prison, he asked Thoreau why he was in jail. Thoreau very indignantly asked Emerson why he was not right there with him, as he too had been opposed to the war for the same reason. How many of us are that ready to put our money where our mouth is!)*
e. When we sidestep the effort and sacrifice required to address the evil condition with the attitude, "I don't want to be bothered; it will put me out too much." ("*I would like to work at the soup kitchen on Tuesdays but it is the day I get my hair and nails done. Or... I am against abortion, but it is just too much fuss to do or say anything about it. Leave that to others!*")
f. When we rationalize with regard to why we cannot engage in actions to address the evil condition by thinking, "If I do that they will have my head on the platter." *("I am very much against the practices of the World Bank because they deliberately charge interest that causes excessive suffering for the poor in Third World countries. If I take any action to speak up in any way, I will be fired from my position at the bank.")*

While social sin is communal, the responsibility belongs to individuals. Social sin is the amassment of our own personal sins. The effects of my sins are limited to those in somewhat close proximity. I sin due to an action or a failure to act and the consequences generally affect a small group of people. Personal sins are healed through the healing sacrament of reconciliation. Social sin, on the other hand, is intricate and ambiguous and affects a much larger group of people. It invades our laws, customs, and practices and thus the repercussions are immense. It is not easily healed as it usually involves a collective blindness. Sometimes social sin is even disguised as socially acceptable. We need to make it our business to see. *(A young man who grew up in New Orleans during the days of segregation was riding his daily bus. He witnessed a scene he had observed many other times: a black woman getting on the bus, only this time she attempted to enter it from the front rather than the rear.*

[96]Robert J. Schreiter, C.PP.S., "Sin," in *CPDBT,* 921–922.

The bus driver hit the woman. For the first time this young man's eyes were opened. He saw the evil of prejudice and its effects.)

The pope maintains that personal sin such as fear, greed, and selfishness is at the core of all social sin and that we must take responsibility for it. We respond to social sin with a communal mindset, an awareness that we are part of the human village. This begins with an inner disposition of solidarity with those who suffer any injustice, asserts the pope. One reason Jesus was killed was because of his unpopular, dangerous support for the poor and marginalized. He shook the status quo. He offered hope to the oppressed and unnerved those who were in positions of power.

The first place to begin to address our participation in social sin is to raise our consciousness to all evil, especially evil that robs human beings of their God-given right to dignity.[97]

Testing

In what way, if any, has your original understanding of sin been stretched, challenged, or affirmed? Was there any new information for you? If so, what was it? Was there anything you found to be uncomfortable about in this teaching? In light of the material just presented, is there any implication for living the Christian life? In what way is this post-biblical teaching related to the scriptures of this Sunday's liturgy? In light of this sharing, how would you articulate a theology or understanding of sin? Is it the same as your first understanding, or has it changed?

Decision

How does this teaching about sin challenge our community? In what way do we as community live the message we just shared? Are there ways we need to grow in our understanding of what was shared? Where are the specific places where transformation is needed? Is there any concrete action I can take to be an agent of change in my community? How does this understanding of sin challenge me personally? How am I living the message? In what way do I need to grow? What is one specific action I can take this week as a response to our sharing?

Refer to chapter 7, "Preparing the Catechetical Session," if you intend to plan your catechetical session at this time.

TRINITY

Natural Sign

In what way have you experienced God in creation? How would you finish the following sentence: "The Trinity is . . ."?

Tradition: Biblical, Ecclesial, and Liturgical Signs

The mystery of the Trinity is essential to our faith. It is unique to the Christian faith: One God in three persons. The Hebrew scriptures do not provide a Trinitarian understanding of God. Israel contributed the concept of a mono-theistic God. In the Hebrew scriptures God is Creator, Author of all Life. Israel depicted God as Word (*dabar*), Spirit (*ruah*), Wisdom (*hokmah*), and Presence (*shekina*).

The New Testament does not clearly define the dogma of Trinity. Rarely is Jesus referred to as God, as it would identify him too closely with the Father. But his divinity is recognized. The word Trinity is not used, but there is a proclaimed experience of Triune God—Father, Son, and Spirit. This is referred to as the economic trinity—the experience of God's action in the world. Matthew's gospel has Jesus exhorting his disciples to go out and baptize all nations in the name of the Father, Son, and Spirit (28:19). The Trinity is experienced in Jesus' baptism in the Jordan when the Spirit descends upon him and the Father's voice is heard.

The apostolic age held fast to the doctrine of one God and defended this against pagan polytheism. There are references to the Trinity in early liturgies prior to a formalized doctrine on Trinity. There is a basic principle that states that from the church's prayer flows its creed (*lex orandi, lex credendi*). The church professed its belief through its prayer. The prayer of the church reflects the lived experience of the Triune God. From the experience of ritual prayer, the church formulated its official creed.

The Trinitarian creed was formulated as a result of heresies that crept into the church early in its history. Language is very limited when it comes

[97]Section on social sin adapted from "Grace and Sin," a presentation by Robert Duggan, North American Forum on the Catechumenate.

to explaining an inexplicable mystery. Notions from philosophical origins helped formulate the theology.

There were two schools of thought emanating from the Greek and Latin Fathers. The two schools were based on the distinctions between immanent trinity and economic trinity. The economic trinity (Greek Fathers) was based on the experience of God in the world, in the history of salvation. Humanity experienced God as creator, Son as redeemer, and Spirit as sanctifier. The term relates to the three "faces" or actions of God's manifestation. Economic trinity refers to the *mission* of God who sent the Son and the Spirit to accomplish the work of salvation.

Immanent trinity (Latin Fathers) refers to the relationship the Father, Son, and Spirit have with one another apart from the actions they have performed in the world. Immanent trinity centers on the "Oneness" of God, one divine nature. The inner life of God is Trinitarian. Outside the inner life, the actions of God are common to all three persons as there is only one nature. No person of the Trinity is less than the others.

The Arian heresy asserted that there was a time when Jesus *was not.* He was created by the Father. The divinity of the Holy Spirit was questioned by other heresies. The Council of Nicea (325 C.E.) resolved the heresies by establishing a creedal statement of faith, the Nicene Creed (proclaimed in every eucharistic liturgy).

The Council asserted that there is one God of three: co-equal and co-eternal. Jesus was begotten, not made. He always was with the Father. There was never a time he was not. He was with the Father, as was the Spirit, at the creation of the world. That is, all three always existed. The three persons are distinct, but not separate. The Son is of the same substance as the Father (*homoousios*). Father, Son, and Spirit work for our redemption. The Council of Constantinople in 553 attested to the one God in three persons (consubstantial Trinity). The Council of Toledo maintained that the "three persons do not share one divinity unto themselves, but each one is whole and entire."[98] They are distinct from one another, yet one. The term used to designate this three persons and their distinctions is *hypostasis.* The Father is not the Son, the Son is not the Spirit, etc. God is one, but not solitary. The divine persons are distinct. They are distinct in the way they are related to each other. The Father generates, the Son is begotten, and the Holy Spirit proceeds.

The official church teaches that the Trinity is an absolute mystery. We do not understand it even after it has been revealed. Mystery transcends the capacity of our ordinary rational and conceptual powers. It goes beyond the scope of human imagination and everyday knowledge.

God as Father

The Father, unbegotten, acts only with the Son and the Spirit. The Father generates the Son and sends the Spirit. Jesus reveals the Father who is Father because of his relationship to Jesus, the Son. Jesus is Son only in relation to the Father.

God as Son

Jesus was eternally begotten of the Father. He was not made. Jesus is of the same essence as the Father—divine and coeternal (he always was). In John's gospel Jesus is referred to as the Word. One possible metaphor for trying to grasp the ineffable mystery is to see it in terms of the WORD image. If Jesus is the WORD of the Father, the WORD was always a part of the Father. God but spoke the Word and a part of Godself came forth from his very being.

It is through Jesus that the Father is expressed to us in our salvation history. The Son is the same unity, substance as the Father—thus it is not Sonship as we understand it in human terms.

God as Spirit

If Jesus is the Word, the truth of God's self that comes from his very being, then who is the Spirit? The Spirit is also God. The Word was spoken and Jesus was begotten. The life force, the breath that came forth from the mouth of God was the Spirit. From the truth of God's existence came the Son, begotten of the Father. From the truth of God as revealed to us by the Son comes love, the Spirit of God. If Jesus is the Word, or Truth of who God is, the Spirit is the action of the Truth: Love.

[98]Linda Gaupin, *Catholic Faith and Life,* 46.

God the Holy Spirit is another divine person who is with Jesus and the Father. The Spirit is given as gift from the Father, given to us through the Son. The Spirit communicates the Father to us and we are able to communicate in a personal relationship with the Father. The Holy Spirit is God communicating with us. Thus, the Holy Spirit is given in love and with that love comes reconciling and renewing power. The Spirit is of the same essence as the Father, but distinct. "The Spirit has the same essence of the Father, and yet is distinct from the Father and the Son. The Spirit proceeds from the Father through the Son. The procession is not a begetting, since this would lead to the supposition that there are two Sons, nor is the Spirit merely a mode [through] which the Son communicates himself to us. The Spirit originates from the Father and the Son, and has a distinct relationship to the Father and the Son."[99] Thus, they are three persons in one God, and the Spirit has a role in the saving mission throughout history.

The symbols of the Holy Spirit show us the nature and the activity of the Spirit in the church. Water signifies the Holy Spirit in baptism and is a sign of new birth. The gestation of first birth took place in water, so too, our birth in the divine life comes through water. Anointing is a sign of the presence of the Spirit. Christ in Hebrew means the *one anointed by God's Spirit.* The Holy Spirit anointed Jesus as "Christ."

By the power of the Spirit Mary conceived and Simeon could proclaim her son messiah. Through the Spirit power went out from Jesus through acts of healing and saving. The Spirit raised Jesus from the dead.

Fire as symbol signifies the transforming energy of the Spirit's actions. Jesus said of the Spirit, "I came to cast fire on the face of the earth, and would that it were already kindled." The tongues of *fire, cloud, and light* are manifestations of the Holy Spirit. They reveal God's transcendence, omnipotence and glory, (e.g., Moses on Sinai, at the tent of meeting, and the wandering in the desert).

The *seal* as symbol of the Spirit is similar to anointing. It indicates the effects of the anointing of the Spirit. The *hand* as sign of the Spirit demonstrates healing power. Jesus invokes the Spirit and heals the sick by the laying on of hands. The apostles would do the same. The *finger* is also a sign of the Holy Spirit. By the finger of God Jesus cast out demons (Lk 11:20). The dove (flood, baptism) is a traditional sign of the Spirit. Noah released a dove and the earth was again hospitable. The Spirit comes "like a dove" and remains in the purified hearts of the baptized (Mk 1:10).

What is the bottom line here? When all is said and done, it is God who created us, who sustains us, who will judge us, and who will give us eternal life. This is a God who is not removed from us. Our God is a God of absolute proximity, who is truly communicated to us in the flesh in history and within the human family. God is with us in the spiritual depths of our existence as well as in our unfolding history. God is in our everyday lives. God is the source of enlightenment and community.

We proclaim the Trinity in the liturgy in the greeting, the sign of the cross, the Gloria, the creed, the eucharistic prayers, the doxology, and the final blessings as well as in all the sacraments. Refer to the *Catechism of the Catholic Church,* #249–267.

Testing

Were there any new insights? How would you articulate an understanding of Trinity? How does this dogma have anything to do with everyday life? Have any of your original assumptions been stretched?

Decision

How does this teaching call us to action? What one action will you take as a response?

Refer to chapter 7, "Preparing the Catechetical Session," if you intend to plan your catechetical session at this time.

TRANSFIGURATION

See Feast of the Transfiguration and Second Sunday of Lent.

[99]Ibid., 49.

Bibliography

Abbott, Walter M., S.J., ed. *The Documents of Vatican II.* New York: The Guild Press, 1966.

Adam, Adolf. *The Liturgical Year.* Collegeville: The Liturgical Press, 1979.

Anderson, Bernhard W. *Understanding the Old Testament.* Fourth Edition. Englewood Cliffs: Prentice-Hall, 1986.

Boadt, Lawrence, C.S.P. *Reading the Old Testament.* New York/Mahwah: Paulist Press, 1984.

Bright, John. *The Kingdom of God.* New York: Abington, 1953.

Brown, Raymond E., S.S. *An Adult Christ at Christmas.* Collegeville: The Liturgical Press, 1978.

———. *The Beatitudes According to Luke. New Testament Essays.* Garden City: Doubleday Image Books, 1975.

———. *A Coming Christ in Advent.* Collegeville: The Liturgical Press, 1988.

———. *Community of the Beloved Disciple.* New York: Paulist Press, 1979.

———. *A Crucified Christ in Holy Week.* Collegeville: The Liturgical Press, 1986.

———. *The Gospel and Epistles of John.* Collegeville: The Liturgical Press, 1988.

——— et al, eds. *The New Jerome Biblical Commentary.* Englewood Cliffs: Prentice Hall, 1990.

———. *Once and Coming Spirit at Pentecost.* Collegeville: The Liturgical Press, 1994.

———. *A Risen Christ in Eastertime.* Collegeville: The Liturgical Press, 1991.

Byrne, Brendan, S.J. *Paul and the Christian Woman.* Mystic: Twenty-Third Publications, 1998.

Camp, Claudia. *The Women's Bible Commentary.* Louisville: Westminster/John Knox Press, 1992.

Cantalamessa, Raniero. *The Mystery of Easter.* Collegeville: The Liturgical Press, 1993.

Carson, D.A. *The Gospel According to John.* Grand Rapids: Eerdmans, 1991.

Cassidy, Richard J. *John's Gospel in New Perspective.* Maryknoll, NY: Orbis Books, 1992.

The Catechetical Documents: A Parish Resource. The Archdiocese of Chicago. Chicago: Liturgical Training Publications, 1996.

Catechism of the Catholic Church. Liguori: Liguori Publications, 1994.

Catholic Household Blessings and Prayers. Washington, D.C.: NCCB, 1988.

Collins, Raymond F. *Preaching the Epistles.* Mahwah: Paulist Press, 1996.

———. *John and His Witness.* Collegeville: The Liturgical Press, 1991.

———. *Preaching the Gospels.* Mahwah: Paulist Press, 1996.

Commetarius in Annum Liturgicum Instauratum. Published by the Consilium for the Implementation of the Constitution on the Sacred Liturgy.

Communities of Salt and Light: Reflection on the Social Mission of the Parish. Washington: NCCB, 1993.

Congregation for Divine Worship. *Actio Pastoralis.* "Instruction on Masses for Special Gatherings." May 15, 1969.

Corbon, Jean. *The Wellspring of Worship.* Matthew J. O'Connell, trans. New York: Paulist Press, 1988.

Crosby, Michael H. *The House of Disciples.* Maryknoll: Orbis Books, 1988.

———. *The Spirituality of the Beatitudes: Matthew's Challenge for First World Christians.* Maryknoll: Orbis Books, 1981.

Days of the Lord, Vols. I–VII. Collegeville: The Liturgical Press, 1991–1994.

De Lubac, Henri. *Catholicism: A Study of Dogma in Relation to the Corporate Destiny of Mankind.* New York: New American Library, 1964.

Documents on the Liturgy. Collegeville: The Liturgical Press, 1982.

Dues, Greg. *Catholic Customs and Traditions.* Mystic: Twenty-Third Publications, 1992.

Dunning, Jim. *Echoing God's Word.* Arlington: North American Forum on the Catechumenate, 1993.

Ellis, Peter F. *The Genius of John.* Collegeville: The Liturgical Press, 1984.

Fink, Peter E., S.J., ed. *The New Dictionary of Sacramental Worship.* Collegeville: The Liturgical Press, 1990.

Flanagan, Neal M., O.S.M. *Mark, Matthew, Luke: A Guide to the Gospel Parallels.* Collegevillle: The Liturgical Press. 1978.

Fuller, Reginald H. *Preaching the Lectionary.* Collegeville: The Liturgical Press, 1974.

———. *Preaching the New Lectionary.* Collegeville: The Liturgical Press, 1984.

Garland, David E. *Reading Matthew: A Literary and Theological Commentary on the First Gospel.* New York: Crossroad, 1995.

Gaupin, Linda, C.D.P., Ph.D. Catechesis for Liturgy, Orlando, Florida, 1996.

———. "Special Certification in Sacramental Catechesis." Diocese of Orlando, Florida, October 23, 1996.

General Catechetical Directory. The Catechetical Documents: A Parish Resource. Chicago: Liturgy Training Publications, 1996.

General Instruction of the Roman Missal, ICEL, 1975. Chicago: Liturgy Training Publications, 1990.

Grassi, Joseph A. *Loaves and Fishes.* Collegeville: The Liturgical Press, 1991.

Gutierrez, Gustavo. *Sharing the Word Through the Liturgical Year.* Maryknoll: Orbis Books, 1997.

Hare, Douglas R.A. *Matthew, Interpretation: A Bible Commentary for Teaching and Preaching.* Louisville: John Knox Press, 1993.

Heschel, Abraham J. *The Prophets.* New York: Harper & Row, 1963.

Himes, Michael. "Jesus: Yesterday, Today and Forever." Workshop, National Conference of Catechetical Leadership, Orlando, Florida, April 13–17, 1997.

Hoffman, Elizabeth, ed. *The Liturgy Documents.* Chicago: Liturgy Training Publications, 1991.

Huck, Gabe. *The Three Days: Parish Prayer in the Paschal Triduum.* Chicago: Liturgy Training Publications, 1981.

Hughes, Philip Edgcumbe. *The True Image.* Grand Rapids: Eerdmans, 1989.

Hynes, Mary Ellen. *Companion to the Calendar.* Chicago: Liturgy Training Publications, 1993.

Jarrell, Stephen T. *Guide to the Sacramentary.* Chicago: Liturgy Training Publications, 1983.

Johnson, Luke Timothy. *The Gospel of Luke.* Sacra Pagina Series, Vol. 3. Collegeville: The Liturgical Press, 1991.

———. *The Writings of the New Testament: An Interpretation.* Philadelphia: Fortress Press, 1966.

Johnson, Sherman E. *Jesus and His Towns.* Good News Studies 29. Wilmington: Michael Glazier, 1989.

Jones, Cheslyn, et al, eds. *The Study of Liturgy.* Revised Edition. New York: Oxford University Press, 1992.

Jungman, Joseph, A. *The Mass of the Roman Rite: Its Origins and Development.* Francis A. Brunner, C.SS.R., trans. Westminster: Christian Classics, Inc., Replica Edition, 1986.

———. *Public Worship: A Survey.* Clifford Howell, trans. Collegeville: The Liturgical Press, 1957.

Karris, Robert J., O.F.M., ed. *Collegeville Bible Commentary.* Collegeville: The Liturgical Press, 1986.

———. *Invitation to Acts.* Garden City: Doubleday and Company, Inc., 1978.

———. *The Pastoral Epistles.* Wilmington: Michael Glazier, Inc., 1984.

Kavanaugh, Kieran, O.C.D. and Otilio Rodriguez, O.C.D., trans. *The Collected Works of St. John of the Cross.* Washington, D.C.: Institute of Carmelite Studies, 1979.

Kealy, Sean P., C.S.Sp. *Jesus and Politics.* Collegeville: The Liturgical Press. 1990.

Komonchak, Joseph A., et al, eds. *The New Dictionary of Theology.* Collegeville: The Liturgical Press, 1990.

Kuntz, J. Kenneth. *The People of Ancient Israel: An Introduction to Old Testament Literature, History, and Thought.* New York: Harper & Row, 1974.

LaVerdiere, Eugene, S.S.S. *Dining in the Kingdom of God.* Chicago: Liturgy Training Publications, 1994.

———. *Luke.* Wilmington: Michael Glazier Books, 1980.

Lee, Bernard J., ed. *Alternative Futures for Worship, Vol. 3; The Eucharist.* Collegeville: The Liturgical Press, 1987.

Liturgy of the Hours. New York: Catholic Book Publishing Co., 1975.

Marrow, Stanley B. *The Gospel of John.* New York/Mahwah: Paulist Press, 1995.

Marthaler, Berard. *The Creed.* Mystic: Twenty-Third Publications, 1987.

Mazar, Peter. *To Crown the Year: Decorating the Church Through the Seasons.* Chicago: Liturgy Training Publications, 1994.

McBrien, Richard P. *Catholicism.* Minneapolis: Winston Press, 1980.

———, ed. *HarperCollins Encyclopedia of Catholicism.* San Francisco: HarperCollins, 1995.

McKenzie, John, L. *The Dictionary of the Bible.* New York: Collier Macmillan Publishing Co., 1965.

Mick, Laurence E., Timothy Fitzgerald DiCello, Kathleen Hughes, R.S.C.J. *Sourcebook for Sundays and Seasons.* Chicago: Liturgy Training Publications, 1995.

Migne, J. P., ed. *The Liturgy of the Hours, Vol. 2.* New York: Catholic Book Publishing Co., 1996.

The National Catechetical Directory. The Catechetical Documents. Chicago: Liturgy Training Publications, 1996.

Perkins, Pheme. *Reading the New Testament.* New York/Mahwah: Paulist Press, 1988.

Perrin, Norman and Dennis C. Duling. *The New Testament: An Introduction.* Second Edition. New York: Harcourt Brace Jovanovich, Publishers, 1982.

Pilch, John J. *The Cultural World of Jesus.* Collegeville: The Liturgical Press, 1995.

Rahner, Karl. *The Great Church Year.* New York: Crossroad, 1993.

Ramshaw, Gail. *Richer Fare for the Christian People: Reflections on the Sunday Readings, Cycles A,B,C.* New York: Pueblo, 1990.

Reid, Barbara E. *Choosing the Better Part.* Collegeville: The Liturgical Press, 1996.

———. "The Gospel of Mark in the Liturgical Year." Workshop: Church of Our Saviour, Cocoa Beach, Florida, 1996.

Richards, Hubert. *The Gospel According to St. Paul.* Collegeville: The Liturgical Press, 1990.

Richter, Klemens. *The Meaning of the Sacramental Symbols.* Linda Maloney, trans. Collegeville: The Liturgical Press, 1990.

Rordorf, Willy. *The Eucharist of the Early Christians.* Matthew J. O'Connell, trans. New York: Pueblo, 1978.

Rybolt, John E., C.M. *Sirach,* Old Testament #21. *Collegeville Bible Commentary,* Robert J. Karris, O.S.M., ed. Collegeville: The Liturgical Press, 1986.

Sanchez, Patricia Datchuck. *The Word We Celebrate.* Kansas City: Sheed and Ward, 1986.

Schneiders, Sandra. *The Revelatory Text.* San Francisco: HarperCollins, 1991.

Scott, Bernard Brandon. *Hear Then the Parable.* Minneapolis: Fortress Press, 1989.

Senior, Donald, C.P. *Invitation to Matthew.* New York: Doubleday Image Books, 1977.

———. *The Passion of Jesus in the Gospel of Matthew.* Wilmington: Michael Glazier, 1985.

———. Workshop: "Gospel of Matthew." Church of Our Saviour, Cocoa Beach, Florida, October, 1995.

Stamps, Mary E., ed. *To Do Justice and Right Upon the Earth: Papers from the Virgil Michel Symposium on Liturgy and Social Justice.* Collegeville: The Liturgical Press, 1993.

Stuhlmueller, Carroll, C.P., ed. *The Collegeville Pastoral Dictionary of Biblical Theology.* Collegeville: The Liturgical Press, 1996.

Talbert, Charles H. *Learning Through Suffering.* Collegeville: The Liturgical Press, 1991.

———. *Reading John: A Literary and Theological Commentary on the Fourth Gospel and the Johannine Epistles.* New York: Crossroad, 1992.

———. *Reading Luke.* New York: Crossroad, 1992.

Talley, Thomas J. *Origins of the Liturgical Year.* Collegeville: The Liturgical Press, 1986.

Tannehill, Robert C. *The Narrative Unity of Luke-Acts: A Literary Interpretation.* Vols. I and II. Philadelphia: Fortress Press, 1986 and 1990.

Wintherop, Ronald D., S.S. *Conversion in the New Testament.* Collegeville: The Liturgical Press, 1994.

Yarnold, Edward, S.J. *The Awe-Inspiring Rites of Initiation.* Second Edition. Collegeville: The Liturgical Press, 1994.

GLOSSARY

Abraham
See Second Sunday of Lent: first reading.

Anamnesis
See Twenty-Sixth Sunday: liturgical context; "Bread," Biblical sign: Easter Vigil; Third Sunday of Easter: liturgical context.

Anointing
The action of touching a person or thing with a substance such as oil, water, mud, blood, or fat in order to bring about a change, either in an external or internal manner. See also "Sign of Oil": Easter Vigil; "Service of Baptism": Easter Vigil (Confirmation); "Confirmation": Doctrinal Appendix; "Reconciliation": Doctrinal Appendix; See Fourth Sunday of Lent: first reading.

Anonymous Christian
See Feast of Christ the King.

Authority
Refer to Twenty-First Sunday in Ordinary Time.

Baptism
See "Symbol of Water": Easter Vigil; Service of Baptism: Easter Vigil; Sundays of Easter; Baptism of the Lord; Twenty-Fourth Sunday: second reading; "Baptism": Doctrinal Appendix; Overview of Easter.

Beatitude
"Technical term for a literary form found in both the OT and NT. A beatitude is a declaration of blessedness on the ground of some virtue or good fortune." (John L. McKenzie, *DOB*, 84) See Fourth Sunday in Ordinary Time.

Bible
From the Greek word *ta biblia* (the books), the Bible is a collection of literary works of various genres that unfold God's relationship with human beings over the course of human history. The Christian Bible is divided into two sections—Old Testament and New Testament. The Old Testament spans the historical experiences of the people of Israel from their beginning around 2,000 B.C.E. until the Maccabean Revolution, around a hundred and fifty years before the birth of Christ (before the Christian era, or before the Common era). The New Testament proclaims the story of Jesus Christ, Messiah, Son of God, Savior of the world, the long-expected One foretold by prophets of old—his kerygma (message) and the life and mission of his followers. See also: "Hebrew Scriptures" (below); "Symbol of Word": Easter Vigil; "Biblical Signs and Themes"—Chapter 2; "Scripture"—Chapter 3.

Bless
To bless in ancient Israel means to "invoke upon the faithful all that God is and all that he has done for his people." (Reginald H. Fuller, *PL*, 27) See *CCC*: 1078–1083, 1669, 2090, 2645. See Ninth Sunday: first reading; Mary, Mother of God: first reading.

Blood
See Palm Sunday: passion exegesis; Holy Thursday: first reading; "Symbol of wine/blood": Easter Vigil.

Bread
See "Symbol of Bread": Easter Vigil; "Eucharist": Doctrinal Appendix; Eighteenth Sunday: first reading, liturgical context.

Christology, John's
See Trinity Sunday.

Church/Community
See Corpus Christi: second reading; Fifth Sunday of Easter; Seventh Sunday of Easter: second reading; "Symbol of Church": Easter Vigil; see also "Church, Mystery of": Doctrinal Appendix; Seventh Sunday: gospel exegesis; Fifteenth, Seventeenth, Eighteenth, and Nineteenth Sundays: gospel exegesis; Twenty-First Sunday; Twenty-Third Sunday: gospel exegesis; Twenty-Fourth Sunday; Twenty-Fifth Sunday; Twenty-Seventh Sunday: first reading.

Cloud
A sign in scripture of divine presence and God's involvement in human affairs. See also *CCC*, 697.

Conversion
Refer to First Sunday of Lent: liturgical context; "Conversion": Doctrinal Appendix; See also Tenth Sunday: first reading; Twenty-Second Sunday: second reading; Christ the King: first reading.

Creation
See first reading from Genesis: Easter Vigil; First Sunday of Lent; Third Sunday in Advent; Fourth Sunday; "Creation": Doctrinal Appendix.

Cross
See Palm Sunday; Holy Thursday; Good Friday; "Symbol of Cross": Easter Vigil; Overview of Triduum; Feast of the Triumph of the Cross; Eighteenth Sunday: second reading; Sundays of the Easter Season; "Paschal Mystery": Doctrinal Appendix.

Day of the Lord
Thirty-First Sunday: first reading; Thirty-Third Sunday: second reading.

Death
See Third Sunday of Easter: first reading; Twelfth Sunday: second reading; Thirty-Second Sunday; Twenty-Eighth Sunday: first reading; "Death:" Doctrinal Appendix.

Desert
In biblical understanding, the desert was a place of encounter with God. See First Sunday of Lent.

Dust
In biblical understanding, dust referred to the dry surface of the ground out of which God fashioned human beings (Gn 2:7). It also meant *the ground of the grave*, which prompted another meaning of commonness and worthlessness, and sometimes death. Refer also to Ash Wednesday.

Ecumenism
Universal mission of the church. See Twentieth Sunday: liturgical context; Twenty-Fifth Sunday.

Election
Refers to the choice by God of a certain group of people. There is no intention to assume superiority or merit. The choice is due to the graciousness of God. Election demands a response in behavior and lifestyle in conformity with God's will. It is a privilege and responsibility. See also First Sunday of Lent; Symbol of Community: Easter Vigil.

Epiclesis
Refers to the action of calling down or invoking the power of the Holy Spirit to bless, consecrate, and transform that which is blessed. In the sacraments it is associated with the action of the laying on of hands. See also Symbol of "Laying on of Hands": Easter Vigil; Symbol of "Bread as Ecclesial Sign": Easter Vigil.

Epistle/Letter
An epistle is a literary composition intended for a wide audience, and not necessarily attached to a specific situation. A letter is a non-literary method of communication between individuals.

Eschatology
Thirty-Second Sunday; Thirty-Third Sunday: second reading; Transfiguration: gospel exegesis; "Eschatology": Doctrinal Appendix.

Eucharist
See Palm Sunday: passion exegesis; "Symbol of Bread/Wine": Easter Vigil; Holy Thursday; Third Sunday of Easter: liturgical context; Corpus Christi; See Eighteenth Sunday: first reading; Twenty-Eighth Sunday; "Eucharist": Doctrinal Appendix.

Eucharistic liturgy, Paul's original sketch of
See Corpus Christi.

Eucharistic prayer
See Seventh Sunday of Easter: gospel exegesis; Eighteenth Sunday.

Evangelization
See Eleventh Sunday: liturgical context; Twelfth Sunday: gospel exegesis.

Expulsion of the Christians from the synagogue
See Thirteenth Sunday.

Faith
See Nineteenth Sunday: gospel exegesis.

Faith/Works
See Ninth Sunday; Tenth Sunday; Eleventh Sunday; Thirtieth Sunday: second reading.

Fear of God
Fear was a common response to deities in antiquity. It involved two almost incongruous elements—terror in the face of transcendence and attraction and love that are expressed in feelings of contentment, guidance, and assurance. As the element of fear subsides, "fear of God" may move into the sphere of piety, religion, worship, and obedience. (*CCC*, 1831)

Finger of God
The finger of God throughout Hebrew Scriptures is a term reflecting God's power. It is similar in usage to the "hand" of God, also a symbol of divine power. The term is used in the New Testament in Luke 11:20 when Jesus drives out a demon "by the finger of God." It is used also as a means to show the ease with which Jesus performed his miracles. St. Ambrose, in the fourth century, made the comparison of the Son and Spirit with the hand and finger of God. There was no intention to minimize their role, or to imply that they were only a small portion of God. "It expresses the unity of power among the three in all their actions." (Dennis M. Sweetland, "Finger of God," in *CPDBT*, 334.) This understanding is articulated in later centuries in the hymn *Veni Creator Spiritus (766–856)*. The Spirit is cited as the "Finger of God's Right Hand." The term *finger of God* is used in the Vatican II document, *Dogmatic Constitution on the Church* #5, quoting a passage of Luke 11:20. It is a reference to the power of Christ's miracles as a sign that the reign of God was firmly established on this earth. See also "Symbol—Laying on of Hands": Easter Vigil. (*CCC*, 700.)

Fire
Fire is a symbol in scripture of the presence, action, and protection of God. It also refers to judgment, anger, testing, and purification. See also "Symbol of Fire/Light": Easter Vigil; Pentecost: first reading during the day; Service of Baptism. (*CCC*, 696)

Flesh
The biblical understanding of *flesh* refers to the way human beings act—positively or negatively. Flesh could honor and obey God, but it could also rebel against God. It represents a person's totality. It also is the stage on which the struggles of the spirit are won or lost—the struggles of human passion. In the NT, *flesh* is also symbolic of the Incarnation, and the elevation of human dignity as a result. However, negative connotations of flesh have been passed on to us from previous generations. Even though church tradition teaches that flesh is not sinful, but created in goodness and sanctified by the Incarnation, vestiges of the heresy which denies that goodness remain with us today. However, one is not to deny the apparent ambiguous mystery—that flesh is mortal, beautiful, and weak. See Palm Sunday: passion exegesis; Corpus Christi: gospel exegesis; Fourteenth Sunday: second reading.

Forgiveness
See Pentecost; gospel exegesis; Twenty-Third Sunday: gospel exegesis; Twenty-Fourth Sunday; Sundays of Lent.

Garment
See "Symbol of Garment": Easter Vigil; Service of Baptism; Holy Thursday: gospel exegesis; Twenty-Eighth Sunday: gospel exegesis; Thirty-Second Sunday (wedding garment represents acts of righteousness and good deeds); Holy Family: second reading; Thirteenth Sunday, Cycle C.

Gehenna
The final place of eternal punishment in the Bible. The root of the word means "valley of Hinnom." This valley, located southwest of Jerusalem and running into the Kidron, was at one time the boundary between the tribe of Judah and the tribe of Benjamin. At one time this valley had the reputation of evil due to the idolatrous cult that offered religious sacrifices, including children, to the god Moloch. Jeremiah brought judgment and condemnation upon the Valley of Hinnom, which was later remembered by those who associated the valley with fiery damnation, hell, and the locus for final judgment. The NT made a clear distinction between Hades and Gehenna. Hades was a place where the ungodly were sent for temporary punishment. Gehenna was the place of final judgment and permanent punishment. Gehenna was the destination of those who refuse to accept the reign of God.

Grace
"Grace means favor, God's favor toward us. It can be creative, redemptive, or eschatological." (John J. Pilch, "Grace," in *CPDBT*, 397) According to NT understanding of *grace*, the favor (*grace*) God gives is God's Son, Jesus Christ. Grace is God revealing godself to human beings. See Tenth Sunday: gospel exegesis; Twentieth Sunday: second reading; Twenty-Fifth Sunday; "Grace": Doctrinal Appendix; Third Sunday of Lent: second reading.

Hand
See "Symbol: Laying on of Hands": Easter Vigil; "Service of Baptism": confirmation; "Confirmation," "Reconciliation": Doctrinal Appendix. (*CCC*, 699)

Heart
The heart is at the center of a person's entire life—the place where he or she meets God. In biblical anthropology the heart is the source of feelings, desires, longings, understanding, and decision, and conversion (*metanoia*) results in positively changing all of these. The antithesis consists in closing one's mind and heart, resulting in "hardness of heart." (Thomas P. McCreesh, O.P., "Heart"; Diane Bergant, C.S.A., "Hardness of Heart," in *CPDBT*, 424, 408)

Hebrew Scriptures
For Jewish people, there is only one canon—the Hebrew Bible. "Old Testament" is a Christian designation to distinguish between the first and second testaments. The Hebrew Bible is one book composed of three parts—the Law (Torah), the Prophets, and the Writings. Since the Jewish Hebrew Bible and the Christian Old Testament are fundamentally the same, except for the arrangement, many scholars today prefer the more inclusive term—Hebrew Scriptures—as a reference for the Old Testament. Some books not included in the Hebrew Bible were, at one time, read enthusiastically and regularly by the Jewish people but, for some reason, were not included in their canon. These were included in the Christian Bible, however. The early Christians were Greek-speaking people. They read the scriptures of the Old Testament, known as the *Septuagint*, from a Greek source originating in Alexandria, Egypt around the third century B.C.E. The arrangement of books in this translation was different from the arrangement in the Hebrew Bible. "The Prophets" were placed last, and some of the books that did not make their way into the Hebrew canon were included.

After the Reformation, Protestants restricted the number of books in the canon of the Old Testament to only those included in the Hebrew Bible. The books not included were put in a special section called the "Apocrypha" (hidden or secret works), with the explanation that they are worthy of reading, but are not on the same par as the rest of the scriptures. The Catholic Church, on the other hand, officially determined that the above mentioned books are deserving of canonical recognition. Thus, the Catholic canon is seven books longer than the Protestant and Jewish canons. Eastern Orthodox churches recognize the seven extra books as well. See also: "Symbol of Word": Easter Vigil; Biblical Signs and Themes: Chapter 2; "Scripture": Chapter 3. See also Holy Family: first reading.

Hermeneutics
The science of interpretation—the principles by which a statement or text is interpreted.

Holy Spirit
See Baptism of the Lord; Triduum; Sundays of Easter; Pentecost; Trinity Sunday; Good Friday: gospel exegesis.

Hospitality
Ancient cultures believed that the extension of hospitality, especially to strangers, was a religious act. Hospitality was a very important responsibility for Israel. The people knew well what it meant to be a stranger in a foreign land. Divine hospitality was a common metaphor for God's protection and care for Israel. The NT extends this hospitality a step further by insisting that the poor, oppressed, outcasts, and marginalized are to be recipients of hospitality. Offering such hospitality is the same as offering it to Christ himself. Lack of hospitality has serious implications, as indicated by the story of Sodom and Gomorrah (see below). See "Bread—Biblical Sign": Easter Vigil; Third Sunday of Easter: gospel exegesis; Eleventh and Thirteenth Sundays: gospel exegesis; Twenty-Eighth Sunday: first reading.

Human Dignity
See Easter Vigil: first reading; Easter Sunday: second reading; Christmas, Mass at Midnight: liturgical context; Fourth Sunday of Lent: second reading; Twelfth Sunday: gospel exegesis; Easter Vigil: first reading; Seventeenth Sunday: second reading; Trinity: gospel exegesis.

Incarnation
See Second Sunday of Advent; Overview of Advent and the Sundays of Advent; See Overview of the Christmas Season and the Sundays of the Christmas season; Trinity Sunday; Twenty-Sixth Sunday: second reading; "Incarnation": Doctrinal Appendix.

Jubilee Year
Israel established a jubilee year in order to bring about economic and social justice in Israel. "The law freed Israelite slaves and returned ancestral land to its original owners. Although the law may never have been practiced, the Jubilee became a symbol of hope in OT literature and in the Gospel of Luke." (Kathleen M. O'Connor, "Jubilee Year," in *CPDBT*, 501)

Judgment
See also Seventeenth Sunday; Thirty-First Sunday: first reading; Christ the King: first reading

Justice, biblical
See Fourth Sunday; Twenty-Fifth Sunday: gospel exegesis; Thirtieth Sunday; Second and Third Sundays of Advent; "Justice": Doctrinal Appendix; *hesed*: Holy Family, first reading; Symbol of Community: Easter Vigil.

Kerygma
The message of the gospel—the word that was originally proclaimed. See First Sunday of Advent: second reading; Twelfth, Seventeenth, Twenty-First, and Thirty-First Sundays: gospel exegesis.

Kingdom of God/Reign of God
Jesus' death and resurrection signaled the end of an age and the beginning of the messianic age. The purpose of Jesus' mission was to establish God's reign on earth until he returns in glory. The reign of God is both a present and future reality. The intention of the parables is to proclaim the reign of God. Scholars suggest that rather than refer to the *kingdom of God*, we call it instead the *reign of God*. Kingdom refers to a place where someone lives. Reign, as it is described in the parables, suggests a *way to live*. See Fifteenth Sunday, Seventeenth Sunday: gospel exegesis; Twenty-Seventh Sunday: first reading; Twenty-Eighth Sunday: gospel exegesis; Second Sunday of Advent; "Kingdom of God": Doctrinal Appendix.

Law
Fourth Sunday of Lent: first reading; Seventh Sunday: gospel exegesis; Twenty-Ninth Sunday: gospel exegesis.

Light
See "Symbol of Light/Fire": Easter Vigil; Epiphany; Christmas Overview; Sundays of Christmas Season; Fourth Sunday in Lent; Thirty-First Sunday: first reading; Second Sunday of Advent: second reading.

Love of God/neighbor
Seventh Sunday: first reading; Thirtieth Sunday; Twenty-Third Sunday: second reading.

Manifestation
See Epiphany, Sundays of Christmas Season; Pentecost, Mass During the Day: first reading; Sundays of the Easter Season; Nineteenth Sunday: gospel exegesis.

Mary, Mother of God
See Solemnity of Mary, Mother of God, Immaculate Conception; "Mary, Model for the Church": Doctrinal Appendix.

Meal/Banquet/Feast
See Twenty-Eighth Sunday: first reading: Eighteenth Sunday.

Meekness
See Fourth Sunday; Fourteenth Sunday: first reading.

Miracles
See Signs/Miracles below.

Morality
See Sixth Sunday of Easter: gospel exegesis; Fourth Sunday: gospel exegesis; Twenty-Second Sunday: second reading.

Mountains
Sixth Sunday of Easter: gospel exegesis.

Name, biblical understanding
See Mary, Mother of God.

Non-Violence
See Seventh Sunday; Twenty-Third Sunday: gospel exegesis.

Oil
"Symbol of Oil": Easter Vigil; Sacraments of baptism, confirmation, penance; Thirty-Second Sunday.

Paranesis
A moral exhortation or instruction and common literary form of the ancient Hellenistic, Christian, and Jewish world. Christian tradition freely employed this common form of moral imperative. See Third Sunday of Advent: second reading.

Parousia
See First Sunday of Advent.

Paschal Mystery
See Triduum; Symbol of Cross: Easter Vigil; Third Sunday of Easter: liturgical context; Sundays of Easter; Twelfth Sunday: second reading; Thirteenth Sunday; Fifteenth and Eighteenth Sundays: second reading; Twenty-First Sunday: gospel exegesis; Twenty-Second Sunday: second reading; Overviews of Triduum, Easter Season; "Paschal Mystery": Doctrinal Appendix.

Pentateuch
The first five books of the Old Testament: Genesis, Exodus, Leviticus, Numbers, Deuteronomy.

Pericope
The particular portion or segment of scripture that is chosen for a specific proclamation.

Poverty
See Fourth Sunday.

Prayer
See Nineteenth Sunday: gospel exegesis; Trinity Sunday.

Prophets and Prophecy
Prophets—ministers of God's word—were trained for their service. They did not just sit and wait for the Lord to speak to them. Some prophets were trained to serve in the temple and were known as temple prophets. Even though some prophets were trained professionally for their service, others did emerge outside the system (see Amos 7:14–15). Prophecy was in the form of warning, encouragement, judgment, praise, thanks, exhortation and reassurance, prediction of future events, and interpretation of past events. Prophets were messengers of the Lord and delivered God's word to the people. See also Third Sunday of Easter: gospel exegesis; Epiphany: first reading; Thirty-First Sunday: gospel exegesis.

Religious Intolerance
See Sixteenth Sunday.

Resurrection
Triduum; Sundays of Easter: Pentecost; Ascension; Trinity Sunday.

Revelation
See Trinity Sunday.

Sacrifice
See Fifth Sunday of Easter: second reading; Tenth Sunday: gospel exegesis; Eighteenth Sunday.

Shepherd
See Fourth Sunday of Easter; Feast of Christ the King: first reading and gospel exegesis.

Signs/Miracles
Hebrew Scriptures: Signs are evidence of God's presence and power. They are the way in which God communicates to people. They need to be interpreted. "A sign is a vehicle of communication—an action, condition, quality, occurrence, visible object, or linguistic unity—that conveys meaning. Most often it is a significant event, action, or other vehicle of communication that reveals God's intention or presence." (John J. Pilch, "Sign/Symbol," in *CPDBT*, 911) "The purpose of a sign is to make visible, to confirm dramatically, the truth and power of Yahweh's word spoken by the prophet. A sign does not necessarily have to be a miracle, in our sense of the word, for its significance is not so much in the unusual character as in its power to confirm a prophetic word spoken in threat or promise." (Bernard W. Anderson, *UOT*, 331–334)

New Testament: Much of John's gospel is intent on authenticating Jesus' identity. His miracles play a key role in that discussion. The scriptures provide us with various perspectives regarding Jesus' miracles. Luke/Acts proposes a positive view of Jesus' miracles. In Luke's gospel and in the Acts of the Apostles, Jesus' miracles are the impetus for faith (Lk 4:31–5:11). The disciples' miracles proclaim and promote the growth of the faith (Acts 3:1–4:4; 5:12–14; 8:6–8; 13:4–12). Mark's view is not as positive as Luke/Acts. He reflects a negative perspective. Mark reminds us that Jesus' miracles are not accepted by everyone. He reminds us that our faith is not to be completely based on Christ's miracles, but also on the power of the cross (Mk 8:14–21, 22–26, 27–31). John's gospel posits a complex, multivalent understanding of Jesus' miracles, called signs. They sometimes elicit faith (4:53; 10:41–42; 11:45, 47–48; 14:11). Not everyone believes in Jesus because of his miracles. Signs are often ambiguous (10:25–26; 11:45–48). Some people are interested in Jesus' miracles or signs simply for their own self-interest (physical benefits, 6:26). Some see them as a threat to Israel's security (11:46–48). Some believe that Jesus' signs are not from God because his regular behavior does not conform to certain standards (9:16, 30, 34). Scripture anticipated the rejection of Jesus' signs (12:37–40). People who accept Jesus' signs often possess some initial faith (2:11; 4:46–54; 20:30–31; 21:6–7). Sometimes the contrary is true, however (2:23; 3:2; chap. 9; 11:45). If faith already exists, Jesus' miracles strengthen and deepen it (2:11; 4:46–54; 20:30–31). The early Christian community believed that they shared Jesus' power and thus were agents of his miracle-working activity. John's community believed that they were agents of Jesus' signs continued in the life of the community. However, the miracles, in and of themselves, do not authenticate Jesus' mission. (Charles H. Talbert, *RJ*, 103–104) See also Fourth Week of Advent: first reading.

Sin

See Sundays of Lent; Seventeenth Sunday; Thirty-First Sunday: first reading; Overview of Lent; "Sin": Doctrinal Appendix.

Sodom and Gomorrah

See Genesis, chapters 18, 19. Don C. Benjamin asserts that the story of Sodom and Gomorrah is about hospitality: "...strangers appear, Lot's household protects them, and they bless it with life." There was a definitive protocol regarding hospitality in antiquity. It helped to test whether a person was a friend or an enemy. In the story of Sodom and Gomorrah, the strangers pass the first test with flying colors when they decline the first invitation. They become official guests with the gesture of foot washing. Another test was to observe the stranger's table manners. If they responded appropriately it was apparent that they understood the mores of their host. However, in this instance, before the test is completed, the young warriors and men in leadership gather and decide on their own that the visitors are enemies. Their punishment would be rape (similar to what was experienced by David's messenger before he was released by the Ammorites). The sexual implications in that culture were not understood as they are today. Sexual activity was considered to be part of the realm of contractual agreement. Monarchs had hundred of wives because they were in contractual agreement with other nations. Homosexual or heterosexual rape was a sign of a broken treaty. We are understandably shocked when Abraham offered his daughters in return for the strangers' lives. While not certain, scholars believe that this was an act of offering Abraham's own self to save the guests. It was believed that dead parents live on in their children. Since it is the children who must care for aged parents, by offering his daughters he was in essence saying, "Here, take my only hope of survival. I will be destined to live a life of poverty and destitution because of the death of my daughters." The sin of Sodom and Gomorrah was its refusal to extend hospitality to the strangers.

Son of Man

"In the OT Son of Man is a synonym for a human being. In Daniel 7:13 Son of Man is used to indicate that of a symbolic figure of the last days in human experience. In the NT Jesus seems to have used Son of Man in two different ways: as a way of referring to himself, and in reference to Daniel 7:13. After Jesus' death and resurrection, his followers expressed their expectation that he would come again by identifying him with the Son of Man of Daniel 7:13. Outside of the gospel tradition Son of Man was little used by the first-century Church. It was revived in the Patristic era as an expression of Jesus' humanity." (Terrance Callan, "Son of Man," in *CPDBT*, 937)

Soteriology
The study of salvation—the discipline that examines the mystery of salvation embodied in the passion, death, resurrection, ascension of Jesus. See Twenty-Second Sunday: second reading; Twenty-Eighth and Twenty-Ninth Sundays: gospel exegesis; Christ the King.

Stewardship
See Thirty-Third Sunday: gospel exegesis; Eighth Sunday.

Submission of wives
Holy Family: second reading.

Suffering
See Second Sunday of Lent: second reading; Second Sunday of Easter: second reading; Fourth Sunday of Easter: second reading; Sixth Sunday of Easter: liturgical context; Seventh Sunday of Easter: second reading; Fifteenth and Sixteenth Sundays: second reading.

Symbol
A sign that embodies what it is intended to signify. It is almost synonymous with sacrament. It is a sign which is intimately connected to that which it signifies. For further explanation refer to the section of the Easter Vigil that explains symbols. See also *CCC*, 1146–1149.

Temptation
See First Sunday of Lent: gospel exegesis.

Time
See Seventh Sunday of Easter: gospel exegesis; Chapter 8: sacred time, liturgical calendar; see Overview of Ordinary Time.

Trinity
See Sixth Sunday of Easter: gospel exegesis; Easter; Trinity Sunday; Mary, Mother of God: first reading; "Trinity": Doctrinal Appendix.

Typology
Typology is a way of interpreting the scriptures in light of God's plan of salvation, understood as having begun with people and events of past generations. Typology asserts that some of those people and events looked forward to (foreshadowed) future events, truths, and realities. For example, OT persons or events foreshadowed a New Testament truth, event, or reality. In the Book of Hebrews the Old Testament liturgy foreshadows the heavenly liturgy inaugurated by Jesus. "In the Church's pastoral and liturgical tradition typology emphasizes the continuity between the Testaments. It also underscores the abiding presence of God among those who believe." (Demetrius R. Dumm, O.S.B., "Type," in *CPDBT*, 1026) See also Epiphany: first reading; Holy Family: gospel exegesis; Eighteenth Sunday: gospel exegesis.

Water
See "Symbol of Water": Easter Vigil; Easter Vigil Readings; Pentecost Vigil: gospel exegesis; "Baptism": Doctrinal Appendix; See Third Sunday of Lent.

Word
See also Easter Vigil: fifth and sixth readings; Third Sunday of Easter: liturgical context; "Hebrew Scriptures" (above); Symbol of Word: Easter Vigil; Fourteenth Sunday: gospel exegesis; Fifteenth Sunday: first reading, liturgical context; Seventeenth Sunday: gospel exegesis; Thirty-First Sunday: gospel exegesis; Biblical Signs and Themes: Chapter 2; "Scripture": Chapter 3; Overview of Cycle A.

DOCTRINAL INDEX

This index of doctrinal topics lists relevant church documents and official sources. Document titles are abbreviated; for more information on these sources, see the listing of documents that follows the index.

DOCTRINAL TOPICS

Note: This is by no means an exhaustive listing of topics or documentation for the topics listed. This index merely scratches the surface and serves as a point of departure for those interested in further exploration of such topics.

DOCUMENTS

AA — *Apostolicam actuositatem:* The Decree on the Apostolate of the Laity, Vatican Council II, November 18, 1965. (Can be found in *The Documents of Vatican II,* edited by Walter M. Abbott, S.J., New York: Guild Press, America Press, Association Press, 1966.)

AG — *Ad gentes:* Decree on the Church's Missionary Activity, Vatican Council II, December 7, 1965. (Can be found in *The Documents of Vatican II,* edited by Walter M. Abbott, S.J., New York: Guild Press, America Press, Association Press, 1966.)

BT — *Basic Teachings for Catholic Religious Education,* NCCB, 1973. (Can be found in *The Catechetical Documents: A Parish Resource,* Chicago: Liturgy Training Publications, 1996.)

CB — *Ceremonial of Bishops,* ICEL, 1989. (Can be found in *The Liturgy Documents: A Pastoral Resource,* Chicago: Liturgy Training Publications, 1990.)

CCC — *Catechism of the Catholic Church,* USCC-Libreria Editrice Vaticana, 1994.

DH — *Dignitatis humanae:* Declaration on Human Freedom, Vatican Council II, December 7, 1965. (Can be found in *The Documents of Vatican II,* edited by Walter M. Abbott, S.J., New York: Guild Press, America Press, Association Press, 1966.)

DOL — *Documents on the Liturgy 1963–1979, Conciliar, Papal and Curial and Liturgical Texts,* Collegeville: The Liturgical Press, 1982.

DV — *Dei verbum:* Dogmatic Constitution on Divine Revelation, Vatican Council II, Nov. 18, 1965. (Can be found in *The Documents of Vatican II,* edited by Walter M. Abbott, S.J., New York: Guild Press, America Press, Association Press, 1966.)

EJFA — *Economic Justice for All,* NCCB, 1986.

EN — *Evangelii Nuntiandi:* On Evangelization in the Modern World, Paul VI, December 8, 1975. (Can be found in *The Catechetical Documents: A Parish Resource,* Chicago: Liturgy Training Publications, 1996.)

GIRM — *General Instruction of the Roman Missal,* ICEL, 1975. (Can be found in *The Liturgy Documents: A Parish Resource,* Chicago: Liturgy Training Publications, 1990.)

GCD — *General Catechetical Directory,* Sacred Congregation for the Clergy, 1971. (Can be found in *The Catechetical Documents: A Parish Resource,* Chicago: Liturgy Training Publications, 1996.)

GS — *Gaudium et spes:* The Pastoral Constitution on the Church in the Modern World, Vatican Council II, December 7, 1965. (Can be found in *The Documents of Vatican II,* edited by Walter M. Abbott, S.J., New York: Guild Press, America Press, Association Press, 1966.)

HLS — *This Holy and Living Sacrifice for the Celebration and Reception of Communion under Both Kinds,* USCC, 1985. (Can be found in *The Liturgy Documents: A Parish Resource.* Chicago: Liturgy Training Publications, 1990.)

LG — *Lumen gentium:* Dogmatic Constitution on the Church, Vatican Council II, 1965. (Can be found in *The Documents of Vatican II,* edited by Walter M. Abbott, S.J., New York: Guild Press, America Press, Association Press, 1966.)

LM — *Lectionary for Mass: Introduction,* second editio typica, ICEL, 1985. (Can be found in *The Liturgy Documents: A Parish Resource,* Chicago: Liturgy Training Publications, 1990.)

NCD — *Sharing the Light of Faith: National Catechetical Directory,* NCCB, 1978 (Can be found in *The Catechetical Documents: A Parish Resource,* Chicago: Liturgy Training Publications, 1996.)

OCF — *Order of Christian Funerals,* ICEL, 1990.

PO — *Presbyterorum ordinis:* Decree on the Ministry and Life of Priests, Vatican Council II, 1966. (Can be found in *The Documents of Vatican II,* edited by Walter M. Abbot, S.J., New York: Guild Press, America Press, Association Press, 1966.)

RA — Rite of Anointing and Pastoral Care of the Sick, *Rites of the Catholic Church,* ICEL, 1976.

RBO — Rite of Blessing of Oils and Rite of Consecration of Chrism: Introduction, *Rites of the Catholic Church,* ICEL, 1976.

RCIA — *Rite of Christian Initiation of Adults,* ICEL, 1988.

RC — Rite of Confirmation, *Rites of the Catholic Church,* ICEL, 1976.

RMa — Rite of Marriage, *Rites of the Catholic Church,* ICEL, 1976.

RP Rite of Penance, *Rites of the Catholic Church,* ICEL, 1976.

RO Rite of Ordination of Deacons, Presbyters, and Bishops, *Rites of the Catholic Church,* ICEL, 1976.

SC *Sacrosanctum concilium:* Constitution on the Sacred Liturgy, Vatican Council II, December 4, 1964. (Can be found in *The Documents of Vatican II,* edited by Walter M. Abbott, S.J., New York: Guild Press, America Press, Association Press, 1966, OR *The Liturgy Documents: A Parish Resource,* Chicago: Liturgy Training Publications, 1990.)

UR *Unitatis redintegratio:* The Decree on Ecumenism, Vatican Council II, November 21, 1964. (Can be found in *The Documents of Vatican II,* edited by Walter M. Abbott, S.J., New York: Guild Press, America Press, Association Press, 1966.)

TJD *To Teach as Jesus Did,* NCCB, 1972. (Can be found in *The Catechetical Documents: A Parish Resource,* Chicago: Liturgy Training Publications, 1996.)

FOOTNOTE CODES

ACC	Brown, Raymond E., S.S. *An Adult Christ at Christmas.*
AIRI	Yarnold, Edward, S.J. *The Awe-Inspiring Rites of Initiation.*
BAL	Brown, Raymond E., S.S. *The Beatitudes According to Luke.*
CBC	Karris, Robert J., O.F.M., ed. *Collegeville Bible Commentary.*
CBP	Reid, Barbara E. *Choosing the Better Part.*
CC	Hynes, Mary Ellen. *Companion to the Calendar.*
CCA	Brown, Raymond E., S.S. *A Coming Christ in Advent.*
CCC	*Catechism of the Catholic Church.*
CCHW	Brown, Raymond E., S.S. *A Crucified Christ in Holy Week.*
CCT	Dues, Greg. *Catholic Customs and Traditions.*
CD	*The Catechetical Documents: A Parish Resource.*
CHBP	*Catholic Household Blessings and Prayers.*
CNT	Wintherop, Ronald D. *Conversion in the New Testament.*
CPDBT	Stuhlmueller, Carroll, C.P., ed. *The Collegeville Pastoral Dictionary of Biblical Theology.*
CR	Marthaler, Berard. *The Creed.*
CSL	*Constitution on the Sacred Liturgy.*
CSM	McBrien, Richard P. *Catholicism.*
CWJ	Pilch, John J. *The Cultural World of Jesus.*
DL	*Days of the Lord (Vols. I–VII).*
DOB	McKenzie, John L. *The Dictionary of the Bible.*
DOL	*Documents on the Liturgy.*
DV(II)	Abbott, Walter M., S.J., ed. *The Documents of Vatican II.*
EEC	Rordorf, Willy. *The Eucharist of the Early Christians.*
EGW	Dunning, Jim. *Echoing God's Word.*
GAJ	Carson, D.A. *The Gospel According to John.*
GAP	Richards, Hubert. *The Gospel According to St. Paul.*
GCD	*General Catechetical Directory.*
GCY	Rahner, Karl. *The Great Church Year.*
GEJ	Brown, Raymond E., S.S. *The Gospel and Epistles of John.*
GIRM	*General Instruction of the Roman Missal.*
GJ	Ellis, Peter F. *The Genius of John.*
GL	Johnson, Luke Timothy. *The Gospel of Luke.*
GNLY	*General Norms for the Liturgical Year and Calendar.*
HCEC	McBrien, Richard P., ed. *HarperCollins Encyclopedia of Catholicism.*
HD	Crosby, Michael H. *The House of Disciples.*
HTP	Scott, Bernard Brandon. *Hear Then the Parable.*
IA	Karris, Robert J., O.F.M. *Invitation to Acts.*
IM	Senior, Donald, C.P. *Invitation to Matthew.*
JGNP	Cassidy, Richard J. *John's Gospel in New Perspective.*
JHT	Johnson, Sherman E. *Jesus and His Towns.*
JHW	Collins, Raymond F. *John and His Witness.*
JP	Kealy, Sean P., C.S.Sp. *Jesus and Politics.*
KG	Bright, John. *The Kingdom of God.*
LF	Grassi, Joseph A. *Loaves and Fishes.*
LK	LaVerdiere, Eugene, S.S.S. *Luke.*
LTS	Talbert, Charles H. *Learning Through Suffering.*
LY	Adam, Adolf. *The Liturgical Year.*
MI	Hare, Douglas R.A. *Matthew, Interpretation: A Bible Commentary for Teaching and Preaching.*
MML	Flanagan, Neal M., O.S.M. *Mark, Matthew, Luke: A Guide to the Gospel Parallels.*
MRR	Jungman, Joseph A. *The Mass of the Roman Rite: Its Origins and Development.*
MSS	Richter, Klemens. *The Meaning of the Sacramental Symbols.* Linda Maloney, trans.
NCD	*The National Catechetical Directory*
NDSW	Fink, Peter E., S.J., ed. *The New Dictionary of Sacramental Worship.*
NDT	Komonchak, Joseph A., Mary Collins, Dermot A. Lane, eds. *The New Dictionary of Theology.*
NJBC	Brown, Raymond E., S.S., et al, eds. *The New Jerome Biblical Commentary.*
NTI	Perrin, Norman and Dennis C. Duling. *The New Testament: An Introduction.*
NULA	Tannehill, Robert C. *The Narrative Unity of Luke-Acts: A Literary Interpretation* (Vols. I and II).

OCSP	Brown, Raymond E., S.S. *Once and Coming Spirit at Pentecost.*
OLY	Talley, Thomas J. *Origins of the Liturgical Year.*
PAI	Kuntz, J. Kenneth. *The People of Ancient Israel: An Introduction to Old Testament Literature, History, and Thought.*
PCW	Byrne, Brendan, S.J. *Paul and the Christian Woman.*
PE	Karris, Robert J., O.F.M. *The Pastoral Epistles.*
PG	Collins, Raymond F. *Preaching the Gospels.*
PJGM	Senior, Donald, C.P. *The Passion of Jesus in the Gospel of Matthew.*
PL	Fuller, Reginald H. *Preaching the Lectionary.*
PNL	Fuller, Reginald H. *Preaching the New Lectionary.*
PTE	Collins, Raymond F. *Preaching the Epistles.*
PW	Jungman, Joseph A. *Public Worship: A Survey.* Clifford Howell, trans.
RCE	Brown, Raymond E., S.S. *A Risen Christ in Eastertime.*
RCIA	The Rite of Christian Initiation for Adults.
RF	Ramshaw, Gail. *Richer Fare for the Christian People.*
RJ	Talbert, Charles H. *Reading John.*
RL	Talbert, Charles H. *Reading Luke.*
RM	Garland, David E. *Reading Matthew: A Literary and Theological Commentary on the First Gospel.*
RNT	Perkins, Pheme. *Reading the New Testament.*
ROT	Boadt, Lawrence, C.S.P. *Reading the Old Testament.*
RT	Schneiders, Sandra. *The Revelatory Text.*
SB	Crosby, Michael H. *The Spirituality of the Beatitudes: Matthew's Challenge for First World Christians.*
SIR	Rybolt, John E. *Sirach. Collegeville Bible Commentary, Old Testament #21,* Robert J. Karris, O.F.M., ed.
SL	Jones, Cheslyn, Geoffrey Wainwright, Edward Yarnold, S.J., and Paul Bradshaw, eds. *The Study of Liturgy, Revised Edition.*
SWTLY	Gutierrez, Gustavo. *Sharing the Word Through the Liturgical Year.*
TCY	Mazar, Peter. *To Crown the Year: Decorating the Church Through the Seasons.*
TDJR	Stamps, Mary E., ed. *To Do Justice and Right Upon the Earth.*
TFC	Lee, Bernard J. *The Future Church of 140 B.C.E.*
TGJ	Marrow, Stanley B. *The Gospel of John.*
TI	Hughes, Philip Edgcumbe. *The True Image.*
TLD	Hoffman, Elizabeth, ed. *The Liturgy Documents.*
TWOW	Corbon, Jean. *The Wellspring of Worship.*
UOT	Anderson, Bernhard W. *Understanding the Old Testament,* Fourth Edition.
WBC	Camp, Claudia V. *The Women's Bible Commentary.*
WNT	Johnson, Luke Timothy. *The Writings of the New Testament: An Interpretation.*
WWC	Sanchez, Patricia Datchuck. *The Word We Celebrate.*